C0-FZT-619

The Quality Yearbook

1995

The Quality Yearbook

1995

James W. Cortada
John A. Woods

McGraw-Hill, Inc.
New York San Francisco Washington, D.C. Auckland Bogotá
Caracas Lisbon London Madrid Mexico City Milan
Montreal New Delhi Paris San Juan Singapore
Sydney Tokyo Toronto

McGraw-Page Library
Randolph-Macon College
Ashland, Virginia 23005

Copyright © 1995 by McGraw-Hill, Inc. All rights reserved. Printed in the United States of America. Except as permitted under the United States Copyright Act of 1976, no part of this publication may be reproduced or distributed in any form or by any means, or stored in a data base or retrieval system, without the prior written permission of the publisher.

1 2 3 4 5 6 7 8 9 0 AGM/AGM 9 0 9 8 7 6 5 4

ISBN: 0-07-024046-9

ISSN: 1072-9135

The sponsoring editor for this book was James H. Bessent, Jr., and the production coordinator was Claire Huismann. It was composed at Impressions, a division of Edwards Brothers, Inc.

This book is printed on recycled, acid-free paper containing a minimum of 50% recycled de-inked fiber.

Contents

Preface

Welcome to the 1995 edition of *The Quality Yearbook*. We would like to thank all of you who purchased the first (1994) edition. Your support has made this book one of our publisher's real success stories. This tells us that we have met a need, and this is gratifying, but we also know we cannot stand still, and we have made several changes in the 1995 version. Before we describe them, it is a good idea to reiterate the purpose and goals of *The Quality Yearbook*. It has two purposes:

1. To provide an *annual documentation* of the most useful ideas, tools, and articles in quality.
2. To serve as an *annual comprehensive reference* for finding information on activities, publications, awards, and organizations dealing with quality management.

We set several goals for ourselves in developing this book. The most important include:

Create a Clearinghouse. Because there is so much coming out in quality, McGraw-Hill and the editors of this book perceived a need for a kind of "clearinghouse" to which people from all different organizations might turn as a starting place to learn about current thinking in quality. *The Quality Yearbook* includes the best and most useful selection of information available. Its utility is founded on this premise, and its success will be a testament to how well we fill this need.

Create a Book of Lasting Value. Because it will be revised annually, *The Quality Yearbook* will focus on information that has come out in the period immediately preceding its publication. While currency is one of its strengths in this fast-changing field, each edition also is intended to have lasting value. Managers will find articles throughout the book that will continue to be applicable for several years as they go about implementing quality in their organizations. However, for all those actively engaged in the quality revolution, each year's edition will give them updates on all the book's content areas plus selected new topics that reflect the latest developments in the field.

Develop an Authoritative Review. Yet another goal for *The Quality Yearbook* is to help develop clearer thinking about and implementation of the principles of quality management. By providing managers and others interested in quality with an authoritative review of the latest discussions about the applications and extensions of these principles, each edition can help to standardize the categories for exploring this important set of principles and practices.

Organization

Like last year, we have divided the book into four parts:

Part One, Background for Quality, includes "Classics in Quality" and a new section, "Contemporary Thoughts on Quality Management." Our aim here is to give you some thoughtful background reading on TQM in general before we get to articles that are more focused on specific industries and practices.

Part Two, Quality by Industry, covers TQM as practiced in manufacturing, services, and four different areas of the public sector—government, health care, higher education, and K-12 education.

Part Three, Implementing Quality, presents the best articles and ideas from the past year on the theory and techniques of quality management. We have broken the readings into four categories:

1. Quality Transformation
2. Quality Tools and Techniques
3. Functional Processes
4. Standards and Assessments

Part Three provides a wide spectrum of articles that explain the whys and hows of implementing quality including many different examples from different industries.

Part Four, Quality References, includes a wide variety of material to help you further your exploration of TQM. You will find a comprehensive bibliography of quality articles and books that have come out since the last edition (this is current through the fall of 1994), a guide to quality organizations, a directory of quality magazines and journals, and a review of quality awards. For reflection and use in preparing speeches and reports, we have included a 25-page section "Quotes on Quality," which should stimulate thinking on many issues. You will also find a profile of the 1994 Baldrige Award winners in this part and a review of the changes in the 1995 Baldrige Award criteria.

What's New in the 1995 Edition?

Practical and Process-Oriented. We have made a conscious effort to include more case studies and "how-to" articles in this edition. We want the book to provide you, our readers, with practical guidelines and answers to questions you might have about implementing quality management. We have chosen to stress the idea of process management and measurement. Each year we launch the yearbook with an essay by one of the editors dealing with a theme we think is important. This year Jim Cortada takes up the topic of process management and reengineering, with a review of the various approaches to continuous improvement. Nearly every survey of quality practices we have seen suggests (a) that almost all the top 1,000 companies in the United States now have a quality emphasis with process management and improvement at the heart of their efforts, and (b) that schools of thought have cropped up as to the best way to approach this effort from evolutionary improvement to radical reengineering. Throughout the book, you will see several articles that deal with this subject. This includes a new section in Part Three on process management and measurement, with five different articles.

References. We have expanded the reference section with a more complete listing of magazines and journals covering quality topics, a completely updated section on quality awards (including an extended section on international awards), a new section listing on-line quality services, a review of 25 books that we think would make up a basic library in quality management, and a short how-to piece on benchmarking. And despite the fact that the Baldrige Awards were announced less than three weeks before this book went to press, we were still able to include profiles of the winners.

We have included once again the comprehensive glossary of terms found in the 1994 edition because we want to make these available to new users of the yearbook. Readers who have found this a helpful reference will be interested to know that there will be a much expanded version published in spring 1995 as the *McGraw-Hill Encyclopedia of Quality Concepts and Terms.* This will include more detailed definitions, examples, illustrations, and a list of books where you can find additional information on each term. Because we have included the glossary for two years running, it is likely we will replace it with a new section in the 1996 edition. That will either be more articles or new reference material. You can help us decide by filling out the feedback form in the back of this book.

Consulting Editors

Assisting us in the preparation of this edition were six consulting editors, prominent in their fields, who made suggestions for articles and who contributed original articles themselves. We are very proud to have them associated with the book, and you will find their articles in the beginning of each subsection in Part Two. These individuals are:

- **Manufacturing: B. Joseph Pine II,** founder and president of Ridgefield, Connecticut-based Strategic Horizons, Inc., a management consulting firm specializing in helping companies envision and then realize their future. Joe is the author of the highly acclaimed book *Mass Customization: The New Frontier in Business Competition,* which the *Financial Times* named one of the top business books of 1993. He has also written articles for a number of magazines and journals, including the *Harvard Business Review, The Wall Street Journal, Planning Review,* the *IBM Systems Journal, Chief Executive,* and *CIO.*
- **Services: Ron Zemke,** president of Performance Research Associates, a Minneapolis-based consulting and training company specializing in service quality audits and service management programs. Ron is also senior editor for *Training* Magazine and editor

of *The Service Edge* Newsletter. He is author or co-author of several best-selling business books, including *Service America! Doing Business in the New Economy, Managing Knock Your Socks Off Service, The Service Edge: 101 Companies that Profit from Customer Care,* and *Sustaining Knock Your Socks Off Service.* Zemke received the 1994 Mobius Award for his contributions to the customer service profession.

- **Health Care: Sherry Bright,** senior vice president for strategy at General Health System in Baton Rouge, Louisiana. This is a private nonprofit customer-driven company that provides a wide variety of services to meet the health care needs of its market. Sherry's responsibilities include managing the change process at General Health, leveraging new learning in areas such as quality, systems dynamics/thinking, and interactive planning. She serves as the chair of the Executive Committee for the Quality Management Network, a group of more than 32 health care organizations working on improving quality internally and sharing.
- **Government: Joseph Sensenbrenner** is president of Sensenbrenner Associates and works in the application of private sector TQM approaches to public-sector service delivery. In 1988 he was recognized as one of the "Ten Most Influential Figures in Quality Improvement." Joe was a three-term mayor of Madison, Wisconsin, serving from 1983 to 1989, during which time he pioneered service improvements in virtually very municipal activity. He is the author of articles that have appeared in the *Harvard Business Review, Quality Progress,* and *Nation's Business* in the area of implementing TQM in government.
- **Higher Education: Ronald Heilman** is a member of the school of business faculty at the University of Wisconsin, Milwaukee, and head of the Center for Quality, Productivity, and Economic Development at that university. He is also a member of the education committee of Milwaukee: First in Quality (MFIQ) and past president of the MFIQ Executive Committee. Ron is a senior member of the American Society for Quality Control. He is president and founder of the National Educational Quality Initiative, a nonprofit corporation dedicated to improving the quality of the U.S. educational system. Besides Ron's article on the state of quality in higher education, we have also included an article by him in the process management part of the book.
- **Education, K-12:** We have a team of consultants in this area: **David Bayless, Gabriel Massaro,** and **Nancy Roche**. This team, working with Joiner Associates, created the revised version of the best-selling *The Team Handbook* designed for educators. **David Bayless** has had 25 years of professional experience as a statistician and spent 10 years as vice president and study area director at Westat, Inc., in Rockville, Maryland, specializing in large-scale

surveys of various types for local and national educational systems. He is now president of Bayless Associates and serves as consultant to various schools districts seeking to implement TQM in the classroom and in administration. **Gabriel Massaro,** a research associate at Westat, Inc., has more than 25 years experience in education. He was an associate superintendent of schools for curriculum and instruction, an elementary and high school principal, college professor, elementary and high school teacher, and educational researcher and consultant. He now specializes in consulting and training in the area of TQM implementation in schools. **Nancy Roche** is an educational consultant working with Westat, Inc. Nancy has designed and presented workshops, conferences, and seminars on quality leadership, tools, and team building. She has been a teacher, a curriculum specialist, and a school principal.

We appreciate the help of these professionals and commend their articles to you to better understand the state of TQM in their respective areas.

Feedback From You

What we put in next year's edition can depend either on our judgment alone or in partnership with you. Please use the feedback forms at the back of the book to tell us what you think of this year's edition and what you want in the next. It only takes a minute, but it allows us to hear your voice, something we take very seriously. This is our way of making sure *The Quality Yearbook* meets your needs. So take advantage of this chance to shape this book to better meet your needs.

Acknowledgments

This book was a big undertaking for us, and we are indebted to many people who have played a role in its coming together. Our editor at McGraw-Hill, Jim Bessent, has been very supportive and helpful in many ways, and we appreciate having him on our team.

We want to thank the editors and publishers of the several magazines, journals, and books from which we drew the articles that make up the heart of this book. All were very forthcoming in supplying the permissions that allowed us to reprint the pieces you see here. This group represents a wide spectrum of opinions and the leading publishers on quality topics today.

Bob Chapman, Jan Kosko, and Ann Rothgeb at the National Institute of Standards and Technology assisted us by supplying information on the Baldrige award winners and criteria changes for 1995. They were also helpful in the preparation of this year's quality awards directory. We thank them for their responsiveness to our needs.

Our production schedule for this book is an extraordinarily quick two months, and at our production house, Impressions, we were fortunate to work again on this edition with Claire Huismann and David Nelson. Their conscientious work made production go very smoothly and finish on schedule.

Our wives, Dora Cortada and Nancy Woods, have also been very supportive of our efforts as we shuttle between our houses doing the myriad chores involved in delivering this book to you. Their contributions are as important as any we have had.

Finally, we want to thank those who have found the 1994 edition of this book a useful addition to their shelf of quality resources and to those of you who are new buyers this year. Without you, *The Quality Yearbook* wouldn't exist.

James W. Cortada
John A. Woods

PART ONE

Background for Quality

Total Quality Management is often thought of as a special approach to managing, something to try when things are not going as well as you would like. This is somewhat of a misunderstanding of TQM. It represents, rather, a more informed approach to facilitating organizational success. Its methods and techniques simply make the most sense when we view an organization as a system. From this approach, we begin to understand the importance of *managing processes* and improving them, to the benefit of the business, its customers, and other stakeholders. The approach to management suggested by TQM is not arbitrary. As a manager, you are responsible for making sure your company's processes work as well as possible and that they improve. Traditional management techniques, based on hierarchies and a focus on individual employees and short-term events, are, quite simply, a lousy way to make a system run well.

In the 1995 edition of *The Quality Yearbook,* we are putting more emphasis on the idea of process management. You will find new sections on that topic as well as on measurements and teamwork, all important aspects of making processes run smoothly and improving them through time. Thus, to start off this edition, we include an essay, "The Status of Process Management Today," that introduces this important topic. We hope this stimulates your thinking about how your organization is doing in terms of documenting and improving the processes by which work gets done. The essay is followed by a selection of "Classics in Quality," articles that also emphasize this idea of process management. Finally, in Part One of the book, we include two articles in a new section called "Contemporary Thoughts on Quality Management" to help you further understand and justify the TQM approach to managing an organization.

The Classics and Contemporary Thoughts

We have chosen four items for this edition's classics section. The first is *The New York Times* obituary of Dr. W. Edwards Deming, published in December 1993. We include this because it is a succinct and well-written summary of Dr. Deming's life, work, and approach to management (he always said he did not know what "quality management" was). This is followed by a listing of his 14 Points and 7 Deadly Diseases in his words, because these, more than anything else, capture his understanding of effective management. Making decisions based on these points will, according to Dr. Deming and many others, help managers do their best to look out for the organizations they are responsible for.

Following Dr. Deming's material, you will find excerpts from the books *Kaizen* by Masaaki Imai and *Quality Is Free* by Philip Crosby. Imai's piece introduces the idea of kaizen, the Japanese word for continuous improvement, as the foundation of Japanese management. Crosby's piece presents his definition of quality. This serves as the foundation of all his ideas on the practice of quality management.

We conclude Part One with articles from *Quality Progress* and *Sloan Management Review.* Richard Spitzer's piece, "TQM: The Only Source of Sustainable Competitive Advantage," provides a rationale for financially justifying in any company the quality approach to management. Robert Grant, Rami Shani, and R. Krishnan provide a thoughtful review of TQM in comparison with traditional management thought.

We hope Part One helps further your understanding of the basis of TQM. If you have read some of this material before, we hope it refreshes your memory.

The Status of Process Management Today

James W. Cortada

An important addition to the 1995 edition of The Quality Yearbook *is an emphasis on process management, with new sections of articles on that subject and on measurement. This article provides you with background on this important aspect of managing for quality.*

One of the central themes of modern quality management practices is the application of process management techniques for governing the conduct of work activities. In a quality-focused enterprise, management recognizes that the organization is a system composed of interrelated activities with the purpose of serving customers. The idea of a "system" acknowledges that nothing happens in isolation. Things that one department or group does within a company affect what occurs in other parts of the organization. That view of organization work has led to two realizations: (1) the need to have measurements, incentives, and rewards that encourage efficient and effective coordination of activities within all parts of the business, in short, better "working together" relationships (hence, for example, the interest in teams) and (2) the need to manage activities across multiple departments, not just within departments. This second requirement has led to the application of process management techniques, and that is what this article is about.

What Brought About the Interest in Process Management?

Historically, we have structured our organizations around functional departments, with each department devoted solely to its particular activities. Generally, the efforts were quite manageable unless the volume of work was too much or resources were inadequate. Billing, for example, has often been seen as a self-contained set of activities, or process, to be fully managed by members of one department. Other activities, such as product development, have involved multiple departments. However, department managers could affect and improve only what they were responsible for, with little regard for how this affected other related work in other departments. For example, customer service, which may begin by taking an order from a customer, moves to the fulfillment of that order, followed by billing, and then collection, could cut across a minimum of three departments: order processing, distribution, and accounting. Each department could work hard on improving its little piece of the process and yet, overall, the effect on the customer might not be dramatically improved, costs to the company could still be too high and, of course, there may be errors and miscommunication among people and departments.

As companies began to look at all the things that happen from the initial contact with a customer until completed transaction, several problems emerged that make it obvious that there has to be a better way to manage work involving these different departments and functions. First, computer technology was speeding up certain activities while creating problems (usually bottlenecks) for other departments. For example, computers can speed up order taking, but in the process generate a bottleneck in fulfillment, if the company is not staffed to handle this new volume of orders (even as the bill arrives before the merchandise!). Second, because of the department view of business activities, improvements in order entry would make that department appear to be performing well, despite the effect on the unprepared shipping department. Clearly, there had to be a better way to cut across multiple functions. Third, new views of business responsibility dictated the need for different approaches. These included such ideas as cycle time reduction (getting things done faster for competitive reasons) and customer impatience with delays and faulty execution resulting in lost sales. Finally, as companies downsized in the 1980s and 1990s, they discovered that *how* things got done needed to be changed.

Executives admonishing people to stop doing things that did not "add value" to the company or to customers sounded good, but until they applied some methodology for making real improvement, work just piled up for employees who remained. This led to fundamental breakdowns in the ability of a company to perform the basics, and at the same time drove down employee morale. Examples we are all familiar with include the failure of a customer center to answer your telephone call within three to four rings, the inability of a company to give you a reliable delivery date on an order right on the spot, or long delays in getting a response to a letter of inquiry.

For decades there have been little pockets of industrial engineers and statisticians who have worked on improving work flows by looking at all the tasks involved. They have sought to refine the steps in various processes. They have tried to eliminate steps that seemed to make a process more complicated than necessary, rearranging processes to make them easier to execute, and measuring the effects of these changes. These exercises were usually limited to such areas as engineering projects, then later to shop floor activities (and even here not extensively until the 1970s), and always to highly technical projects such as those associated with defense systems, some medical applications, and space travel.

Beginning in the 1950s, and finally with a loud voice by the late 1970s, concepts developed by these experts began to be shared more widely. Perhaps no individual more dramatically publicized this view of management in the United States than Philip Crosby who, in 1979, published *Quality Is Free,* a book in which he argued that the elimination of errors, reruns, mistakes, and so forth, would more than offset the cost of rooting out these problems. His book received wide attention in the business community, particularly in American and European companies. In Japan, 20 years earlier, a similar phenomenon had started with the teachings of an American statistician,

Dr. W. Edwards Deming. He argued the case for a more "scientific" or method-based look at work activities through lectures and consulting, not publishing his ideas in book form until 1982 in *Out of the Crisis*. He built a very strong case for looking at the totality of an organization's activities, not simply discrete elements. By the late 1980s, Dr. Deming's ideas were beginning to be widely received in American and European circles, while the Japanese had already embraced them as basic principles of their management activities by the early 1960s.[1]

Others had worked in narrower areas, primarily in the specifics of manufacturing activities both in the United States and Japan. The three most notable examples were Armand V. Feigenbaum and Joseph M. Juran in the United States and Kaoru Ishikawa in Japan. Beginning in the 1950s and working constantly over the next four decades, they and their disciples filled in many of the details on how to look at specific tasks and functions. They produced a large number of important, sometimes lengthy, volumes and papers on how to look at organizations holistically as systems, how to manage specific processes within them, and built business cases to justify these approaches. They added to our understanding of how to measure, assess, and improve processes, and apply them increasingly to a broader array of business activities.[2] Thus, by the start of the 1980s, primarily in manufacturing, a new view of how to manage complex operations has developed that has become the philosophical and tactical basis for much of the "quality movement" of the 1980s and 1990s.

The reason for going through this history is to understand that "quality" or "process management" is not a fad, but is based on specific research and experiences created over a half century. In fact, if we step back a full century, we see other forces were at work that insured the inevitable application of the scientific approach to work. The rise of statistics all through the late nineteenth and twentieth centuries, the convenience of data gathering and manipulation (made possible by the computer over the past half century), and technological changes in production, transportation, and communications are all forces of large historical proportions transcending any notion that process management is a fad.[3]

So focusing on process management is here to stay. Work gets done through interconnected steps in processes that have repercussions throughout the organization on everyone's performance. It is the most intelligent and realistic approach to management, and has developed a body of practices that work. Some organizations apply these well, and others do not. But managers

---

1. Philip B. Crosby, *Quality Is Free* (New York: McGraw-Hill, 1979); W. Edwards Deming, *Out of the Crisis* (Cambridge, Mass.: MIT Center for Advanced Engineering Study, original edition 1982, but the most widely read edition is 1986).

2. See, for example, Armand V. Feigenbaum, *Total Quality Control Handbook* (New York: McGraw-Hill, 1983); Joseph M. Juran, *Juran on Planning for Quality* (New York: Free Press, 1988), and with Frank M. Gryna, Jr., *Quality Planning and Analysis* (New York: McGraw-Hill, 1986).

3. James W. Cortada, "Quality Movement is Here to Stay," *Total Quality Review* (March/April 1994) pp. 7–9.

ignore the ideas surrounding process management at their peril. They can be sure that some of their competitors are implementing these practices to gain strategic advantage with customers. In some industries, TQM and process management are *de rigueur,* the normal way to run a business; others have yet to discover these concepts.

Disagreements over Process Management Approaches

Once discovered, the process management approaches become more complicated because there are schools of thought on how best to manage your process. Keep in mind that many of the tactical steps, for example, flowcharting, data gathering, interviews, and so on, are essentially the same from version to version. However, you need to be aware of some fundamental strategies that can be applied to these tasks because they affect the final outcome of work. To a large degree, disagreements over how to manage processes boil down to what extent an organization is prepared to make changes. There are three general schools of thought. The first holds that you take an existing process and continuously improve it. The second says you blow it up and replace it with a radically new one. The third argues that you replace the guts of a process with a piece of software and then reengineer its front and back ends. Each has its proponents who practice and preach their approach, have published articles and books, and who generate considerable debate.

The most widely practiced process management strategy involves taking an existing process, cutting out redundant or "nonvalue added" steps, and tightening up its overall operations with better measurements, more fact-based decision making, and simpler work steps. The assumption here is that an existing process has some value, but could provide more if cleaned up. A large body of literature has grown up in support of this strategy explaining how this is done.[4] Almost all quality management consultants teach and practice continuous improvement. Perhaps the most widely read proponent of this approach today is James Harrington who, in multiple publications, has explained the rationale for this approach and the steps one should take.[5] What makes Harrington's ideas attractive is his linkage of process improvement work with the business objectives of the corporation. By improving processes within the context of what the business is attempting to accomplish, process management remains relevant.

Continuous Improvement

The continuous improvement school of thought holds that by improving an existing process, you reduce the risk of failure, while still getting productive work out of a process. Incremental improvements become possible across

4. For some examples, see Peter R. Scholtes, *The Team Handbook* (Madison: Joiner Associates, 1988); James H. Saylor, *TQM Field Manual* (New York: McGraw-Hill, 1992); Ellis R. Ott and Edward G. Schilling, *Process Quality Control* (New York: McGraw-Hill, 1990); V. Daniel Hunt, *Managing For Quality: Integrating Quality and Business Strategy* (Homewood, Ill.: Business One Irwin, 1993).

5. H. James Harrington's most widely read book, which incorporates his ideas from his earlier writings, is *Business Process Improvement* (New York: McGraw-Hill, 1991).

many processes; thus, in aggregate, the entire organization can improve 10 to 20 percent compounded each year. Your corporate culture is more likely to accept this incremental improvement approach over other, more radical ones. Proponents like Harrington argue that most processes do not need replacement, just improvement. In fact, dramatic improvements can be achieved in such areas as reduced cycle time, reduced labor content (for example, fewer signoffs and audits), and a greater focus on results. Both efficiency and effectiveness can be improved. Critics of the continuous improvement approach complain that the changes achieved are not radical enough, particularly in those industries where competition is very intense and change has to come very fast.[6]

There is still an ongoing debate about which processes should be continuously improved and which should be completely replaced. The debate is an important one because both approaches frequently make sense in many companies. However, if there is a pattern developing it is the following:

1. Organizations new to a focus on process management tend to try process improvement first. That way they get their feet wet, perform the demonstration projects, and identify potential areas of opportunity for further work.
2. Organizations new to a focus on process management find that the vast majority of training available on quality, TQM, and process management is about continuous improvement strategies and tactics and, thus, know no other way.
3. As organizations mature, they begin to differentiate between process improvement and process reengineering, having multiple projects of both types underway.

Once a process has been reengineered, these enterprises then impose continuous improvement management methods on the new processes.

4. The evidence suggests that continuous improvement across the board is generating more benefits than a few, dramatic reengineering projects.

Reengineering

The second school of thought holds that processes should be obliterated, totally replaced. Proponents of this approach argue that you must start with a clean sheet of paper, with new ideas, and be prepared for dramatic change right from the start. Given the changing nature of organizations (such as growing flatter, more geographically dispersed, more "virtual"), no other option exists, they claim. With rapid response to competition becoming more of a reality, the need for order of magnitude change becomes imperative. Examples are constantly touted of profound changes leading to significant benefits. The

6. The loudest critics are Michael Hammer and James Champy, *Reengineering the Corporation* (New York: HarperBusiness, 1993); but see also Rosabeth Moss Kanter, Barry A. Stein, and Todd D. Jick, *The Challenge of Organizational Change* (New York: Free Press, 1992).

term "reengineering" has come into its own to apply to replaced processes, corporate cultures, organizations, and business strategies (we include various articles on this idea in the process reengineering section of *The Quality Yearbook*). The term is also often used when someone simply means continuous improvement.

The most widely recognized proponents of this approach are Michael Hammer and James Champy who, in 1993, published a book, *Reengineering the Corporation,* which sold over 300,000 copies in its first year. The authors received considerable attention from the business press through interviews, speeches, and articles, all laced with dramatic language about the need to throw out old approaches and replace them with radically new ones. They have argued "that American corporations must undertake nothing less than a radical reinvention of how they do their work."[7] To describe the extent of change they call for, the authors have used such words as "fundamental," "radical," and "dramatic." The kinds of radical process redesign called for include, for example, billing procurement processes where organizations move from using 500 people to 5, from completing the design of a new car in months instead of many years, of using different companies to do work that the company formerly did for itself.

Characteristics of projects requiring reengineering are different from those simply needing improvement. The more dramatic change is usually a one-time event with a process, not a continuous replacement. The application of technology is almost always central to the redesign rather than simply an add-on. Management is always intimately involved with reengineering, while with continuous improvement, management normally just supports and provides resources for others making the improvements. The speed with which change must come is greater with a reengineering project. The risk of failure with reengineering is greater, but so are the rewards of success. Proponents of reengineering argue that it is a strategy applicable to all kinds of companies (for example, those in trouble, those about to be in trouble, or those doing well that want continued success). In fact, the best reengineering projects are those carefully chosen based on their own merits, process by process.

Using Technology to Improve

The third school of thought is a hybrid of these two extremes. It essentially calls for the application of technology to deliver the bulk of the performance of a process, with tasks reordered in front of and behind the technology and appropriate changes to organization, staffing, etc., made to accommodate the change. Results can be incremental or dramatic. Typically, this kind of process change is done by installing application software or some technology (for example, computer networks, or high powered software and computers to help manage and monitor an operation) and reordering the activities surrounding the approach. A computerized scheduling and order system for a manufacturing process would be an illustration. Such software helps track the need

7. Hammer and Champy, *Reengineering the Corporation,* p. 5.

for components in the manufacturing process, monitors inventory, and dispatches orders when more are needed. This approach helps companies develop just-in-time inventory control.

Perhaps the most widely read proponent of this approach today is Thomas H. Davenport, who wrote *Process Innovation: Reengineering Work Through Information Technology*. He argued that information technology is the enabler of dramatic improvements in process work.[8] For example, the use of information technology (IT) made it possible for IBM to reduce the time it takes to provide purchase quotes for large computers from one week to less than one day by using computers to perform most of the necessary calculations (something we should expect from IBM). Like the other proponents of process improvement strategies, he cites many examples across numerous industries and functions to back up his position. The published literature on process improvement is beginning to provide many other examples of this strategy being employed. They cover the extended use of marketing databases, groupware for teams, and exploitation of a broad range of telecommunications, from cellular telephones to PCs.[9] Both Harrington and Hammer might argue that his approach is theirs.

Trends in Process Management

Regardless of the approach selected, there are already discernable trends that suggest all three are being applied. Work is becoming more mobile as workers, customers, and offices move around in cars and through electronics. Information technology is being applied in more delegated ways than ever. We can see that by the enormous increase in the use of PDAs, PCs, and employees operating out of their own homes and cars. Local area networks support more computing power than traditional computer centers. We also see companies downsizing, flattening hierarchies, and reducing fixed costs. It seems every week some major corporation is announcing that it will reduce its workforce by tens, hundreds, or thousands, depending on size. To do that requires restructuring work, not simply getting rid of it.

New strategies for operating organizations have taken hold that call for new ways of doing work. The two most popular are the concepts of the "virtual corporation," where you do only that which you are very good at and everything else gets farmed out.[10] The other is the concept of gaining competitive advantage by reducing the amount of time it takes to do something (known as cycle time reduction).[11]

---

8. Thomas H. Davenport, *Process Innovation: Reengineering Work Through Information Technology* (Boston: Harvard Business School Press, 1993).

9. For recent bibliography see James W. Cortada and John A. Woods, *The Quality Yearbook* (New York: McGraw-Hill, 1994) and the 1995 edition; James W. Cortada and John A. Woods, *McGraw-Hill Encyclopedia of Quality Concepts and Terms* (New York: McGraw-Hill, 1995).

10. On "virtual corporations" the best is James Brian Quinn, *Intelligent Enterprise* (New York: Free Press, 1992).

11. The best description of this strategy is George Stalk, Jr., and Thomas M. Hout, *Competing Against Time: How Time-Based Competition Is Reshaping Global Markets* (New York: Free Press, 1990).

Where Process Innovation Is Taking Place

The question of process management is becoming increasingly important as companies look for models to emulate, and as they worry about what their competitors are doing and benchmark themselves against others. The published literature on this topic is rapidly growing, but at the same time is spotty on what processes are being worked on and in what industries.[12] Ernst & Young has published several industry surveys that show process improvement strategies are a major component of quality programs. These industries include computer hardware, automotive, health, and finance. Industry-focused surveys on best practices have been few and far between so far.[13]

Several patterns of behavior have emerged that offer lessons for all companies seeking to more effectively manage their processes for improvement and strategic advantage:

1. Companies in industries experiencing tremendous change or competition are more likely to apply process improvement and reengineering across the entire enterprise. Examples include computer and automotive manufacturers and telecommunications. These companies tend to have the longest experience managing a wide body of processes. They are also the source of so many well-known case studies: Toyota, Ford, IBM, Motorola, Xerox, GE, and AT&T.
2. Companies just now experiencing some change or deregulation are conducting their initial process improvement projects. Frequently, these are demonstration projects to illustrate the process of improvement, and often are done on processes perceived by everyone to be broken. These usually are too big for an initial project, but are done anyway. This pattern holds in such industries as gas and electric utilities and insurance.
3. Companies are performing more continuous improvement than reengineering, although many people are confusing the terms, calling their work efforts reengineering when they really mean incremental improvement. Also evident is the continued heavy application of information technology to distribute work, speed up transactions, and facilitate movement of large quantities of data. Radical reengineering projects are relying overwhelmingly on the application of IT in creative ways.
4. What is being reengineered is all over the board with no discernable pattern. That means a company can probably find others who are improving processes similar to each other either in the same or other industries. For all intents and purposes, the Fortune 1000 companies all have process improvement projects currently underway.

---

12. See bibliographies in Cortada and Woods, annual editions of *The Quality Yearbook*. Each has a detailed bibliography by industry, quality practice, and organizational function.

13. For examples, see David K. Carr and Ian D. Littman, *Excellence in Government: Total Quality Management in the 1990s* (Milwaukee: ASQC Quality Press, 1990); M. Daniel Sloan and Michael Chmel, *The Quality Revolution and Health Care* (Milwaukee: ASQC Quality Press, 1991); Stephen S. J. Hall, *Quality Assurance in the Hospitality Industry* (Milwaukee: ASQC Quality Press, 1990).

5. There are not comprehensive, convenient sources of information on best practices, despite the enormous efforts of such organizations as the American Productivity and Quality Center (APQC) and the American Society for Quality Control (ASQC) to gather and disseminate information of this kind. Major consulting firms that do process improvement and reengineering work obviously feel a profound sense of reluctance to share publicly their experiences for reasons of client confidentiality.
6. Companies are finding three major sources of information: management consultants, published accounts of process work, and telephoning admired companies either in their industry or outside for advice. This last approach is proving to be very effective, particularly within one's own industry where management knows which companies are most progressive. How to undertake these benchmarking exercises is now the subject of many books, articles, and seminars.[14]

If we look at the published literature on process work, it becomes obvious that the most comprehensive process improvement work has occurred in manufacturing, product design, military and defense related activities, equipment repair operations, and logistics (customer fulfillment). Many of these have been under construction or renovation for over a decade. They are heavily concentrated in manufacturing. However, in the past five years, service industry process improvement projects have come into their own. Order entry and fulfillment across many industries is the most obvious. Billing and accounts payable are now well understood. Hotels have reengineered many of their front desk and billing processes. Customer survey processes have now proliferated across all industries to help in doing this.

Public sector industries have as varied a pattern of performance as the private sector. The leading users of process improvement are hospitals and other health care facilities, which, over the past decade, have had to drive down operating costs and improve effectiveness, particularly in the United States. (See essay by Sherry Bright and other articles in health care section of this book.) As a result, health care today probably has the most comprehensive published documentation on best practices, standards of performance, and documentation on effective processes.[15] This does not suggest that there is not much more to be done in this area. American state governments are rapidly increasing their use of process management methods in such areas as welfare, civil rights enforcement, and labor relations. Public sector projects tend to be publicized more than private sector projects, so researchers are often left with the impression that the creativity leadership is coming out of

14. Robert C. Camp, *Benchmarking: The Search for Industry Best Practices That Lead to Superior Performance* (Milwaukee: ASQC Quality Press, 1989); Gregory H. Watson, *Strategic Benchmarking: How to Rate Your Company's Performance Against the World's Best* (New York: John Wiley & Sons, 1993).

15. *Striving Toward Improvement: Six Hospitals in Search of Quality* (Oakbrook Terrace, Ill.: Joint Commission on Accreditation of Healthcare Organizations, 1992).

local, state, and national government when, in fact, the public sector has hardly started to manage its activities as collections of processes.

Quality award winners invariably have a large body of processes that have been documented, continuously improved, or radically changed. Because of the requirements to publicize results, award winners remain primary sources of innovative examples that other companies rely on. Baldrige, Deming, and European quality award winners universally appear eager to share their work. Process improvements in these firms usually cut across all functions, from understanding customers to designing and manufacturing products. The overwhelming majority of winners are still manufacturing, although that is beginning to change as service sector award candidates arrive on the scene (for example, hotels, credit card companies, and insurance). Each of the organizations managing award programs track how many companies are requesting and using their award criteria. Since application for an award must also include demonstrated results of applied quality practices, we know that process management has been rising steadily for nearly a decade.[16]

What functions are not doing much? If you look hard enough, there is activity in all functional areas. Some functions were addressed sooner rather than later. For example, manufacturing activities were subjected to process management as early as the 1960s. However, only since the late 1980s have companies attempted to improve sales and marketing through process management. In fact, a debate is going on whether sales is being reengineered or simply loaded up with technology, such as laptops and car phones.[17] Several key personnel areas are now also being subjected to process management: training, performance assessments, rewards, and compensation.[18] Customer surveys and logistics have also come into their own as highly successful areas for process management.[19]

On the plus side of the ledger, the introduction of ABC (Activity-Based Costing) accounting methods is beginning to cause process changes in accounting, although hardly enough at this point to claim that accounting departments are applying process management to their work. We do not see any important work underway with process improvement in strategic planning or finance. Most legal departments in corporations and law firms are also way behind, despite their aggressive use of technology for case management and data query applications. Accountants, strategic planners, lawyers, and the

---

16. Curt W. Reimann and Harry S. Hertz, "The Malcolm Baldrige National Quality Award and ISO 9000 Registration: Understanding Their Many Important Differences," in Cortada and Woods, *The Quality Yearbook* (1994) pp. 611–627.

17. James W. Cortada, *TQM for Sales and Marketing Management* (New York: McGraw-Hill, 1993) pp. 155–177.

18. Calhoun W. Wick and Lu Stanton Leon, *The Learning Edge: How Smart Managers and Smart Companies Stay Ahead* (New York: McGraw-Hill, 1993); Helga Drummond, "Incentive Schemes in a Quality Culture," *Work Study* (March–April 1993) pp. 25–27; Peter R. Scholtes, "Total Quality or Performance Appraisal: Choose One," *National Productivity Review* (Summer 1993) pp. 349–363.

19. Bob E. Hayes, *Measuring Customer Satisfaction: Development and Use of Questionnaires* (Milwaukee: ASQC Quality Press, 1992); Les Gould, "New Warehouse Payoff. A 200% Jump in Productivity," *Modern Materials Handling* 48, no. 3 (March 1993) pp. 40–42.

banking community have hardly started to use basic process management tools such as data analysis, statistical process control, or process measurements.

An Assessment

Management is finding process improvement strategies to be an effective tactical approach for strategic business transformation. It answers the question, "How do I transform work, culture, and results?" Proven methods for performing this work exist and are well documented. Yet, while a debate is raging over improvement versus radical change, most are opting for continuous improvement approaches. Documentation on successes and failures remains quite limited, along with practical collections of information on best practices. There appears to be almost no evidence of any significant research on process management coming out of the business schools in either the United States or Europe. The lack of academic interest is startling by its absence despite some weak efforts to correct this problem.[20] The best work is being done by business consultants and line management in American and Asian companies. They are actually doing the process improvement work and, periodically, reporting on results in print and at seminars. In fact, line management and its process teams are doing almost all the reporting on experiences evident at seminars. In the United States in 1993, there were over 1,000 conferences at which such reports were made; it appears that 1994 will have had the same number of presentations.

Documented results suggest that most process improvement efforts have been worth doing, although much remains to be done to establish what range of expectations in improvements one might expect from redesigning work processes. One problem facing managers is that organizations that meet with difficulty in improving or reengineering processes are not reported on publicly. The only negative press seems to be on problems companies have in implementing various Total Quality Management activities.[21] Such accounts do not necessarily focus on process management issues per se.

The quality gurus of the 1970s and 1980s generalized about expectations for quality improvement being in the range of 10 to 40 percent, but they relied heavily on the reduction of repeat work, valueless activities, and error elimination—all very important benefits of process management. However, we are learning that this is too narrow a list of benefits to be derived from both continuous improvement or reengineering efforts. In short, the gurus may

---

20. The ASQC launched *Quality Management Journal* in 1993 to provide an outlet for formal academic research on the subject. IBM Corporation in 1992 awarded nine U.S. universities multi-million dollar grants for the purpose of conducting research on quality practices, to develop their own internal programs by which universities could be run, and to provide for training.

21. For example, Selwyn W. Becker, "TQM Does Work: Ten Reasons Why Misguided Attempts Fail," *Management Review* 82, no. 5 (May 1993) pp. 30, 32; Mark Graham Brown, "Why Does Total Quality Management Fail in Two Out of Three Tries?" *Journal for Quality and Participation* (March 1993) pp. 80–89.

have understated the benefits of process management. There is growing evidence that the benefits are closer to 40 percent than to 10 percent. As additional improvements are made in how work activities are measured, these figures should settle into more predictable patterns.

The Role of Measurement in Process Management

Measurements are taking on a greater role than a decade ago because of the influence of process management techniques and quality practices. Measurements are also becoming the subject of debate in business literature.[22] The number of measurement options is also growing. Not just a collection of financial numbers, or counts of how many things were made or done correctly, other groups of measures are making their way into process management. These include surveys on employee and customer satisfaction and measures of results of a process, of quality, of waste, of cycle time, and of flexibility.

Understanding the relationship among these measures, that is to say, how one influences another, is the true genius in understanding the effectiveness of a process. Increasingly, evidence is pointing to a growing level of sophistication in the application of measurements and the use of statistical process control.[23] As various measures of a process's performance are tried out, people learn which measures affect performance of people and the process, and how one measure influences another. Over time, they usually experiment with many combinations and ultimately reduce them to a mighty few that scientifically give insight on performance and meaningful data on results.

The Future

Perched here at the start of 1995, one can look back with satisfaction at the enormous expanded use of process management techniques across Western Europe, all of North America, and the industrialized portions of Asia. Those companies that do not use such approaches are rapidly becoming the exception, while little application is more the norm in the public sector. The most rapid expansion in the application of process management methods in the past three to five years has been in the service sector and, increasingly, in small companies. Practical guides to process management are available in articles, books, seminars, and consulting firms, while organized "best practices" databases remain too sparse. My expectation is that the growing interest in using benchmarking techniques will contribute to fixing this problem.

---

22. Christopher Meyer, "How the Right Measures Help Teams Excel," *Harvard Business Review* (May–June 1994) pp. 95–103; Brian L. Joiner, *Fourth Generation Management: The New Business Consciousness* (New York: McGraw-Hill, 1994) pp. 117–178.

23. Wayne A. Taylor, *Optimization and Variation Reduction in Quality* (New York: McGraw-Hill, 1991); Steven M. Hronec, *Vital Signs: Using Quality, Time, and Cost Performance Measurement to Chart Your Company's Future* (New York: Amacom, 1993).

CLASSICS IN QUALITY

On the Death of Dr. W. Edwards Deming

John Holusha

This piece is the obituary for Dr. Deming, published on December 21, 1993, in The New York Times. *This gives a short background on Dr. Deming's life and his approach to management. It is a fitting tribute to the person who has come to symbolize an uncompromising approach to sound management practice based on a commitment to customers, employees, and society in general.*

W. Edwards Deming, an expert on business management who advised Japan on how to rebuild its shattered industries after World War II and urged American corporations to treat their workers as associates rather than adversaries, died early yesterday at his home in Washington. He was 93.

The cause was cancer. Although he was ill in recent years, Mr. Deming continued to work, conducting the last of his four-day seminars on quality-management in the Los Angeles area from Dec. 7 through Dec. 10.

Mr. Deming's theories were based on the premise that most product defects resulted from management shortcomings rather than careless workers, and that inspection after the fact was inferior to designing processes that would produce better quality.

He argued that enlisting the efforts of willing workers to do things properly the first time and giving them the right tools were the real secrets of improving quality—not teams of inspectors.

Initial Success in Japan

Mr. Deming was an obscure statistician in this country in 1950 when research he had conducted during World War II came to the attention of some Japanese

Copyright © 1993 by The New York Times Company. Reprinted by permission.

industrial leaders. At their request, he then gave a series of lectures in Japan on his quality-control principles, and he and his message were eagerly embraced. The Japanese, who lacked many natural resources or a colonial empire, were a receptive audience because they believed they would prosper only if they could sell products on world markets.

His advice to Japan made Mr. Deming the leader of a generation of specialists on product durability and reliability who were then sought by American companies trying to catch up to Asian competitors. But his renown in the United States never matched the reputation he achieved in Japan.

After the application of his methods brought enormous commercial success to some Japanese companies, the Japanese created a Deming Prize for companies that made striking advances in quality. Mr. Deming was described by many commentators as the best-known and respected American in postwar Japan after Gen. Douglas MacArthur.

William Edwards Deming was born on Oct. 14, 1900, in Sioux City, Iowa, to a family whose roots in America reached back to the Revolutionary War. He grew up in strained financial circumstances in Powell, Wyo., where his father worked as a part-time lawyer and land developer.

Mr. Deming attended the University of Wyoming in Laramie, working at odd jobs while he studied engineering. He later earned a master's degree in mathematics and physics from the University of Colorado and was awarded a doctorate in physics from Yale University in 1928.

Mr. Deming used the later years of his long career to try to reform American management, for considerable fees, sometimes as much as $100,000 a year from a single client. A tall, formal man who habitually wore frayed three-piece suits and spoke to senior executives as if they were schoolboys, he delighted in telling corporate chieftains who asked him to help solve a company's problems that they were a significant part of the problem.

"Can you blame your competitor for your woes?"he would intone to groups of corporate managers. "No. Can you blame the Japanese? No. You did it yourself."

"Can you blame your competitor for your woes?" he would intone to groups of corporate managers. "No. Can you blame the Japanese? No. You did it yourself."

Although the core of his method to improve quality was the use of statistics to detect flaws in production processes, he developed a broader management philosophy that emphasized problem-solving based on cooperation. He exhorted managers to "drive out fear," so that workers would feel free to make improvements in the workplace.

Mr. Deming denounced management procedures like production quotas, performance ratings and individual bonuses, saying they were inherently unfair and detrimental to quality. He said customers would get better products and services when workers were encouraged to use their minds as well as their hands on the job.

A frugal man in his personal life, Mr. Deming drilled companies to work relentlessly to reduce waste—anything from parts sitting unused in inventory to motions by a worker that did not add value to the final product. One of his daughters recalled that he had dated the eggs in his refrigerator with a felt-tipped pen so that the oldest would be eaten first and none would go to waste.

Success at Ford and Xerox

His blunt approach offended many executives, who turned elsewhere for advice. Yet some companies, including the Ford Motor Company and the Xerox Corporation, sent hundreds of their top-level managers to his lectures and seminars. "He said the only way to bring about change was to have direct contact with senior management," said James K. Bakken, a former vice president at Ford.

Well into his 90's, Mr. Deming maintained an active travel schedule, criss-crossing the country to conduct seminars and consult with companies he considered sufficiently motivated to benefit from his attention. He also lectured at Columbia University's Business School and taught continuously at New York University's Stern School of Business from 1946 until the end of the spring term this year.

Integral to Mr. Deming's approach was an emphasis on sensitivity to customer needs. Everyone has a customer, he said, either inside or outside the organization. Although he developed his methods in an industrial setting, Mr. Deming insisted that his approach was applicable to institutions generally, even those in service and nonprofit businesses.

After Mr. Deming's first trip to Japan, the Japanese Union of Scientists and Engineers assembled his lecture notes and published them as a book, "Elementary Principles of the Statistical Control of Quality."

Prize Established by Japanese

Mr. Deming refused to accept royalties from the book and suggested that the funds be used to promote quality. The group thus established the Deming Prize for achievements in quality, which quickly became one of the awards most sought by Japanese companies.

Yet Mr. Deming remained little known in the United States, where wartime efforts to establish statistical quality-control methods fell before the heading rush to push products out of factories. The prevailing sentiment in American industry from the 1950's until the late 1970's was that more quality meant more cost and that consumers did not want to pay for higher-quality products.

That attitude began to change when Japanese products with brand names like Sony and Panasonic drove the American consumer-electronics industry almost out of business while reliable, fuel-efficient Toyotas and Hondas gnawed away at the domestic auto industry.

One of the first large American corporations to seek Mr. Deming's help was Ford Motor. Ford officials persuaded him to visit their headquarters in Dearborn, Mich., in February 1981, when the company's sales were faltering and it was losing hundreds of millions of dollars.

Ford executives were expecting a slick presentation on tricks to improve quality. Mr. Deming, instead, insisted on questioning the company's culture and management philosophy. Eighty-five percent of quality problems, he told them, are the result of management errors.

"The first thing he said was, 'Do you have a constancy of purpose?' We were not quite sure what to make of him."

"We were sitting there with our pens poised to write down the prescription for what we should do about quality," Mr Bakken recalled. "The first thing he said was, 'Do you have a constancy of purpose?' We were not quite sure what to make of him."

Because Mr. Deming was sponsored by Donald E. Petersen, Ford's president at the time, the relationship survived the executive egos bruised by these early encounters, and statistical control charts blossomed in the company's factories. In the 1980's, Ford led the domestic auto industry in quality improvements.

No Formal Organization

As Ford's success became obvious, demand for Mr. Deming's services grew. He kept his client list short and refused to have anything to do with companies not willing to make top executives available to him. Among the companies that turned to Mr. Deming and his disciples were Dow Chemical, Procter & Gamble, American Telephone & Telegraph and the New York Times.

Unlike other quality experts, like Joseph Juran and Philip Crosby, Mr. Deming never built a formal organization. He continued to work as a solo practitioner out of an office in the basement of his modest home in Washington. But he did develop an informal alliance of followers and often required clients to hire a member of his circle to teach statistical methods and instill his philosophy.

Mr. Deming developed that philosophy in the 1920's and 30's while working at A.T.&T.'s Hawthorne manufacturing plant in Chicago and as a protégé of Walter Shewhart of Bell Laboratories. Mr. Shewhart was a pioneer in the use of statistics to control manufacturing processes.

Although his academic training was in mathematics and physics, Mr. Deming had mastered statistical theory and practice, in part by taking a one-year leave of absence from the Agriculture Department in the mid-1930's to study under a pioneer of the discipline, Sir Ronald Fisher of the University of London.

In the 1930's, Mr. Deming helped design the sampling techniques used by the Census Bureau. And in World War II he helped military planners apply statistics to the production of supplies for warfare.

Changing the Culture

Companies that sought to improve their quality by adopting Mr. Deming's methods often found they had to change their entire culture. To convince workers that managers really did want to enlist them as partners, many companies eliminated cherished management perquisites like special parking spaces and executive dining rooms because shop-floor workers found them offensive.

One Deming lesson to designers and engineers was to change the way they thought about quality. Traditionally, specifications for almost any physical object were set at a desired value with a certain allowable deviation.

Anything within the deviation limits was considered a good part, anything outside the limits bad.

But Mr. Deming's statistical studies showed that with complex products these allowable deviations could add up to a defective final product. The message to managers was that simply being within specification was not good enough. Processes must be continually honed, he taught, to reduce the variability from part to part.

Mr. Deming's first wife, Agnes, died many years ago. His second wife, Lola, died in 1986. He is survived by two daughters, Diana D. Cahill of Palos Verdes, Calif., and Linda D. Ratcliff of Potomac, Md.; five grandchildren, and three great-grandchildren.

John Holusha is a writer for The New York Times.

The 14 Points for Management and the 7 Deadly Diseases

W. Edwards Deming

Deming is most famous for articulating the ideas captured in his 14 Points and 7 Deadly Diseases. He revised his 14 Points in 1990 from the original version published in 1986, and to help you better understand the evolution of his thinking, the two versions are reproduced here. Sometimes the revisions make specific changes, and sometimes they just make the point more concise. The 7 Deadly Diseases were not revised and are included as originally written. We include this material here, appropriately, to once again affirm the wisdom of Dr. Deming's approach.

Origin of the 14 Points

The 14 Points are the basis for transformation of American industry. It will not suffice to solve problems, big or little. Adoption and action on the 14 Points are a signal that management intend to stay in business and aim to protect investors and jobs. Such a system formed the basis for lessons for top management in Japan in 1950 and in subsequent years. [What follows are the 14 Points, first the original version published in *Out of the Crisis* in 1986 followed, point by point, with the 1990 revision.]

1. Create constancy of purpose toward improvement of product and service, with the aim to become competitive and to stay in business, and to provide jobs.
   Revised Version: Create and publish to all employees a statement of the aims and purposes of the company or other organization. The management must demonstrate constantly their commitment to this statement.
2. Adopt the new philosophy. We are in a new economic age. Western management must awaken to the challenge, must learn their responsibilities, and take on leadership for change.
   Revised Version: Learn the new philosophy, top management and everybody.

Reprinted from *Out of the Crisis* by W. Edwards Deming by permission of MIT and the W. Edwards Deming Institute. Published by MIT, Center for Advanced Engineering Study, Cambridge, MA 02139. Copyright © 1986 by W. Edwards Deming.

3. Cease dependence on inspection to achieve quality. Eliminate the need for inspection on a mass basis by building quality into the product in the first place.
   Revised Version: Understand the purpose of inspection, for improvement of processes and reduction of cost.
4. End the practice of awarding business on the basis of price tag. Instead, minimize the total cost. Move toward a single supplier for any one item, on a long-term relationship of loyalty and trust.
   Revised Version: End the practice of awarding business on the basis on price tag alone.
5. Improve constantly and forever the system of production and service, to improve quality and productivity, and thus constantly decrease costs.
   Revised Version: Improve constantly and forever the system of production and service.
6. Institute training on the job.
   Revised Version: Institute training.
7. Institute leadership. The aim of supervision should be to help people and machines and gadgets to do a better job. Supervision of management is in need of overhaul, as well as supervision of production workers.
   Revised Version: Teach and institute leadership.
8. Drive out fear, so that everyone may work effectively for the company.
   Revised Version: Drive out fear. Create trust. Create a climate for innovation.
9. Break down barriers between departments. People in research, design, sales, and production must work as a team, to foresee problems of production and in use that may be encountered with the product or service.
   Revised Version: Optimize toward the aims and purposes of the company the efforts of teams, groups, staff areas.
10. Eliminate slogans, exhortations, and targets for the work force asking for zero defects and new levels of productivity. Such exhortations only create adversarial relationships, as the bulk of the causes of low quality and low productivity belong to the system and thus lie beyond the power of the work force.
    Revised Version: Eliminate exhortations for the work force.

11a. Eliminate work standards (quotas) on the factory floor. Substitute leadership.
Revised Version: Eliminate numerical quotas for production. Instead, learn and institute methods for improvement.

11b. Eliminate management by objective. Eliminate management by numbers, numerical goals. Substitute leadership.
Revised Version: Eliminate Management by Objective. Instead, learn the capabilities of the system, and how to improve them.

12a. Remove barriers that rob the hourly worker of his right to pride of workmanship. The responsibility of supervisors must be change from sheer numbers to quality.

12b. Remove barriers that rob people in management and in engineering of their right to pride of workmanship. This means, *inter alia,* abolishment of the annual or merit rating and of management by objective.
Revised Version: Remove barriers that rob people of pride of workmanship.

13. Institute a vigorous program of education and self-improvement.
Revised Version: Encourage education and self-improvement for everyone.

14. Put everybody in the company to work to accomplish the transformation. The transformation is everybody's job.
Revised Version: Take action to accomplish the transformation.

Enumeration of the Deadly Diseases

1. Lack of constancy of purpose to plan product and service that will have a market and keep the company in business, and provide jobs.
2. Emphasis on short-term profits: short-term thinking (just the opposite from constancy of purpose to stay in business), fed by fear of unfriendly takeover, and by push from bankers and owners for dividends.
3. Evaluation of performance, merit rating, or annual review.
4. Mobility of management; job hopping.
5. Management by use only of visible figures, with little or no consideration of figures that are unknown or unknowable.
6. Excessive medical costs.
7. Excessive costs of liability, swelled by lawyers that work on contingency fees.

KAIZEN, The Concept

Masaaki Imai

Kaizen, continuous improvement, is the foundation of Japanese management. This excerpt from Chapter 1 of this book contrasts the Kaizen approach to managing with traditional Western practices.

KAIZEN Values

Back in the 1950s, I was working with the Japan Productivity Center in Washington, D.C. My job mainly consisted of escorting groups of Japanese businessmen who were visiting American companies to study "the secret of American industrial productivity."

Toshiro Yamada, now Professor Emeritus of the Faculty of Engineering at Kyoto University, was a member of one such study team visiting the United States to study the industrial-vehicle industry. Recently, the members of his team gathered to celebrate the silver anniversary of their trip.

At the banquet table, Yamada said he had recently been back to the United States in a "sentimental journey" to some of the plants he had visited, among them the River Rouge steelworks in Dearborn, Michigan. Shaking his head in disbelief, he said, "You know, the plant was exactly the same as it had been 25 years ago."

He also spoke of his recent visit to Europe, where he had led a group of businessmen on a study of European tile-manufacturing plants. As they roamed from one plant to another, the group members became increasingly restless and dismayed at the "archaic" facilities.

The group was surprised to find that these plants were still using belt conveyors, and that not only the workers but even visitors had to walk over or under them, indicating a general lack of safety precautions. One member said, "There is no management if they don't care about the worker's safety." It is rather rare to see belt conveyors in modern Japan. Even if they are still used, they are designed so that people do not have to walk over or under them.

In spite of these observations, Yamada also noted that he had found the facilities at Western universities and research institutions far more advanced, and Western research projects rich in originality and creativity.

I was recently traveling in the United States with Fujio Umibe, chief specialist at Toshiba's Research and Development Center. Umibe told me of a recent encounter with a co-worker from one of Toshiba's outlying plants in Japan. Upon hearing that Umibe had not set foot in the plant for over ten

---

Reprinted from *KAIZEN: The Key to Japan's Competitive Success* by Masaaki Imai, by permission of McGraw-Hill, Inc. Copyright © 1986 by the KAIZEN Institute, Ltd. (KAIZEN is a trademark of The KAIZEN Institute, Ltd.)

years, the man chided him: "You really should come out and see the plant. You won't recognize it today!" By way of substantiation, I have been told that a quarter of the production lines at one Toshiba plant were changed while the plant was shut down for the week-long summer holiday in 1984.

These conversations set me to thinking about the great differences in the ways Japanese and Western managers approach their work. It is inconceivable that a Japanese plant would remain virtually unchanged for over a quarter of a century.

I had long been looking for a key concept to explain these two very different management approaches, one that might also help explain why many Japanese companies have come to gain their increasingly conspicuous competitive edge. For instance, how do we explain the fact that while most new ideas come from the West and some of the most advanced plants, institutions, and technologies are found there, there are also many plants there that have changed little since the 1950s?

Change is something which everybody takes for granted. Recently, an American executive at a large multinational firm told me his company chairman had said at the start of an executive committee meeting: "Gentlemen, our job is to manage change. If we fail, we must change management." The executive smiled and said, "We all got the message!"

In Japan, change is a way of life, too. But are we talking about the same change when we talk about managing change or else changing management? It dawned on me that there might be different kinds of change: gradual and abrupt. While we can easily observe both gradual and abrupt changes in Japan, gradual change is not so obvious a part of the Western way of life. How are we to explain this difference?

This question led me to consider the question of values. Could it be that differences between the value systems in Japan and the West account for their different attitudes toward gradual change and abrupt change? Abrupt changes are easily grasped by everyone concerned, and people are usually elated to see them. This is generally true in both Japan and the West. Yet what about the gradual changes? My earlier statement that it is inconceivable that a Japanese plant would remain unchanged for years refers to gradual change as well as abrupt change.

Thinking all this over, I came to the conclusion that the key difference between how change is understood in Japan and how it is viewed in the West lies in the KAIZEN concept—a concept that is so natural and obvious to many Japanese managers that they often do not even realize that they possess it! The KAIZEN concept explains why companies cannot remain the same for long in Japan. Moreover, after many years of studying Western business practices, I have reached the conclusion that this KAIZEN concept is nonexistent, or at least very weak, in most Western companies today. Worse yet, they reject it without knowing what it really entails. It's the old "not invented here" syndrome. And this lack of KAIZEN helps explain why an American or European factory can remain exactly the same for a quarter of century.

The essence of KAIZEN is simple and straightforward: KAIZEN means improvement. Moreover, KAIZEN means ongoing improvement involving everyone, including both managers and workers. The KAIZEN philosophy assumes that our way of live—be it our working life, our social life, or our home life—deserves to be constantly improved.

The KAIZEN philosophy assumes that our way of life—be it our working life, our social life, or our home life—deserves to be constantly improved.

In trying to understand Japan's postwar "economic miracle," scholars, journalists, and business people alike have dutifully studied such factors as the productivity movement, total quality control (TQC), small-group activities, the suggestion system, automation, industrial robots, and labor relations. They have given much attention to some of Japan's unique management practices, among them the lifetime employment system, seniority-based wages, and enterprise unions. Yet I feel they have failed to grasp the very simple truth that lies behind the many myths concerning Japanese management.

The essence of most "uniquely Japanese" management practices—be they productivity improvement, TQC (Total Quality Control) activities, QC (Quality Control) circles, or labor relations—can be reduced to one word: KAIZEN. Using the term KAIZEN in place of such words as productivity, TQC, ZD (Zero Defects), *kamban,** and the suggestion system paints a far clearer picture of what has been going on in Japanese industry. KAIZEN is an umbrella concept covering most of those "uniquely Japanese" practices that have recently achieved such worldwide fame. (See Figure 1.)

The implications of TQC or CWQC (Company-Wide Quality Control) in Japan have been that these concepts have helped Japanese companies generate a *process-oriented* way of thinking and develop strategies that assure continuous improvement involving people at all levels of the organizational hierarchy. The message of the KAIZEN strategy is that not a day should go by without some kind of improvement being made somewhere in the company.

The belief that there should be unending improvement is deeply ingrained in the Japanese mentality. As the old Japanese saying goes, "If a man has not been seen for three days, his friends should take a good look at him to see what changes have befallen him." The implication is that he must have changed in three days, so his friends should be attentive enough to notice the changes.

The belief that there should be unending improvement is deeply ingrained in the Japanese mentality.

After World War II, most Japanese companies had to start literally from the ground up. Every day brought new challenges to managers and workers alike, and every day meant progress. Simply staying in business required unending progress, and KAIZEN has become a way of life. It was also fortunate

---

**Kamban* as a word simply means signboards, cards, or chits. With just-in-time production, a worker from the following process goes to collect parts from the previous process leaving a *kamban* signifying the delivery of a given quantity of specific parts. When all the parts have all been used, the same *kamban* is sent back, at which point it becomes an order for more. Because this is such an important tool for just-in-time production, *kamban* has become synonymous with the just-in-time production system. The just-in-time system was first employed by Toyota Motor Corp. to minimize inventory and hence cut waste. The underlying principle is that the necessary parts should be received "just in time" for the manufacturing process.

Figure 1. **The KAIZEN umbrella.**

that the various tools that helped elevate this KAIZEN concept to new heights were introduced to Japan in the late 1950s and early 1960s by such experts as W. E. Deming and J. M. Juran. However, most new concepts, systems, and tools that are widely used in Japan today have subsequently been developed in Japan and represent qualitative improvements upon the statistical quality control and total quality control of the 1960s.

KAIZEN and Management

Figure 2 shows how job functions are perceived in Japan. As indicated, management has two major components: maintenance and improvement. Maintenance refers to activities directed toward maintaining current technological, managerial, and operating standards; improvement refers to those directed toward improving current standards.

Under its maintenance functions, management performs its assigned tasks so that everybody in the company can follow the established SOP (Standard Operating Procedure). This means that management must first establish policies, rules, directives, and procedures for all major operations and then see to it that everybody follows SOP. If people are able to follow the standard but do not, management must introduce discipline. If people are *unable* to follow the standard, management must either provide training or review and revise the standard so that people can follow it.

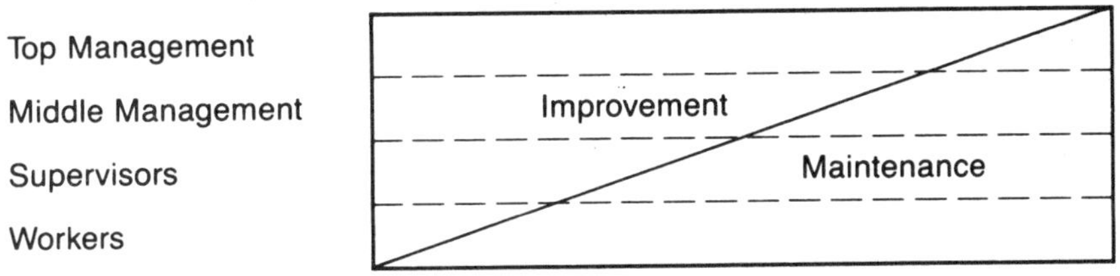

Figure 2. **Japanese perceptions of job functions (1).**

In any business, an employee's work is based on existing standards, either explicit or implicit, imposed by management. Maintenance refers to maintaining such standards through training and discipline. By contrast, improvement refers to improving the standards. The Japanese perception of management boils down to one precept: maintain and improve standards.

The Japanese perception of management boils down to one precept: maintain and improve standards.

The higher up the manager is, the more he is concerned with improvement. At the bottom level, an unskilled worker working at a machine may spend all his time following instructions. However, as he becomes more proficient at his work, he begins to think about improvement. He begins to contribute to improvements in the way his work is done, either through individual suggestions or through group suggestions.

Ask any manager at a successful Japanese company what top management is pressing for, and the answer will be, "KAIZEN" (improvement).

Improving standards means establishing higher standards. Once this is done, it becomes management's maintenance job to see that the new standards are observed. Lasting improvement is achieved only when people work to higher standards. Maintenance and improvement have thus become inseparable for most Japanese managers.

What is improvement? Improvement can be broken down between KAIZEN and innovation. KAIZEN signifies small improvements made in the status quo as a result of ongoing efforts. Innovation involves a drastic improvement in the status quo as a result of a large investment in new technology and/or equipment. Figure 3 shows the breakdown among maintenance, KAIZEN, and innovation as perceived by Japanese management.

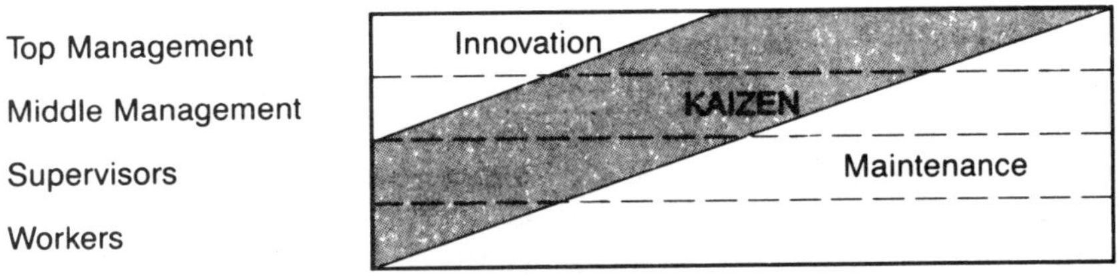

Figure 3. **Japanese perceptions of job functions (2).**

On the other hand, most Western managers' perceptions of job functions are as shown in Figure 4. There is little room in Western management for the KAIZEN concept.

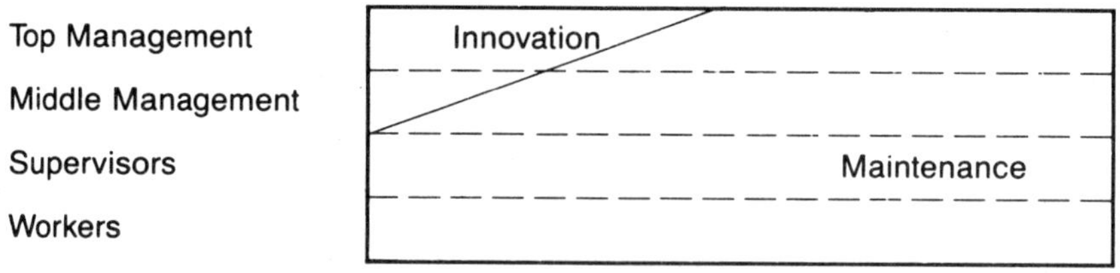

Figure 4. **Western perceptions of job functions.**

Sometimes, another type of management is found in the high-technology industries shown in Figure 5. These are the companies that are born running, grow rapidly, and then disappear just as rapidly when their initial success wanes or markets change.

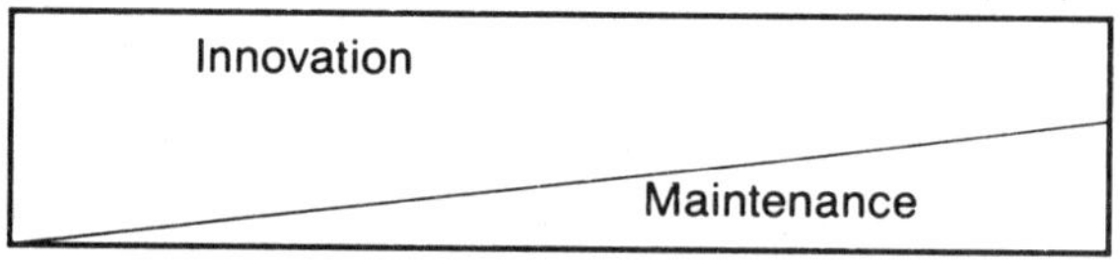

Figure 5. **Innovation-centered job functions.**

The worst companies are those which do nothing but maintenance, meaning there is no internal drive for KAIZEN or innovation, change is forced on management by market conditions and competition, and management does not know where it wants to go.

Since KAIZEN is an ongoing process and involves everyone in the organization, everyone in the management hierarchy is involved in some aspects of KAIZEN, as shown in Figure 6.

Top Management	Middle Management and Staff	Supervisors	Workers
Be determined to introduce KAIZEN as a corporate strategy	Deploy and implement KAIZEN goals as directed by top management through policy deployment and cross-functional management	Use KAIZEN in functional roles	Engage in KAIZEN through the suggestion system and small-group activities
Provide support and direction for KAIZEN by allocating resources	Use KAIZEN in functional capabilities	Formulate plans for KAIZEN and provide guidance to workers	Practice discipline in the workshop
Establish policy for KAIZEN and cross-functional goals	Establish, maintain, and upgrade standards	Improve communication with workers and sustain high morale	Engage in continuous self-development to become better problem solvers
Realize KAIZEN goals through policy deployment and audits	Make employees KAIZEN-conscious through intensive training programs	Support small-group activities (such as quality circles) and the individual suggestion system	Enhance skills and job-performance expertise with cross-education
Build systems, procedures, and structures conducive to KAIZEN	Help employees develop skills and tools for problem solving	Introduce discipline in the workshop	
		Provide KAIZEN suggestions	

Figure 6. **Hierarchy of KAIZEN involvement.**

The chapter goes on to make further distinctions between Kaizen and other management approaches and ideas. The book itself systematically explains the implementation of Kaizen in any organization. See reference section on a quality management library for the complete table of contents of Imai's book.

Quality May Not Be What You Think It Is

Philip B. Crosby

Crosby is one of the leading figures in the quality movement. His approach to quality management, with a special emphasis on the delivery of defect-free products and services that conform to specifications, is explained here.

There is not doubt in my mind that those who pick up this book are hoping it will contain some single piece of information that will permit immediate clarification and ultimate resolution of all their problems with quality. Perhaps some wise and perceptive sentence, like: "Quality is ballet, not hockey."

I wish it could be so. Unfortunately, the business of quality management is not all that easy. It isn't all that hard either, but it does encompass more than a single gulp of philosophy. It also requires unblinking dedication, patience, and time. The problem of quality management is not what people don't know about it. The problem is what they think they *do* know. It is made difficult by the conventional assumptions about quality that people develop over years of successfully making a living in some line of work other than quality management.

In this regard, quality has much in common with sex. Everyone is for it. (Under certain conditions, of course.) Everyone feels they understand it. (Even though they wouldn't want to explain it.) Everyone thinks execution is only a matter of following natural inclinations. (After all, we do get along somehow.) And, of course, most people feel that all problems in these areas are caused by other people. (If only *they* would take time to do things right.) In a world where half the marriages end in divorce or separation, such assumptions are open to question.

It is difficult to have a meaningful, real-life, factual discussion on sex, quality, or other complicated subjects until some basic erroneous assumptions are examined and altered. The only ones who are usually willing to take that step are those who are ready to admit they are in trouble, or have an intellectual interest in improvement. I have had hundreds of discussions with operating managers over the years and can state absolutely that their interest in quality is proportional to the amount of profit-deteriorating situations they are experiencing at that exact moment. I can't speak for their attitudes toward sex.

Reprinted from *Quality Is Free* by Philip B. Crosby, by permission of McGraw-Hill, Inc. Copyright © 1979 by Philip B. Crosby.

Given the chance to explain quality management to people who will listen, regardless of their motives, it is possible to make a case for becoming deeply involved. No other action a manager can take will generate improved operations, increased profits, and reduced costs so quickly with so little effort. But before all that can occur, we have to examine the thinking processes that lead some to believe that quality is merely goodness that always costs more.

No other action a manager can take will generate improved operations, increased profits, and reduced costs so quickly with so little effort.

In discussing quality, we are dealing with a people situation. The entire concept of quality management in this book is oriented toward that thought. People conduct the business of every company, whether it is a foundry or a hotel. Each individual performs an individual service. This service has been identified, described, and assigned by the management. If the service is constructed and performed correctly, it follows that the operations of the company should be successful. That applies to any industry or technology. I am not differentiating between manufacturing quality and service quality. All the quality actions we are talking about apply, regardless of the business of the company. There are technological differences, but they really involve only the last few percentage points of involvement. The programs defined in the following chapters permit you to deal with those exceptions in a planned fashion.

To understand those programs, and quality itself, in the most practical terms, it is necessary that we deal with five erroneous assumptions that are held by most management individuals. These assumptions cause most of the communication problems between those who want quality and those who are supposed to effect it.

The first erroneous assumption is that quality means goodness, or luxury, or shininess, or weight. The word "quality" is used to signify the relative worth of things in such phrases as "good quality," "bad quality," and that brave new statement "quality of life." "Quality of life" is a cliché because each listener assumes that the speaker means exactly what he or she, the listener, means by the phrase. It is a situation in which individuals talk dreamily about something without ever bothering to define it.

That is precisely the reason we must define quality as "conformance to requirements" if we are to manage it. Thus, those who want to talk about quality of life must define that life in specific terms, such as desirable income, health, pollution control, political programs, and other items that can each be measured. When all criteria are defined and explained, then the measurement of quality of life is possible and practical.

In business the same is true. Requirements must be clearly stated so that they cannot be misunderstood. Measurements are then taken continually to determine conformance to those requirements. The nonconformance detected is the absence of quality. Quality problems become nonconformance problems, and quality becomes definable. All through this book, whenever you see the word "quality," read "conformance to requirements."

If a Cadillac conforms to all the requirements of a Cadillac, then it is a quality car. If a Pinto conforms to all the requirements of a Pinto, then it is a quality car. Luxury or its absence is spelled out in specific requirements, such as carpeting or rubber mats. The next time someone says someone or something has "lousy quality," interrogate that person until you can determine just exactly what he or she means.

Quality is precisely measurable by the oldest and most respected of measurements—cold hard cash.

The second erroneous assumption is that quality is an intangible and therefore not measurable. In fact, quality is precisely measurable by the oldest and most respected of measurements—cold hard cash. Ignorance of this fact has led many managements to dismiss quality with a wave of the hand as something beyond handling. They are thinking of quality as goodness and spend their time having emotional discussions which make it impossible for management to take specific, logical actions to attain quality.

Quality is measured by the cost of quality which, as we have said, is the expense of nonconformance—the cost of doing things wrong. These costs are divided into prevention, appraisal, and failure categories. But they all are a result of not doing things right the first time. You can spend 15 to 20 percent of your sales dollar on such expenses without even trying hard. A company with a well-run quality management program can get by with less than 2.5 percent of sales, which is spent on the prevention and appraisal activities necessary to make certain the company is maintaining its standards of excellence. Measurements should be established both for measuring the overall cost of quality and for determining the current status of specific product or procedure compliance. These measurements should be displayed for all to see, for they provide visible proof of improvement and recognition of achievement. Measurement is very important. People like to *see* results.

There are those who will assume that some tasks are just plain unmeasurable. To them, you must raise the question of just how they know which people are the best at what jobs, whom to fire, and whom to reward. Anything can be measured if you have to do it.

The third erroneous assumption is that there is an "economics" of quality. The most-offered excuse managers have for not doing anything is that "our business is different." The second is that the economics of quality won't allow them to do anything. What they mean is that they can't afford to make it that good. This of course, is an indication that they don't understand quality and that they are just wishing you would go away. Pressed, they will relate some case of "goldplating," where a designer made a product unsalable by insisting on adding some luxury component. At that time, it is proper to explain the real meaning of the word "quality" and point out that it is always cheaper to do things right the first time. If they want to make certain that they are using the least expensive process that will still do the job, they should get deep into process certification and product qualification. These are part of a mature quality program. We mustn't get faked out by words that have no meaning, and "economics of quality" certainly has no meaning.

The fourth assumption that causes problems is the one that says that all the problems of quality are originated by the workers, particularly those in the manufacturing area. It is hardly possible to find a business magazine that doesn't have some sort of article about the falling standards of workers and how lousy the quality is on the assembly line. Few quality professionals can discuss product conformance for very long without emphasizing how people don't perform the way they used to. In reality, the people in the shops work as well as they ever did and much more productively than in the past. They contribute a lot less problems than their white collar brethren.

It is a matter of record that just as much crime is committed per person by middle and upper-class individuals as by people from the lower economic classes. In fact, the most expensive rip-offs, such as computer crimes, are committed exclusively by the well educated. Yet it is accepted without question by most people that ghettos produce criminals as routinely as tomato patches produce tomatoes. People "prove" this by pointing to prisons, where primary occupancy is by people from low-income backgrounds.

The real reason for this is not that most crimes are committed by the poor, but that the police tend to look for crime in areas where people are less mobile, more easily identifiable, and less liable to offer a significant defense. (Of course, there are a lot of people around ghetto areas who do wrong things. But almost every successful executive I have ever met claims to have originated in some "tomato patch" or other—so the tomato patch can't be all that bad.) The quality control people have much the same conditioning as the police. They march blindly past the defects of accounting, engineering, computer programming, and marketing on their way to the manufacturing ghetto to look for errors. And, by golly, they find a lot of them out there. It is an important place to look for ways to lower unnecessary costs. But the people in the manufacturing ghetto can contribute only a little to the prevention of problems because all planning and creation is done elsewhere. And it is the "elsewheres" that need attention when it comes to reducing the cost of quality. You will find the causes of most of our expensive problems at the other ends of pencils and telephones.

The fifth erroneous assumption is that quality originates in the quality department. Unfortunately, most quality professionals feel that they are responsible for quality in their company, so this assumption is really entrenched. However, the high attrition rate of quality management people who insist on being responsible for quality problems should make us think a little. People who insist that "quality problem" means that the quality department made a mistake of some sort are laying a clear, if inaccurate, track back to their teepee. They must learn to call problems by the names of those who cause them: accounting problem, manufacturing problem, design problem, housekeeping problem, front-desk problem, etc. Otherwise they will be held responsible for resolving problems over which they have no control.

Quality department people should measure conformance by the various means at their disposal; they should report results clearly and objectively; they should lead the drive to develop a positive attitude toward quality improvement; they should use whatever educational programs can be helpful. But they should not do the job for others, or the others will not change their evil ways.

This is the primary weakness of modern professional quality management. The desire to be actively involved in the creation, production, marketing and managing of a company's product or service is almost irresistible. But it only takes a little involvement to destroy the objectivity that is the quality professional's most precious possession. Once integrity is compromised, it does not return to its original pristine state.

It is not an easy thing to refuse a good friend who tearfully begs for just one more drink. But you must do so if you are to keep that person alive. Similarly, you do no one a favor when you create new "temporary" requirements on the spot. The designated requirements are either met or they are not. If we don't need a criterion, and the customer doesn't need it, then have the requirements officially changed—but go through the system and make certain that no step has been left out.

Now let's get to the business of what quality management *can* do for a company. It may be helpful to begin with an analogy. Each day, thousands of people board hundreds of airplanes and fly to dozens of cities. With few exceptions, these planes arrive and depart as planned and few injuries occur. Meals are served and consumed; movies are projected and viewed; drinks are offered and drunk; storms are spotted and avoided; and many personal services are provided. You are safer riding in a commercial airliner than sitting in your home.

However, suppose that these same activities took place with the pilots and other crew members not on the plane. Suppose the crew were in an office building somewhere, flying and managing the aircraft by remote control. Suppose they first issued each order to subordinates who then transmitted the instructions to the autopilot equipment.

Suddenly, we are faced with a new equation. The concept of flying has changed dramatically. Under the present system, the pilot goes along with you. If you crash, the pilot crashes. When the pilot is subject to the same fate as the passenger, he or she is bound to be personally concerned with every detail. But if the pilot were managing from an office, he or she would not crash when the plane went down. The pilot might be investigated after a crash, but it would never be all that clear whether the pilot, a subordinate, the system, or perhaps one of the in-flight passengers was at fault.

If you were going to travel under those circumstances, you would want to make certain that every plan, every control, every consideration was tested, controlled, and audited. You would want the most competent and professional management of every aspect of the flight. You would want to make certain that everything was done exactly right—the first time.

Quality management is a systematic way of guaranteeing that organized activities happen the way they are planned.

Quality management is a systematic way of guaranteeing that organized activities happen the way they are planned. It is a management discipline concerned with preventing problems from occurring by creating the attitudes and controls that make prevention possible.

Quality management is needed because nothing is simple anymore, if indeed it ever was. Our sophisticated business world is like those planes flying by remote control with instructions filtered through layers of subordinates. The people who really control activities do so from offices, laboratories, studios, and other remote places. The further the administrator gets from the administered, the less efficient the administration becomes.

Although individuals at lower levels can add to the deterioration of a process, there isn't a great deal they can do to improve a product or service. It makes you wonder why so much attention is given to improvement in those areas and so little to management and administration. If effective quality management is to be practical and achievable, it must start at the top.

CONTEMPORARY THOUGHTS ON QUALITY MANAGEMENT

TQM: The Only Source of Sustainable Competitive Advantage

Richard D. Spitzer

This article takes you through a step-by-step argument for why aggressively implementing TQM is the best way to "maximize a firm's value through maximizing customer satisfaction at the lowest possible cost." If you have ever wanted a theoretical justification for implementing TQM, this article provides a starting place.

With less regulatory intervention in an increasing number of industries and the privatization of many industries in the world market, the effects of Adam Smith's model of capitalism have become more widespread and obvious.[1] During the last 15 years, the United States has witnessed almost complete deregulation of transportation industries, such as airlines, buses, trucking, and railroads. Electric and gas utilities, financial markets, and telecommunications (including cable television) companies have also experienced dramatic changes in regulation. Furthermore, the political changes occurring in Eastern Europe are likewise an exercise in massive deregulation.

Reprinted with permission from *Quality Progress*, June 1993. Copyright © 1993 ASQC, Milwaukee, WI.

Most economists would concur that deregulation has, on the whole, been a success, demonstrating the superiority of the competitive market over government planning. Consumers benefit from competitive prices. For example, as a result of deregulation, the average airline fare dropped about 29%, trucking rates went down about 20%, and long distance rates dropped 40% to 45%—all in real terms.[2]

With increased competition, today's senior executives must continue to search for a sustainable source of competitive advantage that will let their companies earn abnormal rates of return—that is, profits that more than cover the opportunity cost of capital, sometimes referred to as economic rents. The principles of modern corporate finance, espoused by such financial economists as Richard Brealey, Stuart Myers, and Merton Miller, deliver the message that shareholder value is increased only through investments that earn economic rents. However, classical microeconomics suggests that, when an industry settles into long-term competitive equilibrium, all of its assets are expected to earn their opportunity cost of capital—no more, no less. If they earned more, firms in the industry would expand or firms outside the industry would try to enter.

Opportunities to earn economic rents typically arise only when a given company has some special advantage, such as being first in the market with a new, improved product for which customers are prepared to pay premium prices (until competitors enter and squeeze out excess profits). Other advantages can arise from patents, proprietary technology, or production cost advantages that competitors cannot match, at least for several years. Unfortunately, little can prevent others from imitating or even improving an invention or other potential sources of advantage. Competitive strategists insist that, for outstanding performance, a company has to beat the competition consistently. Unfortunately, the competition is equally aware of this notion. Consider the following:[3]

- *New product development.* Competitors obtain detailed information about 70% of all new products within a year of their development. Furthermore, patenting usually fails to deter imitation and, on average, imitation costs a third less than innovation and is 33% quicker.

- *Production.* New processes and incremental improvements to old processes are more difficult to protect than new products. Sixty percent to 90% of all process intelligence or learning ultimately diffuses to competitors.

- *Marketing.* Nonprice measures are usually deemed more potent than price changes, partly because they are more difficult to match. Opponents often react to a given maneuver by adjusting their entire marketing mix. These responses tend to be fierce, yet available data on advertising suggest that the moves and countermoves frequently cancel out.

Literature on business strategies is replete with accounts of why a sustainable competitive advantage is necessary. All of these accounts, however, beg the question: Which advantages tend to be sustainable and why?

Researching Sustainable Advantages

Pankaj Ghemawat states that sustainable advantages fall into three categories.[4]

1. *Size in the targeted market.* Size advantages exist because markets are finite. If a business can commit to being large, competitors resign themselves to remaining smaller. They fear that, if they were to match the leader's size, supply might exceed demand, making the market unprofitable for every company.

   Commitment to being large means making durable, irreversible investments. To exploit commitment opportunities, a business must be able to preempt its competitors. The business, however, has to be especially wary of environmental changes that can erode the value of its early investments. Size can be an advantage only when there are compelling economies to being large, such as economies of scale, scope, or experience.
2. *Superior access to resources and customers.*Advantage through preferred access to resources, information, or customers can give a business a sustainable advantage that is independent of size. The advantage persists because competitors are held back by an investment asymmetry: They would suffer a penalty if they tried to imitate the leader. Access will lead to sustainable advantage if two conditions are met: the advantage must be enforceable over the long term and it must be secured under better terms than those the competitors will be able to obtain later.

   Enforceability can come from ownership, binding contracts or self-enforcing mechanisms, such as switching costs. Without enforceability, the terms of access shift with the overall market conditions, wiping out any competitive differences. Enforceability, however, can be a double-edged sword. In pursuing sustainable access advantages, a company risks obtaining worse terms than those available to its rivals.
3. *Restrictions on competitors's options.* Restrictions on the options available to competitors might occasionally arise, hamstringing their ability to imitate the leading company's strategy. Rivals can be frozen into their current positions for several reasons including public policies, inability to defend their positions, and response lags.

   With respect to public policy, government intervention always affects the workings of markets—that is its avowed purpose. Often government intervention will go so far as to affect competitive positions within an industry. Government interventions include patents (which try to protect innovators from imitators), antitrust laws (which prevent large businesses from being as aggressive as smaller competitors), and handouts (which some companies get while others do not). A company that is on the right side of a public policy can exploit its position to build sustainability against companies that are on the wrong side.

   A business can also sustain an advantage if its competitors are restricted in their ability to defend their positions because of previous investments.

If imitation threatens the cash flow from those investments, disadvantaged competitors might stay put and defend them, thereby giving the innovator an opportunity to take the lead.

The final restriction of rivals' options comes from response lags. One business can be as efficient as another in terms of potential size or access without being equally prepared to make a specific move. In that event, the nimbler of the two can count on a lag in its competitor's response—in other words, a period of sustainability. A longer response lag is better because the existing advantages stretch out and opportunities to create new ones multiply. Lag times vary considerably. Rivals typically respond quickly (weeks) to price changes but respond much more slowly (years) to nonprice measures, such as research and development and quality improvement.

Easily duplicated strategies can lead to insecure competitive advantages. Competitors' replication of such strategies can quickly undermine a seemingly successful plan. Some success stories revolve around contestable advantages; a company's competitors might be stupid some of the time, but history indicates that the company cannot rely on the competitors being stupid all of the time. This is why sustainable advantage commands ongoing attention.

Evaluating Sustainability

While Ghemawat outlines intriguing factors that can affect the sustainability of a competitive advantage, a more useful analytical tool comes from research by David Feeny and Blake Ives.[5] Feeny and Ives discuss a pillared model that serves as an idea-filtration tool for assessing the sustainability of competitive advantages based on information technology. The tool, however, can be used for more extensive applications.

The model defines three pillars supporting sustainable advantage: generic lead time, competitive asymmetry, and preemption potential (Figure 1).

Generic lead time is the time it takes a competitor to approximately duplicate the prime mover's strategy given similar starting points. Lead time is the time span from when the prime mover launches the project (the prime mover must take some preliminary actions—performing internal and external assessments followed by planning—before the strategy can be fully deployed) until a competitor has a substantive response in place. The response might be immediate and the lead time nonexistent, depending on:

- Competitor discovery—the amount of time that elapses before the competitors become aware of the prime mover's competitive initiative.
- Competitor acknowledgment—the time it takes to analyze the initiative, determine that a response is necessary, and gain approval for a planned response.
- Competitor response—the time it takes to bring the approved plan to life.

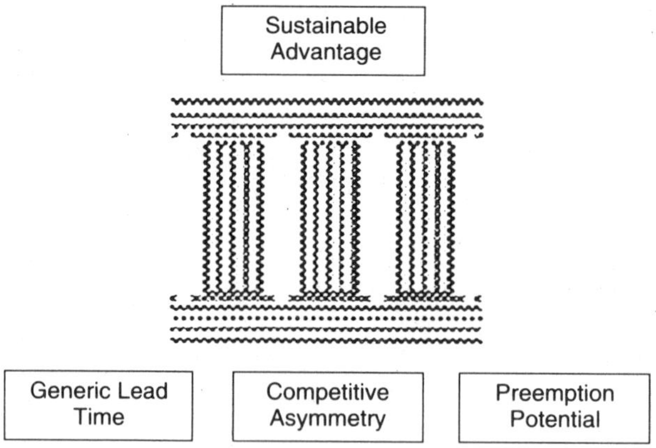

Figure 1. **The model.**

Obviously, generic lead time will vary considerably from industry to industry, depending on the level of competition. Highly bureaucratic businesses will tend to be more sluggish in responding to initiatives and will therefore offer more opportunity for lead time advantage to the prime mover.

The second pillar, competitive asymmetry, addresses exploitable differences existing among industry rivals. E.H. Chamberlin used the team "monopolistic competition" to describe industry competition between businesses that possess significant unique features within their resource and asset bases.[6] He demonstrated that monopolistic competition is associated with some industry participants achieving superior financial returns for sustained periods (i.e., economic rents). The implication is that heterogeneity is a potential source of competitive advantage, and companies should seek to base their strategies on such distinctive capabilities. Thus, a strategy that leverages differences between the prime mover and its likely followers makes it difficult or impossible for the followers to mount an effective response.

There are three categories of asymmetry: competitive scope, organizational base, and information resources. In essence, scope is the range of markets, locations, channels, and products within which the firm chooses to compete. Michael Porter notes that competitive scope can have "a powerful effect on competitive advantage."[7] Differences in scope can provide powerful starting points for leveraging various strategic initiatives. While competitive scope takes an outward look at the firm (focusing on its products, target markets, and degree of integration), a look at the organizational base (structure and culture) can also yield exploitable opportunities. In addition, information resources (existing data bases and knowledge bases) present a rich source of leverageable uniqueness.

The last pillar, preemption potential, is concerned with the potential of the prime mover to seriously preempt retaliation by the follower. In other words, once a competitor has retaliation in place, will it do any good? Some best known examples of preemptive successes include Merrill Lynch's Cash Management Account, American Airlines' SABRE system, United Airlines' APOLLO system, and more recently, Microsoft's Windows Operating System. The Federal Trade Commission's level of activity in its investigation of American Airlines and Microsoft reveals the significance of the preemption potential of both SABRE and Windows, as their competitors beg for government intervention.

Total Quality Management

Total quality management (TQM) has come to mean many things to many people. Unfortunately, it has come to be associated more often with statistical methods, such as statistical process control and design of experiments, than with a method of management. In its truest sense, TQM is a means of operating a business that seeks to maximize a firm's value through maximizing customer satisfaction at the lowest possible cost. Maximizing customer satisfaction at the lowest possible cost is achieved by continuously improving all processes within a company and empowering employees. One of the best descriptions of a TQM system is the system espoused by the Malcolm Baldrige National Quality Award criteria.

In its truest sense, TQM is a means of operating a business that seeks to maximize a firm's value through maximizing customer satisfaction at the lowest possible cost.

The argument for the proposition that TQM is the only source of sustainable competitive advantage is that TQM is not only a process that seeks excellence but also is the only way to achieve ongoing success in highly competitive industries, where there are a large number of suppliers relative to customers. Today, many companies claim sustainable competitive advantage through the use of isolated fixes, such as a computer system application or the adoption of a best-in-class practice in a functional area. Admittedly, many of these fixes have provided advantages to the companies, but these benefits are only temporary if the companies do not have continuous improvement systems in place. Furthermore, the improvements achieved through the fix might prove to be fictitious if the voice of the customer has not been incorporated into the improvement process.

As mentioned previously, Ghemawat proposed that there are three general categories of sustainable competitive advantage: size, access to resources, and limited options. While the argument for these categories appears to be valid on the surface, further analysis reveals that the underlying logic is flawed. Consider his argument regarding size. Size is not a cause leading to the effect of sustainable competitive advantage. Typically, size is an outcome of successful operations; a business cannot experience sustained growth if it is operating inefficiently or is not focusing on the customer. Therefore, size alone does not beget sustained advantage. This logic can also be used to invalidate Ghemawat's other two sources of sustainable competitive advantage.

This same logic can also be used to invalidate the monopoly argument posed by economists. Economists argue that monopolies are temporary phenomena unless the monopoly is imposed by the government.[8] If companies making up the monopoly rely simply on their large size and overlook the customers, competitors will create alternatives to the monopolized goods, making the monopoly obsolete. Therefore, regardless of their size, superior access to resources, or restrictions on competitors' options, those companies will not sustain a competitive advantage.

Does TQM help companies sustain a competitive advantage? Two means exist for answering this question: correlating highly successful companies with the use of TQM and evaluating TQM via the Feeny and Ives framework.

MVA, EVA, and TQM

To correlate highly successful companies with the use of TQM, a definition is needed for the term "highly successful companies." For the purposes here, it will mean those companies that have succeeded in maximizing customer satisfaction at the lowest possible cost, thereby maximizing the firm's value. Modern corporate finance theory provides the proper analyses for determining successful companies—i.e., those that consistently increase their value. Joel Stern and G. Bennett Stewart have introduced two metrics of performance derived from modern corporate finance theory: market value added (MVA) and economic value added (EVA).[9]

Conceptually, MVA is the market's verdict on the dollar amount that management has added to (or subtracted from) the funds that creditors have lent to the business and that shareholders have provided over the years in the form of paid-in capital and retained earnings. MVA is the absolute spread between a company's market value and its capital. It reflects how successfully a company has invested capital in the past and how likely it will successfully invest capital in the future. If investors, as a group, expect a company simply to earn the required rate of return appropriate to the nondiversifiable riskiness of its business and its capital structure, MVA should be zero. This means that the stock should be worth exactly what investors have contributed over the years. If investors expect returns to exceed a company's cost of capital, MVA will be positive. If management has not been customer oriented or has made other blunders, MVA will be negative. In other words, MVA measures how well corporations have created value for shareholders by satisfying their customers in the most efficient way possible.

The second metric of performance, EVA, is an innovative measure of annual operating results. Instead of looking at raw earnings, EVA considers the after-tax cash flow from operations minus the required rate of return on the capital used in the business. Thus, EVA is a measure of excess returns or economic rents. In theory, MVA represents the present value of all future EVAs.

While MVA is a measure of the value investors expect a company to create in the future, EVA is a measure of what happened in any given year. In essence, EVA tells investors whether a company is in the process of creating value. Increases in EVA should be accompanied by increases in MVA. These measures address the most fundamental question facing managers of all types of companies: How capably are managers using the capital in the business? Stewart notes that "The reality of the stock market is that all managers are in essentially the same business: putting scarce capital to its most promising uses. To increase their companies' stock price, managers must earn rates of return on capital that exceed the return offered by other equally risky companies that also are hungry for funds."[10]

The Performance 1,000—a new way of ranking companies based on the MVA and EVA metrics—rates the largest nonfinancial companies in the United States in terms of how much value they have created for shareholders.[11] It is based on the proposition that the stock market is a highly efficient arbiter of corporate performance. It provides both absolute and comparative measures of how well a company's managers have rewarded owners over time and for individual years. Rankings come out very differently when performance is the gauge. General Motors (GM), a high ranking company in measures of corporate heft such as total sales or assets, ranks dead last (No. 1,000) in the 1992 Performance 1,000, with an MVA of negative $23 billion—meaning GM's market value is $23 billion less than its invested capital. Wal-Mart, on the other hand, takes the No. 1 slot, with a $59.9 billion MVA, indicating that it has created about $60 billion in market value wealth for its shareholders. Sears, Roebuck & Co., which uses considerably more capital than Wal-Mart, ranks No. 994, with an MVA of negative $3.1 billion.[12]

Other financial sages agree that the Performance 1,000 is extremely useful in comparing corporate performance. Michael Jensen, a Harvard Business School Professor who is a luminary of modern financial theory, said "It makes sense to take into account the investment outlays to maintain and generate earnings and the required return on those outlays."[13]

Figure 2 lists the 50 most successful U.S. corporations ranked by MVA.[14] Quality professionals should be quite familiar with the corporations on this list, particularly Walt Disney.

Walt Disney, which ranked No. 27, demonstrates that management can make a powerful difference on value additivity. Chairman Michael Eisner is attributed to putting the magic back into the kingdom. When greenmailer Saul Steinberg launched his assault on Disney in 1984, the company's EVA was just more than $500 million—up slightly from where it had been in 1980. After nine years with Eisner at the helm, the MVA is up to $10.3 billion, pushed along by a string of hit movies and the management of the company's theme parks. Recent movie successes such as *Aladdin* and *Beauty and the Beast* should bolster this remarkable level of performance.

At Disneyland in Anaheim, CA, customers are referred to as "guests" and employees are called "cast members." *We Create Happiness*, the Disneyland orientation program handbook, explains the language of the land:

"Producing the Disneyland Show for our Guests requires the talents of a diverse group of people, more than 12,000 performing in more than 400 different roles. Although our individual jobs vary, we all work from the same script, speaking the same language—the language of Disney show business.

"You already know you've been Cast for a Role, not hired for a job, and you'll work either On Stage presenting the Show or Backstage preparing and supporting the Show. As Cast Members, we're Hosts and Hostesses to our

Rank	Company	Market Value Added (in millions)	Economic Value Added (in millions)
1	Wal-Mart	$59,977	$858
2	Merck	57,318	1,595
3	Philip Morris	55,036	2,349
4	Coca-Cola	49,419	871
5	Bristol-Myers Squibb	37,727	1,600
6	General Electric	37,185	544
7	Johnson & Johnson	30,455	651
8	Abbott Laboratories	24,500	614
9	Procter & Gamble	22,774	500
10	Amer. Home Products	22,516	989
11	Exxon	21,236	−4,736
12	Pfizer	20,749	98
13	PepsiCo	18,912	534
14	Microsoft	17,951	412
15	Eli Lily	17,603	850
16	Waste Management	17,351	−73
17	Kellogg	13,128	336
18	3M	12,814	140
19	GTE	12,697	−55
20	The Home Depot	12,441	107
21	At&T	12,227	−1,494
22	Anheuser-Busch	11,534	338
23	Schering-Plough	10,885	433
24	Sara Lee	10,859	64
25	Gillette	10,800	160
26	General Mills	10,354	288
27	Walt Disney	10,336	−7
28	Syntex	9,268	322
29	Amgen	9,189	163
30	Schlumberger	9,111	1
31	Emerson Electric	8,582	56
32	McDonald's	8,357	187

Figure 2. **The 50 most successful U.S. corporations ranked by market value added.**

Source: "The Stern Stewart Performance 1,000," *Corporate Finance*, October/November 1992, p. 33.

Rank	Company	Market Value Added (in millions)	Economic Value Added (in millions)
33	The Limited	8,220	124
34	Campbell Soup	7,957	119
35	Dun & Bradstreet	7,939	220
36	Novell	7,911	158
37	Du Pont	7,900	−3,232
38	Food Lion	7,878	110
39	H. J. Heinz	7,260	290
40	BellSouth	7,195	−917
41	Warner-Lambert	7,149	46
42	Rhone-Poulenc Rorer	7,086	374
43	Toys R Us	6,908	34
44	The Gap	6,907	143
45	UST	6,327	190
46	Baxter International	6,264	73
47	ConAgro	6,137	366
48	Boeing	6,020	1,112
49	Pacific Telesis Group	5,939	−406
50	Archer-Daniels-Midland	5,912	−9

Figure 2. ***(Continued)***

Guests—not customers—and they're an Audience, not a crowd. We don't have rides, we have Adventures and Attractions, each carefully 'Imagineered' to provide family entertainment unparalleled anywhere in the world."

The Disney attitude is not a facade—it is pervasive throughout the organization. All elements of the Disneyland park focus on the guest, including the park's design, the cast training program, and maintenance of the facilities. These elements make the slogan on the Disneyland sign, "The happiest place on Earth," no empty promise.[15]

Minnesota Mining and Manufacturing (3M), ranked No. 18, is another outstanding performer quite familiar to quality practioners. 3M excels in many areas, most notably new product development and technology transfer. It has a vast array of products, from Post-It notes to medical lasers. David P. Sorenson, executive director of corporate technical planning and coordination, explains that, because technology is the lifeblood of 3M, the company takes particular care to ensure all employees have access to it. All of 3M's scientists, engineers, and technicians belong to its Technical Forum, a technology fraternity divided into 23 chapters, each of which specializes in one field, such as polymers or imaging. This system of spreading knowledge around the organization has worked well for 3M.[16]

Emerson Electric, ranked No. 31, is often benchmarked for its asset management, which focuses on statistical process controls, just-in-time inventory, and make-it-right-the-first-time tactics. Steve Walleck of McKinsey and Co. notes: "Emerson does this more efficiently than anyone. A lot of people have recognized that Chuck Knight's (Emerson's chief executive officer) planning process—the way he operationally plans companies at Emerson—is a model for industrial business management. It gives them a competitive advantage with respect to lower costs, more reliable delivery, and higher quality."[17]

Merck, a well-known drug company that is No. 2 on the list, rewarded its shareholders with an increase of $22 billion in MVA during the 1980s while increasing its total capital by just $3 billion. Similarly, Merck's EVA exploded from $218 million in 1980 to $1.6 billion in 1991. That translates into Merck earning $1.6 billion more than its cost of capital in 1991.

Excellence in new product introduction has resulted in Merck's research scientists designing 18 prescription drugs that now boast sales of more than $100 million each.[18] Merck Sharp & Dohme (MSD), a U.S. pharmaceutical marketing unit for Merck, is considered the benchmark for employee training. It is consistently rated No. 1 in *Sales & Marketing Management*'s annual ranking "America's Best Sales Force." "We never stop looking for ways to train people better," says Jerome C. Keller, vice president of sales at MSD. "We have people who do nothing but look for new and better ways to train."[19]

At MSD, new recruits undergo an intensive three-phase training program that lasts an entire year at a cost to MSD of about $40,000 per trainee. Established MSD representatives receive three to five weeks of training each year, and they are tested quarterly. Customers are the main reason for the emphasis on training. "Doctors can make tough customers," said Keller. "By keeping them [sales representatives] at the razor's edge of medicine, they can converse with physicians in such a way that they are highly credible."

In 1991, a portion of MSD's training program was completely rewritten. "Even though the competition says we're the best trained in the industry," said Keller, "I don't."

General Electric, which is No. 6 in the Performance 1,000, is a well-managed corporation that focuses on satisfying customers. During the 1980s, chairman Jack Welch transformed the industrial giant from a jumble of more than 100 businesses into 13 streamlined units that all rank either No. 1 or No. 2 in their respective markets.[20] At the beginning of 1980, its stock commanded an MVA of just $860 million; by 1992, its MVA soared to $37.2 billion.

As a group, merchandisers ended the decade as the fourth largest value creators with an aggregate MVA of $60.8 billion.[21] By 1990, every dollar invested in Wal-Mart was worth $4.15. The Limited, another master of merchandising, vaulted from No. 382 to No. 50 over the course of the decade; in 1992, its MVA was $8.2 billion. Walter Loeb of Loeb Associates, an investment advisory boutique, notes "Retailers that scored high on the list should not only be considered merchandisers but also information processors. They perceive ever-changing customer demands and provide high-tech feedback to manufacturers."[22]

The Limited, Wal-Mart, General Electric, Merck, Emerson Electric, 3M, and Disney are but a few of the top performing companies that use TQM principles to operate their businesses. Although they might not call what they do TQM, it is apparent that they do rely on its key elements.

The Feeny and Ives Model and TQM

As previously discussed, Feeny and Ives evaluate sustainable competitive advantage using the three pillars of generic lead time, competitive asymmetry, and preemption potential. Consider the pillar of generic lead time as it is associated with TQM implementation. Feeny and Ives argue that the more lead time afforded by strategy being deployed, the better the chances for sustaining the advantage enjoyed by that strategy. The lead time in implementing the TQM strategy is relatively long because most companies have voiced a commitment to quality for marketing purposes (regardless of actual practice). Therefore, a proclamation of commitment to TQM will likely fall on deaf ears and raise minimal response from competitors. Acknowledgment and response are not likely to occur until the effects of this commitment have become painfully obvious—which can be as long as 10 to 20 years, as evidenced by the auto industry.

TQM will also help leverage competitive asymmetries associated with competitive scope, organizational base, and information resources. Implementing TQM is a difficult process, and the complexity of organizational and competitive issues facing the implementer grow geometrically with the number of industries in which the implementer competes. Thus, the more narrowly defined companies (in terms of the number of industries in which they compete) should be able to accomplish the implementation process much more expeditiously than their multi-industry counterparts.

Finally, TQM most certainly possesses preemption potential due to the typical sluggish response of competitors. Today's highly competitive markets are driven by the customers. These same customers are making obsolete the notion of brand loyalty, a practice in which they are expected to stay with the producer regardless of the superiority of competitors' products.

Today, customers are more informed and make purchases on the basis of value. Therefore, if a given competitor were to consistently outperform all others in an industry in terms of customer satisfaction, the economic buying power of the customers will squash those not performing up to current standards. Customers do not care about which company survives and which does not. There will always be entrepreneurs willing to replace the defeated. The point is that preemption potential does exist because of the velocity of information flow regarding outstanding producers and the economic power of value-seeking customers.

If a given competitor were to consistently outperform all others in an industry in terms of customer satisfaction, the economic buying power of the customers will squash those not performing up to current standards.

TQM: The Only Mechanism

TQM is not an option but rather a reality for companies doing business in a capitalist society. The discipline of competition arising from the free market requires the elements found in TQM: customer-driven quality, strong quality leadership, continuous improvement, full employee participation, management by fact, companywide application, quality and operational results, and systematic quality strategies, methods, and practices. TQM is the only mechanism to either sustain competitive advantage or survive competitive disadvantage. The capitalist model guarantees this much.

References

1. The essence of Adam Smith's model of capitalism is that, through the free market system where individuals voluntarily participate in economic exchange, both parties benefit and productive efficiency is achieved. That is, if an exchange between two parties is strictly voluntary, it will not take place unless both believe they will benefit from it. As industries become globalized and deregulated, the increasing competition among suppliers for participation in the marketplace heightens the consumers' power of choice and provides increasing discipline in the marketplace to the demands of the consumer.
2. "Conversations for the '90s—The Deregulation Experience," *Harris Conversations for the '90s,* Harris Bank, Chicago, IL.
3. Pankaj Ghemawat, "Sustainable Advantage," *Harvard Business Review,* September-October 1986, p. 53.
4. Ibid.
5. David F. Feeny and Blake Ives, "In Search of Sustainability: Reaping Long-Term Advantage From Investments in Information Technology," *Journal of Management Information Systems,* Summer 1990, Vol. 7, No. 1.
6. E.H. Chamberlin, *The Theory of Monopolistic Competition* (Cambridge, MA: Harvard University Press, 1933).
7. Michael Porter, *Competitive Advantage* (New York, NY: Free Press, 1985).
8. Ross D. Eckert and Richard H. Leftwich, *The Price System and Resource Allocation,* 10th edition (Hinsdale, IL: Dryden Press, 1988).
9. G. Bennett Stewart, *The Quest for Value* (New York, NY: Harper Business, 1990).
10. Ibid.
11. Sarah Smith, "The Best and Worst Performers in Corporate America," *Corporate Finance,* March 1991, p. 32.
12. Laura R. Walbert, "Capital Choices," *Corporate Finance,* October/November 1992, p. 22.
13. Smith, "The Best and Worst Performers in Corporate America."
14. "The Stern Stewart Performance 1,000," *Corporate Finance,* October/November 1992, p. 33.
15. Brad Stratton, "How Disneyland Works," *Quality Progress,* July 1991, p. 17.
16. Alexandria Biesada, "Benchmarking," *Financial World,* Sept. 17. 1991, p. 40.
17. Ibid.
18. Smith, "The Best and Worst Performers in Corporate America," p. 34.
19. Biesada, "Benchmarking," pp. 41–42.
20. Smith, "The Best and Worst Performers in Corporate America," p. 33.
21. Smith, "The Best and Worst Performers in Corporate America," p. 37.
22. Ibid.

Richard D. Spitzer is senior consultant with Booz Allen & Hamilton in its Dallas, Texas, office.

TQM's Challenge to Management Theory and Practice

Robert M. Grant, Rami Shani, and R. Krishnan

This thoughtful article from the Sloan Management Review *suggests that TQM requires not only the adoption of new practices, but a new mindset and understanding of managers' roles. It systematically contrasts traditional approaches to managing an organization with those suggested by TQM, showing the superiority of TQM for facilitating organization success.*

The success stories of total quality management (TQM) are well known. They include such companies as Xerox, Allen-Bradley, Motorola, Marriott, Harley-Davidson, Ford, and Hewlett-Packard. These companies committed themselves wholeheartedly to TQM; they made fundamental changes in their management practices and philosophies and improved product quality and company performance.

But more often, companies that have tried to implement TQM have not achieved such dramatic benefits. They may have produced some tangible improvements in product and service quality, but the quality improvement programs ultimately fell apart. In many of these companies, the TQM programs lost momentum because disagreements over goals and implementation procedures surfaced, upper-level managers turned their attention to other priorities, and employees became increasingly skeptical about organizational commitment to the programs. In other companies, quality programs clashed resoundingly with other strategic initiatives.

Consider the case of Kodak. In 1983 and 1984, Kodak embarked on a companywide quality campaign in response to increased competition, high silver prices, and an overvalued dollar. The company's "corporate policy quality statement" committed Kodak "to be world leader in the quality of its products and services. We will judge this quality by how well we anticipate and satisfy customers needs."[1] During the next few years, Kodak trained employees in statistical techniques, held annual worldwide quality conferences, involved top management in quality programs, disseminated reports of quality improvement experiences throughout the company, and required managers to formulate personal quality improvement projects.

Reprinted from *Sloan Management Review*, Winter 1994, pp. 25–35, by permission of publisher.
Copyright 1994 by the Sloan Management Review Association. All rights reserved.

Yet despite considerable improvements in operational and competitive performance, Kodak's disappointing financial performance led to increased pressure for more drastic corporate restructuring. During the 1990s, top management became increasingly confused by the dilemma of managing continuous, incremental improvement while making radical, top-down change. A $1.6 billion restructuring in 1991 incurred massive early-retirement costs but did little to yield longer-term savings in operating costs. In January 1993, Kodak appointed Christopher Steffen from Honeywell as chief financial officer in order to enhance shareholder value through more aggressive financial controls. Conflict between Steffen and Kodak's CEO, Kay Whitmore, led to Steffen's departure after eleven weeks, only to be followed by Whitmore's departure in August. Underlying the top management discord at Kodak is the conflict between two unreconcilable approaches to change management.

The recent histories of Alcoa and McDonnell Douglas point to similar conflicts. At Alcoa, incoming CEO Paul O'Neill viewed Alcoa's TQM program as a barrier to more radical change, while, at Douglas, the massive downsizing in 1991 and 1992 emasculated a once-ambitious TQM effort. These experiences support our basic message: TQM inevitably conflicts with established Western management practices. Its assumptions and theories are quite different from those underlying conventional practices, and therefore TQM will not succeed in a firm unless conventional practices are transformed. The tendency for TQM to create dissension within firms arises not only because TQM conflicts with conventional management ideas, but also because TQM conflicts even more violently with other contemporary trends in management thinking. If TQM is one new management paradigm forcing a rethinking of management concepts and practices, the other is what we call the "economic model of the firm," which is based on the principles of maximizing shareholder value. We argue that TQM and the economic model are inherently incompatible, and that companies will need to choose, implicitly if not explicitly, between the two. To that end, we explore the differences between TQM and conventional management practices, particularly those influenced by the economic model of the firm.

TQM inevitably conflicts with established Western management practices.

What's Different about TQM?

TQM comprises a group of ideas and techniques for enhancing competitive performance by improving the quality of products and processes. Although TQM has been disseminated throughout Japan, North America, and Europe, we are particularly interested in its profound impact on U.S. businesses since the early 1980s. The techniques and philosophy of quality management can be traced to W.A. Shewhart's *Economic Control of Quality of Manufactured Products*, published in 1932, but rapid dissemination of quality management in the United States did not become a phenomenon until the 1980s. W. Edwards Deming's appearance on a CBS documentary broadcast on 24 June 1980 was a turning point; "If Japan Can . . . Why Can't We?" triggered a surge of interest in the quality management methods that had originated in the United

States but that Japanese companies had applied and developed in the preceding twenty-five years.[2]

TQM's origins and pattern of diffusion are quite different from those of other management and organizational innovations that have swept through the business world during the postwar period, innovations such as management by objectives, time-based management, and the strategic management of core competences. Four distinctive features of TQM stand out (see Table 1).

Table 1. **Development and Diffusion of TQM and Other Management Methods**

	TQM	Other Management Methods
Intellectual Origins	Statistical theory: sampling and variance analysis.	The social sciences: microeconomics, psychology, and sociology in particular.
Sources of Innovation	Industrial engineers and physicists working in industry and government.	Leading business schools and management consulting companies.
National Origins	International: developed in the United States, transferred to Japan, subsequently diffused and extended within North America and Europe.	United States, then transferred internationally.
Dissemination Process	Populist: smaller companies and middle managers have played a prominent role.	Hierarchical: from leading industrial corporations to smaller, less prominent companies; and within companies from top management down.

■ *Intellectual Origins.* Most contributions to modern management theory and technique originated in the social sciences. Microeconomics is the basis for most financial management techniques (e.g., discounted cash flow analysis, security valuation, and accounting principles); psychology has guided the development of marketing techniques and decision support systems; and sociology provides the conceptual basis for much of organization design. The theoretical basis of TQM, however, is statistics. At the core of TQM is statistical process control (SPC), which is based on sampling and variance analysis.

■ *Sources of Innovation.* The R&D centers for most modern management ideas and techniques have been the leading business schools and management consulting companies. In contrast, the pioneers of TQM—Deming, Shewart, Joseph Juran, and A.V. Feigenbaum—worked primarily within industry and government rather than in universities. Their backgrounds were mainly industrial engineering and physics, and they had few links either to business schools or to consulting companies. Consequently, business schools have not been in the vanguard of the quality movement, and business school faculty have been students of TQM rather than the teachers. In fact, Motorola and Milliken opened their quality training programs to university professors in 1991.

■ *National Origins.* TQM's development pattern is also atypical. Most concepts and techniques in financial management, marketing, strategic management, and organizational design have emerged in the United States and subsequently diffused internationally. TQM, by contrast, represents one of the first truly global management techniques. It began in the United States, was developed mostly in Japan, and, during the 1980s, developed further as it diffused throughout North America and Europe. TQM thus integrates American technical and analytic skills, Japanese implementation and organizational expertise, and European and Asian traditions of craftsmanship and integrity.

The quality movement has been a populist one. Smaller companies were the original leaders in TQM.

■ *Dissemination Process.* The dissemination of most modern management innovations has been hierarchical. Typically, the pioneers are leading industrial corporations such as General Electric, IBM, and General Motors. Within companies, dissemination has been a top-down process from chief executive officers to divisional heads and down through the managerial ranks. The quality movement, by contrast, has been a populist one. Smaller companies were the original leaders in TQM. Nashua Corporation was the first U.S. company to employ Deming as a consultant. Other pioneers were Milliken, Florida Power and Light, Allen-Bradley, First National Bank of Chicago, and Marriott. The Growth Opportunity Alliance of Lawrence, Massachusetts, a consortium of more than fifty mostly small companies, was an early convert. Malcolm Baldrige National Quality Award winners have included Globe Metallurgical and Wallace Company.

In addition, the CEO has not always been the prime driver for implementing TQM within companies. Departmental and divisional managers have often been the initiators. At Ford, William Scollard, general manager of the auto assembly division, brought Deming to the attention of Ford president, Donald Petersen.[3]

Implications of TQM for Management Practice

To understand the broad implications of TQM, it's useful to consider how statistical process control, a technical tool of control, evolved into TQM, a philosophy that affects all functions of the firm, at all levels of management.

SPC's Impact

There is nothing revolutionary about SPC. It applies sampling theory to production processes in order to detect malfunctions faster than is possible with final inspection. SPC is consistent with Taylorist principles of scientific management; in fact, it represents a significant advance in scientific management.

But whereas SPC in its basic form simply determines when output is falling outside the boundaries of "acceptable quality," Feigenbaum, Deming, and Juran developed SPC into a tool for systematically analyzing variations and defects and, ultimately, for redesigning production processes to reduce variability. This has had important implications for the way work is done.

First, it implies that the individual operator rather than a quality control engineer is best placed both to identify unacceptable variation and to take remedial action. This leads to changes in operations management that reverse trends of the past half-century such as deskilling, specialization, and increased supervision. SPC requires operator training and gives the operator more responsibility for performance, innovation, capital equipment, and the work environment.

The individual operator rather than a quality control engineer is best placed both to identify unacceptable variation and to take remedial action.

Second, SPC's emphasis on identifying and correcting the sources of variation directs attention to the linkage between production activities. Implementation of SPC requires detailed analysis of the production process, typically using process flow analysis charts. As a result, the manufacturing process is perceived as a single integrated system, and operators and line managers have to communicate and share knowledge in order to diagnose and correct problems. This emphasis leads naturally to the view of a production chain as a series of supplier-customer relationships.

From SPC to TQM

Whereas SPC is a precise set of quality improvement techniques, TQM extends quality improvement methods to all functions and all management levels; TQM is a companywide philosophy of quality improvement. This philosophy contends that the firm's primary goal is to better meet customer requirements by improving the quality of products and processes. The implications for management are fundamental and far reaching.

■ *The Role of Management.* In addition to the decentralization of operational decisions, TQM typically increases participation in higher-level decisions among those in the lower echelons. These two trends—self-management and participative decision making—constitute a substantial change in managers' roles. Traditionally, managers, by virtue of their training and experience, were responsible for gathering information, making decisions, and applying the incentives and sanctions needed to implement those decisions. Under TQM, managers' priorities are reordered: their decision-making and control functions contract, and their roles as consultants and coaches grow. Thus, jobs become less specialized not only horizontally, but also vertically. The distinction between "those who think" and "those who do" is blurred.

Under TQM, managers' priorities are reordered: their decision-making and control functions contract, and their roles as consultants and coaches grow.

Diffusion of decision making is matched by diffusion of coordination. Under TQM, shop-floor teams become involved in communication and coordination with teams in other departments and units. Flows of information and communication become less vertical, more lateral.

These changes can have profound effects on organizational structure. Within the formal structure, they tend to widen managers' span of control, which permits the removal of whole layers of middle management and corporate staff. A flatter organizational structure results. In addition, an informal parallel structure may emerge. At Texaco, for example, a "corporate quality steering committee" and a "total quality task force," supported by a "quality resource center," lead a number of quality groups that have been established throughout the company.[6]

■ *The Effects of Integration.* Some of the most significant effects TQM has on an organization arise from its effectiveness in promoting coordination and integration of productive activity. Juran's contributions to TQM are particularly important in this regard.

To Juran, quality management is not simply the task of identifying and eliminating variation. It is serving customer needs. This has a number of implications. First, TQM focuses the entire company on customers; it gives the company one externally focused goal that all departments and functions can support. Many companies, such as Baldrige Award winner Globe Metallurgical, have emphasized increased employee interaction with customers.[7] By 1990, 24 percent of *Fortune* "1,000" corporations had one-half or more of their employees involved directly with customers.[8]

Second, this customer focus provides not only an objective for the company but also a mechanism that unifies processes. Serving the external customer may be viewed as the final link in a chain of supplier-customer relationships that extends throughout the company from R&D and purchasing to sales, distribution, and customer support. Under such a system, the requirements of the final customer drive a demand-pull sequence of relationships, where the goal of each stage is to satisfy the requirements of the subsequent stage.

Third, quality management is more than a unifying objective and mechanism, it is a philosophy. It is the company's *raison d'être,* and it integrates the entire management of the company.[9] Juran's approach links quality improvement and control with quality planning, thus extending quality management from the realm of operations into that of strategic planning. As a result, quality management is not the preserve of the quality assurance department or even operations management; it is the primary responsible of top management.

These organizational changes, deriving from the focus on customers, have had wide-ranging effects. For instance, the principles of identifying and measuring quality variables, establishing targets, introducing accountability, and promoting innovation and continuous improvement have been applied to work that has previously been considered virtually unmeasurable. Indeed, some of the most startling management changes and performance improvements have occurred in nonmanufacturing activities—customer service, sales and marketing, even finance. The application of TQM to Hewlett-Packard's marketing and sales functions is particularly interesting. The company developed a system performance.[10] The sidebar, "Accounting and TQM," explains how TQM has triggered fundamental change in management practices in accounting.

Another area that has been greatly affected is product design. Taguchi's work on building quality into design has extended TQM beyond operations

ACCOUNTING AND TQM

Of all the organizational functions, accounting has probably seen the most intense conflict between TQM and established management practice. Critics charge that, with the traditional accounting system, management does not focus on the "real" costs of poor quality because these costs are hidden in many different operating expense items. Accounting may capture internal rejects and customer returns, but it does not capture downtime that occurs because of poor quality parts and materials. It is also argued that the failure of conventional management accounting systems to include many of the benefits of improved quality results in underinvestment in capital equipment, new technologies, and training.

Accounting data focuses on reducing the cost of materials and direct labor. Typically these items are the least affected by TQM. Conversely, critical performance improvements made by TQM go undetected, including indirect cost savings arising from lower inspection and maintenance, reduced lead time to market, improved customer satisfaction and reputation, flexibility in making product changes, and future reductions in warranty costs. In the absence of broader-based accounting measures, companies have frequently failed to perceive the true benefits of quality circles and other quality management initiatives.* Tektronix, Hewlett-Packard, and IBM have introduced activity-based costing to uncover hidden costs associated with products and processes. Activity-based costing demands minute understanding of the company's operations, and its successful implementation requires that accountants actively participate in the operational details.† Another approach is to move to a set of multiple performance measures using a "balanced scorecard" approach.‡ Despite the development of these techniques, integrating the benefits of quality improvement into accounting systems and the guidelines of accepted accounting practices remains an elusive goal.§

*P. F. Drucker, "The Emerging Theory of Manufacturing," Harvard Business Review, May-June 1990, pp. 94–102.
†K. Kelly, "A Bean Counter's Best Friend," Business Week, 25 October 1991, pp. 42–43.
‡R. S. Kaplan and D. Norton, "The Balanced Scorecard—Measures That Drive Performance, Harvard Business Review, January-February 1992, pp. 71–79.
§R. S. Kaplan, "Measuring Manufacturing Performance: A New Challenge for Managerial Accounting Research," The Accounting Review 58 (1983): 686–705.

management.[11] Taguchi views quality from a customer performance perspective; he emphasizes consistent performance of the final product within specified tolerances. Building quality into design also requires a close linkage between market information and the design process. Quality function deployment (QFD) is an especially powerful technique for closing the gap between design and marketing so that the design properly represents the customer's needs and wants.[12]

The Challenge to Management Theory

We have shown how TQM induces extensive and fundamental change throughout the corporation. But TQM's impact goes beyond management practice. Embedded in the work of Deming, Juran, and other TQM theorists, such as K. Ishikawa, is a philosophy that embraces the purpose of the corporation, the role of work, and human nature. Inevitably, therefore, TQM also carries implications for the principles and theories of management. The conflicts we have observed between TQM and top management-directed plans for strategic change and organizational restructuring are more than a clash of incompatible *management practices*—they also reflect deep-seated incompatibility between the *theoretical principles* implicit within these practices.

Conflict within management theory is no new phenomenon. For much of the past half-century, management theory has coalesced around two broad schools: a "rationalist" school based on the principles of scientific management and the theory of bureaucracy and a "human relations" school based on the role of the organization as a social system, emphasizing psychological and social needs. The differences between these approaches have been caricatured by the labels "Theory X" and "Theory Y."

Some management writers have argued that TQM can bridge these schools. TQM's scientific approach is consistent with the theories of the rationalist school and its work design, and structural components are consistent with the human relations approach. Drucker argues that TQM's ability to link the warring schools of management arises from a critical element—information is fed back to individual employees rather than flowing up to management.

> *By aligning information with accountability, SPC resolves a heretofore unresolvable conflict. For more than a century, two basic approaches to manufacturing have prevailed, especially in the United States. One is the engineering approach pioneered by Frederick Winslow Taylor's "scientific management." The other is the "human relations" approach developed before World War I by Andrew Carnegie, Julius Rosenwald of Sears Roebuck, and Hugo Munsterburg, a Harvard psychologist. The two approaches have always been considered antitheses, indeed, mutually exclusive. In statistical quality control, they come together.*[13]

If TQM is bridging the historical divide between scientific management and human relations management, how do we explain the intensity of conflict we have observed between TQM and other strategic and structural initiatives of the 1980s and 1990s? The reason, we believe, is that the intellectual battlelines have been redrawn. As companies seek to respond to the challenges of our turbulent era, the primary conflict is no longer between "Theory X" and "Theory Y" but increasingly between TQM and approaches to management based on the economic model of the firm.

The economic model has grown out of conventional management theory and standard microeconomics, but it reflects several theoretical developments of the past two decades: agency theory, contract theory, shareholder value maximization, and transactions cost theory. All of these developments share a set of premises:

- the objective of the firm is to maximize shareholder wealth;
- individuals are self-interested, rational decision makers driven primarily by economic goals;
- the economic relationships between individuals are governed by contracts, which may be complete and short term as in the case of market contracts, or incomplete and long term as in the case of employment contracts and the "relational contracts" that govern intrafirm relationships; and
- cost efficiency determines contractual form and institutional structures, whether directly through managerial decision making or indirectly through the forces of competition (i.e., competition is a "selection mechanism" through which inefficient institutional forms are eliminated).

The result is a model of the firm that rests on clear theoretical foundations; shows a high degree of internal consistency; offers predictions that, to a great extent, are consistent with observations; and yields clear and unambiguous normative implications.[14] The corporate restructuring movement of the past decade is a clear example of these normative implications.

TQM, on the other hand, has no explicit theory. Indeed, one of the reasons business schools have been unable to comprehend TQM's power and potential is that it appears intellectually insubstantial. Deming's "Fourteen Points," for example, combine seemingly common sense principles of management ("institute training," "institute leadership," "break down barriers between staff areas," and "end the practice of awarding business on price tag alone") with a number of folksy, yet quirky, maxims ("drive out fear," "eliminate slogans, exhortations, and targets for the workforce," "eliminate numerical quotas," and "adopt the new philosophy"). However, we argue that a set of theoretical assumptions does underlie the principles and techniques of TQM. Together, these assumptions constitute a management paradigm that contrasts sharply with the economic model.

Organizational Goals

Basic to the conflict between TQM and the economic model are fundamentally different goals. At the root of the economic model is profit maximization, which has been redefined more precisely to mean maximization of shareholder wealth. This principle is legally sanctioned in the requirement that boards of directors operate public corporations in the interests of shareholders. The shareholder value approach has yielded a set of management principles and decision rules that extend well beyond its first fruits—the development of discounted cash flow analysis during the late 1950s. Shareholder value has extended into both strategic and operational analysis on the basis that all management decisions must ultimately be related to the issue of whether they are creating value for shareholders.[15] During the past ten years, shareholder value analysis has exerted a powerful influence on diversification, divestment, and financial strategies.

TQM views long-run profitability as an *outcome* of serving customers rather than as a driving force.

TQM emphasizes that the firm's primary objective is providing customer satisfaction. TQM does not reject the notion that a primary objective of the firm should be the pursuit of profit maximization, but it views long-run profitability as an *outcome* of serving customers rather than as a driving force. The risk of using shareholder value maximization to guide decisions is that the firm loses touch with its *raison d'être*—serving the customer. Deming is critical of short-term profitability as a guide to business performance and "the futility of management by the numbers."[16] Thus, although shareholders take a backseat in quality management, their long-term interests are seen as convergent with quality goals: "What value is a 25 percent increase in the quarterly dividend to a company that is out of business five years from now?"[17]

Convergence and Conflict

These differing goals are critical determinants of company environments. In the economic model, conflict is axiomatic: every individual seeks to maximize his or her economic welfare. For owners, it is wealth maximization; for employees it is maximizing income and non-income benefits and recognizing the disutility of work. Inevitably there is conflict over rent appropriation. Who receives the surplus that the firm earns? The traditional view is that it belongs to the firm's owners. Yet to the extent that human capital, rather than physical and financial capital, is the firm's critical strategic resource, the division of surplus is more complex than a simple conflict between labor and capital.

Quality improvement can lower costs and give consumers the dual benefit of improved performance and lower prices.

TQM envisages a convergence of the long-term interests of employees, shareholders, and customers. By improving quality, the organization creates a secure future for itself and its employees. This convergence encompasses both economic and noneconomic goals. Quality improvement can lower costs and give consumers the dual benefit of improved performance and lower prices. Such gains enhance the competitive advantage for the organization, thus offering economic benefits to owners and employees. At the same time, TQM recognizes that individuals are motivated by more than economic gains. As Simon argues, people are "socially dependent creatures" who are "tractable, manageable, and above all, teachable."[18] By encompassing the common interests of consumers, employees, and owners, and by taking account of social welfare rather than a narrower economic welfare, TQM may be viewed as a mechanism for optimizing the firm's contribution to society.

One of the human needs that TQM recognizes is the need to create. Quality is a form of perfection that has intrinsic value; a quality product is a work of art in the sense that it embodies the human quest for perfection. In this sense, TQM represents a return to the values of craftsmanship that have fallen victim to twentieth-century management methods. It is management techniques, rather than production technology, the are primarily responsible for the depersonalization of the production process in U.S. companies: financial management views the firm as a system for maximizing financial returns, marketing management focuses on ephemeral differentiation rather than on consumers' basic needs, and production management has been dominated by the imperative of cost minimization.[19] TQM reasserts the notion that products and services embody the effort, creativity, values, and collective personality of their producers. To this extent, TQM builds on the tradition of sociotechnical systems analysis, drawing in particular on the evidence from many Japanese and Scandinavian manufacturers that advanced production technology is compatible with traditional values of craftsmanship.

Organizational Design

These philosophical differences have implications for organizational structure. In the economic model, agency theory provides a central principle for the design of organizational structure. According to the economic model, each agent (employee) is pursuing self-interested goals. Therefore, the organizational structure must be designed to induce agents to pursue the firm's interests. The agency problem has been analyzed principally in relation to the conflict of interest between shareholders and top management.[20] However, the problem of agency is general to all manager-subordinate relationships. The implication is that the central management problem is to devise incentives and sanctions that align employee behavior with the organization's goals. Two solutions exist. One is to create a hierarchy of principal-agent relationships where, at each level, managers monitor subordinates' performance and apply rewards and penalties. The other is to introduce market forces within the firm; profit centers and internal contracting arrangements align individual, departmental, and firm goals by diffusing the goal of profit maximization.

But if we accept that quality creates a common goal for individuals who strive for social interaction and acceptance, then our organizational structure will be very different. It will allow employees to coordinate their activities for the common good without organizational impediments. Although little progress has been made in rigorously analyzing the implications of TQM for organizational design, many companies are reconceptualizing their structures. Several companies have inverted their hierarchical structures, reinforcing the notion that top management and corporate staff provide service support for the front-line units. Other companies have moved toward team-based structures. British Petroleum has conceived of its structure as a series of "eggs within eggs"—Quinn Mills identifies this as a "cluster organization."[21] TQM is also conducive to the interactive, nonbureaucratic structures described by Burns and Stalker's "organic" form and Mintzberg's "adhocracy."[22]

However, the critical difference in the conceptualization of organizational structure between the two paradigms is the economic model's adherence to a hierarchical structure with owners and their representatives at the apex and TQM's view of the firm as a system oriented toward serving customers. TQM conceptualizes the firm as a chain of linked processes whose end point is the customer. This emphasizes horizontal structure and coordination of activities rather than vertical structure. Moreover, it points to a departure from the specialization-based approach of grouping similar activities along functional lines. Juran's analysis of product "procession" in which "the product progresses sequentially through all departments, each performing some operation that contributes to the final result" provides a basis for a macro view of organizational structure.[23] Business process reengineering reflects this desire to align organizational structure with the business processes the company performs.[24]

The Role of Information

Within the economic model, the manager's primary role is to prevent and detect shirking by employees. Therefore, managerial access to information is critical to control.[25] Under TQM, information is also essential to decision making, control, and performance, but the information flow is different. If it is assumed that employees are motivated to pursue organizational goals and can make decisions about their own work, then a key requirement is to provide them with sufficient information and feedback to optimize their behavior and interactions. Computer networks have been an important element in making non-hierarchical structures technically feasible.[26]

Dynamic vs. Static Optimization

Like Kodak, a number of firms are implementing large-scale corporate restructuring. The economic model of the firm, with its emphasis on increasing shareholder value, underlies these strategic changes. Corporate restructuring is primarily a top-down process involving vigorous cost cutting though the elimination of under utilized resources, divestment of "peripheral" business and assets, a redrawing of the firm's boundaries through increased vertical deintegration and use of outside vendors, and a stronger orientation toward profitability through tight financial controls.

Both TQM and corporate restructuring are responses to the volatile business environment. Increased international competition, market turbulence, and technological change have necessitated lower costs, increased attention to customers, innovation, and faster responses. But these solutions—TQM and corporate restructuring—are quite different because their underlying philosophies have different orientations toward time.

The microeconomic principles that underlie the economic model are static, and the extension of static, constrained optimization techniques to multiperiod settings (e.g., DCF, multiperiod capital asset pricing) fails to capture the dynamics of complex systems. In several respects, the economic model's view of the efficient organization of production has extended little beyond Adam Smith's classic description of pin manufacture. Thus corporate restructuring emphasizes static efficiency gains through cost cutting, outsourcing, and divestment of underperforming assets.

In contrast, TQM emphasizes dynamic performance improvement. Juran devoted his 1964 monograph, *Managerial Breakthrough,* to analyzing what he perceived as the two modes of management: control and breakthrough.

Whereas conventional management theory is primarily concerned with control, breakthrough, which involves "a dynamic, decisive movement to new, higher levels of performance," represents the company's basic urge for survival.[27] It is the means by which managers, over the long term, make their greatest contribution to company performance. Hayes, Wheelwright, and Clark identified the contrast between management as a process of static optimization and of seeking continuous improvement as the critical difference between U.S. and Japanese management and as the fundamental flaw in the "modern management methods" developed and applied in the United States during the greater part of the post-war era.[28]

One of the dangers of the economic model is that it has reinforced conventional preoccupation with sources of static efficiency at a time when some of the most influential ideas relating to the strategy, structure, and competitive performance of firms, including population ecology and resource-based theory, are concerned with competition as a dynamic process. Recent work on resources and corporate capabilities places special emphasis on dynamic aspects of competitive advantage—investing in irreplaceable, nontransferable assets and upgrading the basis of competitive advantage through innovation and the development of new skills.[29] These ideas are quite compatible with the dynamic orientation of the TQM paradigm.

Dynamic and static optimization also have different implications for organizational structure. Managing for maximization of productivity and minimization of cost in the short term imply the following: specialization; individual incentives linked to quantitative performance in the short term; parsimony in investment and the use of assets; the imposition of short-term financial targets on divisions and business units; and active management of the asset portfolio and divestment of poorly performing assets. By contrast, managing for innovation involves creating organizational conditions conducive to the creation and diffusion of new knowledge.

The Blurring of Boundaries

In the economic model, the distinction between firms and markets is central to analysis of the capitalist market economy. The price mechanism (the "invisible hand") governs external transactions, and administrative processes (the "visible hand") govern internal transactions. The distinction between firms and markets ("islands of conscious power in a sea of market transactions"[30]) is determined by relative costs. Where the administrative costs of hierarchy are less than the transaction costs of market exchange, transactions will become internalized within firms.

TQM's focus on customer requirements blurs the boundaries between companies. Both suppliers and distributors are part of the production system, and conventional contracts are an inadequate basis for governing their relationships. TQM requires continual interaction, including information sharing and collaboration in technology and design. Within companies, coordination does not consist simply of managerially directed rules and decisions; it is also a process of interaction involving managerial direction, market relations (e.g.,

Table 2. **Emerging Management Paradigms: TQM and the Economic Model of the Firm**

	TQM	Economic Model of the Firm
Organizational Goals	Serving customers needs by supplying goods and services of the highest possible quality.	Maximizing profit (i.e., of shareholder wealth).
Individual Goals	Individuals motivated by economic, social, and psychological goals relating to personal fulfillment and social acceptance.	Individuals motivated only by economic goals: maximization of income and minimization of effort.
Time Orientation	Dynamic: innovation and continual improvement.	Static optimization: maximizing the present value of net cash flow by maximizing revenue and minimizing cost.
Coordination and Control	Employees are trustworthy and are experts in their jobs—hence emphasis on self-management. Employees are capable of coordinating on a voluntary basis.	Managers have the expertise to coordinate and direct subordinates. Agency problems necessitate monitoring of subordinates and applying incentives to align objectives.
Role of Information	Open and timely information flows are critical to self-management, horizontal coordination, and quest for continual improvement.	Information system matches hierarchical structure: key functions are to support managers' decision making and monitor subordinates.
Principles of Work Design	System-based optimization with emphasis on dynamic performance.	Productivity maximization by specializing on the basis of comparative advantage.
Firm Boundaries	Issues of supplier-customer relations, information flow, and dynamic coordination common to transactions within and between firms.	Clear distinction between markets and firms as governance mechanisms. Firm boundaries determined by transaction costs.

serving the internal customer), and voluntary collaboration. (Table 2 summarizes the differences between TQM and the economic model of the firm.)

Such boundary blurring suggests the need to reconsider the nature and functions of corporations and the theory of organization. But on a practical level, manifestations of boundary blurring have included the following:

- the replacement of arms's-length supplier-customer relationships (which are based on competitive bidding, aggressive negotiation of contract terms, maximization of bargaining power, and strategic games involving secrecy and bluff) with dependent relationships;

- the emergence of collaborative partnerships and internal networks within firms in place of hierarchically governed relationships;
- the growth of formal collaboration between firms, including franchises, joint ventures, and various types of licensing agreements; and
- the growth of informal collaboration between firms in bilateral relationships and multilateral network relationships.

Conclusion

Why have experiences with TQM been so variable? At Harley-Davidson and Xerox, TQM has transformed competitive performance; in many other companies, TQM efforts have spluttered and died. Given the nature of TQM, as described in this paper, we maintain that TQM is a revolutionary philosophy that requires radical and pervasive change within the firm. The very popularity of TQM has impeded top management's deep understanding of its ideology and consequences.

TQM's origins and dissemination pattern are quite different from those of almost every other management innovation of the past half-century, and it has bypassed the leading business schools and management consulting companies. As a result, many companies have misunderstood and misapplied it, and it has not received the careful academic scrutiny that has served to give credence and authority to other innovations in organization and management.

TQM calls for systemic changes in management practice, including the redesign of work, the redefinition of managerial roles, the redesign of organizational structures, the learning of new skills by employees at all levels, and the reorientation of organizational goals. Implementation of TQM therefore provides challenges similar to those involved in the management of other revolutionary transitions. The management problem with TQM is analogous to the problems associated with introducing representative democracy into former autocracies and introducing equal rights into racially segregated societies: Once we get it going, how do we keep the lid on it? When the upper echelons of management relinquish their traditional rights and powers, can the process be arrested or reversed? The long TQM road takes companies into a new landscape where authority, decisions, and innovation are much more widely shared. Once a company enters this new territory, it is hard for top management to respond to circumstances that seem to demand sudden strategic shifts. As McDonnell Douglas and Kodak have found, several years of TQM make it difficult for top managers to inaugurate rapid downsizing or divestment.

Implementation of TQM provides challenges similar to those involved in the management of other revolutionary transitions.

Thus the first stage in managing companywide TQM programs is to recognize their revolutionary character. The companies that have been most successful in obtaining long-lasting performance benefits from TQM—Xerox,

Hewlett-Packard, Nashua, Banc One, and Allen-Bradley—have permitted their quality programs to drive systemwide changes. Top managers must become agents of change, redefining management roles and structure and accepting their own loss of power in the process. Attempting to foster quality improvement in production operations and the lower echelons of the organization while maintaining conventional top-down strategic planning, financial control systems, and active asset management inevitably creates conflict.

But TQM's revolutionary impact goes still deeper. TQM represents a challenge not only to conventional management practices but also to the assumptions and theories on which those practices are based. The theories underlying TQM and the economic model of the firm are inherently incompatible. There are a few examples of companies in which corporate restructuring and TQM have coexisted, but closer examination suggests that the approaches have been used sequentially rather than simultaneously.

Western managers have traditionally prided themselves on being pragmatic, eclectic, and open-minded, but the conflicts between these philosophies suggest that managers and their companies will increasingly need to choose, implicitly if not explicitly, to which school they belong.

References

We acknowledge financial support for our research from Northern Telecom's University Interaction Program.

1. Kodak Annual Report, 1984.

2. For an account of the origins and development of quality managment, see: D.A. Garvin, *Managing Quality: The Strategic and Competitive Edge* (New York: Free Press, 1988).

3. M. Walton, *The Deming Management Method* (New York: Dodd, Mead. 1986), pp. 140–144.

4. Ibid.

5. G. Bushe and A.B. Shani, *Parallel Learning Structures* (Reading, Massachusetts: Addison-Wesley, 1991).

6. *Annual Report, 1988,* Texaco, Inc. (White Plains, New York, 1989), p. 24.

7. B. Rayner, "Trial-by-Fire Transformation: An Interview with Globe Metallurgical's Arden C. Sims," *Harvard Business Review,* May-June 1992, pp. 117–129.

8. E.E. Lawler, S.A. Mohrman, and G.E. Ledford, *Employee Involvement and Total Quality Management* (San Francisco, Jossey-Bass, 1992), p. 96.

9. J.M. Juran, *Quality Control Handbook* (New York: McGraw Hill, 1974).

10. *HP Measures of Marketing Excellence,* Hewlett-Packard, January 1989.

11. G. Taguchi and D. Clausing, "Robust Quality," *Harvard Business Review,* January-February 1990, pp. 65–75.

12. W. Lazer, S. Murata, and H. Kosaka, "Japanese Marketing: Toward a Better Understanding," *Journal of Marketing* 49 (1985): 69–81.

13. P.F. Drucker, "The Emerging Theory of Manufacturing," *Harvard Business Review,* May-June 1990, pp. 94–102.

14. The best exposition of the economic model of the firm can be found in: P. Milgrom and J. Roberts, *Economics, Organization, and Management* (Englewood Cliffs, New Jersey: Prentice-Hall, 1992).

15. A. Rappaport, *Creating Shareholder Value: The New Standard for Performance* (New York: Free Press, 1986); and T. Copeland, T. Koller, and J. Murrin, *Valuation: Measuring and Managing the Value of Companies* (New York: John Wiley, 1990).

16. See Walton (1986), p. 55.

17. Ibid.

18. H. Simon, "Organizations and Markets," *Journal of Economic Perspectives* 5 (1991): 35.

19. R. Hayes, S. Wheelwright, and K. Clark, *Dynamic Manufacturing: Creating the Learning Organization* (New York: Free Press, 1988).

20. M.C. Jensen, "The Eclipse of the Public Corporation," *Harvard Business Review,* September-October 1989, pp. 61–75.

21. See R.M. Grant, *Strategic Change and Restructuring within the Oil Industry* (Milan: Franco Angeli, 1993), pp. 128–150; and D. Quinn Mills, *Rebirth of the Corporation* (New York: Free Press, 1991), pp. 91–107.

22. T. Burns and G.M. Stalker, *The Management of Innovation* (London: Tavistock, 1961); and H. Mintzberg, *The Structuring of Organizations* (Englewood Cliffs, New Jersey: Prentice-Hall, 1979).

23. Juran (1974), pp. 203–204.

24. M. Hammer and J. Champy, *Reengineering the Corporation: A Manifesto for Business Revolution* (New York: HarperBusiness, 1993).

25. A. Alchian and H. Demsetz, "Production, Information Costs, and Economic Organization," *American Economic Review* 62 (1972), pp. 777–795.

26. J.F. Rockart and J.E. Short, "IT in the 1990s: Managing Organizational Interdependence," *Sloan Management Review,* Winter 1989, pp. 7–17.

27. J.M. Juran, *Managerial Breakthrough* (New York: McGraw-Hill, 1964).

28. K. Clark, R. Hayes, and S. Wheelwright, *Dynamic Manufacturing* (New York: Free Press, 1988).

29. R.M. Grant, "The Resource-Based Theory of Competitive Advantage: Implications for Strategy Formulation," *California Management Review,* Spring 1991, pp. 114–135.

30. R. Coase, "The Nature of the Firm," *Economica* 4 (1937): 386–405.

Robert M. Grant is professor of management, School of Business Administration, Georgetown University. Rami Shani is professor of management and R. Krishman is professor of marketing, California Polytechnic State University.

PART TWO

Quality by Industry

While quality management principles remain the same for all types of organizations, different industries apply these principles in ways particular to their businesses. Part Two provides a diverse collection of articles on how quality management is making a difference in various industries. We have clustered this collection around *manufacturing, services*, and *the public sector*. In selecting articles for each sector, we sought a balance between principles and applications, with an emphasis on the application of these ideas.

Another goal we have had in gearing up for *The Quality Yearbook* has been to garner the assistance of consulting editors to review and briefly summarize their perspective on the application of quality principles in their areas. We are fortunate this year to have had the assistance of experts in manufacturing, services, and the four public sector areas covered in Part Two. Each of them has written an original article for the 1995 edition: B. Joseph Pine II (consultant and author of *Mass Customization*) for manufacturing; Ron Zemke (author, consultant, and senior editor at *Training* Magazine) for services; Joe Sensenbrenner (consultant and former Madison, WI, mayor) for government; Sherry Bright (senior vice president for strategy and quality implementation at a major health care delivery system in Louisiana) for health care; Gabriel Massaro, Nancy Roche, and David Bayless (consultants in quality education) for K–12 education; and Ron Heilman (head of the Center for Quality and Productivity at the University of Wisconsin, Milwaukee) for higher education. We commend their articles to you. They provide wonderful perspective on the value of the quality approach to succeeding in their respective areas.

In the rest of Part Two, here's what you'll find:

Manufacturing

The two most studied and discussed automotive manufacturing operations in the United States today are Chrysler and Saturn. We have included two articles that provide a comprehensive review of how these companies are using the principles of TQM to make their internal operations more efficient (and humane) places to work and to deliver cars that meet and exceed customer expectations. You will also find articles on how a company that supplies boxes for consumer products and a chemical company are implementing TQM in their operations.

Services

Besides Ron Zemke's piece, we have selected three other articles for this section, two of which speak to the importance of managing the interface between the company and its customers. This interface provides the impressions on which customers will make judgments about quality excellence and, to sustain market position, it is vital that the impression be positive. You will also find an article profiling AT&T's Universal Card Service, which makes customer delight the basis of all its actions.

Public Sector

Organizations of all types are now beginning to appreciate the value of TQM principles for helping them fulfill their mission. For the four areas of the public sector, besides the contributions of our consulting editors, we have selected a variety of pieces that demonstrate how quality management is being applied in these areas. Some articles we especially recommend include Vice President Al Gore's introduction to the National Productivity Review in the government section, the piece on Shodo Management and its relevance to health care, and the review of TQM at Babson College.

* * *

For additional material on TQM by industry, please consult the bibliography in Part Four. It includes a detailed, annotated list of materials across several industries, of which the articles in Part Two are only a small sample.

Challenges to Total Quality Management in Manufacturing

B. Joseph Pine II

This original article by Joe Pine, consulting editor in manufacturing and author of Mass Customization: The New Frontier in Business Competition, *discusses the challenge to manufacturers of mass customization and the importance of understanding this approach as a natural part of the practice of TQM.*

Much of the press on quality in the past year has been surprisingly negative. Several past exemplars of Total Quality Management have fallen on hard times, such as Wallace Co., Globe Metallurgy, and the IBM AS/400 division—quality award winners all. While thousands of manufacturing companies have successfully embraced TQM, the *Wall Street Journal*, *Business Week*, *Fortune*, and other publications have reported on scores of manufacturers that have failed to achieve any lasting gains and, indeed, may be falling even further behind their competitors. The corporate mood today appears to be one of increasing dissatisfaction with TQM, particularly in relation to the seemingly unbounded potential of each new management idea that hits the boardroom.

Reengineering and mass customization are two such ideas to which many manufacturers are turning, and are the ones that seem to provide the greatest challenge to the TQM philosophy. This article will help reduce the confusion surrounding these concepts and provide TQM adherents with a way of meeting the challenges without throwing out the philosophy.

Total Quality Management

TQM is a philosophy or paradigm that, as John Woods described in the lead article of the 1994 edition of *The Quality Yearbook*, portrays how a company operates, affects how people in the company behave, and explains the results they get. Its basic tenets are (1) that a business exists to satisfy customers; (2) the company is a system that transforms inputs to create products that customers value; and (3) the system's processes have to be explicitly managed well to deliver what customers perceive to be high quality products.[1]

Described in this way, Total Quality Management seems almost unassailable. Who could disagree with the above? But if so, why has TQM lost some of its luster in the past year or so, at least with the popular business press? A number of stories are behind the headlines:

- *Implementation.* Despite the tremendous progress made across a wide variety of companies, many managers and executives still "don't get it." They don't understand that TQM is a philosophy, not a set of techniques and technologies that can be picked up and applied willy-nilly. When this happens, training is given short-shrift, the need for buy-in discounted, and isolated improvements remain unconnected.

- *Follow-through.* Quality is a journey, one on which managers must remain diligent and unswerving to maintain success. TQM cannot be set in motion and then left to its own devices; it requires constant care and feeding lest old ways of doing business come home to roost. But the difficulty and time it takes to successfully nurture a long-lasting TQM program is resulting in growing impatience, particularly among senior executives.

- *Connected.* TQM must be connected to any manufacturer's *raison d'etre*: to profitably provide products that customers value. Some companies chase awards rather than customer wants and needs, or pursue internally generated numerical targets rather than first understand what customers truly value. In a recent article on this issue, *Business Week* discussed the quality program at Varian Associates Inc., a maker of scientific equipment, which made tremendous progress on its internally defined quality measures only to find true customer service—and profits—wane.[2]

- *Differentiation.* For the very reason that many companies have made tremendous progress, within many industries high quality no longer has the distinctiveness required to be a clear differentiator in the marketplace. Many managers report that manufacturing defect-free products—the traditional way of defining quality—is now "jacks to open" in the industry. Even Joseph Juran has stated that defect rates are becoming so low in some industries that soon customers will no longer be able to clearly differentiate between even orders of magnitude differences in quality. In the professional hand tool industry, for example, virtually all customers expect very high degrees of quality; every

1. John A. Woods, "TQM: What's It Really All About?" *The Quality Yearbook 1994,* James W. Cortada and John A. Woods, editors (New York: McGraw-Hill, 1994), pp. 3–13.
2. David Greising, "Quality: How to Make It Pay," *Business Week,* August 8, 1994, pp. 54–59.

major player (Snap-on, Craftsman, Proto, etc.) offers unconditional replacement guarantees and has moved on to other areas for a source of competitive advantage, including delivery, service, and new products.

■ *Turbulence.* TQM is a philosophy that grew in an environment of relatively stable markets. As it has been practiced, its adherents have assumed that customer needs can be aggregated into large pockets of demand, that defects and satisfaction surveys can show where processes must be improved, and that customers care most for low prices and high quality. Unfortunately, in many, if not most, manufacturing industries, these premises no longer hold as markets become increasingly fragmented and turbulent. As a special issue of *Fortune* related last fall,

> Whether you sell $100 million planes or 79-cent pens, your buyers have changed enormously in the past few years. Their demands are lengthening; their patience shrinking. Epochal shifts in the global economy have given them a sultan's power to command exactly what they want, the way they want it, when they want it, at a price that will make you weep. You'll either provide it or vaporize. . . . In the words of one gloomy retailer, "The customer isn't king anymore. The customer is dictator."[3]

With the first three issues, it is "simply" a matter of the management and employees administering, observing, and executing the precepts of the TQM philosophy. Of course, that is anything *but* a simple matter, and many of the articles in *The Quality Yearbook* can show you how companies have been able to achieve it. Here, however, let us focus on the last two issues—differentiation and turbulence—where manufacturing companies that *have* successfully embraced the TQM philosophy are being challenged.

Reengineering

Many see reengineering as the proper response to these issues, and in many ways see it as the opposite of TQM. Exactly what is reengineering? As defined by its leading proponents, Michael Hammer and James Champy, it is "the fundamental rethinking and radical redesign of business processes to achieve dramatic improvements in critical, contemporary measures of performance, such as cost, quality, service, and speed."[4] While Total Quality Management starts with stable processes and strives to continuously improve them, reengineering throws away how things are being done today, and starts over with a blank slate to design new processes and organizational structures that are

---

3. "Meet the New Consumer," *Fortune* Special Issue: The Tough New Consumer, vol. 128, no. 13, Autumn/Winter 1993, p. 6.

4. Michael Hammer and James Champy, *Reengineering the Corporation: A Manifesto for Business Revolution* (New York: HarperBusiness, 1993), p. 32.

designed, in one fell swoop, to achieve dramatic improvements in performance.

Reengineering assumes a fundamental disconnect between a company's current course and speed and what is required for success in the industry and marketplace.

Reengineering assumes a fundamental disconnect between a company's current course and speed and what is required for success in the industry and marketplace. As such, reengineering may very well be required both of those companies that never got on the quality bandwagon and of those whose markets have become increasingly turbulent, changing more rapidly than average TQM programs have thus far been able to handle.

But while TQM is a philosophy that guides ongoing processes, structures, and decisions, reengineering is a *tool*—a means, not an end. Without first knowing to what end it should be aimed—without combining the potential of reengineering with the reality of a philosophy such as TQM—it has very little hope of lasting success. At one materials manufacturing company, a reengineering project became a "bloodbath" (in the words of the president) when it came time for implementation. Only when it was integrated into the company's existing TQM program, was the project salvaged. Using the quality philosophy as a lever for change, significant progress was then made in reengineering the business processes and organizational structures.

A second mistake companies often make is to turn over too much of their reengineering activity to a legion of outside consultants, eliminating the possibility of taking advantage of the deep process knowledge of those working in the company. At one telecommunications equipment provider, consultants who successfully developed and used a reengineering approach for cutting costs were asked to increase innovation and customization as well. Assuming the same approach would work and desiring to control everything about the project to increase (in their minds) the chances of success, the consultants effectively cut out much possibility of input from those who knew the products and development processes best. The end result was a dismal failure.

Manufacturers who have embraced TQM must meet the challenge of reengineering by integrating the two, using reengineering as a means for TQM's end: profitably providing products customers value.

Mass customization builds upon the traditional TQM foundation of low costs and defect-free production by adding another requirement: customizing products and services in response to individual customer wants and needs.

Mass Customization

However, as markets become increasingly turbulent and defect-free products less of the differentiator they once were, many manufacturers across a wide variety of industries are finding that they are constantly having to increase the amount of variety and customization they offer. They are finding that *mass customizing* their products is a key to success in today's environment. Mass customization builds upon the traditional TQM foundation of low costs and defect-free production by adding another requirement: customizing products and services in response to individual customer wants and needs. Some of its practitioners include:[5]

5. For further examples and a better understanding of what mass customization is, see B. Joseph Pine II, *Mass Customization: The New Frontier in Business Competition* (Boston: Harvard Business School Press, 1993).

- Bally Engineered Structures, Inc., whose modularized and modifiable panels and accessories can be put together in a virtually limitless number of ways, including in walk-in coolers, freezers, insulated outdoor structures, refrigerated warehouses, environmentally controlled rooms, cold storage buildings, and blast chillers—every one of which is customized to each buyer's exact specifications.

- McGraw-Hill, Inc., whose Primis endeavor produces customized college textbooks at a plant in Harrisonburg, Virginia.

- Motorola's Paging Products Group in Boynton Beach, Florida, which mass customizes pagers in lot size of one from over 29 million combinations.

- Lutron Electronics Co. of Coopersburg, Pennsylvania, which designs and manufactures lighting controls (switches, dimmers, and systems to control sets of lights) for residential and office environments. It manufactures over 11,000 different controls, 95 percent of which have annual shipments of less than 100 units.

In many ways, mass customization is a natural extension to Total Quality Management, an evolution in business competition that has progressed from success being based on innovation and tailoring (craft production), to low costs (mass production), to low costs *plus* defect-free products (which some call Total Quality Management or lean production), to low costs, no defects, *and* individual customization (mass customization). TQM allows companies to get out of the "vertical silos" so prevalent and so restricting in mass production, to reduce cycle times and setup times, and begin to build the necessary flexibility and responsiveness into processes required to increase variety. It seems just a matter of ensuring that quality is to be found in the eyes of *individual* customers for a manufacturer to embrace mass customization from within the TQM philosophy. In other words, mass customization should be the natural outcome of a company seeking to practice TQM. Such companies take advantage of new technologies, organizational structures, and operational capabilities to maximize satisfaction to individual customers while minimizing the costs of doing so.

It seems just a matter of ensuring that quality is to be found in the eyes of *individual* customers for a manufacturer to embrace mass customization from within the TQM philosophy.

Unfortunately, TQM has not always been understood in these terms.[6] Even Toyota Motor Company—heretofore a paragon of TQM—has found it difficult to implement mass customization, finding that people became more allegiant to their teams than to the company overall ("horizontal silos"), that increasing robotization reduced their ability to continuously improve, and that product proliferation became engineering-driven rather than customer-driven.

6. For more details on this, including on the Toyota example, see B. Joseph Pine II, Bart Victor, and Andrew C. Boynton, "Making Mass Customization Work," *Harvard Business Review*, September–October 1993, pp. 108–119.

Companies that have embraced TQM to meet the challenge of mass customization must make some potentially very jarring changes in how they have been practicing the art of quality, including the following:

- *Markets.* While TQM has, in the past, depended upon relatively stable marketplaces where processes, and by extension products, could be fine-tuned over time, mass customizers must thrive on turbulent markets by finding and serving very small market niches, right down to the individual customer.

- *Teams.* While cross-functional teams have tended to be very stable and long-lasting (like the markets they serve), to fully achieve mass customization requires "instant teams" whereby people and processes are brought together to respond to a particular customer or market opportunity, and stay together for only as long as it takes to serve that customer or fulfill that opportunity.

- *Focus.* TQM organizations to date primarily focus on and measure "customer satisfaction," which, as it is generally practiced, really means *market* satisfaction—periodically surveying a representative sample of customers to gauge their satisfaction relative to competitors. Mass customizers must focus more on *customer sacrifice*—continuously measuring and reducing the gap between what the company can provide and what individual customers really want and need—and deserve.

- *Learning.* Flowing from the focus, companies that embrace the TQM philosophy have primarily learned through *process failures*, ensuring that a defect never recurs. Companies that further embrace the need to mass customize must learn more through *capability failures*, continuously renewing their processes and products whenever confronted with a gap in customer sacrifice.

As can be seen, these changes—and more that could be cited—are stark. Perhaps the reason so many managers are becoming increasingly dissatisfied with TQM and grasping at reengineering is because the requirements for mass customization are so great. But their dissatisfaction really represents a misunderstanding of TQM as a set of procedures rather than a philosophy—one that emerges from viewing the organization as a system with the purpose of serving customers through effective management processes. Mass customization is a dramatic step forward on the journey of those who practice TQM. Without understanding the organization as a system, neither TQM nor mass customization stands much chance of success.

As the need for differentiation and the turbulence of markets continues to increase, the requirements for successful practitioners of TQM also increase. Toyota now realizes that to maintain its competitive advantage over all rivals, it indeed must figure out how to move beyond its traditional advantages, grounded in its decades-old tradition of lean production. Tatsuro Toyoda, the CEO of Toyota, was recently asked what more the company can do with the Toyota Production System. In reply, Toyoda said that while their primary objective today was further reducing costs, "Clearly, the next manufacturing horizon beyond leanness is greater flexibility, so that the same line can produce many variations at an affordable cost."[7] Taken to its limit of a variation for every customer, that is the challenge of mass customization.

7. "Toyota dodging 'big company disease'," *USA Today*, May 23, 1994, p. 7B.

Is Saturn Competitive?

Robert R. Rehder

This article explores just how well Saturn is doing. The company has adopted a number of techniques and approaches identified with TQM, but it is still working to become profitable. However, given the high fixed cost of starting this company, and the very traditional company culture from which it started, it seems worthwhile to give Saturn more time to prove itself. This article provides an excellent overview of such issues. Try to answer the question posed by the title when you complete this article.

Both General Motors and the United Auto Workers already knew they were in serious trouble in the early 1980s. They just didn't know how much. GM was losing market share to the Japanese. It was also having a difficult time financially because the U.S. economy was in a lengthy recession. Several hundred thousand GM employees were being released, plants were closing, and the UAW was rapidly losing its dues-paying members.

For several decades, Detroit had failed at its attempts to build an inexpensive, world-class, small automobile that could compete with the market-dominating Japanese and turn a profit. Remember the ill-fated Omni, Gremlin, Vega, Pinto, and Chevette? The Chevette cost GM an estimated $300 per unit. The Pinto carried the risk of a gas tank fire if rear-ended. None of these cars could come close to matching the high quality standards of Japanese automobiles.

On November 3, 1983, GEO Roger Smith announced with great pride and stars-and-stripes fanfare that Saturn would prove GM could profitably build a small automobile in the U.S. that would beat Japanese competition. Clearly GM and Roger Smith were placing their reputations on the line with Saturn, much like Toyota had when it opened its first transplant, NUMMI, in Fremont, California.

On December 19, Donald Ephlin, vice president of the UAW, and Alfred Warren, Jr., GM's vice president of industrial relations, announced the creation of a new GM/UAW study center to review new relationships and approaches to the operation of the Saturn project. Two months later, an unprecedented "group of 99" was formed, made up of a wide range of GM and UAW people, including plant managers, staff production workers, and union personnel. The "group of 99" immediately divided itself into research teams to determine through worldwide benchmarking field studies how to build a

Reprinted from *Business Horizons* March-April 1994. Copyright 1994 by the Foundation for the School of Business at Indiana University. Used with permission.

world-class automobile. The teams visited more than 100 benchmark companies and traveled more than two million miles throughout the world. During these field studies, the following common concepts emerged as keys to a highly successful company:

- Quality was a top priority to maintain customer satisfaction. The customer was number one, whether it was the next group receiving parts or services (the internal customer) or those receiving final products or services (the external customer).
- Everyone in the company has ownership and is responsible for its successes and failures.
- Equality is practiced, not just preached.
- Barriers to doing a good job have been eliminated.
- People are the company's most important asset.
- Union and management are partners, sharing responsibility for ensuring the success of the enterprise.
- People have authority to do their jobs.

Saturn soon learned that to accomplish these ambitious goals, it would have to change not only its production system, but also its organization, manufacturing, industrial relations, suppliers, and retail systems. It had to fundamentally change the very way it does business. At this time, however, corporate GM was still convinced that the way to beat the Japanese was through lights-out automation, which it was using at its Hamtramck plant.

Saturn learned it would have to change not only its production system, but also its organization, manufacturing, industrial relations, suppliers, and retail systems.

Another historic decision made by Roger Smith in 1983, eight months earlier than his formal announcement of Saturn, was to form a joint venture with Toyota, New United Motors Manufacturing Inc. (NUMMI) in Fremont, California. The influence NUMMI would have on Saturn during their parallel development is unmistakable and profound. NUMMI was to be managed by Toyota, who pioneered the Japanese lean system. This was Toyota's first American transplant and the first UAW-organized Japanese transplant. GM wished to learn Toyota's manufacturing system; in return it would market its Corolla-based automobiles under the GM nameplate Nova and, more recently, Prizm.

In September 1983, the UAW and NUMMI signed an unprecedented 17-page letter of agreement that formed the basis of a new nonadversarial management-labor relations system. There is little doubt that the agreement greatly influenced the development of the joint GM/UAW Saturn Study Center, whose primary goal was to review new labor-management relationships. The Study Center and the research and deliberations of the "group of 99" produced an historic 11-page labor agreement between GM and the UAW in July 1985 establishing a partnership for the joint development and operation of Saturn. This partnership agreement, while strongly influenced by Toyota's nonadversarial labor relations agreements and system, went much further. It required a working partnership of Saturn management and UAW officers and members at all levels of decision making during Saturn's development and all throughout its operation.

SATURN'S STATEMENT OF PHILOSOPHY

We, the Saturn Team, in concert with the UAW and General Motors, believe that meeting the needs of customers, Saturn members, suppliers, dealers, and neighbors is fundamental to fulfilling our mission.

To meet our customers' needs . . .

- our products and services must be world leaders in value and satisfaction.

To meet our members' needs, we . . .

- will create a sense of belonging in an environment of mutual trust respect, and dignity;
- belive that all people want to be involved in desicions that affect them, care about their jobs and each other, take pride in themselves and in their contributions, and want to share in the success of their efforts;
- will develop the tools, training, and education for each member, recognizing individual skills and knowledge;
- believe that creative, motivated, responsible team members who understand that change is critical to success are Saturn's most important asset.

To meet our suppliers' and dealers' needs, we . . .

- will strive to create real partnerships with them;
- will be open and fair in our dealings, reflecting trust, respect, and their importance to Saturn;
- want dealers and suppliers to feel ownership in Saturn's mission and philosophy as their own.

To meet the needs of our neighbors, the communities in which we live and operate, we . . .

- will be good citizens, protect the environment, and conserve natural resources;
- will seek to cooperate with government at all levels and strive to be sensitive, open, and candid in all our public statements.

This state-of-the-art union/management collaboration extends from the office of the CEO to workers on the assembly line. It is based on joint decision making from strategic planning to shop-floor problem solving. The agreement clearly sets new standards for industrial democracy in the U.S. auto industry, like those in Northern Europe. This joint GM/UAW decision-making process, for example, is similar to that found in the joint union-management development and operation of Volvo's Uddevalla plant in Sweden.

Though it was not specifically revealed to me during my field studies exactly how much soft or hard technology was transferred from NUMMI and Uddevalla to Saturn, the Saturn "group of 99" did include the two firms in their benchmark plant visits. They were most impressed with these organizations' recognition that their team members at all levels best support the systems and structures they help develop and implement. As previously discussed, the Japanese lean system has, for the most part, limited joint UAW/management decision making to lower operational levels, except for the joint development of their industrial relations system.

The Saturn memorandum of agreement, like the NUMMI agreement, is separate from the standard GM/UAW 8-inch thick boilerplate with its legalistic and adversarial language. It states the joint Saturn mission and philosophy and describes the new organization and management systems necessary to develop and manufacture world-class automobiles. Local 1810 was charted at Saturn in June 1986, when Saturn emerged as a separate wholly owned subsidiary of GM.

The Mission, Philosophy, and Values of Saturn

Saturn placed great emphasis on the joint management-union member development of its mission and philosophy.

Saturn, like NUMMI and Uddevalla, placed great emphasis on the joint management union member development of its mission and philosophy. The statements, in fact, are quite similar to those of the other two plants. Representing the foundation of such nontraditional firms, these value-laden statements are a major departure from the dehumanizing and technological emphasis of the traditional assembly line. They substitute a new set of fundamental values with which future decisions are made. Underlying their broadly participative development is the common belief that people at all levels want to be involved in decisions that affect them.

Saturn's founding team, after lengthy discussions, developed a mission statement with the following two distinct, highly ambitious, and challenging goals:

1. To market vehicles developed and manufactured in the United States that are world leaders in quality, cost, and customer satisfaction by integrating people, technology, and business systems; and
2. To transfer knowledge, technology, and experience throughout General Motors.

The team supported its mission statement with a statement of philosophy, shown in the box on page 78 that identified its partnership with its critical stakeholders—much like the Japanese lean system. The team further developed a statement of five fundamental values:

1. commitment to customer enthusiasm;
2. commitment to excel;
3. team work;
4. trust and respect for the individual; and
5. continuous improvement.

The values, philosophy, and mission statements bear an unmistakable resemblance to those of Toyota's lean system first transplanted at NUMMI. Even the collaborative union/management team processes by which they were jointly developed are very similar. In an article published in 1986 after my year-long field research at NUMMI with Marta Smith, we listed the following seven goals developed by NUMMI's management and union members:

- search for constant improvement (*kaizen*);
- develop full human potential;
- pursue superior quality (*jidoka*);
- build mutual trust;
- develop team performance;
- make every employee a manager;
- provide a stable livelihood for all of its employees.

These goals support their stated shared vision that "together we can build the best subcompact automobiles in the world."

Mike Bennett, head of Saturn's UAW Local 1853, said during a recent field study visit, "Saturn is basically built upon the Japanese lean system." A further examination of the firm's partnership, consensus-based organization, and management system will reveal that although it was perhaps important psychologically for the founding team to start with a fresh approach to achieve a sense of ownership, it nevertheless ended up with an American adaptation and planned improvement of the Toyota lean system. This, in turn, was a Japanese adaptation and improvement of the American system.

In addition, Saturn adapted parts of the northern European, highly participatory, industrial relations system along with several technical innovations, such as Opel's moving-pallet assembly line. Unlike Volvo's Uddevalla system, though, Toyota and Saturn have retained two key characteristics of the American system: the moving assembly line and the narrowly defined and closely measured job analysis and short cycle time. However, unlike the American system, teams—not management—now primarily do time analysis, statistical quality measures, and constant improvement. Toyota, for example, took Frederick Taylor's time-and-motion work standardization methods out of managers' hands and gave them to their work teams to allow them to continuously analyze and improve their own performance. The team standardization of tasks at NUMMI, for example, is no less exacting than even Taylor could have wanted.

Unlike the American system, teams—not management—now primarily do time analysis, statistical quality measures, and constant improvement.

According to Adler's field studies at NUMMI (1993), the teams' own employment of these scientific management tools is a central reason for their success, along with their efforts to build a communitarian culture around trust and common purpose. Adler argues that the Taylorist time-and-motion work standardization discipline required by management to be employed by NUMMI's teams within its paternalistic bureaucracy is essential for quality and efficiency. He allows that this work does not have much intrinsic value, and even quotes a NUMMI worker who calls it a "lousy job." Nevertheless, he rationalizes that NUMMI workers are realistic and recognize that they "had an unlucky draw in terms of education and opportunity."

The question remains as to whether their "lousy job" is any better with the group doing their own work analysis, standardization, and enforcement of this rigidly structured discipline than when management did it. Adler argues that the answer is unequivocally yes, not only in terms of the quality and productivity of their output, but also because it enhances their expertise, self-esteem, and pride in their work.

Although the transfer, adaptation, and improvements of these complex social technical systems represent a major breakthrough for GM, they do not quite ring true with the "All-American hot dog, apple pie, and Saturn" image. This image was sold ahead of its product by the Hal Riney Advertising Agency, which was selected to be Saturn's "communication partner." In many ways, Riney's Saturn theme was similar to the one it created for President Reagan's 1984 reelection campaign, "It's morning in America." This time it was, "It's spring in Spring Hill, Tennessee," and it portrayed the new Saturn corporation as the new hope, the reawakening of a sleepy America, and a return to all the fundamental American values that made this country great.

No mention was made of Saturn's collectivist Japanese lean system heritage or its North European co-government, management/labor relations system adaptation. Like America, the Saturn Corporation, its new process, and its product have been born with a diverse human and technological heritage. The corporation's new automobile does qualify as "all-American," with its relatively few Japanese and other foreign parts; however, much of the soft and hard technology that produced it are global.

Constant Improvement through a Balanced Sociotechnical System

Although the Saturn organization is built upon the Toyota lean system, from its core team philosophy and structure to its stakeholder partnerships, it has attempted to make improvements all along the line. Unlike its parent corporation, GM, in the early 1980s Saturn recognized the importance of a balanced social-technical system from its benchmarking studies of Toyota's lean system and Volvo's Kalmar and Uddevalla systems. Saturn understood that it must design its systems to ensure a balanced development of its people and technology as an essential part of a successful constant improvement, or *kaizen,* system.

Saturn understood that it must design its systems to ensure a balanced development of its people and technology as an essential part of a successful constant improvement, or *kaizen,* system.

Saturn improved the Japanese system by employing the North European concept of management-union collaboration in decisions at all levels to design and operate on an ongoing basis its integrated systems. The union-management partnership at Saturn, for example, designed and operates its comprehensive education and training center programs—called Saturn U.—to enable its team members to stay ahead of its technology. This is essential for autonomous teams engaged in constant improvement. Saturn's assembly equipment, like that at NUMMI, is relatively low-tech and people-oriented. This is not surprising—considering it was a broad team of managers and workers who chose it and then spent up to 750 hours of retraining long-term GM veterans to ready the job.

A Highly Integrated Manufacturing and Assembly System

Saturn, which is headquartered in the Detroit area, retains its planning and design functions there. This somewhat constrains its communication and integrated team approach to reducing total product cycle time because its manufacturing complex is located in Spring Hill, Tennessee. The highly integrated, four-million-square-foot manufacturing and assembly complex was built in the middle of Tennessee's beautiful, rolling farm country. Saturn sought to protect and preserve this beautiful area through careful design and placement of its facility. The plant cannot be seen at all from the highway, for it is set well back in the middle of a large farm in a small valley.

The entire complex is most attractive inside and out and is fully air-conditioned—including the foundry. The plant can match or better any of the new Japanese transplants in appearance, but it does not compare to the attractive work environment of Volvo's Uddevalla facility, which had windows, soft colors, natural light, and an extremely quiet interior. (Volvo, however, closed Uddevalla for a number of political-economic reasons.)

The Saturn complex has three integrated subunits:

- powertrain: from lost-foam castings to fully dressing engines and transmissions;
- body systems: stamping, fabricating, and painting of its unique spaceframe and panels;
- vehicle systems: assembly of its final product.

The noisy conveyor belts and assembly lines, similar to Japanese transplants, betrays its Fordist and lean heritage. Its skillet system method of assembly, unique in the U.S., was adopted from the Opel facilities in Russelsheim, Germany, after two years of management-union group meetings to reach a consensus. The team member rides along on the skillet or platform with the automobile as long as necessary to complete the task cycle. Unlike the lean system's average one-minute work cycle time, Saturn's cycle time averages a much less stressful seven minutes—nowhere near Uddevalla's several-hour-long work cycle. However, Saturn is estimated to be putting approximately 30-35 work-hours per vehicle in final assembly; the better Japanese transplants require almost half that many hours. This is well above Saturn's own target of 20 hours.

Thus, serious questions arise about the long-term competitiveness of Saturn. *The Wall Street Journal* called it a $5-billion financing quagmire, with losses estimated at more than $700 million last year ("Swollen GM . . ." 1992). Although Saturn's integrated manufacturing and assembly process greatly facilitates its "just-in-time system," it also remains vulnerable to parts shortages caused by strikes because it is one of the highest UAW parts-content automobiles in the GM family.

The UAW, in its war with the Big Three's outsourcing strategy, has increasingly used what the union calls "apache strikes" at key supplier locations such as the Lordstown, Ohio metal stamping plant. The September 1992 shutdown of the Lordstown plant by the UAW forced the almost immediate shutdown of Saturn, which maintains a one-day supply of parts with its lean system. Saturn's workers were not laid off, however; they continued their training and maintenance—a practice that is traditional in Japanese lean transplants.

Saturn's Technological Innovations

Saturn's lost-foam casting process, which uses extensive and intricate polystyrene patterns, is a first in the industry on this scale. The process greatly reduces costly machining and produces castings with precise tolerances. Saturn was the first American automobile company to assemble four versions of manual and automatic transmissions on the same assembly line—still behind the newest Japanese plants. Saturn also pioneered large-scale applications of thermo-plastic technology for rustproof, dent-resistant, polymer bodyside panes. Its skillet method of assembly, already mentioned as the first such system imported to the United States, has been further improved.

All these technological initiatives have been achieved by involving team members early in the design stage. They have been further improved in use on the shop floor by keeping people and technology development in balance. With more than 150 U.S. patents granted or pending, combined with product innovations and a constant improvement process, Saturn has the potential to fulfill a key part of its mission: "to transfer knowledge, technology, and experience throughout General Motors." Saturn's dealer and marketing system has already been identified as the model for the Oldsmobile division of GM.

All these technological initiatives have been achieved by involving team members early in the design stage.

Saturn's Business Systems

The state-of-the-art business systems at Saturn give people throughout the firm critical information for making collaborative decisions about every aspect of the business, from design to dealers. GM's Electronic Data Systems (EDS), acquired from Ross Perot, provided most of the expertise and hardware. A close Saturn/EDS partnership was critical from the start. Because Saturn represented an attempt to develop a totally new organization as well as product, using a cleansheet approach provided EDS and Saturn with an opportunity to develop a completely new and fully integrated business system as well. Such an approach is essential to a high-performance Japanese lean system.

Saturn developed the following principles, which enabled it to achieve accurate real-time data for all essential business needs:

- functional applications would process on a single corporate platform;
- database structures would be relational;
- data entries would be defined in a central repository;
- rigorous standards would be established regarding presentation and data modeling.

To ensure that such a sophisticated management information system would provide consistency in Saturn's social-technical systems and empower people throughout the company—not just automate for a select few—a business system action council was established. This council included members from all the functional areas of Saturn, resulting in a highly integrated system. It provides accurate real-time information for all of Saturn's business functions: human resources, finance materials management, manufacturing, product engineering, corporate communications, sales and service, and marketing (including Saturn's partnership dealer system). Without this fully integrated business information system, the critical horizontal coordination among these functional areas would not be possible. The potential value of Saturn's business systems to other GM divisions is very great.

The potential value of Saturn's business systems to other GM divisions is very great.

Saturn's Team-Based Organization Structure, Training, and Development

Saturn's organizational structure is represented by a series of linked concentric circles. Saturn and UAW advisors are represented at every level, beginning with the work unit, the work unit module, the business unit, and three action councils: manufacturing, technical development, and customer. These action councils convene in the strategic action council, which establishes strategic goals and oversees the entire organization. All the councils are assisted by flexible and involved critical resource teams of highly qualified professionals who move from business team to business team adding expertise and providing an active coordination role in the overall decision-making process.

The basic building block of Saturn, as is characteristic of all lean organizations, is the self-directed team, referred to at Saturn as a "work unit." Whereas the Japanese instinctively build their organizations around teams because of their collectivist culture, Saturn spent years and millions of dollars researching and developing its self-directed work unit. This is understandable. Saturn's parent, General Motors—the world's largest private-sector, traditional bureaucracy—used "management prerogatives" and well-defined, mindless job classifications. Saturn nowadays would reject its parent's very individualistic way of doing business, adopting the group structure and "every worker is a manager" philosophy the Japanese have perfected in their lean system.

Some have argued that Saturn took a very long time to reinvent the Japanese lean system when it had NUMMI to study and experience in detail during development. Conversely, Toyota took more than a quarter of a century to develop its team-based lean system. Saturn also had to unlearn almost a century of traditional values, norms, and practices that GM had practiced and perfected. Its years of studying and benchmarking resulted in volumes of research publications, manuals, and training guides. More significantly, Saturn developed a refined variation on the team-based lean organization that validates one of its key findings and philosophies: "People will support what they help create." Team members at Saturn spend from 250 to 750 hours in intensive training, with a large portion of this time devoted to such topics as team and consensus building, leadership, problem identification and solving, and total quality management.

Saturn's investment of millions of dollars in ongoing team-member training is contrary to the American view of the worker as a mindless, narrowly trained, expendable, single-purpose machine tool. The lean system depends on constant improvement, and as yet, machines cannot constantly improve themselves. Saturn's lengthy and expensive development costs (estimates range from $3–5 billion), however, have created very real financial problems today.

Every work unit at Saturn assumes the responsibilities of a supervisor in a traditional organization, with the support of two external co-advisors: one from management and one from the UAW. A charter team member forms the team, hires the members, teaches the philosophy, and assists in the members' development of the skills and knowledge essential to carry out the team's tasks and goals. Team members are salaried and have high levels of job security; they continue their training if the plant is not operating for any reason.

Every work unit at Saturn assumes the responsibilities of a supervisor in a traditional organization.

Continuous training is essential at all lean organizations because each work unit has the following functions: resolving conflicts; planning and making operational decisions; designing and exchanging job assignments; shifting leadership roles; controlling inventory; maintaining records; setting new improvement goals; performing repairs and housekeeping; assisting in developing and delivering training; and scheduling meetings inside and outside the work units.

The compensation and incentive system for Saturn's UAW members is also unique. Saturn and the UAW have contracted to share in the rewards of the company's overall performance if jointly set goals are met, as well as put 20 percent of the workers' compensation at risk if these targets are not met. This risk-reward sharing system is designed to encourage teamwork and continuous improvement by providing common overall goals rather than facilitating conflict through individual or group performance goals.

During 1992 the jointly set goals were tied to the teams' completion of a comprehensive training schedule—not productivity. Given Saturn's high number of work hours per automobile, this may well need re-examination. Saturn's training strategy is measurable and competency-based, which means the goal is to have everyone trained as a trainer. The "subject areas include: philosophy; mission and goals; computer and business skills; quality; business systems; human skills; product process; dealer sales and service; machinery equipment; health and safety; and generic technical. By far the largest percentage of time (42 percent) is spent on human skills training, which includes such topics as managing conflict, decision making, task analysis, time management, team excellence, project management, and trainer education. This again is a significant departure from the traditional American system.

Saturn's Supplier and Dealer Partnerships

On the supplier input side of Saturn's stakeholder-partnership, the goal was to establish a long-term, single-source, partnering relationship based on the just-in-time system. Saturn supplier partners are selected by consensus by a product development team composed of members from manufacturing, engineering, finance materials management, quality management, and the

UAW. The product development team then continues to work closely with the supplier partner to ensure continuous improvement in quality, costs, and just-in-time standards.

Saturn has been an industry leader with its electronic data interchange system (EDI), which allows direct communication with more than 300 suppliers. This system greatly facilitates planning and shipping schedules as well as materials and inventory coordination. It is also used for supplier payments through electronic fund transfers (EFTs). Several Japanese suppliers are now Saturn partners, and management may wish to have many more. GM suppliers' UAW-dictated average wage and benefit cost of $34 an hour is almost twice what independent competitors pay. But despite Saturn's compelling need to cut costs by more than $100 million, suppliers continue to be chosen by a joint management/UAW team.

Saturn is caught in the same web of noncompetitive GM/UAW suppliers as is GM, which itself is desperately seeking to cut its billions in losses by restructuring top management, downsizing, and attempting to shift parts work to more competitive outside suppliers. Because quality is still a serious problem with some suppliers, Saturn's union-management team is asking its suppliers to help in raising quality standards and just-in-time reliability.

Again, Saturn has borrowed the Japanese dealer-partner relationship and has sought to extend its philosophy and lean system to retailers and valued customers. Technology and training are teamed to transfer Saturn values, know-how, and information. Saturn dealer employees are given extensive training at Spring Hill or in local dealership.

Each Saturn dealer is equipped with elaborate computerized information systems linked by satellite for two-way data and one-way video information sharing. This system has streamlined vehicle and parts ordering and quickly spots problem repair areas. It facilitates prompt recall coordination, as when Saturn's dealers reported a surge in water pump changes caused by a defective coolant. Saturn's prompt and generous response turned a potentially disastrous public-relations crisis into a positive, widely publicized example of Saturn's responsive and extensive warranty system.

Saturn has established large and exclusive market areas for its dealers in order to avoid what it sees as counterproductive competitive price shopping in the industry. Its pioneering one-price, no-haggling marketing has proven highly successful, and is now being tried by many dealers in the industry. In Saturn's clean, attractive showrooms are highly trained sales representatives who treat customers less like one-time targets of opportunity and more like partners in a long-term relationship. The remarkable success of this new, no-pressure Saturn buying experience speaks for itself.

The Enigmatic Question of Saturn's Success

Depending on one's perspective, the answer to the question of Saturn's success could be yes, no, or maybe. Saturn the automobile has unquestionably been a sales, quality, and marketing success. It has achieved what made Japanese automobiles gain rapid market share in the 1980s: quality, reliability, competitive prices (though to date highly subsidized by GM), and courteous service.

Following a brief shutdown at Saturn caused by a GM supplier strike, many customers were willing to wait months for their Saturns while competitive Japanese models were readily available with rebates. In 1993, Saturn's sales reached 196,000 units, matching Toyota's Corolla. As measured by external and internal audits and dealer and customer-satisfaction indexes, Saturn has the potential to join the world's top quality leaders.

As measured by external and internal audits and dealer and customer-satisfaction indexes, Saturn has the potential to join the world's top quality leaders.

The problems, however, are centered on productivity, costs, and profits—and those problems are significant. Industry analysts maintain that Saturn is much less productive than Honda's or Toyota's transplants. GM estimates that Saturn lost approximately $700 million in 1992, and although it broke even in 1993, this was only made possible by creative accounting: $3 billion of its start-up costs will go on GM's books rather than on Saturn's.

The Saturn Corporation borrowed heavily from the Japanese lean system and North European co-management systems. It is now increasingly evident that it was hardly lean when its new plant, technology, management systems, and products took its union-management systems, and products took its union-management team almost a decade to develop. Nor is its present work force lean enough to be competitive, according to Robert Boruff, Saturn's manufacturing head. Boruff stated he would like to eliminate from the present work force many of the 1,000 additional people needed for the third shift, which was added in spring 1993 to increase production from 200,000 to 320,000 units (White 1992). Saturn had already trimmed its engineering staff 38 percent during 1992, which should help stem costs. With the third shift added, production could meet the 300,000-unit output needed to break even. But current sales are declining and production is now being cut back. Saturn estimates that it will need to produce 400,000 or possibly 500,000 automobiles per year to meet its profit goals. As such, it is considering expanding the Spring Hill facility or converting existing GM plants.

It is encouraging to note that some Saturn team members freely admit they don't have enough to do and have offered to trim their team numbers without fear of job loss. The pace of work at Saturn in no way resembles the intensity found in a typical Japanese transplant. But it does remain highly repetitive and stressful. In the past, 10-hour days, often five days a week or more, in rotating day and night shifts were not uncommon. Significant changes in the work schedule were designed to reduce worker stress. Since June of 1993, three crews rotate on two 10-hour shifts six days a week. Each of the three crews works four 10-hour shifts a week with no overtime, even on Saturday. This innovative rotating schedule creates 16 five-day "weekends" per year for workers.

In summer 1992, Saturn's salaried team members were earning the highest wages in the industry—about $45,000 annually when their bonus increases were included. The Saturn/UAW co-management system, while giving new meaning to union-management collaboration in the United States, also contributes somewhat to its high overall cost structure. The fact that Saturn managers earn much more than their UAW partners—with whom they often share equal responsibilities—also causes friction. Vice presidents at Saturn can earn up to $125,000, their UAW partners often less than half that amount. When you add to the overstaffing Saturn's extraordinarily high development costs and overhead, its large percentage of expensive GM supplier parts, and its low productivity, Saturn faces a difficult challenge in proving that it can be profitable. The productivity improvements made recently will be a major test of the promising co-management system and will be closely watched by union and management traditionalists and revisionists alike.

The productivity improvements made recently will be a major test of the promising co-management system.

Saturn clearly has a long way to go to achieve its goal of becoming a world leader in costs. However, it is doing much better in reaching its other stated goals of quality and customer satisfaction as measured by customer demand and independent quality measures, despite a string of recalls in the last several years. It is clear that Saturn's quality out the door is good, but the amount of costly internal rework necessary to achieve this goal is as yet less certain.

Saturn is also achieving its second major goal by providing GM with valuable knowledge, experience, and technology—not only in dealer and marketing systems but in its collaborative union-management partnership, autonomous work teams, electronic data systems, and new production technology. The question remains, however, how much this experience and technology will be successfully transferred to and used by GM in its efforts to revitalize and transform itself. GM has already slowly and painfully learned from Saturn that observation and study of the Japanese lean system and other innovative organization and management systems is one matter; building a lean-based system that is less stressful, more democratic, and still competitive is quite another.

Another Measure of Saturn's Success: Quality of Work Life

There is a growing understanding—albeit with significant backsliding during periods of economic decline—that the development of workers who are more fully involved and committed to constant change and creative improvement are key parts of the new, flexible, learning organization essential in today's competitive environment. However, this necessitates much more than changing only employee behavior. Totally new organizations are needed in which workers are more autonomous and far less controlled and managed, sharing more equitably in rewards. Omar Aktouf, in his far-reaching article on humanistic theory (1992), underscores this position:

> From corporate culture to management by symbols, from champions of the product to total quality, the aim is to change only one thing: the behavior of employees, with no thought that the context must also be changed. . . . How then can the transition to more cooperative and vital work be made? It can be made by moving toward a form of organization where candor, symmetry, equity, and sharing would provide the grounds for humanizing the firm.

Saturn has reduced the stress of the traditional assembly line worker through its skillet or platform system. However, it has kept the constant pacing, fragmentation, standardization of work, repetitive motion, and excessive noise. Saturn's rotating shifts and 10-hour work days—like the American and Japanese systems, often demanding a great deal of overtime—create high levels of worker stress at home and on the job.

Team members have also raised questions about how fairly union officials were selected and how well they truly represented team members' interests. Future union votes on whether to abandon the innovative labor memorandum of understanding in favor of a more traditional contract will be closely watched. Despite a close election concerning UAW Local 1853 leadership in spring 1993, union votes to date at Saturn have been highly supportive of Saturn's innovative labor management partnership.

Saturn remains a paradox, both humanistically and competitively.

Saturn remains a paradox, both humanistically and competitively. The answer depends on one's perspective. Like Uddevalla and, to a lesser extent, the Japanese lean system, Saturn has taken steps in the right direction away from the repetitive, passive-obedient Taylorist system (in which employees are treated as a mechanistic means to economic ends) toward a more cooperative, fully involved, and sharing organization. It has achieved limited success in achieving greater organizational and manufacturing flexibility than the traditional American system, but it has retained the inherent flexibility problems and many of its assembly-line stressors.

Some industry analysts and academicians argue that Saturn remains overstaffed, its work pace slack, its team members not fully employing the disciplined time-and-motion work standardization systems needed for constant improvement. In addition, the aging Saturn car has sales falling short of production. And there is evidence of less support from both corporate GM and the UAW. At a time when the Japanese are once again changing their lean organization and production systems to achieve far greater flexibility and less worker stress, Saturn still remains unprofitable, relatively inflexible, and stressful. At the same time, it has achieved resounding organizational, technological, industrial relations, and product and marketing innovations and successes. Its innovations are extensive and comprehensive, including product development and supplier and market relationship similar to the Japanese lean system.

Saturn, Toyota, and Uddevalla all represent highly innovative, nontraditional manufacturing organizations that are invaluable prototypes.

Saturn, Toyota, and Uddevalla all represent highly innovative, nontraditional manufacturing organizations that are invaluable prototypes in the ongoing search for even more productive, flexible, and collaborative organizational and management systems. The nirvana of flexible production is known in the automobile industry today as a lot size of one (the ability to make a completely different vehicle every time) but at a unit cost that equals that of the most competitive mass production system. If human dignity, development, and industrial democracy were added to process, it would indeed become a worthy quest for the next century. Volvo's Uddevalla system met two of these criteria; but in its short time of development it did not attain world-class competitiveness. To date, neither has Saturn.

A recent book by Barry Bluestone, a respected economist at the University of Massachusetts, and his father Irving Bluestone, a retired senior UAW officer (1993), cites Saturn as the American benchmark corporation. It points out the essential role of the independent union: to avoid the work force's total dependence on the goodwill and personal philosophy of management. Without such a union, the authors argue, employee input into relatively low-level decisions within the autonomous team on the shop floor can be little more than another scientific tool to foster corporate productivity and profits and eliminate jobs. Perhaps there is still hope for a positive answer to Erich Fromm's question: "Must individuals be passive and dependent in order to have strong, well-functioning organizations?"

References

Paul Adler, "Time and Motion Regained," *Harvard Business Review*, January-February 1993, p. 106.

Omar Aktouf, "Management and Theories of Organization in the 1990s: Toward a Critical Radical Humanism," *Academy of Management Review, 17, 3* (1992): 424.

Larry Armstrong, "Chrysler's Neon," *Business Week*, May 3, 1993, pp. 119, 124.

Barry Bluestone and Irving Bluestone, *Negotiating the Future: A Labor Perspective on American Business* (New York: Basic books, 1993).

Robert Rehder and Marta Smith, "Kaizen and the Art of Labor Relations," *Personnel Journal*, December 1986, pp. 85–86.

"Swollen GM Finds a Crash Diet Means Uncomfortable Labor Force," *Wall Street Journal*, September 9, 1992, p. A6.

Thomas Thurston, "The Saturn Corporation and the Integration of Production and Consumption: Automotive Postmodernism?" Yale University, unpublished manuscript, 1992, pp. 17–18.

Joseph B. White, "For Saturn Copying Japan Yields Hot Sales But Not Profits," *Wall Street Journal*, October 1, 1992, p. A6.

Robert R. Rehder is a professor of organizational behavior and management at the Robert O. Anderson School of Management, the University of New Mexico, Albuquerque.

Worker Involvement Lights Up Neon

Marc Hequet

The new Chrysler Neon was developed with the full participation of workers from the shop floor. This article documents and provides examples of the worker participation process at the Neon plant in Belvidere, Illinois.

Mary Strang throws windshields for a living. She and her production-line partner at Chrysler's Belvidere (IL) Assembly Plant use a vacuum-clamp fixture to hoist the 28-pound glass trapezoid from a conveyor, flip it for mounting, mounting, maneuver it around production-line machinery, and ease it onto the body of a 1995 Chrysler Neon.

Her new job is a daylong weight-lifting session: One windshield every 45 seconds or so, 72 an hour, eight hours a day, five days a week, plus a couple of Saturdays every month. The Belvidere plant, 75 miles northwest of Chicago, is pumping Neons out the door in anticipation of brisk demand for the subcompact the Japanese media has labeled "the Japan killer."

The windshield job suits Strang, a broad-shouldered brunette in a black T-shirt brilliant with Wilma Flintstone and Betty Rubble in cartoon colors on its front. A week earlier, her job kept her on her hands and knees inside cars all day installing consoles—the receptacle for the shift lever between the front seats.

Strang knew before long that the console job was wrong for her. She told her supervisor, and together with plant safety, the union and upper management, they decided she was the wrong shape to be inside a subcompact on her knees all day. She moved to windshields after just three weeks. "That's a pretty bad job for anybody," the muscular Strang says of the console job. "I had too much upper weight to be on my knees all day long."

A few years ago, Strang could have been on her knees installing consoles for a long time while she waited out a byzantine bureaucratic process known as "getting PQXed" to another job.

Those long days of bending could have wrecked her back and cost the company thousands of dollars in health care, workers comp and replacement-worker costs. Meanwhile some ill-attached consoles might have gone down the line to inspectors, leading to added repair costs and decreased production. Worse, some misfit consoles might have made it out the door and into the

---

Reprinted with permission from the June 1994 Issue of *TRAINING* Magazine. Copyright 1994. Lakewood Publications, Minneapolis, MN. All rights reserved. Not for resale.

marketplace, where they could have turned a promising vehicle into a sour citrus fruit of a car.

PQXed? Strang doesn't even know what it stands for. It doesn't matter anymore. Now, when something needs doing at the Belvidere Assembly Plant, workers speak up—and somebody gets the ball rolling promptly.

Why waste brainpower? "The people on the floor put together have more knowledge than any and all engineers," says Stu Duckworth, an hourly Belvidere employee who now works a desk job as a quality representative. "We've got more than 3,000 people on the floor, and I'm sure they've each got one or two ideas at least."

This is worker involvement: Give people some say-so about their jobs, the philosophy goes, and they will work smarter and better.

Worker involvement is not a new concept in American industry, but U.S. automakers didn't show much interest in full worker involvement until the 1980s, when the Japanese had already made deep inroads into the U.S. auto market.

Now about 50 percent of U.S. companies have some kind of formal worker-involvement program, and the number is growing, says David Lewin, a UCLA professor who studies the subject.

Belvidere is Chrysler's big worker-involvement makeover. The company decided in 1989 to replace its Horizon Omni and Sundance Shadow with a new subcompact.

After looking at several plants, Chrysler chose Belvidere to build the Neon. Among Belvidere's advantages are a veteran work force (average age 48 with 23 years' experience) and the fact that Belvidere had built another small car, the Omni.

In Neon, Belvidere's veterans built, and in fact helped design, a spacious "cab-forward" car with a relatively long wheelbase and wide track that undersells comparable vehicles by up to $4,000.

The first Neon rolled off the Belvidere assembly line Nov. 10, 1993. The current model is known as the 1995 Neon because it meets 1995 federal safety and emission standards.

What makes the story noteworthy?

- Massive worker involvement has been Neon's hallmark. Production workers participated in the design of the vehicle and in decisions about the ergonomics of the production line. Early worker-involvement attempts at Belvidere date to at least 1987, when the plant was still building the Omni, but the pace really picked up in 1989 when worker teams were organized to suggest cost-cutting methods. The full-involvement rollout came with Neon in 1992.

That year, "process teams" of managers and hourly workers flew to Chrysler's Technology Center in Auburn Hills, MI, to sit elbow-to-elbow with engineers and design the vehicle, its parts, the production line and production tools. Then van loads and finally bus loads of workers drove the seven hours from Belvidere to Auborn Hills to spend days at a time working with prototypes and with engineers.

All told, nearly 1,500 of Belvidere's 3,200 employees made the trip to receive technical training on Neon prototypes and to offer suggestions to the engineers. Chrysler still managed to develop the Neon in just 31 months, five ahead of schedule. Indeed, Chrysler says that ties the industry benchmark for vehicle development established by Honda.

■ Workers themselves helped design the 948,000 man-hours of training everybody at the plant went through in connection with the Neon launch—a phenomenal figure that includes all those worker-days with the engineers at the Chrysler Technical Center.

■ Neon was a critical success even before it became commercially available. It was named 1994 Car of the Year by *Automobile* magazine in its January issue. On the other hand . . .

■ . . . in February 1994 Chrysler abruptly recalled all 15,000 Neons it had built to fix an engine problem that sometimes resulted in failure to start. "Recall" has become a dirty word among auto buyers who know the bother and delay of getting a car fixed. But Neon—like Saturn, which has also had voluntary recalls—positions the recall as a badge of honor, a move that shows it's serious about quality.

■ Candor at the Belvidere plant is startling. Employees up to and including plant manager John Felice expound freely on Neon's flaws and what's being done about them. "The defects I'm talking about the customer will never see," says Felice. "We find it, we eliminate it, we prevent it from happening again."

Employees up to and including plant manager John Felice expound freely on Neon's flaws and what's being done about them.

The automotive press touts Neon as the first U.S. vehicle with a real chance to challenge Japanese dominance in the subcompact market. Chrysler is depending heavily on worker involvement—suggestions, problem-solving teams and, most recently, "stabilization" teams—to hold down costs, to produce a defect-free vehicle, and to improve continuously.

Given that Neon retail prices start at less than $9,000, its builders have little margin for error if they hope to produce the rarest of goods—a profitable U.S.-made small car.

But this winsome set of wheels with the come-hither headlamps has people's attention. "The Neon may fail dismally, but my gut tells me it's not going to," says Frank Schuller, coordinator of the International Motor Vehicle Program at the Massachusetts Institute of Technology. "That is a fantastic little car. It has dual air bags, nice acceleration, it's designed with a fair amount of headroom."

And even a cold-blooded scholar like Schuller can't deny the obvious. "I think it's cute," he gushes.

"A Little Bit of Listen"

Chrysler's Belvidere Assembly Plant, built in 1965, could be a dreadful place to work. Against the monotonous northern Illinois farmscape, its gray smokestacks rise like the spires of a desolate Emerald City in a *film noir* "Wizard of

Oz." The administration building is a low-budget clutter of desks, room dividers and wall charts. While the vast, 3.3 million square-foot plant itself is clean and well-lit, its relentless industrial roar and the demands of the production line could soon take their toll—if workers didn't like their jobs.

But they do. Ask Ron Barr, a 29-year plant veteran, to compare life on the production line today with when he started at Belvidere. "You mean like night and day? That's how different it is," says Barr, an inspector now but still an hourly worker. "When we first hired in here it was, 'Do as you're told and keep your mouth quiet.' There was no input from the employees whatsoever. Never any suggestion boxes for ideas on how to make your job easier. It was unheard of. You just did your job."

Garland Jinkins, a bearded, grandfatherly type checking electrical connections under a Neon hood, is more reserved. "It used to be you were told what to do and do it," says Jinkins, an electrical integrity auditor who was worked at the plant for 28 years. "Now there's a little bit of listen. I ain't saying it's 100 percent yet. I'd be lying if I said it was. But it's a lot better than it used to be."

MITs Schuller met workers on a visit to Belvidere in March. "If you compare the way they appear now vs. 10 years ago, they seem very much happier," he says. "There's not a lot of hostility and grumbling. There seems to be a lot more participation on the line." United Auto Workers (UAW) Local 1268 reports that the plant generated 3,000 grievances or more annually before worker involvement. Last year, the number of grievances was 51.

Windshield installer Strang, hard at work on the line, playfully challenges a passing Mike "Bear" Dunlavy to an arm-wrestling match. Dunlavy is a towering veteran whose nickname fits. Nevertheless he might lose such a match because he hasn't been slinging parts on the production line for a while. Like a number of production workers at Belvidere, Dunlavy, while still hourly, has moved into a management-type administrative job.

Every morning at about 5 a.m., Dunlavy picks up worker suggestions from boxes around the plant. His title—product quality improvement communicator—reflects that he's supposed to keep workers in touch with management. Suggestions are called IQPs for Individual Quality Participation—to distance this effort from an earlier, much-ignored suggestion program.

Previously, suggestions straggled up a bureaucratic ladder from worker to supervisor to plant manager. Even if a suggestion was accepted, the line worker who suggested it likely wouldn't get credit.

Now, each suggestion goes to a manager who must refer it within one day to someone in a position to act on it. The second person has two days to respond. On the fourth day, the worker who made the suggestion gets a report on the progress of the idea.

Every day, after an IQP meeting with other hourly workers, Dunlavy gets the first five minutes in a meeting with plant manager Felice and his staff to report on the progress of worker ideas.

Suggestions can be unremarkable. One still pending, for example, is to use three bolts of the same size at one station instead of three different-sized bolts, so workers can make just one trip to the bolt bucket instead of three.

If that seems piddling, it's because Belvidere has already made some big cost-cutting changes. One team of production workers, for example, has saved $5 million in metal processing since 1989. Another saved tens of thousands of dollars by converting suppliers from cardboard shipping containers to reusable plastic.

Change-Master Teams

The suggestion process is a microcosm of the change that has transformed the Belvidere Assembly Plant.

When Chrysler chose Belvidere to build the Neon, worker involvement shifted into high gear. Belvidere established seven permanent "process teams" with about 35 members each; members represented every department in the plant. These teams became the core change masters at Belvidere, sharply upgrading the plant's worker-involvement efforts. The teams worked with engineers at Chrysler's Auburn Hills Technology Center to design the vehicle and production process; they met with suppliers; and they returned to Belvidere to train other workers to build the involvement process and the car that would be called Neon.

The Neon launch generated an unprecedented volume of training at Chrysler. Every worker, hourly and salaried, attended two orientation sessions on the Neon, one in May 1993 before their summer break and another in August or September when they came back and production was about to begin.

Training for Neon began with a 2½-hour program for everybody in the plant, which covered the new car and introduced the new emphasis on quality improvement. Groups of about 60 watched an introductory video that featured plant manager Felice and UAW Local 1268 president Larry Rielly, followed by a 30-minute video on W. Edwards Deming's approach to quality. The training also included 15-minute videos on problem-solving and cause-effect analysis, followed by exercises.

Workers also received training focused on their specialties. Rather than simply delivering training designed by Detroit, eight coordinators helped set up training suggested and designed by the workers themselves. Belvidere posted jobs for people who wanted to work through the three-month 1993 summer layoff scheduling more training for the Neon.

Production workers who took those jobs surveyed other workers before the layoff, department by department, to find out what people wanted to learn. These apprentice trainers did a journeyman's work setting up training, tracking results and keeping records. "A monumental job that was very well done," says Len Frost, Belvidere's training administrator.

Then, experienced process-team members from the production line delivered the training themselves—and that made a difference. "In the past we would have brought in corporate people or retirees or outsiders, and they speak a different language," says Frost. "But we found when we had the process people present the class, you could see a change in people's attitude right there, because these guys can answer any conceivable question."

Experienced process-team members from the production line delivered the training themselves.

Some groups of employees, including repair and utility workers, received almost 80 hours of training, part of it before heading for the Chrysler Technology Center and the rest afterward. Much of the training was on new equipment, mostly in the body shop—20- and 40-hour training programs that taught workers to set up, maintain and repair welding robots. Workers also trained on new metal-stamping equipment installed at Belvidere for the Neon. All told, the training amounted to nearly seven weeks per employee.

Participative Engineering?

Training and vehicle design flowed seamlessly together as the process teams and later other workers traveled to Auburn Hills to work with engineers.

Traditionally, autos have been designed in isolation from manufacturing. Engineers do what they do and throw the plans to manufacturing. If manufacturing has a problem with the design, engineering might grudgingly make a change—if there is still time before the assembly line is overhauled to build a new model.

Chrysler's so-called "platform" approach, however, puts everybody together in the same room at the outset—engineers, manufacturing, and even suppliers.

Chrysler's so-called "platform" approach, however, puts everybody together in the same room at the outset—engineers, manufacturing and even suppliers. And according to Belvidere's worker-involvement philosophy, manufacturing includes production-line operators, the hourly workers.

"Initially this program was really seen as a threat to the engineering staff," says training administrator Frost. "Here we had the people from this cornfield up there giving insight into vehicles that used to be the engineers' bailiwick all by themselves. But as time went along, the engineers could see the value of the program."

The production workers weren't exactly eager at first, either. "There was no trust there," says union local president Rielly. "Our people honestly felt that no matter what they said, the engineers were going to do whatever they wanted. Once our people found out that what they said mattered, and the engineers were going to accept it, it was, 'Hey, if you've got something to say—say it.' "

Videotapes of those early meetings are telling. They show production operators in work shirts at first hanging back from the crowded conference table while white-shirted engineers in neckties lead the meetings and do all the talking. Session by session, however, the production-line operators gradually take their places at the table, poring over parts and talking in gruff bursts.

When engineer and autoworker find common ground, it is obvious even on video. One usually imperturbable engineer suddenly becomes animated when an operator suggests off-center bolt holes on a part to ensure against installing it upside down. That's the kind of thing, evidently, that excites engineers.

Engineers and operators mulled 4,000 different parts of the car that could be designed for quality, ergonomics and ease of assembly. The up-front collaboration on Neon proved fruitful: Potentially costly problems were caught early. For example, operators found they couldn't fit an air gun under the bumper to bolt it down. Engineers redesigned the part.

Does Neon Sound Familiar? Remember Saturn?

The kind of innovation displayed in Chrysler's Neon project marks the curve in the road the U.S. auto industry is following. But Neon is the second milepost. Saturn was the first.

The General Motors Corp., subsidiary that built a car from scratch with wall-to-wall worker involvement invited all of the 700,000 people who have bought Saturns since production began in 1990 to its factory in Spring Hill, TN, in June, 1994 for a sort of automotive Woodstock.

Saturn and Neon will compete head-to-head for market share in the small-car category. Their stories invite comparison:

- Both see recalls as a change to build customer relations. When Saturn recalled more than 352,000 vehicles with potential engine-fire problems, some dealers welcomed owners with barbecues and trips to movies while their cars were fixed. Like Saturn, Neon sees voluntary recalls as a point of honor and as a signal to prospective buyers that it's determined to build the car right. Chrysler recalled all 15,000 Neons it had built by early February to fix a water leak that affected the vehicle's computer and sometimes resulted in cars not starting. Only 1,300 were in customer's hands.
- Workers for both companies are empowered and customer-focused, building vehicles with attention to principles of total-quality management. Saturn teams are self-directed, while Neon follows a more traditional management structure. If you come in late at Saturn, you've got to deal with the team. If you come in late at Neon, you've got to deal with the supervisor.
- At Saturn, no one punches a time card. At Neon everyone—from production to plant manager—punches a time card.
- Saturn, under a special agreement with the United Auto Workers, uses cross-functional work teams. Neon, under a more traditional arrangement with the UAW, keeps workers in more narrowly defined jobs—although in its new stamping plant at Belvidere, IL, all the production workers are under one classification and can do 15 different jobs.
- Saturn's 8,000 workers and Neon's 3,200 share in the profits when their companies make money. Saturn has an additional incentive: To encourage teamwork and continuous improvement 20 percent of pay is "at risk" until workers meet preset performance goals. Neon uses no such incentive.
- Saturn built a plant from scratch at Spring Hill, and must rely on its parent company for funding to expand capacity at the site in order to meet production and profitability goals. Neon is produced in a 29-year-old plant at Belvidere, where workers built Omnis, Horizons and, more recently, the Dynasty, Fifth Avenue, New Yorker and Imperial.

Continued—

Does Neon Sound Familiar? Remember Saturn? (continued)

- Saturns have among the lowest defect rates in the industry. Chrysler, with a worse-than-average defect rate, hopes worker involvement in design and production of the Neon will help it improve.
- Neon prices start at $8,975, whereas 1994 Saturns go for $9,995 and up.
- Neon and Saturn workers comment little about the other guys' car. But when they do, it's a real zinger. "No wonder their car's less expensive than ours," says Jack O'Toole, UAW adviser for people systems at Saturn. "It's a cheaper product."

Ouch! And maybe that's the biggest difference of all. At Saturn and Neon, worker involvement has union members taking potshots not at management, but at the competition.

Collaboration also meant well-trained production workers. The 1,500 workers who made the trip to the technology center had a chance to work on the Neon. Before long, the workers who didn't make the trip also had their own prototype to tear apart and put back together at Belvidere—an unheard-of 14 months before launch.

A Windshield Cracks

Chrysler continues to trail the best automakers in vehicle quality, with an average of 1.35 defects per vehicle, sharply worse than the industry average of 1.07. Its Dodge brand scores even worse, with 1.48 defects per vehicle—twice the number of Toyota's 0.74. The company has made improvement a priority.

At Belvidere, Neon production workers know it—and see some changes. "I think Chrysler's more concerned now with quality than with numbers of cars going out the door," says 28-year veteran Elbert Jordan, whose job is test-driving Neons on the plant's half-mile torture track. "I know from day-to-day operations that a lot of things that probably would have gone out years ago don't go out anymore. We go back and redo it, whatever it takes. And we get our count when we can."

When a relief worker spells windshield-thrower Strang back on the production line, he bumps the glass lightly against the windshield-washer spout. The senior worker at the station notes the minute crack and yells, "Whoa! Take this one out!" The two throwers lift the windshield off again and quickly replace it without stopping the line.

Strang and the senior worker had been doing the job in about 40 seconds, so there is time to replace the damaged windshield and maintain the line rate of 72 cars per hour. But they had stopped the line three times in the previous hour because the wrong glass was coming down the conveyor. "Ten years ago if we stopped the line we'd have got screamed at," says Strang, who came to work at the Belvidere plant in 1984 as a summer replacement before she went full time in 1988.

Now workers are encouraged to stop the line if they see a flaw. Strang likes the new way. "It gives the employees more confidence in what they're doing, because they know if there's something wrong they can change it," says Strang. "Plus the customer is not going to get the problem after it's sold."

Now workers are encouraged to stop the line if they see a flaw.

Strang had a harrowing moment earlier in the day. "This morning I broke a window," she says. "All we did was shift it and it cracked." Who gets the blame? Wrong question. After hearing the report from the production line that windows were cracking from merely being moved around, the window vendor has decided the inner window isn't strong enough, and is working to fix the problem, says Strang.

Belvidere's worker involvement means involvement with suppliers as well—and the plant's collegial culture sometimes befuddles vendors. Last autumn, at a supplier's facility, a Belvidere team spent two hours with the supplier's managers before heading for the plant floor.

Finally the supplier's plant manager stopped the meeting. "He wanted to know who was the boss," chuckles Greg Camp, a salaried employee on the Neon launch team. "It turned out I was the boss, but we didn't tell 'em that when we walked in the door. It shocked 'em, because my hourly people knew as much as I did."

Treating production-line workers like experts is an idea that goes right to the top at Belvidere. Plant manager Felice's team of inspectors, known as "validators," found a piece of window molding that was bulging just a bit on the cars, not sealing perfectly. They tracked it up the production line. Everything upstream seemed to be within specifications. When they came to the worker who pressed the molding into place, they found their clue.

"They feel different," the operator told Felice. "About two weeks ago, they started feeling different." The operator held up two pieces of the mylar molding. "These feel pretty good," he said of one. And of the other. "These don't."

The different feel reflected a difference in elasticity. The good moldings were cracking slightly in place, creating a perfect seal. The other moldings didn't crack, creating the bulge. Having found the root cause, Belvidere now can work with the supplier on getting the right "feel"—something the inspectors never would have learned had the worker not spoken up.

And the worker never would have spoken up about such a mushy piece of evidence unless he knew he'd be taken seriously.

Stretch, Don't Crack

Felice and his staff just hope they don't crack when they're stretched—because they're stretched all over the plant. Worker involvement means anybody can hail the plant manager as he strides by.

On his way to meetings he's stopped five or six times by people, says Felice. What keeps him going during his 14-hour days is the hope that other managers will fully emulate his stop-and-listen approach, and that will gradually take the pressure off him.

His staff gets the idea. "Tom Peters would say that an organization where everybody is empowered is going to be chaotic," says Keith Nelson, Neon launch coordinator. "He's right."

At Belvidere, wouldn't an electronic performance support system help ease the interruptions on the way to meetings? The plant has such a data base in place to answer workers' questions and concerns. But Nelson says a computer terminal at each production-line station would run counter to the plant's involvement principles.

"You have to deal with the soft side of the business," says Nelson. "Not everything can be put on a data base. You have to keep it personal. People build cars. Data bases don't."

UCLA's Lewin believes that as many as one-fourth of companies with worker-involvement programs are facing diminishing returns because of overextended managers. "More and more executives and professionals are coming to our classes with beepers on their belts," says Lewin. "There are good reasons for that, but the issue is upon us and you have to ask the question: How many are spread too thin?"

Are managers stretched too thin? If so, involved workers should be able to do more for themselves.

At Belvidere, Nelson is late for a meeting. But he's not worried. "No individual is critical for any process," Nelson shrugs. "If I'm late, somebody else will start the meeting."

In short, worker involvement is a problem that comes with its own built-in solution: Are managers stretched too thin? If so, involved workers should be able to do more for themselves.

Marc Hequet is an associate editor of Training *Magazine.*

Quality in a Box

Paul Froiland

This article explains how a consumer products box manufacturer has gone about successfully implementing quality management throughout the company, starting in its manufacturing processes. This approach has dramatically increased sales and profitability, and the company has become a benchmark for other companies going in this direction.

Company after company has laid a black wreath over the alleged tomb of total-quality management and stolen away into the hush of the night to wait in quiet embarrassment for the next management bandwagon. Not so Field Container Co. in Elk Grove, IL. Field Container, a privately held family corporation located off the westernmost runway of O'Hare Airport, makes boxes. Fine, shiny cake-mix boxes. Strudel boxes. Spark-plug boxes. Dog-food boxes. And, especially, ice-cream boxes. Field is the world's largest maker of frozen-treat boxes. Dove Bars. Popsicles. Eskimo Pies. Häagen Dazs ice-cream bars.

Field Container is also the fifth-largest of the 450 container manufacturers in the United States, and the largest privately held one. Its explosive growth has averaged close to 30 percent in the last two years, and its revenues have risen from $70 million seven years ago to $400 million today. The company's goal is to hit $1 billion by 2000. And all because of its total-quality-management program.

CEO Larry Field didn't know TQM from tequila mix on the day in the mid-1980s when Pillsbury Co., one of his largest clients, invited him and a salesperson of his choice to a two-day seminar on supplier certification. It was an inconvenient time for Field, and he asked if he could send a substitute. The Pillsbury person told him, "We just wanted the CEO and a salesman," but if he didn't feel like attending, he didn't have to.

With that out of the way, Field went about his hectic day as usual, only to wake up in the middle of that night with a nagging feeling perhaps common to people on the eve of a revolution. Maybe I'd better go, he thought.

And he did. The seminar was confusing and sobering, by turns. Pillsbury was talking about statistical process control (whatever that was), continuous improvement (ditto), and buyer certification (ditto). What Field was quick to notice, however, was that every one of his 13 folding-carton competitors was there.

Reprinted with permission from the February 1994 issue of *Training* Magazine. Copyright © 1994. Lakewood Publications, Minneapolis, MN. All rights reserved. Not for resale.

On the second day of the event, Pillsbury dropped its bombshell: Over the next two years, the company would reduce its folding-carton supplier base from 13 to four, and two years after that, to two suppliers. "That got my attention," says Field. "I was very nervous."

Field returned to Elk Grove and called all his managers into a daylong meeting. The consensus was that the company would rise to meet the challenge. Quality was going to be the biggest issue in the company, and there had to be ways of measuring it. Clearly Pillsbury's intent was to reduce its suppliers to those who could most effectively adopt statistical process control, continuous improvement, and other total-quality strategies. So everyone at Field was going to be trained in quality techniques. Field hired a consulting firm to help with the project, and over the next two to three years, 300 managers and supervisors at the 2,100-employee company attended training sessions. They emerged fired with enthusiasm, but ultimately pessimistic.

Pessimistic? Here's how Field puts it. "They said, 'We'll be honest with you, Larry: It's not going to work here.' " Field asked them why, and they said: " 'The feeling among all of us is that you'll give your money [to the project] but not your time. Neither you nor your father [Eli Field, the company founder] have gone out there [to the training sessions in Nashua, NH,] for the seminar, and until such time as you make a commitment, it's not going to work.' So after being insulted and upset, my father and I went out to Nashua to a three-day seminar, and we bought into it."

Since that time, every employee in the company has had at least a day of training in quality, and two years ago the company hired the first full-time, on-premise trainer in its 51-year history, followed six months later by another. Field is on the verge of hiring full-time trainers at all its sites.

Don't Stop the Presses

The quality thrust began with the idea of continuous improvement.

The quality thrust began with the idea of continuous improvement. Field Container developed process teams: work teams empowered to continuously analyze processes to reduce waste and down time. Each team at the company (and there are about 100 teams at Field locations nationally) is allowed to spend $1,000 without authorization. If a team wants to spend more, it figures out the payback on any capital expenditure it wants to make, and presents a case to the executive steering committee. The committee usually gives approval if the team can demonstrate enough cost savings.

Employees first attacked the enormous sheet-fed printing presses that dominate the shop floor. These presses cost $300 an hour to run, but must be stopped to change inks between each printing run. This process of preparing the press for the next job is called a changeover or make-ready. The printing industry average for make-ready time is an hour and a half per color. So a six-color job would take nine hours to prepare.

The process teams were taught some cycle-time reduction skills. Then, on their own, they came up with the idea of videotaping a changeover to look for inefficiencies. The result? Make-readies were reduced from nine hours to four hours, all due to workers critiquing themselves on tape. There was no management intervention, no coercive "suggestions." The current goal of the process teams is to reduce make-ready time to an hour.

At Field's Westfield plant, a parking lot away from the Elk Grove facility, the company installed high-tech Heidelberg presses, built to need only four hours of make-ready time. Once the process teams took on these presses, however, they were able to reduce make-ready time to less than an hour. They're currently gunning for 30 minutes.

There are other machines on the Elk Grove and Westfield floors: presses that score the sheets of cardboard after they've been printed, and presses that cut individual box forms out of the sheets at a rate of 7,000 an hour. Still other machines glue and fold the boxes, running them along at such a speed that an observer can't tell the product, or even its color, until the computer detects an imperfect glue spot and flicks a box off the line and into the air. When the box shell hits the floor, one can finally see what product it would have held, had it measured up.

Another process team looked at cycle-time reduction for the gluer. The team of line workers pulled out the video cameras again and taped themselves in action. The first thing they noticed was that in any changeover between jobs, there were a lot of different-sized bolts that needed to be tightened, requiring different wrenches. The process was slowed considerably by the fact that the person tightening the bolts was continually looking around for the right wrench. The process team made a dramatic proposal: Shut down the gluer and retrofit it entirely with self-tightening bolts. They were given the go-ahead, and the changeover process was reduced from 45 minutes with wrenches to 10 minutes with bare hands.

John Nolan, corporate director of the Total Quality Challenge, which is what Field Container has named its quality effort, tells other stories about discoveries that process teams made. One ongoing headache with all printing presses is the need to avoid dirt spots (called hot spots) on plates. A process team decided to filter the air and keep it constantly circulating—but more important, the team began to make a point of telling everybody to keep the door closed.

"[Another] of our teams," Nolan says, "was looking at 'white waste,' which is damaged layers of wallboard rolls. [Wallboard is the recycled paper product from which boxes are made.] They identified half-a-million dollars in white waste. They told Larry [Field]: 'We've got the wrong material-handling equipment. If you spend $80,000 on a new roll-clamp truck, you can eliminate it.' Larry said, 'I want that thing ordered today.' "

Improvement = Layoffs?

At most companies, it doesn't take much talk about continuous improvement for the rumor mill to begin guessing about impending layoffs. After all, if you improve a process enough, you ought to need fewer workers to handle it. Field Container had never laid off a worker since the company was founded in 1942—that is, until 1992, when it was forced to lay off some 80 hourly workers at its Elk Grove plant. Six months before the layoffs, in the heady growth period the company had enjoyed over the previous year, scores of new employees were hired. Then business slackened. It was those new hires who were let go.

"It had nothing to do with the continuous-improvement process," says vice president of human resources Tony Grassi, "yet many of the employees felt that *was* the cause of the layoffs. So we sort of shot ourselves in the foot."

At the same time, management could see that continuous improvement and reduced cycle times *would* likely lead to a condition that might be described as WBSA (working by standing around), as processes became ever more efficient. This was distressing, since Field Container still tries to hold to what has become known as the old employment contract: You give over your working career to the company, and the company employs you for life.

The company began to make strategic plans to redeploy workers from departments that had dramatically reduced waste or cycle time to departments that were being created by company growth.

With the training department taking the lead, the company began to make strategic plans to redeploy workers from departments that had dramatically reduced waste or cycle time to departments that were being created by company growth. Director of training and development Scott Ward began identifying workers who were likely candidates for future layoffs. He enrolled them in cross-training courses so that by the time their jobs might be eliminated, they would be ready to move over to new positions.

Training specialist Dan Hobbs began a joint program with two community colleges in the area, Triton and Elgin. He arranged for Triton to offer a course in advanced press work for Field Container employees in groups of about 15. The company reimburses the tuition of each student who completes the course. "Some of these people are just feeder operators," Hobbs says, "but they're learning the press operation. Triton has a new Heidelberg press just like the most recent one we have bought, and our employees are learning the computer console." Many workers who have taken the class have been able to move into higher-paying jobs at the company, he says.

Even more fundamental to the overall training effort is the English-as-a-second-language course offered to all nonnative-English-speaking employees. (Sixty percent of Field Container's Chicago-area work force is Hispanic.) This class is taught by instructors from Elgin Community College.

Educating in Quality

Company executives felt that continuous improvement applied not just to the business, but to the employees' bottom lines as well; that is, workers' incomes should improve along with the company's. Field Container already has a profit-sharing program, which provides some incentive, and a recently formed process team is looking at how a gain-sharing program might be started.

But if employees were to be genuine partners in the success of the business, they had to understand how the business works. They had to learn, for instance, why a cycle-time reduction doesn't always fall neatly to the bottom line. For example, cycle time on the printing presses was reduced enough that the equivalent cost of a new printing press had been saved in worker hours. Yet there was no gain in production figures. The reason? The presses were now so efficient that the plate room, which photographed the plates that went onto the presses, could not keep up. When a press finished its run of one job, the plate room would not be ready with plates for the next one.

The solution to this problem proved to be training. New plate-room workers had previously received on-the-job training by watching the veteran next to them photograph a plate. They would learn the process—along with all the idiosyncrasies and inefficiencies of the veteran. Then they would pass those on—adding some idiosyncrasies of their own—to the next new person following them. The company brought in expert trainers from the equipment-manufacturing company and retrained the whole plate-room work force. End of problem, end of delays.

It Don't Come Easy

The quality path has been neither smooth nor easy for Field Container, despite the company's massive revenue growth. Field learned, as have other organizations, that "quality" is not a single, one-size-fits-all solution to business problems. The key ingredient seems to be management's flexibility and its ability to admit to, and learn from, mistakes.

Field learned, as have other organizations, that "quality" is not a single, one-size-fits-all solution to business problems.

At first, for example, all employees were required to serve on a process team. Gradually the company learned that certain people just didn't want to be on teams—and that they were not necessarily poor performers. The requirement was dropped.

The company also assumed that once a process team was established, it would exist forever. Now most people at Field realize that there is an evolutionary flow to teams. "Some teams dissolve," says Nolan. "Other teams are created when new problems come up. There was one [leader] at the steering committee meeting this morning who said that his team was tired. Our advice to him was: 'Let it go. Let it dissolve. Give them a little rest.' Those who really want to get back into it will get picked up by other teams, or start a new team themselves. It's a constantly evolving process.

"Nothing is forever," Nolan adds, "although we have a couple of teams that I'm sure *feel* like it's been forever."

The company also found that workers sometimes suspected that management didn't take the teams seriously. In some instances, process teams made recommendations and felt that they weren't being followed or even listened to. "That's deadly," says Grassi. "If a recommendation isn't going to be followed or acted on right away, that has to be communicated, so that the process team doesn't feel disempowered."

Not that workers run home weeping in such cases. The level of trust and communication in the company is such that production workers can and do express unpleasant opinions to the bosses and live to tell the tale. "If we do something as management, and on occasion we do, to screw things up," says Grassi, "[people] have no problem calling Mr. [Eli] Field or Larry and saying, 'Hey, this doesn't seem right."

The Fields and other executives "aren't there to defend what we did," Grassi adds, "but rather to understand why you're upset with it. And often we *did* screw up, and we'll change it. You just get the problems resolved and move on."

Some of the quality efforts at Field are above and beyond the call of any container manufacturer. In an effort to develop a better partnership with its customers, for instance, the company had itself certified by the American Institute of Baking (AIB), which certifies Field's *customers* for the purity of their food products. As a result, everyone who works on the fluing and folding line wears a hair net, against the remote chance that a stray human hair might end up in a box shell that will leave the plant with no food product in it. It's unnecessary, but Field's customers love the extra protection against possible liability.

The AIB certification also requires that all presses, machines and other equipment be placed at least 18 inches from any outside wall. Along this demilitarized zone sits a line of rat traps, which never have and probably never will catch a rat, since rats don't eat wallboard. But, again, the customers are happy that Field is AIB-certified.

Aw, Shucks

One of the most disarming and enjoyable things about a visit to Field Container is the earnestness of its striving and the modesty of its managers regarding the company's success. Behind that modesty is the conviction that things could always be improved—what Grassi calls a "restless dissatisfaction."

Larry Field takes slight exception to the suggestion that Field Container is an exemplar of TQM done right. "We don't hold ourselves up that way," he says. "I don't think we're an example of 'Boy, it's really working here!' We've had a culture change from traditional and autocratic to an environment of teamwork and communication, [but] I think we've got a long way to go." He does allow, however, that he thinks "we're getting successful at it."

So successful that the giant and widely admired Chicago-based printing company R. R. Donnelly recently decided to use Field Container as a benchmark. But not successful enough that Field intends to sit back and rest anytime soon. The company asked the University of Chicago's graduate school of business to do a mock Malcolm Baldrige quality review in 1993. Field came out with a score about in the middle range of companies that actually do apply for the award. The most startling comment made by the "review" team was that there was actually too much empowerment and teamwork on the floor, and not enough direction from management.

As a result, the company is now putting a member of management on each of the process teams to help focus the teams on companywide goals and projects.

The next major challenge is to quantify the company's administration and sales functions so that they can be measured by a total-quality yardstick.

The next major challenge, according to chief operating officer Larry Nussbaum, is to quantify the company's administration and sales functions so that they can be measured by a total-quality yardstick, just as the production areas are now measured. This represents a profound change in the *nature* of the indicators by which performance is gauged. "We're beginning to measure much more cultural types of things," he says, "the measurement of hourly training per employee, the measurement of customer satisfaction, of on-time delivery."

The company has developed an internal Malcolm Baldrige Committee to systematize its future path to continuous improvement. In December 1993, half of all Field Container managers nationwide attended a six-hour training session on the plan that the internal Baldrige Committee put together to map the future. The other half were to attend the course last month.

"This is really the next generation," says Nussbaum.

Think about that when you unwrap your next Dove bar.

Paul Froiland is an associate editor of Training *Magazine.*

Early Steps on the Road to Quality at Quaker Chemical

Ira R. Dolich, Matthew K. Frick, and Jan Wolring

This article by three mangers of Quaker Chemical talks about the way this company has gone about implementing TQM. It emphasizes the importance of top management commitment in this process and gets very practical about steps they took.

Quality is a simple, three-syllable word. Yet legions of practitioners have labored on and continue to fashion an elaborate framework to take advantage of a very human desire. Few people start out any task with the expectation and wish that it will turn out poorly. People like to do a job right the first time. People know when a job is done right, they look for it, they know it when they see it, and they pay money for it. The "it" is quality. And "it" is a chameleon that changes colors as quickly as customer needs change.

Whether hailed by advocates or elevated to fad status by critics, the concept of quality plays, and will continue to play, an integral part in today's competitive business arena. To survive in today's world, you have to provide a product or service that consistently meets, anticipates, or even exceeds a customer's needs 100 percent of the time, the first time.

A Chinese proverb sagely advises that the longest journey starts with a single step. Quaker Chemical Corporation's journey of continuous quality improvement started with three steps. Commitment was the first step. Commitment to quality is difficult to maintain when short-term concerns such as ever-changing customer requirements test the organization's vision. The only way to sustain this effort is through senior management's unrelenting focus. The second step recognized the need to build and organize systems that would allow employees to do the best possible job. These systems required, in some cases, significant change on the part of the organization and individuals. As much of the recent literature shows, superficial application of "quality techniques" without attendant underlying values rarely works. But management commitment helped in achieving the longer-range goal of lasting, improved quality. The third step was to develop a general process that would integrate

From *National Productivity Review*, Spring 1994, copyright © 1994. Reprinted by permission of John Wiley & Sons, Inc.

and guide efforts leading to a total quality environment and allow the company to measure its progress.

Building Commitment and Involvement

If there is one area of total agreement among quality practioners, it is that the commitment and involvement of senior management are essential to a successful continuous quality-improvement program. According to a popular saying, a plate of ham and eggs is the best way to visualize the difference between involvement and commitment. Although the chicken is clearly involved in the production of the egg, the pig is truly committed in its contribution.

If there is one area of total agreement among quality practioners, it is that the commitment and involvement of senior management are essential.

How then did Quaker establish a framework for commitment and involvement for all members of its management team, as well as its employees? It would be nice to be able to state that the company's continuous quality improvement programs today are the result of a long-standing grand design. But in reality, they were the result of a number of disparate steps taken over a period of time and forged into a long-range plan over the last few years.

Quaker Chemical Corporation, headquartered in Conshohocken, Pennsylvania, and with a worldwide family of affiliates and licensees, is one of the largest companies in the world devoted primarily to the production of chemical specialty products for the aerospace, automotive, bearing, can, construction, metalworking, pulp and paper, and steel industries. In the early 1970s, it became apparent to Quaker's management and its board of directors that operations should be guided by a well-articulated statement of basic objectives. It was felt that the typically stated objectives to earn a profit, to achieve growth, and the like, were superficial, unless seen in a broader, strategic context. This led to the development of a statement of corporate philosophy, which was reviewed and revised by the board of directors and returned to management for further consideration. Ultimately the statement included the various internal and external interests to be served by the organization. The corporate philosophy sets the tone for corporate planning by noting that *"A resolute commitment to excellence and the quality of our products and services, in satisfying customer needs consistent with the Company's Code of Ethics, will enable Quaker Chemical to achieve its basic purpose of growth. . . ."*

Although that statement has been modified over the years, the basic thrust of the corporate values remains unchanged. Although quality and excellence were not hot topics in the 1970s, Quaker had serendipitously taken the first step of weaving these themes into the company's fundamental planning process. Yet quality and excellence remained undefined, dimensionless, and relatively invisible to the organization.

Involvement in quality-improvement activities becomes a daunting task if it is viewed only as time expended in addition to normal work assignments. It becomes easier when it is built into daily work life. The path chosen at Quaker was to make quality a strategic planning element and to continually focus on it at every opportunity. Indeed, Quaker's CEO uses the twin themes of globalization and total quality management in virtually all communications and activities with company stakeholders. This has been further promulgated in each annual report since 1990.

To establish some dimension and mass to the quality-planning process, a quality policy was formulated. As currently defined, the policy states that Quaker will *"meet, anticipate, and even exceed customer expectations 100 percent of the time, the first time."* The aim is *not* one of perfection; rather, it is to understand what customers truly expect and then try to meet those expectations all the time. This policy applies to business planning, product and service development, and raw material selection. It extends through manufacturing, product movement and shipment, administrative functions, and final use of the product by the customer. The policy is relatively clear and lends itself to setting quantifiable goals. Indeed, Quaker has found that measuring corporate performance on customer performance items has made it a bit more modest about the way it performs. Not everything the company does seems to be on target.

Focusing on customer needs greatly accelerated the commitment and involvement process. By the mid-1980s, more and new quality requirements were placed on Quaker by its customers, particularly the steel industry. They initiated demands for quality system certification, statistical process control (SPC), and a host of other methodologies not practiced at Quaker at the time. These requirements stemmed from pressure on Quaker's steel mill customers from their customers, the automotive industry. Responding to the impact of the Japanese automakers, the automotive industry in the United States and in Europe started to mandate total quality for their suppliers and sub-suppliers. Although Quaker does significant business with the automotive industry, its products are consumed during their production process and do not leave the factory on or in the vehicle. Until recently, these automotive customers had always regarded Quaker as an indirect, or non-production, supplier. With total quality at almost full throttle, Quaker is now being required to meet automotive supplier quality systems directly. At first, these extra requirements were a nuisance. When business results are good, it is not enough to convince senior management that a new paradigm, one of total quality management, is required. Nevertheless, by 1986, significant resources were being spent on meeting specific customer quality system requirements.

Encouraging Employees to Do Their Best

With all the attention now being directed to quality and corporate transformation, it became apparent that even more information and focus were required. U.S. managers from several parts of the organization attended seminars led by Deming and other quality experts. In Europe, Crosby seminars began to provide similar focus for Quaker managers there. Additional research convinced a senior executive that the TQM phenomenon would not go away. Clearly, it offered Quaker real competitive value in the marketplace to improve customer satisfaction.

In March 1987, a group of senior officers and department managers joined the Philadelphia Area Council for Excellence (PACE). One of the nation's oldest and largest regional excellence councils, PACE was founded in 1983 as a Council of the Greater Philadelphia Chamber of Commerce. PACE put together several roundtable groups of Delaware Valley businesses to study and practice total quality management.

The Quaker group participated in full-day, once-a-month seminars for about eighteen months. In these seminars, senior and key department managers were exposed to and used problem-solving techniques, SPC, team dynamics and facilitation, visionary leadership, and other TQM skill sets. Soon after joining PACE, the Quaker management group formed an "I-Team" (Implementation Team). The purpose of the I-Team was to communicate and implement the skill sets acquired at the PACE roundtable throughout the organization. At this point, the I-Team's focus was directed to Quaker's North American Operating Region and did not extend to the rest of its global organization. Under the roundtable's guidance, the I-Team started using short-term quality project teams (STQPs) to tackle specific interdepartmental processes where breakthrough improvements were needed. The STQPs were led by PACE-trained team leaders and facilitators and following Deming's PDCA (Plan, Do, Check, Act) cycle to direct their chosen projects.

The first STQP was composed primarily of I-Team members and some in-house process experts. They were charged with improving the customer-supplied sample technical service operations at Quaker. This project was chosen for a number of reasons. It was an important part of the sales support system, and Quaker's performance was often perceived to be slow by its customers. Also, it consumed a significant amount of resources, and the payback was uncertain. Finally, tangible and measurable achievements were expected. The project proved to be only a qualified success, but the STQP process itself was proven, and more teams were commissioned to start in 1988. The projects chosen were to

1. Minimize off-specification production in one of Quaker's product lines;
2. Redesign Quaker's process by which no-charge samples get to the customer;
3. Establish a mission for the pilot plant and reconfigure its work processes to achieve the mission; and
4. Imbed the total quality theme in all Quaker publications and training programs.

Two of the four were extremely successful, one missed the mark and was subsequently recommissioned, and one was moderately successful (however, its work served as a template for very successful techniques being used in Quaker's process control and corrective action systems today).

Each project team had a trained leader and facilitator, as well as a pair of I-Team advisors who oversaw the progress of each team. Activities were assessed both in an ongoing fashion and in two formal milestone reviews made before the final team presentation of results and additional recommendations to the full I-Team. In this way, management review, visibility, and involvement throughout the process were high. In addition, because the individuals having overall management responsibility for the various processes being improved by the STQPs were all on the I-Team, the open flow of information prevented many of the turf issues that might otherwise have resulted.

Team members were selected by the project team leaders, with recommendations by the I-Team members considered. Team members represented all levels (sub-operator level through top management) and all functions pertinent to the process under STQP redesign. Team meetings were generally weekly. The better teams were able to keep the meetings brief and to the point with most of the work being done outside the meetings. All team members were trained in team mechanics, the PDCA cycle, and a sample of the continuous improvement tools available to them. When the need arose, experts in tools such as SPC and cause-and-effect analysis were brought in to provide more extensive training.

The better teams were able to keep the meetings brief and to the point with most of the work being done outside the meetings.

Over twenty-five STQP's have been in operation since 1987. Three are active today, as are variants of STQPs—Employee Involvement Groups (EIGs), where the focus is departmental rather than interdepartmental—and a number of standing groups, such as Quaker Detroit's Quality Board and Quaker Conshohocken's Process Improvement Team.

Quaker's STQPs have been directly responsible for the company's current ISO 9001 and 9002 certifications in the United States. More than 150 of the approximately 400 employees in the Quaker North American region have served on STQPs, EIGs, or other project teams. In addition, those trained in the process have continued to use the tools learned through their STQP experiences in many ad-hoc situations.

Quaker has learned and achieved a great deal through its STQP experiences. Focused, trained, cross-functional teams are an indispensable element in a total quality management system. However, the company also experienced several pitfalls in applying (or misapplying to be more accurate in a case or two) those teams.

One of the first lessons that Quaker learned was that STQPs and project teams per se are not enough, because directly involving only 150 of 400 people in the total quality transformation is insufficient to generate critical mass. Because 100 percent involvement is required, biannual quality awareness seminars were established for all Quaker employees to attend. Also, in 1991 a visionary planning process was established. Through it, department visions are created to support the company vision and quality policy. By working on goals to achieve their departmental visions, which they developed under I-Team review, all employees have become involved in the process.

The company also realized that the scopes of some of the STQPs were too broad. Teams could not complete their missions in a reactively short period of time (less than six months). It was then necessary to refocus the objectives of some teams after much work had already been done. Problems also cropped up when the team's goals did not align with management's vision. In selecting the processes that were to be worked on, it was necessary to select projects that were important to the company's success and in alignment with the strategies and business plans in operation at the time. When the team's mission and these business realities diverged, management interest in successful outcomes for an STQP's success was reduced and, as a result, some recommendations were never wholeheartedly implemented. Moreover, the same key employees were always in demand to be on teams, and several of them found it difficult to adequately serve on multiple teams and accomplish their departmental and personal business and quality objectives.

Managing Total Quality

As the 1980s drew to a close, Quaker committed itself to ensuring that its quality systems would excel when measured by such customer and industry quality standards as Q-1, GM's Quality Target for Excellence, ISO 9000, and others. To build on prior successes and establish a global quality perspective, several initiatives were undertaken.

Quaker's experience with the I-Team clearly underscored the fact that quality improvement must include everyone in all parts of the organization. To help ensure total participation, the company formed a Corporate Quality Steering Committee (CQSC). This group consists of all senior managers throughout the organization, including the chairman of the board. The mandate of the group was to ensure that within each business unit:

- Leadership and involvement exist at all levels of management.
- Short-term expectations are consistent with long-term goals.
- Corporate quality objectives are defined and communicated through the organization.
- There exists a long-term commitment to improvement of product and service quality.

As Quaker went from being an international company to a global organization, management and quality councils were created in other geographic areas. Commercial pressures were building in many areas for supplier quality improvement programs. The European steel industry was no less under the gun than the U.S. steel industry for quality improvements for their principal use group—the automotive industry. Additionally, another force for organized quality systems emerged in Europe—ISO 9000 certification.

To meet these demands, Quaker's European management team formed the European Quality Council. In some respects, this group mirrors the North American I-Team. These groups share certain characteristics that contribute to the management of Quaker's quality-improvement system. For example, most of the teams are multifunctional and composed of line managers and officers. Responsibility for success is never positioned solely with a quality department; rather, it becomes each department's responsibility to ensure that their processes operate in accordance with corporate quality goals and appropriate customer and industry standards.

Although making sure that total quality "happens" is the responsibility of everyone in the organization, management must be involved or the quality program will eventually fizzle out. Although Quaker is still refining its process of management involvement, several key drivers have emerged from the company's experiences.

1. *Provide education and training in quality for all employees. Learn and apply the same skills being taught throughout the organization.* At Quaker, all senior mangers attended a four-day workshop on business process improvement (BPI) or process re-engineering. The group re-engineered and greatly simplified the corporate budgeting process using the acquired skills. These actions were widely communicated and launched numerous BPI training and implementation activities throughout the organization. Interestingly, the selection of the budgeting process was not a random choice. This was an outgrowth of an earlier SPC charting training exercise for senior managers that showed variability in the budgeting process. Senior managers have also been trained regarding the setting and significance of product specifications to better assess progress on meeting corporate goals. If quality improvement as a concept is to succeed long-term, there must be total buy-in at all levels. Management invests to give all employees the tools to succeed. Over the last four years, a core curriculum has been developed for all employees to increase basic skills and knowledge of the business. These programs range from seminars for understanding corporate business values to problem-solving and project management skills.
2. *Schedule periodic quality reviews with direct reports.* Quaker's Corporate Quality Steering Committee consists of senior managers and has met approximately every six weeks for the last two-and-one-half years. This group sets yearly corporate quality goals and reviews individual business unit progress toward meeting these goals on a periodic basis. Additionally, major quality initiatives, such as achieving ISO 9000 certification for all business units, internal quality promotional activities, and significant quality skill set training issues, are developed by this group.
3. *Develop and review strategic quality plans and objectives on an ongoing basis.* To reinforce the link between quality and strategic business planning activities, each senior and middle manager has one or more personal quality improvement goals. These are reviewed annually and a portion of the manager's variable compensation package is based on their attainment. This program is the latest version of the president's goal program. At the beginning of the company's focused quality activities, the president of Quaker required that *all* employees submit to him a personal quality-improvement goal on a yearly basis. Progress toward achieving this goal was reviewed on a quarterly basis and comment made to each employee. Significant quality improvements were acknowledged and communicated throughout the corporation.

4. *Clarify and set specific responsibilities for quality.* Along with all other employees, the CEO has specific quality-improvement goals. He reports on them to Quaker's board of directors.
5. *Monitor and continually improve the defect and error rate of internal processes and systems.* Specific measures of first-run quality performance are charted monthly and reviewed by management at the CQSC. Results are widely communicated throughout the organization and corrective action plans established.
6. *Monitor and continually improve the level of customer satisfaction.* Senior managers regularly report on their customer visits. Partnering quality-improvement activities are also established during these visits. Additionally, the CEO has aggressively pushed for customer satisfaction level assessments. A pilot program has recently been completed in the United States, and other affiliate operations have conducted their own surveys.

Measuring Organizational Performance

There has to be some structure to a continuous quality improvement process and some indicators of progress. Meaningful measurements of quality based on customer satisfaction can be difficult to devise, however. Indicators can focus on certain activities that can make the organization look good, but reveal little about what customers are thinking or how they are reacting to the company's actions.

The structure of Quaker's quality programs was provided by the quality policy and implemented through a corporate quality plan. The purpose of the plan is to document a simple process that integrates and guides efforts leading to a total quality environment. Suggesting the basic items that promote and initiate continuous quality improvement at all business units, the six points of the plan enable individual business units to link their departmental and individual quality-improvement goals to overall business planning and to the corporate quality planning process. The six points are as follows:

1. Adopt, communicate, and implement corporatewide quality and attitude value programs.
2. Develop a work process applying quality management tools to continuously improve all company processes.
3. Maintain safety, health, and environmental guidelines consistent with local, state, and federal regulatory policy.
4. Proved products and services that focus on customer satisfaction by conforming to customer expectations at all times, the first time.
5. Link total quality improvement into all business planning elements, such as products/service quality, competitive status, organizational mission, and culture, including values.
6. Improve constantly and forever.

Each year, several items linked to the quality plan are fashioned into quality performance-improvement goals. Each corporate business unit reports on specific action plans to meet these goals and progress to date. The overall process and progress against goals are guided by the Corporate Quality Steering Committee.

Quaker has taken to heart the adage that you can't manage what you can't measure. Therefore, the last critical piece of its overall quality improvement process if "Measure Up." Quaker's way of keeping score, Measure Up is driven by the following actions:

1. Find out exactly what the customer wants.
2. Provide the product or service the customer wants right the first time.
3. Continuously improve the way we make and sell the products and services the customer wants.
4. Link all programs of corporate performance improvement indicators.

Four key measurement programs are incorporated into Measure Up. The first one is the Quaker Quality Index (QQI), a Dow Jones-type index for quality. It consists of several operating elements that provide a tracking mechanism to see how Quaker measures up to customer expectations 100 percent of the time, the first time. It is basically a first-run yield of the company's quality systems.

The second program tracks what it costs to fix things gone wrong. This program follows the approach of the Crosby Price of Non-Conformance (PONC) and contains such elements as the cost of returned goods, the cost of scrapping raw materials and finished products, and the cost of issuing and the value of credits given to customers for unsatisfactory company performance. The QQI and the PONC index are tracked by each Quaker business unit and reported on quarterly throughout the corporation.

The third part of the program is internal auditing, which was started in compliance with ISO 9000 certification requirements. The key issues here are determining the level of conformance to standards or expectations and reporting findings to a level of management that has the authority to take corrective action. Verification that corrective action has taken place in a timely manner is part of the measurement index.

Customer assessments and customer satisfaction levels are an integral part of the program.

The most important part of Measure Up is the voice of the customer. Therefore, customer assessments and customer satisfaction levels are in integral part of the program. Customers exist in many forms—those who form the base of the commercial enterprise and those who make up the organization. Each comes to the table with needs and expectations. Of necessity, those expectations seek performance, a key dimension of the quality formula. A product or service that does not meet performance expectations will not satisfy the customer. Customers also exist inside the organization—the employees.

For assessing external customer satisfaction, Quaker has embarked on a major project to benchmark steel industry customers' levels of satisfaction with the company's products and services compared to the competition. The objectives were to provide a customer satisfaction baseline on an anonymous basis and to tie these measures into the QQI and PONC programs to fine-tune Quaker's continuous quality-improvement process. These programs will be repeated on a yearly basis as a continuing embodiment of the quality policy to "listen to the customer" and to help the company design a process that will delight the customer.

When each employee ensures that the quality of his or her work meets the needs and expectations of those internal customers serving the outside world, then the expectations of the ultimate customer, the external customer, should be assured. But what are employee opinions and attitudes about quality, competitiveness, and management performance?

In 1991, Quaker hired an outside consulting firm to assess and compare opinion patterns on a number of subjects among different employee groups, departments, and locations. Quaker would also be compared with strategic/peer organizations, and benchmarks would be developed against which to measure the impact of changing employee opinions over time. Results of employee attitude surveys at the that time revealed some interesting information. One of the more significant findings came from comparing the views of employees at the "best-run companies" sampled with the remainder of the database. Clear differences in a number of areas attested to the fact that something was operating in these organizations at the human level that differentiated them from the pack. Most noteworthy here: Employees in these companies give more respect to top management; they also feel that they get more respect themselves. In addition, they voice more positive feelings about the quality of products and services from their organizations.

Employees in these companies give more respect to top management; they also feel that they get more respect themselves.

A second Quaker employee attitude survey was recently completed, and improvement is notable on many questions concerning performance orientation and quality. The value of these programs cannot be understated. For example, according to the first survey, employees thought that the work-flow process at Quaker was not very well organized. This one issue gave rise to the incorporation of business process improvement or re-engineering in training programs for all Quaker employees. These particular programs are just now beginning to filter throughout the organization and, when the next survey is conducted two years from now, Quaker hopes to see significant improvement in this particular rating. Most gratifying to the organization are the significant improvements noted in employee attitudes about the quality of the company's products and services compared to the last survey, and an extremely high overall rating regarding quality of product and service delivered by Quaker Chemical Corporation. Ancillary to that is that most employees said that company training programs adequately prepared them to carry out their job functions.

What of the future? Quaker seems to have a fairly firm anchor on management involvement and integrating quality into its business planning. Albeit embryonic, systems to measure the effectiveness of the company's actions are also in place and generating information.

What is abundantly clear to some but not yet to all is that the implementation of lasting quality must forever change the nature of work life. Standards never stagnate. Future standards will include more and more focus on results. Fancy systems that do not yield greater customer satisfaction, reduce variability, and improve productivity will fall by the wayside. Getting this message out is Quaker's next challenge.

Ira R. Dolich is vice president, quality, at Quaker Chemical Corporation in Conshohoken, Pennsylvania. Matthew K. Frick is manager of quality for Quaker's North American Operations and is in charge of all quality assurance laboratories in this area. Jan Wolring is managing director of Quaker Chemical B. V. in the Netherlands.

Services Sector

Service Quality Circa 1995: A Play with Many Acts

Ron Zemke

What's the state of service quality today? Ron Zemke, consulting editor in the area of services, writes in this original article about the importance of the service component in any business. Zemke reminds us that in every industry, the service industries included, service is not one thing but many things, and only those companies that "get with the program" are likely to create or maintain any kind of competitive advantage. Zemke is also represented in the "Teams and Teamwork" section of the yearbook with a thoughtful article on the value of teams in organizations.

Five words capture what today's customers want from the organization they do business with: faster—better—cheaper—my way. There is no mistaking the message. The company than can shave delivery and turnaround time, provide better quality, and tailor its products and services to the customer's precise needs is a company to be reckoned with. Add one more dimension, and you have a company with an insurmountable edge on the competition. That dimension?

High Quality Customer Service

Providing outstanding customer service as part of the "package" you present to your customer pays and pays well. Studies done by business economists over the last five years[1] show that companies rated high on the quality of their customer service:

- Keep customers longer—50 percent longer or more.

- Have lower sales and marketing costs—20 percent to 40 percent lower.
- Experience higher return on sales—7 percent to 12 percent higher.
- Have better net profits—7 percent to 17 percent better.

We are also learning that there is another economic dimension to good service. When customers are pleased with the way they are treated, employees are frequently more satisfied with their jobs and content to stay with the organization.[2] Why? Simple! Who wants to spend their working hours in an organization customers hate? And who isn't motivated by a customer's thanks—and manager's "job well done"?

In principle, quality customer service is pretty simple: Make sure you know what your customer wants and expects of you; be flexible in meeting those demands; treat customers like partners rather than as adversaries or end-users; and work like heck to make it easy for the customer to do business with you.

Why is providing great service so difficult—more difficult, some would say, than making a great product? It is a mission easier to describe than to mount and master; a practice that requires resolve and skill to maintain over more than the shortest span. Think about the simple haircut, a service so common and ordinary we take it for granted. It is a good illustration of just how different and difficult creating world-class, customer-pleasing service can be.

If you are a barber/beautician/stylist, you are very much at the behest of whoever walks in the door. No rejecting the raw material or sending it back to the vendor. No way to say, "I'm sorry, sir/ma'am, but your head is out of round and your hair is just too thin. We don't work with substandard material." Nor do you have more than partial control over standards. The customer controls the standards. And the one who walks in the door with a copy of *Esquire* or *Vogue* or *Self* or *Fortune* with a favorite photo of Madonna or Whitney Houston or Bruce Willis or Eddie Murphy circled has a clear vision of the end results in mind, realistic or not—and will hold you to them. On top of that, customers don't leave their heads for you to work on and come back at 5 p.m. to survey your work. Oh, no, they hop up in the chair, look into the back bar mirror, and "help" you do your job: "Careful! Not too short" . . . "Now don't make the part too wide" . . . "Not too close on the sideburns, full on the sides though." They stay right there in your service factory and tell you how to take care of business for them.

And when you've finished, they are only conditionally satisfied with the job you've done. The final, final evaluation must wait until they see how their spouse, family, friends, coworkers, and casual passersby react to the "new do"—and until they've had a crack at reproducing your styling excellence in their own bathroom mirror after a hot steamy shower.

That, oversimplified, is the reality of delivering quality service today. It must be done one customer and one encounter at a time, each and every time, to the specifications of that one customer—if you are going to have a chance of getting that customer back again.

Managing the Service "Act"

Because service is such a public performance, and so "obvious" when it is delivered well, recent times have seen an explosion of expert pronouncements regarding the necessary and sufficient conditions for successful service delivery. Indeed, well meaning but service inexperienced product quality experts routinely look upon service quality as a "lesser" practice; a simple subset of "real" quality improvement. In fact, the intangibility and variable nature of service quality, as well as its dependence upon customer perception for validation, make consistent service quality an extremely difficult deliverable to manage.

Pioneering service quality researchers Leonard Berry, A. "Parsu" Parasuraman, and Valarie Zeithaml recently cut through the din of good and bad advice and synthesized ten fundamental "lessons" or truisms that emerge from their decade of studying efforts to create and manage service quality in America:[3]

1. *Listening* is fundamental; quality is defined by the customers—no other standard is meaningful. "The goal is to become a 'listening company,'" they assert.
2. *Reliability*, doing what is promised dependably, accurately, is the cornerstone of service quality. Of all the demands cited by customers, this is paramount. Produce what you promise or perish.
3. *Mastery of the basics* is all most customers are looking for. "In all our customer research, we have yet to find any evidence of extravagant customer expectations," say these eminent researchers.
4. *Service design*, mapping out the way your service delivery system should (or does) work, in great detail is critical to flawless performance—and to improvement.
5. *Service recovery*, solving problems immediately and effectively, is important to customer retention.
6. *Surprising customers* with "uncommon swiftness, grace, courtesy, competence, commitment, or understanding" can go far toward distinguishing an organization in the customer's eye.
7. *Fair play*, treating customers in an ethical and above-board way, is fundamental. "Fairness is not a separate dimension of service, but, rather, touches the essence of what customers expect."
8. *Teamwork* among service providers, and up and down the service "chain," is critical not only to effectiveness but to employee motivation and stress management.
9. *Employee research*, asking your employees to assess internal service quality, to call out conditions that act as barriers to service customers well, and to be alert to systems breakdown, keeps the organization ahead of marketplace problems.

10. *Service leadership*, asking/expecting managers to "serve the servers" and "walk the talk," is critical to bringing an organization's service quality aspirations to fruition. Manager as role model and leader, communicator and coach is fundamental to success.

Emerging Issues

The study of service as a critical commercial distinguisher and a systematically manageable outcome has lagged behind the "disciplines" of product quality. As a result, there continue to be emerging issues in the design, delivery, and sustenance of superior quality service. At least three issues have begun to receive serious attention in the last year.

1. Strategic Variety in Service Differentiation

Until very recently, "service" was assumed to be a single variable. Evaluation of service quality has routinely been limited to the assessment of a few simple variables, such as promptness of product delivery, courtesy of customer contact personnel, and recovery quality.

But as serious researchers such as Berry, Parasuraman, and Zeithaml and a few others have worked to unbundle and quantify the idea of quality service, it becomes harder and harder to specify what exactly it means to say we are concerned with the design and delivery of "high quality, distinctive customer service." As more options for creating distinction arise, the selection, creation, and delivery of distinctive service becomes more of a ponderable strategic issue.

As these options arise, we need better tools for sorting and sifting the possibilities and matching them to our existing opportunities.

As more options for creating distinction arise, the selection, creation, and delivery of distinctive service becomes more of a ponderable strategic issue.

One such tool—or the potential for one—appeared in the January/February 1993 issue of *Harvard Business Review* in an article titled, "Customer Intimacy and Other Value Disciplines" by Cambridge, MA, consultants Michael Treacy and Fred Wiersema.[4]

Treacy and Wiersema contend that companies that have gained a leadership position in their industries have done so by narrowing their business focus to one of three "value disciplines" dubbed Operational Excellence, Customer Intimacy, and Product Leadership. The "so what" to their treatise is that "companies that push the boundaries of one value discipline while meeting industrial standards in the other two gain such a lead that competitors find it hard to catch up." They claim it's the rare company that can excel in more than one of the three at the same time. Only Toyota, USAA, and Staples (a large office supply firm) make their dual-strategies successful, say Treacy and Wiersema.

The three value disciplines are fairly self-explanatory.

Operational Excellence: Providing customers with reliable products or services at competitive prices and delivering them with minimal difficulty or inconvenience. Think of it as the "Amazingly-Easy-to-Do-Business-With" strategy.

Customer Intimacy: Segmenting and targeting markets precisely, then tailoring offerings to exactly match those demands. This is the "Make-Me-Feel-Unique-and-Special" approach. It is also the home of one-to-one customer relationships and high value added.

Product Leadership: Offering customers leading edge products and services that make competitive products obsolete and distinguish the buyer as cutting edge. It is the "You-Are-the Best-and-the-Brightest-So-You-Deserve-the Best" appeal to customers.

My reaction when first exposed to Treacy and Wiersema's categories was to test their robustness by seeing where currently popular service distinguishers fit. Six sigma quality? Easy—Product Leadership. How about service guarantees? Easy again—Operational Excellence. Same for exceptional recovery processes and systems reengineering. Customer intimacy seems an easy home for partnering, customer education, and all those efforts to create unique "dazzlement experiences" for customers. According to my little litmus test, the only odd variable is frequency marketing, practices such as frequent user programs, buyer clubs, and the like. I can see these fitting into either Operational Excellence or Customer Intimacy approaches.

Peter Drucker said, "The purpose of a business is to create and retain customers." He didn't say, "create perfection" and he didn't say "create and keep busy a quality department." He said create and retain customers. Let me be so bold as to suggest that unless you and the average employee in the average frontline service job can unequivocally place your organization in one of Treacy and Wiersema's three buckets, your service quality program is probably anchorless and adrift. If you want to excite people about the prospect of "We're number one!" it helps if they know what they're going to be number one at.

Peter Drucker said, "The purpose of a business is to create and retain customers." He didn't say, "create perfection" and he didn't say "create and keep busy a quality department."

2. Customer and Supply Chain Partnering

One of the common tattoos of the last half decade has been that of "exceeding customer expectations" and creating customer "dazzlement." What Berry et al. call "surprising the customer." At the same time, a realization that this upwardly spiraling goal has some real drawbacks has set in. "Innovate or Die" as a slogan usually leads to organizational exhaustion, even in the entertainment industry. The alternative is to create a different relationship with the customer—that of colleague and partner, rather than court magician. Partners co-invent a mutually profitable future. They succeed or fail together, not at one another's expense.[5]

The idea of a partnered relationship has gained significant appeal in situations where the "customer" of a product or service is not the end-user or final recipient of that product or service. We increasingly hear terms like "supply chain partners" used to denote the realization that some buyer-seller, provider-customer relationships are, in fact, only intermediary relations between the creator of the product or service and the actual recipient of the product or service. Most important about this realization is the notion that success for any single member of the supply chain partnership is dependent on the success of all the members of the chain, and alternately, the satisfaction of the eventual end-user.

How do you establish a partnership with a customer? How do you find a common ground for mutual success? At Baxter Healthcare,[6] it's done by sharing with customers the company's resources and expertise in everything from hazardous waste disposal to their quality process. In the late 1970s, the suburban Chicago-based health-care products manufacturer came to the conclusion that partnering with the company's primary customers—the hospitals, clinics, and HMOs of the U.S. health-care delivery system—was vital to the long-term success of both.

Partnering at Baxter often takes the form of experience sharing. "If one of our account executives has a customer with a finance problem or an operations problem, he may simply arrange for a Baxter financial operations person to talk common problems and solutions with that client." David Auld, vice president of quality leadership, says. "Sometimes we don't have the expertise but can help arrange for it in a way the customer can afford. Waste elimination is a big issue. We didn't have any expertise, so we enlisted Waste Management Corp. to work with our customers, through us, on the issue."

Beginning around 1984, Auld and his staff of 50 quality professionals became one of those "sharable" resources. Today, Auld and his people, in addition to their in-house work, provide consulting, training, and general quality program assistance to 200 hospitals and other health-care providers nationwide. His group's experience is a good example of the benefits of turning "customer-ships" into partnerships. "We charge for our services. It would be a violation of the law not to, but our primary goal is to improve the quality process for all—Baxter as well as for the individual hospitals we are consulting with." Partnering resources and services are provided to customers no strings attached, save the cost of the quality consulting and other resources. And no full-court press from account reps follows a big partnering activity, such as the instituting of a Baxter-aided quality program. But there are significant core business payoffs. First, there is the lowering of barriers between Baxter and its customer/partners and an improvement in understanding and communication. Says Auld: "As a result of our working with these hospitals on quality issues, we've come to know each other better in general. We can work more comfortably on joint problems."

Second, there is the establishment of a vocabulary for common problem-solving. In one case, a customer who had been sticky and contentious with Baxter for years became a booster when a problem-solving team concluded that they had been using terms very differently. They learned, for example, that they had very different definitions of what constituted an "on-time" delivery.

And finally, there have been measurable changes in the business relationship for both members of the partnership. Auld is reluctant to give exact figures, but does say that, "We track the relationship. We compare the business we were doing together before partnering and after. The return is significantly higher now. It's always in the area of a double-digit increase."

Here is an old Wall Street maxim: "Bears make money. Bulls make money. Pigs always get slaughtered." Perhaps there is an appropriate addendum—"And partners always prosper together."

3. Managing Internal Service Quality Leads to External Quality Service

Increasingly, organizations are accepting the message that there is a direct relationship between the way employees feel about their work and the way customers feel about the organization. In the parlance of the day, employees who feel well-serviced by the organization, serve their customers well. The working metaphor is that everyone in an organization is a customer and a supplier, working in an internal chain of relationships that, ultimately, services the customer. That is not an entirely new message. Indeed, industrial psychologists and sociologists interested in job satisfaction have long spread that contented employees produce more product.

The core approach to measuring internal customer satisfaction is the question: "What happens in this organization that makes it harder for you to satisfy your customers (inside and out) than it should be?"

The new news is that internal service is a more complex issue than traditional job satisfaction. Job satisfaction, traditionally, has focused on issues such as pay, working conditions, supervision, and promotional opportunities. Internal service satisfaction, though sometimes touching on job satisfaction, is much more concerned with tools and conditions employees perceive as important to fulfilling this role in satisfying customers. The core approach to measuring internal customer satisfaction is the question: "What happens in this organization that makes it harder for you to satisfy your customers (inside and out) than it should be?"

At San Diego Gas and Electric Corp.,[7] there is a strong internal belief that smooth hand-offs and good communications between sales and service areas or engineering and production, are critical to wringing out ineffectiveness and creating the kind of seamless operation invisible to the customer—but critical to external customer satisfaction. Acting on this belief, SDG&E measures as well as gives incentives—on the basis of an 11 item internal service survey. The items, internally developed, respond to very practical indicators SDG&E employees cite as evidence of a positive internal service attitude. Some items are very procedural:

"They respond to my phone calls and messages."

Others have to do with colleague competence:

"They have the knowledge and skill to give me what I need."

Other items deal with perceived attitude:

"They show a sincere desire to help."

To be important to SDG&E, this focus on internal service must result in a customer payoff, says Patricia Kuhl, service consumer research analyst. According to the company's continuous customer satisfaction tracking programs, it does; customers who say they are "very satisfied" with the utility's service have tracked upward in step with increases in internal satisfaction since the program was instituted in 1982.

Service Quality Tomorrow

The emerging art of managing service quality is just that—an intact field of study. As customer service and service quality increase in import to customers worldwide, the practice will grow and mature. Its limits are, most surely, nothing more nor less than the combined imaginations of customers and providers, partnering for progress.

Notes

1. Chip R. Bell and Ron Zemke, *Managing "Knock Your Socks Off" Service* (New York: AMACOM Books, 1992).

2. J. L. Heskett, and L. A. Schlesinger, "Putting the Service-Profit Chain to Work," *Harvard Business Review*, March–April 1994, pp. 164–174.

3. Leonard A. Berry, A. Parasuraman, and Valarie Zeithaml, "Improving Service Quality in America: Lessons Learned," *Academy of Management Executive*, vol. 8, no. 2, 1994. (See reference section "A Quality Management Library" for information on Berry et al.'s book, *Delivering Quality Service*.)

4. Michael Treacy and Fred Wiersema, "Customer Intimacy and Other Value Disciplines," *Harvard Business Review*, January–February, 1993.

5. Chip R. Bell, *Customers As Partners: Building Relationships that Last* (San Francisco: Berrett-Koehler Publishers, 1994); Rosabeth Moss Kanter, "Collaborative Advantage: The Art of Alliances," *Harvard Business Review*, July–August 1994, pp. 96–108.

6. Ron Zemke, "Turning Customers into Partners," *The Service Edge* Newsletter, Lakewood Publications, September 1991.

7. Randy Johnson, "Internal Service: How One Company Uses Pay Incentives to Create Enduring Change," *The Service Edge* Newsletter, Lakewood Publications, June 1993.

Managing the Evidence of Service

Mary Jo Bitner

Service providers need to be concerned that the image they project in their interactions with customers provides "evidence" to these customers that they can deliver on their promises. A messy desk of a travel agent says this person is unreliable, whether that is true or not. This article describes how to manage customer interaction to make sure the image and the reality of the services delivered coincide.

When a company offers an intangible service, how do consumers choose it, evaluate it, and assess its quality? On what evidence is an intangible service judged? For example, how do consumers choose between two different dentists, and how do they judge whether they are satisfied with the services of a particular car repair business? Research and theory suggest that customers rely on a variety of cues or surrogate indicators of service to choose among alternatives and judge quality.

Intangibility and Service Evidence

The primary characteristic that distinguishes goods from services is the relative intangibility of most services. While a manufactured good can be seen, felt, and touched, most services cannot be, and therefore they must be experienced by consumers before they can be evaluated. Clearly, tangibility exists along a continuum, and all products exhibit some tangible as well as intangible qualities.[1] However, services *tend* to be more intangible, while goods *tend* to be more tangible. It has been suggested that because of their intangibility, it is more difficult for consumers to evaluate services prior to purchase, to compare different service alternatives, and to judge the quality of service even after it has been experienced.[2]

Research suggests that customers rely on the tangible evidence of service, or perhaps surrogate indicators of service, when they are unable to judge the actual quality of service. For example, one study suggested that first impressions of a firm's reception area design will influence consumers' overall impressions of the firm.[3] Another study showed that travel customers' beliefs about and satisfaction with a travel agent were influenced by whether the

---

Reprinted, with permission of the publisher, from *The Service Quality Handbbook,* edited by Eberhard E. Scheuing and William F. Christopher. Copyright © 1993 AMACOM, a division of the American Management Association. All rights reserved.

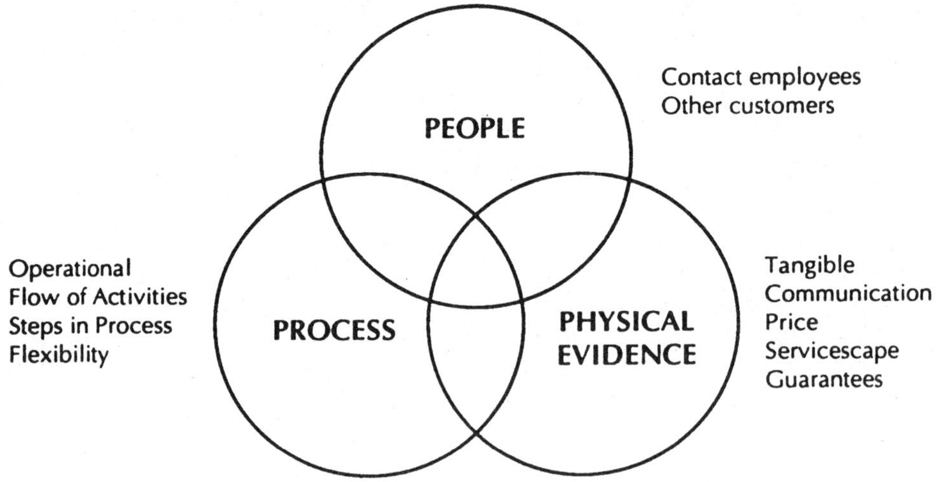

Figure 1. **The evidence of service.**

travel agent's office was organized or disorganized.[4] And another study showed that airline customers were likely to perceive an airline as having lower safety standards if there were coffee stains on its tray tables. Research on service quality across a variety of service industries suggests that above and beyond the basic reliability of service, consumers rely on cues such as employee responsiveness, empathy, assurance, and tangibles to assess quality.[5]

Beyond the basic reliability of service, consumers rely on cues such as employee responsiveness, empathy, assurance, and tangibles to assess quality.

Clearly, the reception area decor, the travel agent's desk (organized vs. disorganized), the coffee stains on the tray table, and the empathy of a service provider can and may be totally independent of the objective quality of service. That is, the disorganized travel agent *may* in reality have an outstanding record of reliable service and provide better quality overall than competitors. However, customers are likely to rely on cues like office clutter in the absence of other criteria on which to choose or judge a service. The process or operational flow of activities by which the service is delivered is also critical in forming perceptions of the service.

Figure 1 depicts the three major categories of service evidence as experienced by the customer: people, process, and physical evidence. Together, these elements constitute what is referred to here as the "evidence of service." All three elements, or a subset, are present in every encounter a customer has with a service firm.

People

All of the human actors involved in the delivery of a service provide cues to the customer regarding the nature of the service itself. This includes the employees of the service firm and other customers in the service environment. How these people are dressed, their personal appearance, and their attitudes and behaviors all influence the customer's perceptions of the service. The service provider or contact person can be very important. In fact, for some services, such as consulting, counseling, teaching, and other professional relationship-based services, the provider *is* the service. In other cases, the contact person may play what appears to be a relatively small part in service delivery, for instance, a telephone installer, an airline baggage handler, or a hotel bellperson. Yet research suggests that even these providers may be the focal point of service encounters that can prove to be critical for the firm.[6]

Other customers can also influence perceptions of the service. Prior to purchase, a person may use other customers as a cue to the type of service being offered and the market segment. For example, before entering a restaurant, a potential customer may peer through the window to see whether he or she "fits" with the other customers already in the restaurant. The decision to go in or not is partially determined by the other customers and the evidence they provide regarding the type of restaurant and market segment. Frequently, the service experience itself is influenced by other customers, since in many instances, for example, in classrooms, hospitals, retail stores, airplanes, and restaurants, customers experience the service together. The experience of one customer may easily influence the experiences of many others. Sometimes, the needs of one customer may even conflict with the needs of another.[7]

Process

The actual steps the customer experiences, or the operational flow of service, will also provide him or her with evidence on which to judge the service. Some service operations are very complex, requiring the customer to follow a complicated and extensive series of actions to complete the process. Highly bureaucratized services frequently follow this pattern, and the logic of the steps involved often escapes the customer. Another distinguishing characteristic of the process that can provide evidence to the customer is whether the service follows a production-line/standardized approach or whether the process is an empowered/customized one.[8] None of these characteristics of the process are inherently better or worse than others. Rather, the point here is that these process characteristics are another form of evidence used by the consumer to judge service. For example, two successful airline companies, Southwest (U.S. airline) and SAS (Scandinavian airline), follow extremely different process models. Southwest is a no-frills (no food, no assigned seats), no exceptions, low-priced airline that offers frequent, relatively short-length, domestic flights in the United States. All of the evidence they provide (from their price, to their people, to the standardized process they follow) is consistent with their vision and market position. SAS, on the other hand, focuses on the business traveler and is concerned with meeting individual traveler needs. Thus, its process is highly customized to the individual, and employees are empowered to provide nonstandard service when needed. Both airlines have been very successful, and in both cases the evidence of service that is showcased in their operational process is highly compatible with the firm's goals and the needs of the identified market segment.

Physical Evidence

The physical evidence of service includes tangible representations of the service such as advertising and other forms of communication, including billing statements, letters, and business cards; service guarantees; price; and the physical environment in which the service is delivered and the customer and the firm's employees interact.[9] When consumers have little on which to judge the actual quality of service, they will rely on these cues, just as they rely on the cues provided by the people and the service process. Physical evidence cues provide excellent opportunities for the firm to send consistent and strong messages regarding the firm's purpose, the intended market segments, and the nature of the service.

In many service industries, the service setting, or "servicescape," provides a particularly prominent representation of physical evidence. The servicescape is defined as the "built environment, or the human-made, physical surroundings of the service."[10] The servicescape plays a variety of roles with respect to both the customers and the employees of the service firm. For example, the servicescape serves as a "package" for the service offering in a way not unlike that of a product's package. Product packages are designed to portray a particular image to the consumer as well as evoke a particular sensory or emotional reaction.[11] In a service setting, the servicescape does the same thing through the interaction of many complex stimuli. The service package can also convey the values of the organization and the ideals it hopes to achieve.

The physical surroundings may also serve to differentiate a firm from its competitors and signal who the intended market segment is. In strolling through any large shopping mall, one quickly notes the environmental distinctions between clothing stores catering to the youth market and those aimed at older market segments. Even without examining the merchandise, a shopper instinctively knows that neon signs, bright lights, and loud music signal a youth market segment. Similarly, legal clinics and legal chain operations intended for price-sensitive, middle-income persons can effectively use their physical environments to distinguish themselves from large, corporate law firms. By keeping furnishings relatively simple and functional, the legal clinics signal both intended market segment and price level to potential customers, and simultaneously differentiate themselves from the large firms.

A final role of the servicescape is that of facilitating the individual and interdependent actions of persons in the environment, namely the customers and employees. How the environment is designed enhances or inhibits the efficient flow of activities in the servicescape. A well-designed, functional facility can make the service a pleasure to experience from the customer's point of view and a pleasure to perform from the employee's viewpoint. On the other hand, poor and inefficient design may frustrate both the employee and the customer as they seek to carry out their respective plans. Similarly, the servicescape can encourage and nurture certain social behaviors between and among customers and employees. For example, Benihana restaurants and

Club Med facilities show how servicescapes can be designed to enhance employee/customer and customer/customer interactions. On the other hand, airport waiting areas and university classrooms are notorious for discouraging interpersonal interaction through the way they are designed and laid out.

Identifying the Evidence

Service evidence will communicate to the consumer, whether the messages sent are intended or unintentional, planned or accidental. This section of the chapter proposes a way of thinking about service evidence that can enhance the strategic value of all three types of evidence cues.

Mapping the Service

The three categories of service evidence—people, process, and physical evidence—may be more or less important for a particular service firm or industry.[12] Thus, a first step in determining evidence strategy would be to identify the relevant forms of evidence presented to the customer in a given context. Service mapping, or blueprinting, provides a useful tool to begin assessing and identifying evidence opportunities.[13]

A service map visually displays the service by simultaneously depicting the process of service delivery, the roles of customers and employees, and the visible elements of the service. The service map provides an excellent starting point for isolating evidence opportunities. Figures 2 and 3 show service maps for two different services: express mail and an overnight hotel stay. (The blueprints are deliberately kept very simple, showing only the most basic steps involved in the process. Complex diagrams could be developed for each and every step, and the internal processes could be much more fully developed, if desired.) The horizontal lines of the blueprint separate (1) the actions of the customer from those of the contact person, and (2) those contact person steps that are visible from the invisible process steps. A service map may be read horizontally from left to right to understand the actions or steps that must be performed by either the customer or the contact employees of the firm, or it may be read vertically to understand the structural relationships that exist to support the actions of the customers and employees.

For example, in reading the express mail blueprint, the customer actions are simply three: phone call, turn over package, receive package (a different customer). The visible contact employee actions are minimal as well: pick up package, deliver package. A significant number of complex steps and procedures must occur behind the line of visibility, however, to ensure that these two actions can be performed accurately and reliably. In fact, customers are usually fascinated to see the complexities of the express mail process, and Federal Express frequently invites its customers to tour its sorting and delivery facilities in order to further make tangible this seemingly simple service.

Federal Express frequently invites its customers to tour its sorting and delivery facilities in order to further make tangible this seemingly simple service.

Evidence Opportunities

The maps presented in Figures 2 and 3 help in visualizing the three types of evidence and provide a common ground for beginning to assess and identify

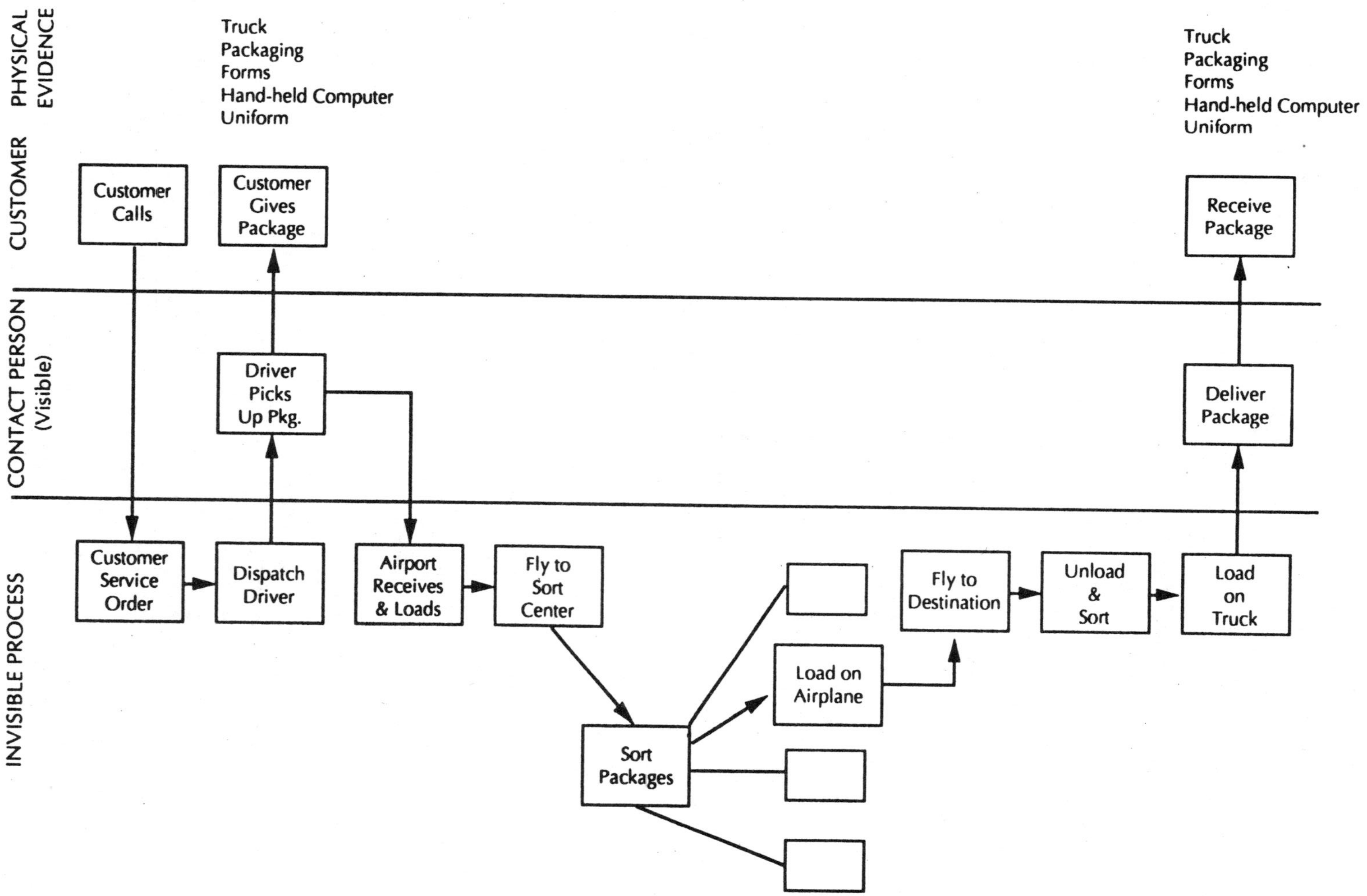

Figure 2. **Express mail delivery service.**

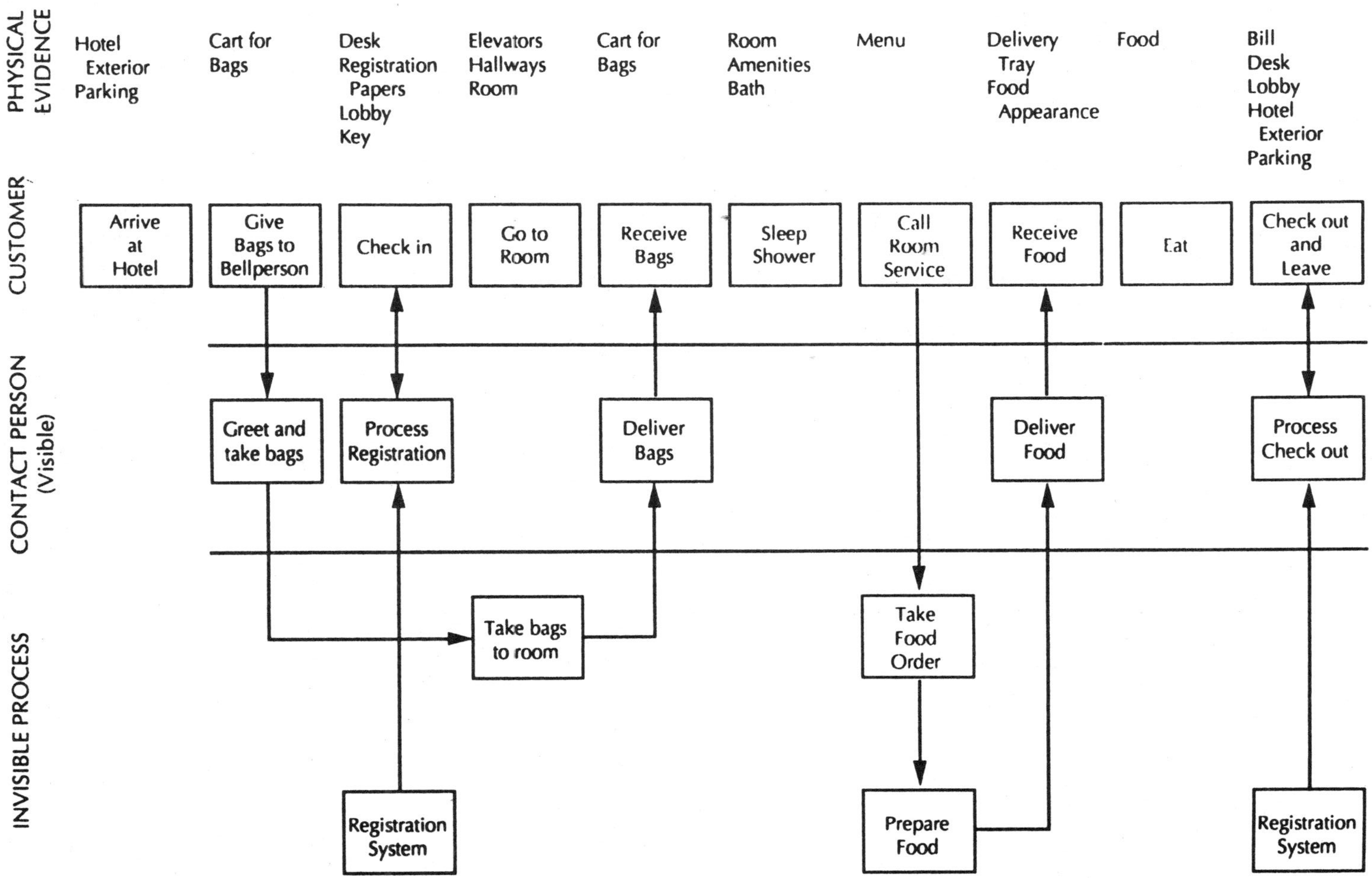

Figure 3. **Overnight hotel stay.**

evidence opportunities. For example, the complexity of the *process* and the actual steps involved from the customer's point of view are clearly evident reading horizontally across the top section of the blueprint. From the customer's point of view, the process of staying overnight at a hotel is more complex and interactive than the process of using an express mail service. The *people* who interact with the customer are also clearly identifiable by reading across the line of interaction and noting each crossover point where there is an interaction with an employee of the firm, whether or not the customer sees that employee (i.e., whether there is a face-to-face interaction or a phone conversation). There are many more points of human interaction in the hotel example than in the express mail example. In both cases, it is clear from the blueprint exactly whom the customer interacts with and at what steps in the process. Each of these interaction points is a potential opportunity for providing service evidence. The *physical evidence* of service, while not typically shown on a blueprint, can easily be added, as it has been in Figures 2 and 3. This was done by analyzing each step in the process (from the customer's point of view) and adding relevant evidence that the customer would evaluate at that step.

Each of these interaction points is a potential opportunity for providing service evidence.

The two case examples will be described in a bit more detail to illustrate the uses of the blueprints.

Express Mail

In examining the express mail map in Figure 2, it is clear that from the customer's point of view there are only three points at which evidence of the service is provided: when the phone call is made, when the package is picked up, and when the package is delivered. The visible evidence at each of these points of interaction is depicted on the blueprint and can be analyzed for its consistency and ability to communicate clearly the firm's image and purpose. In the specific case of Federal Express, the employee's uniform, the forms and packaging used to transmit the package, the truck driven by the employee, and the hand-held computer carried by the employee are the "tangible evidence" of the service. In this case, the servicescape does not play a role with respect to the customer, since the customer would not routinely see the airplane, the sorting facility, and the customer service center where much of the actual service delivery process is carried out. From the customer's point of view, the *process* is simple (three steps) and relatively standardized, the *people* that perform the service are the phone order taker and the delivery people, and the *physical evidence* is composed of the document package, the transmittal forms, the truck, and the hand-held computer. The complex process that occurs behind the line of visibility is of little interest or concern to the customer.

Once the evidence of service has been identified through the mapping approach, then opportunities for change can be evaluated. Is enough evidence of service provided so that the customer *knows* that the service has actually been performed? Is the evidence compatible and consistent? Does the evidence communicate the desired image? Does the evidence fit the needs and preferences of the target market?

Overnight Hotel Stay

In the case of the overnight hotel stay depicted in Figure 3, it is clear that the customer is more actively involved in the service than he or she is in the express mail service just described. Even in this simple overnight hotel stay, the customer performs a number of actions in experiencing the service. The guest must first check in, then go to the hotel room, where a variety of steps take place (receiving bags, sleeping, showering, eating breakfast, etc.), and finally check out. Imagine how much more complex this process *could* be and how many more interactions might occur if the service map depicted a week-long vacation at the hotel, or even a three-day business conference. From the service map it is also clear (by reading across the line of interaction) whom the guest interacts with and thus the *people* who provide evidence of service to the customer. Several interactions occur with a variety of hotel employees, including the bellperson, the front desk clerk, the food service order desk, and the food delivery person. Each of the points of interaction is an evidence opportunity. In addition, the servicescape plays a *major* role in service delivery. The hotel facility itself is critical in communicating the image of the hotel company, in providing satisfaction for the guest through the manner in which the hotel room is designed and maintained, and in facilitating the actions and interactions of both the guest and the employees of the hotel. In the hotel case, the *process* is relatively complex (although again somewhat standardized), the *people* providing service evidence are a variety of front-line employees as well as other guests in the hotel, and the *physical evidence* includes everything from the guest registration form to the design of the lobby and room, to the uniforms worn by front-line employees.

Again, as with the express mail case, once the points of evidence are identified through mapping, opportunities for change can be assessed. Given the importance and complexity of the servicescape in the hotel industry, special attention will be focused on the facility design from the perspective of *both* employees and customers.

Guidelines for Evidence Strategy

Given the relative intangibility of most services, the strategy for managing the evidence of service is critical. And customers will react to the company's evidence whether or not an evidence strategy exists. That is, the tangible evidence of service will communicate to customers, whether or not its power to do so is recognized and planned. The following guidelines capture the essence of a plan for evidence strategy.

Given the relative intangibility of most services, the strategy for managing the evidence of service is critical.

Recognize the Strategic Impact of Evidence

Before an evidence strategy can be effective, it must be linked clearly to the company's overall goals and vision. Thus the first step is to know what those goals are and to determine how the evidence strategy can support them. At a minimum, the basic service concept, the target markets (both internal and external), and the firm's broad vision of its future must be identified.

Map the Evidence of Service

The next step is to map the service. Everyone should be able to *see* the service process and the existing elements of evidence. An effective way to depict service evidence is through the service map. While service maps clearly have multiple purposes,[14] they can be particularly useful in visually capturing evidence opportunities. People, process, and physical evidence can be seen in the service map. From the map, one can read the actions involved in service delivery, the complexity of the process, the points of human interaction that provide evidence opportunities, and the tangible representations present at each step. Employees, customers, and managers can all be involved in constructing the service map, which will then give them common ground for moving ahead to identify opportunities.

Clarify Roles of the Servicescape

Sometimes the servicescape has no role in service delivery from the customer's point of view. This is essentially the case with express mail, where the customer rarely sees the actual facilities where service is provided. However, in many cases, such as hotels and health care, the servicescape plays multiple roles with respect to both customer and employee actions and attitudes.[15] Clarifying the roles played by the servicescape in a particular situation will aid in identifying opportunities and deciding just who needs to be consulted in making facility design decisions.

Assess and Identify Evidence Opportunities

One question to ask is: Are there missed opportunities to provide service evidence?

Once the current forms of evidence and the roles of the servicescape are understood, then possible changes and improvements can be identified. One question to ask is: Are there missed opportunities to provide service evidence? For example, the service map of an insurance or utility service may show that little if any evidence of service is ever provided to the customer. A strategy might then be developed to provide more evidence of service to show the customer exactly what he or she is paying for. Or it may be discovered that the evidence provided is sending inconsistent messages that don't serve to enhance the firm's image or goals. For example, a restaurant might find that its high price cue is not consistent with the design of the restaurant, which suggests "family dining" to its intended market segment. Another set of questions to address concerns whether the current evidence of service suits the needs and preferences of the target market. And, finally, does the evidence strategy take into account the needs (sometimes incompatible) of both customers and employees? This question is particularly relevant in making decisions regarding the servicescape.[16]

Be Prepared to Update and Modernize the Evidence

Some aspects of the evidence, particularly the servicescape, require frequent or at least periodic updating and modernizing. Even if the vision of the company doesn't change, time itself takes a toll on physical evidence, necessitating change and modernization. Organizations clearly understand this when it comes to advertising strategy, but sometimes other elements of physical evidence can be overlooked.

Conclusion

In presenting itself to the consumer, a service firm is concerned with communicating a desired image, with sending consistent and compatible messages through all forms of evidence, and with providing the type of service evidence the target customers want and can understand. Frequently, however, evidence decisions are made over time and by various functions within the organization. For example, decisions regarding employee uniforms may be made by the human resources area, servicescape design decisions may be made by the facilities management group, process design decisions are most frequently made by operations managers, and advertising and pricing decisions may be made by the marketing department. Thus, it is not surprising that the evidence of service may at times be less than consistent. Service mapping, or blueprinting, is presented here as a valuable tool for communicating within the firm, identifying existing service evidence, and providing a springboard for changing or providing new forms of evidence.

Notes

1. G. Lynn Shostack, "Breaking Free From Product Marketing," *Journal of Marketing* 41 (April 1977), pp. 73–80.

2. Valarie A. Zeithaml, "How Consumer Evaluation Processes Differ Between Goods and Services," in *Marketing of Services,* James H. Donnelly and William R. George, eds. (Chicago: American Marketing Association, 1981), pp. 186–190.

3. Suzyn Ornstein, "First Impressions of the Symbolic Meanings Connoted by Reception Area Design," *Environment and Behavior* 24, no. 1 (January 1992), pp. 85–110.

4. Mary Jo Bitner, "Evaluating Service Encounters: The Effects of Physical Surroundings and Employee Responses," *Journal of Marketing* (January 1990), pp. 71–84.

5. A. Parasuraman, Valarie A. Zeithaml, and Leonard L. Berry, "SERVQUAL: A Multiple-Item Scale for Measuring Consumer Perceptions of Service Quality," *Journal of Retailing* 64, no. 1 (1988), pp. 12–40.

6. Mary Jo Bitner, Bernard H. Booms, and Mary Stanfield Tetreault, "The Service Encounter: Diagnosing Favorable and Unfavorable Incidents," *Journal of Marketing* 54, no. 1 (January 1990), pp. 71–84.

7. Boas Shamir, "Between Service and Servility: Role Conflict in Subordinate Service Roles," *Human Relations* 33, no. 10 (1980), pp. 741–756; Charles L. Martin and Charles A. Pranter, "Compatibility Management: Customer-to-Customer Relationships in Service Environments," *Journal of Services Marketing* 3, no. 3 (Summer 1989), pp. 5–15.

8. David E. Bowen and Edward E. Lawler III, "The Empowerment of Service Workers: What, Why, How, and When," *Sloan Management Review* 33, no. 3 (Spring 1992), pp. 31–39.

9. Leonard L. Berry and A. Parasuraman, *Marketing Services* (New York: The Free Press, 1991), Chapter 6.

10. Mary Jo Bitner, "Servicescapes: The Impact of Physical Surroundings on Customers and Employees," *Journal of Marketing* 56, no. 2 (April 1992), pp. 57–71.

11. Michael R. Solomon, "Packaging the Service Provider," *Services Industries Journal* 5, no. 1 (1985), pp. 64–71.

12. Stephen J. Grove, Raymond P. Fisk, and Mary Jo Bitner, "Dramatizing the Service Experience: A Managerial Approach," in *Advances in Services Marketing and Management: Research and Practice, Vol. 1,* Teresa A. Swartz, David E. Bowen, and Stephen W. Brown, eds. (Greenwich, Conn.: JAI Press, Inc., 1992).

13. G. Lynn Shostack, "Designing Services That Deliver," *Harvard Business Review* 62 (January–February 1984), pp. 133–139; G. Lynn Shostack, "Service Positioning Through Structural Change," *Journal of Marketing* 51 (January 1989), pp. 34–43; Jane Kingman-Brundage, "The ABC's of Service System Blueprinting," in *Designing a Winning Service Strategy,* Mary Jo Bitner and Lawrence A. Crosby, eds. (Chicago: American Marketing Association 1989), pp. 30–33.

14. Kingman-Brundage, "The ABC's of Service."

15. Bitner, "Servicescapes."

16. Ibid.

Mary Jo Bitner, Ph.D., is associate professor of marketing at Arizona State University and focuses her research on customer evaluation of service encounters.

Creating and Maintaining Elegant Service Delivery

Chip R. Bell

This article by the coauthor of Managing "Knock Your Socks Off" Service *suggests that today's winning companies understand that "simply having a quality product or outcome are table stakes" to play in a game where customers choose the winner, and service is their criteria. Bell documents how companies can create great memories of themselves in the minds of their customers that keep them and their friends coming back.*

The absolute world ruler of all awesomely mechanized fast food restaurants lets me down! My wife, son, and I wheeled in, placed our order at the drive-in microphone and drove to the window attendant, who collected our money and gave us our to-go order. As we were about to turn back onto the interstate, my son suddenly pleaded: "Go back! They forgot to put in my ice water, and I have nothing to drink."

I returned, parked the car, fought the slow line inside and confronted the counter clerk. She handed me the missing cup of ice water, offering her show-stopping explanation: "Ice water is free, so it doesn't show up on our screen!" Final score: Service Delivery System 1. Customer 0.

We live in a time when customers' service expectations are growing just as fast as their quickness to ire when those expectations fall short. Customers marvel at the magic of Walt Disney World, the miracle of Federal Express and the thoroughness of Home Depot. With these types of excellent encounters, their evaluation bars are forever raised for all service providers. Today's "golly gee-whiz" becomes tomorrow's "just adequate." Customers devote their assets and allegiance to those service providers who can deliver service dazzlement.

What do the service greats do to keep ornery, picky customers not only coming back but good-mouthing them to the neighbors? Front-row service leaders recognize the importance of creating and maintaining service-delivery system elegance—a philosophy of being easy to do business with. No matter whether customers effectively get their needs met, the hoops they must negotiate shape the grade they enter on their mental report card. The Department of Motor Vehicles *did* give you a zero defects driver's license and the

---

Reprinted with permission from *Quality Digest*, January 1994. Copyright © 1994 QCI International. All rights reserved.

mortgage company *did* give you an error-free mortgage. Even though customers usually get the end result they seek, the service delivery processes they must endure are fodder for countless across-the-backyard-fence hate stories.

Even though customers usually get the end result they seek, the service delivery processes they must endure are fodder for countless across-the-backyard-fence hate stories.

The Anatomy of Elegance

Elegance has countless definitions—classy, artistic, high-quality—but the pervading concept is one of flow—an unencumbered ease that makes spectators look back with awe. Hotels by Ritz Carlton, cars by Rolls-Royce, music by Handel, poetry by Browning, art by Monet, architecture by Wright—all pronounce elegance with confidence and ease. But what of service-delivery systems? They must make the difficult-to-near-impossible look easy.

Service quality is, bottom line, whatever the customer says it is. And service excellence, unlike product perfection, requires a focus on uniqueness, not uniformity. As with art, one customer's masterpiece is another customer's junk. However, several dimensions commonly pepper customers' votes for the service delivery most likely to succeed:

- The simple, accurate and efficient delivery system that makes customers feel "confident," "secure," and "relieved."
- The magical, engaging, and participative delivery system that makes customers feel emotions like "glee," "joy," and "giddy like a kid."
- The personalized, partnered, and individual delivery system that makes customers feel "special," "cared for," and "pampered."
- The self-service delivery system that makes customers feel "independent," "in control," and "self-sufficient."

If service providers can paint elegance in one of these four shades, they probably can produce a service-delivery system catering to their customers' unique preferences.

The Domino's Model

The service-delivery architecture of Domino's Pizza, as well as others like Jiffy Lube and Federal Express, rests on the principles of simple and predictable.

The service-delivery architecture of Domino's Pizza, as well as others like Jiffy Lube and Federal Express, rests on the principles of simple and predictable. We rarely call Domino's for gourmet pizza—we just want a reasonably acceptable pizza delivered "in 30 minutes or less or $3 off." We count on the pizza. But how does Domino's ensure that "simple and predictable" always happens?

First, the Domino's clerk asks you for your address to make sure you've called the nearest store. Second, the clerk states the time as a kind of public "on your mark, get set, go." Third, Domino's mechanized production cycle enables the delivery person to be out the door with the right pizza in time to arrive at your house without driving recklessly. And, fourth, if you say the pizza is late, then the pizza is late never: "According to our clock . . ."

But what constitutes simple and predictable? If, as a service provider, you want to invent simple and predictable, you would build the following into the process:

- *Fine-tune customer data collection.* First, find out customers' critical success factors (their priorities for the service experience). Then learn their exact standards for those factors. Build into the data collection a way to perpetually update your service standards and performance.
- *Eliminate even the smallest detractor in the customers' path.* Simple and predictable means getting what we want without a lot of hassle, fanfare, or clutter. Take an "empathy walk"; try to see your delivery system through your customers' eyes. Notice any potholes or blind alleys in your delivery system that may sidetrack customers.
- *Remember that small is beautiful and minimal matters.* Try to strip the service experience of everything unrelated to meeting the customers' specific needs. Examine the customers' experience from end to beginning. Add only those things customers want and expect.

The Disney Model

Walt Disney Co. has one of the most magical service-delivery systems in the world. They started with a desire to create a fantasy experience and then designed their delivery system to create that. Walt Disney envisioned going far beyond the ordinary carnival or garden-variety circus to create "the most wonderful place in the world." He used a delivery system crafted to enliven the senses and engage the emotions.

The spirited and emotional approach to service can be as powerful as the simple and efficient. The following key steps lead to such a delivery system:

- *Choose the emotion carefully.* While fun and magical works for Disney, fun and silly works for Chuck E. Cheese, and folksy and friendly for Southwest Airlines. Once you identify the emotion you hope to foster, take it apart. Assume the emotion is "excitement." Ask questions like, "What exactly does exciting look like to our customers?" "What do customers see, smell, hear, taste and touch that communicates excitement?" "What other experiences do our customers pursue for excitement, and what can we learn from them?" and "How can you find and retain service people who demonstrate excitement?"
- *Encouraging the creative experts in your company.* Remember the movie *Big* with Tom Hanks? He became a hero of the toy manufacturer where he worked because, being really a child, he was an expert on toys. Who are the creative experts in your company, and how can you tap into their wisdom to create or reinvent your service-delivery system? What novel and dramatic ways will reinforce your chosen emotion to all? Chuck E. Cheese produced an annual report for their target market—six- to 12-year-old kids. It sent a powerful message to all employees about the perspective

to take in managing their service-delivery system. Instead of worrying about graffiti in the bathrooms, they installed chalkboards.

The Ritz-Carlton Model

The Ritz-Carlton model doesn't focus on luxury (although the Ritz *is* luxurious); it focuses on a "we do it your way" type of service. The driving force is to help the customer feel pampered, uniquely cared for, and treated with trust and class. This includes fostering employees' confident, attentive deference—service associated with an experienced butler or a maitre d' in an upscale restaurant. Legendary stories of Nordstrom department stores communicate this type of delivery system. Saturn dealerships often convey the same tone.

San Antonio, Texas-based USAA insurance and financial services only sends customers product information the company thinks relates to their situation and lifestyle. Their computer looks up as many as 140 personal variables about each customer and matches the data against known buying profiles. This helps them predict likely purchasing trends based on life events such as moving, promotion, birth of a child, and college expenses. USAA, Ritz-Carlton, and others all practice well-honed approaches that leave the customer feeling cared for. They include:

Ritz-Carlton's ethic of "ladies and gentlemen serving ladies and gentlemen" is far more than a sentimental slogan for ceremonies; it is a cultural reality.

- *Treat employees exactly as you expect them to treat customers.* Ritz-Carlton's ethic of "ladies and gentlemen serving ladies and gentlemen" is far more than a sentimental slogan for ceremonies; it is a cultural reality.
- *Record data about customers' unique needs and requests.* Train all customer-contact people to be attentive to customers' special requirements and provide them with a way to input that information into the system. Find subtle ways to update the information. Develop a two-way dialogue through a newsletter or a customer club. Use coupons in ads or direct mailers so that customers can provide personal information. Include a few focused questions that build your data base on these customers.
- *Rewrite your organization's policies with an eye toward trust.* Get rid of policies that make customers prove they're not crooks. Trusting customers starts with trusting employees. Examine your internal procedures to isolate ones with a "guilty until proven innocent" tone. Rewrite or weed out rules that "apply to all in order to catch the few." Replace ones that have the leading theme "prove it to me first" with "we trust you implicitly."

The Kinko's Model

The 1990s has become the era of speed. Customers work more hours, earn more disposable income, and enjoy less leisure time. The combination fuels a strong drive for "save me time" convenience. People choose the automated teller machine over the long, slow teller line. Window shopping has taken a back seat to catalog browsing. Faxes replace mailed letters, on-line computer dialogues replace telephone conversations. "Shop for me," "cook for me" and "clean for me" services are exploding cottage industries. Customers respond more quickly to a 24-hour 800-number in a catalog than to a retail store's latest white sale.

This has ushered in a greater reliance on service providers who major in easy, quick, and "you're in charge." Quick-print chain Kinko's epitomizes this type of delivery system. In most locations, Kinko's is open 24 hours a day, 7 days a week. The trained staff helps customers help themselves do a myriad of office-support functions, from photocopying and collating to layout and desktop publishing. Their "we help you help yourself" approach combines a sensitivity to the customers' clock and their sense of control.

You can help build this same commitment to customer service when you:

- *Define easy access in the broadest manner possible.* For instance, bank-by-mail is the traditional view, bank by e-mail the '90s view. What if hospitals eliminated universally applied visiting hours? Can you serve better if you eliminate allegiance to hours, to location, to people? Would a drive-up window make a difference? How would adding 24-hour delivery service impact your business? What if all your service people had beepers? Can customers easily reach you on Sunday afternoon?
- *Ask customers to help you reinvent your service-delivery system.* Since customers don't know why you can't do it, they can better tell you how you could do it. Create a customer advisory team to assist in streamlining, simplifying, and expediting.
- *Measure and monitor cycle time.* How long does an activity really take? What would you need to do to cut the turnaround time in half (and what would happen)?

Create a customer advisory team to assist in streamlining, simplifying, and expediting.

The Path to Great Memories

The heyday of "knock your socks off" service has of late yielded rich dividends. Customers now willingly pay more for service. And today's customers tell pollsters that service in general is improving in most industries. Car buyers now care as much about J.D. Power results on quality as they do *Consumer Report's* rundown on worth. Disposable plays a back seat to dependable; value rules over cost.

Today's winning organizations recognize that simply having a quality product or outcome are table stakes—the minimum price of admission into the game. Organizations win the service game by producing superior, memory-making processes. When today's hospital patients rate "How was I treated" as having a higher priority than "Did I get well," you know that they assume end results as a given and the process for getting that result as the key distinguisher.

Organizations win the service game by producing superior, memory-making processes.

The four models outlined above by no means exhaust the possibilities. Choosing the right strategy should be grounded in an intimate knowledge of customers—their needs, expectations, hopes, and desires. Once chosen, make the process elegant (and thus positively memorable) by consistently following a path perpetually honored by customers.

Chip R. Bell manages the Dallas office of Performance Research Associates Inc., a consulting firm that specializes in service quality training. He authored or coauthored nine books, including Managing "Knock Your Socks Off" Service *(with Ron Zemke, AMACOM Books, 1992).*

Courting Customers— and Employees

Jeffrey Heller

It is not an accident that AT&T's Universal Card Services won a Baldrige Award in only its third year of existence. The credit card company rated near the top of the list in an Equitrends survey of customer satisfaction—right up with Lexus, BMW, and Mercedes Benz. This article documents how UCS goes about making customer service its number one priority.

In the world of customer service, no news is usually considered good news. "The fewer complaints we hear," say many companies, "the better we must be doing."

However, one division of AT&T has been setting new standards for customer service by insisting that the mere absence of complaints is no measure of success. "Simply satisfying your customers' needs is not enough," said Paul Kahn, then-president of Universal Card Services (UCS), when the division was formed in 1990. "You've got to absolutely delight in your customers."

The AT&T Universal Card is a credit card and long-distance calling card which UCS has loaded with tempting features. When the card was introduced, UCS pegged its variable interest rate to the prime rate, a first for the credit card industry. Since 1990, this rate has been lowered five times and currently is three points below the industry average.

Customers were further enticed by the prospect of having one card for obtaining cash advances at banks and ATM machines, and for making long-distance calls in the US and around the world. Also, customers who accepted the AT&T Universal Card in its first year were told they never had to pay an annual fee as long as they used the card for one transaction—one phone call, purchase, or cash advance—every year.

However, the AT&T Universal Card was entering a market saturated with credit cards. In 1990, AT&T estimated that more than 6,000 national, regional, and local cards were scrambling for customers in the US. To make itself known and loved, the Florida-based UCS decided to court customers so aggressively that only one word would describe the reaction they wanted to elicit: delight.

Apparently, UCS has succeeded in its mission. UCS received 270,000 telephone calls on its very first day. For one 30-month period, the AT&T Universal Card averaged 10,000 new accounts per day. By 1992, more than 12

Reprinted with permission from *The Total Quality Review*, January/February 1994. Copyright ©1994 by Cambridge Strategy Publications. All rights reserved.

million domestic users were spending more than $15 billion using the AT&T Universal Card, which made it second in sales volume in the entire credit card industry.

The ripples created by delighted customers were soon picked up by the pollsters. In 1991, the independent research firm Equitrends conducted a customer satisfaction study that rated UCS fourth in quality among 130 products and services surveyed. The top three companies were Lexus, BMW, and Mercedes Benz. No other credit card company rated above number 42. The next year, UCS still ranked first in the Equitrends survey among credit card companies.

Today, even marginal cardholders seem happy with UCS. The credit and collections group (which operates under the motto, "Make 'em happy and make 'em pay") routinely asks delinquent customers who have finally paid to rate UCS's handling of the collection process. Nearly nine out of ten say they would recommend the AT&T Universal Card to a friend.

One to One Courtship

UCS decided to delight its customers on two levels: as an organization, determined to rewrite the rules of the credit card industry to favor the customer; and as individual employees, equally determined to do everything they can to set customers' problems right.

(Stories of the lengths to which UCS employees have gone to delight customers are now legend around the company. Some favorite stories are presented throughout this article.)

Customers told UCS they valued having their problems resolved with only one phone call. Today, UCS can do this 95 percent of the time.

UCS employees work hard to set the pace in customer service for the entire industry. For example, virtually no credit card company took applications over the phone when UCS was formed. But, from the beginning, UCS did, usually in less than four minutes. Says UCS chief quality officer Rob Davis, "Customers have told us they want to do business over the phone, real easily. So that's what we do." Today, UCS applications are processed in an average of three days, versus an average 24 days for the industry.

UCS also initiates billing disputes for customers, again over the phone. Says Davis, "If you've bought something with our card and returned it, and the merchant doesn't want to give you credit, most credit card companies say, 'Write us a letter and explain it all.' We take your information over the phone and print out a letter for your signature. But, when you send it back to us signed, we'll send it to the merchant for you." And once the customer contacts UCS, all disputed charges are immediately suspended until the dispute is investigated and resolved.

Customers also told UCS they valued having their problems resolved with only one phone call. Today, UCS can do this 95 percent of the time.

Courting Customers as an Organization

UCS has recognized that individual employees, no matter how dedicated, can only do so much to court and win the loyalty of customers. So from its earliest days, UCS looked for ways to use the weight of the entire organization to court customers.

It didn't take long to find a worthy target. Early on, UCS discovered that it rejected one in 10 creditworthy applicants because of poor information from credit bureaus. Therefore, UCS pressured the bureaus to open their records to consumer review and correction. When UCS was launched, the credit-reporting industry's accuracy rate was a dismal 36 percent; less than three years later, the rate is up to 98 percent and rising.

UCS also decided to lead the credit-card industry in privacy and solicitation policies, after customers began expressing their concern about being swamped with unwanted mailings and phone calls. UCS contacted customers by phone and by mail, to ask which offers, if any, customers would like to receive. By 1991 UCS had stopped the phone and direct mail marketing of new products and services to customers, who expressly asked not to receive any solicitations. And today, UCS will not share its customer lists with other organizations, inside or outside AT&T.

UCS works with outside groups to educate consumers and to ensure high ethical standards in its policies. The division's consumer affairs work group regularly reviews products and credit policies with consumer advocacy groups. Recently, UCS contributed $1 million to the National Coalition for Consumer Education, which sponsors a multi-year program to teach consumers how to avoid credit pitfalls. Among other efforts, the Coalition sponsors counseling for migrant workers in Indiana and for low-income, inner-city residents in New Jersey.

UCS has also exploited the technological power of its parent company, AT&T, to help fight consumer fraud. Soon after UCS get started, thousands of newly issued AT&T Universal Cards were being diverted from the mails into the hands of professional criminals. UCS became aware of the problem when customers began calling to claim that they had never made the purchases listed on their bills. Some customers make purchases and innocently forget about them. But when customers insisted they had not, and when they had not even received their AT&T Universal Cards, fraud was clearly indicated. Straightening out credit histories and accounts could take months of agony, for UCS employees and customers alike.

UCS tackled the fraud problem head-on by developing a way to safeguard customers' accounts until the cards were safely in hand. Today, new AT&T Universal Cards cannot be used until the cardholder activates them, using a simple series of commands issued over a touchtone phone. Other credit card companies are following this example.

Listening to Customers and Employees

In an industry where information is power, UCS has recognized the need to develop sophisticated systems for gathering and evaluating information from two of its most important audiences: customers and employees.

Today, customers can contact UCS 24 hours a day, seven days a week, through a toll-free 800 number on their AT&T Universal Cards. Customers

Back-to-School

On a key back-to-school shopping day in September, one of the companies hired by UCS to process merchants' requests for authorization suffered a computer failure. As technicians struggled for four hours to restore the system, the transactions of 35,000 AT&T Universal Card holders were denied. Although not at fault, UCS customer associates began a Herculean weekend of authorizing charges manually. On Sunday, senior managers convened to draft a letter of apology, which was mailed to cardholders by Wednesday, along with a $10 service guarantee certificate. UCS takes customer service so seriously that the company whose computer system had failed agreed to pay the half-million-dollar cost of the certificates.

also contact UCS by letter, facsimile, or Telecommunications Device for the Deaf services for the hearing impaired. For customers who prefer to converse with an employee in their native languages, UCS provides translation services for 140 languages through AT&T's Language Line Service.

For customers who prefer to converse with an employee in their native languages, UCS provides translation services for 140 languages through AT&T's Language Line Service.

Typically, UCS makes a strenuous effort to contact its customers before they contact UCS. UCS conducts ongoing phone-contact surveys, which provide insight into recent transactions with, and inquiries from, its customers. Every month, UCS randomly selects for these surveys more than 3,000 customers who have contacted UCS for service. Also, UCS conducts several studies every month to determine its customer rating compared to competitors.

Senior executives, technical staff, and other UCS people who do not speak every day with customers also have plenty of opportunity to hear their comments first-hand. Every month, these "non-contact" employees must listen to at least two hours of incoming customer phone calls. Also, several times a year, senior executives conduct focus groups with customers in cities across the US.

All this quantitative and anecdotal information about customers becomes the fuel for ideas in the monthly meeting of UCS "Customer Listening Post." Here, employees can discuss whether existing procedures or policies (such as the solicitation policy) should be changed, or new ones developed, to meet the immediate and long-term needs of customers.

Quality-Linked Bonuses for Employees

With the information gained from all these sources, UCS also has established accuracy and timeliness measures for key processes performed by employees (see Figure 1). Today, employee performance is tracked by more than 100 quality indicators which are measured every day and displayed on walls and TV monitors throughout UCS hallways and offices.

Employees have more than academic interest in meeting the quality indicators set by UCS. Every UCS employee receives a bonus equal to 12 percent of his or her daily salary, for every day in those business quarters in which

Processes Measured	**Types of Measure**
Customer Inquiries	
18 process measures such as	
Inbound Calling	Average Speed of Answer, Abandon Rate,* Courtesy
Claims Processing	Accuracy, Timeliness
Correspondence Processing	Accuracy, Timeliness
Application Processing	
24 process measures such as	
Outbound Telemarketing	Accuracy, Courtesy
Direct Mail Processing	Accuracy, Timeliness
Credit Approval	Accuracy, Timeliness
Payment Processing	
9 process measures such as	
Address Change	Timeliness, Accuracy
Data Entry	Timeliness, Accuracy
Exception Processing	Timeliness, Accuracy

*Average speed of answer and telephone abandon (hang up) rate are critical customer relationship management measures.

Figure 1. **Customer Inquiries.**

the entire company meets its quality targets. The average employee earns $2,200 in direct, quality-linked bonuses.

Every UCS employee receives a bonus equal to 12 percent of his or her daily salary, for every day in those business quarters in which the entire company meets its quality targets.

Because UCS considers its employees a vital source of information, they are courted as avidly as UCS courts its customers. No example illustrates this fact more vividly than a recent difference of opinion about the quality indicators used to determine employees' bonus money.

At a quarterly breakfast meeting with employees, UCS managers announced that the quality indicators were once again being raised. An employee in the audience stood up and asked the managers point-blank if the standards were being raised only so that UCS could avoid paying more bonus money to employees. On the spot, a manager responded that UCS would continue to raise quality standards, when the company found it necessary.

However, to prove that UCS was not trying to avoid paying bonuses, the manager also stated the figure that UCS had budgeted for bonuses over the next quarter. And he pledged that any money not paid in bonuses would be donated to the United Way.

The fact that this employee was answered honestly and sincerely reflects UCS's commitment to listening to its employees. Says Rob Davis, "We believe that if employees are delighted with UCS, they will do an even better

Lost and Found

Associate Ed Richardson received a call from a desperate card holder whose wife, suffering from Alzheimer's disease, had disappeared in a strange city while on vacation. Local police couldn't find her. After verifying the man's story—to make sure the woman was not a victim of domestic violence, and hiding for good reason—Ed put a block on the woman's card. This way, if she tried to use it, the merchant would have to call UCS. Ed arranged for any such calls to come to him, even if he was off-duty. Five days later, the call came, and the merchant verified that the woman seemed confused. Ed instantly conferenced the call to the woman's husband and the local police. The missing woman was quickly assisted by a medical team and helped home.

job of delighting our customers." In early 1992, for example, UCS began organizing 90-minute "Meetings of the Minds," where senior executives—even the CEO—will talk shop with no more than 10 employees from all job levels. These meetings have become so popular that the Jacksonville headquarters holds an average of four meetings every week.

As UCS's business has grown, so have the number and range of employees' brainstorms for improving it. UCS actively encourages suggestions with cash awards which range from $51 to $10,000, along with gift certificates. In 1991, UCS employees submitted 5,700 ideas to "Your Ideas—Your Universe," the company's suggestion program. In 1992, almost 9,000 ideas were submitted (and employees were rewarded with $42,000 in cash and another $4,000 in gift certificates). In 1993, UCS expected to receive 12,000 suggestions.

UCS actively encourages suggestions with cash awards which range from $51 to $10,000, along with gift certificates.

Until recently, only managers were allowed to evaluate the merits of employees' suggestions before they were approved for implementation. This is because managers were considered the subject-matter experts. But in 1993, UCS realized that its front-line employees are the real experts; as a result employees at all levels now participate in evaluating suggestions.

These anecdotes and accomplishments might make UCS seem rather complacent. But, UCS people seem determined to avoid becoming too satisfied with their progress. Perhaps this determination explains why UCS has done so well at delighting its customers.

"From the beginning," says Rob Davis, "we had a clear vision of the corporate culture we wanted to build at UCS.

That vision included delighting our customers. It's not just a process or a program at UCS. It's an integral part of who we are."

Jeffrey Heller is a freelance writer based in the East Coast. He may be contacted at 178 Cherry Hill, NJ. For additional information on UCS, contact Rob Davies, Chief Quality Officer, Universal Card Services, 8787 Baypine Rd., Jacksonville, FL 32256 (Tel: 904-954-8238).

Public Sector

GOVERNMENT

The Big Picture: The Third Revolution in Government Change

Joe Sensenbrenner

This article by consulting editor in government Joe Sensenbrenner (former mayor of Madison, Wisconsin, and expert in applying quality management in government) talks about the evolution in the management of government and the value of quality management principles in making government both more efficient and responsive.

During the last ten years, a fundamental change has begun in how people understand how to improve government. This change is only beginning to take hold in a few government organizations, but has radical implications for everyone who depends on government. In my opinion, it offers the prospect of reducing the conflicts burdening the development and implementation of public policy as well as increasing the delivery of services that are most broadly needed by society.

These changes were initially borrowed from the private sector and defined broadly under the phrase Total Quality Management. Because government provides an environment that is different in significant respects to the private sector, practices had to be adapted and tailored for government. In this process a new conception of government and its relationship to the public it serves is beginning to change. This change may be represented as evolving from two prior predominant ways of looking at government improvement, as shown in Figure 1.

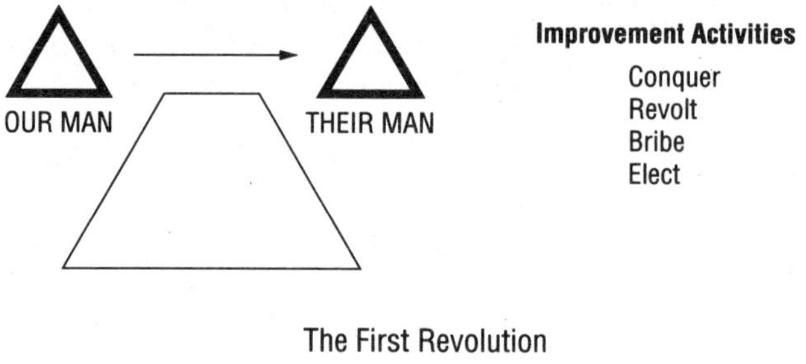

Figure 1. **How to "improve" government through 1960.**

The First Revolution

The First Revolution saw government as a rather weak structure dominated by the top person. All of the action involved substituting one leader for another through such "improvement activities" as military action, bribery, or election. The theory is akin to the great person theory of political history: Great changes are perceived as the result of decisive and singular action by a truly gifted person. Historically, those who sought government "improvement" have embraced this theory and its attendant practices exclusively. Widely practiced abroad, the theory was largely replaced in the United States in the 1960s by the Second Revolution, as shown in Figure 2.

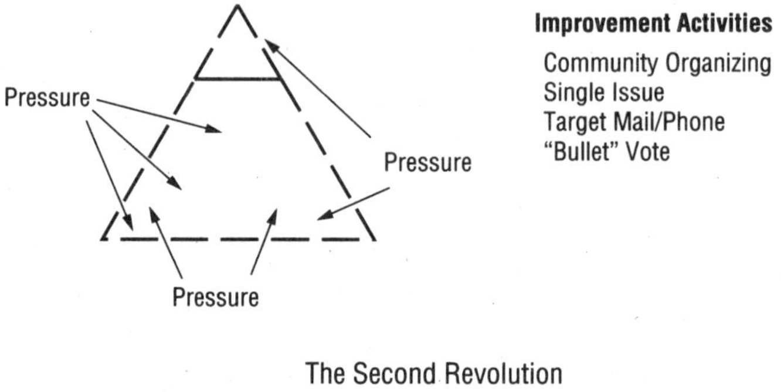

Figure 2. **How to "improve" government 1960s through 1990.**

The Second Revolution

This second stage emerged when citizens recognized the potential power of those *in* the government and made the bureaucracy's work more important but also more susceptible to "pressure" tactics. Both civil servants and elected officials became targeted by those outside for "improvements." Community organizer Saul Alinsky helped spread this approach based partly on his premise that "no one with power shares it voluntarily." The result was often sharply adversarial, promoting a public perception of government bureaucracy as, at best, indifferent and often hostile to the interests of the general public itself.

While this strategy could achieve limited objectives, these outsiders were often perceived as the "squeaky wheels" or "special interests": self-serving people who ignored larger community needs. Occasionally, rather fluid coalitions of special interests would be formed, but the basic model remained confrontational and narrowly focused.

The Third Revolution

A Third Revolution has taken place in some locations. The causes for these changes are many. Of principal importance are the sheer growth in the size of government and the increasingly independent critical skills of frontline workers. These factors place the frontline supervisors and workers in a potentially new role (see Figure 3). They are sufficiently far from the top of the organization that "command and control" is impractical. Further, the expertise of the frontline workers exceeds that of their boss at least 90 percent of the time, Russell Ackoff estimates. These institutional and technological factors create a new potential role for government and its workers.

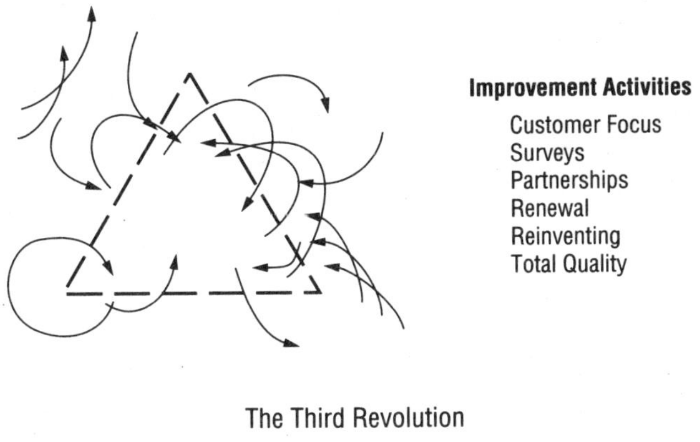

Figure 3. **How to "improve" government 1990s to the future.**

In governments leading the Third Revolution, workers charged with the responsibility to provide a public service can initiate the most important organizational activity. They can initiate dialogue with the intended beneficiaries of their services. Using the strategies discussed elsewhere in this volume, these workers are making dramatic improvements in service delivery and efficiency and, doing so, creating goodwill among the very citizens who depend upon or support their activities. They are the pioneers and models for effective government improvement of the future.

This revolution is based upon continuous civic involvement by those who serve the citizens, a practice that lies at the core of American values. Moreover, the practices imply a continuing improvement in service and cost. And each day, we know better who the new leaders are and how to help them sustain their efforts.

Conclusion

We know that methods of accelerating learning about quality improvement are both important and growing in popularity. Difficult to institute, the practices have integrity at their core and a staying power that have only been glimpsed. The emergence of this new conception of government is tailored by the practices of our better public leaders. It is shaped by the dual needs of American society to meet global challenges in an economically resurgent world abroad and the demands of an increasingly restive economic underclass at home.

To meet these challenges, government must alter both how it reacts to surrounding changes and how it changes itself. It must change how it changes, and move past the First and Second Revolutions in Government Improvement. We must now continue to invent and perfect the Third Revolution.

This revolution is the best hope for all levels of public organization to overcome institutional barriers, build on solid principles of adult learning, and contribute to a vision of government for the entire country. How government responds will determine the contours of the American position in the world for the next century. If we fail to improve, I am convinced that existing structures and paradigms will prevent America from getting the public investments and human capital it must have for a successful future. These early efforts merit our support.

Introduction to the National Performance Review

Vice President Al Gore

Vice President Gore's task to reinvent government is daunting, as this excerpt from the National Performance Review points out, but it is also vital. The principles for change recommended here are those based on TQM: customer-focus, improving process efficiency, and empowering employees. It is hard to say if this effort will be successful or fall by the wayside as other such efforts have, victims of politics or neglect. Nevertheless, this excerpt gives one reason to be hopeful and provides a good basis for understanding the task and challenge for governments of all levels to become more responsive and efficient.

> Our goal is to make the entire federal government both less expensive and more efficient, and to change the culture of our national bureaucracy away from complacency and entitlement toward initiative and empowerment. We intend to redesign, to reinvent, to reinvigorate the entire national government."
>
> President Bill Clinton
> Remarks announcing the National Performance Review
> March 3, 1993

Public confidence in the federal government has never been lower. The average American believes we waste 48 cents of every tax dollar. Five of every six want "fundamental change" in Washington. Only 20 percent of Americans trust the federal government to do the right thing most of the time—down from 76 percent 30 years ago.

We all know why. Washington's failures are large and obvious. For a decade, the deficit has run out of control. The national debt now exceeds $4 trillion—$16,600 for every man, woman, and child in America.

But the deficit is only the tip of the iceberg. Below the surface, Americans believe, lies enormous unseen waste. The Defense Department owns more than $40 billion in unnecessary supplies. The Internal Revenue Service struggles to collect billions in unpaid bills. A century after industry replaced farming as America's principal business, the Agriculture Department still operates more than 12,000 field service offices, an average of nearly 4 for every county in the nation—rural, urban, or suburban. The federal government seems unable to abandon the obsolete. It knows how to add, but not to subtract.

The federal government is not simply broke; it is broken.

And yet, waste is not the only problem. The federal government is not simply broke; it is broken. Ineffective regulation of the financial industry brought us the savings and loan debacle. Ineffective education and training programs jeopardize our competitive edge. Ineffective welfare and housing programs undermine our families and cities.

We spend $25 billion a year on welfare, $27 billion on food stamps, and $13 billion on public housing—yet more Americans fall into poverty every year. We spend $12 billion a year waging war on drugs—yet see few signs of victory. We fund 150 different employment and training programs—yet the average American has no idea where to get job training, and the skills of our workforce fall further behind those of our competitors.

It is almost as if federal programs were *designed* not to work.

It is almost as if federal programs were *designed* not to work. In truth, few are "designed" at all; the legislative process simply churns them out, one after another, year after year. It's little wonder that when asked if "government always manages to mess things up," two-thirds of Americans say "yes."

To borrow the words of a recent Brookings Institution book, we suffer not only a budget deficit but a performance deficit. Indeed, public opinion experts argue that we are suffering the deepest crisis of faith in government in our lifetimes. In past crises—Watergate or the Vietnam War, for example—Americans doubted their leaders on moral or ideological grounds. They felt their government was deceiving them or failing to represent their values. Today's crisis is different: people simply feel that government doesn't work.

If the vehicle designed to carry out policy is broken, new policies won't take us anywhere.

In Washington, debate rarely focuses on the performance deficit. Our leaders spend most of their time debating policy issues. But if the vehicle designed to carry our policy is broken, new policies won't take us anywhere. If the car won't run, it hardly matters where we point it; we won't get there. Today, the central issue we face is not what government does, but how it works.

We have spent too much money for programs that don't work. It's time to make our government work for the people, learn to do more with less, and treat taxpayers like customers.

President Clinton created the National Performance Review to do just that. In this report we make hundreds of recommendations for actions that, if implemented, will revolutionize the way the federal government does business. They will reduce waste, eliminate unneeded bureaucracy, improve service to taxpayers, and create a leaner but more productive government. They can save $108 billion over 5 years if those which will be enacted by the President and his cabinet are added to those we propose for enactment by Congress. Some of these proposals can be enacted by the President and his cabinet; others will require legislative action. We are going to fight for these changes. We are determined to create a government that works better and costs less.

A Cure Worse Than the Disease

Government is not alone in its troubles. As the Industrial Era has given way to the Information Age, institutions—both public and private—have come face to face with obsolescence. The past decade has witnessed profound restructuring. In the 1980s, major American corporations reinvented themselves; in the 1990s, governments are struggling to do the same.

In recent years, our national leaders responded to the growing crisis with traditional medicine. They blamed the bureaucrats. They railed against "fraud, waste, and abuse." And they slapped ever more controls on the bureaucracy to prevent it.

But the cure has become indistinguishable from the disease. The problem is not lazy or incompetent people; it is red tape and regulation so suffocating that they stifle every ounce of creativity. No one would offer a drowning man a drink of water. And yet, for more than a decade, we have added red tape to a system already strangling in it.

The federal government is filled with good people trapped in bad systems: budget systems, personnel systems, procurement systems, financial management systems, information systems. When we blame the people and impose more controls, we make the systems worse. Over the past 15 years, for example, Congress has created within each agency an independent office of the inspector general. The idea was to root out fraud, waste, and abuse. The inspectors general have certainly uncovered important problems. But as we learned in conversation after conversation, they have so intimidated federal employees that many are now afraid to deviate even slightly from standard operating procedure.

The federal government is filled with good people trapped in bad systems.

Yet innovation, by its nature, requires deviation. Unfortunately, faced with so many controls, many employees have simply given up. They do everything by the book—whether it makes sense or not. They fill out forms that should never have been created, follow rules that should never have been imposed, and prepare reports that serve no purpose—and are often never even read. In the name of controlling waste, we have created paralyzing inefficiency. It's time we found a way to get rid of waste and encourage efficiency.

The Root Problem: Industrial-Era Bureaucracies in an Information Age

Is government inherently incompetent? Absolutely not. Are federal agencies filled with incompetent people? No. The problem is much deeper: Washington is filled with organizations designed for an environment that no longer exists—bureaucracies so big and wasteful they can no longer serve the American people.

From the 1930s through the 1960s, we built large, top-down, centralized bureaucracies to do the public's business. They were patterned after the corporate structures of the age: hierarchical bureaucracies in which tasks were broken into simple parts, each the responsibility of a different layer of employees, each defined by specific rules and regulations. With their rigid preoccupation with standard operating procedure, their vertical chains of command, and their standardized services, these bureaucracies were steady—but slow and cumbersome. And in today's world of rapid change; lightning-quick

Town Meeting with Vice President Gore

During Vice President Gore's town hall meeting with employees of the Department of Housing and Urban Development (HUD), the following exchange took place:

Participant: *We had an article in our newsletter several months ago that said—the lead story was "I'd rather have a lobotomy than have another idea." And that was reflecting the problem of our Ideas Program here in HUD.*

Many of the employees have wonderful ideas about how to save money and so on, but the way it works is that it has to be approved by the supervisor and the supervisor's supervisor and the supervisor's supervisor's supervisor before it even gets to the Ideas Program . . .

Many of the supervisors feel threatened because they didn't think of this idea, and this money is wasted in their office, and they didn't believe or didn't know it was happening and didn't catch it. So they are threatened and feel that it will make them look bad if they recognize the idea.

Vice President Gore: *So they strangle that idea in the crib, don't they?*

Participant: *And then they strangle the person who had the idea.*

information technologies, tough global competition, and demanding customers, large, top-down bureaucracies—public or private—don't work very well. Saturn isn't run the way General Motors was. Intel isn't run the way IBM was.

Many federal organizations are also monopolies, with few incentives to innovate or improve. Employees have virtual lifetime tenure, regardless of their performance. Success offers few rewards; failure, few penalties. And customers are captive; they can't walk away from the air traffic control system or the Internal Revenue Service and sign up with a competitor. Worse, most federal monopolies receive their money without any direct input from their customers. Consequently, they try a lot harder to please Congressional appropriations subcommittees than the people they are meant to serve. Taxpayers pay more than they should and get poorer service.

Politics intensifies the problem. In Washington's highly politicized world, the greatest risk is not that a program will perform poorly, but that a scandal will erupt. Scandals are front-page news, while routine failure is ignored. Hence control system after control system is piled up to minimize the risk of scandal. The budget system, the personnel rules, the procurement process, the inspectors general—all are designed to prevent the tiniest misstep. We assume that we can't trust employees to make decisions, so we spell out in precise detail how they must do virtually everything, then audit them to ensure that they have obeyed every rule. The slightest deviation prompts new regulations and even more audits.

Before long, simple procedures are too complex for employees to navigate, so we hire more budget analysts, more personnel experts, and more procurement officers to make things work. By then, the process involves so much red tape that the smallest action takes far longer and costs far more than it should. Simple travel arrangements require endless forms and numerous signatures. Straightforward purchases take months; larger ones take years. Routine printing jobs can take dozens of approvals.

This emphasis on process steals resources from the real job: serving the customer. Indeed, the federal government spends billions paying people who control, check up on, or investigate others—supervisors, headquarters staffs, budget officers, personnel officers, procurement officers, and staffs of the General Accounting Office (GAO) and the inspectors general. Not all this money is wasted, of course. But the real waste is no doubt larger, because the endless regulations and layers of control consume every employee's time. Who pays? The taxpayer.

Consider but one example, shared with Vice President Gore at a meeting of federal employees in Atlanta. After federal marshals seize drug dealers' homes, they are allowed to sell them and use that money to help finance the war on drugs. To sell the houses, they must keep them presentable, which includes keeping the lawns mowed.

In Atlanta, the employee explained, most organizations would hire neighborhood teenagers to mow a lawn for $10. But procurement regulations require the U.S. Marshals Service to bid out all work competitively, and neighborhood teenagers don't compete for contracts. So the federal government pays $40 a lawn to professional landscape firms. Regulations designed to save money waste it, because they take decisions out of the hands of those responsible for doing the work. And taxpayers lose $30 for every lawn mowed.

Regulations designed to save money waste it, because they take decisions out of the hands of those responsible for doing the work.

What would happen if the marshals used their common sense and hired neighborhood teenagers? Someone would notice—perhaps the Washington office, perhaps the inspector general's office, perhaps even the GAO. An investigation might well follow—hindering a career or damaging a reputation.

In this way, federal employees quickly learn that common sense is risky—and creativity is downright dangerous. They learn that the goal is not to produce results, please customers, or save taxpayers' money, but to avoid mistakes. Those who dare to innovate do so quietly.

This is perhaps the saddest lesson learned by those who worked on the National Performance Review: Yes, innovators exist within the federal government, but many work hard to keep their innovations quiet. By its nature, innovation requires a departure from standard operating procedure. In the federal government, such departures invite repercussions.

The result is a culture of fear and resignation. To survive, employees keep a low profile. They decide that the safest answer in any given situation is a firm "maybe." They follow the rules, pass the buck, and keep their heads down. They develop what one employee, speaking with Vice President Gore at a Department of Veterans Affairs meeting, called "a government attitude."

The Solution: Creating Entrepreneurial Organizations

How do we solve these problems? It won't be easy. We know all about government's problems, but little about solutions. The National Performance Review began by compiling a comprehensive list of problems. We had the GAO's 28-volume report on federal management problems, published last fall. We had GAO's *High-Risk Series*, a 17-volume series of pamphlets on troubled programs and agencies. We had the House Government Operations Committee's report on federal mismanagement, called *Managing the Federal Government: A Decade of Decline.* And we had 83 notebooks summarizing just the tables of contents of reports published by the inspectors general, the Congressional Budget Office, the Agencies, and think tanks.

Unfortunately, few of these studies helped us design solutions. Few of the investigating bodies had studied success stories—organizations that had solved their problems. And without studying success, it is hard to devise real solutions. For years, the federal government has studied failure, and for years, failure has endured. Six of every ten major agencies have programs on the Office of Management and Budget's "high-risk" list, meaning they carry a significant risk of runaway spending or fraud.

The National Performance Review approached its task differently. Not only did we look for potential savings and efficiencies, we searched for success. We looked for organizations that produced results, satisfied customers, and increased productivity. We looked for organizations that constantly learned, innovated, and entrepreneurial public organizations. And we found them: in local government, in state government, in other countries—and right here in our federal government.

At the Air Combat Command, for example, we found units that had doubled their productivity in 5 years. Why? Because the command measured performance everywhere; squadrons and bases competed proudly for the best maintenance, flight, and safety records; and top management had empowered employees to strip away red tape and redesign work processes. A supply system that had once required 243 entries by 22 people on 13 forms to get one spare part into an F-15 had been radically simplified and decentralized. Teams of employees were saving millions of dollars by moving supply operations to the front line, developing their own flight schedules, and repairing parts that were once discarded.

A supply system that had once required 243 entries by 22 people on 13 forms to get one spare part into an F-15 had been radically simplified and decentralized.

At the Internal Revenue Service, we found tax return centers competing for the best productivity records. Performance on key customer service criteria—such as the accuracy of answers provided to taxpayers—had improved dramatically. Utah's Ogden Service Center, to cite but one example, had more than 50 "productivity improvement teams" simplifying forms and reengineering work processes. Not only had employees saved more than $11 million, they had won the 1992 Presidential Award for Quality.

At the Forest Service, we found a pilot project in the 22-state Eastern Region that had increased productivity by 15 percent in just 2 years. The region had simplified its budget systems, eliminated layers of middle management, pared central headquarters staff by a fifth, and empowered front-line

PRINCIPLES OF THE NATIONAL PERFORMANCE REVIEW

We will invent a government that puts people first, by:

- Cutting unnecessary spending
- Serving its customers
- Empowering its employees
- Helping communities solve their own problems
- Fostering excellence

Here's how. We will:

- Create a clear sense of mission
- Steer more, row less
- Delegate authority and responsibility
- Replace regulations with incentives
- Develop budgets based on outcomes
- Expose federal operations to competition
- Search for market, not administrative, solutions
- Measure our success by customer satisfaction

employees to make their own decisions. At the Mark Twain National Forest, for instance, the time needed to grant a grazing permit had shrunk from 30 days to a few hours—because employees could grant permits themselves rather than process them through headquarters.

We discovered that several other governments were also reinventing themselves, from Australia to Great Britain, Singapore to Sweden, the Netherlands to New Zealand. Throughout the developed world, the needs of information-age societies were colliding with the limits of industrial-era government. Regardless of party, regardless of ideology, these governments were responding. In Great Britain, conservatives led the way. In New Zealand, the Labor Party revolutionized government. In Australia and Sweden, both conservative and liberal parties embraced fundamental change.

In the United States, we found the same phenomenon at the state and local levels. The movement to reinvent government is as bipartisan as it is widespread. It is driven not by political ideology, but by absolute necessity. Governors, mayors, and legislators of both parties have reached the same conclusion: Government is broken, and it is time to fix it.

The movement to reinvent government is driven not by political ideology, but by absolute necessity.

Where we found success, we found many common characteristics. Early on, we articulated these in a one-page statement of our commitment. In organizing this report, we have boiled these characteristics down to four key principles.

1. Cutting Red Tape

Effective, entrepreneurial governments cast aside red tape, shifting from systems in which people are accountable for following rules to systems in which they are accountable for achieving results. They streamline their budget, personnel, and procurement systems—liberating organizations to pursue their missions. They reorient their control systems to prevent problems rather than simply punish those who make mistakes. They strip away unnecessary layers of regulation that stifle innovation. And they deregulate organizations that depend upon them for funding, such as lower levels of government.

2. Putting Customers First

Effective entrepreneurial governments insist on customer satisfaction. They listen carefully to their customers—using surveys, focus groups, and the like. They restructure their basic operations to meet customers' needs. And they use market dynamics such as competition and customer choice to create incentives that drive their employees to put customers first.

By "customer," we do not mean "citizen." A citizen can participate in democratic decision making; a customer receives benefits from a specific service. All Americans are citizens. Most are also customers of the U.S. Postal Service, the Social Security Administration, the Department of Veterans Affairs, the National Park Service, and scores of other federal organizations.

In a democracy, citizens and customers both matter. But when they vote, citizens seldom have much chance to influence the behavior of public institutions that directly affect their lives: Schools, hospitals, farm service agencies, social security offices. It is a sad irony: Citizens own their government, but private businesses they do not own work much harder to cater to their needs.

3. Empowering Employees to Get Results

They fit together much like the pieces of a puzzle: If one is missing, the others lose their power.

Effective, entrepreneurial governments transform their cultures of decentralizing authority. They empower those who work on the front lines to make more of their own decisions and solve more of their own problems. They embrace labor-management cooperation, provide training and other tools employees need to be effective, and humanize the workplace. While stripping away layers and empowering front-line employees, they hold organizations accountable for producing results.

4. Cutting Back to Basics: Producing Better Government for Less

Effective, entrepreneurial governments constantly find ways to make government work better and cost less—reengineering how they do their work and reexamining programs and processes. They abandon the obsolete, eliminate duplication, and end special interest privileges. They invest in greater productivity, through loan funds and long-term capital investments. And they embrace advanced technologies to cut costs.

These are the bedrock principles on which the reinvention of the federal bureaucracy must build—and the principles around which we have organized our actions. They fit together much like the pieces of a puzzle: if one is missing, the others lose their power. To create organizations that deliver value to American taxpayers, we must embrace all four.

Our approach goes far beyond fixing specific problems in specific agencies. Piecemeal efforts have been under way for years, but they have not delivered what Americans demand. The failure in Washington is embedded in the very systems by which we organize the federal bureaucracy. In recent years, Congress has taken the lead in reinventing these systems. In 1990, it passed the Chief Financial Officers Act, designed to overhaul financial management systems; in July 1993, it passed the Government Performance and Results Act, which will introduce performance measurement throughout the federal government. With Congress's leadership, we hope to reinvent government's other basic systems, such as budget, personnel, information, and procurement.

Our approach has much in common with other management philosophies, such as quality management and business process reengineering. But these management disciplines were developed for the private sector, where conditions are quite different. In business, red tape may be bad, but it is not the suffocating presence it is in government. In business, market incentives already exist; no one need invent them. Powerful incentives are always at work, forcing organizations to do more with less. Indeed, businesses that fail to increase their productivity—or that tie themselves up in red tape—shrink or die. Hence, private sector management doctrines tend to overlook some central problems of government: its monopolies, its lack of a bottom line, its obsession with process rather than results. Consequently, our approach goes beyond private sector methods. It is aimed at the heart and soul of government.

The National Performance Review also shares certain goals with past efforts to cut costs in government. But our mission goes beyond cost-cutting. Our goal is not simply to weed the federal garden; it is to create a regimen that will *keep* the garden free of weeds. It is not simply to trim *pieces* of government, but to reinvent the way government does everything. It is not simply to produce a more efficient government, but to create a more *effective* one. After all, Americans don't want a government that fails more efficiently. They want a government that *works*.

Our goal is not simply to weed the federal garden; it is to create a regimen that will *keep* the garden free of weeds.

To deliver what the people want, we need not jettison the traditional values that underlie democratic governance—values such as equal opportunity, justice, diversity, and democracy. We hold these values dear. We seek to transform bureaucracies precisely *because* they have failed to nurture these values. We believe that those who resist change for fear of jeopardizing our democratic values doom us to a government that continues—through its failures—to subvert those very values.

Our Commitment: A Long-Term Investment in Change

This is not the first time Americans have felt compelled to reinvent their government. In 1776, our founding fathers rejected the old model of a central power issuing edicts for all to obey. In its place, they created a government that broadly distributed power. Their vision of democracy, which gave citizens a voice in managing the United States, was untried and untested in 1776. It required a tremendous leap of faith. But it worked.

Later generations extended this experiment in democracy to those not yet enfranchised. As the 20th century dawned, a generation of "Progressives" such as Teddy Roosevelt and Woodrow Wilson invented the modern bureaucratic state, designed to meet the needs of a new industrial society. Franklin Roosevelt brought it to full flower. Indeed, Roosevelt's 1937 announcement of his Committee on Administrative Management sounds as if it were written today:

> The time has come to set our house in order. The administrative management of the government needs overhauling. The executive structure of the government is sadly out of date. . . . If we have faith in our republican form of government . . . we must devote ourselves energetically and courageously to the task of making that government efficient.

Through the ages, public management has tended to follow the prevailing paradigm of private management. The 1930s were no exception. Roosevelt's committee—and the two Hoover commissions that followed—recommended a structure patterned largely after those of corporate America in the 1930s. In a sense, they brought to government the GM model of organization.

By the 1980s, even GM recognized that this model no longer worked. When it created Saturn, its first new division in 67 years, GM embraced a very different model. It picked its best and brightest and asked them to create a more entrepreneurial organization, with fewer layers, fewer rules, and employees empowered to do whatever was necessary to satisfy the customer. Faced with the very real threat of bankruptcy, major American corporations have revolutionized the way they do business.

Confronted with our twin budget and performance deficits—which so undermine public trust in government—President Clinton intends to do the same thing. He did not staff the Performance Review primarily with outside consultants or corporate experts, as past presidents have. Instead, he chose federal employees to take the lead. They consulted with experts from state government, local government, and the private sector. But as Vice President Gore said over and over at his meetings with federal employees: "The people who work closest to the problem know the most about how to solve the problem."

Nor did the efforts stop with the men and women who staffed the Performance Review. President Clinton asked every cabinet member to create a Reinvention Team to redesign his or her department, and Reinvention Laboratories to begin experimenting immediately. Since April 1993, people all across our government have been working full time to reinvent the federal bureaucracy.

The process is not easy, nor will it be quick. There are changes we can make immediately, but even if all of our actions are enacted, we will only have begun to reinvent the federal government. Our efforts are but a down payment—the first installment of a long-term investment in change. Every expert with whom we talked reminded us that change takes time. In a large corporation, transformation takes 6 to 8 years at best. In the federal government, which has more than 7 times as many employees as America's largest corporation, it will undoubtedly take longer to bring about the historic changes we propose.

Along the way, we will make mistakes. Some reforms will succeed beyond our wildest dreams; others will not. As in any experimental process, we will need to monitor results and correct as we go. But we must not confuse mistakes with failure. As Tom Peters and Robert Waterman wrote in *In Search of Excellence,* any organization that is not making mistakes is not trying hard enough. Babe Ruth, the Sultan of Swat, struck out 1,330 times.

With this report, then, we begin a decade-long process of reinvention. We hope this process will involve not only the thousands of federal employees now at work on Reinvention Teams and in Reinvention Labs, but millions more who are not yet engaged. We hope it will transform the habits, culture, and performance of all federal organizations.

Some may say that the task is too large; that we should not attempt it because we are bound to make mistakes; that it cannot be done. But we have no choice. Our government is in trouble. It has lost its sense of mission; it has lost its ethic of public service; and, most importantly, it has lost the faith of the American people.

In times such as these, the most dangerous course is to do nothing. We must have the courage to risk change.

Reengineering Experiments in Three Federal Organizations

Jay Chatzkel and Paul R. Popick

Adapting quality management techniques to the bureaucracies of government invites the idea of process reengineering in the fullest application of that idea. It is not easy, but this article documents the beginning efforts in three government agencies.

There are many reasons why business process reengineering (BPR) has become the hot topic in federal agencies and departments. For starters, there is a new administration in Washington, agency budgets are in crisis, the public is increasingly vocal in its dissatisfaction with government's performance, and a number of private sector organizations, shaken by changing global competitiveness—have seen BPR as essential to keeping their ships afloat in stormy seas. At the same time, a number of public managers have an intense desire to turn their agencies into outstanding public service organizations—and see BPR as a critical vehicle for accomplishing needed changes. Yet, there is only limited information about the reengineering practices that are taking place in federal organizations.

The "Assessing Quality Initiatives in the Context of Redesigning Government" project of the National Academy of Public Administration (NAPA) and IBM's Federal Systems Company Management Consulting Group have explored current uses of reengineering in three departments. The cases present a snapshot of reengineering efforts at these federal organizations. The exploration identifies key building blocks of the reengineering projects. A year-long project on business process reengineering is also beginning at the Academy's Center for Information Management, and will involve rigorous research on government reengineering practices.

Three site-specific explorations of reengineering—at the Internal Revenue Service (IRS), the Department of Defense (DoD), and Department of Veterans Affairs (VA)—indicate the diversity of federal reengineering projects. These projects range from the IRS effort to transform its entire organization, to Defense projects involving specific core business processes and VA projects with a limited process span.

Reprinted from *The Total Quality Review*, March/April 1994, with permission of the authors.

These investigations into reengineering practices in the federal environment are described in the following three case studies. The key building blocks of the reengineering projects are highlighted at the end of each case. The explorations are intended to generate or suggest key issues needing in-depth systematic examination and research which will be conducted at the Center for Information Management.

How Can Business Process Reengineering Make a Difference?

According to Michael Hammer *(Reengineering the Corporation: A Manifesto For Business Revolution),* "Reengineering is about changing business practices, envisioning new ways of working, selling that vision to the organization, and getting the organization to change." Business process reengineering is considered a radical, dramatic process which discards the practices of the past and uses a blank sheet of paper to create the new process to replace them.

Why Business Process Reengineering Now?

Reengineering has appeal because it provides the possibility of great gains in productivity and effectiveness. While agencies and departments have been struggling to get a 5 percent to 10 percent increase in effectiveness, BPR may allow for a leap of 50 percent or more in quality, quantity produced, time saved, and cost reduction. According to Joe Movizzo, vice president of IBM Consulting Group, "organizational and cultural change, when taken in conjunction with business process and information technology change, create a multiplier effect resulting in orders of magnitude improvements."

Internal Revenue Service

The Internal Revenue Service is an organization of 118,000 people. It is the chief supplier of income for the federal government. At a time when reducing the deficit is a central issue, the IRS is faced with growing pressures to improve tax compliance and general effectiveness of operations while, at the same time, maintaining a customer focus.

The IRS is the only large federal organization attempting to reengineer all of its major operating systems as parts of one overall, structured, and simultaneous process.

Sometimes it can take a near-death experience for a person or an organization to make radical change. The IRS experienced a near crash of its computer systems in 1985 during a failed computer system transition, from which it took several years to recover. The silver lining was that the IRS began to seriously rethink what was necessary for a successful IRS. One element of rethinking was its joint IRS/National Treasury Employees Union Quality Improvement initiative, started in 1985. Another major element was the 12-year information systems upgrade which started in 1987 and, in turn, fostered the development of a third major element, the Tax Systems Modernization (TSM) program, which began in 1990.

In 1987, Commissioner Fred Goldberg, recognizing that the IRS needed to deal with its issues systematically, started the IRS effort to develop a business vision and strategy for the organization. Since then, the IRS has strived to transform its processes so that it can "dramatically reduce the burden on taxpayers, generate substantial additional revenue through improved voluntary compliance, and achieve significant quality-driven productivity gains throughout the IRS."

Although the IRS established an overall business vision in 1987, the different parts of the organization worked diligently, but separately at achieving their individual goals. IRS has a huge complex of information systems, one of the biggest in the world. One fundamental difficulty in transforming those systems was getting the functional managers to participate in determining their own departmental information requirements. By 1990, the information technology and quality efforts were still separate efforts. At this time Tax Systems Modernization began. TSM started as a fully integrated effort to modernize IRS's systems framework and by 1992 developed a series of three studies (at national, district, and service center levels) which provided a growing awareness of how the IRS actually operated. The studies presented the organization with major opportunities for restructuring its business processes and organizational structure so that the IRS can increase effectiveness and responsiveness, reduce the burden to the public, and reduce its costs.

The quality and information technology efforts, which started as separate entities during the 1980s, began to be reworked in 1990. The new overall effort, called Core Business Systems, began to integrate the five IRS business strategies:

- Tax Systems Modernization,
- Total Quality Organization,
- Compliance 2000,
- Ethics, and
- Diversity.

Core Business Systems tries to address all these areas and use them to measure business reengineering need and effectiveness.

Early in TSM, a key issue emerged in accomplishing the IRS business vision. The problem, according to Hank Philcox, IRS chief information officer, was that while technology and information systems improved, plans called for business processes to stay the same. Some change began when IRS Deputy Commissioner Michael Dolan engaged the University of Tennessee to train IRS staff in the "core business process" approach. Core business systems were named, each having a system owner. While this was a great advance, the emphasis in the core systems continued to focus on incremental improvement, and the incremental change approach did not effectively integrate information technology capabilities. At the same time, IRS analysis showed that the technology effort would only accomplish 50–60 percent of the potential for needed change in the organization. The IRS information technology staff had identified powerful possibilities for change that provided motivation for the organization to look at itself. One result was a recognition of the need to mesh the IRS human resource development plan with the information technology and business operations plans. All of these changes were necessary to optimize the potential for improvement.

Currently, a huge amount of tax-related information still has not been captured by IRS computers. That information is warehoused in files and then must be retrieved in individual pieces for review of returns. IRS knows that it has to develop the ability to acquire that information so that it can reduce the time and effort required to process and investigate tax returns. The important thing is to develop a common data repository. If that is not done, said Philcox, different IRS business units working with incompatible data bases will compute taxes "each in their own way."

Larry Westfall, the TSM executive, is responsible for cutting across all lines to coordinate and oversee the integration of IRS core business systems activity. The IRS is completing a full business plan to prioritize the TSM budget and align it with the IRS business strategy. IRS will then be able to implement the business process redesign.

IRS now has a systems focus and can use business process reengineering to ask how it can restructure the organization. The original quality and core business systems work and business process reengineering have turned out to be complementary. The massive technological upgrade is proceeding and a revised Tax Systems Modernization process is integrating all the requirements that flow out of the six core business IRS systems. This work has deepened the IRS's capabilities to carry out the strategic plan that began in 1987. IRS is putting together teams now to implement the business process reengineering initiative.

IRS now has a systems focus and can use business process reengineering to ask how it can restructure the organization.

IRS discovered that its issues were similar to those of other organizations, both larger and smaller, and benchmarked to learn how to make quantum leaps in performance. For example, IRS benchmarked the Xerox Corporation and discovered Xerox was engaged in a dual effort of quality and reengineering in order to make quantum leaps in productivity to meet foreign competition. Xerox integrated reengineering with information technology and connected those radical changes with its already existing quality program. Xerox also aligned line management with its core systems, increasing line managers' responsibility for the overall effectiveness and customer responsiveness of core processes. The IRS is working with the lessons learned from Xerox to fit all of its processes together, to draw out and recombine the best of both its quality and reengineering initiatives for maximum effect.

IRS is working with the lessons learned from Xerox to fit all of its processes together.

One of the most striking things about the IRS effort is that it has developed a human resources (HR) master plan that is closely tied into the overall business process redesign effort. The IRS is redesigning its organization as a triangle in which the success of the business plan, located at the top, is supported by technology and human resources development at the base of the triangle. According to David Mader, HR chief at IRS, not only is the HR component trying to redesign IRS's human resource capability to support the business vision, it is also seeking to reengineer its own processes so that current HR staff time requirements are reduced by 25 percent in the short term.

Effective labor-management relations are important to the IRS redesign. The relationship with the National Treasury Employees Union (NTEU) has been a key part of the quality and business process reengineering efforts from the beginning. NTEU National President Robert Tobias sits in on senior staff meetings and has full knowledge and participation in reshaping IRS processes.

Mader says that the IRS is reorganizing to become a learning organization. To best accomplish its redesigned approach to tax administration, the Service recognizes that as it redesigns its work, the roles of managers and employees will change and new knowledge, skills, and abilities will be required. Consistent with that view, IRS sees that effective communications are critical and has started an office of internal communications to foster accurate, immediate flow of necessary information throughout the IRS system.

The IRS realizes it must determine the new kinds of equipment and employee education necessary to enable its workforce to meet its organizational business goals. To determine how well the Service is achieving its goals, IRS is establishing new performance measures.

The IRS will be relating differently to its external customers, the taxpayers, as well. To best accomplish its mission of effective, voluntary compliance it intends to rely on continuing education and assistance.

The scale and scope of the IRS effort is enormous, and the experience of getting it underway is helping IRS staff to increasingly grasp the nature of their task. Mader, HR chief at IRS, says that the planning stages of the business process improvement already have been wrenching, leading him to wonder what the experience of actually implementing the proposed reengineering will be like.

Key Building Blocks of IRS Reengineering:

- Recognizing core business processes.
- Aligning BPR with the organizational quality initiative.
- Building an alliance between the human resources and technology efforts in support of the business plan.
- Benchmarking best practices.
- Redesigning for a common data repository.
- Developing a learning organization.
- Enhancing communications through continuing education and assistance.
- Using information technology as an enabler of the reengineering process.
- Using the system integrator to work with the business client in the final formulation of the project.
- Developing performance measures to determine effectiveness.

Department of Defense

Today DoD faces new missions, it needs to maintain technological superiority, and it needs to do more with less. To accomplish these ends requires that Dod change its business practices.

One indicator of the DoD interest in BPR is its Corporate Information Management (CIM) component. A CIM credo is that "Improvement requires a total commitment to reinventing policies, organizations, people, culture, processes, resources and systems. Isolated changes to one or another element of the enterprise inevitably fail to achieve overall goals."

The CIM project is changing from an initial focus of building open information systems to one of integrating CIM goals into leadership, policy, plans, organization, cultures, resource management, and measures of performance. The CIM project is creating the policy, principles, processes, training and infrastructure to achieve these changes.

Mike Yoemans of the DoD's CIM office says the problem is "we are left with business processes that we did not engineer, that are enormously expensive, and that are out of control." Although some changes to agencies and departments may require legislative change, "most requirements coming out of BPR require changes to the internal regulations which have become institutionalized over time," Yoemans adds.

The changes Yoemans envisions involve changing DoD's processes, culture, and technology. Strong upper-level management commitment sustains the impetus for change, while retraining and personnel incentives are key to establishing the changes. To date, 150 process improvement projects have been undertaken; many have reached the implementation phase.

A centerpiece for the CIM effort is the methodology, or template, for change. CIM is continuously integrating leading-edge approaches as the building blocks for its overall methodology. Quality management along with the enterprise model, Activity Based Costing, and functional economic analysis are important co-partners in its business process reengineering approach. Yoemans makes a major point that CIM is trying to use off-the-shelf software and specific consultants where they will be of particular advantage to "provide the fresh perspectives necessary to rethink the way things are done."

Quality management along with the enterprise model, Activity Based Costing, and functional economic analysis are important co-partners in this business process reengineering approach.

The following three narratives describe applications of CIM-developed BPR methodology.

US Army Integrated Facilities System

Leo Oswalt of the Integrated Facilities System of the US Army is using CIM materials for a series of "proof of concept" tests at Ft. Eustis, VA, Ft. Bragg, NC, and Rock Island, IL, to determine real costs of doing business at these army bases. Previously, the true costs of activities were buried in various, apparently unrelated, budgets. The bases now are getting to know the actual costs of operation. The bases' differences of size and diversity of mission have demanded a template model that tolerates a diversity of operations, but the basic tenets of the CIM template have held. By examining base activities at the grass roots, with a relatively simple but systematic approach, significant areas of opportunity for improvement have clearly shown themselves. While efforts are geared to discover areas of opportunity for improvement, the project teams have begun to get base personnel to see that their organizations do have "business activities" and those activities form core processes.

The project goal is to get the template to be as universally applicable and simple to use as possible, allowing the department to bring down the costs of application considerably.

Finance Systems at Degree-Granting Institutions

Another CIM initiative involves redesigning the budget and finance systems at the 20 DoD degree-granting institutions. Sandy Rogers, who heads the project for CIM feels, that "the principal problems facing the academies are that their organizational models are academic institutions dating back to the 17th century, and that is the key stumbling block to change." The project started with the United States Military Academy (USMA), the Naval Academy and the Air Force Academy. Project drivers have been:

- lack of cost data or comparative cost data,
- downsized budgets, and
- the need to comply with the chief financial officer legislation, and Office of Management and Budget planning requirements.

The project's goals are to eliminate duplication and save resources. For the goals to be accomplished, CIM sees that it is necessary for the services to begin to understand that they are operating business processes and that they develop a viewpoint that the data base is owned by the whole organization.

The CIM effort organizes and manages the process. It brings in consultants to facilitate how functional managers analyze "as-is" processes and to work with staff to develop the "to-be" phase of process. Through process mapping, the USMA team found that it took 209 steps to buy a PC. That process was redesigned down to 14 steps. Further, the cross-cutting team mapped 31 stovepipe systems at the Military Academy which are now open to review. CIM will stay with the academy teams through the implementation stage to develop a new business process and the systems integration necessary to implement needed change.

Through process mapping, the USMA team found that it took 209 steps to buy a PC. That process was redesigned down to 14 steps.

Although the initial focus of the project was budget and finance, other relevant areas, including installation management and community services, began to come under the umbrella of exploration since they are naturally affected by the budgeting system. At the Military Academy alone, the teams may be able to save $1 million of a $5 million budget annually. Rogers says the teams estimate that 75 percent of the changes proposed could be done without requiring any outside approvals or legislation. Key to success, for Rogers, "is that there has been buy-in from senior staff."

While the project has made significant headway, it is still a work in progress. One team participant mentioned a problem of not knowing enough about existing best practices. CIM has made strenuous efforts to benchmark, but at this early stage it is not always easy to find working alternatives, leaving a danger of spending excessive time on reinventing wheels that already exist.

Defense Investigative Services

The Defense Investigative Services (DIS) has nearly completed its starter reengineering project to convert paper personnel security questionnaires to electronic records. CIM worked with DIS to develop the business case, conduct the Activity Based Costing workshops, and define new processes. A cross-functional team of functional managers and information technology (IT) managers drew up the departmental requirements and oversee project implementation.

John Donnelly, the director of the project at DIS, notes that "the functional managers are identifying the process improvements and the IT people love it. Before, IT staff never got specific project requirements but still had to come up with a workable IT system regardless." Now work related to the questionnaire processing is proceeding at an accelerated pace. Begun in March 1992, it is expected to be deployed in the first quarter of 1994. The management team has begun to resolve organizational problems in a new way.

Trent Bowen of DIS notes, "Now management takes a different view when they run into a problem. They organize workshops to analyze the process." DIS is getting to the point where it has institutionalized a set of skills methods and a common language that allows this new orientation to work. This approach counters the tendency for moving toward the quick fix that does not get to fundamental causes. While DIS did not have an existing quality management program, the CIM process proved remarkably similar to many quality programs. Team building, work process simplification, benchmarking, firm leadership commitment, and the development of a working strategic plan were fundamental parts of the success that DIS is having.

Key Building Blocks of DoD/CIM Reengineering

- Employing a common skill set, overall methodology, and language.
- Recognizing the functional manager as key to the change process, with the information technology as support.
- Making a business case for change.
- Identifying and improving core business processes using process modeling, data modeling and simulation tools.
- Developing strategic planning to determine priorities for reengineering.

Veterans Affairs

According to Bob Woods, deputy assistant secretary for information resources management (IRM) at the Department of Veterans Affairs, a year from now the VA will be reengineering its organization with a customer service orientation, dealing more with outcomes and performances. Woods thinks a major hurdle for change in VA is that federal government is not organized for customer service, but for control and regulation. One limiting factor in the transformation process is that authorization for any major change at VA must come from many constituencies, both governmental and non-governmental. Even with necessary legislative and oversight approvals, the task of carrying out significant change in a large and diverse federal agency is still enormous. While Woods is in charge of the IRM component of this $35 billion department, he feels the core solution to the problems at the VA is attitude change, moving to a "service to the citizen" orientation, and becoming more competitive. Pursuant to that, Woods is establishing four or five major priorities and consistent themes of cutting cycle time and improving quality.

A major hurdle for change in VA is that federal government is not organized for customer service, but for control and regulation.

Woods' vision is a focus on improving the VA as a customer-oriented organization that is the catalyst in using information technology to change the way VA does its business. The goal is to enable more effective and efficient delivery of high quality, timely service and for VA to serve as a model for the public and private sectors. Woods has ongoing initiatives directed at improving customer service. One is an Outreach Kiosk Pilot Project which has placed VA information kiosks (booths) in places readily accessible to veterans, such as shopping centers and military bases. Private sector companies provided the kiosks to VA at no cost and the sites donated the space. The kiosk project illustrates how VA is moving to partner with private sector organizations to improve access and make a difference in the lives of veterans.

Woods plans to use an array of strategies to bring about desired change at the VA. Continuous improvement through the existing quality management effort will be used to upgrade existing processes, with reengineering employed for specific business processes that are determined to be fundamentally flawed.

Woods acknowledges that the VA cannot do business process reengineering without a strategic plan that encourages the VA to operate as a system of business processes. This means that eventually the VA might reshape its organization into a system of related business units.

Some beginning efforts are underway and have produced significant changes. Using a business process reengineering principle that different aspects of processes do not necessarily have the same requirements, the VA targeted the time period involved in purchasing computer hardware. Donald Neilson, director of IRM planning, acquisitions and security service, states "Several improvements in the IRM acquisition process have taken place as we continue our efforts to become a value-added, more service-oriented organization." The first step taken was improving business by streamlining the original procurement process from 120 days to 14 days, depending on the complexity of the project. The second step was to raise the organizational threshold for required approvals from $50,000 to $250,000. Under this process, each individual staff office and administration is granted procurement authority to make acquisitions of federal information processing equipment, software and services up to $250,000. The third step was to bring into effect three separate levels for signature authority, which recognized that the requirements for the various levels were different and divided responsibilities for procurement decisions into three tiers of dollar amounts. Decisions for any purchase up to $1,000,000 are now the responsibility of Don Nielson; decisions for purchases from that break to the level of $2,500,000 are in the hands of Michael Herway, deputy assistant secretary for plans and technology; and any decisions involving sums of $2,500,000 to $10,000,000 are the responsibility of Woods. This assignment of specific procurement responsibilities has allowed direct action to be taken on procurement and reduced the time required for decisions to 14 days.

A second effort was the reviewing of regulations required for VA's information management resource acquisition process. All of the regulations were examined to determine if and how they added any value to the procurement process. One-thousand pages of internally-generated regulations were examined for the value they added to VA requirements. The product of that review is a streamlined and reduced version, laid out in a 26-page, user-friendly, step-by-step publication, called the IRM Planning and Acquisitions Handbook.

The product of that review is a streamlined and reduced version, laid out in a 26-page, user-friendly, step-by-step publication, called the IRM Planning and Acquisitions Handbook.

Making complicated processes simple and customer-focused was not a technological breakthrough. Rather, the accomplishments came out of a determined effort to cultivate "service to the citizen" as the way of doing business at the VA. The statement of new principles at the IRM office says that "IRM is on the move—in partnership with VA organizations, we have cut the red tape, reduced paperwork, and strengthened the process." As an example, the VA partnered with the Armed Forces Communications Engineering and Electronic Association to sponsor a forum dedicated to providing industry information on the information technology requirements of VA. The information enables industry to make informed decisions about pending contracts and to prepare more qualified and cost-competitive proposals.

Making complicated processes simple and customer-focused was not a technological breakthrough. Technology is an enabler where and when it makes a difference.

The drivers of the VA program are leadership commitment, planning, and a performance orientation. Technology is an enabler where and when it makes a difference. Information technology can enable the process in small and large ways. To simplify and respond to requests for proposals, for instance, a data bank will be made available that vendors can access by modem. This will allow a broad population of vendors to have full and immediate access to acquisitions proposed by the VA, and eliminates the need to call or write for specifics, as well as unnecessary trips by vendors or extended waits for mailed documents.

The VA is one of the federal departments touching directly on the lives of millions of Americans. The VA is unusual in that it has a walk-in population and a set of services it delivers. The VA must maintain accurate and current information on veterans and their beneficiaries in order to provide entitled benefits as quickly as possible.

One key to meeting that goal is setting up a master veteran record (MVR). The MVR provides client-focused information to better serve veterans and their beneficiaries. The MVR concept is that of a logical data base or set of interconnected data bases that identifies VA clients, actual or potential, and stores specified data about these veterans. The MVR is being designed to take into account security and privacy concerns. The MVR will lead to data sharing and integration within VA, and will permit improved veteran service. The MVR addresses the current problems associated with the receipt of DoD records, the use of multiple, independent veteran files, and the sharing of client data within the federal government. Instituting the MVR allows VA to achieve three major aims:

- noticeably more reliable, convenient and responsive services to veterans and their families,
- significant time-savings for VA through reengineering routine handling of veteran data and cross-organizational business transactions, and
- the streamlining of MVR interactions with other agencies such as DoD, IRS, and Social Security.

Key Building Blocks of the VA Reengineering

- Adopting a customer-focused approach.
- Increasing responsiveness through more timely and higher quality services.
- Recognizing that many regulations are internally imposed and can be eliminated without legislation or outside approvals.
- Simplifying processes before automation.
- Reallocating responsibilities as a key to major changes in process flow.
- Designing variations of core processes to tune into the requirements of different market segments.
- Crediting the positive effect on the change process by inspired, committed leadership.

Conclusions

Among the motivations for reengineering in these three federal organizations are a declining budget, increasing demands for quality service by constituents, and a determination on the part of people in the organizations to use the most powerful tools available to bring about needed change. To respond, these federal organizations are struggling to incorporate reengineering into their management tool kits. Strategic planning, business process improvement, and business process reengineering increasingly are seen as key elements of the new set of management principles used to address the needed changes.

Each of these federal organizations is beginning to realize that the processes of its organization are *business* processes. Each has come to recognize that it needs to change the ways it does its business and that no single element of an organization can be perceived as operating solely to achieve its own ends, but rather as integral parts of the organization that is gearing to achieve its business plan. For example, while the Department of Defense previously had operated from the assumption of "defense at any price," shrinking budgets no longer make this approach acceptable. Similarly, in the information technology arena, information system designers are beginning to recognize that while their work may have been technologically advanced, it was extremely costly and did not necessarily improve the operating business functions of their organizations. This recognition means that increasingly these systems will be evaluated as either value-added or not for their organizations.

No single element of an organization can be perceived as operating solely to achieve its own ends.

Simultaneously, functional managers now are using methodologies that allow them to have a rigorous enough knowledge of their business processes that they can give working requirements to the information technology side to produce appropriate support systems. Since process costs can be measured, and since technology can be brought into play through process mapping and simulation, a working knowledge of the real effects of process changes for an organization can become known quickly, if not immediately. This means that it is increasingly possible to choose between how things are done now (the "as-is") and what is possible (the "to-be").

Considering the marshalling of interest and effort in these organizations, a central question is how far and how applicable is BPR to these federal organizations? The answer is "It depends." The related bottom-line question is: "How much control do you have of your processes?"

In the private sector, a CEO may have complete control of his or her whole organization, and all its processes. The CEO may have the resources to seek out, or benchmark, what the competition and trends are, both short and long-term, worldwide. That same CEO may hold a position of authority for an extended period of time. Further, the CEO may have authority to redeploy organizational resources (financial, human and material) as well as the ability to reshape organizational turf as needed.

In federal agencies, a broad array of legislative, adjudicative, and regulatory considerations—in conjunction with limited terms for executives—reduce the span of effective control that may be necessary for effecting fundamental, long-term, costly, and potentially traumatic changes.

A question has been raised about whether organizations actually can carry out business process reengineering in its most radical sense. Yoemans of DoD's CIM sees as legitimate a gamut of responses ranging from *continuous improvement, and process redesign,* and *streamlining, to new process design.* Yoemans suggests a softer definition of business process reengineering in public sector organizations to allow for the staging that may need to be done before more radical reengineering can take place. This kind of understanding may require these federal organizations to formulate a public sector version of reengineering to match the life-in-a-fishbowl conditions of public institutions.

Observations

- In public sector organizations, there is a question of how much political appointees with limited tenure are interested in initiating and managing costly, potentially traumatic reengineering efforts that involve fundamental, long-term system changes.

- Where some changes may be made more readily, especially those dealing with internally generated regulations, others which require changes in legislation or those which involve adjudication will be far thornier to accomplish.

- All agencies must cease to be risk averse and inflexible, stovepiped islands of functionality supported by layered organizations and unmanaged overhead, and constrained by outmoded laws and policies. They must become flexible, cross-cutting, flattened entrepreneurial learning organizations.

- BPR is different from many total quality management initiatives in that reengineering efforts focus on a *compelling case for action, an order of magnitude change, periodic intensive effort with equally intense management involvement, a select but broad cross-cutting set of business processes targeted,* and *a probable key role for information technology.* Reengineering will target almost immediately, the kinds of core processes that many quality initiatives may take years to build towards. Reengineering, however, is not a magic bullet. To be successful, it must be integrated with a set of organizational, human resources, and technological enablers. This can involve a major allocation of resources and enormous effort.

- Usually BPR should be focused on the most critical processes because of the time, funding, and other resources that are required to plan and implement it. However, in many cases in federal agencies, there is no operational strategic plan, and business process reengineering projects are being considered for a whole set of reasons, such a "let's deal with the squeakiest wheel" or "this process seems more readily workable than those other ones."

Jay Chatzkel is principal of Progressive Practices, a consulting company located in Vienna, Virginia. Paul R. Popick is a member of the management consulting group of IBM's Federal Systems Company.

Public Sector

HEALTH CARE

The State of Quality in Health Care

Sherry Bright

This article by Sherry Bright, consulting editor in health care, provides background on the state of quality in this field. She discusses the importance and value of implementing Total Quality Management principles in helping health care institutions become more efficient and responsive to the needs of customers and all stakeholders.

Background

While the health care field has long been interested in and committed to quality, for most of its history this focus on quality involved the relationship between physician and patient. With this orientation, it was difficult to improve the overall quality of health care because each situation was viewed as unique.

In the late 1980s, though, TQM began to emerge as a better way to manage health care institutions and deliver higher quality care to patients. During this time, TQM leaders and experts from other industries teamed up with people from health care organizations to explore the potential of this approach in health care. This evolved into the National Demonstration Project, which proved during its three-year tenure that the principles of quality management were as powerful in bringing about improvement in health care as in other industries. From the beginning of the nineties, there has been a concerted effort to deploy the philosophy, principles, and techniques of TQM throughout the health care sector.

Organizations have developed strategies for initiation of TQM that range from strategic alignment with their vision and mission, to the application of tools and techniques, to problem solving, to verbal commitment, but with limited follow-through. In doing this, they encounter special problems within the industry's basic structure. For example, the focus on individual treatment, where each patient and that patient's diagnosis and treatment is looked on as special and unique, has been thought of as the way to deliver the highest quality care. Without losing concern for the individual, the new learning requires we understand how "like" patients flow through the system of care to reduce variations in treatment that add no value to our care.

Without losing concern for the individual, the new learning requires we understand how "like" patients flow through the system of care to reduce variations in treatment that add no value to our care.

Likewise, the historical reliance on specialization and subspecialization has focused attention away from *processes of care* and toward single cases, as if each were absolutely unique. Optimization of *each event* in the diagnostic and treatment process has led to suboptimization of the whole process. The way these issues play out in any given organization has led to diverse approaches in implementing TQM and a variety of results. Still, among those organizations that have disciplined themselves to stick with TQM for the long term, the power of this approach is clear, and the results are there.

The Evolution of Quality in Health Care

Those health care organizations whose managers saw the potential of TQM early on have benefitted from its implementation. The promise of this approach, however, has yet to be fully realized. With the core principles and tools in place, we now see more use of such things as the seven management tools, quality planning and hoshin planning techniques, idealized redesign and reengineering, all incorporated into a systems view of the entire health care delivery process.

All this speaks to many leaders' beliefs that the real benefits of improvement in health care will come as the larger system itself is addressed. This will involve consciously making the public a part of the system. These leaders realize that the frontier in delivering quality health care is the involvement of everyone as part of the system. They know that hospital-based programs are just that—programs. They focus on cures rather than prevention. The latter requires everyone making personal decisions to move toward more healthy lifestyles.

Today we see a desire among health care professionals trying to implement quality to look for breakthroughs and completely reengineered processes. There is a tendency to skip over the immediate opportunities for incremental improvement throughout the current system. Over the next few years, we need to address questions like this and others such as: Should processes be stabilized and controlled *before* their appropriateness is addressed? How much variation in the system should be tolerated? If the fundamental product of institutions is health care, what priority should be given to improving administrative functions that support but are not core processes? How should physicians, who are often acting as independent contractors, be incorporated into the improvement process?

Many organizations are finding themselves at a decision point. They have committed themselves to the quality journey, have gained familiarity and even dexterity with the tools of quality, and have established processes for managing the implementation of the quality plan. Now they must focus their energy on the application of the tools to their reason for being—improving outcomes and the health of their patients with increasingly restricted resources. This shift from organizing and planning for quality to daily management of quality results requires a greater maturity from organizations and their leaders.

With the Joint Commission on Accreditation of Health Care Organizations visibly positioning its "Agenda for Change" on the basis of TQM, the pressure exists to adopt and adapt the principles. There have been questions about the Joint Commission's sincerity in this transition, and even about its value. Still, the Joint Commission is currently the most powerful accrediting body for hospitals and it is reemphasizing its intent to maintain that position. The emerging link between the Joint Commission and the Malcolm Baldrige National Quality Award can reinforce the Commission's new orientation. There is a great overlap between the criteria for accreditation by the Joint Commission and the criteria for judging applicants for the Baldrige Award. Those who make it through the Joint Commission accreditation survey, which takes three years, may have met the initial threshold for the Baldrige. The pressure for results is not limited, however, to the Joint Commission or other accrediting bodies.

Health Reform: A Call to Action

Health reform and its impact on the health industry make it imperative for the industry to figure out how to provide service to more people at lower cost. It is clear that the old ways of managing and even of how we cast our problems will not provide the means for meeting this challenge. The gains in patient care being made through process improvement in key diagnoses and treatments will not be enough. We need to address the leverage points within the system that have to do with patient involvement in prevention of illness and redefine the issue of primary care and its delivery. To do this, we need the skills, tools, and values inherent in a TQM culture more than ever.

We need to address the leverage points within the system that have to do with patient involvement in prevention of illness and redefine the issue of primary care and its delivery. To do this, we need the skills, tools, and values inherent in a TQM culture more than ever.

Quality is not part of the criteria the public uses in most health care purchase decisions; they assume there is equivalent quality among providers. And for those who do look at this issue, there is, as yet, no clear way to discriminate among providers. Report cards that rate competitive providers on various characteristics—including outcome, length of stay, cost, and satisfaction—are clearly not generally available, but some cities, states, and organizations are setting the pace. With quantifiable information that does discriminate between providers, it is expected that the use of quality in purchase decisions will increase. In the interim, the primary basis for competition among providers is cost. TQM can help here by providing the means to reduce cost of service delivery while, at the least, maintaining outcomes in satisfaction, mortality, and morbidity.

Highlights

Some highlights of quality in health care during 1993/94 include:

- The coming together of various networks of organizations focused on quality improvement to synergistically learn and share knowledge.
- Documented successes in clinical process improvement and outcomes.
- Challenges to the pacesetters for breakthrough improvement in health status.
- Growing recognition of the importance of the relationship between the public and health care providers as a system, and the important implications of this for everyone to be more involved with their health.
- Establishment of the concept of "report cards" of system, provider, or health plan performance.

* * *

Few, if any, health care organizations remain in a state of denial over the move to a philosophy of quality improvement. The challenge now is deployment to operations, including a focus on cost-structure improvement, satisfaction of patients and clients, and improved clinical outcomes. The pressure is on, but the standards by which success will be judged are not consistent. The "value" of health care is neither clear nor shared, and ethical questions of access and allocation of resources intrude in the process of improvement. Still, those organizations that have demonstrated constancy of purpose are proving the viability of the concepts. The train is leaving the station, and those who want to be around tomorrow need to climb aboard.

Shodo Management

J. Daniel Beckham

This article discusses the techniques of Shodo management (bringing together thinking and doing) as practiced in Japanese factories and the relevance of these ideas to successfully applying quality management techniques in running a health care facility. It is an insightful and thought-provoking piece.

A hospital is a factory. Admittedly, it's a different kind of a factory. After all, we're providing the most intimate of all human services. And certainly we have a different relationship with our customers. We invent them. But as Willis Goldbeck once observed, "The human body is not wildly variable by zip code."

Hospitals and doctors are in the manufacturing business no matter how much they would like to feel otherwise. The insistence on viewing ourselves as artists and craftsmen joined in a labor of love has done much to retard the benefits of standardization and routinization that are key ingredients in creating quality and value.

Henry Ford took the industrial revolution to new heights by reinventing manufacturing in America. He introduced the rigid assembly line where everything moved through in lock step. You can't argue with the kind of impact Ford's thinking and his approach had in terms of creating world dominance for American manufactured goods. But it had some serious side effects too.

That assembly line sent defects and problems right on down the line where they piled up to be reworked or else got delivered to the customer. It reduced workers to task specialists and moved decisions away from the work. It created a lot of functional silos within organizations largely along departmental lines: Finance, marketing, engineering, and manufacturing became specialty bunkers.

Although hospitals have always viewed themselves as unique, certainly not as factories, many of their approaches to getting work done came right out of Henry Ford's manufacturing plants. Goals are set on the basis of departments. Departmental goals are substituted for process. Delays and errors become inevitable. Different departments with different goals and priorities make problems with hand-offs inevitable. Accountability blurs, the bureaucracy thickens, and costs rise.

Reprinted with permission from *Healthcare Forum Journal* January-February 1993. Copyright © 1993, the Healthcare Forum.

The "Old" Factory

If you go into one of Henry Ford's "old" factories, you'll find similar machines grouped together. All the stamping machines are in one part of the factory, all the drill presses are in another, all the die machines are in another, and the painting all gets done in yet another area. In the old factory, you'll see inventory riding all over on forklifts and big warehouses full of inventory. You'll find that the manufacturing people don't meet with customers and suppliers.

In their book, *The Virtual Corporation,* William Davidow and Michael Malone describe the difference between a US factory and the Japanese version: "Whereas the GM plants' wide aisles were crammed with indirect workers (workers on their way to relieve a fellow employee, machine repairers in route to troubleshoot a problem, housekeepers, inventory runners) adding no value to the actual product, the Toyota plants' narrow aisles were almost deserted. Practically every worker in sight was adding value to the car."

Further, the Toyota plant had only about one hour's inventory on hand. (There was no warehouse.) Any worker could stop the line, yet none needed to and there were no defective cars awaiting rework or repair. At the GM plant, only senior managers could stop the line, yet it stopped frequently because of machinery breakdowns and parts shortages (despite weeks' worth of inventory on hand). The GM rework area was jammed with cars. All along the Toyota line, the workers were busy, while at GM some were working as others sat around waiting. The Toyota workers were described as purposeful, the GM workers as dispirited.

You don't have to look far to find the indicators of an old factory well entrenched in just about every hospital in America.

You don't have to look far to find the indicators of an old factory well entrenched in just about every hospital in America. Do we have similar machines all grouped together? Do we have inventory riding all over the factory? (Look at it this way, the patient is both customer and inventory.) We wouldn't have gurneys if we didn't have inventory on the move. And to deal with capacity constraints, we add beds. The hospital functions as a warehouse. There'd be no such thing as "average length-of-stay" if this weren't the case.

Do our "manufacturing people" meet customers and suppliers? Actually, this is an area where we do pretty well because doctors, nurses, and other caregivers have a lot of contact with customers. It's in administration where we typically fall down on this one. When was the last time you sat in the emergency room for an hour and just watched and listened? When was the last time you went up and walked on a nursing floor at 3 AM? When was the last time you visited a doctor in her office?

The Reckoning

What happened to manufacturing in America? Well, it fell off the tracks. Rates of productivity and growth dropped. Research and development shifted from steady improvement of products to pure science and big breakthroughs. And the financial guys traded long-term profits for short-term profits.

According to Paul Strebel in his book, *Breakpoints,* "In the early 1980s, one out of every six employees at Ford of Europe was a controller, auditor, or financial person of some kind. Among other things, finance made the decisions about pricing and production scheduling. The operating line managers depended on finance to provide them with the numbers needed for their decisions. In addition, there were monitors to monitor the monitors. Despite or perhaps because of all the control, Ford's production costs remained well above those of its Japanese competitors."

At Ford, the finance people still don't participate on process improvement teams. In fact, they describe any of their colleagues who get too close to manufacturing or engineering people as "going native."

We paid a big price for not moving beyond Henry Ford. David Halberstam has called it "the reckoning." Financially driven American manufacturing ran into a Japanese system built in an environment defined by scarce resources and constant uncertainty. Following Toyota's lead and the lessons set forth by Taiichi Ohno the Japanese had concocted a production system infinitely more flexible and resilient than Henry Ford's. If Ford had forged a revolution, then Toyota and Ohno set loose a counter-revolution.

Ohno's revolution is called "lean production." John Krafcik of the Massachusetts Institute of Technology described lean production in the following way: "Lean production is 'lean' because it uses less of everything compared with mass production—half the human effort in the factory, half the manufacturing space, half the investment in tools, half the engineering hours to develop a new product in half the time. Also it requires far less than half the needed inventory on site, results in fewer defects, and produces a greater and ever growing variety of products."

As hospitals and doctors begin to recognize they are indeed involved in manufacturing and ought to make the best of it, they will have a choice to make—whether to continue to cling to tenets of the "old factory" or to embrace the principles of lean production.

Mind, Body, and Brush

In Japan, operations have always been viewed as strategic. The Japanese don't make the clear distinctions between operations and other parts of the business that we do in the US. There may be some cultural factors at work. Japanese brush calligraphy, called "Shodo," is viewed as much as a philosophy of living as an art form. Shodo describes the art of coordinating mind, body, and brush. There is no line drawn between thinking and doing in Shodo.

There is no line drawn between thinking and doing in Shodo.

The same wholism shapes Japanese manufacturing. You can't separate Japanese manufacturing strategy from its marketing strategy or its human resource strategy or its financial strategy. There is a great deal of interconnectedness.

In trying to understand how the Japanese revolutionized manufacturing and with it the field of management, it's useful to think in terms of four key characteristics. The terms are mine but they describe the essence of the Japanese approach:

1. The Mindful Stream

Margaret Wheatley conveys the power and wisdom of fluidity beautifully in her new book, *Leadership and the New Science,* when she compares effective organizations to a mountain stream: "This stream has an impressive ability to adapt, to shift the configurations, to let the power balance move to create new structures. But driving this adaptability, making it all happen, is the water's need to flow."

Peter Drucker has observed that there are different kinds of teams and some are more fluid than others. A baseball team can accommodate a lot of individual stars. It is routine. Positions are assigned. Everybody has a very specific role to play. The batting order can be juggled, the pitcher replaced, but it is a highly routinized game.

Football is more fluid. There are huddles on the field. There's a playbook but the course of the game and the competitors' reactions are much more uncertain. Football is less predictable and more fluid than baseball.

Basketball is even faster moving, more emotional, less responsive to playbooks. More decisions are made on the court. You don't carry a playbook to the basketball court the way you can to a football game. When a play gets mapped, it gets scratched on a board in front of the bench. Decisions are made on the spot and are driven by immediate circumstances. Basketball is even more fluid than football.

Business, in today's unpredictable environment, requires basketball teams more than baseball teams.

What does a fluid team look like? Well, it shares all the characteristics that constitute any true team. First the team members all share a common purpose about which everybody agrees. There's a mutual vested interest in success. They share information freely. They are loyal to each other and each member of the team adds value. The fluid team has one additional characteristic: It can adjust quickly because team members are not locked into specific roles and structure.

Apply the characteristics of a team to those who work in most hospitals today. How well do we really function as any kind of a team, let alone as a fluid team?

Allan Cox in his book, *The Homework Behind the Teamwork,* defines a work team as "a thinking organism where problems are named, assumptions challenged, alternatives generated, consequences assessed, priorities set, admissions made, competitors evaluated, missions validated, goals tested, hopes ventured, fears anticipated, success expected, vulnerabilities expressed, contributions praised, absurdities tolerated, withdrawals noticed, victories celebrated, and defects overcome."

To encourage fluidity, the Japanese de-layer their organizations and put workers into multifunctional roles. American companies have begun to catch on. The highly successful new Chrysler Viper was built by workers who all fit into one job class—"craftsman." The Viper development team was made small—85 people compared to the typical Chrysler new-product development team of 1,400. Chrysler let suppliers design and build critical parts and components.

At Motorola's cellular phone plant, there's one pay grade. The way workers get a raise is by learning two new skills and staying "defects free" for five days.

Organizational fluidity extends beyond teams of flexible workers. *Fortune* magazine recently described flexibility as Japan's "hot new strategy." It suggests the Japanese are moving beyond product quality to "more and better product features, flexible factories, expanded customer service, and rapid outpourings of new products." The *Fortune* article is illustrated with a photo of two Camrys and a Lexus moving down the same Toyota assembly line.

Fluidity does not mean an abandonment of standardization. Quite the opposite. A Camry and a Lexus share thousands of common parts, hundreds of common workers, scores of common processes. Standardization provides the foundation for rapid fluidity and customization. *Business Week* provided an example of how Ford is now using standardization to increase flexibility: "Ford thinks it has a better idea. First, design V-8 and V-6 engines around a basic building block—in this case, a combustion chamber designed for maximum fuel economy. Then equip factories with machinery flexible enough to build several different models. Ford now plans as many as six new V-8s and V-6s in the Nineties—everything from cast-iron workhorses to high-performance aluminum thoroughbreds."

In a marketplace characterized by constant change and customers who are increasingly responsive to customization of services and products, flexibility is an obvious virtue. Nissan describes its flexible approach as the "five anys." It is preparing itself to make "anything in any volume anywhere at any time by anybody." The mindful stream suggests an organization willing and able to turn on a dime, to abandon the obvious and sack the conventional.

2. August Clouds

The second characteristic of Shodo management recognizes the interconnectedness of things as well as their primacy. What happens on a hot, sunny August day? The sun comes up, heats the ground and water, which gives off humidity, which forms afternoon clouds, which often leads to a storm, which causes rain to fall—and around we go. There are some fundamentals at work here, of course—water, sun, earth, and air—thermodynamics, condensation, gravity. There are processes in play.

Most organizations, it has been suggested, have only five or six fundamental processes. It is these processes that, when improved, create the most leverage. Of course, processes don't exist in splendid isolation. They are themselves interconnected with one another.

Process improvement must begin first with understanding. Understanding of the big picture: what things are fundamental, and how they are interrelated. Without the sun, there would be no clouds, but the same would be

SHODO MANAGEMENT AT MAYO

After spending some time studying the Mayo Clinic in 1990, I concluded that they are a uniquely "Japanese" organization—perhaps the most Japanese of all American enterprises. When I shared that thought with some of the folks in Rochester, I was surprised to learn that not only did they agree with the comparison but they had already concluded the same thing about themselves.

Shodo management reflects the "Mayo way" very well. The clinic has long relied on teamwork as the foundation of good management and makes heavy use of multidisciplinary teams of doctors, physical therapists, and nurses.

It has always demonstrated a strong appreciation of systems thinking. When Mayo recognized a gap in the healthcare services provided in Rochester, it fostered the growth of a thriving (and independent) family practice-based group called the Olmsted Clinic. It also had a clear understanding of the importance of Sunbelt communities in retaining its midwestern patient base. As a result, it launched its satellites in Jacksonville and Scottsdale.

Although Mayo makes decisions based on consensus, it can move fast when it needs to—and when it does, it moves with forceful commitment. It moved south quickly to acquire clinics in Wisconsin and Iowa. No healthcare organization approaches Mayo's ability to move patients and medical records with speed and efficiency.

And few organizations have built their reputation as firmly on being customer-oriented. As Will Mayo frequently pointed out, "The patient's concern is the only concern."

true if there were no water. Without a clear sense of driving processes, all process improvement at subordinate levels is potentially much ado about nothing. By discovering the critical process levers in an organization and its environment, radical improvements can be made on the order of 60 to 70 percent.

By recognizing production processes as circular systems rather than linear chains, smart companies have found that they can link parallel activities instead of integrating results. Boeing has used computers and information systems to design and build airplanes in "waves" instead of in production lines.

The Japanese look at markets as if they are systems. At Sony, acquisition of Columbia put the company into the music and the movie business. Sony envisions its electronic equipment as hardware, and it views music and movies as software. It's a perspective that only makes sense if you take a systems view.

The Japanese concept of "kaizen" is a cornerstone of this approach. Author Masaaki Imai calls kaizen the "ongoing improvement involving everyone—top management managers, and workers. If asked to name the most

PUTTING SHODO MANAGEMENT TO WORK

The Mindful Stream

- Designate team leaders with authority
- Make multidisciplinary teams the standard work unit
- Put decisions where the work is
- Use rotations and internships with customers and on the floors
- Don't play baseball
- Connect with computers and information systems
- Collect information once at the source
- Make suppliers part of the team
- Measure and reward at the team level
- Supply workers with tools
- Break the box with "on-the-spot creativity"

August Clouds

- Create a process map
- Reduce components
- Reduce steps
- Transfer maximum number of tasks to those doing the work
- Quickly trace defects to their cause (shut the line down)
- Ask the "five whys"
- Award ownership of the whole process
- Give those who use output ownership of the process
- Make performance indicators highly visible
- Push for radical rates of improvement

On Falcon's Wings

- Use zero-base work design
- Obliterate processes wherever possible
- Offer waves of new services
- Use time as a critical metric
- Go for 2 to 3 times the speed
- Keep job classes fluid
- Wipe out layers and increase span of control

Kami Sama

- Reorganize around customers and processes
- Bring customers onto the team
- Become an anthropologist
- Put work teams into regular customer contact
- Set target prices first
- Give pricing to those closest to the customer and the work
- Put a rep with your biggest customers
- Customize service to the customer
- Put the computer to work for the customer
- Exceed customer expectations
- Move beyond quality
- Lead the customer
- Combine marketing and production

important difference between Japanese and Western management concepts I would unhesitatingly say, 'Japanese kaizen and its process-oriented way of thinking versus the West's innovation and results-oriented thinking.' In business, the concept of kaizen is so deeply ingrained in the minds of both managers and workers that they often do not even realize that they are thinking kaizen."

Kaizen is not a linear phenomenon. It is circular. Improvements give rise to improvements, which give rise to more improvements and ultimately to increased customer satisfaction.

3. On Falcon's Wings

Speed represents a third characteristic of Shodo management. Speed has emerged as potentially the most important metric of the Nineties. The new imperative is to offer the highest quality, the lowest cost, in the least amount of time.

Speed, like quality, creates a seeming paradox. Just as it was once assumed by many that higher quality costs more (when it actually costs less), it has also been assumed that as you pick up the pace, costs will rise and quality will fall. After all, "haste makes waste," right?

Cycle time relates to how long it takes to complete a task or activity. If, for example, it takes one hour to complete a task and you decide to cut cycle time by 30 percent, haste may indeed make waste unless you build in a feedback loop reinforcing the learning and improvement generated from each cycle. If you complete three cycles within the time period previously required for one then theoretically the amount of learning and improvement should increase significantly over the time period (there are now three feedback loops compared to one).

George Stalk, with the Boston Consulting Group, has popularized the importance of speed in the US. He has some rules that apply to speed. There's the ".05 percent to 5 percent" rule, which suggests that products and services receive "value" only .05 percent to 5 percent of the time they are in an organization's system. The other 99.5 percent to 95 percent of the time they are simply waiting. They are waiting for the service or product ahead of them to be finished. They're waiting for physical or intellectual rework to take place. Or they're waiting for management to say it's okay to go on to the next step.

There's also the "¼ to 20" rule, which suggests that for every quartering of time consumption there is a doubling of productivity and a 20 percent reduction in cost.

Finally, Stalk talks of the "3 × 2" rule. If your organization grows at three times the average rate of its industry, then it will usually enjoy twice the profits.

In Japan, auto lots full of new cars are rare. Most cars are still sold door-to-door and to a lesser extent in showrooms, which usually have only one car in inventory for every model available. In reality, most cars in Japan are manufactured to order and there is no excess inventory sitting in the lots.

The familiar American car lots are a testament to the lack of speed in the sales and distribution system. It's not unusual for one heavy equipment manufacturer to spend 45 days preparing an order and then 16 hours assembling the product. Those 45 days represent a lucrative target for increasing speed, productivity, and profits.

Speed can be a tremendous competitive advantage in the marketplace. Toyota introduces four new car models for every three Detroit brings to market. In the late Seventies, Honda honed its Falcon speed on Yamaha. Yamaha made the mistake of threatening to displace Honda as the leading motorcycle company. Honda responded by swamping Yamaha with new motorcycle models. In 18 months, it introduced 113 new motorcycles, eventually forcing Yamaha to surrender.

American companies have learned to play the game too. In Japan, Coke introduces a new product every month. They have to be prolific and fast in a market where 1,000 new soft drink products are introduced each year. Harley-Davidson has applied speed to its manufacturing process and reduced the average time needed to manufacture a motorcycle from 360 days to less than three.

4. Kami Sama

The fourth characteristic of Shodo management is "kami sama," which in Japanese means simply that the "customer is God." It reflects a saturation of the organization with the customer perspective.

Ford knew how to handle customers. He let the dealer do it. Ford viewed his dealer network as a buffer for his manufacturing process. He wanted to smooth his production and did that by loading up dealers with inventory. That set the stage for a long, strained relationship between manufacturers and dealers. And it puts customers outside the manufacturing circle, isolating them from the processes that created value.

One reason the Japanese are outpacing us in marketing these days is because we're still practicing socioeconomic market segmentation while the Japanese are practicing lifestyle segmentation. The Japanese go at marketing like anthropologists. They wander around parking lots. Go to picnics. Attend baseball games.

They spend a lot of time watching what people do instead of listening to what they say. Customers will lie to you. There's an old saying that the Japanese adhere to: "If you want to understand a man, watch his feet, not his lips."

Mazda monitors the pulse rate of people who drive its cars. The Japanese now are not just trying to satisfy customers but striving to delight them. Mazda wants to build cars that "wink at you." Honda wanted its redesigned Accord to be positioned like a "rugby player in a suit." In Japan, there is now a push to build cars that require exactly the same pressure to flip a turn signal, open a door, press a latch or a trunk lid.

There is also an overt effort in many Japanese organizations to push the customer perspective deep into manufacturing with what they describe as "kansei" engineering: the absolute awareness of both reason and emotion.

Closeness to customers is the hallmark of the Japanese anthropological approach to marketing. Toyota is reported to be considering entering the light aircraft business. They began their investigation of the industry by spending

$10 million to buy a "fixed base operator." Those are the folks who fuel and service light aircraft. What better way to get to know the potential customers for new light aircraft?

The Japanese also ignore accounting reports in favor of market experience. They've demonstrated a consistent willingness to accept lower profits to build market experience and customer closeness. They set prices based on what they view as market realities rather than turning pricing over to accountants.

When Canon decided to bring a copier to market in the US, it set its target price first (less than $1,000), then engineered backwards from the price. When they cost out components, the Japanese have them costed by those who are most familiar with the work rather than by financial types in a distant corporate bureaucracy.

For the Japanese, winning in a market or an industry is the objective, not profits. There is a difference. The philosophy in Japan is that profits follow market success, not vice versa.

The Japanese recognized early the importance of customization: fine-tuning products and services to meet the unique needs of each customer. Panasonic can produce 11 million variations on 18 models of racing and mountain bikes in 199 color combinations.

If you want to buy a Panasonic custom bike, you go into the shop and get fitted the way you would get fitted at a custom tailor. They feed specific information into a fax machine and within an hour it's input into a computer in Japan. A blueprint is produced within a matter of minutes. (It used to take three hours to produce a blueprint.) A bar code is then assigned to you as a customer and that bar code will be on every component piece that goes into your bicycle. Then it goes into assembly.

It takes 90 minutes for mass-produced bicycles to be manufactured. It takes three hours for a custom bike. There's a little bit of difference in price, however. A mass-produced bike runs $250 to $510; a custom bike is $540 to $3,200.

It's Our Turn

While America has lost pre-eminence in many industries—automobiles, electronics, office products—in healthcare, we are still regarded as the best in the world. That puts us in pretty much the same position as the American auto industry in the Seventies.

In healthcare, we have not yet faced foreign competition or the power of the thinking that undergirds Japanese management. We have never experienced the unrelenting competitive pressure that has been heaped on other American industries.

Of course, we have more pressing imperatives for changing the way we deliver healthcare in America than preparing ourselves for the prospect of global competition. Skyrocketing costs, uncertain results, and impatient buyers create an environment hungry for dramatic results. Yet too often our response has been to simply improve the conventional and hot-wire the status quo.

As we look to reshape and reform American healthcare, we should do so with a clear understanding that we are in the business of manufacturing care, that we must consider radical redefinition of how we get our work done, and that there are lessons aplenty in factories throughout the world.

To contend that we are different—somehow immune from the powerful new practices that are revolutionizing other industries—reflects a dangerous myopia.

J. Daniel Beckham is president of the Beckham Company of Whitefish Bay, Wisconsin, a health-care consulting firm focused on strategy and integration. He is a regular columnist for the Health-care Forum Journal.

Reengineering Service in an Acute Care Hospital

Edward Deevy and Peg MacInnis

This article discusses how TQM and the reengineering of processes to better serve customer needs have made a difference in the quality of care one hospital delivers.

This emphasis on speed and responsiveness presents a major challenge for institutions that were originally designed to operate in a stable and predictable environment. These institutions, characterized by a tribal culture and a high degree of organizational complexity, are often incapable of quickly making the changes needed to gain competitive advantage. The need to redesign service delivery will increase as hospitals become more dependent on revenues generated by outpatient services.

This article reviews how Hale Municipal Hospital, an acute care hospital, set about reengineering its emergency room (ER) delivery system and the lessons learned from the experience. Hale Municipal Hospital, has been providing acute care services to the Haverhill, Massachusetts community for almost 100 years. The present hospital is a modern 150-bed facility, owned by the City of Haverhill and managed by Quorum Health Resources.

Begin, Pause, Begin Again

The process of bringing about a cultural transformation was initiated five years ago when HCA/Quorum took over the management of the hospital. A survey of management attitudes had revealed very low self-esteem among middle managers and a strong tribal culture.

Two off-site management development sessions provided an opportunity for catharsis and letting go of the old culture that empathized dependence and control. The process of empowering the middles was begun at these sessions.[1]

After the initial efforts to transform the culture in 1987–88, there was a hiatus, and it was not until 1990 that management was able to refocus its energies in this area. A small group of managers received special training in the concepts and techniques of continuous process improvement. These management practices, sometimes referred to as total quality management (TQM), were introduced to all managers in a two-day off-site training session.

Reprinted with permission from the *Journal for Quality and Participation*, January/February 1994.
Copyright © 1994 the Association for Quality and Participation.

Building a Vision

The development and training in quality techniques provided a backdrop for a visioning session that included top and middle management. Participants agreed that:

- The hospital's success would ultimately depend on its ability to compete in the marketplace . . .
- All our improvement efforts would need to be directed towards building customer loyalty and to enhancing the perception of service delivery in the local community . . .
- There was a concern, expressed by several managers, that the mistakes made by other hospitals in introducing quality improvement programs be avoided.

What emerged was a consensus that management move beyond the talking stage and get involved with some specific improvement projects.[2]

Selecting an Area for Improvement

Shortly after the visioning session the first team was established to study the emergency room process for improvements. The emergency room (ER) selection was a result of several factors:

- It was clear that the ER provided a major opportunity for improving the reputation of the hospital in the community . . .
- Feedback from former patients and from the community revealed a less than favorable perception of ER services.

The mandate of the team was to look at work flow and everything that could affect smooth and efficient delivery of services to patients. This would require not only mapping each step in the reception/triage/emergency room area but also mapping the work flow in X-ray, laboratory and respiratory therapy, since each of these departments are integral parts of the total ER delivery system.

Such process mapping, we decided, could best be accomplished by a team of employees who had intimate knowledge of the processes based upon their daily work. Each department head nominated one of their staff members to serve on the team. A department head from outside the ER system who had training in group facilitation skills was invited to serve as leader/advisor for the team.

Reengineering ER Service Delivery

The reengineering process in our emergency room was divided into two phases:

1. The diagnostic phase in which the disconnects and redundancies in the current delivery system were identified.
2. The remedial phase, which is still in progress and involves implementation of the redesign recommendations developed during the diagnostic phase.

Diagnosis and Process Mapping

Hospitals are typically viewed vertically as a set of divisions which are, in turn, made up of a set of departments. This structure identifies how people relate to each other administratively but it fails to show how work flows. This vertical view of hospitals reinforces a culture of tribes operating in functional isolation, optimizing themselves, but perhaps suboptimizing the total business.

An end-to-end process view of a hospital delivery system enables everyone to examine how work flows, what happened between departments, and most importantly, how patients relate to the total process (see Figure 1).

As first step in developing the end-to-end view, training was provided in process mapping. By the end of the second meeting team members were already comfortable in using this technique. A high level of trust and mutual respect quickly developed. Members of the group consulted with co-workers between the weekly meetings so that they could accurately describe each step of the process. At the end of ten weeks the team had identified the intricacies and complexities of the ER delivery system.

As the team developed the process maps, using large sheets of newsprint and stick-on notes, the focus began to shift to what a reengineered delivery system could look like. With guidance from the team advisor, the group categorized their improvement/redesign ideas into three areas: the physical layout of the reception/triage area; the information flow between intact work groups and the disconnects at critical points in the system.

Design recommendations relating to the layout of the reception area were communicated directly to the architectural consultant. Some specific improvement ideas, such as the introduction of electronic pagers, were introduced with the approval of department heads affected by the changes.

Selling and Implementing the Reengineered ER Delivery System

During the diagnostic phase the team focused on the proverbial cow path, the time honored practices that were carried out as the patient moved through the system. It was agreed that team members would be involved in selling the changes to the managers who would have the responsibility for implementations. We refer to the implementation of the various changes as a process of reengineering.[3] The initial presentations to hospital administrators and middle management were well received. The Board of Trustees also responded positively and suggested that changes be implemented as soon as possible.

Resistance comes in many forms . . . It was at this time that resistance began to appear:

- Several managers at the upper and middle levels suggested that since conventional TQM guidelines had not been followed, the process was somehow flawed . . .[4]
- One of the key department heads was openly critical of the work of the team . . .
- A change in hospital leadership had the effect of diverting the attention of management.

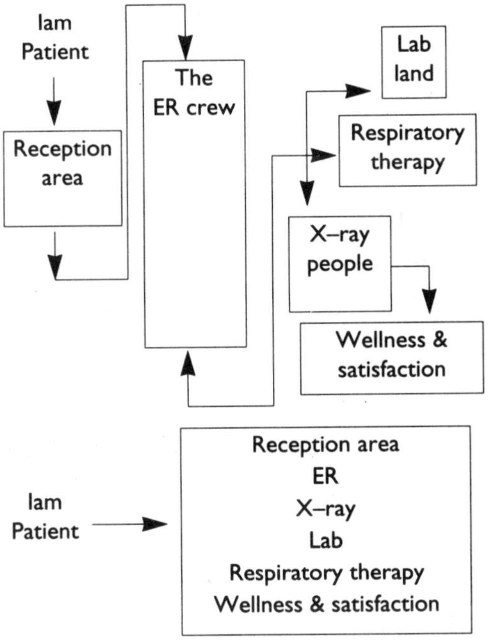

Figure 1.

Despite some management resistance, it is likely that most team recommendations will be implemented. Money has been set aside for the redesign and refurbishing of the reception room area. A senior manager has been given oversight responsibility. Perhaps, more importantly, there is a growing awareness of the need for the hospital to make significant improvement in delivery of ER services.

There is a growing awareness of the need for the hospital to make significant improvement in delivery of ER services.

Gradually, middle and upper level managers are coming to see this project as an integral part of the strategy to increase the competitiveness of Hale Hospital.

Learning from Our Experience

While this project is still in progress, it is possible to make some general observations.

A key success factor during the diagnostic phase was the fact that the leader/advisor was capable of quickly building trust and cohesiveness among team members.

Some additional factors contributing to the success of the diagnostic phase include the fact that:

- The starting point and ending point of the system under study was defined . . .

- Team members had intimate knowledge of the steps in the process . . .
- The team was not burdened with a lot of jargon . . .
- Process mapping can be used effectively as a tool for building interdepartmental cooperation and for promoting teamwork . . .
- Participating in the process mapping made it possible for team members to see the total delivery system and to develop a greater appreciation for the interdependence of the different employee groups within the system . .
- We recommend including someone on the team with expertise in information technology (IT).

The most difficult challenge in reengineering a service delivery system is managing the politics of implementation. In hindsight, we believe that resistance could have been reduced by involving the department heads at the beginning of the diagnostic phase.

Two Keys to Reengineering

We believe that there are two keys to reengineering a service delivery system. The first is an understanding of current processes that identifies redundancies, non-value added work, disconnected flow between departments and other built-in impediments. This process knowledge provides the basis for the integration and refashioning of the entire system. It allows for a holistic approach to improvement that includes work processed, communication and changes in the physical environment.

It is not enough to simply focus on work processes or copier technology or on re-designing the work space. The total delivery system needs to be put under the microscope if significant changes are to take place.

The total delivery system needs to be put under the microscope if significant changes are to take place.

The second key to reengineering a service delivery system involved building political support for the changes at the middle and upper levels of management. The fact that employees develop innovative ideas for improving work flow is no guarantee that these ideas will implemented.

The challenge at Hale Hospital is to be able to deliver a service to patients that is perceived to be as good or better than the service available from other providers. Like many other hospitals, Hale faces the challenge of open competition from organizations that are smaller and more capable of adjusting to change. Reengineering is the tool that can be used by Hale Hospital and other hospitals to reduce complexity and develop the responsiveness needed in today's healthcare marketplace.

References/Notes:

1. More detailed description of the cultural transformation at Hale Hospital can be found in "Ready for Quality? How One Hospital Introduced the Deming Method" by John Albert, Kathleen Gilligan and Edward Deevy in *Hospital Topics,* Spring 1990, Vol. 68, number 2.

2. There is growing concern that TQM, in its various forms, will end up becoming another panacea that failed to deliver on its promises. See "Why Total Quality

Management Can Fail" by Edward Deevy and Kathleen Gilligan in *Networking,* Spring/Summer 1992.

3. The term reengineer, as used by Michael Hammer and others refers to the automation of delivery systems. We define reengineering broadly as re-designing of work so as to improve its effectiveness and efficiency. Business process reengineering (BPR) refers to the simplification of processes in business so as to reduce the work content and thus, reduce cost, improve the quality, and increase the speed to market of a product or service.

4. The danger of hospitals taking an overly rigid approach to continuous process improvement (CIP) is discussed in an article by Karl Albrecht in *Modern Healthcare,* January 4, 1993. Albrecht suggests that hospitals avoid becoming "bogged down in the total quality management process."

Edward Deevy is a partner in the consulting firm of Deevy Gilligan International. Peg MacInnis is chief dietician for Nutrition Services and a Quality Improvement Coach at Hale Hospital.

Public Sector

HIGHER EDUCATION

TQM in Higher Education: 1994

Ronald L. Heilman

This article by Ron Heilman, consulting editor in higher education, discusses the current state of quality management practices in this area and provides some ideas for its future implementation, suggesting greater cooperation between industry and colleges and universities.

A review of TQM, or CQI (Continuous Quality Improvement) as it is more popularly labeled by educators, in higher education in 1994 reveals the movement is gaining momentum and with that momentum, legitimacy. This is probably best summarized in two publications of the American Association For Higher Education (AAHE): *CQI 101: A First Reader for Higher Education* and *25 Snapshots of A Movement*.

In the opening paragraph of the introduction to *CQI 101* Steve Bringham, director of AAHE's Continuous Quality Improvement Project, states:

> Two years ago, there was hardly a reason to put a book like this together. Total Quality Management (TQM)—or, as it is more commonly known in higher education, Continuous Quality Improvement (CQI)—was only on the periphery of campus concerns. Where there was an awareness, it tended to be superficial; actual practice of CQI principles was rare. But during 1992 and 1993, all that changed. As 1994 begins, we find an explosion of interest in CQI, including heated debate about its virtues and a rising tide of campus activity exemplifying both the best and worst of quality management practice.

The challenge implied is to learn from both those best and worst practices and continue to propel the movement forward.

It was to facilitate learning from some of the best examples that AAHE published *25 Snapshots*. Each "snapshot" is a brief profile (four to six pages) of a campus implementing CQI. The information presented is all the result of a survey conducted during spring 1994 and presents perspectives of these institutions, which are at various stages in their respective quality journeys, in a common format. That format is:

The Institution
Reasons for Embracing CQI
Getting Started
Strategic Framework
Obstacles
Key Successes
Academic Activity
Faculty Resistance to CQI
Next Steps
Hindsight

At the end of each profile is the name and address of a contact person.

Although the tone of *25 Snapshots* is generally upbeat, it is abundantly clear that institutions of higher education are generally in an early phase of the transition to a new way of conducting "business." Therefore, there remains a great opportunity for developing creative means of overcoming obstacles and both increasing the number of institutions embracing the change to a total quality orientation as well as accelerating the transition among those having begun their journey.

There remains a great opportunity for developing creative means of overcoming obstacles and increasing the number of institutions embracing the change to a total quality orientation.

A tactic frequently employed to accelerate the transition in the business world has been to "steal shamefully" from the experiences of those organizations more advanced in the transition. Successful use of this tactic usually requires *adapting* rather than adopting.

Higher education does not have a tradition of looking to its supplier, i.e., the K-12 system, for experiences from which to learn. Given the uncharted waters now being entered, perhaps it is time to broaden the search to include this previously overlooked potential resource.

In a article entitled "Can TQM in Public Education Survive Without Co-Production?" appearing in the July 1994 issue of *Quality Progress*, author Robert T. Chappell (see Education K-12 section, where that article is reprinted) asserts that the concept of co-production is particularly applicable to K-12 education. Chappell states:

> . . . co-production is based on the notion that the person providing the service and the next-in-line customer receiving the service share the responsibility for the quality and outcome of that service.

Chappell concludes that the co-producers of a quality K-12 education should be educators, students and parents. This conclusion, coupled with the premise that continually improving education is a fundamental need, leads to the recommendation that improvement strategies should be TQM based and characterized by these three groups sharing the responsibility for the quality of teaching and learning.

To operationalize a definition of quality education, Chappell cites the workplace competencies and foundation skills deemed necessary for entry-level workers in a high performance workplace. These were reported in *Learning A Living: A Blueprint for High Performance*, a report from the U.S. Department of Labor Secretary's Commission for Achieving Necessary Skills (SCANS). These two sets of workplace know-how are:

1. *Workplace Competencies—Effective workers can productively use:*
   Resources—They know how to allocate time, money, materials, space, and staff.
   Interpersonal Skills—They can work on teams, teach others, service customers, lead, negotiate, and work well with people from culturally diverse backgrounds.
   Information—They can acquire and evaluate data, organize and maintain files, interpret and communicate, and use computers to process information.
   Systems—They understand social, organizational, and technological systems; they can monitor and correct performance; and they can design or improve systems.
   Technology—They can select equipment and tools, apply technology to specific tasks, and maintain and troubleshoot equipment.
2. *Foundation Skills—Competent workers in the high-performance workplace need:*
   Basic Skills—Reading, writing, arithmetic and mathematics, speaking and listening.
   Thinking Skills—The ability to learn, to reason, to think creatively, to make decisions and to solve problems.
   Personal Qualities—Individual responsibility, self-esteem and self-management, sociability and integrity.

The foundation skills are based on a previous study, *America and the New Economy*, a joint effort of the American Society for Training and Development (ASTD) and the U.S. Department of Labor (DOL). This provided a broadened view of the "basics." The traditional definition of the basics consisted of the "three Rs: readin', 'ritin', and 'rithmetic. The ASTD/DOL study broadened the definition to include:

Learning to Learn—The ability to acquire the knowledge and skills needed to learn effectively, no matter what the learning situation.

Listening—The ability to heed the key points to customers', suppliers', and co-workers' concerns.

Oral Communications—The ability to convey an adequate response to those concerns.
Problem-solving—The ability to think on one's feet.
Creative Thinking—The ability to come up with innovative solutions.
Self-esteem—The ability to have the pride in one's potential to be successful.
Goal-setting/Motivation—The ability to know how to get things done.
Personal and Career Development Skills—The awareness of the skills needed to perform well in the workplace.
Interpersonal Skills—The ability to get along with customers, suppliers, and co-workers.
Teamwork—The ability to work with others to achieve a goal.
Negotiation—The ability to build consensus through give and take.
Organizational Effectiveness—The understanding of where the organization is headed and how one can make a contribution.
Leadership—The ability to assume responsibility and motivate co-workers when necessary.

All of these essentially constitute the customer specifications or satisfaction criteria for the attributes of an entry-level worker. An objective review of these reveals they are arguably equally applicable to graduates of postsecondary educational institutions. Accepting this argument leads to the question: If institutions have parallel objectives, will the same strategy serve them equally well? Specifically, will the K-12 co-production model suggested by Chappell have equal applicability for postsecondary education? If so, an opportunity to "steal shamelessly" exists.

Will the K-12 co-production model have equal applicability for post-secondary education? If so, an opportunity to "steal shamelessly" exists.

Recall that successful use of this tactic tends to require adapting rather than adopting. For postsecondary institutions, it is clear that educators, students, and parents will not constitute the co-producers. As students pass through the postsecondary educational system, they are "cutting apron strings." Thus, parental influence is typically greatly diminished. However, the future employer arises as a significant next-in-line customer and leads to the conclusion that the business community should share the responsibility for improving post-secondary education. (This does not exclude responsibility at the elementary and secondary levels.)

The challenge implied by acceptance of the educator, student, business community co-production model is designing win/win relationships. Visionary and management guru Peter F. Drucker stated in 1989:

> Today, we are in the early stages of a social and technological revolution that should drastically and irrevocably change the meaning of education and the art of teaching in our society. In fact, education will have to change more in the next three decades than it has since the modern school was created by the appearance of the printed book over 300 years ago.

Among the specifics he foresaw are internship programs as a regular part of the curriculum. Interestingly, the April 25, 1994, issue of *USA Today* reported "Last year, 26 percent of all graduates hired by companies worked as interns, vs. 9 percent the year before . . ." according to Northwestern University data. Also, a well-structured internship program is totally consistent with an education, student, employer co-production model. However, if Drucker's view of the future is correct, a great deal of change is forthcoming. Channeling some of that change through a co-production model for improvement could contribute significantly to the quality of future postsecondary education.

The growing momentum of the TQM/CQI movement in higher education should not be a signal for its advocates to relax. Although CQI has gained in acceptance, recognition, and level of activity in 1994, continued growth cannot be assumed. Rather, continued growth for CQI should be facilitated through the development of new, creative win/win partnerships with the business community within the context of the co-production model described, i.e., these new relationships need to be characterized by a shared responsibility for the quality of education. Investing in developing such relationships now will pay dividends far into the future. Thus, as leaders in higher education engage in planning for 1995 and beyond, they need to think CQI, think strategically, think partnerships, think shared responsibility, and think creatively. And, those in business who care about their respective competitive positions need to think in a parallel manner. By working and learning together, the educational objective of preparing the student for lifelong learning and business' objective of continuous improvement can both be more readily achievable. The synergy from combining these efforts can secure a future in which this country's most precious assets, our youth, are prepared to maintain our position of leadership.

Shaping America's Future

Julie E. Horine, William A. Hailey, and Laura Rubach

This article summarizes research done on the extent of the implementation of TQM in higher education. It suggests that TQM is finding a role in our colleges and universities, especially in administration, but that among faculty it has a way to go.

Since *Quality Progress* printed its first survey of quality management efforts in educational institutions two years ago, the total quality management (TQM) movement has exploded, capturing the attention of educators at all levels. This year, 139 universities and 46 community colleges responded to the survey.

Across the country, colleges and universities are reporting successes gained through applying TQM principles. There are reports of increased employee empowerment, customer satisfaction, teamwork, and cultural change. However, institutions are noting that managing continuous improvement requires a willingness to change and a considerable amount of time and training.

For many, the academic side of schools remains the hardest to change. Respondents surveyed at these institutions suggest that successful implementation of TQM requires overcoming barriers such as skepticism and inertia at all levels, the noncollaborative hero culture, and the lack of top management support and commitment.

Both two- and four-year institutions report less than 25% employee involvement throughout the institution in TQM efforts.

This year's survey examines the maturity of TQM efforts in institutions in two areas: the administrative side as measured through employee involvement, quality councils, improvement efforts, and teams, and the academic side as measured through the integration of TQM into curricula.

Maturity in Quality Management

Most institutions (78% of universities and 70% of community colleges) report that they are in the early stages of TQM. They indicate that their institutions have been using TQM in administrative applications for two years or less. Both two- and four-year institutions report less than 25% employee involvement throughout the institution in TQM efforts. Some institutions note that their TQM efforts are not campuswide and are currently concentrated in a single site, such as the business or engineering school.

Reprinted with permission from *Quality Progress*, October 1993. Copyright © 1993 ASQC, Milwaukee, WI.

INTEGRATING TOTAL QUALITY MANAGEMENT

Beginning with the 1993–94 school year, business schools across the country seeking accreditation will be required to demonstrate to the American Assembly of Collegiate Schools of Business (AACSB) how they use continuous improvement concepts to improve critical processes related to curricula, faculty, and administration.

Milton R. Blood, AACSB Managing Director and Director of Accreditation, said, "The new guidelines challenge schools to pursue continuous improvement." The guidelines "Achieving Quality and Continuous Improvement Through Self-Evaluation and Peer Review: Standards for Business and Accounting Accreditation" replace the old guidelines that were viewed as rigid and prescriptive.

"The new AACSB accreditation guidelines are truly a breath of fresh air for management educators," says Scott S. Cowen, dean of the Weatherhead School of Management at Case Western Reserve University in Cleveland, OH. "The revised standards not only encourage innovation and experimentation in curriculum design, but also have established a norm of continuous improvement, quality, and excellence for all of our educational activities.

Approximately 680 member schools participate in AACSB activities with approximately 45 schools involved annually in initial or continuing review.

Quality Councils, Officers, and Centers

Approximately half of the institutions (50% of universities and 41% of community colleges) have quality councils, officers, or centers to coordinate their TQM efforts. Top administrators such as William F. Glavin, president of Babson College in Babson Park, MA, are taking the lead in establishing quality councils at their institutions. Glavin established Babson's Office of Quality in 1992. Samford University in Birmingham, AL, began its quality effort with the establishment of its Office of Quality Assessment, and Maricopa Community College District in Phoenix, AZ, established a quality officer, quality council, and individual campus quality administrators to coordinate its quality efforts. While the common means of coordinating TQM efforts are quality councils, officers, and centers, some schools report coordination efforts through facilitator teams and ad hoc groups that report directly to senior administrators.

The greatest concentration of process improvement efforts is in the administrative area of the institution.

Process Improvement Efforts

The greatest concentration of process improvement efforts is in the administrative area of the institution (67% in universities and 65% in community colleges), followed by teaching methods (50% in universities and 54% in community colleges). A significant difference in the focus of improvement efforts

PARTNERSHIPS WITH INDUSTRY

Many universities and colleges are partnering with industry to integrate total quality management (TQM) principles into courses and curricula as well as into daily operations. Eight institutions—Purdue University, University of Wisconsin-Madison, Tuskegee University, Carnegie Mellon University, North Carolina State University, Georgia Institute of Technology, Massachusetts Institute of Technology, and Rochester Institute of Technology—are participating in the TQM University Challenge (sponsored by Motorola, Inc., Proctor & Gamble, Xerox, Milliken, and IBM), which is aimed at integrating TQM principles into business and engineering curricula and administrative processes.

IBM's $1 million grants to eight institutions in 1992 are resulting in the integration of TQM concepts into undergraduate, graduate, and executive core courses. Institutions receiving the grants are Rochester Institute of Technology, University of Maryland-College Park, University of Houston-Clear Lake, Georgia Institute of Technology, Pennsylvania State University, University of Wisconsin-Madison, Oregon State University, and, jointly, Clark Atlanta University and Southern College of Technology.

between community colleges and universities is reflected in the emphasis placed on student achievement (18% for universities and 43% for community colleges) and communication (17% for universities and 41% for community colleges). Figure 1 (page 208) shows that community colleges are more active in pursuing improvements in five of six categories.

Team Efforts

Institutions were asked to describe their process-improvement team efforts at the central-administration level, across disciplines, within disciplines, and with students. Some institutions have teams active at all levels. For example, El Camino Community College in Torrance, CA, has 33 process improvement teams currently involved in the phases of the plan-do-study-act (PDSA) cycle. Over the past three years, these teams have reduced processing time, reduced customer complaints, and improved responsiveness to college services.

Both universities (45%) and community colleges (41%) report that their greatest area of concentration is with central-administration teams. Central-administration team projects range from reducing purchase order cycle time at California Polytechnic State University in San Luis Obispo, CA, to reducing employee absenteeism at Fox Valley Technical College in Appleton, WI.

Harvard University's Office for Information Technology has more than 40 teams pursuing quality improvement in the administrative area.

Harvard University's Office for Information Technology has more than 40 teams pursuing quality improvement in the administrative area. These teams achieved an 85% reduction in data entry error rate in Harvard's copy services, a 20% productivity gain in data center operations, and an annual

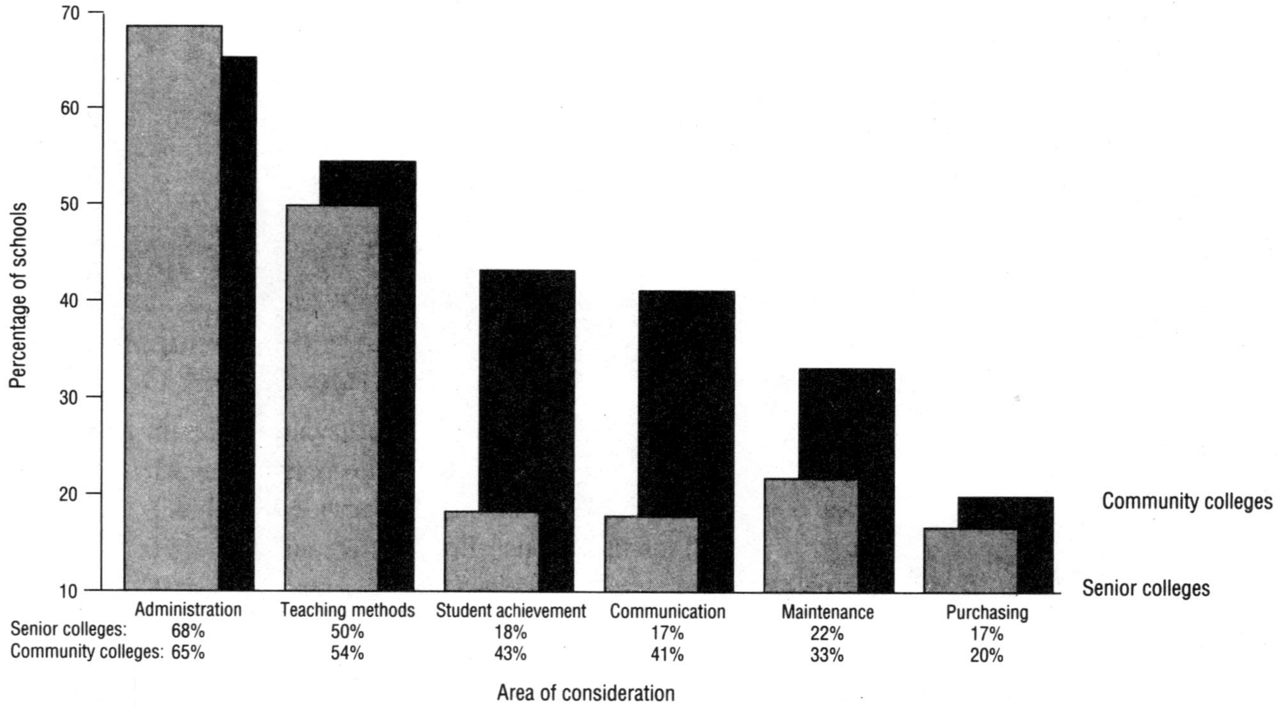

Figure 1. **Areas where process improvement efforts have been concentrated.**

$60,000 savings in expenses on network services area traffic. While teams might not be an integral part of the business school curriculum,[1] the team successes at Harvard illustrate the considerable improvement-team activity in the administrative area.

Campuswide improvement teams constitute the third area of concentration for universities (21%) and the second greatest area of team activity for community colleges (39%). Cross-disciplinary improvement projects range from improving the registration process at the University of Minnesota-Twin Cities in Minneapolis, to reducing advising errors at Pellissippi State Technical Community College in Knoxville, TN.

Unit teams within disciplines represent the second area of concentration for universities (29%) and the third area of concentration for community colleges (28%). Unit-team improvement activities span such projects as reducing application cycle time at the University of Chicago's Graduate School of Business to reducing the complexity of the faculty grade check system at El Camino Community College.

Student teams represent the least active area in both universities (12%) and community colleges (17%). Student-team improvement projects range from improving the budgeting process for student government at St. John Fisher College in Rochester, NY, to improving the use of TQM principles in the classroom at George Stone Area Voc-Tech Center in Pensacola, FL.

At American River College in Sacramento, CA, the focus of student teams is radically different. Business-area TQM classes concentrate on teaching students to work and live in a team environment in the classroom. Approximately 75 student teams of six to 10 students collaborate on both presentation of class material and active application of learned TQM principles through real-life applications. Several teams work on improving the procurement acquisition policies for the state government of California, while other teams work with the Office of State Printing, state controllers, the franchise tax board, and other agencies. "A unique aspect of this program," according to Del Nelson, chair of American River College's Management Department, "is that the majority of the students enrolled in the 15-credit-hour TQM certificate program already have a four-year degree and are working full-time in industry."

Maturity in Quality-Related Courses

The greatest concentration of quality-related courses for universities is currently offered through schools of management (77%), followed by divisions of statistics (51%), engineering (49%), continuing education (29%), and education (14%). Community colleges, however, provide their greatest offering of quality courses to community businesses and organizations through continuing education (52%), followed by schools of management (50%), statistics (43%), engineering (41%), and education (15%). TQM courses range from the more traditional courses in statistical quality control and design of experiments to courses in quality management, team building, problem solving, quality tools, benchmarking, ISO 9000, and the Malcolm Baldrige National Quality Award criteria.

A number of institutions are adopting the new management principles of TQM and are experimenting with radical departures from traditional curricula. Babson College began integrating TQM into its undergraduate and graduate curricula four years ago following a quality forum. Babson's new 1993–1994 master of business administration (MBA) curriculum focuses heavily on teamwork and problem solving and incorporates faculty from different disciplines to deliver courses in five thematic areas. Marian College in Fond du Lac, WI, reports 14 courses in its quality and productivity management program, ranging from ISO 9000 to employee involvement.

A number of institutions are adopting the new management principles of TQM and are experimenting with radical departures from traditional curricula.

Maturity in Quality-Related Degrees

More than one-fourth (28%) of the universities returning surveys offer quality-related master's degrees, 15% offer quality-related bachelor's degrees, and 8% offer quality-related doctorate degrees. California State University-Domingues Hills in Carson, CA, offers a master's degree of science in quality assurance through its School of Science, Math, and Technology that attracts degreed engineers from industry. Dowling College in Oakdale, NY, offers a post-master's degree certificate in TQM. A number of institutions offer quality certificates, such as the Ecole de Technologie Supérieure (University of Québec) in Montreal, Canada, which offers a 30-credit-hour certificate in quality management and assurance.

Approximately half (48%) of the community colleges responding to the survey offer a quality-related associate's degree, and 33% offer a quality-related certificate. Aims Community College in Greeley, CO, offers a 90-credit-hour quality management certificate through its continuing education division; more than 40 members of the faculty and staff hold certifications in the program. Other quality-related certificates or degrees range from quality control technology at St. Louis Community College at Florissant Valley in St. Louis, MO, to manufacturing quality control at Mesa Community College in Mesa, AZ.

Many institutions are breaking away from the traditional formats of graduate programs. For example, Fordham University in New York offers an innovative W. Edwards Deming Scholars MBA Program. In this program, which was initiated in the fall of 1992, students spend their first days of class attending Deming's four-day seminar and follow a team-oriented curriculum based on the PDSA learning cycle. Innovative programs such as Fordam University's are creating environments that promote cooperation and interdisciplinary interactions.

References

1. John A. Byrne, "Harvard B-School," *Business Week*, July 1993.

Julie E. Horine is an assistant professor of educational leadership at the University of Mississippi in Oxford. William A. Hailey is a professor and holder of the H.F. McCarty Chair of Management at Millsaps College in Jackson, MS. Laura Rubach is an editor with Quality Progress.

Can Higher Education Learn from Factories?

Dean L. Hubbard

This article provides a detailed review of how Northwest Missouri State University operates after having adopted TQM as its management philosophy. This is one of the few universities in the United States to have quality management as its operating principle. The author describes many positive results that have emerged from this approach.

American industries have dramatically improved their effectiveness by applying total quality management (TQM) principles. But are TQM concepts applicable to the unique environment of higher education? Can TQM techniques be applied without compromising traditional academic values, such as academic freedom? In sum, can higher education learn from factories?

In 1984, Northwest Missouri State University began exploring these issues. Northwest is a typical comprehensive, co-educational, publicly supported, regional university. It has a student enrollment of 6,000 and a faculty of 235. The majority of students live in on-campus housing (67%) and come from within a 100-mile radius of the campus, which is located in Maryville, MO, a community of 10,000. The university offers 112 undergraduate degrees, 26 master's degrees, and an educational specialist degree.

Implementing TQM in a University

Northwest decided to pursue TQM, particularly in the academic side of the enterprise. The first step in developing Northwest's TQM plan, called the Culture of Quality, involved an approach frequently used by industries: benchmarking. In his book *Benchmarking,* Robert Camp defines the concept as "the [continuous] search for . . . [the] best practices that lead to superior performance."[1]

Of all the techniques used in TQM, benchmarking is the easiest fit to education and the most important for two reasons. First, it raises expectations, and high expectations are the foundation on which quality is built in any setting. Second, without benchmarks, goals have a tendency to be self-serving and preserve the status quo. Stated more bluntly, comparisons of one's students or programs with those of other institutions is the best antidote for the inertia that plagues most campuses.

Reprinted with permission from *Quality Progress,* May 1994, ASQC, Milwaukee, WI.

In keeping with Camp's definition, Northwest benchmarked several sources, beginning with the institution's own faculty and students, who were asked to submit ideas for creating a quality culture on campus. While different individuals and groups on campus spent a semester formulating ideas, a steering committee culled ideas from so-called "educational reform" literature that had appeared in the previous decade. Various data regarding student characteristics and performance were gathered and compared to national norms. The 200 ideas gleaned from all of these sources were synthesized and incorporated into a document titled "Reviewing the Reviews: Suggestions for Reforming Higher Education." Of course, not all 200 ideas should be applied at Northwest, nor were all of equal value. In fact, some were mutually exclusive. Ultimately, 42 were selected as the goals to make up the Culture of Quality plan.

Applying the Principle of Parsimony

Planning efforts in higher education are usually too global, involve too many goals, and fail to differentiate between the crucial and the trivial. One way to overcome this tendency is to apply the principle of parsimony, which involves rigorously pruning even good ideas and programs until only the vital few remain.[2] While one will not encounter the expression "principle of parsimony" in TQM literature, the concept is frequently used. For example, Nam Suh, professor of engineering at the Massachusetts Institute of Technology, avouched as an axiom: "The perfect design is associated with the assemblage of the fewest parts."[3] At Northwest, this means fewer and more sharply focused goals, clearer definitions of quality appropriate to the task at hand, fewer administrative layers, fewer programs, and fewer evaluative metrics.

A secondary but equally essential benefit is that pruning generally results in an organizational structure that more sharply reflects the mission.

Northwest started by applying this principle to its mission. It adopted a sharply focused statement that commits the university to "place special emphasis upon agriculture, business, and teacher education, particularly as these professions contribute to the primary service region." Further, the mission states: "All of the university's programs build upon comprehensive general education requirements."

A sharpened mission provided half of the context needed for selecting a mutually supporting cluster of goals that reflect the university's basic values. The steering committee produced the second half by examining 15 major research reports to identify a set of planning assumptions. The committee's findings were categorized into six areas: demographic, economic, social, political/legal, technological, and competitive. Again, the principle of parsimony was applied. Five megatrends particularly germane to Northwest were extrapolated from these assumptions:

- The emerging global economy will give rise to a global community characterized by increased communications across national borders, not only in business, but also in education, entertainment, science, and the arts.
- Technology will penetrate even deeper into people's daily lives.

- Information will increasingly become the capital, or raw material, of economic activity. The ability to receive, analyze, and transmit information in oral, written, and numeric form will be crucial.
- The need for specialists will increase since nearly every successful enterprise operates within a rather narrow market niche.
- The rate of change in all areas will accelerate. Those who have learned how to learn will be best equipped to capitalize in such an environment.

The principle of parsimony was applied for a third time to the organizational structure itself. Concomitant with the announcement of plans to shift to a TQM approach, corporations frequently announce plans to flatten the organizational structure by significantly reducing administrative positions. While cost savings is probably the primary driver of such moves, from a TQM standpoint, eliminating administrative layers facilitates involving employees in defining and managing quality in their own work settings. (Since line administrators justify their existence by pointing to decisions they make and since there are only so many decisions to go around, reducing the number of administrators frees up decisions that can then be pushed down the organizational structure.) A secondary but equally essential benefit is that pruning generally results in an organizational structure that more sharply reflects the mission.

At Northwest, seven colleges were consolidated into four that more accurately reflected the commitment to "place special emphasis upon agriculture, business, and teacher education, particularly as these professions contribute to the primary service region." Thirty-one programs were eliminated along with four full-time dean positions and two vice president positions. The result was a reallocation of $1.9 million (more than 6% of the education and general budget) away from administration and academic support areas to quality improvements in instruction.

Finally, the principle of parsimony was applied to the number of support services the university would attempt to manage. The result was outsourcing the management of the custodial, grounds, and maintenance functions and the power plant to a private corporation. (Food service and the bookstore had previously been contracted out.)

Focusing on the Customer

Despite the intuitive appeal of adopting a focus on the customer, faculty members generally have difficulty understanding how such an approach would play out in the classroom. In fact, at some universities, TQM efforts have been aborted because of this issue. Northwest concluded that, in the classroom, the students along with the instructor are "suppliers" who produce a "product" (knowledge) that future "customers" (employers or graduate schools) will evaluate. Since the instructor and students must cooperate to understand and satisfy the customers' needs, the students must be involved in instructional design and evaluation and be empowered to assume more control over their own education. In other settings on campus, students are customers in the typical sense.

In the support services at Northwest, a customer orientation was readily adopted. A permanent Continuous Quality Improvement Committee was established to identify and prioritize opportunities for improvement and to establish expectations. The committee, chaired by a department director, includes faculty and students. One of its first accomplishments was to develop and post the pledge shown in Figure 1 around the campus.

The students must be involved in instructional design and evaluation and be empowered to assume more control over their own education.

Various assessment instruments have been adopted to understand and monitor customers' needs, expectations, and perceptions, including regular focus group sessions. (The student senate sponsors an annual "Gripe Day" to garner reactions and an "I Love Northwest Week" to celebrate successes.) Maintenance and custodial personnel regularly survey administrators, faculty members, and students regarding the perceived quality of their services. In addition, monthly building inspection tours are conducted at sites selected by a member of the university president's cabinet.

Conducting Assessments for Prevention

Historically, industries ensured the quality of products by placing inspectors at the end of the assembly line. Assessment (to use educational parlance) under such conditions consisted of ranking and sorting what the workers produced.

This system has several problems. First, it is very expensive. The cost of not making products right the first time includes wasted labor and raw materials needed for rework, warranty costs for marginal products that were shipped, lost customers, and damaged reputation. Second, the use of inspectors suggests that workers are not trusted to do their jobs right the first time, thus lowering workers' expectations and aspirations. As is often the case, expectations become self-fulfilling prophecies. Finally, the presence of inspectors highlights differences between management and labor. Under such circumstances, workers tend to focus their attention on turf protectionism, cumbersome work rules, and other adversarial strategies.

All of these negative consequences can also be observed in education. Yet, it is incontrovertible that assessment and feedback are critical to the improvement of any process. Less obvious is the link between assessment systems and attempts on the part of those being assessed to beat the system. Sometimes that means distorting numbers. Other times, it leads to focusing solely on that which is easily measurable while ignoring more important goals (for example, simple recall rather than critical thinking skills). Since assessment, by its very nature, clarifies minimum standards, minimums often become maximums. Once participants—be they students or employees—realize that their performance is being measured so that they can be sorted and ranked, they will shift their energies toward finding ways to circumvent the system.

This conundrum led Philip Crosby to advocate that inspectors be taken off the assembly line and that the focus be on prevention instead.[4] W. Edwards Deming concurred with Crosby, but went even further, stating: "Eliminate

Culture of Quality
Commitment to Service

Northwest Missouri State University recognizes that quality service is an essential component of a quality university. Furthermore, we acknowledge that all of us—students, faculty, staff, and administration—are at times providers and at other times recipients of services.

Accordingly, we pledge our best efforts to provide quality service to you by:

- Treating you with respect, fairness, and honesty
  - Making you feel important and earning your trust
- Performing our tasks with competence and skill
  - Giving you confidence in the quality of what we provide
- Communicating clearly and courteously the services provided
  - Making it easy for you to know what you can expect
- Listening actively to your requests, comments, and concerns
  - Making it easy for you to tell us what you need
- Being flexible and open to new ideas
  - Accepting you and valuing your knowledge
- Providing what we agree to deliver in a timely manner
  - Enabling you to depend on us to help meet your goals

Figure 1. **The Pledge**

work standards (quotas) on the factory floor. Substitute leadership. Eliminate management by objective. Eliminate management by numbers, numerical goals. Substitute leadership."[5]

In higher education, most assessments are inspections at the end of the assembly line for purposes of ranking and sorting; relatively little diagnostic testing is done. Further, the primary beneficiary is the instructor who uses the results to assign grades, not prevent failures. The key to at least attenuating these problems lies in shifting the primary focus of assessment away from ranking and sorting toward improvement.

At Northwest, two assessment approaches were incorporated into the Culture of Quality plan to focus the results on raising expectations and preventing errors rather than simple ranking and sorting.

At Northwest, two assessment approaches were incorporated into the Culture of Quality plan to focus the results on raising expectations and preventing errors rather than simple ranking and sorting. First, an assessment program deliberately designed to raise expectations has been put in place. Freshmen are asked to come to the campus for a week-long orientation before school begins each fall. During that time, in addition to being introduced to the Culture of Quality, they are tested along several dimensions using a combination of locally developed and nationally normed tests. The information obtained is used for placing students in appropriate classes and later used as a benchmark against which progress is measured.

At the end of the sophomore year, one of the nationally normed tests administered during freshman orientation is readministered to plot progress. In addition, a writing sample is analyzed. Various departments also administer their own tests, examine portfolios, and the like before students are formally admitted to advanced standing. Three benefits accrue from such a program:

1. An opportunity is provided to solve problems while there is still time.
2. Freshmen encounter a salutary kind of anxiety as they look forward to this hurdle.
3. A more homogeneous upper-division environment is created that facilitates teaching higher-order thinking skills, such as analysis, synthesis, and evaluation.

This approach also avoids the problem encountered with administering senior exams that are part of graduation requirements: namely, the reluctance to deny graduation after four years of promotion and presumed satisfactory performance.

Just prior to graduation, additional tests are given. The results are used to evaluate program effectiveness. Finally, five years after graduation, alumni are surveyed to gain additional feedback.

A second, less traditional use of assessment focuses on improving both teaching and learning. In his book *Higher Learning,* Derek Bok suggests that testing drives students' study habits." The first thing that students do when beginning a course is find out how they will be tested. They ask the instructor, query former students, and study the syllabus. Once they have a feel for the types of questions they will be asked, they adjust their study habits accordingly. Therefore, if instructors ask questions that force students to use higher-order cognitive skills, such as analysis, synthesis, or evaluation, students will prepare themselves for those tasks. On the other hand, if all the instructor demands is recall and understanding, students will study in those modes.

Since few college instructors have ever systematically learned how to construct questions that test different cognitive levels, Northwest focused on that task. Specialists were brought on campus to hold weekend workshops on the topic of how to teach and test students on higher-order cognition. Participation was extensive and enthusiastic. Thus, the stigma often associated with assessment was avoided, assessments were moved in the direction of prevention, the quality of instruction was improved, and the expectations of students were raised.

Training

While it would be impossible to implement TQM without training, training should not be treated as an end in itself nor should success be judged by how many participate in specific training exercises. Over the years, Northwest has sponsored many training programs dealing with everything from statistical process control to how to handle telephone conversations. Through the George Washington University National Satellite Network, the university has participated in video conferences featuring Deming, Crosby, Peter Drucker, Joseph Juran, and Peter Scholtes.

TQM in Support Services

Most colleges and universities that have attempted to apply TQM concepts have started with support services, in the hope that the academic side will emulate what is working successfully in these more amenable areas. In fact, some have advocated that this is where the process should start.

Northwest took the opposite approach. It worried that starting with support services might trivialize the whole effort and would be akin to an automaker sprucing up the factory and cleaning up the cafeteria while still turning out inferior cars. So, it started with the academic program. Within a year, the Support Staff Council asked why it couldn't be a part of the Culture of Quality. Since that time, all of the support services (custodial, grounds, maintenance, and power plant) and the traditional student services (registrar's office, student finance office, cashier's office, and the like) have been involved.

An Ongoing Process

Continuous quality improvement is one of the pillars of the TQM faith. In that spirit, managing quality, like quality itself, must be viewed as a receding horizon. Hence, Northwest does not claim to have arrived at the quality gate. In fact, the Culture of Quality plan is currently being evaluated and expanded in the context of the latest Malcolm Baldrige National Quality Award criteria.

Educators, like their counterparts in industry, need to remind themselves that plans are not static, nor are they ever complete. (In this sense, the notion of total quality management is a misnomer.) Some action steps involve initiating activities that are ongoing and thus never completed. A lecture series that supports general education would be an example. Other action steps are complex and require several years to pilot, test, and refine before it can be said that they have been fully implemented. Northwest's assessment program would fit this category. Also, some departments begin implementing some action steps earlier than others. And, of course, in the process of implementation, refinements or adjustments are frequently made in the original action step.

Educators, like their counterparts in industry, need to remind themselves that plans are not static, nor are they ever complete.

Results of TQM at Northwest

Following is a summary of some major accomplishments realized as a result of the Culture of Quality program so far:

- The first comprehensive electronic campus in the nation was installed. It includes a computer workstation, two dedicated television channels, and a telephone that accesses a computer-generated voice in each residence hall room. (The computer-generated voice makes it possible to listen to stored information instead of reading it on a monitor). The network has more than

2,400 terminals, 400 microcomputers in 15 labs, 200 software applications, and a computerized videodisc and interactive voice-synthesizer tutorial system.

- Major writing assignments have increased 72% as a result of an across-the-curriculum writing program and the electronic campus.

- The semester was lengthened from 15 to 17 weeks. The net effect of this change was the addition of one month of instruction to the school year, or 16 weeks to the four-year college experience.

- A research program for undergraduates is in place, which has had remarkable success. Since 1990, top students have been required to participate.

- More than 50 events designed to integrate students' extra-curricular lives with learning activities are sponsored each year. Examples include guest lecturers, art gallery exhibits, music master classes, Black History Month speaker, and Greek Week presentations.

- A Student Services Center was established with the goal that students be able to transact 90% of their business with the university at a single location. In other words, instead of going to different buildings or offices to cash checks, pay bills, buy tickets, and so forth, students can do all of that at one centrally located counter.

- Registration, which used to take one or two days, can now be accomplished from the student's room on the electronic campus in less than 15 minutes.

- A set of 17 "Institution-Wide Instructional Goals" was adopted by the faculty. These goals provide a context for all other action steps.

- An assessment program was initiated. In this program, multiple measures are used to gauge students' attitudes and performance.

- General-education core courses were adopted. Core courses encompass the basic knowledge and skills necessary for successful completion of college and later for functioning as a literate, educated citizen. Core courses must be completed by the end of the sophomore year.

- Freshmen experiencing difficulty in selected courses now have the opportunity to participate in supplemental instruction activities that not only help them in the targeted course, but also provide instruction in note taking, using a textbook as a learning tool, test taking, and similar topics. The result is that, instead of spending three hours per week, for example, studying chemistry, students might spend four or five hours per week.

- Advanced-standing requirements are being developed whereby students will be formally evaluated at the end of their sophomore year.

- Workshops are regularly conducted to help faculty develop pedagogical strategies for extending writing, thinking, and listening skills across the curriculum.

- A faculty committee created a uniform course outline/syllabus format to ensure that the university's Institution-Wide Instructional Goals are integrated into the objectives of core courses.

- An applied research program encourages faculty to experiment with alternative teaching and learning strategies.

- More than half of all departments have adopted or developed comprehensive senior exit exams.

- Yearly workshops are conducted to help faculty members who are inexperienced at teaching at the college level.

- A new faculty evaluation system was developed by the faculty.

Of course, most of these initiatives could have been implemented in the absence of TQM, but they weren't. Northwest's experience suggests that doing things better does, in the end, pay off. Specifically, the dollar impact of Culture of Quality changes is dramatic:

- A $962,000 deficit in the education and general budget in 1985 was erased in four years and has been replaced with a $1.3 million surplus.

- The number of students choosing to move out of the residence halls at the end of their freshman year dropped by 50%.

- The university went from technical default on its auxiliary bonds to a $1.7 million surplus—a surplus realized while the residence halls were being renovated, new furniture was purchased, and occupancy rates went from 60% to 100%.

- Faculty salaries increased at nearly twice the rate of inflation (39.3% vs. 21.3%), and operating and equipment budgets were substantially increased.

- The portion of the university's education and general budget allocated to instruction grew from 48.5% (the national average) to more than 59%.

- Computed in fiscal year 1992 dollars, $3.1 million (10%) of the education and general budget was shifted from physical plant, administrative, and academic support services to instruction. At the same time, these services were improved.

- Despite a severely declining population in its catchment area, enrollment grew 26% until it hit capacity.

- Foundation assets grew from $1.4 million to $3.7 million.

- A six- to 18-month backlog on maintenance projects was eliminated. A campus beautification program was implemented. At the same time, campus maintenance costs were reduced by $1.7 million per year.

Observations and Lessons

Colleges and universities are exceedingly complex organizations. A typical campus encompasses a bookstore, dining establishment, hotel operation, police force, construction company, athletic club, and entertainment center, all of which supposedly support and complement a collection of fiercely competitive (internally) academic departments that deliver the institution's core product. Each segment shares attitudes and technologies common to its industry, albeit tempered by its association with the others and with the traditions and expectations of academe. The assertion that a single concept can be applied in this multifarious environment seems exceedingly heroic. Indeed, any attempt to slavishly apply Deming's, Crosby's, Juran's, or any other guru's model to every segment of an educational institution is probably doomed from the outset. Nonetheless, the system in all of its diverse dimensions—from the registration of students to the presentation of ideas—can be managed in ways that maximize quality outcomes. Furthermore, while there are identifiable differences between manufacturing a product, teaching a course, and delivering a service, many of the principles and techniques used in managing manufacturing quality can be applied to managing educational quality. Likewise, some of the principles that undergird quality education have trenchant potential for manufacturing (for example, designing assessments to raise expectations).

Many of the principles and techniques used in managing manufacturing quality can be applied to managing educational quality.

Higher education can learn from factories. Principles for ensuring quality—principles that are grounded in a clear sense of mission, concern for people, and high expectations—can and should be emulated. John Gardner's observation applies to education just as surely as it does to other segments of society:

"In a society of free men, competence is an elementary duty. Men and women doing competently whatever job is theirs to do tone up the whole society. And the man who does a slovenly job—whether he is a janitor or a judge, a surgeon or a technician—lowers the tone of the society . . . .

"Those who are most deeply devoted to a democratic society must be precisely the ones who insist upon excellence, who insist that free men are capable of the highest standards of performance, who insist that a free society can be a great society in the richest sense of that phrase. The idea for which this nation stands will not survive if the highest goal free men can set themselves is an amiable mediocrity."[7]

References

1. Robert C. Camp, *Benchmarking: The Search for Industry Best Practices That Lead to Superior Performance* (Milwaukee, WI: ASQC Quality Press, 1989), p. 12.

2. The principle of parsimony was introduced in the book *The Quest for Quality: The Challenge for Undergraduate Education in the 1990s* by Dean L. Hubbard, Lewis B. Mayhew, and Patrick J. Ford (San Francisco, CA: Jossey-Bass, 1990).

3. L. D. Albano and Nam P. Suh, "The Information Axiom and Its Implications," Proceedings of the ASME Conference on Intelligent Concurrent Design, DE-Vol. 66, December 1993, pp. 1–11.

4. Philip B. Crosby, *Quality Is Free* (New York, NY: McGraw-Hill Book Co., 1979).

5. W. Edwards Deming, *Out of the Crisis* (Cambridge, MA: Massachusetts Institute of Technology, 1986), p. 24.

6. Derek Bok, *Higher Learning* (Cambridge, MA: Harvard University Press, 1981).

7. John Gardner, *Excellence,* second edition (New York, NY: Harper & Row, 1971), pp. 193–194.

Dean L. Hubbard is the president of Northwest Missouri State University in Maryville.

TQM Thrives at Babson College

Scott Madison Paton

This article profiles how TQM is changing the way one small but highly regarded business school has taken TQM to heart and to practice. The administration has embraced TQM for the same reason as many businesses have: limited resources, increasing competition, and the need to more effectively and efficiently meet the needs of its customers.

How does a tiny and fiercely independent college in Wellesley, Massachusetts, gain a reputation as the nation's leading business school? Babson College did so by conducting an experiment in higher education that's shattering paradigms about traditional teaching, coaching and working together.

By using total quality management (TQM) in every facet of its organization, Babson College is learning new ways to run an organization that produces world-class products: Students who have the necessary skills to compete in the global marketplace. Babson teaches TQM, integrates TQM throughout its curriculum, conducts leading-edge TQM research and uses TQM in its administrative processes.

Babson holds semester-long courses in TQM at the graduate and undergraduate level. In addition, TQM is woven throughout the curriculum, including 14 courses with TQM content. Ten percent of the faculty conducts TQM research, including benchmarking, quality function deployment, ISO 9000 and information systems. Six faculty members are collaborating on a TQM textbook.

While other schools also conduct TQM research and teach TQM, Babson is unique for the way it integrates TQM principles into its curriculum and runs the institution.

Why TQM?

Babson must provide the best "service" to its "customers" to compete in the "market."

Why would Babson go to such lengths to implement TQM? Since its founding in 1919, the highly prestigious business school has turned out many of the world's leading businesspeople and entrepreneurs. Why the change? Despite its small size (3,100 students, 117 full-time and 63 part-time faculty members, and 400 staff members) Babson must provide the best "service" to its "customers" to compete in the "market."

Reprinted with permission from *Quality Digest*, September 1993. Copyright © 1993 by QCI International. All rights reserved.

"We looked at our MBA program and realized that we're not serving our customers well—both students as customers and companies as customer," says Phyllis Schlesinger, assistant professor of management. "Our students weren't coming out with the kind of skills we felt they need to solve problems and look at managerial problems as integrated pieces."

In addition to making "products" that don't meet the demand of today's organizations, Babson faced an increasingly crowded marketplace. The number of schools granting business degrees has more than doubled to 800 in the past 20 years while the number of students has decreased. Gone, too, are the days of endless tuition hikes. Babson's president has pledged not to raise tuition (already in the $18,000-a-year range) more than 1 percent to 1.5 percent above the Consumer Price Index.

Faced with many of the same problems corporate America faced in the mid-1980s, Babson chose the same solution: TQM. Already more than half of the college's staff has received TQM training and participates on teams. About 10 percent of the faculty has recently begun quality training. Students assimilate TQM as an integral part of the "Babson experience."

"In the broadest sense the goal is survival," explains George Covino, Babson's co-director of quality. "That survival will be brought about by satisfying the customer."

Quality from the Top

Babson's commitment to quality starts in the president's office. William F. Glavin became Babson's president in July 1989 after a 34-year career in industry that began at IBM and ended at Baldrige award-winning Xerox.

"When Glavin came to Babson, he realized that higher education in general (not just Babson) was in a crisis mode, particularly if you compare education across industries and cost increases," says Susan West Engelkemeyer, co-director of quality and assistant professor of management. "Health care gets the bad name, but higher education has really experienced higher cost increases over the past 10 years."

Glavin's first act at Babson was to hammer out a four-year strategic plan with the President's Cabinet (Babson's top management) and more than 100 members of the Babson community, including faculty, administration, students, alumni and trustees.

Next, Glavin and his cabinet underwent TQM training, attended a TQM retreat and met as a group to review the college's goal- and objective-setting process using TQM tools. The cabinet flowcharted the process and then interviewed senior and mid-level managers to confirm customer requirements.

In June 1992 Glavin established Babson's quality office, which consists of two co-directors of quality: Covino, who serves as the primary trainer and administrator of Babson's quality process, and Engelkemeyer, who was released from half of her teaching responsibilities to work with the faculty on TQM training and implementation in academic programs.

LIBRARY TEAM IMPROVES PROCESS

It's no surprise that the people who run Babson's state-of-the art Horn Library are involved with the TQM process. The library's 30 employees work on four quality improvement teams. One of those teams has made substantial improvements to the library's serials-acquisitions process.

The team began their project by brainstorming for problems within the serials-acquisitions area. They narrowed their list of 14 problems to tracking incoming shipments from the time they arrived until they go to cataloging. Next, they flowcharted the entire serials-acquisitions process. After looking at the process on paper, they immediately identified areas for improvement.

They then benchmarked their process against other college and university libraries they considered to be world-class. Much to their surprise, only nearby Wellesley College's library had enough knowledge of their own process to even answer their questions.

Team members say the quality process:

- Creates order out of otherwise chaotic processes.
- Gives the team a structure for change.
- Provides for more efficient work to meet customer demands better.

"We had a host of things that we needed to address," recounts Engelkemeyer. "Everything from the infrastructure, to developing a new technoculture, to a reward-and-recognition system, which was heavily oriented toward individual achievement of goals. We now expected people to work in groups."

Covino and Engelkemeyer are developing a TQM infrastructure and strategic quality plan for Babson. Their primary duty, however, has been to train faculty and staff in a series of three-day TQM introductory workshops. They began by training nine "quality specialists" who serve as internal quality consultants, form the quality steering committee, act as facilitators to Babson employee involvement teams and conduct TQM training.

Babson's vice president chose the quality specialists, who went through nine days of intense quality training. Up to 25 percent of their time may be spent working with the quality office and with teams. The quality specialists have three primary roles:

- Train people in the introductory workshops.
- Serve as team facilitators.
- Act as resident quality "experts" within their divisions.

Babson holds its introductory workshops for natural work groups within different departments and organizations. The training familiarizes these groups with quality principles and problem-solving methods.

"We train people in 'family' groups that come from a particular department or area," explains Engelkemeyer. "As part of their training, they identify a process that they want to work on improving. That's their first project."

Each team begins its first project during the three-day training by flowcharting a process within their organization. Using the tools learned in the training, they then improve upon that process.

"Their first project is fairly low-level, but it is designed for them to learn the tools and practice them in familiar territory," adds Engelkemeyer.

Since the teams form among natural work groups and their first project revolves around a fairly straightforward problem all team members can relate to, initial success is almost guaranteed.

"The problem now is how to get people to move from something that is pretty well self-contained in their work area and identify problems that are larger in scope and more difficult to tackle," notes Engelkemeyer. "So we're looking at not only training and education using tools and techniques, but also continuing the momentum—how to get people involved in second-level teams and how to start solving the big problems that we face at the institution."

The college currently has about 35 teams at work, about half of which are facilitated by a quality specialist. As the number of teams increase and TQM continues to spread throughout the Babson community, the need for quality specialists increases.

The college currently has about 35 teams at work, about half of which are facilitated by a quality specialist.

"As more of the Babson community is educated about TQM, there is a greater need for quality specialists to act as facilitators, provide interventions and get groups going," explains Elizabeth Lemons, director of human resources and a quality specialist. "I think a lot of people have good intentions, but they don't know how to get going. That is the facilitator's role."

One team project entails redesigning the performance-appraisal system. The team is responsible for the research, design and delivery of the new program. Although Babson's current performance-appraisal system was designed before they implemented TQM, it does contain many TQM elements.

"It was designed with the anticipation that the TQM program would be implemented at Babson," explains Lemons. "The factors that employees are evaluated on included buzzwords you would hear in a TQM program. You are evaluated on teamwork, customer service, initiative, accomplishment of goals and objectives, employee development and employee empowerment."

The Babson Quality Office works with a $130,000 annual budget, which does not include salaries and quality specialists' time.

Faculty Reaction

While Babson's staff has embraced the TQM effort, faculty reaction has been a bit more reserved, a situation common in many academic institutions. At most schools, not just Babson, initial faculty resistance to quality is common, according to Allan Cohen, Babson vice president of academic affairs and dean of the faculty. Cohen says he believes academic institutions encounter faculty resistance due to three factors:

- Faculty is suspicious of anything that comes from industry. "The general feeling is that there must be something wrong with it if it comes from the business world," says Cohen.

Quality Should Be Used Everywhere in Education as in Business

William F. Glavin

I came to Babson College in July 1989 after a 34-year career in industry, having begun with IBM and ended as vice-chairman of Xerox Corp. I was the first Xerox executive to attend the Crosby Quality College, and I insisted that David Kearns, chairman of Xerox, attend a class right away. I was the impetus behind Xerox's commitment to use quality as a program to change the culture of the organization.

Quality and all it encompasses can and should be used everywhere in education just as in business. Higher education is in a financial crisis that too many institutions are ignoring or, at best, treating as a short-term event.

Revenues—endowment income, annual giving, investment income, etc.—are much lower than in the '80s. But the major crisis is that our customers (students and those who pay the tuition bills) will no longer put up with continuing tuition increases totally outside the realm of reason. We can no longer increase tuitions at unjustifiable rates. The time has come to limit increases to no more than 1 percent to 1.5 percent above the Consumer Price Index.

With reduced tuition increase, we in education must use new ideas and methodologies to contain costs and improve effectiveness. Therefore, I believe the total quality management approach for academic institutions is a necessity, not a luxury.

We must listen to our .customers and meet their requirements, not just our own self-interests.

William F. Glavin is president of Babson College.

- Faculty experiences difficulty adjusting to students as customers. "The biggest stumbling block is that faculty has problems thinking about students as customers because they get so hung up on the fact that customers are always right," says Covino. "That doesn't work with a student who doesn't understand what his or her needs, wants or expectations should be."
- "Introducing" a quality process makes many faculty members feel as if management doesn't think they have been oriented toward high standards and doing things well all along.

While Babson isn't immune to the same faculty resistance that plagues other schools, it has had moderate success integrating TQM into the faculty arena.

While Babson isn't immune to the same faculty resistance that plagues other schools, it has had moderate success integrating TQM into the faculty arena.

"We are different from a lot of other institutions," says Cohen. "As a business school, our faculty is far more tuned to the outside world than in most other academic institutions."

The President's Cabinet set the standard for how quality would filter through the faculty. Instead of mandating faculty involvement, they set an example of how well teams work by going through the training and becoming a team first.

"I argued vigorously when the cabinet went through its training that we could not be a totally top-down organization," explains Cohen. "It would never work. But we couldn't just wait for it to rise from below, either. We decided to use a top-down, bubble-up approach. We decided not to force faculty to go through training and to use it. Instead, we made training available to anyone who's interested."

Faculty members have begun taking the training and several teams have formed. Cohen sees full integration of the TQM process into the faculty as a five-year process.

"I do not expect a quality revolution in the faculty to happen overnight," says Covino, echoing Cohen's prediction. "There are light bulbs going on in their heads and connections are being made. We're looking for little victories."

One faculty team has been using brainstorming and affinity diagrams to make improvements to the advising system. Another team, comprised of the deans and chairs, is working on Babson's load system, which determines how much faculty members should be teaching.

The TQM process has also given faculty a means to track progress and institute change. "Academic institutions move at glacial speed, if they move at all," jokes Cohen. "Faculty members are wary of being burned by doing hard work on things and having them disappear."

A Curriculum for the 21st Century

Babson's use of TQM has led the institution to focus on its customers: students, parents, businesses, society. This customer focus recently led the college to scrap its entire two-year MBA program and replace it with a zero-based curriculum that's light years away from the traditional classroom experience. Instead, students go through four modules that simulate the product life cycle, work on real problems in mentor companies, and live and work internationally.

Students go through four modules that simulate the product life cycle, work on real problems in mentor companies, and live and work internationally.

"The main focus is to have the students follow what we feel is the business life cycle during the first year," says William Makris, associate dean and director of admission. "They will learn different skill sets that they need in different types of businesses from inception of the idea through midterm to long-term growth."

The program's first year traces the business development cycle from the invention or discovery of a product or service, through assessing the business opportunity, into creating the marketing and delivery systems and on to further development of products in the cycle. The first year also includes participation in the Business Mentor Program, which pairs students with businesses and offers them real business problems to evaluate.

The second year builds upon the first-year MBA experience as students expand their knowledge via nine elective courses and required international course work. Babson requires all U.S. citizens enrolled in the MBA program to participate in one of three academic programs: the International Management Internship Program; a semester abroad at one of Babson's four sister institutions; or an intensive three-week elective in one of these cities: Lausanne, Switzerland; Paris; Prague, Czech Republic; St. Petersburg, Russia; or Quito, Ecuador.

Babson's grading process is as innovative as its new curriculum. Students receive one grade for each of the four modules. Each module consist of a series of graded, integrated exercises and case discussions. A faculty jury evaluates students' understanding of each module. Performance is assessed on an individual and group basis. In addition, class participation is an essential part of the program.

The four modules are divided as follows:

- *Module I—Creative Management in Dynamic Organizations*

  This introductory module encourages students to develop new ways of thinking about management behavior. Students have the opportunity to explore topics such as leadership, ethics, innovation and creative problem solving. Students work individually and in groups to apply these ideas to managerial situations. Through team-building exercises in the great outdoors, to assisting with a community-based project, to helping a colleague perfect computer skills, or simply thinking about leadership in a new way, Module I lays the intellectual and motivational foundations for the Babson MBA.

- *Module II—Assessing Business Opportunities*

  The second module introduces students to the analytical tools necessary to master industry analysis and assess a company's competitive position. Students will be assigned a mentor company in Module II and will complete their first mentor company project presentation, which requires students to evaluate their company's financial data and compare it with their company's competitors.

- *Module III—Designing and Managing the Delivery System*

  In Module III students look at processes from an operations perspective—how they work, how much they cost, how they affect customer value. They then evaluate whether to design or redesign the delivery system. Two themes help create cross-functional cohesion in the module: total quality management and strategic fit. Students collaborate with their mentor company to recommend the design or redesign of a delivery system.

- *Module IV—Growing and Renewing Business*

Module IV reinforces concepts from previous modules and introduces new concepts necessary for managing effective enterprises in the short and long term. Students will assess managing large or small organizations under condition of growth or adversity; examine internal and external forces driving change; develop a complex set of strategies to lead an adaptive organization; and evaluate the operation of global enterprises.

TQM Continues Babson's Tradition of Excellence

Babson's TQM implementation and its new MBA curriculum have resulted in an organization that can compete with any business school in the nation. *U.S. News & World Report* agrees, naming Babson the best business specialty school in the nation in its recent feature, "America's Best Colleges."

Perhaps more important has been the reaction of faculty, staff and students to Babson's quality process.

"I have been affected by it as a faculty member because things seem to be running more smoothly in areas where people have done their homework on quality issues," says Schlesinger. "Admissions has been much better. Dates are better met. Everybody seems to have ownership of something rather than one person. The environment is a lot better."

Reaction to the quality process among Babson's staff is similar. "It has really allowed us to focus our attention on what we should be doing," says Rick Mickool, director of user services for the Information Technology and Services Division. "TQM asks us, what are we really in business for? What are those businesses? How do we do them? How do we document them? and How are we going to do them even better?"

Babson plans to involve students directly in its TQM process via a new program called Quality Camp.

Babson plans to involve students directly in its TQM process via a new program called Quality Camp. The camp will put student leaders through the same three-day training that faculty and staff receive.

"Obviously, students have a part to play in this community," says Jane McSweeney, director of student activities. "They should be doing things in a quality manner as well. After all, we are trying to speak in quality terms and using quality concepts with the students; they should know what we mean.

The Quality Camp training will also provide student leaders the opportunity to address problems in the student community. "Obviously, we can't fix problems like student social life and a missing sense of tradition," explains McSweeney. "Now the students will have the quality tools to work on those problems themselves."

The involvement of faculty, staff and students in Babson's quality journey as well as its commitment to providing the best-possible education continues Babson's tradition of excellence.

Scott Madison Paton is the editor-in-chief of Quality Digest *Magazine.*

Public Sector

EDUCATION K–12

Educational Reform and Quality

Gabriel Massaro, Nancy Roche, and David Bayless

This article by our consulting editors in K–12 education provides some background on how quality principles came to be applied to education and gives some examples of successes. The principles of quality management can play an important role in improving education in this country, but the application of these ideas in this field is still in its infancy.

Again the push for reform is upon us. As the productivity of our competitors increasingly outdistances our own, America's ability to compete in world markets is questioned. At the same time that jobs requiring little skill are automated or moved out of the country and the demand for skilled workers in American industry increases, the national pool of educated and skilled people grows smaller, and the number of unemployed rises. In this new economic age, the challenges to educational institutions are similar to those faced by American industry years ago. At that time, many companies decided to implement the philosophy and methods of management espoused by W. Edwards Deming, the architect of Japan's postwar economic revival.

Dr. Deming, whose ideas are said to be nothing less than a third wave of the industrial revolution, advocated managing using the concepts and techniques of quality improvement. To improve quality, management must demonstrate its commitment to quality and accept responsibility for improving it. The quality environment encourages teamwork, communication, joint

The authors wish to acknowledge Dr. David Romstad, superintendent of schools in the Parkview District of Wisconsin for several contributions to this article.

problem solving, trust, security, pride in work, and never-ending improvement. The extended process is constantly improved because a true cooperative spirit prevails.

History

In 1987, Dr. Jacob Stampen of the University of Wisconsin, Madison, wrote how Deming's ideas for improving quality through better management compare to ideas from the research dealing with the effective schools movement.[1] He wrote that Deming's ideas for improving the quality of products and services in industry seem adaptable, at least on a conceptual level, to the management of education. Deming's 14 Points offer similar guidelines as those emerging from the effective schools and school improvement literature.

Currently, the quality movement in public education in this country is at a sort of crossroads. It is true that there are many places where serious and systemic efforts are underway to engage students, staff, and parents in continuous improvement activities. However, it is also true that there is an emerging awareness among many early quality pioneers that the school system's ability to sustain deep and meaningful change is constrained by the limited access to, and involvement of, parents and other external customers in the business of schooling.

Central to the next wave of quality involvement in the public school will be the direct and dynamic involvement of all customers in decision making, design of process improvements, and development of both the strategic priorities and the qualitative and quantitative indicators that will gauge the ongoing degree to which strategic priorities are being met. This involvement will increasingly be found in the systems where customers have been involved right from the start.

Central to the next wave of quality involvement in the public school will be the direct and dynamic involvement of all customers.

Students and staff at the Mt. Edgecumbe High School in Sitka, Alaska, have successfully implemented and adapted Deming's philosophy and underlying points to an educational setting. In this boarding school of about 200 students and 15 teaching faculty, the students have taken charge of their education.[2] One of the former teachers, David Langford, attended a session dealing with the quality movement. He read as much as he could and followed up by meeting with executives who were part of companies implementing Total Quality Management programs. Langford concluded that Deming's ideas could be applied in education. He convinced his superintendent and began by introducing Deming's ideas into his classes in business and in a special course he called "continuous improvement." He prepared worksheets for the students to use to develop data on their study habits. The result was that as students' enthusiasm, drive, and efficiency improved, they learned much more, faster. As this new process spread throughout the school, the culture of the school began to change. Other staff members became interested in adopting some of the quality principles. Teachers began to work with each other more cooperatively and with parents. The school has begun a journey of continuous improvement.

The Parkview School District in southern Wisconsin is an example of a district that went straight to the customers. Parents, students, staff, and citizens developed, in their own language, the strategic imperatives that will guide all efforts in the district for the next five years. Additionally, this cross-functional strategic team (Parkview Community Strategic Development Group) also designed the specific, results-driven protocols that will continuously feed data back into the system specifically engineered to align with the strategic imperatives of the district and community. In short, Parkview customers not only developed agreements on specific strategic goals, but also designed the ways in which they continuously will be able to know whether, and to what extent, the strategies are successful.

All these kinds of efforts represent a dramatic departure from the traditional long-range planning schemes where customers are surveyed for their input but also where the development of both specific plans, and the summary evaluations of progress toward implementation, remain the responsibility of professionals inside the organization. This is not necessarily bad. However, it sustains the old (i.e., current) paradigm in which organization insiders continue to roll out plans for process improvements. The new paradigm, and the only real hope for public education, is one where the customers and the education service providers are linked together right from the start—and stay linked—all the way out to implementation and continuous evaluation.

Although there seems to be a cry to improve student outcomes, we might do better to concentrate on setting goals and improving the current state of the art. Both the Association for Supervision and Curriculum Development and the American Association for School Administrators have devoted many articles in their journals to this theme. One entire journal issue of *Educational Leadership* was devoted to Total Quality Management. Many of the articles endorsed the implementation of the philosophy and practices related to quality. Bayless and Massaro have written several articles related to the successful implementation of Total Quality Management in the state of Louisiana and four southern school districts.

Some Examples of Schools Implementing Quality

As in industry, commitment from school system district leadership is necessary to create a successful process. When applying quality management to education, educators claim that quality moves far beyond the paradigm by endorsing total participation, motivation, and systems theory. In the Kate Sullivan Elementary School in Tallahassee, Florida, for example, staff and parents explored ways in which they could lead. The principal, Nancy Duden, changed her leadership paradigm. She supported a great deal of dialogue with the teachers and parents. By taking time, and allowing people to state questions and get responses, much of the fear that accompanies change was quelled. She met the challenge of working cooperatively, a major tenet of quality.

Another premise, which is part of Deming's philosophy, is that all people have an intrinsic drive to do well. He maintains that in a supportive environment people will strive to reach their potential without any need for external motivators. At Kate Sullivan School, Nancy Duden provided constructive alternatives to the traditional grades. Self-evaluation by students, portfolios of students' work, and parent-teacher conferences replaced report cards. Parents, teachers, and students have begun to realize that these new "grading" processes help better measure student progress and assist all in working together in a continually growing and learning environment.

Two other Florida schools have also implemented the quality principles. The Brown Barge Middle School in Pensacola involves students and parents in all facets of students' learning. In Tallahassee, the Deer Lake Middle School began to apply quality principles acquired through training. They investigated student achievement. After reviewing test data, they looked at student classroom placement. The use of statistical tools enabled them to make easier comparisons and a more detailed analysis. Students and parents became more actively involved in the education process. Classroom organization resulted in a redefinition of success. The students, parents, and staffs of the schools cited have taken a very important step to redefine successful educational practices.

In Williston, Vermont, at the Swift House of Williston Central School, an educational reform is in progress that is authentic in the way it achieves the aim of involving and meeting the needs of "customers" of the education system (students, parents, the community) to improve the quality of learning. Swift House includes approximately 100 learners within the larger Williston Central School. These learners are ages 9 to 13, and there are four learning leaders and three associated support staff in this effort. Their efforts involve the implementation of a continuous improvement approach to meet the individual needs of students and have resulted in a completely transformed approach to teaching and learning that better meets the needs of all participants.

Their efforts have resulted in a completely transformed approach to teaching and learning that better meets the needs of all participants.

The Richmond County School System in Augusta, Georgia, is another interesting example of an organization attempting the shift to community-driven strategic planning. The community has been involved from the very beginning in framing the strategic imperatives for the community's education. Leadership in the school system has been bold in its willingness to support community-driven improvements in total quality in all of its services and processes. This delicate, yet vital, blend of executive commitment and community-based involvement is, we believe, essential for achieving the kind of paradigm-busting, breakthrough thinking that can support continuous and lasting improvement in public schools that demonstrably satisfy all internal and external customers.

A Final Caveat

Much recent attention in journals and books has been given to the nefarious role played by boards of education that are constantly changing in membership and focus. It is typically posited that this phenomena is a hurdle of such magnitude that schools will never be able to achieve the higher goals of TQM while board's change their minds like the winds. The authors believe that this thinking is irrelevant. In settings where the voice of the customer is allowed to enter the planning and management process in authentic and complete ways, barriers such as whimsical boards of education become less important. The key is to involve the customers with dignity, integrity, and openness. The force of quality is the voice of the customer.

Notes

1. Jacob O. Stampen, "Improving the Quality of Education: W. Edwards Deming and Effective Schools," *Contemporary Education Review*, Winter 1987, vol. 3, no. 3, pp. 423–433.

2. Myron Tribus, "The Application of Quality Management Principles in Education at Mt. Edgecumbe High School, Sitka, Alaska," *American Association for School Administrators*, 1991.

Transforming Schools

Julie E. Horine, William A. Hailey, and Laura Rubach

This article from Quality Progress *summarizes research done in 1993 on the state of total quality management in K–12 education. TQM is slowly finding a place in the management and delivery of education in this country, but it still has a long way to go.*

Great strides are being made by educators using total quality management (TQM) to improve America's schools. This is abundantly clear in the responses from 105 of the nation's public and private school districts. Compared to the 65 respondents in last year's survey, a growing number of schools are embracing the process, principles, and tools of TQM.

Like many companies that have successfully launched quality efforts, schools are creating quality councils, quality improvement teams, and customer-supplier partnerships. Perhaps more salient is the paradigm shift, occurring in many schools, that reflects the wisdom of an old African proverb: "It takes a whole village to raise a single child." The essence of the proverb is reflected in the growing number of educators adopting a systems perspective for improving and using the collaborative efforts of students, parents, teachers, administrators, taxpayers, and other who hold a stake in the success of the school community.

Like many companies that have successfully launched quality efforts, schools are creating quality councils, quality improvement teams, and customer-supplier partnerships.

Districts often express their frustration with how painfully slow and time consuming it is to implement TQM. Others emphasize that cultural change takes time, requires the development of a total systems approach to restructure for quality, and must be ongoing and never ending for meaningful change to occur. The greatest challenge to implementing quality management for many districts can be summed up in four words: trust, shared vision, and leadership.

The greatest challenge to implementing quality management for many districts can be summed up in four words: trust, shared vision, and leadership.

This article summarizes the deployment of TQM principles in districts as measured by senior leadership and employee involvement, improvement efforts, team activities, and partnerships.

Leadership and Employee Involvement

Most districts are in the early stages of implementing TQM. The difference between last year's and this year's survey findings is that a greater number of schools are exploring TQM principles and tools. The majority (79%) report that they have been using TQM principles and tools in their administrations

Reprinted with permission from *Quality Progress*, October 1993. Copyright © 1993 ASQC, Milwaukee, WI.

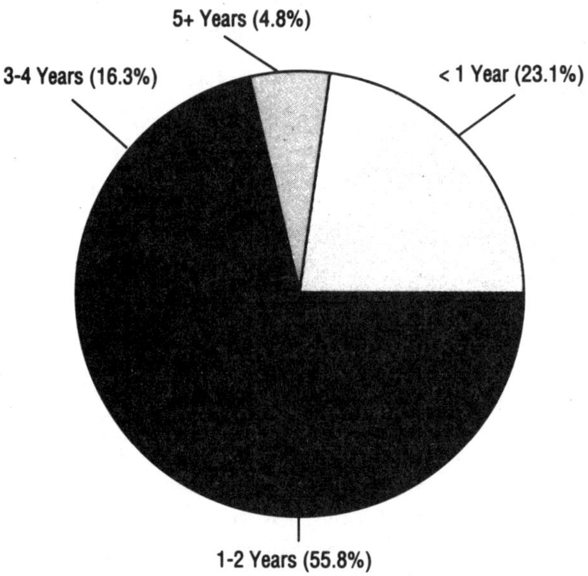

Figure 1. **Number of years school district has been using TQM principles and tools in administration.**

for two years or less. Roughly one-fourth of the districts (23%) report that they are still in their first year of TQM awareness, and over half (56%) are in their second year of TQM. Only a few districts (5%) note a maturity level of five years or more (see Figure 1).

More than half of the districts (53%) report relatively low levels of employee participation in their quality efforts (25% or less). This is probably because many districts are just beginning to use TQM. Groups most actively involved in district TQM efforts are administrators, followed by teachers, staff, school boards, and students (see Figure 2).

Quality councils and quality officers are quickly becoming an integral part of the operation of the districts pioneering in TQM. To coordinate their quality efforts, more than half of the districts (53%) have quality councils, and more than one-third (36%) have quality officers. In many cases principals or teachers, committed to quality management principles, are seizing the opportunity to coordinate district TQM activities.

Improvement Efforts

Although more than half of the districts (62%) report that their TQM activities are focused districtwide, considerable efforts are taking place at single sites (24%) and with pilot projects (27%). Pilot projects, in many cases, are being used by state departments of education to lead the implementation of TQM education. South Carolina, for example, is implementing total quality education within six pilot school districts. South Carolina's Department of

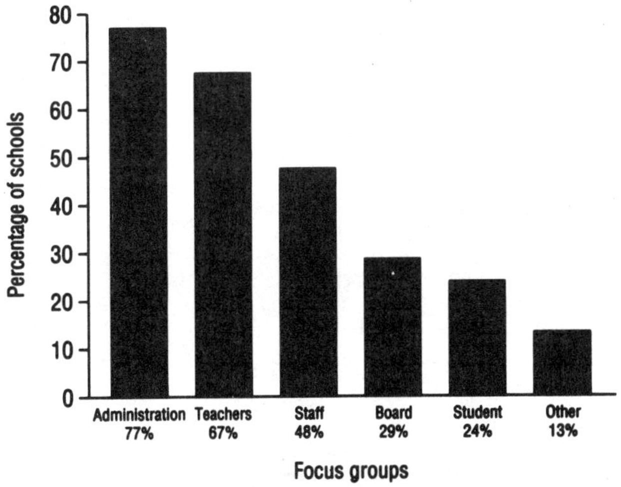

Figure 2. **Groups involved in district TQM efforts.**

Education is walking the talk through its own rigorous training and improvement team efforts that range from improving communication between the Department of Education and the school districts to improving the process of assessing school standards.

State mandates, such as the 1993 Massachusetts Education Reform Act, require schools to use participatory management and involve all customer groups in the improvement process. One of Massachusetts' comprehensive laws requires the establishment of school councils at each school site that consist of teachers, parents, business, and other constituent groups.

Districts report that their improvement efforts are focused primarily on the administrative side of the organization, followed by teaching methods, student achievement, communication, food service, transportation, maintenance, and purchasing (see Figure 3). Districts also report improvement efforts in the following areas: discipline, attendance, community relations, school grounds safety, evaluation, planning, school design, paper flow, tardiness, and problem solving.

Team Activities

The initiation of process-improvement team activities throughout districts suggests that a growing number of districts are realizing the benefits of focusing on process improvements. The greatest concentration of teams is at the building-site level, followed by the central office, districtwide, and student levels. The number of teams at multiple levels ranges from zero to 40 teams (see Figure 4).

Building-site team projects address a variety of problems, including reducing cycle time for special program referrals at Waco Independent School

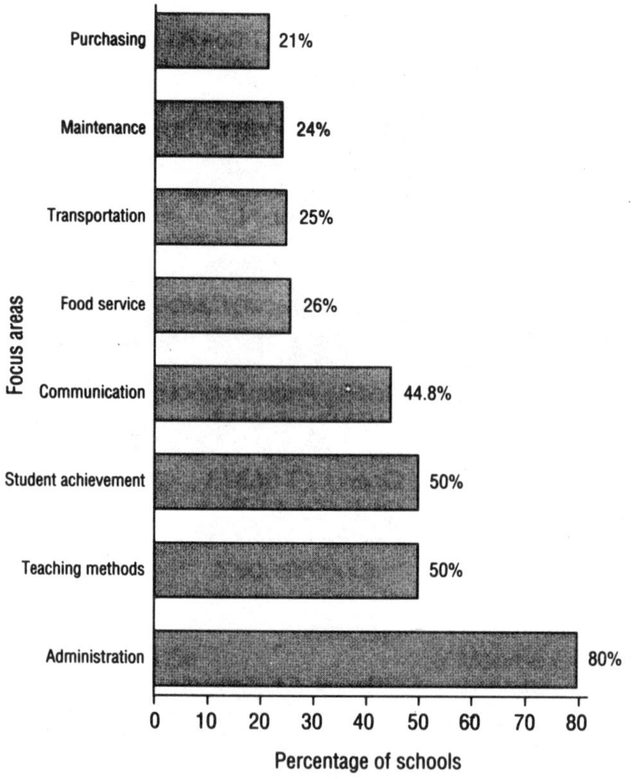

Figure 3. **Focus areas of district process improvement efforts.**

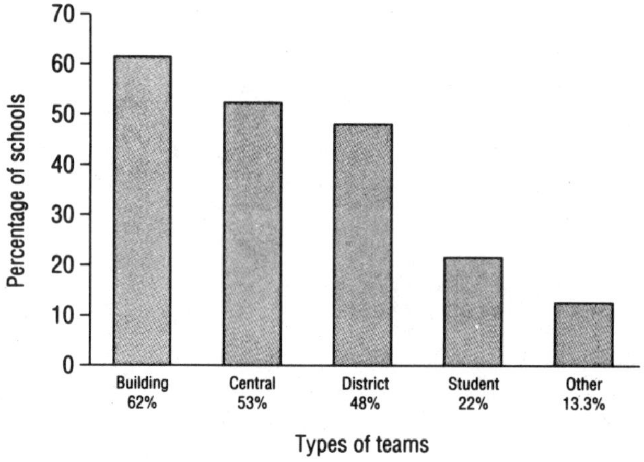

Figure 4. **Types of TQM-trained teams working on process improvement.**

District in Waco, TX; reducing student tardiness at Southbridge Public Schools in Southbridge, MA; and improving school safety at Sacramento County Office of Education in Sacramento, CA. Rappahannock County Schools in Sperryville, VA, has 28 teams at the building-site level that focus on projects such as reducing the number of fourth-grade students requiring math remediation.

Central-office team projects encompass problems like reducing the cost of tax collection at the State College Area School District in State College, PA, and improving the hiring and selection process at the School District of Brodhead in Brodhead, WI. Examples of other team projects include improving intraoffice mail services, purchase order procedures, and telephone communications.

Various districtwide team projects include increasing staff involvement in curriculum issues at Cherry Hill School District in Cherry Hill, NJ; improving program evaluation at Forrest City School District in Forrest City, AR; and improving student achievement at Fort McMurray Catholic Schools in Alberta, Canada.

Approximately 500 students at St. Pius X Elementary School in New Orleans, LA, are participating in a homework improvement system.

Some student team projects focus on such items as developing a process for student portfolios at Mt. Edgecumbe High School in Sitka, AK; improving student follow-up procedures and reporting at Francis Tuttle Voc-Tech Center in Oklahoma City, OK; and concentrating on improving student achievement and accelerating learning time at Birmingham Public Schools in Birmingham, AL. Student teams at Beloit Turner School District in Beloit, WI, are using quality tools to improve student government. Approximately 500 students at St. Pius X Elementary School in New Orleans, LA, are participating in a homework improvement system, which is a result of their input during a brainstorming session to identify reasons for not completing homework.

Other process-improvement team activities were mentioned by districts. One example is the creation of company teams in Millcreek Township in Erie, PA, that allow students to work with industry in applying quality processes.

Pat Konopniki, director of the Office of Vocational Education in Virginia Beach City Public Schools, reflected the enthusiasm of many administrators regarding the quality management process when she said, "Teacher and classroom involvement has been phenomenal. The bottom-up approach from the classroom has worked the best . . . once teachers get excited, there is no stopping them."

Quality education also requires the improvement or redesign of external processes linked to other educational institutions, state agencies, community social systems, and family units.

Partnerships in Quality

Educators committed to a systems perspective of TQM recognize that quality education does not flow naturally from the improvement of existing internal processes such as transportation, registration, curriculum, and teaching methods. Quality education also requires the improvement or redesign of external processes linked to other educational institutions, state agencies, community social systems, and family units. This knowledge has led, in part, to the growth of district partnerships with industry and other community entities.

More than two-thirds (71%) of the districts report partnerships supporting their TQM efforts. These partnerships include state efforts such as Minnesota's Partners for Quality Education Initiative and Xerox Corporation's Loaned Executive program, which provides districts such as the Rappahannock County School District in Sperryville, VA, with training and consultation. Wichita Falls Independent School District in Wichita Falls, TX, is an example of a district partnering with a variety of community entities ranging from the local Chamber of Commerce to the Sheppard Air Force Base Quality Office. The diverse and extensive partnership list for districts suggests that a number of communities are rolling up their sleeves and working together to improve their educational systems.

Julie E. Horine is an assistant professor of educational leadership at the University of Mississippi in Oxford. William A. Hailey is a professor and holder of the H. F. McCarty Chair of Management at Millsaps College in Jackson, MS. Laura Rubach is an editor with Quality Progress.

Education—From Vision to Strategies

Al Anderson

This article by an administrator in Canada discusses how one district in Alberta went about implementing TQM. In reading the article, you will see the difficulties the district faced, and yet the importance of sticking with it to see results.

While some international comparisons report that Canadian students are comparing reasonably well against other industrialized nations, other do not and, regardless, the confidence of Canadians in their educational system is waning. According to a recent survey, 46 percent of the people think that "education is worse today than it was 25 years ago."[1] Private and home schools, in particular, show impressive increases in their student populations. However, Canadian educational organizations have not been in a position to refute the charges of poor quality, mainly because of a lack of reliable data. We talk about excellence and quality but have not really defined it. We have not planned for improved futures and have not involved the customers. When a system of education vouchers or choice is introduced, some jurisdictions [school districts] may disappear because they have not planned for quality. This paper presents two Canadian school jurisdictions' strategic plans for addressing quality, within the educational environment. It offers, as one possible solution to quality in education, a systems approach to improvement, with a focus on the student and other customers. The plan involves a characterization of the student within the vision and mission of the jurisdiction, emphasizing the importance of quality indicators, standards, data systems and strategies.

Introduction

Twin Rivers School Division No. 65 was Alberta's newest jurisdiction in September, 1989. Carved from two existing county school authorities, it is located in an oil, gas and woods resource area, bordering the foothills of the Rocky Mountains of Alberta, Canada. The new board and administration were intrigued with the notion of creating an improved future for students, particularly with the notion of strategically planning for obtaining measurable growth now and continuing to the year, 2000 A.D.

Reprinted with permission from *The Total Quality Review,* March/April 1994. Copyright © 1994 Cambridge Strategy Publications, MCB University Press.

The second jurisdiction, Camrose Roman Catholic School District (RCSSD) No. 60, is a small, two-school system interested in taking the systems approach to continuous improvement and adding the spiritual and customer focus.

Michael Fullan, a Canadian authority on change, says that "for an institution to sustain substantial reform requires a shared and deep understanding about the nature of the desired end."[2] This thinking led Twin Rivers people to struggle with their vision and mission. Who are the students of the future? What will their needs be, given the uncertainty of the living, learning and workplace environment? Systems thinking suggest that we should not be content with narrow views or a smorgasbord choosing of things to track and attack. We did not want the shoot-in-all-directions strategy that produces hit-and-miss results. The following emerged from our early planning:

Systems thinking suggest that we should not be content with narrow views or a smorgasbord choosing of things to track and attack.

Vision

- "Education for Tomorrow . . . Today"

Mission

- To view the child as the center of the educational process.
- To instill in each student an appreciation for and an awareness of self worth and quality of life.
- To develop in students responsible citizenship and an understanding of learning as a lifelong process.
- To foster within students, staff and community, a commitment to academic, personal, physical, social and cultural development.

Goals

Academic

- To increase the power of the learner to achieve levels of knowledge and skills consistent with his/or her abilities.
- To achieve and exceed provincial standards.
- To provide programs that nurture creative and critical thinking, problem solving and process skills.
- To encourage the pursuit of independent and lifelong learning.
- To implement curriculum and instructional programs that foster the ongoing pursuit of excellence.

Personal and Physical

- To design programs that develop a positive self concept which translates into positive relationships with others in the school and community.
- To emphasize the importance of physical and emotional well being.
- To relate work and leisure activities to quality of life.

- To nourish the development of ethical conduct and moral values, including societal ideals such as knowing right from wrong, the use of one's personal faith as a guide, and recognition of and regard for the dignity and worth of all humanity.

Social and Cultural

- To develop the knowledge, attitudes and behaviors that lead to an openness to positive change and a willingness to take corrective and adoptive action.
- To adopt world view programs which are considerate of the importance of active community involvement, the rights and responsibility of citizenship, understanding and accepting other cultures and societies, and the development of responsible attitudes and behaviors towards the global environment.

The vision, mission and goals are not unlike those identified by other school jurisdictions. They speak of the whole child in terms of the academic, personal, physical, social and cultural components. But how were we to plan for a realization of our vision? If we understand quality improvement to be a process, not an event or program, what would such a plan look like?

Our decision was to develop an indepth characterization of the student. What we were looking for would have to link with the vision, mission and goals of the jurisdiction. We called these essential linking characterizations, *quality indicators.* From a search of the literature and from discussions with other jurisdictions, about 120 possible quality indicators were identified. That number of indicators was not only unmanageable but many of the items were unrelated to our requirement that they must link to the stated goals, mission, and ultimately, the vision. In the end, 11 quality indicators and an additional 14 tracking factors were selected. The tracking factors were things that were important for us to know, but did not merit the status of quality indicators. We were now in new territory. Our quality indicator schema is shown in Figure 1 (page 244).

The quality indicators were tested with parent, business and industry customers as well as our professional staff. While staff had been involved in examining the original set of indicators, other customers had not been part of the exercise. In retrospect, bringing a broader range of customers in earlier would have improved our process. A ranking of the indicators from most to least important revealed significant consensus among the participants Figure 2 (page 245).

In retrospect, bringing a broader range of customers in earlier would have improved our process.

Quality Standards

Quality Indicators were not enough in themselves. We needed to describe and expand upon each indicator in detail and establish expected levels of performance. We chose the term *standard* to describe a level of expectation for each quality indicator. If we had followed the corporate TQM analogy, we might have substituted the term *outrageous goals.* The necessity of adding meaning

Figure 1. **Quality Indicators and tracking factors.**

to the quality indicators and standards became clear, as did the need to specify criteria or expected levels of performance for each of the indicators. Defining standards in terms of what we wanted students to accomplish, instead of attaching numbers or percentages to desired outcomes, appeared to be the preferred approach Figure 3 (page 246).

Data Collection

The next step in the strategic plan was to identify the present levels of student performance relative to the accepted standards. In this the data collection phase, instruments were devised to gather information from students at selected grades. Where possible, we clustered the quality indicators and cycled the administration of instruments so as not to overload the teachers and schools with data gathering. For example, the same instruments were used to gather student data on learner empowerment, love of learning, and lifelong learning. Another assessment cluster was environmental conscience, global view, and futurism.

Complex thinking skills and academic achievement are examined yearly, while other indicators and clusters are assessed every two years.

Grade levels are sampled with one grade from each of the elementary (grades K–6), junior high (grades 7–9) and senior high (grades 10–12) included for each indicator. The assessment cycle is illustrated in Figure 4 (page 247).

Data Gathering Cycle

We were in new territory again when it came to collecting data relative to both the quality indicators and the tracking of Twin Rivers students. Alberta

Quality Indicator	Percentage of Agreement Parents	Staff	Business	Priority Parents	Staff	Business
Learner Empowerment	97%	97%	94%	1	1	2
Increased Scores on Provincial Testing Academic Achievement)	67%	50%	62%	11	11	11
Communication Skills	94%	95%	98%	2	2	1
Complex Thinking Skills	92%	91%	86%	5	4	4
Life-long Learning	91%	91%	80%	4	5	6
Love of Learning	85%	85%	74%	8	8	8
Wellness Lifestyle	90%	87%	85%	6	6	5
Positive Self Esteem	93%	95%	92%	3	3	3
Environmental View	90%	78%	71%	10	10	9
Global View	80%	81%	65%	9	9	10
Environmental Conscience	87%	86%	75%	7	7	7

Respondents assigned values of: Very Important = 5, Important = 3, or Not Important = 1. If everyone, for example, ranked a quality indicator as a 5, the percentage of agreement would have been 100 percent.

Figure 2. **Customer Rating Of Quality Indicators**

colleges and universities were not accustomed to providing detailed participation, scholarship, and other data, to individual school divisions. The specific tracking areas are as follows:

- Student Promotion and Retention Rates
- Student Arrivals and Departures
- Upgrading Statistics
- High School Graduation Patterns
- High School Course Enrollment
- Employment and Unemployment Patterns
- Staff Retention
- Special Education Statistics
- Pupil/Teacher Ratio
- Scholarships
- Post Secondary Enrollment
- Post Secondary Completion Rates
- Student Attendance

Quality Indicator	Definitions	Standard
Learner Empowerment	Empowered learners are independent and self directed and have the necessary concepts, skills, attitudes, tools and opportunities to learn.	Students in the Twin Rivers School Division will become empowered learners.
Communication Skills	Students who are skilled communicators have the ability to comprehend and evaluate others' ideas, feelings and attitudes by listening and viewing; and to identify and express their own ideas, feelings and attitudes through writing, speaking and actions.	Students in the Twin Rivers School Division will become skilled communicators.
Positive Self Esteem	Positive self esteem exists when a student has a favorable perception and evaluation of him/her self with respect to behavior, ability, body and worth as a person.	Students of the Twin Rivers School Division will have positive self esteem.
Complex Thinking Skills	Students who are skilled complex thinkers can take sensory information and filter it through knowledge and experience to create meaningful thinking and awareness.	Students of the Twin Rivers School Division will be critical and creative thinkers.
Lifelong Learning	A life-long learner approaches learning as an ongoing process from birth to death and is characterized as one who has a plan for personal and professional development, is a consumer of technology, models behavior, volunteers, continually pursues new learning experiences, participates in numerous leisure activities and is a leader of others.	Students of the Twin Rivers School Division will become lifelong learners.

Figure 3. **Indicators, Definitions and Standards.**

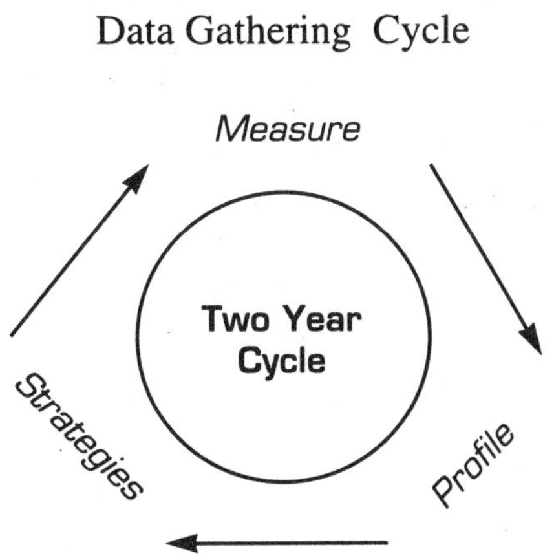

Figure 4.

The importance of sufficient and reliable data has become increasingly clear. With information available on each quality indicator in terms of standards, strategy alignment was to become the next task. What should we begin doing, and what do we stop doing? How should we prioritize our actions to achieve positive change? This phase of the strategic plan was to be the next phase.

The author's subsequent move to a dual role of contracting superintendency services to the Camrose RCSD District 60, and functioning as an associate at the Canadian Centre for Quality Improvement (CCQI) and Quality Improvement International (QII) is resulting in some modifications to the original quality improvement strategy.

Present directions include integrating the total quality management (TQM) processes of Deming, Juran and others, to strategic planning in education. An introductory course, based on the work to date, including a framework for long-term quality improvement, with a focus on customers, is being offered. In the process of such planning and development, we continue to learn. We are further ahead than we were, and each time the process is recycled, the strategies realigned, and the components tuned, we will move closer to achieving customer satisfaction and loyalty. Reversing the trend of decreasing Canadian confidence in the education system will not be easy. Redirection, however, is a must.

Future directions will not stop with the systems planning as illustrated in the Camrose RCSSD District 60 model in Figure 5 (page 248). We must find new ways to turn the learning organization into the learning community. Here, shared vision of "quality of life," with accompanying systems planning, will result in new linkages and positive outcomes for both youth and adults. Perhaps then Canadians, as both contributors to and benefactors of, this learning community, will return their confidence to the educational scene.

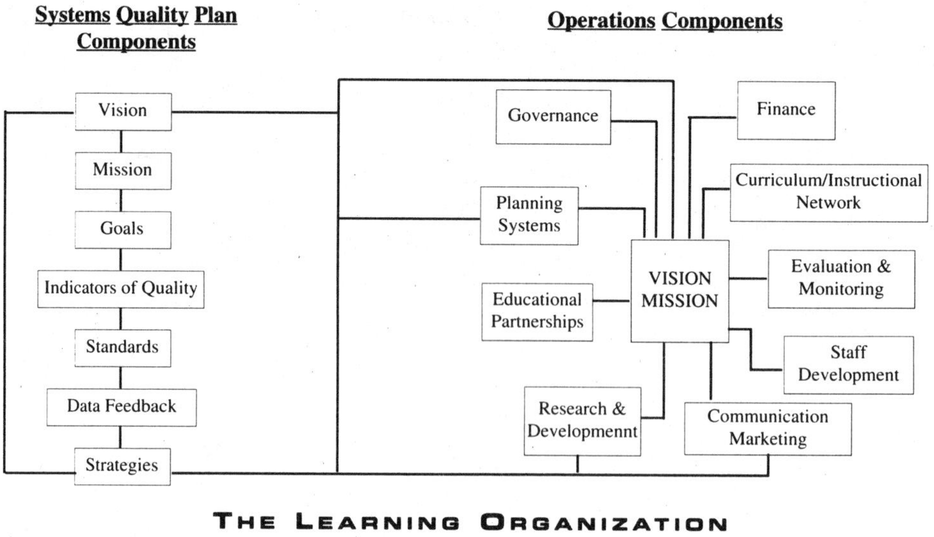

Figure 5. **Linking quality systems planning with operations.**

References

1. Fennel, Tom, "What's Wrong at School?" *Maclean's,* Vol. 106, No. 2, January 11, 1993, pages 28–32.

2. Fullan, Michael, "A Conference Presentation," Association for Supervision and Curriculum Development (ASCD), National Conference, San Diego, February, 1991.

Additional Sources

Anderson, Al and Zimmer, Jerry, 1991–1992 *Quality Indicator Profile Report,* Twin Rivers School Division No. 65, September, 1992.

Scanlan, David, "Education System Falling Apart, Canadians Believe," *The Edmonton Journal,* February 13, 1993, (Newspaper article based on an Angus Reid-Southham Poll).

A. L. (Al) Anderson, Ph.D., is contracting superintendent of schools for Camrose RCSSD District No. 60. He is also education associate with the Canadian Centre for Quality Improvement (CCQI) and Quality Improvement International (QI).

Can TQM in Public Education Survive Without Co-Production?

Robert T. Chappell

This article explores the importance of having students, parents, and teachers intimately involved in the process of education for TQM to realize its full potential. Chappell explains why this is true and how TQM can be implemented in a school setting.

Learning a Living: a Blueprint for High Performance, a SCANS Report for America 2000 is the U.S. Department of Labor's contribution to educational reform following a decade-long stream of criticism of public elementary and secondary education.[1] SCANS—The Secretary's Commission for Achieving Necessary Skills—is the first document produced by the U.S. government that specifically details how public education should be changed to prepare students for the 21st century workplace. The centerpiece of the *SCANS* report is "Workplace Know-How," a set of workplace competencies and foundation skills that all entry-level workers must possess in a high-performance workplace.

Graduates entering the work force, according to *SCANS*, will be expected to have competencies in managing resources, managing information with computers, monitoring their own performance, improving systems, and selecting and applying technology. They will also need to have interpersonal competencies, such as the ability to work on teams and serve customers. Graduates will still need basic arithmetic and communication skills, but *SCANS* will also expect workers to have reasoning and problem-solving skills and personal qualities necessary for responsible self-management.

Among *SCANS'* recommendations is that U.S. schools "must be transformed into high-performance organizations," a trait that characterizes our most competitive companies. *SCANS* challenges school administrators to apply W. Edwards Deming's 14 points.[2] Educators, students, and parents should use total quality management (TQM) to co-produce quality educational services. If students use TQM to improve the quality of their school work, they should enter the work force with the workplace know-how identified in

Reprinted with permission from *Quality Progress*, July 1994. Copyright © 1994 ASQC, Milwaukee, WI.

SCANS, which includes working on teams, serving customers, solving problems, monitoring and correcting performance, and improving systems.

Public Schools Use TQM

By 1993, more than 100 U.S. school districts had implemented some form of TQM.

An increasing number of American public school districts are looking to TQM to improve services to their customers—the students. By 1993, more than 100 U.S. school districts had implemented some form of TQM.[3] The American Association of School Administrators formed a quality network in June 1991. More than 400 public school districts have representatives in the network.

There is great variation in the content and length of TQM training for educators. Some districts provide as little as a checklist on how their schools should operationalize Deming's 14 points. Some offer a partial-day, in-service training. And others provide several days of intensive quality training on customer service, team problem solving, and quality improvement.[4]

There is also considerable variation in the way TQM is implemented in school settings. In a study by Julie Horine, William A. Hailey, and Laura Rubach, it was found that of school districts using TQM, 80% use quality tools to improve administrative services, 50% use the tools to improve teaching methods, and 50% use them to increase student achievement.[5] At least one district has mandated that all employees serve on problem-solving teams and quality improvement teams to improve instructional and support services.[6]

Evaluating TQM in Schools

TQM efforts in public education have not yet produced dramatic results. There have been no claims of massive increases in student achievement or decreases in student dropout rates. The Horine, Hailey, and Rubach study, however, cited positive results of TQM use by several school districts, such as reduced cycle time for special-education referrals, reduced student tardiness, reduced school safety problems, reduced need for remedial math instruction, improved student achievement, and reduced tax-collection cost.[7]

In 1990, a Virginia school district, Rappahannock County, began providing several days of TQM training for all teachers, bus drivers, secretaries, cafeteria workers, custodians, and administrators. This was made possible through a partnership grant with the Xerox Corporation and the Virginia Department of Education. Three years later, a study of the effects of TQM implementation in that district found that 89% of all school employees used aspects of the quality training in their work with students and parents; 72% thought administrators had increased efforts to meet employee needs; and 66% felt a greater sense of empowerment.[8] Nearly 80% of parents who responded to the survey said that school district employees had increased their efforts to meet the children's needs. Students also participated in a quality improvement team with bus drivers, parents, teachers, and administrators to reduce parents' dissatisfaction with district transportation services from 34% in 1991 to 11% in 1993.

A fair question to ask, however, is "How can we be certain that school districts that report implementing TQM are really using TQM?" Corporations might vary in their approaches to TQM, but those wishing to gain recognition for their quality efforts must submit to the stringent evaluation of the Malcolm Baldrige National Quality Award. Currently, there is no similar process to assess TQM efforts in public schools, but legislation that contains provisions for a Baldrige Award in education in currently under consideration by the U.S. Congress (Senate Bill 4, House Bill 820).[9] If the Baldrige Award criteria are applied to education, there will be an objective process to evaluate whether applicant school districts are fashioning customer-driven services and procedures. Until a standardized evaluation process is developed, there can be no assurance that schools are really using TQM.

Cost of Quality

From a cost-of-quality perspective, superintendents and principals cannot point to increases in corporate profits as evidence that quality makes a difference. A school district's market share, however, might be an indicator of whether TQM is making a difference. Market share in K-12 public education can be measured as a percentage of the total resident-student population being served by a school district. Parents who think their children's needs are not being served by public schools might send their children to private schools or provide home instruction. Students who don't like school might drop out or purposely get expelled.

When a district's average daily membership decreases, its share of state revenues shrinks. Take, for example, a school district with 25,000 school-age children (5 to 18 years old) (see Figure 1). If the district receives $3,000 in state aid for each student but 5,000 resident children are not enrolled in the district, the district loses out on $15 million (5,000 students multiplied by $3,000 each). The district's market share is 80% (20,000 of 25,000 students enrolled). If the district improves the quality of its educational services, its market share should, consequently, rise.

K-12 school district market share

A	Number of children ages 5-18 residing within a district	25,000
B	Number of children in district in private/parochial schools	1,250
C	Number of children in district receiving home instruction	375
D	Number of children in district who have dropped out	3,125
E	Number of children in district long-term suspensions/expelled	250
	Total not enrolled	5,000

Market-share formula $\frac{A - (\text{sum of B, C, D, E})}{A} \times 100 = \text{market share}$

$$\frac{25{,}000 - 5{,}000 \text{ (children not in school)}}{25{,}000} \times 100 = 80\% \text{ of district's market served by district}$$

Figure 1.

Customer Satisfaction Surveys

To detect and correct causes of dissatisfaction, some school districts distribute customer satisfaction surveys (Figure 2). Surveys can show how well parents and students like the services provided by the school and can generate baseline data to help measure changes in attitudes toward school services. Surveys typically do not measure, however, the effectiveness of instruction.

Teachers often take the view: "No matter how much I improve the way I teach students, if they don't want to learn, I can't make them." Some students, on the other hand, say, "Why should I try? I don't want to be in school anyway." This debate points to a major issue of the schools' next-in-line customers, the students. Who is responsible for educational quality or improvement? Are teachers the only accountable parties or should the students be held equally accountable? And what about the responsibility of parents, principals, superintendents, and school boards?

Please answer the following questions using the scale below. Any comments that you wish to add may be placed at the end of the form.

	5 Strongly agree	4 Agree	3 Neither	2 Disagree	1 Strongly disagree
1. The academic program provided by the Rappahannock County Public Schools will prepare my child/children for the world of work in the 21st century.	☐	☐	☐	☐	☐
2. The various educational programs of the Rappahannock County Public Schools meet the needs of my children.	☐	☐	☐	☐	☐
3. There is open communication between our children's teachers, administrators, and the family.	☐	☐	☐	☐	☐
4. The cleanliness of the school buildings and grounds is acceptable.	☐	☐	☐	☐	☐
5. Discipline in the Rappahannock County Public Schools is fair and consistent.	☐	☐	☐	☐	☐
6. The major emphasis of the Rappahannock County Public Schools is a strong academic education of its students.	☐	☐	☐	☐	☐
7. Parents and students are dealt with by school personnel in a friendly and respectful manner.	☐	☐	☐	☐	☐
8. The transportation services that are offered by the Rappahannock County School Board are excellent.	☐	☐	☐	☐	☐
9. Everything considered, I am satisfied with the Rappahannock County Public Schools.	☐	☐	☐	☐	☐
10. Extracurricular offerings (athletics, clubs, and field trips) are adequate.	☐	☐	☐	☐	☐

11. Comments and suggestions: ______________________________

____

____

Sample parent satisfaction survey used by the Rappahannock County Schools, Sperryville, VA. Reprinted with permission.

Figure 2.

The Concept of Co-Production

When TQM was gaining acceptance by U.S. corporations, academicians in public administration developed the concept of co-production.[11] The theory of co-production is based on the notion that the person providing the service and the next-in-line customer receiving the service share the responsibility for the quality and outcome of that service.

Gordon Whitaker describes co-production in three service settings:

> Education or health care or crisis intervention have as their primary objective the transformation of the consumer. Others may benefit from a child's education or a worker's good health or the pacification of a husband or wife in a heated argument, but the primary beneficiaries are the clients themselves. In delivering services, the agent helps the person being served to make the desired sorts of changes. Whether it is learning new ideas or skills, acquiring healthier habits, or changing one's outlook on family or society, only the individual served can accomplish the change. He or she is a vital co-producer of any vital transformation that occurs.[11]

The theory of co-production is based on the notion that the person providing the service and the next-in-line customer receiving the service share the responsibility for the quality and outcome of that service.

No one in the school system can guarantee that every child will be taught well. There is too much variation in teaching styles and teacher preparation programs. Nor can educators issue a warranty that all students who get solid instruction will learn well. Students don't enter the classroom with equal interest or readiness for learning. What public education can do is work to improve the system. One way to improve the educational system is for educators, students, and parents to work together.

Educators, students, and parents can and should learn to use the tools and strategies of TQM to co-produce quality educational services.

Co-production Model for TQM in Public Education

Educators, students, and parents can and should lcarn to usc the tools and strategies of TQM to co-produce quality educational services. The co-production model for TQM is based on the premise that educators, students, and parents should receive training in TQM to help them learn to work together, solve problems, serve customers, monitor and correct performance, and improve systems.

These are the steps to follow to implement the co-production model for TQM in a school district:

1. *Get leadership from the top.* If a co-production model for TQM is to be implemented in an entire school system, the change should be led by the superintendent or deputy superintendent with the support of the school board.
2. *Adopt a quality mission statement or policy.* For example: "School district employees will strive to continuously improve services to students, parents, and fellow employees. Each employee will participate in team problem solving and quality improvement efforts. Students will learn and use quality improvement tools and strategies to help them co-produce

their education. Parents will be invited to learn and use quality improvement strategies to help them co-produce their children's education.

3. *Select a TQM training program.* Corporations might be willing to underwrite part of the cost of TQM training. Consider training all school employees, starting with volunteers. Invite parents to participate in training. Determine the appropriate grade levels and training content for students.
4. *Organize a quality coordinating committee.* This committee can:
   - Coordinate internal (employees) and external (students, parents, community, employers, and colleges) customer surveys.
   - Form quality teams composed of school employees, students, and parents to address problems and improve educational service quality.
   - Advise and assist quality teams on how to use the TQM process.
5. *Institute a process for quality teams to measure, report on, display, and evaluate their results.*

Suggested TQM Training Topics

Areas of TQM training that might be considered are:

- What is quality?
- What is a customer? Are parents and students the school's customers? When do teachers and parents become the students' customers? What are some methods to provide good customer service? How are customer requirements negotiated?
- What is continuous improvement? What are the steps and tools used in a data-oriented, team-based problem solving and quality improvement process? How are statistical tools, such as cause-and-effect diagrams, control charts, and Pareto charts, used in quality improvement? How can students use these to improve behavior and academic performance?
- What is co-production? What are the roles and responsibilities of educators, students, and parents in improving educational services and the educational system? How can brainstorming, negotiation, and consensus be used to facilitate this partnership?
- What are the *SCANS* workplace competencies and foundation skills? How will TQM help students develop competence to work on teams, serve customers, solve problems, monitor and correct performance, and improve systems?

Shared Responsibility for Results

The emphasis in the TQM co-production model is based on shared responsibility for the quality of teaching and learning. The educational system must take the lead in designing and delivering quality and continuously improving instructional services that consider the needs of its customers. Parents have a responsibility to facilitate their children's learning through the provision of a calm, supportive environment. Parents should also demonstrate their commitment to improvement by supporting cost-effective school budget requests, serving on school quality improvement teams, and volunteering to help in the schools. Students are responsible for working hard, behaving appropriately, and continuously improving their work.

As students learn their roles in the co-production model, they should become TQM literate. TQM training for public school students might provide the workplace know-how that *SCANS* expects of entry-level workers. If educators, parents, and students learn to work together to co-produce quality educational services, public schools and the U.S. work force might both reach the high performance level envisioned by *SCANS*.

As students learn their roles in the co-production model, they should become TQM literate.

Notes

1. *Learning a Living: A Blueprint for High Performance, A SCANS Report for America 2000,* U.S. Department of Labor, 1992.
2. W. Edwards Deming, *Out of the Crisis* (Cambridge, MA: Massachusetts Institute of Technology, 1986).
3. Julie Horine, William A. Hailey, and Laura Rubach, "Transforming Schools," *Quality Progress,* October 1993, p. 23.
4. Robert T. Chappell, *The Effects of the Implementation of Total Quality Management on the Rappahannock County, Virginia Schools,* doctoral dissertation registered with Dissertation Abstracts International, Virginia Tech University, November 1993.
5. Horine, Hailey, and Rubach, "Transforming Schools."
6. Chappell, *The Effects of the Implementation of Total Quality Management on the Rappahannock County, Virginia Schools.*
7. Horine, Hailey, and Rubach, "Transforming Schools."
8. Chappell, *The Effects of the Implementation of Total Quality Management on the Rappahannock County, Virginia Schools.*
9. David M. Gangel, "Expansion of the Baldrige Award Eligibility to Education," *QED News,* October 1993.
10. Gordon Whitaker, "Co-Production: Citizen Participation in Service Delivery," *Public Administration Review.* May-June 1980. pp. 240–242.
11. Ibid.

Robert T. Chappell is the assistant superintendent and a quality coordinator at Rappanhannock County Public Schools in Sperryville, VA.

PART THREE

Implementing Quality

Part Three presents a collection of articles and excerpts from books, almost all published in 1994, that deal with the strategic and tactical issues surrounding the implementation of Total Quality Management. Reflecting what organizations have learned over the past several years, we have organized this material into four logical groupings: *Quality Transformation, Quality Tools and Techniques, Functional Processes*, and *Standards and Assessments*. Within each of these groups, you will find practical advice and techniques relevant to all types of organizations.

Quality Transformation

Quality management is *not* just a set of techniques to add to your management repertoire (as we discussed in the article that opens this book). It requires a long-term commitment at the top and a disciplined, informed transformation of company culture. Managers *must* focus on supporting and developing the people who carry out the interrelated processes that characterize organizational work. This section includes an array of articles on *leadership, cultural change, customer focus, training*, and *teams and teamwork*. Our selection is designed to give you a clear sense of the attitudes and approaches necessary to successfully manage for quality while understanding the problems and opportunities this approach poses to businesses. It is not easy to build a culture based on the values of quality management. Implementing Deming's 14 Points is a challenge for everyone in a business, and it is easy to fall back on more traditional command and control methods. But facing that challenge is worth it, as the articles in this section demonstrate.

Quality Tools and Techniques

In the 1995 edition of *The Quality Yearbook*, we have emphasized the idea of *process management*. To that end you will find a variety of articles on what process management is all about. Under the category of process management we have selected two practical pieces. One discusses a technique for aligning organizational processes with strategic objectives. The other is a brief excerpt from Brian Joiner's book, *Fourth Generation Management*, that explains the importance of understanding and properly responding to process variation—throughout the organization. We also include some useful articles discussing the importance of measurement in managing processes.

This section also includes a thoughtful review of what reengineering is and its history, as well as a critique of this technique, which suggests that the revolutionary rhetoric of reengineering is inappropriate and self-defeating.

Functional Processes

Important work is underway is many industries at the functional level (e.g., accounting, sales and marketing, and human resources), making it possible to begin documenting their successes and procedures. We have noted this and chosen to highlight six areas: *suppliers and purchasing, information technology, sales and marketing, accounting, legal,* and *human resources.* Our guideline here was thoughtful practicality, and these articles describe how quality principles can help shape and improve practices in all these areas. We especially commend Jim Cortada's article on using the Baldrige criteria to evaluate and improve sales processes.

Standards and Assessments

We conclude Part Three with a collection of articles that provide further explanation of ISO 9000 certification issues and discuss the Baldrige approach in assessing the state of quality in organizations.

* * *

We again want to refer you to the detailed bibliography in Part Four. You will find an extensive listing of current articles and books covering all the topics taken up in Part Three.

Principle-Centered Leadership and Change

Stephen R. Covey and Keith A. Gulledge

In this thought-provoking article, the authors provide real insight into how to lead change. They point out that this involves both change in external organizational structures, but equally important are the internal changes in personal behavior and attitudes to sustain change and improvement. Leaders understand this, and it makes all the difference in the success of an organization and the people who are a part of it.

The CEO of a Baldrige Award winning firm was asked over lunch, "What was the most difficult thing for you about winning the Baldrige?" He thought just a moment and then readily replied, "It was changing myself. I had to change my leadership style to release people. I realized I couldn't control them; I had to let them go."

The Need for Change

One common denominator characterizes virtually all organizations: the need for change. In many cases, dramatic, fundamental change is required, even for very successful companies and institutions. Unfortunately, many leaders have not yet internalized the lesson shared by this enlightened chief executive. The change required must start with leaders changing themselves before they can effectively influence change within the organization.

Survival induced change. . . Frequently change, like quality itself, is unavoidably thrust upon organizations due to major market dynamics, including

Reprinted with permission from the *Journal for Quality and Participation,* March 1994. Copyright © 1994 by the Association for Quality and Participation.

the suddenly realized requirement to reduce costs or die. In other cases, forward thinking leaders envision essential changes before others inside the organization, or even the industry, are fully aware:

- In early 1992, the chairman and CEO of a multi-billion dollar, profitable telecommunications company shared his vision of the year 2000 with a gathering of senior officers and employees of the firm. Instead of describing the glowing future the group had expected, the CEO began his talk with this disturbing theme: "Ladies and gentlemen, I am deeply concerned about our company's viability in the year 2000. We must make substantial changes in the way we are doing business if we are to survive."

- Referring to a recent 1993 cover of *Fortune,* depicting General Motors, IBM, and Sears as dinosaurs, the head of a major manufacturing division of one of the nation's most admired corporations told a group of their senior leaders, "If we don't change our culture and the way we are doing business, we are going to wind up on the cover of *Fortune* as a dinosaur!"

- As the head of a major, century-old life insurance company put it in their 1993 annual officers meeting, "The old ways of doing business don't work any more."

Corporate America is not alone . . . New ways of doing business are being thrust upon virtually every segment of our society: healthcare institutions, public and private school systems, the military establishment, and government at all levels.

Quality-focus induced change . . . It is axiomatic that quality, innovation, and continuous improvement require organizations to change. Powerful external and internal environmental factors may dictate the pace, but the effectiveness of organizational change for quality reflects the quality of organizational change.

Change We Must, but How?

Once the need for change is recognized, regardless of its source, the questions of how and how well begin:

- What roles must leaders play to assure that the changes involved will be the right ones to obtain the right results in the right way at the right time—successfully and sustainably?
- Why it is usually so difficult to accomplish . . .
- How such change can be effectively created and maintained.

To find some answers to these often asked questions, we will look at:

- The fundamental nature of organizations
- Two basic types of change within organizations
- A cycle for creating effective change
- Why organizations resist change
- *Principle-centered leadership,* including the *Seven Habits* as a foundation for quality change.

The Nature of Organizations

In our July/August 1992 *Journal for Quality and Participation* article entitled "Principle-centered leadership: mission, vision and quality within organizations," we discussed the *principle-centered leadership paradigm* as a fundamental way of understanding organizations (Figure 1).

Every organization—and every sub-unit of larger organizations—functions according to natural laws or principles, regardless of the leaders' awareness of them. Understanding these governing principles and their interaction with all components of the organization is essential to maximize effective quality change.

Every organization functions according to natural laws or principles, regardless of the leaders' awareness of them.

Change takes place throughout four levels or dimensions within any organization. The degree of concurrence and integration *throughout all four dimensions* will govern the degree of sustainable long-term quality change effectiveness.

Change at the organizational level . . . Organizational level change relates to fundamental mission, vision, or values of the organization; shifts in strategic choices, goals, or action plans; reorganization of basic structures and systems; and the degree of alignment between all organizational elements.

Change at the managerial level . . . Managerial level change reflects new task definitions or changes in:

- How we do our present job . . .
- Skill sets and management styles . . .
- How people relate to each other in doing their jobs . . .
- The nature and degree of empowerment throughout the management and labor work force.

Every organization (and every sub-unit of larger organizations) functions according to natural laws or principles, regardless of the leaders' awareness of them. Understanding these governing principles and their interaction with all components of the organization is essential to maximize effective quality change.

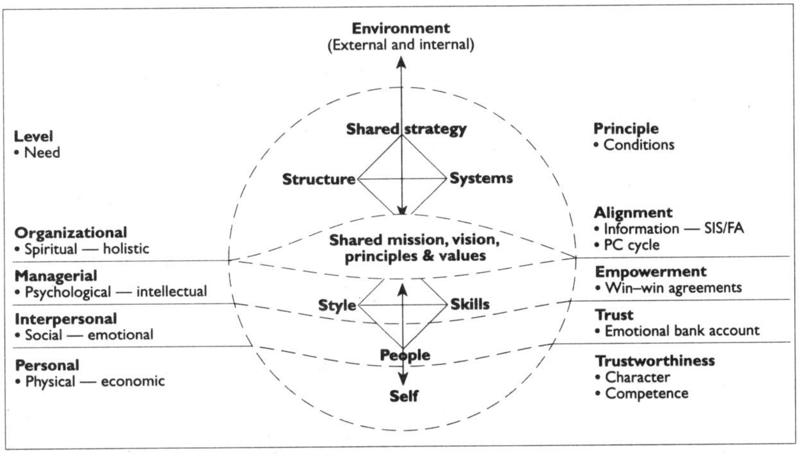

Figure 1. **The principle-centered leadership paradigm.**

Change at the interpersonal level . . . Interpersonal level change means altering the way people relate to each other as human beings, how they communicate, their behavior patterns, including the degree of trust throughout the organization.

Change at the personal level . . . Personal level change indicates the degree of individual commitment to new or different thought processes, behavior patterns, and values that ultimately govern how the entire organization operates; the degree of personal trustworthiness reflected in both the character and competence with which people view each other within the organization.

Effective leaders recognize two primary types of change: from the outside-in (structural) and from the inside-out (cultural/behavioral).

Quality change requires integrated change throughout all four of these dimensions. Let's look at what leaders typically regard as organizational change and why it is frequently necessary, but always insufficient, for long-term quality effectiveness.

Change from the Inside-Out

Structural versus Cultural Change

Effective leaders recognize two primary types of change: from the outside-in (structural) and from the inside-out (cultural/behavioral). The first is more readily accomplished than the second, yet the key to sustaining the first is the second.

Structure and R-word management . . . Often, when a new leader is appointed in any organizational unit with a challenge to fix things or to get this organization back on track, he or she typically implements one or more of the following *R-words* to accomplish the task:

- Reorganize . . .
- Restructure . . .
- Reinvent, or in current jargon . . .
- Re-engineer.

These structural changes might be as radical as re-engineering (rethinking the processes, systems, and organizational components of the entire organization from the ground up) or dramatic changes in strategy or personnel as General Motors and IBM have undertaken recently. Some examples of such changes in structures, systems, or strategy are:

- Flattening the organization . . .
- Downsizing (or rightsizing) . . .
- Shedding or acquiring divisions . . .
- Taking new strategic directions . . .
- Embarking on bold new initiatives in product development or marketing . . .
- Creating new compensation or performance management systems, or making significant personnel shifts.

Structural change, while the most visible and tangible type of change, and often the manager's first target when trying to accomplish their most significant objectives (including their quality programs) is frequently necessary but always insufficient alone.

Organizational change is cultural change . . . Organizations are more than structures, they are held together and accomplish goals through people working together with a common purpose and sharing certain resources.

There is really no such thing as organizational behavior, only the collective result of individual behavior. Therefore, there is no such thing as *organizational* change without *personal* change. *Organizational* change means collective individual change.

There is no such thing as *organizational* change without *personal* change.

It is *cultural change*—the change of collective behavior of the individuals personally and interpersonally within the organization—which will ultimately sustain and make effective the structural change at the organization and managerial levels.

This type of change means changing not only the behaviors, but also the paradigms, attitudes, management and leadership styles, and the personal and professional relationships between people throughout the enterprise.

Inside-out personal change . . . Structural change is *outside-in:* personal change must be *inside-out*. Long-term, sustainable organizational change (structural and cultural) requires inside-out personal change. And it is changing people from within that is the challenge which makes organizational change so difficult and painful (as the Baldrige winning CEO noted at the beginning of this article). Another corporate executive told us that he once worked for a boss who believed that it is easier to change *people* than it is to *change* people.

Once leaders realize they cannot change other people—they can only change themselves—they then establish the beginnings of significant cultural change within their organization.

The Leader's Change Objective: Interdependence

Total quality through both systemic, structural change and personal, individual change, requires the transformation of independent me-*thinking* to interdependent *we-thinking*. The task of developing interdependence systemically and interpersonally is compounded by the realization that many organizations function at the level both systemically and personally of *dependence* (Figure 2, page 264).

As the *Seven Habits Maturity Continuum* illustrates, neither people nor organizations can become effectively interdependent until they have developed sufficient capability to first become independent. Breaking down barriers between departments, tearing down functional silos, and cooperating instead of competing internally all necessitate building new and stronger synergistic relationships among key organizational stakeholders. The *Seven Habits*, lived in all dimensions, form the powerful basis for such relationships.

The Cycle of Effective Change

How can leaders bring about not just change or transition, but the genuine cultural transformation to support synergy for developing and implementing successfully new strategies, systems and processes? Let's examine the change

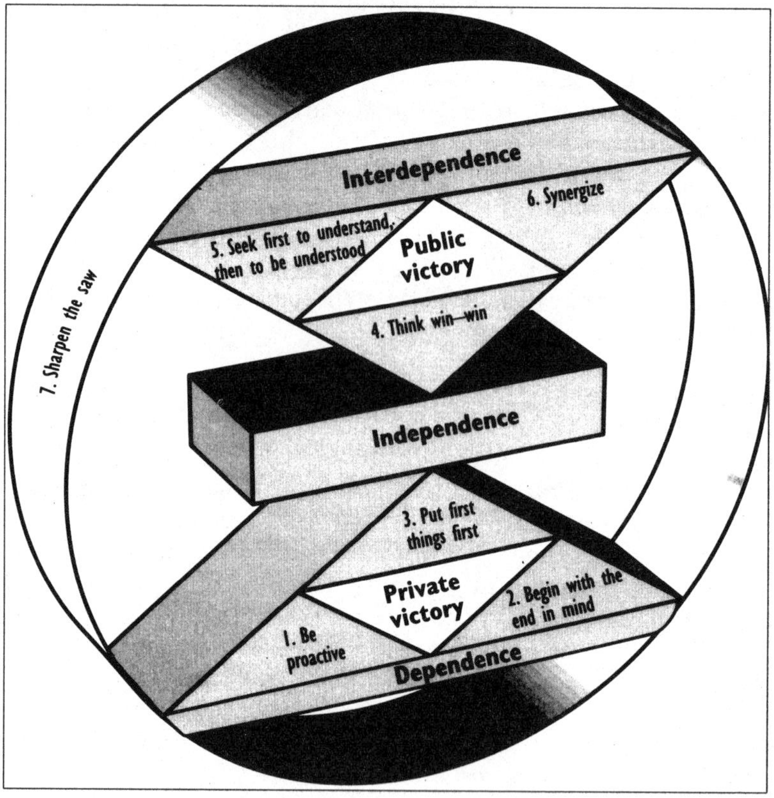

Figure 2. **The Seven Habits Maturity Continuum.**

cycle figure to better understand principles of effective, transforming change (Figure 3).

Which Principles for the Transformation process?

The first issue is, "What *principles* will guide our change decisions?" Managers think they are in control; ultimately, they are not. Principles will govern the change. Will these principles include:

- Communication?
- Involvement?
- Interdependence?
- Alignment?
- Empowerment?
- Trustworthiness and trust?

Or will the change be based upon:

- Top-down control directives?
- Urgency and crisis? Isolation and independence?

When the significant paradigms of leaders, managers, and workers shift — their fundamental thought processes, assumptions, and mental maps really change — we have the beginnings of meaningful, powerful cultural transformation within organizations. People will behave differently when they see differently. When leaders see their organization and its environment differently, they will make the changes in systems and processes that will in turn support the different behaviors and cultural habits that will produce different results.

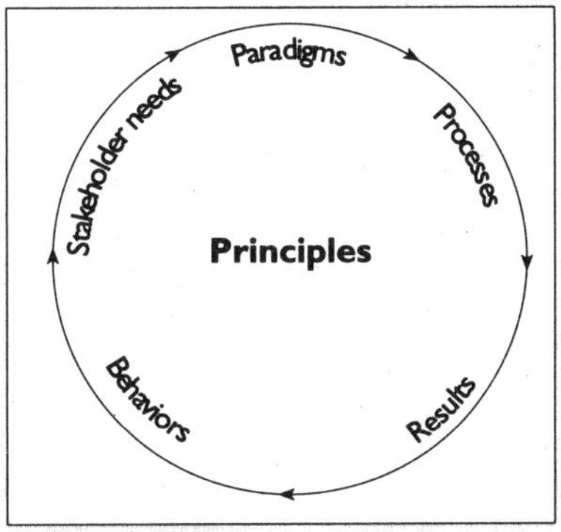

Figure 3. **The change cycle.**

When the organization feels pain, management should ask, "What principles are being violated?"

Results versus Needs

The results produced by an organization mean little in isolation; they must be compared to stakeholder needs to measure effectively the nature and extent of necessary quality improvement.

Management by objective concentrates on desired results, on establishing goals and measurements of effectiveness and efficiency in achieving them. Performance improvement, however, is realized more directly through focusing on changing the human behaviors necessary to achieve the objectives, including communications, exhortations, and skill training.

Systems and Processes

More substantial change is created if management alters the organizational systems and processes (the structure) which influence employee behavior. Understanding that the vast majority of problems are systems related (*common cause* rather than the result of individual worker negligence or mistake (*special cause*) is core to the quality movement's focus on continuously improving, or radically re-engineering systems and processes.

For instance, most organizations realize that changing the compensation system from salary to commission, or from piece rate to profit sharing, will significantly influence the behavior of people within the system.

Paradigm Shift

Neither the focus on results (MBO) through individual behavior change, or concentration on systems and process improvement is wrong. Both are essential—but alone are invariably incomplete. Change of structure and systems may drive temporary behavior, but unless paradigms are shifted, ultimate, effective, enduring systems and behavior change will struggle to take place.

Substantial, sustainable change originates at this earlier stage. When the significant paradigms of leaders, managers, and workers shift—their fundamental thought processes, assumptions, and mental maps really change—we have the beginnings of meaningful, powerful cultural transformation within organizations. People will behave differently when they see differently. When leaders see their organization and its environment differently, they will make the changes in systems and processes that will in turn support the different behaviors and cultural habits that will produce different results.

Unless paradigms are shifted, ultimate, effective, enduring systems and behavior change will struggle to take place.

For instance, management's current and fundamental paradigm of customer service quality wasn't shifted by quality consultant's advice, it shifted when competitive pressures forced them to reevaluate the basic principles upon which they had established and run their businesses for decades. Improved systems, more effective behaviors, and higher quality results is a function of that paradigm shift.

Paradigm shift in healthcare. . . Paradigms change for varied reasons, frequently because of crises and intense attack on the status quo. Healthcare practitioners and institutions today, for instance, are being severely challenged by coming changes in health care reform. The fundamental rethinking, reevaluation of the nature of healthcare services and economics—from allocation of healthcare based on economics to universal coverage—will result in substantial changes in systems, processes, behaviors and results. Absent this fundamental paradigm shift towards universal coverage, many necessary and beneficial reforms in the healthcare system would probably not occur.

To pursue this example further, imagine what changes in institutional systems, individual behaviors, and overall results would occur if a paradigm shift were to take place among our national leaders that the healthcare focus should change from cure to prevention.

With the principle of paradigm shifts underlying sustainable organizational change, let's examine what gets in the way of making the shift and why people resist other forms of change in systems and structure.

Why Organizations Resist Change

Typical American management style targets quality goals or objectives, develops a strategic or operational game plan, and turns loose the driving forces of money, training, technology, reorganization, public relations, and so forth, to achieve them. Frequently leaders fail to address adequately the restraining forces—what holds back people within the organization from accepting, much less enthusiastically embracing, the intended quality changes (Figure 4).

Leaders accelerate their organization towards quality by stepping on the gas—but fail to take their other foot off the brake.

Leaders accelerate their organization towards quality by stepping on the gas—but fail to take their other foot off the brake.

Organizations Don't Resist Change: The People within Them Do

People don't resist change so much as they resist being changed and the uncertain, unknown consequences of change. The larger or more significant the

People don't resist change so much as they resist being changed and the uncertain, unknown consequences of change. The larger or more significant the perceived change — more substantial the departure from the status quo — the more the resistance seems to mount.

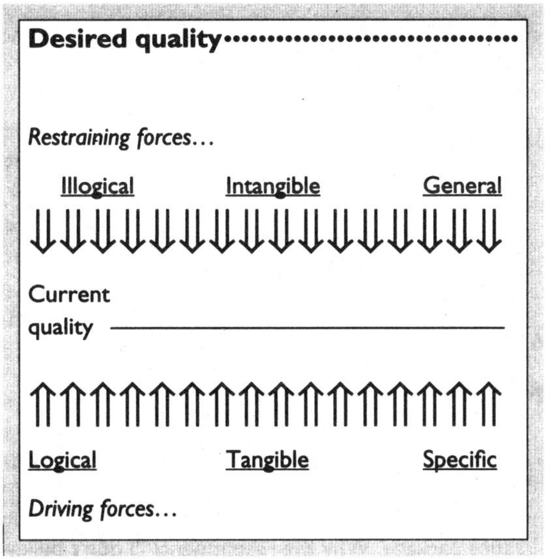

Figure 4. **A force field illustration of resistance to change.**

perceived change—more substantial the departure from the status quo—the more the resistance seems to mount.

Lack of trust . . . In our experience the most pervasive restraining force, the most formidable obstacle, to effective, sustainable quality change within organizations is lack of trust. A survey we conducted in 1991 of 3,500 people from all sectors of the American economy bears out our direct consulting experience.

Workers do not trust management, middle management does not trust upper management, upper management does not trust the work force or sometimes each other, and few people trust *the system*. And what replaces lack of trust? Not just distrust but fear, including fear of change (Figure 5, page 268).

People don't trust what consequences (intended or unintended) the change will bring; they don't trust the motives behind the change; and they don't trust that the change is either the right thing to do or will be done right.

At its best, change threatens the comfort zone in which people have found security: at worst it is perceived as harmful as jobs are eliminated and worker economic well-being is destroyed—and the negative effects plague organizations for years afterward.

This breakdown of trust, replaced by fear, is like organizational AIDS which attacks and frequently destroys the organizational immune system. Mistakes, problems, and difficulties which might otherwise be handled in stride are allowed to become major problems, validating in the minds of employees and other stakeholders the extent of the fear and untrustworthiness and thus contributing to it. And the cycle of disintegration spirals downward, with organizational integrity its victim.

Workers do not trust management, middle management does not trust upper management, upper management does not trust the work force or sometimes each other, and few people trust "the system." And what replaces the lack of trust? Not just distrust — but fear, including fear of change.

Figure 5. **What's holding back quality?**

Barriers to Change

Against this backdrop of distrust and fear, leaders encounter related barriers and inertial restraining forces such as the following as they initiate structural and cultural quality change in their organizations:

Insufficient, untimely two-way communication . . . Management typically first fails to seek sufficient understanding of the problems, barriers and restraining forces opposing the change, and therefore does not adequately address them. Then management fails to explain adequately in open dialogue with employees and other stakeholders the issues and solutions as they assess them.

Too often difficult decisions such as reducing the work force are formally announced after rumors are already spreading, and people feel trust has been violated because leaders have not candidly discussed the situation in a timely fashion, giving people adequate time to understand and adjust.

Inadequate understanding . . . Without effective communication, people fail to reach shared understanding. Unless trust in the leadership is extraordinarily high, there will be little acceptance of the proposed change, much less genuine commitment towards it. Employees neither understand the full nature of the change nor the reasons for it—the *what* and the *why* behind it. What people do not understand, they frequently distrust, fear . . . and resist.

People affected by change who are not involved in the analysis or decision making process concerning the change feel violated when asked to accept or implement the change, even if it is beneficial. They resist not so much the

A worker in the middle of a highly complex technical process was informed by her boss that upper management was changing the procedures for systems interface with another department.

Ultimately, the new approach proved beneficial for all. Enormous amounts of management time were spent in the initial implementation phase, however, addressing concerns and overcoming resistance to the change.

The worker's comment was common to her colleagues: "Why didn't they talk to us about our ideas? Don't they think we care and understand how to do our jobs?"

Figure 6. **A lack of involvement scenario.**

A telecommunications employee told of his resentment towards senior management when a small reduction in force for commonly supported and justifiable reasons was announced well in advance, including a generous severance package. Why the resentment? "I don't believe their story. I wouldn't bet management will follow through on the severance package commitment. I don't trust them." Why not? "You wouldn't believe the lousy way they treated workers in a similar situation the last time." When was the last time? "Six years ago."

Figure 7. **Memory of past trust violations.**

change itself, but are offended at the perceived lack of respect for their input regarding the process (Figure 6).

No shared ownership or commitment . . . Inadequate communication, insufficient understanding and involvement, result in no deeply shared ownership commitment to the change. A *they are doing it to us* attitude develops rather than *this is our commitment to quality* change requirements.

Memory of past trust violations . . . Current employees remember with bitterness two, five or ten years or more afterwards trust violations, such as a reduction in force or change in benefits, in which management was perceived to act precipitously, unfairly, or at worst, deceitfully, in misrepresenting situations or in violating promises and established expectations. The destroyed trust lingers for years afterwards, undermining support for future difficult management decisions (Figure 7).

The primary source of employee security is directly threatened by structural change.

Ever-changing structures threatened security . . . People need security, and change threatens the source of that security. How so? In what elements of an organization do people find security? In the structures and systems, traditionally rigid and resistant to change. So where do leaders usually focus their change management efforts? On structures and systems and applying the *R-words:* reorganize, re-engineer, restructure, reinvent. The primary source of employee security is directly threatened by structural change.

Structure and systems should support the organization's strategic action plans, not vice versa. Since strategy must be flexible in order to adjust to changing environmental circumstances, organizational structure and systems must also be flexible and adjustable. And yet most employees find their source of security in the structures and systems of the organization. When change occurs, particularly radical change such as re-engineering, the very source of employee security is threatened.

When people do not understand the complex external environment; have no shared mission; are confused as to strategy; and management begins reorganizing structures and systems, what do people say about upper management? "They don't know what they're doing!" "What is going on with those people?" Trust in management declines further.

When the quality paradigm is perceived as a cost reduction strategy . . . For many organizations, employees equate quality change, including re-engineering, as a euphemistic threat meaning cost reduction and downsizing. "I'm supposed to help re-engineer myself out of a job." People resist being manipulated and used when they perceive that they are expected to contribute to their own, or their co-workers', employment demise.

Inertia outweighs driving forces . . . People will support change if their pain is so acute that they see almost anything to be better than the present condition. People will not support change when the resisting inertia of the known status quo is more powerful than the forces driving the uncertain change. But people generally need to believe that the benefits of the change outweigh its pain and cost; that there are identifiable first steps that are reasonably doable; and that management is sufficiently trustworthy to lead the change effort successfully.

Management defends their own creation . . . Sometimes upper management resists change because they defend the systems they created that put them into their current position.

A middle-level manager serving as a member of a task force examining major alterations of the corporate performance management system (including grade classifications, compensation, and the performance review process) asked a senior executive his view of their recommendations. After a brief discussion, the senior executive commented, "You know, I don't really understand why you people are working to make these changes. The system's always been good to me!"

No paradigm shift . . . When people do not understand the change, are not involved in the decision making process, do not see benefits of the change, feel threatened by the unknown consequences of change, or do not trust senior management in making the change, there is no paradigm shift by employees to embrace the change. When fundamental paradigms do not shift, structural change may occur but cultural (behavioral) change may be superficial and short-lived.

Principle-Centered Leadership: Foundation to Quality Change

Structural change may be forced upon employees through management's reorganization decisions. But for cultural change to take place, an inside-out process must occur: each individual must internalize new paradigms, principles and behavioral habits. Each person must take personal ownership for committing to the new order.

Principle-centered leadership focuses on living the *Seven Habits of Highly Effective People* in all four dimensions of an organization.

Principle-centered leadership is activated in an organization:

- By individuals personally and interpersonally in interacting with themselves and each other . . .
- By people doing their jobs at the managerial level . . .
- By the organization through its collective behavior and through its strategy, structure and systems.

The result of living all *Seven Habits* in all four dimensions is a culture of trustworthiness and trust throughout the organization.

Let's look more at how living the *Seven Habits* breaks down barriers to change and provides the foundational principles and processes by which trust can be developed in all dimensions of any organization.

Habit 1: Pro-active, Responsible Acceptance

Pro-active leaders and employees accept responsibility for their own behavior without blaming and accusing others; act according to values and principles they identify and commit to live by; and focus on their circle of influence, wherein they can make a difference, as opposed to spending time in their circle of concern, where they have little ability to contribute.

When they are involved in change, pro-active leaders and followers (we all play both roles) assess true principles and their own values and act accordingly—accepting their own responsibilities, and working within their circle of influence to fulfill them. They don't pass the buck and point fingers; they are doers, not complainers. Rather than resist change, they involve themselves in assessment, creation, and effective implementation to the maximum degree possible.

Security lies in the clearly identifiable mission, vision and principles that are constantly reflected in the behavior of leaders and managers.

Habit 2: Security through Shared Mission, Vision, Principles, and Values

Where should people find their security within organizations? Not in changeable and temporary structures and systems.

Security lies in the clearly identifiable mission, vision and principles that are constantly reflected in the behavior of leaders and managers. Employees place trust in the constancy of that mission and in the unchanging principles embodied throughout the organization. When people feel secure in the mission and principles of the organization, they feel less threatened and thus offer less resistance to change in structure and systems.

The leader as facilitator . . . Leaders are responsible to facilitate the development of deeply shared mission and vision within the organization, including each sub-unit. The habit of beginning with the end in mind applies personally as well as organizationally. When people within the organization recognize a common overlap between their personal values and mission and those of the organization they serve, the ground is prepared for growth and development of the people who control all the other resources of the organization.

Habit 3: Prioritized Joint Commitments

It is not only important for people to understand the mission, vision, principle, and values of the organization, but also to understand and share through involvement and commitment its strategic action plans. The difference is the understanding that strategy will change with the changing environment and internal resources, while core mission and principles will be more constant and stable.

Effective strategy is commitment to putting first things first . . . First things first items definitely include the following:

- Planning and prioritizing the allocation of resource . . .
- Understanding and prioritizing stakeholder needs
- Focusing time and energy now on important though not yet urgent requirements of creating opportunities . . .
- Developing relationships . . .
- Innovative thinking.

When people are clear as to their roles, strategic roles and their action plan to achieve them, they appreciate that change is essential to long-term success. They are better able to accept change as normal rather than resist the movement from their current comfort zone.

Habit 4: The Paradigm of Mutual Benefit

Trust is built when people see by constant practice that leaders seek mutual benefit for employees and other key stakeholders in all their quality change decisions and initiatives. True win-win thinking requires seeking to understand needs and wants of stakeholders and synergistic creation of third alternatives that cooperatively balance competing needs and scarce resources.

When the paradigm of internal cooperation and common benefit permeates a culture, change initiatives and quality improvement requirements receive early support, not suspicion. Through this paradigm a framework is created for open dialogue on the genuine merits of change and the most effective options for implementation, rather than on defusing private agendas and overcoming the fear and distrust around a *what are they going to do to me now?* attitude.

Habit 5: Stakeholder Information System Feedback

Central to effective change based on win-win thinking is the constant openness of two-way communication between all participants in the organization through a stakeholder[1] information system *(SIS)*: This two-way communication process includes:

- Management with employees . . .
- Upper management with middle management . . .
- Departments and divisions with each other . . .
- Headquarters with the field . . .
- The main organization with external stakeholders, and they with each other.

Understanding comes before being understood . . . The key to being understood (and essential to building trust and acceptance) is first to understand. When leaders demonstrate consistent commitment to: 1) understanding their stakeholders' needs, desires and ideas before making decisions, and 2) effectively facilitating stakeholder understanding and commitment to those decisions, a paradigm of genuine dialogue and synergy is developed. With such understanding, change is more readily accepted and implemented.

The more timely, accurate, and relevant the information feedback leaders receive from all key stakeholders, the better prepared they are to initiate and implement change in structures and in cultural norms that represent the realities of the environment and the constraints of organizational resources.

Such 360° feedback through *SIS*, and then widespread distribution, analysis, and discussion concerning the feedback results, can provide management and decision makers invaluable capability to foresee trends, to better meet stakeholder needs, to make organizational strategic adjustments, and then to modify systems and structures as necessary both to address problems and to create and take advantage of critical opportunities.

Habit 6: Constant Synergistic Dialogue

Synergy is the fruit of win-win thinking and empathic communication. Through constant synergistic dialogue, the creative capabilities of the organization are unleashed through the involvement of all appropriate parties to:

- Access and evaluate organizational strengths, weaknesses, opportunities, and threats pertaining to meeting stakeholder needs . . .
- Develop and implement solutions addressing any and all of them.

Calling upon data developed through *SIS*, the organization empowers itself through synergy to energize its collective intelligence, experience, and wisdom to make the right moves, in the right way, at the right time. When

---

1. Internal organization stakeholders include all categories of employees, such as upper and middle managers, union members, non-union workers, members of various departments, and in many cases owners. External stakeholders include customers or clients, owners, suppliers, distributors, community organizations, government regulators, and the public generally.

When people within organizations commit to the principle that the status quo means continued innovation and progress, they reduce resistance to change.

people are shown respect and honor through meaningful involvement in analysis, decision making, and implementation, the change resistance is transformed to support for change.

Habit 7: Continuous Personal and Organizational Improvement

Continuous improvement means continuous change. When people within organizations commit to the principle that the status quo means continued innovation and progress, they reduce resistance to change and look forward to making the next series of structural and process improvements even more significantly effective.

As with any complex ecosystem, organizational effectiveness and quality comes through balance . . . Change for the sake of change alone, and change so frequent that it becomes disruptive, uneconomical, and inefficient as well as ineffective, does not constitute quality. Leaders must never be afraid to institute change; but they must also never be afraid to conclude that staying the present course is, indeed, the best course.

Summing Up

Effective leaders focus on the need for cultural change, inside-out, as a core to sustaining structural (or outside-in) change. They address the restraining forces holding back change, not only the driving forces to initiate it.

Through the processes of living and applying the *Seven Habits* in four levels *(personally, interpersonally, on the job managerially, and throughout the organizational strategy, systems, and structures)* leaders create a viable and effective environment of trustworthiness and trust wherein change can be positive and positively received.

Stephen R. Covey is founder and chairman of the Covey Leadership Center and is the author of The Seven Habits of Highly Effective People *and* Principle-Centered Leadership *(Simon and Schuster). Keith A. Gulledge is the managing editor of the client services division of the Covey Leadership Center.*

Ten Mistakes CEOs Make about Quality

Willard I. Zangwill

This article covers many standard ideas about TQM in a systematic format. It reminds managers once again that they must focus on improving the system to better serve customers. The article talks about how CEOs often mistake their role and their responsibility to lead.

The winners of the Malcolm Baldrige National Quality Award and other firms noted for excellent quality programs think differently about quality than most firms. A professor of management science and students at the University of Chicago interviewed executives at a number of firms that have excellent quality programs. These interviews revealed 10 mistakes that many corporate executive officers (CEOs) make that might prevent their companies from developing excellent quality programs.

Mistake 1: Failing to Lead

When CEOs strive to be leaders and to inspire their employees to excel, many adopt an approach that almost always fails. They recall movie scenes in which great leaders give powerful and highly motivating speeches, such as Knute Rockne inspiring his football team or Gen. George Patton spurring his troops to success. Leadership to these CEOs becomes management by exhortation and inspiration. Speeches, high goals, slogans, and campaigns are supposed to motivate employees and propel the organization toward competitive victory.

This misguided Hollywood style of leadership almost always fails. Jack Stack, CEO of Springfield Remanufacturing, which remanufactures engines in Springfield, MO, recalls when he took over a division and gave a powerful speech designed to rouse and inspire the workers.[1] At the end of the speech, he asked if there were any questions, and one worker in the back yelled out, "How old are you, anyhow?" The workers had often been exhorted with motivational speeches and campaigns, slogans, and goals. They were cynical because of repeated failures and knew from experience that little real change would occur.

Although speeches and exhortations might produce a brief flurry of activity, soon people go back to the same management, systems, and procedures

Reprinted with permission from *Quality Progress,* June 1994. Copyright © 1994 by ASQC, Milwaukee, WI.

as before. Repeatedly, CEOs make speeches, set goals, wage a big campaign, and then wonder why this leadership produces little lasting change.

Movies, in an effort to create a dramatic effect, confuse the issue. Prior to their speeches, Rockne and Patton thoroughly planned, organized, equipped, trained, and prepared their men. That was the main substance of their leadership and created the success. The motivational speech was the final encouragement and, perhaps, was not even necessary.

Good leadership must produce results, which means that the actual work done in the offices or factory must change. Exhortations rarely accomplish that. Change requires a new infrastructure in which the organization's steps, procedures, and techniques are improved. This requires new systems, planning, incentives, and training. Improvement in the way work is done is what quality systems accomplish and is the substance of real leadership.

Mistake 2: Thinking That Planning Devolves from Financial or Marketing Goals

Planning, in many organizations, starts with top management setting goals for financial growth (profit, earnings per share, and return on investment) and market growth (sales). These overall financial and sales goals then get broken down into specific goals and budgets for each department or area.

Planning should start with the customer, and the centerpiece of planning should be customer satisfaction.

What is often neglected in these goals, however, is the customer, who makes the purchase and pays the bills. Planning should start with the customer, and the centerpiece of planning should be customer satisfaction. This is true of the Baldrige Award winners. Westinghouse Commercial Nuclear Fuels Division, for example, has quality goals that directly relate to customer satisfaction issues. The senior management level has eight goals, which are divided into subgoals in lower levels of the organization. Even the individual worker or work team has goals that relate to the overall customer satisfaction goals. Each month, Xerox Business Systems sends out 40,000 surveys to its customers and to people who bought from the competitors, and the data from these surveys strongly influence corporate goals. Motorola has overarching goals for improving quality and cycle time, which are directly derived from customer satisfaction issues. All of the Baldrige Award winners examined, such as Globe Metallurgical, IBM Rochester, and Federal Express, have systems to ensure that customer satisfaction drives their goals.

Peterson Products, a metal stamping firm near Chicago, IL, was about to launch a marketing campaign to elevate sales. Instead, it decided to improve on-time delivery to the customer. When the percentage of on-time delivery went up, the salespeople were ecstatic because for the first time they could promise delivery. Sales rose 25% because the customers were getting what they wanted, and Peterson was able to drop the plan for the marketing campaign.

Another example is Cooper Tire in Findlay, OH. Building a reputation as a reliable supplier with modern plants, it aimed its marketing directly at the customers. It has doubled its market share and enjoys a profit growth rate of

22% per year. According to the *New York Times*, it is the envy of giants like Goodyear, Bridgestone, and Michelin.[2]

In most firms, planning is a vertical process that is driven from the top down or from the bottom up. Planning should be a horizontal process, however, starting from the customer and working inward. Financial goals are also necessary, but the customer should drive the goal-setting process, and every department and functional group should have goals that positively affect customer satisfaction. As Bob LaBant, IBM vice president, said, "My goal is to make our customers successful. If I had one measure, it would be their success."[3]

Mistake 3: Believing That Being Close to the Customer and Planning for Customer Satisfaction Is Sufficient

The top executives at many companies believe that their firms have a strong customer focus. They might have oriented their planning systems to better satisfy the customer. They might also maintain complaint hotlines, have extensive warranties, and conduct customer satisfaction surveys. These techniques, while helpful, still do not constitute a total customer focus because customer satisfaction is not something that concerns only some parts of the firm. Each and every group in the firm should have goals and incentives that are tied into enhancing customer satisfaction. This requires a carefully conceived management system that involves all parts of the firm in improving customer satisfaction.

Each and every group in the firm should have goals and incentives that are tied into enhancing customer satisfaction.

Why is this done so infrequently? Perhaps the most pervasive reason is that many companies lack a systematic approach to customer satisfaction. The executives believe that a system isn't needed and that they already understand the customers and know what they want. Almost always, however, that belief is false. Motorola, for example, is well aware of this fact and requires its executives to visit its customers' firms. The executives are required to speak not just to the firms' executives, but also to the workers who actually use the Motorola product. Experience has shown that almost everyone has distorted ideas about what customers truly think, and a systematic approach is needed to overcome this.

Steps to Overcome the Problem

How should such an approach be developed? The first step is to conduct an analysis of all the interactions a customer might have with the organization. Most organizations collect customer satisfaction information on the products or services they provide, but an organization provides far more than just a product or service. It also provides a complicated set of interactions with the customer, all of which should be top notch. For example, a firm must have knowledgeable salespeople, on-time delivery, accurate information, error-free invoices, courteous and helpful employees who quickly answer phones, and accurate and understandable technical manuals. Data should be collected on all customer interactions because total customer satisfaction means meeting or exceeding customer expectations in all areas.

Once the data are collected, the information must be used to improve the system. For example, the complaint department might handle a customer's complaint well, but once the customer's specific problem is resolved, a deeper issue arises about what happens next. Many firms do not try to find the cause of the complaint and change the system to prevent the problem from recurring. Using customer information merely to resolve the immediate problem or error is not sufficient; the underlying system must be improved.

The failure to properly use customer information often occurs in the design of a new product. The marketing department might collect a great deal of customer-related information, but the design engineers might not use it. For instance, marketing might discover that customers want a car with good acceleration, but the engineers need to know whether that means acceleration for passing on a highway, acceleration from 0 to 60 miles per hour, or acceleration to make the tires squeal. Each situation requires different engineering design choices, but marketing often does not obtain information in a form that the engineers can use.

One way to overcome this problem is to give the right people direct access to the customers. Ingersoll Rand in Pittstown, NJ, did this in the design of a new hand-held air grinder. A cross-functional new product development team was formed consisting of people from the marketing, engineering, and manufacturing departments. This team conducted focus groups with customers throughout the country. It was able to develop the new grinder in one-third the usual development cycle time. The grinder has sold well and won an award from the Industrial Design Society of America.[4]

While exposing decision makers to customers is a good first step, more formal techniques should be developed to drive the customer information throughout the company. Quality function deployment (QFD) is used by a number of companies, including Hewlett-Packard, Ford, and General Motors. QFD obtains detailed lifestyle information from the customer. This information is then deployed throughout the product design process to ensure that the final product fits the lifestyle of the customer, who then will feel comfortable with it.

A good customer satisfaction system gets the right information to the right people to improve the underlying process.

A good customer satisfaction system does far more than obtain information. It gets the right information to the right people and ensures that the information is used not just to correct a specific error, but to improve the underlying process.

When the System Breaks Down

Even a very good system might not be sufficient under times of stress and strain. The system is often abandoned and customer-oriented goals are sacrificed to achieve other business objectives. To meet end-of-period goals, for example, a great rush often takes place in which defective products are shipped or services are cut. This happens because executives are driven to reach their numerical goals, to ship a specified amount of product, or to make a certain profit. When a crunch comes and the numbers might not be reached, the customer-oriented standards are likely to be abandoned first.

What can be done about this? Robert Galvin, chairman of Motorola's executive committee, said one of his most important roles was to stand up for quality.[5] He served as the guardian and maintained the status of quality and customer focus even in times of stress and pressure, when others would have sacrificed them. That is a role that top management cannot delegate, and it is the foundation of any successful total customer satisfaction system. Only the CEO can ensure, even in times of great pressure, that quality and customer satisfaction are preserved.

Mistake 4: Believing That Quality Means Inspection

Many executives view quality narrowly and believe that it refers only to manufacturing process control and inspection. Inspection, however, is the antithesis of quality. In fact, quality's ultimate goal is to eliminate inspection. Inspection should not be needed if the process is successful in producing the product without defects. Inspection is only necessary if the production process is faulty and producing defects. In this circumstance, final inspection might be necessary, but it should be viewed only as an interim procedure.

There are three problems with inspection. The first is that inspection only eliminates a percentage of the defects. Joseph M. Juran, W. Edwards Deming, and others suggest that inspection will, as a rule of thumb, eliminate 80% of the defects, and 20% of the defects will still get through to the customer.[6]

Second, an inspector might be able to find defects when the defect rate is at a few percent, but when there is one defect per 25,000, he or she cannot hope to find a defect. Today's marketplace demands such high quality levels, often a few defects per million, that final inspection is not a practical method for achieving those levels.

The third major problem with final inspection is that it is expensive; the cost of inspectors, equipment, and correcting the defects at the final stage at high. At worst, the defective product must be scrapped, totally wasting the item. Even when the item can be salvaged, the rework and repair adds substantially to the cost.

Quality improvement efforts in many companies have shown that inspection is an inadequate approach. It is much better and less expensive to produce the product correctly in the first place. The key to this is error cause removal, which means identifying the cause of the defect or error and then eliminating it. Once the cause is eliminated, the defect cannot occur. Systematically done, this approach is far less expensive and is the best way to achieve virtually zero defects.

For example, billing invoices for domestic pagers from Motorola had 450 errors out of 22,000 total invoices. The errors included wrong or omitted serial numbers, freight amounts, or carriers. In just one year, the error rate was cut to nine out of 20,000. this would have been impossible to do by inspection. Instead, the causes of the defects were rooted out one by one. The team working on this problem noticed that some of the information was already in the computer and did not need to be recopied, which eliminated the possibility of error in that step. Other information was available from the bar coding system, and form simplification cut the remaining errors.[7]

Another example is from the People's Bank of Bridgeport, CT, which had a high error rate for its tellers in the proofing department. For each error found, a special correction notice had to be issued, which was expensive. To solve the problem, extra inspection, training, and management encouragement were attempted, but that did not help the situation. Finally, the bank tried to eliminate the root causes of the errors. It discovered that the tellers had to know how to do 78 operations. The bank standardized documents and reorganized the system so that the tellers needed to do only 12 operations. The errors virtually disappeared.

Whether in manufacturing or service activities, defects are rarely cut by increasing inspection.

Whether in manufacturing or service activities, defects are rarely cut by increasing inspection. Getting rid of the root causes of the errors is usually cheaper and more effective.

Mistake 5: Believing That Quality Improvement Is Too Expensive

Many executives believe that quality improvement is too expensive when, in fact, the opposite is true—quality cuts costs. Quality requires doing the right job right the first time, and doing the right job is cheaper than doing the wrong job. Any task that must be redone or product that must be reworked adds cost. Any waste of people's time, such as having to wait an excessively long time for top management to make a decision, adds to the cost. The more right things that are done right the first time, the more money that is saved. That is why quality saves money, and all of the Baldrige Award winners have documented proof of this.

One of the curious facts about quality is that costs tend to go down more rapidly than expected.

One of the curious facts about quality is that costs tend to go down more rapidly than expected. This is because quality improvement in one area often cuts costs in other areas, thereby reaping multiple savings. For example, a firm decided to improve the quality of the information generated by its computerized inventory system.[8] Its computers would show that a product was in inventory when, in fact, there was no such product on the shelf, or they would show that a product was unavailable when there were still several in stock. Even though this happened only a small percentage of the time, people often had to call the warehouse to check whether an item was in stock or not.

To improve this system, the firm set up a special team to get rid of the defects. Any time a problem arose, the team would count the inventory and check out what had gone wrong. Many problems were found and resolved. Part numbers were simplified and corrected, storage was rearranged, and the computer software was improved. After a couple months of effort, the computerized inventory system was made reliable, dependable, and accurate. An immediate savings was in the elimination of phone calls checking whether an item was in stock.

Then came an unexpected twist. Twice a year the firm took physical inventory and counted everything in stock. Soon after the computerized inventory system was corrected, a physical count was made. The numbers from the physical count, however, were different from those that the computer reported. The physical count showed the computer count to be wrong. The quality team was upset and felt demoralized. After all of the effort to improve the computerized inventory system, the team members thought that it had failed.

The quality team, however, decided to check the physical count. Since everyone in the firm helped do the physical count, it turned out that many people made errors because they did not understand the parts number system or the storage system. The physical count, therefore, was wrong, and the computer count of the inventory was more accurate. The biannual physical inventory was stopped, since it was not as accurate as the computer system, and the computer data were then used for all financial reporting.

In addition, the accounting department had two computer programmers developing software for the physical count, which was necessary because of the firm's changing product mix, consisting of a variety of electronic test and computer equipment. Now, with the physical count eliminated, the programmers were no longer needed for that task.

The people who had started the project of correcting the errors in the computer system had no concept that other savings would result. Phone calls from people trying to find out what was in stock, physical counts of inventory, and the need for revisions to the inventory computer program were eliminated.

Most systems consist of many parts or steps in which one part feeds information or material to the next. As the quality of one part of the system improves, it sends higher-quality information or material to the subsequent steps in the process. That higher-quality input produces a cost reduction in those steps. Since the interconnection of systems is often complex, sometimes, as in the inventory example, it is difficult to foresee exactly where the cost reductions will occur. But as quality improves in one operation, costs almost always drop not only in that operation, but also in other operations.

Mistake 6: Managing by Intuition and Not by Fact

Most CEOs strongly believe in their judgment. After all, that is the essence of being a CEO—having the background, judgment, and intuition to make good decisions. Research, however, tells a different story. Many behavioral science studies have verified that intuition and judgment are not nearly as sound as we are led to believe. In effect, people's brains "lie" to them and tell them their judgment is much better than it really is.

The book *Decision Traps* by J. Edward Russo and Paul J. H. Shoemaker, for example, details some of the fallacies that people's brains tell them.[9] In December of one year, executives were asked to predict sales for the following year. More than a year later and after the actual annual sales figures were shared with everyone, the executives were asked to recall their predictions, and they remembered them as being much closer to the actual outcome than they really were. In essence, once the actual figures were known, the brain subconsciously distorted and recalled the predictions as closer to the actual outcome.

Once a person knows an outcome, his or her brain adjusts its memory. The person then thinks that his or her judgment was far better than it actually was. Judgment also gets distorted because the brain tends to pay more attention to recent, unusual, or emotional events.

Management by fact, not intuition, strives to surmount this predicament. One of the most common areas for misjudgment is in assuming to know the needs of customers. Almost all presumptions about customers are wrong. Whitman Corporation in Chicago, IL, was concerned that its customers were upset because of damage to goods during shipment. It launched a project to reduce the shipping damage and succeeded after some effort. Only later did it learn that the customers were disappointed and thought the old shipping method was better. Although the new packaging protected the contents well, it was extremely hard for the customers to open.[10]

At First National Bank of Chicago in Illinois, the managers thought that the most important thing to customers was fast, courteous service. When the customers were surveyed, however, that item ranked fourth in importance. The customers' biggest concern was employees who said they would get back to them on an issue, but then did not.[11]

The need for management by fact extends not just to customers, but to any action or decision that can be made, as demonstrated in the following examples. A firm was proud that it had reduced its defect rates to 5% from 15%. When asked for the facts, it produced some charts that showed a 5% defect rate for several months. There was no indication, however, that the defect rate was previously 15%. When pushed further, someone recalled that someone else had said the defect rate was at least 15% at some point last year. Someone else then recollected that when new machines were installed the defect rate shot up briefly, and perhaps, that unique occurrence accounted for the 15%.[12]

Another firm was proud of the new sales techniques its salespeople were using. When questioned, however, they could produce no proof of increased sales and justified it by replying that the salespeople had only recently been trained so it was too early for proof. When the training was investigated, it was discovered that only 60% of the salespeople had attended the training session. When those attendees were questioned, most thought the training was useless and too theoretical, so they never implemented it.[13]

Compaq computer also searches for facts and, according to Vice President Hugh Barnes, continually uses sanity checks and cross-checks.[14] Just because an executive says something, that does not mean the statement is gospel. Suppose an executive predicts that the sales for a product will be 5,000 units. That statement is questioned, and the facts are sought. Is it the person's surmise? Is it based on market surveys? Is it based on firm orders? The degree of validity of the statement is thereby determined.

The mind, behavioral scientists know, searches for evidence to confirm its beliefs and denies the validity or existence of contrary or additional evidence. The best antidote to these distortions is management by fact. The facts are usually easier to obtain and considerably more useful than most people believe. Baldrige Award winners tend to collect a great deal of information and use it extensively in their decision processes.

Mistake 7: Using Misguided Incentives and Developing a Distorted Culture

CEOs often sincerely try to institute beneficial changes, such as launching a quality program. They allocate resources, train people, and establish goals. But after a year of waiting, they have gained little in return for their time and money. Why does this occur?

Obtaining a sizable change in an organization requires a major revision in the culture, and a CEO's program to improve quality will have little impact if the incentives are wrong for the culture. This frequently occurs, for example, when managers are encouraged to attain monthly production quotas, even if it means shipping poor-quality products.

Baldrige Award winners tend to collect a great deal of information and use it extensively in their decision processes.

Another common incentive is the promotion of managers who are deemed good crisis or fire-fighting managers. The manager who is considered a star is the one who marshals the resources, gets everyone to work overtime, and resolves crises. Top management hears of these heroics and promotion occurs. Rarely does anyone ask, however, why this manager permitted so many crises to happen.

One important tenet of quality is to keep the system under control so that defects or crises rarely occur. The best executives follow this philosophy and work to reduce the number of crises. Without the crises to get top management's attention, however, these people might work with little honor or promotion.

Trouble might also ensue if the overriding culture is based on cost reduction. Some managers will cut back on training, maintenance, and new product development. Those actions cut cost, but they have no chance to positively influence the company. This manager will keep costs very low, look good to top management, and receive a promotion in 18 to 24 months. The manager after him or her, however, is left with depleted resources and the inability to compete. Implementing a quality program often means making careful investigation of the cultural aspects of the organization that might defeat it.

Mistake 8: Changing Targets Each Year

Most CEOs have an annual planning process, similar to management by objectives, in which goals are established for the next year. The overall goals are set by top management, and then lower levels get their goals after some debate and discussion in a cascading process. In theory, if managers have reasonable goals and incentives, then most goals will be accomplished. In actual practice, however, high levels of accomplishment rarely occur.

To achieve any really important and challenging goal requires training, investment, management reviews, incentives, worker involvement, and cultural changes. All of this takes time and effort to implement. If new goals are instituted annually, management gets involved with new goals and directions before it can get fully underway on the old goals.

How can a CEO overcome this? Although some of the annual goals can change yearly, a few should be so fundamental and crucial that they persist into the foreseeable future. Motorola has instituted three such goals for the entire firm: quality, cycle time, and cost reduction. It took years to develop and implement the systems to ensure progress on these goals and for some people to realize that the CEO was really serious about them.[15]

Although some goals will have to be revised annually, changing too many goals too fast will confuse middle management and employees. Instead, top management should identify the fundamental factors that underpin the firm's success. To implement these factors, top management should include a few cardinal goals as well as the systems to achieve them (training, management reviews, and incentives).

Mistake 9: Failing to Follow the Best Practices

Near the end of the 1970s, Xerox was confronted by formidable competition from Japanese firms. The Japanese were selling copiers at a cost comparable to Xerox's manufacturing cost. Xerox's market share was plunging. After years of disregarding its Japanese competition, Xerox had to confront reality.

Although Xerox launched several programs in its counterattack, perhaps the most crucial was benchmarking. With benchmarking, employees in the organization determined the best practices in the industry. They learned about these best practices, implemented them, and became the best at them. All functions of the firm, not just manufacturing, were required to benchmark, including shipping, internal auditing,, treasury, and training. Xerox, like most manufacturing firms, had most of its costs not in manufacturing, but in overhead and general administration. Therefore, all parts of the firm had to benchmark and learn how to become the best at what they did.[16]

An important aspect of benchmarking is to look for the best practices not just inside one's industry but also outside. For warehousing, for example, Xerox benchmarked against L. L. Bean. Going outside one's industry might, in fact, be easier because direct competitors are less likely to share information. IBM Rochester, a Baldrige Award winner, for example, benchmarks itself against 200 other leading firms from both inside and outside its industry.[17]

Benchmarking is a powerful concept. But despite the obvious value of learning from the best, many managers will perceive the process as threatening and deny its value. They will object that other firms are different and not comparable and argue that what another firm does is not relevant. At Xerox, people gave repeated rationalizations and justifications for not benchmarking, such as the fact that the Japanese have a different culture, get government support, and have a better school system. Denial of the situation was rampant, and Xerox leadership had to convince people that they could learn and improve by studying other organizations.[18] The most difficult part of benchmarking is not the process itself, but in getting people to do it.

Benchmarking requires leadership to help people face the fact that they are not the best and must therefore improve. It also requires hard work to know one's own process thoroughly and to understand and learn from the benchmarking process. Most of all, it requires a CEO who knows that world-class success cannot be achieved with second-class operations.

Mistake 10: Believing Baldrige Award Examiners Are Stupid

The Baldrige Award is an award given for outstanding quality to companies applying in three categories: manufacturing, service, and small business (no more than 500 employees). To apply, companies must complete the Baldrige Award examination process, which requires making detailed descriptions of the company's total quality systems. Many firms, however, make the mistake of submitting material that resembles a public relations piece. This might occur because of the company's natural enthusiasm for its achievement. More likely, it is because the company lacks well-defined, well-documented, and measurable quality systems.

A rule of thumb for determining whether a good quality system exists is to audit the process. An audit will determine whether the company is making progress in a particular area and what to do if it is not. A poor system, for example, will likely have one or more of the following problems: no clearly established goals, no means to measure progress toward the goals, and no well-defined process of identifying and correcting problems.

Most Baldrige Award applicants have fairly good systems in the processes that directly generate the products and services. The weak systems are generally seen in leadership, planning, product development, and administrative activities. The lack of systems in these areas often becomes apparent in applicants' responses to questions asking how these processes are improved. The companies might respond by indicating that they have meetings or that a particular person, such as the division manager, has responsibility for the activity. Or they might try a public relations approach such as, "We at the XYZ company are always looking for ways to improve our strategic quality planning process. We believe that quality is one of the most important components of our business plan, and thus, quality is an integral part of our strategic planning process." The company however, never directly describes how the process is systematically improved.

Another example is an organization's description of a "process that ensures that customer service requirements are understood and responded to throughout the company."[19] An inadequate response would be: "We believe that a customer focus is a key element in our continued success. Every customer contact department has signs posted stating 'Service and courtesy are our business.' In addition, all internal stationery for memos has 'Treat the Customer Right' imprinted prominently in the letterhead." Again, there is no discussion of the system.

Virtually every issue addressed in the Baldrige Award criteria asks for a description of the management system or process the company uses for that issue. This means how the process is monitored, how it is improved, and what the results have been both in terms of improvements over time and in comparison to competitors and world-class companies. When no system exists, it is tempting to resort to public relations statements about the importance of quality and customer satisfaction. The Baldrige Award examiners, however, are not stupid enough to be fooled.

Acknowledgment

The author wishes to thank George Easton, University of Chicago, for his extensive help in writing this paper.

References

1. Lucien Rhodes with Patricia Amend, "The Turnaround," *Inc.,* August 1986, p. 42.

2. Johnathan P. Hicks, "A Tire Outdistances Its Rivals," *New York Times,* May 8, 1990.

3. "IBM Rochester, 1990 Winner of the Malcolm Baldrige National Quality Award," IBM, Rochester, MN, 1990.

4. N. R. Kleinfield, "How 'Strykeforce' Beat the Clock," *New York Times,* March 25, 1990, p. 1.

5. Robert Galvin, chairman of the executive committee, Motorola, Guest Lecture at Graduate School of Business, University of Chicago, Feb. 13, 1991.

6. Joseph M. Juran, editor in chief, and Frank M. Gryna, associate editor, *Juran's Quality Control Handbook* (New York, NY: McGraw-Hill Book Company, 1988), Section 18.

7. Paul Noakes, vice president, Motorola, private conversation, March 18, 1991.

8. J. Timothy Fuller and Willard I. Zangwill, "Repealing the Law of Diminishing Returns for Quality," Report, University of Chicago Graduate School of Business, Nov. 3, 1989.

9. J. Edward Russo and Paul J. H. Shoemaker, *Decision Traps* (New York, NY: Simon and Schuster, 1989).

10. William Naumann, vice president, Whitman Corporation, Guest Lecture at Graduate School of Business, University of Chicago, Nov. 30, 1992.

11. Aleta Holub, vice president, First National Bank of Chicago, personal interview, Jan. 18, 1992.

12. William Naumann, vice president, Whitman Corporation, Guest Lecture at Graduate School of Business, University of Chicago, Nov. 30, 1992.

13. Tim Fuller, lecturer, Special Seminar, University of Chicago, Winter 1991.

14. Hugh Barnes, vice president, Compaq Computer, personal interview, May 18, 1992.

15. Paul Noakes, vice president, Motorola, private conversation, March 18, 1991.

16. Barry Bebb, retired vice president, Xerox, personal interview, Jan. 29, 1992.

17. "IBM Rochester, 1990 Winner of the Malcolm Baldrige National Quality Award," IBM, Rochester, MN, 1990.

18. Barry Bebb, retired vice president, Xerox, personal interview, Jan. 29, 1992.

19. George Easton, professor, Graduate School of Business, University of Chicago, personal interview, May 18, 1991.

Willard I. Zangwill is a professor of management science at the Graduate School of Business, University of Chicago.

On Arrogance and Participation

Edward Cohen-Rosenthal

This article eloquently explores how arrogance on the part of leaders, the need to be right, to run the business, is a formula for failure in the long run. The author explains the value of people working together to solve problems, to learn, and to lead organizational success. Readers will find this a nice addition to the ideas of Covey and Gulledge.

The reasons for unsuccessful empowerment mostly boil down to variations on one theme—arrogance. You can call it authoritarian culture or you can tag it as management or union resistance but the central issue if that someone feels as if they can't trust ordinary workers to deal with more than garden variety problems.

The source of deepseated cynicism . . . At its very base, the notion of employee involvement and worker participation is an attack on arrogance. Each and every day, workers confront workplaces and work situations that put them down, demean their capabilities and defy their common sense:

- They see bosses who order them to do things they know to be wrong and wasteful . . .
- They see their *superiors* using their positions as weapons . . .
- They see *professionals* who use their *professional* status to ignore their ideas.

It is that powerful experience that breeds deep cynicism and resentment into the workplace.

At the very heart of employee involvement is an acknowledgement of the humility of the workplace.

Humility and employee involvement . . . At the very heart of employee involvement is an acknowledgement of the humility of the workplace where common struggle and learning replace slavish attachment to any notion or any person that promises the one right way. Stephen Covey, author of *Principle-Centered Leadership,* calls humility "the mother of all virtues—because it promotes stewardship."

Humility and Fallibility in Knowledge and Science

The notion of fallibility is a human necessity, a fundamental epistemological principle. In simple terms, no one does or can know it all:

Reprinted with permission from the *Journal for Quality and Participation,* March 1994. Copyright © 1994 by the Association for Quality and Participation.

- All answers are approximations . . .
- The only thing I am certain of is the lack of certitude.

The *Heisenberg Uncertainty Principle* applied in workplaces would be that all things carry a certain amount of uncertainty. Heisenberg's original physical principle says that you cannot fix both the velocity and direction or vector of change in a sub-atomic particle but only describe it in terms of probabilities.

It is similarly true in the workplace that the speed of change and where it is going cannot be predicted exactly but we can aim in the right direction. Strategic planning doesn't guarantee the future but projects an organization towards more desirable goals. Reading through past strategic plans can make us cynical when we recognize how off the mark most were or it can remind us that precision is a fool's virtue when getting going in the right direction is what counts in reality.

Science Provides Us with Metaphors which Shape Our Reality

Admittedly one can overdraw scientific and social analogies, but our understanding of our world shapes how we think about our social reality.

It doesn't matter whether scientific formulae describe accurately social phenomena. What matters is that these concepts shape how we think about our world.

In the Newtonian worldview *action = reaction* translates into *I say = you do.* These equations don't work so neatly in the real world.

Working in a Newtonian workplace . . . In the Newtonian world-view *action = reaction* translates into *I say = you do.* These equations don't work so neatly in the real world and leave much that needs to be explained. People are constantly vexed and perplexed over why there is a mismatch between orders given and what is actually done.

Usually we ascribe the problem to poor communication. I assert that the situation can be improved through better communication but it will never be solved. The vain attempt at absolute compliance is best replaced by a common understanding of where you are aiming your goals.

The impact of "new science" on how we think about the world . . ." Even the science of today is not so sure of itself as it once was. Margaret Wheatley in *Leadership and the New Science* observes:

"In our past explorations, the tradition was to discover something and then to formulate it into answers and solutions that could be widely transferred. But now we are on a journey of mutual and simultaneous exploration. In my view, all we can expect from one another is new and interesting information. We can not expect answers. Solutions, as quantum reality teaches, are a temporary event, specific to a context, developed through the relationship of persons and circumstances. There will be no more patrons, waiting expectantly for our return, just more and more explorers venturing out on their own."

Wheatley links the understanding of science's limitations to the importance of participation:

"Participation, seriously done, is a way out from the uncertainties and ghostly qualities of this nonobjective world we live in. We need a broad distribution of information, viewpoints and interpretations if we are to make sense of the world."

Scientific Management and Certainty

The belief in the power of industrial science is a case in point in the workplace of arrogant systems whose underlying logic subverts even the good intentions of many of its practitioners.

At the heart of Taylorism (a.k.a. scientific management) there was a profound belief in the correctness of *science*. Coming to prominence in an era of enormous advances in science and technology, Frederick Winslow Taylor had a deep conviction that application of workplace science would result in the *right* answers that had objective validity to both management and workers. Each employee would be able to see the consummate logic of the engineered system. Taylor writes:

"Among the various methods and implements used in each element of each trade there is *always one method and one implement which is quicker and better than any of the rest.* And this one best method and best implement can only be discovered through a scientific study and analysis of all the methods and implements in use, together with accurate, minute motion and time study. This involves *the gradual substitution* of science for the rule of thumb . . ." (*Italics* added for emphasis)

That arrogation of rectitude, or the assumption of eternal correctness, due to the assumed scientific validity of the work method and the fundamental belief that it would then work as designed are the major traits (and fallacies) of Taylorism. Both personally and by philosophy, Taylor represented an arrogance that caused major counter-reactions in many workplaces then and now. The following comments of Taylor on matching people to their technology demonstrates both arrogance and why people reacted against his system:

"Now one of the very first requirements for a man who is fit to handle pig iron as a regular occupation is that he shall be so stupid and so phlegmatic that he more nearly resembles in his mental make-up the ox than any other type."

"It is impossible for the man best suited to this type of work to understand the principles of this science, or even to work in accordance with these principles without the aid of a man better educated than he is."

The industrial engineer is the high priest of the workplace. Now that is arrogance.

Taylor believed that managers were stuck in their old ways, relied on coercion more than reason, engaged in cronyism and did not act in their own best interest. He thought that the unions too were beholden to old traditions, restricted output, acted stubbornly and clearly didn't understand how their members could make more money and be treated more fairly if only they vigorously adopted scientific management.

There was a fervency to the new management science that led to a Babbit-like belief in its possibilities for transforming industry.

Indeed it wasn't only American capitalists who came to embrace modern, *scientific management*, Vladimir Lenin venerated Taylorism and believed that together *scientific management* and *scientific socialism* would lead to the communist nirvana. He was wrong, of course.

Totalitarian scientific versus democratic, empowered workplaces . . . There is, I believe, a direct connection between the belief that *someone on high has the right answer*—whether that be a dictatorship of the boss or the proletariat—and that leads directly to totalitarian workplaces. Democracies and empowered workplaces are much messier than the false sirens of controlled approaches. Both the long term results and the underlying integrity of the values speak on democracy's behalf.

Post-Taylorism . . . Indeed it fell to Taylor's disciples during the 1930s to recognize that science, even good science, needs to be tempered with due process and democratic participation.

The post-Taylorists developed alliances with the labor movement and demonstrated bold experiments in new work design including the Hart, Schafner and Marx menswear activities with the Clothing Workers and the Cleveland joint projects with the Ladies Garment Workers Union. Unions in a variety of industries hired industrial engineers to help make their employers more efficient and to assure that standards were fair to their members.

Quality and the Pursuit of Certainty

The total quality management (TQM) movement also risks supporting arrogance in the workplace. Its underlying message is that quality is everything and fervency of belief in its superordinate role will make it happen.

Control charts can inform judgment, not replace it.

It too often displays the same derisive view of managers and unions that Taylor displayed. Granted Dr. Deming provides tremendous insight and wisdom about the functioning of modern organizations but the turning of Deming into a demigod where the 14 points become equivalent to received revelation is going way too far. The brashness with which Dr. Deming chided managers runs the risk of an arrogant dismissal of many sincere efforts and alternative solutions that can and do work. Statistical process control (SPC) charts too often are treated like ancient runes with their deciphering allegedly unlocking the secret answer to all problems. Control charts can inform judgment, not replace it.

Were QWL and quality circles too lowly or unscientific? For some time in America, the quality movement has derisively dismissed the contribution of quality circle and quality of worklife (QWL) efforts. Yet, when quality improvement teams started they looked, tasted, smelled, felt and acted like quality circles.

The replacement for circles and QWL, total quality, was to be management driven. When the cascading TQM reached the workers they were to implement the quality commitment and decisions of those above them. This too was a dismal failure.

Quality is a total organizational imperative and employees need to be involved in the full range of decisions; not just figuring out how to dot someone else's *i's* and cross someone else's *t's*. When employees heard they were being empowered through quality; they wondered whether it was a new paternalism or the real thing.

In the mid-1980s when quality efforts came to prominence in many organizations like AT&T and General Motors, it was defined as not being the soft quality of worklife joint efforts of the past but a more scientific, management driven approach.

For too long, participative approaches had let the underlings or the union run the show; quality was to be spread by those who know more and reinforced with databased science. It was a reassertion of managerial and expert power in the organization.

This arrogance in the organization was fought by those who viewed quality as a good goal and early *imperial* efforts were toppled in favor of broader based initiatives.

The Newest Arrogance: Reengineering

Even more frightening is the current fascination with reengineering. Promising to start from a clean slate, it chooses to *obliterate* previous systems and fix them relatively quickly. This is the neutron bomb for organizational change that leaves the financial structures standing while the people are terminated.

Potential employment disasters aside, it is an incredibly arrogant set of presumptions about the ability to construct efficient organizations as if it were as simple as a computerized erector set created by consulting cognoscenti. The lip service given to self-management is not a means of real empowerment but a fiat for efficiency.

The lip service given to self-management is not a means of real empowerment but a fiat for efficiency.

It is an extremely sanctimonious sneering at current organizations for the tangles they were stupid enough to get themselves into. Michael Hammer, the reengineering guru, says *(in the Wall Street Journal)*: "A lot of people embark on reengineering but don't go anywhere because of failures of intellect or courage." Indeed its own proponents admit that over 80 percent of the efforts fail according to their own standards.

While failure can be blamed on clients unwilling to go the extra mile, the sheer magnitude of its arrogance may be its biggest flaw. It promises the right answers and expert decisions on using correctly available technology. This is a seductive mix for American managers looking for a quick fix. Reengineering may not be so much a bad idea—that we need to rethink systems at work—as it has a case of bad *we know better* attitude.

Humility of Position

Titles and positions in organizations carry with them levels of power. The critical question is what kind of power. The traditional use of power in a hierarchy is power *over*. There are people *who work for* their boss.

SOMETIMES ARROGANCE JUST HAS TO BE OUTWITTED. . .

I remember hearing the story in Eastern Airlines where workers tried to do their work right on a numerically controlled lathe by making their own tapes.

The engineering department insisted on regularly sending a faulty tape back to the machine shop.

Frustrated by the worker's lack of obedience to the chain of command, management placed a lock on the machines to prevent the workers from doing the work correctly, more timely and less costly.

The workers left a fake lock on the machine so that the engineers would have an illusion of control.

Philip Crosby, noted quality consultant, says that you pick them out easily:

"The signs of arrogance are not subtle:

- The boss dominates all meetings
- The boss is usually late
- The boss is out of touch
- The boss follows different rules than everyone else
- The boss rejects those who do not agree continually."

Crosby also observes that "the difference in whether people enjoy their jobs or cringe when it is time to go to work lies in the way they are treated. Arrogant managers or management teams make life miserable for people."

Who do you really work for? The assumption of a position in an organization is an expression of trust; trust that the person will perform their role well. It is a power to *accomplish* carrying with it certain resources.

In some organizations, the hierarchy has been inverted and instead of having subordinates, managers treat the employees who work with them as their *customers* helping them to accomplish their goals and better meet the end customer's needs.

When managers feel as if they have to have all of the answers, they are being set up for a fall both personally and professionally.

Employee participation is a direct attack on *bosses* because it admits that others have wisdom in the organization. It is this confrontation with the arrogance of managerial power that most frustrates the advance of employee participation. When advocates talk about middle management resistance to employee participation it is a polite euphemism for their stubborn hold onto what is perceived as power.

The Dangers of Arrogance to Its Practitioners

Yet arrogant management is a distorting and dangerous notion for the managers involved themselves. Autocracy and arrogance in the workplace are the forward face of mistrust and fear.

When managers feel as if they have to have all of the answers, know everything that is going on and control every aspect of the work, then they are being set up for a fall both personally and professionally. This kind of superperson—*ubermenschen*—approach leads to heart attacks and other stress related diseases as well as serious dysfunction at home. Workers who are under the thumb of such managers wait for opportunities to see them fail and frequently set them up to trip over themselves.

On the other hand, managers who recognize and nurture the strengths of those who work with them, learn from those they are responsible for, breed confidence and improved capability of other employees and are more effective managers and healthier people.

Learning while helping or guiding . . . As a consultant, frequently I find clients looking for the expert with the cookbook answer. Even when there are some sort of answers, they are looking for the simple quick fix. But a consultant must use his or her position to help an organization identify and then develop insight, questioning and competency that leaves it more sure of its own capabilities. We must learn together.

I find that I learn from every consulting encounter. Even when profferred, I prefer to downplay the expert role. That does not mean that I don't have ideas and something to offer or that I don't get frustrated when the client doesn't *listen* and do what I suggested. But at the core. I need to remember that the client must take charge and be part of an unfolding dynamic of organizational change.

My role is to help uncover options and help facilitate choice in the client organization. Expert power can help an organization learn or it can rob it of its ability to innovate and sustain change.

The Problem of Imperialistic Professionalism

It is uniformly (though not universally) true that the most difficult groups to work with in work redesign projects are the professionals. Through their schooling they have been invested with the mantle of knowledge. They wear it as if draped in academic robes. The problem is when gaps in knowledge are filled by *professional imperialism.*

What one doesn't know is always larger than what one does know. Indeed the pace of growth of knowledge makes schooling an entry point to professionalism, not a laminated license. For example, in many fields a freshman engineer is out of date on many practices by the time he or she gets a first job. The half-life of data or even processes is so short it seems to rival the expiration dates on yogurt containers. This realization should contain smugness about current knowledge. Yesterday's expert can become today's relic with alarming speed.

Professional shrouds cannot be used to cover-up lack of knowledge. Instead, professionalism can mean a spirit of inquiry and a way of attacking a problem. But it is not a synonym for *know it all.*

Beware of the Trap of Professional Arrogance

Professionals of most any stripe fall into the trap of professional arrogance:

- Nurses look over the shoulders of doctors and quietly check patient care to compensate for the doctor's oversights . . .

- Construction tradespersons routinely adjust for the mistakes of haughty architects . . .
- Secretaries running the office is no exaggeration. Legal secretaries in particular know that lawyers left unleashed can nit-pick a process to death and have difficulty cooperating.
- Engineers send down drawings or designs that need to be adjusted so that they can work.

Harvard professor Chris Argyris has studied the thinking process among professionals and observes that when "their learning strategies go wrong, they become defensive, screen out criticism and put *blame* on anyone and everyone but themselves." He goes on to state: "Put simply, people consistently act inconsistently, unaware of the contradiction between their espoused theory and their theory in use, between the way they think they are acting and the way they really act." Indeed perceived arrogance by the receiver is often a genuine belief in correctness by the professional sender and often meant with good intention. However when challenged, the professional frequently lashes out defensively.

This is not to say that professionals don't know important things or that thinking processes learned in schools and through professional experience can't be helpful; but it does not entitle them to belittle and dismiss those who work with them. We need the value added of professionals; not the value hogging.

We need the value added of professionals; not the value hogging.

Labor—Management Loftiness

There are two forms of union-management arrogance that need to be attacked and dismantled: the exchange of management's right's clauses for union recognition and intra-union paternalism.

The Arrogance of Rights for Recognition

The spread of management's rights clauses after World War II provided management with the mantle of *it's my choice right or wrong*. In the heady days after the war, when the world was America's oyster, a sweetheart deal was cut. In exchange for union recognition clauses that guaranteed union dues, labor agreed to look the other way when it came to the management of the enterprise.

In those days, labor and management could get away with it. Expanding markets, domestic application of new technology, rising standards of living and the ability to absorb cost increases through higher prices or productivity made the deal workable.

The great unraveling . . . But this arrangement began to unravel at the end of the 1970s. American economic hegemony over Europe, Asia and Latin America eroded and those who doggedly stuck to their old path, management and labor, have paid dearly for their shortsightedness. The arrogant belief that we could remain the top of the heap is written on the tombstones of many communities and companies who refused to adapt to change. Blind faith in management or blind blame of management both contributed to the fall.

A Personal Lesson in Humility. . .

Some years ago I was conducting a study of worker participation in Africa and Asia. I had an interview set up with the leader of the Self-employed Women's Association (SEWA), Ela Bhatt, in Ahmedabad India.

SEWA, a union of the poorest of the poor including women who comb the streets for scraps of fiber to sell at the mills, is one of the premier examples of successful development activity anywhere in the world through their self-help activities for healthcare, banking, skills training, childcare and other pressing concerns of its members.

I came prepared with my interview guide. But upon meeting Mrs. Bhatt, I recognized that the canned questions wouldn't work and tossed the interview sheets aside.

We talked about how she, a Brahmin Gujerati in the Ghandian tradition, led this band of desperate women. Her answer came not from a control orientation but from one of humility. But it was humility based on the middle ground between assertion of self and selflessness. This simple but profound truth has helped me to understand that lack of arrogance is not abrogation of principled response. Mahatma Gandhi himself said, "I am my people's leader. There go my people. I must follow."

Workers who adopt either attitude are at risk when they don't recognize that they have to be part of the solution or they will become its victims. In the words of one steelworker union president, "Management is too important to leave to management." By the end of the 1970s, we were beginning to learn that "I told you so" or "it's not my job" was an insufficient answer for everyone and anyone. *Management right or wrong* clauses are suicidal for both parties.

Union Paternalism

The union side also displays arrogance when some union leaders act paternalistically toward their members' wishes. Well intentioned or not, it breeds a view of the union that distances it from its membership. Arrogance of this sort also mars the public image of the union from being an instrument of worker's will to the pawn of *union bosses.*

In essence, a good cooperative process at work humbly admits that managers are not always right, workers are not always right, but by working together they are more likely to be right.

Backroom deals that are not aligned with the interests of the members rob the union of its real base of support—its membership. While I believe that managers are not always right, the same is true of the union and of workers whether union or not. Romanticism about the wisdom of workers is misplaced. Sure every worker has ideas but not all of them are good ideas. Some of them are half-baked, misinformed or just plain wrong.

In essence, a good cooperative process at work humbly admits that managers are not always right, workers are not always right, but by working together they are more likely to be right.

Working Class Solidarity or Division?

Arrogance in the workplace does not just occur between levels of the organization or just from management to workers. Workers themselves are also guilty of many of the same sins.

Classification systems were enshrined in labor contracts under Taylorism to combat the capriciousness of supervisors. Too often, such rigid classification systems instead of creating solidarity and fairness or protection against capriciousness, have devolved into discord and undue segmentation of work.

Skilled trades elitism . . . One of the principle values of the labor movements has been solidarity; yet arrogant attitudes and practices among workers themselves undermine solidarity in the workforce and weaken worker power.

Too often skilled trades workers in maintenance areas carefully guard their prerogatives and block advances by production or clerical workers. The notion of skilled trades as labor's aristocracy is prominent. This occupational elitism is bad enough but when it is combined with racism and sexism it takes on an even uglier complexion.

The overapplication of seniority frequently divides workers by forcing newcomers to *pay their dues* through undesirable work. This breeds resentment among many younger workers. Skilled trades workers have a right to feel good about their autonomy, quality, problem solving capability, compensations and craft—but so do the rest of the people at work. The answer to poor working conditions is not to ration them to particular industrial castes but to make them better for all.

It is sad to see when people define themselves by what they are not rather than by who they are. Finding someone else to look down upon doesn't build up esteem, it steals it from everyone. When managers' and workers seek to lay the blame on the other guys, the result is that little gets done, and no one is respected.

In truly empowered workplaces, self-directed teams blur the lines between production and maintenance, salaried and hourly, line and support staff. Everyone contributes to solving problems, to learning from others in their group and sharing what they know. When any member of the team feels that he or she is better than the others then the whole team is disrupted. Teamwork is not some version of Maoist leveling but a way to recognize, encourage and draw upon a diversity of capabilities, ideas and talent. Work teams needn't make everyone in the group an interchangeable part but can provide support and backup to deal better with work's uncertainties and to create new community at work.

Teamwork is not some version of Maoist leveling but a way to recognize, encourage and draw upon a diversity of capabilities, ideas and talent.

Humility As an Alternative to Arrogance

Earlier I discussed the scientific metaphor that often underlies workplace change. But there is also an equally powerful alternative theological frame—work—it's the concept of humility. The notion of humility is a central theme in most religious traditions. In Christianity, Judaism, Islam and many other religious traditions, the notion of man as imperfect is a fundamental tenet. If one accepts humility as a concept or organizing principle, the assumption of omniscience becomes fundamentally a blasphemous act. To believe that any one person has the lock on truth, knows it all, and can control it all presumes to individuals a god-like quality that they do not and cannot deserve. Who gave anyone the right to be *bosses* or *prima donnas?* Who has the right to invest themselves with such absolute authority? Listed at the head of the list of seven deadly sins is the sin of arrogance or prideful behavior.

Humility in both West and East . . . In Christian theology, humility is a fundamental principle of meritorious behavior. In the Jewish tradition, the Talmud observes that there is no room in the world for both arrogance and God. The *Book of Proverbs* contains a number of scathing attacks on pride and arrogance including the admonition that "pride goes before destruction and a haughty spirit before a fall" *(Proverbs 16:18).*

Indeed reviews of failed companies almost always include stories of arrogant and prideful behavior of senior leadership that toppled their organization into the abyss.

This idea that inflation of the ego is harmful is not a Western concept alone; it is clearly expressed in Eastern traditions as well. Maori tribal artists in the South Pacific deliberately make mistakes in their artwork and sculpture to affirm human imperfection.

Assertion Not Arrogance

The answer to the problem of arrogance is not withdrawal or denial of expertise or belief. In an organization each person must contribute to the fullest of his or her ability for it to be successful.

There are people in the organization with special knowledge, talent, skills and motivation. These need to be employed as part of the tapestry of the organization. Managers, supervisors or union leaders who refuse to provide leadership and share their vision and concerns do those who depend on them no favor. Assuming total control thinking that it enables and helps out often winds up creating total dependence. Leaders need to listen for the sounds and the underlying themes that their constitutents are communicating and for the often silent pleas for inclusion and understanding.

Leaders need to listen for the sounds and the underlying themes that their constitutents are communicating and for the often silent pleas for inclusion and understanding.

Final Thoughts

Struggling with arrogance is a difficult, ongoing personal and organizational effort:

- It requires understanding that knowledge has its limits . . .
- It asks us to recognize that organizational authority enables us to achieve larger goals and build competence and confidence among those with whom we work . . .
- Above all, recognizing that arrogance kills participation, the antidote is open, broad and deep involvement of others in a common search for better solutions.

In a truly empowered organization, each of us will bring to the table what we have to offer and elicit from those we work together with what they have to offer as well. When we have ideas they will be open to challenge and improvement and when we act we will be willing to acknowledge when we have made mistakes and learn from them. And that, I humbly submit, is continuous improvement.

Edward Cohen-Rosenthal of Cornell University is co-author of Mutual Gains: A Guide to Union-Management Cooperation *(2nd Ed., Ithaca, ILR Press, 1993).*

Quality Transformation

CULTURAL TRANSFORMATION

Alignment: How It Works and Why It Matters

Donald Tosti and Stephanie Jackson

The authors of this article explain in detail how organizational strategy, objectives, and activities must parallel organizational values, practices, and behaviors if a company is to make sure that its culture and its mission are properly aligned. They present a clear and simple model for understanding that this is vital for any company seeking to move from a traditional hierarchical management approach to TQM.

What you do, these days, may be less important than how you do it—if you want to stay in business over the long term. The press is full of examples of how hard it is to stay on top. Small companies plunge, almost overnight, from stunning success to failure. Giant companies that once seemed permanent fixtures of the business landscape are now struggling. Even the finest products, the best services, or the most advanced technology now give organizations only a short-lived edge over their competition. Sustained success depends on an organization's people—because it is people who determine the way those products and services are delivered.

Until recently, the proposition that people are organization's greatest asset has received little more than lip service in most companies. But a number of factors—globalization, spreading technology, shorter product life cycles,

---

Reprinted with permission from *Training* Magazine, April 1994. Copyright © 1994. Lakewood Publications, Minneapolis, MN. All rights reserved. Not for resale.

tougher competition, and customers' increasing demands for high-quality goods and services—have made it clear that lip service isn't enough. Consequently, there's been a growing interest in organizational culture and its influence on people and their performance.

The *Oxford American Dictionary* defines culture as "the customs . . . of a particular group." In their 1982 book *Corporate Cultures,* Terrence Deal and Allan Kennedy describe culture as "the way we do things around here." Culture is not just about *what* people do—the tasks they perform—but also about the way they do it—how they behave as they perform those tasks. Culture refers primarily to behavior patterns that people tend to bring to *any* task or decision. Changing an organization's culture, then, would seem to have the potential for greater long-term, sustained benefits than changing its products services or delivery methods.

Much of the literature on organizational culture has focused on categorizing different types of cultures. Terms like "myths" and "heroes" and "rituals" are used to describe key components of these various cultures. This literature is both interesting and informative; it has taken the understanding of corporate culture far beyond what used to be called "the informal organization."

But categorization schemes are not particularly helpful in determining what one can *do* about an organization's culture. Myths and rituals can be meaningful signals of the nature of a culture, but remember that culture ultimately is *behavior*—it is the way people in the organization tend to behave as they go about their work. Culture change, then, is behavior change. And the technology of behavior change is not new.

Remember that culture ultimately is *behavior*—it is the way people in the organization tend to behave as they go about their work. Culture change, then, is behavior change.

Values

So if culture is behavior, why is it so much more resistant to change than most other behavior? We suggest that most of the difficulty results from two key characteristics of behavior patterns that are part of a group's culture:

- *They are groupwide.* Almost everyone in the group will exhibit the behavior pattern. Therefore, the prevailing norms, expectations and rewards support the behavior—and behavior that does not fit will be punished. It becomes very hard for people to change culturally determined behavior unless the behavior of others around them changes at the same time. This means that the environment must change in a way that supports the new behavior.

- *They are value-driven.* Culture-based behavior is usually linked to an underlying belief or value. People will be reluctant to change behavior that is part of the culture, or will find it difficult, unless they see the new behavior as compatible with some key value.

For example, it is relatively easy to get someone to change specific behaviors relating to a particular task—organize the information in a business case differently, say, or assemble equipment in a new sequence. This kind of change will not usually fly in the face of prevailing norms. But if someone is

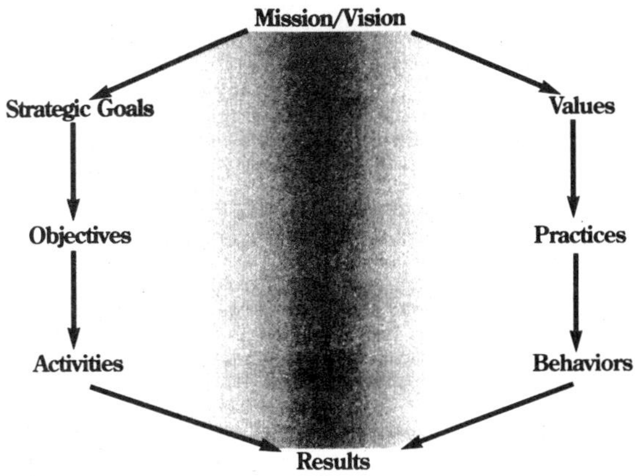

Figure 1.

asked to work differently with others (consult with people in other departments before preparing the business case, or share equipment-assembly tasks with workers from another unit or team) the change may violate norms, values or expectations about how things "have always been done."

Another factor that may contribute to the difficulty of changing cultural behavior is lack of a clear picture of the role that culture plays in achieving business goals—the relationship between an organization's culture and its performance. The model shown in Figure 1 provides a framework for examining that relationship.

The model describes two interdependent paths for providing direction—for helping people move from the global statement of the organization's mission and vision to specific business results.

- *The left-hand path is strategic.* It emphasizes *what* needs to be done: the broad strategic goals the organization will work toward; the objectives that groups and individuals must accomplish to carry out those strategies; and the activities that must be performed to meet those objective.

- *The right-hand path is cultural.* It emphasizes *how* things should be done: the values implied by the mission and vision; the practices that reflect those values; and the specific, day-to-day behaviors that will represent the values and practices to others as people go about their work. Note that these values have to do with the way the organization conducts its business—not with people's personal values about home, family, religion or personal relationships.

Alignment

The key implication of this model is that any significant change—whether strategic or cultural—must take into account "organizational alignment."

Alignment refers to compatibility *between* the strategic and cultural "paths," and consistency *within* them. The organization's values should be compatible with its strategic goals; a group that strongly values stability should not be setting goals around the pork-futures market. And people's day-to-day behaviors should be consistent with the values that they and the organization espouse; the behavior of a group that claims to value responsiveness to customers should not include responding to requests with, "Sorry, that's not part of my job."

Alignment refers to compatibility *between* the strategic and cultural "paths," and consistency *within* them.

Organizations traditionally have concentrated their thought and energy on the strategic path. Most companies invest considerable time and effort in defining strategic goals and objectives. Fewer explicitly address the cultural path with clearly defined, published statements of values. Fewer still make a consistent effort to examine and support the practices and behaviors that represent those values. Yet our behavior patterns—the way we do things—are just as important as our activities—what we do—in determining the results we achieve.

In other words, values—like strategic goals—are business necessities. For example, achieving and maintaining market share requires setting relevant goals, and testing actions and decisions against those goals. But it also requires supporting relevant organizational values, and checking typical practices and behaviors against those values. If we value "openness" and "innovation," these values are supposed to encourage certain behaviors to achieve a goal. For example, we use new ideas and information to create a level of customer satisfaction that will help increase our market share.

Both strategies and values provide important direction and contribute to organizational success. In recent years, with increasing competition and decreasing differences in the technological and product advantages of different companies, the "values" side of the model—the side most strongly associated with the culture of the organization—has assumed a greater role. When customers perceive fewer differences between our products and those of our competitors, they begin to place more importance on how those products are delivered and supported.

Here is a description of each of the components of the organizational alignment model.

- *Mission and vision* represent the organization's *intent*. They provide guidance about our purpose, expressed in terms of what we are in business to do (our mission), and the expected impact of our performance (our vision).

For instance, here is a mission statement for a hypothetical financial-services company: "We provide products and services to business customers that help them make well-informed, timely financial decisions."

The vision statement for the same company might read: "We see our customers developing a well-founded confidence in their financial decisions and increasing security about their financial future."

Those statements are supposed to guide and inspire everyone in the organization as they make choices about strategies, customers, markets, products and services.

■ *Strategic goals and values* provide further direction about where the organization is going, and by what route. Strategic goals define, in broad terms, how the organization intends to allocate resources to accomplish the mission and vision. Values define how it intends to behave as it does so.

A strategic goal might be "to provide a full line of financial services to small and mid-size organizations" or "to gain a competitive advantage through top-quality customer service." Statements like those provide guidance to people about where they should allocate resources, and how they should invest their time and effort.

In addition, the organization can make statements about the values it considers important—values such as partnering ("We work in partnership with our customers, freely sharing information, ideas and plans") or empowerment ("We encourage people at all levels to take initiative to meet customer needs, and support them in doing so").

Statements like those provide guidance about how people should behave in working with customers, and how managers should behave toward employees.

Mission, vision, value and strategy statements thus serve to tell people "what we are about," and to guide us all in setting priorities and choosing how to behave.

■ *Objectives and practices* are what "institutionalize" our strategies and values. They represent decisions about how we're going to execute the strategies. "Objectives" refer to the kinds of goals people set for themselves and the results they expect of their work units. "Practices" are the typical ways in which people interact with customers and others both within and outside the organization.

If we've made a strategic decision to market to small and mid-size organizations, managers might support that decision by setting specific sales objectives for those markets, or setting product-development objectives around the needs of small and mid-size customers.

Managers might support a *value* of partnership by a practice such as holding regular joint meetings with clients. They might support a value of empowerment by practices such as ensuring that front-line customer-service people have all the resources they require and the authority to take action in meeting customer needs.

Managers might support a value of empowerment by practices such as ensuring that customer-service people have all the resources they require and the authority to take action in meeting customer needs.

■ *Activities and behaviors* are the execution of the organization's intent—the ultimate determinants of its performance. They are what really happens in the organization on a day-to-day basis: the kinds of activities on which people choose to spend their time, and the way they behave as they perform those activities. Missions, visions, values and strategies are meaningful only insofar as they are translated into action through activities and behaviors.

A strategic decision to build a competitive edge through customer service becomes real when people throughout the organization engage in activities such as inviting and acting on customer feedback, looking for ways to meet unusual customer needs (rather than explaining why they can't be met), and

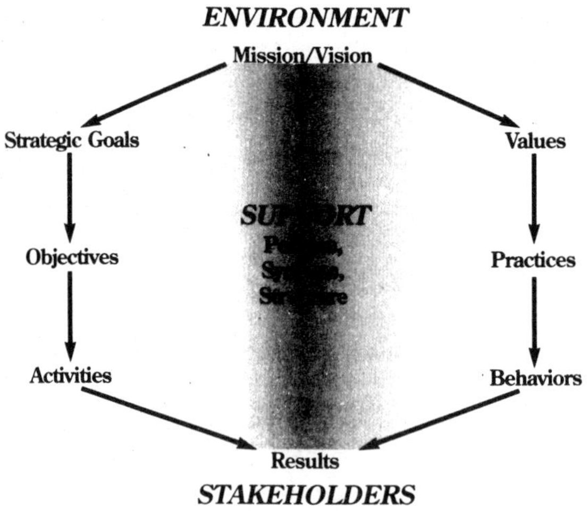

Figure 2.

testing decisions made everywhere in the organization for their potential impact on customers.

Values of partnership and empowerment become real when people engage in behaviors such as inviting employees from other groups to planning meetings or taking action to meet needs as they arise, rather than waiting for approval.

■ *Results* are the outcomes produced by the sum of all the activities and behaviors that go on within the organization. Results can be measured in a variety of ways: profits, product-quality measures, customer satisfaction and retention, sales measures, employee- and customer-attitude surveys, changes in market share and so on. The way an organization chooses to measure its performance will determine its ability to stay on track, and its ability to develop support systems and policies that are in line with values and strategies.

An organization that looks at results exclusively in terms of sales volume and annual profit will have a picture of its short-term success, but will lack information that may be critical to its long-term health, such as customer-satisfaction and retention measures.

Influences

The two parallel paths described in the model do not operate in isolation. They interact with the external environment in which the organization operates, with its internal support systems, and with its stakeholders. If we add those factors, we get an expanded model like the one shown in Figure 2.

■ The *external environment* includes factors over which the organization has limited influence, such as the economy, the sociopolitical environment, competition, governmental policies and regulations, and the state of technology. Any or all may influence our choice of strategy or values.

For instance, fierce competition in the large corporate market, and the fact that expensive technology is required to penetrate it, may enter into our decision to concentrate on the small and mid-size business market. Increasing recognition of our organization's impact on the physical environment may lead us to place greater importance on social responsibility as a value.

■ *Stakeholders* are groups significantly affected by the organization's performance, such as customers, shareholders, suppliers, and even the general public. These groups have different relationships with the organization and different expectations of it. Understanding these expectations is a key factor in decision making.

For example, while shareholders and financial analysts may judge us strictly in terms of our growth or profits, customers may be evaluating us on factors such as responsiveness, quality and range of services or environmental sensitivity. We need to take both sets of expectations into account.

■ *Support* mechanisms are systems, policies and structures that function as "performance levers." These mechanisms may help or hinder people in carrying out the activities and behaviors required to execute strategies, uphold values, and produce the desired organizational results. Support mechanisms include such things as reward and recognition systems; information and measurement systems; performance-appraisal systems; compensation and benefits plans; the design of the physical environment; organizational structure and reporting relationships; training and development; job definitions and work design; administrative policies; and so on.

For instance, compensation systems for salespeople that focus exclusively on reaching revenue targets can create pressure to violate values about the treatment of customers or to ignore strategic plans for penetrating selected markets. Similarly, centralized control policies designed to bring about consistency can get in the way of responding to customer needs unless those policies are flexible and are balanced by reward systems that support responsiveness to customers.

The goal should be to achieve a level of compatibility and consistency that allows people to devote most of their energy to achieving key results—instead of to overcoming obstacles.

■ *Organizational alignment* occurs when strategic goals and cultural values are mutually supportive, and when key components of the model are linked and compatible with each other. Market strategies should be consistent with organizational values—and perceived as such by all of our employees. Group objectives should be derived from the overall business strategy and supported by management practices. People's day-to-day activities and behaviors should be consistent with our mission, strategy and values. Systems and policies should support those activities and behaviors.

It's unlikely, and even undesirable, that any organization will reach perfection in all these areas. The goal should be to achieve a level of compatibility and consistency that allows people to devote most of their energy to achieving key results—instead of to overcoming obstacles. Some effort always will be devoted to the kind of healthy dissent that can help an organization continue to grow and adapt.

Why Another Model?

The number of possible organizational-performance "models" is probably infinite—and the number that already exists in the literature is beyond counting. In introducing yet another model, our intent is not to claim that this one is right, and others wrong. Models should be judged in terms of their usefulness, not their "correctness."

This organizational-alignment model has proven useful in several projects involving large-scale changes, both strategic and cultural. It has helped to:

- *Set a context for change.* Because the model is both comprehensive and relatively simple, it helps people focus on the "big picture" during the change efforts. Managers and others who must make decisions and communicate about change have used the model to provide a rationale for specific change efforts, to clarify the relationships among multiple-change efforts in an organization, and to recognize the potential implications of a change for other aspects of the organization.

- *"Demystify" culture.* People often think and speak about culture almost exclusively in terms of either broad, global principles ("Customer service is the watchword around here") or highly specific behaviors ("We *always* start meetings on time around here"). Focusing at either level can prove frustrating. It's hard to deal with big, squishy concepts like "trust," "integrity," or "customer service," but it's also easy to get lost in a welter of detail, focusing on specific behaviors. This model can help people to move between the two levels, look at specific behaviors and see what they imply about the things the organization really values, and identify behavioral practices that will exemplify broadly stated values or principles.

- *Adapt successful programs from other settings.* When a company is particularly successful in bringing about a desired change, it often gets a good deal of attention in the business press. Other companies quickly try to imitate the paragon, but somehow the formula fails to transfer. The organizational-alignment model has helped executives view success stories about organizations as they should be viewed: good sources of ideas, but not blueprints to be followed. The model has helped managers increase their understanding of what *their* organizations need to do to create an effective "quality" effort or to implement "concurrent engineering."

The resources and effort invested in organizational alignment—to get all or most of the organization headed in the same direction—offer enormous potential payoffs to the organization, its people and its customers. Alignment *matters.* It pays off in the profits, in job satisfaction, in quality of service, and in long-term organizational health.

Donald Tosti and Stephanie Jackson are principals in the Vanguard Consulting Group in Larkspur, CA.

The Age of Intangibles

Frank K. Sonnenberg

This article reminds managers one more time that what is important for success within and without the organization are the intangibles—passion, service, creating change, responsiveness, trust, and flexibility. These are characteristics of a quality culture, and the author does a good job of summarizing these from his book, Managing with a Conscience.

The Industrial Age brought us cars, refrigerators, washing machines and computers—equipment that can be seen, touched and demonstrated. The information Age, in contrast, is characterized by intangibles—those resources that involve the intellect and the ability to gather analyze, transmit and synthesize information.

The Information Age is characterized by intangibles—those resources that involve the intellect and the ability to gather analyze, transmit and synthesize information.

Just as you cannot measure liquids in pounds or nuclear fusion in quarts, you cannot use yesterday's standards of measurement to gauge the results of empowering your workforce; creating an environment that encourages risk and discourages fear, eliminating waste and improving business processes; encouraging continuous education and training of employees; communicating in an open and honest manner; building trust among employees; nurturing long-term relationships with suppliers and clients; working hard to develop an impeccable reputation; living according to sound business ethics; and unifying your organization around a mission and shared values.

There are eight critical success factors for competing effectively in the 21st century. You won't find these attributes in an annual report because they are intangible and difficult to quantify. But that doesn't make them any less important to an organization. These so-called soft issues are all very much like the tree that falls in the woods. In the Information Age, if we don't believe that there was a noise, maybe it is time to get our hearing checked.

Generate Passion

Results. . . Results. . . Results. In the turbulent, frenetic, dog-eat-dog times of the past decade, many believed the only way to achieve success was to get the business done—no matter what. Like slum lords, some corporations let their assets deteriorate by mistreating employees, squeezing suppliers and taking advantage of customers. What they forgot in the pursuit of short-term profits, of course, was that this significantly damages the ability of both individuals and organizations to perform in the long term.

Reprinted by permission of publisher from *Management Review*, January 1994. Copyright © 1994, American Management Association, New York. All rights reserved.

The loss of employee commitment is rampant in American business today. When investigators recently examined the situation, the number of American workers who said they were currently working to their full potential was shockingly small—23 percent. The researchers, Yankelovich and Ammerwahr, also discovered in their random sampling of American workers that "nearly half (44 percent) say they do not put any more effort into their jobs than is required to keep them. The overwhelming majority (75 percent) say that they could be significantly more effective in their jobs than they are now." The implications for productivity are startling.

There are a few companies today, however, that do offer employers and employees an idyllic match. In these companies, employees feel proud to work there. These organizations have values and viewpoints compatible with those of their employees. They are oriented toward the long haul, working toward the prevention of ills, not only curing the symptoms. They care about morals and ethics, doing what is in the best interests of their clients. They care about their impact on the environment.

Why shouldn't employees be able to work somewhere where they feel they are making a meaningful contribution? Where procedures, policies and protocol are never more important than results? And where building bonds between people is considered as important as the bottom line. Employees hope that such an organization will also care about them?

In return, companies can count on everyone pitching in when there is a crisis. When sacrifice is needed everyone should be willing to step forward. When management needs that little something extra, people should want to help. People won't have to be cajoled, they won't have to be threatened, and they certainly won't have to be bribed. They will only have to be asked.

Constantly Reinvent Yourself

An organization's ability to generate and act on new ideas can make the difference between a winner and an also-ran.

When was the last time that someone from your organization came up with a good idea? Do ideas come from a select few or is it everyone's responsibility to contribute? Does your company reward innovation or smother and stifle it with politics, protocol and procrastination? Do you welcome ideas with outstretched arms or do you listen because you have to? Do you have a formal plan for stimulating ideas or just allow them to happen? Do senior managers break down old barriers or construct new ones? Do you encourage the exploration of new ideas as a corporate philosophy, or do you do so only when you are forced to?

In this new age of competitive intensity, an organization's ability to generate and act on new ideas can make the difference between a winner and an also-ran. But just as capital equipment must be properly maintained and repaired to protect its value, creativity—an organization's most important natural resource—must be nurtured if it is to provide the greatest benefits.

Creativity makes a difference at every level and in every type of organization—either in creating new products and services, managing an advertising relationship, or finding ways to solve long-standing problems that seem unsolvable until someone with imagination throws an old ball with a new twist.

In order to stimulate creativity, organizations must first analyze the internal climate, norms and personal biases that inhibit innovation. Then they must create an environment where new ideas are welcomed and allowed to flourish—one where ideas are evaluated on their individual merits rather than the status of the person introducing them. People should be encouraged to look for "the good" in every idea and try to add value to it rather than shoot it out of the sky.

According to Rosabeth Moss Kanter, "Wise executives worry more about invisible mistakes—failing to take risks, failing to innovate, failing to create new value for customers." They know that when people aren't making mistakes they're probably not trying anything new. Everyone should recognize that being right all the time is an enormous barrier to innovation. When organizations foster a risk-averse climate, creativity will be stifled. Making mistakes, and then learning from them, is an important stage in the learning process. Employees need confidence and assurance that experimentation resulting in failure won't have repercussions.

If employees don't know where the company is heading, don't expect them to sacrifice themselves for the organization's benefit.

Build Concentration and Focus

In order to be successful, an organization must focus its efforts on those factors that are critical to its success. If you randomly select 50 people in your organization and ask them basic questions about the direction and priorities of the company, would their answers be similar? For example, what is our organization's mission? What factors are most important to our future success? How does someone get ahead in our organization? Who are our competitors and how do we differentiate ourselves from them? What are our major initiatives this year? How do you think our industry will change over the next few years, and how will our company respond to those changes?

If employees don't know where the company is heading, don't expect them to sacrifice themselves for the organization's benefit. They won't get excited about what they're doing, or put down their swords and stop their political bickering, and they won't be passionate about their careers or the future of the organization. Unless you can get common answers to the most basic questions, you foster waste, redundancies, inefficiencies, confusion and anxiety.

Importance of Internal Communication

According to a study conducted by the Columbia Business School and Dunhill Personnel Systems Inc., "When 225 middle managers were asked the top on-the-job stress points, 43 percent of the respondents pointed to a lack of information, while 31 percent of the respondents cited conflicting information."

Employees are saying that they need information today because it will be obsolete tomorrow; they are saying that it must be customized to meet their specific needs or they're just not interested. This immediate need to know more information is driven by the belief that in an age of abundant data and rapid change, you can't be productive by waiting till the end of the month to get a generically written, watered-down newsletter that doesn't provide relevant facts. While that may have been satisfactory yesterday, when everything wasn't so time sensitive, in today's global economy, it just isn't enough.

To succeed in today's competitive marketplace, organization must give internal communication the priority that it deserves. They must view it as an avenue to release the creative genius of an organization, not as a bothersome chore. After all, communication acts as a powerful agent of change, a source of continuous improvement, and a catalyst for moving the organization forward. And finally, organizations must address their internal and external audiences with a single voice to avoid sending mixed messages to the marketplace.

The difference between products will be so infinitesimal that much more will be needed to win the loyalty of the marketplace.

Devote Yourself to Service Excellence

Today's accounting systems do not accurately reflect the true costs and benefits of client relationships. For example, they ignore cash flows over the lifetime of the relationship because accounting practices do not reflect the fact that it is easier and five times cheaper to keep an existing client than it is to recruit a new one. As a result, many people think of each sales transaction as an isolated event, rather than as an investment in building a lifelong relationship with a customer; they believe if a transaction is handled badly, the cost is the loss of a single sale.

Due to global competition, companies have placed so much emphasis on, and have made such great strides in, the production process that it will be very difficult in the future to differentiate products solely on the basis of workmanship. The difference between products will be so infinitesimal that much more will be needed to win the loyalty of the marketplace. There will be growing emphasis on intangibles as the way to satisfy customers.

If organizations are to deliver service excellence, their employees must learn to recognize the value of building long-term relationships with clients and understand the consequences of not doing so. They must abandon the view that clients represent nothing more than immediate sales transactions and a quick way to increase commission checks. Instead, they must treat clients based on the potential business that they may receive over the years. They must learn to see themselves through their customers' eyes rather than focusing inwardly. They must go beyond playing a selling role, offering advice and information that provides added value to buyers and recognizes their ongoing needs. They will concentrate on building ongoing relationships with a few clients instead of endlessly searching for new prospects and then losing them as they focus on yet newer leads.

Adapt to Change

We are living in a time of unparalleled change, turbulence and uncertainty that is transforming our lives at work and at home. Can you remember the last week that your favorite news magazine or news show did not tell you about a startling new development? The speed of new information that seemed to have reached the upper limits in the 1980s has not abated. In fact, according to General Electric CEO Jack Welch, "The pace of change in the '90s, will make the '80s look like a picnic, a walk in the park."

Companies must tap all of their employees, encouraging them to be catalysts of change rather than just react to it. Instead of employing change-management techniques in response to change, then waiting for the next wave of change to arrive, the ability to change must become an everyday occurrence—it must become part of every employee's mind-set.

Change has become so constant that companies can ill afford the length of time between the development of an idea and its implementation; as soon as new approaches are introduced, they start becoming obsolete. Just as manufacturers search for faster ways to bring new products to market, companies must search for better and faster ways to institute change in their organizations. They must create a working environment where employees modify and renew themselves every day.

In addition, the way companies are managed has itself evolved. In any age of empowered workers and dismantled layers of management, companies can no longer bear to have only a few select decision makers. In the past, once decisions were made by management, employees were expected to conform. Today, such attempts will cost the commitment of employees, something empowered companies cannot afford.

In a world in which change is an everyday occurrence, business-as-usual is a guaranteed recipe for failure. To succeed, tomorrow's company must go beyond coping with change; it must embrace it. Rather than react to change, it must learn to anticipate it. Those who cling to the past will meet change with apprehension and anxiety. Only those prepared to meet the challenges of change will be rewarded with unparalleled opportunities. The payoff will go to those employees who are not only committed, but ready to lead the effort.

Respond with Speed

Time is a precious resource that cannot be replenished: It is a constant that cannot be changed. Unlike money, which flows in and out and can earn different rates of return, time is finite. We cannot get more time, but we can learn to manage the time that we have better. In the 1980s, resources were abundant enough that we seldom had to face the consequences of waste. Today, this isn't true. We can't make up for lost time by throwing resources at problems. If your competitors build products with 20 percent fewer people and aggressively market them while yours are still in the testing stage, if people are more comfortable doing things the traditional way rather than inventing a better way, if precious time is wasted in countless meetings, if innovative ideas are tied up in the approval process and if creativity is stifled by procedures, your organization will not be competitive in the 1990s.

In bureaucracies, the individual employee doesn't matter because he or she has just a single voice, and individual customers don't matter because their voices are never heard by the people who determine policy. People choose the political solution rather than the best answer. Promotions are earned through political savvy rather than performance. The "show" becomes more important than content, and rumor becomes the primary form of communication. This causes organizations to focus inward and lose touch with reality.

Just as car manufacturers design aerodynamic racing cars with as little wind resistance as possible, companies that want to finish first have to expose and then eliminate all of the nonessential business activities that add drag rather than value. To succeed, bureaucratic obstacles must be eliminated, and speed, simplicity and continuous improvement emphasized. Operational units must remain small. People must get out of their offices and in front of customers. Ad hoc task forces, composed of multifunctional groups, should be set up to tackle issues. Ideas should be chosen based on merit rather than an individual's place in the pecking order. Activities that do not add value to the client should be eliminated.

Be Flexible

Organizations must remain flexible in order to succeed; they must create an organizational structure and operating style that permits the company to take advantage of new opportunities. In the past, conventional wisdom decreed that multiple vendors increased competition and enhanced performance, and playing one supplier against another was good business. Today's collective wisdom suggests quite the opposite. As organizations focus more of their efforts on the things they do best and those that are critical to their success, they will rely more and more on external resources, outsourcing, strategic alliances and building strong external relationships.

The only way to ensure that those relationships will last is to start with honorable intentions, make a commitment, and expend the time and effort so everybody wins. To do this, keep in mind that formal contracts don't make successful relationships, people do . A partnership is successful to the degree that it replaces the traditional "we versus them" mentality with a new "we" that allows everyone involved to grow and reach their full potential. A partnership will succeed in the long run when both sides work for their common good rather than trying to get the upper hand. When greed takes over, supposed partners spend all of their time trying to out-negotiate each other and both end up losing. Moreover, in these situations, one of the organizations is likely to come out noticeably ahead of the other, ultimately causing jealousy and resentment.

Build Trust

"Workers simply don't trust management," according to a 1992 *Industry Week* survey. While 87 percent of the workers polled think it is 'very important' that 'management is honest, upright, and ethical,' only 39 percent believe that it is."

If businesses are to thrive in the global marketplace, trust must be more than something that is talked about; it must be at the core of everything that is done. Trust is not an abstract, theoretical, idealistic goal forever beyond our reach. Trust—or a lack of it—is inherent in every action that we take and affects everything that we do. Organizations cannot be jungles where only the fittest survive, living in a state of battle readiness in order to meet the grueling tests of everyday corporate life.

Just as high levels of trust reduce friction among employees, increase productivity and stimulate growth, low levels of trust adversely affect relationships, stifle innovation and hamper the decision-making process. Employees in organizations marked by low levels of trust usually operate under higher levels of stress, spend a great deal of effort covering their backsides, justifying past decisions, and conducting witch hunts or looking for scapegoats when something doesn't work out. This prevents them from focusing on the work they should be doing and the free exchange of ideas that results in innovative solutions. The constant need to prove one's worth promotes short-term fixes rather than long-term solutions.

Organizations cannot be jungles where only the fittest survive.

Trust in an organization is like love in a marriage: It bonds people together and makes them strong and effective. Trust in a relationship increases security, reduces inhibitions and defensiveness, and frees people to share feelings and dreams. Trust makes you free to put your deepest fears in the palms of your colleagues' hands, knowing that they will be treated with care. Trust allows you to be yourself and maintain your own values without worrying about acceptance. Trust makes colleagues willing to spend time together and make sacrifices for one another. Trust is an expression of faith that makes it easy for colleagues to have confidence in one another's ability to perform well and to know that they will be there if needed. Trust means that promises made will be kept, and it also means that when a promise is not kept, it was probably for good cause. And finally, trust means that a relationship will last not because it is good business, but because the relationship itself is valued.

Frank K. Sonnenberg is a marketing expert and a writer. This article is based on his book, Managing with A Conscience *(McGraw-Hill, 1993).*

Quality and Jobs Are Synonymous

Armand V. Feigenbaum

Feigenbaum, one of the pioneers of quality management, argues forcefully here for the connection between the practices of quality management and the creation of jobs in the American economy. We place it in the "Cultural Transformation" section of the yearbook because it provides food for thought for those responsible for creating and sustaining a culture that supports quality. If a manger needed any incentive for implementing TQM, it should be growth and the creation of jobs, making everyone winners.

Experience in this country and abroad clearly demonstrates that there is an inseparable relationship between quality and jobs. In fact, quality leadership is the best single job creation program in this intensely competitive world. This is equally true for small and large firms. Strong quality programs have been proven to be essential in small and medium-size firms in export as well as local markets, because value means quality to today's consumer—from the homemaker to the industrial company. Today, when a customer is satisfied with quality—likes what he or she buys—that customer tells eight people; when the customer is dissatisfied, he or she tells twenty-two. That's the hard arithmetic of quality's effect on sales growth in the U.S. marketplace.

International quality leadership is essential to domestic quality leadership for a business today—even though there may not yet be much import competition or interest in exporting on the part of the company. The U.S. Commerce Department estimates that 70 percent of all products manufactured in the United States are now targets for strong import competition; General Systems Company studies indicate that nearly 100 percent of all American nondefense manufactured products will be vulnerable to import competition within this decade.

Services are not far behind. A communications satellite is indifferent to whether jobs of the back office of a financial intermediary or an information processor are in New York, Tokyo, or Bombay, as long as they are quality-efficient. In the Far East, software development in such English-speaking countries as the Philippines, India, and Malaysia costs only one-tenth to one-twentieth of similar developments in the United States, and these countries are aggressively positioning themselves with the quality capability for this

---

Reprinted by permission of John Wiley & Sons, Inc, from *National Productivity Review*, Spring 1994. Copyright © 1994 by John Wiley & Sons, Inc. All rights reserved.

kind of job creation and business development. This means that U.S. companies will face many more "Japans" in the 1990s. Murphy's Law, internationalized, says that if a company can face foreign competition, it will.

There is a certain type of leadership needed to implement total quality as a fundamental way of managing competitive improvement, not merely as a loose collection of quality technique projects and fireworks-display motivational seminars that has so constricted quality development in the past. Total quality leadership today is based on the total rejection of a false management doctrine that dominated many public- as well as private-sector organizations throughout the 1970s and much of the 1980s. According to that doctrine, good management and successful improvement meant getting the ideas out of the boss's head and into the hands of the workers plus regular doses of management cheerleading, underwritten with extensive technique-based seminar programs. But the reality was that when employees returned to their jobs to use what they'd heard, they continued to face (1) ambiguous management processes that they couldn't influence, (2) having to thread their way through organizations that were a group of separate departmental silos, and (3) the reality that they were still being nickel-and-dimed to death in their work. In such an environment only incremental improvement could, at best, be hoped for. This is a principal reason why some of the great companies that were this country's business pacesetters of the 1980s are now urgently searching for fundamental changes in their ways of working. And it is a major reason why some of the admirably intentioned national public-sector improvement programs from the Hoover and Grace Commissions on down gradually died and were buried without autopsy.

This means that U.S. companies will face many more "Japans" in the 1990s. Murphy's Law, internationalized, says that if a company can face foreign competition, it will.

Today we know that good management means reintroducing into the U.S. workplace what these management practices of the 1970s and 1980s overlooked or even purged—that is, the fundamental improvement strength that comes from giving workers the freedom to innovate, letting them solve problems democratically, and encouraging teamwork. The improvement centerpoint of many of the private-sector companies that are America's business leaders today is built around a form of organizational populism that encourages human strengths combined with strong management leadership. This kind of management has the personal know-how to establish the organization's quality playbook of the work and teamwork processes that guide improvement and then to quarterback the implementation practices that help every person in the organization think, decide, and act on how to accelerate quality service.

There are several basic infrastructure obstacles blocking management quality improvement in the United States today. The first is a change in fundamental human values and expectations. This is most apparent within the U.S. marketplace and in the slow growth in many U.S. markets. While the value trends are of the American as a consumer of private-sector products and service, he or she is also the taxpayer with similarly escalating quality expectations for public-sector services.

One of the fundamental but little recognized reasons for the dismal sales results in some U.S. markets during these past few years has been what can best be described as a buyer's quality strike. Sales remain stubbornly low, even though buyer disposable income that could be spent on the products and services remains at high levels. For many years General Systems has been surveying consumer patterns in major U.S. markets, and the data have shown that buyers have continued to make quality a progressively more important consideration than price in their purchase decisions. As the 1990s have proceeded, there has been a fundamental sharpening of this attitude as buyers have become convinced by the widespread advertising and media attention to quality that any private- or public-sector organization can provide essentially perfect quality service if it is properly managed. Survey data for the year 1992 show that nine out of ten buyers now make quality their primary purchasing standard, but in these days of economic constraint, they express this as affordable quality—quality, price, time-saving considerations, and service—not simply as a tradeoff between quality and price.

The data have shown that buyers have continued to make quality a progressively more important consideraton than price in their purchase decisions.

This is a statement of the fundamental social and economic change that has been escalating throughout the United States in the past decade. The economic stability and the lifestyles of consumers, as well as the work processes and business velocity of companies, now depend almost completely on the reliable, predictable operation of products and services, with little tolerance for the time and cost of any failures—something very different from the past.

The organizations that understand today's user values and expectations recognize that in today's markets quality leadership depends on accelerating the increase in the things gone right that consumers want—total quality—not merely reducing the things gone wrong—traditional quality control. For example, in the private sector, routinely washing automobiles after a dealer service call is a factor that many consumers identify as a principal dealer service value differentiator, because they perceive that it shows care and because it saves them time and effort. They assume—rightly or wrongly—that any responsible dealer can accomplish any technical tasks, such as an emissions check, about as well as any other. Quality expectations in the 1990s aren't merely measured in such traditional terms as quality defects, zero or otherwise. They are, instead, measured in terms of the total user perception of quality service.

Quality expectations in the 1990s measured in terms of the total user perception of quality service.

Another infrastructure issue is that, with some notable exceptions, quality improvement is only now entering America's service sector in a major way. Over the past decade, the emphasis on quality in the United States has been largely centered in the manufacturing sector, with such positive results as the economic revival of the U.S. automobile industry. Over this same period, however, some U.S. service organizations have grown out of touch with the rapid changes in U.S. values, employee attitudes, and management approaches. These disconnected organizations are increasingly isolated from the service quality that their users want, because the attitude change that helped to place U.S. automobile manufacturers back on the growth track—acceptance that quality is what the user, not the manufacturer, says it is—is not yet recognized in many service organizations. It remains very difficult for service providers in health care, education, or environment, for example, to accept the principle that in the 1990s service quality is the call of the service receiver, not the service provider. This difficulty is compounded by the fact that, although manufacturers can sometimes unscramble broken eggs by fixing or replacing a defective part, the option of a service defect recall isn't open to services.

But service-sector leaders in industries ranging from financial intermediaries to hospitality providers have now begun to demonstrate that there is no more effective way to return this hidden organization to effective capacity than through systematically improving service quality. The service providers that have been doing this have achieved 25 percent and more additional high-quality output with their existing resources.

In the face of these and other infrastructure issues, why the durability of total quality, especially when the media report that queasiness about quality continues to grow; when some business, education, and government institutions hear about the white, the yolk, and the albumen of total quality, but not about the total quality egg itself; and when there are generalized discussions about quality programs, but no coupling with an explanation of the hard-edged improvements they accomplish? The durability in the face of all this is because total quality is the competitive connector today—it connects organizations with their customers, service receivers, employees, and suppliers in volatile times. By doing so, it helps create jobs—a top priority if we are to cast off today's economic doldrums.

President of General Systems, Inc. in Pittsfield, Massachusetts, Armand V. Feigenbaum, Ph.D., is the originator of total quality control. He is also founding chairman of the International Academy for Quality Control and the first American to receive France's Georges Borel Prize for preeminence in quality.

Can the U.S. Army Become a Learning Organization?

Margaret J. Wheatley

This article reviews Wheatley's experience as a consultant to the U.S. Army and demonstrates that even an organization as tradition-bound as the Army can and must transform itself into a more efficient and effective organization. The principles of TQM, while not specifically discussed in this article, inform all the changes Wheatley describes.

Strong stereotypes of military leadership abound; it's a system of *yes-sirs* where rank and privilege create carefully structured relationships and status, where spans of control are tight and narrow, and where if the leader says "Charge" everybody blindly follows.

Whatever the historic accuracy of these stereotypes, the US Army is faced with as great a need to change as any other organization. Since the end of the Cold War in 1989, and the Gulf War in 1991, the Army has been asked to adjust to a set of new realities. Changing and declining resources, available technologies, and an expanded mission have all bombarded the organization.

Since the Gulf War, the Army has downsized by over 400,000 people; it is operating with a 40 percent smaller budget than projected five years ago; it has withdrawn over 100,000 soldiers from overseas bases and become a primarily US based force capable of projecting itself anywhere in the world on short notice, and must now be prepared to serve in several new ways.

The stable Cold War era of a known enemy, whose moves and thoughts could be studied and countered after careful analysis, has shifted to a fluid, turbulent world stage of increasing complexity and unpredictability.

Whereas in the past the Army was either fighting a war or maintaining itself in peace, now it is increasingly called on to intervene in a category of activities labeled *operations other than war.*

New roles and goals: operations other than war . . . These new activities for the Army range from counter-drug actions, to earthquake, riot, hurricane and flood relief, to nation building and peace keeping activities. Last year, a group of highly trained special forces found themselves offering educational

Reprinted with permission from the *Journal for Quality and Participation,* March 1994. Copyright © 1994 by the Association for Quality and Participation.

activities in oceanic bio-diversity to a West African nation as part of their nation-building activities.

The pace of Army activities is also increasing dramatically. In the Spring of 1990, 6,100 soldiers were active in 45 countries. Now, nearly 21,500 soldiers are operating in more than 70 countries—nearly a 300 percent increase in operational tempo.

The range of potential enemies (or allies) includes:

- Armies of agrarian societies, religious groups, tribes, guerrilla bands, and clan leaders. . .
- Industrial armies of nation-states. . .
- High-tech forces of post-industrial, knowledge-based societies.

Battles may occur in any number of cultural, climactic, and political environments.

Jazz management. . . Given this incredible mix of unpredictable new activities that exist in a fuzzy range somewhere between war and peace, Army Chief of Staff General Gordon R. Sullivan has adopted the metaphor of jazz management.

He believes that soldiers still must be classically trained, but then be able to improvise in these widely divergent operations. In 1992, he stated that the Army was facing: "Perhaps our greatest challenge since WW II: to master the elements of change and retain our world-class, qualitative edge into the 21st Century."

The Central Change Questions

The questions which have been the focus of attention for the Army's senior leaders for the past few years include:

- How do you take an institution like the US Army and reinvent it for the 21st Century?
- How do you create a force that is not only flexible and prepared to serve at a moment's notice, but also is able to grow in its range of activities?
- How do you build in versatility to such a large institution?
- How do you move from rigid and protective hierarchies and rank to a learning organization?
- And as a commanding general, what is your role in leading and inspiring such profound changes?

Working with a sense of urgency in an organization which, in terms of its mission, has very little margin of error, they have established a number of creative initiatives. Each of these is an attempt to cut across stove pipes, to get away from planning and appropriation cycles that traditionally take from eight to 15 years (or more,) and to build in feedback loops to learn immediately from its experiences in a rapidly shifting global environment.

An invitation to observe, comment and assist. . . During the last months of 1993, I was invited to observe several major Army commands, and to comment on what I thought of their change efforts. I was both surprised and impressed by what I saw (I had no prior experience with the Army as an organization,) and a bit awed at the degree of change required of them.

Change efforts currently underway vary from fundamental redesign of functions and processes, to pushing decision making down, to development of sophisticated data bases to facilitate planning to total quality initiatives. But I was especially intrigued by innovations focused on developing the capacity for the Army to become a rapid-response learning organization. (General Sullivan states that the Army is and must be a learning organization.)

I was especially intrigued by innovations focused on developing the capacity for the Army to become a rapid-response learning organization.

Critical Organizational Learning Factors

In observing their initiatives at creating such an organization, I looked for certain factors. I believe that learning can only occur in an organization that is rich in connections and relationships that make it possible to *know what it knows:*

- The organization has to have the kind and quality of information and relationships that make its experience available to itself . . .
- It needs to have access to itself everywhere in order to learn from its own experiences . . .
- It also needs to have a culture that supports action followed by reflection, rather than analysis that never ends, or actions that are never understood.

Assessing learning capacities . . . I assess the learning capacity of the organization on three key variables: information, relationships and self-reference:

- For any initiative, I want to understand how the innovation treats information:

  Does it create means for the expansion and liberation of knowledge?

  What kinds of opportunities are there for the creation of new information, and for increasing access to information by more and more of the organization?

- I also look to see how the proposed change affects relationship.

  Does it weave together people who formerly were isolated from one another?

  Does it include more and more people who were once considered outsiders to the organization?

  Does it understand that by creating new relationships it creates valuable new information, and thereby extends its capacity to flex and change as required?

- Lastly, I want to understand how the innovation affects the identity of the organization.

  Do activities contribute to building a strong core in terms of values, mission, competencies?

  Is a self-referential capacity being developed, so that the organization understands who it is in the midst of turbulent and changing demands?

  When making a decision to change, what does it reference?

  Can it use its history and traditions to make sense of new information, without staying locked in that history?

  Is it building new traditions from its present activities?

Three Army Learning Innovations

In observing many areas of innovations in several commands of the US Army, I have been intrigued by the types of questions noted above. In the Army I observed, the imperative to change is felt everywhere, and there are many serious and important innovations occurring in different places. I'd like to describe three that I feel are significant in terms of increasing the Army's capacity to learn and adapt continuously.

After Action Reviews

In the late 1970s, the Army instituted a process of self-examination whose only parallel, in the words of one general, is in Maoist cell groups. *After Action Reviews (AARs)* occur after every training event or actual battle.

During an *AAR* soldiers and their commanders gather to probe in detail:

- What went on . . .
- What actions occurred . . .
- What actions should have occurred . . .
- Who did what.

Every participant in these *AARs* is under a microscope, being called to accountability by their colleagues for their decisions and actions during the time under review. Behaviors of the leader, individuals, and the group ar all analyzed. They are equals, engaged in *discovery learning*. Soldiers describe these sessions as brutal, sweat-inducing—and absolutely necessary for their learning.

The process has become so ingrained that during the Gulf War *AARs* would be held spontaneously in the rear of a truck—called by anyone independent of rank.

These AARs have fostered an expectation that behaviors and decisions will be reviewed, and that everyone will benefit from the learning, no matter how difficult it is to hear at the time.

Other armies have looked at this process, recognized its value, yet been quite clear that nothing in their culture would support these soul searching processes.

As I observed one AAR, I was struck by the benefit that any organization could achieve by these detailed self-examinations, and yet how swiftly most would flee from them. But for the Army, the need is quite clear: "Learning is less fearful than failure in battle." Learning has a higher value here; it's recognized as a source of safety.

Tradition of teamwork supports the process . . . This mutual exploration of failures also is possible because of the Army's strong tradition of teamwork. Unlike corporate teams, soldiers and leaders know that they must be able to depend on one another for their lives. There is a quality of mutual support and respect among soldiers and between them and their leaders that non-military organizations can only envy.

Teamwork and compassion . . . Putting drill sergeant stereotypes to rest, nowhere in my organizational wanderings have I observed more compassionate and caring leadership than in the Army.

Nowhere in my organizational wanderings have I observed more compassionate and caring leadership than in the Army.

This true comradeship was beautifully captured in a letter I was shown on my first visit to the Army. The letter was written during the Civil War, from General Sherman to General Grant (near Memphis, March 10, 1864.) In one phrase, Sherman summed up the essence of this spirit of love and reliability:

"I knew that wherever I was that you thought of me, and if I got in a tight place, you would come, if alive."

The Louisiana Maneuvers

The second major initiative that dramatically creates conditions of a learning organization is the *Louisiana Maneuvers (LAM),* an initiative begun by Chief of Staff General Sullivan in 1992 to "change the way we change." *(In 1941, 400,000 troops were massed in Louisiana in order to test out concepts of doctrine and battle strategies and gain insight into equipment and organizational alternatives for World War II.)*

In reviving this historic event, but giving it a modern day spin by also using technology rather than large troop exercises, the Chief of Staff created "an evaluation vehicle to assess new ideas in *real-time* and shortcut Cold War policy decision methodologies."

Virtual reality and live simulations. . . The modern LAM is an approach to supporting greater and greater versatility in the Army—finding ways to operate outside the existing structure in *real-time* to test out broad, future-focused issues.

Using a mix of simulations, virtual reality, new and untested technologies and live field tests, the 1990s LAM attempts to gain immediate and accurate information about those challenges that will most affect it in the future. This is paradoxical work; as one general remarked: "We need to apply technologies to paradigms we don't yet know."

In its first year, *LAM* resources were applied to ten issues a year, chosen from among an initial 200 issues discussed in two days of electronic dialogue among all Major Generals, and then decided upon and championed by the Senior General Staff (who meet every six months to review progress.)

In 1993, these issues covered a broad area, from detailed exploration of advanced technologies for the *digitized battlefield* to developing better procedures for tracking equipment. *(Studying processes for moving and inventorying of equipment led the Army to study the work of Schneider Trucking, Hunt Brothers and United Parcel Service. Within two months they achieved "total asset visibility" equal to UPS.)*

Soldiers in Somalia and Europe recently have used state-of-the-art technologies for both humanitarian and peace-keeping missions that were tested quickly, without traditional R & D, or test and evaluation procedures.

LAM facilitates quick study and response, using all available resources as "a forcing function to get available technologies into the hands of soldiers."

Cutting through stovepipes and silos. . . Whatever the area under study, *LAM* calls upon resources throughout the Army, irrespective of rank or function. Soldiers are directly involved in the experiments and solutions that they will be called upon to execute. In ignoring traditional barriers, *LAM* forces the organization to mobilize itself in new ways. And its activities always result in changes in products or procedures with a speed new to the Army.

Soldiers are directly involved in the experiments and solutions that they will be called upon to execute.

Historically, weapons development and procurement bogged down the Army in a planning to execution cycle that took eight to fifteen years. Now, those staff assigned to *LAM* move freely through the Army's structure, causing things to happen in record time. "We are," as their leader says, "very flat, brainy, and go for it."

Leadership and Battle Labs

A corollary set of activities, built on the same laboratory/testing model, is the third initiative of note. These are the *Battle Labs,* begun under the guidance of General Frederick R. Franks Jr., Commanding General of the Training and Doctrine Command (TRADOC).[1] The creation of the *Battle Labs* contains a crucial lesson for all leaders intent on change. There came a point, General Franks commented, "when I couldn't wait any longer. I decided to act as if the organization was already where it needed to be.

Five laboratory environments were then created; places where issues specific to the changing dynamics and requirements of battle could be experimented with, and their results moved swiftly into practice.

A whole systems approach to warfare. . . Battle Labs look at war under a microscope by creating combined teams, with all disciplines represented, to look at horizontal integration across the commands, or sometimes across the armed services. The areas chosen reflect the profound change in the concept of battle; strategy now involves an integrated view of warfare, an area known

1. (TRADOC began in 1973 as an institution to rethink warfare, and examine the entire spectrum of war fighting needs, form doctrine, to training, to organizational requirements. It is the largest educational system in the Western world, operating the equivalent of many universities for officers, along with literally hundreds of training centers.)

Experimenting with the Art of Command. . .

I was particularly struck by one *Battle Lab* that experiments with the art of battle command. With a slight shift in language, this lab is grappling with issues that plague all leaders today, whatever the organization.

Their purpose is to find ways to develop "agile, versatile, intuitive leaders not fixed in place," who have access to all information and who can thereby maintain *situational awareness.*

In defining the new roles of battle commanders, this lab works to understand the appropriate balance between technology and face-to-face leadership skills, realizing that the human factor in technology is the key variable.

Their central question is: "How does the commander obtain the cohesion of trust necessary for sharing danger while leveraging technology?" And their orientation towards solutions is also instructive. No longer searching for the perfect answer developed after years of paralyzing study, they now seek to get it *nearly right.*

The commander's job is also to be in the right place, at the right time, and to get it *about right.* (The Army works under another prime, perhaps reverse principle. In the words of military historian Michael Howard, the Army "can't get *it* too badly wrong.")

as *battle space. (Battle space continues to expand, from the 3 km that Napoleon had to be concerned with, to the more than 300 kilometers that modern ground weaponry can reach. With heavy reliance on satellites, space has become the fourth dimension of battle.)* The Gulf War was fought by a *Celestial Army;* The first instance where combat forces largely were deployed, sustained, commanded and controlled through satellite communications.)

The work of the *Battle Labs* is more specific than that of *LAM,* but they work in close concert with the *LAM* approach, feeding results and technologies into *LAM's* global issues (*LAM* then conducts large scale maneuvers where many ideas and technologies can be tested simultaneously.)

Labs create breakthroughs in product development cycle time. . . These labs have resulted in some spectacular results, notably in bringing new technologies into use with amazing speed.

Bringing a new Forward Looking Infrared Radar on-line in record time. . . For example in determining how best to create the next generation of *Forward Looking Infrared Radar (FLIR),* a *Battle Lab* did joint testing of several emerging technologies with other branches of the armed forces in February 1993. They learned that they could use a common module that would fit 79 systems with only the development of interface kits. On bid, four vendors created products that fit the Army's needs. These are now in the budget and the equipment will be fielded no later than early 1996.

Battle Labs facilitate radical change in vendor relationships. . . This *Battle Lab* process also represents a new way of working with vendors. No longer are specifications developed, prototypes developed, modifications ordered and then equipment produced. In the *Battle Labs,* before anything gets documented, it is tested and defined through use. Documentation, which used to absorb countless years and costs that escalated sometimes by as much as 100 times, now occurs only after the system has been tried and tested by soldiers.

Battle Labs absorb and process information from many sources. . . Information from the *Center for Army Lessons Learned,* where past battle and training experiences are collected and analyzed, are combined with futures studies and emerging technologies. The end products of a *Battle Lab's* work are specifically defined requirements in doctrine, training, leader development, organization design, and material—all integrated horizontally across the force.

Each of the *Battle Labs* works across the organization, involving real soldiers in the solutions they will be asked to use. Procedures and organization charts get lost in the shuffle.

The Battle Lab and re-inventing government. . . The work of each lab is integrated through one integrative battle lab, and through a database that combines a work of all. These labs have now become a prototpye model for the Department of Defense in its *Re-inventing Government* activities.

Structures and Processes That Facilitate Learning

Each of these three major initiatives, I believe, contribute important learning about structures and processes that can facilitate an agile, versatile, and well-prepared army.

Integrators, Not Incubators

While *Battle Labs* and *LAM* may appear to be *incubators*—special organizations removed from the fray of day-to-day constraints—on closer look they do not operate in that mode. Each of them works across the Army, identifying useful resources wherever they exist. But they can work with those resources in new ways, outside of existing procedures and boundaries.

What makes these three ventures successful at achieving both quality decisions and speed is that they:

- Stay within the existing organization, but with the mandate to force new relationships, and to engage in activities that generate rich and diverse information. . .

- They involve members and resources of the organization, but ignore its structures and standard operating procedures. . .

- They combine and recombine the elements of the organization to effectively test a new weapons systems, or a new doctrine. Any part of the organization potentially can be part of the laboratory.

Currently only the *After Action Reviews* exist everywhere in the organization—which at this point, represents a major shift in the culture.

Both *LAM* and *Battle Labs* are demonstrating to the whole Army its capacity for quick and smart decisions. In modeling this behavior, they demonstrate that this level of thinking and responsiveness is possible in such a procedure-bound organization.

Leadership and Inspiring Change

I believe that through the continued use of these processes the Army will gradually create a new belief system, one that will change the Army's sense of itself. Through these three processes, they are demonstrating:

- The conditions under which good thinking and fast response occur. . .
- The intelligence that exists in the Army, intelligence that becomes even smarter as it is joined with others. . .
- That the way the Army has been structured, with its rank, procedures and go slow policies, is not the Army that will continue.

By ignoring its present operating mode, these processes and structures are creating present time experience with a future way of operating. This is what General Franks meant by his strategy of "acting as if the organization was already where it needed to be."

In creating organization-wide laboratory environments, these initiatives underline a key learning for leaders who are trying to inspire change.

With both *LAM* and *Battle Labs,* two commanding generals created the means for the organization to see and experience for itself how it could learn from itself and change. They created important initial conditions for experimentation and learning, and the means for broad involvement.

Inspiring Continued Change

But once those conditions were in place, the inspiration for continued change comes not from the leadership, but from the successes that are occurring in many places around the organization. In this way, the organization provides its own inspiration, and also establishes its own pace of change.

But once those conditions were in place, the inspiration for continued change comes not from the leadership, but from the successes that are occurring in many places around the organization.

People learn what is possible by listening to the experiences of their peers, rather than the inspiring words of their leaders. As they are able to reference more and more of these stories, the organization changes its beliefs about itself. It comes to know itself as capable of change, even in an organization as tradition and policy-bound as the US Army.

How do you take an institution the size of the Army and transform it into a learning organization? I believe you start with these types of high profile, broad reaching initiatives which give the organization opportunities to experiment with new ways of learning.

These efforts build new networks of connections, and new levels of information that enable it to be both responsive and smart. As people notice these efforts, the organization recognizes that it does have new and different capacities for thinking and doing. It comes to know itself as a learning organization because of personal, constant, and visceral experiences with the power of its thinking and its abilities to act. It learns it can be what it needs to become.

References and Resources

Quotes from Army personnel came from author's interview notes, or internal Army reports.

Fred Kofman and Peter M. Senge, "Communities of Commitment: The Heart of Learning Organizations," *Organizational Dynamics*, Fall 1993.

Jack Scarborough, "Revisiting the Military Stereotype," *Journal of Management Inquiry*, September, 1993.

Alvin and Heidi Toffler, *War and Anti-War* (Boston: Little, Brown & Co., 1993).

Margaret Wheatley is president of the Berkana Institute and a principal in Kellner, Rogers & Wheatley, Inc. Her recent book Leadership and the New Science *(San Francisco: Berret-Koehler, 1992) was named "Best Management Book of 1993" in Industry Week Magazine.*

Quality Transformation

VOICE OF THE CUSTOMER

Customer Training: More Than a Sales Training Tool

Margaret Kaeter

Customer education can be one of the ties that bind customers and suppliers. This article shows how companies that show a concern for and then train customers in the use of their products are adding a dimension to their offering that can help sustain their competitive advantage.

From the moment the first ancient craftsman patiently explained to a potential customer why his leather was more durable, his pottery more beautiful, or his tailoring more exact than his competitors', customer education has had a role in the world of commerce. Savvy marketers quickly learned that educating customers on a product's benefits and uses was an integral part of the sales process.

The lesson was enduring: Until recently, customer training almost always boiled down to "selling disguised as training," sayd Michael Wolf, a partner with Booz Allen Hamilton, a New York management consulting firm. In the classic approach, companies produce elaborate product-use seminars, written materials and videos that subtly—or not so subtly—show customers that the sponsor's product is the best solution to a generic problem. This brand of

Reprinted with permission from *Training* Magazine, March 1994. Copyright © 1994. Lakewood Publications, Minneapolis, MN. All rights reserved. Not for resale.

customer education often is informative and can help gain loyalty for a particular product or supplier, but it rarely is designed to do more than simply complement sales efforts.

Today, the story is changing. As companies struggle to develop unique competitive niches in a fast-changing and fiercely competitive world economy, some are discarding traditional product-management approaches in favor of uncovering and responding to their customers' needs. That focus has forced many to look at their customer-education strategies in a new light. In some cases, customer training has become the very cornerstone of efforts to reorient every facet of the business to respond to customer needs.

"A great deal of today's customer training is an attempt to return to a more personalized approach, where you're in direct contact [with] and understand the needs of customers," says Joyce Doria, vice president of human resources, quality and training systems in Booz Allen Hamilton's Bethesda, MD, office. "People are beginning to see that customers need information and that the impact of providing it is positive for everyone."

"Customer education has been a real linchpin for us as a company," confirms Leslie Ratay, corporate communications manager for the Pewaukee, WI-based printing company Quad/Graphics. The firm offers customer-training activities such as CAMP/Quad, a periodic three-day gathering designed to introduce about 30 customers at a time to the world of printing and Quad/Graphics operations. "It positions us not just as a printing company but also as a research-and-development organization and a know-how company."

In short, state-of-the-art customer-training programs are not so much sales tools as elements of a broader marketing strategy. Some programs view the customer as an actual partner on the business team. "They create a strategic alliance between the customer and supplier," says Wolf, adding that it can be difficult for a competitor to break in once that alliance is solidified.

Some programs view the customer as an actual partner on the business team.

"When you make your customers successful, they'll make you successful," adds Doria. "It's a myth that increased attention to the customer costs more money. [Customer education] is one area where companies are seeing the payback of reaching out to the customer."

Building Distinction

Most of these in-depth and broad-ranging programs are still product-oriented, but they focus on delivering the information customers need to be more efficient users of the company's product—not directly on the company's desire to sell more of the product.

"It used to be that you'd buy a computer and they'd show you how to plug it into the power outlet," says Don Lehmann, a professor of business at Columbia Univesity in New York and executive director of the Cambridge, MA-based Marketing Science Institute, an organization that directs academic research on business issues. "Now suppliers know that you'll be reluctant to replace the familiar with something new unless you get adequate training."

Many companies also find that providing in-depth product-use training actually saves them money. About 40 percent of perceived quality problems occur because the customer doesn't know how to use the product, says John Goodman, president of Technical Assistance Research Program (TARP), a Washington, DC-based consulting company noted for its research on customer-service issues. "Companies are finally starting to quantify the impact on loyalty if the customer has an unplesant surprise," he says. "They're finding that it's much cheaper to prevent the problems through training. It costs five to 10 times more to get a new customer than to keep one you already have."

Many companies also find that providing in-depth product-use training actually saves them money.

Goodman recalls a foreign auto manufacturer that was receiving complaints from customers whose manual-transmission cars wouldn't start on the first turn of the key. The company spent hundreds of hours of engineering time trying to locate the problem. In the end, it discovered the glitch: the clutch had to be depressed to the floor before the car would start. But no one had informed customers. "You can bet that people weren't telling their friends to buy that car," Goodman says. "Yet it wasn't a quality problem at tall. It was a customer-training problem."

Product training also can give companies the chance to explain unique qualities of products that are perceived to have few differences from competitive goods. "Many product categories are more mature today. They've become like commodities," says Lehmann. "As a result, the supplier needs to educate the customer, to tell him or her what is different about this product." Minneapolis-based Aveda Corp., for example, distributes eduational brochures that describe the value of its all natural cosmetics and hair-care products in environmental terms, a tactic that has firmly differentiated its product in a crowded market and convinced many consumers to pay as much as 10 time more for an item that, arguably, does the same job as its cheaper counterparts.

Meeting Complex Challenges

Some organizations, faced with a combination of marketing challenges, have found customer training the most effective way to build a competitive advantage.

St. Paul, MN-based 3M's Occupational Health & Environmental Safety division, for example, manufactures industrial respiratory-protection products as well as sorbent materials and containers for cleanup and handling of oil spills and hazardous chemicals. Because the respiratory-products industry is regulated, products must meet minimum performance criteria set by the federal government. Consequently, manufacturers compete in areas such as product features, advantages and benefits; new technology; product-line depth; sales and distribution networks; and price.

In many cases, however, the clearest factor differentiating one manufacturer from another is customer education. "By educating our customers, our sales force is providing a value-added service as well as selling product," says Stephen Henderson, the 3M division's marketing-communications manager.

The division uses a three-pronged approach to customer training. 3M provides purchaser and end-user training, distributor sales and product training, and extensive training for the 3M sales rep who, in turn, will train purchasers and end users. "Our philosophy is to surround the customer with people who are educated and can help them define issues and areas of opportunity within work processes that will lead to solving problems," says Phil Heinz, the division's training supervisor. "Our key customers, the people who actually make the decision to purchase our product, are the industrial hygienists and safety directors at companies. These are very knowledgeable, well-educated, sophisticated buyers. If we are going to help them, we need this surrounding approach."

Even though the division sells exclusively through distributors, the first prong of the customer-education effort is geared to the needs of industrial hygienists. 3M offers a respirator-selection guide that is updated yearly, a toll-free hot line with technical-service operators on duty during working hours, and a software program designed to aid product selection. (The computer program serves as an added plus for the customer because an audit trail can be printed to show government regulators from the Occupational Safety and Health Administration [OSHA] exactly how a decision was made.) In addition, a quarterly publication updates industrial hygienists and safety managers on regulatory changes, new-product information, and the results of various studies of the product's performance in work settings.

Once the proper respirator has been selected, workers themselves must be trained to use it. In the United States, OSHA requires employees to be trained at least yearly in the selection, fit,use and maintenance of the respirator or respirators they wear. (In countries that have varying regulations and in those that have no regulations regarding respirator-use training, 3M applies the U.S. or European standard.) Large companies, of course, have staffs to deliver this training, but small- to mid-sized operations don't. "It's a major liability concern for these companies," says Henderson. "Half of their concern is finding the right product, but the other half is training employees to use it correctly."

3M developed a program to train its sales representatives to offer end-user training that satisfies OSHA's requirements. Every sales representative receives in-depth training on proper hygiene practices, technical knowledge, government regulations and product applications, "Training programs are in a constant state of evolution," says Henderson. "We update the programs regularly as a way of helping our customers meet or exceed government requirements.

The division also offers a train-the-trainer program for companies that want to take over their own respirator-use training. "We view customer training as a part of servicing the product," says Henderson. "It gains customer loyalty because we are providing a legitimate service to our cusomers."

Ensuring Sales

End-user and purchaser education is only a portion of 3M's commitment, however. Since the division sells through distributors, Heinz figures that the more distributors know about solving their customers' problems—as well as

HOW TO TRAIN A CUSTOMER

Good training is good training. If the students get the message and feel pretty good about the experience, you've probably met your imediate goals. When you're dealing with your company's customers, however, the training event brings nuances that not only affect the quality of the training, but the strength of the sales relationship. Consequently, the trainers and consultants with whom we spoke offered some specific advice on how to make these events a success.

- *Make sure it's optional.* "People do things much more willingly if it's their own idea," says H. B. Fuller's Gerald Mielke. "You can't require that [customers] attend your training."
- *Use enthusiatic trainers.* OK, that's a good rule for any training program. But when you're dealing with customers, the last thing you want them to associate with your product is boredom. "I like trainers to be genuinely enthused about working with the customer," says Mielke. "People can spot a phony."
- *Be flexible.* Since most customer groups include various levels of expertise, avoid canned presentations. "You have to be able to adjust to the needs of the audience more quickly than when training a homogeneous group," says Mielke.
- *Be diplomatic.* In an employee-training session, it's rather simple to tell someone tht his or her question isn't on the subject. When the event involves customers, though, you may need to accomodate the digression, at least briefly, then tactfully get back on track.
- *Know the industry well.* You'll often be training people who are in the front line of their industry, says Mielke. They'll be able to tell immediately if your knowledge isn't current, which will lead them to conclude that none of the information you're providing is as solid as their day-to-day experience.
- *Know as much as possible about the customer's operation.* In other words, don't limit your understanding to the piece of the process with which your product or service is concerned. "We have to know the machines, the adhesives that we supply, the paper, the inks, the folding, the warehousing, and the environmental effects on the paper, because that can affect how the adhesive works," says Mielke. "It also affects other aspects of these people's jobs."
- *Make it a company effort.* Although many organizations prefer to have a sales representative deliver product training, most work with the training department or the technical experts to develop the sessions. At Quad/Graphics, for example, every employee is responsible for customer training. "When the customer gets the informaton directly from the person doing the job, it means more," says Leslie Ratay. "It's more believable."

Continued—

How to Train a Customer (continued)

- *Have credentials behind you.* Mielke is a chemist. 3M's industrial hygienists are ready to answer questions at a moment's notice. SmithKline Beecham doesn't hesitate to send a company veterinarian or animal scientist to a training program, if necessary. Although it's great if the expert can attend a customer-training session, these companies say it's usually enough just to let attendees know that an expert helped train the trainer and develop the materials.
- *Do some homework on the group.* "You may be walking into a hostile environment," says Mielke. Are you training workers who just settled a bitter union negotiation? Has the company just downsized or announced unpleasant news such as a pay freeze?
- *Consider the cost.* Even though customer training is traditionally offered free of charge, the customer doesn't always view it that way. "It may not have a direct cost, but people are still taking time off from work," points out Booz Allen Hamilton's Michael Wolf. "You still have to be viewed as the least-cost alternative."
- *Provide more than they could get on their own.* "The greatest strength of our distributor training is the depth and focus we provide," says 3M's Phil Heinz. "The distributor may see 15 different experts during one training event." Likewise, the strength of SmithKline Beechman's program is its delivery of multidisciplinary information in one package—the cattle producer doesn't need to attend separate seminars on animal health, animal nutrition, and cattle-working techniques.
- *Make the products secondary.* Unless you're giving product training to a distributor or retailer, customer training is more effective if you focus on skills—how to use the product or general selling strategies, for example. Although the people who use a 3M respirator are trained on exactly how to use that particular respirator, the fact that it's a 3M product is rarely mentioned in the training. Likewise, Mielke doesn't talk about H. B. Fuller when training book-binding machine operators on how to use a new adhesive—he concentrates on the job at hand.

product features, advantages and benefits—the more product 3M will sell. Consequently, for the last decade Heinz and his staff have offered courses to distributors that mirror the offerings the division's own sales reps receive. Distributors can attend classes that teach them about the products, basic selling skills, advanced selling skills, or even sales management.

"As we develop classes for our own people, we also make them available to our distributors' sales representatives," says Heinz. "This gives them better selling skills, which can only help us, because if we do a good job on this training, they'll do a better job providing solutions to end users."

3M isn't alone in realizing the benefits of training distributors. Although companies have long offered basic product-information seminars to distributors and retailers, many of today's programs seek to raise the professionalism of the distribution chain on all counts. Some companies have developed training for their distributors and retailers on employee relations, advertising, management-information systems—virtually any area of expertise that large suppliers can offer smaller distributors. "A lot of companies are viewing this type of training as the only way they can make sure their products are sold well," says Wolf. "They view their distribution networks as an extension of their own sales force, so they give it the same attention they give their own people."

"They view their distribution networks as an extension of their own sales force, so they give it the same attention they give their own people."

Training also helps create loyalty among distributors, a factor that is becoming increasingly important as the number of distributors and retailers decreases and the survivors wield more buying power, says Lehmann. Distributors and retailers are gaining power over manufacturers, he says, and they're demanding that the manufacturers "do more than was traditionally asked of a transaction agreement." A retailer, he says, "can basically tell Coca-Cola when it will run promotions. And it can say, 'If you want to sell Coke here, you have to tell me how to merchandise and inventory soft drinks.' "

Helping Customers Survive

While some customer-education programs help build and maintain loyalty in a complex marketplace, other training is designed to ensure that customers are in business tomorrow. "If our clients win with our help, then we win," says Gerald Mielke, summing up this philosophy. Mielke is an industry specialist for St. Paul, MN-based H. B. Fuller's book-binding and graphic-arts strategic-business unit, which supplies adhesives used in the book-binding industry.

Mielke and the company's sales representatives try to ensure that a client's book-binding machine operators understand every nuance of their jobs, not just the factors that relate to H. B. Fuller's products. "We don't just tell them that two plus two is four," says Mielke. "We tell them why it's four." When operators understand what they are doing and why, H. B. Fuller's problem-solving recommendations become more meaningful, he explains.

Some customer training has little chance of directly increasing sales; instead, it's an investment made to ensure the survival of a market.

By training a company's entire staff of operators at one time, Mielke often can forge greater efficiencies for his customer. He recalls one case in which the client company had started with a single machine operator who had very little training; he learned most of his job through trial and error. As the company grew, this operator trained new operators, who trained still others, and the original inefficiencies were passed from one generation to the next. After the operators attended H. B. Fuller's basic "how to" seminar, the group's supervisor reported that production increased 50 percent virtually overnight. "He asked me what I did," says Mielke, "and I told him all I did was try to get them to fly in formation."

Some customer training has little chance of directly increasing sales; instead, it's an investment made to ensure the survival of a market—and, not coincidently, the sponsoring company's share of the customer base.

This was the rationale for Exton, PA-based SmithKline Beecham's educational campaign for beef producers. Although the company's U.S./Canada animal-health division has run many educational programs in the past on how to use a specific product to prevent or cure a specific disease, it now offers customer training with a new goal: helping all cattle producers, including those who don't use SmithKline products, produce better beef.

"Rather than selling a product, we're more interested in selling a solution to a problem over the long term," explains John Landon, marketing manager for the company's cow/calf products. "We aren't interested in a one-time sale. We want to be a long-term partner with these people."

In 1991, several beef-packing plants had reported problems with meat quality because some cattle vaccines had been incorrectly administered. "Because we manufactured some of those products, we felt a challenge to train the customer in the proper use of the product so the image of beef wasn't damaged," says Landon. "The producer's livelihood depends on that image, and ultimately ours depends on it, too."

The campaign didn't stop at telling beef producers how best to administer vaccines though. "We looked at it as an opportunity to train the customer on other, common sense practices for working cattle to produce the best end product," says Landon. Topics include the value of good facilities, how to make sure animals don't become bruised when they're being handled, and how to process cattle with as little stress on the animal as possible.

The educational program is offered nationwide through state cattle producers' associations, nonprofit groups that disseminate information to their members. It includes a wall chart, a video, a slide show, a brochure, and other written materials. While the materials can be used alone, SmithKline's sales reps also deliver the seminar, showing exactly what they're talking about by working with a live animal. "The best thing about this program is its flexibility," says Landon. "We can get the information out to everyone because we have so many options.

The initial program was so well received—40 states took advantage of it—that the company has since added a second program for producers who raise calves and a third that presents the advantages of communication among various groups in the industry. "Personally, I find that these programs clearly testify to the company's commitment to the beef-cattle industry," says Mike Smith, director of animal health and education for the Denver-based Colorado Cattle Feeders Association, one of the groups that has helped set up presentations. "It's a bold step to offer this to noncustomers, but I think it sets up a win-win situation for the entire industry."

Added Benefits

As companies continue to delve into this "holistic" approach to customer training, they discover some unexpected benefits.

Quad/Graphics, for example, finds that customer training complements the company's other customer needs-analysis activities. "Clients will discuss problems and challenges during the training sessions that wouldn't get discussed in the normal course of a business relationship," says Ratay. "That helps us develop products and services that better meet their needs." And that, in turn, provides an opportunity for the company to bring customers back in for more training.

Likewise, it gives the company's clients a chance to network and benchmark with one another. "It brings together people who might not be willing to share ideas in another setting," she says.

In some cases, customer training has allowed clients to hire less-experienced people and bring them up to speed quickly, says Ratay. "The fact that they can send a novice and know he or she will return knowing the job has helped us land some customers."

The simple fact that the training opportunity exists can send important signals to customers, says H. B. Fuller's Mielke. "If we put this time and energy into training them, and we show them that we know what we're talking about by helping solve their problems, then they know that same kind of thought has been put into product development. They know they've chosen a good supplier."

Margaret Kaeter is a freelance writer from Minneapolis who frequently writes on quality topics for different publications.

The Voice of the Customer: More Than a Distant Echo

Tracy Benson Kirker

Not just customer satisfaction, but delivering customer delight is what this article suggests is the single most important way to develop your competitive advantage. The article discusses the wisdom of extraordinary guarantees in this quest to delight those who pay the bills. The article following this one elaborates further on this idea.

What would it be worth to you to routinely overhear your customers say: "I wouldn't even consider doing business with anyone else." Your right arm? Your entire advertising budget? How about 1% of sales and some blood, sweat, and tears? That's what companies that have implemented extraordinary guarantees are forking over in return for customer delight.

Before you dismiss the notion of "customer delight" as so much management jargon, consider what AT&T researchers discovered about customer loyalty. Customers who rated the company's products or services below five ("outstanding") on a five-point scale were found to be at risk. "When I say I'm satisfied," notes Richard C. Whiteley, co-founder and vice chairman of Forum Corp., Boston, "what I'm really saying to you is that I find your product acceptable. That is not a strong enough platform upon which to crcatc a competitive advantage."

Creating a sustainable competitive advantage means positioning the purchase decision as just one small step in a long-lasting and profitable relationship.

Creating a sustainable competitive advantage involves overcoming the traditional point-of-purchase mindset. Whether your company is a consumer manufacturer, an OEM producer, or a wholesale distributor, it means positioning the purchase decision as just one small step in a long-lasting and profitable relationship. While the offer of a product or service guarantee is generally designed to reduce the purchase risk on the part of the customer, says Christopher W. L. Hart, president of the Boston-based TQM Group, "a guarantee that's ironclad makes tangible in some sense what is otherwise highly intangible." When a company offers an extraordinary guarantee, Mr. Whiteley agrees, what it is saying to the customer is, "Fundamentally, when you have a relationship with us, we're going to stand behind what we do for you. And if it doesn't work, we'll make it right."

Reprinted with permission from *Industry Week*, January 17, 1994. Copyright Penton Publishing, Inc., Cleveland, Ohio.

Companies that ignore the long-term nature of the customer relationship will ultimately find themselves hostage to a frantic case of industrial keeping-up-with-the-Joneses. What it really comes down to, believes Robert Hunter, president of Delta Dental Plan of Massachusetts and a veteran of the extraordinary guarantee, is a question of raising the bar. "I think once you get into the game of customer satisfaction, the next logical step on the continuum is delighting them," says Mr. Hunter. "If you're able to satisfy your customer and your competition can't quite get there, and you wait for them to catch up with you—you're going to be in trouble. We're surprised, quite frankly, that [our service guarantee] has been in place this long and no one has matched it. We didn't expect it to last that long."

While ultimately a tool to build market share, the real power of the extraordinary guarantee can help an organization identify its customers' current and future needs, and provide managers a detailed road map to ensure that the company's processes are designed to exceed those needs.

Mr. Hart suggests using the extraordinary guarantee internally, just as a manufacturer might pursue just-in-time: to introduce pain into the organization. "If you want to do JIT, you are going to have to get your manufacturing operation debugged, in sync, capacity-balanced, and so on, or you won't have product coming out on the other end."

Likewise, when considering whether to offer an extraordinary guarantee, managers and employees should first do the necessary research to know what the customer really wants. Once the customer-focused vision is articulated, the organization needs to ask itself: "What do we need to do internally before we can offer this guarantee?" By doing that, says Mr. Hart, a company can begin to see where it falls short. The next step is to prioritize those processes that need to be addressed, estimate the cost and time involved, and begin to reengineer them accordingly. The key is that even if a company never takes its guarantee to the marketplace, it is accessing the voice of the customer at every step along the way.

Once the customer-focused vision is articulated, the organization needs to ask itself: "What do we need to do internally before we can offer this guarantee?"

Of course, determining what customers *really* want isn't nearly as easy as it might sound, as companies from General Motors to IBM will attest. In fact, the debate over just how much a customer *can* tell an organization about his future needs is heating up. On the one hand, market researchers tout focus groups and customer surveys as the marketing equivalent of the crystal ball. On the other, CEOs such as Intel Corp.'s Andy Grove argue against weighing customer input too heavily.

As he told executives during the American Society for Quality Control's most recent Quality Forum, "Breakthroughs come from an instinctive judgment of what customers *might* want if they knew to think about that."

Whether a company is creating the next generation microprocessor or processing aluminum ingots, the bottom line when it comes to customer satisfaction is to focus on the aspects of the product that are meaningful to the customer. "Exceeding expectations about things that don't matter a whole lot to customers is a waste," notes Forum's Mr. Whiteley, author of *The Customer Driven Company* (Addison-Wesley, 1991).

Even in the stodgiest and most conservative industries, customer delight can indeed transform the relationship between a supplier and its customers. Take the case of AT&T Universal Card, a winner of the Malcolm Baldrige National Quality Award. Accepting customer delight as a benchmark was probably the most difficult step, notes TQM Group's Mr. Hart. After all, "how do you get customer delight from a credit card? Get it to tell your fortune when you pull it out of your wallet?"

Gradually the company realized its only opportunity to affect the nature of its relationship with customers was either when a customer called with a question or a problem or when an AT&T representative called to collect on a delinquent account. In the case of the former, notes Mr. Hart, "they've done a tremendous job of training their people to go above and beyond, to make that [phone call] a special moment." In the case of the latter, the company began by challenging deeply held assumptions about the very purpose of a delinquency department. It managed to transform the mission of the department from collecting from "deadbeats" to helping customers work through their credit problems.

Once a company adopts a mission of delighting customers, an extraordinary guarantee serves double duty as both a built-in dissatisfaction radar and continuous-improvement mechanism. The more specific the guarantee, the more precise an organization can be about just which aspects of the product or service are not up to par. And the easier it is for customers to invoke the guarantee, notes Mr. Hart, the more likely the company is to unearth processes that need to be improved.

Once a company adopts a mission of delighting customers, an extraordinary guarantee serves double duty as both a built-in dissatisfaction radar and continuous-improvement mechanism.

Making it easy for the customer to collect on an unfilled promise is only the beginning. Even more difficult is training employees to view such occasions as an opportunity to retain a customer for life rather than as a blemish on their performance record. Ironically, says Mr. Hart, the companies that find it the hardest to convince employees to seek opportunities to pay on an unfulfilled guarantee are the ones in which there are high levels of employee loyalty. The reason: "They don't want to give the company's money away—they figure the customers are cheating.

"The fact is, it doesn't matter," Mr. Hart declares. Research performed by Hampton Inn showed that "those who had a problem and invoked the guarantee were to much more likely to come back and to refer Hampton Inn to others than those who had problems and didn't invoke the guarantee." To reap the full benefit of the guarantee, "the task becomes finding those people who have a problem and [inducing] them to invoke the guarantee, because the long-run interests of the organization demand it. The [potential] stream of future revenue is to much greater than what we might pay them today."

Aside from tracking payouts, some companies have gone so far as to actually reward employees for paying out on unfulfilled guarantees. Beyond ensuring that the systems work, such tactics demonstrate managers' commitment to improving customer satisfaction. "One of the problems with quality," Mr. Hart reflects, "is, as you go down the line, employees' belief that senior executives are committed and involved drops off. Committing to an

Extraordinary Guarantees in Action

Below is a sampling of extraordinary guarantees in place in a variety of companies.

MacInTax Personal Edition by ChipSoft Personal Products Div.: "If you are assessed an IRS penalty because of a calculation error by MacInTax, we'll pay the penalty. . . . If MacInTax doesn't have a form you need to do your taxes, we'll refund your money. . . . If you don't agree that MacInTax is faster than doing your taxes by hand, we'll refund your money."

L. L. Bean: "Everything we sell is backed by a 100% unconditional guarantee. We do not want you to have anything from L. L. Bean that is not completely satisfactory. Return anything you buy from us at any time for any reason if it proves otherwise."

Saturn Corp.: "Saturn offers a bumper-to-bumper warranty, which covers virtually everything from the front bumper to the rear for the first three years or 36,000 miles, whichever comes first. . . . In addition, Saturn offers a limited 30-day/1,500-mile money-back guarantee. If you don't want the car, simple return it in the condition in which it was delivered, without damage or excessive wear and tear."

Quicken® software by Intuit: "Try Quicken risk-free for 60-days. . . .Guaranteed to work with any printer and monitor supported on the Macintosh or your money back."

extraordinary guarantee with Draconian payout provisions is putting management's money where its mouth is. I don't know of any stronger single signal that a management team can send to its organization about how serious it is about quality and about making sure that its customers are satisfied."

A note of caution: For managers who see the extraordinary guarantee as a motivational quick fix, "the assumption is that people aren't working hard enough or right enough," says Mr. Whiteley. "But quality issues today are not about motivation. They're about processes that don't work." Likewise, organizations that approach extraordinary guarantees as an external marketing gimmick without examining their internal process can expect customer apathy at best and at worst a mass exodus over the long haul.

"Guarantees are a method for putting rigor into the process," says Forum Corp.'s Mr. Whiteley. "But what I'm really describing here is an ethic that is developing that says, 'It is just uncomfortable for us as suppliers for customers to have products of ours that don't work.' "

Learning from the Service Sector

From the beginning, recounts Robert Hunger, president of Delta Dental Plan of Massachusetts, the board of directors adopted a philosophy of superior customer service. (Prior to breaking away as an independent in 1985, Delta Dental was administered by Blue Cross-Blue Shield of Massachusetts.) "When Chris Hart's article came out in the *Harvard Business Review* ["The Power of Unconditional Service Guarantees," July-August 1988], we already knew we had differentiated service," Thomas Raffio, senior vice president, recalls. "We are actually looking for a way to highlight that to the marketplace, as well as to develop a program that would simultaneously help us continuously improve."

"We also realized," Mr. Hunter adds, "that in the insurance industry, whose reputation is one step above the self-service gas station, we could make a small move, but it would actually be a gigantic step." So began Delta Dental's groundbreaking mission to guarantee the quality of its services to all three groups of customers—dentist, company accounts, and individual subscriber patients.

Delta Dental's Guarantee of Service Excellence (GOSE), organized around seven basic services, drives almost every aspect of the company's business, from recruiting and training (which is ongoing) to the physical layout of the customer-service department.

The company's promise to resolve questions immediately over the phone, for example, prompted significant changes both in technology and design. "It used to be that our customer-service reps would sit in an office and would have to page through four or five screens to get through a normal call," Mr. Raffio notes. "Now there's one screen."

Moreover, customer-service reps now operate from stations that are centrally located. Sophisticated technology tracks incoming calls, automatically routing them to available representatives, and feeds relevant information to an electronic overhead sign that is visible throughout the department. The absence of tall dividers between stations allows the customer-service manager to spot bottlenecks and to assist employees who need additional help.

"The focus of the guarantee," Mr. Hunter reflects, "is to bring the customer loop right in to every employee in the company. [The employees] can literally hear the customer speaking to them through these guarantees."

GOSE has undoubtedly helped Delta boost its market share, but Mr. Hunter says guarantees ought not to be used as a marketing ploy. "I couldn't understand why [the guarantee] wasn't catching on in the industry until I heard some of our competitors saying, 'Well, we've checked the market, and we don't need that.' That's not the idea at all. It's not a message to the market—it's the other way around. We're trying to get information out of the market."

Mr. Hunter cautions managers not to mimic successful programs without first addressing their environment. "You've got people in here at every level of the company who really want to succeed. And they love to come to work every day." Without that sense of commitment and a desire to make the system work, "it would be hard for them to deliver what we promise to customers."

Mr. Raffio thinks the systems are just as important as the culture. "You can have the most customer-oriented customer-service reps, but if your online system doesn't have all the information, if he or she has to put the person on hold, run to five different files, come back and transfer the call to another department, it doesn't work."

Ongoing training occurs at every level and addresses a multitude of needs. A fully equipped on-site training center offers courses ranging from basic math and dental terminology to diversity training. Employees, notes Mr. Raffio, "can't do the work unless they know what they're doing. You can't say you're empowered and then walk away and expect them to make the right decision."

Tracy Benson Kirker is a writer for Industry Week *Magazine.*

Phenomenal Promises That Mean Business

Barbara Ettorre

This article continues to discuss the idea of offering unconditional guarantees as a way of delighting customers beyond expectations and to make good on those guarantees. It shows how guarantees are not only good for customers, but for the company as well. Only those companies completely committed to delivering quality to customers can afford to make such promises in the first place.

It is not for nothing that the best ideas are often the simplest.

Take a look at the notion of unconditional guarantees. A company offers a product or a service to its customers with a variation of this guarantee: If any of what we have promised fails to measure up, we will do whatever it takes to satisfy you the customer, no questions asked. And you the customer will have a hand in determining what that action would be.

The essence of simplicity, no?

Those enterprises that are able to offer peerless products and service might give out a resounding, "Yes." Others—especially those that lag in world-class-level quality and efficiency—might be more ambivalent.

They might cite top management's reluctance, a corporate culture that wouldn't accept such a thing, or employees that would never be coaxed into going along with such an absurdity. They might point to their distribution, invoicing or manufacturing systems, for example, saying that these would have to be overhauled to accommodate an unconditional guarantee. They also might say that an unequivocal guarantee of service—with few restrictions and with the customer defining the terms—would seem like financial suicide. After all, wouldn't customers abuse the guarantee? And, they would say, think of the expense, especially if the customer calls the shots. The naysayers would be correct to believe that an unconditional guarantee would not work for them. In fact, it would irreparably harm their companies. If a business is not at the top of its form—its processes, products and services in the highest echelons of quality and efficiency and with all employees committed to continuous improvement—that company would do better to improve itself than to offer an unconditional guarantee it could not hope to honor.

Reprinted with permission of publisher from *Management Review,* March 1994. Copyright © 1994, American Management Association, New York. All rights reserved.

"The guarantee has to be quality-driven, or else you're committing suicide," says Eric Bruno, staff specialist, branch market assessment, at GTE Corporation. "Not only would it bankrupt the company, but it would ruin its image." GTE's Telephone Operations division is in the midst of extensive reengineering and has been introducing various unconditional service guarantees in increments to its business and residential customers. But, Bruno points out, GTE embarked on its top-down quality program in 1984 and has had nearly a decade to reach its current quality levels.

Indeed, the experts stress that unconditional guarantees must come as the culmination of a lengthy commitment to quality. They say that any company that enacts an extraordinary guarantee must be prepared to put its reputation on the line for its customers indefinitely. Such a guarantee, they insist, is not a fad, not a marketing gimmick, not the latest notion from the CEO. And they agree that these kinds of guarantees are not for most American businesses since too many products and services are mediocre.

Unconditional guarantees must come as the culmination of a lengthy commitment to quality.

The professionals also caution that a company should not enact a guarantee that it can't deliver. Domino's Pizza Inc. recently learned this the hard way. The company was forced to cancel its guaranteed of 30-minute delivery on all telephone orders when a St. Louis court awarded $78 million to a woman who had been struck by a Domino's driver in 1989.

The guarantee—enacted in 1984 and the catalyst for Domino's phenomenal growth—originally stipulated that late-arriving pizzas would be free (later amended to $3 off the order). The jury's award albeit large, should not have taken the company by surprise: There have been numerous lawsuits charging that Domino's drivers, in the eagerness for speedy delivery, had been driving irresponsibly and had injured or killed individuals.

In the 1980s, when quality movements began to take hold, unconditional guarantees began to proliferate in the marketplace. In his book, *Extraordinary Guarantees* (AMACOM, 1993), Christopher W. L. Hart explains that first-rate service establishments—restaurants, hotels and the like—began to put guarantees in writing as a marketing tool and found that the idea revitalized their operations throughout. Note, however, that these companies were already at the top of their industries.

Hart, president of the Boston-based TQM Group and a former examiner for the Malcolm Baldrige National Quality Award, is a longtime proponent of extraordinary guarantees. He defines it as going beyond industry standards, beyond what competitors are doing and beyond what customers would dream of—even, he says, "beyond what the company itself at first thought was feasible." The concept of extraordinary guarantees is part of what he calls "management by commitment," and he offers an example from a recent trip to Japan:

A 19-year-old employee was pointed out to Hart while he was visiting a manufacturer of integrated circuit boards. While driving home from work one day, she had noticed the rumble of a nearby train and had wondered if the movement of the train as it passed the factory could cause product defects. She expressed her concern to her supervisor who passed it along to the process engineers. They laboriously collected three years of back data from the railroad and, sure enough, there was a correlation between defective goods and the times when trains went by.

The story illustrates deep loyalty by employees at all levels, Hart stressed. The underlying fear of losing face—which motivated all those workers—is so great that the Japanese do extra things to make commitments they [seemingly] cannot meet or to avoid not honoring commitments they've already made, he says. Hart then makes an intriguing analogy for non-Japanese companies: An extraordinary guarantee can be the device used to achieve this level of commitment in an organization that does not have the Japanese ethos.

That these guarantees can galvanize employees, empower them, bond them into a team and commit them to company goals is understood by the experts—and by those to whom an unequivocal guarantee often is the only constant in a shifting world.

"A well-conceived guarantee is, among other things, an act of fairness," says Leonard Berry, director of the Center for Retailing Studies and J.C. Penney Professor of Retailing Studies at Texas A&M University. "While it is a tangible indication from a company to a customer, it also can be a powerful cultural shaper for employees." Berry goes on to say that a guarantee "puts teeth into management rhetoric" about improving quality and is a positive reinforcer, contributing to the company culture that binds employees together.

A guarantee "puts teeth into management rhetoric" about improving quality.

That's why internal guarantees, an interesting variation on the theme of extraordinary guarantees, are becoming so prevalent. In an internal guarantee, one area of a company issues a guarantee to other areas in the company—its customers. An example is GTE's management executive training operations in Norwalk, Conn. It trains about 18,000 GTE management personnel annually, starting with front-line supervisors. If seminars don't live up to attendees' expectations, the training division will refund their tuition or find some other way to satisfy them. The seminars are paid for by company funds—each attendee pays with departmental money. But the refund comes out of the seminar operations and is reflected in its budget.

"The guarantee is a great way to market ourselves and a continuous way to monitor the relevancy of our training programs," says Jerold Tucker, GTE's director of corporate education and training. "It puts a hard dollar measure on a soft science."

Power Tool

One company learned what a powerful tool a guarantee can be to its employees in a telling way. First Image Management Company, a computer services output concern based in California, was bought by a much larger company in 1990 and was moved to Atlanta. At the time, First Image had two years' experience with an unconditional service guarantee.

First Image went through dramatic and anxiety-causing changes in values, culture and processes during the buyout and move, recalls Robert Gregory, vice president of production. Only two people in leadership roles survived the purchase of the company. "We found that the power of an unconditional guarantee affects all the employees," says Gregory. "It cuts through all the events when a company is bought because it is a resolute and insistent focus. It kept alive our reason for existing as a company."

According to Gregory, the guarantee provided a certainty ("Deliver on our promises or there will be consequences," as he says), even during a time when employees were unsure where their loyalties lay or to whom they reported. They were even worried that the new owners would discontinue the guarantee.

"In the three years of being swallowed by a new parent, tripling in size, and losing our name and logo, the one thing that tangibly represented our identity, the one anchor, was the guarantee," Gregory asserts. "Not only did our parent *not* take away that service guarantee, now there are other parts of the company looking at it."

It would seem that an extraordinary guarantee is a sort of magic charm: Apply the guarantee and, lo, customers start smiling. A win-win situation all around. But if a company says it will do whatever it takes to make a customer happy, can it still make money? And, how can it stop customers from invoking the guarantee unfairly?

Overwhelmingly, those companies have implemented phenomenal guarantees say that abuses are rare. They maintain that the payback in retained and new customers far exceeds any costs incurred in honoring their guarantees.

The payback in retained and new customers far exceeds any costs incurred in honoring their guarantees.

In fact, Baldrige award criteria experts are now stressing guarantees as a key element in relationship management. "The cost of getting and retaining a customer is so high that guarantees are part of the psychology of commitment," says Curt Reimann, director for quality programs at the National Institute of Standards and Technology and director of the Baldrige award. "The retained customer has long-term value," he continues. "Guarantees are a safety valve; they keep us on our toes and allow us to get a good snapshot of validated practices."

Indeed, without an unconditional guarantee, a company can believe it is doing a very good job when customers may think that job is only average. A good example is GTE Telephone Operations. Prior to implementing its guarantee, the company looked at its 1991 internal statistics on commitments met for its small business customers. The division said it had a 93 percent rate, according to Robert Coens, staff administrator, marketing strategy at GTE Telephone Operations. But he noted that the surveys showed customer perceptions averaged only 79 percent, a large variance.

The GTE guarantee says that if the company doesn't meet its commitment for installation or repair, the customer gets up to a $100 credit, no questions asked. All customer representatives are empowered to invoke the guarantee. "We are holding our breath right now," says Coens. "We are reengineering our processes that deal directly with customers at the same time we are delivering the guarantee program. The guarantee will give us a sanity check. Quality cannot drop. It's real challenge."

The Extraordinary Guarantee

In his book, Hart cites the example of Oakley Millwork, a Chicago supplier of construction industry products. Between 1988 and 1991—when housing starts in its area fell 41 percent—Oakley's sales rose 33 percent. Why? The company had implemented an extraordinary guarantee—if any item ordered from its catalog was out of stock and unavailable for immediate delivery, the customer would get the item free. In pleasing its customers and attracting new ones, Oakley improved its operations and efficiencies. The guarantee "transformed the company," Hart writes.

An unconditional guarantee may well change a company for the better, but human nature being fallible, wouldn't customers take advantage of it? After all, customer demands clearly increase over time as the service improves. Not so, says Professor Berry: "Our research shows convincingly that while customer expectations are rising, these expectations are quite reasonable—a hotel that is quiet, clean and safe, for example, or a car repair shop that fixes the car right the first time. Demands are not becoming extravagant."

We Got the Shoe Right Here

One company that knows firsthand about customers that stretch the customer guarantee somewhat is L.L. Bean Inc., the outdoor and sporting retailer based in Freeport, Maine. There are L.L. Bean customers who have sent back a pair of boots or a jacket that had been worn for years, even decades, for a refund or an exchange—usually honored under the company's unconditional guarantee. The story of Leon Leonwood Bean, the company's founder and namesake who made a Maine hunting shoe in 1912, is now legend. He marketed the waterproof shoe to hunters for $3.95 a pair and borrowed money to send out refunds when 90 of the first 100 pairs were returned because faulty stitching caused them to leak. L.L. Bean then set about to improve the shoe.

The company—today with $750 million in sales, primarily from its mail-order operation—liberally publishes its guarantee of "100 percent satisfaction in every way," stating that, for whatever reason, L.L. Bean will replace an unsatisfactory purchase, refund its price or issue a credit, whichever the customer wants. Such a policy can be expensive, since the company estimates that each return costs $8 in processing, postage and labor. (L.L. Bean will not, however, divulge the number of returns received per year.)

All returns are considered to be under that guarantee, and fewer than 2 percent of them in any year are regarded as abuses of the guarantee, says spokesperson Catharine Hartnett, "The customers who clean out their closet and send back all the L.L. Bean merchandise they found are fairly rare."

Does a company have to put its extraordinary guarantee in writing, as L.L. Bean does? Not always. Nordstrom Inc., the Pacific Northwest retailer, has an implied guarantee of 100 percent customer service and satisfaction at its 73 stores nationwide. Its employee handbook consists of one page, which includes the goal of "outstanding customer service" and "Rule #1: Use your good judgment in all situations." There are no additional rules.

Because decentralized Nordstrom has more than the normal number of salespeople on the floor and because each of them can act independently without approval from a supervisor, the store has a longstanding reputation for peerless customer service. "You don't just guarantee customer service, you *do* it," says Joe Demarte, vice president of personnel at Nordstrom. "The guarantee has to be genuine; people have to want to do it." He notes it doesn't take long for an employee to be a convert. "When you give the trust, no one is looking over your shoulder," he says.

Put Your People on the Line

When considering extraordinary guarantees, there seems to be no end to what well-run companies will do to satisfy their customers.

When considering extraordinary guarantees, there seems to be no end to what well-run companies will do to satisfy their customers.

An example is the Tech Van program implemented by AGCO, the Georgia-based manufacturer of farming combines and other sophisticated machines. Each combine can cost upwards of $150,000 and include up to 15,000 parts. Many companies—including Allis-Chalmers, one of AGCO's predecessors—have mobile repair crews to follow combines as they move north from Texas to North Dakota and Montana during the May-to-September wheat harvest season. A breakdown can cost a combine operator $100 to 200 an *hour* in lost time in a choreographed harvesting season in which, as one moves northward, wheat ripens approximately 23 miles per day.

For its "combine caravan," AGCO has outfitted two semitrailers, each with a parts warehouse and a computerized office. Combine customers call a toll-free number and are immediately connected with the trucks who then dispatch one of several service vans equipped with parts and cellular phones and who work along a 200- to 300-mile radius.

During the off-season, the company has stockpiled additional parts at key AGCO dealerships along the way, "as explorers cached supplies running for the North Pole," says Larry James, manager of combine engineering and product tests as AGCO's engineering group.

"We keep improving this system annually," says James, noting that the 1993 harvest saw a computerized system in place in which a customer could call, request a part, and be told immediately if the part is in stock and where to get it.

James says that many of AGCO's best technicians are in the field more than 100 days a year in rotating teams of 12 to 15. If the combine repair is under warranty, it is usually free to the customer. Otherwise, the closest dealership gets the sale; the technicians do not hand out bills. There are about 17 Tech Van stops per season, each lasting one to three weeks. The routes and phone numbers are given out to AGCO customers at custom harvester meetings in the off-season. A part of the win-win that occurs with AGCO's Tech Van guarantee are the trip reports faxed to James every day. If there are chronic breakdowns, for example, "I know instantly if a part is mismanufactured, and we make sure we don't still do that," he says.

Certainly, one of the best features about unconditional guarantees is the conduit of customer information that flows back to the company as an immediate "How are we doing?"reality check. L.L. Bean, for instance, handles 11 million customer calls a year including orders. Positive and negative customer comments are keyed into the computer and routed to the appropriate department for immediate action.

One of the best features about unconditional guarantees is the conduit of customer information that flows back to the company as an immediate reality check.

When the guarantee invoked at GTE, the particulars are logged and tracked in the company's internal operating system and routed to the appropriate area. GTE's Bruno says the data are examined as to how the process can be improved in the future.

The future, in general, will see unconditional guarantees that are as imaginative as their creators can devise. The best of them will reflect the companies that engendered them, constantly pushing the human limits of quality and customer satisfaction. And, just as with all valid quality movements, others will follow the leaders.

Barbara Ettorre is a writer with Management Review *magazine.*

Measuring Customer Satisfaction in Business Markets

Warren R. Hayslip

This article provides several practical guidelines for undertaking surveys of business-to-business customers. He points out that when done properly, customers like to provide feedback for such surveys because that helps guarantee they will get what they expect.

The rapid emergence of customer satisfaction surveys in the past decade has been a truly remarkable development. In the early 1980s, relatively few leading edge companies and market research firms used customer satisfaction surveys; in the 1990s, however, this specialized analytical discipline has become an essential component of quality management activities in many U.S.-based manufacturing and service companies.

The Malcolm Baldrige National Quality Award criteria clearly indicate the high level of importance that quality management professionals place on this specialized market research activity. Category 7, Customer Focus and Satisfaction, carries more points than any other award category, with a point value of 300 out of the possible 1,000 points.

With annual growth rates estimated at 30%, the CS survey segment is now identified as one of the fastest growing segments of the $2 billion U.S. market research industry.

Further evidence of the growing acceptance of customer satisfaction (CS) surveys is seen in a recent study. The study estimates that the segment for CS survey work alone accounts for $100 million in consulting/research revenues for major U.S. market research firms.[1] With annual growth rates estimated at 30%, the CS survey segment is now identified as one of the fastest growing segments of the $2 billion U.S. market research industry.[2] But with all of this hoopla about CS measurements and their role in the quality management process, not everything is perceived as satisfactory in the CS business. In recent years, knowledgeable customers, suppliers, and survey practitioners have expressed doubts about the state of the "art" of measuring customer satisfaction. They have voiced a number of critical concerns, including the misuse of telemarketing and other data-gathering media, the proliferation and excessive use of surveys, and the overall effectiveness of CS research as an ongoing analytical discipline.[3]

Reprinted with permission from *Quality Progress*, April 1994. Copyright © 1994 by ASQC, Milwaukee, WI.

In spite of these important issues, it does seem improbable that CS surveys will fade from the corporate management scene anytime soon. On the contrary, because CS surveys potentially offer the most efficient and objective means of measuring customers' perceptions about the quality of products and services, it seems very likely that their use will continue to grow well into the future. So, instead of asking whether these surveys should be used, the relevant question is actually: How can the value of CS surveys be improved?

One area of the CS survey discipline that seems to be a particular source of confusion and is critically important to many corporate managers is the use of CS surveys in business-to-business markets.

Over the past decade, I've had ample opportunity to study and work in this particular survey area. From my experience, initially as a corporate manager in charge of customer surveys for a large international manufacturing company and later as a full-time consultant in the CS field, I have learned a number of lessons that can benefit professionals who are involved in developing customer surveys and other managers who are involved in the quality management process.

In particular, I've learned that there are common mistakes made in business-to-business surveys (or simply, business surveys) that can easily be avoided. Many of these mistakes, which can be very costly in terms of results, occur simply because people lack an awareness of basic survey principles. This is unfortunate because the understanding of business surveys should not be reserved for a small cadre of survey professionals; it is a subject that is relevant to a large number of corporate managers.

I've learned that there are common mistakes made in business-to-business surveys (or simply, business surveys) that can easily be avoided.

By virtue of the fact that almost all companies participate in business markets either as suppliers or customers, it is inevitable that many of these companies will be involved in business CS surveys. So, the goal of understanding and improving business survey work is a legitimate priority not only for business suppliers but for corporate customers as well.

Differentiating Consumer and Business Markets

When taking a closer look at business surveys and their potential problems, it is important that a fundamental differentiation be made between business markets and the better-understood sector of consumer markets. This is a critical distinction in customer survey work because the major structural differences between consumer and business markets lead to important differences in how CS surveys should be designed and executed.

While most survey professionals and corporate managers seem to understand the nature of consumer markets and surveys, many seem quite unaware of how they differ from business markets and surveys. But the differences are not only real, they are in some respects rather profound. There are five key factors that highlight some of the critical differences between consumer and business markets:

- Size of customer populations
- Magnitude of purchase volumes

- Purchase transaction complexities
- Customer knowledge of supplier offerings
- Nature of customer-supplier relationships

Structural Characteristics of Consumer Markets

Using the five key factors to profile the major structural characteristics of consumer markets, some remarkably consistent findings emerge:

- Size of customer populations: Most consumer markets are composed of large numbers of customers in which no single customer has a significant share.

- Magnitude of purchase volumes: The majority of consumer purchases are for products and services that are relatively small in actual dollar amounts.

- Purchase transaction complexities: The purchase of most consumer items is a relatively simple process involving an individual's decision to buy or not to buy.

- Customer knowledge of supplier offerings: As a general rule, consumers are not very knowledgeable about the products and services they purchase or the suppliers' operational processes to produce and deliver those items.

- Nature of customer-supplier relationships: In the majority of consumer markets, suppliers and customers essentially maintain an arm's-length relationship in which they do not share proprietary information or collaborate in any significant way.

To confirm the validity of these characteristics, a detailed study is not needed, just common sense. If people simply reflect on their daily experiences as consumers and how they typically interact with the suppliers of the products and services they purchase, they can see that the structural characteristics just suggested are indeed, evident in the majority of consumer markets in which they participate, including retail and grocery stores, mail order, food service, health care, transportation, insurance, hotels and lodging, and entertainment.

Furthermore, these consumer market characteristics are significant. They essentially describe a predominant market structure in which large suppliers sell on a nonnegotiated basis to many less-knowledgeable customers. This is very important because the bargaining arrangement in this marketing structure substantially affects the extent and flow of communication between suppliers and customers and, ultimately, dictates how suppliers choose to listen and relate to customer needs and expectations in CS surveys.

As a result, while the typical supplier of consumer products or services might want to spend time with each customer to understand his or her needs and expectations, that course of action is impractical if not impossible. Except for those businesses that provide customized products and services, consumer marketing (and its related measurement of customer satisfaction) typically requires the understanding of the composite perceptions of relatively large numbers of customers.

Assessing the Needs of the Many

As a direct result of these structural conditions, consumer CS surveys tend to take on attributes that respond directly to problems and opportunities of surveying large customer populations. There are at least three important survey attributes that are common in consumer CS surveys:

1. *Selective-sample orientation.* Because suppliers cannot survey every customer, they rely heavily on selecting and analyzing representative samples that constitute rather small percentages of the total population.
2. *Tracking the "larger herd."* Because consumer CS surveys are ultimately focused on understanding the big picture, survey practitioners often use small samples and quantitative techniques (i.e., statistical inference) to predict the composite perceptions of large populations.
3. *One-way data gathering.* Since customer populations are generally very large and supplier-customer relationships are not very close, survey practitioners to not usually worry about "selling" the survey to respondents. Even with low response rates, consumer CS surveys can almost always collect samples of sufficient quantity and quality for analysis.

These three attributes are evident in the vast majority of consumer surveys, whether the supplier is a credit card company, consumer electronics manufacturer, or power utility. In fact, the most visible and well-known example of consumer surveys is the polling of voters in an election year. In this type of survey, pollsters routinely select "small" population samples (maybe a few thousand respondents), use the sample data to estimate the voting patterns of many millions of voters at specific confidence levels and margins of error, and commonly use computer-assisted telephone centers as a basic means of high-volume data gathering and analysis.

Structural Characteristics of Business Markets

The structural characteristics of business markets consistently differ from those in consumer markets and, in may cases appear to be opposite:

- Size of customer populations: Many business markets are composed of relatively small numbers of customers of which a few buyers might have a substantial share or dominant position.

- Magnitude of purchase volumes: A large number of business purchases are for products and services that are relatively large in actual dollar amounts.

- Purchase transaction complexities: The decision to purchase major business products and services is usually a relatively complex process in which numerous decision makers and decision influencers negotiate terms and specifications with suppliers.

- Customer knowledge of supplier offerings: In many cases, customers have significant interests in the products and services they purchase and, as a result, tend to acquire substantial knowledge of the products and services they buy and the suppliers' internal operational processes.

- Nature of customer-supplier relationships: Particularly in recent years, customers tend to actively develop close working relationships with their key suppliers. This relationship involves sharing proprietary information and developing joint work efforts.

By comparing the structural characteristics of consumer and business markets, it becomes clear that the bargaining balance between suppliers and customers significantly differs. As opposed to consumer market conditions, in which suppliers sell to many customers, business market suppliers routinely sell on a negotiated basis to fewer, more knowledgeable, and more powerful customers.[4]

Furthermore, this dramatic difference in the bargaining balance has a very tangible effect on the extent and flow of communication; it certainly affects how CS surveys should be designed and executed in business markets. This is particularly true in heavily concentrated market segments, in which a handful of key customers can dominate a supplier's competitive sales environment.

Many business CS surveys have the oportunity to be much more comprehensive in scope and can include significantly higher percentages of their customer populations in survey samples.

Assessing the Needs of the Few

As a result of the structural characteristics in business markets, many business CS surveys tend to take on attributes that are much different from those typically seen in consumer surveys:

1. *Selective-census orientation.* As opposed to consumer markets, in which customer populations can easily exceed 100,000, business markets frequently have customer populations well below a thousand or even a few hundred. In fact, it is not unusual for a large supplier to have fewer than 50 customers in a single market segment. As a result of the smaller populations, many business CS surveys have the opportunity to be much more comprehensive in scope and can include significantly higher percentages of their customer populations in survey samples.

   Some companies actually take the opportunity to survey all of their customer accounts. For example, Milliken & Co., a perennial leader in the textile industry and a past Baldrige Award winner, uses an exhaustive approach in its CS survey sample selection. It monitors virtually 100% of the active accounts in many of its key textile market segments. Other companies, while stopping short of a total census, achieve a partial census by subdividing their customer segments into customer peer groups (based on sales volume or other criteria) and seeking a 100% response rate from those peer groups that contain the large and important customer accounts.

2. *Tracking the lead steer.* One of the recurring difficulties of surveying business markets is targeting and segmenting respondents. As opposed to consumer markets, in which most, if not all, qualified respondents are assumed to have essentially equal knowledge and buying clout, business markets have an altogether different situation. In these markets, respondents differ greatly in terms of knowledge of products and services (due to different management functions and experiences) and buying clout (due to large differences in purchase volumes among various customers).

   As a result, suppliers must be mindful of differences in respondents' qualifications. They must design the surveys so that the responses of critical respondents are not lost in the aggregation of data. As opposed to consumer surveys, in which the focus is almost exclusively on the composite picture of customer perceptions, business surveys have a legitimate concern about individual perceptions of key survey respondents.

   For example, in CS survey I recently directed for an industrial supplier to the hosiery industry, great value resulted from separating out the responses of the top five customers (which accounted for 90% of sales) and profiling the comments of key decision makers within these companies. These ratings and comments indicated that the large customer accounts held views that were different from the survey averages in certain critical respects. This was an important finding because it clearly indicated that customer quality priorities were not homogeneous in the marketplace and that the major accounts required customized improvement programs.
3. *Two-way communication.* In business markets, customers and their key suppliers are increasingly developing close partnerships to improve quality, responsiveness, and other performance attributes. When measuring customer satisfaction within this type of close working environment, the survey process cannot be conducted behind closed doors.

   As compared to consumer surveys, in which suppliers can quietly probe into isolated population sample, business CS surveys are much more open to market scrutiny because important customers are usually aware of these surveys. The key decision makers at these companies are usually not passive respondents. Not only is their active participation critical to the successful execution of the CS survey, but they also have a real interest in the ultimate outcome. The improvement of products and services (which is a legitimate concern) must be the supplier's primary purpose for conducting the survey.

   As a result, large customers in business markets do not view CS surveys as a stand-alone activity conducted for the sole benefit of suppliers; rather, thoughtful corporate customers see these surveys as part of the overall quality improvement process and ongoing partnership.

   Unlike consumer markets, in which there is almost an endless sea of potential respondents, business markets must depend rather heavily on the responses of a relatively small number of qualified respondents. Thus, qualified business respondents are a scarce and valuable resource and should be treated accordingly.

Common Mistakes in Business CS Surveys

From start to finish in the business survey process, problems can occur. Here are common errors to be avoided:

1. *Sloppy introduction.* One of the worst sins in business CS surveys is to attempt to interview important customers in a manner that is either unprofessional or below the quality of the ongoing partnership. Too often, in the interest of reducing costs or shortening turnaround times, survey practitioners resort to inappropriate telephone techniques, such as high-volume cold calls. Surprise interviews are improper for key business decision makers and, accordingly, receive low response rates. This problem is frequently compounded by using interviewers with little or no business experience, who muddle through the interviews in a rote questioning manner.

   In business CS surveys, initial communication is highly critical to the overall success and deserves a lot of management attention. Since there is only one chance for a first impression, companies should make sure that it is a positive one. Failure to do this will, at best, lower the quality of responses in business surveys and, at worst, project an inferior communications image that can damage an important customer relationship.
2. *The never-ending interview.* This major flaw in business CS surveys becomes evident to respondents after they have agreed to be interviewed. To their growing displeasure, the "quick" interview (as promised by the telephone interviewer) eventually stretches into a 40-minute interrogation of tedious and redundant questions. This is a sure sign of poor questionnaire design; the interviewer is simply asking too many questions.

   Over the years, I have found that in business CS surveys, about 25 to 30 well-designed questions are quite adequate in addressing the key performance attributes of most suppliers. Once the interview exceeds this threshold, respondent fatigue sets in and the quality of responses decreases proportionately, particularly in telephone interviews. Survey practitioners should be sensitive to this fatigue factor as they design and execute customer surveys.
3. *Misapplied statistics.* While reliability statistics are critically important in all types of market surveys, they can easily be misapplied in business surveys. A major reason is that the implicit "one man, one vote" rule in consumer surveys is not necessarily acceptable in business surveys, particularly in highly stratified markets in which small customers purchase only thousands of dollars of products while large customers purchase millions of dollars' worth. Companies cannot assume that the response from all of their customers are of equal weight and importance.

   Recently I was asked to evaluate a large U.S. manufacturer's CS survey program. The market research group in charge of the survey claimed "excellent" results in the latest survey, touting a 5% precision interval at the 95% confidence level. But I later discovered that the survey was less than excellent, as it only received a disappointing 30% overall response rate and failed to get responses from many of the company's large and influential customers.

Clearly, in this case, the use of reliability statistics presented a misleading picture because it strongly implied that all of the survey respondents were equal in standing (and thus, substitutable) and that the small calculated margin of error indicated survey success. To use reliability estimates effectively, the research group should have first segmented the large, stratified sample into customer peer groups and then calculated margins of error.

4. *Stuck on the aggregate.* It is true that, for management purposes, business CS surveys should ultimately provide bottom line index numbers to gauge overall customer satisfaction. But it is also important that suppliers go beyond these aggregate calculations and understand the essential components.

Unlike consumer surveys, in which the analysis of individual responses has limited value, business surveys provide a special opportunity to evaluate the response of important and knowledgeable customers. Important customers, by and large, see CS surveys as a critical element of their ongoing partnerships and use the survey medium to openly communicate their opinions and perceptions.

Important customers, by and large, see CS surveys as a critical element of their ongoing partnerships and use the survey medium to openly communicate their opinions and perceptions.

Because important customers deserve special attention, surveys should be designed to accommodate them. Otherwise, vital information about these key customers can get lost in the aggregate.

5. *Solutions without value.* Business CS surveys provide powerful and useful information on how suppliers can improve their quality performance. Occasionally, however, these surveys provide customers a new forum to register petty complaints, and to request product and service improvements that simply might not make economic sense.

As a result, suppliers must manage CS survey projects carefully and use the findings with considerable business judgment. In particular, they should not make major decisions based on survey findings alone; rather, they should look for other corroborating data and use other analytical tools—such as internal quality measurements (statistical process control data) or external analyses of system economics—to give them added insights into the potential problems that might surface in routine CS surveys. When used in conjunction with these other data and management tools, the true value of CS surveys is substantially enhanced.

Ultimately, business CS surveys must be oriented toward finding ways to create economic value for customers and suppliers alike and not naively pursuing customer satisfaction as if it were some kind of Holy Grail. If suggested quality improvements do not create real economic value for one or both parties, the importance of pursuing these initiatives should be questioned.[5] Companies that incorporate this kind of insightful economic questioning into their management reviews routinely get the greatest value from business CS surveys.

6. *The broken record.* Many companies that conduct business CS surveys want to have CS data that are consistent and comparable over time so

that their quality progress can be measured over several years. In fact, quite a few of these companies award bonuses and other forms of compensation using a survey-based formula that compares business performance from one period to the next. Unfortunately, once a survey-based formula is set in place, these companies are reluctant to make any changes in their survey processes because such moves can be perceived as jeopardizing the survey continuity.

While it is certainly commendable to establish long-term CS measurement objectives and to use effective formula-based management techniques, companies should be careful about institutionalizing survey programs that are cast in stone for years. Unless a company is confident that its CS survey methodology produces valid, adequately detailed, and reliable data, it runs the risk of locking itself into a particular survey process. Because a set survey-based formula might be producing inexact or even erroneous findings, the company might, unwittingly, be diminishing the value of its CS surveys.

Furthermore, CS surveys should be kept within the perspective of total quality. Continuous improvement does not just apply to a company's products and services; it also applies to its application of management techniques, including surveys. Since most companies are still in the learning phases of designing CS surveys, it seems prudent that corporate managers keep their survey options open as they continue to discover new survey improvements and learn from each other.

An Effective Tool

Many companies use CS surveys in their business markets; unfortunately, some of them use surveys incorrectly. To have effective surveys, they must:

- Understand the differences between business and consumer markets and address these differences in survey development
- Avoid the six common mistakes in survey administration

By understanding these differences and avoiding these mistakes, companies can develop an efficient and objective means of measuring customers' perceptions about the quality of their products and services.

References

1. Laura Loro, "Customer Is Always Right: Satisfaction Research Brooms," *Advertising Age,* Feb. 10, 1992, p. 25.

2. Kenneth Wylie, "Dollars Grow Tight in U.S., But Foreign Research Blossoms," *Advertising Age,* June 22, 1992, p. S2.

3. "Six Myths About Telemarketing," *Sales & Marketing Management,* October 1992, pp. 108–111; Christine L. Mehta, "Too Many Surveys, Too Many Numbers Add Up to Confusion," *Automotive News,* Nov. 5, 1990, p. 13i; John A. Goodman, Scott M. Broetzmann, and Colin Adamson, "Ineffective: That's the Problem With Customer Satisfaction Surveys," *Quality Progress,* May 1992, pp. 35–38; "Measuring Customer Views: Is D-I-Y Wise?," *Business Marketing Digest,* Fourth Quarter 1991, pp. 31–38;

and Valerie Rice, "The Art and Science of Customer Surveys," *Electronic Business*, Oct. 7, 1991, pp. 141–144.

4. For readers who are interested in further studies in business marketing, the Institute for the Study of Business Markets (ISBM) at Penn State University is a leading research center in the field and has sponsored a significant amount of literature. Contact Irwin Gross, executive director, ISBM, Penn State University, Delaware County Campus, 25 Yearsley Mill Rd., Media, PA 19063.

5. Irwin Gross, "The Perils of Customer Satisfaction," *Marketplace: The ISBM Review*, Spring 1991.

Warren R. Hayslip is the president of Priority Metrics Group, Inc. in Spartanburg, SC.

Motorola: Training for the Millennium

Kevin Kelly and Peter Burrows

Motorola has always been a leader in its commitment to training. This article from Business Week *explains this commitment and why the company expects to expand its training to nearly 160 hours per year for each employee.*

Motorola Inc. hardly seems in need of a makeover. It's marching from strength to strength in cellular and paging gear. Its chip business is straining to meet demand. And its profits—excluding special charges—leaped 77% last year, to $1.02 billion, as sales surged 28%, to $17 billion. Helping power this performance has been Motorola's Six Sigma defect-reduction program, which made it the first large company to win a Malcolm Baldrige National Quality Award in 1988. Indeed, Motorola has one of the finest reputations for quality in Corporate America.

After quality, though, what? Motorola's leaders fear that by the turn of the century, rivals will have caught up, and quality will have changed from a goal to a given. In the business wars of the coming decade, they believe, the most crucial weapons will be responsiveness, adaptability, and creativity.

To develop those attributes, Motorola is gearing up a new campaign built around lifelong learning. Under a program conceived by Robert W. Galvin, the 71-year-old former chairman who heads the board's executive committee, Motorola will dramatically increase training of all employees, from the factory floor to the corner office. The goal is a workforce that is disciplined yet

Reprinted from the March 28, 1994 issue of *Business Week* by special permission, copyright © 1994 by McGraw-Hill, Inc.

free-thinking. The initiative will aim to inculcate them with company procedures so they're a well-oiled machine but also to develop the knowledge and independent-mindedness that Motorola will need to conquer rapidly changing technologies and markets.

"Off the Scale"

The learning campaign will demand huge resources. Motorola already gives all employees at least 40 hours of training a year, one of the heavier commitments in U.S. industry. It hopes to quadruple that, perhaps by 2000. That "would put them way off the scale," says Anthony Carnevale, chief economist of the American Society for Training & Development (ASTD). It might also cost $600 million a year—the same as a big chip factory. Motorola is even pushing its methods in pubic schools to prepare the next generation of employees (page 160).

Motorola already gives all employees at least 40 hours of training a year, one of the heavier commitments in U.S. industry. It hopes to quadruple that, perhaps by 2000.

Such a commitment doesn't get made without the strong support of top management. Galvin's son, President Christopher B. Galvin, is a booster. So is Chief Executive Gary L. Tooker, who concedes that he doubted the concept when it came up in the early 1980s. Tooker, who ran Motorola's chip business with an iron hand, was seen by some as a tough guy who might dismiss training as costly fluff. But when he took over last December, after George M. C. Fisher left for Eastman Kodak Co., Tooker made it clear that he would stay the course. "If knowledge is becoming antiquated at a faster rate, we have no choice but to spend on education," he says. "How can that not be a competitive weapon?"

One reason Motorola dares to make such a commitment is that its training to date has paid off handsomely. The company's quality depends on employees from the shop floor up using tools such as statistical process control. That procedure, which involves tracking error rates, requires arithmetic and a bit of algebra. But the company found in 1985 that 60% of its workforce had trouble with seventh-grade math. Around that time, Bob Galvin, then chairman, decreed that 1.5% of payroll would be spent on training—a proportion that has risen to 4%. The company also founded Motorola University, its teaching center, and tightened up on hiring. It now requires seventh-grade math proficiency for all new hires, more for technical jobs.

Several other big companies train a lot, too. But Motorola stands out in how it binds education to business targets. For instance, it will set a goal to reduce product-development cycle time, then create a course on how to do it. This is not learning for its own sake: Students are drilled in specific tasks until they get them right, whether it's operating a tool or being more persuasive with customers. "The intimacy between education and business strategy is tighter at Motorola than anyplace I know," says Donald K. Conover, AT&T's recently retired vice-president for education and training.

"The intimacy between education and business strategy is tighter at Motorola than anyplace I know."

A good example came two years ago, when Fisher decreed that the company had to do better at software. Motorola University organized a three-day seminar at which 30 vice-presidents mapped out a plan of attack. It also taught the vice-presidents how to form project teams and techniques for fostering change. As a result, the veeps decided to let software engineers work at home more often and dress casually in the office. The engineers also started getting banquets and awards—laurels once preserved for the hardware side. And Motorola tried harder to patent software. Pleased executives won't discuss results, except to say that the annual number of patents has risen 20%.

Symbolic of the commitment is Motorola U., with headquarters in Schaumburg, Ill., 14 branches from Tokyo to Honolulu, and a budget of more than $120 million. Courses designed by "instructional engineers" cover such topics as critical thinking, problem-solving, management, computers, remedial English, and how to run a robot.

Motorola U. also propagates the company's culture—regimented, efficient, and more than a little driven. Executives of Nextel Communications Inc., the upstart cellular-communications company, ran head-on into those qualities when they negotiated a deal for Motorola to supply them with equipment and buy a stake in their company. "It was 18 months of agony," says Nextel Chairman Morgan E. O'Brien. A united front of Motorola negotiators followed procedures on every detail, from contract to press release. "It's bureaucratic," says O'Brien, "but that's what makes them efficient."

Establishing consistency is essential to a company that gets more than half its revenue from overseas and is increasing foreign production. "We're a unifying force," says Motorola U. President William A. Wiggenhorn. For example, Motorola U. helps ensure that the commitment to equal opportunity for women applies around the world, including Japan, where Motorola is one of the few companies in which women engineers instruct men.

"Empowerment"

Translators make sure courses communicate the same message across cultures. In Asia, for example, the sports metaphors in U.S. course materials are replaced with stories about families. Other aspects require uniformity. For instance, "empowerment" is a key word in Motorola's vocabulary, but many languages—Japanese, Chinese, and German among them—have no exact equivalent. So Motorolans in those countries use the English word.

Motorola doesn't train only its own either. It learned long ago that it couldn't hit quality targets if it got bad parts. Yet some suppliers pretended they knew how to use quality methods and agreed to specifications they couldn't meet. "We used to usually end up hating each other," says Christopher Magnella, process-engineering manager at the Austin (Tex.) chip plant. The remedy: Magnella helped develop a class for suppliers on statistical process control.

Training for people outside the company can have other benefits, too: In central China, Motorola U. offers courses to students studying at the Nanjing Institute of Posts & Telecommunications. That helps it spot potential hires and educate potential customers. In Japan, Motorola is putting together courses to explain the new PowerPC microprocessor to salespeople, engineers, and customers. It's not all education for export either. One course on quality methodology originated in Singapore and is now being used in the U.S.

Those who doubt that learning is a competitive weapon need only look at the new Austin chip plant, MOS-11. It makes some of the most sophisticated chips in the world, with circuit lines measuring a half-micron across—1/200 the width of a human hair. Leading chip plants often take three to four years to open, but Motorola needed just 18 months. Says Operations Manager Bill Dunnigan: "We surprised everybody, including ourselves."

The secret was "away teams"—120 people sent around the world to become expert on the equipment that would fill the plant. Technician Steven Henderson spent his first 13 months with Motorola on the road: "People in the office didn't even know who I was," he says. Much of his time was spent at a Motorola plant in Phoenix and at a San Jose (Calif.) supplier of wafer-processing gear, Silicon Valley Inc. The Motorola team helped Silicon Valley build a production mock-up. For realism, the team used thousands of $100 to $150 wafers—and then discarded them. While expensive, this let operators and technicians learn the gear, get the bugs out, and write training documents for Austin.

For realism, the team used thousands of $100 to $150 wafers—and then discarded them.

Thus prepared, MOS-11 set a company record for yield of good wafers in just its third lot. (It won't disclose the numbers.) With the new capacity, Motorola has emerged as the leading supplier in the fast-growing market for very fast static RAMs, which go into personal computers and other products.

Training is also the *sine qua non* for Motorola's team approach to manufacturing. At a factory for pagers and two-way radios in Swords, Ireland, outside Dublin, 80% of employees belong to teams, where membership requires seven days of training. The Waste Watchers team was in the plant cafeteria early one recent Tuesday, calculating how to save $250 a week by using smaller shipping boxes. It's much the same at the cellular-products factory in Arlington Heights, Ill., where workers schedule production and can veto the hiring of specific individuals. Corporate Vice-President Richard Chandler has been able to shift technicians and supervisors off the shop floor and into research, design, and customer service. "How could I do any of this if I didn't train my workers?" he says.

Give-and-Take

Naturally, some employees balk at going back to school. Chandler concedes that he has had to threaten some with firing to get them to do it. But most incentives are positive. For example, the new skills can qualify employees for promotions. To keep classes interesting, problems are derived from situations at Motorola. Instructors use a lively give-and-take. And students who fall behind get tutoring. If some employees still don't learn what's required, though, they may be demoted.

Actually, classroom training is only part of the learning at Motorola. Even more important is "embedded learning," or apprenticeship. In Arlington Heights, for instance, new employees earn regular wages while learning tasks under a more experienced worker's guidance. ASTD's Carnevale says Motorola is a national leader in that style of learning—which is in addition to the 40-plus annual hours of formal instruction.

Even more important is "embedded learning," or apprenticeship.

An Insider's Lexicon

Motorola uses a specialized language to bind its employees together and describe its unique methods. Here's a sample:

ADAPTIVE MANAGERS Managers who tailor their approach to subordinates by taking account of individual needs.

SIX-HATTING Putting on six different hats to look at a problem from different perspectives.

SIX SIGMA An accuracy range—plus or minus six standard deviations from a norm—that means only 1.2 parts per billion are defective. Since processes deteriorate over time, Motorola considers 3.4 defects per million as six sigma.

RONA Return on net assets. A basis for bonuses.

TOTAL CUSTOMER SATISFACTION 1. Motorola's guiding slogan. 2. An annual team competition for ideas to improve customer satisfaction.

DATA: MOTOROLA INC.

Motorola is taking a risk by throwing so many resources into training, since there are few reliable yardsticks to measure its effectiveness. A mid-1980s study purported to show that each training dollar delivered $30 in productivity gains within three years. And Motorola claims that problem-solving teams and other work groups have saved around $4 billion. But such numbers are soft: After all, what savings might have been achieved anyway? More to the point is the assessment of Gary Langely, manager of organization and human effectiveness in Austin: "We take it on faith and strong belief that it is improving our bottom line." When factories are running 365 days a year, Langely says, "there's no time to slow down to see if it's making a difference."

The lack of hard evidence is unusual in a company that has "metrics" for everything down to catered lunches. An obvious question is whether training could go too far. Another is whether Motorola could stifle initiative by teaching a procedure for every jot of the working day. Nextel Chief Executive Brian McAuley notes that while the Motorola deal took 18 months to conclude, a deal with MCI Communications Corp. took 4 1/2 days. "Motorola couldn't have done that," he says. Some Motorolans also argue that instructors don't spend enough time on such emerging issues as promoting creative thinking or workplace diversity.

Tunnel Vision?

Motorola's leaders know the dangers of turning inward. Tooker vows not to repeat the mistake of Six Sigma several years ago, when the company focused so hard on defect reduction that it nearly lost sight of overall customer satisfaction. The company shifted its focus outward after being stung by the results of an independent survey of customers.

There may be no way to prove that a commitment to learning will sustain Motorola into the next century. But it's not a bad bet. With change rendering an engineer's knowledge obsolete every five years, Tooker sees little choice. For a company that seems to keep statistics on everything, the biggest lesson from education may be that sometimes you just have to rely on intuition.

Kevin Kelly and Peter Burrows are correspondents for Business Week.

Action Learning: Taming Real Problems in Real Time

Paul Froiland

Action learning is, at its heart, about turning a company into a learning organization. It has to do with identifying problems, creating teams to work on improvements to solve those problems, and learning from the experience. In a way, it is PDCA given the label of training. This article documents this approach to training, which is hands-on, action-oriented.

There's a problem at the Grinchling Co., maker of amazing Grinchling Chocolate Bars, which have taken the American candy market by storm. Phenomenal demand for the new chocolate bar has persuaded the company to hire scores of workers at its domestic plants and to begin construction of new plants in Stuttgart, Germany, and Manila, the Philippines. But the managers who will be in charge of the international plants are command-and-control types with no training in managing workers of other cultures.

Mr. Grinchling, the company president, brings in Nosweat Consultants to run a two-week training program for the future international managers, featuring such films as "Ich bin ein Stuttgarter" and "Say Hello to Manila." The managers get a great deal of generic information about managing Germans and Filipinos. Six months later, the foreign plants are ready to begin production, and the managers have forgotten all the sure-fire tips they learned in training. They institute their old, familiar command-and-control methods at the new plants. Workers at Grinchling Schokolade in Stuttgart rebel and go on strike. The workers in Manila call in sick in hordes, and production falls severely.

Action learning, say its proponents, is as old as the medieval craft-guild system: You learn by doing.

What went wrong?

It may be an overdrawn case of When Training Doesn't Work, but it is quite the opposite of what happens when action learning works. Action learning, say its proponents, is as old as the medieval craft-guild system: You learn

Reprinted with permission from the January 1994 issue of *Training* Magazine. Copyright © 1994, Lakewood Publications, Minneapolis, MN. All rights reserved. Not for resale.

by doing. A real work challenge is the centerpiece of an action-learning experience. Teams or work groups take an actual problem to the training program, work on solving it, commit to an action plan, and are accountable for carrying out the plan.

Of course, real-life applications of the method are not always so clear-cut. Action-learning programs often encompass a variety of other elements. Some practitioners, for example, consider personal development an essential component of action learning. Participants may attend outdoor experiential courses where they climb ropes or rappel down cliffs. Or they may be placed in situations that require them to confront viewpoints unfamiliar—and sometimes opposed—to their own. Some action-learning courses involve high stakes for participants—executives may have to bet their annual bonus on their solution to a problem, for example—while others involve little or low risk.

In contrast, Grinchling managers attended classroom training that depicted hypothetical instances of cross-cultural interaction. The training was not framed in terms of a real problem or challenge, such as how can I make the Stuttgart plant run profitably and smoothly within 60 days? The managers were not held accountable for putting into practice what they learned in training. So they tackled their foreign assignments by conducting business as usual. And they nearly ruined the company.

Noel Tichy, of the University of Michigan's business school in Ann Arbor, is one of the foremost proponents of action learning. Michigan, in fact, uses action learning in its MBA program so that students "get their hands dirty," learning the curriculum by taking on real-life work challenges at area businesses. Tichy also has used action learning to help such companies as General Electric and Ameritech overturn and rebuild their corporate cultures.

"The problem with management is that we treat it as a quasi-scientific thing," Tichy says. "Management is a clinical practice. You don't train heart surgeons by having them read Harvard cases. Management development has to get much closer to the real world. How do you train people in the crafts? That's all we're talking about. The basic principles apply all the way to the shop floor."

Management is a clinical practice. You don't train heart surgeons by having them read Harvard cases.

John Murphy, formerly corporate director of executive education and quality education at GTE Corp. in Stanford, CT, implemented an action-learning approach to problem solving during the '80s that the company continues to use today. Now president of Executive Edge Inc., a Fairfield, CT, consulting firm, Murphy defines action learning as the opposite of the classroom-training model, which assumes that training or "development" is a discrete activity that precedes the real work it is intended to shape; that is, first people receive training, then they go out and achieve business results. That, he says, is backwards; rather, "You put [people] in a legitimate work situation [intending] the achievement of results for which they have accountability. Then, in collaboration with them, you provide them with the just-in-time learning that everyone needs in order not to make a disaster out of the responsibility they have."

How It Works

A typical action-learning project involves groups of between six and 30 employees (sometimes including vendors and customers). There are a few variations on how the groups are composed. Some groups include a single "stakeholder" for the work problem that is being dealt with; the rest of the participants come from different businesses within large corporations or different functions within smaller ones. These nonstakeholders are included to provide the group with fresh perspectives on the problem at hand. Sometimes all the participants have a stake in solving the problem—in other words, they all work in the same department or division of the company. Or, in a multistakeholder group, participants from a variety of divisions focus on their own particular issues, taking turns examining each others' problems.

One example of a multistakeholder action-learning group is the ongoing "Gap Group" process, used for leadership development at AT&T in Morristown, NJ. The name came from each group's goal of identifying and surmounting the gaps in performance or output that a division faces. High-potential managers each bring in a business problem confronting their division and work in small groups with six or seven peers from other divisions. The process lasts seven days; one day is dedicated to each manager's business problem.

The stakeholder for each problem presents the issue for two hours. The group then wrestles with the problem and tests the "definition" that the stakeholder has presented. Participants propose alternative ways to look at the problem, as well as possible solutions. The group receives guidance either from a group-process expert, usually a consultant, or from subject-matter experts, often business-school professors. When the group settles on a possible solution, the stakeholder makes out an action plan for his problem. He is accountable for producing the results the action plan calls for within the time period he designates. The group may meet informally after that to check progress, or just stay in touch by telephone. The manager of the leadership program will also call participants at intervals to remind them they are accountable for solving the problem.

Gap Groups are composed of as diverse a membership as possible. "We tried it once the other way," says Joe Galarneau, executive education director at AT&T. "We tried having people who were all from sales, for example, and they would always say, 'I've tried that; I've tried that' to every suggestion that was raised."

Group members at AT&T also make action plans for personal behavioral changes that they wish to make based on insights gained during the Gap Group process, but there is no mechanism that makes them accountable for these.

Probably no two companies use action learning the same way. One key difference is between those who use "accountability" strictly in the honor-system sense vs. those who use accountability combined with risk. In the second type of application, you stand to lose money or at least face if you don't carry out your action plan.

At AT&T, an example of the first type of company, the members of an action-learning group are held "accountable" for producing the result their action plan specifies. Should they fail to produce it, however, it is up to them to find out why. They are trusted to do this and don't face any particular risk.

In the second type of group, there is accountability *and* risk. Tichy describes it best: "The key in action learning is you have to create performance anxiety [with] the illusion of pretty high risk," he says. "So [your group] did a crummy report; you're not going to lose your job, but you're going to be professionally embarrassed. And that's usually enough inducement to pull the all-nighters. And when you put people under that kind of pressure, you can see what kind of team members they are and how effective [they are]."

Another example of risk may be the loss of a bonus for executives if they fail to take appropriate action and produce results. Yet another type of risk: getting kicked off the action team for failing to do what you said you would on the problem.

GE Medical Systems in Milwaukee uses the action-learning model that Tichy introduced throughout the corporation. Teams are composed of about two-thirds stakeholders and one-third high-potential people whom the company wants to develop, according to John Christman, training manager. Team members who will become facilitators for GE's famous Work-Out sessions are trained in the action-learning process. (The Work-Out sessions themselves could be considered a form of action learning: Teams of knowledgeable stakeholders are chartered to develop action plans for solutions to resolve business issues or improve processes. They are then empowered to enact these solutions.) Work-Out facilitators are not allowed into the action-learning course unless they have a problem, an owner of the problem, and a date already scheduled to begin meeting on the problem.

Corning Inc. in Corning, NY, offers an elective course in action learning to teach work teams how to apply the method. Corning owns a large plant in State College, PA, that manufactures glass for TV picture tubes. Employees wishing to get into an action-learning training group there must come from a work team that is trying to solve a real business problem, such as how to improve employee-to-employee relations. "They bring their own real problem with them," says former director of education and training J. Edwin O'Brien, "and as they're learning the process, they're applying it to a back-home operation. The team has the responsibility to solve the problem."

Action-learning groups at State College are gender- and race-balanced, and deal with what often become highly volatile issues of sexual and racial harassment.

Corning also uses action learning for diversity training at its State College plant. Action-learning groups at State College are gender- and race-balanced, and deal with what often become highly volatile issues of sexual and racial harassment—who can touch whom where, for example, and whether it doesn't really matter because they both know it's kidding. (It's *not* kidding and not welcome, according to women in two of the groups that O'Brien observed.) The action that has resulted from the groups is a monitoring system for employee complaints about other employees or supervisors. The system is used to determine whether there is a racial or gender component to complaints, an issue that had not been considered before the action-learning project was started.

Other companies try to create action-learning groups that represent as diverse a spectrum of employees as possible, and some even include willing clients. Cigna International Property and Casualty Corp., the Philadelphia insurance company, puts people in action-learning groups that work 40 hours a week for four to five weeks. Each group is assigned a single problem that faces just one of Cigna's divisions. Usually only one or two people in the group will be from that division; every other division president will also send one or two people.

Cigna's most recent group was charged with evaluating the entire business strategy of one segment of the company, according to Marilyn Gardner, vice president for corporate training in Philadelphia. The property-casualty business that was under examination was losing money, and the group was supposed to determine whether the business's current strategy was viable.

The first week the group immersed itself in the particulars of the business in question. After that, group members went out into the field and interviewed customers, competitors, employees and intermediaries who helped sell that business, to determine the soundness of the current strategy. Following that, the group gathered again and listened to the advice of an expert from Harvard Business School and another from the Wharton School of Business. The group concluded its charge with a recommendation for a new business strategy, and the business is now acting on that strategy. (See accompanying box for a participant's view of that group.)

Going Global

Some organizations use action learning for larger issues, such as refocusing a company along global lines.

Whirlpool Corp., in Benton Harbor, MI, held its first-ever worldwide leadership conference in 1990 in Switzerland, bringing in 140 top executives, according to Tom Helton, corporate director of organization and leadership development. The issue they faced: global integration after Whirlpool's acquisition of N.V. Philips, a European subsidiary that had plants in Germany, Italy, France and England.

During the conference the 140 participants brainstormed and generated a list of 300 projects that they saw as advancing the integration of the now international company. The CEO and executive committee picked 15 of these projects, which they labeled Whirlpool 1 company challenges. Each project had American and European co-chairpersons, and project leaders divided all 140 members among their teams. The 15 projects were chartered at the meeting—with deliverables required—and the teams were sent off to work.

One of the 15 projects included the articulation and detailing of the process by which the company created products. Other projects included the global-management reporting system that has since been instituted at the company, and the development of a quality initiative. According to Helton, results from the more successful of the projects are "still reverberating through the company."

If the Training Fits . . .

Many companies use action learning at the executive level. John Lawrie, president of Applied Psychology Inc. in Crawfordsville, IN, thinks that there is a natural fit between executives, who are doers, and action learning, which is learning by doing.

"At [executive] levels you get a natural selection of people who know how to fix things, because things always get screwed up," Lawrie says. "Now if you put people who have been rewarded for this action style into an academic setting, what happens is that [the learning] falls through the cracks. If the trainee is a 'Do it! Jump on it!' type, then that's what we should do instead of talking about it."

Many agree with Lawrie's view that action learning is the natural province of executives. Michael Gilliam, vice president and general manager of the Global Business Center for Cigna, believes action learning is best done with managers "on a fairly high level," although he thinks any group of people can benefit from it.

Larry Ward, manager of executive development for the Dow Chemical Co. in Midland, MI, conducted a needs analysis of Dow's top 300 executives across the world to find what they perceived their development needs to be. "The feedback was so generic that I couldn't figure out where the heck you could go with it," he says. "I got things back like 'dealing with ambiguity.' " As a result, Dow called in a consultant, who sat down with the top 17 executives and asked them what key issues Dow needed to deal with in order to survive the next 10 years. Action-learning groups were formed around such issues as Dow's commitment to the eco-system, reconsidering the company's internal systems, and clarifying its strategic intent.

The reason that executives and managers seem to thrive best with action learning, according to Victoria Marsick, an associate professor of adult education at Teachers College at Columbia University in New York, is that the types of projects undertaken are usually seen as "more intensely meaningful" to managers and executives, and they are more willing than lower-level employees to take on accountability for the results. "At lower levels," Marsick says, "the project is often handed over to them from some senior manager, and they don't see the intrinsic worth of it."

Consultant Murphy agrees with Marsick. "The top three levels of management, like it or not, are the greatest force for change and accountability in a company," he says.

On the other hand, it *is* possible to use action learning successfully at lower levels. Consultant Lawrie says that for that to happen, one of the ingredients of the action plan must be getting the buy-in of the boss. "One of the critical pieces in [line workers'] environment is their boss," he says. "Part of the plan has to include how the group is going to present its notions to the boss. Which ones is he likely to go for? Which is he likely to turn down? Why?"

Patricia Stacey, a consultant with Action Learning Associates in Ann Arbor, MI, also sees possibilities for line workers using the process. In fact, she

Action Learning in Action

Michael Gilliam, a vice president and general manager of the Global Business Center of Cigna International Property and Casualty Corp. in Philadelphia, spent four intensive weeks in an action-learning group.

"The problem that we were charged with was analyzing the strategies of one of our [property-casualty insurance] business units over the last three years," Gilliam says. The group was not supposed to come up with a new business strategy, just make recommendations as to whether the existing strategies needed minor adjustments, whether they were wrong altogether, or whether they were being implemented incorrectly. The group was required to produce a paper with its recommendations at the end of the four weeks.

Gilliam's group consisted of 11 cross-disciplinary upper- and middle-management members from various divisions of Cigna—Cigna International, Cigna's domestic division, benefits, investment and several others. No two people came from the same division, and there were no vendors or clients included in the group. Group members abandoned their jobs for the duration of the process and met off-site.

"The first week was a mixture of academics, [consultation with] some professors from Harvard and Wharton, plus a briefing from the division staff that had the business problem," Gilliam says. "We absorbed a lot of data about the business problem as well as data on strategy, and [applying] academics to strategy.

"The second week we split into four teams and traveled the country. We conducted about 100 interviews with employees, distributors and customers on a one-to-one basis.

"The third week we assimilated the data," Gilliam continues, "and the fourth week we formed the recommendations and wrote a 40-plus-page paper." At the end of the fourth week, the group presented its recommendation to the president and entire executive staff of the troubled division. The executives were given a few hours to read the paper and then come back and put questions to the action-learning group.

The results? "The [division] executives were very complimentary, open and receptive to our recommendations," says Gilliam. The recommendations are currently being implemented.

Gilliam is extremely high on the action-learning process as he experienced it. "I think participating in this is the best thing I've ever done both from a work and educational standpoint—and the most exhausting thing I've ever done from a physical and mental standpoint," he says. "Generally, we were working in excess of 15 hours a day over the last two weeks. And we were self-managed, so it was our own excitement and adrenalin that was pushing our 15-hour days." Gilliam says he would highly recommend the process to anyone—"if they have the stamina."

Continued—

Action Learning in Action (continued)

One of the most important things that Gilliam believes came from this was "learning the dynamics of teamwork and what can be accomplished with a group of highly skilled people who are truly focused for an extended period. That's hard to duplicate in the classroom or any sort of corporate environment," he says.

"You're basically living with 11 people for four weeks," he continues. "People are burned from a mental standpoint, and they have to learn how to cope and get along. It's exciting to watch the dynamics of that happen."

says, "The problem is that people at the top get these wonderful, grandiose ideas, but have no clue about what's going on at the bottom. If you get the right people in the room who know what the process is, they can fix it."

She suggests that for action learning to work at the line level, workers must make a commitment to their supervisor that, once the problem is mapped out, they will fix it and save either a target dollar amount, or target percentage of cycle time. Then they have to return at the end of the allotted time and demonstrate that they've done it. "Otherwise," she says, "a [rule] of action learning says that if you can't do the job, you have no business being there. People have to be willing to take that risk and make it happen."

Does a lot of this sound like tenets of the total-quality movement? In fact, many of the techniques that quality-improvement teams routinely use to solve problems or improve processes borrow from action-learning methods.

Many of the techniques that quality-improvement teams routinely use to solve problems or improve processes borrow from action-learning methods.

At Whirlpool, line managers run action-learning groups composed of front-line workers. "We have close to 100 percent of our line managers actually conducting the [action] training," says Helton. The role of training and HR people has become largely one of training line managers to be trainers, he says. One incentive for line workers to participate is that they've all become stakeholders in the company since employee stock options were granted a few years ago. Whirlpool was trading at $37 a share when the options were granted; it's trading in the $60 range now. Employees see the results in their pockets when they tackle and solve company problems.

One problem that Whirlpool employees handled using action learning was recovering overpaid duty on compressors that the company was importing from a Brazilian affiliate. Members of the procurement group formed a team that took on the issue of what processes they would need to implement the company's strategies for inventory control and cost reduction. The team found a process that recovers the duty, saving the company hundreds of thousands of dollars a year.

"Whoopee in the Woods"

Although personal-growth training may be extrinsic to a strict definition of action learning, many companies insist that it is one of the keys to making action learning work. The idea is that group members are encouraged to consider other points of view. For this reason many organizations regard a consultant or group facilitator as essential. If the action-learning group were run by someone who already works at the sponsoring company, that someone likely would have a similar perspective to those in the group.

In the pursuit of personal growth and better group dynamics, action-learning groups often are sent to outdoor "ropes" and rock-climbing courses to enhance team trust and harmony. Proponents insist that team-building exercises improve the efforts of a team working on a business problem. Likewise, they contend, individual contributions are enhanced when team members are forced to examine things from new perspectives. According to Marsick, the notion that action learning ought to be merged with personal-development activities began in Sweden, which, along with other European countries, has a much longer history with the process than America does.

"The [Swedish] model typically adds to the project [opportunities] for people to look at things in new ways," Marsick says. "They deliberately try to startle people out of the way they look at things. They may take the group of managers to interview a group of theater people about their ideas of leadership. They are forced to meet with hippies and other fringe groups that Swedish managers wouldn't normally interact with. When you put people in situations that are very different from what they are ordinarily in, it's often uncomfortable for them, and it forces them into new ways of thinking."

In the United States, the startling experiences usually come in the guise of Outward Bound types of courses, which offer team-based challenges and are designed to help group members learn more about each other while they develop a team commitment. "The Outward Bound things contribute a lot to the personal learning," says Marsick, "and they create conditions for a team to work together more effectively. That would jump[-start] the efficacy of the team as a learning group."

At Ameritech, a "Baby Bell" company in Hoffman Estates, IL, action-learning groups not only go through Outward Bound exercises, they also visit soup kitchens. "People learn best when they're out of their comfort zone," says Bob Knowling, vice president and head of the Ameritech Institute.

Ropes and rocks courses are not essential, "but they are a useful social technology for kick starting team development."

Ropes and rocks courses are not essential, says Michigan's Tichy, "but they are a useful social technology for kick starting team development." He often uses such activities with action-learning groups, he says, but only in conjunction with real team issues. "This kind of 'whoopee in the woods' stuff is no different than the sensitivity-training fad in the '60s. You've got to link it to real stuff fast."

Marvin Weisbord, a consultant in Plainfield, NJ, is co-director of a nonprofit organization called Search-Net, which uses action learning to help people program community-planning conferences. According to Weisbord, outdoor courses are just one way of adding to action learning. "You can do it with swings and sliding boards, with hopscotch and jump ropes," he says. "You can do it with coat hangers, stamp collections, rock 'n' roll. All these programs are tied to is getting yourself into a situation in which you are vulnerable and you don't know the answer and the outcome is not assured and bulling your way through." He also cautions, however, that all these exercises have to be tied to the learning task in some way.

Others are less sold on incorporating an experiential element. Whirlpool's Helton says that when his company first experimented with what it thought was action learning, employees went through outdoor courses in conjunction with classroom learning. They always gave the outdoor courses rave reviews. "The problem is, however," Helton says, "when that kind of thing is looked at from a business perspective, the senior leadership here was asking, 'How is that helping me move the company to achieve the goals we've set?' And that's a tough one to answer."

Whirlpool eventually abandoned the outdoors courses and set up an action-learning system that integrated three-level teams: the manager of a unit, his or her direct subordinates, and their direct subordinates. "What you get then," says Helton, "is everybody in the room who's needed to make a change." The teams then undertake a real business problem, have customized workshops, go out to work individually on their projects, then reconvene for more training.

Consultant Murphy is the most outspoken in his disdain for tying outdoor courses and the like to action-learning projects. If the whole point of action learning is to work on real business problems, he argues, what in the world is anyone but a lumberjack or a forest ranger doing out in the woods? "I think ropes courses and rock climbing are a crock," he says. "The company is full of [metaphorical] fields and ropes and rocks: Why isn't *that* the experience in the experiential learning? Nothing builds a team better than the excitement of having met an incredibly difficult goal. If you have to go to a rock pile to get that, you're just not linking the business reality to the training opportunity. To me, taking your employees to a ropes course is saying that you don't know how to do that with your own company."

Nothing builds a team better than the excitement of having met an incredibly difficult goal.

Insecure Executives

Advocates and users of action learning are glowing in their assessments of its possibilities. But some organizations would consider it anathema. "If you don't have the appropriate leadership," says Tichy, "it isn't going to work. I did a massive action-learning process at Honeywell Systems in the early '80s, but they didn't execute. They didn't have the leadership .... In fact, it can probably make your leaders look worse. Companies that have insecure people will find this absolutely threatening. Those are the guys that come in with their body/mind guards and their written scripts, and they do their one-way speech and they're whisked away in a limo. [Action learning] is mix it up, get out there and scrimmage."

Other organizations, Tichy says, *think* they're doing action learning but don't give it enough time, don't choose significant projects, and don't take real risks. "It's kind of a traditional 'We'll pitch it to the CEO,' " he says. "Life goes on. I go back to my division and the program falls apart." You have to real risks. "It's kind of a traditional 'We'll pitch it to the CEO,' " he says. "Life goes on. I go back to my division and the program falls apart." You have to put people at sufficient risk and track their projects, he says, and you have to tie it into the company's measurement and reward systems.

Consultant Lawrie describes another situation in which action learning would be unlikely to succeed: "[When] you have a very authoritarian boss with people who have been with him over the years. They're so conditioned to be told what to do, and he's so conditioned to [telling them] and being rewarded for it, that it would be a mistake to try action learning."

Ready for Takeoff?

Will action learning be the next big movement in training? Perhaps and perhaps not. Joe Raelin, who teaches at Boston College's Carroll School of Management, came upon the European version of action learning while on sabbatical in Lancaster, England. There, he found two major MBA programs similar to Tichy's at Michigan in which students learned by studying real-life problems at companies.

Back in the United States, however, Raelin says he doesn't see any widespread rush to embrace it. Although he considers himself somewhat of a promoter of the process, he says he's been having a hard time launching it in this country. He suspects two reasons for the resistance; "First, it may well be that this country's corporate directors are not willing to have someone poke around in critical problems in their organizations; it's a resistance to culture change.

"Second, action learning is not a product or an outcome; it's a process. And we tend to be outcome-oriented rather than process-oriented," he says.

Tichy, on the other hand, is absolutely bullish on the prospects of action learning. "No question that it's taking off," he says. "It's related not to action learning having been refined or further developed: it's the firing of [CEO John] Akers [by IBM] and [Bob] Stempel [by General Motors], it's the taking out of Paul Lego at Westinghouse and James Robinson [at American Express], and all of a sudden transformation becomes a serious game. Then you ask yourself, 'How the hell am I going to change the culture?' Doing some old way of training isn't going to work. The marketplace is forcing them to change and they're realizing they have to break free of the old stuff."

Or, as John Murphy puts it: "I don't want awareness training; I want to know how to do this damned thing."

That's the essence of action learning.

Paul Froiland is associate editor of Training *Magazine.*

Reengineering the Training Department

Beverly Geber

To be more responsive to their customers and more cost-effective, training departments are rethinking their purpose and methods. Through the use of technology, they are coming up with new methods, as well as new content, for delivering the training vital to keep an organization in the game. This article explains in detail these new directions in training.

It was Claudia Davis' job to grapple with the fallout of the information age. As director of education for Hewlett-Packard Co. in Palo Alto, CA, she had to make sure that the company's legions of software engineers stayed current in a field in which the store of information changes so rapidly that their knowledge becomes obsolete in less than two years.

In the face of such a voracious need for continuing education, the old ways of providing training couldn't cope. By the time Davis' training department could fashion a new classroom course and deliver it to the engineers in the computer company, the information was already getting moldy. The situation was not only logistically vexing; it also endangered the competitiveness of H-P when its engineers did not know quickly about new advances in their field.

Yet that was not the only disadvantage of traditional classroom training. The costs of dragging engineers into classrooms continued to rise. Facilities, materials and instructor time all grew more expensive. But what troubled Davis even more was the time and productivity lost due to taking the company's engineers off the job for training. In the fiercely competitive computer industry, in which profit margins are often as thin as computer chips, the company couldn't tolerate frequent siphoning of its employees' time.

Davis was made vividly aware of all this two years ago when the education department had to teach H-P employees about object-oriented computer technology. Engineers needed to learn it right away, but others in the company needed to know about it as well. Davis calculated that so many people were affected that if she offered classes every day in 12 locations, it would still take more than a year to reach everybody in the company who needed to know.

Reprinted with permission from the May 1994 issue of *Training* Magazine. Copyright © 1994, Lakewood Publications, Minneapolis, MN. All rights reserved. Not for resale.

So she turned to technology. Davis and her instructional designers devised a course on object-oriented technology that was geared to H-P. Then the company promised National Technological University (NTU), a videoconferencing company, that if it would transmit the course, H-P would guarantee that a certain number of subscribers would sign up for it.

That cut the cost of travel, since engineers could now attend the course through downlinks at their own workplaces. But it still meant that the engineers had to go into a room at a particular time to view the telecast. It would be ideal, Davis thought, to distribute the training to the engineers in such a way that they could learn what they needed at their own workstations when they had the time. So she took the next step.

It would be ideal, Davis thought, to distribute the training to the engineers in such a way that they could learn what they needed at their own workstations when they had the time.

Now, by using a three-way linking system that joins a computer, a videocassette player, and the satellite feed from NTU, engineers can record the classes as they're being telecast and watch them later at their desks. They can freeze the screen, which may show the contents of an overhead transparency that the professor is discussing, and use a computer-notes function to add their own comments to what appears on the screen. After the engineers finish watching the broadcast, they can print out their own personally annotated version of the content.

The new setup allows the engineers to move through the material at their own pace whenever they have time, a convenience that contributes to higher productivity. Although it costs money to telecast the classes and provide the engineers with desktop systems to capture it, the company is still saving money by eliminating the direct and indirect costs of classroom training. Currently, each setup used to deliver the training costs several thousands of dollars apiece, and not all engineers have systems. But Davis expects the cost to drop to about $400 within a couple of years, making the system easy to justify to top management.

"It's so overwhelming that nobody even questions it," Davis says. She calculates that in order to deliver five hours of classroom training, about 25 extra hours are needed for travel and incidental time. Multiply that 25 hours by the salary of the individuals involved and there's no need to bother calculating the direct costs of training, Davis says. "I just have to show [executives] the first set of numbers. It can't be worth it to let [trainees] spend 25 hours to get five hours of training."

And Davis believes that learning effectiveness is just as great—maybe better—with the new methods. In the past, a course with just five hours of content would probably be stretched to a couple of days in order to justify the travel. Trainers would undoubtedly throw in some information that trainees would need eventually but perhaps not immediately. Trouble was, by the time they needed to use the bonus information, they'd forgotten it.

The new arrangement may not be the consummate, never-to-be-improved-upon way to deliver training to engineers, but Davis maintains that it's radically better than the old way.

Davis and a growing number of her counterparts at other U.S. corporations are at work to reinvent the way in which training is conceived and delivered within their companies. At the same time, but to a lesser degree, they are also changing the way in which their training departments operate.

The popular term for this is reengineering. Briefly, it means radically changing a process, usually through the use of technology, to realize substantial gains in cost, time or service. In an earlier time, before the word was coined and popularized by Michael Hammer and James Champy, authors of *Reengineering the Corporation,* it was called "doing more with less."

Training directors have always sought ways to wring more value out of their budgetary bucks. But those improvements tended to be modest and incremental, rather than the radical, revolutionary change that is sought today. Several trends have converged recently to bring about that sense of urgency within some corporate training departments.

■ *Time.* As the H-P example attests, it is no longer acceptable for training to be delivered on a sluggish timetable. And it's not just generalized information for certain employee populations, such as object-oriented technology for engineers, that needs to be delivered before it goes stale. Consider, for instance, that many companies, in order to stay competitive, have accelerated their new-product cycles. In some cases, a new-generation widget that is slightly improved through the use of technology can be released less than a year after its predecessor. Ideally, training to support that new-product release should be ready before the product is made if the company wants to sell as many of the widgets as possible during the short shelf life they will enjoy before they, too, are made obsolete by the next generation.

■ *Content.* The content of training courses used to be relatively static. That's still true of many subjects, such as time management. But other courses need to be changed frequently, perhaps because the state of the art of a particular technology changes. This means that companies must have the ability to deliver new content to employees without having to develop new classroom instruction or remaster a course delivered on interactive videodisc. Even so, the implication is that training is always represented by a course. That's not necessarily true these days. In fact, some companies are stretching the boundaries of the word "training." If the term can be described as information and instruction that helps people perform their jobs, then it is a small step to a world in which training departments help develop networked computer-based systems that deliver training modules as well as daily news and information to the desktops of the people who need it. For instance, Federal Express is testing an embedded learning system that will be available to the company's central service agents on their desktop computers. Besides training modules, the system will also carry daily updates that give the agents important information. If, for example, a snowstorm has just hit the East Coast, making it impossible to expedite packages in certain areas, agents would be able to tap a few buttons on their keyboards to find out which areas can be fully served and which can be only partially served.

■ *Place.* Things used to be simple. An instructional designer would create a course which, in due time, would be presented in a classroom. All the people who needed to take it would be ferried to the location in right-sized batches for two or more days of learning. Courses usually lasted at least two days in order to justify the costs of bringing trainees from around the country—or around the world—to a central location. Content could always be found to fill up at least two days' worth of training. And if the trainees did not immediately need the information being thrust at them, they probably would sooner or later. Hopefully, they'd remember it when they needed it. Many companies are deciding now that such gatherings are far too expensive and time-wasting—as well as being an often untimely method of learning—to justify frequent use. Their preference is distributed training, in which information is put at employees' disposal, sometimes through an electronic performance support (EPS) system, at the moment the employee needs it. "Nowadays, if someone wants to do training by satellite or computer, it's considered an exception, and they have to go through all sorts of approvals, whereas it's easy to get approval for a classroom-based course. In the future, the opposite will be true," says Marc Rosenberg, district manager for education and training in AT&T's corporate human-resources department in Somerset, NJ. He is involved in a corporatewide rethinking of the role and delivery of training within the company.

Their preference is distributed training, in which information is put at employees' disposal at the moment the employee needs it.

■ *Technology.* It is, quite simply, the enabler. There is nothing new about the perception of centralized classroom training as expensive and inefficient. Five years go, training directors could envision distributed learning and information on demand, but they couldn't produce it. The technology was a barrier because it was prohibitively expensive and not especially user-friendly. But as the march of technology pushes prices lower, and as more people learn to use computers as something other than fancy typewriters, both those barriers have started to crumble. The result is significant change in the way in which training is delivered. Davis says that up to 65 percent of training at H-P is now delivered outside the classroom. Larry Silvey, managing director of Arthur Andersen Consulting Education in St. Charles, IL, says he has seen major changes just in the past two years in what technology can offer training. His division developed a highly sophisticated, CD-ROM-based simulation that helps teach the company's consultants how to consult. It presents an imaginary client company, along with specifics of the client's situation, and asks the student to give the company some valuable advice. The new course, which takes a typical trainee about 40 hours to complete, replaces a 60-hour program of individual study and classroom instruction. Although it was expensive to create the course, Silvey says that Arthur Andersen saves about $10 million a year in training and payroll costs by delivering the course on CD-ROM.

All of these driving forces have converged to force change within some training departments. "We just don't have the luxury of using the old methodologies anymore," says Maryanne Johnson, director of the leadership center within the Center for Professional Development at U.S. West Inc., in the Denver suburb of Lakewood, CO.

Few training departments are making the kinds of radical changes implied by the term reengineering. More common are situations in which training contributes to reengineering efforts elsewhere in the company by providing instruction that helps employees take on new roles, says George Bennett, CEO of Symmetrix Inc., a Lexington, MA, consulting firm that specializes in reengineering.

It may not be possible for a training department to get maximum benefit from a reengineering effort if the rest of the company isn't doing it, says Bennett. But reengineering the training department can still produce handsome results.

Training departments that are on the reengineering path generally are lodged within large companies that have thousands of far-flung employees. The companies also tend to be high-tech or communications firms, whose employees are already comfortable using sophisticated technology. They might be organizations with visionary leaders who are pushing the training departments toward re-engineering. They might be companies in financial pain, whose leaders are asking tougher questions about the utility of money spent on training.

"Training is a hefty investment," Rosenberg says. "Training and HR have these big bull's eyes on them that say 'overhead.' The training department that says, 'We've trained 20 percent more students than last year,' is in trouble." In other words, a training department concerned only with counting the number of students in seats probably isn't measuring whether students learned anything—or whether the skills they did gain are helping the company at all.

Rosenberg suggests it's essential that the training department begin to think of itself as an educational resource whose goal is to serve customers well with the minimum amount of hassle to them. Starr Eckholdt, president of the Alliance of Organizational Systems Designers, a Winston-Salem, NC, consulting firm that specializes in reengineering efforts, admits that a reengineered training department is easier to describe than to create. First, he says, you figure out what your customer needs. Then you eliminate or reduce cycle times in order to deliver information to employees and give them resources to build their skills. The shorthand version: shorter time frames and higher impact.

It's essential that the training department begin to think of itself as an educational resource whose goal is to serve customers well with the minimum amount of hassle to them.

A reengineered training department, in Rosenberg's vision, is one that knows it delivers value because it measures that value. It delivers its products and services in the way that is most convenient for the user, even if it means delivering training and information to employees' homes. A reengineered training department almost surely uses technology to improve its processes and deliver its services. It probably contains fewer people than it did before, and the ones who remain probably use sophisticated, automated tools for instructional design.

How the Trainer's Job Changes

All this talk of re-engineering the training department brings up a point of intense interest to the average training-department employee: Will my job change and, if so, how much?

The answer to the first question is: Yes. Depending on what kind of job you hold and whom you ask, the answer to the second ranges from "a little bit" all the way to "prepare for whiplash."

Many of the companies already in the midst of re-engineering have seen the duties—and hence, the required skills—of trainers change.

Sometimes the changes have been relatively minor. Almost all the training departments that are making greater use of technology to deliver training are insisting that everyone become much more knowlegeable about technology. Surprisingly, even high-tech companies such as Apple Computer Inc. have found that their trainers needed heavy doses of computer-literacy training in order to prepare them for a new way of delivering instruction. Some companies, such as Arthur Andersen and Co., have had to add more graphic-arts specialists and technological wizards to the training department to be able to produce a new class of computer-driven courseware.

Many training directors believe that the people who populate training departments in the future will hold different occupational titles than they hold now. Classroom instructors, for instance, ought to be beefing up their résumés ASAP.

"One of the things we have to face is that we still have a lot of people in the training community who are oriented toward classroom activities," says Jim Hite, a training manager with Northern Telecom's Learning Institute. Many of these trainers aren't at all comfortable working with technology and can't fathom that there are many topics that no longer need to be taught in a classroom, he adds.

Just 25 percent of the training offered by Apple Computer to its U.S. sales force is conducted in a classroom, which means the company needs many fewer classroom instructors than it once did. As part of its effort to re-engineer, the training department analyzed the skills it now needs in its staffers, rewrote almost every job description, "posted" the jobs within the training department, and hired anew for all the positions. Some people settled into a rough approximation of their old jobs, but others had to scramble to retrain themselves for new positions. For instance, the training department has many more "project managers" than before, a position that requires a wide knowledge of most aspects of training—including technology—and an ability to get a group of specialists, each working on several projects, to meet deadlines.

Continued—

How the Trainer's Job Changes (continued)

But even the instructional designer's job changed at Apple, says Lucy Carter, director of Apple's worldwide performance system. Much more than in the past, instructional designers need to be able to design courses that are delivered by technological means. They also no longer have the luxury of taking 18 months to design a course. Now, Carter says, a course can be designed in about two weeks. How? For one thing, the training department uses a sophisticated instructional-design expert system that allows trainers with no formal instructional-design experience to create a prototype. Then an experienced instructional designer fine-tunes it.

At Federal Express, there has been a big drop in the demand for classroom instructors. Just a few years ago, a classroom instructor may have spent 80 percent of her time in the classroom; today that figure has dropped to 40 percent. Peter Addicott, senior manager of training and development for the company's southern region, says that those trainers are now spending more time doing internal consulting with line managers. The company hasn't had to shrink its training staff, but Addicott notes that the number of training-department employees has stayed constant for six years while the number of workers companywide has doubled in the same period of time.

Will the training department need fewer people in the future? Yes, says Maryanne Johnson, director of the leadership center within the Center for Professional Development at U.S. West. Claudia Davis, director of education for Hewlett-Packard, doesn't believe that fewer trainers will be needed, just smarter ones. For instance, she says, "We don't have instructional designers. We need people who are performance technologists."

Davis sees a rising need for trainers who are better at "scanning the environment" for new information and breakthroughs. "The role of education is scanning for ways to meet the business needs in a shorter time frame," she says.

And, by extension, the role of the reinvented trainer is to find those new ways. It may require other kinds of skill. As Carter puts it: "You can sit in a garage all night, but it won't make you a car. You can be a trainer all your life, but you might not have the skill sets to take you forward in this environment."

According to Eckholdt, a department that wanted to reengineer itself would begin with the question, What are we trying to achieve? It's an old question, he admits, but those in charge of the training function have to take a fresh look at it, freeing their minds of the way things have always been done.

If the training department is trying to produce highly effective employees for the organization, it must map the processes it uses to mold ordinary people into productive, valued employees. "When you look at it this way, you reframe your thinking around the product you're trying to produce. You ask, 'How can we do it better than we've ever done it before?' " Eckholdt says.

Ideally, he says, in this creative stage, training executives should be reaching for breakthrough ideas, not incremental improvements. For instance, the inclination in many quarters would be to streamline the existing curriculum and make it easier for employees to sign up for courses. But, says Eckholdt, what if the training department could come up with a way to meet training needs in a somewhat customized way, within weeks of identifying the need, and take the solution straight to the customers? What might such an arrangement look like? It might not include a curriculum of courses at all.

To date, very few training departments have completely overhauled themselves. Most often, re-engineering begins with one or two significant changes in the way in which training is delivered. It builds from that point, provided that training directors can be convinced that learning is as good or better than before, and provided that the costs and cycle time can be reduced.

Silvey says Arthur Andersen has pinpointed three goals of its reengineering effort. First, it wants to use technology as much as possible to reduce cycle times, increase productivity, cut costs, and improve learning results. It wants to use the best practices it can find in other companies and universities. And it wants to create an electronic performance support system for its employees in field offices.

Despite the heavy technology bent of its strategy, Silvey says that reengineering does not mean that classrooms will be eliminated. In fact, Arthur Andersen's CD-ROM consulting simulation now is used sometimes in the classroom to create a more authentic learning situation. Trainees work in teams to advise the make-believe company contained in the CD-ROM program, just as they would in the real world. Coaches in the classroom help guide them, just as an Arthur Andersen senior partner might in reality.

At Northern Telecom, the communications company in Nashville, TN, the training function set up an EPS system that supplements the five-day training course given to new managers. Jim Hite, a manager for the Northern Telecom Learning Institute, says that the EPS system contains practical information the manager can capture at the moment she needs it. For instance, the system contains detailed information and examples of how Northern Telecom managers are expected to draw up budgets. The EPS system didn't do away with the need for a class to orient new managers, but it reduced dramatically the number of times new managers had to bother someone else for answers to their questions.

A different kind of need at U.S. West led to a laptop-based learning system for almost 400 of the company's top managers. The reasoning is, Johnson says, that if the company is going to compete effectively, in a new technological age, its top decision-makers need to be knowledgeable about wireless and multimedia technology.

Previously, the company brought executives together for a series of informational meetings. But it made more sense to let the executives learn about the new technologies on computers at their own pace, obviating the expense and time of flying everyone to a central location for a course. An executive retrieves the information through a laptop computer that hooks up to a CD-ROM player, fax machine (for reporting test results), videocassette recorder, and the Internet data base.

When the executive begins the program, she takes a pretest that identifies the gaps in her knowledge about technology; that assessment produces a "map" of the learning program that shows the executive how to access information to plug the gaps. The program contains 10 modules, each built around a particular technology. When she is finished, she takes a posttest to measure what she learned.

The company found that it had to make available "coaches," subject-matter experts who could answer any questions the executives might have while going through the material. The coaching system provided the hand-holding some computer-reticent managers needed, as well as providing the course designers with tips on how to improve the program. Eventually, it will be made available to all employees of U.S. West. In the meantime, Johnson says, the company is expecting significant cost savings from delivering the instruction on laptops instead of pulling its most expensive employees off the job for a day or two of classroom training.

The company is expecting significant cost savings from delivering the instruction on laptops instead of pulling its most expensive employees off the job for a day or two of classroom training.

Another high-tech company, Apple Computer Inc., is also busily reinventing the way in which it delivers training. In the process, Apple has drawn together the training, advertising, public relations and documentation functions in order to coordinate all the information that goes to trainees. Lucy Carter, director of worldwide performance systems for the Cupertino, CA-based company, says that when she examined the previous new-product training and information system from the point of view of the company's 20,000 salespeople, she was overwhelmed by the volume of material.

The company released 72 new products last year, and for each one salespeople typically received four or five CD-ROM disks, four or five videotapes, and a huge pile of paper. None of the four departments that sent the information was aware of how much the others were sending. "It was a great amount of information representing a huge amount of time and money, and it wasn't improving anybody's performance," Carter says.

Shc gathered a task force that analyzed how salespeople used their time and learned about new products. She helped organize a benchmarking project to find out whether other companies were using alternative delivery methods. She sent people to conferences about EPS systems. And she convened a worldwide Apple training council to mull how the training function could better meet the needs of trainees.

One of the outcomes of that council was the process that now exists to inform salespeople about new products. Called Apple's Reference Performance and Learning Expert (ARPLE), it is an EPS system that is distributed to individual salespeople through computer file servers in 60 locations around the world. Not only can users call up information on new products, they can also use an expert system to create a presentation for a particular product.

Eventually, says Carter, the sales rep will be able to enter information about a particular client, and have the expert system suggest a strategy for selling to the client.

But the beauty of the new system is that users are no longer inundated with information flowing from three or four pipelines. The PR, advertising, documentation and training departments pool their information to eliminate redundancies before sending the information out to salespeople. It wastes less time and money on the corporate end, and saves the salespeople from wading through useless information.

Carter suggests that what makes ARPLE different from the average EPS system is that it is a multifunctional effort to improve performance that looks at the company's systems from the point of view of the user. "I've seen some EPS systems that look great, but when you look at the target audience, you see they're also receiving 96 other things they have to see and do," she says. "Our effort was not just to make training function differently but to make the organization function differently and to have the organization support the individuals."

Re-engineering typically begins with efforts to improve the process of *delivering* training within the company.

Judging by the path of progress in the companies mentioned so far, re-engineering typically begins with efforts to improve the process of *delivering* training within the company. If those changes lead to improvements in the training department's internal processes, great. But there have been fewer efforts to reinvent the way in which the training department itself functions.

This is entirely understandable. After all, the trainer's charge is to deliver instruction as effectively as can be. If quantum leaps are possible, they ought to apply to the department's core responsibility. Efforts to improve processes within the training department, without radically rethinking the role of training within an organization, may be little more than rearranging the deck chairs on the Titanic. But there have been a few attempts to reengineer the way in which training departments operate, most of them arising from efforts to reengineer the delivery system.

The training department at U.S. West, for instance, is trying to redesign its computerized systems to create one interlocked, fluid system to replace the hodgepodge it now contains. Because several of the systems don't talk to each other, there exists a series of time-wasting, paper-based "hand-offs" that slow down the whole training process.

For instance, one computer system contains employees' training records and another contains reservations for classes; the classes themselves are listed only in a catalog, which is updated and mailed to employees at regular intervals. Employees needed to check the catalog for a course they wanted to take, and reserve a spot. But the trainers had to deal with two different computer systems in order to check to see whether the employee needed the course and schedule him into a class.

With a new system, which Johnson says will be online next year, the employee sits at his desk and taps into one seamless system that contains information about the courses available and what his skill gaps are. Soon, Johnson hopes, the employee will be able to access certain training modules right from the system, without having to attend class. In the meantime, Johnson plans to speed up the scheduling of classes and reduce the need for the catalog.

Arthur Andersen's Silvey says that his department has cut its review times for new training courses by one-third by doing "rapid prototyping" of new courses. In the past, instructional designers may have put together the "perfect" training course only to see it mauled when it went through a sequential review by 10 people. Now, the instructional-design team creating a technology-based course can produce a version that is strictly vaporware, and call together the 10 reviewers in one room to see it and comment. The result is a much shorter time to design a course.

Arthur Andersen has cut its review times for new training courses by one-third by doing "rapid prototyping" of new courses.

Hewlett-Packard has found ways to produce a CBT course in two weeks. Among its tricks is its use of a template that allows it to author more quickly, and its ability to "repurpose" segments of previous training products, Davis says. What she means is that H-P might take a snippet of a course and use it in another way in a new course. Maybe a piece of video used in a performance-appraisal course could be used to buttress a different learning point in a CBT course on diversity. This ability to reuse material in new ways is essential in cutting the time it takes to produce training. "There's not a lot that is new," Davis says. "What's important is our ability to repurpose and reconfigure, which saves time."

Technology has allowed a great many advances in the workings of the training department, as well as the way in which instruction is conveyed to employees. Ten years ago, it was possible to wish for something like an EPS system that would provide brief training modules and coaching available on the spot to employees at their desks; unfortunately, the technology didn't permit it.

Today, it's possible to wish for a learning system that is completely learner-driven and mobile. Perhaps it's a system that gives the learner an unlimited multimedia extravaganza that also automatically links him by e-mail to others learning the same material within the company. The system might be accessible anywhere—including a car. Perhaps it allows the learner to fill knowledge gaps by using public data bases. To accomplish that, of course, there would need to be an as-yet-uninvented piece of software that would allow the user to pluck the precise piece of information he needs from a data base, such as the Internet, without getting bogged down in its labyrinths.

AT&T's Rosenberg acknowledges that it's possible to imagine all kinds of wondrous advances that will bring us closer to the ideal of a true learner-driven training system. Hardly anyone in the training community could disagree with such a vision, he contends. But there are a few potential obstacles to the fruition of such a dream.

First, and most obvious, is technology. In some cases the technology simply doesn't exist yet to make the dream come true. In other cases the technology is available but it carries a shocking price tag.

Peter Addicott, senior manager of training and development for Federal Express' southern region, believes that mobile learning—anywhere, any time—is the key to his company's training future. In fact, he can glimpse it now in the tools used by Federal Express' delivery people. Each courier has a mobile device linked to a central system that can tell her where a package is at any given moment. There is no reason, says Addicott, that those systems can't also deliver an EPS-like learning system. No reason, that is, except for money and the computer hardware and software it will buy. It probably won't happen this year, Addicott says, but he hopes to have such a system in the near future.

Those limitations—money and technology—are the reasons that this potential revolution in learning will be led, once again, by large companies.

Those limitations—money and technology—are the reasons that this potential revolution in learning will be led, once again, by large companies. They are the ones with the deepest pockets and the strongest motives to switch to an electronic learner-driven system.

But there is another barrier that may foil the revolution: the learner. "I think part of what's holding us back as a society is our comfort with the classroom environment," says Apple's Carter.

Northern Telecom's Hite says he often gets requests from line managers wanting to have a performance problem solved. Almost always, he says, the manager wants Hite to put together a classroom-based course. And Northern Telecom is not a low-tech company.

Trainees sometimes resist computer-based training, too, because they're not used to learning in that way. Johnson says that when U.S. West introduced the laptop-based system to teach its top executives about the latest advances in technology, it overwhelmed them at first by delivering the entire collection to them in one chunk. "We gave them the laptop, and the CD-ROM, and the videos, and the paper-based systems, and it was just too much," Johnson says. The company later discovered that some trainees needed to be able to call a coach to talk about the information. U.S. West has learned that it must continue to cater to employees' comfort needs—in other words, their desire for human interaction.

Will this mean that companies will always and forever need to provide a classroom option so that trainees can forge bonds with others? Not necessarily. After all, we have reached a point where romances are carried to the brink of a formal engagement through the use of data-base bulletin boards and e-mail. It's just possible that 15 years from now when Generation Xers have ensconced themselves solidly in corporate America, a tiny fraction of instruction will be delivered in classrooms, and everyone in the training community will look back in wonder at the marvelous inefficiency of the system that exists today.

Beverly Geber is special projects editor of Training *Magazine.*

Quality Transformation

TEAMS AND TEAMWORK

Rethinking the Rush to Team Up

Ron Zemke

Are teams the solution to every organizational problem for improving how work gets done? Ron Zemke, in this thoughtful article, has some interesting answers to this question. The bottom line: We are still learning how to make best use of teams and how to facilitate teamwork in the first place, not an easy thing in the individualistic American culture.

The working world is teeming with teams. Organizations eager to display a commitment to quality, customer service, customer focus, cost containment or you-name-it are slapping the "team" label on every group of workers in sight.

Some enthusiasts have gone so far as to predict that by the year 2000 many companies will be run entirely by teams that report directly to the CEO. At his confirmation hearing earlier this year, Labor Secretary Robert Reich, a big fan of work teams, talked up the idea of making participation and cooperation mandatory.

But even as the team trend continues to gain momentum, gray clouds of doubt and strife have begun to gather.

Reprinted with permission from the November 1993 issue of *Training* Magazine. Copyright © 1993, Lakewood Publications, Minneapolis, MN. All rights reserved. Not for resale.

At Douglas Aircraft Co., the troubled subsidiary of McDonnell Douglas Corp., massive layoffs have put a total-quality campaign and a team-management initiative in jeopardy. News accounts speak of disgruntled and suspicious workers who have come to view cooperating with the team concept as an exercise in assisting one's own executioner.

Florida Power & Light Co., winner of Japan's Deming Prize for quality management, scaled back worker participation when employees complained that team meetings and problem-solving assignments were interfering with the "real work" they were being held accountable for and paid to do.

This summer the National Labor Relations Board (NLRB) ordered Du Pont Co. to disband seven worker-management teams on grounds that they were illegal labor organizations under the terms of the 1935 National Labor Relations Act. The Du Pont teams had been established to address issues such as safety, fitness and incentives. The NLRB declared that such issues are "mandatory subjects of (labor-management) bargaining." The board also ruled that recommendations made by the teams could not be adopted unilaterally by Du Pont; the company would have to bargain with its chemical workers union.

Saturn Corp., the division of General Motors established as a grand experiment in worker participation, teamwork and Deming-style quality improvement, finally turned its first-ever monthly operating profit in May of 1993. But that feat took the combination of a $100-per-car giveback by the dealers and a voluntary six-day workweek, with no overtime pay, at the Spring Hill, TN, manufacturing facility. Financial analysts are questioning whether Saturn ever will be able to turn an actual operating profit, while union leaders grow impatient for the participation experiment to pay off for their members.

While these are sensational examples of disappointing results, they are far from isolated. A recent McKinsey & Co study reported that two-thirds of 30 quality programs studied—programs highly dependent on the team approach to improving quality—stalled or failed to produce the desired results. Another report, this one compiled by Ernst & Young for the American Quality Foundation, concluded that nothing wonderful necessarily happens simply because a company trains its workers in quality techniques, assigns them to "teams," and tells them to go forth and fix something. Further, Ernst & Young's International Quality Study found that forming teams to study and improve products and processes leads to measurable improvement only in organizations currently performing poorly in their markets in terms of profit, productivity and quality. In medium-performing companies, the study found, bottom-line results seem unaffected by team activities. In high-performing companies, the introduction of new team-based work systems actually may be harmful.

In light of all this it may be tempting to ask whether team-based management is a bad idea whose time has come.

In light of all this it may be tempting to ask whether team-based management is a bad idea whose time has come. But instead of leaping ahead to write a premature epitaph for what may be a perfectly sensible concept, perhaps we should back up. If the initial bloom is starting to fade from the rose, it may be a good time to seek clarity rather than repudiation. "Are teams a bad idea?" is almost certainly the wrong question. We might ask at least three better ones.

Question 1: What, Exactly, Is a Team?

The word team, like a nouveau condiment, tends to be applied overgenerously these days to all sorts of groups and working arrangements. Take this magazine article as a case in point. It was conceived and written by a single person. Yet it came to fruition as readable words, set in type on the pages you are holding, through the highly coordinated efforts of a number of people.

An editorial conclave met to discuss, approve and schedule the creation of the original manuscript. That manuscript was worked over by two or three editors of the magazine. Those editors questioned phrases and logic they considered faulty and challenged exposition they found confusing, drab or unclear. Meanwhile, an art director and an illustrator pursued a graphic expression of some part of the article's premise. Then another whole set of highly coordinated efforts went into combining the art, the article copy, and the overall layout plan for the magazine into film flats to be shipped to the printing plant.

So the process of placing this article in your hands depended upon the efforts of a number of people working collaboratively and sometimes collectively. Critical to the success of the process were the needs to communicate clearly, coordinate effort and apply specialized knowledge. But while we think of ourselves as a pretty effective and cohesive bunch, are we a "team" in the revolutionary-new-style-of-management sense? Is the article itself a "team" product? I would be inclined to say no. But you'd get different answers from different people.

Consultant Jack Osburn, president of Osburn Team Works in Rancho San Diego, CA, points out that the word team is now routinely applied to everything from roundtable-discussion groups to quality circles to self-managing work units. In a recent issue of the journal *Performance & Instruction,* Osburn suggests that "teams" in the working world generally fall into three classifications:

Level 1: Management diagnoses a problem and decides, with some input from others, what must be done to correct or improve the situation. Management then informs or mandates actions to be carried out by a specific group (or "team") of employees.

Level 2: A group of people is given a limited problem-solving or process-improvement assignment. These employees diagnose the problem and may recommend or even implement solutions or changes—but with strict management approval.

Level 3: On a daily basis, decision making on processes, projects and operations is done by those closest to the work, based more on expertise than on rank or status.

But are all three of those configurations really teams? Not in many views. Jon R. Katzenbach and Douglas K. Smith, consultants with McKinsey & Co., distinguish teams from ordinary "working groups" in their 1993 book, *The Wisdom of Teams: Creating the High-Performance Organization.* They define working groups as sets of people who "interact primarily to share information, best practices, or perspectives, and to make decisions to help each individual perform within his or her area of responsibility." They then proceed to the separate genus of teams and classify different species, including pseudo-teams, potential teams, real teams and high-performance teams.

They define a "real team" as "a small number of people with complementary skills who are equally committed to a common purpose, goals and working approach for which they hold themselves mutually accountable. Real teams are a basic unit of performance."

Real teams only perform effectively, however, "provided there are specific results for which the team is collectively responsible and provided the performance ethic of the company demands those results." Real teams, according to Katzenbach and Smith, have one of three purposes:

- To recommend things (teams that study and recommend solutions to specific organizational performance problems).
- To make or do things (teams responsible for ongoing operations, not just occasional or episodic projects, in areas such as manufacturing, selling or servicing).
- To run things (teams responsible for management and administration of an entire enterprise or large unit).

Edward Lawler defines a work team as a group of workers who have a whole or meaningful piece of ongoing work to do, receive feedback about the work, and have considerable autonomy in how they accomplish the work.

The team that "makes and does things," is what most of us might think of as an ongoing work team. Edward Lawler, founder and director of the Center for Effective Organizations at the University of Southern California, offers an insightful discussion of such teams in his 1992 book *The Ultimate Advantage: Creating the High-Involvement Organization.* He defines a work team—as opposed to an ad hoc process-improvement team or problem-solving team or quality circle—as a group of workers who have a whole or meaningful piece of ongoing work to do, receive feedback about the work, and have considerable autonomy in how they accomplish the work.

Lawler goes on to cite seven characteristics that distinguish a bona fide work team from other groups of employees who perform various joint activities:

- *Work-flow control.* The team has enough authority over the creation of a product or service that it controls and may be held responsible for a clear input and a clear output.

- *Membership.* Work teams typically include all the employees working in a given area or on a complete process. Team membership is not optional.

- *Decision-making responsibility.* Members of real work teams make important decisions about how the work is done. They perceive themselves to be in control of the process. Self-managed work teams (one species within genus "work team") make all the decisions that would be necessary to run a small business. Semiautonomous work teams (another species) have far less control over resource allocations and personnel decisions than do self-managed teams, but both types qualify as genuine work teams.

- *Training required.* Members of work teams are trained to perform technical tasks and to work collaboratively with other members of the team. Characteristically, team members are cross-trained to perform multiple technical tasks as well as to assume responsibilities that, in a nonteam environment, would be reserved for management.

- *Meetings.* Team members meet frequently to make schedules and review results and processes. Some teams meet to make decisions about hiring, firing and other "management" activities.

- *Supervision.* Formal supervision—or management—has a more remote responsibility for the day-to-day activities of the team than in "traditional" management relationships. Supervisors monitor, give feedback, and try to ensure that the decision-making processes and the internal operations of the team are effective. Lawler tends to characterize the supervisory role as one of "maturing" the team toward a goal of self-sufficiency on a number of fronts.

- *Reward systems.* For Lawler to deem a work group a team, its members' pay must be based on skills. Some sort of pay-for-skill or pay-for-knowledge system must be in effect.

Question 2: Are Teams Always a Superior Way to Go?

The popular rhetoric would lead one to suppose that the performance of teams—all kinds of teams—is invariably superior to the performance of solitary employees or traditionally supervised work groups or special task forces or any other nonteam syndicates of people.

In *The Team Handbook,* one of the best-selling quality-team-development primers, Peter R. Scholtes contends that ". . . rarely does a single person have enough knowledge or experience to understand everything that goes on in a process. Therefore, major gains in quality and productivity most often result from teams."

Katzenbach and Smith, while more reserved than most team-management zealots, wrote in a recent issue of the *Harvard Business Review:* "We believe that teams will become the primary unit of performance in high-performance organizations. We are convinced that every company faces specific performance challenges for which teams are the most practical and powerful vehicle at top management's disposal."

In their book, however, Katzenbach and Smith acknowledge that not all performance challenges are created equal: "If performance at critical delivery points depends on combining multiple skills, perspectives and judgments in real time, then the team option is the smartest one. The key judgment is whether the sum of individual bests will suffice for the performance challenge at hand or whether the group must deliver incremental performance requiring joint work products. Although the team option promises greater performance, it also brings more risk, and managers must be brutally honest in assessing the trade-offs."

Lawler is less esoteric. He argues that ongoing work teams—what Katzenbach and Smith refer to as "teams that make or do things"—are most appropriate when:

- The organization emphasizes quality over other product and service variables.

- Innovation is a key strategy. That is, the organization needs to bring new or novel products to market in a hurry, or must develop highly tailored solutions to meet clients' needs.

- The organization is trying to create a combined-variable strategy, such as speed *and* quality or low cost *and* innovativeness.

Traditional approaches to management—authoritative, nonparticipative, nonteam approaches—are more likely to succeed when the organization competes primarily on a low-cost strategy and when direct labor costs account for the great bulk of the total cost.

And when are work teams not such a great idea? According to Lawler, more traditional approaches to management—authoritative, nonparticipative, nonteam approaches—are more likely to succeed when the organization competes primarily on a low-cost strategy and when direct labor costs account for the great bulk of the total cost of the organization's products or services. He's talking essentially about basic-commodity operations. If your company makes nails, say, and your customers have no need for customized, special-order nails, and you're trying to be the low-cost supplier of nails, you probably have little to gain and much to lose by tying up your production workers in a lot of team meetings. Let them make nails.

Other researchers have found that teams in administrative and management areas generally are less effective than teams on factory production floors or in direct customer-service functions.

Assuming the basic situation is appropriate, Lawler's review of the research on work teams suggests the following positives:

Work teams can effectively handle inventory, scheduling, quality assurance, and some other tasks typically reserved for managers and supervisors.

- Work teams can improve average employee output *if* the team sets production goals and gets feedback on how well it is achieving these goals.

- Productivity can increase *if* team members are extensively cross-trained *and* they choose to help one another *and* they perform their own support work, thus significantly lessening costs for staff and maintenance services. In other words, if workers manage themselves and order their own supplies, you ought to be able to get rid of some supervisors and supply orderers.

- Cohesive groups exert social pressure and can play a role in motivating individual performance. There is also evidence that rewards and punishments are more effective in shaping individual performance when given by a work group rather than by a supervisor.

- Work teams can effectively handle inventory, scheduling, quality assurance, and some other tasks typically reserved for managers and supervisors. Note, however, that these are rather rudimentary management tasks. Work teams are *not* usually well-suited to take on higher-level management roles: deciding whether to build and market a particular model of automobile, running a cost-benefit analysis on where to locate a new factory and so on.

- In small production facilities, supervisor-to-employee ratios can be reduced to 50-to-1—or even 100-to-1—through the use of teams.

Again, all of those points refer to ongoing work teams. What about special-project teams, the kind assigned to solve specific problems or identify new opportunities? Research and experience with group problem solving and group innovation have been going on a lot longer than research on permanent work teams. And the findings are far from universally positive. For instance:

- The quality circle, a type of special-purpose problem-solving team, has a well-documented history of starting strong but quickly losing effectiveness and becoming irrelevant to ongoing quality improvement.

- Research conducted in the 1970s by organizational psychologist N.R.F. Maier suggests that the quality of a group or team decision is often as good as that of a lone supervisor—but not, generally, any better. Maier did find, however, that people are more likely to accept a group decision than a supervisor's—and also more likely to accomplish the task in question.

- In a six-month study of matched groups of clerical workers at the Prudential Insurance Co., traditionally managed groups (in other words, those with little or no worker participation) were compared with participatively managed groups. The traditional groups had higher levels of production. However, the traditional groups also had higher turnover rates, and their performance levels tended to slip whenever a supervisor was absent.

- In a wide range of studies of problem solving in ambiguous situations (that is, where the problems have no single correct answer), individuals have come up with more solutions—and higher-quality solutions—than have groups working toward consensus.

- A number of studies also have demonstrated that "nominal groups" (groups in name only) almost invariably outperform "real" or intact work groups in problem-solving tasks. Researchers have added problem-solving practice, incentives for good solutions, and even different mixes of personality types to the experimental brew, all to no avail. The intact teams continue to fall short of the nominal groups—with one exception. When the problem to be solved is linear—that is, when it must be solved one step at a time—nominal and real groups perform equally well.

The conclusion that tasks decided upon by a group are more likely to be accomplished than those assigned by a supervisor is not an isolated finding but a well-documented phenomenon.

If you are beginning to think that teams may not be the perfect solution to all of your organization's problems, you're probably right. But that doesn't make them a waste of time and energy.

Several legitimate fuels fire the zeal for teams. First, more than 20 years of research testifies to their motivational potential. The conclusion that tasks decided upon by a group are more likely to be accomplished than those assigned by a supervisor is not an isolated finding but a well-documented phenomenon.

Second, as Lawler and others have pointed out, work teams can and do make reasonable decisions over limited, local issues—so long as there are concrete, measurable goals by which to judge performance, and the group receives timely, meaningful feedback.

Third, teams are a democratic alternative to being "bossed." That's not an inconsequential factor during these uncertain times, when organizations are going through wrenching upheaval. True, there is evidence that in uncertain times, strong, task-oriented leadership accomplishes more than "open and caring" leadership. But despite the common perception of work teams as open and caring groups, there is no reason a team can't be strongly task-oriented.

Question 3: If We're Going to Use Teams, How Can We Use Them Most Effectively?

Let's start with special-project teams as opposed to ongoing work teams. Through two decades of research, psychologist Maier found that in problem-solving groups, a well-trained group leader is extremely important. He also found that this leader must function as a facilitator rather than a director. As such, the group leader must:

- Reward and recognize the contributions of the members.
- Remind the group of the range of solutions being generated, and keep track of the offerings.
- Point out connections between the various solutions under consideration.
- Be problem-minded rather than solution-oriented, thus keeping the group from jumping to closure prematurely.
- Protect minority opinion and seemingly oddball suggestions.

Other researchers have found that a group working without an appointed leader can perform effectively *if* the group members agree to 1) mutually enforce a sequence of procedures for their work, 2) adhere to strict time frames for their meetings, and 3) stick to a content agenda—that is, agree that everyone will talk about the same thing at the same time. These are the same points made in most training programs on how to run an effective meeting of any sort. They are well-documented in addition to being commonsensical.

Studies of interpersonal dynamics in small groups suggest that group problem solving is *least* effective when:

- A few members dominate the discussion.
- The group is large (larger groups are easier for talkative individuals to dominate).
- The group is homogeneous, made up of similarly experienced people. Again, nominal groups routinely outperform real groups in generating solutions to ambiguous problems.

And what about ongoing work teams? We've already covered some situations in which they're likely to be more or less effective. But Lawler would add one key point: For enduring work teams, the selection of team members is important. "Work teams are most effective with individuals who desire complex, challenging work," he writes in *The Ultimate Advantage*. "[W]ork teams also require individuals who enjoy social interaction and who value social rewards. Individuals who don't value social interactions, social rewards and meetings won't flourish in a team setting."

The long and short of it? Our reading of the research suggests that on the positive side, ongoing work teams can be highly motivating. They also can be a way to cut overhead costs. (Translation: You can get rid of some expensive bureaucrats, managers and staff-support people.) How long those two benefits will last, however, only time will tell. Bureaucracy can be pruned, but it has a way of creeping back. And if Lawler is right about permanent work teams requiring certain types of personalities, then it is easy to wonder if the motivational effects of teaming up might be short-lived for a great many people.

As for the effect of teams on quality and productivity over the long haul, the evidence is unclear. Best bet: Teams with clear and limited performance targets will meet those targets provided they have the right skills, the right kind of feedback, and the right incentives to perform.

Teams with clear and limited performance targets will meet those targets provided they have the right skills, the right kind of feedback, and the right incentives to perform.

On the downside, don't expect teams to replace any but the most rudimentary of management functions. Likewise, don't count on teams to perform miracles of creativity and innovation; groupthink and resistance to change present the same stubborn problems for teams of workers as they do for teams of managers. And don't expect something for nothing. To be effective, teams need training, and plenty of it.

Teams aren't the answer to every problem in every company, but they certainly are a viable option in many situations. They can be useful and productive. Just make sure your organization's expectations are realistic, its support is well-funded and complete, and management is prepared to be patient with the effort.

Ron Zemke is an author, consultant, and senior editor of Training Magazine *and consulting editor to* The Quality Yearbook.

How to Use Process Improvement Teams

Charles N. Weaver

If Ron Zemke questions the wisdom of teams for attacking every organizational problem, Weaver suggests some reasons why teams break down (among them, lack of supporting culture) and how to make sure they work as effectively as possible.

Day one: Senior management announces that it will implement companywide total quality management (TQM). To accomplish this, it has established a quality improvement council that will organize process improvement teams. The announcement creates a sense of optimism in the work force. Employees expect the teams to devise TQM strategies to lift the barriers that prevent them from doing their jobs as well as they can. Managers are hopeful that the teams will offer straightforward approaches to achieving quality.

Three years later: The use of these teams to help implement TQM brought organizational improvements. But, after a promising start, the program's effectiveness waned. Managers and employees became frustrated and disillusioned. Efforts to achieve world-class quality, based solely on this approach, ran aground as the organization encountered false starts, detours, and dead ends.

This scenario is common, but not necessarily inevitable. For organizations to avoid these types of problems when using process improvement teams to implement TQM, they must first understand the dynamics of TQM.

The Dynamics of TQM

TQM is an organizational development effort that requires two organizational changes.[1] The first is an educational effort to change an organization's culture, which includes how it recruits, trains, and manages its employees; how it selects and deals with its suppliers; and how it relates to its customers. The second is long-term education to increase an organization's effectiveness. Long-term education involves learning new methods for planning, engineering, problem solving, consensus building, communicating, and using process improvement teams.

Reprinted with permission from *Quality Progress*, December 1993. Copyright © 1993 ASQC, Milwaukee, WI. All rights reserved.

One of the best sources on which to base this organizational development effort is W. Edwards Deming's 14 points from his book *Out of the Crisis*.[2]

It is almost impossible to secure significant, lasting gains in organizational effectiveness without supporting changes in culture. For example, a department in a large company changed long, unproductive meetings into effective ones by restructuring the process to include a premeeting consensus on the agenda and a systematic approach to manage unresolved issues. The process worked well until a new chief executive officer arrived and changed the structure of the meetings back to their former unproductive state.

It is almost impossible to secure significant, lasting gains in organizational effectiveness without supporting changes in culture.

Another obstacle to organizational development is the competitiveness between cross-functional departments. Since most processes are cross functional, one might expect that process improvement teams would be a perfect way to mesh the different processes and achieve improvements. Almost all departments, however, are managed vertically rather than horizontally in terms of processes. Consequently, most employees have a strong allegiance to their departments. These feelings are intensified by managers who believe that competition between departments, such as off-duty competitive sports or departmental output measures, bring out the best in their employees.

It is ironic that these same managers who preach competitiveness are the ones who expect process improvement teams to cooperate. Often, team members argue, stonewall, and seek to frustrate old rivals. Before managers can expect team members to cooperate, they must eliminate the competition they foster between their own departments.

False Starts, Detours, and Dead Ends

Due to their ignorance or resistance, senior managers sometimes have no intention of changing their organization's culture. But factors such as foreign competition, reduced market share, increased costs, or customer and employee complaints often force these managers to accept that TQM is needed if their organization is to achieve greater performance.

Many managers ignore Deming's teaching that quality improvements require a broad range of efforts; they believe that fixing processes through process improvement teams will cure the organization's quality problems. And often, senior managers do not take the lead role in quality improvement but delegate the responsibility to cross-functional teams of middle managers.

It is not fair, however, to place all the blame for failed TQM efforts on senior managers. Many TQM consulting firms limit their advice to the effectiveness side of the organizational development equation, such as tactical planning and team building, but seldom make serious efforts to change their clients' cultures.

Teams are manifestations of Deming's third and fifth points.

Managers Don't Understand Teams' Roles

Senior managers who do not understand the need to change their organization's culture usually fail to understand the purpose of process improvement teams. The teams are manifestations of Deming's third and fifth points. In his third point, Deming states that mass inspection is not the way to improve quality. Instead, the production processes should be inspected. Deming's fifth point focuses on continual improvement of processes.

Few senior managers adopt a systematic approach to identifying and improving processes and their components. Instead, they are reactive: They wait for a problem to occur, then direct a process improvement team to fix it. After the problem is fixed, it's back to business as usual. Generally, no further improvement of that process takes place unless another problem occurs.

Some managers use teams for purposes that have little or nothing to do with process improvement. For example, a team developed advertising themes for radio and television commercials. Another team reviewed and appraised TQM consulting firms the company was considering hiring. These are not appropriate tasks for process improvement teams. It is unfortunate that the misuse of these teams often produces successes; these successes make managers think they are on the right path.

Why Teams Can Fail

There are other reasons why reliance on the quality improvement council/process improvement team approach to TQM can, after a run of success, lead to disappointment. One reason is that this approach assumes that success in today's competitive environment can be achieved by fixing and streamlining broken-down bureaucracy. While improving existing processes is important, it ignores many larger issues, such as:

- Has the organization determined whether it really needs the processes that are being streamlined?
- Are there better ways to do the work of these processes?
- Do these processes support a worthwhile mission?
- Even if these processes work well, are they the best way to satisfy customers?

For example, what good would it have done to improve the processes involved in making stagecoaches when the motorized bus was just around the competitive corner? Improving unneeded or obsolete processes can put an organization out of business. Few teams consider innovation or strategic planning parts of the processes they are chartered to improve.

Other Restrictions of Teams

A limitation of process improvement teams is that only a fraction of the work force serves on them, violating Deming's 14th point: "Put everybody in the company to work to accomplish the transformation."[3] Deming endorses the use of teams but suggests that they should do more than what is typically chartered for them. Deming asserts that teams need to engage in many quality-related activities, including understanding where they fit into the overall scheme of things, identifying suppliers and customers, and understanding that they can contribute ideas and plans.

Deming is talking about empowerment, which is far more than using teams to fix processes. Empowerment can turn the traditional tiered organization chart upside down. Yet, there is little in the operation of typical teams that creates this kind of empowerment in terms of horizontal structure, authority, and communication.

Identifying Improvement Areas

Another roadblock in the process improvement team approach is the absence of a simple, systematic mechanism for identifying processes needing improvement. Efforts to identify processes with financial measures, such as the cost of quality and return on investment, are theoretically possible, but busy managers seldom have the time, motivation, or staffing to make the required calculations. Instead, they tend to rely on their own judgments and input from subordinates. While the judgment of managers is usually accurate in identifying the first few processes for improvement, there are three pitfalls in relying on their judgment to identify them.

Deming is talking about empowerment, which is far more than using teams to fix processes.

1. Most boards of directors do not understand that their jobs are to support management actions that will have positive, long-term effects on their organizations' missions. Instead, they pressure managers to improve profitability in the short term. Consequently, most managers target processes for improvement that have the most direct and immediate effects on profits. While this is important, the real key is to select processes that will improve the quality of products and services. Improving quality automatically reduces costs through decreased rework and fewer mistakes, delays, field failures, and warranty charges. Reduced costs increase productivity, which allows organizations to capture markets with better quality and lower prices.
2. In most organizations, certain processes in need of improvements are easily identified, since they have been known for years to reduce cash flow or produce high costs, rework, scrap, and many customer and employee complaints. After dealing with these problems, how can managers pinpoint less obvious ones? There is no easy answer. In fact, identifying and prioritizing the less-obviously flawed processes is so difficult that this is rarely attempted; when it is, it is often done incorrectly.
3. Another problem is suboptimization. When processes in an organization are optimized through improvement actions, there is the danger of the unexpected, and often not immediately known, effect of suboptimizing other processes or the larger system in which the processes exist. This can happen for a variety of reasons, such as having managers who are unaware of their customers' expectations about the quality of products and services. When managers misunderstand these expectations, they might commit time and resources to streamlining less important or even unimportant processes. Suboptimization can also occur when improved processes put enormous and unexpected pressure on downstream processes to handle the sudden increase of input. If bottlenecks and higher

error rates develop in downstream processes, these processes and the larger system can be suboptimized.

The Benefits of Using Teams

While there are many obstacles to using process improvement teams to help implement TQM, there are also many benefits when the teams are used correctly, such as:

- Teams can be a relatively quick and economical way to achieve demonstrable improvements in processes.
- Early process improvements can convince a board of directors that progress is being made in increased short-term profitability and help convince workers that management is serious about TQM.
- The team approach creates a cadre of facilitators whose skills can be of great benefit in follow-up TQM activities.
- Senior managers who are put in charge of teams can learn many aspects of TQM, such as the philosophy of continuous improvement and leadership through consensus, and skills such as team building, facilitating, group dynamics, and flowcharting.

Despite these valuable results, the team approach usually runs out of gas. But teams can build a foundation for a comprehensive and enduring organizational transformation in both culture and effectiveness.

How to Get Started

An organization that uses the quality improvement council/process improvement team approach to implement TQM must first establish the council. The council's responsibilities are to train members of the organization in TQM concepts, provide budgets for teams, allot times for employees to work on the teams, and set up a recognition-and-reward system for team members.[4]

Improvement teams can play a vital role in introducing TQM into every department in an organization. This requires a minor modification in the way these teams are usually deployed. Each team is assigned to the departments that share the processes the team is trying to improve. This begins when a team leader explains the goals and purpose of the team with the department managers by using Deming's second point (adopt the new philosophy), fourth point (don't deal with suppliers on the basis of price tag alone), and fifth point (improve continuously and forever).

Team leaders should ask each manager for one person from his or her department to serve on the team. Team members must be knowledgeable in how the targeted process works in their departments and be optimistic that the process can be improved. Team members will typically spend 25% of their time over a period of one to three months on team activities. They will act as liaisons between their managers and the team.[5]

Over time, a number of teams will be chartered, and department managers will become more involved with improvement activities. This continual involvement with teams and continual education in TQM philosophy by the council will have a great influence on managers and their departments. The organization can begin to go through the changes in culture and effectiveness outlined in Deming's 14 points.

Another important part of the relationship between the teams and departments is that, although the processes are analyzed by the teams, improvement actions are carried out under the direction of department managers. This contrasts with what is taught by most TQM consultants; they teach that teams must advocate remedial actions to the council and that the council decides whether to authorize implementation. Also, it is generally the teams that carry out the approved remedial actions.

A better approach is to ask department managers to work with the teams to carry out improvements in their departments. This is preferable because managers might worry if they are not kept informed of team activities that relate to their departments, and they might feel blindsided by an action the council or team takes. Also, involving managers can get them in the spirit of continuous improvement. As they become more involved, they realize that senior management will not only authorize improvement but is eager for it.

Teams Ensure Continuous Improvement

As managers carry out team-identified improvements in their departments, they might realize that teams need not be the only source of ideas for improvements and that they can also initiate them. It is important that senior management support such initiatives with additional staffing and funding. Unfortunately, senior management rarely does this, opting for initiatives that are budget neutral. But in cases in which initiatives are supported, cultural transformation can begin quickly, increasing efficiency and effectiveness. When all departments are improving, the setting is right for comprehensive cultural change and effectiveness gains. Expanding the involvement of departments in quality transformation requires additional activities, such as:[6]

1. *Understanding the mission.* Employees should understand where their departments fit into the larger organization, especially with respect to customers and suppliers. Employees should be familiar with their departments' mission statements. If a department has no mission statement, one must be created. Employees should be taught the necessity of innovation. They should also be taught to think about their internal and external customers. Teaching these TQM concepts can involve techniques such as viewing videos, problem solving, and role playing.
2. *Developing a performance measurement system.* A simple, but useful, management information system (MIS) can be built into each department to measure a variety of TQM-related enhancements to an organization. Departments build this MIS by reaching a consensus on the measurable components of their departmental mission statements, known as key result areas. For this approach to be successful, managers must understand that the purpose of measures is improvement and not greater control. Managers then develop one or two indicators to measure how well each

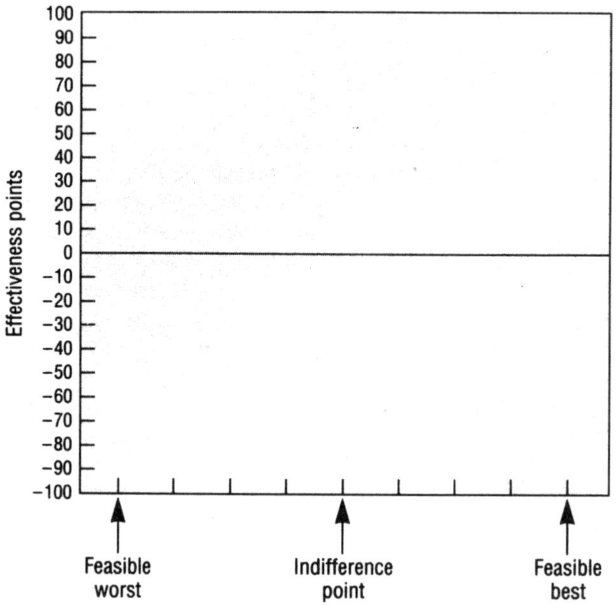

Figure 1. **Feedback chart.**

key result area is being accomplished. Input from customers and suppliers should be used in the creation of key result areas and indicators. Beyond adding to the quality of the process, the inclusion of suppliers and customers can increase cooperation, promote system optimization, and break down barriers.

3. *Using feedback charts.* Departments can develop and automate simple feedback charts that show their consensus on the feasible best, feasible worst, and indifference point for performance on each indicator (see Figure 1). One of the best uses of this MIS is that information about branch performance on indicators is provided in monthly feedback sessions. With this feedback, employees can see how well they are meeting the performance goals and determine what they need to do to accomplish them. With these inputs from employees, managers can remove the barriers that hamper employees' job performance.
4. *Creating the appropriate climate of the feedback sessions.* Managers should create a climate in the feedback sessions in which employees feel free to identify performance barriers. Managers must also accept their responsibility to remove barriers to performance. When this kind of improvement goes on month after month in a series of feedback sessions, large gains in efficiency and effectiveness can occur. To make feedback sessions even more potent, customers and suppliers can participate. They can make valuable suggestions for improvements, and their relationship

to the departments can become more harmonious if their expectations are better understood.

5. *Getting feedback.* When this MIS is developed in a department, indicators should be compared against one another so that the ones most important to the department's mission can be prioritized. By prioritizing indicators, it is possible to prioritize processes, since it is processes that drive indicators. As monthly performance is posted on feedback charts, managers can decide which processes require improvements. Feedback charts can help detect suboptimization as well; negative effects from process improvements will show up immediately on the charts as indicators of other processes.

Process Improvement Teams Can Work

The quality council/process improvement team approach can be a useful beginning to TQM implementation, especially to achieve early improvements of easily identifiable flawed processes and to convince employees that management is serious about improving quality. This approach, however, can be fraught with many false starts, detours, and dead ends. In the long term, it seldom provides the comprehensive approach to quality transformation required for success in today's intensely competitive marketplace. But the systematic connection of teams to departments can help foster an organization-wide quality transformation.

References

1. W.L. French and C.H. Bell Jr., *Organizational Development*, fourth edition (Englewood Cliffs, NJ: Prentice Hall, 1990).

2. W. Edwards Deming, *Out of the Crisis* (Cambridge, MA: Massachusetts Institute of Technology, 1986).

3. Ibid.

4. Joseph M. Juran, *Juran on Leadership for Quality: An Executive Handbook* (New York, NY: Free Press, 1989).

5. For an excellent explanation of the relationships between process improvement teams and departments, see H. James Harrington, *Business Process Improvement* (Milwaukee, WI: Quality Press, 1991).

6. Charles N. Weaver, *TQM: a Step-by-Step Guide to Implementation* (Milwaukee, WI: Quality Press, 1991).

Charles N. Weaver is the C.E. Jurica Distinguished Professor of quantitative management at St. Mary's University in San Antonio, TX, and a Total Quality Management consultant.

Effectively Compensating Teams: A Primer on Pay and Rewards

Donna R. Neusch

A problem every company going to a team-based structure faces is the development of new compensation programs that fit this new structure. The author of this article presents a thoughtful review of that problem and makes some specific suggestions for creating compensation programs that encourage and properly reward working in teams.

If you are "doing teams" you have probably already encountered the compensation crunch. (See Fig. 1.) The current compensation tools you have to reinforce team performance are designed only to reinforce one of two things: individual contribution or individual time. It is time for new compensation tools.

The purpose of this primer is to provide a fresh look at a troublesome topic. It's not meant to give you all the details for team compensation, only the highlights, some differentiators. It will give you a different slant on how to approach compensation for teams.

If you are taking the time to read this short primer on compensation, it's likely that your manufacturing organization fits the following profile:

- You have implemented work teams or are in the process of installing teams.
- The majority of your non-exempt production employees are classified as "hourly" employees.
- Your hourly employees get pay increases in two ways: through general across-the-board increases or cash lump sums that are virtually the same for everyone, and/or through progressive step increases as a result of moving into a higher job classification.
- You are paying for time spent on the job rather than for performance on the job.
- If you do have an hourly performance appraisal system, it is probably perceived to be ineffective because everyone gets virtually the same increase, anyway.

Reprinted with permission from *Target*, vol. 10, no. 1, 1994. Copyright © 1994, Association for Manufacturing Excellence. All rights reserved.

The Compensation Crunch

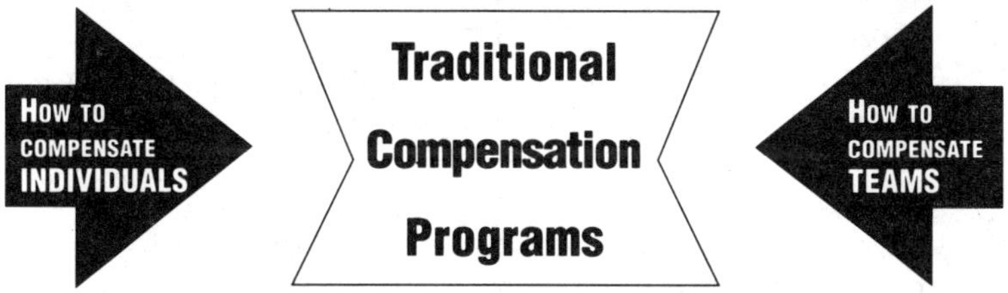

Crunch #1: "First it was teams, then problem-solving and process improvement, now it's formal cross-training — what's in it for me?"

Crunch #2: "This guy is a really skilled hot-shot, so he's earning top dollar, yet he's a lousy team player."

Crunch #3: Another 2 1/2 percent increase across-the-board this year and our team has exceeded all of our performance objectives, yet those guys across the plant seldom even have a team meeting and they all got 2 1/2 percent."

Figure 1.

- The thought of changing your current compensation system to support a team environment and reinforce team performance is either a) not an enjoyable thought, or b) it's a terrifying, paralyzing thought.

"Compensation, that's the last thing we touched because we just didn't know how to go about it." This statement was made by a Fortune 500 presenter at a recent AME event on self-directed work teams. From his audience's questions, they, too, felt just as threatened and concerned about how to tackle the compensation issue.

Yes, companies are loathe to touch it, but compensation is one of the more effective management tools for successfully driving team evolution, maturity, and performance. The fact is, current compensation systems were designed to reinforce individual contribution, not the contribution of teams or individuals on teams. Eventually, all companies wanting a team-based environment are forced to face the compensation crunch. This darned "team thing" has gotten in the way of our hallowed traditional compensation systems.

Compensation is one of the more effective management tools for successfully driving team evolution, maturity, and performance.

Unfortunately, some of the new, highly touted "alternative reward strategies" haven't come to the rescue—most have not fully met the needs of companies serious about transitioning to a team-based environment. For example, what about a pure pay-for-skills approach? It directly reinforces the individual's ability to acquire skills, and only indirectly supports team performance. And sometimes, the race for skills acquisition actually pulls the team apart.

Even broader based team rewards such as gainsharing can produce mediocre results if companies fail to align critical people systems—like jobs, teams, skills development, performance feedback and base pay delivery—with the company's business objectives and initiatives. As a result, no improvement takes place and there is of course no "gain" to share.

Compensation for teams requires a new way of thinking about compensation. It also requires a new approach to designing, developing, and implementing effective compensation systems.

Terminology

First, let's agree on the meaning of some basic compensation terms for our look at effective compensation for teams:

Pay is base pay—the fixed pay rate that a person makes per hour, week, biweekly, etc. It's the rate used as the basis to calculate pay premiums such as overtime and shift differentials.

Reward is variable pay distributed apart from base pay. Generally, rewards are programs designed specifically to reinforce selected business objectives. They are usually team- or facility-wide in application—gainsharing is a widely used example of reward.

Broad Banding is a pay grade structure characterized by broad pay ranges. The broad bands support lateral movement within the band rather than vertical movement up through a hierarchy of grades.

Skill-based pay or **pay-for-skills** is a base pay delivery system that directly links an individual's base pay and increases with the acquisition of defined job skills.

Strategy-based Pay® is a base pay system that directly links an individual's pay increases to team performance, individual performance, and other critical business factors. In a company needing increased flexibility, a critical business factor might be skill acquisition by the individual.

Prerequisites for Team Compensation

If you want to design an effective compensation system that balances rewarding the team and the individuals on the team, do not begin with compensation.

Next, here are some prerequisites for designing team compensation. To begin with, if you want to design an effective compensation system that balances rewarding the team and the individuals on the team, do not begin with compensation. The purpose of compensation is reinforcement. Most companies tackle compensation issues prematurely. They are *not absolutely* crystal clear what needs to be reinforced, and so they do a poor job of reinforcing the right things.

How does one begin, then? The process you use must lay a proper foundation for your compensation systems—your company cannot afford to design new compensation purely for the sake of having new compensation. We use a structured ten-step process to create new pay and reward systems to reinforce a team-based environment. In this process, redesigning compensation doesn't even get addressed until Process Step 7. Companies take the first six process steps, and their pay delivery systems fall naturally and appropriately from the process. To effectively compensate teams, whatever process you select should include steps similar to these six:

1. Create an organizational profile of the future and a migration strategy for getting there. Be clear about the company's direction

and its "future state," and what that will look like in your team-based environment.

2. Analyze and then define the flexibility requirements of your organization. Compensation can be a significant reinforcer of flexibility . . . but only if your flexibility needs are defined.
3. Redesign the way work is done to support the new organization and its flexibility requirements. Do this by broadening job definitions and then defining teams by their roles, scope, and accountabilities.
4. Define the new roles of supervisors and managers. Ensure this is aligned with your new broader jobs, and evolving team definition, maturity, and performance requirements.
5. Formalize skill and competency development. This will activate flexibility in the organization, improve quality performance, and provide structured learning opportunities for your people.
6. Develop a performance feedback system that balances team and individual accountabilities and feedback—a feedback system in which performance factors are directly tied to the company's strategic success factors, operational business objectives, and its world-class initiatives. Now you're ready to tackle compensation. Now you have the solid foundation you need.

Putting It All Together—Taking "Process Step 7"

Once your organization is positioned to address compensation redesign, an early question will be, "Which do we implement first, rewards (gainsharing) or base pay (skill-based pay)?" In general, it is usually more effective to address your base pay system first. However, at this stage of the design process it would be precipitous to say that pure skill-based pay is the system of choice. An effective base pay system reinforcing new broader jobs, skill acquisition, team and individual performance, and the company's world-class initiatives is a critical precursor to any type of rewards program. Fundamental team and individual performance issues must be addressed by an effective base pay system before any type of broad-based reward approach would have an even chance for success.

Once your organization is positioned to address compensation redesign, an early question will be, "Which do we implement first, rewards (gainsharing) or base pay (skill-based pay)?"

There is an exception to this guideline for a union environment. First, there is a reluctance in a union environment to establish consequences for performance, and then there's the difficulty of achieving new, breakthrough base pay systems in the collective bargaining environment. Designing and implementing a broad-based reward system can be a more effective transition toward "team compensation," followed by changes to the base pay that balance team and individual performance.

For example, Kemper Cabinets, a manufacturer of fine kitchen cabinets has been developing a performance-based reward system following a ten-step process. As the joint union and management design team worked through this ten-step process, they determined that they also had an opportunity to

Major Performance Factors (Weights)	
Team Factors	**Individual Factors**
▪ Quality (10%)	▪ Teamwork (15%)
▪ Schedule/Customer Service (5%)	▪ Problem Solving (10%)
▪ Costs (5%)	▪ Work Habits (10%)
▪ Process Improvement (10%)	▪ Flexibility (35%)
Team Weight = 30%	Individual Weight = 70%

Figure 2. **Weight performance factors to support company strategy and to balance team and individual contribution.**

realign their base pay system with the company's need for flexibility through increased skills. The decision was made that after the implementation of their custom-designed gainsharing plan, they would explore a new base pay system that is skill-related.

Paying Teams and Individuals on Teams

For this primer, you can start by developing a new base pay system—one that distributes the annual payroll increases based on individual and team performance related to performance factors that support your company's business objectives. Rather than pre-select one of an assortment of popular pay types, you will focus on developing base pay tied directly to your business strategy. We refer to this approach to compensation as Strategy-based Pay.®

Developing Strategy-based Pay® presupposes you went through something similar to the six process steps described earlier, and that one of your deliverables looks like the chart in Figure 2.

The key to Strategy-based Pay® as a form of base pay for the team environment is the linkage and balance among team performance, individual performance, and the company's various strategic success factors. If the chart in Figure 2 were really yours, there are some assumptions we could make about your strategy: Because this is the first year of your new design, overall performance evaluation will still be weighted on the side of the individual to promote a gradual transition to full team-based performance—only 30 percent for teams, but 70 percent for the individual (next year the balance will shift more toward teams!).

Individual flexibility, reflected in skills acquisition, carries a weight of 35 percent because it's critical as a foundation for the team-based environment and to support the company's flexibility requirements. In fact, all the individual performance factors support the company's move toward a team-based environment. This will make the resulting compensation system "skill-related" rather than pure skill-based pay.

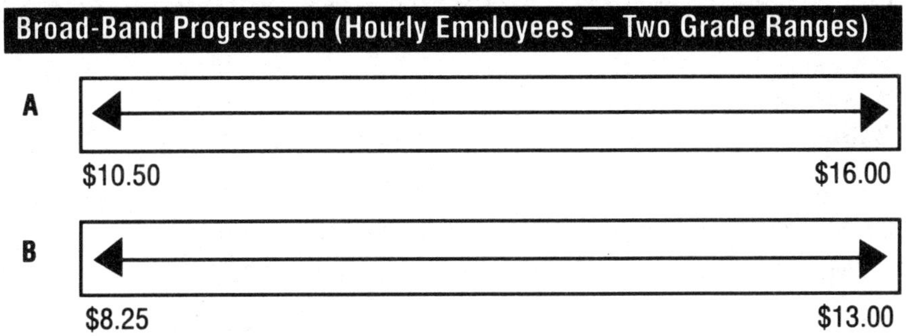

Figure 3.

The major team factors? They are the same for every team in the company, because they represent your strategic success factors of quality, schedule/customer service, cost reduction, and process improvement. However, sub-factors for each major performance factor will differ from team to team depending on the type of work done. Eventually these major team factors will carry an increasingly higher weight as the teams mature and become capable of achieving the high performance and continuous improvement required.

Overall, this chart says clearly not just that you want to pay for performance, but the areas in which you expect performance and how much they mean to the company.

Although Strategy-based Pay® is a different approach to compensation, some traditional compensation tools and guidelines are still used: your company's corporate compensation policy, current labor rates, job evaluation, market surveys, and internal and external equity positions, for example. But how some of them are used will be different.

Job evaluation is still conducted. However, if you've moved from a position of scores of narrow "job" titles to a handful of broad new jobs, job evaluation is a much simpler process—there are fewer jobs. In a broad job environment, slotting of jobs can be an effective approach, as is simplifying an existing point factor system. For example, Schrock WCI went from 190 job titles to five broad jobs. Evaluation of the five broad jobs was completed within a few hours. The result was that the company moved from a pay structure based on ten labor grades to one of two broad bands. Their internal job systems have been greatly simplified and the hours spent evaluating and re-evaluating the 190 job titles were virtually eliminated. Market surveys are still conducted to ensure your organization's competitive position to the market. However, matching the market to new broader jobs takes a few more calculations since the data for the benchmark jobs are consolidated to reflect the newer, broader jobs.

If you've moved from a position of scores of narrow "job" titles to a handful of broad new jobs, job evaluation is a much simpler process—there are fewer jobs.

Another highlight or differentiator of this new approach to pay will be in the pay structure and delivery system. Your pay design team might propose

Performance Matrix

Weighted Performance Rating	1P	2P	3P	4P	5P
4.6-5.0	7%	6%	5%	4%	3%
3.6-4.5	6%	5%	4%	3%	2%
2.6-3.5	5%	4%	3%	2%	1%
1.6-2.5	3%	2%	1%	1%	0%
1.0-1.5	0%	0%	0%	0%	0%

Figure 4. **P = Pentile.**

Broad-Band Progression (Hourly Employees — Two Grade Ranges)

10.50 -11.60	11.61 -12.70	12.71 -13.80	13.81 -14.90	14.91 -16.00
$10.50				$16.00

8.25 -9.21	9.22 -10.15	10.16 -11.10	11.11 -12.05	12.06 -13.00
$8.25				$13.00

Figure 5.

a simplified broad band structure (Figure 3) in which an individual's pay progresses based on his or her weighted performance rating.

Though simple, this approach tends to worry managers because of its "perceived" financial implications. In other words, managers fear that all employees will soon be at the top rates like those of $16.00/hour or $13.00/hour shown in Figure 3.

There are at least two basic techniques a company can employ to control progression through a broad band structure. The first technique uses a performance matrix (Figure 4). The performance matrix is constructed to distribute the company's annual salary budget based on the individual's weighted performance rating and his/her position in the broad band. The intent is to truly differentiate pay distribution based on performance. In our example, the market rate for pay is represented in the 3P or third pentile column, so pay progression begins to slow down once an individual has exceeded the market rate.

The second progression control technique builds off the first. In addition to using a performance matrix to distribute pay increases, the broad band may be segmented into fifths (pentiles), as shown in Figure 5 (page 412), or even sevenths (septiles). The segmentation provides additional structure for controlling progression. Here's how it works.

Using a segmented broad band, control points are established. Such control points often combine skill acquisition and performance for entry into certain segments of the broad band. The control point guidelines will vary by each of the new broad jobs placed in the broad bands. For example, entry into the fifth pentile of band "A" ($14.91–$16.00) might be limited to employees with specific technical skills and that hold a minimum performance rating of, for example, 3.5. Also, employees in a particular job in band "B" might be required to achieve a minimum number of skill points before entering the fourth pentile ($11.11–$12.05). The pay design team will take into consideration the pay levels of the current incumbent population, the skills training and certification requirements, and business needs when developing these control points.

Broad-banding is not the only structure which might flow from a Strategy-based Pay® approach. Other structures and matrix configurations may evolve depending on the results of an organization's first six process steps.

In the final analysis, what's important in Strategy-based Pay® is applying process to compensation redesign. Make base pay a powerful tool to support your company's team-based environment. Quit paying for time spent on the job. Begin paying for performance on the job, and appropriately redistribute the payroll dollars your organization is already spending each year.

Quit paying for time spent on the job. Begin paying for performance on the job.

Rewarding Collective Team Performance

Once the organization's base pay system is realigned with broader jobs, skills development (flexibility), and team and individual performance, it is appropriate to consider the design and implementation of a performance-based reward program such as gainsharing or goal sharing.

Gainsharing plans such as Scanlon, Rucker, and Improshare® have been around for decades. Today, however, many companies are developing a customized approach to performance-based rewards. A wide variety and combination of financial and operational measures are being used to ensure these new plans are self-funding and that they focus and drive team performance.

One caution and a suggestion before reviewing the design process for performance-based rewards. *The caution:* Financial rewards granted at an individual or specific team level, rather than facility-wide, can create competition and animosity among teams. Isolating a large or small team for special treatment almost always sends the wrong message to the team itself, and to other teams in the company.

The suggestion: Explore non-financial recognition systems as a first step in your reward efforts. Simple non-financial rewards can effectively recognize superior performance. One company provided each work team with a budget that represented what the company used to spend on individual recognition efforts—approximately $20 per employee. Each team now uses that budget to recognize the team as a whole, individuals within the team or other teams. They apply their budget to a catalogue of reward options, such as team lunches, movie tickets, T-shirts, and mugs.

And now, some highlights of performance-based rewards for teams. At some level, it is important for all teams to be focused together on supporting the strategic success factors of the organization. This requires that teams working collaboratively take a broader perspective toward the term "performance." A well-designed and implemented performance-based reward system is an effective tool for focusing and rewarding the performance of teams at a facility-wide level.

The customized design of a performance-based reward system is normally carried out by a cross-functional, vertical-slice design team.

The customized design of a performance-based reward system is normally carried out by a cross-functional, vertical-slice design team. Companies follow a variety of processes, but in the end, those with effective performance-based rewards use processes that answer the following questions to several levels of detail:

1. What improvements are desired? Based on the company's strategic direction and vision-into-action package, in exactly what factors is significant improvement required?
2. What initiatives are planned to achieve the improved performance? How will the initiatives improve performance? If the company doesn't know how the improvement is going to be made, is it likely there will be any improvement?
3. How will the improved performance be measured for each factor, when, by whom, and under what conditions?
4. What individual behaviors contribute to improved performance for each identified factor?
5. On which factors will the improvement and reward strategy focus?
6. What is the process for tracking each measure? How will it be tracked? By whom? At what periodicity? Will employees be involved in the tracking?
7. What does performance improvement have to look like to generate a payout? What are the funding formulae?
8. How will payouts be distributed? Who participates? How often? What are the distribution formulae? What's the split among employees, the company, its stake-holders?
9. What special considerations must be made? Set-sides? Pools?

These are not all of the questions that might be asked, but they are the core questions—questions which lead the design team toward a process for designing a performance-based rewards strategy to support the company's business objectives.

Summary

Pay and reward are important management tools. They are not an end in themselves. Effective team compensation flows naturally and appropriately from a process that doesn't begin with compensation. Rather, it's a process that begins by acknowledging the company's strategic direction and "future state," and translates that into a defined chart of major performance factors for teams and individuals. Then the process uses new compensation tools and structures to deliver pay and reward to reinforce team and individual performance.

Donna R. Neusch is a certified compensation professional and partner at Millennium Management Tools, Inc. (MMT) located in Evergreen, CO. She recently co-authored the book, The High Performance Enterprise: Reinventing the People Side of Your Business.

PROCESS REENGINEERING

Reengineering the Organization: A Step-by-Step Approach to Corporate Revitalization

Jeffrey N. Lowenthal

In this thoughtful review of what reengineering is really all about, the author looks at the idea of change, why it is important for managers to understand what change involves in terms of organizational success, why management efforts to lead change often fail, and how to make sure change efforts succeed.

In the business world, change has become the norm. The steady, predictable growth of the 1950s, 1960s, and 1970s has given way to changes that have no historical precedent, such as global marketplace competition, radical technical innovation, limited resources, and major shifts in attitudes about work, employees, and leadership. Today, changes are more frequent and develop faster, and the business world has become more complex and fluid.

Change is one of the foremost issues, if not the foremost business issue, of our day. Change entered the corporate lexicon as a word describing a mixed

Reprinted with permission from *Quality Progress*, January, February, and March 1994. Taken from the book *Reengineering the Corporation: A Step-by-Step Approach to Corporate Revitalization*, Published by ASQC Press, 1994. Copyright © 1994 by ASQC Press. All rights reserved.

blessing. On the one hand, change represents growth, opportunity, and innovation; on the other hand, it represents threat, disorientation, and upheaval.

In response to this rapid change, global leaders have offered suggestions to restore growth and profitability. Many think the government is capable of restoring market leadership and demand that a new global climate be established, allowing their companies to prosper again. Others point at managers to take the lead in implementing change because, today, they must not only do things right but also do the right things.

This book operates from the words of Abraham Lincoln, offered to the nation in a time of crisis and change: "The dogmas of the quiet past will not work in the turbulent future. As our cause is new, so must we think and act anew." And we are in turbulent times. Take, for example, a Russian cosmonaut who spent 313 days in space only to return to a country that no longer existed and a hometown with a different name.

'The dogmas of the quiet past will not work in the turbulent future. As our cause is new, so must we think and act anew."

At a recent meeting, Roberto Goizueta, corporate executive officer of Coca-Cola, told his managers, "If you think you are going to be successful running your business in the next 10 years the way you [did] in the last 10 years, you're out of your mind. To succeed, we have to disturb the present."

Organizations that continuously adapt their bureaucracies, strategies, systems, products, and cultures to the shocks and forces will eliminate their competitors. Such organizations will adapt to crises that bedevil competitors by maximizing their strengths and developing new strengths as change occurs. These organizations are, or will become, masters of organizational reengineering, an approach that helps organizations adapt to change. Change is seldom easy. Further, change can neither be rushed nor dragged out—the key is balance.

A Simple Explanation of Change Theory

Change is a slow and sometimes painful process In the past, inventions and their applications have been ignored by whole populations that had known about them for years. Three historical examples—gunpowder and rifle development, the printing press, and the facsimile, or fax machine—illustrate the slow pace of change in the past.

Five hundred years passed between the first known use of gunpowder and the earliest rifles in Europe. In fact, for 300 years following the development of rifles, so little progress was made in rifle improvement that Benjamin Franklin suggested to the Continental Congress that the American army be equipped with longbows because rifles were inaccurate and gunpowder was hard to obtain. Further, the historical statement, "Don't shoot until you see the whites of their eyes," was made to ensure that every musket shot produced a kill so that gunpowder wasn't wasted.

The second historical example is the printing press. The Arabic people had been aware of the technology of printing from the books of the Jewish scholars and the other religious communities they ruled. Yet, they made no use of the printing press until three centuries after Johannes Gutenberg's invention.

The fax machine, which is indispensable in most organizations today, is the third historical example. Fax machines were invented in the 1950s, but were not widely accepted until the 1980s.

Before the 1800s, change was localized and sporadic. It affected a few people in various places or large numbers in one place, but rarely large populations on a global basis. Changes that did occur were so slow or remote that they were virtually imperceptible. When change occurred at a faster pace, it was typically due to massive social upheavals, such as foreign invasions or the overthrow of a regime. This pattern was profoundly altered by the Industrial Revolution.

Today, change no longer occurs at a slow pace. Many changes can be linked to the rapid application of recent inventions, such as global communications, the microprocessor, new plastics, and other synthetic materials. Word of new technologies and products travels quickly via professional meetings, proliferating scientific journals, or global television. Today, we have the capability of communicating simultaneously with nearly every person on earth, so change continues to evolve.

To understand change, the two basic kinds of change—structural and cyclical—need to be understood.

Structural Change

Structural change involves a fundamental transformation of some activity or institution. After structural change takes place, the activity or institution is considerably different (and can represent either an improvement or a decline from the previous state).

Structural change is radical. For example, the speed of communication increased only slightly as human runners were replaced by messengers on horseback. The telegraph and telephone, however, changed the speed of communication dramatically. Today, we have nearly instantaneous communication. In the future, communication will continue to change, maybe not in terms of speed, but in terms of amount and format.

This type of change is irreversible. Communication systems have undergone a permanent transformation and attained a new state. There might be stability in the new state or there might be a continuing evolution to yet another new state, but the system will not revert to the prior state. The discovery of the new knowledge and the creation of new technology and equipment makes the old system obsolete. Permanent adjustment is required. If an organization does not respond, it will fall behind and be swept under by its competitors.

Structural change could require dismantling old institutions, relationships, and procedures and replacing them with new ones. You cannot expect to move successfully into the future burdened with the baggage from the past.

Cyclical Change

Cyclical change, on the other hand, involves a temporary change from a level or state. Over time, cyclical change tends to follow a discernible fluctuation pattern of returning regularly to prior states. An example of cyclical change can be found in the retail industry. Every year, in late August through the end of December, retailers hire additional personnel to help with the holiday season. This addition of personnel typically requires changes in hiring policies, training, and other administrative tasks. After the season is complete, however, retailers typically return to business as usual.

Cyclical change usually does not cause any irreversible alterations in the structure of the institutions or activities in which they are occurring. Cyclical changes are therefore repeating, nonstructural, and limited, and the required adjustments are temporary. While the pace of change is increasing and becoming limitless and infinite, each type of change has its own pattern, with a discernible direction, amount, pace, and duration.

A Need for Change: Continuous Improvement

Physics teaches us that, for a piece of wood to burn, it must be heated to a temperature at which it ignites; then it burns by itself. The initial heating requires energy, but once the wood is ignited, the flame sustains itself and gives off much more energy than was required to start the fire.

A more intense fire than that of burning wood results from a mixture of aluminum powder and metal oxide. By itself, the mixture is cold and lifeless, but when heated to an ignition temperature, it becomes a source of brilliant light and intense heat that cannot be put out by ordinary means. The mixture will burn under water or in any other environment that would extinguish an ordinary flame. When it burns, the fire is self-sustaining and does not depend on its surroundings for support.

Unfortunately, organizations do not operate like a mixture of aluminum powder and metal oxide; they are not totally self-sustaining. Organizations must rely on both internal and external factors to succeed. Long-term success depends on how well a company can meet and satisfy its customers' shifting demands.

Organizational reengineering is based on two interacting factors: total customer satisfaction and effective and efficient internal processes. A company's success depends on its ability to satisfy its customers' needs. In turn, this ability depends on how well the organization's internal processes work to meet this eternal demand. Therefore, the organization succeeds from the inside out: The commitment and dedication of employees to fulfill customer needs become the self-sustaining flame that perpetuates success. Competing from the inside out means managing employees not merely so they are comfortable within a company, but so they can also compete in the marketplace.

Organizational reengineering is based on two interacting factors: total customer satisfaction and effective and efficient internal processes.

An organization's success in this respect does not result from quick fixes, simple programs, or management speeches. It starts with the identification of an organization's core competencies, which in turn guide management behavior. This guided management behavior then affects the attitudes and values of all employees toward the realization that competitiveness, internal processes, and effective people management are strongly linked.

The reengineering process is only one method to gain a competitive advantage. Its components are not new or innovative; they all have been around for many years, if not decades. What makes the reengineering process so powerful is the blending of the various components into a synergistic whole.

Business Process Reengineering

Business reengineering, or business process reengineering, is a term that recently entered the business lexicon; now it appears everywhere.

The term is being grossly misused and even abused in a variety of industries. It is being slapped onto projects hungry for funding, from traditional automation and systems rebuilding efforts to incremental quality improvement schemes. Many suppliers also have adopted the term to market their same old products and services.

What makes the reengineering process so powerful is the blending of the various components into a synergistic whole.

The business world today differs dramatically from the one that existed just a few years ago. For example, there is a rising global competitiveness and a demographically transformed work force. Further, customer demands have become more intense, such as requiring ever-shorter time frames for delivery. Organizational reengineering, business process reengineering, and total quality management are among the strategies some corporations are using to deal with those changes.

Most change processes, such as total quality management, are focused on enhancing products and services for both customers and suppliers. Total quality management requires incremental changes over several years, and those changes are usually small and take place within the current corporate culture. Some companies, however, have recognized the need for more extensive, almost radical, changes in operations. Organizational and business process reengineering are the processes used to design those radical changes. They have generated many huge successes.

When a reengineering effort succeeds, companies reap big benefits. For example, a major automobile company reengineered its invoice processing and reduced the number of employees who work in that department by 75%. Similarly, a major telecommunications company reengineered part of its service department and cut costs by almost a third.

What Is Organizational Reengineering?

Many business process reengineering firms define their product as a process by which companies become world-class competitors by remaking their information systems, organizations, ways of working together, and the means by which they talk with each other and their customers. This is a good starting point for defining organizational reengineering, but it is not complete. A historical perspective is needed to more fully understand the term reengineering.

A Historical Look

Exactly how organizational reengineering started is a contentious subject among the industry's professionals. Some claim that the reengineering process started a few years ago as a blending of several methodologies. Others claim that organizational reengineering started in the 1980s when the American auto industry, battered by Japanese rivals, began to integrate car design with assembly-line automation. At that time, American automobile manufacturers embraced the ideas of just-in-time (JIT) manufacturing (delivering supplies just when the factory needs them rather than warehousing inventories) and total quality management (continuously improving the quality of operations and customer service).

Organizational reengineering is several products rolled into one. It can be compared to a multisymptom cold medication. Just like the various brands of cold medicines, consulting firms that offer reengineering services combine their own ingredients in different formulations. They use marketing strategies to differentiate themselves from each other. Whatever the mixture of services, however, reengineering efforts usually have four major components:

1. A greater focus on the organization's customers (both internal and external)
2. A fundamental rethinking of the processes in the organization that lead to improvements in productivity and cycle time (known as process improvement or business process reengineering)
3. A structural reorganization, which typically breaks functional hierarchies into cross-functional teams, such as team building and organizational development activity
4. New information and measurement systems, which use the latest in technology to drive improved data distribution and decision making, such as quality and information technology

When viewed from this perspective, it becomes apparent that reengineering's foundation has had a long history over the past 100 years.

Process design and the scientific study of work can be traced to the days of Frederick Taylor (1856–1915). The theories of organizational structure and dynamics date back to Henri Fayol (1841–1901), Alfred P. Sloan Jr. (1875–1966), and Peter Drucker (1909–present). Information and measurement systems were addressed by Georg Siemens (1839–1901). Finally, the emphasis on customer focus was established by Robert E. Wood (1879–1969).

This brief history reminds us that the past holds valuable lessons concerning the principles underlying the reengineering process. These lessons from the past can help prevent future problems.

Darrel Rigby, author of *The Secret History of Process Reengineering,* illustrates the value of one of these historical lessons. His example focuses on breaking functional hierarchies into cross-functional teams, which is a major component of reengineering. According to Rigby, the battle between the merits of function-based organizations and process- or product-based organizations is well documented. Functional organizations offer the following benefits:

- They maximize development and utilization of specialized skills.

- They offer cost-effective divisions of labor and provide economies of scale in plant and equipment.
- They allow for effective hiring of employees and offer clear career paths for specialized experts.

On the other hand, Rigby says that organizations with cross-functional structures provide better coordination and integration of work, offer quicker response times, and provide for simpler cost controls. This latter type of organization also offers higher levels of employee creativity and greater job satisfaction.

Which type of organizational structure is better? According to Rigby, leading-edge companies vacillate between structure types. They usually start with functional organizations, then shift to a process-focused structure, then to a one-or-the-other status, next to a combination of both, and finally they start the cycle again. To illustrate his theoretical discussion, Rigby provides the following example of the schizophrenia of American businesses in choosing an organizational type.

During the late 1940s, the predominant choice for organizational structure was the functional one. During the next decade, as organizations pushed decision making down to the lowest levels possible and the hierarchical structure flattened, organizations shifted gears. With this shift, staff size was reduced and organizations focused more on using cross-functional work teams. The 1960s brought another shift, this time to situational leadership and structure.

In other words, organizations would choose the most appropriate structure, either functional or cross-functional, that the situation required. Thus, organizations attempted to adopt the best of all worlds: matrix management. Matrix management was the new and innovative structure type of the 1970s. Matrix management, however, typically resulted in total confusion because managers had extreme difficulty shifting between functional and cross-functional structures on an as-needed basis.

As the cycle continued, the early 1980s brought sharp criticism of the matrix structure, and many large organizations shifted back to a functional structure. Most managers realized, however, that the functional structure of organizations was not flexible enough for a fluid and dynamic business environment. Thus, it became increasingly clear that the most appropriate organizational structure is the process- or product-based organizational one.

Organizational reengineering requires that tasks be compressed and integrated rather than fragmented into specialized and repetitive tasks.

A Working Definition

Learning from these historical examples, organizational reengineering negates nearly all of the premises on which previous organizational structures (functional, matrix, and situational) have been based. Organizational reengineering requires that tasks be compressed and integrated rather than fragmented into specialized and repetitive tasks. Thus, a working definition of organizational reengineering is:

The fundamental rethinking and redesign of operating processes and organizational structure, focused on the organization's core competencies, to achieve dramatic improvements in organizational performance.

In other words, organizational reengineering is a process by which a company can redesign the way it does business to maximize its core competencies. In turn, this redesign results in significantly higher profits, greater customer satisfaction, lower expenses, consolidated activities, and increased productivity.

Organizational reengineering redesigns the way work flows through an organization, which often leads to system and infrastructure changes. Further, this process focuses the organization on its core competencies, in addition to cultural aspects of change, which separates organizational reengineering from business process reengineering.

An organization's core competencies are its collective knowledge, including the processes by which it coordinates and integrates diverse production skills and multiple streams of technology. In essence, core competencies are the systems that enable an organization to identify and use the knowledge embedded within its organization to its best competitive advantage.

Organizational reengineering involves reorganizing work flows, cutting waste, combining process steps, and eliminating repetitive tasks. It will not work within the typical corporate culture because it changes the corporate culture itself. The process replaces the traditional culture with a new set of organizational principles by which leaders can rebuild their business. Reengineering strives to break away from the old rules about how organizations are structured and the way they conduct business. Reengineering involves recognizing and rejecting old methods and finding imaginative new ways to accomplish work. New rules will emerge from the redesigned processes to govern the organization. The redesigned processes and the new rules produce a quantum leap in the performance of an organization.

Organizational reengineering does not lead to incremental improvements, which are usually associated with traditional quality improvement programs. Instead, it produces breakthrough improvements in operating and financial performance. Reengineering goes to the heart of the ways in which organizations work. It is not just automating or reautomating existing business processes, it is discarding conventional ways of working and replacing those ways with entirely new ones.

As stated earlier, organizational reengineering centers on the radical redesign of business processes to better meet customer need through a focus on core competencies and cultural change. It focuses on processes that create something of value for either internal or external customers. Reengineering can be applied, for example, to new product development processes that turn an idea into a manufacturable and marketable prototpye or to order fulfillment processes that begin with the receipt of an order and end when the customer has received and paid for the product. Thus, reengineering examines processes that are cross-functional. Target processes transcend the boundaries between sales, marketing, manufacturing, finance, and research and development. Processes are neglected in traditional structures because most companies focus on functions while processes fall between the cracks.

Organizational reengineering might focus on process redesign, but it doesn't end with process redesign. A radical change in the structure of a process inevitably entails dramatic change in all other aspects of the organization, which include the content and definition of jobs, the shape of organizational structure, and the values and beliefs that people have about what is important to the organization.

In summary, organizational reengineering rethinks the way work is completed inside an organization; it does not simply try to improve existing processes. Organizational reengineering changes processes completely so that they are logical, efficient, and driven by an organization's core competencies.

Organizational reengineering changes processes completely so that they are logical, efficient, and driven by an organization's core competencies.

The Reengineering Process: An Overview

The reengineering process presented provides a holistic approach to the redesign and rebuilding of an organization. It is broader than the model for reengineering business processes, which is only a component of the model presented. This model provides action steps for the strategic, cultural, and technical aspects of reengineering an organization (see Figure 1).

Reengineering business processes is not a substitute for strategic direction. For example, reengineering will not help to perfect a flawed process. But when an organization has a clear strategic direction with a focus on core competencies, reengineering will help it better achieve its goals by creatively strengthening and combining customer opportunities.

Note, however, that any process change will be met with resistance inside an organization unless cultural factors such as employee buy-in and job satisfaction are considered part of the change process. Internal resistance could cause great internal pain and potentially result in failure of the reengineering effort. Thus, the model strongly emphasizes the preparation of employees for change.

Embracing Change

In early 1983, the book *In Search of Excellence* offered the business community examples of organizational excellence that others could follow. Authors Thomas Peters and Robert Waterman set specific organizational standards and rated a variety of companies against these standards. Three companies—Levi Strauss, Texas Instruments, and Digital Equipment Corporation—received high marks and were presented as models of excellence. Less than two years later, *Business Week* carried a cover story titled "Who's Excellent Now?", which described the difficulties that several companies featured in the book faced.

The article stated that Levi Strauss was caught unprepared when customers' tastes changed; Texas Instruments attempted to become a major manufacturer in home computers; and Digital Equipment Corporation, resting on

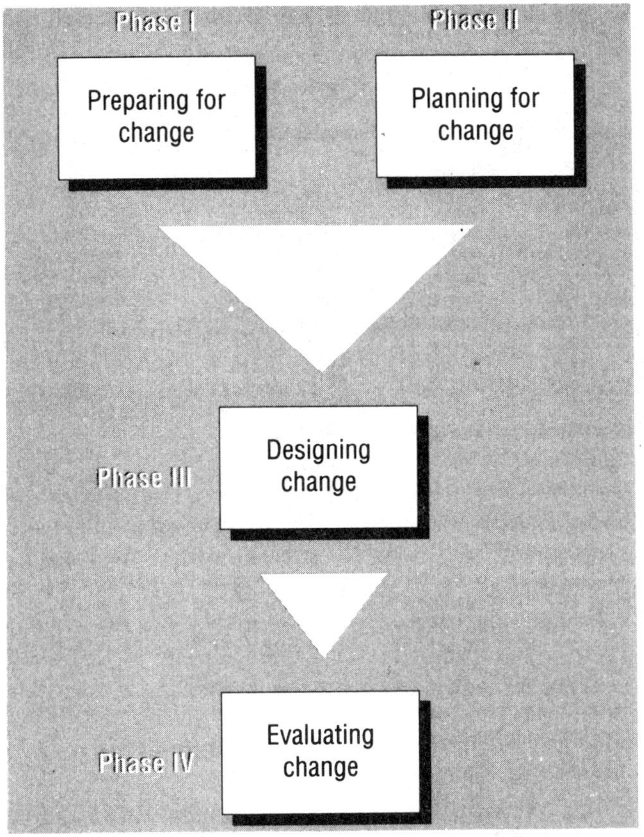

Figure 1. **Reengineering model overview.**

the laurels it had won in the development of minicomputers, missed significant opportunities as the computer market shifted to personal computers. Specifically, these three companies had failed to live up to their touted excellence.

Many business professionals wanted to know what happened to these companies. The critical issue was not that these three companies fell short of the standards that Peters and Waterman had set for them; instead, it was that they had failed to prepare for and embrace change. In fact, it could be said that all three were resistant to organizational change.

An organization must have a built-in ability to make rapid changes in response to internal and external environments. Further, it must do so with a minimal disruption of services. This ability of an organization to transform itself with little or no distress or disruption sets the leaders within a particular industry apart from the competition. Organizations that have this transformation ability exhibit two primary characteristics: responsive awareness (the ability to relate to a changing external environment) and focused flexibility

An organization must have a built-in ability to make rapid changes in response to internal and external environments.

(the ability to remain focused while reconfiguring to meet the change required by the external environment). These two change characteristics help reduce distress and disruption in the workplace. The process of developing these two characteristics, however, can be time consuming and expensive.

Many companies expect that after this round of downsizing is over, they will be able to resume their regular management practices. It was these management practices, however, that created the need for downsizing.

For example, many American companies are now suffering through the difficult process of downsizing. Many companies view downsizing in a negative light, and they are operating as though their work-force reduction were a one-time activity. They expect that after this round of downsizing is over, they will be able to resume their regular management practices. It was these management practices, however, that created the need for downsizing. These organizations are not building on the ability to adapt to change and, therefore, will probably have to repeat the downsizing process over and over until nothing is left to lose. Further, their operations might have been disrupted significantly because of the employees' fears of losing their jobs.

Clearly, many organizations are shortsighted because they are not building the two positive change characteristics of responsive awareness and focused flexibility. Lacking this flexibility, employees experience change as painful, which in turn causes avoidant behavior that inhibits the change process. If properly handled, however, the pain associated with a change process can be avoided, so organizations will be able to better weather future storms of change.

The Fallacy of Programmatic Change

Most change programs don't work because their guiding paradigm is flawed by a common belief that change begins with the knowledge and attitudes of individuals. Thus, according to this paradigm, a successful change effort must begin by changing employee attitudes, which leads to changes in individual behavior. When this change is repeated by many people, the ultimate result will be organizational change.

In a four-year study regarding organizational change, Michael Beer, Russell A. Eisenstat, and Bert Spector found that while senior managers understand the necessity of change to cope with new competitive realities, they often misunderstand what it takes to bring about change. These senior managers tend to make two assumptions about change. First, they assume that companywide programs, such as the development of a mission statement, training courses, and a new performance appraisal system, will suddenly transform an organization. The second assumption, which is driven by the prior assumption, is that employee behavior is changed by altering a company's formal structure and system. Thus, this type of change is like a conversion experience—once people "get religion," changes in their behavior will surely follow. According to the study, these two assumptions constitute the fallacy of programmatic change.

An example of this fallacy occurred recently at a Midwest-based publisher. In the early 1990s, a Big Six management-consulting firm was hired to help streamline the production operations in a division that grossed more than $100 million. A divisionwide change effort was announced through a series

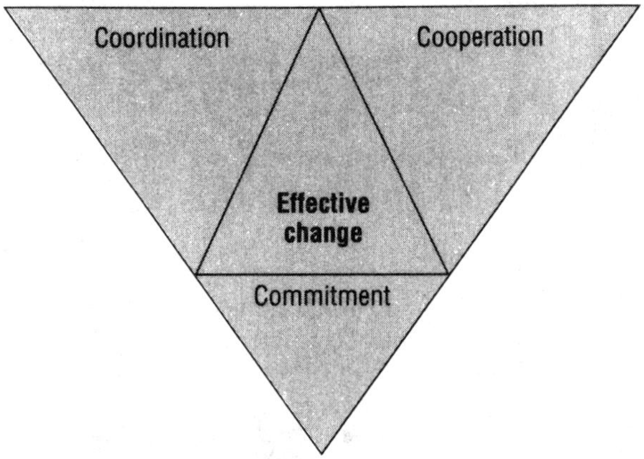

Figure 2. **Elements of effective change.**

of town-hall meetings, departmental meetings, and a division newsletter. The change was precipitated by the division's profits, which had been slipping during the late 1980s and early 1990s. Further, employees were making serious mistakes that were costing the company tens of thousands of dollars to correct. The solution, as decided by executive management, was to change the way the division operated, and the place to begin was at the top.

The general manager of the division, working with his staff, articulated the division's core competencies, mission and vision statements, and guiding principles. These items were published and distributed to all employees. The manager also undertook a divisionwide effort to redesign the work flow and push change in accountability and responsibility down throughout the organization. He also initiated a new performance appraisal system.

According to several presentations, the work-flow changes would take between six and 12 months to complete. Eighteen months later, however, behavior hadn't changed and serious mistakes were still occurring. What went wrong? Why did this change effort stall? The answer to the first question is everything. Every assumption made by the consulting firm and the divisional leadership staff about who should lead the change effort, what needed changing, and how to go about precipitating the change was wrong. In essence, change was attempted by first changing individual behavior and then shifting the organizational structure.

The most effective way to change behavior is to put people into new roles within the organization, which would impose new responsibilities and relationships on them.

A new paradigm of change, as proposed by Beer, Eisenstat, and Spector, is that individual behavior is shaped by the roles that people play in the organization. Thus, the most effective way to change behavior is to put people into new roles within the organization, which would impose new responsibilities and relationships on them. This creates a situation that forces new attitudes and behaviors to emerge in people.

Figure 2 shows three interrelated factors that are needed to change an organization effectively: coordination, commitment, and competencies. Coordination of effort, or teamwork, is especially important if an organization

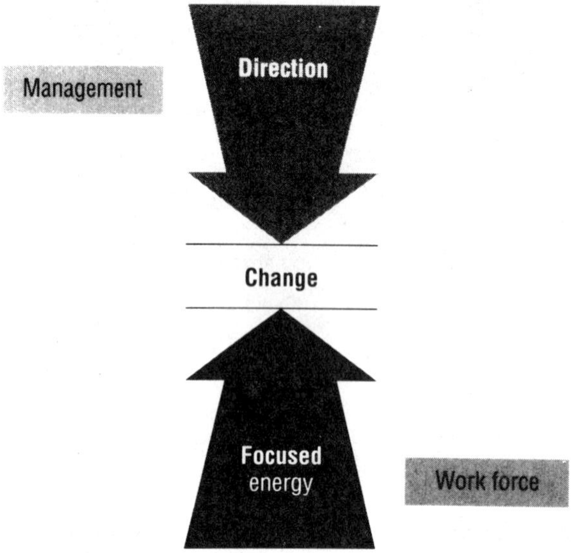

Figure 3. **Internal pressures to change.**

wants to benefit from the existing synergy of employee knowledge and understanding. With proper coordination of effort, an organization can discover cost-reduction, quality-improvement, and product-development opportunities. Commitment to change is essential if management wants employee cooperation and effective implementation of the changes. Finally, new competencies, such as knowledge of the business, analytical skills, and interpersonal skills, are required if employees are to identify and solve problems as a team. If any of these elements are missing, the change process will break down.

Most business professionals think of training programs as the principal method to propose change. The problem with training programs is that management generally fails to support the new skills learned in the training session. That is, training programs only focus on competence (i.e., skill building). Since there is a lack of commitment in the organization, when employees get back on the job, many of their new skills go unused. Therefore, many employees experience frustration and view the training as a waste of time. This undermines whatever commitment to change a program might have aroused in the first place.

Another problem with most companywide change programs is their narrow focus. Typically they focus either on commitment or cooperation, but rarely on both, and almost never on competence. For example, if senior management develops vision and mission statements that specify teamwork, teams will not spontaneously form, and employees will not necessarily know how to function within the teams.

New merit compensation programs, which are designed to implement change, can also be counterproductive. In these programs, managers must differentiate between better and poorer performers. But they are not always trained to carry out the skill development or competence needed to effectively carry out the new compensation system. Thus, the system could actually inhibit cooperation.

Corporatewide merit programs have an additional problem. They are designed to cover everyone and everything. Thus, they usually don't cover anything particularly well. They are so general and standardized that they don't address the daily realities of particular units or employees.

Training or companywide programs are not necessarily inappropriate; both can play a valuable role in supporting an integrated change effort. The key is to have an integrated approach to change, training, and compensation. The preceding publisher example had all the right programs for development, such as division direction (vision and mission statements), organizational structure redesign, and a new performance appraisal system. The various programs, however, were used in isolation and individually failed to achieve their goals. When programs are used in isolation, at best they are viewed as irrelevant, time consuming, and a fad. At worst, this lack of integration can inhibit change. In the publisher example, change was inhibited because the programs were not integrated. But the question remains: How does an organization carry out effective change?

Most successful change efforts take place at the periphery of the corporation—in a few plants and divisions far from corporate headquarters.

The Paradox

Most individuals believe change efforts should start at the top of the organization and be driven downward. According to Beer, Eisenstat, and Spector, however, most successful change efforts take place at the periphery of the corporation—in a few plants and divisions far from corporate headquarters. In addition, the successful change efforts were led by the general manager of the local unit rather than the corporate executive officer or corporate staff people. Beer, Eisenstat, and Spector's findings help explain why change in some companies has had very little positive impact, even with wave after wave of programs that are designed to induce change.

In successful organizations, the leaders did not focus on formal structure and systems; instead, they addressed concrete business problems. By aligning employee roles, responsibilities, and relationships, they focused energy for change on the work itself and not on abstractions such as participation or culture.

Successful managers need to lead a nondirective change process. That is, managers need to create a climate for change and provide the general direction in which the company should move without insisting on specific solutions. The work force, on the other hand, needs to focus its energies on resolving specific business issues and providing input for directional change based on its frontline experiences (see Figure 3).

Managers need to create a climate for change and provide the general direction in which the company should move without insisting on specific solutions.

A first-tier automotive supplier located in the Southeast experienced a downward turn in business due to increased overseas competition. The president of the company decided that the organization's core competencies would allow the company to expand into the aerospace and agribusiness markets, which would help counterbalance its troubles in the automotive business. The president set the general direction (that is, the two new markets) and allowed the organization to build a critical mass for change by preparing the work force for the changes about to occur.

The formal change started in a small South Carolina plant, where the plant's management and the work force together figured out how to change. The president, who saw this demonstrated success, resisted imposing this successful change on the other parts of the organization (the paradox) and instead simply shared this success with other areas of the company. Shortly, two other plants, in Ohio and Pennsylvania implemented the techniques used at the first plant and successfully changed. Word spread fast, and as other parts of the company started to change, the president realigned the corporate structure and system to the new management practices that had been developed in the periphery. If the president had imposed a structure or a system at the beginning of the change or had attempted to push his own style of management, the tension between these dynamic units and static top management could have caused the change process to break down.

Jeffrey N. Lowenthal is the author of Reengineering the Corporation: A Step-by-Step Approach to Corporate Revitalization, *published by ASQC Press, 1994.*

The Hocus-Pocus of Reengineering

Paul A. Strassmann

In its more extreme form, reengineering, according to Strassmann, is a nearly mindless "throw out the old and bring in the new" approach to change and "improvement." Strassmann presents a compelling case against this form of reengineering, rejecting its radical, warlike rhetoric for a more deliberate approach to process improvement. While this article may seem to argue for the validity of a continuous improvement approach over reengineering, the real difference may have to do with the rate of change and the way managers go about reengineering. As Strassmann properly implies, it doesn't make a lot of sense to throw out the baby with the bath water. It seems to us that a more studied approach to reengineering includes keeping the best of old and incorporating the best of the new in a way that involves and enhances the commitment of employees while making the company more efficient and effective.

Make no mistake: Reengineering is a great idea as well as a clever buzzword. What manager wouldn't support the notion of taking something that is defective and fixing it? Industrial engineers, methods analysts, and efficiency experts have done it for years.

Naturally, reengineering is too good to be new. A contemporary repackaging of tried-and-true industrial-engineering methods, this cure now is being administered in large doses to business enterprises that to survive must instantly show improved profits.

In one important way, though, reengineering differs from past incremental and analytic methods and allies itself with more suspect movements: In political terms, it more closely resembles a coup d'etat than a parliamentary democracy.

Those applying the label "efficiency through reengineering" advocate the adoption of radical means to achieve corrective actions. This extremism offers seemingly instant relief from the pressure on corporate executives to show immediate improvements. It calls for discarding all existing institutions and reconstituting an organization on the basis of completely fresh ideas: the new business model is expected to spring forth from the inspired insights of a new leadership team.

Reprinted with permission from the author and from *Across the Board*, June 1994. Copyright © 1994 by Paul A. Strassmann.

THE WISDOM OF MICHAEL HAMMER

To fully understand the intellectual roots of reengineering, let its guru speak for himself:

"American managers . . . must abandon the organizational and operational principles and procedures they are now using and create new ones. . . . Business reengineering means starting all over, starting from scratch. . . . It means forgetting how work was done. . . . Old job titles and old organizational arrangements . . . cease to matter. How people and companies did things yesterday doesn't matter to the business reengineer. . . . Reengineering . . . can't be carried out in small and cautious steps. It is an all-or-nothing proposition."

Reengineering the Corporation

"On this journey we'll carry our wounded and shoot the dissenters. . . . I want to purge from the business vocabulary: CEO, manager, worker, job."

Forbes ASAP, September 13, 1993

"It's basically taking an ax and a machine gun to your existing organization."

Computerworld, January 24, 1994

"What you do with the existing structure is nuke it!"

Site Selection, February 1993

"Reengineering must be initiated . . . by someone who has . . . enough status to break legs."

Planning Review, May/June 1993

"You either get on the train or we'll run over you with the train. . . . The last thing in the world that reengineering does is enhance the manager's sense of self-importance, because one of the things that reengineering says is that managing isn't so important."

Across the Board, June 1993

"Reengineering . . . will require a personality transplant . . . a lobotomy."

Computerworld, June 1, 1987

"Don't try to forestall reengineering. If senior management is serious about reengineering they'll shoot you."

Management Review, September 1993

The reengineering movement's tone is set by its most prominent proponent, Michael Hammer, co-author of *Reengineering the Corporation* (HarperBusiness). He consistently invokes violence and revolution in rhetoric and practice. "The way you deal with resistance [to reengineering] is . . . a bloody ax," he told *Across the Board* a year ago. "Al Capone once said, 'You get a lot further with a gun and a kind word than with a kind word alone'."

Matching new prophets' ideas with past patterns helps determine whether their proposals simply repackage what has been tried before. Hammer's dogmatic pronouncements—as well as his sentence structure—resonate with the radical views put forth by political hijackers like Robespierre, Lenin, Mao, and Guevara. By replacing some of Hammer's nouns, one can produce slogans attributed to those who gained power by overthrowing the existing order (see box).

It is an unlikely coincidence that the most widely read book on reengineering carries the provocative subtitle *A Manifesto for Business Revolution* and claims to be a "seminal" book comparable to Adam Smith's *An Inquiry into the Nature and Causes of the Wealth of Nations*—the intellectual underpinning of capitalism. Keep in mind that another popular polemic, also bearing the title "Manifesto," successfully spread the premise that the only way to improve capitalism is to obliterate it.

Competing Moralities

Much more is at issue here than reengineering itself; the question is one of the morality of commerce against the morality of warfare.

The morality of warfare—of vengeance, violent destruction, and the use of might—has been with us ever since primitive tribes competed for hunting grounds. Societies have recognized the importance of warfare by sanctioning a class, subject to some rules, to kill, while the redeeming code of loyalty and self-sacrifice for the good of all would prevail.

The morality of commerce, with us since 500 B.C. or so, is based on shunning force, developing voluntary agreements, collaborating even with strangers and aliens, respecting contracts, and promoting exchanges that benefit both the buyers and the sellers.

Reengineering's radical promoters have succeeded in gaining at least temporary respectability, successfully translating 1960s radicalism—with its socially unacceptable slogan, "Do not reform, obliterate!"—into a fashionable, money-making proposition.

Nearly every large-scale tragedy of the last few centuries can be traced to the substitution of the morality of warfare for the morality of commerce, under the guise that this will lead to greater overall prosperity. Hammer's adoption of the nonredeeming expressions of military morality crosses the line of acceptability. Reengineering, an activity in the commercial domain, should be bound by its morality, with military language and thinking left to those who must confront the prospect of getting shot at.

Reengineering's radical promoters have succeeded in gaining at least temporary respectability, successfully translating 1960s radicalism—with its socially unacceptable slogan, "Do not reform, obliterate!"—into a fashionable, moncy-making proposition. Thcir clarion call for overthrowing the status quo is similar to that trumpeted by the students who occupied deans' offices across the United States. Now those arguments are parlayed into lucrative consulting assignments.

Leaders of revolutionary political movements since the French Revolution have been fixed on seizing power under whatever slogan could be sold to those hoping to improve justice, freedom, or profit. And those same leaders—mostly intellectuals who rarely delivered more than pamphlets and speeches—have consistently worsened conditions after taking over the Establishment.

Reengineering fits neatly into patterns of past revolutionary movements: In each case, the leaders call for uncompromising destruction of existing institutions. Only through this kind of attack on customs, habits and relationships can newcomers gain influence with little opposition. The common characteristic of the elite that agitates destructively for positions of leadership is an arrogance that they are the only ones with superior insight, the only ones deserving of trust.

The Solution: Business-Process Improvement

To be effective, any way to improve the way people work must be *evolutionary,* not revolutionary. The long history of miscarriages of centrally planned radical reforms, in addition to reengineering's as-yet-dismal track record (as acknowledged by Hammer himself in an interview last summer), suggest that evolutionary approaches deliver better and more permanent improvements. Evolutionary change stimulates morale and imagination, creating conditions for rewarding organizational learning and for inspiring employees to discover innovative ways to deal with adversity and competitive challenges.

Evolutionary change stimulates morale and imagination, creating conditions for rewarding organizational learning and for inspiring employees to discover innovative ways to deal with adversity and competitive challenges.

I call this more-moderate approach "business-process improvement" (BPI).

The first step—one that reengineering proponents generally skip—is gaining widespread support for change; after all, lasting improvements in business processes can be made only with the support of those who know the business. Leadership's primary task is creating conditions for continuous, incremental, and adaptive change.

Too often companies signal impending change poorly: by downsizing. Abrupt cutbacks responding to a steadily deteriorating financial situation are a sure sign that management has been incompetent or asleep. Dismissing employees on a large scale, accompanied by incentives for longtime employees to resign voluntarily, paralyzes the survivors with fear and an aversion to taking initiative. It forces out those most qualified to find employment elsewhere.

Getting rid of people whose skills have become obsolete reflects the organization's failure to innovate and learn. Liquidating a company is easy and profitable, but rebuilding it for growth pays off in the long term.

While reengineering requires the company to take outside consultants' advice, BPI depends on employee commitment and imaginative cooperation, relying heavily on in-house know-how to find conditions that will support the creation of new jobs—even if that means that many existing positions will disappear.

BPI calls for applying rigorous methods to charting, pricing, and process-flow analysis of "as is" conditions. Process improvement continues for the lifetime of a company, with each major improvement bringing forth new payoff opportunities. The objective is to create a learning environment in which renewal and gain will be an ongoing process instead of just a one-time shock therapy. Adopting formal process-flow methods and a consistent technique for tracking local improvements allows the company to alter combined processes initially isolated for short-term, local productivity gains.

In BPI, the people directly affected by the potential changes study the "as is" conditions and propose "to be" alternatives to achieve the desired improvements. In BPI everybody with an understanding of the business will be asked to participate.

In BPI, the people directly affected by the potential changes study the "as is" conditions and propose "to be" alternatives to achieve the desired improvements.

For example, a government agency incurs internal charges of $10.05 per employee paycheck issued due to layers upon layers of bureaucracy. By comparison, a local commercial-services company—with integrated, streamlined processes—incurs charges of only $1.67. To bring down that $10.05 figure, employees are helping to compile "as is" work-flow diagrams showing who does what and when and how. Upon entering the diagrams into a computer, they will know that the paycheck costs so much because it has to go through, typically, the controller, then the personnel department, then the regional processing center, then the auditors.

The next step will be to complete a "to be" diagram showing how much money and time is saved when one link—say, the controller—is removed. Then the organization can determine how to skip that element, finding that the controller can preapprove checks and doesn't need to see them. After that it's a simple (though grueling) matter of examining each process in turn.

BPI balances the involvement of information managers, operating managers, and subject-matter experts. Cooperative teams are assembled under nonthreatening circumstances in which much time is spent, even wasted, in discussing and evaluating different viewpoints. Unanimity is not what business process is all about: Differences are recorded, debated, and passed on to higher levels of management for resolution.

BPI requires that you perform a business-case analysis, which not only calculates payoffs but also reveals the risks of each proposed alternative. This is not popular because current computerized methods of analysis have too little integrity to be acceptable to financial executives.

Reengineering: The Autocrat's Salvation

Business-process improvement's advantage over reengineering lies in its approach to managing organizational change. A relatively slow and deliberate process-improvement effort is more in tune with the approach that people normally use to cope with major changes.

Every day should be Process Improvement Day—that is how organizational learning takes place and how you gain employee commitment. At each incremental stage of process improvement, your people can keep pace with their leaders, developing the same understanding of the business. They are allowed the opportunity to think about what they are doing. They are not intimidated by precipitous layoffs that inhibit their sharing of ideas on how to use their own time and talent more effectively.

As currently practiced, reengineering assumes that your own people cannot be trusted to fix whatever ails your organization. It requires you to accept what the experts, preferably newcomers to the scene, tell you.

Every day should be Process Improvement Day—that is how organizational learning takes place and how you gain employee commitment.

In reengineering the consultants recommend what the "to be" conditions ought to look like, without learning the reasons for the "as is" conditions. Reengineering's credo is to forget everything you know about your business and start with a clean slate to "reinvent" what you would like to be.

But what applies to individuals or nations certainly applies to corporations: It is never wise to disregard your people, relationships with customers, assets, accumulated knowledge, or reputation. Versions of the phrase ". . . throw history into the dustbin and start anew" have been attributed to every failed radical movement of the last 200 years.

Reengineering proponents worry little about formal methods. They practice emergency surgery, typically amputation and tourniquet-like remedies to stop the flow of red ink. Reengineering may be appropriate under emergency conditions of imminent danger—but only as long as management understands that work-force demoralization means the patient may never fully recover. Hammer's simple methods, much swifter than BPI's more-deliberate approach, are preferred by the impatient and those not compelled to cope with the long-term consequences of what happens to the quality and the dedication of the work force.

In reengineering, participation by most of the existing management is superfluous, because what is in place will be junked anyway. Under such conditions, for instance, bringing in a successful cookie-company manager to run a computer company makes perfect sense. In reengineering, debate is discouraged since the goal is to produce a stroke of insight that will turn everything around in a flash.

Autocratic managers leap at the opportunity to preside over a reengineering effort, as do chief information officers (CIOs) with propensities to offer technological means as a way of introducing revolutionary changes. In recent national meetings, computer executives have offered reengineering as the antidote to the slur that CIO stands for "Career Is Over."

Reengineering conveys a sense of urgency that does not dwell on much financial analysis, and certainly not on formal risk assessment: managers who tend to rely on bold strokes rebel against analytic disciplines. Business-case analysis brings forth the traditional confrontation of the tortoise and the hair—the plodders versus the hip-shooters. Though the hip-shooters sometimes win, the odds are against them in an endurance contest.

Slow and Steady Wins the Race

Reengineering offers neither the time nor the opportunities for an organization to adapt smoothly to changing conditions. It imposes changes swiftly, by fiat, usually from a collection of people imported to make long-overdue changes. Even if the new approach is a superior one for jarring an organization out of its ingrown bad habits, it is difficult to implement because those supposed to act differently now are reluctant to do their creative best in support of the transition from the old to the new.

Reengineering has the advantage of being a choice of last resort when no time is left to implement business-process improvement. In this sense, it is akin to saying that dictatorship sometimes is more effective than community participation. The drastic cure may have lingering, even fatal, side effects.

Despite occasional reversals in fortune, constitutional democracies have never willingly accepted dictatorship as the way out of their troubles, and the record of drastic, last-ditch attempts to deal with crises in governance is dismal. Despite occasional short-term improvements, extreme solutions often destroy past accumulation of human capital, and retrospectively, these eras of violence are always viewed as times of retrogression.

Paul A. Strassmann, a longtime chief information-systems executive, is now Visiting Professor of Information Warfare at National Defense University.

Quality Tools and Techniques

PROCESS MANAGEMENT AND MEASUREMENT

The Alignment Matrix

Ronald L. Heilmann

This article describes a method for aligning processes throughout the organization with its goals and strategy. The author advocates looking at internal relationships among employees in terms of commitments and needs. This helps define employee interactions in a way that opens communication and facilitates continuous improvement.

Successfully implementing a total quality management (TQM) system in any organization requires the alignment of every member's efforts with the aim of the organization. This alignment is especially critical for members of the management team, who are responsible for leading the transformation process. Individually and collectively, the management team members must serve as role models, and they must continually convey clear and consistent messages about the organization's aim. To ensure consistency, the alignment must be measured continually; a system to make this monitoring feasible must be established.

The alignment matrix facilitates this measurement. It is specifically designed to develop a consistent direction within a hierarchical organizational structure.

Reprinted with permission from *Quality Progress*, January 1994. Copyright © 1994 ASQC, Milwaukee, WI. All rights reserved.

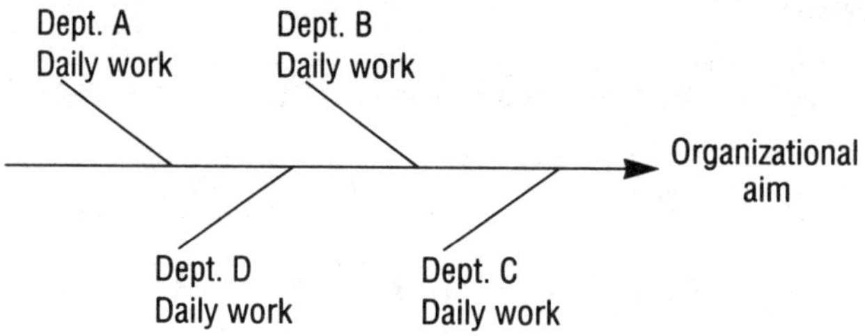

Figure 1. **Ideal alignment: a causal relationship between daily work and achieving an organizational aim.**

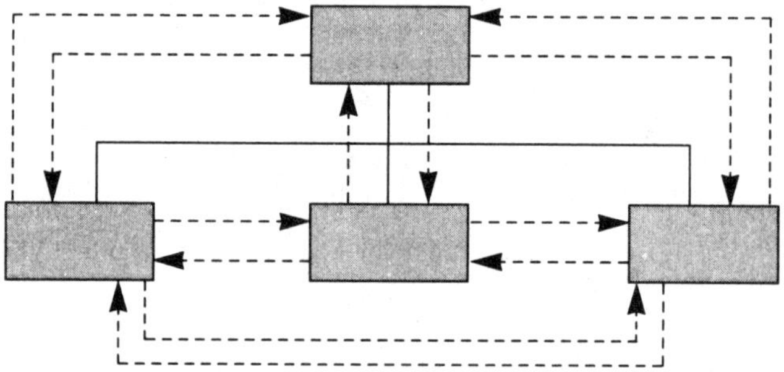

Figure 2. **Organizational diagram of a manager and three subordinates.**

Development of the Tool

The simple cause-and-effect diagram in Figure 1 depicts the notion that, within a totally aligned organization, the daily work performed by every subunit affects the achievement of the organization's aim. Although this notion is obvious, most organizations are unable to achieve this relationship.

Figure 2 shows a simple organization diagram depicting a manager and three subordinates. Superimposed on the structure are the possible communication flows within this small subunit. The diagram could be further complicated by indicating that each member has the opportunity to communicate with higher or lower levels of the organization beyond those shown. The flow of communication can become even more complicated when larger organizations are considered. Achieving consistent communication throughout complex networks requires a standard basis for that communication. Communication based on facts or data is most likely to produce the desired consistent results. Such communication will not eliminate misinterpretation, but it should minimize the opportunity for misinterpretation because it inherently increases objectivity and decreases ambiguity. Since such communication is a new phenomenon within most organizations, it must be modeled by members of the management team.

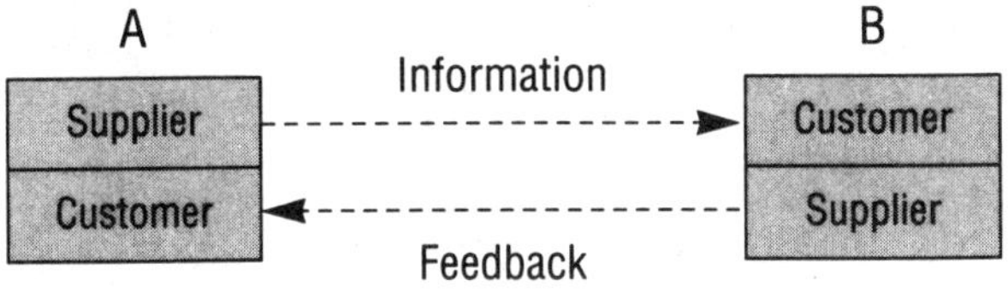

Figure 3. **Role reversal in a simple two-node feedback loop.**

Communication flow within an organization is essential to aligning every employee's work with the organization's aim. Without an effective process of communication within an organization, it is highly unlikely that the people within the organization will truly share a common understanding of that aim. It is axiomatic that conflicting views of an organization's aim will result in inefficiencies that harm its competitive effectiveness.

Communication flow within an organization is essential to aligning every employee's work with the organization's aim.

The benefits of the ideal alignment depicted in Figure 1 are fully realized when the concept of the internal customer permeates an organization. Only when every employee realizes that his or her efforts both support and are supported by the efforts of others can the full cooperation inherent in an aligned organization occur. In this case, full cooperation means committing to satisfy the needs of internal customers with the same fervor as that devoted to satisfying external customers. In an environment characterized by full cooperation, positions are often mutually supportive; every employee has a reciprocal relationship with every other employee as both a customer and supplier. An example of mutually supportive positions is within a firm that has a customer-focused team composed of members from sales and sales service departments. In this team, members share customer information to create an environment that eliminates surprises for everyone: Everyone's job is made easier.

Consider the simple two-node feedback loop in Figure 3. The person staffing Node A is a supplier of information and a customer of feedback; in contrast, the person staffing Node B is a customer of information and a supplier of feedback. Such relationships are commonplace and might be horizontal or vertical within a hierarchical organizational structure. In the ideal environment of full cooperation, the horizontal/vertical orientation causes no difference in the ability to reverse internal customer/supplier roles. In most organizational environments, however, a vertical orientation gets in the way of people who try to achieve fully reciprocal relationships; this undermines the alignment process.

A better understanding of any working relationship can minimize and ultimately eliminate barriers to full cooperation. One approach for increasing understanding is to view positions in terms of needs and commitments. Needs are those things that must be received to enable fulfilling a responsibility. Commitments are those things that must be delivered to fulfill a responsibility. Thus, for any given position(s), needs relate to the customer mode and commitments relate to the supplier mode. This relationship is depicted in

A better understanding of any working relationship can minimize and ultimately eliminate barriers to full cooperation.

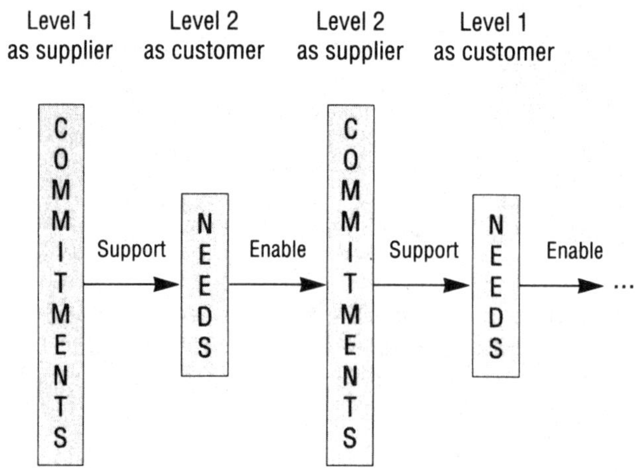

Figure 4. **Needs/commitments relationships between levels of management.**

Figure 4. A needs/commitments view of positions in an organization helps its members recognize the necessity of intersupportive behavior. Such intersupportiveness matures into the fully reciprocal relationships inherent in an aligned organization. This will be described in the following section, "The alignment matrix."

Recognizing the critical roles of alignment, open communication, and a needs/commitments view of an organization led to the design of the alignment matrix. It is not intended to be a prescriptive tool; rather, it is designed to be tailored to a given situation.

The Alignment Matrix

An alignment matrix consists of sets of needs and commitments, together with commensurate performance measures, that define a specific internal customer/supplier relationship. An internal customer/supplier relationship exists whenever responsibility for a task, outcome, or objective is shared. Given that the fundamental intent of an alignment matrix is to continuously monitor alignment, the performance measures used should be readily available or easily collectible. Effective use of these performance measures offers at least a partial replacement for the annual performance review; W. Edwards Deming labels performance reviews a deadly disease and says they should be eliminated.

One way of using these data is to share the measurements in regularly scheduled "How are we doing?" meetings. The question applies equally when two levels of management are involved. By making the opportunity to evaluate one's supervisor or manager an integral part of this monitoring process, the negative connotations of the word "boss" can be eliminated, a greater

Employment
- Blue collar: 100 (unionized)
- White collar: 30

Operation
- Shifts: three
- Work week: five days
- Partial shifts most Saturdays

Corporate structure
- Multiplant, vertically integrated, geographically scattered
- (The plant produces final product)

Plant organizational structure
- Traditional hierarchical

Quality steering committee
- Totally vertical (hourly through plant manager)

Figure 5. **Plant profile.**

sense of team emerges, and empowerment is reinforced by permitting constructive criticism to flow upward in an organization. Such bilateral evaluation is unlikely to deteriorate into a traditional reward-and-punish system of evaluation when undertaken in an environment of focusing on alignment. Indeed, it is likely to quickly evolve into a process of coaching and reverse coaching in which workers and their managers help each other do better work.

Such bilateral evaluation is likely to quickly evolve into a process of coaching and reverse coaching in which workers and their managers help each other do better work.

An Application

An effort to develop a quality-focused culture throughout a small manufacturing plant with a history of autocratic management had been under way for more than two years. (A profile of the plant—a stereotypical manufacturer—is shown in Figure 5.) During the first year, the Quality Steering Committee had rewritten the plant's mission statement, had undergone team-building and problem-solving training, had successfully completed a visible process improvement project, and had begun initiatives oriented toward cultural change. Approximately 25% of the work force had undergone training in team building and problem solving, and five teams had successfully completed projects—of which four had focused on process improvements.

During the second year, a focus on quality in daily work was initiated through mandatory training on the quality assurance components of all manufacturing jobs. This led to the formation of highly visible quality improvement teams addressing office processes and the first broadly cross-functional team.

Although significant progress had been achieved, it was clear that extra effort was needed to help the supervisors become role models for the work force. The supervisors needed to bond as a team and to convey clear and consistent messages about how the assignments they gave to the hourly workers

Superintendent's commitments as supplier	Supervisor's needs as customer	Supervisor's commitments as supplier	Superintendent's needs as customer
Provide support and recognition of team involvement	Provide training and continuous opportunities for experience	Support, create, and lead project teams	Achieve continuous improvement of all processes
Yes/no	Yes/no	Level of team activity	Plant performance measures
Provide leadership and consistent direction	Support of supervisor's decision in the eyes of the work force	Lead the work force	Achieve plant goals
Supervisor's perceptions	Supervisor's perceptions	Plant performance measures	Plant performance measures
Trust supervisor's data as basis for decisions	Provide training and continuous opportunities for experience	Use data-based communication regularly	Develop basis for good business decisions
Yes/no Level of perceived use	Yes/no	Yes/no Level of activity	Plant performance measures

Figure 6. **An alignment matrix.**

supported the firm's aim. They needed to become more comfortable with basic problem-solving tools so they could serve as resources to hourly workers who were on problem-solving teams in their units. Their decision-making capabilities needed to be enhanced to enable them to deal comfortably with the increased responsibility at their level inherent in a firm committed to TQM. One skill common to all of these developmental needs of the supervisors is data-based communication. Therefore, special attention needed to be devoted to developing that capability.

Recognition of the critical role of the supervisors in the firm's TQM initiative led to integrating the supervisors' development into the firm's quality plan. The outcome of this effort is the alignment matrix in Figure 6. The plant superintendent and each supervisor chart those measures pertinent to him or her. The plant superintendent is responsible for charting the aggregate performance measures. Progress on each measure is shared at monthly meetings between the plant superintendent and the supervisors.

As an example of how to use the alignment matrix, look at the first row of Figure 6. Working from right to left parallels the why-why-why approach to determining root causes.

The content of the right-hand cell in the fist row indicates that the plant superintendent must continuously improve processes (on-line as well as off-line) if the performance targets established as part of the annual plan are to be achieved. Daily and weekly measures of performance—such as units produced, machine downtime, percent of scheduled preventive maintenance performed on time, and sales credits issued for returned items—are charted and displayed by the superintendent as ongoing feedback to everyone in the plant.

The second cell from the right shows that a key component of the strategy to achieve continuous improvement of all processes is to have the supervisors committed to using the talents of the work force through quality improvement (QI) teams. Supervisors must create such teams when needed, encourage and support those teams when formed, and, in some instances, lead those teams. The extent of the effective use of the QI teams has been incorporated as a significant factor in the evaluation process for the supervisors. Thus a supervisor's compensation and promotability are partially determined by the superintendent's evaluation of his or her role in developing teams. The superintendent's evaluation is charted for each supervisor and shared with him or her during monthly meetings.

Recognition that the supervisors must be given training opportunities if they are to be able to identify opportunities for QI teams, serve as effective resources to the teams, and lead the teams is shown in the third cell from the right. At present, a simple yes/no measure is tracked for each supervisor for each pertinent voluntary training opportunity. Supervisors are rewarded for participating in training when they are evaluated by the plant superintendent.

The left-hand cell of the first row indicates that it is the plant superintendent's responsibility to help supervisors develop their ability to work with QI teams and their capacity as members of the supervisory team. The superintendent must take advantage of every opportunity to provide support and recognition for those supervisors exhibiting the desired team-oriented behavior. Simply acknowledging this behavior in periodic performance reviews is insufficient. Therefore, a measure of the superintendent's performance is the supervisors' perception of whether the superintendent is providing timely and adequate feedback pertaining to team activities. This yes/no assessment, shared by each supervisor during the monthly meetings, also facilitates reverse coaching. A variation of the simple yes/no measure shown in the left-hand cell of the first row was a logging of Zapps and Sapps. This proved to be more emotionally laden than fun and was therefore discarded. (The book *Zapp! The Lightning of Empowerment* by William C. Byham and Jeff Cox had been read by the entire management team. In it, a Zapp is defined as any force that energizes people and a Sapp is the opposite—any force that drains people.)

Referring again to Figure 6, note that the measures in the right-hand cell of each row are plant performance measures; that is, those global measures that track how well the entire organization is progressing toward established targets.

The design was reviewed by the supervisors and initiated only after they all signed a statement committing to use the tool to help achieve the plant's mission.

A plan-do-check-act process was used to implement this new tool at the firm. The process began with individual interviews with the plant superintendent and the six supervisors. The firm's consultant initially designed the program working with the plant superintendent. The design was reviewed by the supervisors and initiated only after they all signed a statement committing

Our mission

As members of this organization, our mission is to be the leader in our industry for providing value to our customers through service, quality, and innovative products. Our internal objective is to develop trust and communication throughout our plant to provide a superior work environment permitting all members to achieve personal goals.

Our method

The mission will be accomplished through the combined efforts of all members. We will focus on a customer/supplier relationship (both internal and external) through continuously improving our training and standard operating procedures. A team concept allowing for self-direction will be used based on the trust of members' decisions.

Our pledge

We, the undersigned members of the management team, pledge our commitment to achieve the mission statement. Our contribution to accomplishing this mission will be to provide the drive, energy, and dedication to continuously improve our individual capabilities. We commit to actively use these skills to continuously improve our environment and working relationships. We commit to building trust within our group by applying the concept of customer satisfaction to fulfill the respective needs as detailed on the attached page.

We commit to participate in a monthly mutual update meeting during which we will openly communicate feedback on our current performance on the objectives. We accept that our ability to fulfill the respective needs listed will be considered in the annual performance appraisal we each receive.

Figure 7. **Agreement document.**

to use the tool to help achieve the plant's mission (the statement appears in Figure 7). It includes the plant mission statement to ensure proper alignment. It also formally introduces the internal customer satisfaction concept into the appraisal process but does not eliminate the annual performance appraisal.

The alignment matrix has been in place for about 18 months. The start was rocky due to unfamiliarity and lingering fear, which stemmed from the history of autocratic management mentioned earlier. Because there had been no change in the management team, the alignment matrix is being attempted through a new commitment by the team to change to a new way of doing business. Earning the trust of the work force and convincing the workers that the change is real will take time. But despite its short history, some encouraging results have emerged. Primarily, the supervisors have bonded as a team despite turnover of one member. Also, there has been a growing use of the basic problem-solving tools and data-based communication throughout the plant. And, although not directly attributable to the use of an alignment matrix, production records have recently been set at the plant.

At the pilot site, the alignment matrix has facilitated progress in the TQM transformation process. The mere process of drawing the matrix depicting the interdependencies helped clarify what was meant by alignment, helped focus on the plant's aim, and helped establish the role of alignment in achieving the aim. Much remains to be done. But, as benefits accrue over time, it is expected that they will reinforce the emerging buy in. And, as the supervisors grow in confidence and become role models, the transformation process is expected to accelerate.

Bibliography

Badiru, Adedeji B., "A Systems Approach to Total Quality Management," *Industrial Engineering*, March 1990.

Byham, William C., and Jeff Cox, *Zapp! The Lightning of Empowerment* (Bridgeville, PA: Development Dimensions International Publications, 1989).

Deming, W. Edwards, *Out of the Crisis* (Cambridge, MA: Massachusetts Institute of Technology, 1986).

Fishman, Nina, and Lee Kavanaugh, "Searching for Your Missing Quality Link," *Journal for Quality & Participation*, December 1989.

Kerr, Jeffrey L., and Ellen F. Jackofsky, "Aligning Managers With Strategies," *Strategic Management Journal*, Summer 1989.

Schiemann, William A., "Strategy-Culture-Communication: Three Keys to Success," *Executive Excellence*, August 1989.

Ronald L. Heilmann is the director of the Center for Quality, Productivity, and Economic Development at the University of Wisconsin-Milwaukee.

Management Reactions to Variation

Brian L. Joiner

This excerpt from Joiner's book Fourth Generation Management: The New Business Consciousness *looks at the value of control charts to better understand and deal with business processes. Joiner believes that many problems in organizations come from "tampering," treating common-cause variation (variation due to the way the system works) with special-cause solutions (solutions suited to problems brought about by causes outside of the system). In a few examples from his book, he discusses what happens when managers make this mistake and what the proper response should be in these common cause situations.*

Although the concepts of comon causes and special causes may sound logical when reading about them, their value doesn't really hit home until you see them in action. This chapter provides several case studies that will help you become more familiar with how these ideas are applied in practice.

Case Studies

Case #1: Unpaid Invoices

Camille, the manager of accounts payable, walked through the department, pleased by the hum of activity. She entered her own office and got settled at her desk. A few minutes later, Carlos entered, hesitating a bit at the door.

"What's up, Carlos?" she asked.

"Well, I just finished the figures for last month . . ." he said.

"And how do they look?"

"Uhhh, you're not going to like this . . ."

Camille steeled herself, then said, "Just give it to me straight. What's the news?"

Carlos checked the paper he was holding and said, "It seems we're having a problem getting our suppliers paid on time. We had more than five percent of invoices unpaid last month."

From *Fourth Generation Management: The New Business Consciousness* by Dr. Brian L. Joiner (McGraw-Hill). Copyright © 1994 by Joiner Associates Inc. All rights reserved. Reprinted with permission.

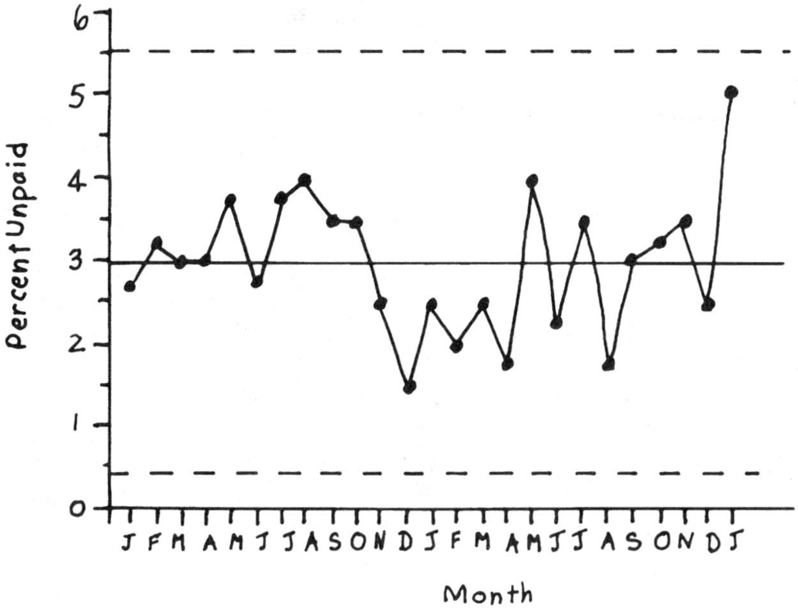

Figure 1. **Data on unpaid invoices.**

> *"Over five percent! We haven't seen that in a long time. We used to hold invoices to help our own cash flow, but we're not doing that any more. What's going on out there? Let me look at those figures."*

Look at the chart of Camille's figures on unpaid invoices. Here are the options she is considering. What would you recommend?

1. Look at each invoice that was not paid and find out who worked on that invoice. Have the employee involved go through further training.
2. Figure out what was different last month compared to other months. Were there more invoices? Were new or different services being paid for the first time? Were there new employees in the department?
3. Dig up all the invoices that had to be reprocessed in the past few months and categorize the causes of the problems. Look for patterns.
4. For several weeks, have people working on each major step in the process keep data on how many and what kinds of errors occur in their steps.
5. Change the account payables software.

The chart of Camille's data shows that this is a stable process, that there is no evidence of special causes. This means her best options are #3 and #4:

they both represent common cause strategies. Option 1 is tampering: Camille needs to look for patterns across all the data. Training would be appropriate only if she found systematic differences between people who were trained differently. Option 2 is a special cause reaction: it assumes something was different or important about the last data point, which the control chart shows was not the case. Option 5 is a potential reaction but is premature at this point. Camille's available data do not show that the software is the cause of the problem.

Long-held beliefs are hard to overcome. Experience has shown that most people, when presented a situation like this, are tempted to hedge their bets. They'll use one of the common cause approaches, but *also* ask the special cause question, "What was different last month?" This is particularly tempting when data points get near the control limits. All our instincts scream: "DO SOMETHING! Things will get worse if we don't act!" On some occasions, a data point near the limits may indicate the presence of a special cause, but *far more often* these points are due to common causes, and subsequent data points fall back well within the limits.

Case #2: Increased Impurities

"Del, do you have a minute?"

"Sure, Aaron," said Del. "What can I do for you?"

Aaron handed Del a lab report.

"Eileen just finished measuring the impurities in the batch we're about to load into the trucks, and it doesn't look good. We've got an impurities measure of .23%. I know that we've got customers waiting for this shipment, but that's way above what we usually ship out."

"Let me think a minute," said Del. "That's more than one-and-a-half times what we had with the last batch. I thought we had been doing a good job lately of holding the impurities down."

Del paced the room several times then turned to Aaron. "Call the people waiting for this stuff and see if they can still use it. Otherwise we may have to scrap the whole batch. . . . I also want to see our data for the past few months so we can decide what else to do."

Look at Del's data in the chart. Here are the options he's considering. What would you recommend?

1. Blend material from this batch with material from a different batch that has a lower impurity level. The combined mixture will yield an acceptable level of impurities. This will save the material from being scrapped.
2. Look at the data by shifts, days, sampling machines, vessel types, and so on. See if there are patterns.
3. Send out a memo to all staff with information regarding the higher than normal impurity level. Note that there has been a bad batch, and that operators should be more careful in the future. Post the

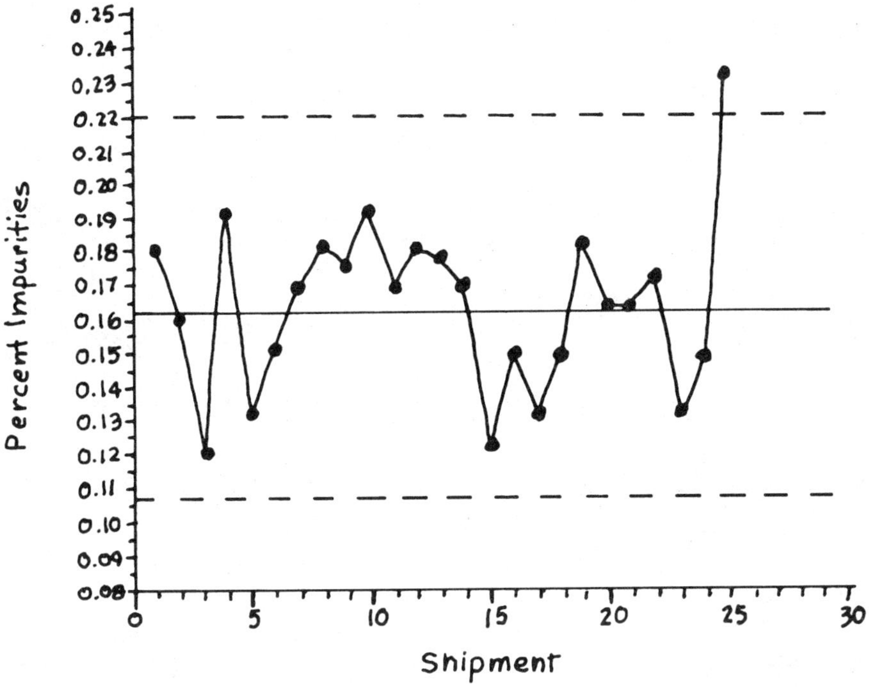

Figure 2. **Data on impurities.**

control chart with the memo in the processing area so all employees can see what is being shipped and what is expected of them.

4. Make some educated guesses about possible causes, and change settings on the machines to see what happens. Have all pipes and vessels cleaned. Monitor the effect.
5. Have employees investigate what was different about this batch relative to other batches. Was this batch processed differently? Were the measurements taken differently? Is there a new supplier?

The best option for Del is #5, which represents the only special cause approach here. The control chart shows that the last impurity measure was well beyond the control limit: something had changed the system. Option 1 might be necessary but could be dangerous because that action alone will not solve the problem, and customers may suffer unintended side effects that you may or may not ever learn about. Options 2 and 4 represent common cause strategies (stratification and experimentation, respectively); they would help you find factors within the system, but would not show you what was different in the last batch. Option 3 is perhaps the worst option: improvement does not come from exhortations or slogans. Until we know what has happened in

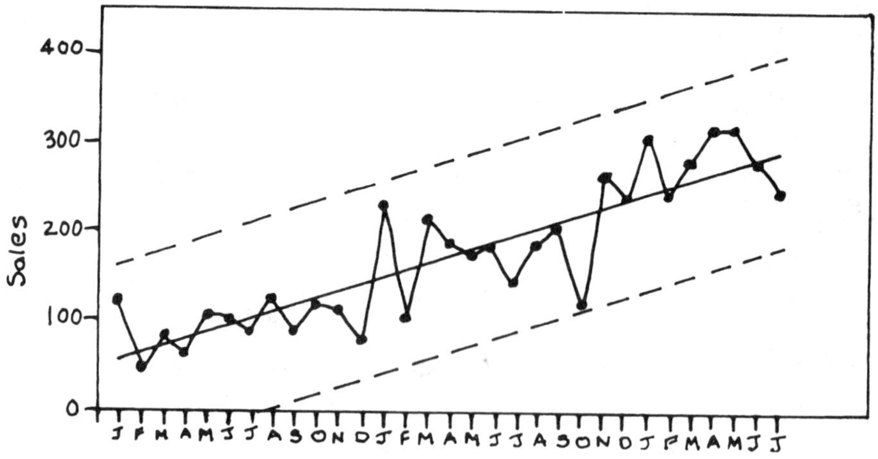

Figure 3. **Trend in sales data.**

the process, employees are likely to end up tampering in an attempt to make improvements.

If you have looked carefully at the chart of Del's data, you may have also noticed that there was a special cause—a series of eight points above the centerline (points 7 to 14)—that appeared earlier and went undetected because no one was charting the data at the time. If Del is lucky, he may still be able to track down the source of that special cause, and if he's luckier, it may be related to the latest event. But his chances now are much slimmer than if he had known when the special cause appeared and been able to initiate an immediate search for the cause. The trail grows cold quickly.

It's useful to pause a moment and think about what our reactions might have been in these two cases had we not charted the data. Then think about the work environments throughout our organization. On how many processes do we have no data at all? How many times do people look at just the latest result, in isolation? Just the latest two results? Appropriate use of figures requires charts like these.

Case #3: Rising Sales

Any number of times I've heard managers describe seasonal patterns in sales or trends in other figures. In a big percentage of cases when we sat down and looked at the plots of the data, the trends and seasonality didn't materialize. Only common cause variation was evident. Our human tendency to see patterns and trends where there are none continues to amaze me. It reminds me of the Rorschach tests in which psychologists work with clients by analyzing images they see in ink blots. Plotting the dots changes a lot of perceptions.

But sometimes there is real seasonality or a real trend—real structural variation.

Figure 3 is a control chart for product sales. These data have structural variation: an underlying trend that in this case is shown by an overall increase over time. The limits show the width of common cause variation, but they are not flat. These points require a slightly different calculation from the one we did earlier, but the interpretation is the same. There is a stable process on top of the structural variation, and therefore no reason to interpret the latest dot. There are no lessons to be learned from comparing high dots with low dots. We have some confidence in predicting the next few months' sales.

Without seeing this chart, a manager might react to the "steady drop in results" the last two months, or to the sharp drop several months earlier. The chart helps keep us from overreacting by reminding us this is most likely just common cause variation. No reason to tamper—to put on a sales campaign or otherwise deviate from our basic strategy. This chart will also help us see if any of our initiatives really *change* the pattern; most do not.

This chart will also help us see if any of our initiatives really *change* the pattern; most do not.

Case #4: Construction Projects

"To control costs, project managers shall report on the costs of all projects that are 10% or more off from budget."

What are your reactions to this policy? Does your organization have policies like this? What are some of the effects?

Let's look at this policy from a 4th Generation perspective. To analyze the policy, it would be useful to have some data. Here are the cost variances that a company collected for 20 projects.

Just having the data available changes our evaluation. You can see that five projects required explanations. There's a better way to look at these numbers, as shown on the control chart on page 452.

For almost everyone, the control chart does a far better job facilitating understanding of these cost variances than does a simple list. As you can see,

Project	% over or under	Project	% over or under
1	-12.5	11	-0.7
2	0.1	12	-7.8
3	-6.1	13	0.7
4	10.1	14	-5.7
5	10.1	15	3.5
6	9.5	16	-9.1
7	-12.5	17	-5.2
8	1.3	18	9.1
9	-0.7	19	0.7
10	30.0	20	-5.9

Figure 4. **Cost variances on the last 20 projects.**

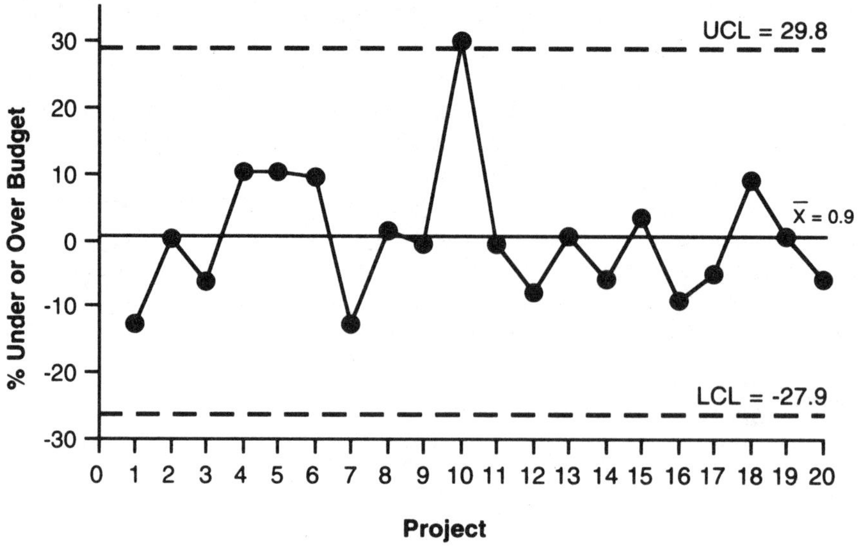

Figure 5. **Control chart of cost variances.**

only one project was outside the limits, and therefore only one for which we would recommend the special cause strategy:

For almost everyone, the control chart does a far better job facilitating understanding of these cost variances than does a simple list.

- *Get timely data:* These data were only looked at eight months after that project was completed.
- *Take immediate action* (a Level 1 Fix): Not applicable; it's too late.
- *Search for what was different.* The project leader had written a report, but it didn't contain any information that helped them understand how this project was *different* from others. The only hope of discovery rests in people's memories (an unreliable source of accurate information!).
- *Find a long-term remedy:* Not possible here since "what was different" had been lost.

How about the rest of the projects? Should we be satisfied because the process is stable? Should we focus particular attention on those outside the 10% "action" limits? There are no other points beyond the control limits, no other signals of special causes—and therefore nothing special about the projects beyond the 10% limit. All the data points are relevant. It would not be effective to focus special attention (as had been done) on those outside the 10% managerial limits. Instead we should use the common cause strategy.

One company that looked at similar data discovered a relationship between the project size and the percent variance as illustrated in the following chart:

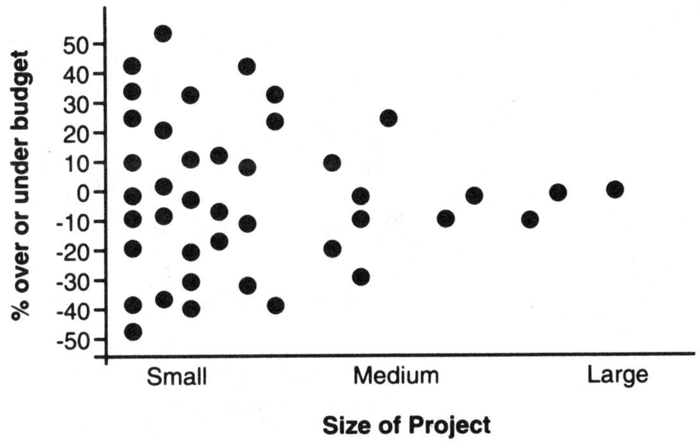

Figure 6. **Relationship of percent variance to project size.**

The chart shows that larger projects had smaller percent variances even though their dollar variances were larger. This provides important insight: a policy of explaining variances greater than 10% for all projects, no matter what the size, no longer seemed relevant. The company decided to keep three different control charts, one each on small, medium, and large projects (each of which naturally had different width control limits).

Still another organization found that the larger variances tended to show up primarily in one type of project, so they focused first on reducing the variances in those projects. As they went deeper they found they were chasing mice when tigers were loose. The big problems were not with cost variances. The trouble arose mainly from poorly planned projects, projects that had sloppy construction that cost millions over the years but came in "on budget": the discovery of these big problems had its roots in trying to understand the system. The company came to see that cost variances were an easy but not very useful indicator of project effectiveness. Part of the solution was to establish a "balanced score-card" that relied on a variety of other indicators.

Should We Manage to Budget?

A key question arises: Do we want people to manage to budget? Most managers unhesitatingly say YES!—for some very good reasons. Among other things, managing to budget:

- Forces fiscal constraint
- Allows us to allocate resources
- Provides a basis for charging the customer
- Helps ensure we make a profit

In some cases, managing to budget can also encourage creativity, providing an impetus to "do more with less."

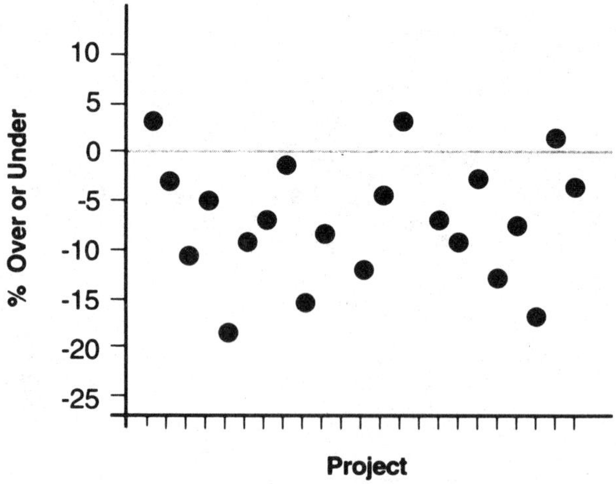

Figure 7. **Budget variances.**

In practice, however, these "benefits" carry a heavy price. Suppose the project manager told you a project had encountered unexpected difficulties and was headed for a 35% overrun. Would you still want her to manage to budget? Some managers say, "Under those circumstances, of course I don't want her to stick with the original budget. I want people to tell me, give me early warning, and we'll adjust the budget." With such responses, I have a hard time understanding what people mean when they say "manage to budget."

But other managers say, "Yes, she must still come in on budget. We only have so much money. You can't overspend your bank account at home." What methods do these managers want the project leader to use to come in on budget? Improve the system, distort the system, or distort the figures? You know what happens. You've been there. You've lived in buildings where this has happened: windows left out; air conditioning system short-changed; hallways too narrow. Or, perhaps it was done just by distorting the figures—by charging expenses to other projects.

What does such behavior do to an organization? It produces substandard output, and perhaps even worse, **keeps executives from seeing the reality of things.** They see the figures they want to see, and the consequences are carefully camouflaged. An organization that does not know its reality is like a ship sailing in a fog, headed for an iceberg. The figures will all look good until one day the holes below the waterline can no longer be concealed, and all of a sudden, one of our "most admired companies" sinks below the surface. This is not news. We've all seen it before; I've said it before. It's all around us.

One company charted the outcomes for its projects. Their chart looked like Figure 7.

It's a stable process, centered at −8%, meaning that the projects come in an average of 8% under budget. Only three projects came in over budget, and then only slightly. Looks good, doesn't it. Don't you want projects to always come in under budget? But what's really happening in this company? Managers make conservative estimates, sacrificing opportunities to invest the capital elsewhere, year after year . . . a good way to go out of business. That company had made it clear to people that they should come in under budget. Promotions depended on it. So they distorted systems and figures and came in under budget.

The disadvantages of managing to budget are numerous:

1. Promotes short-term business decisions; optimizes the piece, the cost of the individual project, at the expense of the whole (the company's overall performance)
2. Customers, quality, and perhaps even safety receive short shrift
3. Stifles creativity (except in encouraging people to find creative ways to meet their figures)
4. People spend whether they need to or not
5. Leads to tampering

A good first step is to stop doing counterproductive things. So suppose you were the manager in charge of construction projects, and the chart on page 455 was your chart. Would you go back to your staff and say: "I have read this wonderful book and I now understand that all the variation in our project costs is due to common causes. So from here on out, you only have to investigate and identify the causes of the cost variances when the variances are more than 29%"? Would you feel happy about that statement? Would you feel nervous about issuing such a policy? Why does it make you feel nervous? Because it seems like you're giving your employees permission to be off by 29%, endorsing sloppy estimation and work. As the manager I quoted before said:

> *"There's a major difference between whether you feel comfortable with* that amount of variation *as opposed to being comfortable with* that approach to dealing with it."

He was unhappy with the amount of variation he found in his processes and wanted less; but he realized that plotting the data, and using the common cause and special cause strategies was the best way to go about reducing that variation.

Brian L. Joiner is CEO of Joiner Associates Inc., a consulting and training firm located in Madison, WI.

Learning the Meaning of Measurement

Michael Barrier

At Granite Rock Co., a Baldrige Award winner, measurement is not an extra, but a vital part of its management practices. Once, when asked how the company found the time to measure, and wasn't it awfully time consuming, the Granite Rock manager responsed, "You have to understand—that's what we do."

Think of quality management as a brightly colored hot-air balloon—a dazzling thing that seems always just about to shoot into the stratosphere, propelled by gassy rhetoric. Fortunately, there is a tether that binds it firmly to earth.

"Measurement is what it's all about," says Val Verutti, quality-support manager for Granite Rock Co., in Watsonville, Calif. "If you set goals and lofty ideals, without means of measuring, you're just kidding yourself. You've got to have ways of finding out if improvements really are improvements."

Granite Rock is a 386-employee, family-owned company that manufactures construction materials of many kinds: aggregates, ready-mix concrete, gravel, asphaltic concrete, and so on. The volume and accuracy of its measurements, among other things, won it a Malcolm Baldrige National Quality Award in 1992, in the small-business category.

The criteria for the Baldrige award were in fact a wake-up call to Granite Rock's managers, Verutti says; as they began applying those criteria to the company, they came awake to the need for better measurements. "When they start asking for three years of trend data," Verutti says, "and you don't have one measure in place, that gives you a clue right away."

Measurement is now mandated throughout Granite Rock. In the aggregate division, for example, mixtures of different kinds of rock are subjected to statistical process control, a quality-management technique used to ensure that each batch is as nearly identical to every other batch as possible. "Our parameters are getting narrower and narrower," Verutti says, as the range of permissible variation shrinks.

Granite Rock measures the cubic yards and tons of material moved per hour. It measures not just its own profit performance but also its market share. It checks the reliability of its technical data by having its own laboratory's

Reprinted by permission, *Nation's Business*, June 1994. Copyright © 1994, U.S. Chamber of Commerce.

measurements monitored by outside labs. It benchmarks—that is, measures itself against other firms—extensively.

None of this measuring is done for its own sake. Jack Leemaster, general manager of Granite Rock's southern concrete and building materials division, told a Baldrige award conference last year that the company attaches great importance to selecting the right information to be tracked because the data "organizes the quality process for the entire company."

The company attaches great importance to selecting the right information to be tracked because the data organizes the quality process for the entire company.

Granite Rock didn't hire any consultants to initiate that quality process, or base its program on the ideas of any one authority. Rather, Verutti says, Bruce W. Woolpert, president and CEO, "had a lot of ideas when he came here in 1986, and he started making changes right away." Woolpert "scared everybody half to death," Verutti recalls, "Because the company was successful"—the need for far-reaching changes wasn't immediately apparent.

Woolpert started by setting about a dozen "baseline goals" as measures of the company's performance; the number grew to 57 in 1992 and 66 in 1993. The baseline goals, Woolpert says, "are the specific action areas that we're going to focus on" every year in support of Granite Rock's nine corporate objectives. "This is what makes the corporate objectives come alive."

Through customer surveys, Granite Rock identifies the factors most important to its customers—not just throughout the company but in each of its markets as well. Because those surveys have shown that on-time delivery is its customers' highest priority, Leemaster said, "we measure delivery of every load and carefully track the results."

On-time delivery is more important to customers than getting the lowest price, because a late delivery can mean that the customer has an idle crew, and the cost of paying those idle workers can rapidly eat up any price advantage.

Granite Rock went outside its industry to benchmark its on-time performance because it couldn't find a noncompeting concrete company in some other part of the country whose performance was good enough to hold up as a standard. Granite Rock benchmarks instead against Domino's Pizza, which has a store in each of the northern California cities where Granite Rock does business, and which until recently guaranteed delivery within 30 minutes.

To give its customers complete control over delivery times, Granite Rock instituted what it calls an "automatic loadout system" at its crushed-rock quarry (the largest west of the Mississippi River). The system works like a bank's ATM machine—the customer simply drives up in a truck, inserts a card, and tells the machine how much of which material is needed. The truck is loaded automatically, and a bill follows later. Granite Xpress, as it's called, is open 24 hours a day, seven days a week, so a customer can load up and start work on a project before the quarry opens in the morning—or keep working after the quarry closes.

Granite Rock has been successful at measuring customer preferences accurately—it stayed profitable and almost doubled its market share during the severe California recession—but doing so is not a simple matter. The company has constantly tweaked its customer surveys to produce a better picture of its customers' opinions; it switched from a numerical-grade system to a letter-grade system for rating its services, for example, and found that customers were more likely to express strong positive or negative feelings through the letter grades.

"If you work hard at it," Woolpert says, "you can eventually come up with a customer survey that tells you how your customers place you vs. your competitors"—particularly as customers become convinced that the company really does want their opinions and will respond to them. "We've worked for seven years to get our surveys to the point that we feel pretty good about them."

Val Verutti worked for 30 years as a chemist for a cement company before he joined Granite Rock, and he appreciates such difficulties. "Measurement is my forte," he says. "That's what you do in a laboratory. But two very important things, human-resource relationships and customer satisfaction, are hard to measure."

In other words, the more directly people are involved, be they employees or customers, the trickier it is for a business to make accurate measurements. Where employees are concerned, that is true in large part because in business, as Aubrey C. Daniels writes in *Bringing Out the Best in People* (McGraw-Hill), measurement "is most often an antecedent to punishment."

The measuring tools themselves are good ones, Daniels says: "The ability to measure is not now, nor has it ever been, the problem. We can measure any performance. The problem in measurement comes from the way it is used. If it is used to punish, people will go to extraordinary lengths to avoid being measured."

The problem in measurement comes from the way it is used. If it is used to punish, people will go to extraordinary lengths to avoid being measured.

Moreover, Daniels says, they will corrupt the measurements that *are* made: "Falsification of data is a more common problem than many upper managers realize, and its main purpose is to avoid punishment."

Such hazards are why quality-management thinkers emphasize so strongly that measurements should be not of people, but of *processes.* Such measurements, when combined with other ingredients of effective quality management—employee empowerment, self-directed teams, and the like—can make the measuring of people a largely superfluous exercise.

The idea, Verutti says, is to present the measurements to employees in a graph format that they can understand. "Once they realize that they can affect that graph by their own actions and that there's no stigma attached to making a mistake, they'll try things, and if it goes in the wrong direction, they'll correct it in a hurry," he explains.

Used in that way, "data sets people free," says Michael D. Pugh, a hospital executive who has sparked rising interest in quality management among businesses in Pueblo, Colo. "I've seen employees stand up and talk with the greatest confidence about some process because they had the data and they knew what was going on."

In 1991, Pugh's hospital, Parkview Episcopal Medical Center, stopped measuring its employees through performance appraisals. "When people find out we don't do performance appraisals here," Pugh says, "they look at me like I'm from Mars." But "most performance appraisals are not objectively based," he says. "They can't be. There's no way to separate the influence of the system from the influence of the individual's effort."

Granite Rock does not measure its employees' performance, either—but it does measure the progress of most of its workers, through a program that the company calls the Individual Personal Development Plan (IPDP). The IPDP is mandatory only for salaried employees; it is voluntary for the approximately 250 unionized workers. Nonetheless, overall participation stands at 83 percent.

Granite Rock does not measure its employees' performance, but it does measure the progress of most of its workers, through a program that the company calls the Individual Personal Development Plan (IPDP).

The personal-development plan spells out work-related objectives—acquiring new skills, in particular—on which participating employees and their supervisors agree.

"We don't stop there," chief financial officer Rita Alves said at the Baldrige conference. "In the last section, we outline how we're going to accomplish those goals," with "observable measures" of how well those objectives are being accomplished. "We actually know if we got there or not. It's not a wishy-washy thing."

Granite Rock does not consider the IPDP an appraisal or evaluation; in Alves' words, meeting the objectives of the development plan "is not directly tied to compensation." Val Verutti puts it this way: Evaluations look back, whereas the IPDP looks forward.

To help its employees reach their objectives, Granite Rock in one recent year spent almost $1,600 per employee on training—more than 10 times the average for the construction and mining industries, the company says. (And the expense was well worth it, Bruce Woolpert adds, pointing to an annual savings of $2 million in workers' compensation premiums that he attributes to such training.)

To test the effectiveness of its training, Granite Rock measures not just the percentage of IPDP goals attained—88 percent in 1992—but many other numbers: the number of employees cross-trained, the number applying for open positions, and so on. Because the IPDP prepares employees to assume greater responsibilities, Granite Rock promotes heavily from within: The number of openings filled from within the company rose from 30 percent in 1988 to 50 percent in 1991.

Measurement, no longer a tool for exercising control over employees, has instead become a tool for helping employees improve their own performance.

Verutti recalls that an executive with another company asked him how Granite Rock managers found time to devote to IPDPs. "They look awfully time-consuming," the executive said, "and a lot of our executives are working 60 hours a week now." Verutti's reply: "You have to understand—that's what we do."

At Granite Rock, much of what passes for "managing" at other firms has been delegated to self-managed teams, and managers have become tutors and coaches. Measurement, no longer a tool for exercising control over employees, has instead become a tool for helping employees improve their own performance.

"If managers are viewed as evaluators, as opposed to people who encourage other people to be better," Bruce Woolpert says, "it's real hard for someone to come up and say, 'I can't read.' "

Woolpert had a specific incident in mind—one that says something about the benefits that can flow from Granite Rock's approach to measurement. Early in 1992, he asked Paul Bush, a Granite Rock driver, to reduce to writing the substance of a conversation they had had. Bush, who suffers from dyslexia, told the hundreds of people in the Baldrige conference audience last year that he had then admitted to Woolpert that he could not read or write.

"I felt very small," Bush said, but Woolpert responded by asking him "if I would like to do something about my problem. I didn't really want anyone else to know, but I said yes."

Bush began attending a class for adult dyslexics once a week, and it "turned my life around," he said. "It convinced me that I could learn almost anything."

Michael Barrier is a senior editor with Nation's Business *Magazine.*

Proactive vs. Reactive SPC

Christopher Wozniak

Proactive SPC goes with proactive TQM—it is part of the culture and what people do as part of their jobs to continuously improve processes and quality. In this article, the author discusses this idea and contrasts it with reactive SPC, which is arbitrary and simply done because someone thinks it is a good idea, but not an important part of the culture.

In the last five years, I have played a part in implementing three statistical process control (SPC) programs and have learned that the implementation of SPC can unfold in two different directions. One direction is proactive; the other is reactive.

In essence, the proactive SPC path is the textbook approach espoused by quality leaders, educators, and consultants. Proactive SPC can be described very simply as actively seeking ways to improve the processes that are important to customers.

The reactive SPC path is what is left when the proactive path is not taken. It is simply an SPC program with ambiguous direction and serendipitous accomplishments. Instead of seeking solutions to problems, companies sometimes use the reactive path to blame others for their problems.

Reactive SPC is simply an SPC program with ambiguous direction and serendipitous accomplishments.

The Birth of Reactive SPC

It is not enough to throw valuable resources into the establishment of an SPC program. Without a system to perpetuate the program, SPC implementation might stop completely or be carried out for ulterior motives.

For instance, in an upper-management-driven program, lower-level managers might misinterpret the decision to start other programs, such as just-in-time manufacturing or quality function deployment, as an end to the SPC program. Instead of, "Here is another good idea coming from headquarters," lower-level managers are more apt to say, "Hey look, SPC is no longer important."

As a result, the lower-level managers might stop the program or simply not actively promote SPC activities, yet have their staffs continue monitoring processes for several reasons. First, they might believe that upper management will someday have a renewed interest in SPC and, hence, they must be prepared. Second, they might have discovered that control charts can be used as a weapon to ward off customers' claims that a process has changed or to

---

Reprinted with permission from *Quality Progress*, February 1994. Copyright © 1994, ASQC, Milwaukee, WI. All rights reserved.

blame suppliers for quality problems by saying, "Our process hasn't changed, so your materials must have." Finally, when customer certification agreements or less informal exchanges of information are established, it might be awkward to abruptly stop them.

Another situation that can stop or slow SPC implementation is when the task is assigned to one person, such as an SPC coordinator. Management and employees alike might consider SPC as someone else's job, and their commitment to the program becomes low or nonexistent. Similarly, when SPC is thought of as a task rather than an ongoing process, a time will come when the task is assumed to be completed.

All of these situations lead to reactive SPC.

The Problems

Reactive SPC is bad business. Reactive SPC leads to:

- A poor return on investment. Training, computer software, and other resources are spent on maintaining the status quo.
- An eventual loss of business. A competitor might be improving its products through proactive SPC and eventually take away customers.
- A demoralized and distrustful work force. For example, I approached a "quality fixer"—a person who repairs defective machine parts found during inspections—about his ideas on how to solve a particular problem. He replied, "I've been telling you guys for over a year what I think the problem is, and nothing has been done. Do you think I care anymore?"

Nurturing Proactive SPC

To keep SPC proactive, a system that encourages and institutionalizes SPC must be developed.

If something is important enough to do, then it is important enough to do right. To keep SPC proactive, a system that encourages and institutionalizes SPC must be developed. Here are some suggestions for developing that system:

1. *Incorporate SPC into job procedures and standard operating procedures but allow for flexibility.* In one case, a process engineer did a good job of creating a measurement system for a critical process but failed to document any procedures for it. Subsequently, when he left the company, the system broke down. Control charts were abandoned, people forgot test procedures, and accountability disappeared. The next process engineer had to start from scratch. He wrote procedures, trained employees from the production, lab, and inspection functions, and worked closely with his team until everyone understood the procedures and their roles in the process. Yet, he allowed for flexibility in the system. When new things were learned or better methods suggested, he changed the procedures to reflect them.
2. *Establish job performance measures that relate to specific SPC goals for all levels of management.* Successful performance objectives can be stated

DO YOU HAVE A REACTIVE SPC PROGRAM?

Here is a short test to help you determine whether your statistical process control (SPC) program is reactive or proactive. Answer the following questions either "yes" or "no":

1. Do all employees involved in the SPC program clearly understand who their customer is?
2. Do all employees clearly understand the customer's needs and how their process meets those needs?
3. Is there regular contact with the customer, and is information shared with all production employees involved with the process in terms that they understand?
4. Have the critical measurements important to the customer been translated into meaningful measurement systems? In other words, is there a real relationship between what the customer wants and what is being measured?
5. Are the measurement systems in control and capable?
6. Are there control charts for the critical measurements?
7. Do the employees taking the measurements actually plot the control charts, or does their manager do it?
8. Are the people closest to the process (e.g., production employees) involved in investigating out-of-control conditions?
9. Are there formal or informal procedures in place for training new employees and assessing retraining or continuing-education needs?
10. If an out-of-control condition occurred:
    - Would employees learn of the problem before management does?
    - Would the problem be communicated in a timely manner to all involved?
    - Would the employees understand how the out-of-control condition affects the customer?
    - Would everyone involved in the process know what his or her role was in correcting the problem?
11. Are control charts shown to upper management without first "cleaning them up" by manipulating data to make the chart appear to be in control or removing out-of-control plots and recalculating control limits?
12. Is there a formal channel, such as a weekly team meeting, through which SPC opportunities, objectives, and results are communicated?

If you answered "yes" to all of the questions, your SPC program is on the right track. A "no" answer to any question might indicate a reactive approach and should serve as a warning.

in specific terms, such as "a 10% reduction in customer complaints" or "a twofold increase in process capability." Sometimes general objectives, such as "make a presentation to upper management of a success story," are sufficient.

Employees' commitment and involvement can be greatly enhanced if they are given the opportunity to see problems firsthand.

3. *Engage people.* Employees' commitment and involvement can be greatly enhanced if they are given the opportunity to see problems firsthand. One production employee, for example, would not buy into a new corrective-action method I was proposing. I didn't want to say, "Just do it," knowing that the employee would go back to the old way as soon as I wasn't looking. Instead, I asked him to help with an experiment to test the old method against the new method. The employee replied that it was a waste of time because he already knew the old method was better. By the end of the experiment, however, he had become the most vocal proponent of the new method. It was easy for him to change his opinion since he had done the work that proved it was better.

   There are numerous other ways employees can be engaged. Employees can visit customer locations to see the customers' needs firsthand. They can be shown defective products returned by customers. Employees' suggestions can be solicited and implemented; if an idea can't be implemented, however, the person making the suggestion must be told why it can't be used.
4. *Create team protocol aimed at encouraging teamwork.* When working on a team, the key is to make sure everyone understands his or her role. Employees' roles in teams can be informally communicated or documented in procedures. Employees must know who is participating in the team, what they are to work on, when and where to meet, and how to conduct meetings.

   Without protocol, the danger is having a team without teamwork. For example, one manager learned this lesson when he divided his employees into four groups and called them teams. After several weeks, the team concept was abandoned because the groups were teams in name only.

   On the other hand, a group of people working together might not even consider themselves a team but, in reality, work as one. For example, several people from different departments worked to improve a process but didn't consider themselves a team. The informal team leader rallied everyone around an out-of-control process by explaining the importance of the process, showing them examples of defects, and defining how the members could help. The protocol was informal, but everyone's role was well-defined. Feedback on the process's performance and on how each team member contributed to the improvement was constantly communicated. Within six months, the process's capability improved from a C_{pk} of 0.15 to a C_{pk} of 0.95.
5. *Learn from mistakes.* Of course, no company wants to institutionalize bad policies and procedures. Thus, a proactive SPC program requires constant examination to weed out the ineffective elements and to re-create successes. This should be done at each level of management. The result will be a constantly evolving process rather than a static, obsolete program.

Get Excited

When I was working on my first SPC program, a plant superintendent told me, "Don't get too excited about this SPC stuff. I've been around for 15 years, and I give SPC a year before the next program comes along." He was right. The program started to fizzle out. Soon after, however, a companywide commitment was made to SPC, and the proper system was developed. The SPC program has since flourished.

It is not enough to ask for involvement in and support of the SPC effort. Ultimatums and directives are not enough, either. If system changes are not implemented, the result will be reactive SPC.

Christopher Wozniak is the process improvement specialist at Milliken & Company in Saluda, SC.

The Key Problem with TQM

John A. Goodman, Gary F. Bargatze, and Cynthia Grimm

This article suggests that companies simply are not customer-oriented enough and that most still don't have good ways in place to measure customer satisfaction. The authors then suggest a method for dealing with this problem and gathering more data on customers.

Total quality management (TQM) is getting a bad reputation due to poor results. Consider these examples:

Scenario one: The chief executive officer of an international travel and leisure company complains, "I've spent $1 million on training and quality improvement and have little to show for it."

Problem: Training is often used as a quick, satisfying fix—a Band-Aid that can be contracted out. It is a way to avoid the time and effort needed to develop more effective, permanent strategies, such as empowerment and response rules, incentives, and measurement systems to support the implementation of the incentives.

Many companies fritter away their resources on the wrong quality improvement activities. A shotgun approach is encouraged. Managers believe that everyone must be involved in some activity even if it's not important to the primary mission of serving the customer. For example, the vice president of quality of a company that won the Malcolm Baldrige National Quality Award said, "I knew we were in trouble when we found a quality team meeting on where to locate the water cooler."

Scenario two: An office equipment company receives complaints about late installation of copiers, but internal quality data show a high on-time delivery rate. Internal arguments on whether there is a problem continue until reports of lost sales from sales representatives instigate further investigation. It is then found that delivery does not mean installation.

Problem: Quality impact tends to be gauged by internal measures over the short term; market impact is usually gauged only over the long term. The value of a quality improvement activity to the marketplace is not documented. Often, there is operational impact but no additional value to the

Reprinted from *Quality Progress*, January 1994.

customer. Therefore, by the time a company measures market impact, it is impossible to discern what did and did not work.

The bad name that TQM is receiving is a matter of execution, not intent. Well-intentioned executives think their TQM efforts are customer driven, but they are not. The two basic problems that exist in most TQM efforts are the manner in which priorities are set (if they are even set at all) and the lack of rigorous measurement of results.

The two basic problems that exist in most TQM efforts are the manner in which priorities are set and the lack of rigorous measurement of results.

Setting Priorities

Instead of being customer driven, many companies' priorities are based on management's perception of key customer problems (perceptions that are often wrong) or on poor interpretation of data on customers' problems. As a result, TQM starts with a rational objective and arrives at an irrational conclusion.

Not setting priorities based on what is important to customers is the result of two situations:

1. *Problems with data.* Companies now obtain data on quality from many internal and external sources, such as surveys, customer complaints, comment cards, field reports, warranty repair data, and mystery shoppers. Often, measuring quality using multiple information sources is good, but this can be too much of a good thing. Each data source uses a different method for collecting and classifying data. Combining different data sources can result in lots of data but no actionable information because the data conflict. How the data are combined often has more to do with internal corporate politics than the true nature of customer quality.

   The problem of multiple data sources is rooted in customers' behavior: Most customers don't complain or request assistance.[1] Those who do speak out but are not assisted in their first contact never contact the company gain.

   Customer complaints vary in meaning based on where the complaint is directed. For the average company, only one complaint is received at headquarters for every 50 to 250 problems in the marketplace. This ratio decreases to one complaint for every 20 to 50 problems when there are field representatives. An 800 number will evoke about one complaint for every 10 to 50 problems, depending on the phone number's visibility and the type of product. Retailers tend to hear about half of all problems but usually do not pass the information up the line. Only about one in three persons with a broken product will bring it back for repair. Comment cards evoke one complaint for every 100 problems.[2]

   In addition, customers report problems to different people and at different times in the product life cycle. This leads to conflicting indications of what is failing and how often. Figure 1 shows at what points problem data can be generated in the product life cycle.

   Internal and survey-generated problem data are easier to interpret but are often more trouble to gather. Repair data, such as warranty repairs,

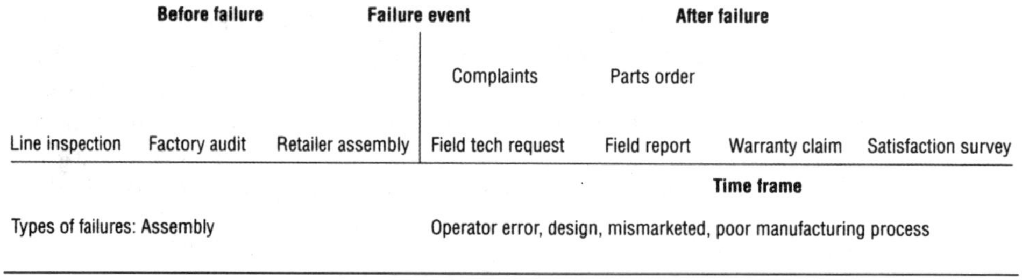

Figure 1. **Problem data come from different sources.**

are usually viewed as financial rather than quality data. Survey data are only collected annually in many companies and therefore fail to reflect current marketplace experience.

Combining information from different data sources requires careful analysis by someone who understands the data-gathering processes used for all of the sources and knows how to interrelate the results.

2. *No feel for what drives customer loyalty.* There are two reasons why managers often do not know what drives customer loyalty. First, as previously noted, there are multiple priorities due to multiple data sources. Second, there is a lack of information on which problems cause market damage—that is, loss of customer loyalty.

   Managers usually determine what is important to customers by applying their intuition or by asking customers what is important. Both approaches are dangerous, as illustrated by the following examples:

■ An international airline knew via management intuition that on-time departure was the most important driver of satisfaction. On long flights (over 10 hours), however, data showed that clean bathrooms and the quality of the food were better predictors of ongoing loyalty than on-time departure statistics.

■ A hotel chain found that improving service in the coffee shop produced significant enhancements in loyalty, while the same effort in the lounge did not.

■ A high-tech company focused on the quality of its products even though its products already had very low failure rates. In reality, most of the customers' problems concerned the sales and distribution functions.

■ A bank believed that interest rates were the key to winning the loyalty of business loan customers. But, in fact, the major factors causing loss of customers were related to the accessibility and responsiveness of the customer relations managers. Chief financial officers were willing to forgive high interest rates but not unreturned telephone calls.

■ In an insurance company, consumer focus groups and management intuition both identified the timeliness and accuracy of its claims process as most important. A survey of 5,000 customers who had recently filed claims, however, found that the clarity of the claims' explanations was a better predictor of customer loyalty than the claims' accuracy or timeliness. Even consumers did not assign importance to "clarity of explanations" when, in an academic setting, they were asked a hypothetical question on their rationale for choosing an insurance company. Therefore, hypothetical, nontransaction-based discussions can produce misleading quality priorities.

Measuring Results

The results of TQM efforts are often not tracked in a way that allows companies to separate what does and does not work in the marketplace. Most companies believe that monthly measures of customer satisfaction and quality are too expensive and that a yearly "Do you love us?" survey is sufficient. While financial data and sales data are reported on and scrutinized weekly and monthly, most companies believe that quarterly or yearly quality reviews are sufficient.

While financial data and sales data are reported on and scrutinized weekly and monthly, most companies believe that quarterly or yearly quality reviews are sufficient.

This approach has three weaknesses:

1. Management attention to satisfaction is sporadic.
2. When quality initiatives are implemented, their impact cannot be evaluated for a long period of time, and causality is lost.
3. Frontline staff are forced to fall back on internal measures, which are not as credible. The lack of monthly customer-based measurements causes companies to focus on internal measures instead of on customers' needs.

A Better Approach

A results-oriented approach to quality improvement and customer loyalty is needed. Here is a five-step process to effectively set quality priorities and respond to customer needs:

Step 1: Inventory sources of data. List all of the functions that receive customer complaints, inquiries, and comments, such as the headquarters executive office, consumer affairs, customer service, field sales district offices, and frontline retail and operational offices. Functions that handle routine transactions should also be included.

Step 2: Determine the number of problems. List the frequency of reported problems by type of problem from each function. Use a multiplier to project the actual number of problems in the marketplace. Research indicates that the number of problems reported by customers to headquarters is a small percentage (0.1% to 5%) of the actual number of problems experienced in the marketplace. This percentage, of course, varies by the types of products and the organization of companies within industries.[3] Through research, a company can determine the appropriate multiplier. For example, if research shows that 5% of customers with a problem complain to headquarters, the multiplier is 20, meaning the number of complaints received must be multiplied by 20

Relative market damage of customer problems with loans

Problem type	Frequency	Loyalty damage*	Loan customers at risk
Understanding loan application	5%	40%	2%
Delay in approval	20%	16%	3%
Loan status information	30%	26%	8%
Branch payment	15%	27%	4%
Payment book	13%	9%	1%
Payment credit	20%	26%	5%
Phone service	30%	22%	6%

*Percent who "probably will not" or "definitely will not" get next loan from this bank

Figure 2. **Example of market damage.**

to estimate the number of similar problems in the marketplace. Thus, if headquarters received 40 complaints, it should assume that 800 customers had similar problems.

Step 3: Identify what is important to the customer. In addition to identifying the number of customers who had problems, a survey should also be conducted to estimate the loss of loyalty that these problems are causing (i.e., market damage).[4] In terms of maintaining or losing customers' future business, the most frequent problem is not necessarily the most important problem. Figure 2 shows an example of market damage in a banking environment.

Step 4: Develop a focal point and methodology to reconcile the data. A single function should be charged with collecting and reconciling internal quality data, data on customers' problems, and survey results. Without the focal point, data conflicts will ensue.

Reconciliation of data requires an examination of data collection methodologies and classification schemes. The goal is to identify the key drivers of customer satisfaction—that is, those product and service attributes that, if done poorly, are most likely to cause a loss of customer loyalty. Company resources should be concentrated on fixing problems and maintaining high quality as it relates to these attributes. Many companies assign this responsibility to a quality function; however, most quality functions tend to focus on internal causes and not on external causes, such as distribution, marketing, and customer behavior.

Step 5: Track impact results monthly. Most companies fall into two measurement pitfalls. First, they only track loyalty and satisfaction once a year with a customer survey. Second, they depend on monthly internal operational and cost data to evaluate quality initiatives. But internal operational and cost data do not indicate whether quality initiatives have an impact on the marketplace. Once the key drivers of customer satisfaction and loyalty and their impact on revenue have been identified using effective baseline customer research, these key attributes should be measured monthly.

Companies That Have Avoided the Pitfalls

Only a few companies have effectively addressed the problems of creating customer-driven priorities and measuring TQM efforts' impact on customer loyalty. Apple, Avis Europe, Bank One Cleveland, Cathay Pacific Airlines, Ford Credit, and Toyota are among those that have enhanced the success of their quality programs as well as their success in the marketplace.

Only a few companies have effectively addressed the problems of creating customer-driven priorities and measuring TQM efforts' impact on customer loyalty.

To ensure that their priorities were customer driven, Apple, Toyota, and Cathay Pacific Airlines surveyed a large number of customers and gathered data on their problems, complaint behaviors, and the impact of specific problems on loyalty. They then set priorities based on market damage. Here is what happened:

- Apple conducted surveys of its product users and those who contacted Apple for service. Apple identified the key problems that purchasers encountered. In addition, for those who contacted the company for service, Apple found a significant drop in loyalty if a request was not handled on the first call.[5]

- Toyota found that the sales process is critical in satisfying customers and maintaining their loyalty. Its priorities now focus on helping sales representatives achieve a professional demeanor by providing incentives and by measuring their progress.[6]

- Cathay Pacific Airlines found that on flights longer than 10 hours, customers were more concerned with bathroom cleanliness, food quality, and continuous information on the status of flight operations than with exact on-time arrival of their flight.[7]

To ensure the integrity of their data analyses, Toyota and Avis Europe made a senior officer responsible for customer satisfaction. These officers direct, or have influence over, all satisfaction measurements, complaint handling and data collection, and internal/field quality data collection (e.g., warranty and operations data). This allows them to achieve a consistent approach to information collection and integrated analysis. Their staffs act as internal consultants to the rest of the organizations, providing information on how to improve performance. Through their analyses, they communicate the probable bottom-line benefit of specific improvements to the line managers, thereby creating a positive incentive to act on problems.

Apple, Bank One Cleveland, and Ford Credit analyze customer complaints and their internal service system data to identify the types of problems and questions that their service representatives could not fully answer on first contact. After they determine which problems cause the most market damage, they increase frontline representatives' expertise, access to information, and authority to ensure a higher closed-on-first-contact rate. Using this approach, Apple achieved a dramatic 50 percentage point increase in satisfaction among customers calling with problems.[8] Bank One Cleveland reduced its customers-at-risk rate by 80% and recently won the 1992 Better Business Bureau award for service excellence.[9] Ford Credit not only retained 40,000 customers who otherwise would have been lost, but also reduced the number of customer service staff by more than 15%.[10] It really is cheaper to give excellent service rather than mediocre service.

Both Avis Europe and Toyota have installed monthly tracking reporting systems that analyze the performance of each local operating unit (for example, a station or dealer) on customer problem areas. Both systems use mail surveys, which are inexpensive and usually achieve a respectable response rate of 30% to 35%. (Avis Europe is currently achieving a 55% rate.) At Avis Europe, the results are reported monthly in a format that can be understood by the local manager in 90 seconds. At Toyota, data are distributed electronically in real time.

In 1992, Toyota gained in both absolute sales and market share.[11] Avis Europe has seen a 22% increase in customer retention and was a finalist for the European Quality Award.[12]

Specific Recommendations

Here are several suggestions to help companies set customer-driven priorities and measure results effectively:

1. *Determine what is important to customers by using baseline market-damage surveys.* Identify the full range of problems that customers encounter, where and how often they complain, and the impact of problems on repurchase. While customer focus groups are helpful, don't depend solely on them because they deal with the hypothetical. As illustrated in the insurance company example, focus groups—like management intuition—can suggest priorities that do not contribute to loyalty.
2. *Decriminalize and solicit complaints.* Complaints are good; by complaining, a customer is giving the company a chance to retain his or her loyalty. What is bad are customer problems. Use complaints as a source of data, not as a quality measure. Use the results of monthly surveys about problems as the quality measure. Solicit complaints via several channels. The solication can be positive. For example, Shell Canada puts this statement on its gasoline pumps: "We can only solve problems we know about."
3. *Integrate and reconcile problem data, starting with satisfaction and survey data.* Complaints and surveys can be reconciled by determining how many incidents occurred in the marketplace. This estimate can then be improved and confirmed with an examination of internal quality and operations data. Finally, the total market damage can be calculated in dollars by multiplying the best estimate of the total number of problem instances in the marketplace by the lost loyalty per incident based on the data collected.
4. *Track the results of quality initiatives.* Measure the quality of recent transactions that can be linked to particular units or processes. Focus on

the performance of the five to eight opportunities for success—that is, the problem areas. Focus on customers' market actions (e.g., purchasing the product again and recommending it to friends) rather than on customers' satisfaction.

5. *Educate staff on the link between customer problems and customer loyalty, extra costs, and employee frustration.*

In summary, management must effectively use internal and external customer data during TQM initiatives to maximize increased revenues and decrease internal costs. The customer data analyses provide the targets for quality improvement.

References

1. "Executive Summary" in *Consumer Complaint Handling in America: An Update Study* (Washington, DC: U.S. Office of Consumer Affairs, 1986), and J.A. Goodman, "The Nature of Customer Satisfaction," National Quality Forum IV, Oct. 5, 1988.

2. Based on research conducted across many industries from 1980–1993 by Technical Assistance Research programs, Inc.

3. Ibid.

4. For more information on this type of research, see John A. Goodman, Scott M. Broetzmann, and Colin Adamson, "Ineffective—That's the Problem With Customer Satisfaction Surveys," *Quality Progress*, May 1992, pp. 35–38.

5. Apple baseline market-damage research, 1988.

6. Toyota analysis of its New Vehicle Sales and Delivery Survey, 1991.

7. Cathay Pacific Airlines baseline market-damage research, 1992.

8. Based on Apple baseline and ongoing satisfaction tracking research, 1988–1992.

9. Based on Bank One Cleveland baseline and ongoing satisfaction tracking research, 1990–1993.

10. Based on Ford Credit internal financial analysis, independent of its baseline survey process, 1993.

11. Presentation by Robert Schrandt, vice president, Toyota Customer Relations and Satisfaction, April 6, 1993.

12. Based on Avis Europe financial analysis as reported by Linda Lash, Avis Europe director of customer satisfaction, 1992.

John A. Goodman is the president of Technical Assistance Research Programs, Inc. in Arlington, VA. Gary F. Bargatze is the senior vice president of Technical Assistance Research Programs, Inc., in Arlington, VA. Cynthia Grimm is the vice president of Technical Assistance Research Programs, Inc. in Arlington, VA.

Functional Processes

SUPPLIERS AND PURCHASING

Creating Trust in Customer-Supplier Relationships

Kerry Humenuik and Sharon Hamilton

These authors view the customer-supplier relationship as a dance in which both parties get something. Sometimes one leads, sometimes the other, but the goal is always to create relationships that result in more effectively and efficiently serving the needs of the final customers.

When developing long-term customer-supplier relationships with expectations that those relationships will be both effective and adaptable, a culture change is not only important, it is essential. As in any culture change, old paradigms must be discarded and a totally new way of viewing relationships must be adopted. The new paradigm we are speaking of is needed today for tomorrow's success. That paradigm will depend upon, and lead to the outcomes of mutual trust, respect and understanding for and between both parties.

Changing paradigms—Traditionally, we have viewed the customer-supplier relationship as one which awards business based mainly on price. As W. Edwards Deming points out in point number four of his famous fourteen

Reprinted with permission from *Journal for Quality and Participation*, January/February 1994.
Copyright © 1994 the Association for Quality and Participation. All rights reserved.

points: "End the practice of awarding business on the basis of price tag. Instead, minimize total cost. Move toward a single supplier for any one item, on the long term relationship of loyalty and trust."

It is up to each organization to determine which elements are necessary to achieve a successful, well-functioning customer-supplier relationship: a cookbook approach won't work. The elements for a successful relationship must be carefully chosen from among an almost infinite selection; for such a decision, a well-defined process is required. While the elements of each relationship may be unique, the elements needed to guide the customer-supplier relationship building process are known.

What are the elements of a successful customer-supplier relationship building process? Through both research and experience we have found the following to be excellent guides to creating a customer-supplier relationship based upon mutual trust:

- Price alone does not a good criteria make. . .
- Partners set clear priorities. . .
- Expectations are clearly defined. . .
- Partners build an environment of dynamic communication. . .
- Accept communication as a dynamic process. . .
- Be courteous. . .
- Use proper closing techniques. . .
- Keep your options open. . .
- Partners commit to a spirit of performance.

The remainder of the article will flesh out each of these guides.

Price Alone Does Not a Good Criteria Make

Awarding business largely on the basis of price excludes many of the elements of quality. This not only interferes with the actual decision making process, but it also impairs our ability to implement a continuous quality improvement process. In other words, we start at a lower level of quality and deny ourselves the opportunity to improve it.

Awarding business largely on the basis of price excludes many of the elements of quality.

The traditional business orientation is one where the customer and supplier are stanced so that there is a winner and a loser. This competitive orientation must give way to one which is more cooperative.

Perhaps in today's world, a better analogy would be to compare the relationship to a dance. In some situations, the partner attempts to maintain dominance, and such a position is not acceptable to the other (and it rarely is), the dance becomes less engaging. If this persists, it is inevitable that one partner will pull away. The dance may end there. A dance is enjoyable when both partners understand beforehand which steps are expected. So, too, is the relationship between suppliers and customers.

While this is intuitively acceptable, it is also supported by various studies. To see which characteristics of this relationship were most influential, we interviewed thirty customers and suppliers. Four elements were quickly identified as essential for a successful relationship. These elements were:

1. Partners set clear priorities. . .
2. Expectations are clearly defined. . .
3. Partners build an environment of dynamic communication. . .
4. Partners commit to a spirit of performance.

Each of these elements brings clarity to the relationship, and while interrelated, each has much to offer on its own merits, and should be examined separately.

Partners set clear priorities—Although price may be one priority, it should not be the only priority in establishing the customer-supplier relationship. Consider the following:

- A good price means nothing if the product or service needed is not available when trying to meet a customer's time requirements.
- A company negotiates a great price, with year-end bonuses, however, when the goods are received they do not meet the specifications. You are left empty handed while your customer waits. Now, instead of calculating the savings you will calculate how much it cost in terms of lost sales/replacement costs.

It's partnering, not parry and thrust. . . As has often been said, an ounce of prevention is worth a pound of cure. In the new paradigm, the other party is your partner, not your adversary. Although one hides his or her plans and intentions from an adversary, one freely shares these with a partner. It is particularly critical to share each other's mission, vision and values.

This sharing can benefit everybody; if there is a commonality of purpose the partnership can proceed and grow. On the other hand, if there is not, it is best to find out early that the arrangement will not work. Remember your business could depend on who you choose as a supplier.

The mission, vision and values of the partnership should be the basis upon which the issues are prioritized. With clear priorities, the partners can evaluate, and if appropriate, build a mutually satisfying long-term relationship. Otherwise, one can find one's partner planning for a waltz and the other for a cha-cha.

Expectations are clearly defined—Clearly defining expectations is essential to protect the quality process. If priorities explain what is important to me, expectations explain what results I anticipate, and specifically, how my partner will contribute toward those results.

Margo Walker from Lanier Worldwide, Inc. has provided one of the most succinct and meaningful statements of expectation which totally supports the quality process. She says: "Both partners need to agree to focus on business through the eyes of the customer, and to respond accordingly."

Clearly defining roles. . . Implicit in defining expectations is the definition of the role(s) of each partner. Where a process ends for one partner and begins for the other partner needs to be clearly understood and the processes themselves need to be well-managed.

A well-managed process has an owner. The process owner can be an individual, or a team, but it is clear as to who is responsible for analyzing, measuring performance, improving and documenting the process to eliminate bottlenecks and inconsistencies. Documentation is an integral component of ownership, rather than an afterthought. Once the documentation is complete, the process owner must insure that the information is conveyed to all who interact or interface with that process.

Establishing norms. . . Norms must be established for all aspects of the relationship. This includes everything from how meetings will be conducted to determining procedures for follow-up.

Establish a positive orientation. . . A partnership has every potential to be satisfying, rewarding and enjoyable. Commit to learn, grow and succeed together from the very start.

A key component to any successful supplier partnership is to develop a method to measure a supplier's performance against established norms. This performance measurement system must be shared with the supplier as a primary means of communicating results. This feedback will help both parties focus on continuous improvement.

A key component to any successful supplier partnership is to develop a method to measure a supplier's performance against established norms.

Partners build an environment of dynamic communication—Communication is what changes a coincidental sharing of purpose into a relationship.

Each partner feels that his or her needs are as important as the other's, so it is important to understand your partner's needs. It is only fair, that each partner acknowledges the other's sense of priority. Understanding your partner's position provides a foundation for communication.

Implement effective communications skills. . . Communications is not a spectator sport—effective communications skills are not passive in nature.

- Listen actively and provide feedback to the person communicating. . .
- Focus on both verbal and non-verbal communications—all messages have components of each. . .
- Restate the message—whether sending or receiving, it is appropriate to restate to ensure clarity and mutual understanding. . .
- Ask questions to obtain complete understanding of what is being said—if there is any doubt, ask for clarification. A question can not only lead to better understanding, but might also lead to improvement of the initial idea. . .
- Obtain formal feedback—ask (in writing) "How an I doing?" Use the feedback to improve your next interaction. Remember that negative feedback provides the most opportunity for improvement.

Good dancers (and partners) practice more than they perform. . . In the customer-supplier dance, communication is one of the basic steps. Highly perfected communication, like any other skill, requires practice; when you're convinced that you've perfected the technique, practice one more time.

Ginger Rogers and Fred Astaire did not become famous by trying a dance step only until it was good enough, but by aspiring to perfection. Just as they scheduled their rehearsals, you can schedule practicing communication skills. For example, you may decide to contract with yourself to use active listening skills a minimum of three times a day, then increase to five times a day, et cetera.

Accept communication as a dynamic process—Communication must be dynamic since every customer-supplier relationship is going to change as the situation changes and as quality is continuously improved. Likewise, as your criteria for choosing a supplier are more focused on quality, the change you may need to be ready for is changing partners. The success of your business is your number one priority. Don't allow yourself to become complacent in your thinking—your supplier of today may not be the best choice for your needs tomorrow.

> *"Courtesies of a small and trivial character are the ones which strike deepest in the grateful and appreciating hearts."*—Henry Clay

Be courteous—Unfortunately, courtesy or civility seems to be a lost art form—a casualty of the drive for efficiency and competitiveness. Courtesy is consistent with quality improvement because it improves relationships and communications.

Use proper closing techniques—Summarize the events of meetings, reiterate action items and determine who will be responsible for them. Ensure that each party knows what they need to do, and when it is expected to be completed.

Responses should be timely (read IMMEDIATELY).

Responses to inquiries. . . Responses should be timely (read IMMEDIATELY). Follow up in writing. Use thank you notes (handwritten is not only acceptable, but more personal as well).

Keep your options open—It's always good to keep the door open to options. Offer alternatives when requirements cannot be met as originally stated. Re-negotiate if necessary.

The customer-supplier six step. . . Re-negotiating is one of the more intricate dance steps in the customer-supplier relationship, it goes like this:

1. Customer states requirement. . .
2. Supplier discovers requirement cannot be met (or, perhaps, they can be exceeded!). . .
3. Supplier explains circumstances to the customer. . .
4. Customer and supplier brainstorm alternatives together. . .
5. Customer and supplier reach consensus on new requirements. . .
6. New requirements documented.

Partners commit to a spirit of performance—Both the customer and supplier can set the framework for a successful relationship. A big portion of this is an attitude which expects success. If you approach someone on the dance floor with a positive attitude, the offer to dance will probably be accepted, and enjoyed by both parties. A positive attitude is easily communicated (after all, 70 percent of our communication is non-verbal) and is quite infectious.

This is such a fundamental element of quality that it should not even have to be stated. Employees know the best way to improve the process; managers only need to understand and support them to enable and empower their ideas for the organization's success.

Final Thoughts

It's time to overcome the outdated, win-lose, price-based paradigm for choosing a supplier. Today's market demands a proactive participative customer-supplier relationship. The elements discussed here have shown the way to enter the customer-supplier dance.

Since we all know what happens to wallflowers, it's time to stand up, take a deep breath and ask your intended partner to accompany you to the center of the dance floor.

Kerry Humenuik is the coordinator of quality management for support services at The Cleveland Clinic Foundation. The Foundation is a world renowned healthcare facility and health resource. Sharon Hamilton is the employee involvement programs manager at Picker International—a leader in the diagnostic imaging industry.

The Rules of Purchasing Are Changing

Patrick Flanagan

While the new rules seem to suggest more cooperation with less adversarial relationships between suppliers and their customers, there is still a way to go. Price is still important, and trust is a delicate matter. Further, for commodity-type products, price is still the main concern of most purchasers. This article presents some sobering thoughts on where purchasing seems to be today in many companies. While Deming's point about not buying on the basis of price but on value is indeed valid, there is still controversy among purchasers over how to value one supplier's offerings over another. This article suggests some of the rules during the transition period. Compare this article with the one that preceded it and the one that follows it.

Suddenly management is focusing on purchasing. "Maybe it's because there's no more room for downsizing," carps one recently laid-off executive. The reason is more complex than that, but the fact that labor is only a small part of overhead in the typical nonservices company is a long overdue realization.

"The single biggest expense in most companies is goods and services from outside suppliers, and too few managers still seem to care," says Mary Lu Harding. The image of purchasing executives and staff as being faceless paper pushers is fading, according to Harding, who is a co-author of *Purchasing* from the National Association of Purchasing Management and a consultant/lecturer based in Bristol, Vt. "Neglect purchasing at your own peril," she warns.

One industry that hasn't been neglectful is auto manufacturing. The furor that occurred when General Motors' José Ignacio López de Arriotua jumped to Volkswagen AG is one recent example that made headlines and showed the value of a top-notch procurement executive. A few months later, *The Wall Street Journal* gave Chrysler's vice president of purchasing, Thomas T. Stallkamp, the full-feature treatment. *The Journal* credited him with helping Chrysler "do something no other U.S. automaker could do [in 1992]: make money."

Few others get such accolades. In fact, criticism is more likely to be on the menu. The reason is a growing level of contention between buyer and seller. Management is leaning heavily on purchasing to negotiate, or if that

---

Reprinted by permission of publisher from *Management Review*, March 1994. Copyright © 1994 American Management Association, New York. All rights reserved.

fails some say "extort," more favorable terms and conditions, as well as lower prices, with suppliers. Suppliers are crying foul and fighting back by citing antitrust laws that have little applicability. The upshot is adversarial relationships, both internally and externally.

Retail Wars

This is seen particularly in retailing. The purchasing power of discount chains and super stores is awesome. This gives them a way around both legal and customary purchasing practices. The legal issue is the Robinson-Patman Act, an antitrust law enacted in 1936 to prevent large companies from obtaining preferential prices from smaller suppliers. This so-called Magna Carta for small businesses has since evolved into a much broader, and confusing, interpretation that forbids businesses from selling similar commodities to different buyers at different prices.

This is where the mass retailers gain the edge. The quantities they purchase create new categories of pricing in terms of volume discounts, or other concessions. Donald S. Clark, secretary of the Federal Trade Commission, which is responsible for enforcing Robinson-Patman, cites a hypothetical situation where a peanut butter manufacturer sells $1 jars of its product to grocery stores for 80 cents, after discounts and promotional allowances. This same manufacturer then turns around and sells shrink wrapped, four-jar packages exclusively to club stores for $2.40, or 60 cents a jar. Is this illegal? Clark isn't sure. Instead of answers, he raises questions: Is the manufacturer meeting competition? Is there some cost justification? Assuming the packaging to be "special," which is not a foregone conclusion, do grocery stores actually compete with club stores? Is there some countervailing reason why the club stores would get the four-packs?

What the FTC secretary is saying in so many words is that Robinson-Patman is largely unenforceable, even when taken to the courts, because of the difficulties of proving an antitrust violation. Leslie Marell, an attorney in Tarzana, Calif., who specializes in purchasing law, is more plain spoken: "You have to prove an adverse impact on competition between customers because of price discrimination. The answer in virtually all instances is you absolutely cannot." The reason is that a harmed party has to prove through a market analysis that a competitor that buys goods at a lower price affects your ability to sell in the marketplace. "Then, you have to get a judge and jury to believe you,"she adds. Marell and others do agree on certain actions that are blatantly illegal, although not always easy to prove. Following are some shady tactics used by purchasers to leverage their buying power:

- *Lying about the price available from another supplier.* Savvy purchasers won't say that "I can get it from X company for $1.50, instead of the $1.60 you're bidding." Instead, they say, "I'll pay $1.50, take it or leave it." Even if the purchaser lies, it's difficult to impossible to prove since neither the purchaser nor the competitor will provide documentation of the lower price.

■ *Collusion to agree not to buy or sell.* Competitors cannot get together and agree to blackball a particular company if it doesn't sell goods at the desired price. This raises sticky questions for purchasing associations where potential competitors band together to buy in high-discount quantities. Otherwise, purchasing associations legally have more buying clout in terms of gaining quantity discounts.

■ *Demanding prices that are not obtainable by others.* A buyer that is interested in buying in high-volume usually can negotiate a heavy discount, but the seller has to make sure that it can still make an adequate profit. For example, if a retailer wants to buy 100,000 items for $10 each, that price must also be available to other interested buyers. However, if it is unlikely that in your particular business no other companies would be interested in buying such large quantities, then the seller has to determine if the price demanded by the purchaser provides an adequate profit margin or meets other business goals such as funding expansion and increasing marketshare. If not, the seller should keep negotiating.

There are those who do find one everyday use for Robinson-Patman: It's often cited in negotiations, particularly when special pricing advantages are demanded. While such posturing works occasionally with unsophisticated purchasing managers, it's rarely successful with anyone who knows the ins and outs. Many do, if attendance at seminars such as Purchasing and the Law, which the National Association of Purchasing Management in Tempe, Ariz., offers regularly around the country, is any indication.

Although purchasing clout and the adversarial relationships it creates get a lot of attention, there's another aspect that builds solid buyer-seller relationships. The discounters have little concern about brand loyalty, or product quality. They sell strictly on price. If the club store is not stocking Tide, it will buy another brand of detergent, if the price is low enough. When a product, say a snow blower that's on sale, is poor quality, the consumer complains to the manufacturer, not the discounter.

For these, and many other reasons, purchasing has quite a different look in brandname manufacturing. This is particularly true of components that are integral to product performance and quality, as well as savings related to just-in-time inventory programs. However, when it comes to office and cleaning supplies, or other largely commodity-type goods, the dickering over price and quantity can be as aggressive as with a mass merchandiser.

Sole Sources

The latest trend is to actively seek out sole source suppliers. According to Robert Bretz, director of corporate purchasing for Pitney Bowes, "This is much simpler. There's less effort on the part of the seller and it's easier to resolve issues." He also likes the leverage that committing to a single supplier provides in terms of payments, costs and deliveries. "It's a win-win situation for everyone involved." However, a single source arrangement shuts out the other two or three suppliers that would otherwise share in the corporation's purchasing power. The corporation also is vulnerable should a sole source supplier suddenly develop problems.

For this reason, when developing sole source agreements, purchasing managers put on a stern face. "We do upfront prevention," says Bretz. This includes reviewing detailed financial information on the possible supplier, checking references and "ferreting out all types of potential problems in advance." When problems do occur, the purchaser stays committed to the supplier. "We try to get to the core of the problem. There's no sugar coating, but we want to resolve the issues, not change suppliers," he says.

In these sole source relationships, Bretz points out that problems can arise on both sides, particularly when the buyer does not uphold the company's end of the bargain and is unreasonable about delivery, quantity or quality issues. One example is agreeing to accept a 30-day delivery period and then demanding a 10-day delivery. "We in purchasing often act as a referee between requisitioners and suppliers," he finds.

Cost can still be a sticking point with sole source agreements. Unlike the mass merchandisers that have little concern whether or not a seller stays financially healthy, manufacturers go to some length to assure that key suppliers earn a reasonable profit through cost-plus agreements and long-term contracts. The most visible advocates of this approach are the American automotive companies. "When you start to see your suppliers as the experts, then they become valuable partners instead of a switchable commodity," says Chrysler's Stallkamp.

The result is what Detroit calls "lean production" methods at parts suppliers, a process GM pioneered in the United States, but learned from the Japanese automakers. Part of the GM lean production effort was adversarial when the now departed Lopez ran the show. He dispatched "efficiency experts" to shape up suppliers, demanded double-digit price reductions, and at times tore up contracts when he didn't get them. Chrysler took a lesson from GM and dropped its adversarial stance, including mandated price cuts, which were still being announced as late as 1989. Instead, it eliminated for many suppliers the process of competitive bidding and the writing of detailed specifications. Now, suppliers are relied upon to design and build parts that are high quality, meet general specifications and are low in cost. In fact, when a supplier finds a way to lower prices, Chrysler and the company split the savings and the supplier most likely gets a long-term contract.

When a supplier finds a way to lower prices, Chrysler and the company split the savings and the supplier most likely gets a long-term contract.

This more enlightened approach to purchasing is spreading. It's rare to find a major manufacturer that isn't using terms such as strategic trading partners, preferred suppliers and key vendors. Still, undercurrents of distrust continue to buffet relationships. One reason is that conflicts between buyer and sellers are eternal. Another is that not enough buyers and sellers run well managed operations.

Purchasing Pitfalls

Therefore, the potential for conflict is large. Attorney Marell warns of several traps. The first is the sole source arrangement where one party, usually the seller, suddenly changes the terms. Having a supplier say, "I'm raising the price by 25 percent or I'm taking a hike" means a total loss of buyer leverage because there's no secondary source. Marell finds this most often happens when the contract does not discuss the ability to inspect the books for information about pricing. "This is the reason why more and more sole-source contracts are done on a cost-plus basis," she explains.

A second pitfall is bankruptcy. It's increasingly common for the buyer to loan the seller equipment or tooling, particularly with strategic partnerships. Providing financing, or progressive payments, to retool or expand production is also becoming more prevalent. Should the supplier declare bankruptcy, however, the buyer is stuck.

The third trap involves ownership of drawings, particularly when suppliers are given a degree of freedom to develop engineering plans and specifications. "The buyer needs to have a contractual right to get at a supplier's proprietary information in a worst case scenario," advises Marell.

Locking the Barn Door

Why these and other untoward events occur is easy to understand once the damage is done. "You have to anticipate up front what can go wrong while everyone still loves one another," says Marell. This is easier said than done. Most supplier/purchaser relationships evolve, rather than being created from scratch with organizations that are unknown to each other. "As a practical matter, I question how often there is a strategic alliance and how often it's just a convenience," she says.

There's a need to review existing supplier relationships for viability in terms of profit margins, quality and responsiveness.

Interviews with a number of companies reinforce Marell's point. The rules of the game are changing. There's a need to review existing supplier relationships for viability in terms of profit margins, quality and responsiveness. At the same time, there are growing numbers of potential suppliers that want a foot in the door and a chance to prove themselves. This is particularly true of minority- and women-owned companies, as well as new businesses that have been started by downsized executives with entrepreneurial urges.

"We try to make room for everyone," says a purchasing manager who wants to remain anonymous. The reason is not totally altruistic. His company is heavily dependent on single source suppliers and "bringing in minority- and women-owned suppliers is a way that can't be criticized to keep single source suppliers on their toes." This helps to resolve the back-up problem as well. "If a supplier suddenly develops financial problems or tries to hold us up for a price increase, we already know an alternative and we can feel good about giving them the business."

Despite all the talk of working together, or no longer bludgeoning suppliers into submission, what matters is cutting costs. The lean production approach of the auto industry works in some instances. The brute force of the mass retailers works in others. "There's still a lot of fat in the procurement system and purchasing doesn't always have the clout to do something about it," says a Fortune 1000 company purchasing executive.

Part of the problem is that purchasing clout is spread around the company. Engineers in particular get a lot of criticism. "They get wined and dined and come to purchasing saying 'buy from so-and-so,' and we don't have a choice and not enough effort is made for us to understand what we're buying," says a high-tech company purchasing manager. This means that purchasing takes the blame when thing go wrong and gets little or no credit when right decisions are made.

Both Sides Now

What's the answer? It depends whether you're a buyer or a seller in the purchasing chain. In reality, virtually every company is both. It's rare that sales and purchasing coordinate activities. While the fictional peanut butter producer in FTC Secretary Clark's example is a seller, it's also a buyer. When a number of purchasing executives were presented with this example, they advised forcing suppliers to bite the bullet. According to one, "peanut butter, is peanut butter and who knows what goes into it?" Another said, "They should not be concerned about antitrust violations. What we do is make discounting decisions on an actuarial basis, not on a legal basis." In other words, the odds of getting caught by the FTC are the same or less than selling a $1 million life insurance policy to someone at age 30 and having that individual die six months later.

It's rare that sales and purchasing coordinate activities.

There's a lot of practical advice available from those on the front lines on both sides of the buyer/seller battlefront:

- *Learn the legal basics of antitrust, contracts, forms, terms and conditions, bankruptcy, and possession of proprietary/engineering properties.* Too many don't, and try to bluff their way through the basics.

- *Know your costs and profit margins.* A one-time deal that loses money can be a lesson, but a long-term contract that results in red ink translates into going bust, or extended litigation.

- *Beef up management information systems, not only to provide better and faster cost and profit reports, but also to permit EDI transactions.* More and more purchasers are doing business electronically, and having these systems in place gives an edge over competitors, particularly for smaller companies.

More and more purchasers are doing business electronically, and having these systems in place gives an edge over competitors, particularly for smaller companies.

- *Learn negotiating techniques that resolve differences.* Compromising when feeling squeezed never works. Present a strong case in terms of your costs, terms and conditions in a way that the buyer understands. Opening your books is a two-edged sword, but one that pays benefits.

- *Have a better idea.* Blindly accepting a purchaser's specifications creates a lowest bidder situation. Instead, respond with design, raw materials, manufacturing or other ideas that save money, improve quality or otherwise add value.

- *Stress ethics and training.* Luxury box seats at sporting events, golfing outings, lavish dinners and other freebees still exist. Avoiding possible accusations of improper dealings is imperative in today's business climate.

- *Be fair, particularly when you have clout in the marketplace.* Adversarial relationships rarely pay off in the long run. Testing the legal boundaries is possible, but you could end up in court and be labeled in the press as a "bad guy."

The rules of the purchasing game are changing. Many think it's for the good of both buyer and seller. "Being more competitive is what counts today and tomorrow," says Don Taylor, executive director of the West Texas A&M University Small Business Center in Canyon, Texas. "The seller needs to sell the product and the buyer has to sooner or later make a decision," he says.

It's in the middle ground where differences occur. Taylor has a bit of pragmatic advice that's hard to ignore: "Don't dig in your heels; negotiate." Don't expect it to be easy to negotiate either. Pitney Bowes' Bretz is active in promoting minority- and women-owned businesses as well as building long-term sole source supplier relationships. He's also active in purchasing management professional organizations. Still, Bretz is a businessman. When asked what guidelines his company follows in purchasing, his answer was direct and simple: "Get the best price possible."

Patrick Flanagan, a former editor/writer for Money *Magazine, is a business writer who specializes in high-tech and management issues.*

The New Golden Rule of Business

Myron Magnet

While the preceding article suggests a lingering wariness between purchasers and suppliers, this article from Fortune *shows the kinds of changes going on now, especially in those companies committed to TQM. They are creating long-term, mutually beneficial relationships based on competence, value, and trust. The watchword for all involved is continuous improvement. Neither suppliers nor purchasers can stand still. While these new relationships make life better for all concerned, no one can afford to relax.*

In that battle-scarred landscape where supplier and their corporate customers meet and deal, lions are lying down with lambs, and swords are being beaten into plowshares. Hard-nosed businessmen use embarrassingly romantic terms to describe the new order in supplier-customer relationships. "It's like a marriage," croons a big-league purchasing executive. Says a less sentimental top industrial manager:"It's like committing to one relationship instead of sleeping around."

You already know why business people are talking this way: Close customer-supplier relationships help trim costs in today's predatory world economy. They improve quality by disseminating quality-enhancing management techniques across company boundaries and by enlisting each supplier's technological expertise in helping to design and make parts. Moreover, interdependency boosts speed, essential in a world of ever faster product cycles.

But you may not be aware just how far certain companies are going. Take a look at some dramatic examples of successful new-style customer-supplier relationships. These make clear what it takes to set up such partnerships and manage them well. They show, too, what hefty payoffs these relationships can yield—and not just for customer firms taking reduced costs out of suppliers' hides, but for suppliers too.

Start on a recent Saturday afternoon in the life of Rudy Gassner, vice president for capital goods at AMP, a manufacturer of electrical and electronic connectors. As Gassner was savoring a day off at home in Lemoyne, Pennsylvania, catching up on his reading, the phone rang. It was Silicon Graphics executive Greg Podshadley. Gassner's eyebrows shot up. Sure, Silicon Graphics was a big, valued customer in a closed partnership with AMP, but Podshadley had never butted into his weekend at home before.

Reprinted with permission from *Fortune* Magazine, February 21, 1994. Copyright © 1994 Time Inc. All rights reserved.

What Podshadley had to say was equally unexpected. He was in trouble. An electrical connector going into a new workstation was proving so undependable that it threatened major quality problems for the product. No, it wasn't one of AMP's connectors; it was made by a competitor. But could Gassner supply a substitute—and at once? The snafu had brought the whole project to its knees, shutting down the line.

Gassner called his sales manager and sent him and his colleagues to the distribution center to hunt down the needed parts. Combing the cavernous, deserted facility, they hit pay dirt: the right connectors, and enough of them to put Podshadley's line back in business. Trouble was, they needed to use a dauntingly complicated forklift to get the parts, and none of the managers could work it. So, lucky that no underling was around to watch the comedy, they taught themselves by trial and error, picked up the connectors, and drove them to the airport. Silicon Graphics assemblers were soldering them onto circuitboards in California the next day.

Gassner did all this with zero paperwork—and without hinting that that's what happens when you buy from an AMP competitor. Nor did he charge Silicon Graphics a premium for the service. "This is an IOU to collect sometime," says he. Not surprisingly, Podshadley says he owes Gassner a big one: A lot was at stake. "This business is so fast," Podshadley says, "and the technology is so cutting-edge, that there are going to be problems. You can point fingers, and relationships can deteriorate very quickly. You have to work as a team and do what has to be done, or you lose the market."

You can point fingers, and relationships can deteriorate very quickly. You have to work as a team and do what has to be done, or you lose the market.

Companies that succeed at partnerships like this usually set them up routinely, not as exceptions, and with customers and suppliers alike. Sitting in the middle of a web of such relationships is Bailey Controls, an Ohio-headquartered, $300-million-a-year manufacturer of control systems for big factories, from steel and paper mills to chemical and pharmaceutical plants. To spin its web, Bailey, a unit of Elsag Bailey Process Automation, goes a step beyond the AMP-Silicon Graphics style of teamwork. It treats some suppliers almost like departments of its own company.

Bailey has physically plugged two of its main electronics distributors into itself. Montreal-based Future Electronics is hooked on with an electronic data interchange system. Every week, Bailey electronically sends Future its latest forecasts of what materials it will need for the next six months, so that Future can stock up in time. Bailey itself stocks only enough inventory for a few days of operation, as opposed to the two to three months' worth it used to carry. Whenever a bin of parts falls below a designated level, a Bailey employee passes a laser scanner over the bin's bar code, instantly alerting Future to send the parts at once.

Arrow Electronics, headquartered on Long Island, is plugged in even more closely: It has a warehouse in Bailey's factory, stocked according to Bailey's twice-monthly forecasts. Bailey provides the space, Arrow the warehouseman and the $500,000 of inventory.

The benefits? For Bailey, these arrangements shift inventory costs and management to the distributors, who also discount parts Bailey buys exclusively from them. The distributors expect to gain more in high volume—20% to 30% higher, Arrow reckons—than they lose in lower prices. Transaction costs go down for everyone, since Bailey's purchasing department can do other tasks and its distributors don't need many salesmen to service the Bailey account. As volume goes up for the distributors, slimmer fixed costs mean fatter profits.

Looking in the other direction, at Bailey's dealings with its own customers, you can see in its relationship with paper manufacturer Boise Cascade how dramatically new-style customer-supplier partnerships shift the focus from price to more substantive issues of quality and technological improvement. For using Bailey exclusively, the eight out of ten Boise plants that signed on to participate in the partnership get a predetermined discount on equipment and engineering services. Regular reviews make sure the terms of the deal keep pace with changing business conditions so neither party gets hurt by the unforeseen.

You can see how dramatically new-style customer-supplier partnerships shift the focus from price to more substantive issues of quality and technological improvement.

The companies quickly found that dumping the rituals of competitive bidding, with fat specification books to be prepared and reviewed, cut costs enough to make up for the discounts. Liberated from ceaseless bargaining, the partners pour their energy into using Bailey's equipment and know-how to squeeze maximum performance out of Boise's operation. For example, Bailey has traditionally used an independent software company's algorithms (or computer programs) to control the complex papermaking machine. Though long aware of that software's limitations, Bailey had no incentive to boost its intelligence, lest the software company turn around and license the enhancements to Bailey's competitors.

But to junk the existing software and build a new and better set of proprietary algorithms from scratch, Bailey would need a paper mill to serve as guinea pig—while safeguarding Bailey's technical secrets. Says Bailey senior vice president Gabe Rosica: "You have to do it with someone you know and trust." The new Bailey-Boise relationship gives Bailey its ideal partner, and the software is taking form. Bailey will benefit by selling it not just to Boise but to other papermakers; Boise will gain by having it well before the rest of the industry.

So untraditional are the principles underlying the relationship that Rosica once warned a Boise plant's top brass not to buy an upgraded control console that Bailey's own salesman had persuaded them to purchase. The salesman had done everything right—but Rosica knew that if the plant waited awhile, it could buy a better kind of console that Bailey was developing. "If this was a competitive bid, I would never have raised the issue and jeopardized getting the order," Rosica says. "But because this was a partnership alliance, there was no risk."

Scott Paper, which specializes in different kinds of paper than Boise Cascade manufactures, started aggressively managing its purchasing a year and a half ago. By radically trimming the number of suppliers and forming partnerships with the survivors to concentrate them on Scott's concerns, Scott found it could spend less and get more than the simple service or commodity it was paying for.

Scott wins its price reductions in part by a process called activity-based costing. The supplier opens his company books to the customer, laying out his cost structure: so much for materials, assembly, labor, sales, marketing, and so on. In turn, the customer can wave away whole categories of cost. No need to pay for sales and marketing, for instance, since the partnership arrangement makes them unnecessary.

By radically trimming the number of suppliers and forming partnerships with the survivors to concentrate them on Scott's concerns, Scott found it could spend less and get more than the simple service or commodity it was paying for.

Increasingly widespread in close customer-supplier partnerships, this process works when the partners really trust each other—and really are trustworthy. But activity-based costing is the element that most frightens suppliers about the idea of such partnerships: It lays them open, they fear, to strong-arm abuse. They don't want to be told, as some suppliers have been told, that they must sell at 10% over their cost of manufacturing, with no allowance for research and development, technical support, or other activities they consider essential to their businesses. They worry, too, that once they've agreed to a profit 10% above their manufacturing costs, a powerful customer, knowing their innermost cost secrets, will bully then down to 5%. "That's happened several times," says Patrick Byrne, a managing director of the Chicago-based A.T. Kearney consulting firm, "and it's left a sour taste."

For customers, the danger is that in a laudable effort to cut costs they will deny themselves invaluable supplier expertise. As with every management technique, there's a right and a wrong way to use this one. The key to successful activity-based costing seems to be simple prudence: Know you partner well before you reveal all, and make sure you are getting all the value the supplier has to offer you.

As customers like Scott Paper learn to get more out of suppliers than mere commodities, suppliers like Betz Laboratories, a Pennsylvania-based maker of industrial water-treatment chemicals, learn to give customer-partners a bonus of expertise along with the goods they buy. When customers order Betz powders and potions, they pay for the druggist, so to speak, and get the doctor almost free.

Take Betz's partnership with AlliedSignal. Formerly, Betz just sold AlliedSignal the chemicals to keep the water in its plants from gunking up pipes or corroding machinery. Now Betz presides like some Roman river god over all the water as it flows through the entirety of a plant. Is it as safe as possible for the equipment? Does it meet environmental standards? Is it being used in the least wasteful, most cost-effective way?

Betz cures a defect of the old system just by setting up high-level teams that combine its own and AlliedSignal's engineers and managers, and empowering them to go over every inch of the plants, looking at the water as a single unified system. In the past a departmental manager might have seen ways of improving water usage, but since it would be an improvement of the whole operation, rather than for his particular piece of it, he wasn't inclined to allocate any of his budget to achieve it.

In less than a year the team in one AlliedSignal plant has pinpointed $2.5 million in potential annual cost reductions, chiefly by using filtered river water instead of buying city water and by recycling water instead of dumping it into the sewer and incurring a sewer charge. By using recycled water in the plant's cooking tower, for example, Betz was able to save 300 gallons of water a minute, which adds up to an annual savings of over $100,000 at the cost of only some new valve controls. "Ours is a specialized niche," says Betz senior vice president Bob Moore. "This expertise is just not in AlliedSignal."

By such methods, Betz aims to reduce the total cost of water and water treatment in 34 of AlliedSignal's U.S. plants 6% a year for the next three to five years. And it will reduce costs further by giving AlliedSignal a discount as part of the exclusive partnership. Betz's own fortunes will improve even as AlliedSignal's overall use of water treatment chemicals drops: As sole supplier, Betz's sales to AlliedSignal will more than double.

All the technical skill in the world won't avail, however, without the more fundamental human qualities essential to make a partnership flourish. When Honda picked Donnelly Corp. in 1986 to make all the mirrors for its U.S.-manufactured cars, Honda managers well knew that the company, based in Holland, Michigan, had never made exterior mirrors and had no factory for making them. But Honda people had known Donnelly for many years as an interior-mirror supplier, and they liked what they'd seen.

They knew that Donnelly's values and culture squared perfectly with Honda's. They liked the way Donnelly involved and empowered its workers, making use of their intelligence and imagination as well as their manual skill. They knew, as CEO Dan Ciampa of the Rath & Strong consulting firm puts it, that "unless an organization knows how to foster collaborative relationships internally, it won't be good at making such relationships outside."

If a supplier understands the difference between a partnership and an adversarial relationship, Honda managers believe, you can teach everything else. Accordingly, the company developed a mini-reengineering program aimed at strengthening its suppliers, with Donnelly one of its first grads. Early in the partnership, Honda sent engineers swarming over two Donnelly plants, scrutinizing the operations for kinks in the flow. "The goal," says Jim Wehrman, a Honda purchasing manager, "is to give almost a consultant's outside view of the operation." One night, carrying out what the program had prescribed, overall-suited Honda and Donnelly manufacturing engineers descended on a section of the plant and reorganized it completely. Honda hopes Donnelly will reduce costs about 2% a year, with the two companies splitting the savings.

If a supplier understands the difference between a partnership and an adversarial relationship, Honda managers believe, you can teach everything else.

With only a handshake to mark the birth of the new partnership, Donnelly built an entirely new plant to make Honda's exterior mirrors—a plant putting Donnelly in competition with some customers, for which it made exterior-mirror glass. Actions like this are light-years away from a conventional supply contract: They mark a commitment between two entire corporations, not between a salesman and a purchasing manager.

The payoff is big. From $5 million in sales the first year, the partnership will grow to $60 million by 1997. And as a Honda manager explained to a Donnelly executive: "To Honda, long term means forever—assuming you're doing the job."

Motorola adds a canny refinement to Honda-style supplier relationships. Like the carmaker, it looks for partners that share its values. Then it sharpens their skills by teaching them its own Total Quality Management techniques, even requiring them to take courses in cycle time reduction, customer satisfaction, and so on at an education program it calls Motorola University. But while nurturing long-term partnerships, it fans gentlemanly competition among partners by giving grades, even more often than schools give report cards.

Motorola teams tour suppliers' plants every two years, grading them on how well they stack up against their competitors on quality and timeliness. On top of that, Motorola's so-called commodity managers rate suppliers monthly on an index that combines cost and quality, once again comparing them with their competitors (listed anonymously) and showing how much of Motorola's business each competitor gets. Says Motorola procurement chief Tom Slaninka: "The better performers should earn a greater share of our business." In this way, the heat stays on.

Not surprisingly, says Slaninka, "in the first go-round, five years ago, there was apprehension on the part of suppliers, and the way to get buy-in was to emphasize not the score but the opportunities identified for improvement." What Motorola is truly instilling, after all, is a way for supplier companies to gain. "We're teaching and coaching and pushing them in a direction that's been successful for us," says Slaninka: "toward a culture and a mindset that show that quality and cycle times have a direct relation to the cost of the product. " Motorola has started pushing suppliers to analyze how much quality defects add to their own costs. "It's a real eye-opener," Slaninka says. "They find 12% to 20% cost-reduction opportunities." If the whole exercise boosts suppliers' profits, so much the better, in Motorola's view.

Motorola gets its suppliers to help from the very start in designing a part and figuring out how to make it. Larry Groves, CEO of Targ-It-Tronics, a Florida outfit that makes flexible circuit assemblies for Motorola, explains that a supplier understands, often better than the customer, how to design specialized high-tech parts to minimize their material and manufacturing cost. It also knows how to skirt design flaws that make them apt to break.

For example, says Groves, a Motorola division new to the partnership objected that Targ-It-Tronics' bid on a particularly complex circuit was 30% higher than a competitor's. Groves countered that the other supplier probably failed to grasp how labyrinthine the design really was. Sure enough, when Motorola went back for clarification, the other supplier hurriedly hiked its bid 20% above Groves's.

Distraught, the Motorola managers came back to Groves to say they were already way over budget: Could Targ-It-Tronics help? Some radical alterations of the design and the recipe for manufacture and assembly by Groves's engineers and—*voilà!*—a 35% cost reduction.

So much has Motorola come to value its suppliers' ingenuity that it has established a 15-member council of suppliers to rate Motorola's own practices and offer suggestions for improving, for example, the accuracy of production schedules or design layouts that Motorola gives them. Says Motorola's Slaninka: "This will reduce cost, because every time we make an error it takes people at both ends to correct it."

Intimate and innovative as these buyer-supplier relationships have become, you can be quite sure they will go further. They have to. Says Joe Romasco, executive vice president of Intecolor, the exclusive supplier of control-panel computer monitors to Bailey Controls: "With companies like ourselves and Bailey forming networks of related companies, the marketplace is providing an answer in an American fashion to the Japanese networks of companies." In other words, U.S. companies are learning to cooperate in order to take on the real competition.

Myron Magnet is a writer for Fortune *Magazine.*

Functional Processes

INFORMATION MANAGEMENT

ELM: A Holistic Approach

John Teresko

ELM stands for enterprise-logistics management. This article provides a brief overview of this important concept for using information technology to more successfully coordinate logistics throughout the organization to more reliably deliver the goods to customers.

As an acronym "RTGIELM" would likely relegate real-time global-integrated enterprise-logistics management to paradigms lost, thinks Thomas G. Gunn, author of *In the Age of the Real-time Enterprise: Managing for Winning Business Performance Through Enterprise Logistics Management* (Oliver Wight Publications Inc.).

In his new book, Mr. Gunn has settled on ELM as his acronym of choice for enterprise-logistic management, a new step in the passage of manufacturing from art to science. "ELM may not be the best new acronym, but it will [serve the purpose] if it helps manufacturing management understand how to use enterprise integration as a competitive tool." He defines ELM as "a holistic approach to managing operations and the value-added pipeline or total supply chain—from suppliers to final customers."

As a perplexing management problem, the issue of integrating the organization is not entirely new, except in the urgency with which it is being sought

Reprinted with permission from *Industry Week*, June 20, 1994. Copyright © Penton Publishing, Inc., Cleveland, Ohio.

by companies that are hoping to establish a more nimble and profitable position in the marketplace. To Mr. Gunn, the primary driver is the relentless quest for customer satisfaction. "That's certainly No. 1." He says the second is the recognition of the need for real-time management. "Without that capability, growth and global operations are flawed advantages. The third driver is a manufacturing company's need to perform in a world-class manner. Recognition of the role of logistics in the process may well be the most important finding of modern business theory."

Superior logistics management—rather than just-in-time alone—is increasingly being cited as the new strength of Japanese manufacturers. While JIT and labor costs may have explained Japan's early successes in automobile manufacturing, the Japanese are taking a more sophisticated approach to information technology to guarantee their future—one called dispersed-autonomous manufacturing by researchers at Systems Science Institute, Tokyo.

Superior logistics management—rather than just-in-time alone—is increasingly being cited as the new strength of Japanese manufacturers.

"This post-JIT environment places an emphasis on information systems—not only those that communicate customer design orders, but also on electronic production-control systems," says Prof. Jichiro Nakane. The point is to achieve superior management of the total flow of information, from customer order to delivered product, with an integrated, enterprise-wide system.

While some companies have only begun to recognize the need for this philosophy, others have made substantial progress. For example, Mr. Gunn cites Xerox Corp. where implementing the principles of ELM has reduced inventory by a third, or $650 million, and pared supply-chain cost by another $150 million while increasing customer satisfaction. (Xerox created the position of corporate vice president-integrated supply chain, reporting directly to its chairman and CEO.) Inventory reductions of more than $700 million were made possible at Digital Equipment Corp. And at Sun Microsystems Computer Corp., manufacturing cycle time was reduced from 280 days to 175 days, freeing up $1.2 billion in cash.

Xerox created the position of corporate vice president-integrated supply chain, reporting directly to its chairman and CEO.

"The winners are preparing new plans with production data in minutes, not hours or days," Mr. Gunn says. "They can communicate, either within the corporation or with its external business partners—customers, suppliers, or information utilities—at the speed of light."

Mr. Gunn's preoccupation with speed and real-time hands-on management extends to the beginnings of the manufacturing-software company he now leads as president and CEO. "It was 1984 and the soon-to-be founders of what is now Enterprise Planning Systems Inc. [located in a suburb of Ottawa, Ont.] were struggling to get an MRP system to replan more quickly, and they came up with an idea that became the beginnings of this company," he recalls.

"To gain the advantage of speed, they designed and developed a proprietary parallel processor and wrote special software for it. MRP replanning runs that typically ran 10, 20, or 30 hours could then be done in minutes. That gave customers the capability to run MRP at least once a day, if not several times in an hour. They could use MRP in a variety of ways that never had been envisioned. It really opened up the potential of MRP as a significant competitive tool."

But by 1989 the company founders concluded that their proprietary parallel processor was beginning to work against them. "Large RISC-based UNIX machines had emerged from hardware vendors such as HP and IBM, and IS managers began to see little logic in buying yet another specialized piece of hardware from a relatively small, unknown, and Canadian company," Mr. Gunn says. "And evolving company strategies began to avoid buying proprietary computers that did not mingle well with their legacy systems." Fortunately, when the company's applications were ported over to the RISC boxes, they discovered that the software ran almost as quickly—and in some cases just as quickly. Today the company still positions itself as a supplier of fast MRP, coupled with a suite for advanced applications the speed allows.

Mr. Gunn wears another hat as president of Gunn Associates Inc., a Bryn Mawr, Pa., firm specializing in consulting to manufacturing management. In that now more-limited role, he seems critical of the way today's software providers are approaching the issues of enterprise integration.

For example, he sees shortcomings in today's software solutions for meeting the challenge of providing customer satisfaction. "It seems that no one vendor seems to have it all," he says. "In the case of MRP vendors, some may not have DRP [distribution resource planning] as a front end. Also missing may be some associated distribution-management tools such as warehouse analysis, freight and transportation analysis or the ability to move international goods through customs."

At the back end of many MRP products, he sees a lack of sophisticated procurement applications from at least three points of view: vendor rating, global sourcing, and procurement history. "A good purchasing-software base will include all three things, and most MPR vendors haven't put them together yet."

He cites another shortfall in order entry: "Since that business process tends to be unique to a company, most order-entry systems present little more than a shell of what any company needs." But he says the problems go beyond those functional aspects "into how all of that is integrated, plus the issue of being able, in real-time, to track material through the entire manufacturing process. . . . We need to create and recreate plans quickly. And we also need to track how we're doing against the plan."

Mr. Gunn believes a successful ELM system should address two fundamental business processes in a company's logistics business process: "One is the customer-order-to-delivery process, and the other is the materials-management and operations-scheduling business process."

Mr. Gunn sees a strong case for open, distributed systems and believes that any increased costs are just a short-term event. "Two benefits are overwhelming. One is the ease of creating applications or enhancements. It's as much as eight times faster than in the old COBOL environment. The other is the shortened learning curve that comes with the productivity of the new, intuitive graphical user interfaces."

Ironically while dramatic cost benefits are attributed to an open, distributed architecture, cost allocation tends to become obscured. "With a centralized IS department, the figures are automatically presented by the accounting system as a budget line item," Mr. Gunn says. "When computing is diffused throughout an organization—as open, distributed systems do—it is much much harder to collect or even understand all of those costs."

But neither system captures the totality of IS spending in a corporation, Mr. Gunn believes. "It is generally understood that IS costs in the old mainframe world could be as much as 4% of sales—or even higher—but that can be very misleading. What conventional accounting systems don't generally capture is the cost of engineering computing, telecommunications, the computing on the shop floor—the cell controllers, the CNC machines, and the process controllers.

There is ample evidence that the total cost of spending on information systems in a typical company may represent 30% to 40% of its capital spending.

"Nor do conventional accounting systems realistically capture the cost impact of PCs as they proliferate throughout a corporation. There is ample evidence that the total cost of spending on information systems in a typical company may represent 30% to 40% of its capital spending. While most companies might be surprised to make that discovery, they might be even more surprised to learn that in their catch-up mode, they're not spending enough."

John Teresko is a writer and editor for Industry Week *Magazine.*

MIS + TQM = QIS

Richard B. Keith, Jr.

Like the other two articles in this section, Keith's article points out the important role of information in implementing quality management and goes on to explain how one company revamped its management information systems to create "quality information systems."

"Computer integration cannot be a world-class goal. Anything a computer does is in the same class as what a hammer does."[1]

"Despite years of impressive technological improvements and investment, there is not yet any evidence that information technology is improving productivity or other measures of business performance on a large scale."[2]

These quotes advocate a business revolution that could threaten the huge investments of corporate information technology departments. Quality initiatives, such as total quality management (TQM), stress a new set of values for today's management, chief among them being an emphasis on customer satisfaction through quality and rapid, continuous improvement.

The last item—rapid, continuous improvement—is getting today's management information services (MIS) departments in trouble. How can MIS be expected to spec, design, code, test, document, deliver, train, troubleshoot, and enhance when users keep changing their minds about how they want to transact their business? In fact, a computer system is the last thing TQM-inspired users want to worry about. The Japanese figured out a way to run huge production plants with little colored cards.[3] Who needs a computer at 20,000 times to 100,000 times the cost of little colored cards?

The following details the Lithonia Lighting Company's response when its MIS department was faced with this dilemma and its efforts to integrate the activities of MIS with the company's quality initiatives.

Integrating MIS with TQM

Lithonia, located in Conyers, GA, is a lighting product manufacturer. Its fiscal year 1992 sales were near $700 million, and the company employs about 4,500 people. In the late 1980s, senior management implemented TQM in its manufacturing and distribution facilities. By 1990, it became apparent that, while significant gains were being made in product quality, supplier development,

Reprinted with permission from *Quality Progress,* April 1994. Copyright © 1994 ASQC, Milwaukee, WI. All rights reserved.

and cost reduction, there were no substantial gains made in the office environment. Specifically, the general business processes of the company were being maintained in status quo while all of the TQM focus was on the plant floor. Management realized that for MIS to remain a strategic component of the business, it must play a key role in the company's TQM movement. MIS must be combined with TQM to create a quality information system (QIS). The success of combining MIS with TQM, management reasoned, would be a new understanding of system and service.

Management realized that for MIS to remain a strategic component of the business, it must play a key role in the company's TQM movement.

To most data processors, a system is a series of computerized steps that accept an input, perform an action, and produce an output. The computer system, however, is only a component of the real business system. Data processors tend to focus on user-defined computer inputs, processes, and outputs; the business that surrounds them is often of little consequence. To create a QIS, the data processors' scope must be expanded to include the entire business process. To break the paradigm of data processing, one must first examine those who hold the paradigm dear.

The careers of data processors have been built on their ability to make a computer process perform a specific task that is a piece of a larger process in which they might or might not be involved. In the QIS world, data processors must be retrained to analyze or facilitate the analysis of the larger process.

Additionally, the QIS analyst must assist in the development of improved processes that might have nothing to do with a computer system and could result in the elimination of a computer system. The traditional professional data processor must be transformed into a QIS specialist who functions as a businessperson first and a computer expert second.

QIS requires the systems department to develop, implement, and champion a methodology that looks at the business goals and develops activities that might or might not include a computer system to meet those goals. Service should be the MIS department's deliverable product. This service should include setting goals, facilitating and participating in process improvement, and implementing computer systems.

MIS Takes Over Reengineering

The MIS department took over the company's business reengineering activities. A business engineering department was formed as a sister group to the applications development, training, and computer services departments within MIS. This department contained senior business analysts from technical and nontechnical backgrounds and applications development experts.

The business engineering department began with three objectives:

1. *Everyone must understand the TQM/QIS initiative.* TQM-oriented companies stress organizational and process alignment to serve their customers with high-quality products and services. If MIS is to have effective TQM participation, anyone who deals with an internal or external customer must understand TQM. Although MIS typically does not communicate with external customers, it must apply the same philosophies

to its service as those who do. This requires the same level of understanding of TQM philosophies as other company departments have. Additionally, MIS must tell its customers that it wants to become involved with TQM initiatives and be included in TQM discussions and meetings.

2. *MIS is uniquely suited to facilitate process improvement efforts.* When it comes to analyzing existing processes, MIS has a clear edge over other departments due to the time it spends detailing computer flowcharts and processes. This same approach works as well for a noncomputerized process. A formal methodology was developed that considers the company's approach to TQM, the existing corporate culture and climate, and the resources required to hold an effective process-improvement session.

   Keki R. Bhote's book, *Next Operation as Customers,* suggests 10 steps to consider when planning process improvement[4]:

   1. Establish an improvement team.
   2. Define the missions and objectives of the team.
   3. Identify outputs and major customers of the service provided.
   4. Make a flowchart of the entire macro process.
   5. Analyze the chart for highest-priority opportunities.
   6. Identify the customers of those steps and their requirements.
   7. Develop measurements of those requirements.
   8. Measure conformance.
   9. Continuously improve the performance of the process chosen.
   10. Return to Step 5.

3. *The goals of the company must be the goals of MIS.* If the daily tasks of MIS are not geared to achieving the company's goals, the rest of the company might perceive MIS as uncommitted or uncooperative. MIS management and staff should understand the financial and operational goals of the company and support efforts to achieve them. These efforts include process-improvement facilitation, which results in information technology projects. It also includes developing process measurements, providing data analysis tools that allow users access to key performance information, and, most important, consistent, high-quality customer service to organizations and individuals whose job is to communicate with external customers.

Department Finds Success

The business engineering department found success in its first business reengineering activity. One of the company's smaller divisions, RELOC Wiring Systems, devoted most of its marketing personnel to processing business; thus, there was little time left to prospect for new business. If this trend continued, the outlook for generating future business volume would be bleak. The consensus within the division, however, was that the cumbersome process was the best it could be and that the solution was to add more people. But the recession in the commercial building industry prevented the company from continuing at its current head count, much less hiring additional workers.

At the direction of executive management, and in conjunction with division management, the business engineering department analyzed the division's existing processes, including developing and monitoring key performance measurements. A team of RELOC management and staff from all functional areas of marketing was formed.

Using methodology adapted from Bhote's book and Geary A. Rummler's and Alan P. Brache's book, *Improving Performance*,[5] the team decided on a goal: to optimize the division's estimating and quotations processes to increase sales and best meet external and internal customers' needs. It soon became apparent, however, that to be effective, the scope of the objective needed to be expanded to include order entry and processing. Flowcharts were developed to depict the customer/server relationships and the corresponding processes currently being performed.

These flowcharts were based on performance metrics and standards that focused on key processes of providing price quotes to customers, developing installation drawings, and entering orders. For the next 11 weeks, the RELOC marketing staff time-stamped documents when they entered and exited various stages of the process. The documents were collected, the times graphed, and the results published for analysis. The team and the division's management were shocked to see that the numbers indicated that the process bottlenecks were in areas thought to be relatively efficient and that the process originally thought to be the primary culprit was the one area that consistently came closest to the set standard. The numbers surprised the group so much that the measurements were kept for an additional eight weeks to verify the findings.

The team and the division's management were shocked to see that the numbers indicated that the process bottlenecks were in areas thought to be relatively efficient.

The division's performance metrics clearly indicated poor performance in the order-development area. None of the standards set by the team were met once an order was received. The first indicator of a problem was in the development of the installation drawings. Only 85% of the drawings were complete by the specified date, and just 75% were finished within five days. Since the rest of the order development and entry processes had to wait for this phase to be completed, any delay in developing a drawing could bring order entry to a halt. The manual processes performed after the drawing was complete were equally substandard. Cumulative averages for these processes ranged from 30% to 50% below the level of satisfactory performance.

One of the problems within the marketing department was what theorists call functional silos: Each organizational entity had its own set of responsibilities (quotations people quote, estimators estimate, and so on). This problem was mainly in the area of responsibility to the customer. No one in the division was responsible for a job's quality in quotations or order development. Oftentimes, it was required that management temporarily take over a job to deal with problems that could not be resolved, given the authority level of nonmanagement individuals.

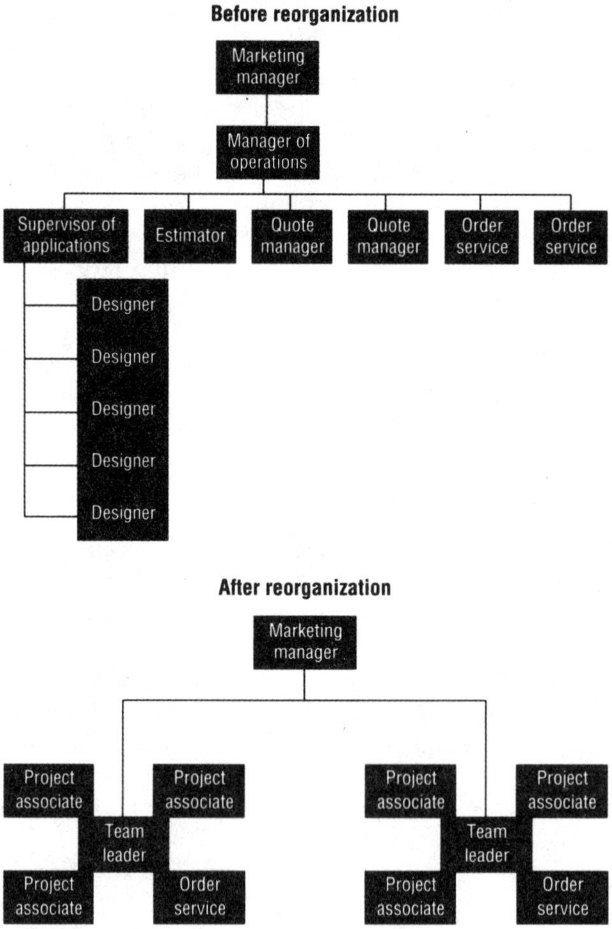

Figure 1. **RELOC marketing before and after reorganization.**

Division Is Reorganized

The division and the business engineering department developed a number of key moves that resulted in significant improvements in customer service, accuracy, efficiency, and quality. As shown in Figure 1, the division was reorganized from a more traditional organization to one with a new alignment of responsibilities.

The quotations, estimating, and drafting positions were reorganized into a number of job cells similar to manufacturing cells and were assigned geographical territories and/or customers. Each cell was charged with total responsibility for any job within its assigned area from start to finish. Division management agreed to empower the cell with authority levels sufficient to handle 90% or more of the issues that might arise. Each cell was measured and held responsible as a team for errors, quality problems, and substandard performance. Order-service representatives were also added to the cell. The representatives provided continuity for the entire job and essentially closed the organizational loop.

Once the cells were properly trained and empowered, there was little need to have a supervisory position between the cell and the marketing manager. The elimination of this position, which was identified as a procedural bottleneck, resulted in less organizational stratification and more information flow between the company and the customer.

Long-term considerations for procedural improvement were focused in two areas:

1. *Education of the customer.* This education enabled customers to know what they needed, and it allowed the agent or contractor to develop simpler installations, requiring less communication with the factory and reducing the overall cycle time in ordering a product.
2. *Automation of the remaining streamlined process.* New systems were developed and installed that read the computer drawing generated for installation guidelines and automatically created a manufacturing order on the company's mainframe. This system eliminated hours of manual order entry and nearly 100% of the product nomenclature conversion errors. From a customer perspective, the order-service representative became more responsive to status inquiries and change requests.

One of the most important aspects of this reengineering effort was the buy-in to the changes by division management and staff. Their support and commitment were the keys in implementing the new organization and procedures within the company. Six months after the changes were implemented, the prime objectives were being met in all categories.

Six months after the changes were implemented, the prime objectives were being met in all categories.

MIS Can Be a Leader in Quality Initiatives

Through direct and continuous participation, the MIS department can become a leader in the TQM movement. Meeting QIS objectives can result in a new synergy between customers and systems personnel. By working together toward common goals and taking advantage of the systems group's resources and services, people can achieve higher productivity levels and improved product and service quality. This, in turn, enhances competitive advantage and positively influences the bottom line. The combination of QIS and an improved bottom line creates a win-win situation for everyone.

References

1. Richard Schonberger, *Building a Chain of Customers* (New York, NY: The Free Press, 1990).

2. Gary Loveman quoted by Tom Peters, *Liberation Management* (New York, NY: Alfred A. Knopf, 1992).

3. Yasuhiro Monden, *The Toyota Production System* (Norcross, GA: Industrial Engineering and Management Press, 1993).

4. Keki R. Bhote, *Next Operation as Customer* (New York, NY: AMA Membership Publishing Division of the American Management Association, 1991).

5. Geary A. Rummler and Alan P. Brache, *Improving Performance, How to Manage the White Space on the Organization Chart* (San Francisco, CA: Jossey-Bass Publishers, 1991).

Richard B. Keith Jr. is the manager of business engineering at Lithonia Lighting Co. in Conyers, GA.

Is Data Scatter Subverting Your Strategy?

John H. Lingle and William A. Schiemann

Lots of organizations have lots of information available from many sources to let them know how well they are performing. The problem is the poor coordination of this data and its frequently nebulous connection with the organization's purpose. This article explores this problem and suggests tactics for creating systems and processes that overcome it.

When viewed as data processing systems, most organizations are Balkanized environments. Bits and pieces of data are scattered in the often conflicting jurisdictions of MIS, marketing, finance, human resources, sales and operations. Organizations have a 21st century computing capacity and a 1960's approach to transforming data into useful information. The results all too frequently turn into "data scatter."

Viewed from the perspective of data scatter, the problems of the multi-billion-dollar division of a Fortune 100 chemical company become all to clear. The quality assessment process seemed to be moving along smoothly. The top team conducted a Baldrige assessment, collected customer data, set the appropriate strategy, gave pep talks and festooned walls with rah-rah posters, and reengineered crucial production processes. The team might have merited the corporate equivalent of a gold star. Instead, 11 months into the program, half thc scnior tcam—including the division president—was shown the door.

In the end, executives on the quality-assessment team did a terrific job making sure the right data was collected—reams of it. But the data was never integrated, never really analyzed for strategic implications, and never used to set division priorities.

While one team was busy completing a series of Baldrige evaluations, another initiated an employee survey, and a third decided to undertake a number of reengineering studies. The teams did not interact with one another, and there was no plan to integrate the data from each source. Had they done so, the top team would have gained a much-needed coherent picture of the "as is," and a handle on how the entire plan was progressing.

Without this, members of the top team latched on to their own favorite study, drew their own conclusions, and then used the data as ammunition to

Reprinted by permission of publisher from *Management Review*, May 1994. Copyright © 1994, American Management Association, New York. All rights reserved.

advance a personal position or refute someone else's. This top team became a house divided.

Data scatter results from the poor job organizations do in managing and transforming data into the integrated information needed to drive success.

Data scatter results from the poor job organizations do in managing and transforming data into the integrated information needed to drive success. If information and knowledge have replaced raw materials and physical labor as the key assets for determining competitive advantage, then solving the data scatter problem is an urgent task for top management.

Data scatter may not always be as visible as the squabbling executives at the chemical company. Sometimes the problem remains hidden, a kind of organizational iceberg lying in wait. Here are three symptoms that should alert you to the potential for trouble ahead.

Symptom 1: Strategy Silos

Call it "strategy silos" or "vertical vision." You sense it when you probe just below the surface of the top team's understanding of the overall strategy. The CEO of a major publishing conglomerate was confronted with stalled strategy implementation efforts at his company. Interviews with the 13 members of the top team showed the reason: Six different strategies were driving the business.

Each executive defined the future based on separate marketing figures, his or her own competitive analysis, and a different way of segmenting principal product and market categories. Strategy was created in the self-image of functional and operational executives, each based on different subsets of data. Not surprisingly, the corporate strategy went nowhere.

The early days of telephone deregulation provide a classic example of strategy silos. The strategies of many of the regional telephone companies were developed on the basis of solid marketplace data but tended to overlook data about existing organizational capability. Data on customer requirements and operations and human resources capabilities was often divided into separate functional fiefdoms. The result: gutsy new marketing initiatives faltered because they were built on insufficient data about organizational culture and capabilities.

Is your organization compromising its overall strategy by compressing its thinking and its data gathering into silos? These five questions should provide an answer:

- If you were to ask each executive to describe briefly the overall business strategy, together with the most crucial data to support it, how similar would the responses be?
- Does the business plan from each function use a common database to assess the cross-impact of each of the other functions on what it plans to accomplish?
- How much "talk time" do the major business units and functions such as marketing, finance, operations and human resources spend interacting with one another during the planning process?

- If you were to ask executives to identify the three or four most important organizational requirements for successfully implementing their strategy—such as decentralized decision making, sufficient cash flow, culture change, rapid new product introduction—would their responses be similar?
- Do the heads of each function clearly know what data and criteria will be used to measure the strategic success of each of the other functions?

Too many negative answers suggest low levels of data-sharing and a high probability that your organization is stuck in strategy silos.

Symptom 2: Data Wars

If knowledge is power, then data is one of the most important weapons in a manager's arsenal. Weapons pointed at colleagues, however, quickly start family feuds.

In a large healthcare company, three-quarters of one board meeting revolved around minute questions on the source, validity and reliability of data on a marketing problem that was under discussion. One executive kept shoring up his position by referring to data other board members hadn't seen. Another offered several microanalyses that would have reduced the usefulness of the data to near zero. Another kept questioning every conclusion offered. No one was willing to integrate the discussion to tame the beast.

In a large healthcare company, three-quarters of one board meeting revolved around minute questions on the source, validity and reliability of data.

Data wars corrupt data as executives seek to defend their positions. The data hoarding that inevitably accompanies data wars deprives decision makers of vital information. And, when data wars begin, costs typically skyrocket as each function insists on collecting its own information.

To determine whether or not healthy data verification is slipping into the initial salvos of a data war, ask yourself these four questions:

- In board meetings, is more time spent discussing key strategic and operational implications than spent arguing about the validity of minutiae?
- Do function heads share data with other functions or do they "spring" data on one another at crucial decision points?
- Does each function use the same supplier to collect and analyze similar types of data? If not, do their separate suppliers work together to integrate information?
- Do functions involve one another in the planning of major data collection initiatives or wait until the results are in before disclosing the project?

Data wars can escalate into one of the most destructive forces within an organization and can result in a third symptom, "decision jerk."

Symptom 3: Decision Jerk

When data is well-integrated, it forms a solid basis for setting priorities, making decisions and planning. There is no abstract calculus you can use to determine whether or not you have sufficient data or whether it is properly integrated. However, two useful questions that test data sufficiency in decision making are: Have we taken into account information about objectives and alternatives from all relevant functions? What new information would cause us to change this decision?

Decision jerk can occur when the "chunks" of data used to make decisions are too small, resulting in multiple misguided efforts.

Decision jerk occurs when management zigs and zags with each piece of data, continually shifting priorities or piling on new initiatives. This can occur when the "chunks" of data used to make decisions are too small, resulting in multiple misguided efforts.

A Fortune 50 company in the retail industry simply could not establish a clear list of priorities. The corporate planning process would begin each March with a preliminary financial plan. Marketing data and customer information arrived semi-annually in June and December. Data from the employee survey typically became available in the fall. The companywide business plan was due each January. Planning reviews and assessment efforts invariably generated a new set of initiatives that were overlaid on whatever else had been started based on the last set of data. In many cases, individual initiatives conflicted in their goals, timing and day-to-day demands on managers. Everyone complained about unmet objectives, a lack of clear priorities and the number of times today's decision got reversed by tomorrow's "action of the day."

Decision jerk causes loss of management credibility. "Here we go again" cynicism sets in. Managers down the line become gun-shy about committing to a decision they know may be quickly reversed or abandoned. Consistency, in turn, requires rational decisions based on well-integrated data sources.

To test for decision jerk, ask these four questions:

- Do decisions tend to be made on the basis of a balance of information sources that are reviewed before each strategic or major operational decision?
- Is there a balanced set of measures used to plot the success of each major initiative undertaken at the company?
- If you asked each employee what this year's top three priorities are and how success in these initiatives is being measured, would the answers be similar? Would each employee know his or her role in achieving each priority?
- When you look back at the end of the year, what percent of the initiatives outlined in the original year's plan get implemented successfully? Do rewards follow accomplishment?

Building Critical Success Gauges

The speed at which information technology is improving suggests that the data scatter challenge is growing, not subsiding. Given the information revolution, it is easy for organizations to get buried in a data blitz and fall into the data scatter trap. So, what's the solution? The key word is *focus.*

Recently, managers in the information systems department at a major financial institution were involved in a quality-improvement initiative.

FIVE MEASURES OF SUCCESS

You get what you measure. Measure the wrong thing and you get the wrong behaviors. Stories of measuring the wrong thing are legion: One package delivery company discovered its drivers circling the block at the end of the day trying to hit gas consumption targets on the nose. These five measurement principles help ensure success in combatting data scatter.

1. *Strategically anchor gauges.* One way to think about gauges of critical success is to assume they are the only gauges a company has available. In such a situation, it is paramount that the dozen or so gauges be solidly anchored in the business strategy. One way to test if this is the case is to see whether someone can determine the strategy by examining only the gauges. To the degree this can be done, the gauges capture the essence of the strategy.

2. *Reflect the outcomes—not the activities.* The more limited the number of gauges, the more important it is that they reflect strategic outcome, not activities. If the available data is limited, the most crucial information is whether the race is being won, not how fast a runner's legs are moving.

3. *Create a counterbalance.* Most gauges have both a light and a dark side. Improvements in one area can result in degradation in others. For example, as the airlines have repeatedly demonstrated, increased revenue can be realized at the cost of shrinking margins; increased employee productivity can be achieved at the price of employee burnout. If a company relies only on a limited set of gauges, these must be counterbalanced to warn when success in one area is being achieved through failure in another.

4. *Ensure responsiveness to change.* One of the most difficult challenges in controlling spacecraft is the lag in communication time—each instrument reading reflects action that occurred in the past. The longer the lag, the more difficult it is to react in time to prevent disaster. The best gauges provide warnings when something is first beginning to go wrong, as opposed to confirming a situation that has taken on crisis proportions.

5. *Exhibit strong signal-to-noise characteristics.* In sound and radio technology, there is always a desire to maximize the "signal"—the true message being communicated—while minimizing undesirable background static that interferes with the message. The same requirements hold true in managing organizations. True changes must be captured effectively in the measurement system, while minimizing extraneous information that is either transitory or unrepresentative of the underlying process.

These managers were tracking 142 separate department performance measures, but no two managers could agree on which half-dozen measures were strategically most important. Such data proliferation would have been impossible 15 years ago. Given the speed of innovation in information technology, this department may well be able to easily track 500 measures in the not too distant future.

But would the department's managers be wise to do so? Probably not. The winning organizations in the rapidly changing '90s will be those that can most effectively focus efforts to bring about value-added change in the quickest manner possible, not the ones that can track the most measures. This means limiting the number of measures an organization deploys. With fewer crucial numbers to track, it is easier to ensure that everyone understands the numbers, together with their role in improving them.

The winning organizations in the rapidly changing '90s will be those that can most effectively focus efforts to bring about value-added change in the quickest manner possible.

Several measurement approaches to help organizations improve their focus have received recent attention. Our research supports an approach that employs a focused set of success indicators. There are six areas to be of vital importance to long term, successful strategy implementation:

- **Market:** How are we doing in meeting customer or marketplace expectations?
- **People:** How well are we deploying our human resources, including employees, partners and suppliers?
- **Finance:** How are we doing in meeting investor expectations?
- **Operations:** How efficiently are we operating the enterprise?
- **Adaptability:** How effectively are we adapting to changing requirements both within and outside the organization?
- **Environment:** How well are we dealing with environmental or regulatory forces that define our playing field?

These strategic performance areas are stakes in the ground that measure results within the boundaries of a company's strategy. Sub-par performance at any point represents a threat to long-term profitability and survival.

Within each of these six areas, an organization must establish three or four gauges that best define strategic imperatives. These gauges will differ from organization to organization, depending on strategic intent.

Because development of the gauges requires the top executives to translate the division's strategy into measurable objectives, the senior team will need to put to rest differences in beliefs about the best way to make the business grow. This can be done by "cascading" the gauges through the division, having each manager discuss with his or her employees their role in helping to improve performance on the strategic measures.

To maintain focus, it is important that an organization track only a limited number of gauges. Begin by looking at your organization's strategy and asking what three or four gauges must be in place in each of the strategic performance areas.

When these measures are updated regularly and accepted by the management team, they accomplish several things:

- Force the management team to clarify the organizational strategy to a level of specificity at which its implementation can be measured and tracked.
- Help reduce information overload by bringing together into a single report crucial elements of an organization's strategic agenda.
- Help managers understand interrelationships in performance by illustrating how improvements in one area can have an impact on other areas.
- Improve communication by providing a common language and reliable information about current organizational strengths and weaknesses.
- Focus an organization's attention toward where it is going, rather than backwards toward where it has been.

Today's organizations are vast storehouses of information. To the extent they can avoid data scatter, they will be able to tap into that storehouse, convert data on information and convert information to new knowledge for serving customers in a more innovative way than their competitors.

John H. Lingle is a principal consultant, and William A. Schiemann is president, of Wm. Schiemann & Associates Inc., a Somerville, N.J., management consulting firm specializing in strategic assessment and measurement-driven organizational change.

Functional Processes

SALES AND MARKETING

Integrating a Baldrige Approach into a Sales District's Management System

James W. Cortada

This article by co-editor James Cortada explains how to use the Baldrige Award criteria as standards for measuring, evaluating, and improving the performance of sales people. These criteria provide concrete direction for developing a sales organization that is more responsive to the needs of customers and the company.

There is a profound change underway in the conduct of business. Much of that change involves the concept of total quality management (TQM) or simply "quality." Its gurus, Deming, Juran, and others, are now virtual celebrities, and it is sweeping through businesses of more than fifty employees. A number of awards are being created to recognize success in the implementation of this new management approach. They are being offered by states, U.S. government agencies, and industry associations. Some individual companies are even recognizing suppliers with quality awards. The most important

Reprinted with permission of John Wiley & Sons, Inc., from *National Productivity Review*, Spring 1994. Copyright © 1994 by John Wiley & Sons, Inc. All rights reserved.

award in the United States is the Malcolm Baldrige National Quality Award, which emphasizes achievement in seven major categories ranging from leadership to fact-based management, from quality assurance of goods and services to results. All have a strong bias in favor of satisfying customer requirements. Over the past several years the number of copies of the Baldrige criteria in circulation has been going up dramatically. This suggests strong interest in the model's potential for improving the effectiveness of a business. But can the Baldrige criteria be applied to a sales organization or are they only useful in manufacturing?

Baldrige Comes to Sales

Over the past half decade, implementation of quality as defined by the Baldrige criteria occurred largely in manufacturing and processing plants. Less was attempted in offices, services, or in sales organizations. But that is changing. Companies are benefiting from implementing statistical quality control, moving from reactive to preventive responses to issues, redesigning the ways they do business (reengineering in today's quality parlance), delegating more authority to employees lower in the organization and closer to customers (empowerment), and methodically identifying their customers' needs. Many firms are now applying TQM to all parts of their enterprises, including sales—perhaps the largest and most important part of the organization previously untouched by the new approach.

But why apply the Baldrige criteria to sales? In an important survey of twenty Baldrige applicants with high scores, a 1991 U.S. government study found that practitioners enjoyed average improvements of sales per employee of 8.6 percent each year, gained 13.7 percent market share, and increased customer satisfaction by 2.5 percent. The study reported that these achievements required coordinated actions on the part of manufacturing and sales together. Good products alone did not sell themselves. In a 1992 unpublished internal study by IBM, management found that sales organizations that embraced Baldrige criteria outperformed those that did not. The successful ones generally achieved 30-or-more-percent growth in sales, market share, and profitability over those that did not. Thus, for example, an IBM sales organization that expanded market by 2 percent and did not apply Baldrige principles essentially failed to gain an additional 1 percent growth in market share. The evidence was so dramatic across multiple continents that the corporation insisted that all sales organizations worldwide speed up their implementation of quality practices.

A 1991 U.S. government study found that practitioners enjoyed average improvements of sales per employee of 8.6 percent each year, gained 13.7 percent market share, and increased customer satisfaction by 2.5 percent.

Baldrige increasingly became the de facto quality model for many other sales organizations as well. Its applicability is evident in many large corporations that have already implemented Baldrige in sales, such as Xerox, Motorola, and Milliken. But empirical evidence of the extent of application in sales organizations for smaller companies—those with fewer than one hundred employees—is lacking. There is, however, some anecdotal evidence that small sales organizations also benefit from Baldrige approaches.

An important research issue remains: to what extent does the Baldrige approach apply to various sizes of sales organizations? How should these practices vary? It seems that the smaller the enterprise, the more naturally some Baldrige practices—such as more customer focus and faster decision making—occur, but also that some disciplines—such as statistical measurement of activities and processes—are not applied. A 1991 IBM sales district survey of one thousand mid-size manufacturing companies in Wisconsin showed that 33 percent of the CEOs considered TQM issues one of the top three facing them in the 1990s, and 63 percent were involved in TQM-related activities, but only a handful reported that these actions were in sales departments.

Once convinced that the Baldrige model represents a practical way to view the activities of a sales organization, the essential challenge for management is to marry the values and measures required of Baldrige to their own operations. No two firms ever do it the same way or in the same amount of time. But a process seems to be emerging that shows how to do it. It involves a combination of education, changes in measurements, and evolution in processes.

How does a sales executive implement quality practices using the Baldrige model? The strategy proposed here is to use the Baldrige assessment method to gauge the quality health of the enterprise, take the results and formulate measurements of current activities catalogued by the seven Baldrige criteria, then use the data to set the agenda for reforms of processes in the enterprise. By reviewing the questions asked in such an assessment and measuring how the organization is doing in these areas, managers can draw conclusions about strengths and weaknesses, and where effectiveness and efficiency can be improved.

Stages of Baldrige in Sales

The first step is to understand the various stages of application of the Baldrige criteria that sales organizations experience over time. That helps management determine what tasks have to be performed and suggests how.

The initial stage of quality implementation for sales organizations typically lasts one to three years, with eighteen months the average. It invariably involves the senior executive, usually a district sales manager, and sometimes a higher-level sales executive, committed to learning about—and teaching sales management about—Baldrige, quality, and process improvement. Awareness education involves understanding the principles involved, the need for the enterprise to change the way it does business, and a sampling of how it is done. It is not unusual, for example, to see one- and two-day seminars on total quality management and some experimentation with application of process improvement techniques.

Salespeople and their first- and second-line managers often initially think that Baldrige is a waste of time, and not applicable to their operations.

Salespeople and their first- and second-line managers often initially think that Baldrige is a waste of time, and not applicable to their operations. Therefore they typically resist such education. In more than a dozen instances in IBM sales organizations, this was a problem. Sales managers at Xerox say that in the beginning of their quality journey, similar problems existed. In a seminar on TQM for sales taught to some one hundred companies between 1991 and 1993, the overwhelming feedback was that sales had resisted exposure to TQM and to its implementation. An organization's quality champions are so frequently challenged that they often entertain doubts. But if they can survive and endure, they begin to get the interest of a few individuals and that grows over time. The resistance caused by lack of appreciation for the relevance of Baldrige accounts for the bulk of the time spent in this first stage.

As interest grows, the organization reaches the second stage, which involves additional training on process improvement, teams, and empowerment. Doses of statistical process control are also now typically applied. It is at this stage that elements of Baldrige that bear some relevance to sales come into play.

A practical and common step many take at this point is to do their initial Baldrige self-assessment. Treated typically as a one-time event, a sales organization conducts an assessment using either a corporate version of Baldrige or the actual Baldrige documentation. This task usually involves a group of managers sitting around a table answering questions from each section of the seven chapters of Baldrige criteria. Table 1 (page 516) lists the seven major Baldrige categories. It includes a few subheadings of some sales-oriented categories to illustrate the applicability of the chapters.

That exercise usually results in a poor score, often between 200 and 300 points out of a possible 1,000. In one case at IBM involving fourteen Baldrige assessments by sales organizations for the first time, all self-assessment scores were between 200 and 230 points. Informal conversations with dozens of sales executives in other corporations confirmed that their initial assessments were also under 300. As one sales vice president at a manufacturing company put it, the assessment was "a humbling experience."

In one case at IBM involving fourteen Baldrige assessments by sales organizations for the first time, all self-assessment scores were between 200 and 230 points.

The issues discussed in such an assessment that are acknowledged as directly relevant to the sales organization are

- To what extent do we understand what our customers want?
- How do we know how well we are performing our services?
- To what extent are we giving our employees the right skills or empowering them to do their jobs?
- How much leadership is the sales district manager providing?
- To what extent are our reps probing for customers' needs?
- Are reps following up their sales with personal visits?
- To what extent are our first-line field sales managers providing salespeople with individualized consideration? Do they limit their leadership to correcting subordinates when sales figures are down?
- To what extent are sales personnel helping to improve the overall efficiency and effectiveness of their sales organization?

An enormous number of questions arise at this stage. Asking the questions is the single most important event that occurs, because it increases

Table 1. **Examination Categories with Sales and Marketing Examples**

1. Leadership Management leadership on vision and strategy Pursuit of excellence and service Involvement in community/corporate activities	95
2. Information and Analysis Market segmentation analysis Opportunity identification process Competitive analysis	75
3. Strategic Quality Planning Sales strategy planning process Sales training plans Employee sales performance planning	60
4. Human Resource Development and Management Skills development process Personnel performance plans Salespersons compensation/bonus/recognition Employee morale and well-being	150
5. Management of Process Quality Introduction of sales programs Sales delivery and support processes Customer-fulfillment processes Business partner quality Quality of activities assessment process	140
6. Quality and Operational Results Sales and service results Customer delivery and support processes Sales (revenue) and profit results	180
7. Customer Focus and Satisfaction Customer expectation: current and future Sales relations with customers processes How commitments to customers are made Customer satisfaction survey process Customer satisfaction results with sales/products Comparisons of customer satisfaction	300
Total Points	1,000

awareness of issues that might not have been addressed in the past. At this point managers realize that they are doing some things well by accident, but also that much can be improved.

The next phase typically involves a commitment to change. Education of employees continues, and managers start paying for more than revenue. They change performance and compensation plans by pay bonuses for quality improvements, for levels of customer satisfaction as measured by surveys, and for the ability and willingness of people to become team players. Quotas often are changed, with part of a salesperson's compensation coming from how the entire sales district performs, not just one's office or territory. It is at this stage that customer satisfaction surveys begin to proliferate and people are measured on results. Initial process reengineering occurs. It is often ineffective but improves such areas as telephone responsiveness, billing accuracy, proposal generation, and quality of sales personnel's knowledge of products. A recent case study on IBM's operations in Wisconsin showed that management worked carefully over many months to craft new terms and conditions for the sales compensation plan along the lines described above and also paid careful attention to the education program needed to facilitate the transformation.

Quotas often are changed, with part of a salesperson's compensation coming from how the entire sales district performs, not just one's office or territory.

The major personnel issue at this point, for which we do not yet have good answers, is the role of the individual in the new world of quality. If salespeople have spent years selling products with an emphasis on transactions and now are also required to develop long-term relationships to sell more than products (for example, services), what do they do?

If measured the old way (just on products sold) and organized with the same kind and size territory as before, calling on the same people as before, nothing changes. Management asks for new behavior and does not get it. Tension and frustrations grow between salespeople and their managers. First-line managers, being held accountable for sales volumes but also being told to change their behavior and take on new responsibilities (for example, improving procedures, empowering, and delegating to employees their authority), are also frustrated.

Employee morale drops, sales can too, and doubts about the quality movement become very evident. Anecdotal evidence and interviews with sales managers after the fact suggest that if there is a lesson here, it is that management needs to define as early as possible the new roles and how these functions will be measured. The first step they usually take is to measure more activities than ever before. The IBM experience indicated that this was a good step. Other companies have made similar reports.

Introduction to "Top Sheet" Measurements

At this stage (usually in year two or three) management wants to move toward a "top sheet" set of measurements on the health of the enterprise that reflect many of the values and concerns of the Baldrige model. Table 2 is an example of a "top sheet" measurement package. The best are simple and understandable by all employees. This approach is lifted directly out of the experience of many manufacturing organizations that post a set of indicators of success on bulletin boards and within departments. It dates back to practices at the turn of the century and, thus, has a long history of being an effective vehicle for communicating with employees and reminding them of what is important.

Using indicators beyond revenue or profit to measure business health represents a watershed cultural change for most organizations.

Using indicators beyond revenue or profit to measure business health represents a watershed cultural change for most organizations. It leads to a variety of other changes in the way the enterprise operates. Common examples include

Table 2. **"Top Sheet" Measurements**

CUSTOMER SATISFACTION	
—Quality of sales representative	88% satisfied
—Accurate invoices	78% satisfied
EMPLOYEE MORALE	
—Commissions/compensation	64% satisfied
—Recognition	40% YTD participation
—Skills plan	90% plan in place
—Overall satisfaction	84% satisfaction index
QUALITY	
—Baldrige assessment	309 points
—Sales rep buy-in	73%
—Employee participation	23% submitted suggestions
FINANCIAL CONTRIBUTION	
—Sales revenue quota	95% YTD
—Revenue growth	8% year-to-year
—Market share	16% share index
—Profitability	28% YTD pre-tax

- Paying sales personnel bonuses for improving personal skills and customer satisfaction
- Putting sales personnel on a district-wide quota, not just their own, paying commission on both (for example, 50/50)
- Writing requirements to participate in process improvement into their performance plans and holding them accountable for this activity
- Statistically measuring all major sales processes and then making decisions on improvements based on that data
- Developing processes to
  —improve skills
  —reduce sales cycles
  —enhance telephone responsiveness
  —perform regularly scheduled customer satisfaction surveys
  —implement market segmentation studies
  —perform service-level audits
  —conduct tactical and strategic planning linked to manufacturing plants
  —conduct customer-sales-manufacturing requirements reviews

Picture a model of what the business does including all the key processes that underpin its activities. Figure 1 illustrates a model of a sales district's role. With such a model, one can look at all processes, test their effectiveness and robustness against the Baldrige framework, and grade them on an ongoing basis. Often, however, such a model is not defined because the sales organization lacks confidence to identify all its activities from the perspective of a

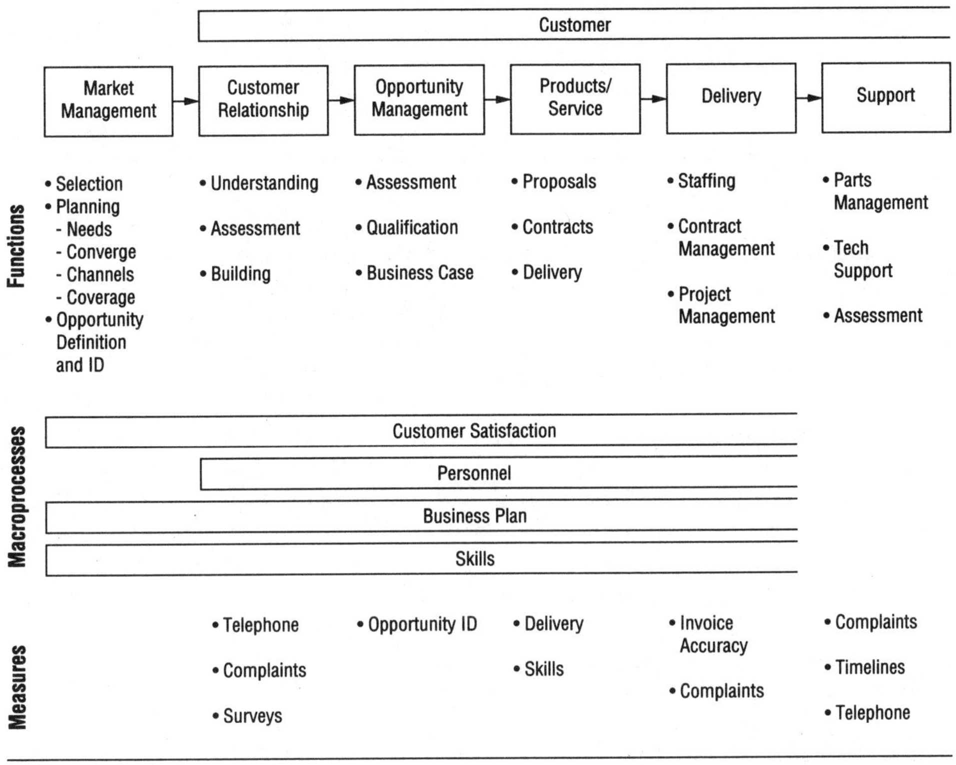

Figure 1.

process map. But such maps enormously enhance the speed with which processes are identified and prioritized for improvement. Therefore, at this stage sales personnel and their management should attempt to draw a process map of the organization, prioritize what needs fixing or replacement, and apply process improvement practices. The map can be modified—and usually is—as the enterprise gains a collective understanding of what it really does and what is most important.

Institutionalizing Baldrige Measurements

By this stage—usually in year three—the enterprise is heavily involved in process reengineering and complaints about uncoordinated activities resound. Quality councils exist in sales offices or in the sales district, giving feedback to management, possibly driving quality education efforts, and providing leadership for much process reengineering. Management quickly realizes the need for greater coordination of work. This is particularly urgent if, as occurs in many enterprises, management has been dismantling levels of supervision and bureaucracy, thereby increasing spans of control, lessening direct supervision, and increasing delegation and empowerment of employees. Who is responsible for booking business? For running the place? These questions are

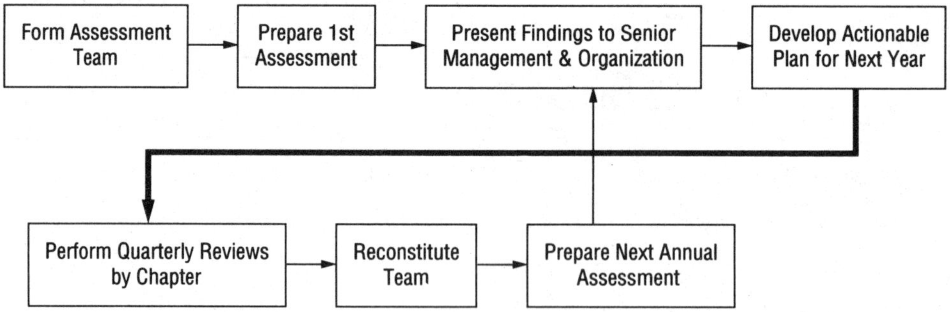

Figure 2. **Baldrige assessment process.**

always asked, especially when management begins to note changes that not everyone fully understands.

Sales personnel experience extraordinary pressures at this time. Their roles have been changing from transaction-focused to relationship-based. Their sales plans and compensation systems have undergone more change recently than ever before. Their managers typically do a poor job of communicating what is going on (for they are experiencing the same kinds of turmoil). Both managers and salespeople are confused about career development as well.

On the other hand, some time-honored inefficiencies are being fixed. These typically are in the areas of time reporting paperwork, pricing, and proposal writing. Investing in such technological aids as laptop computers and cellular telephones becomes easier to justify, because they improve speed of operations and responsiveness to customers. Educational programs extend beyond product knowledge to personal development, for example, strategic planning, process improvement techniques, and communications and interpersonal relations.

Investing in such technological aids as laptop computers and cellular telephones becomes easier to justify, because they improve speed of operations and responsiveness to customers.

To move through this stage managers can fall back on what their manufacturing counterparts have been doing for a number of years: turning their annual Baldrige self-assessment into a process of its own. Once an organization has conducted an initial self-assessment—and, if done properly, it was a written one—a baseline exists. Figure 2 shows how the assessment exercise appears when it is an ongoing process.

Work can begin on identified problems. A year later a second assessment is performed to determine how much progress was made. It is not surprising to see improvements of only 50 to 100 points on a base of 200 to 250. That is because of the start-up time involved in making changes and because the Baldrige criteria value results more than good intentions.

Once the enterprise decides to use Baldrige as its management system, the pieces begin coming together. Problems identified in self-assessments help managers select processes for reengineering. Measures of individual and organizational performance move toward skill development, customer satisfaction, and process improvements.

From Baldrige Assessment to Management Process

To accomplish this transition, assign each of the seven Baldrige chapters to a different manager in the sales district for a minimum of one year. They, in turn, put together small teams to help with their assignment. The teams should include representatives from sales, administration, and other services. During that year managers must collect data on their subject and report regularly to the entire management team on progress and problems. They should also make recommendations to enhance the effectiveness of the sales organization from the perspective of their chapters, and then participate in the annual group self-assessment.

This approach allows a management team to look carefully at several issues. The skills that their sales personnel must have become better defined. What and how to compensate and reward to reinforce behavior that reflects the values espoused in the Baldrige criteria are better appreciated. One concern becomes how to draw salespeople into process improvements that are relevant to them. Management usually knows what processes are critical to the organization's success and often tied to its business strategy, such as the faster development of easier-to-use proposals.

At a senior staff meeting each month, the seven managers in charge of these assignments—"chapter owners"—report on progress; decisions are made about who should fix problems or improve current activities. It becomes clear that all key processes should have "owners." Different people must "own" billing, skills development, opportunity identification, communications, business tools, and so forth. In some enterprises, process owners do not have to be managers. In one instance, ownership of the process to improve sales plan terms and conditions went to a team led by a non-manager. Ultimately management still owned responsibility for determining how to pay salespeople, but they did not necessarily have to own the tasks associated with the improvement of the compensation plan. Process owners are pressured into improving their processes by the principles of good process reengineering and by the audits of their activities.

The seven chapter owners should collectively determine two things:

- What "top sheet" indicators will help the entire enterprise focus on things important to their chapters?
- What needs to be improved?

As their teams begin to function, the sales district manager can ask each to make specific recommendations that, if implemented, would result in numerically measured improvements in next year's self-assessment. For example, suppose the lack of a formal customer satisfaction survey in this year's assessment cost the enterprise the opportunity to score 50 points higher. A plan to develop and implement such a survey could lead to a higher grade in chapter seven. Actions taken as a result of survey data would be worth additional points, and so forth.

Together, chapter owners and senior managers can set a numeric goal for the next year's Baldrige assessment. For example, if this year's assessment

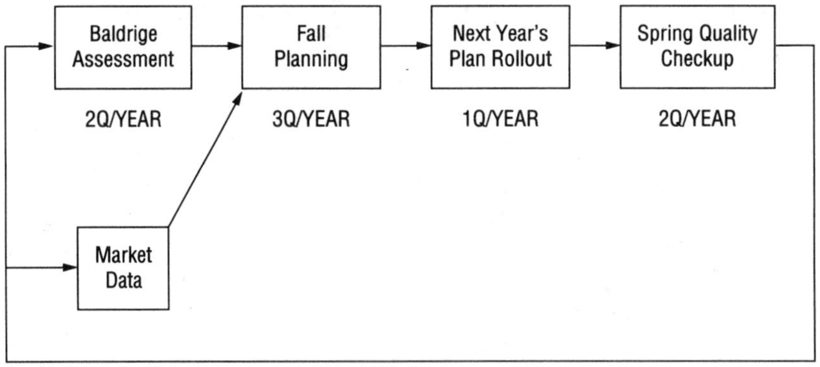

Figure 3. **Baldrige and strategic planning integration.**

yielded 350 points and action plans led managers to forecast a total additional yield of 75 points for next year, the goal would be 425 points. Then chapter owners track each plan element within the seven chapters all year, similar to tracking sales volumes. A year or two of such efforts will cause Baldrige values and measures to become part of the fabric of the business. Any nervousness about focusing so much attention on the Baldrige score goes away; in hindsight the score will be seen to have been a means to an end consistent with the culture of a sales organization understanding numeric targets better than simply worded quality goals. Ultimately the activities associated with each chapter can become part of the organization's planning process. Figure 3 shows the Baldrige assessment process integrated into a sales organization's planning cycle. Although few organizations have gone so far as to weave it into their planning efforts, those that have consider it compatible with the overall task of managing sales activities.

Some companies have taken the process one step further by insisting that all sales district offices perform annual self-assessments. At IBM, for example, division-size organizations must perform such assessments, and executives are partially appraised and compensated on the quality progress their organizations have achieved. Xerox does the same.

Certification of a Sales Organization

As all organizations perform self-assessments, audits should occur just as in accounting.

As all organizations perform self-assessments, audits should occur just as in accounting: Trained individuals who understand the Baldrige process should conduct them. When properly done, the feedback to management by the auditors is highly prized, forming a major component of the following year's improvement strategy.

The next step that can be taken is sales district certification. The concept borrows heavily from an old idea used by government licensing agencies and industry certification bodies. A sales district must have a minimum level of quality, measured in Baldrige terms, to be certified as functioning acceptably.

Those that pass their audits are funded and those that do not are either helped to improve or enjoy the company of a new district manager. Those that excel are invested with funds to reward quality achievers or to support additional skills training. When business volumes rise, more investments flow to those districts as a matter of good business sense.

Each year divisional or corporate management can set a quota for quality, along with the usual expense and revenue targets: a Baldrige point value that a sales district must achieve. The first year it might be 300 points, the second 400, the third 525, and so forth.

But how fast can a sales organization improve from stage to stage? We are so new at applying the Baldrige criteria that we do not yet understand what to expect, so problems of setting a Baldrige score quota that has no basis in reality may occur. Just as we know that sales quotas should be based on attainable stretch objectives, we must learn to do the same with the Baldrige criteria. Because the certification process and setting of quality quotas in a sales organization are in infancy, we are asking how much improvement one can expect annually. Does it take longer to go from 300 to 400 points than, say, from 500 to 600?

We know that the better the organization, the tougher it becomes to earn more points. Those who have won the Baldrige Award will argue that getting from 800 to 875 points is more difficult than going from 300 to 500. At 300 obvious things are not working well; at 500 all the basics are being handled properly. In fact, there are Baldrige winners whose performance has slid sharply after receiving the award.

Challenges and Difficulties, Opportunities and Strengths

Clearly this is not an easy process. At the heart of the effort is a profound change in the culture of most sales organizations. It is very difficult to implement TQM principles in sales organizations. The transition to a Baldrige-based measurement system bring with it a number of frustrations.

First, you can count on about a fourth of your sales force never to change; they may have to be shifted to other jobs or encouraged to leave the company. Independently minded, bred to operate on their own, and confident of what has worked in the past, they will resist. The same applies to sales managers. However, the implementation provides its own solution: Change the organizational structure in which they function so that they have no choice but to alter their behavior and practices, then reward new behavior through compensation, commissions, bonuses, awards, and promotions. Most sales forces respond more to direct stimulation—defining their jobs and linking compensation to specific objectives—than to altruism.

Second, W. Edwards Deming spoke often of the need for a "constancy of purpose" as one moves through a multiyear change. In sales, which is so used to personnel turnovers, his notion is difficult to implement. The lack of constancy of purpose is caused by this turnover, particularly at the sales district manager's level. From the first stage onward the problem exists. It is chronic and can only be dealt with by multiple layers of management. "Staying the course" is the single most important challenge facing a sales organization.

All sales organizations profoundly underestimate the effort required to implement a Baldrige view of the business.

Third, all sales organizations profoundly underestimate the effort required to implement a Baldrige view of the business. All processes have to be catalogued and changed; a mindset that says nothing worth doing goes without measurements has to be implemented; all decisions have to based on hard facts; skills must be continuously improved; personnel practices must lead to a learning environment in which mistakes are allowed if they are instructive; responsible risk taking must be encouraged; and salespeople must be encouraged to work as teams, not as individuals. That change is very hard for most U.S. sales personnel. Beyond people not liking change, it is a struggle to confidently identify what needs to be changed. Overall, sales is in its infancy in learning to apply TQM, let alone use Baldrige criteria effectively.

There are some positive factors at work, however. First, Baldrige values support customers and reflect their wants. That concept has long been endorsed by salespeople who often argue that their management has not always subscribed to the same values. So success must be linked directly to improving relationships between the enterprise and its customers. The focus for salespeople and headquarter staffs alike should be on improving skills that support that strategy.

Second, sales personnel will alter their behavior and their results most easily when compensation plans are changed. Also, modifications in behavior are most likely to occur when sales personnel help define what those changes need to be.

Third, because recognition is a primary motivator among salespeople, appropriately changed attitudes and behavior should be rewarded with awards, publicity, and other forms of recognition.

Finally, sales organizations like a good contest with winners. Baldrige is an award that a company can aspire to. Management can create internal Baldrige-like awards that sales offices, districts, and divisions can aspire to win. This is an effective strategy applied by many American corporations.

The Baldrige model has only recently become a viable assessment and measurement system for sales. There is little empirical evidence describing its dynamics. But some lessons are being learned. The customer focus required by the Baldrige process is validating the pioneering work done by A. Parasuraman, Leonard L. Berry, and Valarie A. Zeithaml on customer requirements. It forces the linking of activities across the company as described by Richard J. Schonberger and Christian Gronroos. But many questions remain unanswered and will require additional work over the next several years:

- How do you convince first- and second-line managers of the benefits of the kinds of changes that the Baldrige model requires?
- What measurements should be altered and in what order to speed up change across the entire sales enterprise?
- How do manufacturing companies change from their "native" culture to one focused more on service?

- In what order should processes be changed in a sales organization?
- What is the rate of change that sales organizations experience?

Evidence about the extent of improvements at the process level remains anecdotal. Thus, we cannot yet say with confidence that if one were to implement a particular process it would have a greater or lesser effect on profits, revenue, or a Baldrige assessment than some other process. Anecdotal data would suggest that the Baldrige approach is applicable in all sizes of organizations; but empirical research has yet to validate that observation.

Nevertheless, sales organizations are weaving the Baldrige criteria into their practices, so these questions will begin to be answered over the next several years. We also know that significant changes in processes and behavior do result in increases in market share, profitability, revenue, customer satisfaction, and employee morale.

Reinventing the Sales Force

Wally Wood

Like Cortada's article, this one also suggests methods for improving not just the sales force but the sales "process." It includes ideas on successfully teaming up and issues such as compensation and becoming "customer centric."

Most problematic sales organizations once were successful, aggressive, and market-driven, says David J. Cichelli, senior vice president of The Alexander Group Inc., a Scottsdale, Ariz.-based sales-consulting firm. What changed? After start-up and rapid growth, salespeople begin to say things like, "My customers tell me what they want to buy," or, "We have to cut prices if we're going to maintain volume." If a company has a hundred salespeople, it can have a hundred sales strategies. The marketing and sales organizations clash—repeatedly—over strategy and tactics. The only way to keep mature firms on track, argues Cichelli, is to reinvent.

Reinvent, not reorganize, which managers have been doing to sales forces ever since there have been salespeople—this even though most of the changes have been, as the saying goes, like shifting deck chairs on the titanic. Reinvent, not reengineer, which is undoubtedly the most fashionable management mode of the moment. According to Jerome A. Colletti, president of The Alexander Group, while reengineering often focuses on taking costs out of the sales and services processes, reinventing means making the right investments in the sales function at the right point in its life cycle.

For New York-based Bristol-Myers Squibb Co., one of those points was at the presentation stage. "In the past we trained our salespeople to go out and give presentations," says Michael F. Iafolla, vice president of managed health care and national accounts for the company. "But now we're teaching them that each presentation has a dollar value. Each physician or HMO [health-maintenance organization] has a certain ability to provide income, so the salesperson needs to take the tools available and adjust them based on the individual customer. That's a big change.

"We are also expanding the range of control a great deal," Iafolla continues. "We are having district managers that formerly had 10 or 11 people reporting to them now have 15 or 20 report, plus [we are] giving these managers accounts they have to call on themselves." The changes mean at least two

---

Reprinted with permission of the author from *Across the Board,* April 1994. Copyright © 1994 by Wally Wood. All rights reserved.

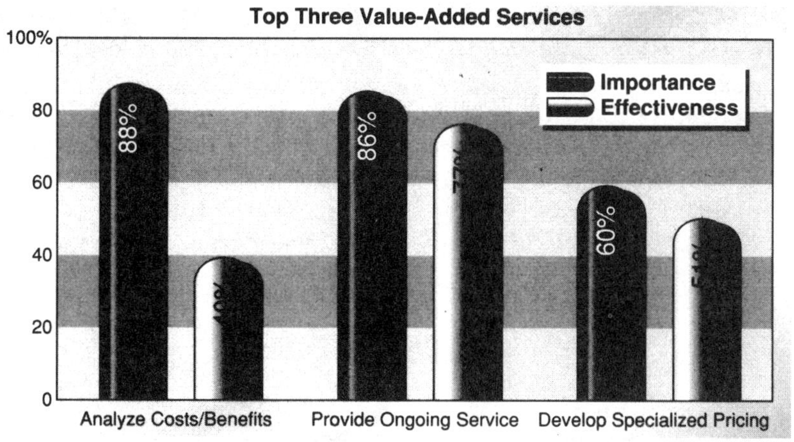

things: Managers understand the reps' problems in a way they did not in the past, and they don't have time to solve a rep's trivial problems.

"Marketing has always wanted to control the bottom-line P&L-pricing, all allocation of resources, etc.," says Iafolla. "Over the past year, I've finally been successful in moving to joint P&L responsibility. In essence both marketing and the account executive are responsible for an account within a segment. We've also tried to tie the bonus structures to customer performance across all the disciplines, which we've never done before."

Most companies haven't been as comprehensive—yet. On that line of thought, Michael Hammer, considered one of the "fathers" of reeningeering, brings up some interesting points, but understandably, he also makes his own distinction between reorganizing and reengineering. He sees it as the difference between moving boxes on an organization chart and looking at everything that happens between identifying a prospect and signing an order.

Hammer says that to date the three sales-related processes companies have reengineered most aggressively are order fulfillment, after-sales service, and new-product development. "Very few organizations have gotten to the order-acquisition process, which is a term we sometimes use because 'sales' is the name of the department," he notes. "There's a related process that companies often call 'customer engagement,' which is before order acquisition. Customer engagement is a process that turns a suspect into a prospect, and order acquisition turns a prospect into an order. Not many organizations have addressed these processes but my radar is starting to pick up that they are starting to do so now."

Very few organizations have gotten to the order-acquisition process.

Of course, before top executives take a tip from management gurus and start to reinvent their sales organizations, they should first explore the source of their sales problems. They must identify weaknesses in the company's cost structure. Changing the sales process will not help if the company is trying to sell goods or services that don't satisfy customer needs or are overpriced, or if the company isn't set up to ship on time.

PRODUCT-PUSHERS OR CONSUMER ADVOCATES?

The Alexander Group Inc. surveyed 53 companies on value-added sales services, asking them to rank the most important services and rate the effectiveness of their sales forces in providing those services. The results indicate that the biggest area for improvement is analyzing costs and benefits, probably because too many sales reps still function as "product-pushers" and not "consumer advocates," The Alexander Group found.

Yet even with quality products, competitive pricing, and exceptional services, a company actually may be sowing the seeds of tomorrow's failure as it reaps the immediate rewards of sales success. The flourishing company that falls on hard times because it has lost touch with its market—IBM Corp., General Motors Corp., Wang Laboratories Inc.—is a business cliché. That's where reinventing the sales organization comes in.

Knocking Down Departmental Walls

Do you recognize the following process? A sales rep communicates news to the district manager, who passes the information to the regional sales director, who then tells a vice president. If the issue is related to distribution or marketing, the vice president of sales has to talk to the vice president of distribution or marketing, who then passes the information down through several levels in the organization until it reaches someone who can act.

Yes, it's a giant game of Telephone, and at best it results in mangled or incomplete information. At worst, it delays responses and aggravates customers.

"We must develop processes that allow people who provide customer support—no matter where they exist in the organization—to communicate directly with the sales reps," Iafolla says. The sales strategies devised by Bristol-Meyers Squibb's U.S. Pharmaceutical Division focus on creating value, which does not necessarily relate directly to the product but can relate to other services—on-time delivery, quality, variety and selection, and more. To develop these strategies, management should include representatives from any part of the company that may be able to add value to the package. "In our company," says Iafolla, "marketing, medical, distribution, and customer service all provide input into the development of the strategic plans for each key customer. This is the only way to ensure that you use your company's resources to maximize your position on a specific account."

Top management should be prepared to overhaul the entire organization's structure and sales-support systems, if necessary, to build closer cooperation among all internal groups.

Top management should be prepared to overhaul the entire organization's structure and sales-support systems, if necessary, to build closer cooperation among all internal groups. The goal is to knock down departmental walls internally—between sales, marketing, manufacturing, finance, and any other department involved in satisfying the customers—and to become closer to prospects and customers. This may require team selling; it may require a new organization chart. It certainly requires a new mind-set.

The sales department figures prominently in the sales process, but in most companies—especially industrial organizations—it is not the only department involved.

"From the time you have a prospect until you have a closed deal," Hammer points out, "the sales rep may be in the lead, but finance is involved for pricing. Product design may be involved; engineering may be involved for technical support or for making product modifications; manufacturing and distribution get involved to plan capacity and give delivery commitments. Sales cannot be addressed purely within the confines of the sales department." This may seem self-evident, but many companies are getting the message only now.

Particular attention should be paid to forging a strong partnership between sales and marketing. This can be difficult since sales and marketing organizations typically are managed, measured, and compensated differently—a gap that may keep them from efficiently meeting customer needs. Two key steps here are to set common goals that support the partnership and to create an explicit sales and marketing process that outlines the kinds of information everyone needs (and why they need it).

Because of turf concerns or physical distance, functional managers tend not to consult their counterparts in other parts of the organization. Mel Ingold, general manager of Impact Planning Group, a Greenwich, Conn.-based consulting firm, has found that marketing managers can usually learn 90 percent (or more) of what they need to know about customers and competitors simply by asking the sales force—but they rarely do so.

Marketing managers can usually learn 90 percent (or more) of what they need to know about customers and competitors simply by asking the sales force—but they rarely do so.

The Tricky Business of Team Compensation

One outgrowth of the reinvention process has been that teams have replaced the lone salesman—and teams mean team-compensation plans. This is where things get dicey.

Sales reps often are harder to influence by financial incentives than many other executives, Hammer says. "The first time I heard this I couldn't believe it, but I've seen it so often that even though it's very counterintuitive, I do believe it. The traditional view is that money talks when you're talking to sales reps. It turns out that's not very true.

"At one insurance company, for example, a reengineering process had the potential to increase the agents' earnings but there was a trade-off: It was going to require them to work in a different way and to work somewhat harder," Hammer continues. "They said: 'We'd rather stay the way we are. We don't want to change.' This is partly because many sales reps are quite well-compensated and partly because they have diverse agendas."

Add to that the fact that sales organizations can be very defensive about their turf and not enthusiastic about teaming up with the back office—especially when experience has made them feel that the backoffice is the enemy that screws up the orders they generate. The idea that salespeople have to team with the engineering, manufacturing, finance, or distribution departments and work together on a cross-functional process is not something they necessarily will embrace.

According to Mark Blessington and William A. O'Connell of the Princeton-based organizational-effectiveness and compensation-consulting firm Sibson & Co. Inc., when a company tries to pull together one of these team-compensation plans, it often fails, further reinforcing the sales force's initial skepticism that team selling would work.

Blessington and O'Connell cite the case of a commercial-furniture company. To foster a more collaborative selling approach, the company offered to split credits on a case-by-case basis according to the contribution of each individual on the selling team. With salespeople who tended to specialize by product line and customers who bought from all these lines, the company wanted salespeople to help each other close deals in all product lines. But instead, most salespeople tried to close their deals alone to get all sales credit and avoid contentious negotiations with other salespeople.

To find out how to prevent these types of breakdowns, Sibson & Co. benchmarked seven large sales forces with successful team-compensation plans. A pay plan was defined as successful when salespeople, sales management, and competitors had a high regard for it, and the plan was at least 3 years old. Blessington and O'Connell's primary finding surprised them. It was that team compensation does not have to be hard—companies make it hard because they are not fully committed to the concept, or they have not figured out exactly when and how to use it.

Team compensation does not have to be hard—companies make it hard because they are not fully committed to the concept, or they have not figured out exactly when and how to use it.

Some of the companies they studied have found effective solutions. Monroe, Mich.-based Monroe Auto Equipment Co. uses a 100 percent team plan. The company decided that freeloaders were a sales-management problem, not a sales-compensation issue, and it pays each team member equally, based on the success of the team, not the performance of individual contributors. This approach has proven very effective for Monroe: the sales force consistently secures the highest market share and the best margins in their category.

Weber Marking Systems Inc., an Arlington Heights, Ill.-based manufacturer of on-site labeling systems, uses a split-credit formula whenever bill-to and ship-to locations fall into different sales territories, while Vernon Hills, Ill.-based Rust-Oleum Corp., a consumer paint-products company, avoids credit splits and uses a double-credit system for national-account sales volume.

Blessington and O'Connell conclude that the challenge for a reengineered sales force is to have clear rules for when to use teams and how to handle sales credit. And those rules, they say, must be managed as absolutes—and less as starting points for constant negotiation.

Are You Customer-Centric?

Ingold once asked a group of research-and-development managers at a specialty chemical company whether they had day-in/day-out contact with customers. One manager said she spoke with six to eight customers daily and two days a week visited plant sites to help customers apply the chemicals her company offered.

Ingold asked, "Do the customers give different information about the company's products and their needs than what the sales force reports?" Yes, came the answer—and the sales force is more interested in price per ton and how many carloads the company could ship; salespeople did not really care about the customers' problems. Ingold then asked, "How does this company use the valuable customer input gleaned by R&D in planning the business?" It doesn't, was the response.

Gary S. Tubridy, senior vice president of The Alexander Group, points out that reinventing focuses on customizing resources to meet the needs of the most valued customers, and that emphasis is consistent with the death of the mass market. Specialized sales and service attention is the focus now.

Reinventing focuses on customizing resources to meet the needs of the most valued customers, and that emphasis is consistent with the death of the mass market.

One first step in the process is segmentation—divide the company's activities by product, by customer, and by distribution channel, and then focus on those that offer the best return. Consider the medical-products company that had both a rigid sales organization and a rigid product organization. In the product group, one product manager was promoting her medication to hospitals across the board, demanding that the sales organization obtain at least one hospital per sales territory. When Cichelli's Alexander Group segmented the customers of the company, it became obvious that the preferred market for this particular product manager's drug was teaching hospitals, not just any hospital.

"Suddenly it was no longer necessary to have every salesperson learn how to sell that product. All we had to do was target 100 hospitals—not 1,000—because that was where the real sales took place," Cichelli says. Reinventing led to a more efficient use of resources by the company's employees.

Similarly, Hewlett-Packard Co.'s Computer Systems Organization in Cupertino, Calif., has become, in the words of Manuel Diaz, vice president, worldwide sales and marketing, a "customer-centric" organization. Diaz's group has identified about 1,000 "Global Accounts" (large, worldwide presence, high-growth potential), 32 of which get dedicated sales teams. These teams ask repeatedly, "What are the things that will help these accounts be successful?" As part of these efforts, Hewlett-Packard will rent an office in a key customer's headquarters building and station an account manager in it.

Immersing a sales force in satisfying customer needs can translate into higher profits. When the construction industry went into a major slump in the late 1980s, "We found ourselves fighting on price and chipping away at profits just to stay in the game," says Doug Chance, training and recruiting manager for Atlanta-based Georgia-Pacific Corp.'s building products distribution division. "What we needed to do was utilize the full breadth of our product and service offerings to meet more of our customers' needs, as well as improve our profitability."

Georgia-Pacific began training its sales representatives and district managers in 1991 in two of the company's dozen districts, focusing on developing a more thorough understanding of customer needs and analyzing how Georgia-Pacific's services compared with competitors'. "Our salespeople learned not only to identify the competitively distinct benefits we bring to the table," says Chance, "but also to recognize that we could expect to be paid for the additional value we offer the customer."

Now Georgia-Pacific's salespeople are "much more skilled at developing a relationship with our customers, and we're more knowledgeable about our markets," Chance says, "We're capitalizing on our uniqueness, not just selling the most boards for the least price."

Putting Sales On-Line

Many mistakenly think that computers come first in the reinventing process. George Colombo, the founder of Merrimack, N.H.-based Influence Technologies and the author of *Sales Force Automation* (McGraw-Hill), says that he has talked to unnumbered sales managers who have said something like, "We got laptops for all our salespeople a year ago and nothing happened."

When a sales-automation system is mandated by the top ranks, salespeople often see it not as a sales-productivity tool but as a management-control tool and "they resist it vigorously," Colombo says. The most successful companies have involved salespeople early in the process of implementing a sales-automation system, he adds.

A company must first have a plan before investing successfully in technology, Colombo says. "The only purpose of technology is to support a sales process that's structurally sound," he adds. "If you automate a mess, all you'll have is the ability to make your mistakes much more quickly."

If you automate a mess, all you'll have is the ability to make your mistakes much more quickly.

If the sales process is sound, then sales automation can increase productivity because it saves salespeople administrative time—time they can spend with prospects and customers, "which is, after all, what we pay them to do," Colombo says.

One company Colombo interviewed for his book scrupulously measured this change and found its salespeople "gained, on average, two full days of selling time per month because of the administrative overhead that was taken off them." Sales automation also helps sales productivity by reducing sales-order cycle time from days—sometimes weeks—to minutes and hours. A salesperson can dial up headquarters, poll inventory, place an order, and obtain shipping dates for a customer on the spot.

Automation also provides the most comprehensive resource for damage control. When a top salesperson leaves, it's important that customers not experience any discontinuity, and having complete customer histories immediately available helps. It's just as important, says Colombo, to know your prospects—the people in the loop you haven't closed yet. A sales-automation system will provide prospect data, "and that can be very, very valuable when a salesperson leaves."

The third advantage is having accurate, timely information—Where are things selling? Where are salespeople most effective? Which sales people need attention?—on which managers can base decisions. "By the time it's a month old, it likely isn't going to do you much good," Colombo notes. "The government doesn't send out a list of *trailing* economic indicators." An automated sales system provides the information that managers need: it provides more information, better information, and it provides it quickly.

Finally, any sales-automation system reduces training costs for new salespeople. "Companies that have automated their sales systems have found that you can get a salesperson out and productive much more quickly than you could previously because there's an automated track to run on," Colombo says.

Leadership and Power Plays

Every reinventing effort runs into the universal, human resistance to change. Hammer notes that some people resist change because they lose power, status, money, or the kind of environment in which they're effective. Some people simply are uncomfortable with things that require new behaviors from them. And some people fear a future that's not entirely clear.

Only if top management leads the way can an organization overcome this resistance. In so doing, management must make clear to everyone affected why the changes are necessary. "I find that people are jaded over internal initiatives", says Impact Planning Group's Ingold. "You must use external-market criteria to change everyone's internal behavior. If everyone understands the external-market conditions, and why the changes will allow the organization to be successful in the future, that's a good starting point."

If everyone understands the external-market conditions, and why the changes will allow the organization to be successful in the future, that's a good starting point.

Ingold and Cichelli agree that the biggest single obstacle to the successful reinvention of the sales organization is past success. Says Cichelli, "things that have worked well in the past preclude organizations from adopting these new practices." Ingold adds: "If you've done it this way for a while and it's worked, people now say: 'Why do we have to change? Why should we do it this way?' " Roll the words "sales relic" over your tongue a few times and you'll probably have the answer.

Wally Wood is a business writer based in Sandy Hook, Conn.

Functional Processes

ACCOUNTING AND FINANCE

All About EVA

Daniel J. McConville

EVA, economic value added, is a new (or not so new depending on your perspective) financial measure of business performance. It seems to be an insightful way to determine how well a company is performing and to enhance the sense of ownership in employees.

Manitowoc Co. Inc., a diversified Wisconsin manufacturer, sliced $55 million from parts inventories. CSX Corp.'s intermodal division got rid of 50 locomotives. Harnischfeger Industries Inc., the mining and paper-mill machinery maker, melted down receivables by 30%. These are not businesses in decline. On the contrary, they're coming on stronger than ever, thanks in part to EVA—economic value added—a financial tool that enables companies to do more with less by spotlighting the cost of capital. When used as a yardstick, EVA can help shape virtually every corporate decision from acquisitions to employee compensation. As a compass, it is merciless: A simple EVA calculation can determine whether or not a company should be in business at all.

Stock prices seem to move in tandem with EVA calculations. "We calculated our EVA back to 1984 and found an almost perfect correlation with the price of the stock," says James Meenan, CFO of AT&T's long-distance unit.

Obviously, EVA is an accountant's delight. But it is not the exclusive turf of finance departments. Anyone with fourth-grade arithmetic skills can do it; no calculator is needed, let alone a computer.

Reprinted with permission from Industry Week, *April 18, 1994. Copyright Penton Publishing, Inc., Cleveland, Ohio.*

To determine the EVA of any operation—the corporate whole, a division, or any activity within a division—simply subtract from the net operating profit after taxes the value of the capital employed to produce that profit. Value is increased by earning a return greater than shareowners or lenders require; EVA is diminished when the return is less. Taken a step further, EVA really gets interesting because it's being used increasingly to equate managers' salaries and bonuses with performance, replacing ROI (return on investment), sales goals, or budget-based percentages. Harnischfeger, which once limited bonuses to 40% of base pay on all but top company officers, has now adopted an EVA compensation plan, as has Manitowoc.

To determine the EVA of any operation simply subtract from the net operating profit after taxes the value of the capital employed to produce that profit.

"We've gone to EVA for our incentive plan," says Manitowoc CFO Robert R. Friedl, "and it goes much farther down through the ranks than previously. We have about 60 people in the program." One of the wonders of EVA or EVA-like measurement systems is that almost any company—large, small, public, private, even a sole proprietorship—can put it to use.

Coca-Cola Co.'s Chairman Roberto C. Goizueta affirmed that things go better with EVA by shedding a passel of business units whose ROI was in the 7% to 8% range compared with Coke's nearly 30% return on capital. The soft-drink maker's cost of capital averages 15%.

For the last two years, AT&T CEO Robert Allen has been pushing his unit managers to segregate their businesses into profit centers, not so much for a reading on profit and loss as to see how their EVA measures up. "The effect is staggering," reports Mr. Meenan. " 'Good' is no longer positive operating earnings. It's when you beat the cost of capital."

Beating the cost of capital is a primary concern of Quaker Oats Co. CEO William Smithburg. To drive that cost down, he has launched an EVA-like program he calls "controllable earnings coupled with empowerment."

By leveling out production schedules at its big Danville, Ill., plant, the cereal and snack-food maker was able to schedule incoming shipments of raw materials and packaging supplies with more JIT-like precision, thus cutting the need for warehouse space. Last year, Quaker reduced inventories from $15 million to $9 million and eliminated five of 15 warehouses. "I used to treat inventories like they were free," declares Steven Brunner, the Danville plant manager. "Controllable earnings makes me act like an entrepreneur."

Quaker's new financial discipline did not go unnoticed in the marketplace. When it withdrew its customary yearend sales promotions, sales tanked, profits plunged, and the stock price withered. But the company's controllable earnings program prevailed and performed just as it was designed to. Quaker stock now trades in the mid-60s, up 30% since its laissez faire inventory system ended.

Quaker stock now trades in the mid-60s, up 30% since its laissez faire inventory system ended.

EVA and its look-alikes are not new. Rather, they're further proof that great ideas never die. Alfred Sloan, the General Motors Corp. patriarch, knew EVA—though not by name—in the 1920s; General Electric Co. was flirting with return-on-capital systems in the 1950s.

Accountants have long known a closely related acronym—RI, or residual income, whose formula looks like this:

RI = Net operating income − (minimum rate of return on investment × operating assets)

GE dropped its EVA precursor "when the stock market appeared to be focusing on earnings per share, which they couldn't tie into," says G. Bennett Stewart, who is credited with the current revival of value-based management systems. A Princeton-trained electrical engineer, he earned his M.B.A. at the University of Chicago's business school, then went on to become a Chase Manhattan wunderkind in the 1970s. In 1982, he and Joel Stern formed Stern Stewart & Co., a consultancy headquartered in New York. "Back in the 1980s, restructuring and LBOs were such a dominant force that you never heard much about EVA," he recalls. "But when LBOs faded from the marketplace, we retooled our practice." And retool Stern Stewart he did, spreading the gospel of EVA after witnessing the wonders it worked for Coca-Cola.

"Coca-Cola is the longest-standing user of EVA," Mr. Stewart says. Today, his firm is to EVA what Coca-Cola is to Coke. Though other consultants market similar programs, only Stern Stewart can claim the EVA acronym as its own, since it holds the trademark. As Mr. Stewart fluently depicts EVA, its keystone is the carrot—executive compensation. All else is the stick. To set the stage, he declares, "What gets measured gets managed. If you change the way a company measures performance, you will change [executive] behavior. Most companies lose track of capital accountability. There is too little concern about managing the assets on the balance sheet."

All EVA does is subtract one more expense, the cost of financing the assets on the balance sheet. What is left over is a measure of how efficiently the business is being managed.

Then comes a familiar aphorism: you don't wash a leased car. Owners, he points out, are more caring than managers. "They manage with a sense of urgency. Their identification with the company is personal and visceral. What we try to do is give the managers a piece of the EVA action and have them get paid like owners through a bonus plan."

Mr. Stewart rounds out his introduction with a factoid: Earnings are easiest. "Easiest to understand perhaps, but misleading," he says.

"Take sales, deduct operating expenses, and you have earnings. All EVA does is subtract one more expense, the cost of financing the assets on the balance sheet. What is left over is a measure of how efficiently the business is being managed and how to assess new capital projects."

Of great importance, he says, is that EVA is an internal process that can change corporate governance. When put into practice, EVA will "make every manager, not only the CEO, responsible for creating value. It can also silence the corporate critics concerned about the absence of links between pay and performance."

Mr. Stewart lists but one caveat for any company considering EVA: It must be a going concern. "It is least applicable to start-ups, true venture companies," he explains. "At that point they're not managing a business as much as bringing a new product to the marketplace."

EVA has its critics, however. Alfred Rappaport, an adjunct professor at Northwestern University's Kellogg Graduate School of Management and chairman of the Alcar Group, a Chicago management consulting firm that often goes head-to-head with Stern Stewart, assails EVA as a flawed concept, at least from a shareholder's view.

"EVA is a short-term measure based on sunken cost—historical investment—which is irrelevant if you're buying 100 shares in the company," he declares. "EVA can report value increases while the business is investing below the cost of capital, or value destruction while the business is actually investing above the cost of capital."

Adds Bruce D. Keener, executive vice president for Kepner-Tregoe, a Princeton, N.J., systems consultant, "I don't buy into EVA completely. It speaks only to the financial side of the business. Every company has an investment in people that doesn't show up on the balance sheet. Furthermore, EVA fails to look forward."

Mr. Keener cites Northern Telecom Inc.'s ill-fated decision some years ago to cut back on R&D. "They lost their competitive edge. Their savings caught up with them, and they quickly began losing money for the first time in the history of the company. Numbers don't always tell the whole story. Besides, I feel that anything tied too much to executive compensation tends to push the greed button."

Not necessarily, retorts Frank A. Jacoby, vice chairman of customer services for New York-based accountancy-consultant BDO Seidman. "EVA can be a good tool not only for executive compensation but also for gainsharing among nonexecutives. EVA can be taken all the way down the line. I see it as a reasonable way to share the wealth among members of a team—all of the team."

Stern Stewart's Mr. Stewart concedes that EVA can be misapplied "if management doesn't use it realistically or doesn't properly tie it into an incentive. In advising clients, we attempt to understand the unique nature of every client's business and anticipate changing conditions."

At Harnischfeger Industries' headquarters in suburban Milwaukee, CFO Francis M. Corby says EVA created a whole new navigation system for his company, but it didn't happen quickly. "We started talking about it two years ago," he says. "First, our management-policy committee showed some interest, and eventually the board's finance and strategic-planning committee approved it and passed it along to the human-resources committee, which also gave it the O.K. Then it went to the full board, which approved it."

"EVA has really changed the culture here," says Mr. Corby. "It's given our managers more options. They're thinking like entrepreneurs.

Harnischfeger's operating and fiscal health have improved considerably since EVA kicked in last year. For one thing, receivables are down 30%, far more than previous declines in the 11% to 17% bracket. That's because under EVA, management is working to achieve an aftertax profit that meets or beats Harnischfeger's cost of capital.

Consequently, managers are now rethinking operating procedures, reconsidering expansion projects, and weighing equipment purchases in a far different light. A materials-handling subsidiary was jettisoned late last fall, not because it was unprofitable; it simply failed to meet the EVA criterion. (Not incidentally, Harnischfeger posted an aftertax profit of $15.4 million through the sale.)

Beginning this year, EVA will be the yardstick to measure an incentive compensation plan for 199 Harnischfeger executives throughout the world. "EVA has really changed the culture here," says Mr. Corby. "It's given our managers more options. They're thinking like entrepreneurs. We're excited about EVA."

So is Tom Hoppin, a spokesman for CSX Corp., the big (assets $13 billion; estimated 1994 revenues $9 billion) Richmond-based transportation conglomerate. "Costs always mattered, but there was no easy way to define what they meant and how they got translated to the bottom line of the business," he says. "In theory and practice, EVA gives us the ability to do that." Citing CSX Intermodal, Mr. Hoppin recalls a $48 million loss in 1987, the year its operations were first separately broken out—and the year the company adopted EVA. "We're not sure what revenues were back then, but I can say that last year they were $793 million and the Intermodal unit posted an operating income of $53 million, which indicates better than a $100 million turnaround in its business."

Thanks to EVA, the CSX Intermodal picture began to brighten when it discarded underutilized routes and the terminals and equipment required to service them. "Once we determined that no amount of investment could turn them around, we phased them out," Mr. Hoppin says. As a result, a vast assemblage of rolling stock was returned to the parent company, including 50 locomotives.

Now that EVA has been guiding Manitowoc's game plan for three years, savings have dropped off. "Once we began measuring things by the cost of capital, it was easy to see early on where the big cuts could be made, like in our receivables," says Mr. Friedl.

No product development or sales expansion at Manitowoc (1993 sales $270 million) goes forward without considering the cost of capital involved. "We're not a huge company," Friedl says, "but we're growing steadily and profitably. That's what happens when managers' incentives are based on operating earnings minus the cost of capital rather than on operating results [alone]."

Daniel J. McConville is a contributing editor to Industry Week *Magazine.*

Breaking Down the Walls

Connie Beal and Joanne Wiswell

This article describes how one company, Storage Technology Corporation, went about improving its accounts receivable processes by implementing sound process management techniques. It affirms the value of these techniques in all processes throughout an organization.

StorageTek became acutely aware of the importance of cash and cash flow during its period in Chapter 11 bankruptcy. "Cash is king" became an operating axiom throughout the recovery process. Following our successful emergence from Chapter 11, we have not forgotten the need for continued focus on this fundamental business principle.

A key component of cash flow analysis is the receivables cycle. Historically, we have regarded the invoice as the beginning boundary of the process and cash receipt as the ending boundary. As such, StorageTek has measured the receivables cycle in terms of days sales outstanding or percentage of dollars over 60 days.

In an effort to further improve our cash management, it became apparent that we needed to concentrate our efforts further upstream in the cycle. How long was it taking us to generate an invoice? Were there any opportunities for improvement?

Team Focus

The Billing and Collections Process Improvement Council, sponsored by corporate vice president and controller, David Lacey, was formed in June 1991, to explore those opportunities. This council is still in existence today with membership consisting of the regional administration managers from StorageTek's five US regional offices and managers in headquarters that provide support services for those administrative departments.

Many quality improvement teams, quality action teams, quality resolution teams, and quality circles are in place countrywide that affect billing and collection processes. The council's charter is to understand and coordinate those quality activities, ensure that all recommended changes to a process have a positive effect on overall process, and communicate ongoing activities, improvements and results.

Another equally important objective of the Improvement Council is to define and establish measurements for our processes.

Reprinted with permission of Juran Institute, Inc. Copyright by Juran Institute. All rights reserved.

Defining Metrics

The concept of measurement was not new; the concept of *process* measurement, however, was new.

Our Core Quality Training (the three-day class that provides StorageTek employees with a common understanding and approach to quality improvement) teaches us that there are three places to measure within a process—inputs, in-process and outputs. Measuring inputs to the process helps us to determine if our internal supplier is meeting our requirements and allows us to have discussions based on real data with these suppliers. This supports an often-used quote at StorageTek, "without data, you're just someone else with an opinion!"

This supports an often-used quote at StorageTek, "without data, you're just someone else with an opinion!"

Measuring process outputs helps to assess if the output is meeting customer requirements. We are most familiar with these types of measurements and have many in place; unfortunately, they are the least helpful in telling us anything about the problems within the process. In the past, we dealt mostly with results measurements—percentage over 60 day receivables, days sales outstanding, invoicing accuracy reports.

In-process measurements help to evaluate the quality within the work process by measuring critical success factors and other significant checkpoints. Ideally this measurement should be close to the beginning of the process in order to facilitate prevention versus rework. It is believed by many that a key measurement of process performance is cycle time—the elapsed time between the beginning and completion of a process or activity. Inspection points, errors, and rework loops lengthen the process and will be reflected in a cycle time measurement.

These three areas of measurement may be grouped into two catgories—effectiveness and efficiency. Effectiveness denotes how well the process satisfies customer requirements. Efficiency is a valuable criteria for the process owner, in essence, how well the process works. Cycle time, though primarily considered an efficiency metric, has definite implications in customer satisfaction. Reducing invoice generation cycle time specifically, while optimizing cash flow and freeing resources for the corporation, also provides the customer with a prompt, accurate invoice.

Collecting Data

Having reviewed the types of measurement and purposes of each, we began collecting cycle time data about the invoice generation process. The beginning boundary was defined as the installation of our equipment with the ending boundary the generation of the invoice. This process is cross-functional and flows horizontally through marketing, customer services (field engineering) and administration.

The initial task was to develop a timeline of subprocesses involved in generating an invoice to the customer and establish cycle time metrics for each.

[Figure 1] illustrates that there are three sequential subprocesses crossing functional work groups inherent in the invoice generation process.

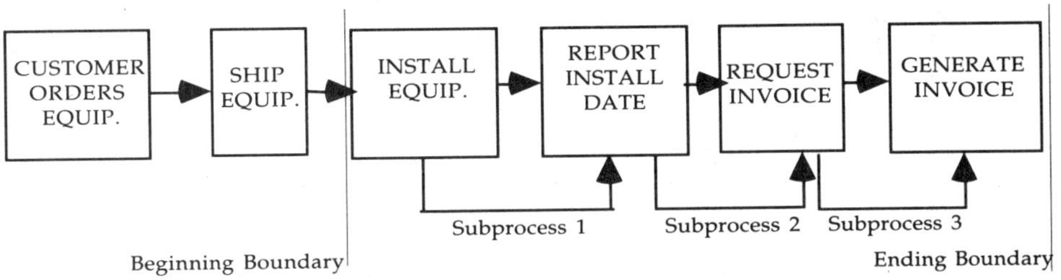

Figure 1.

Subprocess 1: Cycle Time of Reporting an Installation

This measurement captures the number of days from equipment installation to the date the activity is reported in our order entry/billing system. Until this date is reported, an invoice request will not be scheduled.

Subprocess 2: Cycle Time from Reported Install Date to Invoice Request

This measurement captures the number of days from the time the installation is recorded in the system to the release of an invoice request to billing. In some instances, units are shipped to a customer under contractual conditions not yet satisfied (e.g., evaluation of equipment). Since we do not invoice the customer until those conditions have been met, this portion of cycle time includes the waiting period between installation and customer acceptance.

Subprocess 3: Cycle Time from Invoice Request to Invoice Generation

This cycle time incorporates the review of the invoice request and includes any rework time due to error detection/correction.

Once we had established this timeline, our next step was to gather the data within and between each subprocess. Gathering the data was a relatively easy task since our database carried all of these date parameters and had two years of historical information.

Once the data was extracted, we began the process of data validation—an arduous task! Whenever you go back in time and look at data that may not have been used (or validated) you may be in for some clean-up activity. For example, one transaction showed a cycle time of over 3,000 days! A date had been keyed in as 1981 rather than 1991. We spent several months fine-tuning our criteria and validating the data.

Using the Data

From our quality training we learned that it is the transformation of data into information that permits us to make competent decisions about our processes. Our next challenge became how best to convert this data into a meaningful display of information.

Traditionally we have used trend charts (plotting actuals over time) as our primary method of presenting data. The problem with using the trend chart is that although it easily showed the variation in our cycle times, it didn't

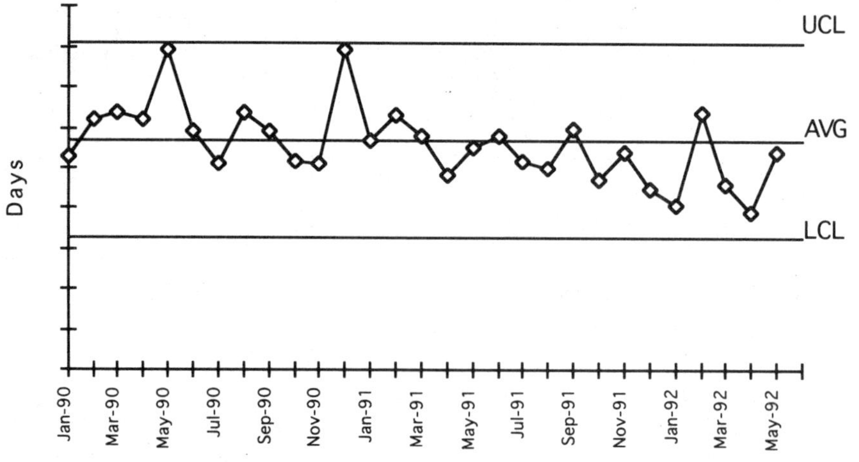

Figure 2. **Average total cycle time.**

help us to determine if that month's activity was unusual. Using the individual control chart, we were able to add upper and lower control limits which provided guidance in determining whether a month was unusual and worth investigating. Control limits are calculated from the cycle time data and provide an indication of the expected (or common cause) variation in the process. If the cycle time falls outside the control limits, it is an indication of a special cause, something unusual. When that occurs, we need to investigate to determine what happened that month.

In selecting the control chart as the tool for our cycle time analysis, we realized that historically we had been guilty of "process tampering."

In selecting the control chart as the tool for our cycle time analysis, we realized that historically we had been guilty of "process tampering." We measured cycle time monthly and each month would analyze the results—if we saw improvement, we patted each other on the back and tried to determine what we had done in that month that resulted in the improvement. If the next measurement period showed cycle time increase, we would scratch our heads in puzzlement and try to determine what or who had failed. Not until we put these results in a control chart did we realize our performance was within the control limits, and we had wasted our efforts trying to explain something that was nothing more than normal process variation [Figure 2, Figure 3].

Our results indicated that total cycle time and cycle time subcategories were stable processes affected only by common cause variation. Therefore, in order to improve cash flow by reducing our total cycle time, the process would have to be changed.

Where Does One Begin?

Since the processes involved in generating an invoice resided in the regional offices, it was agreed a necessary first step was to establish cross-functional

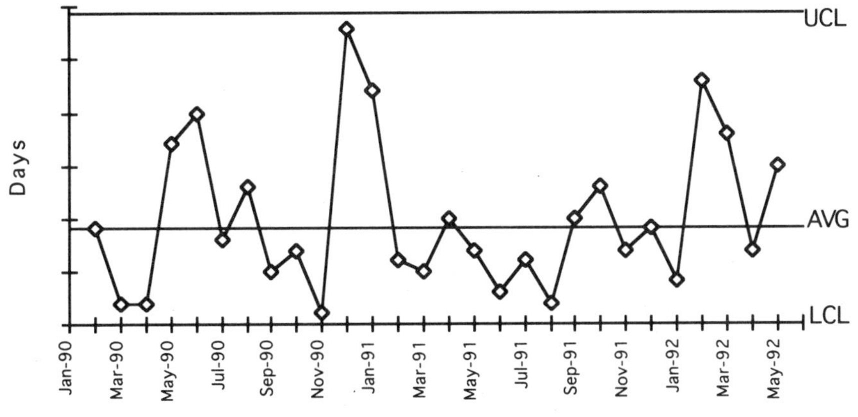

Figure 3. **Average moving range of total cycle time.**

teams consisting of marketing, customer services, and administrative personnel within each region.

Building on our original data collection efforts, the teams wanted to analyze this data in more manageable components. Our invoice generation activities were segmented into four primary business events each with unique requirements and processes:

- physical installation of equipment
- physical de-installation of equipment
- initiate maintenance activities
- discontinue maintenance activities

After displaying our cycle time results by business event category, we were not too surprised to learn that each activity did indeed have varying cycle times. This helped determine which business event had the longest cycle time and should be tackled first.

In an effort to identify and prioritize improvement opportunities, it was important for the regions, using a team approach, to apply StorageTek's nine-step quality improvement process. For example, although the functional areas had previously flowcharted their own process (step 1[in Figure 4]), here was an opportunity to share these process flows and to integrate them; here was an opportunity to communicate!

Obstacles Encountered

Fear of Measurements

We are conditioned that one of the purposes of measurements is to evaluate the performance of an individual or department. This gets in the way when defining process measurements. A common reaction is: "That situation is out of my control; it's not fair to include those days in my cycle time." It's important for everyone to understand that we are measuring the process; the customer will still count those days even if no one else does!

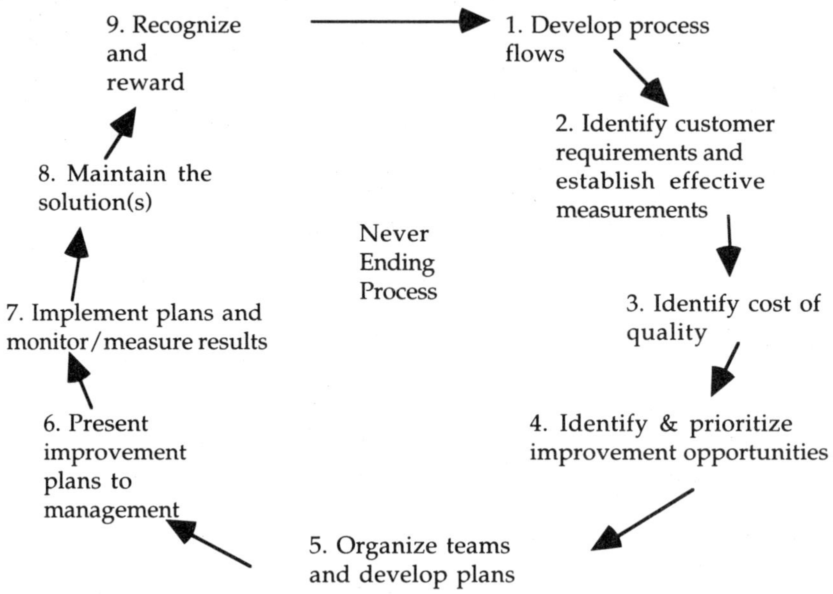

Figure 4. **StorageTek 9-step quality improvement process.**

Establishing Criteria

It's more difficult than it may appear to define the criteria for a measurement. All we wanted to do was to measure the elapsed time between the beginning and ending of a process. We agreed that our starting boundary would be the point at which the customer services engineer installs equipment. Our ending boundary would be the generation of an invoice to the customer. Sound simple enough? It wasn't. We had to agree on how to handle certain anomalies in the business. For example, a date discrepancy arises when the paperwork to initiate an activity is generated after the activity has occurred. When does the clock start ticking?

Depending on the criteria we agreed upon, our cycle time numbers would produce varying results.

Dr. Deming teaches us that nothing has true value. "Any physical measurement is the result of applying a given procedure. It is to be expected that two procedures for measurement will give different results. Neither of the two figures is right or wrong."[1] To further illustrate this point, consider counting the number of people in a department. Even this seemingly easy exercise could yield different results. Should you count Mary who is on medical leave or Jane who is scheduled to start on Monday? How about John, the temporary? Depending on the criteria we agreed upon, our cycle time numbers would produce varying results.

Regardless of the criteria selected, a primary goal is to establish a baseline measurement that can be consistently and continuously applied to monitor the process and evaluate the impact of any changes.

Long Distance Communication

Communication is key to process improvement and can be difficult even when there is a close proximity between work groups. It is further complicated by distance. The Billing and Collections Process Improvement Council conducts a meeting twice a month via conference calls. Other quality action teams addressing billing issues have both headquarters and regional participants and also have meetings via teleconferencing. The regional cross-functional teams face this same problem as their members are located in various cities throughout the region. The commitment to process improvement provides the momentum to overcome this obstacle.

Resource Allocation

Establishing appropriate metrics, collecting data, validating the data, selecting the best way to present the data takes commitment, time and resources. In a time of growth and change, there are many priorities, many schedules to meet, many fires to fight. However, StorageTek is committed to the belief that the quality improvement process, rather than being an adjunct to our day-to-day business, is at its very core. It's been demonstrated that if resources and time are allocated to improve the process, the result is less rework and reduced waste of resources—resources that can be utilized more effectively by continuing to improve the process versus fire-fighting. This parallels Dr. Juran's teachings that the investment in improving the process does increase every participant's workload. This investment in added work must precede the return on investment; however, that return on investment is remarkable!

Although in hindsight it seems elementary, it became obvious that it was impossible to improve our cash management situation without expanding the scope to incorporate all activities related to the process.

Lessons Learned

Setting Targets

Expected levels of achievement cannot be established in a vacuum. Process capability had not been a consideration in setting cycle time expectations. For instance, we set an MBO goal for the administrative staff that each subprocess should not exceed a cycle time of five working days and measured the performance of each function against that requirement. We did not use our data, however, to understand if each particular subprocess was capable of achieving a five day throughput. Not too surprisingly, these arbitrary MBO goals were never met.

Measuring the Entire Process

Initially we measured only the administrative cycle time of this process that was within our span of control, inadvertently narrowing the focus to only a portion of the entire process. We neglected to incorporate those components of the process impacted by the marketing rep and the customer services engineer. Although in hindsight it seems elementary, it became obvious that it was impossible to improve our cash management situation without expanding the scope to incorporate all activities related to the process.

The Value of Process Measurements

Armed with data regarding the cycle time of the total process as well as cycle time data for each segment of the process, we were able to obtain a commitment from executive management in the regions and in headquarters to provide the necessary resources (mostly in the form of people's time) to address this issue. The general managers from each region chartered cross-functional teams to focus on cycle time issues.

The Value of Cross-functional Teams

The process of generating an invoice, not unlike many administrative processes, flows horizontally throughout, and is impacted by several organizations. However, problems were often addressed or elevated only through each organization's vertical chain of command, thereby pre-empting communication between organizations. With the creation of cross-functional teams, the vehicle is now in place to share processes and identify improvement opportunities.

Conclusion

Defining metrics, collecting meaningful data, creating and sharing process flows, forming cross-functional teams, identifying improvement opportunities—it's a start. We've learned a lot, yet we know we still have a lot to learn. Like the unraveling of a mystery novel, each new development uncovers more clues, questions, and answers, making us eager to discover what lies ahead.

Reference

1. Deming, Dr. W. Edwards, *Out of the Crisis.* p. 279.

Connie Beal, Manager, Process Transition and Support, Storage Technology Corporation.
Joanne Wiswell, Manager, Data Administration and Reporting, Storage Technology Corporation.

Functional Processes

LEGAL

Legal Eagles Become Quality Hawks

Rolf Hoexter and Mariesa Julien

This short article describes how TQM and process management are as important in improving the performance of lawyers and their staffs as in any other field. Though the ideas are basic, the point is well made.

The quality of the services delivered in a law firm has a dual nature: quality in fact and quality in perception. Preparing the perfect brief is an example of quality in fact. If, however the client is unhappy with communications with the firm and its staff, quality in perception will be affected. A law firm will retain its clients and gain new ones only when it delivers quality service both in fact and perception.

While the complete introduction of total quality management (TQM) is a long-term process, some results can be seen within the first year. It doesn't take long to regain some of the costs of the TQM program by working on items that add no value and are signs of poor quality, such as missed schedules, lost clients, duplication of effort, or poor training.

To introduce a TQM system in a law firm requires several steps: forming a steering committee, instituting training in quality concepts and problem solving, organizing problem-solving teams, developing action plans, and implementing and testing solutions.

Reprinted with permission from *Quality Progress*, January 1994. Copyright © 1994, ASQC, Milwaukee, WI. All rights reserved.

The Steering Committee

First, a firm must form a steering committee of partners. The purpose of this committee is to manage and guide the firm's quality improvement activities. This guidance is extended to enhance job and service quality, promote staff involvement, improve problem-solving capabilities, and establish an ongoing program for improvement.

The steering committee must define which problems require solutions and prioritize them. To do this, committee members must understand that all work is a process with an input from a supplier and an output to a customer. For example, the mail-room clerk's supplier is the legal secretary; the clerk's customer is the postal worker who picks up the mail. Process output, in terms of productivity and delivered quality, should be measured through the perceptions of the service user (the client) rather than the service provider (the attorney).

Process output, in terms of productivity and delivered quality, should be measured through the perceptions of the service user (the client) rather than the service provider (the attorney).

Most employees never deal directly with the firm's external customers, but all have internal customers. It is important to define internal suppliers and customers and discern what they need. Employees might be surprised to learn how many customers there are and what can be learned by talking to them.

Since 80% of errors made are due to systems and procedures and only 20% are due to human error, quality can be improved substantially by improving the system and not by blaming employees.[1] Some problems that require system improvements are:

- Poor telephone etiquette, such as a rude and abrupt operator, misdirected calls, and unreturned calls and messages
- Lack of detailed billing information on a client's invoice
- Inability of partners and associates to use electronic research facilities
- Not keeping clients updated on the status of their cases in a timely manner

Training and Teams

The managing partners should be instructed in quality awareness. This instruction should be followed with an overview of team problem-solving techniques and the skills and tools required for measuring quality.

Next, the firm should form a problem-solving team consisting of staff members, associates, and support personnel and start a training program to teach team members problem-solving skills. As training proceeds, assign the team a problem to solve, such as telephone communications with clients. By soliciting ideas from all participants, without criticism or discussion, the team can generate a cause-and-effect diagram (Figure 1).

This diagram can help sort out the causes of a problem and organize their mutual relationships. The construction of the diagram focuses the discussion and allows participation from all members of the team. The team members

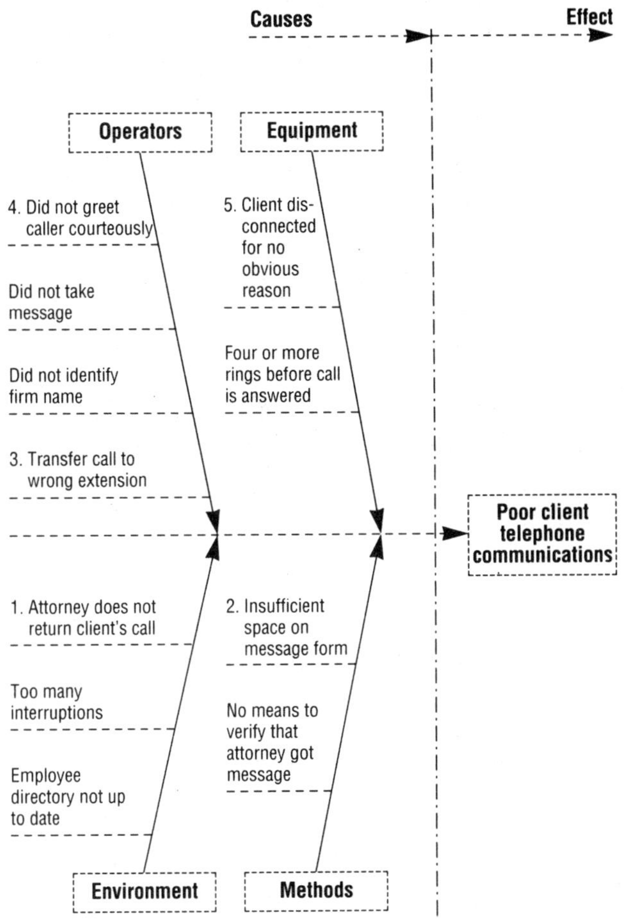

Figure 1. **Cause-and-effect diagram.**

then rank the proposed causes from highest (10) to lowest (1) and calculate the sum of the rankings for each cause. Those with the highest totals have the highest priority. The team can prepare a matrix of the rankings, which looks something like this:

Cause:
Attorney does not return client's call within 24 hours.
Sum of rankings:
210
Cause:
Insufficient space on message form to write message
Sum of rankings:
150

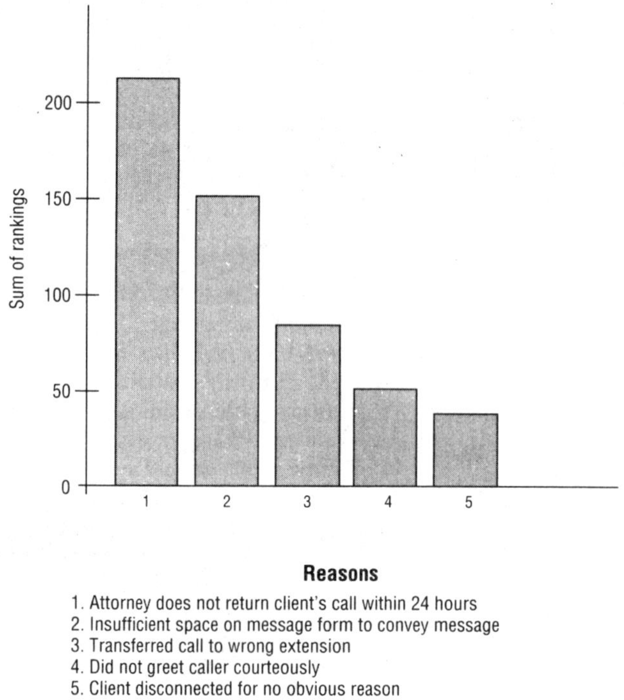

Figure 2. **Reasons for poor client telephone communication.**

A graphic representation of these rankings is shown in Figure 2. The chart illustrates which problem requires the most attention and will yield the most quality improvement.

Action Plans

The team is now able to create various action plans. Each plan should be recorded carefully on a form with a description of the plan, key dates, who is responsible, and so on. (This can be set up in a computer data base so that status information is available to everyone.)

A team member is then assigned to investigate the highest priority item. Since this item was generated during a brainstorming session of internal team members, the team must ascertain whether the item, returning a call within 24 hours, correctly reflects clients' expectation. This is a good opportunity for attorneys who have client contact to find out what clients expect in telephone turnaround time. The attorneys might discover other causes of poor client telephone communications and, even more important, concerns in the area of perceived quality, of which the firm might not have been aware.

The team member investigating the adequacy of 24-hour turnaround presents the data to the team at the next meeting. Surprisingly, all clients surveyed by the attorneys said they would be satisfied if someone called them back within 48 hours. The team then works on improving the process.

Reason:	April 1	Week of April 7	April 14	Total	% of Total
Had nothing to report	II	III	I	6	12.7
Did not have time	IIII	卌	卌 I	15	31.9
Forgot	I	I	0	2	4.4
Did not get dated message	卌 II	卌	卌 IIII	21	44.6
Out of town	0	I	II	3	6.4
				47	100.0

Figure 3. **Reasons for not returning client's telephone call.**

The team member asks the attorneys what they think the reasons are for not returning clients' telephone calls within 48 hours. With this information, he or she can create a check sheet (Figure 3). Next, the team member asks each attorney's secretary to compare the written telephone message forms with the date and time that the attorney returned the call. Each call not returned within 48 hours is noted on the appropriate area of the check sheet. After three weeks of data collection, the results are tabulated and reported to the team.

As it turns out, 44% of the time, the person answering the phone and completing the message form does not enter the date and time of the call. Thus, the recipient of the message form has no idea when the client called. The office manager, a member of the team, agrees to add an area on the form where the time and date can be entered.

The team suggests that to further reduce the number of unanswered calls after 48 hours, the attorney's secretaries, who keep a log of the attorneys' calls, could add a check mark for calls requiring a return call. If the attorney is too busy to return the call, the secretary can make a copy of the original message form and submit it to the attorney as a reminder.

Implementing and Testing Solutions

The next step is to verify whether the two proposed solutions significantly reduce the number of unreturned calls. The team again issues a check sheet to the attorneys' secretaries to monitor whether the number of unreturned calls has been reduced substantially. When the results are tabulated, they are better than expected. The reason for this is, because of the publicity, nobody forgot to return their calls. The team selects a date to retest the new procedure to prevent regression.

The team is now ready to tackle the next most important item and suggest potential solutions. Before instituting any solution, the team carefully plans all actions, including making economic evaluations. If the solution is practical, a test of the solution is run and evaluated. If the solution is sound, it is instituted firmwide. After the solution has been implemented, tests are made to verify whether quality or productivity have actually improved.

This problem-solving process is known as managing with facts. The procedures in this process hold true whether the team is evaluating the purchase of a new postage meter or planning to install a new billing software program. When one item is solved, the team goes on to the next one, and so on. This never-ending procedure is known as continuous improvement.

Quality Improvements Are Difficult to Judge

Measuring improved quality and productivity in the service area is more difficult than in a manufacturing environment. Some of the reasons for this difference include:

- The lack of a quantifiable definition of quality and productivity in a service environment. Quality of a manufactured product can be more easily expressed in measurable terms, such as size and color. In service industries, however, time of completion or how many clients were delighted with the receptionist's manners can be the critical measurements.

- Conventional attitudes often maintain that it is difficult, if not impossible, to improve service productivity and quality. Improvements require the support and leadership of the managing partners to overcome these attitudes.

Substantial gains can be made in service quality and productivity in a professional service organization. Not only are improvements possible but, considering the current economic situation, they might be the only key to prosperity and competitiveness.

Reference

1. Joseph M Juran, *Juran's Quality Control Handbook,* fourth edition (New York, NY: McGraw-Hill Book Company, 1988).

Rolf Hoexter is a senior consultant with the East Hill Group in Englewood, NJ.
Mariesa Julien is a senior consultant with the East Hill Group in Englewood, NJ.

Functional Processes

HUMAN RESOURCES

New Ways to Pay

Donna Brown Hogarty

As organizations move to quality management, seeking to cut waste (and costs) from their processes while enhancing quality for customers, they are looking for compensation programs that are more consistent with the value of the work delivered. This article describes three such programs at three different organizations.

At progressive companies across America, there's a quiet revolution going on every payday. Smart managers are examining their compensation plans, and realizing that the tried-and-true merit pay packages tied to small annual raises based on seniority, do little to retain talented employees—and even less to motivate them and improve productivity.

"Over the past few years, companies have been seeing that the existing pay system doesn't work very well," says James Nickel, leader of the alternative rewards practice team at William M. Mercer Inc., a benefits consulting firm in New York. Many managers up and down the company ladder are troubled at the lack of flexibility built into the traditional pay system: The annual raise—small as it has been of late—is seen as an entitlement, with talented employees often getting an increase that is only a percentage point higher than that of mediocre performers.

And as more companies try to empower their workforces, the old pay systems don't work since traditional merit pay doesn't promote teamwork. "Companies need a system that will cause employees to think more collectively about the company's success, rather than their own," says Nickel.

Reprinted by permission of publisher from *Management Review*, January 1994. Copyright © 1994, American Management Association, New York. All rights reserved.

As a result, innovative companies have begun to pay employees in clever ways. Here are a few of the most common new methods:

- *Variable pay.* A certain percentage of employee pay is put "at risk," generally allowing exceptional employees to doubly recoup their potential losses.
- *Skill-based pay.* Companies grant raises on the basis of skills that the employee has mastered.
- *Gainsharing.* A formula-based plan that pays for productivity and cost-saving.
- *Lump sum merit pay.* Awarded in a single check and not added into salary, thus avoiding future compounded interest.

According to a 1992 survey of more than 2,000 employers 61 percent of companies have some form of results-sharing in place.

More and more American firms are using new forms of pay to motivate and retain employees. According to a 1992 survey of more than 2,000 employers by Hewitt Associates, a benefits consulting firm based in Lincolnshire, Ill., 61 percent of companies have some form of results-sharing in place. (Results-sharing is defined by Hewitt Associates as performance-related awards that must be re-earned each year and do not increase base salary.) This figure is up from 57 percent in 1991 and 44 percent in 1989.

"Employees are expected to share the power and authority for making decisions, and they already share in the company's risk—if the company doesn't do well, they can lose their jobs," says Peter LeBlanc at Sibson & Co, a human resources consulting firm in Princeton, N.J. "It only makes sense to let them share in the company's rewards, as well."

But caution is the byword when it comes to changing any pay program. "Lots of companies like to jump on the latest fad," says Don Lowman, vice president of Towers Perrin, a New York-based consulting firm. "Before adopting any plan, you must do a needs assessment."

The idea is to use pay strategically to help your company reach its goals. For instance, the city of Hampton, Va., recently adopted a new pay plan to help augment the city's massive restructuring. "We've taken out layers of supervision, changed the way in which work is designed and instituted self-managed teams," explains Tharon Greene, director of human resources. To reinforce these changes, the city has several new pay programs: team pay for self-managed teams; variable re-earned performance increases in lieu of traditional raises; and cash bonuses and nonmonetary awards for innovative ideas.

In the three case studies that follow, top management carefully reflected on the company's goals and long-term strategy, and designed pay programs to fit the company's mission.

Rocky Mountain High

Although its pay program is plain vanilla gainsharing—only 10 percent of employee pay is at-risk—Colorado Memory Systems shows how a pay plan can be used strategically.

In October 1992, when Hewlett-Packard bought the small Loveland, Colo., computer component manufacturer files, the computer giant was faced with an immediate problem. How could it ensure that Colorado Memory retained its entrepreneurial spirit? "What we didn't want to do," says Roger Archibald, the Hewlett-Packard exec who oversaw the acquisition, "was to come in with a stack of employee manuals and say 'Here's how you're going to do business.' We wanted them to continue their corporate culture."

This task was difficult because Colorado Memory was about to go public at purchase time; and many Colorado employees, in keeping with their entrepreneurial roots, had plans to buy a piece of the company. When the news of the Hewlett-Packard purchase reached employees, "there was an overall sense of disappointment," says Carl Norcross, Colorado Memory's director of human resources. "Employees were looking forward to the company being publicly traded.

While wrestling with this issue, Archibald, along with Colorado Memory's top management, hit upon an ideal solution: variable pay. The notion of an innovative pay scheme was quite comfortable for Archibald, since Hewlett-Packard has had profit-sharing in place for more than 30 years. But Hewlett-Packard's profit-sharing plan, which pays out twice a year after it exceeds certain profit targets, seemed too tame for the new staffers. "The employees at Colorado Memory are risk takers," Archibald explains. "They came into a company with enormous growth potential, and expected to share, financially, in the company's success."

In addition, Hewlett-Packard was already faced with a need to bring Colorado Memory's pay up to Hewlett-Packard's base pay standards. In some cases, workers at Colorado Memory were working for 30 percent less than their counterparts at Hewlett-Packard. Ultimately, however, "This discrepancy worked to our advantage," says Peter LeBlanc, the Sibson consultant who helped to mastermind Colorado Memory's variable pay plan. "The company could add incentive pay without compensation levels being overly high and still attain parity within the Hewlett-Packard family."

The final result, which came after extensive focus groups composed of 10 percent of the company's employees, explains Archibald, is a classic gain-sharing pay program. Dubbed "success sharing," it works like this: all employees were given raises so that their base pay equalled at least 90 percent of their Hewlett-Packard counterparts. Then, each employee's salary was put at a 10 percent risk. After Colorado Memory's financial performance is analyzed at the end of each quarter, the at-risk portion is distributed—or withheld—based on company earnings. If Colorado Memory does well, employees can earn the 10 percent they put at risk as a bonus, earning 110 percent of their counterpart's pay. If Colorado Memory exceeds its target, the employee can earn an additional 10 percent.

In the first quarter that the program was in place, the company did exceed its goal, resulting in a 20 percent quarterly bonus to all employees. Naturally, the employees love it. "Rather than being suspicious, they see the pay program as a positive thing," says Archibald. "It enabled us to rise above the 'rape and pillage of the people' stereotype that employees of small companies have when they are acquired by a large corporation."

The real test lies ahead, on the day quarterly profits are down and the employees don't reap financial benefits. Company execs, however, are convinced that employees will continue to support the pay plan.

Instant Rewards

Polaroid, the camera company based in Cambridge, Mass., introduced skill-based pay following a major downsizing. In 1988, the company cut staff by 20 percent through severance and early retirement, and also started to redesign work on the factory floor, streamlining its manufacturing process and encouraging workers to work in teams. What made the transition particularly difficult, explains Richard Terry, compensation manager at Polaroid, was the age of many of Polaroid's workers. "We're in a technologically sophisticated, dynamic business, and we've got a mature population. In order for the teams to work, our employees needed to learn and develop new skills," he explains.

In order to earn more pay, employees must learn new skills.

Polaroid found the answer in skill-based pay, and in April 1990, instituted a companywide program. Basically, the program works like this: In order to earn more pay, employees must learn new skills—for instance, how to operate a new machine, or inspect a completed product—and then apply those skills on the job. To keep the process from being haphazard, a Polaroid management team—usually the worker's supervisor, a human resources consultant and a redesign consultant—work with the employee, redesigning and upgrading the employee's job, and targeting the new skills to be learned. "Instead of just becoming a more proficient and knowledgeable machine operator, a worker might begin to pick up some chemical mixing skills, or decision-making and leadership skills," explains Terry. The benefits to Polaroid are obvious: Workers perform more tasks, work better in teams and speed up the assembly process.

"The workers don't have to wait for somebody else to do something," says Terry. Instead, they can simply do it themselves. Some employees, who had long since "topped out" on Polaroid's pay scale for their jobs, have increased their pay by as much as 10 percent.

How has skill-based pay affected the bottom line? Terry explains that isolating the effect of the pay is difficult: "There are so many variables," he explains. "We've moved and improved equipment and changed assembly methods. So if an operation previously required 10 workers, but now requires only six, it's hard to pin down whether the improvement is a result of the equipment change or skill-based pay."

But Terry is convinced that skill-based pay has saved the company money. The workforce has remained 8,000 workers for the past five years, despite steadily climbing sales. And, Polaroid has recently begun marketing two new products—the Captiva camera and Helios, a dry imaging product for use in medical diagnosis—without having to add to its labor pool.

According to a Towers Perrin survey, Polaroid's success with skill-based pay is typical. From a sample of 80 skill-based pay programs, 70 percent reported measurable productivity improvements, with the remaining 30 percent terming the improvements significant. And 71 percent of the firms surveyed noted lower operating costs.

Food for Thought

Like countless factories throughout the United States, the West Bend Company, a major manufacturer of consumer appliances based in West Bend, Wis., used a piece-rate incentive system. "If an employee could run pieces at the rate of 150 an hour, as opposed to the average rate of 100, he or she would receive 50 percent more pay," says Clem Jacak, coach for the West Bend Beverage Makers division, manufacturers of percolators, hot pots and vegetable steamers. But with increasing international competition and demands for higher quality, West Bend had to change. "We're really driven by our big accounts, such as K Mart and Wal-Mart, and we constantly have to do things cheaper, better and quicker for these customers," explains Jacak.

West Bend's response was to break down the company into small operating units, including West Bend Beverage, which became what Jacak calls "a factory within a factory." The parent company decentralized most other corporate functions, such as engineering, purchasing and quality, so that each division is self-contained and operates independently. In addition, West Bend Beverage Makers started to synchronize manufacturing, and adopted just-in-time processes, to minimize inventory and improve quality.

At this point, the company ran into trouble. With the production line trimmed to current orders, worker pay plummeted. "Some employees lost as much as $2 an hour, and morale dropped. We didn't feel that was fair," Jacak recalls. As a result, employees were understandably reluctant to support the new program.

To resolve this, manufacturing at West Bend Beverage set up a rocky alliance with the company's union, forming a task force to study alternative ways to pay workers. Four-fifths of the task force members came from within West Bend Beverage—most of them from the factory floor. The group also included office workers, a member of the corporate bargaining committee, an employee from corporate finance, and the president of the union. "We ended up talking about many issues, including how to support the overall objectives, and achieve a high level of quality," Jacak explains. At one point, management even opened the company's books, to help build trust with workers and demonstrate why the factory needed to reorganize the work.

After a full year of hard work, the task force came up with a goal-sharing program that covers all workers in the beverage unit.

Finally, after a full year of hard work, the task force came up with a goal-sharing program that covers all workers in the beverage unit, including Jacak and other office workers. To determine pay, management measures production costs, overhead, quality control, productivity and customer service into a formula, comparing how well the unit did on each measure with a pre-set target. If the unit has achieved its goals, workers receive 100 percent of their pay. However, if goals have not been reached, "50 percent of everyone's pay is at risk," explains Jacak. If workers exceed their goals, then pay increases by a corresponding percentage.

The new pay plan went into effect in 1990, and has been a huge success. Each year since, workers have exceeded their goals, resulting in an average payout of 4 percent above their current standard pay. West Bend Beverage managers claim the investment in employee pay has been more than worthwhile. "As workers became more proficient, the factory floor employees began to know and understand operations better than the office staff," says Jacak. "We used to have supervisors and a foreman to police the floor. Now we have self-managed work groups, setting their own production goals, and maintaining quality."

Today, West Bend Beverage is a state-of-the-art factory. "We have a 70 percent improvement in our total quality efforts, just in the past three years," says Jacak. The factory has also reduced inventory by 50 percent, and scrap by 70 percent. But most important, the factory has re-won employee loyalty.

Donna Brown Hogarty is a frequent contributor to Management Review.

The Rating Game

Matthew Budman and Berkeley Rice

Performance appraisals—how to handle them in an organization practicing some version of TQM is always a challenge. This article reviews what several different companies are doing. As you will see, there is no easy answer here. However, one thing seems certain, with the disappearance of hierarchies and empowered employees, the traditional performance appraisal is on its way to being history.

Like those of the purely hierarchical organization, the days of the top-down performance review are numbered. The annual or semiannual employee-appraisal process is undergoing a slow conversion.

While some companies have simply tinkered with their appraisal forms or offered training on how to give better reviews, others are seeking fresh alternatives to the traditional top-down appraisal model. Companies are beginning to take into consideration feedback from employees' team members, co-workers and customers (both internal and external). Applying information from all of these sources is known as 360-degree feedback.

"Over the next four to five years, the great majority of organizations will find a way to incorporate data and feedback into the appraisal process other than just the manager's," says Richard Wellins, senior vice president at Development Dimensions International (DDI), a Pittsburgh-based management-consulting company.

The end result, experts say, will be an evaluation process initiated and directed by the employee himself. "The individual him- or herself," Wellins says, "should be the major person in charge of the process—the primary person responsible for collecting, synthesizing, and evaluating their own performance. I think employees want to have control over their own evaluations."

The end result, experts say, will be an evaluation process initiated and directed by the employee himself.

That control, of course, traditionally has been solely in the manager's hands, and like many of the changes wrought by American industry's move toward increased democracy and empowerment in the workplace, the power shift will require significant rethinking—especially for managers who find themselves under subordinates' scrutiny as part of a company's new appraisal process.

Timing and Trust

For those companies contemplating a more inclusive appraisal system, pacing is the key to success, experts say. Employees often are troubled by the idea of

---

Reprinted with permission from *Across the Board*, February 1994. Copyright © 1994, The Conference Board, Inc. All rights reserved.

having to criticize some of their peers. And although managers may find traditional reviews burdensome, they often feel insecure about relinquishing control over the process, and outright hostile about being appraised by their subordinates. "All managers want to be loved, and it's hard when they find out they're not," says Dick Beatty, a professor at the Institute of Management and Labor Relations at Rutgers University in New Brunswick, N.J.

Training on giving and receiving feedback can help allay fears, but participatory appraisals "need to be introduced slowly, and a certain level of trust needs to be built," Wellins says. "If you're moving to self-directed teams, appraisals are not the first thing I would put on the agenda. It takes time. There's no magic to how to build trust."

Beatty recommends that companies plan for a transitional period of two to three years. "What you want to build is candor," he says. "Without candor, you won't have trust. Without trust, you won't have risk-taking. And without risk-taking, you won't have creativity and innovation."

If the process is rushed, Wellins says, "you get what I call a washed-over appraisal: Either everyone gives only positive feedback or people just won't participate."

The dramatic shift all the way to self-based evaluations requires even more adjustment, says David DeVries, a management consultant and former executive vice president of the Center for Creative Leadership in Greensboro, N.C. "Having the employee drive the process is not as simple as it seems. It's a profound shift; historically, we've never asked employees to think this way." DeVries' experience has shown that "it takes five to 10 years before people really can engage in a subtle self-evaluation system."

Increasingly the workplace issue to be evaluated is no longer, 'Are you keeping busy?' but, 'Are you making a strategic contribution?'

Even then, he says, "the organization has to enter the process. Increasingly the workplace issue to be evaluated is no longer, 'Are you keeping busy?' but, 'Are you making a strategic contribution?' The employee doesn't know the answer to that: the manager does. The manager represents the company, and it's his job to say what's important to the company."

Planning the Change

Executives have begun to realize that, "The traditional performance appraisal really doesn't fit the way organizations are going, as we get people more involved and more interested in the success of the organization," says Jay Schuster of Schuster and Zingheim Associates Inc., a Los Angeles-based consulting firm that specializes in compensation issues.

While most companies have taken only tentative, if any, steps toward expanding the standard top-down appraisal process, many intend to do so in the near future, according to a recent survey studying companies' current evaluation practices and plans for future practices. "The future trend," says Wellins, who helped prepare the report, "is that a large number of companies plan to use customer input, team input, and peer input anywhere from often to very often."

The study, "Performance Management: What's Hot—What's Not," sponsored by DDI and the Society for Human Resource Management, found that:

- Relatively few companies currently train managers or nonmanagers in performance appraisal; nearly all plan to do so. "Participants obviously feel they need more training to make their performance management system work," the report reads.

- Few companies use measurements or evaluations to hold managers accountable for performance-appraisal effectiveness, but most intend to begin doing so. "Performance appraisals are treated as tasks," one respondent wrote about his company's current evaluation process. "There is no effort made to determine if they are actually doing any good." Companies can determine effectiveness through climate surveys, employee-satisfaction surveys, or focus groups, says Phyllis Misitano, DDI's project coordinator for the survey. "It's hard to get to quantitative data."

- Many companies plan to institute "upward input," employees appraising their managers—one of the touchier subjects being discussed in boardrooms.

- Slightly fewer companies plan to give employees numerical ratings (usually on a one-to-five scale) than do so now. "I would prefer just a narrative with no corresponding numbers used," wrote one respondent. "I don't feel an effective evaluation is one that makes people feel belittled by giving them a rating or number," another wrote. "An evaluation should be specific" as to an employees' accomplishments; a simple number, while certainly specific, is seen as narrow and vague.

- Companies expect their use of peer and team appraisals to almost double, though the total number for each still is not particularly high.

Letting It Slide: Quaker

Not surprisingly, peer reviews tend to be most successful where employees are accustomed to a participatory, rather than authoritarian, culture, and where employees have a fairly high degree of team interaction and can make informed judgments about their performances. Sometimes, though, even that doesn't work; pioneering companies that have eschewed top-down management in favor of teams since their foundings have seen dramatically mixed results with regard to peer evaluations. While W.L. Gore & Associates Inc.'s system continues to flourish, a Quaker Oats plant found its system deteriorating and eventually collapsing after a decade.

The appraisal system at the Quaker pet-food plant in Topeka, Kan., calls for workers' performances to be reviewed strictly by their peers on criteria such as team spirit, communication, problem-solving skills, and general attitude toward work. Most of the Quaker plant's 250 employees are supposed to participate in self-directed 20-member work teams that meet weekly to discuss production and personnel issues.

There's just one problem: The system has crashed.

The plant opened in 1971 with peer evaluation "one of the basic premises," according to consultant and former plant manager Herman Simon. "In the early days we put a fair amount of work into the appraisal process; now, unfortunately, we don't. The process is no longer working the way it should."

The problems arose, he says, when workers began to downplay criticism of each other. "When we started, people were honest and reasonably strict. After about 10 years, it began to fall apart; there was no incentive for people to be strict about it. Soon *everybody* was top-rated; everybody got good grades, unless somebody really stepped out of bounds. For the last decade, the average individual on the line has gotten no feedback at all."

Only recently has the problem been addressed; over the past year or two, the Topeka plant has been putting together a major reworking of the system. "The program was management-invoked, but what evolved is by the people," Simon says. "Both behavior—like chronic tardiness or attitudinal problems—and sheer technical ability will be part of the evaluation process."

The question is obvious: Why did it take 10 years for management to tackle the subject of performance evaluations? "Why wasn't there a strong push to change anything?" Simon asks. "Because productivity never slacked off. That's the strange part of this."

And why, if the Quaker plant continues to prosper under the current system, is a new process necessary? "Because it's the right thing to do," responds Simon, who says Quaker is looking into instituting a pay-for-performance system. "We think it's important that people know how well they're doing. If people are achieving, it should be recognized, and one way they can be recognized is through pay."

Keeping It Going: Gore

At W.L. Gore, the Newark, Del.-based maker of Gore-tex fabric (among other things), the team-based appraisal system first conceived by founder Bill Gore in 1958 "still works well for us, because we are still focused around teams and projects," says Cheryl Nelson, Gore compensation coordinator for the United States.

Gore associates (*not* employees) are organized in work teams that handle performance problems as well as other traditional personnel functions, such as hiring and firing.

Gore associates (*not* employees) are organized in work teams that handle performance problems as well as other traditional personnel functions, such as hiring and firing. Formal appraisals are company-wide affairs conducted for compensation purposes. At appraisal time—March and September—team members submit rankings and written comments about those peers whose work they're familiar with. The comments are compiled by committees composed of six to 10 volunteers who rank each team member according to his relative contribution to the team. Eventually, these rankings are blended into a master list, broken down by function, of the relative contributions of each associate.

Separate committees determine compensation, largely by where an individual falls in the functional ranking, as well as by comparisons with associates at other Gore plants and employees of companies in "the outside world." Associates are shown most of their co-workers' written comments, but rankings are kept strictly confidential.

CONFIDENCE MEN

Many companies promise that evaluations of supervisors will be given anonymously and reserved for the manager's eyes only, issues that stir vigorous debate among personnel executives and consultants in the field. Some feel that the process can be effective only with "open reviews," in which supervisors and subordinates meet face-to-face to discuss the results. But others insist it is unrealistic to expect subordinates to evaluate their bosses honestly without some guarantee of confidentiality.

"It's surprisingly hard to get negative feedback," says management consultant David DeVries, who advocates anonymity. "This is particularly true if the stakes are high enough. The manager can figure out who gave them a bad rating" and retaliate, DeVries says.

Tod White, former CEO of the management-consulting firm Blessing/White Inc. in Princeton, N.J., counters that "confidentiality is nonsense" in subordinate reviews. "If a manager's job is to help his subordinates succeed, he has to know how well he is meeting their specific needs," White says. "The real value of reverse reviews for a manager is not just in getting the feedback, but in discussing it with the subordinates. The most important thing is how a manager responds to individual needs, and you just can't do that anonymously."

At Milwaukee Mutual Insurance Co., feedback is given to managers anonymously—a practice that's endured since the company instituted upward appraisals as a management-development tool in 1984—and managers are encouraged but not required to share the results with their subordinates. (At least several do share, according to Milwaukee Mutual's Mike Herro.) As an official part of the performance appraisal, however, the results are seen by the manager's superior and count toward a manager's compensation and advancement. "We think that's where the rubber hits the road," Herro says.

This process goes somewhat beyond labor-intensive, Nelson says. "We ask each of the associates to do a contribution list in January and February, and it takes a tremendous amount of time in mailing out requests for lists. I collect thousands and thousands of sheets of paper during contribution-list time. And then each of the compensation-committee members collect contribution lists on their own."

The burden has become so "cumbersome" that the company recently tried reducing the number of associates asked for contribution lists in September. "We do have a business to run," Nelson says. But few associates appear to resent the effort the appraisal system requires; the family atmosphere at Gore, where a percentage of every associate's salary buys company stock, fosters the type of independence and loyalty a participatory-appraisal system needs to succeed, she says.

At times, naturally, even Gore associates find themselves too time-strapped by other obligations to put much effort into the evaluation process, and their financial ties to the company give priority to Gore's fiscal fortunes. "We all have our pocketbooks in Gore," Nelson says. "When the economy is good and unemployment rates are low, associates are willing to spend more time on the process. When, like right now, people are beating down our doors for jobs and our profits are going down, associates are less willing. They want to spend their time making money for the company."

Both Gore and the Topeka plant are quick to point out that their uniquely designed systems aren't easily transferable to other companies, or even to other groups within the same organization. Gore's labor-intensive ranking process already has stymied many would-be imitators, says Trish Hearn, until recently a company spokesperson. "We have people come in who spend a half to a whole day with us on compensation, and they leave and they love the philosophy, but they can't believe how much work we put into it."

Similarly, Simon says that while other Quaker Oats operations have borrowed ideas from Topeka's appraisal system, "It would be looking for disaster to say, 'Do something exactly the way Topeka is doing it' and dump it into Cedar Rapids," where Quaker headquarters are located. "However, there isn't any reason why it *couldn't* work; it depends on what the needs and culture are elsewhere."

Can Peers Be Fair?

While most companies aren't prepared to turn the appraisal system over to employees to manage, more and more appear headed in that direction. Milwaukee Mutual Insurance Co., which uses a combination of supervisor, self-, and peer assessment in what it dubs its "consensus review process," also has found that this system produces more meaningful appraisals.

"There was a bit of trepidation at first," says Mike Herro, vice president of human resources. "Some people had difficulty believing that peers would be fair and objective in a review. But the feedback from our employees indicates that they feel the process more appropriately measures their performance. They feel their co-workers have a better feel for how they're doing than the manager does."

Milwaukee Mutual began consensus appraisal in 1990 as part of an employee-empowerment program stressing self-directed work teams. In that spirit, the employees themselves designed the process and appraisal forms, and negotiate as teams with their managers over how each source of feedback will be weighted. The system, applying to everyone in the organization, includes "upward appraisals" in which subordinates give feedback on managers' communication and team-building skills.

Since many supervisors balk at receiving criticism from those they manage, companies often gain their cooperation by limiting the use of upward appraisals to career-development purposes only. AT&T Co., for example, uses subordinate reviews as one means to evaluate its management-training program in employee involvement. "We first identified the key skills managers need in order to involve their employees," says Ed Bancroft, a consultant who helped develop the program. "Then we used reverse appraisal to see how well we trained managers in these skills."

Milwaukee Mutual began using upward feedback in 1984 solely as a developmental tool, Herro says, and encountered little resistance when it began including it in appraisals two years ago. "If we had started out using upward feedback on performance reviews, it would have carried too much weight," he says. "But the way we did it, it hasn't been a problem. People appreciate the feedback."

Polling the Customer

An often-overlooked dimension of 360-degree feedback is the customer or client review; in fact, many companies have left customers out of the equation altogether. "A lot of companies talk about 360 degrees," Rutgers' Beatty says, "but if they don't include customer feedback, they're using only 270 degrees at best."

Xerox Corp. uses results from periodic customer-satisfaction surveys in performance reviews of its sales and service representatives, and to help determine bonuses for sales and service managers. But "customers" also can refer to those being served within the company: In a manufacturing plant, say, a production manager might be considered an internal customer of someone in R&D or purchasing who regularly supplies him with information or materials.

Xerox Corp. uses results from periodic customer-satisfaction surveys in performance reviews of its sales and service representatives.

Milwaukee Mutual includes feedback from internal and/or external customers, depending on the department. "At performance-review time, everyone routinely surveys their customers for satisfaction." Herro says.

One reason companies have been slower to incorporate customer reviews into their appraisal process than other feedback sources is the time and inconvenience involved in going outside the department or company for data. But companies that neglect customer feedback do so at the expense of the appraisal's effectiveness, says Beatty, who calls customer feedback the "most powerful" motivating force at a company's disposal.

"Customer-backed data creates very real discrepancies between how we see ourselves and how those we have to serve see us," Beatty says. "It's pretty easy to blow off the things that your boss is telling you about your performance. It's much more difficult to say that the customer is wrong. They may be wrong, but they're also your customer, so you can't just dismiss that."

Changing Culture

For the moment, alternative forms of performance review remain a new frontier for most of American industry, and the accuracy of the predictions of DDI's Wellins that experimentation will begin in earnest over the next five years depends in large part upon how quickly the notions of teamwork and self-management take root. In many companies, those principles still are invoked as trendy buzzwords rather than applied as meaningful elements of corporate policy.

Many believe that companies that commit to employee empowerment will institute performance-appraisal reform sooner rather than later—after all, a new appraisal-and-reward system carries a tangible message of cultural change, one that employees may need to take company pledges seriously. But those urging patience have a point: Adding a volatile new element to the working relationship will throw off the balance of power between employer and employees. Everyone involved, Wellins says, should be prepared adequately. "To some extent the situation is like getting married," he says. "In marriage, I think it's usually best to wait a few years before having kids—before introducing a new person into the equation."

Matthew Budman is an assistant editor of Across the Board. *Berkeley Rice is a freelance writer and a senior associate editor at* Medical Economics *magazine.*

Hewlett-Packard's Core Values Drive HR Strategy

Jennifer J. Laabs

Hewlett-Packard is known as a progressive company that has adopted Total Quality Management as its operating principle. This includes the processes traditionally identified as human resources. This article documents how the HR processes at H-P have been improved to lower costs and increase service to its customers—the company's 90,000 employees.

You can always tell who the winners are. They never settle for less than the best. They're motivated more by inner conviction than outside influences. And they willingly learn from their own mistakes. But winners aren't made in a day. Neither was Hewlett-Packard Co.'s personnel department.

Despite the commitment of co-founders Bill Hewlett and Dave Packard to create an environment in which employees can fulfill their natural desires to do good, creative work, they refused to establish a personnel department until 1957—18 years after they founded the electronics manufacturer in Palo Alto, California, simultaneously creating Silicon Valley. A personnel professional wasn't allowed to run the department until 1989, when F.E. (Pete) Peterson became vice president of personnel after a 24-year career in human resources, 17 of them at H-P. "My getting this job was unique," Peterson says, "because the company had a tradition of filling the top personnel job with a general manager on his or her way to something bigger and better."

As with many roads paved with good intentions, H-P's way didn't always take it to the best of places. The company got a late start on its personnel department because both Hewlett and Packard believed that line managers should care about their people and handle their own personnel issues. And because big bureaucracies often inhibit creativity, the late-blooming personnel function, like the rest of the organization, was decentralized as much as possible. Ironically, by 1990 the firm had an inflated roster of 1,800 personnel staffers, for 90,000 total employees worldwide, which represented twice the industry norm. Moreover, H-P's line managers were relying increasingly upon these personnel staffers, with diminishing returns. "I didn't see morale going up [and] I didn't perceive that managers were getting any better at people management," Peterson recalls.

Reprinted with permission from *Personnel Journal*, December 1993. Copyright © 1993, ACC Communications, Costa Mesa, CA. All rights reserved.

That era has ended. Today, H-P's core values are evident in sweeping changes in how the $16.4 billion (sales) electronics firm's human resources are managed. In only three years, the personnel-to-employee ratio has dropped from 1:53 to 1:75—and while Peterson has set no new goals for slimming his department, he's keeping an eye on other firms that boast ratios as low as 1:200.

But reducing numbers are only the beginning. That they've been attained without violating H-P's long-standing no-layoff ethic is equally important. At the same time, Peterson's staff has launched a campaign to provide better service to the organization by carefully reexamining virtually every personnel process. Thus, they're searching out opportunities to consolidate activities that can work better either in a single global center or in a few regional locations. New computer technologies are putting information in the right hands—whether it's a staff professional, line manager, employee or job applicant—more quickly than ever. Wherever possible, they're taking personnel out of the decision-making loop, assuming a consultative role, re-empowering line managers to take responsible action on people issues and returning their attention to staying at the top of the list of preferred employers. And through it all, they're trying to preserve the best of Hewlett-Packard's past practices. "We're moving the pendulum back in the [right] direction," says Peterson. Once again, personnel is becoming a complement to management, not a substitute for it—and it's looking a lot like a winner in the process.

Wherever possible, they're taking personnel out of the decision-making loop, assuming a consultative role, re-empowering line managers to take responsible action on people issues.

New Personnel Leadership Leads to New Strategy

After Peterson took the top personnel position in 1989, he spent six months gathering data and developing a plan of action. He met with all 50 of H-P's senior managers in addition to benchmarking the best practices of other companies. Peterson concluded that H-P's personnel function was on the right track in several areas, but still could benefit from some changes that would more closely link personnel with the organization's goals, processes and strategies. "Identifying, prioritizing and resolving issues was something we already did well," he says. "What was lacking was a clear definition of the role of HR in the '90s and how we add value to the organization."

"What was lacking was a clear definition of the role of HR in the '90s and how we add value to the organization."

Part of the answer lay in returning to the founders' original vision of making line managers responsible for people issues. "I think of ourselves more as consultants than as counselors," he says. Instead of being involved in the day-to-day people problems, H-P's personnel professionals are taking on a broader consulting and coaching role to train managers how to be more effective in people management.

"There's a lot more coaching and counseling that managers could do that personnel has been happy to do [in the past]," says Tom Pierson, H-P's HR planning, staffing and relocations manager. Anybody can sit down and become familiar with H-P's transfer policy, for example, and make an employee and his or her family feel comfortable about transferring. Getting personnel out of the loop allows managers more responsibility over this process and others. "You provide the tools to managers that allow them to do it themselves or make it easier and so much fun that they want to do it themselves," says Pierson.

In 1990, Peterson called upon his worldwide personnel team to *create the environment* by increasing value, providing higher quality and utilizing resources more effectively. Moreover, as part of its new role, personnel at H-P is serving as a business partner with line managers. "HR will become an increased source of competitive advantage and will become more involved in business strategy through the '90s," says Peterson. "How you help your organization become more competitive in a rapidly changing business environment is by far the No. 1 issue."

To translate this revised vision of personnel's role into specific actions, Peterson designed Project '93, a set of specific goals for personnel. In addition to reducing the personnel-to-employee ratio, some of these goals were to:

- Reengineer, define, standardize and continuously improve H-P's personnel processes
- Implement information technology such as a worldwide employment-management system and an international-employee master file and to improve efficiency and effectiveness
- Stimulate change in such areas as teamwork, organizational effectiveness, quality and people development.

To accomplish these goals, Peterson focused the personnel department's attention on its own processes. The first order of business for H-P's personnel department in learning how to use its resources more effectively was to decrease the personnel-to-employee ratio. The goal was meant to help the department streamline its operations and increase its effectiveness both to employees and to the company's managers.

Over the years, the personnel function had grown both in numbers of people and as a percentage of the work force. The largest gain in personnel professionals was in the area of personnel generalists or personnel liaisons. Peterson had to find ways to reduce personnel headcount, while still being a value-added function at H-P. Basically, it was a matter of doing more, better, with less. By May 1993, the department had shrunk to 1,335, a 25% reduction in personnel staff worldwide that will yield an overall savings of more than $35 million a year for the company.

For H-P, streamlining the personnel function to its present level has been an important step in its reengineering process. After considerable debate, the department decided to monitor ratios annually, but not to set new ratio goals for the future so that it can focus on other parts of Project '93. One of those has been the consolidation and regionalization of certain personnel services.

This move came as the result of the personnel department looking at its processes, which were highly decentralized worldwide. Virtually all of Hewlett-Packard's 50 divisions and 120 sales offices had their own on-site personnel staff, which took care of all their HR needs, both administrative and strategic. Peterson decided that there had to be a better way. There was.

Peterson's strategy was to consolidate duplicated or redundant personnel operations wherever possible while keeping those activities that require local attention at the site level. Some operations were centralized at the corporate level, others were concentrated into regional personnel centers, while still others remained the responsibility of on-site personnel staffs that could be responsive to business needs.

Over the past few years, for example, personnel has consolidated disability-claims management into a disability service center, medical transactions into a medical response center and relocations into a relocations center.

The disability service center was consolidated into a single site in January. Previously, there were 26 personnel staffers responsible for disability-claims processing. Instead, managers now own the process by submitting the initial information about an employee who's out on disability leave. "[The new process is that] wherever possible, decisions should be made by the people who know the most about it," says Sally Dudley, compensation, benefits and systems manager.

Peterson's strategy was to consolidate duplicated or redundant personnel operations wherever possible while keeping those activities that require local attention at the site level.

Some of the other major personnel consolidations at H-P have taken place in the U.K., Italy and H-P's European multicountry region. H-P's Australasia location, which includes Australia and New Zealand, has gone to one personnel function for both sites, instead of having two. In the U.S., a large number of field offices have consolidated many of their people-related processes, most notably in the San Francisco Bay Area.

The Bay Area includes 13 different sites and more than 15,000 employees. Since Project '93 started in 1990, the area's 200 personnel employees have incorporated most human resources functions into one regionalized center called the Bay Area Personnel Services (BAPS) Regional Center. This consolidation is expected to be completed by the end of fiscal year 1994.

The regionalized personnel services include operational activities such as records, benefits and staffing and organizational activities, such as employee-relations issues and organizational design projects. Personnel site managers primarily are responsible for these operational and organizational activities at all of Hewlett-Packard's business sites, including the Bay Area.

In addition, BAPS personnel plans to add another component to the 13 Bay Area business sites which will give managers access to common human resources materials such as personnel forms, training and education schedules and employee-records forms. These components will be known as personnel-service centers.

One of personnel's new goals is to contribute to business decision making and facilitate changes that are consistent with H-P's basic values. By maintaining on-site personnel professionals who can consult with managers on business-specific issues, personnel can be more involved in correlating personnel knowledge and practice with business challenges. These on-site groups, called management support teams, include personnel managers, personnel support managers, function specialists and administrative assistants.

Each of H-P's business sites may have different needs. For example, one site may need customer training that must be designed especially for them.

Personnel and management can meet to discuss exactly what's needed and develop a solution according to those needs.

"We learned years ago at Hewlett-Packard that progressive human resources practices don't just occur because you have a group of bright, dedicated people sitting in corporate headquarters thinking up new ideas," says Peterson. That's why H-P opens up the process to managers for suggestions. Ideas are tried out and implemented if they work. If ideas work in one area, they can spread throughout the organization worldwide. For example, Hewlett-Packard pioneered the idea of flexible working hours in its West German division in 1967, and by 1972 it had spread throughout the organization.

The long-term results of personnel's regionalization at H-P are yet to be realized. Personnel expects continued cost reduction, increased effectiveness and greater efficiency of service delivery. Peterson says that he hopes to spread the regionalization of personnel services to wherever it's applicable worldwide.

In addition to consolidating services, personnel has streamlined itself carefully by outsourcing administrative activities when it proves cost-effective and provides a higher-quality service. Outside vendors already handle: 401(k) administration, group universal life program (GULP), COBRA administration and service-award administration.

Technology Helps Personnel Streamline and Get Managers Closer to the People-Management Process

H-P is well on its way to being world-class in human resources information technology systems. Currently, it has several systems in place and several more on the way. These systems are helping the H-P personnel community improve its efficiency and effectiveness in numerous ways.

Before technology improvements could be made, however, it was important for the personnel function first to look at its overall operation. "You can't implement the information technology unless you have process definition. You can't go to consolidated organizations without having systems in place. All three have to move in parallel," says Peterson.

The focus on technology has come as a direct result of Peterson's new direction for the personnel department. In terms of technology, the human resources function had taken a back seat to most other functions at Hewlett-Packard. "We've been kind of the cobbler's children," says Peterson. "We're now very highly funded in long-term information technology."

The company is moving toward a single, integrated system that will serve as the foundation for all people-management processes worldwide—from recruitment through retirement.

H-P's business sites used to manage human resources projects with decentralized personnel technology systems in much the same way as it provided personnel services at each location. Personnel's technology, in some cases, was more than 20 years old. Now the company is moving toward a single, integrated system that will serve as the foundation for all people-management processes worldwide—from recruitment through retirement.

The personnel department scrapped its previous HR technology, which included a distributed-employee database, an HRIS and a payroll system. It now has a new umbrella system called PeopleBase, under which it developed several new personnel applications. These include a telephone-activated benefits system, an employment-management system, a training-management system, a human-resources-management system, an optical-file-imaging system, a personnel-document-management system and an international-employee-master-file system.

In short, H-P intends for PeopleBase to be more than just a personnel information system. It's a vision of people management as an integrated, cross-functional process, rather than a collection of separate, people-related activities.

The employment-management system (EMS) represents one of the personnel department's biggest achievements and is the largest application on the PeopleBase client/server network. The idea for EMS started three years ago with a conversation between Dave Packard and Tom Pierson. They realized that they had a big problem: just to apply for a job at Hewlett-Packard, applicants had to send their resumes to 46 different mailing addresses in the U.S. Each of Hewlett-Packard's business units collected resumes individually. Few, if any, shared resumes with each other.

Pierson has spent the last two and a half years designing, developing, testing and implementing a completely automated staffing system for Hewlett-Packard U.S. and all of its English-speaking foreign divisions. Applicants now send their resumes to one Hewlett-Packard address—H-P's employment response center at its corporate facility in Palo Alto. They're then scanned into the system using advanced, optical-character-recognition technology and are available to all U.S. hiring managers within 72 hours. The system currently is available only to H-P's U.S. personnel staff and its English-speaking divisions, but plans are in the works for similar systems to become available for Hewlett-Packard's non-U.S. operations.

The system, which just went online this fall, can hold as many as 220,000 resumes in the data base. The resumes are kept current—six months old to the present. In addition, EMS can perform a short-list search for applicants in various categories such as the college-recruitment pool, the unsolicited-resume pool or the internal-candidate pool. The system also tracks each resume through the entire hiring process so that any personnel staffer or hiring manager knows at any given time exactly where each candidate is within the H-P system. In addition, EMS automatically sends acknowledgement and regret letters to candidates and tracks affirmative-action information. It even opens an employee file for each new hire as soon as he or she accepts a job offer. The system is expected to save H-P $24 million a year.

In the future, Pierson says that H-P is hoping to put fax machines on each college campus where it recruits so that students can send their resumes directly to H-P's employment-management system. In addition, Hewlett-Packard plans to install kiosks at every H-P building so that employees can submit their resumes for any job opening.

Another bonus for employees is that if they don't currently have a resume, the system will help them write one. EMS even can be accessed by H-P's college recruiters with laptop or palm-held computers so that they can input student-interview reports off-site.

The system also will be compatible with H-P's redeployment program, which matches employees who have lost their jobs because of downsizing or outsourcing with other positions within Hewlett-Packard. "It's reverse engineering," explains Pierson. H-P can match people with jobs rather than jobs with people. "It will provide a lot of added value to be able to rebalance our work force and move people around within H-P to maintain their employment security," he adds.

Line managers also are getting closer to the hiring process with the advent of the new employment-management system. Instead of asking a personnel staffer at his or her particular site to look up all the candidates that fit a certain job description, site managers can look up those candidates themselves in a maximum of five minutes using a key word or key phrase. It takes only a few minutes to learn how to use the system. "Managers are now begging for it because they've heard how great it is," says Pierson. The system will serve managers better, especially those who work alternate shifts and who don't usually have live access to personnel staff members.

Another technology system that's in development is a worldwide data-access system. The system basically is a warehouse in a client/server environment that allows managers worldwide to access employment information across geographics. In the past, when senior management teams wanted information about their worldwide work forces, personnel had to gather each element from each country or entity separately. H-P's international systems don't talk with each other whether it's U.S., European or Asian. "It's very frustrating for the managers," says Pierson.

With the input of managers worldwide, personnel has identified 14 data elements and installed them into what's called an international-employee master file. On the system's first incarnation are such data elements as performance evaluations, payroll and benefits information. The master file will be updated each month with information on every H-P employee worldwide. Managers can access everything from employees' names and employee numbers to payroll information.

Personnel will be adding more data elements to the system each year. Soon it will become so automated that H-P will have one employee master file that contains information on every H-P employee worldwide.

According to Pierson, no other company in the world has HR systems with the capabilities of its EMS and international-employee-master-file systems. They already are proving to be models for the future as other companies call upon H-P to share information about how it developed these systems.

Personnel Links Its Strategy to H-P's Quality-of-Work-Life Strategy

One of personnel's major new initiatives coincides with those of H-P's new chairman, president and CEO, Lewis E. Platt. For 1994, Platt set a strategic planning policy to reassert H-P's position as the best place to work. Hewlett-Packard's past leadership in this area has translated into a significant competitive advantage for the firm in the computer industry, where rapid turnover among highly valued employees is a persistent challenge. H-P's most recent internal surveys, however, show that its employees now believe that the company no longer exceeds industry norms.

To outsiders, this perception may seem off the mark. After all, for the past seven years, the company has been on *Working Mother* magazine's list of the 100 best places to work. It's also featured in *The 100 Best Companies To Work for in America,* the widely acknowledged book by Robert Levering and Milton Moskowitz. And just this year, H-P was ranked as no. 7 on *Money* magazine's list of companies offering the best benefits packages in the U.S.

Nonetheless, some events over the past decade may have tarnished H-P's image with its own employees. For example, a corporate downsizing and an ill-fated program to use part-time workers have taken the luster off its vaunted no-layoff policy. Moreover, the firm isn't making as much progress in managing diversity and promoting women as senior management had hoped.

Once more, the solution was found in refocusing on H-P's traditional values. While putting a fresh emphasis on its internal employee survey, Peterson's staff is working to reverse any weakening of commitment to the Hewlett-Packard Way throughout the organization. This campaign touches on everything from job security to promoting women.

"I'm absolutely convinced that employment security has a lot to do with why reasonably well-educated human beings select a company, are loyal to a company and are good performers," Pierson says. So, H-P has gone out of its way to maintain that employment-security mindset and value system. "It repays itself tenfold," he adds.

The no-layoff policy, however, had changed since 1985, when Hewlett-Packard embarked on a major restructuring, which has been accomplished through voluntary severance, early retirement and redeploymnt plans. Pierson credits the success of the no-layoff policy to good overall management. "H-P has been well managed to the extent that we can see things coming better than maybe some other companies do," he adds.

Another of Hewlett-Packard's personnel programs undergoing change is its flex-force program. Designed to protect the company during recessions while offering employment to non-career workers it was a well-designed program that had some fatal flaws, which personnel discovered three years into the five-year program. One flaw was that the company counted on having an ample labor market of retirees, students and second-income earners who didn't need medical insurance or pension security from Hewlett-Packard.

Within a few years of implementing its flex-force program, personnel realized that there weren't enough people like that to meet its needs. The other problem was that Hewlett-Packard realized that it was taking advantage of contingent workers. The individuals that Hewlett-Packard hired for its flex-force program actually wanted full-time work, but couldn't find it elsewhere. "H-P, the consummate ethical company with uncompromising integrity and high moral standards, said, 'This isn't right,' " explains Pierson. Clearly, it needed a new strategy.

Now, Hewlett-Packard is winding down its flex-force program and is developing partnerships with third-party employment agencies that provide their workers with insurance coverage, benefits and employment security. "These agencies are in the business of making sure they find these people their next job," explains Pierson. "We feel more socially responsible about developing relationships with two or three world-class companies that have a value system similar to H-P."

By effectively managing diversity within Hewlett-Packard, personnel also hopes to help increase the firm's stance as a leading employer. Although the overall percentage of professionals at Hewlett-Packard who are women is a respectable 28%, and the overall percentage of professionals who are minorities is 17%, the upper echelons of management still are experiencing the glass-ceiling effect. Only 4% of senior managers at Hewlett-Packard are female and 5% are minorities. Women managers quit at twice the rate of men at H-P.

Hewlett-Packard has had a management-diversity training program since 1988. The training is given to the company's first- and second-level managers. "What was missing in that program was that it really didn't start at the top," says Emily Duncan, Hewlett-Packard's corporate manager of work force diversity.

The issue of diversity needed top-down emphasis. In June, Hewlett-Packard's CEO and his direct reports participated in an executive diversity-education workshop. This has helped increase awareness of the issue and positioned it as one of the key business policies for the '90s at H-P.

Duncan sees development and retention of women and minorities as the two biggest problems facing H-P in the area of diversity. "We need to ensure that we're providing the right level of support for development activities," says Duncan. In addition, focusing on making sure that the work environment is supportive and is a place where people want to stay and grow will aid retention.

Duncan sees development and retention of women and minorities as the two biggest problems facing H-P in the area of diversity.

Hewlett-Packard has a variety of diversity-education programs for employees and managers. Recent additions to the program include classes on the issues of disability, sexual orientation and harassment. In many cases, employees and managers take diversity-education classes together.

Peterson says that it's important that both senior executives and managers get involved in the diversity process at Hewlett-Packard. "Show me an entity where there's excitement in managing diversity—where there's enthusiasm, results and where people are busting through the glass ceiling—and I'll show you an organization where there's management ownership and responsibility for that aspect of the business," he says. "Show me an entity where it's primarily a compliance program and I'll show you where the personnel function has sole ownership for what goes on in the personnel area." Managers at Hewlett-Packard now must be directly involved in bringing about change throughout the organization.

An important component of H-P's diversity-education process is a 12-month, accelerated-development program for high-potential employees who are in mid-level management positions representing line functions. The program is for all employees, not just minority and women managers, but H-P's goal is to have 38% women and minorities in the program. So far, 38 people have participated in the program, which started two years ago.

The program has four major components: an assessment center, a mentor relationship, a structured work experience and an external education and training program. During the year, managers work (in addition to their normal jobs) on projects that give them a better understanding of H-P's business and help them develop new skills.

Outside the U.S., H-P's diversity program faces special challenges. For example, the management team at Hewlett-Packard's Yokogawa (YH-P), Japan, region has focused on the process of hiring women, people with disabilities and utilizing and motivating its employees who are over the age of 40. Currently, 4.7% of this division's professional work force are women. Its short-term goal is to increase the number to 10% by the end of 1995. Its long-term goal is to have 25% of its professional/exempt positions filled by women.

One of the region's special problems retarding the movement of women into senior management is a labor law that prohibits professional women (except managers) from working after 10 p.m. It's common for professional men to stay until midnight, often giving them a business advantage over women colleagues. The other problem is that the Japanese culture is among the world's most conservative on women's issues. Not surprisingly, it hasn't encouraged women to be as aggressive or as confident as men in moving up the organizational ladder. Focusing on the development of professional women is H-P's goal.

One of the region's solutions is to send an annual interviewing invitation to all of its female employees. Those women who want to move up within H-P then can interview with various managers for higher positions. Other solutions include better training of employees and managers about diversity issues, giving dependent-care leave and offering more flex-time arrangements.

Although Hewlett-Packard's U.S. divisions may be slightly ahead of the game over its foreign counterparts in terms of diversity issues, the company has refocused its efforts to provide its managers worldwide with the tools that they need to build a diverse work force, such as part-time work, job-rotation assignments and telecommuting. Says Duncan: "I think most companies now recognize that this isn't just something nice to do. It creates an important advantage to our business success."

There never is one answer to a problem, and Hewlett-Packard hasn't cornered the market on personnel solutions. However, by not being afraid to reevaluate every HR process and to constantly discard what doesn't work so that solutions emerge, H-P has discovered a winning combination. It very well could be the only way that the human resources profession—and therefore, business—will survive in the '90s.

Jennifer J. Laabs is the senior writer at Personnel Journal.

Building Union-Management Partnerships

Ken Myers and Bob Killeen

This article explores the compatibility of unionism with TQM and suggests 14 benefits for unions and management that emerge from collaborating in the implementation of quality management.

For more than a decade, a quality improvement wave has been sweeping the U.S. private and the public sectors. In many industries, "Made in America" and "Service With Pride" are once again positive marketplace factors. In fact, any debate about the importance of quality appears to have ended. Clearly, quality has become a crucial element in many organizations' competitiveness.

As the revolution grows, organizations are moving from piecemeal quality improvement to more planned, systemic efforts. For example, many organizations are now seeking to implement total quality management (TQM). Successful TQM efforts often require a significant change in management philosophy and action. For example, structures flatten, management becomes more participative, teamwork is encouraged, and the nature of tasks evolves.

For some highly unionized organizations, these philosophical changes have meant finding new ways to engage their unions in the quality quest. Others have struggled down the path with little or no union involvement.

These changes have presented unions with new dimensions, often outside traditional work and contract provisions. Many unions have had to examine their own long-held views of "proper" union-management relationships (and even union-member relationships) and which strategies provide the greatest benefits to members. Not surprisingly, many managers and union leaders continue to hold a largely adversarial view of their relationship and decry any possibilities for transformation.

If an organization is substantially unionized, managers are unlikely to be able to implement TQM alone. Why? Like it or not, most unions exert tremendous influence at the grass-roots level. This is exactly where quality must become an uncontentious way of life. If TQM is to succeed, some form of workable partnership seems to be in the cards. There are steps that managers can take to encourage unions' cooperation and, better yet, gain their active involvement.

If TQM is to succeed, there are steps that managers can take to encourage unions' cooperation and, better yet, gain their active involvement.

Reprinted with permission from *Quality Progress*, April 1994. Copyright © 1994, ASQC, Milwaukee, WI. All rights reserved.

The Setting

The 1980s brought incredible pressures on the public and private sector. Competition, technology advances, acquisitions, government decisions, and a host of other factors helped change the bargaining landscape. Union influence ebbed and flowed in many sectors. At one point, concessionary bargaining became an almost accepted practice.

Post-cold-war industrial transformations, the effects of recession, and increasing global competition are among the many elements that will likely make the 1990s even more complex for management and organized labor. These events will cause the bargaining landscape to continue its evolution. Both unions and management will keep on pursuing their traditional activities; in fact, unions will likely seek to make up lost bargaining ground.

Management and union leaders, however, will face new challenges that will demand innovative responses. Organizations that expect to be healthy at the dawn of the 21st century will unrelentingly seek new structures, improved financial and operating efficiencies, and increased productivity. Almost certainly, these transitions will be fueled by the need to produce higher-quality goods and services to gain and retain customers.

Producing high-quality goods and services must be promoted from within an organization, beginning from the top. Quality, however, rests squarely on the shoulders of employees at the grass roots. Management can plan for quality, promote it, train for it, oversee it, and even reward it. But only an energetic, willing work force can deliver it—a work force that must see why it is in its own best interest to do so. The bargaining unit's influence at this grass-roots level is almost inescapable. Given this, quality would falter in a union-management firefight. Thus, quality excellence is optimally a product of union-management cooperation.

Quality excellence is optimally a product of union-management cooperation.

A contract provision stipulating the value of quality is grossly insufficient. To truly excel requires an active partnership to stimulate and guide grass-roots quality efforts. This is obviously easier said than done. In part, management must examine its own motives and actions that inhibit such cooperation. Often management must take the initiative to encourage union involvement.

Union Objections

Unions don't oppose TQM outright. The majority are painfully aware that quality products and services are their greatest chance for job security. They understand that protective contract provisions mean little when organizations have too few customers.

There is no single, monolithic union response to TQM involvement. Some unions consider active involvement because they don't want to take a position that makes them look like they oppose quality. Employees are consumers. They see first-hand and read about the effects of quality performance in the marketplace. Unless there are very specific reasons to take a hostile position, opposing quality improvement can look like beating up motherhood and apple pie. Employees who are fed nonspecific, unenlightened rhetoric about loss of jobs or management's brainwashing can come to distrust union officials with not-so-subtle results at election time. In addition, refusing cooperation can cast union leaders as reactionary and lacking in vision and initiative.

Some unions have maintained traditional adversarial bargaining positions while embracing quality initiatives. Others take hard-line positions disparaging quality improvement strategies as active, nonconfrontational methods for undermining shop-floor representation. Still others look at management's often poor implementation efforts and conclude that the process is just the latest expensive fad. In any event, policy typically flows from the union's international headquarters, although some local affiliates act independently to best serve their own interests.

Union reluctance is evident. Unions often come to the table with the perspective that much of their success has come through decades of hard-nosed adversarial bargaining. Relationships with management have been strictly defined by contracts, standard procedures, and traditional shop-floor representation. Union leaders are political beings who usually pragmatically represent the wishes of internal hierarchies as well as voting members. Given all of this, when quality efforts begin to emerge in organizations, union leaders are often suspicious of management's motives.

If bargaining units are approached for involvement, they might respond skeptically. In similar manner, if they are ignored, uncertainty can give way to confirmed suspicions. Finding a pathway of mutual trust and cooperation means actively overcoming this initial baggage of suspicion. Here are several common situations that foster union suspicion and thus hamper attempts at promoting joint efforts:

- Unions have experienced a progression of management fads, with senior management often failing to walk its talk.
- The attitudinal- and behavioral-change methods used to facilitate grass-roots quality participation are identical in many respects to those in union-prevention strategies.
- Efforts start in a climate lacking trust or previous collaborative experience.
- Management takes unilateral implementation actions. Quality activities are sprung on the union.
- Efforts are poorly planned and inconsistently implemented with limited follow-through.
- Companies don't provide meaningful awareness briefings, training, or involvement opportunities for union leaders.
- Elements of the quality process and successful outcomes are viewed as upsetting the balance of power between the union and the organization.
- A quality effort is used as ammunition to upset a bargaining unit's internal politics.

- Common quality implementation processes are viewed as manipulative and supportive of an unstated effort to reduce employee allegiance to the union or to redefine hard-won contract provisions.
- Quality initiatives, intentionally or not, permeate activities that infringe on traditional areas for management-union committee resolution and might even make the committee appear peripheral. This is especially true when the nature and structure of work processes as well as the leadership must change if quality is to improve.
- Quality efforts appear to go hand in hand with cost-cutting steps that almost invariably lead to situations in which crafts are diminished or jobs are lost.
- History or other events (such as impending elections) get in the way by encouraging stereotypical rhetoric, posturing, and finger pointing.

Both union leaders and management need to consider each of these issues if any partnership is to become real.

Quality: a Union-Management Opportunity

In any situation, it makes sense to have a range of strategies and tactics. For organizations to prosper in the 1990s and beyond, both management and unions must experiment with alternatives. Traditional adversarial tools need not be sacrificed while new strategies are provisionally adopted. In fact, the experience of American automobile and motorcycle manufacturers and their unions strongly suggests that adversarial bargaining (including strike action) and collaborative quality performance efforts are reasonably compatible.

Experience strongly suggests that adversarial bargaining (including strike action) and collaborative quality performance efforts are reasonably compatible.

A management strategy to foster cooperation must include helping union leaders see the benefits of TQM. Management must provide an understandable rationale that goes beyond "we all must sink or swim together." There are at least 14 potential benefits that might accrue from an active partnership and thus can serve as part of a convincing rationale for its initiation:

1. *Management and union leaders can have greater direct access to each others.* Joint steering committees and similar groups will provide increased opportunity for both parties to make informed personal judgments, present alternate agendas, build trust, and so on.
2. *Management and union leaders can have expanded access to information.* More information is available fortuitously and through active solicitation.
3. *Networking will be facilitated.*One never knows where information can be found or who might be an ally. There can be many unofficial opportunities to make points, season ideas, or send up "trial balloons."
4. *Management and union leaders can both have more control.* Each side has vested interests. Each can maintain its original leverage through

careful joint negotiation of the details and checkpoints. To achieve this, management and union leaders have to sit together on various committees and accede to each other's reasonable requests, even making good-faith concessions to ensure future cooperation. In practice, this is a win-win situation, increasing rather than diminishing control by either party.

5. *Communication will be enhanced.* In most organizations, management communicates with employees through internal media. Similarly, unions communicate with the members through their own publications. Neither gets the opportunity to communicate their viewpoints through the other party. To show good faith, both can at least partially open their communication networks to the other for dialogue that is beneficial to all.
6. *Better performance outcomes will be achieved.* Involvement offers early and direct opportunities for both parties to mutually explore options for task design, structure, and prototyping. Needed changes can be informally discussed away from the heat of formal negotiations. The organization's and union members' interests can be protected while quality-maximizing alternatives are considered.
7. *Knowledge will be gained.* Most managers and union officials are knowledgeable about their own turf. Working jointly on committees, however, provides insight on how both systems operate and what it takes to promote progress.
8. *Better training will be provided.* Internal and external quality training programs provide opportunities for increased awareness and skill building—programs that union officials seldom have access to. When training is made available, union leaders profit, and management typically gains a more skillful partner (and vice versa).
9. *Management and union leaders will better understand each other's organizational functions.* For example, human resources departments are usually responsible for organizations' reward systems—systems that affect employees (union members) and support quality improvement processes. In this area alone, it's beneficial to all to open a dialogue in which each party communicates with the other so both better understand and are open to influence.
10. *Trust will be earned.* Through involvement, both union leaders and management are afforded the chance to see how the other fulfills its promises.
11. *Shared benefits will be realized.* As a result of continued dialogue, union leaders and management have the opportunity to informally negotiate emerging benefits that will likely accrue from quality improvement efforts.
12. *Management and union leaders will work to make changes that are beneficial for both.* Effective changes can bring common-good benefits and benefits unique to each party. Strong players remain strong and are improved by the process.

13. *Early warnings will be sent.* Involvement in the various processes and committees provides a highly effective early-warning system by which either party can detect problems with the partnership.
14. *A good offense will become the best defense.* When quality efforts lead to improvement, everyone can claim the credit. In addition, when tough hurdles must be cleared (such as cost containment), both parties can find viable reasons to take ownership of the process. Alternatives can be jointly researched, and the effect of hard decisions can be minimized and communicated so that those affected by the decisions will be better informed. This will maintain the relationship and avoid sandbagging.

Establish a Workable Partnership

Collectively, the 14 benefits just discussed represent a compelling argument for active union participation in an organization's quality journey. When this argument is tied with local relevant issues, a tentative alliance that covers everyone's interests can be established.

The opportunities and rewards for producing high-quality goods and services are too great to maintain a hostile relationship with unions. Unions contribute infinitely more to quality efforts when they are knowledgeable, willing partners in the creation of processes to satisfy customers. After all, customers are the key to an organization's prosperity and everyone's long-term job security.

Customers don't care about union-management rhetoric or squabbles. They'll just turn to companies that can satisfy their needs. Those companies that can't satisfy customers' needs might well feel the cold embrace of chains and padlocks at their gates.

Ken Myers is the deputy chancellor of the Minnesota Technical College System in St. Paul. Bob Killeen is co-chairman (emeritus) of the Minnesota Council for Quality and a retired United Auto Workers (UAW) representative.

Standards and Assessments

ISO 9000

Quality Standards the World Agrees On

Michael Barrier and Amy Zuckerman

This article clearly explains what ISO 9000 is all about and its benefits. It also suggests approaches to achieve certification for small firms that have limited budgets.

In American business—and small business in particular—there's a quickening interest in the series of international quality standards known as ISO 9000. More and more firms have come to realize that meeting those standards not only can ease entry into export markets but also can lead to significant cost savings.

Canon Virginia, Inc. (CVI)—a Newport News-based firm that assembles copiers, laser printers, and printer cartridges—is a good place to start an assessment of what ISO 9000 can mean to a small company. Not because CVI is in any sense a small company itself—it has 1,200 employees and is an arm of the Tokyo-based international powerhouse, Canon, Inc.—but because it proceeded so smoothly to certification and meeting the ISO 9000 standards.

The ISO 9000 standards were a good fit at Canon Virginia, Inc., because that company, like so many other internationally successful Japanese firms, has a long history of effective quality management. (Canon's version is known as the Canon Production System.) For CVI to be certified as meeting the ISO 9000 standards, it had to make a few changes, says Vice President Tadao Okabe—one of 35 Japanese nationals on the CVI staff—but, he adds, "we

Reprinted by permission, *Nation's Business,* May 1994. Copyright © 1994, U.S. Chamber of Commerce.

didn't find any big gaps" between what CVI was already doing and what ISO 9000 required.

CVI's experience shows that winning ISO 9000 certification can be a relatively simple and painless process for a company that is prepared for it, and that certification can even benefit a company that already has a strong quality program. There is nothing to prevent many small companies from obtaining certification very much the way CVI did.

The ISO 9000 standards were created in 1987 by the International Organization for Standardization (ISO), in Geneva. To date, 95 countries have approved those standards for voluntary application in both the manufacturing and service sectors. In the U.S., almost 2,000 certificates have been issued, to about half as many companies, some of which have obtained certificates for more than one location.

Although ISO issues the standards, it does not regulate the program internationally; that is left to national accreditation organizations like the U.S. Registrar Accreditation Board. RAB and other such boards authorize registrars to issue ISO 9000 certificates.

In Europe, there is some government regulation of these boards, but not in the U.S., where RAB operates with the authorization of a widely respected private organization, the American National Standards Institute, in New York. ANSI is the American representative to ISO.

ISO 9000 certification does not necessarily relate to the quality of a company's products or services but signifies that a company has fully documented its quality-control procedures, whatever they are, and is abiding by them.

ISO 9000 certification does not necessarily relate to the quality of a company's products or services but signifies that a company has fully documented its quality-control procedures, whatever they are, and is abiding by them. (Thus the ISO 9000 mantra: Say what you do, do what you say.)

It's theoretically possible that a company could, while meeting the ISO 9000 standards, turn out consistently inferior products; but it's not likely. Tim Barry, quality-control manager at American Saw in East Longmeadow, Mass., believes that ISO 9000 certification contributed to declines in product defects at the 800-employee, family-owned firm. American Saw's certification, the first in its industry, also improved communication and helped reduce workplace accidents, he says.

For the smallest firms, though—those with only a few dozen employees—the costs associated with obtaining ISO certification can loom larger than the benefits. American Saw's cash outlay for certification was approximately $60,000, Barry says. All of that money went to outside consultants and registrars; the figure doesn't cover Barry's salary or the time spent on certification by other employees.

Costs that are manageable for an 800-employee firm can be daunting for someone like Dick Sunderland, a small manufacturer of customized precision machinery.

Sunderland, the owner of D&S Manufacturing, in Westfield, Mass., just a few miles down the road from American Saw, is seeking ISO 9000 certification "to get a leg up on the competition." Because of the cost of certification, though, Sunderland's ISO 9000 effort has stalled before really getting off the ground.

Through contacts familiar with ISO 9000, Sunderland was able to gain some sense of where his company stood vis-à-vis the ISO standards. An ISO 9000 consultant based in Europe ranked his company close to certification level.

The task remaining for Sunderland before D&S was audited for certification was documenting what he was doing—that is, writing a quality-control manual that would meet ISO 9000 standards.

The problem is that Sunderland says he can't do the work at his current staffing level of 25. He and a foreman can devote an average of five hours a week to the job, not enough to finish in what he considers a timely fashion. He can't afford to hire a full-time quality-control manager.

Sunderland is hardly alone, but there are ways small firms can deal with the costs associated with certification. Among them:

There are ways small firms can deal with the costs associated with certification.

- *Negotiate.* Registrars and ISO 9000 consultants are in business for profit; different registrars charge different amounts. Scott Laney, president of Griffith Rubber Mills, a 430-employee operation in Portland, Ore., advises all companies seeking ISO 9000 certification to try to negotiate a lower price with a prospective registrar; he thinks registrars' prices are trending down. Other factors besides price are important, though: The registrar should be familiar with your industry and have credentials that will be accepted by your overseas customers.

- *Ask customers for subsidies.* Laney also suggests that companies seeking ISO 9000 certification ask their customers to subsidize the cost—especially if the customer is pushing the supplier to get the certification, and the customer obviously values the supplier. One of Griffith's main customers footed the entire bill for its ISO 9000 certification "because they needed our technology," Laney says.

- *Seek alternatives to consultants.* Canon Virginia's Donna Voshell points to growing involvement by community colleges in Virginia and other states in preparing small businesses for ISO certification. She is working with a quality institute at a nearby community college, she says, "trying to get an ISO networking group set up. With ISO becoming so predominant now in the U.S., a lot of people are offering things now at a considerably reduced price from when it was first introduced."

- *Decide if you really need certification.* Ultimately what really matters for many small firms is not getting ISO 9000 certification, but meeting the standards that certification requires. Meeting the standards can be done for a lot less money than getting the certificate.

Other companies see the certification itself as important, however. Canon Virginia's president, Shin-ichiro Nagashima, who decided to seek ISO 9000 certification as a way to gain "worldwide recognition for our production system that we already had in place," says Voshell, who as CVI's calibration supervisor led the certification efforts. (Voshell's job entails verifying that the measuring equipment measures accurately.)

January 1992 was when "we started our investigation of what was required," Voshell says. None of Canon's customers were insisting that it be ISO-certified even though such customer demands are what frequently lead companies to pursue certification. But, says Doug Grossenbaugh, CVI's quality-assurance manager, "we wanted to be ahead of the game."

Voshell herself went through five days of training to be a lead assessor in an ISO-certification audit, and CVI assembled a task force to manage the changes that certification would require. "When we started running into problems that we needed some expert help with," Voshell says, "I made contact with a consultant," choosing one who had already conducted several certification audits. (Consultants can audit as well as consult, but not for the same company.) "Those are the people who are going to understand what's going on," she says.

CVI had the consultant visit several different times, Voshell says, "to evaluate our progress and make sure we were approaching things in the correct manner." Then, near the end of the process, the consultant actually audited CVI's system, in a sort of dry run for the certification audit. The consultant was valuable to CVI "because he offered us various options" — different ways to meet the standards—"instead of just what we had thought of," Voshell says.

Preparing for certification was "basically a matter of putting documentation in place," she says. "We already had a system, and there was nothing wrong with our system—we just needed to document it."

Documenting procedures can be tricky, though, as Voshell says: "When people start writing down what they do, they think, 'Maybe I should add a little more here or a little more there.' That may have been the biggest problem that we ran into."

Aligning documentation with actual procedures was critical to determine if an ISO certificate should be issued.

Aligning documentation with actual procedures was critical to success when the registrar's team showed up to determine if an ISO certificate should be issued. "When the registrar comes in to audit your system," Voshell says, "he's going to audit you to your documentation. Whatever your documentation says you're doing, that's what he's going to be looking at."

Grossenbaugh adds: "Some of the auditors would say, for example, 'Please explain to me how you order paper for your office.' This person would walk over to get the policy, and the auditor would say, 'No, show me how you do it, first, and *then* let's go look at the policy.' " The auditors could then uncover discrepancies between the documented procedure and the way things were really done.

As smoothly as Canon's certification went, the process was still time-consuming—a total of 18 months before a certificate was issued, in June 1993.

Most companies of its size could expect to take even longer, though; 24 months is probably more typical. A smaller company with a strong quality program could conceivably go through the process more quickly, because one of the key elements of the ISO standards is, as Grossenbaugh says, "making sure all the people understand" the quality system; the fewer the employees, the simpler such communication can be.

But if a company already has a strong quality program, can certification really add much to it? CVI's experience suggests that the answer is yes.

Thanks to the more systematic documentation that ISO certification required, Okabe says, CVI's procedures are now more fully accessible by computer, reducing the danger that someone might be relying on an out-of-date manual. "We avoid many conflicts," he says.

Because Canon Virginia is ISO-certified, Okabe points out, it's no longer necessary for a customer like Hewlett-Packard "to come to this plant to check all the details of our quality-control systems, again and again." The savings in money and time are "tremendous," he says.

Two of Canon Virginia's own suppliers are now going through the ISO certification process, and others are gearing up for the effort. "We have recommended to our suppliers that this would be a good thing to go through," says Bob Thomson, CVI's internal audit manager. "That way we can rely on the products that they're supplying to us."

ISO certification can thus bring significant savings by sharply reducing the need for outside quality audits and inspections of incoming products. In addition, as Okabe points out, "systems change, products change, and we have to start all over again to educate our people." The standardized documentation that ISO certification requires "makes it easy to educate them," he says—in effect, there is less to learn, because more remains the same.

ISO certification can thus bring significant savings by sharply reducing the need for outside quality audits and inspections of incoming products.

As a result of meeting the ISO standards, Voshell says, "we're developing more consistency throughout our company. Now that we have the documentation in place, we can see how everybody is performing their individual tasks, and we're trying to get everybody to perform the same way, every time, throughout the whole company."

In keeping with that goal, CVI is consolidating and thus decreasing its documentation; although ISO 9000 led to an increase in paperwork for a while, as everyone wrote down what they were doing, it is now permitting a reduction, by stimulating uniformity in procedures. It is also encouraging a reduction in waste of other kinds: Through the documentation, Voshell says, "you can actually see where there's a duplication of work." In other words, nothing is hidden.

There remains the danger that practice and documentation will slide apart. "People get busy," Voshell says. "They come up with a better way of doing it, and they start revising the policy, but they don't send it around for approval." But CVI has a check on such laxity, she says: "We audit ourselves internally, on a regular basis. If we do forget, we find it in our internal audits."

And if CVI should somehow let a forbidden practice get past its internal audits, it will probably show up in an ISO 9000 audit: The auditors return twice a year. ISO 9000 certification must be renewed annually, and certification can be withdrawn if significant problems show up on one of the semiannual audits.

The internal audits "are eliminating a lot of duplicity," says Jay Bowen, CVI's chemical quality-assurance manager. "Now it seems as if we're all doing the same things and saying the same things."

In weighing those and other benefits of certification against the cost of the process, companies should look to the long term. From that perspective, the expenses may start to look insignificant.

Says Tim Barry of American Saw: "ISO keeps employees involved and aware. The cross-learning is phenomenal. And ISO has been a major marketing advantage. We've picked up a bundle of new clients in the U.S. and Europe."

Michael Barrier is a Nation's Business *senior editor specializing in quality management and related areas. Amy Zuckerman is a free-lance writer in Pelham, Mass. She specializes in foreign trade and is the author of* ISO 9000 Made Easy: A Self-Help Guide to Certification, *published by In/Ex Information Export.*

Is ISO 9000 the Path to TQM?

James P. Corrigan

There is still some confusion about the relationship between ISO 9000 standards and the implementation of TQM. This article succinctly and clearly distinguishes between the two and explains how they can support each other.

During the last decade, there has been an intensified focus on and commitment to total quality management (TQM). TQM has brought varied results to organizations. For some, it was the major reason for their survival. For others, it was a source of frustration that eventually led to abandonment of the effort. Some failed because they had unrealistic expectations and did not appreciate the time and effort TQM required. They embraced TQM as a solution for all corporate problems or the magic key that had led to Japan's industrial success. They were told that if they adopted identical techniques, they would automatically obtain equivalent success.

Similarly, ISO 9000 registration is promoted as the passport required to do business in the post-1992 global marketplace and the only true way to TQM. Unfortunately, overpromotion can raise expectations beyond reality and ultimately cause misapplication, subsequent rejection, and the loss of ISO 9000's excellent objectives and benefits. When rhetoric outstrips reality, consensus quickly moves from approval or adoption to the opinion that it is just another fad.

ISO 9000 and TQM supplement each other. A successful TQM effort will have a quality system that is similar to the ISO 9000 quality system. Therefore, a corporation that has successfully woven TQM into the fabric of its business should need only minor changes to meet ISO 9000 registration requirements.

Although ISO 9000 and TQM supplement and support each other, they do have different objectives, evaluation and improvement processes, and management and success goals. It is essential to understand both approaches and their relationship to each other to ensure that both are applied appropriately so that their benefits can be achieved. When the different aims and focuses of ISO 9000 and TQM are understood, ISO 9000 as a path to TQM can be considered.

Although ISO 9000 and TQM supplement and support each other, they do have different objectives, evaluation and improvement processes, and management and success goals.

Reprinted with permission from *Quality Progress*, May 1994. Copyright © 1994, ASQC, Milwaukee, WI. All rights reserved.

Table 1. **ISO 9000 Standards**

ISO 9000 -	A guideline for the selection and use of quality management and quality assurance standards
ISO 9001 -	A model for the assurance of quality systems for design and development, production, installation, and servicing
ISO 9002 -	A model for the assurance of quality systems for production and installation
ISO 9003 -	A model for the assurance of quality systems for final inspection and test
ISO 9004 -	Guidelines for quality management and quality system elements

Quality Systems

A quality system is designed to ensure the continued repeatability of a set of product and service characteristics that have been explicitly or implicitly agreed to by a customer and a supplier. ISO 9000 is about corporatewide quality systems. Quality systems have existed throughout history and have evolved and matured over time.[1] They have changed because of industrial development and the development of new quality techniques and ideas. The four quality systems—artisan, inspection, statistical process control, and quality assurance—still exist today. The number of systems in use has increased and broadened with each advancement. A disturbing fact, however, is the number of early inspection systems still in operation. Even though it is arguable how adequately some of these systems meet their objectives, they all have the same objectives:

- To achieve and sustain the quality of the product or service
- To give management confidence that quality is being met
- To give the customer confidence that consistency is being delivered in the product or service

ISO 9000 Standards

The ISO 9000 standards define the requirements of a prevention-based quality assurance system. If the system is adhered to, the supplier will always produce and deliver a predictable product or service. As Table 1 shows, ISO 9000 is a set of five primary standards: three address specific quality systems (ISO 9001, ISO 9002, and ISO 9003) and two are guidelines (ISO 9000 and ISO 9004). Additional guidelines have been published for software (ISO 9000-3) and services (ISO 9004-2).

The ISO 9000 standard helps businesses select the appropriate standard (ISO 9001, ISO 9002, or ISO 9003). It defines terms used in the three standards and explains the concepts and use of the standards. It also gives an excellent cross-reference of the elements in each standard.

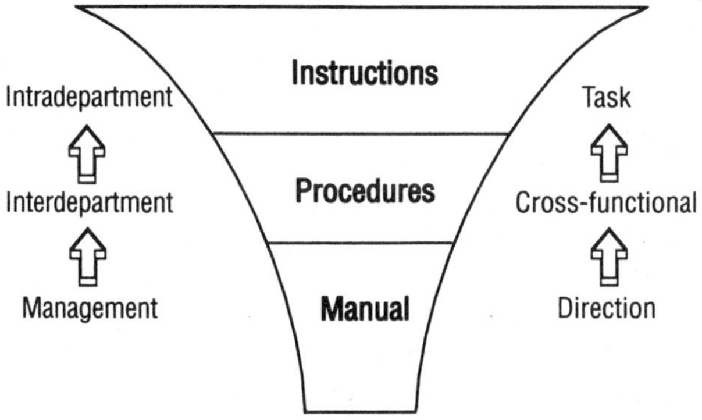

Figure 1. **ISO 9000 documentation system.**

ISO 9001, ISO 9002, and ISO 9003 contain criteria that measure the effectiveness of different quality systems designed to meet customers' requirements. Each standard defines the required elements of its respective quality system. Some elements are discretionary depending on their appropriateness to a supplier's processes or its contractual requirements. Since ISO 9001 has a scope that covers all elements of ISO 9002 and ISO 9003, further discussion of ISO 9000 assumes the use of ISO 9001.

The ISO 9004 standard addresses the role of quality management. It addresses meeting customer expectations and the economic benefit of reducing costs through continuous improvement. Prevention, the need for customer feedback processes, and broader training are highlighted. Public responsibility is also addressed in terms of product safety and liability. The requirements for various elements of the quality system are prescriptive of a TQM philosophy. Some groups advocate that ISO 9001, ISO 9002, and ISO 9003 should reflect ISO 9004 and move toward a TQM measurement. Although that might happen in the future, remember that today only ISO 9001, ISO 9002, and ISO 9003 measure quality systems, not ISO 9004.

The manufacturer defines the quality system and can meet the requirements of the standard's elements through many different processes. These are system standards, not product standards. ISO 9000 standards are essentially paper driven. All of the appropriate elements must be documented, the documentation must cover all of the requirements, and the company must do what it has documented. Adequacy of the system and the producer's adherence to it is measured by auditing against the standard. Therefore, ISO 9000 standards measure neither the efficiency of the system nor how good the product or service is. If third-party auditors or registration services are relied on, the supplier might want to assess the efficiency of the system for itself; third-party auditors can only judge a supplier's adherence to documented procedures.

All of the appropriate elements must be documented, the documentation must cover all of the requirements, and the company must do what it has documented.

The ISO 9001 standard requires a documented quality system that is built on a three-tier set of documents (see Figure 1). Although the three levels are equal in evaluating compliance, the quality manual is the most important because the supplier's procedures and instructions are derived from it. The manual is a management document in which the quality policy and objectives to which the supplier is committed are documented. The manual describes the authority, responsibilities, empowerment, and interrelation of all personnel in charge of implementing the policy. Therefore, it is the guide that defines what will be done and how it will be done. The standard does not explicitly require a formal, documented manual, but it specifies the manual's requirements in great detail and strongly recommends one. It would have been unlikely for a supplier to have its system registered without a manual, and when the updated standards are released later this year, it will be required.

From the quality manual, procedures are developed for each system element. These procedures are interdepartmental. Ideally, they should be developed under the leadership of the organization responsible for the element and agreed to by all dependent and interrelated departments since the scope of the procedures is organizationwide. The following elements must be addressed in the manual:

- Procedures for conducting contract reviews
- Design procedures covering planning, determination of requirements, product specifications, design verification, and engineering change control
- Procedures for controlling the approval and issuance of and changes in all documents related to the standard
- Purchasing procedures covering supplier assessment, definition of ordering data and the assurance of the data's integrity, and product verification by the supplier and the supplier's customer
- Procedures to control the product from consigned product to product identification and traceability, and nonconforming product control and disposition
- Appropriate process control procedures
- Appropriate inspection and testing procedures
- Appropriate equipment procedures to control the calibration and maintenance of inspection, measuring, and test equipment (Although not specified in the standard, similar control procedures could be used for production equipment.)
- Procedures to control the status of product verification (shop-floor control of product)
- Appropriate corrective action procedures
- Handling, storage, packaging, and delivery procedures
- Procedures for the control of quality records
- Internal quality audit procedures (This requirement acts as a control mechanism; it is the one direct, prescriptive element in ISO 9001.)
- Procedures determining training needs and assuring appropriate training levels

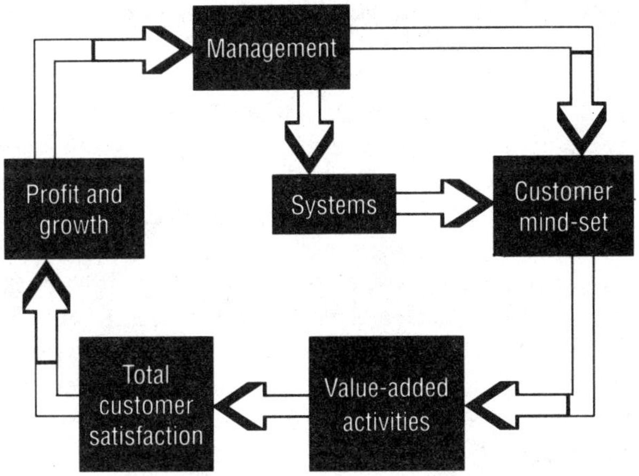

Figure 2. **TQM management system.**

- If they are required, procedures for customer service and procedures for statistical techniques

The procedures lead to the last tier of documents, called instructions, which are departmental, step-by-step directions at the task level.

TQM

There are many definitions of TQM, but the following explains it well: TQM is a management philosophy that builds customer-driven learning or organizations dedicated to total customer satisfaction with continuous improvement in the effectiveness and efficiency of the organization and its processes. This definition describes TQM in a nonprescriptive way with a vision to provide total customer satisfaction through continuous improvement.

To follow this philosophy, management must develop a system similar to the one shown in Figure 2. All members of the organization must be driven to have a mind-set that is focused on satisfying customers' needs and expectations. Such a mind-set leads to concentration on value-added activity directed at total customer satisfaction. Other things being equal, the better the system functions, the more the company's profit and market share will grow.

To build a customer mind-set in employees, management must provide support systems. Assuming the business has an effective quality system in place, the required support systems include continual education and training systems, tailored recognition and reward systems, accessible information systems, and feedback systems. If a TQM system is built without an underlying quality system, it will ultimately fail.

A successful TQM management system weaves these principles into the fabric of the business. TQM, like a house, requires continual care and upkeep to remain viable. Therefore, a "house of TQM" is one in which each function continuously improves the effectiveness and efficiency of its processes, based on customers' needs and expectations. Figure 3 shows a typical house of TQM. The foundation is education, and management is the roof. Each function works to improve the key work or business processes that move toward the goal of achieving world-class performance. For example, development improves development processes, such as design cycle time and design quality: manufacturing improves manufacturing processes, such as implementing just-in-time and self-directed work teams; and support services improve service processes, such as billing and order processing. If customers recognize performance as world-class, it leads to total customer satisfaction. Management must continuously measure both because the parameters that decide world-class performance and total customer satisfaction constantly shift and change with time. Figure 4 illustrates world-class performance and its basic underlying parameters.

ISO 9000 as a Path to TQM

ISO 9000 might not be *the* path to TQM, but it would be *a* path to TQM.

ISO 9000 might not be *the* path to TQM, but it would be *a* path to TQM. ISO 9000 as the path to TQM is incomplete. For example, ISO 9000 doesn't have a sufficient customer focus, doesn't address how good a product or service is, doesn't focus on continuous improvement and the scope of the support systems and processes needed for continuous improvement, and doesn't call for an ongoing evaluation and improvement of the quality system elements. These, however, are not deficiencies. The intent is not to include these elements because ISO 9000 serves a different purpose. It is designed to ensure the adequacy of a given quality system and to use audits to ensure its adherence to it.

TQM requires and assumes that an effective quality assurance system exists and is followed. Unfortunately, this is not always a valid assumption. Any organization starting a TQM effort should assess the adequacy of its underlying quality system. It becomes a baseline from which to start quality improvement activities. Using an ISO 9000 standard for this assessment would provide excellent measurement criteria and a structured approach to periodic evaluation of the quality system. Since a successful TQM effort will continuously force change in the quality system, this advantage could become a long-term critical success factor.

An alternative is to integrate the ISO 9000 standard into TQM from the start. The quality system could be restructured into an ISO 9000 system as part of an initial assessment. The goal would be to use this activity to identify key processes or projects for improvement. It also could serve as the method to start a goal-oriented team activity. By deciding to flowchart the procedures and instructions as part of ISO 9000 restructuring, teams can be directed to improve how the process flows. It would be simple to have the teams identify the required resources and the task-cycle times for a complete flow analysis. They could even be assigned quality improvement goals. The internal auditing requirement also could become the ongoing evaluation and improvement process for the TQM process itself.

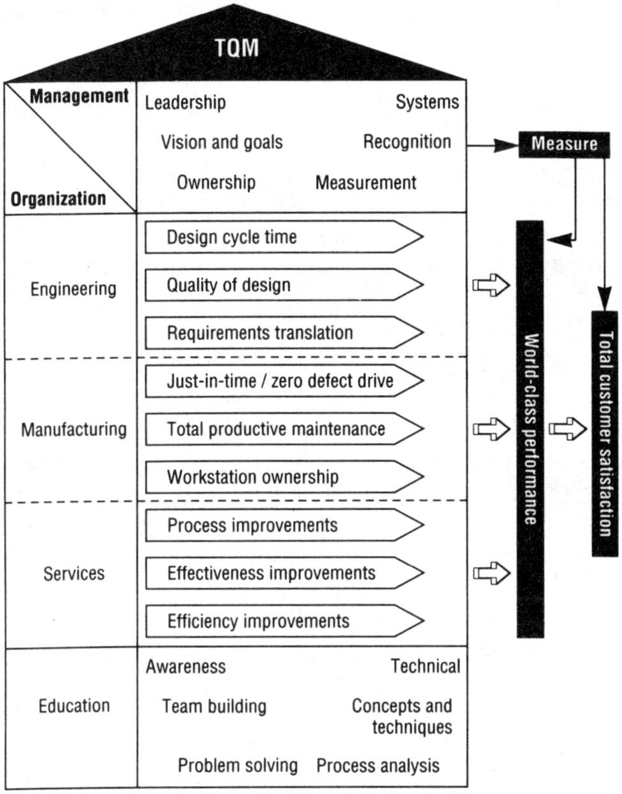

Figure 3. **House of TQM.**

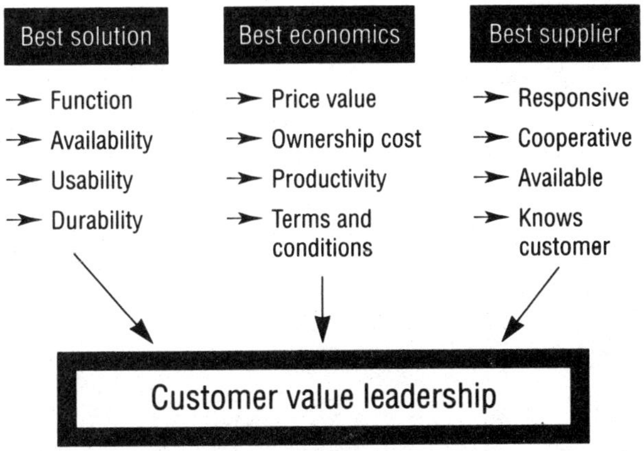

Figure 4. **World-class performance.**

This integrated approach could accelerate the TQM process. It would give quality councils immediate strategic plans. It could also provide greater assurance of early successes and help simplify the cultural acceptance of change. The integration should result in a mutual strengthening of both efforts and ensure that neither effort detracts from the other. It would be a particularly excellent path for those companies that have made significant acquisitions, such as adding new locations with different systems and cultures. It could bring a universal language to amalgamate the separate operations into a consistent corporate system and culture.

Integrate ISO 9000 into the TQM Program

If a company is just starting in TQM or reexamining its TQM effort, it should consider integrating an ISO 9000 assessment into the program. Companies seeking ISO 9000 registration that already have a successful TQM system can manage the activity by making it a quality improvement project. They can develop and implement ISO 9000 procedures and instructions to be consistent with their TQM initiatives.

If a company has no TQM initiative and has no reasons to seek ISO 9000 registration, it should still consider doing an ISO 9000 assessment of its quality system and modifying it as appropriate. Unless a company has supreme confidence in the adequacy of its present quality system and has recently confirmed it, an assessment is as critical to its health as a financial audit. Although the exercise will not be a complete path to TQM, it should increase quality awareness and the need for a solid quality system. This exercise just might result in the enlightenment needed to start a TQM program.

Reference

1. J.M. Juran, ed., *Juran's Quality Control Handbook* (New York, NY: McGraw-Hill, 1951).

James P. Corrigan is a principal at Enterprise Management Services in Katonah, NY.

Teamwork Pays Off for Firm

Jesse D. Freese and Emily Konold

This short article describes how one software company in Minnesota prepared for and achieved ISO 9001 certification. It can serve as a benchmark for other companies seeking certification.

Great team accomplishments don't need to be rare—they need to be understood. One team accomplishment at Help/Systems Inc. is particularly worth understanding: In less than one year the company achieved ISO 9001 registration on its first try.

Help/Systems, a small company in Minnetonka, MN, that provides automation operations software for the IBM AS/400 system, decided to seek ISO 9001 registration. In December 1991, the company's president handed this responsibility to the quality control (QC) specialist. He gave her 15 months to complete the mission.

Knowing little about ISO 9001, the QC specialist attended an ISO 9000 consortium meeting in which she learned that if a company does not already have a quality plan (or manual) in place, it should not put more effort than is necessary into creating one. In other words, the company should create a quality plan that people will use (avoid a big, wordy manual).

Prior to the decision to seek registration, the company's president and QC specialist sought the help of a representative from Fissure, a St. Paul, MN, training and consulting firm. The representative suggested the use of the Software Engineering Institute's (SEI) Capability Maturity Model, which was developed for software producers to use as a framework for total quality management and process improvement. The representative explained to Help/Systems' software engineers the idea of defining processes and measuring them for process and product improvement. Through an open discussion, the software engineers bought into the idea. The representative then presented the plan to train the engineers to perform their own software-development process assessments as part of a continuous quality improvement process.

Getting Started

The key to improvement is in measuring and assessing processes, and the multilayered SEI Capability Maturity Model was selected to do just that (Figure 1). The model measures and assesses a software organization's processes

The key to improvement is in measuring and assessing processes,

Reprinted with permission from *Quality Progress*, May 1994. Copyright © 1994 ASQC, Milwaukee, WI. All rights reserved.

	Level	Characteristic	Key process areas	Quality approach	Results
Process maturity	5 Optimizing	Improvement fed back into process	Changing technology, problem analysis	Quality results from minimizing process variation	Quality and productivity; Risk
	4 Managed	(quantitative) Measurement process	Process measurement, process analysis, quantitative quality plans	Quality results from preventing problems from occurring	
	3 Defined	(qualitative) Process defined and institutionalized	Training, technical practices (reviews, testing), process focus (standards, process groups)	Quality results from early problem finding and fixing	
	2 Repeatable	(intuitive) Process dependent on individuals	Project management, project planning, configuration management, software quality assurance	Quality results from testing at end of project	
	1 Initial	(ad hoc/chaotic)			

Figure 1. **SEI capability maturity model.**

and provides guidance for improving them. It provides a framework for selecting process improvement strategies by identifying the most critical issues to software quality and process improvement. The model uses five process maturity levels to determine an organization's maturity level. Most companies are at level 1; it was believed that for Help/Systems to become ISO 9001 registered, it would need to be at a maturity level of 3 (in actuality, the company was registered at a maturity level between 2 and 3).

Before the company could assess itself, the newly formed assessment team needed training. The training, performed in March 1992, taught the team how to assess its processes and how to use the assessment results within the framework of a six-step process improvement approach:

1. Identify the current processes and standards
2. Compare the existing processes with the devised standards (ISO 9001)
3. Establish areas for improvement
4. Plan the improvement activity
5. Implement the plan
6. Return to step 2

The training also included a practical exercise in performing an assessment. This training convinced the team of the soundness of process measurement and improvement. Next, the SEI assessment questions were tailored to the company's terminology.

An important factor of the training was that it addressed human (soft) issues as well as technical (hard) issues. Addressing these soft issues helped the team overcome resistance to change and become successful. Learning about the soft issues later resulted in the team planning several different activities, such as recognizing and celebrating milestone achievements, a quality manual slogan contest, and a recreational "Quality Olympics" day.

In the assessment kick-off meeting, the goal of reaching ISO 9001 registration and the assessment process were announced to everyone in the company, along with a new product-support guarantee: "If you are not satisfied with our product support for any reason, we will give you one year's product maintenance absolutely free. We want to establish a long-term relationship with you. This guarantee ensures that we will work hard to keep your business in the years ahead."

The product-support guarantee was included in the process-assessment kick-off meeting because it was believed that the idea of customer satisfaction would help everyone better understand the need for process and product improvement. Understanding the need for ISO 9001 was the first step in getting the companywide commitment to reach the registration goal.

The first product assessment took two days. The team compiled the results and presented them to the entire staff. Focusing on strengths, the team pointed out which processes were solid and how to make them better. The SEI maturity level of the company was between 1 and 2, but the team knew that with some minor process changes, significant strides could be made.

Selecting a Path

The next steps in the registration process included creating and implementing a quality manual and getting prepared for the ISO 9001 audit. The manual covered every position in the company connected to the software development and support processes. Rather than just striving to get division procedures certified, the company chose to have every job and procedure in the company open for audit and registration. Everything from software design to the operation of the mail room was fair game.

The manual contained the three areas needed for documentation: top level, detail, and support. New procedures would be generated only when necessary.

To generate the quality manual, the QC specialist and the Fissure representative determined where the SEI Capability Maturity Model could guide the responses to ISO 9001 questions and where new responses would need to be written. Defining the process in the manual required the help of more people. The company formed a software-engineering process group (SEPG) consisting of two software engineers, a customer service representative and a marketing representative.

In April, the following actions were implemented:

- The SEPG analyzed all SEI questions that had been answered "no" and identified the process changes required to make them "yes."
- Individual employees were assigned to one of nine areas in the company's business process.
- A schedule for performing assessments of every job position was set. Individuals or teams with the same job description were interviewed, and detailed descriptions of their work processes were generated.
- As part of process improvement planning, a three-person team attended a project management workshop. The workshop featured computer simulation that allowed team members to experience using project management technical and leadership skills. The team learned how to use technical project-management tools, how to achieve quality, how to lead a team and make it more productive, and how to track and control projects. The team also learned about the human aspects of leadership.

In May, the company chose a registrar, and the assessment dates were set for Nov. 2–4. By the end of May, the first draft of the quality manual's top-level documentation was completed, and it was finalized in the latter part of July.

The company began using the quality manual as a quality and process guide on Aug. 1 and sent a copy to the registrar. By the end of the month, most of the bugs had been worked out of the manual. In October, the registrar called the QC specialist with concerns about the manual. By the time the audit team arrived, the specialist and assessment team had addressed those concerns.

The Audit

Day 1. The audit team arrived and met with the SEPG and top management to explain what it would be doing. The audit team reviewed the company's documentation to familiarize itself with the company's processes. After auditing the purchasing area, the auditors met with the SEPG to report minor findings, which were corrected before the end of the day.

Day 2. The minor findings that were fixed from the previous day were accepted by the auditors. At midday, the auditors reported a serious problem in the design verification area that required significant work and a rewrite of a section of the top-level document.

Day 3. The top-level document was revised that morning. At noon, with the audit nearly complete, the audit team told the QC specialist that, although it was impressed with all departments, it would need to come back in three months for a reaudit. The specialist, who knew that all the problem areas had already been rectified, asked the auditors if they would be willing to register the company if it was able to clear up all of the areas. The auditors agreed.

Later in the afternoon, the audit team signed off on all but one of the noncomformances. The final nonconformance was the result of three different versions of the same document. This was the responsibility of the QC specialist, who asked the team not to hold back registration because of her mistake. The audit team agreed, convinced of Help/Systems' commitment to quality and process improvement, and the company became ISO 9001 registered.

The Keys to Registration

There were many technical problems faced in reaching ISO 9001 registration. Using the SEI Capability Maturity Model and establishing a clear and elevating goal made solving the technical problems easier.

The company's assessment team was another key to success. The team's concerns were addressed early in the registration process. Also, the team was given the proper training to understand process measurement before planning and executing the registration process.

The soft issues (learning about human dynamics) were also important. Recognizing the efforts of the employees by taking "fun" breaks went a long way to the success of registration.

Jesse D. Freese is the vice president of Fissure in St. Paul, MN. Emily Konold is the quality control specialist at Help/Systems, Inc. in Minnetonka, MN.

BALDRIGE CRITERIA/ QUALITY AUDITS

The Evolution of the Baldrige Award

Joao S. Neves and Behnam Nakhai

This article briefly documents how the Baldrige Award has grown and changed over its lifetime. The article's tables and figures are valuable references for anyone interested in the Baldrige Award, either as a potential entrant or to use the criteria to direct and audit their quality management efforts.

Since its debut, the Malcolm Baldrige National Quality Award has substantially influenced the concept of quality and its implementation in organizations.[1] As with any major initiative, this award has received a substantial amount of both praise and criticism.[2] One benefit of this widespread public debate has been the continued refinement of the award's criteria and guidelines by the Baldrige Award organization, which is composed of the National Institute of Standards and Technology, ASQC, and the Foundation for the Malcolm Baldrige National Quality Award.

The Award's Evolution

As with most new projects, many building blocks have been added to the Baldrige Award process in its short lifetime. In particular, the changes introduced have made the 1988 award process pale in comparison to its most recent

Reprinted with permission from *Quality Progress*, June 1994. Copyright © 1994, ASQC, Milwaukee, WI. All rights reserved.

	1988	1989	1990	1991	1992	1993	1994
Framework	Simple						Developed
Examination guidelines						Introduced	Expanded
Performance issues					Introduced	Developed	Developed
Key concepts				6 concepts	10 core values	10 core values	10 core values
Examination characteristics				Incipient	12 areas	Simplified	Simplified
Business factors			Introduced	Detailed explanation	Brief presentation	Simplified	Dropped
Scoring method		Criteria	Dimensions	Dimensions and guidelines	Dimensions and guidelines	Simplified	Simplified
Areas to address	278	192	133	99	89	92	91
Items	62	44	33	32	28	28	28
Subcategories	42	27	-	-	-	-	-
Categories	7	7	7	7	7	7	7

Figure 1. **Changes in the Baldrige Award process from 1988 to 1994.**

version. The evolution of the Baldrige Award process is presented in schematic form in Figure 1. This illustration captures the increasing conceptual richness that has been added over the years. The following is a look at how each element of the Baldrige Award process has evolved.

Categories, Subcategories, Items, and Areas to Address

The seven original examination categories have largely remained unchanged. Although the category titles have changed slightly, their main ideas have not (see Table 1). In all but two categories—human resources and customer satisfaction—the number of items has been reduced and simplified.

In all but two categories—human resources and customer satisfaction—the number of items has been reduced and simplified.

The weights of the seven categories, however, have changed significantly. Less importance is now given to leadership and strategic quality planning, and significantly more weight is given to quality and operational results. Customer satisfaction, the category with the most weight, has always accounted for 30% of the total score.

Subcategories were eliminated from the award guidelines in 1990, which simplified the structure of the award without directly affecting the items and areas to address. The number of items and areas to address has been significantly reduced: from 62 items and 278 areas to address in 1988 to 28 items and 91 areas to address in 1994. This reduction reflects the examiners' increased knowledge of and experience in the requisites of quality.

Scoring Method

The scoring method was not clearly laid out in the 1988 award guidelines. The guidelines only mentioned scoring criteria, which were subsequently transformed into "areas to address" in 1989.

Table 1. **Examination Categories and Their Point Values**

1988	1989	1990
Leadership (150 points) Senior Corporate Leadership Policy Management System and Quality Improvement Processes Resource Allocation and Utilization Unique and Innovative Leadership Techniques	*Leadership* (120 points) Senior Management Quality Values Management System Public Responsibility	*Leadership* (100 points) Senior Executive Leadership Quality Values Quality Values Management for Quality Public Responsibility
Information and Analysis (75 points) Use of Analytical Techniques or Systems Use of Product or Service Quality Data Customer Data and Analysis Distributor and/or Dealer Quality and Data Analysis Employee-Related Data and Analysis Unique and Innovative Information Analysis	*Information and Analysis* (60 points) Scope of Data and Information for "Management by Fact" Data Management Analysis and Use of Data for Decision Making	*Information and Analysis* (60 points) Scope and Management of Quality Data and Information Analysis of Quality Data and Information
Strategic Quality Planning (75 points) Operational and Strategic Goals Planning Function Planning for Quality Improvement Unique and Innovative Planning	*Strategic Quality Planning* (80 points) Planning Process Plans for Quality Leadership	*Strategic Quality Planning* (90 points) Strategic Quality Planning Process Quality Leadership Indicators in Planning Quality Priorities
Human Resource Utilization (150 points) Management and Operations Employee Quality Awareness and Involvement Quality Training and Education Evaluation, Incentives, and Recognition Systems Unique and Innovative Approaches	*Human Resource Utilization* (150 points) Management Employee Involvement Quality Education and Training Employee Recognition Quality of Work Life	*Human Resource Utilization* (150 points) Human Resource Management Employee Involvement Quality Education and Training Employee Recognition and Performance Measurement Employee Well-Being and Morale

In 1990, the concept of scoring dimensions was introduced and has remained largely unchanged since. This concept emphasizes that applicants' quality programs are examined using a three-dimensional gauge: approach, deployment, and results. Since 1993, approach and deployment have been considered linked dimensions.

In 1991, the scoring method was clarified with a table containing scoring guidelines that examiners and companies conducting self-assessments could

Table 1. ***(continued)***

1988	1989	1990
Quality Assurance of Products and Services (150 points) Customer Input to Products and Services Planning for New or Improved Products or Services Measurements, Standards, and Data System Technology Audit Documentation Safety, Health, and Environment Assurance/Validation Unique and Innovative Approaches	*Quality Assurance of Products and Services* (140 points) Design and Introduction of New or Improved Products and Services Operations of Processes which Produce the Company's Products and Services Measurements and Standards for Products, Processes, and Services Audit Documentation Quality Assurance of Operations and Business Processes Quality Assurance of External Providers of Goods and Services	*Quality Assurance of Products and Services* (150 points) Design and Introduction of Quality Products and Services Process and Quality Control Continuous Improvement of Processes, Products, and Services Quality Assessment Documentation Quality Assurance, Quality Assessment, and Quality Improvement of Support Services and Business Processes Quality Assurance, Quality Assessment, and Quality Improvement of Suppliers
Results From Quality Assurance of Products and Services (100) Reliability and Performance of Products or Services Reductions in Scrap, Rework, and Rejected Products and Services Reductions in Claims, Litigation, and Complaints Related to Quality Reductions in Warranty or Field Support Work Unique or Innovative Indicators of Quality Improvements or Economic Gains	*Quality Results* (150 points) Quality of Products and Services Operational and Business Process Quality Improvement Quality Improvement Applications	*Quality Results* (150 point) Quality of Products and Services Comparison of Quality Results Business Process, Operational and Support Service Quality Improvement Supplier Quality Improvement
Customer Satisfaction (300 points) Customer Views of Quality of Products or Services Competitive Comparison of Products or Services Customer Service and Complaint Handling Customer Views of Guaranties/Warranties Unique or Innovative Approaches to Assessing Customer Satisfaction	*Customer Satisfaction* (300 points) Knowledge of Customer Requirements and Expectations Customer Relationship Management Customer Satisfaction Methods of Measurement and Results	*Customer Satisfaction* (300 points) Knowledge of Customer Requirements and Expectations Customer Relationship Management Customer Service Standards Commitment to Customers Complaint Resolution for Quality Improvement Customer Satisfaction Determination Customer Satisfaction Results Customer Satisfaction Comparison

Table 1. ***(continued)***

1991	**1992**	**1993 and 1994**
Leadership (100 points) Senior Executive Leadership Quality Values Management for Quality Public Responsibility	*Leadership* (90 points) Senior Executive Leadership Public Responsibility	*Leadership* (95 points) Senior Executive Leadership Management for Quality Public Responsibility and Corporate Citizenship
Information and Analysis (70 points) Scope and Management of Quality Data and Information Competitive Comparisons and Benchmarks Analysis of Quality Data and Information	*Information and Analysis* (80 points) Scope and Management of Quality and Performance Data and Information Competitive Comparisons and Benchmarks Analysis and Uses of Company-Level Data	*Information and Analysis* (75 points) Scope and Management of Quality and Performance Data and Information Competitive Comparisons and Benchmarking Analysis and Uses of Company-Level Data
Strategic Quality Planning (60 points) Strategic Quality Planning Process Quality Goals and Plans	*Strategic Quality Planning* (60 points) Strategic Quality and Company Performance Planning Process Quality and Performance Plans	*Strategic Quality Planning* (60 points) Strategic Quality and Company Performance Planning Process Quality and Performance Plans
Human Resource Utilization (150 points) Human Resource Management Employee Involvement Quality Education and Training Employee Recognition and Performance Measurement Employee Well-Being and Morale	*Human Resource Development and Management* (150 points) Human Resource Management Employee Involvement Employee Education and Training Employee Performance and Recognition Employee Well-Being and Morale	*Human Resources Development and Management* (150 points) Human Resources Planning and Management Employee Involvement Employee Education and Training Employee Performance and Recognition Employee Well-Being and Satisfaction
Quality Assurance of Products and Services (140 points) Design and Introduction of Quality Products and Services Process Quality Control Continuous Improvement of Processes Quality Assessment Documentation Business Process and Support Service Quality Supplier Quality	*Management of Process Quality* (140 points) Design and Introduction of Quality Products and Services Process Management - Business Processes and Service Production and Delivery Processes Process Management: Business Processes and Support Services Supplier Quality Quality Assessment	*Management of Process Quality* (140 points) Design and Introduction of Quality Products and Services Process Management: Product and Service Production and Delivery Processes Process Management: Business Processes and Support Services Supplier Quality Quality Assessment

Table 1. ***(continued)***

1991	**1992**	**1993 and 1994**
Quality Results (180 points) Product and Service Quality Results Business Process, Operational and Support Service Quality Results Supplier Quality Results	*Quality and Operational Results* (180 points) Product and Service Quality Results Company Operational Results Business Process and Support Service Results Supplier Quality Results	*Quality and Operational Results* (180 points) Product and Service Quality Results Product and Service Quality Results Product and Service Quality Results Company Operational Results Business Process and Support Service Results Supplier Quality Results
Customer Satisfaction (300 points) Determining Customer Requirements and Expectations Customer Relationship Management Customer Service Standards Commitment to Customers Complaint Resolution for Quality Improvement Determining Customer Satisfaction Customer Satisfaction Results Customer Satisfaction Comparison	*Customer Focus and Satisfaction* (300 points) Customer Relationship Management Commitment to Customers Customer Satisfaction Determination Customer Satisfaction Results Customer Satisfaction Comparison Future Requirements and Expectations of Customers	*Customer Focus and Satisfaction* (300 points) Customer Expectations: Current and Future Customer Relationship Management Commitment to Customers Customer Satisfaction Determination Customer Satisfaction Results Customer Satisfaction Comparison

use in their evaluations. The table shows the score—in the form of a percentage of the total points assigned to each area—that a company could get, depending on specific characteristics that should be able to be observed directly.

Business Factors

In 1990, the concept of key business factors was introduced. Key business factors are qualifiers that help examiners compare the performance and achievements of different companies, even though the companies might differ in size, industry, and competitive environment. The 1991 guidelines contained a detailed explanation of how an applicant needed to address the key business factors in each of the examination categories. In 1994, however, this section on key business factors was dropped. Instead, an applicant must now prepare a business overview describing these key business factors:

- The nature of the applicant's business (products and services)
- Principal customers and special requirements; special relationships with customers or suppliers
- A description of the applicant's major markets (local, regional, national, or international)

- Key customer quality requirements for products and services; significant differences by customer or markets
- The applicant's position (relative size and growth) in the industry and key factors in the competitive environment
- The applicant's employee base, including number, type, educational level, and bargaining units
- Major equipment, facilities, and technologies used
- Types and number of suppliers of goods and services
- The regulatory environment within which the applicant operates, including occupational health and safety, environmental, and financial regulations
- Other factors important to the applicant, such as major new directions for the company, major changes taking place in the industry, and new business alliances

Examination Characteristics

In 1991, examination characteristics were introduced. These characteristics further refine how the performance of different companies is to be evaluated by examiners, applicants, and companies pursuing quality improvement through self-assessment.

The examination characteristics were extensively developed in 1992. Concerns about broader issues were presented for the first time, including environmental quality, occupational health and safety, and regulatory compliance. Other issues were also given more prominent display, such as waste reduction, market share, and new technology, products, and markets. Applicants were reminded that there are three bases for comparison: trends from previous years, current levels of achievement, and industry benchmarking.

Applicants were also advised to identify in which phase of the learning cycle (planning, execution, assessment, or revision) each component of their quality programs was involved. Overall coordination of efforts throughout all work units (system alignment) was and continues to be highly valued by examiners.

In 1993 and 1994, the examination characteristics were significantly reduced and simplified.

In 1992, the key concepts were renamed "core concepts and values" and significantly rewritten.

Key Concepts

"Key concepts," which were first introduced in 1991, are embodied in the award criteria, items, and areas to address as well as in the application and examination processes. In 1992, the key concepts were renamed "core concepts and values" and significantly rewritten. For example, the core concepts and values of design quality and prevention, long-range outlook, partnership development, and public responsibility were first introduced that year. One could argue that the most current understanding of the philosophical underpinnings of quality management is presented in this set of core concepts and values. For the applicant, they constitute the best indication of the expected beliefs, attitudes, and scope of application of quality policies and programs.

Performance Issues

Links between the examination characteristics and quality-related corporate issues were introduced in the 1992 guidelines. This section includes extensive discussions in incremental and breakthrough improvements, financial performance, and invention, innovation, and creativity. Companies are explicitly cautioned against giving up the pursuit of breakthrough changes and are encouraged to apply their creativity to all processes and systems, not just technology. Financial performance, although recognized as important, is not a key criterion for obtaining high marks from examiners.

Examination Guidelines

Examination guidelines for examiners and applicants are the latest addition to the Baldrige Award process. Introduced in the 1993 award criteria and expanded in the 1994 edition, this four-page section explains how to put together an application, clarifies the meaning of many terms, defines a style to follow when preparing an application, and informs the applicant of important details (such as the 89-page limit for the application document). It is intended to help applicants meet examiners' expectations.

The Framework

In 1988, the quality framework embodied in the Baldrige Award was simple. As shown in Figure 2 (page 610), most relationships were unidirectional, and a strong quasi-causal dependence was assumed. Management's leadership led to quality efforts, which led to quality results, which ultimately affected customer satisfaction. Feedback information and adjustments were predominantly centered on data analysis, which drove redirected efforts in strategic quality planning, human resources, and quality assurance activities.

Overall, the 1994 framework places more emphasis on results, and results are clearly differentiated from the processes that produced them.

Since 1988, the framework for quality has undergone much revision. New terms such as "driver" and "system" have been introduced. In the 1994 framework (Figure 3), the goal of increasing customer satisfaction is clearly identified outside the framework, along with the additional goals of increasing customer retention and market share. Quality results are explicitly interpreted as internal measures of progress that propel the company to achieving the stated goals. In contrast with earlier versions, most relationships are now reciprocal, signifying that most areas are seen as influencing one another. Overall, the 1994 framework places more emphasis on results, and results are clearly differentiated from the processes that produced them.

Putting It All Together

The Baldrige Award represents an important step for the quality movement. It has introduced a standard for understanding quality and a common reference for quality policies and practices. From a simple enunciation of areas of

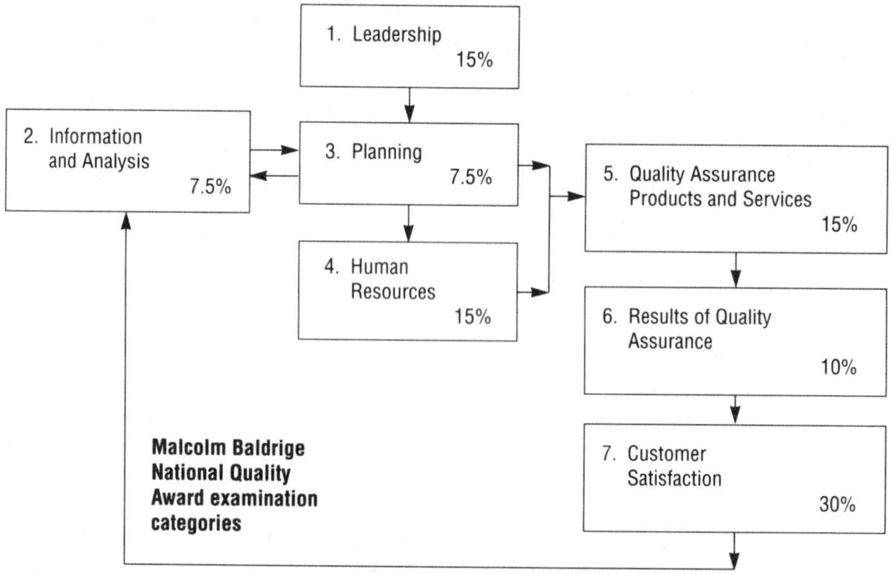

Figure 2. **Quality framework in 1988.**

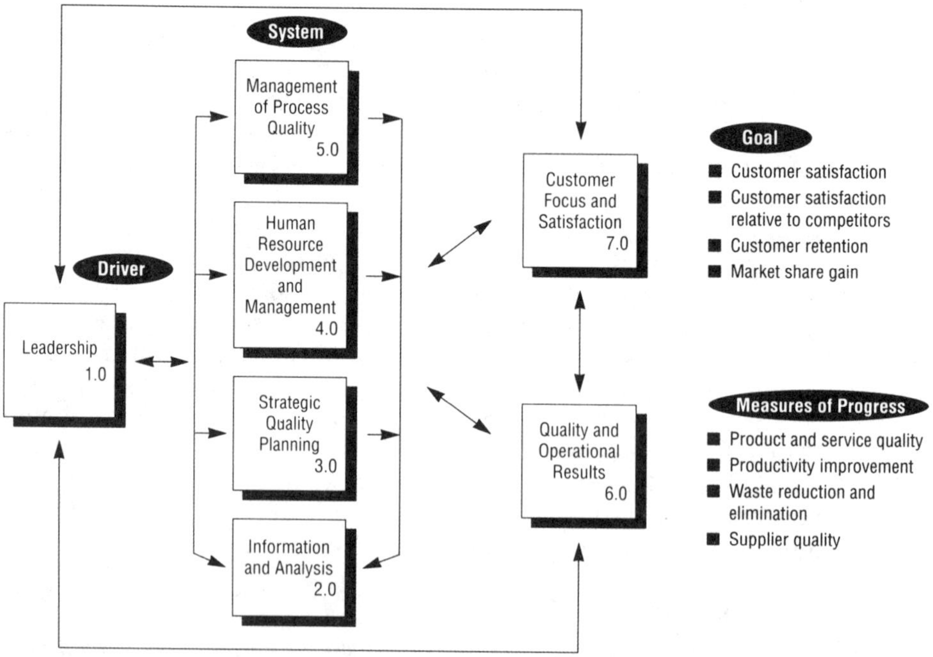

Figure 3. **Quality framework in 1994.**

AWARD OBJECTIVES HAVE BECOME MORE COMPREHENSIVE

Public Law 100-107 of Aug. 20, 1987, states the objectives of the Malcolm Baldrige National Quality Award:

1. Help stimulate American companies to improve quality and productivity for the pride of recognition while obtaining a competitive edge through increased profits.
2. Recognize the achievements of those companies that improve the quality of their goods and services and provide an example to others.
3. Establish guidelines and criteria that can be used by business, industrial, governmental, and other organizations in evaluating their own quality improvement efforts.
4. Provide specific guidance for other American organizations that wish to learn how to manage for high quality by making available detailed information on how winning organizations were able to change their cultures and achieve eminence.

The third objective is the most important. To fulfill this mandated goal, the Baldrige Award organization has continuously reflected on the purpose of the award criteria. In 1988, the Baldrige Award organization stated that the criteria's purpose was to "test all elements of a total quality system."[1] In 1989, the purpose was changed to "permit the evaluation of the strengths and areas of improvement in the applicant's quality systems and quality results."[2]

In 1991, however, two distinct objectives were identified: to be a standard for organizations seeking the highest levels of overall quality performance and competitiveness and to be a framework that can be used by organizations to tailor their systems and processes toward ever-improving quality performance.[3] In 1992, those objectives were further expanded: to help elevate quality standards and expectations, to facilitate communication and sharing among and within organizations of all types based on common understanding of key quality requirements, and to serve as a working tool for planning, training, assessment, and other uses.[4] As stated in the 1994 guidelines, the criteria are now designed to help any firm achieve ever-improving value to customers and improve overall company performance.[5]

As the administration of the award evolved, the purposes of the award criteria were interpreted more broadly and explained more thoroughly. It is apparent that the Baldrige Award organization is now closer to fulfilling its original mandated goal of establishing criteria and guidelines for organizations to follow in their quality efforts.

References

1. *1988 Award Criteria,* National Institute of Standards and Technology, U.S. Department of Commerce, Gaithersburg, MD.

2. *1989 Award Criteria,* National Institute of Standards and Technology, U.S. Department of Commerce, Gaithersburg, MD.

3. *1991 Award Criteria,* National Institute of Standards and Technology, U.S. Department of Commerce, Gaithersburg, MD.

4. *1992 Award Criteria,* National Institute of Standards and Technology, U.S. Department of Commerce, Gaithersburg, MD.

5. *1994 Award Criteria,* National Institute of Standards and Technology, U.S. Department of Commerce, Gaithersburg, MD.

concern in 1988 (organized into the now-famed seven Baldrige Award categories), the Baldrige Award process contains a rich underlying philosophy that is based on adaptations and refinements. Companies involved in quality improvement can benefit greatly from this resource.

References

1. An excellent account of the history of the Baldrige Award is given in Neil J. DeCarlo and W. Kent Sterret, "History of the Malcolm Baldrige National Quality Award," *Quality Progress* March 1990, pp. 21–27.

2. Philip B. Crosby and Curt Reimann, "Criticism and Support for the Baldrige Award," *Quality Progress,* May 1991, pp. 41–44, and David A. Garvin, "Does the Baldrige Award Really Work?," *Harvard Business Review,* January/February 1992, pp. 126–147.

Joao S. Neves is a professor of management at Trenton State College in New Jersey.
Behnam Nakhai is a professor of management at the Millersville University of Pennsylvania in Millersville.

Success Isn't Enough

William H. Miller

The Baldrige Award is evolving. In this short article that includes an interview with Curt Reimann, Baldrige chairman, we learn about the new directions the award is taking and more about its success and current state.

Obviously, the Commerce Dept. has studied what makes the winners of its Malcolm Baldrige National Quality Award tick. Taking to heart a common practice among the award's 19 winners so far—their striving for "continuous improvement"—the department is resisting the temptation to leave well enough alone. It is daring to make a significant change in the award itself, even though the program has been successful far beyond the early modest hopes for it.

Specifically, Commerce intends to transform "the Baldrige"—as the prized trophy has come to be known around industry—from a "competitive" to a "qualifying" award in which any firm meeting the award criteria would be a winner. The limit of two winners per category would be lifted.

Commerce intends to transform "the Baldrige"—as the prized trophy has come to be known around industry—from a "competitive" to a "qualifying" award in which any firm meeting the award criteria would be a winner.

"This does not mean 'come one, come all,' " emphasizes Curt W. Reimann, director of Quality Programs at Commerce's National Institute of Standards & Technology (NIST) and head of the Baldrige effort. "We intend no change in the standards or the degree of difficulty in winning the award. There may, in fact, be no increase in the number of winners."

The proposed change is incorporated in the National Competitiveness Act now in House-Senate conference. Enactment is expected in time to be reflected in the 1994 awards.

Commerce recommended the new approach at the suggestion of the Baldrige program's various advisory organizations. "They felt the limit of two awards per category was artificial and might inhibit cooperation," Mr. Reimann indicates.

"For example," he says, "suppose two companies in different industries are challenging for the award. They should be helping each other with their quality programs. But if only two companies are permitted to win, they might not [help each other] because they want to prevent the other from getting the award."

A main purpose of the Baldrige program, which was conceived by the Commerce Dept. but officially created by Congress in August 1987 and named

Reprinted with permission from *Industry Week*, April 4, 1994. Copyright Penton Publishing, Inc., Cleveland, Ohio.

after the department's late secretary, is to build quality awareness and to foster cooperation and sharing of quality information among companies. "We want to get everything out of the way that might impede cooperation," says Mr. Reimann.

A 32-year NIST veteran who has led the Baldrige program since its inception, Mr. Reimann acknowledges that "conceivably, down the road, an increased number of companies could win the award each year." But that won't happen, he stresses, "without considerable justification. It will have to be based on the strength of the applicants."

Mr. Reimann also acknowledges criticism of the proposed change—usually voiced by those who fear there'll be a weakening of standards. "Nobody intends that," he insists. "In fact, if the standards were to change, it would be very harmful." Besides its current proposal to remove the limit on the number of winners in each category, Commerce also is considering expanding the number of categories. To the current categories of manufacturing, service, and small business, Mr. Reimann reveals, the department is likely to add nonprofit health care and education. (*For-profit* health-care and education firms already are eligible for the award.) The expansion could begin with the 1995 awards.

Striking as these changes seem, they merely continue the tradition of change that has marked the Baldrige program since its inception. For example, Mr. Reimann points out that criteria in the early years of the program focused on product and service quality. Now they're pegged more closely to general business management, corporate strategy, and results. The system used to select examiners and evaluate entries also has been changed. More important, the program has shifted from its original orientation. "In our first two years, more than two-thirds of our entrants were from manufacturing," Mr. Reimann reflects. "But in the last two years we've had a good balance between manufacturing, service, and small-business firms."

In a wide-ranging interview at NIST's campus-like headquarters in Gaithersburg, Md., north of Washington, Mr. Reimann offered these comments on other aspects of the Baldrige program:

The Program's Success

"The fostering of cooperation and sharing—the principal strength of the program—has exceeded our wildest expectations. In the beginning, we expected our award winners to produce a short summary of their applications and share it at maybe a couple of conferences that several companies would attend. Well, our best estimates now are that our winners have participated in upward of 10,000 presentations—reaching millions of individuals and hundreds of thousands of organizations.

We've broken down the barriers within industry and between manufacturing and service.

"And we thought the lessons learned would principally be of interest only to people in the winners' own industries and to their suppliers. But the lessons have become multi-industry. We've broken down the barriers within industry and between manufacturing and service. It's not uncommon for a sharing session by a manufacturer to be attended by people from health care, insurance, and banking.

"Another surprise to us has been the way the program has stimulated other awards related to quality and productivity. There are more than 30 of them now. We're pleased about that, because it helps get the story out. We have helped many of the sponsors get their programs started."

Lower Participation

"Yes, the number of entrants for the Baldrige Award is down. We're concerned, but with a small 'c.' One reason is the number of other awards. In 1987 we were the only award out there. Now, in the aggregate, the count of award applicants is way up.

"Our participation rate also has been affected by the fact that many companies are working on ISO-9000 certification. Although it is a fundamentally different instrument from ours, it is unquestionably diverting their resources, particularly in smaller companies.

"And don't forget, our mission is to build awareness and information sharing. We think the impact we've had in that area has been phenomenal—overwhelmingly more important than the contest itself."

Effect of the Award

"It's hard to get actual numbers, but everywhere I go I see evidence that U.S. quality is up. And I think the Baldrige Award has been a factor. It certainly has built awareness. U.S. quality still has a way to go, but American companies can hold their heads high around the world; they can go toe to toe with the best. In the mid-1980s, there was a feeling that quality was something uniquely Japanese. Now [the nation's] quality models are American. We're not copying anybody else. And there's more optimism, a greater sense that high performance is manageable."

Remaining Quality Challenges

"There's still a lack of sufficient long-term commitment at the executive level, and also for a commitment to the necessary investment in people. Too many companies and organizations are still looking for quick fixes. That's particularly the case among small and medium-size enterprises. . . .

"We're limited in what we can do in this regard with the Baldrige Award, but state and local governments and trade associations can play bigger roles. In larger companies—involved in the rough and tumble of exports—the awareness level and the patience are much higher.

"Also, there's still a lack of awareness on how much better the truly outstanding companies are in quality than the average. Our award winners and award challengers talk about quality in terms of defect levels of parts per million. Yet a lot of companies are still dabbling around with percent levels, or with defect levels of thousands or even tens of thousands of parts per million. That's not going to wash a few years from now.

"And it's costly. Many executives don't appreciate how much more *productive* high-quality companies are in terms of such things as productivity, waste reduction, material and energy conservation, safety, worker's compensation, and achieving environmental goals. The leaders are better at *everything*."

William H. Miller is a senior editor with Industry Week *Magazine.*

PART FOUR

Quality References

We have created *The Quality Yearbook* for your use as an anthology and reference to the quality management movement. Parts One to Three are the anthology part of the book. Part Four is the reference part. Several sections make up this reference, each with its own list of information sources on Total Quality Management. Specifically, you'll find:

- **Comprehensive Annotated Bibliography**. We have ordered this in a similar way to the book's organization. It lists hundreds of articles and books on quality management from a large number of sources. This bibliography is current through the fall of 1994, and it should serve as the first place to turn to find more information on any aspect of quality management in which you have interest. We have selected articles for this section with bias toward pieces that deal with tactics rather than theory. Keep that in mind as you scan the list.

- **Annotated Directory of Organizations**. There are now many U.S. and international organizations that emphasize the study and practice of quality management principles and techniques. This section provides a complete alphabetical listing of all such organizations, both U.S. and international.

- **Directory of Awards**. Many states now have their own quality awards. This section catalogs those awards, with information on the categories for applying, award criteria, and how to get more information. This section also includes two national quality awards, a directory of awards in several countries, and where to write or call for more information on these.

- **Directory of Magazines and Journals**. This section lists 60 different publications that focus on or regularly include articles on quality management. This list rates the magazines according to their usefulness to managers learning about quality.

- **On-Line Quality Services**. This is a new section in the 1995 yearbook and includes a description of five on-line bulletin board services via computer and modem.

- **How to Do Benchmarking**. This is a brief how-to section on undertaking benchmarking projects in any type of organization.

- **Quality Quotes**. We have included a selection of more than 200 quotations from many different people, including writers, philosophers, and practicing managers. These are food for thought, and can be helpful when planning a speech or writing a report.

- **Glossary**. We feel especially good about the quality glossary we have included. This is more comprehensive than any other now available. It is almost like a mini-textbook to help you understand the many concepts TQM has promulgated.

- **The 1994 Baldrige Award Winners and the 1995 Baldrige Criteria.** Despite the fact that the winners and criteria are announced less than three months prior to the publication of this book, we felt it was vital to provide our readers with this information. By special arrangement with our production staff and the publisher, we are able to include this information for you.

- **Index**. We have prepared a detailed index to supplement the Table of Contents. This should be very valuable in helping you find more information on many topics covered in our anthology.

Annotated Bibliography of Quality Books and Articles

This year's bibliography is organized very much like the one in the last edition. We have included bibliographic citations that appeared after we went to press for the previous edition, so you will see some material published late in 1993. We have included references to publications that appeared through early September 1994. In the next edition of *The Quality Yearbook*, we will pick citations that come out after we go to press.

This year the literature began to shift away from basic explanations of what quality is (except for those industries that have been slow to embrace the new management style) and more toward specific case studies of organizational change and process improvements. More articles have appeared this year than before on measurements and cultural change while the number of new books published is actually down from 1993. This edition of the bibliography also includes a larger sampling of "war stories" from Europe and Asia.

MANUFACTURING SECTOR

General Trends

Banerjee, S.N. "Quality Management," *International Engineering Management Conference. Managing Projects in a Borderless World. Pre-Conference Proceedings* (1993): 170–77.

Describes the role of quality management practices in new product introductions. This is a presentation made at a conference held in Delhi, India, December 17–18, 1993.

Chase, Richard B., and Stewart, Douglas M. "Make Your Service Fail Safe," *Sloan Management Review* 35, no. 3 (Spring 1994): 35–44.

Describes the use of poka yoke, or fail safe methods to reduce or eliminate human errors that result in product defects. Argues that the approach also applies in services and that it is part of the product or service design decision in services. Explains how this might be done.

Gunasekaran, A., et al. "An Investigation into the Application of Group Technology in Advanced Manufacturing Systems," *International Journal of Integrated Manufacturing* 7, no. 4 (July–August 1994): 215–28.

GT is described as part of a manufacturing company's efficiency strategy because it allows for reduced setup times, inventory levels, and transportation time. Reviews current literature on the subject.

Hayes, Robert H., and Pisano, Gary P. "Beyond World Class: The New Manufacturing Strategy," *Harvard Business Review* 72, no. 1 (January/February 1994): 77–84ff.

Argues that instead of using TQM, JIT, etc., as a way of getting ahead of competition, a real manufacturing strategy is needed, and that calls for skills and capabilities development that over a long period of time make it possible for your company to do things better than the competition. Leads to different types of decisions than those made in the past.

Jacobs, Derya A., and Clemson, Barry. "TQM and CIM Can Work Together," *Engineering Management Journal* 6, no. 2 (June 1994): 31–39.

Suggests that both be implemented simultaneously since they compliment each other.

Johnson, Russell, and Kleiner, Brian H. "New Developments in TQM," *Work Study* 42, no. 6 (September/October 1993): 5–9.

This is a brief review of how TQM has been embraced and used in the aerospace and defense industries. Includes case studies of U.S. Defense Department support for TQM implementation and inventory reengineering by Martin Marietta Aerospace.

Keller, A.Z., and Kazazi, A. "'Just in Time' Manufacturing Systems: A Literature Review," *Industrial Management & Data Systems* 93, no. 7 (1993): 3–32.

Describes the evolution of JIT manufacturing strategies and then moves on to a review of research that has been done on the implementation and effectiveness of JIT. Research confirms the effectiveness of this approach.

Klassen, R.D., and McLaughlin, C.P. "TQM and Environmental Excellence in Manufacturing," *Industrial Management and Data Systems* 93, no. 6 (1993): 14–22.

TQM is serving as a bridge between corporate business and environmental objectives. Describes how a body of practices TQM offers is used to incorporate environmental considerations in the design and manufacture of products.

Magjuka, Richard J. "Employee Involvement and Continuous Process Improvement (TQM): An Empirical Study," *International Journal of Management* 11, no. 1 (March 1994): 620–28.

Presents results of a survey that studied how manufacturing companies designed and ran employee involvement processes as part of their continuous improvement programs. Results are presented, along with a discussion of their implications for training.

Magrath, Allan J., and Hardy, Kenneth G. "Building Customer Partnerships," *Business Horizons* 37, no. 1 (January/February 1994): 24–28.

Describes why partnerships with customers are formed, five tactical building blocks for such strategies, and the nature of these relationships; a good introduction to the subject.

Owen, Jean V. "Time Is the Yardstick," *Manufacturing Engineering* 111, no. 5 (November 1993): 65–70.

Discusses a large variety of tools and techniques being used by industry to reduce the amount of cycle time it takes to perform work. Presents a case study from the Ford Motor Company of a successful measurement of cycle time.

Shores, A. Richard. *Reengineering the factory: A Primer for World-Class Manufacturing.* Milwaukee: ASQC Quality Press, 1994.

This 93-page book is a quick introduction to improving manufacturing processes at a conceptual level: the issues involved, the agenda to be followed.

Wilkinson, Adrian, Tom Redman, and Ed Snape. "What Is Happening in Quality Management? Findings from an IM Survey," *TQM Magazine* 6, no. 1 (1994): 55–58.

Reports on the result of a survey of 900 individuals on quality management in their own organizations in the U.K. 71 percent reported that quality programs existed in their firms; 11 percent plan to implement one soon (based on 1992 data). Concludes that quality practices were beginning to take hold in British companies.

Wilson, Robert, Jr. "The New Reign of Quality," *Industrial Engineering* 26, no. 3 (March 1994): 48–50.

Argues the case for time compression strategies; time as a competitive edge is described. Also discusses how quality management is implemented and describes the value chain concept.

Automotive

Alonzo, Vincent. "Shifting Gears," *Incentive* 168, no. 8 (August 1994): 76–82.

Describes the current marketing strategies of the three U.S. automotive vendors that emphasize high levels of customer service as their means of obtaining competitive advantage. The comments are specific by vendor: Ford Motor, Oldsmobile Division, and General Motors.

LaBar, Gregg. "Safety at Saturn: A Team Effort," *Occupational Hazards* 56, no. 3 (March 1994): 41–44.

Describes how Saturn Corporation, working with its union personnel, developed safety and health processes and programs at its Spring Hill, Tennessee, facility; it is an outstanding case study of state-of-the-art approaches and results!

Stuelpnagel, Thomas R. "Deja vu: TQM Returns to Detroit and Elsewhere," *Quality Progress* 26, no. 9 (September 1993): 91–95.

Describes Henry Ford's management practices of the 1920s, which are compared positively with TQM practices, and how Ford executives relearned them in the 1980s by reading an old copy of Ford's original guidelines.

Electronics

Anonymous. "Pursuing the Quality Prize," *Manufacturing Engineering* 111, no. 5 (November 1993): 14, 16.

A survey conducted by the American Electronics Association indicates that more than 70 percent of the participating companies use TQM and, of those, nearly half have enjoyed significant benefits. Surveys also a variety of quality prices and programs in use, including Shingo Prize for Excellence in Manufacturing and the ISO 9000 registration process.

Boyett, Joseph H., et al. *The Quality Journey.* New York: Dutton, 1993.

This is an account of how the IBM plant in Rochester, Minnesota, transformed its operations and won the Baldrige Award. It is a detailed case study of the successful introduction of quality management practices in a manufacturing plant; an outstanding book.

English, Michael J. "Evolution: Quality Means Value," *America's Network, Quality Supplement* (1994): 32–33.

GTE Telephone Operations has made quality practices central to its operations. GTE learned, for example, that purchase decisions depend on the correct combination of quality, service, and price. In 1994, focus was on excellence and quality conformance, along with senstivity to customers.

Haycock, T.L. "Applying the TQM Method of Process Characterization to Harris Semiconductor's Spice Model Development and Support," *Proceedings of the Tenth Biennial University/Government/Industry Microelectronics Symposium* (1993): 65–70.

Describes how Harris Semiconductor applied quality practices to reduce the amount of cycle time to get new products to market. Besides application of CAD, this company also used process characterization in its Spice model development and support functions.

Joy, Joseph V. Jr. "Total Quality Analysis Spur Productivity," *Manufacturing Systems* 11, no. 9 (September 1993): 50–53.

This is a case study of how Applied Digital Data Systems (ADDS) applied a Total Quality Management program in order to bring back into the U.S. manufacturing functions from overseas. Includes specific results obtained.

Pulat, B. Mustafa. "Total Quality Management: A Framework for Application in Manufacturing," *TQM Magazine* 6, no. 1 (1994): 44–49.

Describes an eight-element model for the implementation of TQM in manufacturing.

Stratton, A. Donald. *A Quality Transformation Success Story from Storage Tek.* Milwaukee: ASQC Quality Press, 1994.

This is a case study of a company's economic recovery applying such quality practices as Deming's 14 Points, education, and process strategies, complete with lessons learned.

Wussow, N.C. "Quality Improvement: A Progress Report," *APEC '93 Eighth Annual Applied Power Electronics Conference and Exposition. Conference Proceedings 1993* (1993): 854–59.

Baslor Electric, an electronics manufacturer, has been applying quality practices since 1987. Compares results against what the published literature says should be the results of quality management practices. It is a success story, made useful by the fact that this company has been applying the principles for a long time.

Various Manufacturing Industries

Anonymous. "Flynt Fabrics' Quality Program Achieving Significant Results," *Textile World* 144, no. 6 (June 1994): 88.

Describes the TQM efforts of a company applying this approach since 1985. Emphasis of the article is on how this company communicates with its suppliers, deploying a quality conference.

Anonymous. "TQM at Lafayette Graphics," *Printing Impressions* (January 1994): 34.

Describes the application practices at Lafayette Graphics. Emphasis is on explaining how statistics are used by employees in the performance of their daily activities.

Brown, Alan. "Case Study: Quality Management in the Smaller Company," *Asia Pacific Journal of Quality Management* 2, no. 3 (1993): 67–76.

Describes the quality practices at an Australian plastics manufacturing company (Nally (WA) Pty) from its beginning to the present, detailing what issues were faced and how they were handled.

Calderone, F. "Total Quality Management in U.S. Fabrication Shops," *Wielding Review International* (February 1994): 238ff.

This is a good overview of trends in this industry in applying quality practices. The industry is characterized by enormous competition. Calls out the extensive use of ISO 9000. Provides the case for applying quality practices in manufacturing.

Citrano, Virginia. "Message Is Quality at Offices, Factories," *Crain's New York Business* (November 8, 1993): 14.

Describes the case of Rice Aircraft, which used quality management practices to improve market share. A useful overview of the role of senior management in implementing quality practices linked to specific corporate objectives that included solving a major problem: rapid decline in market share.

Idstein, James R. "Small Company TQM," *Management Accounting* 75, no. 3 (September 1993): 39–40.

This is a case study on how a small company of 48 employees implemented TQM. The Kane Graphical Corporation illustrates how one does not need vast resources in order to implement TQM successfully.

Libby, Bill. "Reengineering, by the Book," *Manufacturing Systems* 12, no. 4 (April 1994): 52–55.

Cochrane Furniture applied synchronous manufacturing methods to reduce the amount of time it took to build furniture and to cut inventory expense. It now operates a lean manufacturing process.

Madu, Christian N. "On the Total Productivity Management of a Maintenance Float System Through AHP Applications," *International Journal of Production Economics* 34, no. 2 (March 1994): 201–7.

The article describes how to apply quality management practices of a maintenance float system. Introduces the concept of analytical hierarchy process (AHP) and the Pareto principle.

Petersen, Debbie. "A Brave New World," *American Printer* 212, no. 12 (November 1993): 36–38.

Discusses trends and directions in the printing industry, leading to a new definition of services: that of information service companies. One of the influencing features in this industry will be the application of TQM; digital printing will be another.

Roth, Jill. "Productivity and Quality Improvement: A Special Report," *American Printer* 212, no. 12 (November 1993): 41–46.

Presents the results of a survey of the printing industry's approach to productivity and quality management. Reports little implementation of quality and productivity management practices; only 40 percent were aware of Total Quality Management.

Vanfleet, Rise, and Smith, John S. "The Process of Change," *TQM Magazine* 5, no. 6 (December 1993): 45–48.

This is a case study of the economic recovery of the U.S. Carlisle Tire & Rubber Co. (CT&R), using employee participation and teamwork to revitalize its manufacturing. This is an excellent look at shop floor issues, such as resistance to change, role of managers, and how teams improved dramatically their productivity.

Yeager, Bob. "Where Do We Go from Here?" *Manufacturing Systems* 12, no. 4 (April 1994): 22–28.

Reviews the continuous improvement efforts of Madison Paper Industries; its primary TQM goal is improvement of products and services to external customers.

Various Process Industries

Anonymous. "Baldrige Winner Shares Information on Its Total Quality Program," *Industrial Engineering* 26, no. 7 (July 1994): 9–10.

Describes the quality programs at Ames Rubber Corporation, which won a Baldrige Award.

Anonymous. "Cargill's Field of Dreams," *Prepared Foods* (October 1993): 24.

Describes how the Cargill Eddyville, Iowa, plant is applying Total Quality Management. This plan processes food, such as corn and salad oil, and focuses employee attention on customer satisfaction issues.

Anonymous. "EFQM Viewpoint: Gaining Advantages," *TQM Magazine* 5, no. 6 (December 1993): 13–15.

Reviews Ciba Group's use of TQM practices. This case study of the Swiss chemical company's experience is explained as a series of steps. It is a useful European model of how a company is transforming itself.

Anonymous. "Restructuring Rarely Achieved on the First Cut," *In Vivo the Business & Medicine Report* (February 1994): 10ff.

Describes trends in restructuring and downsizing by companies in the pharmaceutical industry. The changes in who buys, along with the success of previous downsizing efforts, will probably lead to more such efforts in the 1990s. Provides cases studies and statistics on successes.

Juran, J.M. "Quality Woes," *Chemical Marketing Reporter* 246, no. 3 (July 18, 1994): PSR6.

Says chemical companies have hardly engaged in the application of quality practices, but should. The article explains the case for using quality management practices.

Karol, Michael. "TQM Takes the Thorough Technique," *Graphic Arts Monthly* 65, no. 12 (December 1993): 59–62.

While commenting on the role of quality practices in printing, the thrust of the article is on the enormous cultural change that comes with the introduction of quality practices. Describes the major emphasis areas, such as customer focus, process management, and such issues as TQM, ISO, and personnel practices.

Mullin, Rick. "Atochem's New Measurement Code Keys on Stakeholders' Needs," *Chemical Week* 153, no. 20 (November 24, 1993): 40.

This is a case study on how Elf Atochem North America did process reengineering and achieved important improvements in operations.

Mullin, Rick. "Turning the Programs into a Process—Using TQM Polls to Build An Umbrella," *Chemical Week* 153, no. 10 (September 15, 1993): 39–44.

Describes how chemical industry managers are now making a distinction between programs and processes, the latter more of a holistic approach to management. Reviews several cases where successful use of TQM lay in setting specific goals for the entire company and standard approaches to management practices.

Rolfes, Richard J., III. "How We Made TQM Real," *Tapping the Network Journal* 4, no. 3 (Winter 1993/1994): 18–20.

This is a case study on the experience of Camco Corporation, which educated its employees on process management and then began to implement TQM tools. Declares that it now has internal expertise to sustain the efforts.

Wason, Satish K., and Bhalla, Sushil K. "Managing the Technological Process," *Quality Progress* 27, no. 1 (January 1993): 81–85.

Described how the J.M. Huber Corporation's Chemical Division integrated its technology, manufacturing, and marketing activities to improve overall operations using TQM tools. It is a useful case study of the early efforts of a company to implement TQM practices.

Services Sector

Banking and Finance

Anonymous. "Bank's 'Quality' Effort Makes Sound Business Sense," *New Library World* 95, no. 1113 (1994): 17–18.

Describes the role of senior management at American Express in introducing TQM throughout the financial and travel related services operations.

Anonymous. "Help Desk Reshaped for TQM," *Bank Systems & Technology* 31, no. 2 (February 1994): 14–19.

Describes how Continental Bank's cash management is heavily customer focused and applies expert systems as the help desk approach to supporting clients by answering their questions faster and better.

Callis, Juli Anne. "Existing to Serve, Serving to Exist," *Credit Union Executive* 34, no. 2 (March/April 1994): 32–34.

Argues that customer focused services are on the rise and that the use of desktop computing is facilitating the process. The article is less targeted to credit unions and more to businesses in general.

Fry, W. Darryl. "Reinventing a Mortgage Company," *Mortgage Banking* 54, no. 4 (January 1994): 65–70.

ComUnity Lending has used process reengineering techniques successfully since 1991, along with TQM, to improve such operations as mortgage delivery and wire department operations.

Garrett, Panchita. "Get Innovative or Get Dead!" *Texas Banking* 82, no. 9 (September 1993): 3, 26.

Describes TQM implementation at Bank One Texas Trust and at Comerica Bank. Describes how TQM works in banking and several critical success factors for these banks that implemented quality practices successfully.

Griffiths, Gareth. "Emphasis on Customer Service," *Investors Chronicle* 108, no. 1375 (May 27, 1994): 88.

Describes quality practices in the banking industry in Great Britain. Argues they arc becoming niche players and describes how that is coming about.

Lewis, Ken. "Developing Performance Through People," *Banking World* 12, no. 6 (June 1994): 33–34.

The British Cooperative Bank was one of the first English banks to embrace TQM. This is an account of what it did and what issues it currently faces. Emphasis is on training issues.

Lian, Tanja. "Positioning Your Bank in the Customer's Mind," *Bank Marketing* 25, no. 9 (September 1993): 24–33.

Discusses strategic errors banks make. It focuses on the image banks must create in the minds of their customers before tackling TQM.

Lunt, Penny. "Ten Tips Toward 'Total Quality'," *ABA Banking Journal* 86, no. 4 (April 1994): 66–69.

Discusses how First Chicago Corporation applies TQM and, in particular, defect identification. Gives advice on how banks can apply TQM.

McLaurin, Donald L., and Bell, Shareen. "Making Customer Service More Than Just a Slogan," *Quality Progress* 26, no. 11 (November 1993): 35–39.

Describes how Weyerhaeuser Mortgage Company improved customer service by improving interpersonal communication skills. Describes customer requirements analysis and TQM practices that led to improved customer service.

Morrall, Katherine. "Re-engineering: Buzzword or Strategy?" *Bank Marketing* 26, no. 1 (January 1994): 21–25.

First Commerce Corporation uses reengineering techniques to identify who are their customers and what services to provide them. Numerous insights on how to perform successful reengineering are provided.

Muckian, Michael. "TQM 101," *Credit Union Magazine* 60, no. 2 (February 1994): 34–39.

Reports on the growing trend of credit unions applying TQM principles. Says this is difficult to do in this industry because it requires such a major change in culture. University of Wisconsin Business School professor Mark Finster is quoted on the key steps to such a transformation.

Percy, Don. "Measure the Possibilities," *Credit Union Management* 17, no. 6 (June 1994): 12–14ff.

Using the University of Wisconsin Credit Union, the author describes how a "know your customer" strategy was developed and implemented, detailing how the process evolved in 1992 and 1993.

Timewell, Stephen. "Listen to the Customer," *Banker* 144, no. 816 (February 1994): 29–30.

Argues that banks will want to manage customers not products and that the use of surveys is an important tool in understanding them. Market segmentation will cause more varied products and pricing.

Distribution (Wholesale/Retail)

Anfuso, Dawn. "At L.L. Bean, Quality Starts with People," *Personnel Journal* 73, no. 1 (January 1994): 60.

Briefly argues that the company focused on people when it began to implement TQM with great success. Profits and customer satisfaction rose; backlogs and injuries were reduced; and standardization was improved. Changed roles of managers is also reviewed.

Gilman, Alan L. "The Customer Decade," *Chain Store Age Executive* 70, no. 3 (March 1994): 198.

Describes why some chains are implementing preferred customer programs and how these are being done. Refers to programs at Neiman Marcus, InCircle, and Sears.

Hotels

Anonymous. "How the Best Got Better: Marriott Asked Customers for Their Definition of Customer Service," *Industry Week* (March 7, 1994): 27.

Describes how the Marriott in Bethesda, Maryland, used a cross-functional team to improve customer service. Surveying customers led them to devise a faster way to check-in customers, reducing check-in time to under two minutes. Other changes are reviewed.

Anonymous. "Poor Quality Hampers Growth of Chalet Trade," *Travel Trade Gazette* (November 24, 1993): 50.

Complaints about European chalets not being of sufficient quality to appeal to the British customers; discusses ways and whys of the problem. This is a good short piece on changing customer expectations and how an industry is not responding effectively.

Anonymous. "Quality Is . . . Never Having to Say That the Laundry Is Shut!" *New Library World* 95, no. 1113 (1994): 13–14.

Describes quality practices at Scotts Hotels, Ltd., in which practices at Marriott Corporation were introduced. Describes the massive change in practices and the extensive training of the staff required by those changes.

Lyons, Margaret. "Empowerment: How Hotels Get Total Quality Management," *BRW* 3, no. 10 (November 1993): 14–23.

Describes how empowerment works at the Sydney Park Hyatt hotel. It is a detailed case study of how employees treat their customers, the processes involved, and the results achieved.

Verespej, Michael A. "How the Best Got Better," *Industry Week* 243, no. 5 (March 7, 1994): 27–28.

Les Cappetta, director of service development for Marriott Corporation, described quality improvement efforts at his company. Described how a team of employees defined good customer service and then how the company changed its organization and tasks to provide it. Expects to cut operating costs by up to 40 percent.

Insurance

Anonymous. "A Policy of Reengineering: Insurers Are Rethinking Customer Service—and Everything Else, for That Matter," *InformationWEEK* (September 27, 1993): 106.

Argues that the insurance industry is changing many processes in fundamental ways and using healthy doses of IT to accomplish the task. Argues the benefits of several computer-based technologies in reengineering of insurance processes.

DeBow, Yvette. "Making Service Count," *Insurance and Technology* 19, no. 5 (May 1994): 25.

Reports on a seven-point quality program in effect at Delta Dental Plan of Massuchusetts. Describes specific measureable goals for each, such as processing of 90 percent of claims within 15 days and no hassle customer service 100 percent.

DeBow, Yvette. "Taking Service to the Field," *Insurance and Technology* 19, no. 3 (March 1993): 25.

Presents results of a survey on the use of technology in marketing and sales activities to improve customer service. The primary future use of technology was in improving the quality of customer service.

Dauer, Christopher. "Foreign Competition Fuels 'Total Quality' Here," *National Underwriter Property & Casualty* (November 29, 1993): 13ff.

Introduces Total Quality Management principles to the insurance industry, suggesting, for example, that they can help in improving risk management processes.

Harrison, John J. "Database Tech Critical to Insurers," *National Underwriter (Property & Casualty)* (June 20, 1994): 9, 12ff.

A properly constructed database allows a company to gather and analyze data that leads to effective marketing programs and products. Describes what a marketer in the insurance industry can gather and use.

Messenger, Sally J., and Atkins, Tony. "The Prudential Experience of Total Quality Management," *International Journal of Contemporary Hospitality Management* 6, no. 1, 2 (1994): 37–41.

Describes how the Prudential Assurance Co., Ltd., implemented quality management practices, beginning in 1989. Details actions taken, benefits gained, which included lower operating costs and increased productivity.

Mulcahy, Colleen. "Quality Measures Becoming More Standardized," *National Underwriter* 98, no. 21 (May 23, 1994): 31.

Says that performance measurements are coming to risk management activities, displaying the same trends evident in manufacturing in such areas as TQM. Calls for this industry to adopt quality management practices and why, quoting various industry executives.

Transportation and Travel

Anonymous. "Quality Control Vital in Selection—Gray Dawes," *Travel Trade Gazette UK & Ireland* (March 23, 1994): 30.

Over 80 percent of the organizations that asked for a bid on providing services wanted to know what this travel agency's quality program was; describes past achievements and planned invents in the continuing application of TQM.

Caldwell, John H. "Benchmarking: Making It Work," *Business Travel News* (February 7, 1994): 13ff.

Describes how to apply benchmarking to travel business activities. It is a specific, list-oriented discussion of what to do.

Owen, Dave, Bill Hubbard, and Greg Blair. "IE Techniques Improve Productivity at Service Companies," *Industrial Engineering* 25, no. 12 (December 1993): 27–30.

American President Companies, a containerized transportation company, has integrated traditional industrial engineering and TQM practices, leading to creation of actionable data that improves processes in the company. Describes specific quality tools employed by the company.

Utilities

Addicott, G.W., and J. W. Coakley. "Impact of TQM During Top Management Changes and Restructuring," *Proceedings of the American Power Conference 1993* 1 (1993): 350–53.

This case study is about Florida Power's Power Generation Business Unit's experience with TQM. This is an important case study for any industry because it is an example of how TQM was woven successfully into the fabric of the company's culture. Offers specific positive results.

Baim, R.F. "Successful Process Improvement Is Achievable If We Keep It Simple," *Proceedings of the American Power Conference 1993* 1 (1993): 354–60.

The article describes the value of process control as a way to improve operations and then describes a 10-step approach to doing just that.

Bolen, T. "The Quality Initiative at Commonwealth Edison," *Proceedings of the American Power Conference* 1993 1 (1993): 266–69.

Describes the quality effort that began in 1989 at one of the largest U.S. utility companies. This presentation is on activities and results achieved.

Candlin, D.B., and P.J. Day. "Introducing TQM in a Service Industry," *Quality Forum* 19, no. 3 (September 1993): 132–42.

Describes progress made in implementing quality principles at the East Midlands Electricity in Great Britain. Gaps in customer service were identified and action plans layed in place to fix them.

Cavannaugh, H.A. "Re-engineering: Buzz Word, or Powerful New Business Tool?" *Electrical World* (April 1994): 7–9, 12–15.

Besides being another article on the same theme, it includes quotes and discussion of opinions within the utility industry, with examples of projects underway in electrical utilities.

Navaratnam, K.K., and Bill Harris. "Customer Service in an Australian Quality Award Winning Public Sector Service Industry," *International Journal of Public Sector Management* 7, no. 2 (1994): 42–49.

Describes how quality management practices were adopted at the South East Queensland Electricity Board. It is an instructive case study in an industry that is just beginning to understand TQM; this organization has been at it since early 1988.

Sharma, S.P., and W.L. Harrod. "Total Quality Management Process to Achieve Excellence," *APEC '93. Eighth Annual Applied Power Electronics Conference and Exposition. Conference Proceedings 1993* (1993): 29–34.

Reports on AT&T Power Systems' industrial quality management system. A key feature is the extensive use of data and information analysis for planning and improving performance. Describes how that is done and the results obtained.

Other Services

Anderson, Pat. "Service Pints," *Marketing Week (Customer Loyalty Supplement)* (March 25, 1994): 8.

Describes how pub operator Ansells Brewery, Ltd., in Great Britain changed its marketing and operational philosophy after surveying its customers. Focus is now on customer service not beer. The results have been impressive; what the company did is the subject of this short article.

Jones, Peter, and Michael Dent. "Lessons in Consistency: Statistical Process Control in Forte PLC," *TQM Magazine* 6, no. 1 (1994): 18–23.

Reports on the effective use of SPC to improve the quality of a corporate restaurant. It led to other quality practices with positive returns, such as more employee commitment to improved services.

Kasavana, Michael L. "Computers and Multiunit Food Service Operations," *Cornell Hotel and Restaurant Administration Quarterly* 35, no. 3 (June 1994): 72–80.

Describes the application of automation and other forms of technology to improve restaurant operations, particularly management decision making.

Macdonald, John. "Services Is Different," *TQM Magazine* 6, no. 1 (1994): 5–7.

Compares TQM as applied in services vs. manufacturing organizations. Argues that in services, TQM will have to be implemented in a manner different from how it normally is done in a manufacturing company.

Morand, John D. "Total Quality Management," *Economic Development Review* 11, no. 3 (Summer 1993): 3–4.

Argues the case that TQM can strengthen economic development strategies; clearly not a set of management practices currently used by these kinds of organizations.

Scheuing, Eberhard E., and William F. Christoper. *The Service Quality Handbook* (New York: AMACOM, 1994).

A comprehensive review of service quality, with contributions from 57 international experts. Covers all aspects of the subject, with much practical advice. The article "Managing the Evidence of Service Quality" by Mary Jo Bitner in this edition of the yearbook is taken from this book. Highly recommended.

Sill, Brian. "Operations Engineering: Improving Multiunit Operations," *Cornell Hotel and Restaurant Administration Quarterly* 35, no. 3 (June 1994): 64–71.

Describes operations engineering as a method to identify faster and better approaches for providing services in the restaurant business. Provides a logical approach to the management of such variables as layout, time, sequence, persons, methods, and service delivery. It is a process view of managing restaurant activities.

Public Sector

Health

Anonymous. "Business Health Services Increases Markets for Morton Plant Hospital in Clearwater, Fla.," *Health Care Strategic Management* 12, no. 5 (May 1994): 13.

Describes how this hospital signed over 45 managed health care contracts in less than a decade, representing 24 percent of its total revenue. Describes the process used to manage relations and marketing issues with managed health care.

Anonymous. "The Quality March," *Hospitals & Health Networks* 67, no. 23 (December 5, 1993): 52–55.

Says hospitals have been very enthusiastic in embracing quality management principles and practices, and explains why. Presents the results of a national survey showing who is implementing and why quality practices exist in this industry; a major study.

Bebko, Charlene Pleger. "Consumer Factors Affecting the Delivery of Quality Health Care Services," *Health Marketing Quarterly* 11, no. 1, 2 (1993): 19–41.

Presents results of research concerning whether or not a consumer of services can affect the delivery of that service. The answer is yes; considerable amount of attention is paid to methodology and examples.

Bergman, Rhonda. "Reengineering Health Care," *Hospitals & Health Networks* 68, no. 3 (February 5, 1994): 28–36.

Describes the attitude of the health care industry towards reengineering. It is being applied for various reasons including to address performance problems, loss of money and market share, and as a strategy to sustain marketing programs.

Burkhardt, Julie, Patricia Nardone, and Wayne Wandmacher. "Nursing/Pharmacy Interface: A TQM Project," *Nursing Management* 25, no. 3 (March 1994): 38–43.

Applying Deming's 7-step quality improvement process, generation and verification of medical records was improved at North Memorial Medical Center at Robbinsdale, Minnesota. Specific anticipated benefits are described as well.

Burney, Robert. "TQM in a Surgery Center," *Quality Progress* 27, no. 1 (January 1994): 97–100.

Describes the application of TQM at the Virginia Beach Ambulatory Surgery Center: how it was done, the tasks performed, and how it functions today. This is a unique case study of outpatient care facilities using TQM.

Cheung, Ma Hok, and Hugh Koch. "Establishing Continuous Quality Improvement in a Hong Kong Hospital," *International Journal of Health Care Quality Assurance* 7, no. 2 (1994): 19–25.

Presents an excellent case study of the United Christian Hospital in Hong Kong applying TQM principles. The emphasis of the article is on how they launched the effort: its design points and initial tasks.

Curtin, Leah L. "Doing the Right Thing," *Nursing Management* 24, no. 12 (December 1993): 17–19.

Argues that TQM creates the environment necessary for high ethical behavior. Presents a framework for teaching managers how to handle decision making in a value driven way.

Curtin, Leah L. "Quality, the Old Fashioned Way," *Nursing Management* 25, no. 3 (March 1994): 7–8.

Argues that TQM is about doing one's best. In an editorial, the author argues for overhauling the way things are done in nursing without giving up the traditional values of the nursing profession.

Dershin, Harvey. "TQM and Health Care," *TQM Magazine* 6, no. 2 (1994): 30–31.

Says many things that a hospital does is similar to what goes on in a factory and, therefore, the application of TQM offers the same kinds of benefits as in manufacturing.

Dieter, Bryan, and Doug Gentile. "Improving Clinical Practices Can Boost the Bottom Line," *Healthcare Financial Management* 47, no. 9 (September 1993): 38–43.

Defines clinical quality improvement using TQM principles. Details what it does for the organization's culture and efficiency in positive terms. This is an excellent introduction to the topic of TQM in health care.

Holliday, Lynette. "Costing for Quality: A Case Study," *International Journal of Health Care Quality Assurance* 7, no. 2 (1994): 10–13.

Describes how the Dudley Group of Hospitals introduced TQM into its operations. The strategy is described along with the objectives. It is a clearly stated approach applicable to most hospitals; a good read.

Holloway, Beverley, and David Mobbs. "Customer Focus Groups: Developments in Health Care," *TQM Magazine* 6, no. 1 (1994): 13–17.

The author reports that the health care industry is experiencing tremendous turbulence and is increasingly turning to customers to find out how to manage the situation. Describes what health care providers are doing, particularly in Great Britain.

Kim, Pan S., and Delinda D. Johnson. "Implementing Total Quality Management in the Health Care Industry," *Health Care Supervisor* 12, no. 3 (March 1994): 51–57.

Describes the experience with TQM of Sentara Health System in Norfolk, Virginia, since 1990. The article is specific in defining the issues health care organizations face when implementing quality practices and values.

Langenfeld, Douglas E. "In Defense of Total Quality Management," *Healthcare Financial Management* 47, no. 12 (December 1993): 92–93.

Discusses the potential payoff of TQM; argues that this payoff is still to be shown, but that benefits accrue if the slow process is implemented.

Lorence, Daniel. "Benchmarking Quality Under U.S. Health Care Reform: The Next Generation," *Quality Progress* 27, no. 4 (April 1994): 103–7.

Describes a variety of benchmarking projects in health that are drawing interest: billing forms, formatting and submission of data, accreditation standards, remote monitoring, health networks, pharmacy databases, among many.

Merdinger, Wayne J. "Why TQM?-A President's Perspective," *Journal of Management Development* 12, no. 7 (1993): 32–35.

The president of Graham Field Health Products, Inc., describes his experience in implementing TQM. He tells his story beginning before TQM existed at the company, then telling how it was introduced and what he expects from it in the future.

Pehrson, H. Gary. "Give It Time," *Healthcare Forum* 37, no. 4 (July/August 1994): 34–39.

Describes how Intermountain Health Care, Inc., has been practicing clinical quality improvement for over three years. Describes the benefits that have been achieved with this approach. Says this is a long-term commitment, and that is why it has been successful.

Pollack, Sandra, and Aixa Rey. "Applying TQM to Infection Surveillance," *Nursing Management* 25, no. 3 (March 1994): 74–75.

Describes the application of TQM in infection control surveillance at the Coral Gables Hospital.

Potter, C., P. Morgan, and A. Thompson. "Continuous Quality Improvement in an Acute Hospital: A Report of an Action Research Project in Three Hospital Departments," *International Journal of Health Care Quality Assurance* 7, no. 1 (1994): 4–29.

The departments were operating theaters, X ray, and medical records. Demonstrates how a bottoms up audit and quality assessment approach led to many suggestions for how to improve operations.

Sherer, Jill L. "Hospitals Question the Return on Their TQM Investment," *Hospitals & Health Networks* 68, no. 7 (April 5, 1994): 63.

Examines how TQM can generate cost savings for a hospital. Yet 4,500 hospitals have reported in a survey that most have not yet realized their financial targets for TQM programs.

Sherer, Jill L. "Putting Patients First," *Trustee* 47, no. 3 (March 1994): 14–16.

Describes how patient centered care affects operations in a hospital. Presents results of a survey of hospital CEOs: 40 percent said they were implementing or planned to implement patient centered care programs. This was being done to improve services, drive down costs, and as a continuation of quality management programs already underway.

Williams, David M., and Janet M. Williams. "Improving the Quality of Service in an Out Patient Department," *International Journal of Health Care Quality Assurance* 7, no. 2 (1994): 16–18.

Reports on work done by over 150 staff members of the Swansea National Health Service Trust in that part of a hospital that is almost always the point of entry for patients. The results of two years worth of work in an acute hospital outpatient department are documented. Their efforts won the organization major British and European Health Care Quality Awards in 1993.

Education (K-12)

Chappell, Robert T. "Can TQM in Public Education Survive Without Co-production?" *Quality Progress* 27, no. 7 (July 1994): 41–44.

Argues that the U.S. Department of Labor's Commission for Achieving Necessary Skills (SCANS) is in favor of the application of TQM. Describes how this can be done involving students, teachers, parents, and administration.

Feigenbaum, Armand V. "Quality Education and America's Competitiveness," *Quality Progress* 27, no. 9 (September 1994): 83–84.

One of the U.S.'s leading pioneers of quality management argues the case for quality in the education programs of all students, so they think and act in a way that will sustain America's competitiveness in the global market. Accuses American educational institutions of hardly recognizing the value of quality principles.

Fusco, Armand A. "Translating TQM into TQS," *Quality Progress* 27, no. 5 (May 1994): 105–8.

Introduces the notion of Total Quality Schools as a viable form of TQM. Says it would cause management to look at systems rather than micromanaging as they do today; builds the case for applying TQM in elementary and high schools.

Hittman, Jon A. "TQM and CQI in Postsecondary Education," *Quality Progress* 26, no. 10 (October 1993): 77–80.

Argues the case for implementing TQM and CQI in education and tells how this can be done. This is a major strategic piece for any school administrator to read.

Horine, Julie E., William A. Hailey, and Laura Rubach. "Transforming Schools," *Quality Progress* 26, no. 10 (October 1993): 31–38.

Reports on the implementation of TQM in U.S. schools, calling out that the approach is taking off. Presents survey results indicating how and where TQM is being applied.

March, Judith K., Karen H. Peters, and Heidi L. Adler. "Peer Coaching: Empowering Teachers While Accomplishing Management Goals," *Government Union Review* 15, no. 2 (Spring 1994): 44–62.

Reports on a very promising quality management effort in education: the use of peer coaching to improve staff development efforts. Explains the rationale and how it is done.

Rubach, Laura. "*Quality Progress'* Fourth Annual Quality in Education Listing," *Quality Progress* 27, no. 9 (September 1994): 27–79.

This is a compendium of information about the quality activities of 415 schools, colleges, and universities. It lists the areas in which they have quality programs underway, their classroom offerings, names and addresses of contacts.

Schargel, Franklin P. "Teaching TQM in an Inner City High School," *Quality Progress* 27, no. 9 (September 1994): 87–90.

Describes the application and teaching of quality management at the George Westinghouse Vocational and Technical High School in New York City, beginning in 1991. Describes the curriculum, homework assignments, role of the teachers and parents, and what students have learned.

Schargel, Franklin P. "Total Quality in Education," *Quality Progress* 26, no. 10 (October 1993): 67–70.

Calls on schools to teach TQM to students if the United States is to expand its application of quality management practices throughout the economy. Describes the Westinghouse Education Quality Initiative, which is designed to help schools teach quality practices.

Scholtes, Peter R., and Other Contributors. *The Team Handbook for Educators* (Madison, WI: Joiner Associates, 1994).

This is an adaptation for K-12 educators of the most widely used book for teaching teamwork skills. The adaptation was prepared by David Bayless, Gabriel Massaro, and Nancy Roche, consulting editors in the area of K-12 education for this edition of *The Quality Yearbook*.

Higher Education

Gales, Ron. "Can Colleges Be Reengineered?" *Across the Board* 31, no. 3 (March 1994): 16–22.

Answer is yes. Surveys various initiatives in cost cutting, resource sharing with other schools, outsourcing, etc., and suggests other areas of opportunities in higher education.

Helms, Susan, and Coretta H. Key. "Are Students More Than Customers in the Classroom?" *Quality Progress* 27, no. 9 (September 1994): 97–99.

Presents the results of a study done with students at Wright State University in classroom instructions, and calls for TQM to be applied to that process.

Horine, Julie E., William A. Hailey, and Laura Rubach. "Shaping America's Future," *Quality Progress* 26, no. 10 (October 1993): 41–60.

Reports on the results of a survey that indicates success by U.S. colleges and universities in applying TQM principles. Initial successes have been primarily in administration followed by teaching. Most institutions reported that they were still in the early stages of implementation.

Hubbard, Dean L. "Can Higher Education Learn from Factories?" *Quality Progress* 27, no. 5 (May 1994): 93–97.

Describes how Northwest Missouri State University attempted to implement TQM practices. The results were extensive: first comprehensive electronic campus in the United States; major writing assignments up 72 percent;

the semester extended from 15 to 17 weeks; and a quality assessment process put in place.

Meeter, Duane, and Grant Smith. "Student Quality Improvement Projects," *Quality Progress* 27, no. 9 (September 1994): 111–4.

Describes the use of quality progress teams made up of students at Florida State University. They apply quality principles learned in the classroom in projects. Describes the use of students as facilitators helping schools, FSU, hospitals, and private companies apply TQM.

Potocki, Kenneth, Richard Brocato, and Paul R. Popick. "How TQM Works in a University Classroom," *Journal for Quality and Participation* 17, no. 1 (January/February 1994): 68–74.

Describes how TQM principles were taught at the Johns Hopkins University Applied Physics Laboratory; includes details on how TQM was also used to develop and administer the training.

Yarrow, David, and Alex Appleby. "Sharing the Gains," *TQM Magazine* 5, no. 6 (December 1993): 17–19.

Discusses a Best Practices Club for businesses set up and hosted by the University of Northumbria at Newcastle in 1990. Discusses the positive effect this club's activities have had on British businesses over the past three years.

Federal, State, and Local Government

Barra, Ralph. "Paving Roads with More Than Just Good Intentions," *Journal for Quality and Participation* 17, no. 1 (January/February 1994): 26–32.

Describes the application of quality practices at the Maryland State Highway Administration beginning in the mid-1980s, thus making this one of the longest running programs in the public sector. Particularly useful are the descriptions of the various stages of evolution and revolution they experienced over the decade.

Beem, Perry, Daniel Kanouse, and James C. McFarlane. "Combining TQM and Conflict Resolution," *Journal for Quality and Participation* 17, no. 1 (January/February 1994): 54–56.

Useful for describing how to improve labor/management problems leading to partnering activities within the public sector; the case study is the Philadelphia Naval Shipyard's Public Works Department.

Benowitz, Stephen C. "New Age Personnel—Quality Service Delivery in Changing Times," *Public Personnel Management* 23, no. 2 (Summer 1994): 181–85.

The National Institutes of Health has changed its personnel practices to account for smaller staffs and increased focus on needs of stakeholders. How that is being done is the subject of this article.

Berman, Evan M., Jonathan P. West, and Michael E. Milakovich. "Implementing TQM in the States," *Spectrum: The Journal of State Government* 67, no. 2 (Spring 1994): 6–12.

Presents results of a national U.S. survey of corrections, transportation, welfare, health, and education agencies. Results show 59 percent are practicing TQM; 64 percent use top down planning; 60 percent deploy midlevel implementation teams; and 56 percent bottoms up efforts. Most reported benefits from using TQM in decision making and communications.

Bowman, James S. "At Last, an Alternative to Performance Appraisal: Total Quality Management," *Public Administration Review* 54, no. 2 (March/April 1994): 129–36.

Builds the case for not using appraisals of individuals, but rather broader use of TQM, which treats the organization as a system. Finds appraisals of individuals counter to TQM.

Bowman, James S., and Fran L. Wilbur. "We Want to Begin . . . Are We Ready?" *Journal for Quality and Participation* 17, no. 1 (January/February 1994): 34–39.

Details the results of a survey of managers within the government of Florida suggesting partial support for implementing TQM, despite the governor's desire to push forward more aggressively. How those various opinions are playing out in managerial decisions is the subject of this article.

Chalk, Mary Beth. "Implementing Total Quality Management Within Communities," *Economic Development Review* 11, no. 3 (Summer 1993): 5–9.

Argues that TQM practices can help whole communities improve their economic conditions. Describes five lessons applicable to all communities.

Chen, AL Y.S., and Roby B. Sawyers. "TQM at the IRS," *Journal of Accountancy* 178, no. 1 (July 1994): 77–80.

The U.S. Internal Revenue Service has long had a quality management focus, one that recently has been renewed. Describes recent activities within the agency.

Dale, B.G. "A Framework for Quality Improvement in Public Sector Organizations: A Study in Hong Kong," *Public Money & Management* 14, no. 2 (April 1994): 31–36.

Describes the framework public sector managers in the Hong Kong government developed for quality practices in their organizations. Has many of the same features as a TQM implementation plan in the private sector.

Doherty, Linda M., and J. Daniel Howard. "Strategic Transformation in the Department of the Navy: Total Quality Leadership Above and Below the Waves," *Journal for Quality and Participation* 17, no. 1 (January/February 1994): 46–53.

Describes the approach of the U.S. Navy and Marine Corps in implementing quality. They emphasize organizational redesign, describing how they are implementing this strategy.

Duke, Rick, and Elliot Price. "Why Total Quality Management Isn't Just a Tool for Manufacturing: The Case of Metro Augusta, Georgia," *Economic Development Review* 11, no. 3 (Summer 1993): 31–33.

The example of local economic development employing TQM principles is described along with the case study of Augusta, Georgia. General principles for use by all communities are listed.

Durant, Robert F., and Laura A. Wilson. "Public Management, TQM, and Quality Improvement: Toward a Contingency Strategy," *American Review of Public Administration* 23, no. 3 (September 1993): 215–45.

Provides an analysis framework for looking at the spectrum of opinions about the role and implementation of quality management practices in the public sector. This is a detailed introduction to a large number of issues concerning TQM's application by state and federal government agencies.

Ferris, Frank. "Two Views of One Agency: The IRS and NTEU," *Public Manager* 23, no. 2 (Summer 1994): 27–30.

Describes application of TQM at the Internal Revenue Service and at the National Treasury Employees Union for over a decade, making these case studies some of the most mature in the world of quality.

Grandzol, John, and Mark Gershon. "Multiple Criteria Decision Making," *Quality Progress* 27, no. 1 (January 1994): 69–73.

Describes structural alignment changes made at the Physical Plant Department of the U.S. Navy Aviation Supply Office. Describes how TQM was implemented in this office.

Hickman, Edgar P. "TQM in South Carolina," *Business and Economic Review* 40, no. 4 (July–September 1994): 18–21.

Describes the fascinating project that has taken place in Spartanburg where the local Chamber of Commerce promoted TQM as a way of life. The experience has been a very positive one.

Hunt, V. Daniel. *Quality Management for Government.* Milwaukee: ASQC Quality Press, 1993.

This is a major contribution to our understanding of how to apply quality management principles in federal, state, and local government. This is a practical guide on how to implement by a leading expert on quality management practices.

Linden, Russ. "Reengineering to Capture the Customer's Voice," *Public Manager* 23, no. 2 (Summer 1994): 47–50.

Describes what the Department of Labor in Connecticut and Lakeland Regional Medical Center in Florida did to respond to rapid change and to the needs of their clients; both had successes to report.

Loney, Timothy J. "TQM and Labor Management Cooperation: A New Challenge," *Public Manager* 23, no. 2 (Summer 1994): 23–26.

Describes U.S. Executive Order 12871, Labor Management Partnerships, dealing with unions and U.S. government management relationships. Describes the public sector labor environment.

Mathers, Earl F. "Quality Initiatives in Campbell County, Wyoming," *Economic Development Review* 11, no. 3 (Summer 1993): 28–30.

Describes how public and private sectors got together in one community to apply TQM principles to promote local economic development. Emphasizes the role of the local economic development organization applying TQM.

Mukherjee, Sanjoy, and Ashley Braganza. "Core Process Redesign in the Public Sector," *Management Services* 38, no. 6 (June 1994): 6–8.

Describes the benefit of process redesign for the British police force.

Rago, William V. "Adapting Total Quality Management (TQM) to Government: Another Point of View," *Public Administration Review* 54, no. 1 (January/February 1994): 61–64.

Provides a case study of the application of TQM at the Texas Department of Mental Health & Mental Retardation over two years. Concludes that the application of TQM in public sector is possible and that others commenting on the topic have defined incorrectly the problems involved.

Savoie, Donald J. "Looking to Managerialism to Do Better with Less," *Optimum* 24, no. 3 (Winter 1993): 12–18.

Describes efforts underway within the Canadian government to improve the productivity of operations. Based on a survey of 114 project proposals, it becomes clear that managerialism is an important influence. Describes prize winners in a quality award program and what they did.

Schay, Brigitte W. "In Search of the Holy Grail: Lessons in Performance Management," *Public Personnel Management* 22, no. 4 (Winter 1993): 649–68.

This describes three demonstration projects conducted over the past 14 years by the U.S. Office of Personnel Management concerning alternative human resource management approaches, applying Deming's principles. Gives Deming's approach and TQM mixed reviews.

West, Jonathan P., Evan M. Berman, and Michael E. Milakovich. "Implementing TQM in Local Government: The Leadership Challenge," *Public Productivity and Management Review* 17, no. 2 (Winter 1993): 175–89.

Presents results of a survey of U.S. city managers and chief administrative officers on TQM implementation. Reports on critical success factors, e.g., senior management support and rewards.

Wood, Colin, and PaulWalker. "Putting the Customer First," *TQM Magazine* 6, no. 2 (1994): 17–24.

Describes the introduction of quality management practices at the British post office, beginning in 1988.

Nonprofit Associations

Anonymous. "Society for Nonprofit Organizations," *Nonprofit World* 12, no. 3 (May–June 1994): 48–49.

Describes TeamTrack from this society, a workshop to bring employees and board members together to carry out the mission of the organization.

Barrier, Michael. "Raising TQM Consciousness," *Nation's Business* 82, no. 4 (April 1994): 62–64.

Describes how the Chamber of Commerce in Pueblo, Colorado, ran nine workshops to increase local business awareness of TQM practices. Discusses how local businesses were reluctant to invest in TQM training.

Bender, Jodi. "New Model in Educational Programs Unveiled," *Nonprofit World* 12, no. 1 (January/February 1994): 49.

Describes the educational role of the Society for Nonprofit Organizations in helping their members change, apply TQM principles, and empower employees.

Quality Transformation

Leadership

Anonymous. "A Close Look at Organization Restructuring: Is All This Change Necessary?" *Manage* 45, no. 4 (April 1994): 8–11.

Announces a research project by the National Management Association and Louis Allen Associates to study the impact of reengineering in the United States Preliminary results show companies are restructuring reactively, not proactively, and that companies are not forecasting future trends, thus are restructuring ineffectively.

Anonymous. "The New Governance Paradigm," *Chief Executive* no. 93 (April 1994): 40–54.

Describes a roundtable held with CEOs, directors, and institutional shareholders regarding governnance. Among its comments is the observation that quality is a growing factor in governance.

Baum, Ralph A. "It's Either 3 for 3 with Your Customers, Or You're Out," *Journal for Quality and Participation* 16, no. 7 (December 1993): 50–51.

Briefly argues that TQM is a leadership philosophy that values teamwork, trust, and continuous improvement with a heavy dose of customer focus. Explains why this is a good way to run an organization.

Blake, Carmelita. "Value Leadership in Total Quality Management," *Nursing Management* 25, no. 7 (July 1994): 88–89.

Value leadership is the act of adding motivation and a moral dimension to the tasks of a manager. Argues why and adds that TQM is compatible with this perspective.

Boone, Greg. " A Powerful Weapon," *TQM Magazine* 5, no. 4 (August 1993): 55–58.

Discusses how quality programs can become bureaucratic and politicized. The author reviews some steps that management can take to prevent those problems from occurring. The advice is tactical and sound.

Bovet, Susan Fry. "CEO Serves as Chief Communicator of TQM Program," *Public Relations Journal* 50, no. 6 (June/July 1994): 16–17ff.

Reports on the comments made by three CEOs at a recent Conference Board Annual Quality Conference. These leaders discussed how they were using TQM at Allied Signal, PQ, and at Whirlpool.

Capellupo, John P. "The Challenge of Change in This Decade," *Executive Speeches* 8, no. 4 (February/March 1994): 74–76.

Describes how leaders can use such themes as quality management and empowerment to lead operations.

Chandra, Mahesh. "Total Quality Management in Management Development," *Journal of Management Development* 12, no. 7 (1993): 19–31.

Argues the case for implementing TQM and the value of the Baldrige Criteria in meeting and exceeding customer requirements.

Coates, Dennis E. "Retooling TQM," *Appliance Manufacturer* 41, no. 9 (September 1993): 34–36.

Discusses typical problems companies face with implementing TQM and how to get around these problems.

Cullen, Joe. "Visualizing Improvement," *TQM Magazine* 5, no. 4 (August 1993): 33–38.

This is a case study of the Rover Group, a British company, that created a vision and then a process model of its operations, linking the two to implement its business plan. Explains how this automotive company interlocked quality and its business vision.

Dale, Barrie G., and Cary L. Cooper. "Introducing TQM: The Role of Senior Management," *Management Decision* 32, no. 1 (1994): 20–26.

Describes the value of senior management commitment to TQM and then the active role a CEO must play to make TQM happen in an organization. Describes specifically what this commitment must be, e.g., knowledge of TQM, its application, and so forth.

DiPietro, R.A. "TQM: Evolution, Scope and Strategic Significance for Management Development," *Journal of Management Development* 12, no. 7 (1993): 11–18.

Describes the evolution of TQM as an interdisciplinary model for how management can run an organization. Describes the role management must play in the kind of changes called for with TQM.

Grant, Robert M., Rami Shani, and R. Krishnan. "TQM's Challenge to Management Theory and Practice," *Sloan Management Review* 35, no. 2 (Winter 1994): 25–35.

Argues that implementation of TQM requires fundamental changes in organizational structure and management practices. Concludes that the theories underlying TQM and the more traditional economic models of companies are not compatible.

Harber, Doug, Kevin Burgess, and Daphne Barclay. "Total Quality Management as a Cultural Intervention: An Integrative Review," *Asia Pacific Journal of Quality Management* 2, no. 1 (1993): 17–27.

Argues that adoption of TQM is a learning process for individuals and organizations, a response to external forces of change that must be met if the enterprise is to survive and thrive. This is very much a sociological study of the influence of senior management and the dynamics of how an organization changes.

Harrington, H. James. *Total Improvement Management.* New York: McGraw-Hill, 1994.

This is a large book on quality-based management practices. It is intended to cover most aspects of a manager's job and how organizations apply quality practices.

Knotts, Rose, and Sharynn Tomlin. "A Comparison of TQM Practices in U.S. and Mexican Companies," *Production & Inventory Management Journal* 35, no. 1 (First Quarter, 1994): 53–58.

Presents the results of a survey indicating enormous cultural and managerial differences in how companies are managed in both countries. Argues that such differences present problems. However, management practices are quite similar, with the notable exception in Mexico where employee empowerment and participation are lacking.

Long, Carl, and Mary Vickers Koch. "Creating a Vision Statement That Is Shared and Works," *Journal for Quality and Participation* 17, no. 3 (June 1994): 74–77.

Describes the steps the authors went through in helping one company with 1,200 employees develop a strategic vision statement governing subsequent actions.

Macdonald, John. "Putting People First: Making the Most of Human Resources," *Managing Service Quality* 4, no. 3 (1994): 10–13.

Focuses on the cultural changes managers must make personally in order to encourage their employees to subscribe to quality management practices. Encourages management to recognize that their major source of assets is their employees.

Mallinger, Mark. "Ambush Along the TQM Trail," *Journal of Organizational Change Management* 6, no. 4 (1993): 30–42.

TQM and other quality-focused paradigms are suggesting alternative ways to structure management systems. Emphasis is growing on the use of statistics, customer focus, and continuous process improvement. Includes a case study.

Preston, Arthur P., and Ian W. Saunders. "Understanding Quality Leadership," *Asia Pacific Journal of Quality Management* 3, no. 1 (1994): 24–42.

Argues that the key to achieving the benefits of quality-focused management practices lies in the ability of an organization to control and improve both its processes and its products.

Sheehy, Barry, and James D. Robinson, III. "Staying the Course," *Executive Excellence* 11, no. 6 (June 1994): 19–20.

TQM in American companies is in danger of being dropped because some executives and managers are becoming bored with the process, despite the fact that it does lead to significant positive changes. Concludes that the fact remains: TQM works!

Sibsom, Robert E. *Maximizing Employee Productivity: A Manager's Guide.* New York: AMACOM, 1994.

This manager's guide to personnel matters, e.g., motivating, rewarding, etc., is cast in quality management terms.

Wiesendanger, Betsy. "Is Quality Its Own Reward?" *Journal of Business Strategy* 15, no. 2 (March/April 1994): 54–55.

Presents the results of a Conference Board poll of large manufacturing and service companies in the United States showing that 85 percent have formal awards for individuals and groups achieving quality results.

Cultural Transformation

Anjard, Ronald P. "The Quality Dimension as a New Element of the Organizational Behavior Model," *TQM Magazine* 6, no. 2 (1994): 43–44.

Provides a brief historical account of organizational model theories and then suggests another with quality a part of it. This is very much a theoretical piece.

Baden-Fuller, Charles, and John M. Stopford. *Rejuvinating the Mature Business.* Boston: Harvard Business School Press, 1994.

Authors argue that a business can be rejuvinated, along with its industry. Profiles companies that have, including Banc One, Toyota, and British Airways.

Conners, Roger, Tom Smith, and Craig Hickman. *The OZ Principle: Getting Results through Individual and Organizational Accountability.* Englewood Cliffs, N.J.: Prentice-Hall, 1994.

Argues that individuals and organizations both are accountable for performance, and it is that accountability that is the goal of quality management. Not a lot of new news, but a timeless message.

Day, Marie. "Can Organizations Have a Learning Disability?" *Canadian Manager* 19, no. 2 (June 1994): 21–23+.

This summarizes Peter Senge's ideas from his book *The Fifth Discipline.*

Donaldson, Gordon. *Corporate Restructuring: Managing the Change Process from Within.* Boston: Harvard Business School Press, 1994.

Challenges much conventional wisdom about how firms achieve increased efficiency. Illustrates how companies voluntarily restructure themselves and not just because of a fear of a hostile takeover.

Filion, L.J. "Visionary Systems Thinking (VST) as a Support to Creativity in the Quality Management (TQM) Process," *Systems Research* 11, no. 1 (1994): 125–33.

Innovation and new ways of doing things represent one aspect of quality. Describes an approach for integrating these various activities, particularly for supporting use of creativity within the management process.

Filipczak, Bob. "Weathering Change: Enough Already!" *Training* 31, no. 9 (September 1994): 23–29.

Reviews the problems with managers constantly trying to change an organization and the importance of making substantive rather than cosmetic change.

George, Stephen, and Arnold Weimerskirch. *Total Quality Management: Strategies and Techniques Proven at Today's Most Successful Companies.* New York: John Wiley & Sons, 1994.

Part of the Portable MBA Series, this book provides yet another comprehensive review of TQM techniques with emphasis on examples from several large companies.

Gitlow, Howard S., and Shelly J. Gitlow. *Total Quality Management in Action.* Englewood Cliffs, NJ: PTR Prentice Hall, 1994.

An excellent and current review of how to implement TQM, with special emphasis on processes and their analysis and management.

Grossman, Stephen R. "Why TQM Doesn't Work . . . and What You Can Do about It," *Industry Week* 243, no. 1 (January 3, 1994): 57–62.

Announces that interest in TQM is declining, offering as evidence declining interest in Baldrige, and then defends TQM and argues that it will not be adopted widely so long as individuals just worry about fixing existing problems.

Handy, Charles. *The Age of Paradox.* Boston: Harvard Business School Press, 1994.

This is a broad-gauged view of circumstances in which businesses operate; a follow-on to his book, *The Age of Unreason.*

Helzer, T.A. "Envisioning TQM Through Systems Thinking," *Systems Research* 11, no. 1 (1994): 177–83.

Announces that, in general, people have not been able to develop unified sets of concepts for implementing quality practices. Argues that an organization-wide vision does provide a positive and constructive way of allowing many approaches to work together.

Hodgetts, Richard M., Fred Luthans, and Sang M. Lee. "New Paradigm Organizations: From Total Quality to Learning to World Class," *Organizational Dynamics* 22, no. 3 (Winter 1994): 5–19.

Argues the case for organizations becoming learning organizations that apply TQM practices. Describes the concept of the world class organization and what it must be good at.

Joiner, Brian L. *Fourth Generation Management: The New Business Consciousness.* New York: McGraw-Hill, 1994.

Provides a highly readable, practical, and complete review of the basic concepts of quality management. The book is especially valuable for understanding the role of variation and its management as critical in improving an organization. An excerpt from Joiner's book is included in the process management section of this edition of *The Quality Yearbook.*

Lowenthal, Jeoffrey N. *Reengineering the Organization: A Step-by-Step Approach to Corporate Revitalization.* Milwaukee: ASQC Quality Press, 1994.

This is a cookbook approach to corporate revitalization. It offers a discussion of the cultural and organizational issues one has to deal with, and specific planning steps.

Klein, H.K., and P. Kraft. "Social Control and Social Contract in NetWorking. Total Quality Management and the Control of Work in the United States," *Computer Support Coop. Work (CSCW)* 2, nos. 1–2 (1994): 89–108.

Discusses the role of networks as a form of organization control strategies and provides two case studies of how such technical tools redefined control systems in TQM oriented environments.

Maccoby, Michael. "Creating Quality Cultures in the East and West," *Research Technology Management* 37, no. 1 (January/February 1994).

This article points out that people living in Europe and the United States have different values concerning individualism than do workers in Asia, and that both cultures thereby influence how people approach such issues as TQM and teams. Argues that, in particular, Westerners have to deal with their cultural bias when formulating TQM implementation strategies.

Sashkin, Marshall, and Kenneth J. Kiser. *Putting Total Quality Management to Work.* San Francisco: Berrett-Koehler Publishers, 1993.

A short book on the basics, with an excellent section on creating a quality culture.

Senge, Peter M. "Creating Quality Communities," *Executive Excellence* 11, no. 6 (June 1994): 11–13.

A leading expert on quality management practices introduces five operating principles for "learning organizations": they are built by servant leaders; they embody new capabilities; they occur through performance and practice; process and content are inseperable; and all learning can be dangerous.

Senge, Peter, Charlotte Roberts, Richard B. Ross, Bryan J. Smith, and Art Kleiner. *The Fifth Discipline Fieldbook.* New York: Doubleday Currency, 1994.

Carrying on from Senge's book, *The Fifth Discipline,* this work provides more in-depth understanding of organizations as systems and the practical implications of that understanding for learning and improving how organizations and people work.

Sirota, David, Brian Usilaner, and Micelle S. Weber. "Breaking Through the Culture Wall," *Journal for Quality & Participation* 17, no. 2 (March 1994): 74–83.

Summarizes the results of the 1990 GAO study on how companies who applied for the Baldrige Award were successful in implementing TQM.

Sommer, Steven M., and Deryl E. Merritt. "The Impact of a TQM Intervention on Workplace Attitudes in a Health Care Organization," *Journal of Organizational Change Management* 7, no. 2 (1994): 53–62.

Argues that TQM principles are very compatible with long-standing managerial philosophy concerning organizations. Using the health care industry as an example, the author argues that TQM can produce rates of change in organizations faster than more conventional approaches.

Spiro, Leah Nathans. "Quality: How to Make It Pay," *Business Week* (August 8, 1994): 54–62.

With all the naysayers, this article explains how many different companies are using quality management techniques to give direction to their companies, their employees, and improve the bottom line.

Sullivan, Peggy S. "Downsizing with TQM?" *Journal for Quality & Participation* 17, no. 2 (March 1994): 84–90.

Argues that using TQM in downsizing facilitates the process because you rely extensively on open communications, systems thinking process analysis, and employee involvement. Describes benefits of working this way.

Waldman, David A. "Designing Performance Management Systems for Total Quality Implementation," *Journal of Organizational Change Management* 7, no. 2 (1994): 31–44.

Describes how to make a TQM-focused performance management system be compatible with normal organizational structures. It is an important article on measurement and incentive strategies.

Whitney, John O. *The Trust Factor: Liberating Profits and Restoring Corporate Vitality.* New York: McGraw-Hill, 1994.

Reviews the importance of trust in creating a more productive and vital corporate culture. Written by the director of the Deming Center for Quality Management at Columbia University. Recommended.

Whittaker, John. "A New Playing Field for TQM," *Engineering Management Journal* 5, no. 2 (June 1993): 8–12.

Argues that TQM is more suitable for Japanese than U.S. culture and, therefore, will not take root in the United States to the extent it has in Japan. Argues that assembly line workers are resisting it while some in the service sector are not.

Customer Focus

Abromovitz, Hedy Gruenebaum, and Les Abromovitz. *Bring TQM on the QT to Your Organization.* Knoxville, TN: SPC Press, 1994.

This is a primer on TQM for novices, with descriptions about how to apply these practices to problems in customer service. Emphasis is on customer-related issues.

Alonzo, Vincent. "'Til Death Do Us Part'," *Incentive* 168, no. 4 (April 1994): 37–42.

Describes how Harley Davidson, Saturn, and Wal-Mart Stores have built links to their customers through marketing, social interactivity (e.g., product clubs), and other services; all have been successful in growing their business volumes as a result. This is an important article on customer focus.

Barsky, Jonathon. *World-Class Customer Satisfaction: Profits Through Excellence.* Milwaukee: ASQC Quality Press, 1994.

This is a useful guide to linking the desire of an organization to satisfy its customers with more conventional wisdoms about what makes sense for the enterprise. It is a practical guide focusing on what is important to use from the quality world, e.g., benchmarking, retention marketing, and so forth.

Burdett, John O. "The Magic of Alignment," *Management Decision* 32, no. 2 (1944): 59–63.

Describes the success of Wal-Mart Stores, Lawson Mardon Group, Semco, and Toronto Blue Jays to illustrate that all types of cultural transformation approaches of the past decade only worked if all the efforts were aligned.

de Camara, Bob. "Knowing What the Customer Wants," *Flooring* (April 1994): 34.

Presents results of a survey conducted by *Better Homes and Garden* about what Americans want in regard to floor coverings. Describes how this kind of consumer demand survey was conducted.

Finkelman, Daniel P. "Crossing the 'Zone of Indifference'," *Marketing Management* 2, no. 3 (1993): 22–31.

Discusses the what and how of cost/benefit analysis for investments in customer satisfaction and retention. Offers a practical framework for such an analysis, much along the same lines as a capital decision.

Graham, John R. "Customer Service Redefined: It's What You Know, Not What You Sell," *Marketing News* 28, no. 1 (January 3, 1994): 25.

Talks about five types of information and customer expectations that must be matched. Best customer service includes knowledge, information, and expertise, not simply good products.

Greene, Jay. "Competition for Patients Spurs Hospitals' Concern for Serving the Customer," *Modern Healthcare* 24, no. 29 (July 18, 1994): 30–31ff.

Interesting case study of how in one industry management has reacted to the conclusion that customers have choices. Describes what drives customer decisions and the nature of customer surveys to understand these.

Halstead, Diane. "Five Common Myths about Consumer Satisfaction Programs," *Journal of Services Marketing* 7, no. 3 (1993): 4–12.

Reviews five common myths concerning customer satisfaction programs that cause faulty implementation of better services. Specific recommendations are made concerning what to do; an important article on the subject.

Hart, Christopher W.L. *Extraordinary Guarantees*. New York: AMACOM, 1993.

An expert who is widely published on the subject of customer guarantees describes their value, how to create them, and how to deal with "cheaters." This is an excellent book on the process of guarantees.

Helmeke, Todd M. "Exploring the Myth of Customer Service," *Industrial Engineering* 25, no. 10 (October 1993): 16–17.

This describes customer satisfaction surveys, what they are, the kind of data they generate, and how that information is used as part of a TQM strategy. Also describes what kind of corporate culture is most likely to take best advantage of customer satisfaction surveys.

Hiles, Andrew N. "Service Level Agreements," *TQM Magazine* 6, no. 2 (1994): 14–16.

This is an excellent introduction to SLAs, which have become a very popular tool for establishing performance criteria among departments and with customers and suppliers.

Hinton, Tom, and Wini Schaeffer. *Customer-Focused Quality*. Englewood Cliffs, NJ: Prentice Hall, 1994.

A how-to management book with much practical information on how to make the customer the focus of the business.

Innis, Daniel E., and Bernard J. La Londe. "Customer Service: The Key to Customer Satisfaction, Customer Loyalty, and Market Share," *Journal of Business Logistics* 15, no. 1 (1994): 1–27.

To gain customer loyalty, companies usually rely on marketing mix. However, in addition, one can use effective logistics and physical distribution to improve customer satisfaction and market share. Describes how these can be used as competitive strategies.

Johnston, Jo Ann. "Waxing Customer Service and Cars," *Management Review* 83, no. 7 (July 1994): 25–28.

Describes the success of the Scrubadub Car Wash chain in the Boston area. By looking at the service from the customer's point of view, it has done the job well and made it fun and interesting. It has learned seven lessons (e.g, attention to detail, know the customer, fix the problem, etc.), which are described. It is a great little case study!

Lowenthal, Jeffrey N. "Reengineering the Organization: A Step-by-Step Approach to Corporate Revitalization: Parts 1, 2, and 3" *Quality Progress* (January, February, March 1994).

Discusses the holistic nature of effective business transformation strategies. Offers a model of how one might go about implementing such broad changes in an organization. Reproduced in this edition of *The Quality Yearbook*.

Meenaghan, J.A. "Skulls, Subs, Pawns, and Kings: Attitude Cycles in Customer Orientation," *Irish Marketing Review* 6 (1993): 78–82.

Describes a continuum of changes in attitudes that occurs within a company and industry as it moves from a regulated to a deregulated environment. These stages are described.

Mowery, Neal, Patricia Reavis, and Sheila Poling. *Customer Focused Quality*. Knoxville, TN: SPC Press, 1994.

Describes how to integrate quality, marketing, and creativity; ways to understand needs of customers (internal too); how to recover from problems; and how to implement customer-focused customer processes.

Nicholls, John. "Customer Value in Four Steps," *TQM Magazine* 5, no. 6 (December 1993): 49–53.

Defines four stages of implementation for TQM. This particular list by a practioner with experience at Ford Motor Company is very realistic and practical.

Nielsen, Ken. "Managing: Every Complaint Tells a Story," *BRW* 3, no. 9 (October 1993): 41–42.

This is a useful introduction to the nature and benefits of a good customer complaint process, particularly as it applies in the Japanese market where use of such customer feedback mechanisms are considered useful positive processes.

Schlossberg, Howard. "Road to Success Paved with Service That Exceeds Customer Expectations," *Marketing News* 28, no. 1 (January 3, 1994): 22.

Reports on comments made at the AMA Cincinnati Chapter's marketing conference. The universal message was to listen to what customers want; provides specific comments by speakers.

Sepic, Thomas, and David McNabb. "Applying TQM's Golden Rule to Your Support Services," *Journal for Quality and Participation* 17, no. 3 (June 1994): 44–49.

Identifies a wide variety of internal administrative operations as candidates for TQM. These include printing and duplicating, accounting, housekeeping, and financial planning, among many.

Smith, Bob. "Lily Tomlin's Take on Customer Service," *Management Review* 83, no. 7 (July 1994): 17–20.

Describes the comedy characters of this comedian and her recent training videos, all focused on good and bad customer service. She applies humor to change people's perspectives about their job and customer service.

Verity, John W. "The Gold Mine of Data in Customer Service," *Business Week* , no. 3363 (March 21, 1994): 113–14.

Customer service operations represent an effective source of information about customers that can be used to enhance marketing and sales. This data can also be used to drive down field service costs, build closer relations with customers, and generate additional sales.

Zemke, Ron. "Creating Customer Value," *Training* 30, no. 9 (September 1993): 45–50.

Discusses the tradeoffs among good, fast, and cheap products and services to meet customer requirements. Discusses the concept of value creation as the driving force behind customer-focused decisions. It is a useful article on customer relations.

Zemke, Ron and Susan Zemke. "Partnering: A New Slant on Serving the Internal Customer," *Training* 31, no. 9 (September 1994): 37–43.

Reviews the establishment of more productive supplier-customer relationships between staff departments and line departments.

Quality Implementation Strategies and Planning

Alloway, James R., Jr. "Laying the Groundwork for Total Quality," *Quality Progress* 27, no. 1 (January 1994): 65–66.

Discusses problems companies face when adding quality objectives to existing corporate initiatives. Identifies seven problems that occur as a result of not integrating quality practices into the fabric of a corporation's activities.

Anand, K.N., J.N. Bhoraskar, and R.N. Mulye. "Using Policy Management to Implement TQM," *Quality Progress* 26, no. 10 (October 1993): 89–93.

Effective use of policy management makes implementation of quality practices feasible. Takes the reader through a step-by-step approach, and illustrates it with the actions of the Kirloskar Brothers, Ltd., management team in India.

Anonymous. "TQM Programs Making Positive Changes in U.S. Companies," *Industrial Engineering* 25, no. 12 (December 1993): 7.

Reports on the results of a survey conducted by the Conference Board that shows 20 surveys indicate TQM does have a positive effect, but takes a long time, requiring a long-standing corporate commitment.

Barry, Thomas J. *Excellence is a Habit: How to Avoid Quality Burnout.* Milwaukee: ASQC Quality Press, 1994.

This is a very short book on how to develop a strategic plan for quality using a process approach. The author emphasizes strategic rather than tactical approaches.

Brecka, Jon. "QA/QC Services Directory," *Quality Progress* 27, no. 8 (August 1994): 39–128.

This is the seventh annual survey of consultants and firms that can provide assistance in quality management. It surveys the offerings and capabilities of 698 firms and consultants. It is the most comprehensive directory of its kind available, prepared by the assistant editor of *Quality Progress*.

Brown, Mark Graham, Darcy E. Hitchcock, and Marsha L. Willard. "Why TQM Fails and What to Do about It," *Small Business Reports* 19, no. 7 (July 1994): 58–60.

Says once launched, expanding TQM across the company can run into problems caused by old measures, appraisal, and reward processes that are incompatible with TQM. Argues that new organizational structures must then be put in place.

Chalk, Mary Beth. "Measuring the Quality in Corporate Real Estate," *National Real Estate Investor* 36, no. 2 (February 1994): 78, 82.

Describes how Eastman Kodak Co. linked its application of quality methods in its management of real estate holdings to corporate business objectives. This is an important example of how the two activities could be linked, particularly useful since many companies are revisiting whether or not to own the buildings they use.

Covey, Stephen R. "A Total Approach to Total Quality," *Executive Excellence* 11, no. 6 (June 1994): 15–16.

By looking at Solectron Corporation, the author notes the case of one company having to work holistically to implement fundamental cultural changes. Describes how this company implemented TQM practices.

Donovan, R. Michael. "TQM: It's Customer Satisfaction or You Lose," *Industrial Management* 36, no. 2 (March/April 1994): 1–2.

Donovan describes how baselining one quality situation can be done by looking at a company's strategic quality goals and the degree of employee empowerment.

Ehresman, Terry. *Small Business Success Through TQM: Practical Methods to Improve Your Organization's Performance.* Milwaukee: ASQC Quality Press, 1995.

This is a training guide to facilitate acquisition of TQM concepts.

Eskildson, Loyd. "Improving the Odds of TQM's Success," *Quality Progress* 27, no. 4 (April 1994): 61–63.

Keys to success involve making sure you have a clear definition of TQM and, second, a clearly thought-out plan for how an organization will accomplish the changes required. Fuzzy thinking and implementation plans kill TQM's success.

Fisher, Liz. "Total Quality: Hit or Myth?" *Accountancy* 113, no. 1208 (April 1994): 50–51.

Reports on research suggesting only 20 percent of companies could call out significant improvements in performance as a result of TQM practices, making TQM passé and to be replaced with business process reengineering.

Goodman, John A., Gary F. Bargatze, and Cynthia Grimm. "The Key Problem with TQM," *Quality Progress* 27, no. 1 (January 1994): 45–48.

The problems are the manner in which priorities are set and the lack of a disciplined measure of results. Offers a five-step process to insure these problems are avoided; practical and streetwise.

Grossi, Giovanni. "Shortcuts to Paradise," *Internal Auditor* 51, no. 3 (June 1994): 50–53.

Describes those cultural and environmental factors that make TQM a viable way to run a business. Argues the case why quick fixes do not work.

Hamilton, Bruce E., and Preston G. Smith. "Implementing TQM on a Shoestring," *Journal of Management Consulting* 7, no. 4 (Fall 1993): 11–19.

This is the story of how United Electric implemented quality programs. The firm won the Shingo Prize for Manufacturing and is serving as a good role model for other companies.

Hertz, Paul T. "Consultants and the Future of TQM," *Quality* 33, no. 5 (May 1994): 32–33.

Argues that TQM-skilled consultants can play an important role in helping companies new to quality practices get started. Discusses what quality consultants need to do to be effective in helping organizations. These same requirements apply to management guiding their own organizations into the world of quality practices.

Holder, Todd, and Lorin Walker. "TQM Implementation," *Journal of European Industrial Training* 17, no. 7 (1993): 18–21.

Presents the results of a formal study of success elements in the implementation of TQM. Middle management's role and attitudes were considered critical success factors.

Hunter, Laurie, and P.B. Beaumont. "Implementing TQM: Top Down or Bottom Up?" *Industrial Relations Journal* 24, no. 4 (December 1993): 318–27.

Describes the implementation effort of a British-based U.S. manufacturing company; it is a detailed review of a normally successful process.

Jacob, Rahul. "TQM: More Than a Dying Fad?" *Fortune* 128, no. 9 (October 18, 1993): 66–72.

Reports that up to two-thirds of U.S. managers believe TQM has failed within their companies. Also reports that when properly applied, TQM presents useful benefits and offers an effective body of management practices.

Krygier, Alberto. "TQM—A World View," *Journal of Management Development* 12, no. 7 (1993): 36–39.

Describes TQM principles and how they are being applied or affect businesses on different continents. It appears to be targeted particularly to companies that operate on a global basis.

Levine, Constance. "How TQM Worked for One Firm," *Journal of Accountancy* 176, no. 3 (September 1993): 73–79.

The accounting firm of Macdonald, Levine, Jenkins & Co., applied TQM practices to the operation of their CPA firm in Boston, Massachusetts. This case study describes the steps they took and the benefits they received (e.g., what distinguished them from their competitors in the eyes of their clients).

Madu, Christian N., and Chu hua Kuei. "Introducing Strategic Quality Management," *Long Range Planning* 26, no. 6 (December 1993): 121–31.

Introduces a concept called strategic total quality management (STQM) as an extension of TQM. It takes a much broader view of quality practices than normally thought of in TQM; an important new theoretical piece on implementation approaches.

McManus, John J. "Lessons in Quality: Learning from the Japanese," *Managing Service Quality* 4, no. 2 (1994): 10–14.

Describes how Japanese companies implement quality, arguing that unlike British firms that make it an add-on program, the Japanese fully integrate quality practices in all aspects of a company's operations.

Merron, Keith A. "Creating TQM Organizations," *Quality Progress* 27, no. 1 (January 1994): 51–54.

Blames failed TQM efforts not on the tools but on the human dimension. Argues that organizational alignment is a critical first step that must be taken by management and presents a four-step process to accomplish the task. Is specific in its recommendations to senior management.

Miller, Cyndee. "TQM Out; 'Continous Improvement' In," *Marketing News* 28, no. 10 (May 9, 1994): 5, 20.

A Conference Board study shows TQM is being replaced with continuous improvement strategies. TQM only works if practiced by senior management.

Miller, Richard L., and Joseph P. Cangemi. "Why Total Quality Management Fails: Perspective of Top Management," *Journal of Management Development* 12, no. 7 (1993): 40–50.

Identifies six common causes of failure and several strategies for success. To succeed, useful tools include benchmarking, good supplier relations, teamwork, and employee participation.

Morris, Linda. "Organizational Culture and TQM Implementation," *Training and Development* 48, no. 4 (April 1994): 69–71.

Presents the results of a survey of corporate cultures in 34 organizations to determine how they implemented TQM and the results of these efforts.

Povey, Barry. "Continuing Improvements," *TQM Magazine* 5, no. 6 (December 1993): 37–40.

Discusses what an effective TQM program should look like and why for British companies. Critical success factors are reviewed and linked to corporate objectives.

Romano, Catherine. "Report Card on TQM," *Management Review* 83, no. 1 (January 1994): 22–25.

Presents results of a survey conducted by this journal that indicates TQM is not as effective as its defenders argue. Then reviews comments by Robert Galvin, Lewis E. Platt, Rosabeth Moss Kanter, and others about the critical success factors for making quality transformations. They focus heavily on cultural and organizational change and strategic issues.

Ronen, Boaz, and Shimeon Paas. "Focused Management: A Business Oriented Approach to Total Quality Management," *Industrial Management* 36, no. 3 (May/June 1994): 9–12.

Argues that companies that do not implement TQM effectively stand the chance of losing to those that do it right. Focuses on what management must do in general terms; useful as a light introduction for those who know little about the value of TQM as a competitive tool.

Roth, William. "The Slippery Slope," *TQM Magazine* 5, no. 6 (December 1993): 41–44.

Reviews the few basic critical success factors in implementing well quality improvement programs in companies. Argues how important the role of a senior leader is in such a transformation.

Smith, S., et al. "Strategies for Managing the TQ Agenda," *International Journal of Operations Production Management* 14, no. 1 (1994): 75–88.

Presents results of a study of how senior management developed TQM programs in British firms. Offers insights into corporate strategic thinking.

Smolenyak, Megan. "Four Mountains to Cross," *Journal for Quality & Participation* 17, no. 2 (March 1994): 42–45.

Argues that Asian companies also find difficulties in implementing TQM. Mountains to overcome by Asians are their attachment to hierarchy, aversion to risk taking, allegiance to the status quo, and management's attitude toward workers.

Spector, Bert, and Michael Beer. "Beyond TQM Programmes," *Journal of Organizational Change Management* 7, no. 2 (1994): 63–70.

Presents the experiences of three organizations that changed their businesses using TQM. Management must disconnect the organization from its long-standing hierarchical and functional structures, making it more horizontal and cross-functional.

Tague, Nancy R. *The Quality Toolbox.* Milwaukee: ASQC Quality Press, 1995.

Describes 50 quality tools (e.g., brainstorming techniques, scatter diagrams, etc.). This becomes a basic reference tool for process improvement teams.

Thomson, Harvey A., and Richard A. Bobbe. "TQM: Let's Not Do It to Ourselves Again," *Tapping the Network Journal* 4, no. 3 (Winter 1993/1994): 21–26.

Describes what makes for successful TQM implementations: sense of urgency, focus on use of TQM tools and techniques, persistent personal leadership. Describes two cases of office products companies: one that was successful and another that failed.

Weaver, Charles N. *Managing the Four Stages of TQM: How to Achieve World-Class Performance.* Milwaukee: ASQC Quality Press, 1995.

Provides a four-stage road map to implementation. It is a useful introduction to TQM and to its implementation.

Whalen, M.J., and M.A. Rahim. "Common Barriers to Implementation and Development of a TQM Program," *Industrial Management* 36, no. 2 (March/April 1994): 19–21.

Describes eight common barriers the authors have encountered in several firms, such as poor planning, lack of management commitment, and resistance by workers. Argues that execution of a quality philosophy will overcome all of these barriers.

Whittle, Susan. "Strategies for Managing the TQ Agenda," *International Journal of Operations & Production Management* 14, no. 1 (1994): 75–88.

Presents results of a research project on implementation of TQM. Reports on the effect of managerial mindsets and TQM cultures among managers. Offers a TQM methodology built on the research findings.

Communication

Grates, Gary F. "The Subtlety and Power of Communications in Corporate Renewal Initiatives," *Public Relations Quarterly* 39, no. 1 (Spring 1994): 40–43.

Argues that U.S. companies do a poor job in applying good communications when restructuring or changing their businesses. Calls on management to use communications experts to help them get the job done right.

Stern, Gary M. "The New Byword in Internal Communication: Candor," *Communication World* 10, no. 8 (September 1993): 37–40.

Argues that many employees do not feel they get candor from senior management, and that many managers feel knowledge is power and thus are reluctant to share too much of it. The author argues that effective changes in corporate culture requires candor in communicating with employees.

Zairi, Mohamed, and Steve Letza. "Corporate Reporting," *Management Decision* 32, no. 2 (1994): 30–40.

Presents the results of a survey of 100 British firms that show clear communications of goals and vision are essential to success. Presents the concept of 13 variables against which you can measure the effectiveness of a company's communications.

Training

Biech, Elaine. *TQM for Training.* New York: McGraw-Hill, 1994.

A book for human resources professionals involved in providing TQM training. Includes background on TQM and how to implement a TQM training program.

Cassale, Michael. "Multimedia Enhances Quality Control Training," *Information World Review,* no. 82 (June 1993): 15–17.

Describes one of the first TQM training CDs developed so far; done by Skillchange Systems Ltd, a British firm. Full motion video covers three areas: Willing Worker, Tampering, and Customer/Supplier.

Kimmerling, George. "Gathering Best Practices," *Training & Development* 47, no. 9 (September 1993): 28–36.

This is a summary of a benchmarking effort conducted by the American Society for Training and Development concerning best practices in training. This is an important study that should be looked at by anyone conducting training in a work environment.

Thomas, Colin Coulson. "Quality Training: A Waste of Time?" *Training Tomorrow* (March 1994): 26–28.

Describes the various activities management must take to implement various quality-focused activities, such as reengineering. Most of these actions do not change attitudes or behavior. You must begin by understanding stakeholder expectations.

Quality Tools and Techniques

Concepts

Choppin, Jon. "TQM Is Common Sense: A Conversation," *Managing Service Quality* 4, no. 3 (1994): 6–9.

This is a ficticious conversation about the pros and cons of implementing TQM; a wonderful introduction to the case for quality management practices and how to implement them.

Cortada, James W. "Jargon and Business Transformation," *AIXcellence* (July 1994): 10–12.

Argues that quality buzzwords can help an organization transform its practices, if you know what they mean and how to make the concepts work for you.

Cortada, James W. "Quality Movement Is Here to Stay," *The Total Quality Review* (March/April 1994): 7–9.

Drawing upon hundred-year-long trends, the author argues that under the quality umbrella, a major recodification of business practices is shaping how society runs its activities.

Dobyns, Lloyd, and Clare Crawford-Mason. *Thinking About Quality: Progress, Wisdom, and the Deming Philosophy.* New York: Times Books, 1994.

Two well-known experts on Deming have come together on their second book to explain further quality management practices and the relevance of Dr. Deming's approach to the management of work activities in a thoughtful book.

Jordan, P. "Lasting Quality (TQM)," *IEE Review* 6 (November 18, 1993): 269–71.

The author presents the argument in favor of TQM not being a passing fad and that, in fact, it is real and has lasting benefits.

Kolesar, P.J. "The Relevance of Research on Statistical Process Control to the Total Quality Movement," *Journal of Engineering Technology Management* 10, no. 4 (December 1993): 317–38.

Kolesar surveys the history of statistical process control, criticizes research on the topic over the past forty years, and then defines useful research avenues that could be pursued.

Lee, Yoon R., and Harold Lazarus. "Uses and Criticisms of Total Quality Management," *Journal of Management Development* 12, no. 7 (1993): 5–10.

Defines TQM and how it evolved. The author also describes how and where it is being used in general terms.

Mahoney, Francis X., and Carl G. Thor. *The TQM Trilogy: Using ISO 9000, the Deming Prize, and the Baldrige Award to Establish a System for Total Quality Management.* New York: AMACOM, 1994.

The title of this book explains what it is about. It is very technique oriented and somewhat complex, but it has good information and can work with commitment from management.

McCoy, Ron. *The Best of Deming.* Knoxville, TN: SPC Press, 1994.

This is a collection of quotes from Dr. Deming in a 120-page book.

Mitra, Amitaba. *Fundamentals of Quality Control and Improvement.* New York: Macmillan, 1993.

This is a comprehensive, large overview of the philosphies of the key quality gurus, the use of the seven quality tools, statistical process control, and other tools and techniques. Intended as a text for engineering, it is as much a reference book on the subject for all quality practioners.

Pan, J.N., and W.J. Kolarik. "Quality Tree: A Systematic Problem Solving Model Using Total Quality Management Tools and Techniques," *Quality Engineering* 5, no. 1 (1994): 1–20.

This is a detailed view of linkages between management, systems techniques, and Total Quality Management, deploying the concept of a quality tree to describe the linkages between them. Describes the systematic application of the quality tree concept with specific steps.

Sitkin, Sim B., Kathleen M. Sutcliffe, and Roger G. Schroeder. "Distinguishing Control from Learning in Total Quality Management: A Contingency Perspective," *Academy of Management Review* 19, no. 3 (July 1994): 537–564.

Argues that control—an emphasis point in TQM—is not well suited to circumstances where high task uncertainties exist. Offers a broader theory of TQM to account for this factor.

Spencer, Barbara A. "Models of Organization and Total Quality Management: A Comparison and Critical Evaluation," *Academy of Management Review* 19, no. 3 (July 1994): 446–71.

Attempts to bridge between TQM practice and management theory. Calls for additional research on TQM; an academic piece.

Steingard, David S., and Dale E. Fitzgibbons. "A Postmodern Deconstruction of Total Quality Management (TQM)," *Journal of Organizational Change Management* 6, no. 5 (1993): 27–42.

This is a highly philosophical and esoteric discussion of the problems of TQM that continues to declare the death of TQM and describes what will follow.

Waldman, David A. "The Contribution of Total Quality Management to a Theory of Work Performance," *Academy of Management Review* 19, no. 3 (July 1994): 510–36.

Looks at work performance through the lens of a systems view, which is suggested by the TQM approach. Argues that hierarchical levels and autonomy moderate our understanding of the role of individuals within an organization. Discusses the implications for performance management processes.

Wellins, Richard S. "TQM: Forging Ahead or Falling Behind?" *Executive Excellence* 11, no. 6 (June 1994): 10.

This is a very convenient, short definition of Total Quality Management; includes trends in TQM from a recent survey; suitable for management teams. Concludes that TQM is still an evolving strategy, that it does improve performance, that success takes time.

Benchmarking

Bogan, Christopher E., and Michael J. English. *Benchmarking for Best Practices.* New York: McGraw-Hill, 1994.

A comprehensive guide to benchmarking by well regarded consultants and practitioners. Recommended.

Boxwell, Robert J., Jr. *Benchmarking for Competitive Advantage.* New York: McGraw-Hill, 1994.

Provides step-by-step instructions for undertaking a benchmarking study. Includes list of organizations selected "best in class" and industry associations.

Brown, Donald H. "Benchmarking Best Practices," *Computer Aided Engineering* 13, no. 7 (July 1994): 86.

Argues that the lack of benchmarking can contribute to companies failing to implement TQM properly.

Fitzenz, Jac. "How to Make Benchmarking Work for You," *HRMagazine* 38, no. 12 (December 1993): 40–46.

Describes the value and types of benchmarking currently available; a general introduction to the topic.

Kleiner, Brian M. "Benchmarking for Continuous Performance Improvement: Tactics for Success," *Total Quality Environmental Management* 3, no. 3 (Spring 1994): 283–95.

Illustrates how benchmarking is part of a management planning effort. It is particularly useful for learning how to find a benchmarking partner; includes comments on how benchmarking is conducted.

Palat, B. Mustafa. "Process Improvements Through Benchmarking," *TQM Magazine* 6, no. 2 (1994): 37–40.

Provides a brief introduction to the concept and then describes its application by AT&T Oklahoma City Works organization.

Smith, George A., Doris Ritter, and William P. Tuggle, III. "Benchmarking: The Fundamental Questions," *Marketing Management* 2, no. 3 (1993): 43–48.

Describes how benchmarking is used, calling out in particular its applicability in looking at sales and marketing issues. Also catalogs what topics should be benchmarked in sales and marketing.

Reengineering and Improving Processes

Burdett, John O. "TQM and Re-engineering," *TQM Magazine* 6, no. 2 (1994): 7–13.

Reviews critics of TQM, the value of reengineering, relying heavily on the Hammer/Champy nine-step approach.

Center, Kathy. "A New Way to Think about Business Processes," *Tapping the Network Journal* 5, no. 1 (Spring 1994): 22–24.

Describes how an IBM plant developed a business process improvement approach that worked. Its focus is on customers' unique conditions of satisfaction for defining work flows; excellent.

Galloway, Dianne. *Mapping Work Processes.* Milwaukee: ASQC Quality Press, 1994.

This is a how-to book on mapping and documenting processes, complete with exercises and flow charts.

Greengard, Samuel. "Reengineering: Out of the Rubble," *Personnel Journal* 72, no. 12 (December 1993): 48B, 48K+.

This is a useful and practical description of reengineering, which is compared to TQM and process improvement. Describes when process reengineering is needed and why.

Hansen, Gregory A. *Automating Business Process Reengineering: Breaking the TQM Barrier*. Englewood Cliffs, N.J.: Prentice Hall, 1994.

This is a refreshing look at a number of tools and techniques that have recently appeared and that can be used to perform process improvement work. Written by an expert on the subject of process improvement.

Jones, Christopher R. "Improving Your Key Business Processes," *TQM Magazine* 6, no. 2 (1994): 25–29.

Argues that processes are the essential link among all the critical activities of an organization. Provides a general discussion of trends in the application of this approach.

Kinni, Theodore B. "Reengineering: Righting Wrong Organizations," *Industry Week* 243, no. 3 (February 7, 1994): 14–16.

Interviews James Champy, co-author of *Reengineering the Corporation*. Covers the same messages found in the book.

Mattsson, Jan. "Using Service Process Models to Improve Service Quality: Examples from New Zealand," *Managing Service Quality* 4, no. 1 (1994): 47–52.

Describes the use of service blueprinting and service mapping techniques as applied to improving services to customers. The author presents the experiences of three companies that have looked at how their processes support customers.

Roberts, Lon. *Process Reengineering: The Key to Achieving Breakthrough Success*. Milwaukee: ASQC Quality Press, 1994.

This is a how-to book on doing process reengineering and work simplification. It is short and to the point, a practical guide for those who have to do the work of process change.

Strub, M.Z. "Quality at Warp Speed: Reengineering at AT&T," *Bulletin of the American Society for Information Science* 20, no. 4 (April/May 1994): 17–19.

Describes what one organization did after it had been using TQM and needed to enhance it. That involved additional organizational changes and the use of different technologies.

White, Edna M., Mehdi Kaighobadi, and T.J. Wharton. "Process Goal Charts for Quality Improvement Programs," *International Journal of Quality & Reliability Management* ,11, no. 2 (1994): 26–40.

Describes how to link SPC and quality improvement programs in a formal way using process goal charts. Gives examples and a six-step process.

Measurement

Binkley, Mace. "Negotiated Standards: A New Approach to Deming's 11th Point," *Industrial Engineering* 25, no. 11 (November 1993): 56–57.

Describes the discussions held at the Iowa Army Ammunition Plant as it implemented Deming's 14 Points, concerning measurements and measures of employee performance. It is a case study of how Deming's ideas were implemented successfully within a TQM framework.

Crombie, Graem. "Measure for Measure," *TQM Magazine* 5, no. 4 (August 1993): 47–49.

Describes the variety and importance of reasons for implementing quality programs. Argues that the types of measures adopted are affected by the reasons for implementing quality programs in the first place. This is an important article on the issue of strategies for measurements.

Cupello, James M. "A New Paradigm for Measuring TQM Progress," *Quality Progress* 27, no. 5 (May 1994): 79–82.

Argues that one needs to measure planning, screening, control, and diagnositics; that there are four levels of TQM maturity: playing, demonstrating, committed, and actualized performance; and that these need to be measured.

Das, Lachhman. "Performance Measurement Takes Center Stage at Johnson Space Center," *Industrial Engineering* 26, no. 3 (March 1994): 24–28.

Describes the use of performance measurements by JSC's Facility O&M organization over the past several years. How quality management practices are used is also described.

Davies, Paul. "Financial Difficulties," *TQM Magazine* 5, no. 4 (August 1993): 25–28.

Analyzes the nature and causes of false starts with TQM. Argues that it is crucial to measure more effectively results of improvement projects. Defines a four-step strategy for accomplishing this type of measurement.

Dew, John R. "Measuring Total Quality Management," *Tapping the Network Journal* 5, no. 1 (Spring 1994): 6–9.

Martin Marietta Energy Systems developed a set of measures to judge the effectiveness of its quality efforts, using the Baldrige Criteria for the measures. Some of these measures include percent of employees involved in empowered work teams, number of improvement projects started and completed, and percent of employees having completed training in TQM.

Escover, John L. "Focus: Value," *Business Horizons* 37, no. 4 (July–August 1994): 47–50.

Describes the definition and importance of value added in business practices. Argues that all parts of an organization should be assessed by the value-added contributions.

Kaplan, Robert. "Measuring Corporate Performance." Boston: Harvard Business School Management Products, 1994.

This is a collection of four videos (each 30 minutes running time) describing how companies are adopting new performance measurements. Topics include identifying problems with traditional measurements, use of balanced scorecards, and the role of Activity Based Management approaches.

Meyer, Christopher. "How the Right Measures Help Teams Excel," *Harvard Business Review* (May–June 1994): 95–103.

Describes how multifunctional teams' measurements systems can empower a team instead of just management. Discusses how process teams can develop and use measurements.

Sarin, Sanjiv. "Can Work Measurement and TQM Get Along?" *Industrial Engineering* 25, no. 10 (October 1993): 14–15.

Discusses Deming's 11th point concerning work standards and quotas, arguing the case for a partnership on his idea and the practice of TQM.

Taylor, Alan. "Tomorrow's Metrology Technology: Small, Fast, Flexible—And Available to Everyone," *Production* 105, no. 11 (November 1993): 34–37.

Describes the need for metrology tools for TQM teams as they gather vast quantities of data in order to meet customer requirements and ISO certification standards. Shows examples of such tools.

Waldman, David A. "Designing Performance Management Systems for Total Quality Implementation," *Journal of Organizational Change Management* 7, no. 2 (1994): 31–44.

Describes a performance management system designed to be compatible with TQM such that individual and group performance can be managed in some compatible manner; an important academic article.

Wheeler, Donald J. *Understanding Variation: The Key to Managing Chaos.* Knoxville, TN: SPC Press, 1994.

This is a short how-to book on the techniques used in understanding and measuring variation within a process. Gives examples of how to then make changes based on this kind of analysis.

Wilson, Paul F., and Richard D. Pearson. *Performance-Based Assessment: External, Internal, and Self-Assessment Tools for Total Quality Management.* Milwaukee: ASQC Quality Press, 1995.

This short book offers suggestions on organization-wide assessment strategies, with specific recommendations.

Teams and Teamwork

Alschner, W. "The Quality Circle in Total Quality Management," *Qual. Zuverlaessigk.* 39, no. 4 (April 1994): 404–5.

This German article describes the role of individuals, and how quality practices are deployed in quality circles.

Ehin, Charles. "A High Performance Team Is Not a Multi-Part Machine," *Journal for Quality and Participation* 16, no. 7 (December 1993): 38–48.

Argues that the metaphor of work being like a machine, first introduced in the 1920s, no longer is valid. Argues that a new view should be adopted that sees activities through the context of the work being performed.

Fisher, Kimball, Steven Rayner, and William Belgard. *Tips for Teams.* New York: McGraw-Hill, 1995.

A practical handbook with hundreds of short tips for solving common team problems.

Giordan, Judith C., and Angela M. Ahern. "Self Managed Teams: Quality Improvement in Action," *Research Technology Management* 37, no. 3 (May/June 1994): 33–37.

Using teams to do work has helped to reduce the demand for additional employees while increasing the results and outputs of these employees.

Hartzler, Meg, and Jane E. Henry. *Team Fitness: A How-To Manual for Building a Winning Work Team.* Milwaukee: ASQC Quality Press, 1994.

This is one of the latest books on how to form, use, and manage teams, particularly for process work.

Herman, Stanley M. *A Force of Ones: Reclaiming Individual Power in a Time of Teams, Work Groups, and Other Crowds.* San Francisco: Jossey-Bass, 1994.

This book is an antidote of sorts for all those others who argue everything should be done through teams. This author enhances the dialogue by describing how individuals should function and details what their own responsibility is to the new way of doing work.

Rosenthal, Edward Cohen. "On Arrogance and Participation," *Journal for Quality & Participation* 17, no. 2 (March 1994): 58–64.

Argues that the idea of employee involvement and worker participation is an attack on arrogance. Calls reengineering a neutron bomb for organizational change since people are terminated, leaving behind the company. Says teams can fix many corporate problems.

Sexton, Carol. "Self-Managed Work Teams: TQM Technology at the Employee Level," *Journal of Organizational Change Management* 7, no. 2 (1994): 45–52.

Defines a self-managed work team and then provides six conditions necessary for its success. Provides one war story of failure.

Functional Processes

Planning

Casey, I. P. "The Role of GIS in the Quest for Quality," *Proceedings AM/FM International Conference XVI* (1993): 527–37.

The heart of this article is that GIS can benefit from the application of Total Quality Management principles.

Gehani, R. Ray. "The Tortoise vs. the Hare," *Quality Progress* 27, no. 5 (May 1994): 99–103.

In fast-changing environments, traditional planning methods actually slow business transformation. Therefore, management must audit and assess competencies and resources available for change, take into account the strengths and weaknesses of TQM approaches, continuous improvement vs. radical change, and develop plans that rely on corporate competencies based on the capabilities of the employees.

Kajzer, S., and J. Belak. "Corporate Planning as an Instrument of Assertion of the Total Quality," *Systems Research* 11, no. 1 (1994): 167–76.

Describes planning in any quality-focused environment as a holistic process and a major component of management.

Leavitt, Jeffrey S., and Philip C. Nunn. *Total Quality Through Project Management.* New York: McGraw-Hill, 1994.

This is the first book to appear on project management incorporating TQM principles in a practical, how-to form.

Peterson, B.J. "TQM at 3M: Planning with Customer and Staff Input," *Bulletin American Society of Information Science* 20, no. 4 (April/May 1994): 14–16.

Describes how 3M has changed its strategic planning process during the early 1990s to take into greater account the voice of the customer, benchmarking, and staff input. Also describes how the company's TQM efforts were introduced and implemented.

Reyes, Luis. "The Evolution of a Forecasting Department," *Journal of Business Forecasting* 12, no. 3 (Fall 1993): 22–26.

Describes a case study of how forecasting is done at the Warner Lambert Consumer Health Product Group. This is described as an interactive process.

Sales and Marketing

Anonymous. "Sales Force Reengineering and Automation Conference," *American Salesman* 39, no. 7 (July 1994): 22–23.

Argues that reengineering sales processes is the only way today to reduce cost of sales, shorten order and delivery cycles, and improve customer service. Describes basic tenets of an implementation plan (e.g., use of teams, benchmarking, training, etc.).

Barnes, James G. "New Technologies, New Markets, and Changing Marketing Practice," *Irish Marketing Review* 6 (1993): 45–52.

Discussing the future of sales and marketing, the author argues that companies must change fundamentally how they approach marketing. There is the dual challenge of managing marketing information and customer service because more effective practices involve forming relationships with customers, getting away from merely transaction-focused processes.

Brewer, Geoffrey. "Abort, Retry, Fail?" *Sales & Marketing Management* 145, no. 12 (October 1993): 80–86.

Discusses IBM's downsizing as caused by not listening to its customers. Discusses how IBM changed its sales organization and mission over the past several years.

Cortada, James W. "Integrating a Baldrige Approach into a Sales District's Management System," *National Productivity Review* (Spring 1994): 271–85.

The author illustrates phases in the adoption of the Baldrige Criteria in sales, what goes on in each phase, and how to implement them, complete with examples.

Fried, Lisa I. "Information, Please!" *Sales and Marketing Management* 146, no. 3 (March 1994): 29–31.

Describes how the California Cable Television Association applies faxing on demand as a way to disseminate information quickly, satisfying 4,000 customer requests for information in 1993.

Keenan, William, Jr. "Who's on First?" *Sales and Marketing Management* 146, no. 8 (August 1994): 88–95.

Described how Avery Fasson, a manufacturer of paper and film labels, unified two divergent salesforces, improving customer focus and efficiencies.

Lejfer, Sidney C. "Increasing Productivity by Using Sales Automation Software," *Massachusetts CPA Review* 68, no. 1 (Winter 1994): 27–28.

Many CPA firms have applied successfully sales automation tools, giving them timely communication with customers; details the applications.

Lu, Min Hua, et al. "Integrating QFD, AHP, and Benchmarking in Strategic Marketing," *Journal of Business & Industrial Marketing* 9, no. 1 (1994): 41–50.

This is an academic piece that focuses on long-range marketing policy making, applying TQM principles and Kotler's model of three types of marketing strategic orientation.

McCallum, Tricia, and Michael A. Thompson. "Sales Compensation Plans: Cashing in on Performance," *CMA Magazine* 67, no. 9 (November 1993): 17–20.

Describes the trend toward sales compensation plans that balance rewarding sales volumes with altered behavior that improves customer relations and quality. The case for such a changed compensation plan is described.

O'Connell, William A. "Taming the Elite Salesforce," *Small Business Reports* 19, no. 2 (February 1994): 35–42.

Some small companies are finding that treating sales people as an elite group is counterproductive because they can undermine a team-based approach to running the business. Therefore, some are beginning to set limits on how much importance they will ascribe to their salesforce.

Wood, Wally. "Reinventing the Sales Force," *Across the Board* (April 1994): 24–30.

Discusses the implications of TQM in managing the salesforce, including new methods of compensation, teams, and technology.

Logistics and Supplier Relations

Anonymous. "Logistics Processes Viewed as Prime Target as Corporate 'Re-engineering' Takes Hold," *Traffic World* (October 4, 1993): 34ff.

The observations of several consultants on how reengineering is occurring in the area of logistics; includes case studies and specific processes.

Anonymous. "Who Are the Best at 'Quality' Logistics?" *Distribution* 92, no. 9 (September 1993): 12–14.

Discusses the Quality Assurance Institute's effort at forming a Logistics Improvement Forum. Describes how the group is using the Baldrige Criteria to view logistical processes.

Bossert, James L. (ed). *Supplier Management Handbook.* Milwaukee: ASQC Quality Press, 1994.

This is a new revised edition of *Procurement Quality Control.* This fifth edition is comprehensive in discussing all aspects of supplier management processes and issues. Includes material by industry, and how these activities relate to ISO 9000 and the Baldrige Criteria.

Carter, Joseph R., and Ram Narasimhan. "The Role of Purchasing and Materials Management in Total Quality Management and Customer Satisfaction," *International Journal of Purchasing and Materials Management* 30, no. 3 (Summer 1994): 3–13.

Based on a survey, the authors describe what purchasing managers must do to implement TQM: clear quality goals, a purchasing strategy, plan on process improvements, and formal assessments of performance.

Claunch, Jerry W. "Developing World Class Suppliers," *TQM Magazine* 5, no. 6 (December 1993): 33–36.

Discusses the case for having close relations with suppliers, then provides a three-phase view of those relations, and concludes with ideas for how such relations are best managed.

Flanagan, Patrick. "The Rules of Purchasing Are Changing," *Management Review* (March 1994): 28–32.

Reviews new rules of dealing with suppliers, but suggests a cautious note with regard to full cooperation. Emphasizes the importance of managing costs while working with your suppliers.

Humenuik, Kerry, and Sharon Hamilton. "Creating Trust in Customer-Supplier Relationships," *The Journal for Quality and Participation* 17, no. 1 (January/February 1994): 80–83.

Reviews basics of sound supplier-customer relationships.

Lee, Huei, and Dee M. Wellan. "Vendor Survey Plan: A Selection Strategy for JIT/TQM Suppliers," *Industrial Management and Data Systems* 93, no. 6 (1993): 8–13.

All Phase Electrical Supply Company implemented both JIT and TQM, and their experience is described: how it was done, the steps taken, and results gained.

Magnet, Myron. "The New Golden Rule of Business," *Fortune* (February 21, 1994): 60–64.

Discusses how everyone benefits when companies turn a formerly adversarial relationship into a cooperative one.

Miller, William H. "Boeing Gives Credence to Clearwater's Revival," *Industry Week* 243, no. 2 (January 17, 1994): 40–42.

Provides a case study of how one supplier to Boeing turned itself around using TQM techniques to become an award company.

Palaniswami, Shanthakumar, and B.P. Lingaraj. "Procurement and Vendor Management in the Global Environment," *International Journal of Production Economics* 35, nos. 1–3 (June 1994): 171–76.

As companies go global, so too does their procurement of raw materials and parts. Describes how some companies are dealing with this process. The authors focus on manufacturing companies.

Richman, Eugene, and William B. Zachary. "Creating Strategies for Successful Materials Management," *Industrial Management* 36, no. 2 (March/April 1994): 24–27.

Discusses the value of JIT in reducing the amount of inventory needed. Also reviews the concept of Just-in-Time systems.

Stuart, F. Ian, and P. Mueller, Jr. "Total Quality Management and Supplier Relationships: A Case Study," *International Journal of Purchasing and Materials Management* 30, no. 1 (Winter 1994): 14–20.

Presents the result of a study by one firm on supplier relationships applying continuous improvement techniques. This article is interesting because it does not use the automotive industry as its example (while most supplier articles do), and it is an account of a successful effort.

Saunders, Andrew G. "Supplier Audits as Part of a Supplier Partnership," *TQM Magazine* 6, no. 2 (1994): 41–42.

Describes how this is done at Hewlett-Packard in Great Britain, and offers the rationale for how this is performed effectively; a useful case study.

Product Development and Manufacturing

Bischke, Wallace R., and D.N. Prabhakar Murthy. *Warranty Cost Analysis.* New York: Marcel Dekker, Inc., 1994.

This is the first unified analytical treatment of the subject to appear in print. While intended as a text for college use, it is a practitioner's guide to various models, with specific mathematically based examples.

Burkart, Robert E. "Reducing R&D Cycle Time," *Research Technology Management* 37, no. 3 (May/June 1994): 27–32.

Describes a matrix of 45 sources of causes of uncertainty in R&D and how their systematic identification and elimination speeds up R&D. Articulates TQM in an R&D environment.

Ferrin, Richard I. "I Believe I'll Have the Reuben," *Quality Progress* 27, no. 5 (May 1994): 61–62.

Argues the case for understanding what constitutes a product's quality from the customer's point of view.

Gault, Stanley C. "Responding to Change," *Research Technology Management* 37, no. 3 (May/June 1994): 23–26.

Describes how Goodyear Tire & Rubber Company linked its R&D operations to customer wants and needs and to sales and marketing. This is a story of an extraordinary corporate turnaround; includes specific results achieved.

Hall, M.J. "Producibility Management: A Framework for Efficient Product Design," *Simulation in Concurrent Engineering. Proceedings of the 1993 ITEC Workshop on Concurrent Engineering* (London, 1993): 31–49.

Describes the structured process aimed at maximizing a product's marketability, from understanding customer requirements through to design and manufacture. Details various techniques used.

Nakamura, Shigehiro. *The New Standardization: Keystone of Continuous Improvement in Manufacturing.* Milwaukee: ASQC Quality Press, 1993.

The theme of this book is standardization of manufacturing processes, all activities in manufacturing. Describes how this is done as a process in a short book.

Taylor, Rosalind, and Alan Pearson. "Total Quality Management in Research and Development," *TQM Magazine* 6, no. 1 (1994): 26–34.

Describes best practices in R&D quality management and includes a case study from a large corporate R&D operation. Emphasis is on organization analysis techniques to define the goals, standards, and results of R&D.

Information Technology

Braithwaite, Timothy. *Information Service Excellence Through TQM.* Milwaukee: ASQC Quality Press, 1994.

This very brief book (145 pages) is one of the first attempts to describe quality management principles in information services and covers an important selection of management issues.

Brochu, Earl. "Time to Revolutionize Teamwork Approach," *Computing Canada* 19, no. 22 (October 25, 1993): 28.

Announces that TQM and BPR are increasingly being used by MIS organizations. Describes an approach to implementation that the author believes MIS should use.

Criner, James C. "Benchmarking Data Processing Installations," *Capacity Management Review* 22, no. 3 (March 1994): 1–6.

Describes the application of benchmarking by the U.S. Defense Information System Agency to illustrate the effectiveness of comparing its data center operations to those of commercial enterprises.

Edwards, John. "Quality Team Players," *CIO* 16 (June 1, 1994): 86–93.

Argues that a great deal of software is available to help implement TQM. Describes the types of software and calls on CIOs to make these available to their organizations.

Esichaikul, Vatcharaporn, Gregory R. Madey, and Robert Smith. "Problem Solving Support for TQM: A Hypertext Approach," *Information Systems Management* 11, no. 1 (Winter 1994): 47–52.

Hypertext and hypermedia are described as tools that can help decision makers gain access to information, particularly databases. How that can be done is the subject of this article.

Gessford, J. "Object Oriented Cost Accounting System Design," *Journal of End User Computing* 5, no. 3 (Summer 1993): 17–25.

Describes ABC and why it is popular with quality managed companies, and the need for computerization. Details how IS can go about implementing such an application.

Grady, Robert B. *Practical Software Metrics for Project Management and Process Improvement.* Englewood Cliffs, N.J.: Prentice-Hall, 1992.

Describes how metrics can be used to improve the quality of producing software. This is the only conveniently available book that is devoted to the subject of metrics and software and is an extension of the author's early work on the subject. It is practical, explicit, and wise.

Grady, Robert B., and Deborah L. Caswell. *Software Metrics: Establishing a Company-Wide Program.* Englewood Cliffs, N.J.: Prentice-Hall, 1987.

This is an excellent case study of how Hewlett-Packard implemented company-wide software and IS metrics.

Hefley, W. "The Cobbler's Children: Applying Total Quality Management to Business Process Improvement, Information Engineering, and Software Engineering," *SIGSOFT Software Engineering Notes* 18, no. 4 (October 1993): 19–25.

Discusses relationship among business process improvement, business case analysis, information engineering, and TQM. Argues the case that software engineering can be improved through application of all these quality principles.

Heineman, G.T., et al. "Emerging Technologies That Support a Software Process Life Cycle," *IBM Systems Journal* 33, no. 3 (1994): 501–529.

Discusses how to improve the processes used to develop software: types, techniques, trends. Describes research being done on the topic within IBM and with four universities.

Henry, J., et al. "Improving Software Maintenance at Martin Marietta," *IEEE Software* 11, no. 4 (July 1994): 67–75.

They illustrate how to apply statistical methods to assess and evaluate quantitatively improvements in one organization's software maintenance process. Shows where improvements are needed, applying TQM methods.

Kan, S.H., V.R. Basili, and L.N. Shapiro. "Software Quality: An Overview from the Perspective of Total Quality Management," *IBM Systems Journal* 33, no. 1 (1994): 4–19.

This is a brief tutorial on software quality in a TQM context. Describes how software engineering has evolved and the directions it is headed.

Keith, Richard B., Jr. "MIS + TQM = QIS," *Quality Progress* 27, no. 4 (April 1994): 29–31.

Argues the case for combining the two and then describes the role of IS in a TQM environment.

Lingle, John H., and William A. Schiemann. "Is Data Scatter Subverting Your Strategy?" *Management Review* (May 1994): 53–58.

Reviews a variety of problems that emerge from poor management of information and what to do about them.

Malley, J.C., and J.H. Thompson. "Planning Controls in the EDI Environment," *IS Audit Control Journal* 2 (1994): 59–62.

Links EDI and TQM activities in manufacturing, citing the case of the large three U.S. automotive manufacturers. Explains the role EDI is playing in the 1990s.

Marr, J. "Help Desk System Project Tackles Customer Service Issues," *Texas Instruments Technical Journal* 11, no. 3 (May–June 1994): 60–62.

Describes a help desk implementation as a process. While a technical piece for other software development organizations, it is valuable for an IT department attempting to enhance its end user services through a help desk.

Mathieson, Kieran, and T.J. Wharton. "Are Information Systems a Barrier to Total Quality Management?" *Journal of Systems Management* 44, no. 9 (September 1993): 34–38.

Offers a series of techniques to insure that MIS is not a barrier to a company's implementation of TQM. Discusses cultural, managerial, and functional tasks and issues that MIS management must deal with and how.

Merlyn, N. "The TQM/CASE Connection," *Managing System Development* 13, no. 6 (June 1993): 6–7.

Discusses the connection between TQM and CASE. Users of TQM find that CASE usage goes well, then discusses quality management principles in IS.

Redig, G., and M. Swanson. "Total Quality Management for Software Development," *Proceedings of Sixth Annual IEEE Symposium on Computer Based Medical Systems* (1993): 301–6.

Describes a software quality management process being used to meet a government software quality evaluation plan as stipulated by DOD STD 2167A. It is very much a how-to article on implementation.

Swanson, K., and L. Leonard. "Re-engineering for Improved Quality and Productivity," *Object Magazine* 4, no. 3 (June 1994): 34–37, 46.

Provides a case study of the application software factory approach used by Magma Copper, a mining and metals processing company, using a combination of TQM and automation.

Tayntor, C.B. "System Development in a TQM Company," *Management Systems Development* 13, no. 11 (November 1993): 1–4.

Describes what TQM means for systems developers, in what types of environments it works well, and where it creates difficulties.

Teresko, John. "ELM: A Holistic Approach," *Industry Week* 243, no. 12 (June 20, 1994): 39–40.

Provides a brief overview of the concept of enterprise logistics management, a technique for better coordinating organization processes through the use of information technology.

Thompson, K., and P. McParland. "Software Process Maturity (SPM) and the Information Systems Developer," *Information & Software Technology* 35, no. 7 (June/July 1993): 331–38.

Argues that the software development industry is recognizing the need for and value of TQM practices. Describes SPM assessment process to assess the capabilities of an organization's software development process.

Ward, James A. "Continuous Process Improvement," *Information Systems Management* 11, no. 2 (Spring 1994): 74–76.

Introduces the concept to the MIS community and accuses it of not having a development process in place. Describes the basic components of a good process.

Ward, James A. "Meeting Customer Requirements," *Information Systems Management* 11, no. 3 (Summer 1994): 75–78.

Introduces the IS community to the need to understand what their customers want when designing systems and to build in ways of monitoring satisfaction with the products produced.

Wilson, F.A. "Computer Based Systems and Organizational Structures: Designing the Ghost in the Machine," *IFIP Transactions, A Computer Science Technology* A49 (1994): 343–55.

Studies one implementation of information systems and TQM, and suggests that the application of both at the same time will lead to new managerial philosophies.

Zultner, R.E. "TQM for Technical Teams," *Communications, ACM* 36, no. 10 (October 1993): 78–91.

Surveys the components of TQM and how they apply to software development teams. Details what such teams should focus on, with primary emphasis on what users of the software will want.

Research and Development

Singer, Donald C., and Ronald P. Upton. *Guidelines for Laboratory Quality Auditing.* Milwaukee: ASQC Quality Press, and New York: Marcel Dekker, 1993.

This is the best guide to the application of laboratory quality audits available. Written by practitioners, it is intended to help lab directors; includes theory, practical steps, and examples.

Accounting, Finance, and Cost Justification

Awasthi, Vidya N. "ABC's of Activity Based Costing," *Industrial Management* 36, no. 4 (July/August 1994): 8–11.

Defines it, why people are interested in it, and the benefits expected of such an approach; brief and to the point.

Beal, Connie, and Joanne Wiswell. "Breaking Down the Walls," *The Total Quality Review* 3, no. 6 (January/February 1994): 41–45.

A case study of how StorageTek is using TQM to better manage its invoicing system.

Chalker, John A., and Kim Bramer. "Speeding Up the Price Quote System," *Management Accounting* 75, no. 3 (September 1993): 45–49.

Price quotes as a process is presented with a discussion of customer focus issues and the application of TQM principles. Good emphasis is placed on speed of delivering a good quote.

Cytraus, Aldona O. "Reinventing the Internal Audit Process," *OHIO CPA Journal* 53, no. 1 (February 1994): 37–39.

Tells the story of how the internal audit department at Case Western Reserve University began to apply TQM principles. Much resistance was met across the university, but sufficient progress was achieved to warrant further application of TQM.

Duffin, Murray. "The Cost of Indifference," *TQM Magazine* 5, no. 6 (December 1993): 7–9.

Offers a review of how one identifies the cost of nonquality (also known as cost of quality). Discusses the relationship among cost of quality, customer satisfaction, and defects within an enterprise.

Ehrhardt, Michael C. *The Search for Value: Measuring the Company's Cost of Capital.* Boston: Harvard Business School, 1994.

Provides techniques and models for establishing the cost of capital under a variety of circumstances, complete with examples.

Freedman, Julian M. "TQM Applied to Financial Management," *Management Accounting* 75, no. 4 (October 1993): 63.

This summarizes a study by the Financial Executives Research Foundation entitled "Finance in the Quality Revolution: Adding Value by Integrating Financial and Total Quality Management (TQM)." The study concluded TQM is very applicable in financial institutions and practices.

Gessford, John. "Object Oriented Cost Accounting System Design," *Journal of End User Computing* 5, no. 3 (Summer 1993): 17–25.

While intended for IT audiences, this is a clear description of ABC accounting done via computer, giving the case for requiring computers to capture the more extensive data required for activity based accounting.

Hawkes, Lindsay C., and Michael B. Adams. "Total Quality Management: Implications for Internal Audit," *Managerial Auditing Journal* 9, no. 4 (1994): 11–18.

Argues that TQM is incompatible with traditional ideas about compliance; thus, future auditing practices will have to change if quality management procedures are to be implemented.

Jeeves, Andrew. "Accounting for Quality," *TQM Magazine* 5, no. 4 (August 1993): 21–24.

This is a case study of how one company quantified the cost of good and poor quality. Discusses major problem areas, how quantification was done, and their relations to TQM and management styles.

Jeffries, Andrea, and Janice Hankes. "Back to Basics?" *Management Accounting* 72, no. 6 (June 1994): 13–15.

Reports comments by Charles Horngren, a well-known expert on ABC accounting, who is calling for the use of ABC, saying that, like TQM, it would be around for some years.

Julien, Frederick W., and James C. Lampe. "Performance Measures in Internal Auditing," *Internal Auditing* 9, no. 2 (Fall 1993): 66–73.

Describes how TQM is used to improve internal audit responsibilities. Includes a framework for TQM's application and comments from a roundtable on the topic.

Keogh, William. "The Role of the Quality Assurance Professional in Determining Quality Costs," *Managerial Auditing Journal* 9, no. 4 (1994): 23–32.

Describes the difficulties in identifying quality costs, working through two case studies.

McConville, Daniel J. "Start with ABC," *Industry Week* 242, no. 17 (September 6, 1993): 33–36.

Activity Based Costing (ABC) and Activity Based Management (ABM) are called the two most important new concepts to appear since TQM. Explains the rapid adoption of these accounting and management methods and why, particularly by manufacturing companies. Details are given regarding some users.

Oest, Duane, William J.L. Swirsky, and Richard M. Ubinger. "Focus on: ISO 9000," *Journal of Accountancy* 177, no. 2 (February 1994): 60–61.

Discusses the role of accountants and auditors in dealing with ISO 9000. It reviews common myths concerning ISO and things accountants should know about the topic. Also announces that KPMG Peat Marwick intends to be an ISO registrar, the first large accounting firm to do so.

Palmer, Richard J. "Reengineering Payables at ITT Automotive," *Management Accounting* 76, no. 1 (July 1994): 38–42.

Describes ITT Automotive's accounts receivable process and how it improved it.

Shea, John E., and Ilene K. Kleinsorge. "TQM: Are Cost Accountants Meeting the Challenge?" *Management Accounting* 75, no. 10 (April 1994): 65–67.

The result of interviews with accountants and one small business manager covering 10 organizations with quality programs suggests that cost accounting is meeting management's requirements. In many cases this process has been simplified.

Simmons, Cynthia, and Steven G. Sutton. "Audit Quality: An Examination of Auditor Motivation," *Internal Auditing* 9, no. 2 (Fall 1993): 30–37.

Describes how audit departments can help their companies implement TQM. Explores the growing interest in measuring time budgets, and how that is being done.

Stanleigh, Michael. "Accounting for Quality," *Australian Accountant* 63, no. 9 (October 1993): 27–29.

Argues that accountants can do effective root cause analysis and are very good at measuring activities, therefore, they should be used more in TQM. Predicts TQM will affect how accounting is done.

Stoner, James A.F., and Frank M. Werner. *Managing Finance for Quality: Bottom-Line Results from Top-Level Commitment.* Milwaukee: ASQC Quality Press, 1994.

More than strictly a book on quality management practices in finance, it also illustrates how that function is integrated into the broader mission of management of an organization.

Turney, Peter B.B. "Beyond TQM with Workforce Activity Based Management," *Management Accounting* 75, no. 3 (September 1993): 28–31.

Introduces the concept of ABC accounting and workforce activity based management (WABM), what it is, how it is done in conceptual terms, and the kinds of result one might expect.

Human Resources

Adams, M. L. "Quality First. A Model for TQM Implementation and Planning," *IEEE Aerospace*

Electronic Systems Magazine 9, no. 2 (February 1994): 25–27.

Harris Corporation concluded that quality-oriented changes were most profoundly affected by what was done with employees and, thus, human resources must be looked at before doing all the normal quality-oriented activities. Describes their analysis and direction-setting framework that insures personnel issues are addressed up front on any significant project.

Anonymous. "Companies Linking Reward and Quality Programs Report Success," *Industrial Engineering* 26, no. 3 (March 1994): 11–12.

Reports results of a major study on reward programs linked to quality management practices. The study, performed by the Conference Board and the Hay Group, provides substantial evidence of the benefits experienced by large corporations in linking rewards and quality.

Anonymous. "Cutting Workers' Compensation Costs with TQM," *Risk Management* 40, no. 9 (September 1993): 44.

Presents results of a study of a food conglomerate's three plants that looked at the differences in worker compensation costs, concluding it was most influenced by management style. TQM management was a critical influencing factor.

Barnes, James G. "The Role of Internal Marketing: If the Staff Won't Buy It, Why Should the Customer?" *Irish Marketing Review* 1–5 (1994): 55–64.

Argues the case for applying marketing principles to persuade employees about the value of quality management practices. Explains how this might be done. The article covers far more than simply an internal communications process.

Barrett, Colleen. "Service Begins at Home," *Sales and Marketing Management* 146, no. 3 (March 1994): 27–28.

Southwest Airlines solicits advice from its employees for improving operations, encourages employees to have fun on the job, and makes it known that managers are there to serve the employees.

Boje, David M., and Robert D. Winsor. "The Resurrection of Taylorism: Total Quality Management," *Journal of Organizational Change Management* 6, no. 4 (1993): 57–70.

This is a lengthy attack on TQM, arguing that it is nothing more than warmed-over Taylorism of 1911 in which it seeks to control workers' spirits, souls, and bodies.

Budman, Matthew, and Berkeley Rice. "The Rating Game," *Across the Board* (February 1994): 35–38.

Reviews a variety of new approaches for undertaking the appraisal of individual performance.

Caudron, Shari. "Change Keeps TQM Programs Thriving," *Personnel Journal* 72, no. 10 (October 1993): 104–07ff.

Describes the human resource practices of companies that have won the Baldrige Award; shows that HR organizations must partner with other departments to provide effective practices. Cites specific examples from such companies as L.L. Bean, General Motors, and Universal Foods Corporation.

Clinton, Roy J., Stan Williamson, and Art L. Bethke. "Implementing Total Quality Management: The Role of Human Resource Management," *SAM Advanced Management Journal* 59, no. 2 (Spring 1994): 10–16.

HR departments can help implement TQM by leading by example and by recruiting people who can function in a quality-focused environment. Cites management practices HR can model in its own operations.

Crosby, Lawrence A., Douglas B. Grisaffe, and Ted R. Marra. "The Impact of Quality and Customer Satisfaction on Employee Organizational Commitment," *Marketing & Research Today* 22, no. 1 (February 1994): 19–31.

Describes why a concept of employee commitment is influenced by employees, quality, and the customer focus of the company. Research suggests that quality alone will not motivate employees, rather that the value of customer focus is the way to insure the long-term health of the organization.

Hequet, Marc. "Giving Good Feedback," *Training* 31, no. 9 (September 1994): 72–77.

Provides good insights into the process of giving feedback, including the insight that negative feedback can somehow be given so it won't hurt—it will.

Herbig, Paul, Fred Palumbo, and Bradley S. O'Hara. "Total Quality and the Human Resource Professional," *TQM Magazine* 6, no. 2 (1994): 33–36.

Demonstrates that the values long defended by human resource professionals are similar to those of TQM. Argues the case why both have to be linked.

Hogarty, Donna Brown. "New Ways to Pay," *Management Review* (January 1994): 34–36.

Reviews how three companies have come up with new compensation systems.

Hutt, Geoff. "Incorporating Quality Performance Objectives into Performance Appraisal Systems," *TQM Magazine* 6, no. 1 (1994): 8–12.

Citing the case study of AT&T Istel, a European information technology company, the author shows how one company applies Deming's ideas on personnel by making sure employees can excel and know what constitutes achievement, and how a personnel management system evolved around those principles.

Laabs, Jennifer J. "Interactive Sessions Further TQM Effort," *Personnel Journal* 73, no. 3 (March 1994): 22–28.

Describes how Haworth, Inc., a furniture manufacturing company, used roundtable-like meetings called "sensing sessions" at which employees could express their ideas and opinions about company issues directly to senior management. Reports that senior management was now better able to know on what to make decisions and was receiving many suggestions for improvements.

Laabs, Jennifer J. "Specialized Pay Programs Link Employees' TQM Efforts to Rewards," *Personnel Journal* 73, no. 1 (January 1994): 17–18.

Notes the corporate trend of organizations finding new ways to reward and compensate workers functioning in teams applying TQM. Discusses changes in measurements of performance, e.g., away from just financial to also customer satisfaction, process improvement, and team results.

Myers, Ken, and Bob Killeen. "Building Union Management Partnerships," *Quality Progress* 27, no. 4 (April 1994): 95–97.

Describes how to involve union management in a quality transformation process. The article stresses more the benefits of the effort than the mechanics of how that is accomplished.

Neusch Donna R. "Effectively Compensating Teams: A Primer on Pay and Rewards," *Target* 10, no. 1, (1994): 16–21.

A review of an innovative approach for compensating employees who are members of teams.

Parker, Mike, and Jane Slaughter. "Should the Labour Movement Buy TQM?" *Journal of Organizational Change Management* 6, no. 4 (1993): 43–56.

Discusses the negative effects of TQM on workers, yet calls for society to do more than just downsize organizations by rather applying these principles to use all its people effectively.

Parry, Scott. "The Missing 'M' in TQM," *Training* 30, no. 9 (September 1993): 29–31.

Argues that management's performance dictates whether or not quality practices are used by employees. Discusses the role of empowerment, what are the generic competencies required, and the role of training.

Persico, John, Jr., and Gary N. McLean. "The Evolving Merger of Socio-Technical Systems and Quality Improvement Theories," *Human Systems Management* 13, no. 1 (1994): 11–18.

Compares and contrasts socio-technical systems (STS) theory to TQM, concluding that STS is ambiguous and theoretical, while TQM is too prescriptive, emphasizing too many technical aspects and too much pragmatism. Says STS and TQM are slowly converging.

Pfeffer, Jeffrey. *Competitive Advantage Through People: Unleashing the Power of the Work Force.* Boston: Harvard Business School Press, 1994.

Offers practical suggestions on how to shift old management practices, overcoming resistance to changing personnel practices, and implementing practices that bring the best out of employees as a competitive advantage.

Rigg, Michael. "Organization Change and Individual Behavior," *Industrial Engineering* 25, no. 12 (December 1993): 12–13.

Offers five rules of corporate and individual behavior that make implementation of TQM and quality management practices in general work. The focus of the article is on changes in behavior and how that is done.

Rogers, Jerry D., Kenneth E. Clow, and Toby J. Kash. "Increasing Job Satisfaction of Service Personnel," *Journal of Services Marketing* 8, no. 1 (1994): 14–26.

Describes what kind of employees should be hired into services companies and how they should be treated in order to insure high levels of performance and productivity. The key is to improve their job satisfaction.

Troy, Kathryn. "Recognize Quality Achievement with Noncash Awards," *Personnel Journal* 72, no. 10 (October 1993): 111–17.

Reports results of a survey by the Conference Board reporting that companies are moving away from just cash awards and towards other types of recognition. The data is specific as to the types of awards and who participates in identifying recipients.

Legal Affairs

Alberts, Alan. "Deming, TQM, and the Law Office," *Law Practice Management* 20, no. 4 (May-June 1994): 32–33.

Says TQM concepts are new to lawyers; suggests that TQM is a useful way to run a law practice and why.

Hoexter, Rolf, and Mariesa Julien. "Legal Eagles Become Quality Hawks," *Quality Progress* 27, no. 1 (January 1994): 31–33.

Describes how to implement TQM in a law firm. This is a tactical, step-by-step description intended for a legal audience.

Murray, John E. "Total Quality Management and the Law," *Purchasing* 115, no. 4 (September 23, 1993): 32–36.

Describes how purchasing function and legal professionals within a company can work together through the application of TQM. In the world of TQM, lawyers prevent problems by anticipating them before they occur.

Standards and Assessments

ISO 9000

Bradley, Michael. "Starting Total Quality Management from ISO 9000," *TQM Magazine* 6, no. 1 (1994): 50–54.

Reports that over 20,000 companies have registered, but that not all of them have experienced significant improvements through quality management. Describes how one can be successful in the application of TQM.

Chua, Richard C.H. "Is ISO for You?" *Chemical Business* (September 7, 1993): 7ff.

Describes the role of ISO for chemical manufacturers: what it is, why do it, and anticipated results. It is a good survey of the effort involved.

Emmons, Sidney L. "ISO 9001 on a Shoestring," *Quality Progress* 27, no. 5 (May 1994): 49–50.

Describes how Acme Electric Corporation worked with the Underwriters Laboratories (UL) to get registered on ISO 9001. Details the process they went through between 1990 and 1992 to get the job done.

Houser, Bill, and Ken Somers. "The Truth(s) About ISO 9000," *Tapping the Network Journal* 5, no. 2 (Summer 1994): 19–23.

This is a brief description of what ISO 9000 is, its basic elements, how it came into being, and how one normally gains benefit from it.

Johns, Vaughn H. "ISO 9000—Beyond the Myths," *Chemical Marketing Reporter* (April 11, 1994): PSR8-SR9.

Reports that so far 2,000 U.S. companies are ISO certified as compared to 40,000 in Europe, with rapid growth in certification taking place in Japan and in the United States. Reports the results of various surveys on the status of ISO certification; a good update on what is happening.

Lamprecht, James L. *Implementing the ISO 9000 Series*. Milwaukee: ASQC Quality Press, 1993.

This is a clearly written study on how to implement ISO, not simply a description of what it is. The author is a highly respected expert on the topic.

Link, M., and W. Hertz. "Development of Quality Assurance Requirements: An International Comparison," *Kerntechnik* 58, no. 6 (December 1993): 319–26.

Discusses the relationship among TQM, systems assurance, and ISO 9000 with specific reference to their applicability in the nuclear energy industry in Europe.

Owen, Bryn, Tom Cothran, and Peter Malkovich. *Achieving ISO 9000 Registration*. Knoxville, TN: SPC Press, 1994.

Combines ISO 9000 concepts with those of TQM to provide a step-by-step guide for gaining registration. Includes 1994 revisions; serves as a useful guide to the subject in 400 pages.

Pathak, A.K. "ISO 9000—The Quality Standards," *CSI Communications* 16, no. 9 (March 1993): 5–8.

This is an overview of what ISO is, where it fits, and how. This article was published in an Indian journal, yet additional evidence of global interest in ISO standards. This article also contains material on use of IT.

Roos, Gina. "Buyers' New Battle Cry: Get Thee ISO-Certified," *Electronic Buyers' News* (December 13, 1993): E-28.

Describes the effort of Major/Edwards Electronic Supply, Inc., to become ISO certified. The article also discusses the value of ISO 9000 from customers' point of view.

Roussel, Anne Marie. "ISO 9000: A Measure of the Measurement," *Data Communications* 22, no. 14 (October 1993): 55–58.

This is a general description of the ISO 9000 standards and also the process a company goes through to be certified. Explains the benefits of ISO 9000 certification to customers of such organizations.

Voehl, Frank, Peter Jackson, and David Ashton. *ISO 9000: An Implementation Guide for Small to Mid-Sized Businesses.* Delray Beach, Fla.: St. Lucie Press, 1994.

Since most books on ISO 9000 focus on large enterprises, this book is a welcome addition to the literature on the subject. Increasingly, mid-sized companies are applying for certification and are experiencing different issues than larger companies. This book is an attempt to deal with those issues.

Zuckerman, Amy. "Mixed Reviews for ISO 9000," *Iron Age* 10, no. 2 (February 1994): 40–43.

Describes attitudes of steel makers towards this certification process. Those that have TQM programs underway like it more than those that do not. Some challenge the cost of ISO certification and the "free wheeling" certifications underway.

Baldrige Award and Criteria

Deavenport, Earnest W., Jr. "Winning the Baldrige Award," *Chief Executive,* no. 95 (June 1994): 36–39.

Argues that Eastman Chemical Company did not win the award by applying quality management practices, rather it focused on winning customers. One major benefit of the effort, however, was enhanced teamwork throughout the company.

Gradig, Rita M., and John K. Harris. "The Baldrige Award: A Quest for Excellence?" *Review of Business* 15, no. 3 (Spring 1994): 20–24.

Describes the purpose of the award, but then goes on to say many companies are using its criteria to structure their own quality implementations. Managers are using it as another tool with which to run their organizations.

Hart, Christopher W.L. "What's Wrong—and Right—with the Baldrige Awards," *Chief Executive* no. 90 (November/December 1993): 36–47.

Argues that the Baldrige is a useful tool for assessing or launching quality management practices in a company. Describes the controversy surrounding the award from its inception in 1987.

Jordan, Daniel W. "Using the Baldrige Criteria for Self-Assessment," *Engineering Management Journal* 6, no. 2 (June 1994): 16–19.

Argues the case for why the Criteria can be used to assess the performance of an organization. For an example of this approach applied, see Cortada in the preceding "Sales" section.

Triplett, Tim. "Satisfaction Is Nothing They Take for Granite," *Marketing News* 28, no. 10 (May 9, 1994): 6–7.

This is a brief account of the quality work of Granite Rock Co., a construction contractor and building materials supplier, a winner of the 1992 Baldrige Award.

Other Awards, Standards, and Issues

Anonymous. "EFQM Viewpoint," *TQM Magazine* 5, no. 4 (August 1993): 11–12.

Describes the European Quality Award, which is administered by the European Foundation for Quality Management (EFQM). This article describes the award and then shows the links between its guiding principles and the practice of TQM.

Anonymous. "Pros and Cons of BS5750," *Electronics Times* (April 14, 1994): 18.

Describes letters to the editor of this journal complaining about the British standard for quality management systems. Small businesses are protesting the most, losing business to companies that are certified since so many customers are insisting on BS5750 certification.

European Organization for Quality. *The First European Forum on Quality Self-Assessment: The Use of Quality Award Criteria and Models for Self-Assessment Purposes.* Bern, Switzerland: European Organization for Quality, 1994.

This is the first book-length publication to appear on Europe's most important quality award; deals with its application and its criteria.

Loveday, Marion. "Measuring Up to the Top Model," *Managing Service Quality* (September 1993): 41–44.

This is an account of the start and operation of the European Foundation for Quality Management (EFQM) and of the quality award it administers. It is a useful introduction to this important quality award.

Williams, Melanie. "Linking the Results," *TQM Magazine* 5, no. 4 (August 1993): 13–16.

Describes the model presented by the EFQM award with particular emphasis on the requirement to understand business results. Along with the first article in this section of the bibliography, the reader gets a good overview of the European quality model.

A Quality Management Library

There is an intuitive appeal to Total Quality Management that helps explain its popularity. It makes sense to focus your business on delighting your customers and doing that at the lowest cost possible. Making these things happen in a way that helps an organization sustain its strategic advantage in an increasingly competitive global business environment is something else. This takes a deep commitment to and understanding of the principles on which quality management is based and its practices. It is, therefore, helpful to have a library of books to which you can turn to understand this subject. This section of *The Quality Yearbook* has been created to give you some advice on selecting volumes for that library. What you will find here are 25 titles we think can form the core of a sound collection of books on quality management. This list includes classic volumes by Deming, Juran, and several other important thinkers in this field. It also includes books on specific aspects of TQM or its foundational ideas. For each selection, we include basic information about the book, its focus, and then a list of chapters. Including the contents is the most useful way to help you determine if each of these is a book that you might like to have in your quality management library.

First, we have listed each title in alphabetical order by the last name of the author. This list is followed by a more detailed description of each book.

1. Stephen R. Covey, *The 7 Habits of Highly Effective People*
2. Philip B. Crosby, *Quality Is Free: The Art of Making Quality Certain*
3. Thomas H. Davenport, *Process Innovation: Reengineering Work Through Information Technology*
4. W. Edwards Deming, *Out of the Crisis*
5. Stephen J. Frangos with Steven J. Bennett, *Team Zebra: How 1500 Partners Revitalized Eastman Kodak's Black & White Film-Making Flow*
6. Michael Hammer and James Champy, *Reengineering the Corporation: A Manifesto for Business Revolution*
7. H. James Harrington, *Business Process Improvement: The Breakthrough Strategy for Total Quality, Productivity, and Competitiveness*
8. V. Daniel Hunt, *Quality Management for Government: A Guide to Federal, State, and Local Implementation*
9. Masaaki Imai, *KAIZEN: The Key to Japan's Competitive Success*
10. Brian L. Joiner, *Fourth Generation Management: The New Business Consciousness*

11. J.M. Juran, *Juran on Leadership for Quality: An Executive Handbook*
12. J.M. Juran and Frank M. Gryna, *Juran's Quality Control Handbook, Fourth Edition*
13. William Lareau, *American Samurai: A Warrior for the Coming Dark Ages of American Business*
14. Gerald Nadler and Shozo Hibino, *Breakthrough Thinking: Why We Must Change the Way We Solve Problems and the Seven Principles to Achieve This*
15. Burt Nanus, *Visionary Leadership: Creating a Compelling Sense of Direction for Your Organization*
16. B. Joseph Pine II, *Mass Customization: The New Frontier in Business Competition*
17. James Brian Quinn, *Intelligent Enterprise: A Knowledge and Service Based Paradigm for Business*
18. Peter R. Scholtes, *The Team Handbook: How to Use Teams to Improve Quality*
19. Richard J. Schonberger, *Building a Chain of Customers: Linking Business Functions to Create the World Class Company*
20. Peter M. Senge, *The Fifth Discipline: The Art and Practice of the Learning Organization*
21. George Stalk, Jr., and Thomas M. Hout, *Competing Against Time: How Time-Based Competition Is Reshaping Global Markets*
22. Mary Walton, *The Deming Management Method*
23. Gregory H. Watson, *Strategic Benchmarking: How to Rate Your Company's Performance Against the World's Best*
24. Margaret J. Wheatley, *Leadership and the New Science: Learning About Organization from an Orderly Universe*
25. Valarie A. Zeithaml, A. Parasuraman, Leonard L. Berry, *Delivering Quality Service*

Descriptions of Recommended Books

Stephen R. Covey, *The 7 Habits of Highly Effective People,* 358 pages, A Fireside Book, Simon & Schuster, 1989.

Covey's best-selling book (available in trade paperback) is based on understanding that people succeed best when they help others also succeed and when they continuously improve themselves. The ideas Covey promotes are completely consistent with the TQM approach to management, with its emphasis on teamwork, communication, focus on delighting customers, and continuous improvement. (An article by Covey and a colleague is part of the section on leadership in the 1995 yearbook.)

TABLE OF CONTENTS: Part One: Paradigms and Principles Inside Out; The Seven Habits—An Overview; **Part Two: Private Victory** Habit 1. Be Proactive; Habit 2. Begin with the End in Mind; Habit 3. Put First Things First; **Part Three: Public Victory** Paradigms of Interdependence;

Philip B. Crosby, *Quality Is Free: The Art of Making Quality Certain*, 309 pages, McGraw-Hill, 1979.

Crosby demonstrates that doing things right the first time adds nothing to the cost of your product or service. He also shows that doing things wrong is what costs organizations money. Rework, scrap, and repeating services cost companies up to 20 percent of their sales dollars. This book helps managers understand the importance of the idea of defect-free products and services and that delivering such products and services to customers does not add but actually lowers costs. Crosby's book is a pioneering effort in the field of quality management and provides many practical ideas for how a company can develop a management and operational style that helps ensure that defect-free outputs are the norm. Chapter 2 from Crosby's book is included as part of the classics section of the 1995 yearbook.

TABLE OF CONTENTS:

Thomas H. Davenport, *Process Innovation: Reengineering Work Through Information Technology*, 336 pages, Harvard Business School Press, 1993.

This book looks at the central role of information technology in reengineering business processes. Current organizational processes, created before the ability to create and deliver information instantaneously in the organization, are now outmoded and inefficient. This book suggests that the cornerstone to process innovation's potentially dramatic results is information technology—a largely untapped resource, but a crucial enabler of process innovation. Likewise, only by committing to process innovation will management begin to see the value of this technology. This book is a seminal work in the use of IT to facilitate and manage reengineered processes.

TABLE OF CONTENTS:

W. Edwards Deming, *Out of the Crisis*, 507 pages, MIT Center for Advanced Engineering Study, 1986.

This is Deming's summary of how to manage successfully. Deming does not view his teachings in terms of TQM. He always said he was teaching a more informed view of management based on understanding variation and its management for continuous improvement. This book expounds on the ideas captured in the 14 Points and 7 Deadly Diseases (see "Classics" section). It is written as Deming spoke, a not altogether flowing style, but it deserves perusal and use by any manager because it is a standard reference for others in the field. It is best used as a reference to understand Deming's view of management practice on various points.

TABLE OF CONTENTS: 1. Chain Reaction: Quality, Productivity, Lower Costs, Capture the Market; 2. Principles for Transformation of Western Management; 3. Diseases and Obstacles; 4. When? How Long?; 5. Questions to Help Managers; 6. Quality and the Consumer; 7. Quality and Productivity in Service Organizations; 8. Some New Principles of Training and Leadership; 9. Operational Definitions: Conformance, Performance; 10. Standards and Regulation; 11. Common Causes and Special Causes of Improvement. Stable System; 12. More Examples of Improvement Downstream; 13. Some Disappointments in Great Ideas; 14. Two Reports to Management; 15. Plan for Minimum Average Total Cost for Test of Incoming Materials and Final Product; 16. Organization for Improvement of Quality and Productivity; 17. Some Illustrations for Improvement of Living; 18. Appendix: Transformation in Japan.

Stephen J. Frangos with Steven J. Bennett, *Team Zebra: How 1500 Partners Revitalized Eastman Kodak's Black & White Film-Making Flow*, 223 pages, Omneo, An Imprint of Oliver Wight Publications, 1993.

This is the inside story of how the failing black and white film division of Eastman Kodak was given 18 months to turn itself around and how it succeeded beyond expectations. Taking the name "Team Zebra," the leadership of this division implemented teams, reengineered processes, empowered its people, and created a learning organization that quickly began generating results that everyone seemed to own and feel good about. They embraced time-based competition and dramatically reduced costs and waste and improved the commercialization of new products. This book is included as an excellent example of what happens when a company jumps into TQM with both feet.

TABLE OF CONTENTS: Introduction; 1. From Minting Silver Dollars to Squeezing Copper Pennies; 2. Mother Kodak; 3. Flow Is a Go—This Morning; 4. Straight Talk at the Park; 5. Bandages and Tourniquets for a Bleeding Zebra; 6. Racing Down the Data Highway and Other Acts of Empowerment; 7. The Zebra Lives; 8. Formal Strategies for a New B&W; 9. Up the Learning Organization: Building Capabilities in Black & White; 10. The Magic Behind Team Zebra; Postscript: Vision of Black & White.

Michael Hammer and James Champy, *Reengineering the Corporation: A Manifesto for Business Revolution*, 223 pages, HarperBusiness, 1993.

As most people are aware, this was the best-selling business book of 1993, with good reason. It provides managers with real insight into the value of reengineering business processes to improve quality and reduce costs. Reengineering is contrasted with continuous improvement, in which current processes are gradually but continuously upgraded. In reengineering, old processes are thrown out and new ones, often quite different and more efficient, are developed to take their place. This book explains this important idea and includes three detailed chapters from companies that have done this. From a TQM perspective, reengineering is one potentially important tool for reducing costs and improving responsiveness to customers. (James Cortada talks more about this idea in the lead article of the 1995 yearbook.)

TABLE OF CONTENTS:

H. James Harrington, *Business Process Improvement: The Breakthrough Strategy for Total Quality, Productivity, and Competitiveness,* 274 pages, McGraw-Hill, 1991.

Organizations are systems. In systems, work gets done through processes—the goal-oriented steps by which organizations deliver products and services to customers. And, in fact, this is the heart of TQM. This best-selling book by Harrington provides readers with a thorough explanation of the management and improvement of processes. You will find lots of practical guidance on understanding and improving any type of business process from the shop floor to the executive suite and everything in between.

TABLE OF CONTENTS:

V. Daniel Hunt, *Quality Management for Government: A Guide to Federal, State, and Local Implementation,* 384 pages, ASQC Quality Press, 1993.

There are not a lot of books available on quality management in government. This one by veteran author V. Daniel Hunt provides a thorough overview of what TQM is and how to undertake quality initiatives at all government levels. It includes a number of examples that demonstrate how it's being done.

TABLE OF CONTENTS:

Masaaki Imai, *KAIZEN: The Key to Japan's Competitive Success,* 259 pages, McGraw-Hill, 1986.

The word Kaizen means continuous improvement of many little things in an organization's processes that end up making a big difference in efficiency and the quality of outputs delivered to customers. Imai suggests that Kaizen is the foundation of Japan's economic miracle. The book includes more than 100 examples of Kaizen in action, 15 corporate case studies, and 50 charts and graphs. It is well-written and interesting. (An excerpt from this book is included in the "Classics" section of the 1995 yearbook.)

TABLE OF CONTENTS:

Brian L. Joiner, *Fourth Generation Management: The New Business Consciousness,* 289 pages, McGraw-Hill, 1994.

Joiner presents an integrated view of what he calls the "fourth generation" of management: the style of management that emerges from seeing organizations as systems. He hangs his ideas on the "Joiner Triangle," a device to emphasize the three concerns of managers: quality for the customer, teamwork, and the use of measurement, statistics, and science to help the organization continuously improve. The book includes an especially useful presentation of how to manage variation. (An excerpt from this book on this subject is included in the "Process Management" section of the 1995 yearbook.)

TABLE OF CONTENTS: Part One: Getting Better Faster 1. Changing the Way We Manage; 2. Quality vs. Productivity?; 3. The Organization as a System; 4. Rapid Learning, Rapid Improvement; **Part Two: Building a True Customer Voice** 5. Voice of the Customer; 6. Customer-focused Strategies; **Part Three: Managing in a Variable World** 7. Principles of Variation; 8. The Price of Ignorance; 9. Strategies for Reducing Variation; 10. Management Reactions to Variation; **Part Four: Creating and Maintaining Gains** 11. Better Methods, Better Results; 12. Improving Our Ability to Improve; **Part Five: Creating the Environment** 13. All One Team; 14. The Challenges of Performance Appraisal.

J. M. Juran, *Juran on Leadership for Quality: An Executive Handbook*, 373 pages, The Free Press, 1989.

This book presents the Juran Trilogy, planning, control, and improvement in a compelling and practical step-by-step manner. The author's goal is to help those who must lead organizations understand their responsibilities for delivering quality to customers and how to go about that, using the trilogy as the focal point. The book includes criteria for selecting improvement projects and mobilizing teams to carry them out. He emphasizes the role of managers in carrying out such projects. The book includes a variety of real world examples to help make its points.

TABLE OF CONTENTS: 1. Quality: A Continuing Revolution; 2. How to Think About Quality; 3. Quality Improvement; 4. Quality Planning; 5. Quality Control; 6. Strategic Quality Management (SQM); 7. Operational Quality Management; 8. The Work Force and Quality; 9. Motivation for Quality; 10. Training for Quality; Epilogue.

J. M. Juran and Frank M. Gryna, Editors, *Juran's Quality Control Handbook, Fourth Edition*, over 1,000 pages (pages numbered by chapter), McGraw-Hill, 1988.

This is a comprehensive reference book on almost everything you can think of that has to do with quality management. It includes 34 contributed chapters (many by Juran and Gryna themselves plus several other contributors) plus a series of chapters on the state of quality in several countries. Every organization implementing TQM would find it valuable to have this book in their library.

TABLE OF CONTENTS: 1. How to Use This Handbook; 2. The Quality Function; 3. Quality and Income; 4. Quality Costs; 5. Quality Policies and Objectives; 6. Company-wide Planning for Quality; 7. Organizing for Quality; 8. Upper Management and Quality; 9. Quality Assurance; 10. Managing Human Performance; 11. Training for Quality; 12. Field Intelligence; 13. Product Development; 14. Software Development; 15. Supplier Relations; 16. Manufacturing Planning; 17. Production; 18. Inspection and Test; 19. Marketing; 20. Customer Service; 21. Administrative and Support Operations; 22. Quality Improvement; 23. Basic Statistical Methods; 24. Statistical Process Control; 25. Acceptance Sampling; 26. Design and Analysis of Experiments; 27. Computers and Quality; 28. Process Industries; 29. Electronics Components Industries; 30. Assembly Industries; 31. Complex Industries; 32. Job Shop Industries; 33. Service Industries; 34. Quality and Society; 35a. Quality and the National Culture; 35b. Quality in Developing Countries; 35c. Quality in France; 35d. Quality in the Federal Republic of Germany; 35e. Quality in Great Britain; 35f. Quality in Japan; 35g. Quality in the USA; 35h. Quality in Socialist Countries.

William Lareau, *American Samurai: A Warrior for the Coming Dark Ages of American Business*, 336 pages, Warner Books, 1991.

This book is highly recommended for beginners to quality. It provides a dramatic case for moving to TQM. It is written in readable, down-to-earth prose and provides a comprehensive review of the principles and actions any manager practicing TQM should know about. Lareau presents these ideas as 20 Coda for the American Samurai. The table of contents lists these coda (starting with chapter 6) and gives a good sense of the author's style.

TABLE OF CONTENTS: 1. We're Not Number One Anymore; 2. The Myth of American Superiority as the Root of Our Bad Management Practices; 3. The Coming Dark Ages of American Business; 4. The Management Theory and Practice That Is Destroying American Business; 5. The Code of the American Samurai; 6. Management's Obsession with Outcomes Must Be Abandoned; 7. Out-of-Process Defect Inspection Must Be Eliminated; 8. Lies, Damned Lies, and Statistics; 9. Employees Are the Number One Natural Resource; 10. Quality Isn't Number One—It's the Only One!; 11. It's Never "Soup Yet" in the World of Process Improvement; 12. Drive a Stake into the Ground, Not into Your Foot: Benchmarks Instead of Objectives; 13. "Real" Managers Aren't Bosses; 14. Real Employees Do It Their Way!; 15. Real Plans Not 8½ x 11-Inch 10 Pound Doorstops; 16. Training Makes the Money the Old-Fashioned Way—It Earns It; 17. Performance to Specification Costs You Money; 18. You Can't Do It Alone: Suppliers Are Team Members; 19. Performance Appraisals: Why Do We Punish Ourselves? 20. The Letter, as Well as the Spirit, of the Code; 21. Low Tech Is the Right Tech (for Profits); 22. Everybody on Board the Design Train Early!; 23. Consensus Decision Making: The Great Unknown of American Business; 24. Everybody Puts 'em on One Leg at a Time; 25. We March at Dawn (Getting It Done).

Gerald Nadler and Shozo Hibino, *Breakthrough Thinking: Why We Must Change the Way We Solve Problems and the Seven Principles to Achieve This*, 350 pages, Prima Publishing, 1990.

Continuous improvement and reengineering are two important concepts in TQM. This respected book teaches managers and employees how to be more creative in bringing about change and improvement in any organization. It looks especially at using intuitive thinking, rather than just analysis, to come up with solutions to problems that better fit the problem. It emphasizes understanding the organization as a system, and its ideas emerge from understanding the effects of actions throughout the organization. This book reinforces and supplements books by Senge, Wheatley, and others in this list on better understanding what an organization is and thus how to manage it better.

TABLE OF CONTENTS: Part 1: The Conventional You 1. It's Up to You; 2. Problems Beget Problems (and That's Good); 3. Pushing for Breakthrough: Improving Your Chances for Success; **Part 2: Increasing** 4. The Uniqueness Principle; 5. The Purposes Principle; 6. The Solution-After-Next Principle; 7. The Systems Principle: Seven-Eighths of Everything Can't Be Seen; 8. The Limited Information Connection Principle: Don't Become an Expert About the Problem; 9. The People Design Principle; 10. The Betterment Timeline Principle: Know When to Improve It; **Part 3: The Effective You** 11. Holistic Problem Solving: Coordinating the Seven Principles; 12. Welcome to the Future.

Burt Nanus, *Visionary Leadership: Creating a Compelling Sense of Direction for Your Organization*, 237 pages, Jossey-Bass Publishers, 1992.

Leadership is vital for any organization seeking to transform itself using the principles of TQM. Leaders don't tell people what to do, but by their behavior and commitment to principle help create a new and more enlightened business environment to which others willingly adapt. Burt Nanus, director of research as USC's Leadership Institute, describes how great leaders do this, and provides readers with direction for creating and leading the implementation of their vision for quality. Note the special appendix for visionary leadership in the public sector.

B. Joseph Pine II, *Mass Customization: The New Frontier in Business Competition*, 332 pages, Harvard Business School Press, 1993.

Mass customization is the application of mass production technology to the creation of products and services for a market of one. It represents the progression of organizations practicing TQM in their quest to understand and delight their customers. Joe Pine explains this idea in detail in this important book. (Joe Pine is a consulting editor for *The Quality Yearbook*, and you can find more on his thoughts on manufacturing, TQM, and mass customization in the "Manufacturing" section of the 1995 edition.)

James Brian Quinn, *Intelligent Enterprise: A Knowledge and Service Based Paradigm for Industry*, 473 pages, The Free Press, 1992.

Consistent with many other titles selected for this library (Senge and Davenport for two), this book looks at how the use of information can help organizations develop and sustain their competitive advantage in delivering value to customers. It is not the largest companies or even those with superior products that will succeed. It will be, rather, those companies that leverage knowledge to more efficiently and effectively manage their processes to create ever higher-quality outputs. The intelligent use of technology to marshall and deliver information will be vital to any organization to better align its processes and capabilities with customer needs and do this better than competitors. This important book makes a compelling case for the place of knowledge and information to implement quality. In fact, it will only be those organizations that do this particularly well that will succeed, according to Quinn. The author is a three-time winner of the McKinsey award for the best article in the *Harvard Business Review*.

TABLE OF CONTENTS: Part 1: Intellect and Services: Restructuring Economies and Strategy; 1. Services Restructure the Economy; 2. Focusing Strategy on Core Intellectual and Service Competencies; 3. Leveraging Knowledge and Service Based Strategies Through Outsourcing; **Part 2: Knowledge Based Services Revolutionize Organizational Strategies** 4. Revolutionizing Organizational Strategies; 5. Service Based Disaggregation with Strategic Focus; 6. Exploiting the Manufacturing-Services Interface; **Part 3: The Knowledge Based Service Enterprise** 7. The Intelligent Enterprise: A New Paradigm; 8. Managing Knowledge Based and Professional Intellect; 9. Managing the Innovative Organization; **Part 4: Managing the Intelligent Enterprise** 10. Managing Intellect in Mass Services: A Customer Based Quality Focus; 11. Managing for Service Productivity; 12. Managing the "Intelligent Enterprise;" 13. A New Economic and Management Paradigm.

Peter R. Scholtes, *The Team Handbook: How to Use Teams to Improve Quality*, Joiner Associates, 1988.

This is the leading resource for organizations seeking to implement project teams. It is a practical guide, providing many exercises and step-by-step instructions for setting up teams and making sure they succeed. It talks not only about projects and improvement plants, but also about interactions among team members and includes ideas for what to do when things go wrong as well as right.

TABLE OF CONTENTS: 1. Doing Business in a New Business World; 2. The Basics of Quality Improvement; 3. Setting the Stage for a Successful Project; 4. Getting Underway; 5. Building an Improvement Plan; 6. Learning to Work Together; 7. Team-Building Activities.

Richard J. Schonberger, *Building a Chain of Customers: Linking Business Functions to Create the World Class Company*, 349 pages, The Free Press, 1990.

In this book, Schonberger demonstrates how the link between the four main business functions—design, operations, accounting, and marketing—forms a continuous chain of customers that extends beyond those who buy the product or service. He shows that everyone has a customer—the next department, office, shop, or person. It's up to everyone to make sure the "product" or "service" delivered meets their needs and expectations. This idea helps to align processes and minimize rework and, when properly applied, is another useful perspective for implementing TQM.

TABLE OF CONTENTS: 1. The Great Awakening: Earthquakes in the Business Functions; 2. Universal Strategy: The Shattering of Strategic Business Thought; 3. The "Customer-In" Concept; 4. Total Quality: Toward Delighting the Customer; 5. Work Force on the Attack; 6. The Learning Organization; 7. Attack on Nonobvious Wastes; 8. Minimal Accounting and Noncost Cost Control; 9. Pay, Recognition, Celebration; 10. World-Class Product Development; 11. Marketing for Total Gain; 12. Success Formulas for Volume and Flexibility; 13. Elevated Performance Standards. Appendix: Quick (JIT) Response.

Peter M. Senge, *The Fifth Discipline: The Art and Practice of the Learning Organization*, 424 pages, Doubleday Currency, 1990.

In an intriguing, practical, and intellectually engaging manner, Senge presents the important idea of understanding organizations as systems and the benefits of doing that. This is a significant book for any manager because all the practices of TQM emerge from understanding the organization as a system. Senge helps managers to understand that in a system everything affects everything else and that if managers do not understand that, the quality of their decisions will be severely compromised.

George Stalk, Jr., and Thomas M. Hout, *Competing Against Time: How Time-Based Competition Is Reshaping Global Markets*, 285 pages, The Free Press, 1990.

An important part of any process improvement effort is cycle time reduction. Reducing the time it takes to deliver products to the market is central to reducing costs and improving customer satisfaction. This book by Stalk and Hout, two leading thinkers and consultants in using time to competitive advantage, provide a comprehensive and practical review of the role of time in managing processes and how time can help a company better serve its customers.

Mary Walton, *The Deming Management Method*, 262 pages, A Perigee Book, Putnam, 1986.

Where *Out of the Crisis* is cryptic, Walton's book is clear. It is an interpretation of Deming's ideas, done with his blessing, that has found a spot on nearly every list of books those interested in TQM should read. The book thoroughly reviews the 14 Points chapter by chapter and includes several chapters showing how various companies have actually put Deming's ideas to work.

Ford Motor Company, Dearborn, Michigan; 23. Spreading the Deming Work: Growth Opportunity Alliance of Greater Lawrence, Massachusetts; 24. Deming to the Rescue: Malden Mills; 25. Adopting the New Philosophy: Honeywell Information Systems, Lawrence Manufacturing Operation, Lawrence, Massachusetts; 26. Toward a Critical Mass: AT&T, Merrimack Valley Works; 27. The Philadelphia Model: Philadelphia Area Council for Excellence; 29. The Transformation of an American Manager: Microcircuit Engineering Corporation; 30. Lew Springer—The Role of a Zealot: Campbell Soup Company.

Gregory H. Watson, *Strategic Benchmarking: How to Rate Your Company's Performance Against the World's Best*, 268 pages, John Wiley & Sons, 1993.

This is probably the leading and most authoritative books on benchmarking—comparing company processes against those in the best to guide improvement. After beginning with an in-depth discussion of benchmarking fundamentals, this book shows how to put this technique into action. It includes a series of case studies from Hewlett-Packard, Ford, General Motors, and Xerox to demonstrate this technique in a variety of applications.

TABLE OF CONTENTS: 1. Introducing Benchmarking; 2. Linking Strategic Planning with Benchmarking; 3. Understanding the Essentials of Process Benchmarking; 4. Applying Benchmarking Results for Maximum Utility; 5. Doing an Internal Benchmarking Study; 6. Conducting a Competitive Benchmarking Study; 7. Performing a Functional Benchmarking Study; 8. Developing a Generic Benchmarking Study; 9. Expanding Benchmarking for Broader Applications; 10. Creating a Benchmarking Capability; APPENDIXES: A. Benchmarking Code of Conduct; B. Tools of Secondary Research; C. Benchmarking Recognition Award Criteria; D. Sample Benchmarking Procedure; E. Benchmarking Bibliography; F. Glossary of Benchmarking Terms.

Margaret J. Wheatley, *Leadership and the New Science: Learning About Organizations from an Orderly Universe*, 164 page, Berrett-Koehler Publishers, 1992.

This is an insightful treatment of ideas that should be read in conjunction with Senge's book to gain a deeper insight into exactly what an organization is. The point: If you as a manager misunderstand what it is that you manage, what you do will be flawed. Wheatley uses metaphors from modern physics to teach readers about uncertainty, paradox, wholeness, and an unfolding order as relevant to understanding organizations and their management as they are to cosmology or philosophy. The importance of this book for TQM is it helps managers to more clearly understand how organizations evolve and thrive (or die) and the connection between improvement, alignment, and the relationship between the company and its suppliers, its customers, and the world in which it operates. (Wheatley is represented in the 1995 yearbook with an article in the "Cultural Transformation" section.)

TABLE OF CONTENTS: Introduction: Searching for a Simpler Way to Lead Organizations; 1. Discovering an Orderly World; 2. Newtonian Organizations in a Quantum Age; 3. Space Is Not Empty; 4. The Participative Nature of the Universe; 5. Change, Stability, and Renewal: The Paradoxes of Self-Organizing Systems; 6. The Creative Energy of the University—Information; 7. Chaos and the Strange Attractor of Meaning; 8. The New Scientific Management; Epilogue: Being Comfortable with Uncertainty.

Valarie A. Zeithaml, A. Parasuraman, Leonard L. Berry, *Delivering Quality Service*, 226 pages, The Free Press, 1990.

Whether your company is in manufacturing or services, it is important to appreciate that what customers value is the service your offering gives them.

This book by three leading thinkers in the management of services gives readers a clear understanding of what it means to be a leader in delivering services to customers. The authors have developed an influential model that tracks five attributes of quality service—reliability, empathy, assurance, responsiveness, and tangibles—to help managers understand what it is they must deliver to effectively serve customers so they will be around tomorrow to continue doing this.

TABLE OF CONTENTS:

Annotated Directory of Organizations

A growing number of organizations are dedicated to providing information on quality practices, seminars, and publications. Some have existed for many decades, while others are developing as regional support, either as independent nonprofit enterprises or as attachments to local universities.

The following list is in alphabetical order, with brief descriptions of each organization's offerings. This list focuses on organizations in the United States, Europe, and Asia. It includes only organizations that are mainly concerned with quality process improvement and certification. Hundreds of other organizations are beginning to include quality practices in their programs, but those have not been included in the list.

We intentionally have not broken out the list by country for this edition of *The Quality Yearbook* because we wanted readers to see what organizations exist around the world as they look for local ones. The list is selective, including only those of national significance within a country. Many hundreds of very small local organizations are not included here, but as they grow in significance or size, they will be added to our list.

AFAQ
Tour Septentrion, Cedex 9
92081 Paris La Defense
France
Tel: 33 1 47 73 49 49
Fax: 33 1 47 73 49 99
This recently established organization conducts certification of quality practices in companies for the EN29000/ISO 9000 series.

AMERICAN CENTER FOR THE QUALITY OF WORK LIFE
37 Tip Top Way
Berkeley Heights, NJ 07922 USA
Tel: (908) 464-4609
This organization has information, training programs, and does consulting in the area of organizational change and renewal.

AMERICAN INSTITUTE FOR TOTAL PRODUCTIVE MAINTENANCE (AITPM)
P.O. Box 5097
Stamford, CT 06904 USA
Tel: (203) 846-3777, (800) 394-5772
Fax: (203) 846-6883
This organization focuses on Total Productive Maintenance (TPM) quality practices. It sponsors a conference in the fall and publishes the TPM Newsletter.

AMERICAN MANAGEMENT ASSOCIATION
135 West 50th Street
New York, NY 10020 USA
Tel: (212) 586-8100
Fax: (212) 903-8168
The AMA has increasingly taken note of quality practices over the past several years, incorporating these new management methods into its seminars. It publishes the *Management Review, Organizational Dynamics,* and *HR Focus.*

AMERICAN PRODUCTION AND INVENTORY CONTROL SOCIETY (APICS)
500 West Annandale Road
Falls Church, VA 22046 USA

Tel: (703) 237-8344, (800) 444-2742
Fax: (703) 237-1071
This has long been an important organization for manufacturing professionals, providing education and certification programs. In recent years its seminars, publications, annual conferences, and local workshops around the United States have focused on just-in-time manufacturing practices, skills development in capacity management, materials requirements, production, and master production planning. Among its publications is *Production Inventory Management Journal.* APICS is organized through a network of local chapters.

AMERICAN PRODUCTIVITY AND QUALITY CENTER (APQC)
123 North Post Oak Lane
Houston, TX 77024 USA
Tel: (713) 681-4020
Fax: (713) 681-8578
APQC is a quality research center that accumulates information on best practices for all processes. It does client research on who has best practices, supplies copies of articles on processes, conducts seminars, and sells publications. It is the leading center for benchmarking activities in North America. It publishes *Continuous Journey* and administers a benchmarking awards program.

AMERICAN SOCIETY FOR QUALITY CONTROL (ASQC)
P.O. Box 3005
611 East Wisconsin Avenue
Milwaukee, WI 53201-3005 USA
Tel: (414) 272-8575, (800) 248-1946
Fax: (414) 272-1734
This is the most important quality association in the world, with the largest membership. It is also a co-administrator of the Malcolm Baldrige National Quality Award, publisher of several major journals in the field (including *Quality Progress, Journal of Quality Technology, Technometrics, Quality Engineering, On Q,* and *The Quality Review*), has an extensive series of seminars on quality related issues (primarily focused on manufacturing but rapidly expanding to services), and is a major publisher of books on quality themes. It offers a widely respected certification program for quality assurance and other related quality topics, sells books by mail, has local chapters all over North America, and has a variety of technical divisions and committees. If you could only belong to one quality association, this is it.

AMERICAN SOCIETY FOR TRAINING AND DEVELOPMENT (ASTD)
P.O. Box 1443
1630 Duke Street
Alexandria, VA 22313 USA
Tel: (703) 683-8100
Fax: (703) 683-8103
This the major American association for those developing training programs. Increasingly in the last several years, it has concentrated efforts on quality training. It hosts annual conferences in the spring and fall and publishes *Training & Development, Technical & Skills Training,* and *Info-Line.*

AMERICAN SUPPLIER INSTITUTE
15041 Commerce Drive South, Suite 401
Dearborn, MI 48120-1238 USA
Tel: (313) 336-8877
Fax: (313) 462-4500
This organization has skills in implementing Taguchi methods, quality function deployment (QFD), and total quality management (TQM). It offers training programs, consulting, conferences, books and videos, and publishes *ASI Journal.*

ASIAN PRODUCTIVITY ORGANIZATION (APO)
8-4-14 Akasaka, Minato-ku
Tokyo 107, Japan
Tel: 81 3 3408 7221
Fax: 81 3 3408 7220
This is an intergovernment organization with representatives from 18 governments from Asia and the Pacific. It surveys on best practices, offers training programs, and publishes on quality topics. Its purpose is to accelerate economic development through improved economic productivity; it is a major international quality information clearinghouse.

ASSOCIACAO PORTUGUESA PARA LA QUALIDADE
Praca Das Industrias
1300 Lisbon, Portugal
Tel: 351 1 363 6443

Fax: 351 1 364 5081
This association promotes total quality management principles in courses, seminars, conferences and as an information clearinghouse in Portugal. It also administers the Portuguese Quality Award.

ASOCIACIÓN ESPAÑOLA PARA LA CALIDAD (AECC)
92 Calle Zurbano, 1-D
28003 Madrid, Spain
Tel: 34 1 441 7543
Fax: 34 1 441 7390
This is a national quality organization that promotes quality practices, offers educational programs, testing, and maintains ties to quality associations in Latin America.

ASQC QUALITY MANAGEMENT DIVISION
611 East Wisconsin Avenue
Milwaukee, WI 53201 USA
This is an organization with over 30,000 members devoted to promoting quality management as a profession and body of practices and, through a group of committees, to doing research on quality practices. It holds an annual conference in February and publishes the *Quality Management Forum Newsletter.*

ASSOCIATION FOR MANAGEMENT EDUCATION AND DEVELOPMENT (AMED)
21 Catherine Street
Covent Garden
London WC2B 5JS, Great Britain
Tel: 44/71 497-3624
Fax: 44/71 836-0295
This thirty-year old organization concentrates on educational programs for business individuals in Europe. Its focus is on quality; it publishes *AMED Journal* and *AMED News.*

ASSOCIATION FOR MANUFACTURING EXCELLENCE, INC.
380 West Palatine Road
Wheeling, IL 60090-5863 USA
Tel: (708) 520-3282
Fax: (708) 520-0163
Member companies use this organization to determine how to excell in manufacturing through the application of education, documentation, research, and sharing experiences.

ASSOCIATION FOR QUALITY AND PARTICIPATION (AQP)
801-B West 8th Street, Suite 501
Cincinnati, OH 45203 USA
Tel: (513) 381-1959
Fax: (513) 381-0070
It focuses on quality improvement through employee involvement, especially of self-managed teams, labor-management cooperation, redesign of work, and other studies on employee involvement. It sponsors conferences, maintains a library and research service on quality and employee issues, publishes the *Journal for Quality and Participation,* a newsletter, grants organizational team excellence awards, and sells resource materials. It is organized by local chapters in the United States and Canada. It also administers the Annual National Team Competition.

ASSOCIATION FOR THE PRACTICE OF PARTICIPATIVE MANAGEMENT AND TOTAL QUALITY (PRACQ)
(Association pour la Pratique de la Gestion Participative et la Qualite Totale)
Rue Washington 44, BTe. 5
1050 Brussels 5, Belgium
Tel: 32 2 648-0489
Fax: 32 2 649-3269
It fosters productivity improvements of businesses and other organizations in Belgium, primarily through the application of TQM principles. It consults, offers education, and is active in the major European quality organizations, such as the EFQCA and EFQM.

ASSOCIATION FRANCAISE DE NORMALISATION (AFNOR)
Tour Europe, Cedex 7
92049 Paris La Defense, France
Tel: 33 1 42 91 55 55
Fax: 33 1 91 56 56
AFNOR is the the national ISO member organization representing France. It is responsible for promoting the use of ISO standards by French companies.

ASSOCIATION NATIONALE DES DIRECTEURS ET CADRES DE LA FONCTION PERSONNEL (ANDCP)
29, avenue Hoche
75008 Paris, France

Tel: 33 1 45 63 55 09
Fax: 33 1 42 56 41 15
This is an association of personnel managers in France; it operates regional groups, conducts education, and publishes *Personnel.*

ASSOCIATION QUEBECOIS DE LA QUALITÉ
455 St. Antoine West, Suite 600
Montreal, PQ H2Z 1J1, Canada
Tel: 1 (514) 866-6696
Fax: 1 (514) 866-6724
This local quality association has over 2,000 members, holds an annual conference in June, and publishes *Forum Qualité* and *La Qualité Totale.*

ASSOQUALITY
c/o Assolombarda
Via Pantano 9
20122 Milan, Italy
Tel: 32 2 583-70243
Fax: 32 2 583-04951
This is a small organization of management consultants, and its purpose is to promote the use of Total Quality Management principles in Italy.

AUSTRALIAN INSTITUTE OF MANAGEMENT (AIM)
215 Pacific Highway
North Sydney NSW 2060, Australia
Tel: 61 2 929: 7922
Fax: 61 2 922: 2210
While a traditional management development association with a large membership, it increasingly has been exposing its membership to quality-oriented management practices. It publishes *AIM News* and *Management Review.*

AUSTRALIAN ORGANIZATION FOR QUALITY
27 Palmerston Crescent
South Melbourne VIC 3205, Australia
Tel: 61 3 699: 4144
Fax: 61 3 696: 4510
This is the oldest and best recognized quality organization in Australia. It promotes quality practices through education programs and support services.

AUSTRALIAN QUALITY COUNCIL
P.O. Box 298
St. Leonards NSW 2065, Australia
Tel: 612: 439-8200
Fax: 612: 906-3286
This umbrella organization comprises the Enterprise Australia, Ltd., Australian Quality Awards Foundation, Total Quality Management Institute, and the Quality Society of Australia. It hosts seminars and courses on quality, does evaluation consulting, and publishes various resources including *The Quality Magazine* and the guidelines for the Australian Quality Awards.

BRITISH DEMING ASSOCIATION
2 Castle Street
Salisbury, Wiltshire SP1 1BB, United Kingdom
Tel: 44 72 241-2138
Fax: 44 72 233-1313
Its purpose is to promote Dr. Deming's view of quality practices. It has both individual and corporate members and holds an annual conference each April.

BRITISH QUALITY ASSOCIATION (BQA)
Vigilant Pass, 120 Walton Road
London SW1V 1JZ
United Kingdom
Tel: 44 71 931-0607
Fax: 44 71 233-7034
This large organization is the administrator of the British Quality Award. BQA promotes TQM principles, consults, holds seminars, training programs and seminars. It is one of the major European quality organizations.

BRITISH STANDARDS INSTITUTION (BSI)
2 Park Street
London W1A 2BS, Great Britain
Tel: 44 71 629-9000
Fax: 44 71 629-0506
The primary purpose of this organization is to administer the ISO 9000 certification process in the United Kingdom.

BUNDESVERBAND DEUTSCHER UNTERNEMENSBERATOR (BDU) EV
Friedrich Wilhelm Strasse 2
5300 Bonn 1, Germany
Tel: 49 22 823-8055
BDU is composed of institutional members, with a particular emphasis on management and recruiting consultants, and software companies.

CANADIAN NETWORK FOR TOTAL QUALITY
c/o Conference Board of Canada
255 Smyth Road
Ottawa, ON K1H 8M7, Canada
Tel: (613) 526-3280
Fax: (613) 526-4857
This is a newly established organization of quality associations. Like similar structures already in existence in the United States, it promotes coordinated activities to foster the use of total quality management practices.

CANADIAN SUPPLIER INSTITUTE
Skyline Complex
644 Dixon Rd.
Rexdale, Ontario M9W 1J4, Canada
Tel: (416) 235-1777
This organization has skills in the application of Taguchi techniques, quality function deployment, total quality management, and other productivity tools in the area of manufacturing and production. It has training programs, does some consulting, offers an assortment of books and videos, and hosts conferences.

CENELEC ELECTRONIC COMPONENTS COMMITTEE (CECC)
Gartenstrasse 179
6000 Frankfurt 70, Germany
Tel: 49 69 639-171
Fax: 49 69 639-427
It develops the European Standards (ENS) for electronic components and advises on ISO certification in Germany.

CENTER FOR QUALITY AND APPLIED STATISTICS (CQAS)
Rochester Institute of Technology
98 Lomb Memorial Drive
Rochester, NY 14623-5604 USA
Tel: (716) 475-6990
Fax: (716) 475-5959
It offers seminars on quality engineering, quality management and quality standards, applied mathematical statistics, quality and productivity, and custom training programs, using RIT professors who have practical experience. CQAS advises and consults in these areas around the world. It also offers a master's degree in applied and mathematical statistics.

CENTER FOR QUALITY MANAGEMENT
150 Cambridge Park Drive
Cambridge, MA 02140 USA
Tel: (617) 873-2152
Fax: (617) 873-2155
Members of CQM are corporations dedicated to TQM and the dessemination of information on its implementation. CQM sponsors seminars and conferences. It publishes *The CQM Voice*, a bimonthly member newsletter, and *The Center for Quality Management Journal*.

CENTER SATELLITE DEVELOPMENT—INDUSTRIAL COORDINATION CENTER (CSD)
No. 8 Tun-Hwa N Road, 7th Floor
Taipei, Taiwan ROC
Tel: 886 2 751-3468
Fax: 886 2 781-7790
CSD coordinates activities for 25 companies for the purpose of improving the quality of their operations and products. It also offers seminars, publishes on quality, and administers the National Quality Award. It also publishes *CSD Monthly Magazine*.

CENTRUM VOOR KWALITEITSZORG WEST-VLAANDEREN VZW.
Doorniksesteenweg
8500 Kortrijk, Belgium
Tel: 32 2 5620-4723
Fax: 32 2 5625-9684
This organization offers hundreds of courses on quality topics and publishes *Kwaliteit Nu*.

CHINESE MANAGEMENT ASSOCIATION
13th Floor, 4 Roosevelt Road, Section 1
Taipei 0757
Taiwan ROC
Tel: 886 2 396-5207
Fax: 886 2 396-9143
As part of its effort to promote quality management, it offers seminars, consulting, and conferences on the subject, and organizes teams to work on quality-related projects. It publishes *Journal of Management Science* and *CMA Newsletter*, and

administers a quality management award program.

COMMUNITY QUALITY COALITION
c/o Transformation of America Industry Project
Jackson Community College
2111 Emmons Road
Jackson, MI 49201 USA
Tel: (517) 789-1627
This organization promotes quality practices in Mississppi targeted largely at businesses.

CONFERENCE BOARD, INC.
P.O. Box 4026, Church Street Station
New York, NY 10261-4026 USA
Tel: (212) 759-0900
Fax: (212) 980-7014
This nationally recognized council of American businesses is best known for its research on business trends. It also hosts an annual quality conference covering various tools and techniques in the general management of business. It also publishes its research, some of which is related to quality practices.

COUNCIL FOR CONTINUOUS IMPROVEMENT
181 Metro Drive, Suite 500
San Jose, CA 95110 USA
Tel: (408) 283-1300
Fax: (408) 283-1302
CCI's mission is "to develop, document, share, and desseminate data, methodologies, and implementation systems that member organizations use to continually improve their products, services, and operational performance." There are over 160 organizations that are members of CCI. Publishes *The Connection*, a member newsletter.

DANISH SOCIETY FOR QUALITY CONTROL (DFK)
(Dansk Forening for Kvalitetsstyring)
P.O. Box 52
2950 Vedbaek, Denmark
Tel: 45 42 89 13 05
Fax: 45 42 89 08 12
Its purpose is to promote awareness and use of quality practices in Denmark. It holds from four to six conferences annually and administers the Danish Quality Award. It also published *Quality News.*

DANSK STANDARDISERINGSRAD (DS)
P.O. Box 77
Aurejojvej 12
2900 Hellerup, Denmark
This is the ISO 9000 standards association organization for Denmark.

DEUTSCHE GESSELLSCHAFT FUR PERSONALFUHRUNG MBH (DGP)
Niederkasseler Lohweg 16
4000 Dusseldorf 11, Germany
Tel: 49 2115-978
Fax: 49 2115-978 505
It focuses on helping personnel and education functions in German organizations through training programs, consulting, and seminars. It publishes *Personalfuhrung.*

DEUTSCHE GESELLSCHAFT FUR QUALITAT
August-Schanz Strasse 21A
P.O. Box 50 07 63
6000 Frankfurt am Main 50, Germany
Tel: 49 69 9541-240
Fax: 49 69 9542-4133
This is the major German society for quality, has both corporate and individual members, and provides quality programs nationally.

DEUTSCHES INSTITUT FUR NORMUNG (DIN)
Burggrafenstrasse 6
Postfach 1107
1000 Berlin 30, Germany
Tel: 49 30 26-011
Fax: 49 340 260-1231
This is Germany's national ISO member institution, responsible for the implementation of ISO 9000 certification programs in the country.

DIMENSION CLIENTELE
Quebec Customer Service Association
7339 rue Baldwin
Montreal, PQ H1K 3C9, Canada
Tel: (514) 353-4612
Fax: (514) 353-4612
This organization assists members improve customer services, concentrating on companies in

Quebec. It hosts conferences, an annual convention in May, and publishes *Client.*

EUROPEAN FOUNDATION FOR QUALITY MANAGEMENT (EFQM)
Avenue des Pleiades 19
B-1200 Brussels, Belgium
Tel: 32 3 775-3511
Fax: 32 2 779-1237
The EFQM supports the use of quality practices by Western European companies. Membership is by company. It manages the European Quality Award program, begun in 1992; hosts conferences and education programs; and publishes *Quality Link Newsletter.*

FEDERAL QUALITY INSTITUTE (FQI)
441 F Street, NW, Room 333
Washington, D.C. 20001 USA
Tel: (202) 376-3747 or 376-3753
Fax: (202) 376-3765
FQI is the most important U.S. government organization involved in fostering the use of quality practices. It is responsible for helping all U.S. government agencies implement start-up activities in the area of total quality management. It is a government-wide source for information on quality, using the FQI Information Network, which offers to agencies materials such as books, articles, videos, and case studies, all at no cost on-line. It publishes *Federal Quality News* and administers the QIP Award and the Presidential Quality Award.

FINNISH SOCIETY FOR QUALITY
(Suomen Laatuyhdistys ry)
Laaksolahdentie 11A
02731 Espoo, Finland
Tel: 358 0 597-348
Fax: 358 0 509-1807
It promotes all facets of quality applications in Finland, from TQM to quality assurance. It holds an annual conference in April and publishes *Laatuviesti.*

FOX VALLEY QUALITY/PRODUCTIVITY RESOURCE CENTER (Q/PRC)
Fox Valley Technical College
5 Systems Lane (Bordini Center)
P.O. Box 2277
Appleton, WI 54913-2277 USA
Tel: (414) 735-2277
Probably the best-known center for quality practices and education among all community colleges in North America, this is a center for quality education, consulting, and research. Its library on quality management practices is extensive. Its mission is to help local business and nonprofit organizations improve their quality practices through speakers, training, and library resources.

GERMAN ASSOCIATION FOR QUALITY CIRCLES (DQCG)
Am. Puttkamp 27
4000 Dusseldorf 12, Germany
Tel: 49 21 128-4969
Fax: 49 21 168-00168
This organization promotes the use of all kinds of quality practices, runs seminars and conferences for German companies, administers the German Quality Circle Award, and publishes *QC-intern.*

HELLENIC INSTITUTE OF QUALITY
Ipirou 6
104 33 Athens, Greece
Tel: 30 1 822 7430
Fax: 30 1 823 8301
This is a national Greek organization that promotes quality practices among Greek businesses.

HELLENIC MANAGEMENT ASSOCIATION
36, Amalias Avenue
105 58 Athens, Greece
Tel: 30 1 323-2792
Fax: 30 1 322-7048
This organization promotes quality practices, primarily through an extensive TQM education program. It hosts an annual conference in March and publishes *Manager* and *Marketing Review.*

HONG KONG QUALITY MANAGEMENT ASSOCIATION (HKQMA)
P.O. Box 90952
Tsimshatsui Post Office
Kowloon, Hong Kong
Fax: 852 719-3064
It promotes better management through seminars, conferences, and by managing ten specialist clubs. It offers quality certification programs, ad-

ministers the HKMA Quality Award and publishes *Hong Kong Manager.*

HONG KONG Q-MARK COUNCIL
Federation of HK Industries
4/F Hankow Centre
5-15 Hankow Rd., Tsimshatsui
Kowloon, Hong Kong
Tel: 852 723-0818
Fax: 852 721-3494
The Q-Mark Council, within the Federation of Hong Kong Industries, is a council of prominent business, government, and academic leaders. They offer ISO 9000 education, publications and courses, and manage The Hong Kong Q-Mark Quality Award.

HONG KONG QUALITY ASSURANCE AGENCY
1/F, HKPC Building
78 Tat Chee Avenue
Kowloon, Hong Kong
Tel: 852 788-5333
Fax: 852 788-5322
This government agency administers the local ISO 9000 certification process.

HONG KONG SOCIETY FOR QUALITY CONTROL
c/o Manufacturing Engineering Dept.
Hong Kong Polytechnic
Hong Kong, Kowloon
Hong Kong
Tel: 852 766-6591
Fax: 852 362-4741
This ASQC-affiliated society promotes awareness and use of quality practices by local businesses and government agencies. It offers a variety of educational opportunities for business and government, administers ASQC certification programs locally, and publishes a quarterly newsletter.

HUMAN RESOURCES DEVELOPMENT ASSOCIATION OF R.O.C.
No. 51 Chung-Ching S. Road, 17th Floor
Taipei, Taiwan ROC
Tel: 886 2 396-4605
Fax: 886 2 341-7971
This organization promotes quality practices in human resource management. It publishes *Human Resources Development Monthly.*

INSTITUTE FOR HEALTHCARE IMPROVEMENT
One Exeter Plaza, Ninth Floor
Boston, MA 02116 USA
Tel: (617) 424-1800
Fax: (617) 424-4848
The IHI is an independent nonprofit organization created to be a major force for integrative and collaborative efforts to improve health care systems in the United States and Canada. Offers courses and seminars in adopting quality methods to health care management, holds an annual national meeting, and publishes the *Quality Connection* newsletter quarterly.

INSTITUTE OF ADMINISTRATIVE MANAGEMENT (IAM)
40 Chatsworth Parada, Petts Wood
Orphington, Kent BR5 1RW, United Kingdom
Tel: 44 689 875-555
Fax: 44 689 870-891
This is one of the oldest professional associations in Europe; its members are administrative managers. It administers a certification program, offers courses, releases publications, and administers the ATQ Award.

INSTITUTE OF MANAGEMENT SPECIALISTS
58 Clarendon Avenue
Leamington Spa, Warswickshire CV32 4SA, United Kingdom
Tel: 44 71 401-7227
Fax: 44 71 401-2725
It focuses on training in the area of quality assurance, with particular emphasis on TQM, QA, and quality control. It consults on ISO and publishes books, magazines, and videos on quality.

INSTITUTE OF PERSONNEL MANAGEMENT, NEW ZEALAND, INC. (IPMNZ)
P.O. Box 34-620
Birkenhead, Auckland, New Zealand
Tel: 64 9 480-1349
Fax: 64 9 480-0423
This is a personnel management support organization that, in particular, promotes the use of

TQM principles in personnel practices. It hosts a national conference in September and publishes *IPM News.*

INSTITUTE OF QUALITY ASSURANCE
P.O. Box 712
61 Southwark Street
London, SE1 1SB, Great Britain
Tel: 44 071 401-7227
Fax: 44 071 401-2725
One of the oldest quality organizations (founded 1919), it certifies various grades of quality practitioners in a variety of subject areas and provides education on a broad range of quality-related topics. It publishes the monthly *Quality News* and quarterly the *Quality Forum.* It also has a bookstore and training center located at 10 Grosvenor Gardens, London SW1W ODQ.

INSTITUTO PORTUGUES DE QUALIDAD (IPQ)
Rua Jose Estevao, 83A
1199 Lisbon Codex, Portugal
Tel: 351 1 523-978
Fax: 351 1 530-033
IPQ is part of the Ministry of Industry and Energy, and is responsible for implementing national quality programs. It hosts an annual conference in May and publishes *Qualirama* and *Opcao Q.*

INTERNATIONAL ACADEMY FOR QUALITY (IAQ)
P.O. Box 50 07 63
50 Frankfurt am Main W6, Germany
Tel: 49 69 548-0010
Fax: 49 69 548-00133
To be a member, one must be sponsored by three or more scholars operating on at least two continents. Members encourage international understanding of quality issues, promoting research on the philosophy and practice of quality. It also administers the IAQ Award.

INTERNATIONAL ASSOCIATION FOR CONTINUOUS EDUCATION AND TRAINING (IACET)
1101 Connecticut Avenue, NW, No. 700
Washington, D.C. 20036 USA
Its purpose is to provide help in the development and implementation of continuous training programs.

ITALIAN ASSOCIATION FOR QUALITY (AICQ)
Piazza A. Diaz 2
20121 Milan, Italy
Tel: 39 2 720-03460
Fax: 39 2 720-23085
The Associazione per le Qualita promotes the use of quality practices in Italy, its members are corporate enterprises, and it publishes *Qualita.*

JAPAN MANAGEMENT ASSOCIATION (JMA)
Nihon-Nohritsu Kyokai Building
3-1-22 Shiba-koen, Minato-ku
Tokyo 105, Japan
Tel: 81 3 3434-6211
Fax: 81 3 3434-1087
JMA offers courses, seminars, and conferences on all aspects of business; conducts trade shows,and international visits; publishes extensively on all manner of management topics; publishes *JMA Management News, JMA Journal,* and *Human Resource Development;* and administers awards of excellence. Membership consists of over 2,500 corporations.

JAPANESE STANDARDS ASSOCIATION (JSA)
1-24 Akasaka 4-chome
Minato-ku
Tokyo 107, Japan
Tel: 81 3 3583-8008
Fax: 81 3 3583-0698
JSA promotes standardization on quality issues and offers education, all as an organization under the control of the Ministry of International Trade & Industry. It also manages many of the ISO functions in Japan, sponsors a national conference in May, publishes *Standardization & Quality Control* and *Standardization Journal,* and administers the JSA Excellent Standardization Document Award.

JOINT ACCREDITATION SYSTEM OF AUSTRALIA AND NEW ZEALAND
JAS-ANZ Secretariat
P.O. Box 164
Civic Square ACT 2608, Australia

Tel: 61 6 276-1999
Fax: 61 6 276-2117
Formed in 1991, this organization has the mission of developing a unified quality accreditation process for both Australia and New Zealand, while strengthening trade bonds.

JUSE—UNION OF JAPANESE SCIENTISTS AND ENGINEERS
5-10-11, Sendagaya, Shibuya-ku
Tokyo, 151 Japan
Tel: 81 3 352-2231
Fax: 81 3 356-1798
This organization is best known as the administrators of the Deming Prize, Japan's highest quality award. It is Japan's leading quality organization and provides training, hosts symposia, consults, maintains a library and publishes a variety of magazines and journals, including the monthly *Total Quality Control* and *Engineers,* and every two months, *Societas Qualitatis,* which describes activities of JUSE.

KOREAN SOCIETY FOR QUALITY CONTROL
5-2 Soonhwa-dong, Chung-ku
Seoul, South Korea
Conducts research on quality practices, offers educational programs, publishes and distributes materials on quality, and provides channels of communication between local businesses and academia.

KOREAN STANDARDS ASSOCIATION (KSA)
5-2 Soonhwa-dong, Chung-ku
Seoul 100-130, South Korea
Tel: 82 2 772-3417
Fax: 82 2 754-0346
This is the national industrial standardization organization for South Korea. It offers a full compliment of courses and seminars, along with consulting, to organizations seeking quality certifications. It hosts a national conference held in either October or November each year, and publishes *Quality and Management, Standardization,* and *Factory Management.*

MADISON AREA QUALITY IMPROVEMENT NETWORK (MAQIN)
2909 Landmark Place, Suite 201
Madison, WI 53713 USA
Tel: (608) 277-7800
Fax: (608) 277-7810
This very active quality organization is best known for hosting the annual Hunter Conference on Quality, beginning in 1988. Usually held in June, it runs several days, covers all aspects of quality implementation programs, (both in the private and public sector), and is considered one of the more important national quality conferences. Local seminars are also held throughout the year.

MICHIGAN STATE UNIVERSITY INSTITUTE FOR QUALITY AND PRODUCTIVITY
Michigan State University
7 Olds Hall
East Lansing, MI 488824-1047 USA
Tel: (517) 353-0796 or (800) 356-5705
Fax: (517) 353-0796
Typical of many such organizations available in the United States, it offers educational programs in services, business administration, and quality.

MILWAUKEE FIRST IN QUALITY
Metropolitan Milwaukee Association of Commerce
756 North Milwaukee Street
Milwaukee, WI 53202 USA
Tel: (414) 287-4100
This is one of the largest and most active local quality organizations in the United States. It offers a variety of quality skill-building seminars and hosts a major annual convention in the area of quality. Particular focus has been in the area of implementing quality in manufacturing environments, although its offerings are expanding into the service sector.

MINNESOTA COUNCIL FOR QUALITY (MCQ)
2850 Metro Drive, Suite 300
Bloomington, MN 55425 USA
Tel: (612) 851-3181
Fax: (612) 851-3183
This is a very active state council that promotes quality in Minnesota through conferences, seminars, other educational programs and administers the Minnesota Quality Award and the Quality Service Award; it is a model regional quality council.

MOUVEMENT FRANÇIS POUR LA QUALITÉ (MFQ)
5, esplanade Charles de Gaulle
92733 Nanterre Cedex, France
Tel: 33 1 47 29 09 29
Fax: 33 1 47 25 32 21
This is an important French quality association with the mission of promoting exchange and application of information on quality practices by French organizations and companies. It offers training and conferences, runs regional quality circles, administers the Prix Nationale de la Qualité, and publishes *Qualité en Mouvement* and *Regard sur la Qualité.*

NATIONAL ASSOCIATION OF SERVICE MANAGERS (NASM)
1030 West Higgins Road, No. 206
Hoffman Estates, IL 60195 USA
Tel: (708) 310-9930
Fax: (708) 310-9934
This is the oldest association of product service managers in North America. It promotes service quality by businesses, improved practices by service industry organizations, and provides educational programs. It hosts an annual conference in September and publishes *Service Management.*

NATIONAL EDUCATIONAL QUALITY INITIATIVE
P.O. Box 13
Cedarburg, WI 53012 USA
Tel: (414) 229-6259
Fax: (414) 229-6957
This organization exists to promote the adoption of quality principles into all courses taken from preschool through graduate school and continuing education; to incorporate quality principles into all aspects of administration of schools and colleges; and to use quality principles to improve teaching of all subjects at all levels. Sponsors regional and national conferences on quality management in education.

NATIONAL INSTITUTE OF STANDARDS AND TECHNOLOGY
Rt. 270 and Quince Orchard Road
Administration Bldg, Room A537
Gaithersburg, MD 20899 USA
Tel: (301) 975-2036
Fax: (301) 948-3716
This organization, along with the ASQC, manages the Malcolm Baldrige National Quality Award. It is responsible for defining the criteria and point values for the award and also for the judging process.

NATIONAL PRODUCTIVITY BOARD
2 Bukit Merah Central
NPB Building
0315 Singapore
Tel: 65 278-6666 or 279-3721
Fax: 65 278-6665
NPB is part of the Ministry of Trade and Industry with the purpose of creating an outstanding workforce, focusing on quality and productivity in the workplace and in life. Provides training, management guidance, measures of productivity and quality, and publishes *Productivity Digest.*

NATIONAL QUALITY INFORMATION CENTRE
P.O. Box 712
61 Southwark Street
London SE1 1SB, Great Britain
Tel: 44 71 401-7227
Fax: 44 71 401-2725
This very large British quality organization promotes the use of quality assurance practices in British industry through education programs, consulting, publications, and research done jointly with universities. It publishes *Quality News* and the *Quality Forum.*

NATIONAL SOCIETY FOR PERFORMANCE AND INSTRUCTION (NSPI)
1300 L Street, NW, Suite 1250
Washington, D.C. 20005 USA
Tel: (202) 408-7969
Fax: (202) 408-7972
This is a large organization, with members from many countries, dedicated to improving productivity and effectiveness in the workplace. Over 600 chapters meet monthly where one of the more important topics is the science of performance technology, an organized process for solving problems concerning performance. It holds an annual conference in April and publishes *Performance & Instruction* and *Performance Improvement Quarterly.*

NATIONAL SOCIETY FOR QUALITY THROUGH TEAMWORK (NQST)
2 Castle Street
Salisbury SP1 1BB, Great Britain
Tel: 44 722 326-667
Fax: 44 722 331-313
This organization promotes the application of quality principles with particular emphasis on teamwork strategies. It hosts regional member meetings, training programs, annual conferences, and publishes *Executives Brief* and *TeamTalk*. It also administers the Annual Team Excellence Award, Michelin Award, and the Perkins Award.

NEDERLANDS NORMALISATIE-INSTITUT (NNI)
Kalfjeslaan 2
Postbus 5059
2600 GB Delft, Netherlands
Tel: 31 15 690-390
Fax: 31 15 690-190
This is the Netherlands' standardization institute, responsible for promoting the certification of companies by such international standards as ISO; it offers training in industrial quality standards.

NEW ZEALAND ORGANIZATION FOR QUALITY (NZOQ)
P.O. Box 622
Palmerston North, New Zealand
Tel: 64 6 3569 -099
Fax: 64 6 350-5604
This organization is the major quality organization for New Zealand, promoting quality practices as a means of improving New Zealand's competitive posture in the world economy. It hosts a national conference in May, and publishes *Quality New Zealand, Q-NewZ*, and *Software Q-NewZ.*

NORGES STANDARDISERINGSFORBUND (NSF)
P.O. Box 7020
Homansbyen
0306 Oslo 3, Norway
Tel: 47 2 466-094
Fax: 47 2 464-457
This is the national ISO 9000 association member for Norway.

NORWEGIAN SOCIETY FOR QUALITY
Brynsveien 96
1352 Kolsas, Norway
Tel: 47 2 137-775
Fax: 47 2 133-518
This is Norway's primary national quality organization, supporting the quality efforts of businesses within the nation; it administers the Norwegian Quality Award.

PENN STATE MANAGEMENT DEVELOPMENT PROGRAMS AND SERVICES
2790 West College Avenue
University Park, PA 16801-2605 USA
Tel: (814) 865-6341
Fax: (814) 865-7837
Created in 1915 to provide education programs to assist state industries, the bulk of its current programs focus on a broad range of TQM topics for business managers and are delivered around the state. It also offers quality diagnostic services to assess the effectivness of organizations.

PHILADELPHIA AREA COUNCIL FOR EXCELLENCE (PACE)
1234 Narket Street, Suite 1800
Philadelphia, PA 19107-3718 USA
Tel: (215) 972-3977
Fax: (215) 972-3900
PACE promotes the application of Total Quality Management and Deming approaches. It offer educational programs and hosts a four-day Deming seminar. PACE distributes publications on quality and administers the Pennsylvania State Quality Award.

QCI INTERNATIONAL
1350 Vista Way
Red Bluff, CA 96080 USA
Tel: (916) 527-8875
Fax: (916) 527-6983
QCI fosters employee involvement, application of total quality management, and statistical process control techniques. It offers seminars, in-house training, books, and videos for sale, and publishes a monthly magazine called *Quality Digest.*

QUALITY & PRODUCTIVITY MANAGEMENT ASSOCIATION (QPMA)
300 North Martingale Road, No. 230
Schaumburg, IL 60173 USA

Tel: (708) 619-2909
Fax: (708) 619-3383
This network of business professionals focuses on continuous improvement strategies that can be applied in the workplace. It conducts educational programs and workshops, distributes publications, and administers the Annual QPMA Leadership Award.

QUALITY COUNCIL OF ALBERTA
c/o Industry Development Board
Alberta Economic Development & Trade
10th Floor, Sterling Place
9940-106th Street
Edmonton, AB T5K 2P6, Canada
Tel: (403) 427-2005
Fax: (403) 427-5924
This is a newly established organization with the purpose of providing regional support for the application of quality practices in the Alberta region.

QUALITY MANAGEMENT INSTITUTE
5-2 Soonhwa-dong, Chung-ku
Seoul, South Korea
Performs research on successful quality improvement projects, and promotes uses of quality practices. Collects information on worldwide quality activities and serves as an information clearinghouse.

QUALITY SOCIETY OF AUSTRALIA (QSA)
P.O. Box 298
St. Leonards NSW 2096, Australia
Tel: 61 2 906-5788
Fax: 61 2 901-4677
This newly established organization offers networking and recognition of quality activities for its members. It is beginning to offer information on quality practices as well.

SINGAPORE QUALITY INSTITUTE (SQI)
Blk. 18, Ngee Ann Polytechnic
No. 03-08 Clementi Road
2159 Singapore
Tel: 65 467-4225
Fax: 65 467-4226
Like the American ASQC, it promotes quality practices, particularly in business, through seminars, conferences, and publications; it is a clearinghouse for local information on quality. It publishes *QC Focus* and the *SQI Yearbook*.

SIS QUALITY FORUM
Box 3295
103 66 Stockholm, Sweden
Tel: 46 8 613-5320
Fax: 46 8 241-331
It promotes quality practices and, in particular, those of the ISO 9000 standards. It publishes *Nytt om Niotusen*.

STANDARDISERINGKOMMISSIONEN I SVERIGE (SIS)
Box 3295
103 66 Stockholm, Sweden
Tel: 46 8 613-52000
Fax: 46 8 117-035
This is Sweden's national standards organization. Its certification programs are based on ISO 9000, supports training efforts, and publishes the *SIS Quality Forum Newsletter*.

STANDARDS ASSOCIATION OF NEW ZEALAND
181-187 Victoria Street
Private Bag
Wellington, New Zealand
Tel: 64 4 384-2108
Fax: 64 4 384-3938
This is the national standards body for New Zealand with responsibility for promoting quality standards, product certification (S Mark award), and for accreditation under the ISO 9000 banner.

STANDARDS AUSTRALIA
(Standards Association of Australia)
P.O. Box 1055
Strathfield NSW 2135, Australia
Tel: 61 02 746-4700
Fax: 60 02 746-8450
This is Australia's major supplier of independent quality systems accreditation and product certification services. Certification includes AS3900/ISO 9000, and local and regional certifications. It also offers a variety of courses on implementing quality programs.

STANDARDS COUNCIL OF CANADA
45 O'Connor Street, Suite 1200
Ottawa, ON K1P 6N7, Canada

Tel: (613) 238-3222
Fax: (613) 995-4564
This organization acredits quality certification associations and companies. It coordinates the activities of Canada's ISO Technical Committee responsible for ISO certification activities.

SUOMEN STANDARDISOIMISLIITTO (SFS)
P.O. Box 205
00121 Helsinki, Finland
This is Finland's national ISO member association and is responsible for promoting ISO standards within the country.

SWEDISH INSTITUTE FOR QUALITY (SIQ)
Box 5178
Gardatorget 1
402 26 Goteborg, Sweden
Tel: 46 31 773-0875
Fax: 46 31 773-0645
SIQ promotes the study and application of quality principles in business and in other organizations. It does teaching, research, and development, and is the administrator of the Swedish National Quality Award.

TMI FINLAND
Heikkilantie 6
00210 Helsinki, Finland
Tel: 358 0 692-7788
Fax: 358 0 692-7388
This is an association devoted to training and development of human resources, relying on continuous improvement strategies. It also has affiliations and operations in most other European countries. TMI is a defined human improvement process.

TOTAL QUALITY MANAGEMENT INSTITUTE
1st Floor (Fernz Corp)
81 Carlton Gore Road
Box 90-455, Auckland, New Zealand
Tel: 64 9 302-0062
Fax: 64 9 307-3831
Membership is targeted at senior management in the belief that all quality efforts must begin with them. The Institute offers education on TQM, forums, distribution of papers on TQM, and attendance at national conferences. Through the NZ National Quality Awards Foundation, it administers the NZ National Quality Awards, patterned after the Baldrige Award and to which government agencies can also apply.

U-MAN FINLAND OY
Tuusuutarintie 3
00620 Helsinki, Finland
Tel: 358 0 799-266
Fax: 358 0 757-3564
This organization promotes the application of total quality management principles in human resources.

UNI—ENTE NAZIONALE ITALIANO DI UNIFICAZIONE
Via Battistotti Sassi 11
20133 Milan, Italy
Tel: 39 2 700-241
Fax: 39 2 701-06106
UNI establishes and promotes the use of technical standards by Italian manufacturing companies and is associated with ISO. This seventy-two-year-old organization publishes *U&C* and *UNI Notizie.*

UNIVERSITY CONSORTIUM IN QUALITY ENGINEERING
Piazza del Pozzetto 9
56127 Pisa, Italy
This is a recently established group for the purpose of promoting research, teaching and application of quality practices in Italian economic and social actions; members are university and industrial representatives.

WAUKESHA AREA QUALITY/PRODUCTIVITY NETWORK
Waukesha County Technical College
800 Main Street
Pewaukee, WI 53072 USA
Tel: (414) 691-5543
This is an organization of local companies who meet to share experiences in quality practices. It serves as a resource center and organizes local presentations, tours, training, roundtables, and study groups in the Waukesha, Wisconsin, area.

WORK IN AMERICA INSTITUTE
700 White Plains Road
Scarsdale, NY 10583 USA
Tel: (914) 472-9600
Fax: (914) 472-9606

Like other quality associations, it conducts research and member advisory services on productivity (with a special emphasis on employee involvement) and has expertise on labor-management relations and working conditions. It conducts forums, seminars, and site visits; studies company policies; publishes a newsletter called *WORK IN AMERICA;* maintains a library; does research on demand; issues a variety of publications; and has a speaker's bureau and a list of quality consultants.

Directory of Magazines and Journals

This section includes a comprehensive (though not exhaustive) listing of publications that regularly cover issues on quality. Some of them are dedicated to quality issues, and some of them cover quality as part of their regular editorial policy. Many quality organizations, such as the American Society for Quality Control, and others include a variety of newsletters of interest to members, depending on area of specialization. Most local quality organizations also publish their own newsletters. Those publications are not listed here as they are available only to members. You can find out more about these organizations in the state awards section and the quality organizations section of *The Quality Yearbook.*

We have organized this listing into three categories:

1. Magazines, journals, and newsletters dedicated to quality
2. General business magazines, journals, and newsletters that often include articles on quality
3. Industry and special interest magazines, journals, and newsletters that often cover quality issues

All magazines, journals, and newsletters included have something of value to anyone interested in TQM, depending on background and specialty. However, to help you sort through these in terms of their value in learning about and implementing quality, we have developed the following ratings:

★★★ = Highest recommendation, regularly includes very useful information on quality management
★★ = Highly recommended, frequently includes useful articles
★ = Recommended, includes some useful articles

Note: In establishing these ratings, they do not apply to the overall "quality" of the magazines, but to their coverage of quality management topics.

Magazines, Journals, and Newsletters Dedicated to Quality

Healthcare Quality Abstracts

Published monthly except July by COR Healthcare Resources, P.O. Box 40959, Santa Barbara, CA 93140, phone: (805) 564–2177, fax: (805) 564–2146.

Subscriptions: U.S. and Canada: 1 year $98; all other countries: 1 year $110.

This is just what it says it is—a newsletter format abstracting of current articles from a variety of journals all dealing with quality management in health care. The listing is broken up by topic, and the sources for all articles are listed on the back page with addresses and phone numbers of publishers. Rating: ★★

Joint Commission Journal of Quality Improvement

Published monthly under the editorial direction of the Joint Commission by Mosby–Year Book, Inc., 11830 Westline Industrial Drive, St. Louis, MO 63146–3318, (314) 453–4351 or (800) 453–4351.

Subscriptions: $115 per year for U.S., all other countries, $125 per year.

This journal replaced the former journal published by The Joint Commission, the *Quality Review Bulletin*. The goal of this refereed journal is to publish articles that emphasize the improvement of health care quality, which includes the measurement, assessment, and/or improvement of performance in health care quality and delivery. The journal includes how-to articles and case studies. Rating: ★★★

Journal for Quality and Participation

Published seven times a year (January/February, March, June, July/August, September, October/November, and December) by the Association for Quality and Participation, 801-B West 8th Street, Suite 501, Cincinnati, OH 45203, (513) 381-1959.

Subscriptions: Available as part of membership in AQP. Nonmembers: $52 per year in the United States and $75 for international orders.

Includes a variety of practical, detailed articles on implementing quality in different industries and organizations. Articles are nearly always intriguing, useful, and well-written. One of the best magazines available on quality for managers. Rating: ★★★

Journal of Quality Technology

Published quarterly by the American Society for Quality Control, 611 East Wisconsin Avenue, P.O. Box 3005, Milwaukee, WI 53201-3005, (414) 272-8575.

Subscriptions: For ASQC members, annual subscription is $20 in the United States, $38.50 in Canada, and $36 for other international; for nonmembers, $30 annually in the United States, $40 for other international subscriptions.

A technically oriented journal, with heavy use of statistics, emphasizing the practical applicability of new techniques, instructive examples of the operation of existing techniques, and results of historical researches. Useful only to those involved in quality control technology. Rating: ★★

National Productivity Review

Published quarterly by John Wiley & Sons, Inc., 605 Third Avenue, New York, NY 10158, (212) 850-6479.

Subscriptions: United States, Canada and Mexico, 1 year $175; other countries, 1 year $225. Discounts available on multiple copy subscriptions.

A journal that includes practical articles focusing on the implementation of quality in all types of organizations. Divided into three sections: Ideas and Opinions, Features, and Reviews. Rating: ★★★

PI Quality

Published bimonthly by Hitchcock Publishing Co., 191 Gary Avenue, Carol Stream, IL 60188–2292, phone: (708) 665–1000, fax: (708) 462–2225.

Subscriptions: Free to qualified individuals in process industries, or $40 per year in the U.S. and $100 per year for all other countries.

Because it is aimed at qualified circulation, this magazine includes a variety of articles dealing with the use of various technology in the process industries (which include food, beverages, chemicals, pharmaceuticals, soaps, textiles, papers, petroleum, rubber, plastics, stone, clay, glass, leather, and primary metal processing). Articles tend to be short and technology oriented. Rating: ★

Quality

Published monthly by Hitchcock Publishing Company, One Chilton Way, Radnor, PA 19089.

Subscriptions: United States, 1 year $70. Canada and Mexico, 1 year $85. International, 1 year $160.

Includes articles that focus mainly on the technical aspects of implementing total quality management in production and manufacturing environments. Includes reviews and event calendar. Especially of interest to engineers and quality technicians. Rating: ★★★

Quality Digest

Published monthly by QCI International, 1350 Vista Way, P.O. Box 882, Red Bluff, CA 96080, phone (800) 527-8875 or (916) 527-8875, fax: (916) 527-6983.

Subscriptions: 1 year $49, 2 years $78, 3 years $107; $69 for international orders.

Includes a variety of how-to articles and pieces on how various organizations implement quality, especially in people management. Also includes monthly columnists such as Tom Peters, Karl Albrecht, and Ken Blanchard, plus book reviews and other information.
Rating: ★★★

Quality Engineering

Published quarterly by the American Society for Quality Control and Marcel Dekker, Inc. Subscriptions available through Marcel Dekker Journals, P.O. Box 5017, Monticello, NY 12701-5176.

Subscriptions: 1 year $35; add $14 for surface mail and $22 for airmail to Europe and $26 for airmail to Asia.

Dedicated to quality management articles that deal with this message: "What the problem was, how we solved it, and what the results were." Articles tend to be detailed and moderately technical, but quite relevant to quality professionals. Rating: ★

Quality and Reliability Engineering

Published bimonthly by John Wiley & Sons Ltd., Baffins Lane, Chichester, Sussex PO19 1UD, England.

Subscriptions: 1 year $495.

A technical journal with articles designed to fill the gap between theoretical methods and scientific research on one hand and current industrial practices on the other. Highly specialized and mathematical. Recommended only for corporate or university libraries for use by engineers in this area. Rating: ★★

Quality Management in Health Care

Published quarterly by Aspen Publishers Inc, 7201 McKinney Circle, Frederick, MD 21701, (800) 638–8437.

Subscriptions: $134 per year in the U.S. and Canada. For international subscriptions, contact: Swets Publishing Service, P.O. Box 825, 2160 SZ Lisse, The Netherlands.

This is a refereed journal with the purpose of providing a forum to explore the theoretical, technical, and strategic elements of quality management, and to assist those who wish to implement TQM in health care. Articles tend to be practical, somewhat technical, and oriented toward specific tasks in health care management. Rating: ★★

Quality in Manufacturing

Published bimonthly by Huebcore Communications, Inc., 29100 Aurora Road, Suite 200, (216) 248-1125.

Subscriptions: 1 year $75; Canada and Mexico 1 year $95; international 1 year $155. Available free to qualified people in manufacturing (call for sample copy).

A closed circulation large format four-color magazine devoted to reviews and articles about quality technology in manufacturing. Rating: ★

Quality Management Journal

Published quarterly by the American Society for Quality Control, 611 East Wisconsin Avenue, P.O. Box 3005, Milwaukee, WI 53201-3005, (414) 272-8575.

Subscriptions: Available to members of ASQC in the United States at $50 annually, to nonmembers at $60; Canada: $74 to members and $84 to nonmembers; international: $74 to members and $84 to nonmembers.

A peer-reviewed journal designed to present academic research on quality management in a style that makes it accessible to managers in all fields. Rating: ★★★

Quality Progress

Published monthly by the American Society for Quality Control, Inc., 611 East Wisconsin Avenue, P.O. Box 3005, Milwaukee, WI 53201-3005, (414) 272-8575.

Subscriptions: Available as part of membership in the ASQC. $50 per year for nonmembers in the United States and $85 for first class to Canada and international airmail.

This is the foremost magazine on quality management available. It includes a wide variety of general and technical articles plus event calendars, reviews, and many other features. Rating: ★★★

Target

Published bimonthly by the Association for Manufacturing Excellence, 380 West Palatine Road, Wheeling, IL 60090, (708) 520-3282.

Subscriptions: Available to members of AME as part of membership. Cost of annual membership: $125.

Includes many practical articles on how various industries and companies are implementing TQM in manufacturing and management. Also includes reports from regional chapters, book reviews, and event calendar. Practical, accessible, and well-done. Rating: ★★★

The Center for Quality Management Journal

Published quarterly by the Center for Quality Management, 70 Fawcett Street, MS 15/4B, Cambridge, MA 02138, (617) 873-2152.

Subscriptions: $70 per year.

This is a new journal, started in 1992, and it includes a selection of practical articles focusing on the implementation of TQM in different organizations. Rating: ★

The Quality Observer

Published monthly by The Quality Observer Corporation, 3505 Old Lee Highway, P.O. Box 1111, Fairfax, VA 22030, (703) 691-9295.

Subscriptions: 1 year $53, 2 years $90, and 3 years $130; overseas, 1 year $68, 2 years $120, and 3 years $175; libraries, 1 year $90 (2 copies each issues sent to same address); corporations, 1 year $180 (5 copies each issue sent to same address).

Billed as the "International News Magazine of Quality," this is a three-color tabloid-sized publication, with case studies, international news, interviews, and regular columns on quality topics. Rating: ★★

Strategies for Healthcare Excellence

Published monthly by COR Research Inc., P.O. Box 40959, Santa Barbara, CA 93140–0959, (805) 564–2177.

Subscriptions: U.S. and Canada: 1 year $197; all other countries: 1 year $210.

This is a 12-page, two-color newsletter that includes detailed case studies on how specific health care facilities and managers are implementing quality principles in their organizations. Each issue usually includes one long piece followed by other short articles on this subject. Rating: ★★

The Total Quality Review

Published bimonthly by Cambridge Strategy Publications, P.O. Box 26007, Alexandria, VA 22313–6007.

Subscriptions: Introductory subscription in the U.S. available at $135 (regular rate: $165) per year; international: introductory subscription $165 (regular rate: $195) per year.

Organized around differing themes each month, it includes a variety of how-to articles, case studies, and background pieces for understanding the implementation of TQM. Also includes regular news from the Council for Continuous Improvement. Rating: ★★

Total Quality Environmental *Manager*

Published quarterly by John Wiley & Sons, Inc., 605 Third Avenue, New York, NY 10158, (212) 850–6479.

Subscriptions: U.S., Canada, Mexico 1 year $159; other countries 1 year $209.

While aimed at managers and, to some degree, engineers in the environmental area, its articles are practical and cover a broad spectrum in the application of TQM principles to this field. Worth having in the library of any company interested in this field. Rating: ★★★

Total Quality in Hospitality

Published monthly by Magna Publications Inc., 2718 Dryden Drive, Madison, WI 53704-3086, (608) 246-3580 or (800) 433-0499.

Subscriptions: $198 per year, with additional subscriptions to the same organization available at a discount.

A monthly eight-page two-color newsletter covering specific ideas for implementing quality, case studies, and company profiles for the hospitality industry. Rating: ★★

Total Quality Management

Published three times a year by Carfax Publishing Company, P.O. Box 25, Abington, Oxfordshire OX14 3UE, United Kingdom or P.O. Box 2025, Dunnellon, FL 32630.

Subscriptions: Information available by writing to either of these addresses.

An academic journal with a practical bent, it includes articles of practical interest to managers and academics. It covers all aspects of quality management. Rating: ★★

Total Quality Newsletter

Published monthly by Lakewood Publications, 50 Ninth Street, Minneapolis, MN 55402, (800) 328-4329.

Subscriptions: Available at $128 per year; add $10 for Canada and $20 for other international locations.

An eight-page two-color newsletter covering one major topic per issue plus reviews of training materials and short practical articles on what various companies are doing in quality. Rating: ★★

TQM in Higher Education

Published monthly by Magna Publications Inc., 2718 Dryden Drive, Madison, WI 53704-3086, (608) 246-3580 or (800) 433-0499.

Subscriptions: $129 per year with discounts available for additional subscriptions to the same location.

A monthly eight-page, two-color newsletter covering ideas on applying TQM principles, case studies, information on TQM tools, and other practical articles on quality management in colleges and universities. Rating: ★★

General Business Magazines, Journals, and Newsletters That Include Coverage of Quality

Across the Board

Published ten times annually (January/February and July/August combined issues) by The Conference Board, Inc., 845 Third Avenue, New York, NY 10022, (212) 759-0900.

Subscriptions: $20 annually for Conference Board Associates and $40 annually for nonassociates.

A thoughtfully edited magazine on issues of interest to all managers. Includes columns, commentaries, how-to and company profiles, and issue-related articles. Articles occasionally directly related to quality, but nearly all are indirectly related. Rating: ★★★

Business Ethics

Published bimonthly by Mavis Publications, Inc., 52 South 10th Street, #110, Minneapolis, MN 55403-4700, (612) 962-4700.

Subscriptions: $49 per year in the United States and $59 for international subscriptions; available to first-time subscribers for $29.

Includes articles on topics of ethical and social concern to business, all of which are arguably related to quality in one way or another. Occasionally includes articles specifically on quality management and its implementation in socially responsible organizations.
Rating: ★★

Business Horizons

Published bimonthly by JAI Press, Inc., 55 Old Post Road, No. 2, P.O. Box 1678, Greenwich, CT 06836-1678, (203) 661-7602.

Subscriptions: $60 per year in the United States; outside the United States add $20 for surface mail and $30 for airmail.

Published out of the Indiana University Graduate School of Business, there is a diversity of articles of interest to managers, often shorter than found in the *Harvard Business Review*. Rating: ★ (because it only occasionally includes articles on quality)

Business Week

Published weekly by McGraw-Hill, Inc., 1221 Avenue of the Americas, New York, NY 10020, (212) 512-2000.

Subscriptions: Official subscription rate: 1 year $44.95, 2 years $74.95, and 3 years $99.95. Widely available at discounted subscription rates.

The leading business newsweekly in the United States. Gives special attention to quality in one or two issues per year and includes articles on quality management as appropriate during the year. Rating: ★★

California Management Review

Published quarterly by the University of California, Walter A. Haas School of Business, 350 Barrows Hall, University of California, Berkeley, CA 94720, (510) 642-7159.

Subscriptions: 1 year $45, 2 years $80, and 3 years $115; international subscriptions 1 year $68, 2 years $126, and 3 years $184.

A serious journal, but with a practical orientation, often including in-depth articles on quality management theory and implementation. Rating: ★★

Fortune

Published biweekly by Time Warner, Inc., Time & Life Building, Rockefeller Center, New York, NY 10020, (800) 621-8000.

Subscriptions: Official subscription rate: $52.95 1 year, United States and $53.75 1 year, Canada. Widely available at discounted subscription rates.

Provides in-depth reviews of management and other business topics and profiles of executives. Articles do not often focus on quality per se, but they are useful as benchmarks for understanding quality management practices in relation to traditional perspectives on managing. Rating: ★★

Harvard Business Review

Published bimonthly by the Harvard Business School, Boston, MA 02163, (617) 495-6800.

Subscriptions: $75 per year, United States, $95 per year in Canada and Mexico, and $145 in all other countries.

Includes in-depth articles on management techniques in all functional areas by highly regarded researchers and executives. Often includes articles of direct or indirect relevance to those interested in quality. Rating: ★★★

Inc.

Published monthly by *Inc.*, 38 Commercial Wharf, Boston, MA 02110, (617) 248-8000 or (800) 234-0999 for subscription information.

Subscriptions: Available at various rates, often discounted. Currently being offered at $19 for 1 year or $38 for 3 years.

The premier magazine covering issues of interest to small- and medium-sized businesses. Loaded with practical how-to techniques and articles and company and executive profiles. Often covers issues directly related to quality management issues, though it only occasionally uses the word quality to describe this approach. Rating: ★★

Industry Week

Published biweekly by Penton Publishing Company, 1100 Superior Avenue, Cleveland, OH 44114-2543, (216) 696-7000.

Subscriptions: Distributed as a closed circulation magazine to qualified executives in administration, finance, production, engineering, purchasing, marketing, and sales. To those who do not qualify, it is available by subscription at $60 per year or $100 for two years; Canada $90 per year or $150 for two years; international $110 per year or $195 for two years.

Includes articles, columns, and reviews of timely interest to managers on a wide range of business and management topics, with frequent articles on quality management.
Rating: ★★★

Journal of Business Strategy

Published bimonthly by Faulkner Group, Inc., 11 Penn Plaza, New York, NY 10001, (212) 967-7000.

Subscriptions: $98 per year in the United States and Canada and $128 per year in all other countries.

Each edition includes a Special Focus section that provides an in-depth look at one topic of interest in strategic planning and thinking, plus additional articles, columns, and features. Often covers topics on quality management.
Rating: ★★

Management Review

Published monthly by the American Management Association Publications Division, Box 408, Saranac, NY 12983-0408.

Subscriptions: $45 per year in the United States; non-U.S. subscriptions $60 per year.

The official magazine of the American Management Association, it includes a variety of articles of interest to managers and often includes items on quality issues. Rating: ★★

Nation's Business

Published by the U.S. Chamber of Commerce, 1615 H Street NW, Washington, DC 20062-2000, (202) 463-5650.

Subscriptions: 1 year $22, 2 years $35, and 3 years $46; Canadian and international subscriptions add $20 to each rate.

Includes articles of interest to small- and medium-sized business, with frequent coverage of quality management issues. Rating: ★★

Sloan Management Review

Published quarterly by the MIT Sloan School of Management, 292 Main Street, E38-120, Cambridge, MA 02139, (617) 253-7170.

Subscriptions: $59 per year; $79 for Canada and Mexico, and $89 for all other international subscriptions.

Includes practical, yet thoughtful articles on a variety of issues of direct interest to managers. Articles often directly or indirectly related to quality issues. Rating: ★★

Tom Peters On Achieving Excellence

Newsletter published monthly by TPG Communications, P.O. Box 2189, Berkeley, CA 94702-0189, (800) 959-1059.

Subscriptions: United States: 1 year $197 and 2 years $244. Call for international rates.

A slick, readable, and practical 12-page two-color newsletter in the Peters style. Each issue has a theme with lots of short pieces on what different companies and people are doing to solve various business problems. Rating: ★★

Industry and Special Interest Magazines, Journals, and Newsletters that Cover Quality

APICS-The Performance Advantage

Published quarterly by the American Production and Inventory Control Society, Inc., 500 West Annandale Road, Falls Church, VA 22046-4274, phone (800) 444-2742 or (703) 237-8344, fax: (703) 237-1071.

Subscriptions: Included as part of membership package. Nonmembers subscriptions available at $30 per year; $40 in Mexico and Canada, and $50 for all other international subscriptions.

Covers the latest manufacturing principles and practices, case studies, columns, and news. Often includes articles on quality management in its field. Rating: ★★

Change

Published bimonthly by Heldref Publications, 1319 Eighteenth Street NW, Washington, DC 20036-1802, (212) 296-6267 or (800) 365-9753 for subscriptions.

Subscriptions: United States: $31 per year; outside the United States, add $12 per year.

Billed as the magazine of higher learning, it addresses issues of interest to the administration of colleges and universities, and occasionally carries articles on quality management topics. The May/June 1993 devoted an entire issue to this topic. Rating: ★

Educational Leadership

Published monthly September through May, except bimonthly December/ January issue, by the Association for Supervision and Curriculum Development, 1250 North Pitt Street, Alexandria, VA 22314–1453, phone: (703) 549–9110, fax: (703) 549–3891.

Subscriptions: Part of membership package in ASCD. For nonmembers: 1 year $36. Call or write for international subscriptions.

Popular journal for educators and administrators. Occasionally includes articles covering quality principles in teaching and administration. Rating: ★

Healthcare Executive

Published bimonthly by the Amercian College of Healthcare Executives, 840 North Lake Shore Drive, Chicago, IL 60611–9842.

Subscriptions: Write to Processing Center, 1951 Cornell Avenue, Melrose Park, IL 60160. 1 year $45, 2 years $80. For subscriptions outside the U.S., add $15 per year.

Aimed at health care managers, this journal regularly covers quality management issues. Most articles are relatively short and basic. Rating: ★★

Healthcare Forum Journal

Published bimonthly by The Healthcare Forum, 830 Market Street, San Francisco, CA 94102, (415) 421–8810.

Subscriptions: Available as part of membership in The Healthcare Forum or 1 year $45, 2 years $80, 3 years $115. Canada and Mexico add $15 per year; 1 year all other countries $90.

A well-done journal that regularly includes articles on TQM. Articles are often in-depth yet down to earth and readable. Includes many ads on resources for health care managers looking to implement TQM. Rating: ★★

Health Care Management Review

Published quarterly by Aspen Publishers Inc, 7201 McKinney Circle, Frederick, MD 21701, (800) 638–8437.

Subscriptions: $110 per year in the U.S. and Canada. For international subscriptions, contact: Swets Publishing Service, P.O. Box 825, 2160 SZ Lisse, The Netherlands.

A refereed journal that regularly includes articles in the field of health care management. Articles tend to be five to ten pages with references, but nontechnical in nature. Rating: ★★

HR Focus

Published by the American Management Association, 135 West 50th Street, New York, NY 10020, (212) 903-8389.

Subscriptions: 1 year $51.75, 2 years $88, and 3 years $132. Add $10 per year for outside the United States.

Newsletter-like publication, but longer than the average newsletter. Covers a variety of issues and news items of interest to HR managers. Sometimes includes articles on quality subjects. Rating: ★

HRMagazine

Published monthly by the Society for Human Resource Management, 606 North Washington Street, Alexandria, VA 22314, (703) 548-3440.

Subscriptions: Members of SHRM receive magazine as part of their membership. Nonmember subscriptions available in the United States, Canada, and Mexico at 1 year $49, 2 years $79, and 3 years $119. Write for information on international subscription rates.

Dedicated to human resource issues, with occasional articles on quality issues related to HR. Rating: ★

Industrial Engineering

Published monthly by the Institute of Industrial Engineers, 25 Technology Park, Norcross, GA 30092, phone: (404) 449–0461, fax: (404) 263–8532.

Subscriptions: Included as part of membership. Subscriptions available in the U.S. to non-members for 1 year $49, 2 years $82, and 3 years $115; Canada and international subscriptions: 1 year $70, 2 years $120, and 3 years $170.

While aimed at engineers, its articles are nontechnical and oriented toward the application of TQM principles. Includes a regular monthly column on quality. Rating: ★★★

Industrial Management

Published bimonthly by the Institute of Industrial Engineers, 25 Technology Park/Atlanta, Norcross, GA 30092, (404) 449-0460.

Subscriptions: 1 year $32, 2 years $54, and 3 years $80; international subscriptions 1 year $40, 2 years $68, and 3 years $94.

A serious journal with an academic bent that includes quality-oriented articles that are accessible to practitioners. Rating: ★

Integrated Manufacturing Systems

Published monthly by MCB University Press Ltd., 60/62 Toller Lane, Bradford, West Yorkshire, England BD8 9734, phone: 44 274 499–821, fax: 44 274 547–143. In the U.S.: P.O. Box 10812, Birmingham, AL 35201–0812, phone: (205) 995–1567 or (800) 633–4931, fax: (205) 995–1588.

Subscriptions: Call or write for subscription information.

A British journal dedicated to articles relating to the integration of production, design, supply, and marketing functions of manufacturing enterprises. Includes news and review center insert in each edition. Technical, but nonmathematical. Rating: ★★

Journal of Health Care Marketing

Published quarterly by the American Marketing Association Publishing Group, 250 South Wacker Drive, Chicago, IL 60606, (312) 648–0536.

Subscriptions: $50 per year in the U.S., $60 in other countries.

Regularly covers quality issues, especially with regard to customer satisfaction and service quality. Rating: ★★

Management Accounting

Published monthly by the Institute of Management Accountants, 10 Paragon Drive, Montvale, NJ 07645–1760, phone: (201) 573–1760, fax: (201) 573–0639.

Subscriptions: Free to members, nonmembers: $125 per year.

Frequently includes articles on activity based accounting and other subjects related to the implementation of quality principles in accounting processes. For accountants interested in TQM, highly recommended. Rating: ★★★

Manufacturing Engineering

Published monthly by the Society of Manufacturing Engineers, P.O. Box 930, Dearborn, MI 48121, (313) 271-1500.

Subscriptions: Closed circulation magazine sent free to members of the society and others involved with manufacturing. Personal subscription information available by contacting SME.

Covers articles on manufacturing, with some coverage of quality issues, including a monthly column, "The Quality Adviser." Rating: ★

Modern Healthcare

Published weekly by Crain Communications Inc., 965 East Jefferson, Detroit, MI 48207-3185, (800) 678-9595.

Subscriptions: 1 year $110 and 2 years $200; add $48 for all non-U.S. subscriptions.

A health care industry weekly magazine including news articles plus a variety of articles on managing health care facilities. Occasionally includes articles on quality management. Rating: ★

Performance and Instruction

Published monthly except for combined May/June and November/December issues by the National Society for Performance and Instruction, NSPI Publications, 1300 L Street NW, Suite 1250, Washington, DC 20005, (202) 408-7969.

Subscriptions: Available as part of membership; annual subscriptions available to nonmembers for $50.

Includes detailed articles on practical training techniques that will be of direct use to TQM trainers, though the orientation of the journal is not directed to TQM. Rating: ★★

Personnel Journal

Published monthly by ACC Communications, 245 Fischer Avenue, B-2, Costa Mesa, CA 92626.

Subscriptions: $55 per year. For multiyear and international subscriptions, write to the publishers.

An exceptionally well-done journal that regularly includes articles related to quality issues in the area of human resources, including teams and compensation. Regularly includes articles profiling practices at various companies. Rating: ★★★

Phi Delta Kappan

Published monthly except July and August by Phi Delta Kappa, Inc. (professional educators fraternity), 408 North Union, P.O. Box 789, Bloomington, IN 47402, (812) 339–1156 or (800) 766–1156.

Subscriptions: 1 year $35; other countries: 1 year $38.50.

Publishes articles on educational research and leadership with emphasis on trends and policies in education. Occasionally includes thoughtful articles directly relating to quality principles in education. Often includes articles indirectly related. Rating: ★★

Planning Review

Published bimonthly by The Planning Forum, 5900 College Corner Pike, P.O. Box 70, Oxford, OH 45056–0070.

Subscriptions: $95 per year in the U.S. and Canada; $115 for all other countries.

Not dedicated to TQM, but many articles are related to TQM principles or discuss their application. Many issues include a theme such as reengineering or mass customization. Most issues include cases studies of real companies. Rating: ★★

Research in Higher Education

Published bimonthly by Human Sciences Press, Inc., 233 Spring Street, New York, NY 10013–1578.

Subscriptions: For individuals in the U.S.: 1 year $65; other countries: $76.

A refereed journal aimed at planners, faculty, and higher education administrators to better understand how to efficiently and effectively manage these institutions. Articles frequently cover case studies in a particular area at various colleges and universities, with occasional articles on applying TQM. Somewhat technical. Rating: ★

The School Administrator

Published monthly by the American Association of School Administrators, 1801 North Moore Street, Arlington, VA 22209, (703) 875-7905.

Subscriptions: Included as part of membership.

Dedicated to the problems and opportunities of school administrators, occasionally including articles on quality in schools. Rating: ★

The Service Edge

Published monthly by Lakewood Publications, 50 South Ninth Street, Minneapolis, MN 55402, phone: (800) 328–4329 or (612) 333–0471, fax: (612) 333–6526.

Subscriptions: 1 year U.S.: $147; Canada add $100 plus 7% GST; other countries add $20 to U.S. rate.

This is an eight page, two-color newsletter covering specific issues in the delivery of quality to customers and creating company environments where service and quality thrive for everyone. Lots of practical ideas. Edited by Ron Zemke. Rating: ★★

Training

Published monthly by Lakewood Publications, Inc., 50 South Ninth Street, Minneapolis, MN 55402, (612) 333-0471.

Subscriptions: U.S.: 1 year $68, 2 years $116, and 3 years $150; Canada and Mexico: 1 year $78; international: 1 year $89.

Includes articles on issues of interest to corporate trainers, with frequent articles on quality management and training. Articles are practical, well-written, and of interest to all involved in quality management. Often includes articles on quality management.

Rating: ★★★

Training & Development

Published monthly by the American Society for Training and Development, Inc., 1640 King Street, Box 1443, Alexandria, VA 22313-2043, (703) 683-8100.

Subscriptions: Members of ASTD receive this magazine as part of their membership. Nonmember subscriptions available in the United States at $75 per year. International subscription: $135 for surface mail and $165 for air-mail.

Includes articles on training, human resources, and management issues, with frequent coverage of quality management topics in these areas.

Rating: ★★

On-Line Quality Services

This section of the 1995 yearbook provides information on five different national on-line services for managers or anyone interested in TQM. These services provide quick access to information from many different sources and the ability to communicate with other people dealing with quality and ISO 9000 issues.

The Benchmarking Exchange

The Benchmarking Exchange (TBE) is an on-line information and communication service dedicated to support benchmarking in particular and quality management in general. It provides users with access to organizations that have indicated a willingness to enter into benchmarking partnerships. One prominent feature is "the posting board," a database for entry and retrieval of benchmarking projects including contact names, companies, and phone numbers. There are best practices and company profiles databases, among others, and bibliographies of the latest articles from many publications.

TBE is used by individual companies as well as by companies enrolled through benchmarking and quality associations. These include the ASQC's Benchmarking Competency Center, the Strategic Planning Institute's Council on Benchmarking, the Association for Internal Management Consultants, the Benchmarking Centre (UK), and the American Productivity and Quality Center's International Benchmarking Clearinghouse. Members have access to the latest benchmarking and the ability to network with the world's largest pool of benchmarking professionals.

How to Join: For automated enrollment, configure modem in this way: Data: 8, Parity: N, Stop: 1, Echo: Off, Baud: Up to 115,200, Emulate: ANSI, Access # (408) 662–9814, Duplex: Full. Once on line, follow instructions on screen for signing up. You can also contact The Benchmarking Exchange at 7960-B Soquel Drive, Suite 356, Aptos, CA 95003, (800) 662–9801 or (408) 662–9800 for additional information.

Fees: 3 months: $250, 6 months: $440, 1 year: $760. Discounted annual subscriptions offered for multi-users in a company or depending on affiliation with TBE member associations.

Quality Online Forum

The Quality Online Forum (QOF) is a computer on-line service developed and operated by American Informatics, Inc. It is designed to be a one-stop source of information for business professionals who are interested in quality and productivity improvement. For example, if a user was looking for someone who does ISO 9000 consulting, the QOF has a vendor database with a powerful search capability. If a user wanted a video on teambuilding, he or she could enter the Video Conference and post a message, with the likelihood that other users will make a recommendation. The system includes e-mail and other capabilities for networking with people involved in the implementation of quality management.

How to Join: Potential users can receive a free introductory subscription by dialing up the service via their modem. Configure your modem as follows: Data: 8, Stop: 1, Parity: N, Terminal: VT100/ANSI, Baud: 1200 to 14,400. The number is (913) 234–6528. To take full advantage of the system, you need special software that works with Windows and is free on request. You can also contact American Informatics, Inc., P.O. Box 55, Tecumseh, KS 66542, (913) 379–5590 for additional information.

Fees: $60 per year, $21 per quarter, or $10 per month.

The National ISO 9000 Support Group

The services of this group are directed at professionals interested in guiding their companies to compliance with ISO 9000. It is more than just an on-line information service. The services include:

- Fax and modem access to experts on the standard.
- Quick summary reports on all aspects of registration and implementation.
- A monthly newsletter, *Continuous Improvement*, that is filled with how-to articles on conforming to ISO 9000.
- Audio tapes with an overview of the registration process and details on how to prepare a company.
- Up to the minute news on ISO 9000 developments and revisions on line.
- Discounts on books, tapes, training, and other resources.
- Background and cost information on the registration process.
- Information on consultants and registrars.

How to Join: To learn more and to browse the ISO 9000 BBS, configure your modem as follows: Data: 8, Stop: 1, Parity: No, Baud 300 to 14,400, and dial (616) 891–9433. Contact the National ISO 9000 Support Group at 9964 Cherry Valley, Building #2, Caledonia, MI 49316, (616) 891–9114, for additional information.

Fees: $150 per year, includes newsletter and other items as part of membership.

The ISO 9000 Standard Discussion

This is sponsored by the University of Wisconsin-Stout as a moderated and archived distribution list for persons and companies interested in sharing ISO 9000 information and experiences for implementing these standards. Discussion includes: who is doing what; what the successes and concerns have been;

what systems, methods, software, and structures have been beneficial; identified and required solutions; long- and short-term strategies; partnering; educational programs that have been successful; policy issues; assessments; corrective actions; registrar comments and concerns; and so on. Participants are invited to post notes, questions, comments, concerns, ideas, and especially information and suggestions that enable all participants to better understand and use the benefits that the ISO 9000 standards provide.

How to Join: You access the ISO 9000 Discussion List by utilizing Internet, Genie, or CompuServe. To gain entrance to the service, send the following command line:

SEND>LISTSERV@vm1.NoDak.EDU SUB ISO9000 First Name Last Name

Note: That is **your** first name and last name.

Soon after you send this subscription request, you should get one of two messages:

1. "Your subscription to ISO9000 has been confirmed." or
2. "Computer vm1.NoDak.EDU is down." (Please try again in that case.)

For more information contact Nancy Jennejohn, EDA University Center, University of Wisconsin-Stout, Menomonie, WI 54751–0790, (715) 232–5023, e-mail: JennejohnN@UWStout.EDU.

Fees: No fees; the service is free.

The TQM BBS

This is a small service (able to handle two calls at a time) with the purpose of furthering the principles of TQM through education and information exchange. All files (approximately 300 at the time of this writing) are available for downloading. This service is free and run by Tom Glenn. It is accessible at (301) 585–1164. Call (301) 565–8882 (voice line) for additional information.

Fees: No fees; this is a free service.

Directory of Quality Awards

This section of *The Quality Yearbook* profiles quality awards with an emphasis on state award programs. Since the last edition of the yearbook, five more states have established quality awards, and they are included here. We have updated all listings with the best information available on award aspects and on where you can get additional information. If you are interested in learning more about state award programs, we urge you to call or write for details. What you will find here are brief overviews of the criteria for the various state awards. Several states use the Baldrige criteria, but with modifications and different point schedules. For this reason, we have summarized these criteria for each state to provide for comparison and to make it easy for those who just want to read about their state.

We have included new listings for the Shingo Prize and the RIT/USA Today Quality Cup. You will also find a more detailed listing of the quality awards of other countries, with addresses and phone numbers for getting more information. We would be glad to receive information on other quality awards to list in future editions of the yearbook and to receive corrections to any listings now included.

State Awards Directory

ALABAMA

Award: Alabama U.S. Senate Productivity and Quality Award

Categories: There are four categories in which prizes are given:

Small Business. Less than 100 full-time employees.

Manufacturing Sector. Companies or subsidiaries that produce and sell manufactured products or manufacturing processes, including agricultural, mining, or contruction products.

Service Sector (includes government agencies and education). Organizations, companies, or subsidiaries that sell or provide a service.

Special Category. Called *Award of Excellence in Continuous Productivity and Quality Improvement* that previous winners may apply for.

Award Criteria: There are seven areas in which applicants are judged, based on the Baldrige criteria:

1. *Leadership.* Examines senior executives' *personal* leadership and involvement in creating and sustaining a customer focus and clear and visible quality values. (95 pts.)
2. *Information and Analysis.* Examines the scope, validity, analysis, management, and use of data and information to drive quality excellence and to improve operational and competitive performance. (75 pts.)

3. *Strategic Quality Planning.* Examines the organization's planning process and how all key quality requirements are integrated into overall business planning. (60 pts.)
4. *Human Resource Development and Management.* Examines the key elements of how the workforce is enabled to develop its full potential to pursue the organization's quality and operational performance objectives. (150 pts.)
5. *Management of Process Quality.* Examines the systematic processes the organization uses to pursue ever-higher quality and operational performance. (140 pts.)
6. *Quality and Operational Results.* Examines the organization's quality levels and improvement trends in quality, organization operational performance, and supplier quality. (180 pts.)
7. *Customer Focus and Satisfaction.* Examines the organization's relationships with customers and its knowledge of customer requirements and of the key quality factors that drive marketplace competitiveness. (300 pts.)

How to Apply: For information and application forms, contact:

Linda Vincent
Award Coordinator
The Alabama Productivity Center
P.O. Box 870318
Tuscaloosa, AL 35487-0318
Phone: (205) 348-8956
Fax: (205) 348-9391

ARIZONA

Award: The Arizona Governor's Award for Quality (Called "The Pioneer Award")

Categories: Any organization, public or private, may apply for the award, awarded in three categories:
Small (less than 100 employees)
Medium (100–499 employees)
Large (500 or more employees)

Award Criteria: Similar to the Baldrige criteria, applicants are judged on:

1. *Leadership.* Examines senior executives' success in creating and sustaining a customer focus and clear and visible quality values, including how those values are integrated into the organization's management system and reflected in the manner in which the organization addresses its public responsibilities. (90 pts.)
2. *Information and Analysis.* Examines the scope, validity, analysis, management, and use of data collection to drive excellence and improve competitive performance, including the adequacy of the organization's data, information, and analysis system to support improvement in all activities. (75 pts.)
3. *Strategic Quality Planning.* Examines the organization's planning process and how all key quality requirements are integrated into overall organization planning. (60 pts.)
4. *Human Resources Development and Management.* Examines the key elements of how the organization develops and realizes the full potential of work force to pursue the organization's quality and performance objectives. (150 pts.)
5. *Management of Process Quality.* Examines the systematic processes used to pursue ever-higher quality and operational performance, including key elements of process management. (140 pts.)

6. *Quality and Operational Results.* Examines the organization quality levels and improvement trends in quality operational performance, and supplier quality. (180 pts.)
7. *Customer Focus and Satisfaction.* Examines the organization's relationships with customers and its knowledge of customer requirements and of key factors that determine marketplace competitiveness. (300 pts.)

How to Apply: Applicants must submit a written application and must agree to a CEO interview if a finalist. A free copy of the award application is available by contacting:
Dennis Sowards
Arizona Quality Alliance
1221 East Osborn, Suite 100
Phoenix, AZ 85014
Phone: (602) 265-6141
Fax: (602) 265-1262

CALIFORNIA

California has quality awards given by two different organizations. We review both here. One of these organizations is associated with the state government and the other is under the aegis of a private company.

Award: Governor's Golden State Quality Award. This award is administered by the California Center for Quality, Education, and Development.

Categories: There are three categories of awards:
Manufacturing Companies
Service Companies
Small Businesses (fewer than 500 employees)

There are five different awards given:
1. *Quality in Management Award.* Companies that excel in managing their core activity, be it manufacturing, services, or a combination.
2. *Quality in the Marketplace Award.* Companies that excel in translating an approach to quality into improved levels of customer satisfaction and business results.
3. *Quality in the Workplace Award.* Companies that excel in creating a workplace that realizes the full potential of their people to achieve the company's performance objectives.
4. *Quality in the Community Award.* Companies that excel in their interaction with their communities: local, state, and national.
5. *The Governor's Golden State Quality Award.* Companies that achieve excellence in all of the areas.

Award Criteria: To gain the Governor's Golden State Award, applicants are judged in the other four areas, with the distribution of points as follows: Management—300 points, Marketplace—400 points, Workplace—200 points, and Community—100 points. Each of these four awards has criteria based around four areas: Approach 20 percent, Deployment 20 percent, Results 35 percent, and Continuous Improvement 25 percent. Specific criteria are developed for each of these four areas, as specified in the application manual.**How to Apply:** To get more information and to apply for this award contact:
Lyn Wilkinson

California Center for Quality, Education, and Development
425 California Street, 2nd Floor
San Francisco, CA 94104
Phone: (415) 397–0777
Fax: (510) 452–6724

Award: (1) The United States Senate Productivity Award and (2) The Eureka Award for Quality and Service Excellence. Both of these are administered by the California Council for Quality and Service.

Categories: The U.S. Senate Productivity Award is given to:
Large Manufacturing (200 or more employees)
Small Manufacturing (less than 200 employees)

The Eureka Award for Quality and Service Excellence is given to:
Large Service Companies (200 or more employees)
Small Business/Professional Services ((less than 200 employees)
Non-Profit Organizations
Educational Institutions (K-12, Colleges, Universities, Vocational Schools)
Government

Award Criteria: Both awards are based on the Baldrige Award criteria:

1. *Leadership.* Examine senior executives' *personal* leadership and involvement in creating and sustaining a customer focus and clear and visible quality values. (95 pts.)
2. *Information and Analysis.* Examines the scope, management, and use of data and information to maintain a customer focus, to drive quality excellence, and to improve operational and competitive performance. (75 pts.)
3. *Strategic Quality Planning.* Examines the company's planning process and how all key quality and operational performance requirements are integrated into overall business planning. (60 pts.)
4. *Human Resource Development and Management.* Examines the key elements of how the work force is enabled to develop its full potential to pursue the company's quality and operational performance. (150 pts.)
5. *Management of Process Quality.* Examines the key elements of process management, including design, management of day-to-day production and delivery, improvement of quality and operational performance, and quality assessment. (140 pts.)
6. *Quality and Operational Results.* Examines the company's achievement levels and improvement trends in quality, company operational performance, and supplier quality. (180 pts.)
7. *Customer Focus and Satisfaction.* Examines the company's relationships with customers and its knowledge of customer requirements and of the key quality factors that drive marketplace competitiveness. (300 pts.)

How to Apply: To get more information and to apply for this award contact:
Alicia Wszelaki, Adminstrator
California Council for Quality & Service
P.O. Box 880774
San Diego, CA 92168–0774
Phone: (619) 491–3050 or (800) 544–0414
Fax: (619) 491–3055

CONNECTICUT

Connecticut has three awards for quality. Two are administered by Connecticut Quality Improvement Award Inc., which created the first state quality award based on the Baldrige criteria, and one was developed by the Connecticut Award for Excellence. We include descriptions of each.

Award: Connecticut Quality Improvement Award

Categories: There are six categories in which awards are given:
Small (1–100 employees) in *service* and *manufacturing.*
Medium (101–500 employees) in *service* and *manufacturing.*
Large (over 500 employees) in *service* and *manufacturing.*

Award Criteria: The Connecticut award is based on the Baldrige award criteria:

1. *Leadership.* The senior executives' success in creating and sustaining a quality culture.
2. *Information and Analysis.* The effectiveness of information collection and analysis for quality improvement and planning.
3. *Strategic Quality Planning.* The effectiveness of integrating quality requirements into business plans.
4. *Human Resource Development and Management.* The success of efforts to develop and realize the full potential of the work force for quality.
5. *Management of Process Quality.* The effectiveness of systems and processes for assuring the quality of all operations.
6. *Quality and Operational Results.* The results in quality achievement and quality improvement, demonstrated through quantitative measures.
7. *Customer Focus and Satisfaction.* The effectiveness of systems to determine customer requirements and demonstrated success in meeting them.

Award: The Connecticut Small Business Quality Award

Categories: Any organization or component of an organization located in the state of Connecticut with fewer than 500 employees. Eligible organizations include but are not limited to:
Service Businesses
Manufacturing Businesses
Hospitals and Health Care Facilities
Academic Institutions
Non-Profit Organizations
Government Agencies

Criteria: Same as for the Connecticut Quality Improvement Award, but with less detailed documentation.

How to Apply: To get additional information and to apply for either award, contact:
Sheila Carmine, Director
Connecticut Quality Improvement Award, Inc.
P.O. Box 1396
Stamford, CT 06904-1396
Phone: (203) 322-9534
Fax: (203) 329-2465

Award: Connecticut Award for Excellence

Categories: There are six categories, divided into two size ranges, in which awards are given:

Private—Manufacturing. Small-Medium (1–300 employees); Large (300+ employees).
Private—Service. Small-Medium (1–300 employees); Large (300+ employees).
Health Care. Small-Medium (1–300 employees); Large (300+ employees).
Public. Small-Medium (1–300 employees); Large (300+ employees).
Education: K-12. Small-Medium (1,000 or less students); Large (1,000+ students).
Colleges. Small-Medium (1,000 or less students); Large (1,000+ students).

Criteria: The criteria for this award are based on the Baldrige Award:

1. *Leadership*. Examines how senior executives create and sustain a customer focus and clear, visible quality values, along with a management system to integrate all activities of the organization toward quality excellence. (150 pts.)
2. *Information and Analysis*. Examines the scope, validity, management, and use of data and information that underlie the organization's overall quality management system. (65 pts.)
3. *Strategic Quality Planning*. Examines the organization's planning process for achieving or retaining a quality leadership position and how the organization integrates quality improvement planning into overall organizational planning. (60 pts.)
4. *Human Resources Excellence*. Examines the effectiveness of the organization's efforts to develop and realize the full potential of the workforce, including management, and to maintain a work environment conducive and committed to full participation, collaboration, empowerment, quality leadership, and personal and organizational growth. (200 pts.)
5. *Management of Process Quality*. Examines the systematic approaches used by the organization for assuring ever-higher quality of products, initiatives, and services. (125 pts.)
6. *Quality and Operational Results*. Examines quality levels and quality improvement trends based upon objective measures derived from analysis of customer requirements and expectations and from analysis of the organization's performance and supplier quality. (150 pts.)
7. *Customer Focus and Satisfaction*. Examines the organization's knowledge of, responsiveness to, and ability to meet the requirements and expectations of its customers, clients, and constituents. (250 pts.)

How to Apply: To get additional information and to apply for this award, contact:
Ernest J. Nagler, Project Facilitator
Connecticut Award for Excellence
P.O. Box 67
Rocky Hill, CT 06067
Phone: (800) 392–2122
Fax: (203) 258–4359

DELAWARE

Award: Delaware Quality Award

Eligibility: An organization must be in operation within the state for at least three years. For concerns that have other locations nationally or internationally, only Delaware operations are eligible.

Categories: There are five categories of organizations available for this prize:

Large Manufacturing. Companies with 100 or more employees.
Small Manufacturing. Companies with fewer than 100 employees
Large Non-Manufacturing. Companies with 100 or more employees.
Small Non-Manufacturing. Companies with fewer than 100 employees.
Non-Profit Organizations. Organizations of any size.

Award Criteria: As with most state programs, applicants are judged in seven areas, based on the Baldrige criteria:

1. *Customer Satisfaction.* Examines what product or service improvements a company is making that directly result to customer benefit, including changes made to improve the efficiency and effectiveness of the business. (30% weight)
2. *Leadership.* Examines how the principal leader of the organization is involved in the establishment of quality objectives, planning for the implementation of those objectives, establishing measurements, reviewing progress, and initiating adjustments that may be necessary. (15% weight)
3. *Valuing People.* Examines how much time organizations have their employees spend in formal training to learn new skills and techniques. (15% weight)
4. *Operational Processes.* Examines exactly what organizations have done to analyze and improve processes to increase the effectiveness and productivity of the company's operation. (14% weight)
5. *Supplier Enhancement.* Examines if the organization's assessment of suppliers is based on fact versus intuition and the measurement systems used to determine needs. Also examined are the ways organizations interact with suppliers. (10% weight)
6. *Results.* Examines the results of organizations, using such measurements as defect rate reduction, cycle time reduction, and "key success indicators." (11% weight)
7. *Community Impact.* Examines how the entire organization shares quality knowledge and plays a responsible role within the community. (5% weight)

How to Apply: To get additional information and to apply for this award, contact:
Gary Smith
Delaware Quality Consortium, Inc.
Delaware Development Office
99 King's Highway
P.O. Box 1401
Dover, DE 19903
Phone: (702) 739-4271
Fax: (302) 739-5749

FLORIDA

Award: The Governor's Sterling Award

Categories: There are five categories in which awards are given:
Manufacturing
Service
Public Sector
Education Sector
Health Care Sector

Award Criteria: Florida uses the seven Baldrige criteria as a basis for its award, but with special modifications for public and nonprofit organizations:

1. *Leadership.* Includes: Senior executive leadership, management for quality, public responsibility, and corporate citizenship.
2. *Information and Analysis.* Includes: Scope and management of quality and performance data and information, competitive comparisons and benchmarking, and analysis and uses of company-level data.
3. *Strategic Quality Planning.* Includes: Strategic quality and organization performance planning process, and quality and performance plans.
4. *Human Resource Development and Management.* Includes: Human resource planning and management, employee involvement, employee education and training, employee performance and recognition, and employee well-being and satisfaction.
5. *Management of Process Quality.* Includes: Design and introduction of quality products and services, process management, including product and service production and delivery processes, and business processes and support services, and supplier and quality assessment.
6. *Quality and Operational Results.* Includes: Product and service quality results, organization operational results, business process and support service results, and supplier quality results.
7. *Customer Focus and Satisfaction.* Includes: Meeting current and future customer expectations, customer relationship management, commitment to customers, customer satisfaction determination, customer satisfaction results, and customer satisfaction comparison.

How to Apply: To get additional information and to apply for this award, contact:

John A. Pieno, Jr.
Chairman, Florida Sterling Council
P.O. Box 13907
Tallahassee, FL 32317-3907
Phone: (904) 922-5316
Fax: (904) 922-6405

LOUISIANA

Award: U.S. Senate Productivity Award and U.S. Senate Innovation Award

Categories: Private organizations of all types are eligible to apply.

Award Criteria:

For the Productivity Award, judges review:

1. The specific productivity and quality improvement program put in place.
2. The driving force behind the program.
3. The nature and extent of senior management's commitment to productivity and quality improvement.
4. The involvement of the company's work force in the program.
5. The impact of the program on owners, managers, employees, customers, and vendors.
6. The transferability of the productivity- and quality-improvement program to other private-sector business, particularly in the state of Louisiana.

For the Innovation Award, judges review:

1 The specific innovation activity undertaken
2. The driving force behind this activity
3. The nature and extent of the senior management's commitment to activity

4. The involvement of the company's work force in this activity
5. The risks taken in developing this activity
6. The impact of this activity on owners, managers, employees, customers, vendors, and competition
7. The transferability of this specific innovation to other private sector businesses, particularly in the state of Louisiana

How to Apply: For information and to apply, contact:
Edward J. O'Boyle
Selection Board
U.S. Senate Productivity Award
Louisiana Tech University
P.O. Box 10318
Ruston, LA 71272
Phone: (318) 257-3701
Fax: (318) 257-4253

MAINE

Award: Margaret Chase Smith Maine State Quality Award

Categories: Awards are given in five categories:
Manufacturing. Large Business (100 or more employees); Small Business (fewer than 100 employees). Includes SIC codes 01–39.
Service. Large Business (100 or more employees); Small Business (fewer than 100 employees). Includes SIC codes 07, 40–89.
Non-Profit. All sizes of organizations.

Award Criteria: The criteria for Maine's award are based on the Baldrige criteria:
1. *Leadership.* Examines senior executives' personal leadership and involvement in creating and sustaining a customer focus and clear and visible quality values. (95 pts.)
2. *Information and Analysis.* Examines the scope, validity, analysis, management, and use of data and information to drive quality excellence and to improve operational and competitive performance. (75 pts.)
3. *Strategic Quality Planning.* Examines the company's planning process and how all key quality requirements are integrated into overall business planning. (60 pts.)
4. *Human Resource Development and Management.* Examines the key elements of how the workforce is enabled to develop its full potential to pursue the company's quality and operational performance objectives. (150 pts.)
5. *Management of Process Quality.* Examines the systematic processes the company uses to pursue ever-higher quality and company operational performance. (140 pts.)
6. *Quality and Operational Results.* Examines the company's quality levels and improvement trends in quality, company operational performance, and supplier quality. (180 pts.)
7. *Customer Focus and Satisfaction.* Examines the company's relationships with customers and its knowledge of customer requirements and of the key quality factors that drive marketplace competitiveness. (300 pts.)

How to Apply: To get additional information and to apply for this award, contact:
Nancy Werner
Maine Quality Center
Norridgework Avenue

Skowhegan, ME 04976
Phone: (207) 685–3004
Fax: Same, call first.

MARYLAND

Award: United States Senate Productivity Award for Maryland

Eligibility: All organizations, public and private, are eligible for this award.

Categories: There are three categories in which organizations may apply for this award:
Manufacturing
Services
Small Business

Award Criteria: There are five areas in which applicants are judged for this award:

1. *Productivity and Quality Leadership.* Examines senior executives' personal leadership and involvement in creating and sustaining a customer focus and clear, visible quality values. (200 pts.)
2. *Human Resource Excellence.* Examines the ways an organization develops and realizes the full potential of the work force to pursue its quality and performance objectives. (200 pts.)
3. *Productivity/Quality Results.* Examines the organization's quality and productivity trends in quality, both operational and supplier quality, including current quality and productivity levels relative to competitors. (250 pts.)
4. *Customer Orientation and Results.* Examines the organization's relationships with customers and its knowledge of customer requirements and of key quality factors that determine marketplace competitiveness. (250 pts.)
5. *Impact on State and Local Community.* Examines the economic and environmental impact of the organization's quality values on the state and local community. (100 pts.)

How to Apply: This award is sponsored by the two Maryland U.S. Senators. For more information or applications, contact:
Nellie Freeman
Amit Gupta
Maryland Center for Quality and Productivity
College of Business and Management
University of Maryland
College Park, MD 20742-7215
Phone: (301) 405-7099
Fax: (301) 314-9119

MASSACHUSETTS

Award: Massachusetts Quality Award—up to two awards per category will be given in each eligible category.

Eligibility: Any business or appropriate subsidiary located in Massachusetts may apply.

Categories: There are four categories in which organizations may apply for this award:
Manufacturing. Companies that produce and market manufactured products or manufacturing processes and those companies that produce agricultural, mining, or construction processes.
Service. Companies that market services.

Small Business. Complete businesses (not business subsidiaries) with not more than 200 full-time employees. Business activities may include manufacturing and/or service.

Nonprofit. All governmental, educational, health care, social service, and other non-profit organizations.

Award Criteria: Based on the Baldrige criteria, applicants are judged on the following areas:

1. *Leadership.* Examines how senior executives leadership and personal involvement creates and maintains clear and visible values and management systems focused on the customer and sustains an environment for quality excellence. (9% weight)
2. *Information and Analysis.* Examines the scope, validity, analysis, management, and use of data and information to drive quality excellence and competitive performance. (8% weight)
3. *Strategic Quality Planning.* Examines the planning process with particular emphasis placed on the integration of the key quality and overall performance planning requirements in both the short (1 to 2 years) and long term (more than 3 years). (6% weight)
4. *Human Resource Development.* Examines the efforts to develop and realize the full potential of all employees while achieving quality and performance objectives. (15% weight)
5. *Management of Process Quality.* Examines key systemic processes used to pursue every higher quality and organizational performance. (14% weight)
6. *Quality and Operational Results.* Examines the current levels and improvement trends in operations and supplier quality performance, including current quality and performance levels relative to competitors. (18% weight)
7. *Customer Focus and Satisfaction.* Examines the relationships with customers, with an emphasis on the knowledge of customer requirements and key quality factors that determine marketplace competitiveness. (30% weight)

How to Apply: For more information on the Massachusetts Quality Award, contact:

Brendon D. Healey
Executive Director
Massachusetts Council for Quality, Inc.
92 Vernon Road
Scitvate, MA 02066
Phone: (617) 545-6200
Fax: Same

MICHIGAN

Award Quality Leadership Award

Categories Awards are given in six categories::

Manufacturing
Service
Healthcare
Education
Public Sector
Small Enterprise (less than 100 employees)

Award Criteria: The Michigan criteria are based on the current Baldrige criteria, with the same scoring system.

How to Apply: To get additional information and to apply for this award, contact:
William J. Kalmar, Director
Michigan Quality Council
525 O'Dowd Hall
Oakland University
Rochester, MI 48309–4401
Phone: (810) 370–4552
Fax: (810) 370–4202

MINNESOTA

Award: Minnesota Quality Award—up to two awards are given in each of three categories.

Eligibility: Any FOR-PROFIT business or appropriate subsidiary located in the State of Minnesota may apply for an award.

Categories: There are three categories in which companies may apply for this award:
Manufacturing. Companies that produce or sell manufactured products or manufacturing processes and those companies that produce agricultural, mining, or construction products (SIC Codes 01–39).
Service. Companies that sell services (SIC Codes 07, 40–89).
Small Business. Complete businesses (not business subsidiaries) with not more than 200 full-time employees. Business activities may include manufacturing and/or services.

Award Criteria: The Minnesota Quality Award criteria mirror the Baldrige criteria, and applicants are judged on:

1. *Leadership.* Examines senior executives' personal leadership and involvement in creating and sustaining a customer focus and clear and visible quality values. (90 pts.)
2. *Information and Analysis.* Examines the scope, validity, analysis, management, and use of data and information to drive quality excellence and improve competitive performance. Also examines the adequacy of the organization's data, information, and analysis system to support continuous improvement of the organization's customer focus, products, services, and internal operations. (80 pts.)
3. *Strategic Quality Planning.* Examines the organization's planning and how all key quality requirements are integrated into the organization's overall planning, its short-term (one to two years) and long-term (three or more years) priorities for quality and performance. (60 pts.)
4. *Human Resources Development and Management.* Examines the extent of the organization's efforts to develop and realize the full potential of all its employees in pursuing the organization's quality and performance objectives, including the organization's efforts to build and maintain an environment for quality excellence conducive to full participation and personal growth. (150 pts.)
5. *Management of Process Quality.* Examines the key systematic processes the organization uses to pursue every higher quality and organizational performance. (140 pts.)
6. *Quality and Operational Results.* Examines the organization's quality levels and improvement trends in quality, organizational operational performance, and supplier quality, including current quality and performance levels relative to competitors. (180 pts.)

7. *Customer Focus and Satisfaction.* Examines the organization's relationship with its customers and its knowledge of customer requirements and key quality factors that determine marketplace competitiveness, including the organization's methods to determine customer satisfaction, current trends and levels of satisfaction, and these results relative to competitors. (300 pts.)

How to Apply: For more information on the Minnesota Quality Award and information on the Minnesota Council for Quality, contact:
Carol Gabor
Director, Minnesota Quality Award
Minnesota Council for Quality
2850 Metro Drive, Suite 300
Bloomington, MN 55425
Phone: (612) 851–3181
Fax: (612) 851–3183

MISSOURI

Award: Missouri Quality Award, awarded by the Excellence in Missouri Foundation.

Eligibility: Any business or subsidiary of a business that has employees in Missouri and has existed in Missouri for at least one year. Additional eligibility information is available in the award booklet.

Categories: There are two business categories and three size categories in which organizations may apply for this award:

Manufacturing. Includes companies or subsidiaries that produce and sell manufacturing processes, and those companies that produce agricultural, mining, or construction products. (SIC codes 01–39)

Services. Includes companies or subsidiaries that sell services. (SIC codes 40–89)

Size. Organizations are judged in three sizes: Small—less than 100 employees, Medium—100–499 employees, and Large—500 employees or more.

Award Criteria: The Baldrige criteria form the basis for seven areas of the Missouri Quality Award:

1. *Leadership.* Examines senior executives personal leadership and involvement in creating and sustaining a customer focus and visible quality values, including how the quality values are integrated into the company's management system and reflected in how the company addresses the public responsibilities and corporate citizenship. (95 pts.)
2. *Information and Analysis.* Examines the scope, validity, analysis, management, and use of data and information to drive quality excellence and improve operational and competitive performance. (75 pts.)
3. *Strategic Quality Planning.* Examines the company's planning process and how all key quality requirements are integrated into overall business planning. (60 pts.)
4. *Human Resource Development and Management.* Examines the key elements of how the workforce is enabled to develop its full potential to purse the company's quality and operational performance objectives. (15% weight)
5. *Management of Process Quality.* Examines the systematic processes the company uses the pursue ever-higher quality and company operational performance. (140 pts.)
6. *Quality and Operational Results.* Examines the company's quality levels and improvement trends in quality, company operational performance, and supplier quality, including current quality and performance levels relative to those of competitors. (180 pts.)

7. *Customer Focus and Satisfaction.* Examines the company's relationships with customers and its knowledge of customer requirements and of the key quality factors that drive marketplace competitiveness. (300 pts.)

How to Apply: For detailed information about the Missouri Quality Award, contact:
John Politi, Executive Director
Excellence in Missouri Foundation
411 Jefferson Street
P.O. Box 1709
Jefferson City, MO 65102
Phone: (314) 634-2246
Fax: (314) 634-4406

NEBRASKA

Award: The Edgerton Quality Award

Categories: This award is given in two categories. They include for-profit businesses or subsidiaries located in Nebraska in:
Manufacturing Industries
Services Industries

Award Criteria: Similar to the Baldrige criteria:
1. *Leadership.* Examines how senior management creates and sustains a clear and visible quality value and guides the organization's activities toward quality excellence. (10% weight)
2. *Information and Analysis.* Examines the scope and use of the data that underlie the organization's quality management system. (6% weight)
3. *Strategic Quality Planning.* Examines the organization's planning process for achieving or retaining a leadership position compared to its competitors. (9% weight)
4. *Human Resource Utilization.* Examines the organization's efforts to develop and realize the full potential of its employees, including management personnel. (15% weight)
5. *Quality Assurance of Products and Services.* Examines the approaches used by the organization to control the quality of goods and services, including the procured materials, parts, and services. (15% weight)
6. *Quality Results.* Examines quality levels and quality improvement trends upon objective measures derived from customer requirements and expectations and from analysis of business operations. (15% weight)
7. *Customer Satisfaction.* Examines the organization's knowledge of the customer, its overall customer service system, its responsiveness, and its ability to meet customer requirements and expectations. (25% weight)

How to Apply: To get additional information and to apply for this award, contact:
The Edgerton Quality Award Program
Nebraska Department of Economic Development
Existing Business Assistance Division
P.O. Box 94666
301 Centennial Mall South
Lincoln, NE 68509–4666
Phone: (402) 471–4167, (800) 426–6505
Fax: (402) 471–3778

NEVADA

Award: The U.S. Senate Productivity Award

Categories: There are seven categories for different types of organizations. Awards are non-competitive and small businesses will not be judged against larger organizations:

Education
Government
Health and Medical Services
Manufacturing and Mining
Non-Profit
Resort and Travel
Service and Retail

Award Criteria: Matches the Baldrige criteria:

Leadership
Information and Analysis
Strategic Quality Planning
Human Resource Utilization
Management of Quality Process
Quality Results
Customer Satisfaction

How to Apply: For more information, contact:

Katrina Ekedahl, Administrator
U.S. Senate Productivity Award
c/o Quality and Productivity Center
P.O. Box 93416
Las Vegas, NV 89193-3416
Phone: (702) 798-7292
Fax: (702) 798-8653

NEW JERSEY

Award: New Jersey Quality Achievement Award

Categories: Up to two awards may be given in each year in each of the following categories:

Manufacturing Companies or Subsidiaries
Service Companies or Subsidiaries
Small Businesses
Educational Institutions
Government Organizations

Criteria: The criteria for the New Jersey award are based on the Baldrige Award. The points for each category are different for private and government awards.

1. *Leadership.* Examines senior management or public executive's personal leadership and involvement in creating and sustaining a customer focus and clear and visible quality values and fostering a management system to guide the organization toward quality excellence. (95 pts. private; 130 pts. government)
2. *Information and Analysis.* Examines the scope, validity, use, analysis, and management of data and information to drive excellence and improve operational and competitive performance. (75 pts. private; 50 pts. government)

3. *Strategic Quality Planning.* Examines the company or organization's planning process and how all key quality and operational performance requirements are integrated into overall business or organizational planning. (60 pts. private; 60 pts. government)
4. *Human Resource Development and Management* (private); *Human Resource Excellence* (government). Examines the key elements of how the workforce is enabled to develop its full potential to pursue the company or organization's quality and operational performance objectives. (150 pts. private; 175 pts. government)
5. *Management of Process Quality.* Examines the key systematic processes used by the organization to pursue ever-higher quality and operational performance. (140 pts. private; 150 pts. government)
6. *Quality and Operational Results.* Examines the company or organization's quality levels and improvement trends in quality, overall operational performance, and supplier quality. (180 pts. private; 165 pts. government)
7. *Customer Focus and Satisfaction.* Examines the organization or company's relationships with customers and its knowledge of their requirements and the key quality factors that drive competitiveness in the marketplace. (300 pts. private; 270 pts. government)

How to Apply: To get additional information and to apply for this award, contact:

Ed Nelson
Executive Director—Operations
New Jersey Quality Achievement Award
Mary G. Roebling Building, CN 827
Trenton, NJ 08625–0827
Phone: (609) 777–0939
Fax: (609) 777–2798

NEW MEXICO

Award: New Mexico Quality Award

Levels: Rather than award categories, New Mexico has three award levels that recognize progress made in a organization's quality journey. These levels are:

Level One. Pinon Award (Commitment). This level is for organizations that have made a serious commitment to use total quality concepts and principles. Organizations have planted the seed of quality and are working toward the day when they can see the long-term benefits of their efforts. Application at this level requires a description of the business operations and signature of the executive leadership indicating their commitment. The application should contain a 5 to 15 page description of how the organization is approaching the development of an organizational quality system and any results achieved. Applicants must address the seven categories of the Baldrige Award criteria in a general manner.

Level Two. Roadrunner Award (Progress). This level is for organizations that demonstrated, through their commitment and implementation of quality principles, significant progress in building sound and notable processes. Organizations have demonstrated a solid approach to TQM and are "on the run" toward implementing plans and procedures. Application at this level requires a description of the organization and the signature of the executive leadership indicating their commitment. The application should include a 15 to 30 page description of the organization's quality system development, implementation, and results achieved, addressing all the major subcategories of the Baldrige Award criteria.

Level Three. Zia Award (Excellence). This advanced level is for organizations that have demonstrated, through their practices and achievements, the highest level of quality excellence. Applications at this level require the description of the organization and executive commitment as for the other levels plus a description (maximum of 85 pages) of how the organization is applying all the Baldrige Award criteria. The application should address all subcategories of the Baldrige criteria.

How to Apply: For information and application forms, contact:

Mike Silva or Glenn Walters, Award Administrators
Quality New Mexico
320 Gold SW, Suite 1218
Albuquerque, NM 87102
Phone: (505) 242–7903
Fax: (505) 242–2940

NEW YORK

Award: The Governor's Excelsior Award. This award includes special emphasis on the workforce and labor-management relations.

Eligibility: Public and private organizations operating in New York State.

Categories: There are awards in four categories:

Private Sector. For applicants from manufacturing and service organizations, including for-profit health care organizations.

Public Sector. For applicants from state and local governmental entities.

Education Sector. For applicants from public and private schools, colleges, and universities.

Health Care Sector. For applicants who are providers of health care and/or mental health care services (including for-profit and not-for-profit organizations).

Award Criteria: As with many other state awards, this one is similar to the Baldrige award:

1. *Leadership.* Examines senior leaders' personal leadership and involvement in creating and sustaining a focus on customers, developing clear and visible quality values, and fostering a management system to guide the company toward quality excellence. (170 pts.)
2. *Information and Analysis.* Examines the scope, validity, use, and management of data and information to drive excellence and improve competitive performance. (50 pts.)
3. *Strategic Quality Planning.* Examines the company's planning process and how all key quality requirements are integrated into overall business planning, including the company's short-term and longer-term plans and how quality and performance requirements are deployed in work units. (50 pts.)
4. *Human Resource Excellence.* Examines the effectiveness of the company's efforts to develop and realize the full potential of the workforce, including management, and to maintain a work environment conducive to full participation, empowerment, quality leadership, and personal organizational growth, and cooperative interaction between management and labor. (240 pts.)
5. *Management of Process Quality.* Examines the systematic processes used by the company to pursue ever-higher quality and company performance, including the key elements of process management, the design of products and services, management of process quality for all work units and suppliers, systematic and continuous quality improvement, and quality assessment. (100 pts.)

6. *Quality and Operational Results.* Examines the company's quality levels and improvement trends in quality, company operational performance, and supplier quality, including current quality and performance relative to competitors. (150 pts.)
7. *Customer Focus and Satisfaction.* Examines the company's relationships with customers and its knowledge of the key factors that determine marketplace competitiveness, including the company's methods to determine customer satisfaction, current levels and trends in customer satisfaction, and these results relative to the competition. (240 pts.)

How to Apply: To find out more information and to apply for these awards, contact:
The Governor's Excelsior Award
NYS Department of Labor
Averell Harriman State Office Campus
Building 12, Room 540A
Albany, NY 12240
Phone: (518) 457-6747
Fax: (518) 457-0620

NORTH CAROLINA

Award: North Carolina Quality Leadership Award

Categories: The award is given in two sectors and three levels:
Sectors. Manufacturing and Services, for both profit and not-for-profit organizations; Educational Institutions.
Levels. Small (less than 100 employees and less than $5 million in annual sales).
Medium (between 100 and 500 emplyees and between $5 and $40 million is annual sales).
Large (More than 500 employees and more than $40 million in annual sales).

Award Criteria: North Carolina models its award after the Baldrige Award and uses the previous year's Baldrige criteria and training material.

How to Apply: For more information and to apply, contact:
Mette Leather
Director of Recognition Programs
North Carolina Quality Leadership Foundation
4904 Professional Court, Suite 100
Raleigh, NC 27609
Phone: (919) 872-8198
Fax: (919) 872-8199

OKLAHOMA

Award: The Oklahoma Quality Award

Categories: Awards are given in four categories and three organizational sizes:
Sizes: 1–50 Employees, 51–250 Employees, and Over 251 Employees, in the following areas:
Manufacturing. SIC codes 01–02, and 08–09
Service. SIC codes 07, 40–42, 44–81, and 83–89
Government. SIC codes 43, 91–97
Education. SIC code 82

Award Criteria: The criteria for the Oklahoma award are based on the Baldrige criteria:

1. *Leadership.* Examines senior executives' personal leadership and involvement in creating and sustaining a customer focus and clear and visible quality values. (110 pts.)
2. *Information and Analysis.* Examines the scope, validity, analysis, management, and use of data and information to drive quality excellence and to improve operational and competitive performance. (60 pts.)
3. *Strategic Quality Planning.* Examines the company's planning process and how all key quality requirements are integrated into overall business planning. (60 pts.)
4. *Human Resources Development and Management.* Examines the key elements of how the workforce is enabled to develop its full potential to pursue the company's quality and operational performance objectives. (170 pts.)
5. *Management of Process Quality.* Examines the systematic processes the company uses to pursue ever-higher quality and company operational performance. (130 pts.)
6. *Quality and Operational Results.* Examines the company's quality levels and improvement trends to quality, company operational performance, and supplier quality. (170 pts.)
7. *Customer Focus and Satisfaction.* Examines the company's relationships with customers and its knowledge of customer requirements and of the key quality factors that drive marketplace competitiveness. (300 pts.)

How to Apply: To get additional information and to apply for this award, contact:
Michael Strong
Executive Director
Oklahoma State Quality Award Foundation, Inc.
6601 N. Broadway, Suite 244
Oklahoma City, OK 73116
Phone: (405) 841–5295
Fax: (405) 841–5205

OREGON

Award: The Oregon Quality Award

Categories: This award is given in four categories:
Manufacturing
Services
Education
Government

Award Criteria: The Oregon award is based on the Baldrige Award criteria.

How to Apply: To find out more information and to apply for these awards, contact:
Tim Dedlow, Program Manager
Oregon Quality Award
One World Trade Center
121 SW Salmon, Suite 1140
Portland, OR 97204
Phone: (503) 224–4606
Fax: (503) 224–5435

PENNSYLVANIA

Award: Pennsylvania Quality Leadership Award

Categories: Awards are given in four categories:

Large Manufacturing (More than 200 full-time employees)
Large Service (More than 200 full-time employees)
Small Manufacturing (200 or fewer employees, not more than $10 million in sales and $15 million in total assets)
Small Service (200 or fewer employees, not more than $10 million in sales and $15 million in total assets)

Criteria: The Pennsylvania criteria are based on the Baldrige criteria:

1. *Leadership.* Examines the senior executives' personal leadership and involvement in creating and sustaining a customer focus and clear, visible, quality values. (95 pts.)
2. *Information and Analysis.* Examines the scope, validity, analysis, management, and use of data and information to drive quality and improve operational and competitive performance. (75 pts.)
3. *Strategic Quality Planning.* Examines the organization's planning process and how all key quality requirements are integrated into overall business planning. (60 pts.)
4. *Human Resource Planning and Management.* Examines the key elements of how the workforce is enabled to develop its full potential to purse the organization's quality and performance objectives. (150 pts.)
5. *Management of Process Quality.* Examines the systematic processes the organization uses to pursue ever-higher quality and operational performance. (140 pts.)
6. *Quality and Operational Results.* Examines the organization's quality levels and improvement trends in quality, operational performance, and supplier quality. (180 pts.)
7. *Customer Focus and Satisfaction.* Examines the organization's relationships with customers and its knowledge of customer requirements and of the key quality factors that drive marketplace competitiveness. (300 pts.)

How to Apply: To get additional information and to apply for this award, contact:

Beverly M. Centini
Award Administrator
Pennsylvania Quality Leadership Foundation, Inc.
P.O. Box 4129
Harrisburg, PA 17111–0129
Phone: (800) 693–6800 or (717) 561–7102
Fax: (717) 561–7104

TENNESSEE

Award: The Tennessee Quality Award

Eligibility: Any public or privately held organization of any size located in the state of Tennessee.

Categories: Awards are given for four levels of quality, based on where an organization is in its quality transformation:

Level 1, Quality Interest. This is for organizations just starting to express interest in adopting and applying quality principles.

Level 2, Quality Commitment. This is for organizations that have progressed to a point of demonstrating serious commitment to the use of total quality principles.

Level 3, Quality Achievement. This is for organizations who have demonstrated, through their commitment and practice of quality principles, significant progress to building sound and notable processes.

Level 4, Governor's Quality Award. This is for organizations that have demonstrated, through their practices and achievements, the highest level of quality excellence.

Award Criteria: The criteria for the Tennessee Quality Award mirror the Baldrige criteria:

1. *Leadership.* Examines senior executives' personal leadership and involvement in creating and sustaining a customer focus and clear and visible values. (95 pts.)
2. *Information and Analysis.* Examines the scope, validity, analysis, management, and use of data and information to drive quality and excellence and improve competitive performance. (75 pts.)
3. *Strategic Quality Planning.* Examines the company's planning process and how all key quality requirements are integrated into overall business planning, including the company's short-term and longer-term plans and how quality and performance requirements are deployed in work units. (60 pts.)
4. *Human Resource Excellence.* Examines the effectiveness of the company's efforts to develop and realize the full potential of the workforce, including management, and to maintain a work environment conducive to full participation, empowerment, quality leadership, and personal organizational growth, and cooperative interaction between management and labor. (150 pts.)
5. *Management of Process Quality.* Examines the systematic processes used by the company to pursue ever-higher quality and company performance, including the key elements of process management, the design of products and services, management of process quality for all work units and suppliers, systematic and continuous quality improvement, and quality assessment. (140 pts.)
6. *Quality and Operational Results.* Examines the company's quality levels and improvement trends in quality, company operational performance, and supplier quality, including current quality and performance relative to competitors. (180 pts.)
7. *Customer Focus and Satisfaction.* Examines the company's relationships with customers and its knowledge of the key factors that determine marketplace competitiveness, including the company's methods to determine customer satisfaction, current levels and trends in customer satisfaction, and these results relative to the competition. (300 pts.)

How to Apply: For more information and to apply for this award, contact:

Marie B. Williams, Director
Tennessee Quality Award
National Center for Quality
P.O. Box 246
Blountville, TN 37617-0246
Phone: (800) 453-6474 or (615) 279-0037
Fax: (615) 279-0978

TEXAS

Award: The Texas Quality Award

Categories: There are four categories for this award:

Industrial Organizations. Small and Large Industrial.

Service Organizations. Small and Large Service.

Governmental Agencies and Non-Profit Organizations. Small and Large Agenices/Non-Profits.

Educational Organizations. Small and Large Educational Organizations.

Criteria: This is based on Baldrige criteria:

Leadership. The senior executives' success in creating and sustaining a quality culture.
Information and Analysis. The effectiveness of the company's collection and analysis of information for quality improvement and planning.
Strategic Quality Planning. The effectiveness of the integration of quality requirements into the organization's business plan.
Human Resource Development and Management. The success of the organization's efforts to realize the full potential of the work force for quality.
Management of Process Quality. The effectiveness of the system for assuring quality control of all operations.
Quality and Operational Results. The organization's results in quality achievement and quality improvement, demonstrated through quantitative measures.
Customer Focus and Satisfaction. The effectiveness of the organization's systems to determine customer requirements and their demonstrated success in meeting those requirements.

How to Apply: For information and application forms, contact:
Robert Norwood, Executive Director
Quality Texas
P.O. Box 684157
Austin, TX 78768-4157
Phone: (512) 477-8137
Fax: (512) 477-8168

VIRGINIA

Award: The U.S. Senate Productivity Award for Virginia. This award originated to recognize productivity but has now evolved into an award for quality management.

Eligibility: Any organization, regardless of size or profit status, practicing continuous improvement of quality and productivity in the Commonwealth of Virginia.

Categories: The are four categories of awards:
Private Sector Manufacturing
Private Sector Service
Public Sector State and Federal Agencies
Public Sector Local Agencies

Criteria: The overall criteria are derived from the Baldrige Award but have been modified. Applicants are asked to supply information in response to questions in eight areas:

1. *Maturity of Effort.* When was the organization's improvement effort initiated? How was the effort conceived? Is the organization's approach original, or was an existing approach tailored to fit the organization's needs? How extensive is the effort within the company? (140 pts.)
2. *Top Management Commitment and Involvement (Leadership).* Describe resource commitments/allocation. How are the quality values of the organization epitomized by the leaders? What are specific examples of the level of commitment and involvement by top management? (140 pts.)
3. *Employee Involvement and Training, Development and Management of Participation.* How is employee involvement encouraged by top management? What types of quality and productivity training opportunities are provided to employees? How are teams used? To what degree are teams empowered? Are employee training and development plans derived from quality and company performance plans? (120 pts.)

4. *Recognition/Rewards Systems.* To what extent are rewards and recognition systems designed to motivate positive behaviors on the part of all employees? Does sharing rewards follow sharing of information, knowledge, and power? How are contributors to and participants in the quality/productivity improvement effort recognized? Is there an established method for sharing gains? (100 pts.)
5. *Plan for Continuous Improvement.* How does your organization plan? Who is involved? Is there evidence that quality and productivity improvement planning is an integral component of the overall planning system? How do the quality and productivity efforts integrate with the organization's vision, long-range plans, business plans, and human resources programs? Are the individuals responsible for implementing these plans involved in developing them? Are targets for long-term goals established? Are self-evaluations made or conducted against other successful efforts? Does the process link plans to action? And how are plans implemented? (120 pts.)
6. *Performance Measurement Process (Use of Information).* To what extent does your organization utilize measurement to support continuous improvement? To what extent does your organization use measurement for purposes of control? How do you integrate and ensure congruency of measures with quality strategies and actions? How are measures linked to the overall improvement effort? Who "owns" the measurement systems and processes in your organization? To what extent are there systematic and ongoing efforts to improve your measurement systems? What evidence exists to demonstrate that measurement to support improvement is deployed throughout your organization? How are measures communicated to the organization? What types of measures are in place? How are they linked to the overall improvement effort? How do you determine what to measure? What categories of information do you collect? Is the quality of the product or service measured at the customer's and supplier's location? Is quality measured internally from a customer perspective? Is there evidence of statistical thinking? Is competitive benchmarking evident? (120 pts.)
7. *Customer and Supplier Involvement.* How do you involve customers and suppliers in your planning? How do your measures reflect focus on suppliers and customers? To what extent does your organization show evidence of "appreciation for systems" in your leadership and management? How do you assess supplier quality? How are customers and suppliers involved in your organization's ongoing efforts to improve quality and productivity? How are customers and suppliers recognized for their efforts? Is customer satisfaction measured? How? What use is made of this information? (120 pts.)
8. *Results Over Time.* Are quality and productivity improvement efforts, in fact, showing results? What are the specific results from the organization's quality and productivity improvement efforts? Is it probable that performance will continue to improve or is it stable? Is there an appropriate balance between short term, immediate results, and longer term results? Is there evidence that your organization understands the complex cause and effect relationship between quality and productivity improvement initiatives and results over time? Is there an appropriate balance between quality of approach and deployment and impact, and results over time? (140 pts.)

How to Apply: For more information and application forms, contact:

Elizabeth Holmes
U.S. Senate Productivity Award for Virginia

c/o VQPC/ISE
560 Whittemore Hall
Virginia Tech
Blacksburg, VA 24061-0118
Phone: (703) 231-4568
Fax: (703) 231-6925

National Awards Directory

Award: The Shingo Prize for Excellence in Manufacturing

Categories and Eligibility: *Large Manufacturing Companies, Subsidiaries, or Plants* (500 or more employees and at least 50 percent of revenue from manufacturing activities)

Small Manufacturing Companies (Fewer than 500 employees and at least 50 percent of revenue derived from manufacturing activities)

SIC codes eligible: 20–39.

Award Criteria: Applicants are judged on four major criteria:

1. *Total Quality and Productivity Management Culture and Infrastructure.* Examines the system inputs necessary to guide manufacturing strategy, processes, and system integration, leading to world class results, and outcome improvements. Three key elements reviewed: leading, empowering, and partnering. (275 pts.)
2. *Manufacturing Strategy, Processes, and System Integration.* Examines the vision, strategy, processes, and system integration utilized to achieve to world class manufacturing. (425 pts.)
3. *Measured Quality and Productivity.* Intended to provide information about the accomplishments achieved by means of the manufacturing strategy, processes and system integration detailed in criterion 2. (200 pts.)
4. *Measured Customer Satisfaction.* Intended to provide information about measured improvements in customer satisfaction, indicated through any valid approach being used by the company. (100 pts.)

How to Apply: To get additional information and to apply for this award, contact:
Ross E. Robson, Executive Director
The Shingo Prize for Excellence in Manufacturing
College of Business
Utah State University
Logan, UT 84322–3521
Phone: (801) 797–2279
Fax: (801) 797–3440

Award: The RIT/USA TODAY Quality Cup (Given jointly by the Rochester Institute of Technology and USA Today.)

Categories: There are five categories of eligible organizations:

Organizations in these areas with over 500 employees:
Service Firms
Manufacturing Firms
Not-for-Profit Organizations and Institutions (including health care)
Government Units and Agencies of Government
Organizations with fewer than 500 employees in any of the above categories

Award Criteria: This award is unlike the Baldrige or other similar awards. Applications focus on the activities of teams or individuals within organizations to implement quality principles and deliver customer service. The application requests:

1. A brief description (no more than 100 words) that summarizes the quality improvement for which the team or individual is being nominated.
2. In no more than 300 words, describe the process that led to the nominee's accomplishment—how was the problem or opportunity identified; what were its root causes; how was the solution developed and selected; how and by who was the solution implemented? (300 pts.)
3. In no more than 400 words, describe the change brought about by implementing the solution. Identify the internal or external customers affected by the change. Describe how customers benefitted from the change. (400 pts.)
4. In no more than 300 words, describe the way in which the following were measured: (1) the change brought about implementing the solution and (2) the benefits to customers. (300 pts.)

How to Apply: To get additional information and to apply for this award, contact:

Carol Ann Skalski
Quality Cup
USA Today
1000 Wilson Blvd., 22nd Floor
Arlington, VA 22229
Phone: (703) 276–5890

International Awards Directory

This directory includes several more awards than the 1994 edition did. It is based on information provided by administrators of the Baldrige Award and from other sources. It begins with a list of international awards, followed by an alphabetical listing of country awards. We welcome updates and information on awards in countries not covered.

The Deming Prize

This is sponsored by the Union of Japanese Scientists and Engineers (JUSE) and named for W. Edwards Deming. The prestigious award was established in 1951, with categories for *individuals, small companies, factories,* and for *application of company-wide quality control statistical methods.* Organizatons and individuals from any nation may apply. Most winners come from Japan.

For detailed information, contact:

Kohei Suzue, President
The Union of Japanese Scientists and Engineers (JUSE)
5–10–11 Sendagaya
Shibuya-ku, Tokyo 151
JAPAN
Phone: 81 3 352–2231
Fax: 81 3 356–1798

The European Quality Award

Sponsored by the European Foundation for Quality Management. Criteria have some overlap with the Baldrige Award, but with some modifications. For detailed information, contact:

Mike Gallagher
The European Foundation for Quality Management
Avenue des Pleiades 19
B-1200 Brussels

BELGIUM
Phone: 32 2 775–3511
Fax: 32 2 775–3535

International Benchmarking Award

This award is designed to recognize benchmarking excellence by organizations in a variety of specialities, with specific criteria tied to the benchmarking task. For more information, contact:

International Benchmarking Clearinghouse
American Productivity and Quality Center
123 North Post Oak Lane, Suite 300
Houston, TX 77024–7797
Phone: (713) 681–4020
Fax: (713) 681–8578

ARGENTINA

Premio Nacional a la Calidad

Started in 1992, the first award was given in 1994. For more information, contact:

Oscal A. Imbellone, Vice President
Fundacion Empresaria para la Calidad y la Excelencia
Santa Fe 846
2 Piso
1059 Buenos Aires
ARGENTINA
Phone: 54 1 311–8933
Fax: 54 1 312–3228

AUSTRALIA

Australian Quality Prize

Started in 1992 to recognize companies that achieve internationally competitive performance levels. For more information, contact:

Graham Spong, General Manager
Australian Quality Awards Foundation, Inc.
P.O. Box 298
St. Leonards, NSW 2065
AUSTRALIA
Phone: 61 2 439–8200
Fax: 61 2 906–3847

BAHAMAS

National Quality Award

The award was started to encourage quality management, and has various levels at which companies may apply. For more information contact:

Agatha K. Marcelle, Executive Director
Bahamas Quality Council
P.O. Box N-665
Nassau, BAHAMAS
Phone: (809) 328–4130
Fax: (809) 328–4131

BRAZIL

Brazil National Quality Award

The Brazilian award has been patterned after the Baldrige Award. For more information, contact:

Basilio Dagnino, Technical Manager
Brazil National Quality Award Foundation
Ave. Prestes Haia, 773
s/ 1914
Sao Paulo—SP
BRAZIL

BRITAIN

British Quality Award

This national award of Great Britain includes criteria similar to that for the Baldrige. Detailed information is available from:

Director of Awards
The British Quality Association
Vigilant Pass, 120 Wilton Road
London SW1V 1JZ
UNITED KINGDOM
Phone: 44 71 931–0607
Fax: 44 71 233–7034

CANADA

Canada Awards for Business Excellence

The Services to Business Branch of the Canadian government sponsors these awards in several categories including an award for Total Quality. The criteria, briefly, for the quality award include:

1. *Quality Improvement Policy and Plan* (Value 10%)
2. *Implementation of Policy and Plan* (Value 40%)
3. *Results Acheived* (Value 40%)
4. *Future Planning* (Value 10%)

For information, contact:

Canadian Awards for Business Excellence
Industry Canada
235 Queen Street
Ottawa, Ontario K1A OH5
Phone: (613) 954–4085
Fax: (613) 954–4074

CHILE

Chile National Quality Award

For information on this award, contact:

Osvaldo M. Ferreiro, Coordinator
Productivity and Quality Program
Catholic University of Chile
Extension Center
Avda. Bernardo O'Higgins 390

Santiago, CHILE
Phone: 56 2 222–4516
Fax: 56 2 552–5916

COLOMBIA

Colombia National Quality Award

Main criteria are based on 1SO 9004 standards. For more information contact:

Teresita Beltran Ospina
Head of Standardization, Metrology, and Quality Division
Ministerio de Desarrollo Economico
Celle 26 No. 13–19, Piso 34
Bogota, COLOMBIA
Phone: 57 1 334–0542
Fax: 57 1 281–1103

FRANCE

Prix Nationale de la Qualite

The French National Quality Award is designed to encourage and recognize French companies who practice quality mangement. The criteria for this award are similar to the Baldrige Award. For more information, contact:

Mouvement Francaise pour la Qualite-MFQ
5, esplanade Charles de Gaulle
92733 Nanterre Cedex
FRANCE
Phone: 33 1 47 29 09 29
Fax: 33 1 47 25 32 21

HONG KONG

Hong Kong Quality Award

Criteria are generally based on the Baldrige Award. For more informaation, contact:

Elizabeth S.C. Shing
Director General
The Hong Kong Management Association
14/F Fairmont House
8 Cotton Tree Drive
Phone: 852 526–6516
Fax: 852 868–4387

INDIA

The Rajiv Gandhi National Quality Award

Instituted in 1991 and has criteria similar to the Baldrige Award. For more information, contact:

Director General
Bureau of Indian Standards
9, Bahadur Shah Zafa Marg
New Delhi 110 002
INDIA

A second Indian quality award has been instituted by the Institute of Directors, also based on Baldrige criteria. For more information, contact:

Najma Heptulia, National Chairman
Institute of Directors
Madhuban Building
107/55 Nehru Place
New Delhi 110 019
INDIA
Phone: 91 11 642–1668
Fax: 91 11 646–8537

ISRAEL

The Quality Prize

Established by the Association of Electronics Industries, the competition is open to organizations in all industries. For more information, contact:

Avigdor Zonnenshain
Quality and Productivity Director
Association of Electronics Industries
P.O. Box 50026
Tel-Aviv 61500
ISRAEL

MEXICO

Mexico National Quality Award

First presented in 1990. For more information, contact:

Raul Macias G., General Director
Mexico National Quality Award
Heriberto Frias #249
Col. del Valle
Deleg. Benito Juarez
C.P. 03100 Mexico, D.F.
P.O. Box 12700
MEXICO
Phone: 52 5 639–6748
Fax: 52 5 639–6170

NETHERLANDS

The Dutch Quality Award

First awards given in November 1993. For more information, contact:

Jan Balk
Netherlandse Kwaliteit
Postbus 205
2000 AE Haarlem
NETHERLANDS

NEW ZEALAND

New Zealand Quality Award

The first awards were given in 1993. Criteria is based on the Baldrige Award. For more information:

Doug Matheson, Chairperson

New Zealand Quality Awards Foundation
"Karinga" West Bush Road
RD 8
Masterton
NEW ZEALAND
Phone: 64 6 377–4111

NORTHERN IRELAND

The Northern Ireland Quality Award

Established in 1991, the prize uses a version of the Baldrige criteria. For more information, contact:

Roy Adair, CEO/Director
Northern Ireland Quality Centre
Midland Building
Whitla Street
Belfast BT15 1NH
IRELAND

PHILIPPINES

National Quality Award

Joint project with Philippine Society for Quality Control and the National Quality Campaign. For more information, contact:

Philippine Society for Quality Control, Inc.
Suite 607
Campos Rueda Building
Urban Street
Makati
Metro Manila
PHILIPPINES

SINGAPORE

The Singapore Quality Award

The Singapore award uses the Baldrige criteria. For more information, contact:

Lee Siew Hon
The Singapore Quality Award Information Centre
c/o National Productivity Board
NPB Building
2 Bukit Merha Central
SINGAPORE 0315
Phone: 65 279–3708
Fax: 65 278–6667

SPAIN

National Quality Award

Two awards, for companies with more than 250 employees and for companies with less than 250 employees. For more information, contact:

Spanish Association for Quality
Zurbano, 92

1 Drcha.
28003 Madrid
SPAIN
Phone: 34 1 441–7543
Fax: 34 1 441–7390

SWEDEN

Swedish Quality Award

First awards given in 1992 with criteria similar to those for the Baldrige Award. For more information, contact:

Jonny Lindstrom, President
Swedish Institute for Quality
Gardatorget 1
S-412 50 Goteborg
SWEDEN
Phone: 46 31 773–0875
Fax: 46 31 773–0645

TAIWAN

National Quality Award

Begun in 1990, the goal is to award outstanding achievement in TQM and to further the upgrading of quality levels. For more information, contact:

Kao Sin-Yan, Chairman
Center Satellite Development
National Quality Award Section
CSD Industrial Coordination Center
7th Floor, No. 8, Tun-Hwa North Road
Taipei, TAIWAN
Phone: 886 2 751–3468
Fax: 886 2 781–7790

How to Do Benchmarking

James W. Cortada

Benchmarking is a method for finding how to improve processes quickly by learning from others dealing with similar issues. It is a critical tactic used by organizations interested in continuous improvement. It involves the sharing of ideas and descriptions of processes. Benchmarking is done between organizations within an enterprise and also between firms. The latter approach frequently is the most productive since no two firms seem to approach processes quite the same way.

David T. Kearns, former CEO at Xerox, called benchmarking "the continuous process of measuring products, services, and practices against the toughest competitors or those companies recognized as industry leaders." His is a good definition, coming from an individual who has spent his whole life in highly competitive industries and who has a profound knowledge about a wide range of business processes ranging from manufacturing to marketing. In fact, his company is recognized as the leading user of benchmarking because of its own success with it and as a result of some employees writing important books and articles on the topic. IBM's formal definition is "the continuous process of analyzing the best practices in the world for the purpose of establishing and validating process goals and objectives leading to world-class levels of achievement."

Either definition, however, leads to some clear objectives. Benchmarking allows a company to compare its processes with the best, learn from this, and make changes that lead to measurable improvements. By using benchmarking techniques, managers can adopt best practices as their own without having to go through the often laborious and time-consuming process of inventing them on their own.

Many companies that practice TQM have made benchmarking simply a part of their approach to management. It is an efficient way to compare your processes with those of others, either in your own or other industry, and make use of them. Today, nearly half the Fortune 500 companies do benchmarking. Companies and industries are also forming benchmarking consortiums to examine specific issues, for example, the relative cost of some specific set of activities, such as billing and data processing.

In addition to using this approach to see how your processes are doing as compared to those of acknowledged leaders, benchmarking has other uses. It lends itself to objective assessments of the strengths and weaknesses of existing processes. It stimulates thinking and acceptance of new ideas and approaches. Benchmarking frequently helps the process of justifying changes either in quantitative or qualitative ways, even pushing aside internal resistance to change by legitimizing new ideas.

In its simplest form, benchmarking is not a difficult process. First, you define the process to be benchmarked. You measure how you are doing it today, documenting the process. Then select benchmark partners that also have documented a similar process and compare notes, either on a one time or on a regular basis over time. Discussions center around how to improve each other's processes, share what you are learning, and then experiment with improvements. Assessments are fact-based, relying on measurable results. Findings become the basis for changes in your process as you continuously improve your efficiency and effectiveness. This is time consuming, so most firms pick the most critical processes to benchmark.

The process of benchmarking can be just reading an article about a process someone else uses and comparing it to your own. Another approach is to hire a consultant to conduct the benchmarking activity. Often the process owners of two or more organizations will personally lead the benchmarking activities, complete with joint meetings, site visits, and sharing of process documentation. Benchmarking can be of peer organizations within your company (e.g., how one distribution center does against another). Comparing common processes across multiple firms in different industries is useful (e.g., how customer feedback is done). A third approach is to compare your performance against competitors.

Experience suggests some basic rules for effective benchmarking.

1. Train people in the process of benchmarking to insure effectiveness.
2. Make sure company secrets that could damage your firm are not at risk.
3. Coordinate benchmarking with other parts of your enterprise so you avoid two or more groups benchmarking on the same process (a real problem in large organizations enthusiastic about the application of TQM principles).
4. Share benchmarking results widely within your enterprise for the same reasons as in Number 3.
5. Document all benchmarking results in detail so that processes can be improved and lessons learned along the way are not lost.

From a tactical point of view, workable approaches include (1) setting up an internal clearing house for benchmarking information, (2) creating benchmarking teams responsible for carrying out this activity for their processes, (3) designating benchmarking coordinators for various processes, and (4) creating some process for documenting and communicating benchmarking activities. In many large corporations, for example, there now are electronic bulletin boards with databases of such projects.

Benchmarking education becomes a real necessity once an organization has gone down the quality management path for a year or more and is deeply involved in process improvement or reengineering, so offer it to employees as needed. Best practices also involves looking at benchmarking as a process in itself, subject to continuous improvement. Figure 1 is a model of the process,

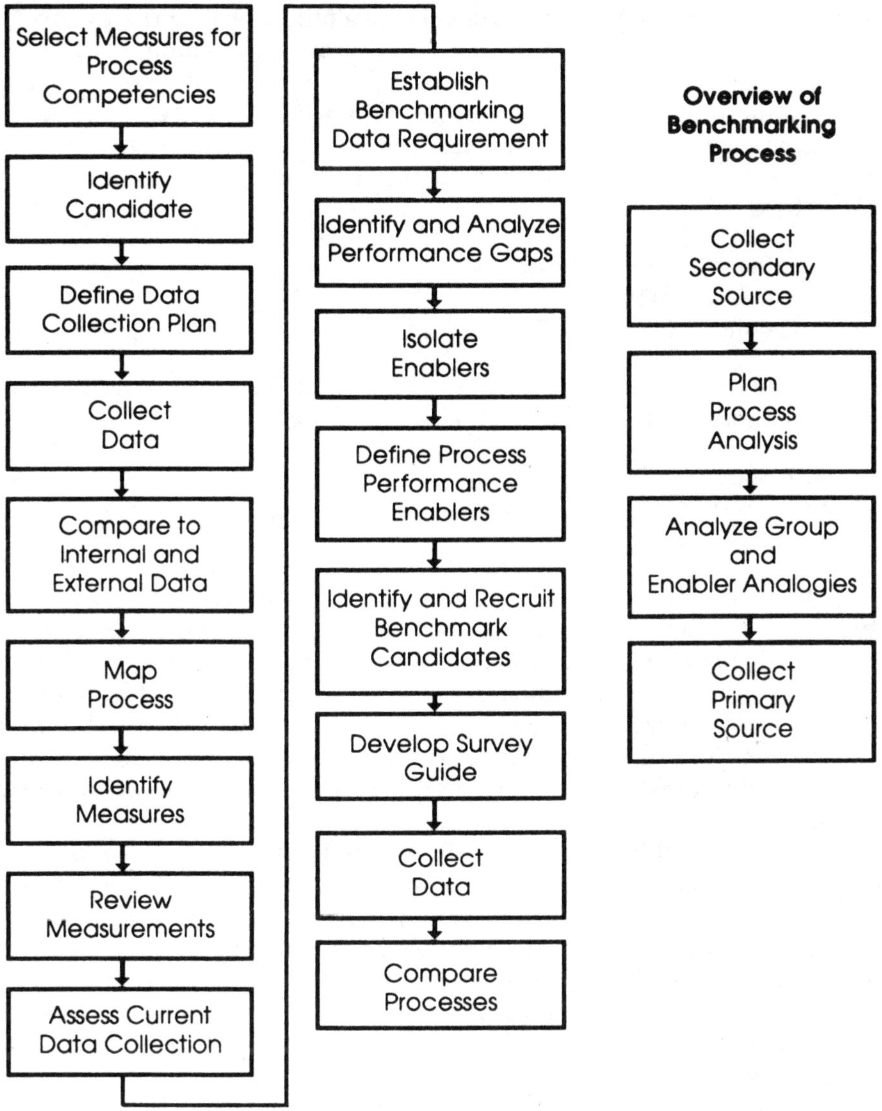

Figure 1.

which incorporates the approaches taken by such companies as IBM, Xerox, and AT&T.

Since the primary purpose for benchmarking is to accelerate the continuous improvement of processes, you should consider using it early in the development of a new process to save time and take advantage of what others have already discovered about best practices. Looking at other processes early on definitely gets your teams thinking in bolder, more effective terms because there is always somebody who has developed a process better than yours. The fastest way to get these ideas is to go to the American Productivity and Quality Center, which has been building a database for benchmarking for many years. As a member of their organization, they will do research on how other people do a process, get you articles, and names and telephone numbers. They work fast and are effective. Process teams find them very useful early-on. Their address:

123 N. Post Oak Lane, Suite 300
Houston, TX 77024–7797
800–324–4673, fax: 713–681–5321

Another resource that is available on-line is The Benchmarking Exchange. You can get additional information on this service at

1960-B Soquel Drive, Suite 356
Aptos, CA 95003
(408) 662–9800

APQC is one of the best things to come along to help those wanting to do process reengineering. They will tell you that over half of the Fortune 500 companies do benchmarking, including many of your competitors. They also can show you that those companies that routinely benchmark have more profitable performance of, on average, a third better than those who do not. The Benchmarking Exchange is a rapidly growing service plugged into many quality organizations, with a great variety of information available through your computer.

Good benchmarking practices follow classic process improvement strategems of Plan, Do, Check, and Act by planning studies, collecting data, analyzing it, and then adopting improvements on a continuous basis.

Benchmarking, while effective with all processes, tends to do best when applied to key business processes, areas causing customer dissatisfaction, applications subject to rapid changes in technology, areas causing employee dissatisfaction and, of course, for the sake of efficiency, with processes that cost more than the benefits they generate.

The common benefits currently being achieved by benchmarking, as based on surveys done on those who have applied this approach, include:

- Leads to stretch objectives.
- Makes goals realistic and actionable.
- Encourages pursuit of excellence and breakthrough thinking.
- Forces study of competition and other firms.
- Focuses attention on customer needs.
- Represents one of the most effective ways to energize process teams.
- Illustrates need for change and how to achieve it in manageable and precise terms.

Benchmarking is in itself a process to be learned, not a single event or a tool. Good process management builds into it continuous benchmarking.

For additional details on benchmarking see Robert C. Camp, *Benchmarking: The Search for Industry Best Practices That Lead to Superior Performance* (Milwaukee: ASQC Quality Press, 1989); Gregory H. Watson, *Strategic Benchmarking* (New York: John Wiley and Sons, 1993); Robert J. Boxwell, *Benchmarking for Competitive Advantage* (New York: McGraw-Hill, 1994); and Christopher E. Bogan and Michael J. English, *Benchmarking for Best Practices* (New York: McGraw-Hill, 1994).

Quotes on Quality

The purpose of these quotes is to provide inspirational insight into what Total Quality Management is all about, to get you thinking about this approach in new ways, and to offer material useful in speeches and presentations. The following quotes are organized loosely by topic. Several of the quotes might have fit in several categories. We tried to put them in the most logical one. But in looking for thoughts on a particular topic, we suggest you still scan the entire section.

The quotes come from eclectic sources, including philosophers, poets, and scientists as well as business writers and managers. There is a reason for this. The ideas of quality management are not unique to this field. They naturally emerge in a variety of forms and contexts whenever people contemplate excellence and high performance in any human endeavor. We may come to see that quality management is ultimately about bringing out the best in all of us to facilitate our mutual success and prosperity. Wise people have appreciated such notions from time immemorial. Consider that as you read these quotes.

The categories we have chosen include: Quality Defined, Quality Management, Quality Leadership, Culture of Quality, Customers, Training, Teams and Teamwork, Process Management, Measurement, Human Resources, Continuous Improvement, and "The Wrong Stuff." Some categories include many more quotes than others. It just seems people have said more quotable statements about leadership, for example, than about measurements.

Finally, if there are other quotes you especially like, we would be pleased to have you send them to us. We will use them in future editions and credit you with their submission.

Quality Defined

Includes thoughts on what quality means to different people.

> Excellence is an art won by training and habituation. We are what we repeatedly do. Excellence, then, is not an act but a habit.
>
> —Aristotle

> Quality isn't something that can be argued into an article or promised into it. It must be put there. If it isn't put there, the finest sales talk in the world won't act as a substitute.
>
> —Charles G. Campbell

> When everything would seem to be a matter of price, there lies still at the root of great business success the very much more important fact of quality.
>
> —Andrew Carnegie

It is man that makes truth great, not truth that makes man great.
—Confucius

I define quality as conformance to requirements. Period. We should perform the job or produce the product as we agreed to do it.
—Philip B. Crosby

Good quality does not necessarily mean high quality. It means a predictable degree of uniformity and dependability at low cost with a quality suited to the market.
—W. Edwards Deming

You do not have to do this; survival is not compulsory!
—W. Edwards Deming

The typical engineering definition of quality is something that is hard to do, is complicated, and costs a lot of money! But that isn't quality; it's incompetence.
—Peter Drucker

There is one rule for industrialists and that is: Make the best quality of goods at the lowest cost possible, paying the highest wages possible.
—Henry Ford

Quality is never an accident; it is always the result of high intention, sincere effort, intelligent direction, and skillful execution; it represents the wise choice of many alternatives, the cumulative experience of many masters of craftsmanship. Quality also marks the search for an ideal after necessity has been satisfied and mere usefulness achieved.
—Will A. Foster

All excellence involves discipline and tenacity of purpose.
—John W. Gardner

Quality is not only right, it is free. And it is not only free, it is the most profitable product line we have.
—Harold S. Geneen

If you really believe in quality, when you cut through everything, it's empowering your people, and it's empowering your people that leads to teams.
—Jamie Houghton

The manufacturing job is mainly to meet standards of cost, quality, and delivery. Any fool or knave can meet any two of these standards *provided* he is allowed to ignore the third. By setting and enforcing standards for all three, we help to ensure a balanced performance.
—Joseph M. Juran

Quality does not happen by accident; it has to be planned.
—Joseph M. Juran

Starting out to make money is the greatest mistake in life. Do what you feel you have a flair for doing, and if you are good enough at it the money will come.

—Lord Rootes

Remember always that the recollection of quality remains long after the price is forgotten. Then your business will prosper by a natural process.

—H. Gordon Selfridge

Quality is not any single thing but an aura, an atmosphere, an overpowering feeling that a company is doing everything with excellence.

—Jack Welch

Quality, a particular and essential character: nature, degree of excellence. . . .

—Webster's Dictionary

Quality Management

Includes thoughts on the concerns of any manager who wants to facilitate quality, including quotes on the idea of an organization as a system.

Chaotic action is preferable to orderly inaction.

—Anonymous

There is no growth except in the fulfillment of obligations.

—Anonymous

A prudent question is one-half of wisdom.

—Francis Bacon

More erroneous conclusions are due to a lack of information than to errors of judgment.

—Louis D. Brandeis

Destiny is not a matter of chance; it is a matter of choice; it is not a thing to be waited for, but something to be achieved.

—William Jennings Bryan

He that wrestles with us strengthens our nerves and sharpens our skills. Our antagonist is our helper.

—Edmund Burke

Money never starts an idea; it is the idea that starts the money.

—William J. Cameron

It is a socialist idea that making profits is a vice; I consider the real vice is making losses.

—Sir Winston Churchill

Knowledge is the only instrument of production that is not subject to the law of diminishing returns.

—John M. Clark

If our factories could, through care, impose the superior quality of our products, foreigners would see the advantage of purchasing French goods and money would flow to our kingdom.

—Jean-Baptiste Colbert

Quality is determined by top management. It cannot be delegated.

—W. Edwards Deming

A system is a network of interdependent components that work together to try to accomplish the aim of the system. A system must have an aim. Without an aim, there is no system. . . . A system must be managed. The secret is cooperation between components toward the aim of the organization. We cannot afford the destructive effect of competition.

—W. Edwards Deming

To find out what one is fitted to do and to secure an opportunity to do it is the key to happiness.

—John Dewey

Most new projects—I can even say every one of them—can be analyzed to destruction.

—Georges Doriot

The effective executive knows that to get strength one has to put up with weaknesses.

—Peter Drucker

Effective executives never ask "How does he get along with me?" Their question is "What does he contribute?"

—Peter Drucker

The increase in productivity has been caused primarily by the replacement of labor by planning, brawn by brain, sweat by knowledge.

—Peter Drucker

Effective executives know that their subordinates are paid to perform and not to please their superiors.

—Peter Drucker

I start where the last man left off.

—Thomas Alva Edison

The reward of one duty is the power to fulfill another.

—George Eliot

If you don't take it for granted that the other man will do his job, you're not an executive.

—William Feather

The competitor to be feared is one who never bothers about you at all, but goes on making his own business better all the time.

—Henry Ford

I learned along the way to delegate. I consider it the height of folly and vanity to try to do something that you can get someone else to do better—and that goes right up to running the business if necessary.

—Robert Fowler

Men for the sake of getting a living forget to live.

—Margaret Fuller

Decision is a sharp knife that cuts clean and straight; indecision, a dull one that hacks and tears and leaves ragged edges behind it.

—Gordon Graham

Capitalism is based on self-interest and self-esteem; it holds integrity and trustworthiness as cardinal virtues and make them pay off in the marketplace.

—Alan Greenspan

There is no way to make people like change. You can only make them feel less threatened by it.

—Frederick Hayes

The way to get things done is not to mind who gets credit for doing them.

—Benjamin Jowett

The will to win is not nearly as important as the will to prepare to win.

—Bobby Knight

A big corporation is more or less blamed for being big; it is only big because it gives service. If it doesn't give service, it gets small faster than it grew big.

—William S. Knudsen

The greatest administrators do not achieve production through constraints and limitations. They provide opportunities.

—Lao Tzu

The problem is that to the unbelievers, to the traditionally minded business people who comprise 99.9 percent of all management, any proof will be shrugged off. They have eyes, but they cannot see. The scales will fall off only when they are struck by a meaningful personal insight into the nature of work, motivation, and competitiveness.

—William Lareau

Good mistakes, those made with careful preparation and understanding of the process in question, are valuable improvement tools. Good mistakes should be encouraged and rewarded as often and as thoroughly as possible.

—William Lareau

True involvement takes more than just pushing only one, two, or three of the four features—power, information, knowledge, and rewards—to all levels of the organization. All four of these features must be moved to the lowest level of the organization.

—Edward Lawler

The aim of all legitimate business is service, for profit, at a risk.

—Benjamin C. Leeming

The game of life is not so much holding a good hand as playing a poor one well.

—H.T. Leslie

The foundation of every noble life are the principles that have shaped it.

—George Lorimer

A company is a multidimensional system capable of growth, expansion, and self-regulation. It is, therefore, not a thing but a set of interacting forces. Any theory of organization must be capable of reflecting a company's many facets, its dynamism, and its basic orderliness. When a company organization is reviewed, or when reorganizing a company, it must be looked upon as a whole, as a total system.

—Albert Low

Republics have a longer life and enjoy better fortune than principalities, because they can profit by their greater internal diversity. They are better able to meet emergencies.

—Machiavelli

The new source of power is not money in the hands of a few but information in the hands of many.

—John Naisbitt

A commander in chief cannot take as an excuse for his mistakes in warfare an order given by his minister or his sovereign, when the person giving the order is absent from the field of operations or is imperfectly aware or wholly unaware of the latest state of affairs. It follows that any commander in chief who undertakes to carry out a plan which he considers defective is at fault; he must put forward his reasons, insist on the plan being changed, and finally tender his resignation rather than be the instrument of his army's downfall.

—Napoleon

What employees are looking for from me—the first word I think is "coxswain"—they want to know that we're headed in the same direction, everyone is given a voice, and each person participates.

—Bill O'Brien

The successful producer of an article sells it for more than it cost him to make, and that's his profit, but the customer buys it only because it is worth more to him than he pays for it, and that's his profit. No one can make a profit producing anything unless the customer makes a profit using it.

—Samuel B. Pettengill

[Reflections while repairing a motorcycle] The overall name of these interrelated structures is *system*. The motorcycle is a system. A *real* system. . . . There's so much talk about the system. And so little understanding. That's all the motorcycle is, a system of concepts worked out in steel. There's no part in it, no shape in it that is not in someone's mind. . . . I've noticed that people who have never worked with steel have trouble seeing this—that the motorcycle is primarily a mental phenomenon.

—Robert Pirsig

Good management consists in showing average people how to do the work of superior people.

—John D. Rockefeller

Take something common and make it uncommon.

—John D. Rockefeller

The best executive is the one who has sense enough to pick good men to do what he wants done, and self-restraint enough to keep from meddling with them while they do it.

—Theodore Roosevelt

Success is journey, not a destination.

—Ben Sweetland

The problem is not to increase quality; increasing quality is the answer to the problem.

—Myron Tribus

I found that the men and women who got to the top were those who did the jobs they had in hand, with everything they had of energy and enthusiasm and hard work.

—Harry Truman

If we let our people flourish and grow, unleash people to be self-confident and take on more responsibility, if we use the best ideas they come up with, then we will have a chance to win. The idea of liberation and empowerment for our work force is not enlightenment; it's a competitive necessity.

—Jack Welch

We have to undo a 100-year-old concept and convince our managers that their role is not to control people and stay on top of things, but rather to guide, energize, and excite.

—Jack Welch

We think in generalities but we live in detail.

—Alfred North Whitehead

The motive of success is not enough. It produces a short-sighted world which destroys the source of its own prosperity. The cycles of trade depression which afflict the world warn us that business relations are infected through and through with the disease of short-sighted motives.

—Alfred North Whitehead

There's a man in the world who is never turned down, wherever he chances to stray; he gets the glad hand in the populous town or out where the farmers make hay; he's greeted with pleasure on deserts of sand, and deep in the aisles of the woods; wherever he goes there's a welcoming hand—he's the man who delivers the goods.

—Walt Whitman

When two men in business always agree, one of them is unnecessary.

—William Wrigley, Jr.

Quality Leadership

Includes thoughts on individual leadership behaviors that bring about the success of all.

True leadership is the art of changing a group from what it is into what it ought to be.

—Virginia Allan

Failing is not falling down; it is remaining there when you have fallen.

—Anonymous

Adversity is sure to bring a season of sober reflection. Men see clearer at such times. Storms purify the atmosphere.

—Henry Ward Beecher

Let people see clearly that it is in your interest to promote theirs.

—Jean de La Bruyere

Men are failures not because they are stupid, but because they are not sufficiently impassioned.

—Struthers Burt

Look at management as a function, not a class. If you go into the role thinking that management is a class, you'll be sorely disappointed when you find that people rebel against you.

—Mike Busch

As I grow older, I pay less attention to what men say. I just watch what they do.

—Andrew Carnegie

Action makes more fortunes than caution.

—Luc de Clapiers, Marquis de Vauvenargues

It is the particular quality of the fool to perceive the faults of others and to forget his own.

—Cicero

If we are to achieve, we must look for the opportunity in every difficulty instead of the difficulty in every opportunity.

—Walter E. Cole

To get the best out of a man go to what is best in him.

—Daniel Consodine

I know a leader when I have followed one.

—John Cowan

In a day when so much energy seems to be spent on maintenance and manuals, on bureaucracy and meaningless quantification, to be a leader is to enjoy special privileges of complexity, of ambiguity, of diversity.

—Max DePree

Whenever you see a successful business, someone made a courageous decision.

—Peter Drucker

Unless a man undertakes more than he possibly can do he will never do all that he can.

—Henry Drummond

The action makes the hero.

—Oswald Dykes

For peace of mind, resign as general manager of the universe.

—Larry Eisenberg

In simplest terms, a leader is one who knows where he wants to go, gets up, and goes.

—John Erskine

Paying attention to simple little things that most men neglect makes a few men rich.

—Henry Ford

Treat people as if they were what they ought to be and you help them become what they are capable of being.

—Johann Wolfgang von Goethe

The very essence of leadership is that you have a vision. It's got to be a vision you articulate clearly and forcefully on every occasion. You can't blow an uncertain trumpet.

—Father Theodore Hesburgh

Fail is made up of fear, apathy, indecision, and lack of purpose.

—Tom Hopkins

Common sense is not sense common to everyone, but sense in common things.

—William James

To be upset over what you don't have is to waste what you do have.

—Ken S. Keyes, Jr.

A leader is best when people hardly know he exists. When his work is done, his aim fulfilled, they will all say, "We did it ourselves."

—Lao Tzu

By staying present and aware of what is happening, the leader can do less yet achieve more.

—Lao Tzu

The genius of good leadership is to leave behind a situation which common sense, even without the grace of genius, can deal with successfully.

—Walter Lippmann

It is not the finding of a thing, but the making something out of it after it is found.

—James Russell Lowell

There is nothing more difficult to take in hand, more perilous to conduct, or more uncertain in its success than to take the lead in the introduction of a new order of things.

—Machiavelli

You have to recognize that every 'out front' maneuver you make is going to be lonely, but if you feel entirely comfortable, then you're not far enough ahead to do any good. That warm sense of everything going well is usually the body temperature at the center of the herd.

—John Masters

Lord, grant that I may always desire more than I can accomplish.

—Michelangelo

Let go the things in which you are in doubt for the things in which there is no doubt.

—Mohammed

Useless laws weaken the necessary laws.

—Montesquieu

So long as men praise you, you can only be sure that you are not yet on your own true path but on someone else's.

—Friedrich Nietzche

All our final resolutions are made in a state of mind which is not going to last.

—Marcel Proust

Be patient with everyone, but above all with yourself.

—St. Francis De Sales

The reward for work well done is the opportunity to do more.

—Jonas Salk, M.D.

Audacity augments courage.

—Publius Syrus

Anyone can hold the helm with the sea is calm.

—Publius Syrus

I've never been poor, only broke. Being poor is a frame of mind. Being broke is only a temporary situation.

—Mike Todd

It is better to aim at perfection and miss than it is to aim at imperfection and hit it.

—Thomas J. Watson, Sr.

The basic philosophy, spirit, and drive of an organization have far more to do with its relative achievements than do technological or economic resources, organizational structure, innovation, and timing.

—Thomas Watson, Jr.

Culture of Quality

Includes thoughts that suggest the attributes of a quality culture.

If you can't win, make the fellow ahead of you break the record.

—Anonymous

A free curiosity has more efficacy in learning than a frightful enforcement.

—Saint Augustine

Management, in the sense of employer, is merely the agent for the public, the stockholders and the employees. It is management's job to preserve the balance fairly between all those interests, that each may have his fair share without imperiling the continuity of the effort upon which the whole depends.

—James F. Bell

The toughest thing about success is that you have to keep on being a success.

—Irving Berlin

Better never to begin than never to make an end.

—Thomas Braxee

I don't want to do business with those who don't make a profit, because they can't give the best service.

—Lee Bristol

You cannot create experience. You must undergo it.

—Albert Camus

The man who removes a mountain begins by carrying away small stones.

—Chinese Proverb

He who heeds not the future will find sorrow close at hand.

—Confucius

A man who had committed a mistake and doesn't correct it is committing another mistake.

—Confucius

Things that are bad for business are bad for the people who work for business.

—Thomas E. Dewey

The secret of success is constancy to purpose.

—Benjamin Disraeli

Enthusiasm is that secret harmonious spirit which hovers over the production of genius.

—Benjamin Disraeli

Results are gained by exploiting opportunities, not by solving problems.

—Peter Drucker

Every great and commanding moment in the annals of the world is the triumph of some enthusiasm.

—Ralph Waldo Emerson

Regardless of circumstances, each man lives in a world of his own making.

—Joseph Murray Emms

The world is full of cactus, but we don't have to sit in it.

—Will Foley

I don't believe in ordering people to do things. You have to sort of grab an oar and row with them.

—Harold S. Geneen

Make your life a mission—not an intermission.

—Arnold Glasgow

Experience is not what happens to a man. It is what a man does with what happens to him.

—Aldous Huxley

In the end, all business operations can be reduced to three words: people, product, and profits. People come first.

—Lee Iacocca

It is the peculiarity of knowledge that those who really thirst for it always get it.

—Richard Jeffries

We realize that we are in a race without a finish line. As we improve, so does our competition. Five years ago, we would have found that disheartening. Today we find it invigorating.

—David Kearns

Where there is an open mind, there will always be a frontier.

—Charles Kettering

To say that a business exists to produce profit for its owners offers no prescription regarding how to do it. Profits are a consequence of business action. They are not a guide to what the action should be.

—Theodore Levitt

Profit cannot be a corporate goal. Indeed, properly viewed, profit cannot even be treated as a consequence of business action. Profit is the requisite of corporate life, just as eating is the requisite of human life. Profit is the food without which corporate life cannot be sustained. Hence to call profit the goal of a corporation is like saying that the goal of human life is eating.

—Theodore Levitt

Six essential qualities that are key to success: Sincerity, Integrity, Humility, Courtesy, Wisdom, and Charity.

—Dr. William Menninger

It is not only what we do, but also what we do not do, for which we are accountable.

—Moliere

To know just what has to be done, then to do it, comprises the whole philosophy of practical life.

—Sir William Osler

Pyramids emphasize power, promote insecurity, distort communications, hobble interaction, and make it very difficult for people who plan and the people who execute to move in the same direction.

—Ricardo Semler

To be content with mediocrity is a tragedy.

—Ruth Smeltzer

When a man's knowledge is not in order, the more of it he has the greater will be his confusion.

—Herbert Spencer

In the long run men hit only what they aim at. Therefore, though they should fail immediately, they had better aim at something high.

—Henry David Thoreau

Apathy can only be overcome by enthusiasm, and enthusiasm can only be aroused by two things: first, an ideal which takes the imagination by storm, and second, a definite intelligible plan for carrying that ideal into practice.

—Arnold J. Toynbee

We should be careful to get out of an experience only the wisdom that is in it—and stop there.

—Mark Twain

Our best ideas come from clerks and stockboys.

—Sam Walton

If we are to get the reflexes and speed we need, we've got to simplify and delegate more . . . simply trust more.

—Jack Welch

The winners of the Nineties will be those who can develop a culture that allows them to move faster, communicate more clearly, and involve everyone in a focused effort to serve ever more demanding customers.

—Jack Welch

Customers

Includes thoughts on the idea of serving customers.

Competition is an economic struggle for survival among businessmen in which the consumer benefits the most.

—Anonymous

The truly market driven company knows that the best product it can produce is a delighted customer.

—John Akers

A customer is the most important person ever in this office—in person or by mail. A customer is not dependent on us, we are dependent on him. A customer is not an interruption of our work, he is the purpose of it. We are not doing him a favor by serving him, he is doing us a favor by giving us the opportunity to do so. A customer is not someone to argue or match wits with. Nobody ever won an argument with a customer. A customer is a person who brings us his wants. It is our job to handle them profitably to him and to ourselves.

—L.L. Bean Credo

Give to the world the best you have, and the best will come back to you.

—Madeleine Bridges

The first thing you as an executive have to find out is what your customers want. Those become your requirements. Then you have to translate those requirements into things your employees and suppliers can understand and do.

—Philip B. Crosby

The customer generates nothing. No customer asked for electric lights.

—W. Edwards Deming

The moral is that it is necessary to innovate, to predict needs of the customer, give him more. He that innovates and is lucky will take the market.

—W. Edwards Deming

I don't worry whether something is cheap or inexpensive, I only worry if it is good. If it is good enough, the public will pay you back for it.

—Walt Disney

There is only one valid definition of business purpose: *to create a customer*.

—Peter Drucker

What the customer thinks he is buying, what he considers value, is decisive—it determines what a business is, what it produces, and whether it will prosper.

—Peter Drucker.

What the customer buys and considers value is never a product. It is always utility, that is, what a product or service does for him.

—Peter Drucker

To supply the wants and needs of a consumer, society entrusts wealth-producing resources to the business enterprise.

—Peter Drucker

The man who will use his skill and constructive imagination to see how much he can give for a dollar, instead of how little he can give for a dollar, is bound to succeed.

—Henry Ford

It is the customer, and the customer alone, who casts the vote that determines how big any company should be.

—Crawford H. Greenewalt

Quality is not what happens when what you do matches your intentions. It's what happens when what you do matches your customers' expectations.

—John Guaspari

Styling and value are what sells cars, but quality is what keeps them sold.

—Lee Iacocca

In matters of principle, stand like a rock; in matters of taste, swim with the current.

—Thomas Jefferson

Marketing is a very special view of the business process. It views the business enterprise as an organized process to create and keep a customer.

—Theodore Levitt

One of the most important lessons of business—the value of concentrating on the customers you have.

—Tom Monaghan

To forget one's purposes is the commonest form of stupidity.

—Friedrich Nietzsche

The way employees treat customers reflects the manner in which they're treated by management.

—James A. Perkins

Good merchandise, even when hidden, soon finds buyers.

—Plautius

It is the greatest of all mistakes to do nothing because you can only do a little. Do what you can.

—Sidney Smith

I am the world's worst salesman, therefore, I must make it easy for people to buy.

—F.W. Woolworth

It's the oldest lesson in the world: Unless you are customer-driven, you go out of business.

—Walter Wriston

Training

Includes thoughts on the importance of training.

If you think education is expensive, try ignorance.

—Derek Bok

Get over the idea that only children should spend their time in study. Be a student so long as you still have something to learn, and this will mean all your life.

—Henry L. Doherty

What we do not call education is more precious than that which we call so.

—Ralph Waldo Emerson

Total Quality Control starts with training and ends with training. To implement TQC, we need to carry out continuous education for everyone, from the president down to line workers.

—Kaoru Ishikawa

No matter how hard Western nations try to engage in QC education, they may not catch up with Japan until the 1990s, since it requires ten years for the QC education to take effect.

—Joseph M. Juran

Teams and Teamwork

Includes thoughts on working together to achieve common goals.

Great discoveries and improvements invariably involve the cooperation of many minds.

—Alexander Graham Bell

Coming together is a beginning. Keeping together is progress. Working together is success.

—Henry Ford

Success is a ruthless competitor for it flatters and nourishes our weaknesses and lulls us into complacency. We bask in the sunshine of accomplishment and lose the spirit of humility which helps us visualize all the factors which have contributed to our success. We are apt to forget that we are only one of a team, that in unity there is strength and that we are strong only as long as each unit in our organization functions with precision.

—Samuel J. Tilden

Process Management

Includes a variety of ideas on process and its management.

A state without the means of some change is without the means of its conservation.

—Edmund Burke

Take away the cause and the effect ceases.

—Miguel de Cervantes

I recommend you to take care of the minutes; for hours will take care of themselves.

—Earl of Chesterfield

It does not matter how slowly you go as long as you do not stop.

—Confucius

If you want your people to do it right the first time, you've got to tell them simply and clearly what "it" is.

—Philip B. Crosby

Doing things right the first time adds nothing to your costs, but plenty to your profits.

—Philip B. Crosby

Instead of setting numerical quotas, management should work on improvement of the process.

—W. Edwards Deming

No amount of care or skill in workmanship can overcome fundamental faults of the system.

—W. Edwards Deming

Defects are not free. Somebody makes them, and gets paid for making them.

—W. Edwards Deming

However certain our expectations, the moment foreseen may be unexpected when it arrives.

—T.S. Eliot

Results should not be too voluntarily aimed at or too busily thought of. They are *sure* to float up of their own accord, from a long enough daily work at a given matter; and I think the work as a mere occupation ought to be the primary interest with us.

—William James

The surest way to be late is to have plenty of time.

—Leo Kennedy

Deal with the difficult
While it is still easy.
Solve large problems
When they are still small.
Preventing large problems
By taking small steps
Is easier than solving them.
By small action
Great things are accomplished.

—Lao Tzu

Live neither in the past nor in the future, but let each day's work absorb your entire energies, and satisfy your wildest ambition.

—William Osler

Method goes far to prevent trouble in business; for it makes the task easy, hinders confusion, saves abundance of time, and instructs those who have business depending, what to do and what to hope.

—William Penn

Set high standards.

—Norman Schwartzkopf

If one assumes a linear model (i.e., no interactions), thinking it correct, then one is a man removed from natural science or reality, and commits the mistake of standing just upon mathematics which is nothing but idealism.

—G. Taguchi

For every thousand hacking at the leaves of evil, there is one striking at the root.

—Henry David Thoreau

It requires a very unusual mind to undertake the analysis of the obvious.

—Alfred North Whitehead

Measurement

Includes ideas on making measurements, collecting data, and understanding and misunderstanding them.

Every man has a right to his opinion, but no man has a right to be wrong in his facts.

—Bernard M. Baruch

Life is the art of drawing sufficient conclusions from insufficient premises.

—Samuel Butler

You can't manage what you can't measure.

—Tom DeMarco

A state of Statistical Control is not a natural state for a process; it is an achievement.

—W. Edwards Deming

Ranking is a farce.

—W. Edwards Deming

Measures of productivity do not lead to improvement in productivity.

—W. Edwards Deming

It is a capital mistake to theorize before one has data.

—Arthur Conan Doyle

Nothing is good or bad but by comparison.

—Thomas Fuller

Facts do not cease to exist because they are ignored.

—Aldous Huxley

Count what is countable, measure what is measurable, and what is not measurable, make measurable.

—Galileo Galilei

I know of scarcely anything so apt to impress the imagination, as the wonderful form of cosmic order expressed by the Law of Frequency of Error. The law would have been personified by the Greeks and deified, if they had known it.

—Sir Francis Galton

In physical science, a first essential step in the direction of learning any subject is to find principles of numerical reckoning and methods for practicably measuring some quality connected with it.

—Lord Kelvin

Far better an approximate answer to the right question, which is often vague, than an exact answer to the wrong question, which can always be made more precise.

—John Tukey

A poorly observed fact is more treacherous than a faulty train of reasoning.

—Paul Valery

Statistical thinking will one day be as necessary for efficient citizenship as the ability to read and write.

—H. G. Wells

Human Resources

Includes ideas on people and the organization and bringing out the best in them.

Success must be sought in business in excellence of performance; and in business, excellence of performance manifests itself, among other things, in the advancing of methods and processes; in the improvement of products; in more perfect organization, eliminating friction as well as waste; in bettering the condition of the workingmen, developing their faculties and promoting their happiness; and in the establishment of right relations with customers and with the community.

—Louis D. Brandeis

There is dignity in work only when it is work freely accepted.

—Albert Camus

Leave my factories but take away my people and soon grass will grow on my factory floors. Take my factories, but leave my people, and soon we will have new and better plants.

—Andrew Carnegie

Reward for good performance may be the same as reward to the weather man for a pleasant day.

—W. Edwards Deming

Lincoln chose his general for his tested ability to win battles and not for his sobriety, that is, for the absence of a weakness.

—Peter Drucker

Executives have good human relations because they focus on contribution in their own work and in their relationships with others.

—Peter Drucker

Ability will never catch up with the demand for it.

—Malcolm S. Forbes

The deepest principle of human nature is the craving to be appreciated.

—Henry James

The problem with most of us is that we would rather be ruined by praise than saved by criticism.

—Norman Vincent Peale

The man whose brain is occupied with utilities, though he will not do much for science, may do a great deal for human life.

—Charles S. Pierce

Continuous Improvement

Includes several thoughts on change and improvement.

The biggest room in the world is the room for improvement.

—Anonymous

What you are must always displease you if you are to attain to that which you are not.

—Saint Augustine

Action and reaction, ebb and flow, trial and error, change—this is the rhythm of living.

—Bruce Barton

Nine-tenths of the serious controversies which arise in life result from misunderstanding.

—Louis D. Brandeis

Like rowing upstream, not to advance is to drop back.

—Chinese Proverb

Competent [people] in every position, if they are doing their best, know all that there is to know about their work except how to improve it.

—W. Edwards Deming

A stumble may prevent a fall.

—English Proverb

A defect is an instance in which a requirement is not satisfied.

—Michael Fagan

When you aim for perfection, you discover it's a moving target.

—George Fisher

Creative thinking may mean simply the realization that there's no particular virtue in doing things the way they always have been done.

—Rudolf Flesch

Nature knows no pause in progress and development, and attaches her curse on all inaction.

—Johann Wolfgang von Goethe

If you add a little to a little and do this often, soon the little will become great.

—Hesiod

So far, evolution has been nothing but staggering from one error to the next.

—Henrik Ibsen

Knowledge rests not upon truth alone, but on error also.

—Carl Gustav Jung

If things always worked the way they should, you could write the history of the world from now on. But they don't, and it is those deviations from the normal that make human progress.

—Charles F. Kettering

When patterns are broken, new worlds can emerge.

—Tuli Kupferberg

Good mistakes, those made with careful preparation and understanding of the process in question, are valuable improvement tools. Good mistakes should be encouraged and rewarded as often and as thoroughly as possible.

—William Lareau

If you want to truly understand something, try to change it.

—Kurt Lewin

How many things served us yesterday for articles of faith, which today are fables to us.

—Montaigne

You don't stand still. You either move ahead or move backward.

—Elisabeth Clairbone Ortenberg

There are no secrets to success. It is the result of preparation, hard work, and learning from failure.

—General Colin L. Powell

To avoid personal obsolescence, we must cultivate the ability to enjoy change rather than to resist it.

—Lelan Russell

Progress is impossible without change, and those who cannot change their minds cannot change anything.

—George Bernard Shaw

A man should never be ashamed to own that he has been in the wrong, which is but saying, in other words, that he is wiser today than he was yesterday.

—Jonathan Swift

The great thing about History is that it is adaptable.

—Peter Ustinov

The only man who can change his mind is a man that's got one.

—Edwards Noyes Westcott

The art of progress is to preserve order amid change and to preserve change amid order.

—Alfred North Whitehead

A mistake is always a value judgment rendered after the fact.

—John Woods

Risky to change. Riskier not to.

—John Young

Think like a wise man but communicate in the language of the people.

—William Butler Yeats

The Wrong Stuff

Includes a variety of thoughts that suggest what happens when people do a poor job of practicing quality management.

He who considers his work beneath him will be above doing it well.

—Alexander Chase

The damn thing won't fly at all until top management people are 100 percent behind it. . . . Where is the bottle neck? Just look at the top of the bottle and you will find it.

—Bill Conway

We are all born with intrinsic motivation, self-esteem, dignity, and eagerness to learn. Our present system of management crushes that all out.

—W. Edwards Deming

Show me a thoroughly satisfied man, and I will show you a failure.

—Thomas Alva Edison

The expert is usually the last to admit change, because he has so much invested in the status quo.

—Charles Hess

Any fool can make a trend out of two points.

—Brian Joiner

Fanaticism: Redoubling your efforts after the original objective is forgotten.

—Joseph M. Juran

Practical men, who believe themselves to be quite exempt from any intellectual influences, are usually the slaves of some defunct economist.

—John Maynard Keynes

There are really only three kinds of people: those who make things happen; those who watch things happen; and those who say, "What happened?"

—Ann Landers

He who accounts all things easy will have many difficulties.

—Lao Tzu

Management is like sex or politics or religion; all of us do it, most of us are convinced that our way is the best, few of us bother to ask if we have met the other's needs and expectations.

—R.J. Moriboys

Only a mediocre person is always at his best.

—W. Somerset Maugham

Ignorance of all things is an evil neither terrible nor excessive nor yet the greatest of all; but great cleverness and much learning, if they be accompanied by a bad training, are a much greater misfortune.

—Plato

The fellow who never makes mistakes takes his orders from one who does.

—Herbert V. Prochnow

Most of our so-called reason consists of finding reasons to go on thinking as we already do.

—J.H. Robinson

When a man does not know what harbor he is making for, no wind is the right wind.

—Seneca

Few tricks of the unsophisticated intellect are more curious than the naive psychology of the business man, who ascribes his achievements to his own unaided efforts, in bland unconsciousness of a social order without whose continuous support and vigilant protection he would be as a lamb bleating in the desert.

—Richard H. Tawney

Managers tend to make their biggest mistakes in things they've previously done best. In business, as elsewhere, hubris is the unforgivable sin of acting cocky when things are going well. As the Greeks tiresomely told us, Hubris is followed inexorably and inevitably by Nemesis.

—Robert Townsend

The cycles of trade depression which afflict the world warn us that business relations are infected through and through with the disease of short-sighted motives.

—Alfred North Whitehead

It is not uncommon to find an MIS department with no formal quality program, whose quality costs are 30 percent or even 50 percent of the annual MIS budget. This is a very expensive and slow way to build software.

—Richard Zulner

Glossary

Over the past decade, the world of quality management has accumulated a growing vocabulary of its own, much like other fields have done. Many of these phrases are common English words, but with slightly new meanings. Phrases used in various fields have crossed over into business and management language. For example, many terms originally found only in engineering or in statistical analysis are now the working vocabulary of managers in human resources, sales, and so forth. Terms from science, psychology, and mathematics have also made this transition. During the early 1990s, the pace of penetration picked up to all corners of business language. By 1994—1995, many of these terms were commonly used in business, not just in science or manufacturing. For that reason, we feel there needs to be a consolidated glossary. It is a vocabulary that is increasing in size each year, reflecting a process of codification underway within quality practices as they become the mainstream of a renewed body of management practices.

Acceptable quality level A level of quality acceptable for a lot or group. These are levels set for purposes of establishing the acceptable quality of inspected samples.

Acceptance sampling Where decisions are made to accept or reject products or services. The term also refers to an approach consisting of procedures or processes by which managers make decisions to accept or reject relying on the results of inspections of samples. Acceptance sampling is designed to avoid having to inspect, for example, all raw material.

Acceptance sampling plan A plan that includes criteria for accepting and rejecting samples. Plans may involve single, double, sequential, chain, multiple, or skip-lot sampling strategies. These also are used in attribute sampling strategy. With variables samples, single, double, and sequential sampling strategies are deployed.

Accreditation Same as certification, it is a formal process that validates the skills of an individual by a recognized organization. This is done, for example, by the Registrar Accreditation Board for ISO 9000 standards, the ASQC for quality experts, and APICS for manufacturing specialists.

Action team (AT) A group of people management has authorized to implement improvement changes to an existing process.

Activities Steps (also tasks) in a process.

Affinity diagramming A technique for organizing a variety of subjective data (such as opinions) into logical topics based on the relationships among individual pieces of information.

Agenda A plan for conducting a meeting. In the quality world, meeting disciplines become a process integral to the operations of an organization. Agendas also include discussion of outcomes expected from a meeting.

American Quality Foundation An independent organization established under the auspices of the American Society for Quality Control for the purpose of fostering the application of quality practices by business and public officials. It also has a research and development mission, responsible for programs to foster U.S. business competitiveness.

American Society for Quality Control (ASQC) One of the world's leading nonprofit professional associations dedicated to the promotion and application of quality-related practices in both public and private sectors. It has over 96,000 individual members and over 700 corporate members in 64 countries.

Analysis of Means (ANOM) A statistical technique used to identify problems in an industrial process and that involves the analysis of experimental designs with factors at fixed levels. This technique was created to help nonstatisticians apply variance analysis techniques.

Analysis of Variance (ANOVA) Used to analyze experimental data, one subdivides the total variation of a set of data into relevant groups that are associated with sources of variation so as to test a hypothesis or to estimate types of variances. Three models are recognized in this process: fixed, random, and mixed when studying hypothesis.

Analytic Hierarchy Process (AHP) A method for making decisions regarding complicated issues through simplifying a natural decision-making approach. You break down a circumstance into its logical components, rank them with numeric values assigned to otherwise subjective data, and then summarize the variables in a prioritized fashion.

ANOM Analysis of means.

ANOVA Analysis of variance.

AOQ Average outgoing quality.

AOQL Average outgoing quality limit.

Appraisal costs Costs incurred in inspecting products to insure they meet customer or your specifications or needs.

ASQC American Society for Quality Control.

Attribute data Also called "go/no-go information," it is a collection of data represented on control charts reflecting attribute data such as a percent, number of affected units, counts, counts-per-unit, quality scores, and demerits.

Augmented product Any product that provides more than a customer expects or normally receives.

Availability A state of being of a machine, product, process, or person to perform a function under predetermined conditions. In a formal definition, it is the ratio of uptime divided by the total of uptime and downtime. Uptime is when something is in active use (such as a machine), while downtime is when it is not active (such as when a machine is being repaired, or retooled).

Average chart Refers to a control chart in which a subgroup average (X-bar) is employed to evaluate the stability of a process's level. This is frequently employed in manufacturing situations.

Average outgoing quality (AOQ) The anticipated quality of output or products that normally occurs.

Average outgoing quality limit (AOQL) The maximum amount of quality of outgoing quality over all possible levels of incoming quality. It is determined by using an acceptance sampling approach that establishes a value for incoming quality of products.

Bar chart A widely used form of a chart that displays events or items in wide horizontal or vertical lines (bars).

Baseline Information that answers the questions, what is the level of our quality now and where are we today? Baselines are created in measurable terms from which future progress on improvements are measured.

Baseline cycle time The amount of time it takes a process to perform the first time it is measured. All future improvements in the speed with which the process is performed is measured against this original cycle time.

Benchmark A quality target that answers the question, where should we be? It can be based on a number of targets: customer requirements, best performing comparable process, or some other goal. It is also a formal process for comparing the performance of a process against that of another process.

Benchmarking The act of continually comparing the performance of one process against that of another, usually of comparable or greater performance. Thus, for example, comparing your billing process to that of a "world class" or "best-of-breed" process, such as that of American Express. Benchmarking is done to determine the effectiveness of existing processes and to find ways to improve those quickly.

Best-of-breed The best example of a process or measurement available usually within an industry, but could be worldwide. Quality is determined by efficiency, effectiveness, value, or defect elimination.

Best-of-class Another way of saying best-of-breed, superior to all comparable goods or services.

Big Q, little q The phrase is used to contrast differences between managing quality in business products and processes (implying many and major) from managing quality in a more narrowly defined scope, such as for one product or process.

Blemish As with a stain on cloth or an imperfection in our skin's complexion, the word refers to a deviation in quality, but not of such a severe type as to constrict the performance of the process or, more frequently, a product.

Blind survey A survey of customers or other individuals in which they do not know who is sponsoring the survey or who are chosen from a pool of candidates. This is a technique often used to compare the performance of one company or process against another.

Block diagram Blocks on a piece of paper each representing a function, process, or task, illustrating interdependencies and operational relationships. These are used to illustrate the flow of work or processes and where things or tasks interface. Functional block diagrams illustrate the flow of a system's subsystems and outputs, and how all relate to each other. Reliability block diagrams are similar except that they emphasize factors that influence reliability of systems, processes, or items.

Brainstorming A widely used technique for generating ideas about how to improve a process or solve a problem. It results in a large number of ideas being created from which a group can pick the best to implement.

Breakthrough Often also referred to as breakthrough thinking, this is the idea of searching for a significant improvement in how a process is designed, implemented, and performs. Emphasis is on a radically new, or revolutionary approach as opposed to the evolutionary improvement in an existing process.

C chart A count chart of any type.

Calibration In the world of quality, it is a comparison of one measurement system or instrument of an unverified accuracy to one that is accurate. This is done to identify variations from a required specification for performance.

Capability index A technique for measuring the odds of failures or defects. It is calculated by dividing current performance by anticipated performance to measure the ability of a process to meet expectations (results) and which has a significant effect on the quality of a process.

Causal analysis This technique concentrates on identifying failures or defects, followed by an analysis of the root causes of those failures, and concludes with recommendations on how to eliminate those defects. It is a popular component of defect prevention activities within a process.

Cause A reason for a specific condition or action.

Cause-and-effect analysis A method used by a group of individuals to study underlying causes. It is often also called fishboning since the output is a fishbone chart.

Cause-and-effect diagram This type of graph illustrates the relationship between one problem and its possible various causes. It is best known as a fishbone diagram because it looks like the skeleton of a fish with each "bone" being the answer to the question Why? It is one of the most widely used and effective quality tools.

Chart A graphical representation of data indicating significant trends and relationships. As a hammer and saw are to a carpenter, a chart is to anyone working with data.

Check sheet This simple recording document is a widely used method for keeping track of data. It is considered one of the formal quality tools. Since the data is tailored to the requirements of the user, it should not be confused with normal checklists or data sheets.

Checklist Refers to a list of steps or actions in a process that are tracked (checked off) as done.

Closed-loop process The notion that activities go through a series of steps in a never-ending, continuous fashion with no beginning or end.

Coach Any individual who serves as a guide leading people through process improvement, usually through the application of Total Quality Management principles. The term is also used to describe a manager who counsels and advises employees instead of telling them what to do.

Commitment Often used in an organization that has developed a vision-based strategic plan or that is embarking on the application of fact-based quality management principles, it refers to the personal resolve to apply TQM-like values and practices.

Common cause Refers to one or more sources of variation in the output of a process that affects all individual results or values of output.

Communication Simply the process for exchanging information. It is also considered a critical process in quality-based organizations.

Competition More than rivalry among vendors, it is also the act of competing among individuals and groups for total customer satisfaction. In the Deming-like view of the world, competition is also considered inefficient and contrary to customer benefit, calling instead for cooperation among vendors to provide best quality goods and services.

Concurrent engineering (CE) A systematic approach to the design of products and their related processes that is integrated and concurrent. That is to say, multiple steps in the process take place at the same time, including manufacturing and product support. The intent of this kind of approach is to lead developers to weigh all elements of a product life cycle from the initial conception of an idea to the final disposition of a product, taking into account such factors as quality, cost, and customer requirements and expectations.

Conformance Refers to a judgment that a product or service has conformed to a predetermined set of requirements, usually drawn from desires of customers.

Consensus A form of agreement reached by a group of people working on a plan or development of a process. It is not a majority vote to adopt a position but rather the state of mind that each individual can live with the decisions of the group and will support and implement them.

Continuous improvement (CI) An important value statement that endorses the notion that all processes and activities can be improved on a regular basis through the application of systematic techniques. It also embraces the idea that there should be a relentless, ongoing hunt for sources of defects to be eliminated. The Japanese call CI "KAIZEN." Another definition calls CI a disciplined process for achieving, first, commitment to excellence and, second, the actual efforts to accomplish ongoing improvements in quality of processes, services, and products.

Control In the world of quality, this word refers to those activities that are performed to maintain a desired state of performance or to correct deviation from standards. It looks at past activity to call out what needs to be changed to return to a predetermined level of performance.

Control chart A graph, a statistical process control method used to track the performance of a process over time expressed in numerical terms. Statistical upper and lower control limits are set within which variance is tolerated. It is one of the most widely used process improvement tools.

Correction Any and all actions taken to reduce or eliminate variations in performance. It is also used to describe similar activities designed to eliminate causes of variation in performance.

Corrective action Refers to actions taken to eliminate problems in products, services, and processes.

Cost of poor quality (COPQ) Expenses generated by providing poor quality goods or services. These are sourced from internal failure costs (from defects before customers get the product), external failure costs (costs after a customer receives the poor product or service), appraisal costs (expenses generated to determine the degree of conformance to quality of a product or service), and prevention costs (expenses to reduce or avoid failures and appraisal costs).

Cost of quality (COQ) More than the cost of quality programs, this refers to all costs for the prevention of defects, assessments of process performance, and measurement of financial consequences. It is used to document variations against expectations and as a measure of efficiency and productivity.

Count chart This type of control chart is used to evaluate the stability of a process by counting events of a particular type that occur in a sample.

Count-per-unit chart This type of control chart tracks the stability of a process by looking at the average count of events within a precise classification per unit occurring in a sample.

Cp Stands for a process capability index. It is calculated by taking the difference between upper and lower control limits and dividing that answer by 6.

Cpk Another popular process capability index.

Criterion A standard by which to base a decision.

Critical path Process owners use this term to describe the shortest distance between the beginning and end of a process or activity. Activities within a process are customarily documented along a critical path.

Critical success factors Activities that absolutely have to go right in order for a process, program, or a team to make its objectives. Traditionally a part of strategic planning, it is frequently a catalog of process elements that must be managed with extra care to insure the overall success of the process.

Cross-functional team A process team made up of people from various departments or organizations affected by their process. This kind of a team works on a specific problem or process that affects multiple departments or organizations, often with the mandate to develop a new or improved process.

Cross plot Another way of saying scatter diagram, used to study the relationship between two variables.

Culture A term used often in the quality world, it defines patterns of shared activities, values, beliefs, and attitudes within an organization. In enterprises introducing quality practices, defining the nature of existing and desired institutional culture becomes an important activity.

Cumulative sum control chart This type of control chart plots a value that is the cumulative sum of deviations of successive samples taken from some target value. Ordinate of each point represents the algebraic sum of the previous ordinates and most recent deviations from a preset target.

Customer Increasingly this word is being used to describe anybody who is the recipient of work that you do, or the next person in a process who receives the output of your work. Often divided into Big C (paying customers) and Little c (fellow employees), it is the concept that everyone should be treated as respectfully and enthusiastically as a paying customer.

Customer delight A phrase to describe the delivery of a product or service that exceeds a customer's requirement. For many organizations, it is a shorthand description of a corporate quality goal.

Customer requirements The things Big C and Little c customers want from a product, service, or process. It is a central concept of quality that all processes and organizations should understand very thoroughly what are the requirements of their customers. Whole processes are implemented to insure that customer requirements are sought and factored into the development and implementation of an organization's processes.

Customer satisfaction Refers to either the delivery of a product or service that meets or exceeds customer expectations or requirements.

Customer/supplier analysis A collection of methods for providing insight into the needs and expectations of customers seen through the relationship between an organization and its suppliers. It is intended to cause the activities between suppliers and vendors to conform to customer requirements.

Customer-supplier partnership Shorthand for a long-term relationship between a buyer and supplier in which mutual trust, teamwork, and dependence are typical. Vendors are considered an extension of a buyer's operations. Buyers use fewer suppliers and commit to long-term contracts and relationships. Suppliers meet quality standards of their customers. This strategy is employed to reduce operating and inspection costs, while improving overall quality of goods and services.

Cycle time The time from beginning to end of a process. It is an important measure of the quality of a process. Many organizations also have found that the reduction in cycle time to get things done represents a significant cost justified benefit of applying quality techniques and values.

D chart Stands for demerit chart (see below).

Data Facts or information presented in descriptive or graphic forms. Information is either measured data (also called variable data) or counted data (also called attribute data).

Data/statistical analysis A collection of techniques and tools for collecting, sorting, analyzing, and presenting information that leads to decisions and process management.

Decision matrix Teams will use such a matrix to analyze problems and possible solutions. Solutions or problems are listed along one vertical column, while criteria are posted along the horizontal. Solutions are ranked 1 to 5, 1 to 8, or 1 to 10 in terms of positive impact and are entered on the grid. Total scores are accumulated vertically to determine which solution is the most attractive.

Defect Any action, error, or circumstance that either does not meet a customer's requirement or fails to make a measurable goal. Examples of defects can be service-oriented (e.g., number of unanswered phone calls) or faulty products (e.g., poorly designed). Defects are usually catalogued into four types (classes) by degree, from 1 to 4: very serious (e.g., can cause injury or major financial problems), serious (significant injury possible or major financial loss), major (in the ability of a product or service to do as designed), and minor (some problem but still capable of performing).

Defect elimination The act of identifying and then eliminating defects in products, services, and processes. It is also a group of techniques for reduction of failures or defects in processes.

Defect prevention process (DPP) A collection of techniques used to understand the causes of existing errors or defects. DPP also includes a method for determing how to prevent these errors in the future. Often the process includes actual implementation of defect prevention actions as an on-going round of error elimination.

Defects per million (DPM) The number of defects (errors) that occurs in one million opportunities. This could be the number of faulty items out of a million or the number of defects (malperformance) in a million times. This measure is widely used and is applicable across all actions of a process, product, or service, hence its popularity.

Demerit chart This type of control chart tracks failures or weaknesses in a process by deducting quality points, which cumulatively is a score of nonconformance.

Deming cycle Another way of saying "plan-do-check-act" cycle in which you plan what is to be done (e.g., in a process, you do it, check to see how it went, and act to improve it). It was developed as a concept by W. Edwards Deming.

Deming Prize Established in 1951 by the Union of Japanese Scientists and Engineers (JUSE), it recognizes companies that have made outstanding progress in improving the quality of their operations. This very important quality prize is named after W. Edwards Deming who, in 1950, first introduced the Japanese to many industrial quality control practices.

Dependability The degree to which a product or service functions and remains capable of doing as required by specifications. Dependability is determined by a judgment of random samples of the process or product and for the time it is supposed to be available. To express it as a ratio, take time available and divide it by the total of time available plus time required.

Deployment Occasionally used in quality circles, the terms refers to the actions taken to implement a consistent or process approach, usually across an entire organization or over multiple departments.

Design of experiments A formal branch of applied statistics that focuses on planning, conducting, studying, and interpreting controlled tests. This is done to evaluate those factors that control values of one or more parameters.

Design phases Three specific phases in the design of a process or product: systems design, parameter design, and tolerance design. The three were designated by Taguchi, a leading Japanese quality expert.

Designing in quality vs. inspecting in quality The notion of prevention vs. detection, in which one improves the quality of a product beginning at the design phase so as to avoid either inspecting the end product or allowing conditions early in a product manufacturing cycle from creating quality concerns further down the process cycle.

Detailed process diagram A flowchart documenting each step in a process.

Detection The act of identifying any nonconformance to some standard after the fact.

Deviation Refers to any departure from a set of desired or anticipated value or pattern of performance. Standard deviation is the measure of the spread for most frequent distributions; used primarily in monitoring process performance.

Diagnostic journey and remedial journey Used together, this is a two-part investigatory process employed by teams to solve chronic quality problems. In the diagnostic phase, a team will go from identification of a symptom to its cause. In the second, it moves from cause to remedy.

Directed survey The opposite of a blind survey, participants know who the sponsor of the survey is. It is an effective approach when asking customers to define how a company or agency can improve its services and products.

Disciplined continuous improvement methodology Another way of saying continuous improvement approaches.

Dodge-Romig sampling plans Developed by Harold F. Dodge and Harry G. Romig, these are four sets of tables: single-sampling lot tolerance, double-sampling lot tolerance, single-sampling average outgoing quality limits, and double-sampling average outgoing quality limit tables.

DOE Short for design of experiments.

Downstream value chain Value chains within consumer and channel organizations and outside of your enterprise.

Driving forces Those circumstances that cause actions leading toward achieving some goal.

Efficient process This phrase refers to a process that generates the results or output desired at the lowest or minimum cost, or in the least amount of time, or with the lowest use of resources (people or ingredients), or other assets. Efficiency is measured by a ratio of required output to cost to produce that result. Cost is defined in a variety of units of resources, such as hours, money, energy, and raw materials.

Efficiency Often this word is used to characterize performance of a process, usually in terms of minimum cost of effort, resources, or money. It is often measured by a ratio of quantity of resources planned for consumption in the execution of the process to resources actually used.

Effect Often applied to a problem or defect that exists within a process or activity.

Effective process A process that generates results that conform to customer requirements or those of the process owner. Lack of effectiveness is the delta between actual and required performance, usually expressed in numeric terms. The delta is always the degree to which results (output) differ from requirements.

Effectiveness Refers to how much the output of a process meets or exceeds expectations or goals. Expectations can be defined by customers or process owners.

80-20 rule Also known as the Pareto Principle, it was rescued from history by J. M. Juran in 1950 to suggest that most effects come from few causes; in other words, 80 percent of all effects come from only 20 percent of possible causes.

Employee involvement A code term for a body of personnel practices in which employees routinely play a critical role in making decisions about operations, priorities, suggestions for improvements, planning, setting of goals and targets, and monitoring performance. It is a major component of modern quality practices.

Empowerment The act of delegating responsibility and authority to employees to make decisions and take actions. In the world of quality, this is a code word for delegation. It embraces the assumption that employees, when properly trained, can often make the best decisions on how to manage and improve a process.

Enterprise processes The major processes of an organization. For example, for a manufacturing company, they could be design, product manufacture, sales, and customer satisfaction. These are typically "mega-processes" that catalog the major activities that support the mission of an organization and become the basis of significant process identification and improvement. Each has many sub-processes, but when added together they constitute the major quality focus items of an organization.

Entitlement Every process, because it exists, has the potential for additional improvement. That potential is called entitlement; additional effectiveness or efficiency if a process is optimized.

Expected product Often a way of explaining a customer's minimum requirements for a product, service, or process.

Experimental design Always a formal (well-documented) plan describing how to conduct a specific experiment.

Extended enterprise An organization that sees its links to members of its value chain in multidimensional ways. Processes and value chains are seen as extending beyond the enterprise into suppliers, customers, or other stakeholders.

External customer Someone or some organization that pays for your goods and services and who is not a formal or legal part of your enterprise.

External failure costs. Costs generated when a defective product or service is delivered to a customer. The expenses to an automobile manufacturer for a recalled vehicle is an example.

External linkages Refers to those linkages that exist between an organization and its suppliers and its customers. Upstream linkages are with suppliers and downstream linkages are with channels of distribution or consumers.

Extrinsic reward Any award or recognition given by other people. This can include recognition of the performance of a process team by another process team.

Facilitator Anyone who helps a process team apply TQM tools and methods. Sometimes the word is used interchangeably with coach.

Fail-safe technique Application of automatic checking devices to capture common problems or errors either in the design or production process. The Japanese call such fail-safe production methods poka-yoke.

Failure mode analysis (FMA) A process for determining which symptoms of a malfunction appear before or after a failure of a critical element or parameter in a process or system. Possible causes are listed and then the product is designed to eliminate the problem.

Failure mode effects analysis (FMEA) A way of taking each potential failure mode in each sub-item of an item to analyze to identify its effect on other sub-items and upon the function required of the process or product.

Failure mode effects and criticality analysis (FMECA) A procedure done after a failure mode effects analysis has been conducted to classify all potential failure effect ranked by severity and probability of occurrence again.

Fishbone diagram This cause and effect diagram is a graphic that illustrates the series of causes of a problem and gets its name from the fact that the lines (representing causes of problems) looks like the skeleton of a fish.

Fitness for use A phrase used to indicate that a service or product is "fit" for customer use, that is to say, meets a customer's requirements.

Flow diagram This kind of drawing defines the steps of a process. It is used to identify areas of problems in a process, redundant and unnecessary steps that complicate a process, non-value-add activities, and where simplification is possible. It is usually a combination of flowcharts and text.

Flowchart A graphical presentation of all the steps in a process. Relying on a technique used in software design, inputs, process, outputs, and decisions are represented in blocks and other symbols. This is one of the most widely used quality tools because it allows one to document easily the flow of activities in a process.

FMA Failure mode analysis.

FMEA Failure mode effects analysis.

FMECA Failure mode effects and criticality analysis.

Focus group A group of customers or users of a process who are brought together in a meeting (or a series of meetings) for the purpose of understanding how they feel about a service, product, or process. Focus groups are also used to generate ideas on how to improve continuously those goods and services.

Focus setting A method employed to concentrate attention on a specific outcome.

Force field analysis A technique used to identify forces that for or against a particular action. Variables for or against might include probability of occurrence or magnitude. Such an analysis can lead to preventitive measures to minimize occurrence of a negative circumstance.

Form-fit-function A phrase used in conjunction with the control of a configuration in which Engineering Change Notices (ECNs) support drawing or component changes that do not affect the "form, fit, or function" of the component or item in the relationship it has to the system in which it is used.

14 Points W. Edwards Deming's management practices designed to improve quality and productivity. They are: (1) create constancy of purpose to improve products and services; (2) adopt the new philosophy of quality improvement; (3) cease dependence on inspection as the way to achieve quality; (4) stop making purchase decisions just on price alone, work instead with fewer suppliers; (5) improve constantly and forever processes for planning, manufacture, and service; (6) have training on the job; (7) practice leadership; (8) drive fear out of the workplace; (9) break down barriers between staffs; (10) eliminate slogans, targets, and exhortations for workers; (11) get rid of numerical quotas for workers and numerical goals for managers; (12) remove obstacles that rob workers of pride of work and eliminate annual merit or rating systems; (13) educate employees and implement self-improvement for all; (14) put everyone to work on transforming the enterprise.

Frequency distribution Used to describe the distribution of a discrete variable and refers to the number of occurrences of individual values over a defined range. When applied to the distribution of a continuous variable, then we have a count of cases that lie between predetermined limits over a range of values that the variable being measured may assume.

Functional administrative control technique Refers to a technique for improving performance by employing a method that combines time management and value engineering. You break down activities into functions and then create teams to solve problems within each function.

Functional organization Refers to an organization responsible for a major part of an enterprise, such as accounting, distribution, legal, marketing, or manufacturing.

Functional team A team made up of representatives from only one functional organization (e.g., only salespeople or accountants).

Funnel experiment This kind of experiment is used to demonstrate effects of tampering. In this one, marbles are dropped through a funnel for the purpose of hitting a flat surfaced target below. This activity is done to illustrate that adjusting a stable process to compensate for an undesirable result or a lucky result will generate a result worse than if no adjustment had been made.

Gainsharing A reward process by which the gains in productivity within a functional organization or company are shared between owners (e.g., stockholders) and employees. In other words, it is a variant of profit sharing and is used to incent employees to improve productivity within an organization.

Gantt chart A type of bar chart often used to display planned and completed activities in specific time periods (e.g., planned sales next to actual sales by quarter).

Gap The delta between how things or processes are today (baseline) and how they should be (your vision or customer requirements).

Gauge repeatability and reproducibility (GR&R) The process of evaluating the accuracy of a gauging instrument by establishing whether measurements taken with the device can be repeated and are reproducible (i.e., roughly the same answer over and over again).

GDT Geometric dimensioning and tolerancing.

Generic product Any basic item or product without any variance or enhancements in features.

Geometric dimensioning and tolerancing (GDT) A method used to minimize costs of production by illustrating dimension and tolerancing on a drawing while taking into account functions or relationships of part features.

George M. Low Trophy This prestigeous award is given annually by NASA to those contracts, subcontractors, and suppliers to this space agency who consistenty mantained and improved their quality performance. Large and small businesses compete in one or the other size category. Previously called the NASA Excellence Award for Quality and Productivity, the award is named after NASA's administrator for almost three decades.

Goal There are many definitions, however, they all generally involve a statement of an achievement or attainment that is desired and leads to actions directed toward its achievement. Goals increasingly are expressed as measurable targets.

Go/no-go This describes the condition of a unit or product in which one of two circumstances prevail: go (conforms to requirements or specifications) and no-go (does not conform).

GR&R Gauge repeatability and reproducibility.

Group Another word for team.

Guideline Increasingly refers to a set of specific suggested practices to encourage conformance to predetermined standards but that are not manditory.

Hierarchical nature of a process Various levels of any process. It is often depicted as a high level flowchart of the major parts of a process followed by other charts illustrating the sub-parts of the high level phases.

Histogram A graphical representation of a distributed set of measurement data. Typically this is a bar graph.

Hoshin planning This Japanese method of planning calls for senior management of an organization, working with various teams of process or unit employees, to establish strategic goals and work on their implementation. It calls for focus on customer satisfaction goals, effectiveness, and efficiency of process work. Goals are set and communicated within an organization and woven into the fabric of employee performance plans, process objectives, and goals for organizations, all of which are measured and improved upon in a disciplined manner. Also often called breakthrough planning of where a company should be in five years.

House of Quality This graphical depiction, widely used by quality experts to illustrate the components of a quality strategy or process, grew out of a formal and rigorous process for identifying customer requirements called Quality Function Deployment (QFD).

Human resources Employees or members of any organization.

Hypothesis Traditionally thought of as an assertion made about some parameter or circumstance in science. Increasingly, the use of hypothesis in the study of business problems and circumstances is becoming popular as a way to focus analysis.

Imperfection A quality departure from requirements or standards. Another word for defect, blemish, or nonconformity.

Improvement methodology Refers to a way of implementing improvements in an organization or process.

In-control process Refers to any process in which variations, by statistical measurements, are within control limits.

Individual involvement The personal role played by individuals in the output of a company, agency, or organization.

Information processing component The component of a value activity that includes recording, use, and distribution of information necessary to perform that activity.

Information system Usually refers to automated (computer-based) systems. Increasingly, this also is becoming a description of the flow of information that allows one to review, analyze, and then take corrective actions within a process.

In-plant Quality Evaluation program (IQUE) The method by which a firm judges the controls over product quality, especially that of a contractor.

Input The injection of energy, information, data, or materials into a process or conversation required to complete an activity to produce an output or work product. The term was borrowed from information processing in which pieces of information (data) were input into a computer.

Input/output analysis A technique used to identify interdependency problems.

Inspection The act of measuring, testing, examining, or gauging one or more characteristics of a product or service and then comparing results to specified requirements. The objective is to determine if conformance by each feature has been achieved.

Instant pudding A slang term employed to illustrate an obstacle to quality. It assumes that quality and productivity improvement can be realized quickly through affirming faith rather than by education and work. Coined originally by James

Bakken of Ford Motor Company, it was more widely used by W. Edwards Deming to criticize an approach.

Institutionalize The act of making something (usually a cultural value or a process) an integral aspect of an organization's way of life.

Internal customer Also known as little c customer, this is a person in an organization who receives the output of another fellow-employee's process work; the opposite of external customer.

Internal failure costs The costs caused by defects found in products and services before they reached a customer outside the enterprise. These are often distinguished from failure or defect costs that are generated by failures once they have reached a customer.

Internal linkages Linkages within a value chain. The effect of an order entry process on delivery costs, for instance, is an internal linkage between a primary activity and a support function.

Intrinsic reward Usually refers to a feeling of accomplishment or satisfaction within an individual caused by doing something satisfactory to a person. The reward is, in effect, given to oneself by mental recognition of achievement. Deming would link this notion to his concept of the "joy of work" in which doing well is something satisfactory and pleasing to all people.

Ishikara diagram A cause-and-effect diagram.

ISO 9000 series standards Constitutes a set of five standards for quality management and assurance documentation to support quality standards. Developed in 1987 by the International Organization for Standardization (ISO), it is intended for organizations in all industries. The ISO standards, however, come to be associated with specific standards for manufacturing companies wishing to market goods and services in 91 countries. For many manufacturing organizations, it is a specialized set of quality criteria.

Just-in-time (JIT) Refers to a body of practices, primarily in manufacturing, that calls for production of goods to be as close as possible to the time when they are sold. Implied is the availability of raw materials within hours of consumption or provision of a service as needed.

Just-in-time manufacturing In pure manufacturing terms, it is a material requirement planning approach used in production in which hardly any inventory of parts or raw materials are kept at the factory and in which little to no incoming inspection of parts or raw material occurs.

KAIZEN This Japanese word is the equivalent of the English phrase "continuous improvement" in which processes are incrementally enhanced to improve overall performance of a process or organization.

Lagging measure A measure issued after the fact it is measuring.

Leadership In the world of quality, it calls for guiding an organization to accomplish its objectives through the application of total quality principles and valuing quality principles. The leadership embraces such values and practices them personally.

Lead team The team that guides or supervises other process teams. Frequently the term is used to describe the senior managers of an organization and their role in guiding other teams.

Leading measure A measure upstream in a process.

Life cycle cost The total cost of a system or product, but may include a process, over its useful life. Costs include acquisition, ownership, and final disposal.

Line chart This kind of chart displays and compares quantifiable data. Often the data presented is amount over time.

Linkage analysis A formal process (tool) for identifying internal and external linkages to identify those activities of value that have a high information processing component or that identify organizations highly dependent on others in delivering or buying services.

Linkages Relationships between interdependent activities within a value chain or between more than one interdependent organization. Linkages are often identified as existing if the effects of the performance of a task on the costs and performance of other actions depend on linkages.

Listening The act of receiving, understanding, and reacting to information, such as customer interests and concerns. In customer feedback processes, the term "listening posts" is often applied.

Loss function Those operations of an organization that study costs related to any variation from the assigned values of any quality characteristic.

Lot A specific quantity of products brought together within conditions considered uniform and for the purpose of sampling.

Lower Control Limit (LCL). The control limit for points below the mid-point horizontal line on a control chart.

Maintainability An old manufacturing term widely used to refer to the characteristics of the design or installation of a piece of equipment that make it possible to repair it later either easily or efficiently. Often replacement products for an earlier generation are designed to improve maintainability to lower costs of support.

Maintenance Always defined as the repair or preservation at a predetermined level of quality of something. In quality, it is usually of a process or body of information.

Malcolm Baldrige National Quality Award The award established by the U.S. Government in 1987 to recognize quality achievements of American companies. It is awarded by the U.S. Department of Commerce and is today the most prestigious quality award in the United States.

Management The collective leadership of an enterprise.

Manufacturing Resource Planning (MRP) Historically, an important system for planning and controlling manufacturing operations. Today, this is seen as a major collection of manufacturing processes.

Margin In the world of quality, this means the difference between total value and combined costs of executing the value activities.

Market-Driven Quality (MDQ) IBM's term for Total Quality Management (TQM). It is the idea that quality is driven by market needs, that a company achieves complete customer satisfaction by delivering defect-free and timely goods and services that effectively meet their needs.

Materials Review Board (MRB) A quality control organization or team, usually employed in manufacturing or process installations, for the purpose of determining how to deal with materials that do not conform to predetermined standards of quality. Members typically are process-control engineers, designers, purchasers of materials, and quality inspectors who are all trying to cause their organization to use materials that meet specific standards of quality.

Mean Any average of a group of data.

Mean time between failures (MTBF) A measure of the average time between successive failures in the performance or quality of a product. For example, it can refer to the number of months between the times when a computer goes down (fails to function). Improvements in design are intended to extend MTBF's from one generation of product to another.

Measurement More than just a major philosophical component of the quality practice's value system, it is an act or process of measuring to compare actual results with intended requirements. Measurements of performance are always expressed in quantitative terms.

Mentor An individual whose responsibility is to advise and guide a process team while serving as an interface between management and teams. Often a mentor is seen as a coach or advisor.

Military standards The specific, documented standards of performance or quality issued by the U.S. Government for any product employed by the military branches (MIL-Q-9858A). Such standards encompass quality measures, performance criteria, statistical sampling reporting (MIL-STD-105E and MIL-STD-45662A), and specifications of components. Since the U.S. military buys almost every kind of product made, their standards often influence design characteristics of commercially available goods.

Mission Usually defined as the intended result of a process. For an organization, it is a statement of its current purpose for existence, what it does.

Mistake proofing A form of quality inspection, it is a technique to avoid human errors from passing through a process; poka-yoke is another name for proofing.

Modeling More than simply a representation of a process, it is a mindset that groups of activities can be described (process), tested, and finally, articulated as approaches.

Moment of truth The moment when someone is face-to-face with a customer providing a product or service. The phrase was originally coined at Scandinavian Airlines (SAS) to describe what happens when an employee sold a ticket to a customer. Now it refers to any customer contact: a telephone call, meeting, letter, and so forth. It embodies the idea that the quality of an organization's performance occurs and is measured at the moment when you deal with a customer.

Multifunctional team This kind of a team has members from various functions, usually to work on a process that crosses more than two organizational functions.

Multivariate control chart This kind of control chart is used to evaluate the stability of a process by looking at the levels of two or more variables, such as a process's characteristics.

n Sample size, such as the quantity of units in a sample.

Need A requirement, often generated from what customers want, desire or is essential. It is also used in design and manufacturing to define a lack of something that must be fulfilled in order for a process to function or a product to be completed.

Noise A slang term for any disruption of a process, system, or function.

Nominal group technique (NGT). An increasingly popular tool or technique for generating ideas in groups. It is used to define business problems and their solution, and to articulate quality measures, goals, and objectives. Ideas are gathered from a group and clustered together by theme or subject, leading to possible definitions and solutions.

Nonconformity The lack of conformity to a prespecified set of standards or customer requirements. Often used as a synonym for defect, imperfection, or blemish.

Nondestructive testing and evaluation (NDE or NDT) Refers to the testing and evaluation techniques that do not damage or destroy what is being tested, such as products or parts.

Non-value-added A descriptive for an activity, process, or task that fails to add any value to a product or service. In process improvement activities, these are sought out for elimination.

Normative performance measurement technique Another quality-oriented group technique, it is a structured workshop method that leads teams through the design of measurement systems that are relevant to their needs. This approach factors in behavioral consequences of a measurement in order to encourage acceptance of a particular measurement.

Number of affected units chart (np chart) This kind of control chart is used to evaluate the stability of a process by looking at the total number of units in a sample in which a certain type or class of event happens.

Objective A desired end result to be achieved within a specified period of time. In practice an objective should always have a schedule for achievement. It is often confused with goals, even used interchangeably.

Operating characteristic curve (OC curve) This kind of graph is employed for determining the probability of accepting lots as a function of the lots' or process's level of quality when deploying a variety of sampling plans. Type A curves show probabilities of the acceptance for a specific lot from finite production; Type B curves measure the probability of acceptance of a lot from some continuous process; Type C curves track the long-run percentage of product accepted during some sampling phase and is applied when using a continuous sampling plan.

Opportunity for error (OFE) This is the number of times any event could possibly have an error. Better known as Total OFE, you calculate this by multiplying the number of units times the OFE per unit.

Out-of-control process A process which, when measured, is performing outside the bounds of acceptable variation. The results of any sample are seen to be caused by chance and not by a controllable circumstance.

Out of spec This slang phrase means something is not conforming to specifications, such as the quality of a product.

Output A term borrowed from information processing and the world of computers; it is a specific result or end work product that emerges from a task or a process. In the world of quality, the nature of that output is defined by the customer (recipient).

Outputs Usually refers to information, but can also be any end result that comes out of a process to customers or users.

Owner That individual who has sufficient authority to change a process without requiring further approval. The term "process owner" is often used to say the same thing.

Ownership The power or ability to control actions and processes. Also used to describe one's personal commitment to actions or values. As employees take on more responsibility for the consequences of actions (empowerment), the concept and use of the word is more frequent.

Parameter design The design of a process or product that results in the performance impervious to variation by moving toward a quality target for quality characteristics or features. Often called robust design. In such a design, performance is considered output of a process.

Parametric design Refers to the design phase during which sensitivity to disruption of a function is reduced or eliminated.

Pareto Diagram or Chart Named after Vilfredo Pareto (1848–1923), who we know because of his 80/20 rule. However, in the world of quality, it is a breakdown of defects, or causes of defects, which are ranked (classified) by their frequency of occurrence or by priority. Problems are classified by cause or phenomenon; the chart looks like the New York skyline with the tallest building being the most frequent occurrence. It answers the question: Which are the most important?

Pareto's Principle The widely known concept that a large percentage of results are caused by a small percentage of causes. Often called the 80/20 rule, approximately 80 percent of all problems are created by 20 percent of the possible causes.

Participation The involvement of employees in decisions or actions that involve both processes they implement or their own work.

People involvement The act of individuals or groups participating in an activity, process improvement, or in making decisions within a process or organization. Another variation of the concept of empowerment.

Percent chart (p chart) A chart in which all data is represented by percentages. Used to measure the stability of a process by the number of samples that conform to expectations.

Performance This widely used word refers to description of an attribute of a task, process, or product. The criteria most commonly associated with performance concern cost or efficiency, quality or effectiveness, and availability or schedule.

Physical component A value component that includes all the actions required to perform one activity.

Pie chart A chart that appears as a circle divided into near triangular shapes to reflect relationships between items and the whole.

Plan Increasingly, this is a detailed list of actions that have a specific, anticipated objective. In the world of quality, plans are increasingly documented, actions measured for effectiveness and efficiency, and results measured as outcomes of performance.

Plan-Do-Check-Act cycle (PDCA cycle) A basic tenet of quality in which you plan an action, do it, check to see how it conformed to plan, make improvements to the process, and do it again. Often this is called either a Shewhart cycle or a Deming cycle, after two quality gurus who advocated this approach.

Poka-yoke A slang term for mistake proofing.

Policy Often a documented statement of principles, values, or beliefs, they represent guides to the management of processes and actions. They increasingly are linked to the attainment of specific goals and have performance objectives. Policies are often used today to facilitate use of quality-based practices and values.

Population In quality and statistics, refers to a collection of data, items, or observations from which findings can be identified and then conclusions reached, leading to decisions. In fact-based decision making, the use of data populations is critical.

Potential product Any product or service that has not yet been developed that could be used to replace an existing product or service that attracts and retains customers beyond what existing products can do. Also known as "follow-on" or "replacement" products once created, they should always exceed performance of predecessor products or services.

Presentation The vehicle for providing data and obtaining approval for action, it is considered a formal way of dealing with important issues. Many of the charts defined in this glossary are used to present data in visually pleasing forms.

Prevention In process management, it is an act taken to avoid a future defect or error in order to improve quality of goods or performance.

Prevention costs Costs incurred in implementing actions to avoid future defects or errors in goods and services.

Prevention vs. detection The contrast between two types of quality-oriented actions. Prevention refers to actions taken to avoid defects, while detection focuses on actions to already existing problems in goods and services. These two approaches are sometimes also called "designing in quality vs. inspecting in quality."

Primary activities Those tasks required to create a product or perform a service, transfer either to a customer, or is a service provided to a consumer after the transfer of a product or performance of a service.

Problem A circumstance or question that is a candidate for resolution. It is also the consequence of not conforming to a quality standard. The word is also used to describe a defect or error that needs to be resolved.

Process A collection of actions or activities that are definable, repeatable, predictable, and measurable. A process is the grouping of actions that lead to a specific result (e.g., billing, customer surveys). All actions are components of processes. Processes are the sum total of an organization's organized activities.

Process Analysis Techniques (PAT) A methodology for defining customer needs, analyzes effectiveness of existing processes, and leads to their improvement. It was most widely defined by IBM and reflects common process improvement techniques.

Process average A measure of a primary tendency, it is calculated by dividing the sum of the values of a collection of readings by the number of readings.

Process capability A measure of the performance of any process as compared to its requirements. Also is seen as a measure of long-term performance after a process has stabilized. Sometimes also called process capability index.

Process control This speaks to a collection of actions used to identify and then eliminate special causes of variation. The intent is to restore stability to an existing process.

Process design Refers to the development of any process.

Process diagram A flowchart or other graphic representation of the various steps in a process.

Process efficiency measurement A ratio of value-add time to total cycle time, it is an attempt to measure the relationship of time in process work.

Process flow analysis This technique is used to identify and analyze important processes. It is particularly useful in identifying specific actions, steps, or roadblocks within processes that can be improved or eliminated.

Process improvement Those activities used to identify and then remove common causes of variation so as to improve the overall performance or capacity of a process. This is not to be confused with process reengineering, which is a total reconstruction or new construction of a process to replace a previous one.

Process improvement and Problem-solving teams Teams brought together for the purpose of either improving a specific process or solving a problem. It is a temporary group that disbands after the problem is solved or becomes permanent if it comes to own the process.

Process logistics All aspects of logistics within an enterprise.

Process management A collection of practices used by management to implement and improve quality management and process effectiveness within an enterprise.

Process map A graphical representation of all the steps in a process. It looks like a flowchart of boxes of steps following one after the other. It may also be a graphical representation of a group of related processes.

Process optimization The act of improving both the efficiency and productivity of a process. Focus is typically on economic issues and more broadly on productivity.

Process owner The person responsible for the implementation of a process and held accountable for its results. Process owners typically are required to establish a set of measurements of success for a process, use continuous improvement techniques to eliminate defects and improve cycle time, while delivering results.

Process performance Refers generally to the effectiveness of a process but, when properly done, is a measure of a process's performance against standards, a benchmark, or customer requirements.

Process reengineering Often used interchangeably with process improvement, in the past several years it has become a distinctive term to describe a body of activities that lead to the creation of a new process radically different from its predecessor. It rapidly is acquiring its own set of tools and techniques, but retains the same criteria for performance sought after in process improvement, only on a more dramatic scale, often by at least one factor of magnitude.

Process review A formal, objective assessment of how well a process has been developed and managed, not necessarily on the output of a process. The intent is to improve both the process being reviewed and the methods used to improve and manage it.

Process simplification The act of reducing the complexity of a process, usually done by eliminating steps, such as redundant activities, multiple signoffs and audits. Removal of non-value-add activities is often the most effective way to improve the quality of a process.

Product More than an item, it is also the output of a process delivered to internal or external customers. This may include systems, equipment, data, services, parts or items for sale.

Product design The activities involved in the development of a product; usually a design process with the voice of the customer very prominent.

Product genealogy Simply an historical record of the components and configuration of a product; it may include data about its manufacture, testing, inspections, and maintenance. The record of quality audits of both components and products is also part of a product genealogy.

Product or service liability The moral or legal obligation of a firm to make restitution to a customer for damage or personal injury caused by that company's products or services. This is often a source of cost justification for quality of products, especially for the cost of safety features.

Production process The collection of activities required to make a product. It often is seen as a collection or family of related manufacturing processes.

Productivity Used widely with various meanings, it generally refers to the ratio of outputs produced, or services rendered, to inputs required for these goods and services. It is also used to explain the desired results or outcomes in terms of quality.

Proportion chart Same thing as a percent chart.

Q chart A quality score chart that may come in various forms.

Q90 series Shorthand for ANSI/ASQC Q90 series of standards, the U.S. version of ISO 9000 standards, adopted in 1987.

Quality While there are many definitions of the term, they all boil down to descriptions of excellence in goods and services and especially to what degree they conform to customer requirements or satisfy customers. Equally important is the notion that all activities and things can be improved upon continuously, and that meeting requirements the first time is a necessary objective.

Quality assurance/quality control Used interchangeably, the terms refer to those activities executed to ensure a high level of quality for a product or service.

Quality audit A systematic inspection by an outside body to determine if quality activities conform to quality plans and expectations. Often the effectiveness of plans and activities is included in the audit.

Quality circle First made popular in the 1970s, this is a small group of employees and their managers who came together voluntarily to identify and solve work-related problems employing structured methodologies. For many American and European firms, this was the first vehicle used to apply quality techniques.

Quality control Just another way of saying quality assurance.

Quality costs Another way of saying cost of poor quality.

Quality engineering The analysis of a manufacturing process or system done to maximize the quality of work done (process) and the output of that work (products).

Quality Function Deployment (QFD) A highly structured methodology for identifying customer requirements, then linking them to the design specifications of goods and services. The primary objective of this disciplined methodology is to solve quality problems before a product is designed. Design engineers and marketing and manufacturing personnel work together to create a product design that most closely meets customer requirements. Survey work on what features customers want (are important) is followed by ranking of features by significance, then by identification of possible problems, and concluding with well-defined engineering specifications. QFD is a widely used approach in manufacturing.

Quality improvement team That team of people responsible for planning and implementing improvements in the quality of processes or organizations.

Quality loss function A parabolic representation of quality loss that happens when a quality feature deviates from its standard or value. The measure is always in monetary terms. The greater the deviation from standard, the more the cost of lost quality increases.

Quality score chart A control chart used to measure the stability of a process. Quality score is the weighted sum of a count of the sums of various classes of events in which each classification is assigned a weight.

Quality team Quality improvement or performance action teams of employees all working on various aspects of a process. Such teams are used for process improvement projects.

Quality trilogy A three-part approach to managing for quality results through planning, control, and improvement. The first focuses on the development of processes and products that meet customer requirements; the second to meet the objectives of products and processes; and the third to continue improving even greater levels of performance.

QUINCUNX This tool creates frequency distributions, often used to simulate manufacturing processes.

Quantitative methods The application of measurements.

R chart Shorthand for range chart.

RAM or R&M. Shorthand for reliability/availability/maintainability. It is a process applied by the U.S. Department of Defense to insure combat readiness of products through reliability and maintenance. This process includes reduction of costs through defined practices.

Random sampling A widely used sampling method by which random samples of units (e.g., products) are chosen such that all combination of these units have an equal chance of being chosen as the sample. This technique is used frequently for selecting products to be inspected for quality.

Range The gap between high and low values of a set of data. Ranges are defined statistically and activities within the gap are variables that are tolerated. Incidents that are recorded beyond the ranges are considered exceptions. It is also more classically defined as the difference between the maximum or minimum values of data in any sample.

Range chart This type of control chart uses R as the subgroup for the purposes of evaluating the stability of variability within a process.

Recognition The attention paid to either an individual or group for outstanding accomplishments. In the world of quality, this is often tendered to teams and in itself is a process designed to reward individuals for embracing and applying effectively quality tools and values.

Red bead experiment This famous experiment was devised by quality guru W. Edwards Deming to show that it was impossible to rank employees by performance for the following year based on last year's performance because differences in performance have to be attributed to a system, not to employees. To perform the experiment, take 4,000 red and white beads of which 20 percent are red, all in a jar, and find six people. They have to produce white beads since their customer does not want red. The first individual starts by stirring the beads and then, after being blindfolded, selects 50 beads. That person next hands the bead jar to the second individual, who repeats the process, then passes the jar on. After all six have selected their 50 sample beads, the number of red beads is counted for each person. Then the limits of variation among them (i.e., employees) attributed to the experiment is calculated. These calculations show that no evidence exists that one person will outperform another in the future. Rather, the experiment demonstrates that management wastes its time trying to determine why a particular employee could gather 10 beads while another could find 20. The lesson is that management should focus on the system for performance (e.g., for selecting the red beads), thus making it possible for everyone to select more white beads. (Deming's own description of this experiment is included in the Classics section of this book.)

Registrar Accreditation Board (RAB) This board evaluates the reliability and competence of organizations that assess and register companies to appropriate ISO 9000 series standards. This board was formed by the ASQC and is governed by members from industry, higher education, and management consulting.

Registration to standards A defined process by which an accredited, independent third-party organization performs on-site audits of a company's operations measuring them against a set of independent standards. Used in certification for ISO 9000 standards, successful audits are rewarded with a certification of compliance to standards.

Regression analysis A statistical technique for calculating the best mathematical expression that describes the functional relationship between a response and one or more independent variables. It is a widely used SPC calculation.

Reliability Often it is defined as the probability of a product or service performing its role under predetermined conditions without failure or problem for a specific period of time. Such a specified statement of performance is frequently made a design requirement for the product or process. First measured in products, it is now increasingly applied to processes and services.

Requirements This is always stated as the needs or wants of customers. Requirements is a profoundly influencing factor in determining the content and output of any process. In addition to this being a statement of what needs to be, it is increasingly also stated as a measurable outcome.

Restraining forces Those realities that prevent a situation from improving. They can be intrinsic to a process or be caused by some circumstance outside of the organization (e.g., economic reality).

Reward A recompense or recognition for something well done. In the world of quality, a distinction is made between external and internal rewards. External rewards are given to individuals or teams by management or peers for quality results. Internal rewards are the personal satisfaction of meeting a challenge, doing a job well, or accomplishing a personal goal.

Right the first time The phrase is used to suggest that it is less expensive and more beneficial to make a product or deliver a service correctly the first time. Taking steps to insure that products and services perform as required is seen as more cost beneficial than having to "do it over again." It is another way of suggesting that defect prevention strategies are more beneficial than defect identification.

Roadblock identification analysis This technique is used to identify circumstances or other obstacles that do or could prevent improvements in performance or that block existing products or services from achieving specified levels of quality. Applying nominal group technique, users identify issues and prioritize them by the degree to which they represent roadblocks to success. Then teams can perform analysis of key barriers and propose ways to remove them.

Robust design Refers to the design of a product or service with minimal losses of quality due to variation from quality expectations.

Robustness One of the most recent entrants into the quality vocabulary, it refers to the condition or quality of a product, service, or process in which performance is relatively stable, with a minimum of variability, despite changes in the environment or operating conditions.

Root cause Refers to the underlying reason why a process does not conform to specifications. The removal of a root cause brings the process back to conformance.

Root cause analysis An important quality process for identifying the source of defects or problems, it is a structured approach that focuses on the ultimate or original cause of a condition. The approach discounts judgment or symptoms about the cause of a problem and relies instead on the collection of possible sources of a problem. It is one of the most widely used and effective approaches in process work.

Rules of conduct A body of guidelines usually established by a team at the start of its process work to govern the behavior and performance of its members. Efficient teams always establish rules of conduct at the beginning of their work.

Run chart A graph that plots performance information over time for processes or defects, for example.

Sample A specific (finite) number of items of a similar type taken from a population or lot for the purpose of examination to determine if all members of the population or lot are conforming to quality requirements.

Sample size A specific number of items of data from a larger body of information.

Sample standard deviation chart (s chart) This kind of control chart takes a subgroup standard deviation, s, and uses it to evaluate the stability of variation within a process.

Sampling The process of collecting a sample of data about the quality of a lot or population of goods, actions, or information as reflective of the patterns of the entire population or lot.

Scanlon committee Refers to a committee made up of various levels of an organization who come together to implement a philosophy of management/labor relations with the intention of improving the productivity of the organization. Specific principles and methods are employed by such committees to facilitate the process. Like many other team-like activities, it relies heavily on employee involvement and responsibility.

Scatter diagram A widely used graphic, it is a technique employed to analyze relationships between two variables. Two sets of data are plotted graphically, with the x axis representing a variable to make a prediction and the y axis to display the variable to be predicted. The illustration shows possible relationships.

Selection grid A tool used to compare each problem, alternative, or opportunity against each other.

Selection matrix This technique is used to rank in importance or effect problems, opportunities, or options based on predefined criteria.

Self-directed teams Teams that work on processes or within functions with little or no management control. They tend to do self-appraisals of each member and have enormous authority over how to use their time and on how to perform their duties.

Seven tools of quality Techniques widely used by enterprises to understand the performance of their processes for the purpose of improving them. They are cause-and-effect diagram, check sheet, control chart, flowchart, histogram, Pareto chart, and scatter diagram.

Shewhart cycle Another name for Plan-Do-Check-Act cycle.

Sharing rallies Meetings in which individuals, but usually teams, are recognized for their contributions and successes with processes. Often these are run like recognition events with awards, motivational speakers, and trips, and are celebrations of progress. Those honored typically have to explain to their audiences what they did and what they learned from the effort.

Signal-to-noise ratio (S/N ratio) This mathematical equation illustrates the extent of an experimental effect above the effect of experimental error caused by chance fluctuations.

Sigma A measure of statistical variability of distributions. In statistical process language, it is a Standard Deviation. In practice, it is a measure of the number of defects per million.

Sigma Capability This sigma measure is of defects per million opportunities.

Simulation The observation of a model or other artificial representation that mirrors a realistic situation and is employed instead of actual direct experimentation for either economic or technical reasons. Often it is a fast way to study the possible performance of an as yet unbuilt product.

Six Sigma One of the most popular forms of measuring performance in manufacturing and also in large corporations. Six Sigma means 3.4 defects, errors, or failures per million occurrences or performances. Such events can be errors in lines of programming, telephone calls missed, or billing mistakes. It is a statistical measure that focuses on virtually no defects as the acceptable level of quality. Popularized by Motorola Corporation, it has proven to be an effective way to translate many types of activities into a measure of defects needing improvements at a very stringent level.

Skills The word today is widely used to refer to someone's experiences, competencies, values, attitudes, and patterns of behavior. Often formally catalogued, they provide an organization with an inventory of capabilities and also for people, a list of possible areas for further training and practice.

Sorting The act of arranging data in some useful order. These may include placing data in classes or categories to provide insight into actions or process performance.

Special cause A source of variation in the performance or output of a process that is unpredictable, intermittent, random, or somctimes unstable. Engineers will often also use the phrase "assignable cause" to mean the same thing; the cause of an exception.

Specification A specific, often documented, description of a product or process, focusing on its features and the results it should produce.

Stakeholder An individual or organization that has an investment (stake) in your success and judges your performance. They are customers, employees, stockholders, the nation, or whoever. They are people or organizations who you have to serve and are interested in your achievements. Another set of examples using schools and universities: students, faculty, employers, alumni, and funding organizations.

Standard deviation The spread of a process, denoted by the Greek letter sigma. In mathematics it is defined as the positive square root of a variance. In quality it is the spread in the variety of output from a process.

Statistic A parameter that can be defined based on quantitative features of a sample, a measure of value. A varient, called inferential statistics, suggests the level of confidence placed on a statement regarding the probability of its accuracy or truth, or about its applicability. The intent is to provide a decision-maker with confidence about a decision to be made after reviewing specific pieces of data.

Statistical control Typically it is used to describe the status of a process from which all special causes of variation have been eliminated, leaving only common causes. When a process is said to be under statistical control, that is another way of suggesting it is stable.

Statistical elimination This analysis of a sample parameter is performed to predict values of a corresponding population parameter.

Statistical estimation This kind of analysis of a sample parameter is done to predict values of its corresponding population parameter.

Statistical methods Refers to the application of the theory of probability to variations or problems. Basic statistical methods are tools and techniques widely used in process work and include such popular items as control charts, capability analysis, and statistical inference. A more sophisticated set of tools, less widely used in normal process work, involves statistical analysis and design of experiments, regression analysis, correlation analysis, and variance analysis. Both sets of tools, however, are evident today in all types of processes and organizations.

Statistical process control (SPC) A body of statistical techniques used to measure the performance of processes. The reason for applying these is to identify specifically areas for improvement in processes and to measure outputs of processes, all leading to actions that will result in continuous improvements and results. Objectives include getting processes to a stable state and to improve their capability or output. Another way of describing SPC is to see it as a management philosophy that seeks out to reduce variation around a predetermined target value and as a disciplined approach to the identification and resolution of problems. Popular SPC tools include fishbone diagrams, graphical representations, Pareto charts, and control charts. All are used to track numerically what a process is doing, analyzing that performance, and suggesting improvements.

Statistical quality control (SQC) Used both in manufacturing and services, it is a methodology for tracking current conditions against a target for quality performance.

Statistics A branch of applied mathematics whose purpose is to describe and analyze observations so as to predict events, leading to decisions that are made in a circumstance of uncertainty. The techniques of statistics rely on the theory of probability, making possible the mathematical study of a problem. Statistics were first introduced into manufacturing processes in the 1920s and after World War II began to appear in office processes. Today the use of statistics is an integral part of any total quality management effort.

Steering committee or group A committee, usually made up of senior management, to oversee and guide a cross-functional or focus activity. It is a widely used mechanism for coordinating the quality improvement activities of an organization at large.

Strategic Total Quality Management Plan (STQMP) The overall plan for introducing, sustaining, and improving the application of TQM tools in an organization.

Strategic Total Quality Management planning cycle A plan for implementing TQM. It includes definition of an enterprise-wide vision, identification of strategic improvement opportunities, their selection, development and maintenance of a TQM plan of action, evaluation of results, and renewal of the plan to reflect changing realities.

Strategy Any broad set of activities to achieve specific goals. Processes, and how they are structured, are often employed to implement strategies.

Structural variation A variation caused by regular, systematic changes in output. These can be, for example, in response to seasonal patterns or to long-term trends.

Subprocess A part of a larger process that can be seen as almost a small process in itself. For example, in a process for renewing a driver's license, a subprocess might be those activities surrounding the written examination or the eye test.

Supplier Anyone or organization who provides input into a process. This can be a high school supplying students to a college, a company delivering raw materials to a factory, or another department, providing you data that you need to do your work. Suppliers are measured on effectiveness and are brought into your processes as a participant rather than simply as a vendor. They may be others within your own enterprise or vendors from other firms.

Supplier/customer analysis This technique is used to gather and exchange data on the needs and requirements of an organization to its key suppliers. It also involves both agreeing to a common definition of what the buying organization's customers needs and expectations are to be fulfilled by both.

Supplier quality assurance A very obvious concept today, it is the expression of confidence that a supplier's quality will match a customer's requirements. This is brought about by a relationship between supplier and customer defined by processes that insure a standard, routine high-level of quality of supplies meeting a customer's needs. This allows a manufacturer, for example, to work with fewer suppliers. J. M. Juran defines nine essential activities to insure supplier quality assurance: (1) definition of product and service quality requirements, (2) evaluation of alternative suppliers, (3) selection of suppliers, (4) conduct of joint quality planning exercises, (5) cooperations with supplier during the execution of a contract, (6) gathering of proof of conformance to requirements, (7) certification of approved (qualified) suppliers, (8) implementation of quality improvement programs as needed, and (9) creation and use of supplier quality ratings.

Support system Refers to a process within an organization for the purpose of guiding the enterprise through the application of TQM principles.

System Used to describe a collection or interdependent processes for the purpose of accomplishing a specific function or goal.

System improvement This method focuses on the improvement or change of any system (often a collection of processes).

Systems (parts) or concept design A design phase whose purpose is the design architecture (materials, size, shape, number of components, etc.). It does this by examining the best available components or technology. Often the phrase used for this kind of activity is "parts design phase."

Taguchi methods Named after Genichi Taguchi, a leading Japanese expert on quality improvement, they comprise a body of techniques for evaluating quality and how to improve it. He pioneered the concept that quality improvements should be measured in terms of cost savings (loss function), arguing that all quality improvements are cost savings.

Tampering In the world of quality, this is an action initiated to compensate for some variation within the control limits of a process. Experimentation has shown that tampering does increase the variability in performance of a process or stable system.

Task A specific action done to complete a task; it is always a component of a process.

Team Much as in sports, this is a group of employees who work together to achieve a common objective. They are typically working on a process or within a department and rely heavily on personal skills applied in a collaborative environment that fosters teamwork and concensus decision-making practices.

Team building Activities for creating, developing, and maintaining a team of individuals who work on a common goal or process. Activities include definition of roles, obligations, and objectives of a team; improvement of relations among team members; enhancing techniques in problem solving, decision making, planning, and resource utilization; reduction of conflict and tension among members; and enhancing the organizational environment in which the team works. Team building is a major activity in a quality-driven organization.

Teamwork The shared responsibility and actions for the completion of any task or process with a common objective by a group of individuals working together.

Timeliness More than just the completion of services or delivery of goods when expected, it is the notion that completion is determined by customer expectations.

Tool In the world of quality, a tool is usually a technique (such as Pareto charts), a discipline (such as SPC), or actually a physical tool (such as software or a device to measure performance of a machine).

Tolerance design A stage in any design process that defines the tolerances of variation in performance that will be acceptable in a final product or service. At this critical phase, where costs of end products can be increased dramatically, designers focus on producing robust designs and products in earlier parameter design phases to contain possible expenses.

Top-down process diagram A kind of chart that defines the major and minor steps in a process.

Top-level process diagram A kind of diagram that displays a complete process.

Top-management commitment The commitment and personal involvement of senior management in the implementation of quality programs. Their roles can include personal participation in quality committees; creation of quality processes, goals, measures, and policies; providing training on quality; and allocation of appropriate resources. Other activities include participation in process teams, inspection of quality progress, rewarding those who have contributed to quality improvements and who are "champions" of quality.

Total More than just another word for complete or everything, it describes the absolute commitment or involvement of everything or everyone in a continuous improvement program.

Total customer service A widely used term, it encompasses all the acts, features, and data that enhance a customer's ability to enjoy the potential capabilities and benefits of a service or product.

Total integrated logistics The integration of all logistics concerning inputs into an enterprise, even all processes within the organization, and the outputs of the enterprise. The purpose of looking at all the inflows and outflows of an organization is to ensure a comprehensive customer support strategy that is optimized for cost and quality.

Total product concept An approach to offer insight into the wide range of possibilities for a product. Such a concept includes a generic product, the anticipated product, an augmented product, and a potential product.

Total production maintenance Refers to a system for all of an organization's maintenance activities.

Total quality control (TQC) Originally conceived by quality guru Armand V. Feigenbaum, it is a system used to integrate quality development, maintenance, and improvement of all parts of an organization so that the manufacture of goods and the execution of services are done most economically while providing excellent customer service.

Total Quality Management (TQM) A body of management and process practices designed to improve the performance of any organization to satisfy customers. TQM calls for the integration of quality activities of organizations and people, applying scientific and disciplined approaches to continuous improvement while fostering customer or market-driven values, and blending the most economical performance while satisfying totally customer needs. It seeks to impose standards, achieve efficiencies, define roles of all individuals within a process and organization, specify controls, reduce errors and defects, apply statistical process control, and employ teams effectively.

Total Quality Management action planning The detailed plan for implementing and managing TQM within an organization.

Total Quality Management philosophy That body of beliefs and general concepts that embraces practices of continuously improving organizations.

Total Quality Management principles The key fundamental rules and practices of TQM necessary to achieve effective implementation of continuous improvement.

Total Quality Management process The process by which all inputs into an organization are transformed into products and services that meet the requirements of internal and external customers; generating a quality output.

Total Quality Management umbrella The integration of all the basic management tools and techniques, and existing efforts at improvement, to create a coordinated, disciplined approach to continuous improvement throughout an organization.

Trainers Individuals who teach TQM principles within an enterprise. Often they are also quality coaches and mentors.

Transactional analysis A series of activities to identify how people and organizations are performing; in other words, what psychological or political games people are playing. The intent is to change people's performance and attitudes so that they may become more effective on their jobs while facilitating cultural transformation in an organization.

Trend control chart A type of control chart that illustrates the deviation of a subgroup average (X-bar) from some expected trend in a process level. The purpose of such a chart is to assess the stability of a process.

Type I error An incorrect decision to reject such items as a statistical hypothesis or a lot of goods when they were acceptable.

Type II error Another type of incorrect decision to accept something, but in this case when it was unacceptable.

U chart A count per unit chart.

Upper control limit (UCL) The control limit for points above the central horizontal line on a control chart.

Upstream value chain The value chains within suppliers to an organization.

Value Considered the amount consumers will pay for a product or service.

Value-adding process Simply put, these are activities that convert an input into a customer-usable output.

Value chain A phrase made famous by Michael Porter, it consists of all the activities performed by an organization that have effects on costs of products or services. Value chain models are used to divide all processes or activities into discrete components that can be identified so as to establish their individual costs (value). Primary value activities might include, for instance, sales or manufacture. Support activities could include personnel management.

Value engineering This kind of organized effort has as its purpose to analyze functions of a system, equipment, services, supplies, and facilities to achieve critical functions at the lowest life cycle cost consistent with defined criteria for performance, reliability, maintainability, manufacturability, quality and safety, and all consistent with requirements of the market (customers).

Value system The total of all actions within all value chains encompassing an organization's suppliers, channels of distribution, and customers.

Variable A variable is a piece of data that has a value when it is within a range exhibiting a specific frequency or pattern. Discrete variables are data limited in value to quantities, such as the number of invoices generated by a billing process, and always relate to attribute data. Continuous variables are measured to a degree of accuracy, such as width of a component, and always relate to variables data. This measurable information is sometimes also called variable data.

Variance Nonconformance to expectations or specifications. In the world of statistics, variance is the square of the standard deviation. But in quality, it is simply how far off the mark something is in meeting customer expectations.

Variation Always a change in data, characteristic, or function caused by one of four possible factors: special causes, common causes, tampering, or structural variations.

Victory-C TQM model A systematic model encompassing an entire organization, and consisting of all the elements necessary for victory (success). It is always focused on total costumer satisfaction.

Vision A concept of an ideal state that an organization would like to achieve at some point in the future (e.g., three to five years out). Vision-based strategic planning is then focused less on today's problems and more on what strategies are required to make the vision come true.

Vital few, useful many J. M. Juran coined this phrase to describe use of the Pareto concept in which most effects come from a few causes, that is, 80 percent of effects from 20 percent of possible causes. The 20 percent of possible causes are the "vital few," the other causes are the "useful many."

World-class This descriptive is often used with such expressions as world-class quality, world-class company, world-class process. It means the best in the world. In the case of world-class company, using the Malcolm Baldrige Criteria, it is a firm that achieves at least 876 points out of 1,000 in its quality appraisal.

World-class quality A standard of excellence that is the best in the world.

X-bar chart Another way of saying average chart.

Zero defects In the world of quality, it is an aspiration but also a way of explaining to employees the notion that everything should be done right the first time, that there should be no failures or defects in work outputs. Developed by Philip B. Crosby, it is the notion that by observing details and avoiding errors, people can avoid almost all errors. It promotes the concept that "close enough" is unacceptable.

1994 Malcolm Baldrige National Quality Award Winners

In 1994, three companies won the Baldrige Award. In services, there were two winners: **AT&T Consumer Communications Services** and **GTE Directories Corporation.** AT&T Consumer Communication Services is the residential long distance services branch of AT&T and is headquartered in Basking Ridge, New Jersey. GTE Directories is one of the world's largest telephone directories companies. The company's primary focus is on publishing and/or selling advertising for white and yellow pages directories for telephone companies within their official franchise areas. The company is located in Dallas, Texas. There were no winners in the large company manufacturing category this year.

In the small company category, the winner was **Wainwright Industries, Inc.,** of St. Peters, Missouri. This is a family-owned manufacturer of stamped and machined products for the automotive, aerospace, home security, and information processing industries.

In 1994, a total of 71 companies applied for the Baldrige Award; 14 companies made the finals and received site visits. The number of applications is down from last year, but this does not represent any diminishing of the award or what it stands for. Part of the reason is that many other quality awards are given at the state and local levels, nearly all of which are based on some version of the Baldrige Award (see awards section of this book for details).

All three winners this year attributed their winning to their focus on customer satisfaction by better tracking what customers desire, adding new products and services to better meet needs, and by making sure they are continuously improving their processes for creating and delivering their products and services.

An especially important consideration in choosing the winning companies is their position as role models for others to emulate. Given the stiff competition and the judges' desire to select those companies that they view as the best role models, these three companies stood out above all other applicants in 1994.

The Real Value of the Baldrige Award

While winning the Baldrige is a visible and public payoff for companies actively implementing Total Quality Management as a philosophy and mode of operating, this is only the frosting on the cake for those firms involved in the process. The real value of the Baldrige Award is its use as a set of guidelines for transforming a company. Thousands of organizations of all types use the Baldrige Criteria to help them proceed down the road to a more realistic, customer-oriented, efficient, and effective management process. Further, the award helps publicize the importance of doing this, and the winners become benchmarks to help others in their quality journey.

As Baldrige winners become benchmarks, we present the following overviews of 1994's winners to give you a sense of what the Baldrige judges determined were outstanding examples of companies that practice Total Quality Management. In doing this, we reproduce the announcement from the National Institute of Standards and Technology citing their reasons for selecting each winner. We then include how you can get additional information on these companies and their individual approaches to managing for total quality.

1994 Baldrige Award Winner, Services Category: AT&T Consumer Communications Services

The following is an edited version of the press release from the National Institute of Standards and Technology announcing that AT&T Consumer Communications Services had won a Baldrige Award for 1994.

AT&T Consumer Communications Services provides domestic and international long distance services primarily to residential customers. Competitors have grown from a handful in 1984 to more than 500 today. Its 44,000 employees serve more than 80 million customers with about 60 percent market share for long distance services. CCS, the largest of some 20 AT&T business units, is based on Basking Ridge, NJ, and has more than 900 sites throughout the United States.

The following briefly summarizes their quality improvement efforts:

- Despite intense competition since deregulation, the company has maintained high market share by constantly focusing on the needs of customers.
- Seventy-five million interactions with customers each day test the company's programs against the goal of perfect customer connection and contact each and every time.
- An integrated business and quality planning system, led by the CCS president and senior executives, focuses on five key customer requirements: call quality, customer service, billing, reputation, and price.
- With part of their compensation based on "customer value added," a composite measure of customer satisfaction, executives regularly use a variety of mechanisms to communicate with the

company's quality and customer-focus values. These include field visits, publications, roundtables, and face-to-face meetings with employees, in which all management and occupational associates participate as equals.

- Teams implement quality improvements, using standardized, AT&T developed tools for planning, executing, and evaluating initiatives to improve performance and customer satisfaction. Process Management Teams include employees from all levels of the company and, as appropriate, suppliers. To ensure a shared focus and commitment across units, internal contracts are used to assign responsibilities and to establish clear improvement goals for each stage of a process.
- Workforce training, skills development, and other elements of human resource plans are systematically integrated into business and quality improvement plans. Annual workforce surveys, employee focus groups, and site interviews provide data for detailed and aggregate views of employee job satisfaction, awareness of company values and goals, perceptions of company leadership, and other topics influencing attitudes, motivation, and performance.
- As is the case throughout much of the telecommunications industry, CCS has made substantial reductions in the size of its workforce. To help employees make the transition, the company has initiated services (such as retraining, preparing resumes, and developing job leads) that associates can use until they find new employment.
- Extensive data and information systems support fact-based management approaches to problem solving, quality improvement, and market development. Customer-satisfaction and operational-performance data are made available throughout the company, providing timely feedback to workers and management on progress toward meeting quality goals. All process and performance measures are linked to overall efforts to meet customer requirements and improve levels of satisfaction.
- Rapid advances in technology have reshaped telecommunications and redefined "service" for CCS customers, so the company invests more than $1 billion annually in developing and installing new technology. For the fourth consecutive year, the 1993 *Data Communications* magazine recognized the company with its Best Overall and Best Technology in Long Distance Carrier Service awards.
- CCS's heavy investment in technology has expanded the capabilities—and enhanced the reliability—of its worldwide telecommunications network. Responding to a cable cut that eliminated service to Manhattan for nearly half a day in 1991, the company overhauled its disaster response system and developed a highly

automated system (FASTAR) that can restore service calling capability within 10 minutes of a major facility outage.

AT&T Consumer Communications Services has prepared a 20-page booklet summarizing their application for the 1994 Baldrige Award. You can receive this booklet and get additional information about AT&T CCS's quality management efforts (and arrange for tours and speakers) by contacting Diane Phelps-Feldkamp, Director, Quality and Business Improvement, AT&T Consumer Communications Services, 295 North Maple Avenue, Basking Ridge, NJ 07920; phone (800) 473-5047.

1994 Baldrige Award Winner, Services Category: GTE Directory Corporation

The following is an edited version of the press release from the National Institute of Standards and Technology announcing that GTE Directories Corporation had won a Baldrige Award for 1994.

With $1.4 billion in revenue, GTE Directories Corporation is one of the world's largest telephone directory companies. The company produces more than 1,200 directory titles in 45 U.S states and 17 countries, including more than 75 different directories in international markets. The company's 5,120 employees work at its headquarters in Dallas/Ft. Worth, Texas, and at other sites in North America, Canada, and overseas.

The following briefly summarizes their quality improvement efforts:

- In a very competitive market—which includes the directory businesses of the Regional Bell operating companies—GTE Directories has sustained increasing revenue growth. In the same period, many competitors have had flat or declining revenues.
- Independent studies show that GTE Directories produces the preferred directory in 271 of its 274 primary markets.
- To meet the company's corporate vision of "100 Percent Customer Satisfaction Through Quality," 14 key customer service requirements have been developed through a Customer Satisfaction Measurement Program. They include professionalism, timeliness, and support for sales functions as well as post-sales and complaint resolution. Key performance measures match each customer service requirement.
- This state-of-the-art measurement process weights the relative importance of different product and service delivery features to each of the company's three distinct customer groups: advertisers,

consumers using the directories, and companies contracting for yellow pages services.

- GTE's Directories Published Error ratio for 1993, just over 350 per 1 million listings, places them as best-in-class according to industry benchmark studies.
- To track and ensure the highest quality supplier performance, the firm relies on supplier evaluations, certification, and recognition plans, supplier base management, supplier and employee communications, continuous benchmarking, and a cross-functional standards and specifications management committee. For example, to remain a qualified supplier, companies must score 8 or above on a 10-point scale that evaluates performance in delivery, customer service, documentation, and product/service value.
- A comprehensive training program is used to provide strong foundations in customer relations skills, team problem solving, and technical job skills. For example, most employees involved in shop-floor printing operations are trained in statistical process control to monitor printing process variability to maintain and improve product quality, decrease waste, and improve productivity.
- Senior executive leadership in quality management is clear. For example, every member of the company's management board personally taught quality tools and techniques to other managers.
- Team-based management is pervasive throughout the company. It is not unusual to find individuals who have served on 10 or more Quality Improvement Teams, even at the manager level.
- A heavy reward system, linked directly to customer satisfaction measurements, serves as a powerful motivator for quality service, with a variety of special awards for individuals and teams supporting quality and operational performance improvement.

For more information on GTE Directories Corporation and their quality management processes, contact Janet Stevens, Public Relations Director, GTE Directories Corp., West Airfield Drive, P.O. Box 609810, Dallas/Fort Worth, TX 75261-9810; phone (214) 453-7751, fax (214) 453-7231.

1994 Baldrige Award Winner, Small Business Category: Wainwright Industries, Inc.

The following is an edited version of the press release from the National Institute of Standards and Technology announcing that Wainwright Industries, Inc., had won a Baldrige Award for 1994.

Wainwright Industries is a privately held, family-owned manufacturer supplying precision components and assembled systems to the automotive, aerospace, and information processing industries. With $30 million in annual sales, Wainwright's major markets are local, national, and, increasingly, international. Wainwright holds top supplier honors from companies like General Motors, Ford, IBM, and McDonnell Douglas. The company won the Missouri Quality Award in 1993. The company's 275 associates are based in St. Peters, Missouri, and in a recently opened plant in Arlington, Texas.

The following briefly summarizes their quality improvement efforts:

- All of Wainwright's associates are involved in the company's Continuous Improvement Process. In 1993, associates submitted an average of 54 suggestions, or 1.25 per week, an unusually high level.
- Senior leaders are highly visible, both inside and outside the company. They act as role models, developing the next level of managers, and strive to personally motivate associates. Executives spend time promoting quality values and quality management to other companies and education and government officials in Missouri.
- Wainwright's commitment to its customers is evidenced by its guiding vision of "Total Customer Satisfaction" and its Customer Satisfaction Index, which measures quality, delivery, communication, and service. For 1993, Wainwright achieved a 95 percent customer satisfaction rating. The company's goal is to reach 98 percent by 1995.
- All company data are linked to the company's five strategic indicators (listed in order of importance): safety, internal customer satisfaction, external customer satisfaction, six sigma quality, and business performance.
- All of Wainwright's business processes are developed with safety of associates in mind. As a result, since 1990 accidents have decreased by 72 percent, lost time due to accidents has decreased by 85 percent, and lost work days have gone down by 87 percent.
- Wainwright Industries believes that public responsibility and environmental stewardship are part of the company's core values. For example, by redesigning processes, developing water-based wash systems, and using organic coolants and lubricants, the company has eliminated all hazardous waste from its facilities.
- Improvement trends in production and delivery areas are positive. For example, reengineering the process used to produce drawn housings has led to reductions in lead time from 8.75 days to 15 minutes, among the best in the industry.
- Wainwright Industries spends up to 7 percent of its payroll on training associates in areas such as basic math and English as well

as more specialized education in statistical process control and computer-controlled machinery operation.

For more information on Wainwright's management approach that led to the Baldrige, contact David Robbins, Vice President, Wainwright Industries, Inc., 17 Cermak Boulevard, P.O. Box 640, St. Peters, MO 63376; phone (314) 278-5850, fax (314) 278-8806.

1995 Malcolm Baldrige National Quality Award Criteria

This section provides you with a summary of the 1995 Baldrige Award Criteria, including changes from the 1994 Criteria, with points given in each category. You can receive a complete copy of the Criteria and the 1995 Application Forms and Instructions (Criteria and Application are two separate documents) by writing to:

Malcolm Baldrige National Quality Award
National Institute of Standards and Technology
Route 270 and Quince Orchard Road
Administration Building, Room A537
Gaithersburg, MD 20899-0001
Phone: (301) 975-2036
Fax: (301) 948-3716

Description of the 1995 Award Criteria

Award Criteria Purposes

The Malcolm Baldrige National Quality Award Criteria are the basis for making Awards and for giving feedback to applicants. In addition, the Criteria have three important roles in strengthening U.S. competitiveness:

- to help improve performance practices and capabilities;
- to facilitate communication and sharing of best practices information among and within organizations of all types based upon a common understanding of key performance requirements; and
- to serve as a working tool for managing performance, planning, training, and assessment.

Award Criteria Goals

The Criteria are designed to help companies enhance their competitiveness through focus on dual, results-oriented goals:

- delivery of ever-improving value to customers, resulting in marketplace success; and
- improvement of overall company performance and capabilities.

Core Values and Concepts

The Award Criteria are built upon a set of core values and concepts. These values and concepts are the foundation for integrating customer and company performance requirements.

These core values and concepts are:

Customer-Driven Quality

Quality is judged by customers. All product and service characteristics that contribute value to customers and lead to customer satisfaction and preference must be a key focus of a company's management system. Value, satisfaction, and preference may be influenced by many factors throughout the customer's overall purchase, ownership, and service experiences. These factors include the company's relationship with customers that helps build trust, confidence, and loyalty. This concept of quality includes not only the product and service characteristics that meet basic customer requirements but it also includes those characteristics that enhance them and differentiate them from competing offerings. Such enhancement and differentiation may be based upon new offerings, combinations of product and service offerings, rapid response, or special relationships.

Customer-driven quality is thus a strategic concept. It is directed toward customer retention and market share gain. It demands constant sensitivity to emerging customer and market requirements, and measurement of the factors that drive customer satisfaction and retention. It also demands awareness of developments in technology and of competitors' offerings, and rapid and flexible response to customer and market requirements.

Success requires more than defect and error reduction, merely meeting specifications, and reducing complaints. Nevertheless, defect and error reduction and elimination of causes of dissatisfaction contribute significantly to the customers' view of quality and are thus also important parts of customer-driven quality. In addition, the company's success in recovering from defects and errors ("making things right for the customer") is crucial to building customer relationships and to customer retention.

Leadership

A company's senior leaders need to set directions and create a customer orientation, clear and visible values, and high expectations. Reinforcement of the values and expectations requires personal commitment and involvement. The leaders' basic values and commitment need to include areas of public responsibility and corporate citizenship. The leaders need to take part in the creation of strategies, systems, and methods for achieving excellence and building capabilities. The systems and methods need to guide all activities and decisions of the company. The senior leaders need to commit to the development of the entire work force and should encourage participation and creativity by all employees. Through their personal involvement in activities, such as planning, communications, review of company performance, and recognition of employees' achievements, the senior leaders serve as role models, reinforcing the values and encouraging leadership and initiative throughout the company.

Continuous Improvement and Learning

Achieving the highest levels of performance requires a well-executed approach to continuous improvement. The term "continuous improvement" refers to both incremental and "breakthrough" improvement. The approach to improvement needs to be "embedded" in the way the company functions. Embedded means: (1) improvement is part of the daily work of all work units; (2) improvement processes seek to eliminate problems at their source; and (3) improvement is driven by opportunities to do better, as well as by problems that must be corrected. Opportunities for improvement include: employee ideas; R&D; customer input; and benchmarking or other comparative performance information.

Improvements may be of several types: (1) enhancing value to customers through new and improved products and services; (2) reducing errors, defects, and waste; (3) improving responsiveness and cycle time performance; (4) improving productivity and effectiveness in the use of all resources; and (5) improving the company's performance and leadership position in fulfilling its public responsibilities and serving as a role model in corporate citizenship. Thus improvement is driven not only by the objective to provide better products and services, but also by the need to be responsive and efficient—both conferring additional marketplace advantages. To meet these objectives, continuous improvement must contain cycles of planning, execution, and evaluation. This requires a basis—preferably a quantitative basis—for assessing progress and for deriving information for future cycles of improvement. Such information should provide direct links between performance goals and internal operations.

Employee Participation and Development

A company's success in improving performance depends increasingly on the skills and motivation of its work force. Employee success depends increasingly on having meaningful opportunities to learn and to practice new skills. Companies need to invest in the development of the work force through ongoing education, training and opportunities for continuing growth. Such opportunities might include classroom and on-the-job training, job rotation, and pay for demonstrated skills. Structured on-the-job training offers a cost effective way to train and to better link training to work processes. Work force education and training programs may need to utilize advanced technologies, such as electronic support systems and "information highways." Increasingly, training, development, and work organizations need to be tailored to a more diverse work force and to more flexible, high performance work practices.

Major challenges in the area of work force development include: (1) integration of human resource management—selection, performance, recognition, training, and career advancement; and (2) aligning human resource management with business plans and strategic change processes. Addressing these challenges requires acquisition and use of employee-related data on skills, satisfaction, motivation, safety, and well-being. Such data need to be tied to indicators of company or unit performance, such as customer satisfaction, customer retention, and productivity. Through this approach, human resource management may be better integrated and aligned with business directions, using continuous improvement processes to refine integration and alignment.

Fast Response

Success in competitive markets increasingly demands ever-shorter cycles for new or improved product and service introduction. Also, faster and more flexible response to customers is now a more critical requirement. Major improvement in response time often requires simplification of work organizations and work processes. To accomplish such improvement, the time performance of work processes should be among the key process measures. There are other important benefits derived from this focus: response time improvements often drive simultaneous improvements in organization, quality, and productivity. Hence it is beneficial to consider response time, quality, and productivity objectives together.

Design Quality and Prevention

Business management should place strong emphasis on design quality—problem and waste prevention achieved through building quality into products and services and into production and delivery processes. In general, costs of preventing problems at the design stage are much lower than costs of correcting problems which occur "downstream." Design quality includes the creation of fault-tolerant (robust) or failure-resistant processes and products.

A major issue in competition is the design-to-introduction ("product generation") cycle time. Meeting the demands of rapidly changing markets requires that companies carry out stage-to-stage coordination and integration ("concurrent engineering") of functions and activities from basic research to commercialization.

From the point of view of public responsibility, the design stage involves decisions regarding resource use and manufacturing processes. Such decisions affect process waste streams and the composition of municipal and industrial wastes. The growing demands for a cleaner environment mean that companies need to develop design strategies that include environmental factors.

Consistent with the theme of design quality and prevention, continuous improvement needs to emphasize interventions "upstream"—at early stages in processes. This approach yields the maximum overall benefits of improvements and corrections. Such upstream intervention also needs to take into account the company's suppliers.

Long-Range View of the Future

Pursuit of market leadership requires a strong future orientation and a willingness to make long-term commitments to all stakeholders—customers, employees, suppliers, stockholders, the public, and the community. Planning needs to anticipate many types of changes including those that may affect customers' expectations of products and services, technological developments, changing customer segments, evolving regulatory requirements, community/societal expectations, and thrusts by competitors. Plans, strategies, and resource allocations need to reflect these commitments and changes. A major part of the long-term commitment is developing employees and suppliers, fulfilling public responsibilities, and serving as a corporate citizenship role model.

Management by Fact

A modern business management system needs to be built upon a framework of measurement, information, data and analysis. Measurements must derive from the company's strategy and encompass all key processes and the outputs and results of those processes. Facts and data needed for performance improvement and assessment are of many types, including: customer, product and service performance, operations, market, competitive comparisons, supplier, employee-related, and cost and financial. Analysis refers to extracting larger meaning from data to support evaluation and decision making at various levels within the company. Such analysis may entail using data to reveal information—such as trends, projections, and cause and effect—that might not be evident without analysis. Facts, data, and analysis support a variety of company purposes, such as planning, reviewing company performance, improving operations, and comparing company performance with competitors' or with "best practices" benchmarks.

A major consideration in the use of data and analysis to improve performance involves the creation and use of performance measures or indicators. Performance measures or indicators are measurable characteristics of products, services, processes, and operations the company uses to track and improve performance. *The measures or indicators should be selected to best represent the factors that lead to improved customer, operational, and financial performance. A system of measures or indicators tied to customer and/or company performance requirements represents a clear and objective basis for aligning all activities with the company's goals.* Through the analysis of data from the tracking processes, the measures or indicators themselves may be evaluated and changed. For example, measures selected to track product and service quality may be judged by how well improvement in these measures correlates with improvement in customer satisfaction and customer retention.

Partnership Development

Companies should seek to build internal and external partnerships to better accomplish their overall goals.

Internal partnerships might include those that promote labor-management cooperation, such as agreements with unions. Agreements might entail employee development, cross-training, or new work organizations, such as high performance work teams. Internal partnerships might also involve creating network relationships among company units to improve flexibility and responsiveness.

External partnerships may be with customers, suppliers, and education organizations for a variety of purposes, including education and training. An increasingly important kind of external partnership is the strategic partnership or alliance. Such partnerships might offer a company entry into new markets or a basis for new products or services. A partnership might also permit the blending of a company's core competencies or leadership capabilities with complementary strengths and capabilities of partners, thereby enhancing overall capability, including speed and flexibility.

Partnerships should seek to develop longer-term objectives, thereby creating a basis for mutual investments. Partners should address the key requirements for success of the partnership, means of regular communication, approaches to evaluating progress, and means for adapting to changing conditions. In some cases, joint education and training initiatives could offer a cost-effective means to help ensure the success of an alliance.

Corporate Responsibility and Citizenship

A company's management should stress corporate responsibility and citizenship. Corporate responsibility refers to basic expectations of the company—business ethics and protection of public health, safety, and the environment. Health, safety and environmental considerations need to take into account the company's operations as well as the life cycles of products and services. Companies need to address factors such as resource conservation and waste reduction at their source. Planning related to public health, safety, and the environment should anticipate adverse impacts that may arise in facilities management, production, distribution, transportation, use and disposal of products. Plans should seek to prevent problems, to provide a forthright company response if problems occur, and to make available information needed to maintain public awareness, safety, and confidence. Inclusion of public responsibility areas within a performance system means meeting all local, state, and federal laws and regulatory requirements. It also means treating these and related requirements as areas for continuous improvement "beyond mere compliance." This requires that appropriate measures of progress be created and used in managing performance.

Corporate citizenship refers to leadership and support—within reasonable limits of a company's resources—of publicly important purposes, including the above-mentioned areas of corporate responsibility. Such purposes might include education improvement, improving health care value, environmental excellence, resource conservation, community services, improving industry and business practices, and sharing of nonproprietary quality-related information. Leadership as a corporate citizen entails influencing other organizations, private and public, to partner for these purposes. For example, individual companies could lead efforts to help define the obligations of their industry to its communities.

Results Orientation

A company's performance system needs to focus on results. Results ought to be guided by and balanced by the interests of all stakeholders—customers,

BALDRIGE AWARD CRITERIA FRAMEWORK
Dynamic Relationships

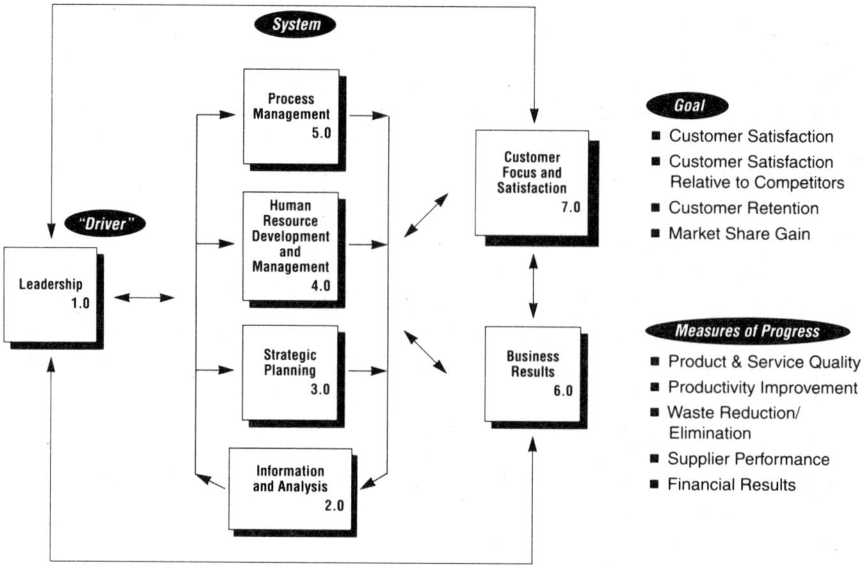

employees, stockholders, suppliers and partners, the public, and the community. To meet the sometimes conflicting and changing aims that balance implies, company strategy needs to explicitly address all stakeholder requirements to ensure that actions and plans meet the differing needs and avoid adverse impact on the stakeholders. The use of a balanced composite of performance indicators offers an effective means to communicate requirements, to monitor actual performance, and to marshal support for improving results.

Award Criteria Framework

The core values and concepts are embodied in seven Categories, as follows:

1.0 Leadership
2.0 Information and Analysis
3.0 Strategic Planning
4.0 Human Resource Development and Management
5.0 Process Management
6.0 Business Results
7.0 Customer Focus and Satisfaction

The framework connecting and integrating the Categories is given in the figure above.

The framework has four basic elements:

Driver

Senior executive leadership sets directions, creates values, goals, and systems, and guides the pursuit of customer value and company performance improvement.

System
The system comprises the set of well-defined and well-designed processes for meeting the company's customer and performance requirements.

Measures of Progress
Measures of progress provide a results-oriented basis for channeling actions to delivering ever-improving customer value and company performance.

Goal
The basic aims of the system are the delivery of ever-improving value to customers and success in the marketplace.

The seven Criteria Categories shown in the figure are subdivided into Examination Items and Areas to Address:

Examination Items
There are 24 Examination Items, each focusing on a major requirement. Item titles and point values are given on page 20. The Item format is shown on page 43.

Areas to Address
Examination Items consist of sets of Areas to Address (Areas). Information is submitted by applicants in response to specific requirements of these Areas.

Changes from the 1994 Award Criteria
The Criteria continue to evolve in four major ways: (1) toward comprehensive coverage of overall performance, including customer-driven quality performance; (2) toward better integration of overall performance, including employee performance, with business strategy; (3) toward further strengthening of the financial and business rationale for improvement priorities; and (4) toward increasing emphasis on results. The Criteria for 1995 are more future oriented, and more directed toward business strategy and competitiveness requirements. At the same time, the Criteria requirements are more focused and aligned, permitting a 40 percent reduction in the number of Areas to Address.

Key Themes Strengthened in the 1995 Criteria
- emphasis on key business drivers, derived from strategic and business planning, integrated into the Criteria framework. The key business drivers address business development and revenue growth, as well as cost reductions stemming from improved operational performance.
- emphasis on financial data in setting priorities for performance improvement
- emphasis on high performance and more flexible and responsive organizations and work systems as well as on the critical requirements, such as effective senior executive leadership, to build and sustain them
- emphasis on investment in developing work force capabilities as a key part of strengthening company competitive fitness

- emphasis on continuous learning as well as continuous improvement. The learning theme is particularly strong in four areas: strategy development; customer and market knowledge; employee development; and information and analysis systems.
- emphasis on business results, including financial results

Many changes have been made in the Criteria and in the Criteria booklet to strengthen key themes and to clarify, focus, and link requirements. Major changes are:

- The number of Examination Items has been reduced from 28 to 24.
- The number of Areas to Address has been reduced from 91 to 54. As a result of this reduction, the application page limit has been reduced from 85 to 70.
- The Description of the Award Criteria has been expanded to cover all Categories, Items, and Areas to Address.

Major changes, by Category, are:

Leadership

- Senior Executive Leadership (Item 1.1) is better focused on the efforts by senior executives in building the leadership system, setting strategic directions, and creating performance excellence goals.
- The title of Item 1.2 has been changed to Leadership System and Organization. The major thrust of this Item is toward flexible and responsive organizations and leadership systems—major themes of the 1995 Criteria.

Information and Analysis

- The title of Item 2.1 has been changed to Management of Information and Data. The scope of the Item is broader than Item 2.1 in the 1994 Criteria. The Item stresses alignment of information and data with user needs and with the key business drivers. A major thrust of the Item is that data and information need to support the more flexible and demanding needs and decision making of high performance work units.
- Item 2.2, Competitive Comparisons and Benchmarking, now focuses more on targeting benchmarking on company priorities and effective benchmarking practices rather than on scope.
- Item 2.3 emphasizes further the critical importance of company-level analysis in support of decision making and priorities. More examples of the use of cost and financial data are given. The Item is intended to serve as the key link between operational and customer-related performance and overall financial performance.

Strategic Planning

- The title of this Category has been broadened (from Strategic Quality Planning) to put major emphasis on business strategy as the most appropriate view-of-the-future context for managing performance. This change is intended to place more attention on the operational performance requirements derived from strategic initiatives. The Category stresses that customer-driven and operational performance excellence are key strategic business issues.
- The titles of the two Items in this Category have also been changed. They are now: Item 3.1, Strategy Development; and Item 3.2, Strategy Deployment.
- Strategy Development (3.1) plays a central directional role in the Criteria. The Item addresses how the company develops its view of the future taking into account the key factors in the environment—competitive, societal, and technological. The Item also addresses how strategy is developed and translated into actionable key business drivers which serve as the basis for **operationalizing** and deploying requirements.
- Strategy Deployment (3.2) addresses how the company's key business drivers are deployed. An important consideration in the Item is the establishment of measures that permit alignment of requirements throughout the company. The Item emphasizes that productivity and cycle time improvement should be included among the key requirements.

Human Resource Development and Management

- The title of Item 4.1 has been changed to Human Resource Planning and Evaluation to emphasize that this Item is the key link between company planning and overall human resource practices. **Evaluation** is crucial to maintaining the alignment between human resource management and company directions. This concern makes Item 4.1 the focal point for evaluating overall human resource systems in relation to business objectives, so that these systems become part of a coordinated strategy.
- A new Item, High Performance Work Systems, has been created to examine work and job design, and how promotion, compensation and recognition support such design. The Item stresses that full participation, high performance, and flexibility depend upon effective work and job designs. That is, participation and active contributions are design issues as well as motivational ones. The Item is thus concerned with the important alignment between incentives and work design. The new Item (4.2) replaces Items 4.2 and 4.4 from the 1994 Criteria.
- The title of Item 4.3 has been changed to Employee Education, Training, and Development to emphasize the larger, more continuing issue of **development.** Development is needed to support the

more demanding high performance work and job systems. The Item is concerned with how education and training are designed, delivered, reinforced, and evaluated, with special emphasis upon on-the-job application of knowledge and skills. The focus is on both company performance and employee development. The scope of this Item is broader than the 1994 version, covering overall education, training, and development.

Process Management

- The title of this Category has been changed (from Management of Process Quality) to minimize confusion that sometimes results from multiple meanings of "quality." The Category addresses all key aspects of effective process management.
- The title of Item 5.3 has been changed to Process Management: Support Services. This change emphasizes that the processes to be described are those which support the key production and delivery processes, but which are not usually designed with them. For this reason, the Item addresses how the support processes are designed, as well as how they are maintained and improved.
- Item 5.5 (Quality Assessment) from the 1994 Criteria has been dropped. Item 1.2 deals with reviews of company performance. Process assessments and related review activities should now be described in Area 1.2c.

Business Results

- The title of the Category has been changed (from Quality and Operational Results) to reflect greater emphasis on business-oriented results to encourage companies to report data that demonstrate impact on customers, markets, and business and financial performance.
- The number of Items in this Category has been reduced from 4 to 3. This change is made by combining Items 6.2 and 6.3 from the 1994 Criteria.
- The new Item, Company Operational and Financial Results (6.2), examines overall company operational and financial improvements from all processes. Results indicators include generic and business-specific ones. The intent of the change is to focus better on company-level improvements and to eliminate reporting of results that might not actually reflect better overall company performance. This change is thus consistent with the more holistic approach to performance emphasized in the Criteria. Human resource results, such as safety, absenteeism, and satisfaction, are now reported in this Item because of their key contribution to operational performance. The point value of Item 6.2 has been increased greatly to emphasize the importance of operational and

financial performance results and the use of these results in guiding performance improvement.

Customer Focus and Satisfaction

- The title of Item 7.1 has been changed to Customer and Market Knowledge. This Item now has a broader scope, a more analytical approach, and an ongoing learning requirement compared with the 1994 version. Particularly important in this Item are the company's key listening and learning strategies—those that provide key information about customers and markets on an ongoing basis.
- Item 7.2, Customer Relationship Management, has been narrowed in scope to better distinguish it from Items 5.2 and 5.3. It is now more nearly customer response management, including responses to complaints. Its title reflects the fact that the Areas addressed stress relationship building.
- Item 7.3 from the 1994 Criteria (Commitment to Customers) has been dropped. The Item dealt primarily with guarantees and warranties. Guarantees and warranties are product and service features and/or elements of company strategy. As such, they are addressed or implied in other Items. Their inclusion in the 1994 Criteria perhaps implied that guarantees and warranties are basic performance requirements. In many instances, guarantees and warranties may be useful marketing or management tools, but they are not necessarily basic requirements.

On the next page you will find the 1994 Award Examination Criteria—Item Listing with the points assigned to each item.

1995 Award Examination Criteria—Item Listing

1995 Examination Categories/Items			Point Values
1.0	**Leadership**		**90**
1.1	Senior Executive Leadership	45	
1.2	Leadership System and Organization	25	
1.3	Public Responsibility and Corporate Citizenship	20	
2.0	**Information and Analysis**		**75**
2.1	Management of Information and Data	20	
2.2	Competitive Comparisons and Benchmarking	15	
2.3	Analysis and Use of Company-Level Data	40	
3.0	**Strategic Planning**		**55**
3.1	Strategy Development	35	
3.2	Strategy Deployment	20	
4.0	**Human Resource Development and Management**		**140**
4.1	Human Resource Planning and Evaluation	20	
4.2	High Performance Work Systems	45	
4.3	Employee Education, Training, and Development	50	
4.4	Employee Well-Being and Satisfaction	25	
5.0	**Process Management**		**140**
5.1	Design and Introduction of Products and Services	40	
5.2	Process Management: Product and Service Production and Delivery	40	
5.3	Process Management: Support Services	30	
5.4	Management of Supplier Performance	30	
6.0	**Business Results**		**250**
6.1	Product and Service Quality Results	75	
6.2	Company Operational and Financial Results	130	
6.3	Supplier Performance Results	45	
7.0	**Customer Focus and Satisfaction**		**250**
7.1	Customer and Market Knowledge	30	
7.2	Customer Relationship Management	30	
7.3	Customer Satisfaction Determination	30	
7.4	Customer Satisfaction Results	100	
7.5	Customer Satisfaction Comparison	60	
	TOTAL POINTS		**1000**

Index

1995 *Quality Yearbook* Feedback Survey

Please cut this form out, fill it in, and mail it to us. We need your feedback. On a scale of 1 to 5 (1 = poor, 5 = outstanding), please respond to the following questions:

1. Overall, how would you assess the value of this book to you? ____ (Rate 1–5)

   Please describe how it has been valuable or not valuable to you. ____________

   ____

   ____

   Why? ____

   ____

2. How would you assess the value of Part One to you? ____ (Rate 1–5)

   What did you find valuable about this part and why? ____________

   ____

   ____

3. How would you assess the value of Part Two to you? ____ (Rate 1–5)

   What did you find valuable about this part and why? ____________

   ____

   ____

4. How would you assess the value of Part Three to you? ____ (Rate 1–5)

   What did you find valuable about this part and why? ____________

   ____

   ____

5. How would you assess the value of Part Four to you? ____ (Rate 1–5)

   What did you find valuable about this part and why? ____________

   ____

   ____

6. What changes and improvements would you like to see in the 1996 yearbook?

   ____

   ____

▲ Tape Here

▼ Fold on line

No Postage
Necessary
If Mailed
in the
United States

BUSINESS REPLY MAIL

FIRST CLASS MAIL PERMIT NO. 3769 NEW YORK, NY

POSTAGE WILL BE PAID BY ADDRESSEE

ATT QUALITY YEARBOOK EDITOR
McGRAW-HILL INC
11 W 19 ST
NEW YORK, NY 10114-0003

▲ Fold on line